May 19–22, 2013
Montréal, Québec, Canada

Association for
Computing Machinery

Advancing Computing as a Science & Profession

SIGSIM-PADS'13

Proceedings of the 2013 ACM
SIGSIM Principles of Advanced Discrete Simulation

Sponsored by:

ACM SIGSIM

Association for
Computing Machinery

Advancing Computing as a Science & Profession

The Association for Computing Machinery
2 Penn Plaza, Suite 701
New York, New York 10121-0701

Notice to Past Authors of ACM-Published Articles
ACM intends to create a complete electronic archive of all articles and/or other material previously published by ACM. If you have written a work that has been previously published by ACM in any journal or conference proceedings prior to 1978, or any SIG Newsletter at any time, and you do NOT want this work to appear in the ACM Digital Library, please inform permissions@acm.org, stating the title of the work, the author(s), and where and when published.

ISBN: 978-1-4503-1920-1 (Digital)

ISBN: 978-1-4503-2281-3 (Print)

Additional copies may be ordered prepaid from:

ACM Order Department
PO Box 30777
New York, NY 10087-0777, USA

Phone: 1-800-342-6626 (USA and Canada)
+1-212-626-0500 (Global)
Fax: +1-212-944-1318
E-mail: acmhelp@acm.org
Hours of Operation: 8:30 am – 4:30 pm ET

Printed in the USA

ACM SIGSIM-PADS 2013 Chairs' Welcome

On behalf of the Organizing Committee, it is our great pleasure to welcome you to the *2013 ACM SIGSIM Conference on Principles of Advanced Discrete Simulation (SIGSIM-PADS).* Building upon 26 years of history and the reputation for high quality papers of the PADS Workshop (Workshop on Principles of Advanced and Distributed Simulation), the new SIGSIM-PADS focuses on the intersection of computer science and modeling and simulation.

This year's Conference continues its tradition of being the premier forum for presentation of research results in this field of research, including high-quality papers in all aspects of simulation technology. The program includes a wide selection of technical presentations, plenary and invited speakers, and a collection of state-of-the-art presentations and articles related to research, development, and applications of Theory of Modeling and Simulation.

The Call for Papers attracted 75 Full Paper submissions from Algeria, Argentina, Australia, Austria, Belgium, Brazil, Canada, Chile, China, France, Germany, Iran, Israel, Italy, Korea, Netherlands, Norway, Poland, Portugal, Serbia, Singapore, Spain, Sweden, Turkey, United Arab Emirates, United Kingdom and United States, making it a truly International event. The program committee accepted 29 of those Full Papers. Also, 11 Work-in-Progress papers and 3 Invited Papers are included in the program. This year's sessions include new topics in the field: Automation in Generation of Simulation Models, Heterogeneous Parallel Simulation, Theory and Emergent Behavior, Parallel Simulation in Multicore Architectures, Management of Activity in Simulation and a Panel on Grand Challenges in Modeling and Simulation. Also, advanced papers on Parallel Simulation algorithms, Agent-Based Simulation, Distributed Simulation, Simulation with Hardware-in-the-loop and varied Applications including Networking and Communications, Logistics, and Biology.

This year we have organized the First *ACM SIGSIM-PADS Ph.D. Colloquium and Poster Session.* During this session, students will have the opportunity to discuss their research with top experts in the field. A Best Colloquium Award will be presented to the best presentation.

The Awards Committee chose the top-five Conference Best Papers, and, based on the reviewer's evaluations and the Committee evaluations, the Best Paper Award has been selected, which will be announced during the Conference and posted in the Conference webpage after the event.

We extend our gratitude to the Symposium Steering Committee members, Technical Program Committee Members, Session Chairs, to all authors for their invaluable contributions, effort, and time. We sincerely express our appreciation to the numerous technical reviewers and the various Review Committees for their thorough work (which includes over 205 reviews), making the Proceedings a high quality and useful document. The efforts, diligence, and thoroughness of the reviewers are gratefully acknowledged.

On behalf of the Conference Committee, we welcome you to Montréal, and we very much hope you enjoy the conference.

Margaret L. Loper
ACM SIGSIM-PADS 2013 General Chair

Gabriel A. Wainer
ACM SIGSIM-PADS 2013 Program Chair

Table of Contents

Activity Management

Session Chair: Yiping Yao *(National University of Defense Technology)*

Parallel Simulation Algorithms

Session Chair: Chris Carothers *(Rensselaer Polytechnic Institute)*

Distributed Simulation

Session Chair: George Riley *(Georgia Institute of Technology)*

Theoretical Aspects and Emergent Behavior

Session Chair: Gabriel A. Wainer *(Carleton University)*

Hardware-in-the-loop Simulation

Session Chair: Kalyan Perumalla *(Oak Ridge National Lab)*

Applications: Logistics

Session Chair: Richard Fujimoto *(Georgia Institute of Technology)*

Optimistic Parallel Discrete-Event Simulation

Session Chair: Richard Fujimoto *(Georgia Institute of Technology)*

Work-in-Progress Session 1: Theoretical Aspects

Session Chair: Olivier Michel *(Université Paris-Est)*

Work-in-Progress Session 2: Parallel Simulation

Session Chair: Jean-François Santucci *(University of Corsica)*

Work-in-Progress Session 3: Agent-based Simulation

Session Chair: Alex Aravind *(University of Northern British Columbia)*

Work-in-Progress Session 4: Distributed Simulation

Session Chair: Kevin Jin *(University of Illinois at Urbana-Champaign)*

Invited Paper

Session Chair: Simon Taylor *(Brunel University)*

2013 ACM SIGSIM Conference on Principles of Advanced Discrete Simulation (PADS)

General Chair: Margaret L. Loper *(Georgia Institute of Technology, USA)*

Program Chair: Gabriel A. Wainer *(Carleton University, Canada)*

Tutorials/Workshop Chair: Levent Yilmaz *(Auburn University, USA)*

Publicity Chair: Richard Fujimoto *(Georgia Institute of Technology, USA)*

PhD Colloquium Chair: Kevin Jin *(University of Illinois at Urbana-Champaign, USA)*

Steering Committee:
Osman Balci *(Virginia Tech, USA)*
Paul Fishwick *(University of Texas at Dallas, USA)*
Richard Fujimoto *(Georgia Institute of Technology, USA)*
Drew Hamilton *(Auburn University, USA)*
Jason Liu *(Florida International University, USA)*
David Nicol *(University of Illinois at Urbana-Champaign, USA)*
George Riley *(Georgia Institute of Technology, USA)*

Program Committee:
Khaldoon Al-Zoubi (*Blackberry, Canada*)
Michele Amoretti (*Università degli Studi di Parma , Italy)*
Osman Balci *(Virginia Tech, USA)*
Fernando Barros *(University of Coimbra, Portugal)*
Wengtong Cai *(Nanyang Technological University, Singapore)*
Chris Carothers *(Rensselaer Polytechnic Institute, USA)*
Rodrigo Castro (*University of Buenos Aires, Argentina*)
Olivier Dalle *(INRIA/University of Nice Sophia-Antipolis, France)*
Andrea D'Ambrogio *(University of Rome "Tor Vergata", Italy)*
Umut Durak (*Roketsan Inc. System Simulations, Turkey*)
Roland Ewald *(University of Rostock, Germany)*
Tony Field *(Imperial College, UK)*
Paul Fishwick *(University of Texas at Dallas, USA)*
Richard Fujimoto *(Georgia Tech, USA)*
Drew Hamilton *(Auburn University, USA)*
David Hill (*Blaise Pascal University, France)*
Jan Himmelspach *(University of Rostock, Germany)*
Xiaolin Hu *(Georgia State University, USA)*
Shafagh Jafer (*University of Milwaukee, USA*)
David R. Jefferson *(Lawrence Livermore National Lab, USA)*
Cameron Kiddle *(University of Calgary, Canada)*
Franziska Klügl *(Orebro University, Sweden)*
Hillel Kugler *(Microsoft Research, UK)*
Jason Liu *(Florida International University, USA)*
Qi Liu *(IBM Watson Research Center, USA)*
Emilio Mancini (*INRIA Sophia-Antipolis, France)*

Program Committee (continued):

Mohammad Moallemi (*Carleton University, Canada*)
David Nicol *(University of Illinois at Urbana-Champaign, USA)*
Libero Nigro (*University of Calabria, Italy*)
James Nutaro *(Oak Ridge National Lab, USA)*
Francesco Quaglia *(University of Rome "La Sapienza", Italy)*
Martin Quinson *(LORIA, France)*
Ernie Page *(MITRE Corp., USA)*
Kalyan Perumalla *(Oak Ridge National Lab, USA)*
George Riley *(Georgia Tech, USA)*
Hessam Sarjoughian *(Arizona State University, USA)*
Thomas Schulze *(University of Magdeburg, Germany)*
Mamadou Diouf Seck *(TU Delft, Netherlands)*
Steffen Strassburger *(TU Ilmenau, Germany)*
Claudia Szabo *(University of Adelaide, Australia)*
Simon Taylor *(Brunel University, UK)*
Andreas Tolk *(Old Dominion University, USA)*
Mamadou K. Traoré *(Blaise Pascal University, France)*
Carl Tropper *(McGill University, Canada)*
Bruno Tuffin *(INRIA, France)*
Chuck Turnitsa *(Columbus State University, USA)*
Adelinde Uhrmacher *(University of Rostock, Germany)*
Brian Unger (*University of Calgary, Canada)*
Kurt Vanmechelen *(University of Antwerp, Belgium)*
Philip Wilsey *(University of Cincinatti, USA)*
Yiping Yao *(National University of Defense Technology, China)*
Levent Yilmaz *(Auburn University, USA)*
Enver Yücesan *(INSEAD, France)*
Gregory Zacharewicz *(University of Bordeaux - IMS, France)*
Brenda Zhuang *(The MathWorks, USA)*

Additional reviewers:

Fernando Asteasuain
Arne Bittig
Franco Cicirelli
Pau Fonseca I Casas
Soroosh Gholami
Hao Jiang
Frank Krüger
Esteban Mocskos
Lisandru Muzy
Francesco Pupo
José L. Risco-Martín
Hesham Saadawi
Damian Vicino
Wei Wei
Haidong Xue

Sponsor: SIGSIM

The ACM SIGSIM mission is to promote and disseminate the advancement of high quality state-of-the-art in Modeling and Simulation (M&S) across a broad range of interests and disciplines.

Semi-Automatic Extraction of Software Skeletons for Benchmarking Large-Scale Parallel Applications

Matthew Sottile* mjsottile@gmail.com

Amruth Dakshinamurthy† amruth.rd@knights.ucf.edu

Gilbert Hendry‡ ghendry@sandia.gov

Damian Dechev†‡ dechev@eecs.ucf.edu

*Research and Engineering
Galois, Inc.
Portland, OR 97204

†Department of EECS
University of Central Florida
Orlando, FL 32816

‡Sandia National Laboratories
P.O. Box 969
Livermore, CA 94551

ABSTRACT

The design of high-performance computing architectures requires performance analysis of large-scale parallel applications to derive various parameters concerning hardware design and software development. The process of performance analysis and benchmarking an application can be done in several ways with varying degrees of fidelity. One of the most cost-effective ways is to do a coarse-grained study of large-scale parallel applications through the use of program skeletons. The concept of a "program skeleton" that we discuss in this paper is an abstracted program that is derived from a larger program where source code that is determined to be irrelevant is removed for the purposes of the skeleton. In this work, we develop a semi-automatic approach for extracting program skeletons based on compiler program analysis. We demonstrate correctness of our skeleton extraction process by comparing details from communication traces, as well as show the performance speedup of using skeletons by running simulations in the SST/macro simulator.

Categories and Subject Descriptors

D.2.10 [**SOFTWARE ENGINEERING**]: Design—*Methodologies*
; D.2.8 [**SOFTWARE ENGINEERING**]: Metrics—*performance measures*
; D.1.2 [**PROGRAMMING TECHNIQUES**]: Automatic Programming—*program transformation, program verification*

General Terms

Algorithms, Performance, Design, Experimentation, Human Factors, Verification

Keywords

Program Skeleton, Static Analysis, Dependency Analysis, Simulation, Source-to-Source Code Generation

1. INTRODUCTION

The design of new computers requires benchmarks and proxy applications that designers can use to evaluate the ability of these new systems to achieve the performance goals of their ultimate end users. Traditional approaches based on generic benchmarks provide a limited view into the workloads that high-performance computing platforms will be faced with in production environments. Ideally, the set of benchmarks available to system designers will include exemplars of specific applications that are critical to the groups purchasing the new machines. Unfortunately, the creation of benchmarks from specific applications is a time-consuming and tedious process. In this paper, we propose a semi-automatic approach to generating these custom benchmarks based on large scale applications through the use of program analysis and code generation.

The creation of application-specific benchmarks or miniature applications ("miniapps") is work intensive as it requires the creator to not only understand the important performance aspects of the application, but how the entire source code base relates to program elements that contribute to that performance aspect. Performance aspects that are commonly of interest in high-performance computer design include message passing patterns, memory traversal footprints, I/O activity, and numerical computation load. Given an arbitrary line of code in a large parallel program, it is difficult to manually discern what role (if any) it plays for a given performance aspect. Modern static analysis and compilation tools make it possible for a machine to aid in answering these kinds of questions, such as "does this line of code affect the value of the payload for an MPI function?"

Our work presents a step towards automating the skeleton generation process. We employ the ROSE compiler framework to gain access to program analysis algorithms and code generation tools to implement a source-to-source translator. Due to the limited information available to the tool from the raw source code, we take a semi-automated approach to generation in which the user of the skeleton generation tool provides information that cannot easily be obtained through pure static analysis. In this paper we will discuss both the analyses that the prototype skeleton generator uses, as well as the mechanism by which the tool user introduces guidance in an iterative process. Our results presented in Section 6 demonstrate what can be achieved with a small number of iterations through the tool with user guidance.

Skeleton Driven Simulation

It is common to use simulation to predict the performance of systems before they are available. Simulation of a full parallel application would be prohibitively expensive given that most production applications take a significant amount of time to execute on the bare system itself. The efficient utilization of large-scale parallel event simulators such as SST/macro [4] requires that skeleton models of underlying software systems and architectures be created. Implementing such models by abstracting the designs of large-scale parallel applications requires a substantial amount of manual effort and introduces human errors. Our approach reduces both the effort and likelihood of errors in the skeleton by using established algorithms for program dependency analysis and code generation. These skeleton models can then be combined with appropriate models of the software stack and system hardware to generate a wealth of information about execution pattern such as application communication characteristics and network utilization for high-performance computing architectures. This information is useful in understanding the impact of various design decisions concerning hardware or software and will enable co-design practices to be applied to the design of future exascale systems and provide an environment to prototype ideas for future programming models and software infrastructure for these machines.

Our primary target for this work is within the hardware-software co-design community concerned with designing next-generation (and beyond) high-performance computing (HPC) systems. Simulation tools are used extensively in the design of computing systems, especially in a co-designed way, to overcome the lack of compiler tools, well-defined ISA features, or complete micro-architectural definitions [4].

2. RELATED WORK

The work described in this paper focuses on using program analysis to derive program skeletons from large-scale parallel applications with the goal of using these skeletons for performance analysis and prediction. Modeling the behavior of a large-scale application in terms of performance metrics is challenging since these applications are often executed in new and dynamic environments. The process is complicated by extremely limited feedback between application development and machine design [9]. A current activity in high performance computing is to come up with a hardware-software co-design methodology where there is a tighter integration between application development and machine design. Simulation plays a critical role in this methodology.

A number of approaches have been proposed for implementing an effective hardware-software co-design methodology. All approaches use simulation extensively since it is cost-effective and does not demand high-end hardware to be available as in the case of direct execution of an application [4]. A trace-based approach where the full program is executed in order to understand the program's behavior suffers from the cost of high execution times to obtain the traces. Simulation using program skeletons provides a number of advantages over direct execution and trace-based approaches when performing coarse-grained studies of large-scale parallel applications. Skeletonizing allows designers to gauge performance without large costs, and a semi-automated approach allows multiple skeletons to be derived from a single source application relative to specific performance aspects of the program. These aspects could include usage of MPI calls, I/O calls, or the memory access pattern of the code.

The practice of studying reduced applications instead of full parallel programs is not new. The use of kernels or miniature applications in performance analysis is well established, and collections of common kernels are accessible for use by the high performance computing community. Two well known collections are the NAS Parallel Benchmarks (NPB) [2] and the PARKBENCH suite [3]. The individual kernels in these suites are intended to represent a common computational pattern that can be found in a broad number of full-scale parallel applications. Examples include sorting algorithms, the Fast Fourier Transform, matrix-based numerical algorithms and so on. While these suites represent simpler implementations of important algorithms than full scientific codes, they still are challenging to use for studying specific performance properties since they contain code for numerical computation as well as message passing and I/O. Furthermore, they represent a generic algorithm implementation that lacks any nuances that would be found in specific application implementations. Our skeletonization approach seeks to overcome both of these issues by allowing irrelevant code to be removed, and to allow skeletons to be derived directly from application implementations.

Scalability of a large-scale parallel application is often largely determined by the communication model it employs. This is most apparent in problems that exhibit strong scaling, where the size of the overall problem handled by each processor shrinks as the processor count increases. Most of the computations that are part of a program are generally executed on individual nodes and have little influence on the program's scalability. Eliminating code that forms the computational part significantly reduces execution time of the program [1]. The work described in this paper focuses on programs that use communication patterns that are not sensitive to the data computed within the program. Programs that exhibit a data and computational decomposition amongst a set of processors that is determined by runtime data properties are significantly more challenging to skeletonize since computational code cannot simply be removed. Programs of this sort are not included in the set of target applications we are concerned with in this paper.

Deriving skeletons from large-scale programs manually requires a significant programmer effort, and is prone to human errors. Some efforts have investigated automatically synthesizing application skeletons from communication traces [10], but this requires extensive trace collecting, and may not capture behavior produced with particular application parameters. For example, a program with a static communication pattern for a given number of processors may have different patterns for different processor counts. A trace represents only one instantiation of the communication pattern. A program skeleton that retains the branching logic that selects communication operations based on the processor count retains the ability to reflect the behavior of the program across a range of scales.

It has also been shown that static analysis techniques can be used to identify computations or routines that do not influence the performance of a program significantly [1]. Automated methods have been demonstrated for transforming parallel scientific applications through the use of both dynamic runtime information in the form of MPI communication patterns and static information about the program [6]. That work uses similar analysis tools as the work we present in this paper, but has a different goal of transforming and optimizing programs versus generation of reduced applications for simulation-based performance analysis.

3. METHODOLOGY

We begin with a discussion of the key components that make up the core of our automatic skeleton extraction framework. The components are presented in brief along with their functionality.

3.1 ROSE Compiler Framework

ROSE is an open source-to-source compiler infrastructure for building a wide variety of customized analysis, optimization and transformation tools [5]. It enables rapid development of source-to-source translators from C, C++, UPC, and Fortran codes to facilitate deep analysis of complex application codes and code transformations. ROSE consists of front-ends for parsing code, a mid-end for code analysis, optimizations and transformations, and back-ends to generate source code [5]. The currently available front-ends are the Edison Design Group (EDG) front-end for C and C++, and the Open Fortran Parser (OFP) front-end for Fortran. Using ROSE program analysis techniques, we have developed an early version of a source-to-source translator to automate the extraction of skeleton applications from their parent applications containing MPI communication patterns.

3.2 Program Skeletons

A program skeleton is an abstract form of its parent application where we retain only those portions of the code that are relevant to the performance dimension that the skeleton is intended to probe. In the case of message passing behavior over MPI, the skeleton is intended to be consistent with the original program flow such that it retains the communication patterns of the original application. To achieve this, a skeleton is essentially a sliced version of the original program that is constructed by removing fragments of redundant or irrelevant computations and message data whose values do not affect application scalability, but retaining those code fragments specific to the set of properties of interest for performance analysis.

Applications that utilize high performance computing systems often implement compute and time intensive computations that form the content of messages passed between parallel processors at runtime, but the message passing pattern that the program exhibits often is independent of the values that these computations produce. This observation that some portion of the computational load is irrelevant when considering performance aspects such as message passing patterns is the basis of our work. However, there do exist a number of complex applications where the message passing pattern is determined by the computations that are performed. Common examples of this include programs that utilize unstructured data in which the decomposition of data across compute elements changes as its state evolves. Addressing programs where dynamic message passing patterns are present driven by the results of the computational part of the program is a topic of ongoing research.

Due to the complexity of large parallel applications, and the limits of purely static analysis for languages like C, C++, and Fortran, we adopt a semi-automated approach where the programmer is involved in the skeleton generation process through program directives and other parameters that guide skeleton generation tools. Once a satisfactory skeleton is created, it can act as a model to enable scalability studies using the SST/macro simulator or other performance analysis and simulation tools to emulate systems under design, such as interconnection networks, for systems containing millions of cores.

3.3 SST/macro Discrete Event Simulator

The SST/macro discrete event simulator is an open source simulation package that enables evaluation of large-scale parallel machines [4]. The simulator is implemented in C++ with a modular design, permitting multiple computation and communication models to be employed. SST/macro is extensible by supporting user-defined network topologies, allocation and scheduling strategies, and performance models by externally linking to the simulator core. It can be driven either by direct execution of application code using communication libraries like MPI, HPX, or OpenSHMEM, or through communication traces like the DUMPI format that is included in the distribution. The MPI implementation and network congestion models have been validated against current HPC machines, including a Cray XE6. The simulator enables us to investigate the effects of varying environment parameters such as type and tuning of network topologies, hardware layout (e.g. processors per node) and system parameter choices (e.g. bandwidths, latencies).

4. APPROACH

Our approach follows a process in which the tool performs analysis and static slicing of the code with the aid of user-provided annotations. This process is applied iteratively by the user until they are satisfied with the resulting skeleton code. The key components of our skeleton generator and how they fit together is shown in Figure 1. The ROSE compiler serves as the base framework for constructing program analysis modules by providing a suite of common forms of program analyses such as dependence analysis, control flow analysis, and call graphs. The SST/macro simulator provides the environment for executing parallel programs with model choices provided by the user. The target MPI application annotated with program directives is fed as an input to the ROSE front end. The front end parses the input source code and generates an Abstract Syntax Tree (AST) called Sage III Intermediate Representation (IR). This AST serves as the input to subsequent analysis and transformation steps used by our skeleton generator.

The primary activity performed by the skeleton genera-

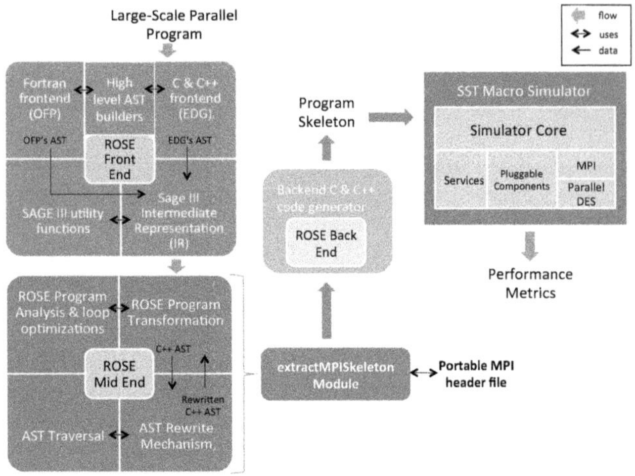

Figure 1: Software components involved in program analysis, skeleton generation, and performance simulation.

tor is the identification of code that can be removed based on constraints provided by the tool user. These constraints are externally provided instead of hardwired into the tool because they directly relate to the specific performance dimensions that the skeleton is intended to probe. This separation allows our skeleton generator to be applicable in a broader set of contexts than MPI-only APIs. For example, the set of API function calls preserved for a skeleton representing MPI activity is completely different from one representing disk I/O operations. The constraints that the user specifies are expressed in two forms. First, one or more API specification files that contain information about the API functions that should be preserved are provided. Second, a set of in-source directives in the form of compiler pragmas are available for targeted control over the internal decisions made by the generator. The MPI API specifications is predefined and provided to the user with the tool.

The skeleton generation tool that we designed has the following overall structure:

- The program code is put into Static Single Assignment (SSA) form, allowing def-use analysis to be performed.
- API calls of interest are identified within the program abstract syntax tree and used to identify code that they depend upon that must be preserved leading up to the calls. This analysis uses the def-use information obtained via the SSA form.
- Programmer directives are processed to override information obtained by analyzing the def-use chains based solely on the API of interest. These directives include overriding choices to exclude or include code, both to overcome limitations in the current dependency analysis algorithms used and to inject knowledge about the desired skeleton that the programmer has that cannot be inferred from syntax alone.

We use the ROSE-provided SSA analysis to compute the SSA form of the program AST, which simplifies the process of def-use analysis to determine all uses of a variable from its definition without any other intervening definitions. The skeleton generator then implements a form of *program slicing*. Slicing relative to one or more statements uses dependency analysis to determine all program elements that the statements depend on to execute correctly. Any code that these statements are not dependent upon can be removed.

Our skeleton generator implements a specialization of slicing in which we do not treat all dependencies equally. Dependencies are classified by a "role" that they play relative to the API that we slice relative to. In MPI programs, we distinguish dependencies that influence the contents of a message from those that influence the message passing communication pattern. This allows us to transform code based on its role—in some cases, we preserve the dependency code with no change as in traditional slicing. In other cases, we may replace the dependency code with a surrogate that aids in reducing the complexity of the skeleton. For example, we may preserve all code that relates to message passing topology, but will replace code related to the message payloads (that can be shown to not influence the topology) to insert initialization to constant values in place of compute-intensive numerical computations.

4.1 API Specification

The skeleton generator skeletonizes programs relative to one or more API specifications. This means that functions that are part of the API are required to be preserved in the skeleton, and further code is preserved based on their dependencies. Each function that we would like to treat as part of the API is specified by the function name, number of parameters, and a list of dependency types for each parameter. The dependency types allow us to categorize code based on how it impacts the API functions. For example, in the case of MPI, we will have code related to the data that is sent (the "payload"), and code that is related to the communication end-points and abstract communicators used within the program. Code that influences these parameters to the API functions is often very different, and the API specification allows the tool to tag program elements based on their role. This information is not currently used in any detail other than distinguishing code by role for role-specific removal or preservation. Deeper analysis of code that takes on certain roles (e.g., payload creation) is the subject of further work. For example, symbolic simulation techniques may be useful for replacing code with a simpler surrogate instead of removing it entirely if the payload data is important in determining the communication pattern.

An example of a small portion of the API specification for MPI is provided below.

```
(api-spec MPI
  ( dep-types payload topology tag other )
  ( default_deptype other )

  ( (MPI_Init          2 )
    (MPI_Finalize      0 )
    (MPI_Abort         2 )

    (MPI_Comm_rank     2  (topology 1) )
    (MPI_Comm_size     2  (topology 1) )
    (MPI_Comm_split    4 )

    (MPI_Send          6  (payload 0 1 2)
                          (topology 3)
                          (tag 4) )
  ) )
```

Each API is labeled by name via the api-spec tag. This is followed by an s-expression that contains a list of dependency types, prefaced with the dep-types tag. The names of the dependency types are user-specified, allowing roles of arguments to API functions to be analyzed at different levels of detail. For example, if the tag role is not of interest to the skeleton generator, it could be eliminated and absorbed into another category. This flexibility allows the user to tune the generator based on what they know is important about their program and how it uses the API. The other category is a special category that is a catch-all for arguments that are considered irrelevant for skeletonization.

Each API call is described by its name, argument count, and an enumeration of arguments by position that are to have roles associated with them. Arguments not listed are by default placed in the other category.

```
(API_FUNCTION_NAME ARGUMENT_COUNT (deptype argA ..)
                                  (deptype argB ..)
                                  ...)
```

For example, on MPI_Send above, we see that it has 6 arguments, the first three of which are related to payload, the fourth is topology, and the fifth is tag. Note that argument numbering is zero-based. The sixth argument is not specified, and therefore takes on the default dependency type "other".

Given a set of API specifications, we then allow an API collection to be specified that is used by the skeleton generator to know what set of APIs to skeletonize relative to, and how to do so. For example:

```
(api-spec-collection
 (include-api "mpi_api.spec" (omit-deps payload))
 (include-api "stdio_input.spec" (omit-deps buffer))
)
```

This tells the tool to include API specifications for MPI and a subset of C STDIO functions. This is important in practice since skeletons frequently require parameter files to be read that are used to configure the application. Given that this code often is performed outside the MPI API, we must allow the skeleton generator to be aware of additional APIs that are important in generating a legitimate skeleton. For each API, a specification of the dependency type to use for selecting code for elimination is also provided. In the example above (provided for illustrative purposes only), code that relates to computation of payload data for MPI calls is eliminated, and buffer management code is eliminated that relates to the STDIO API. This allows a user to have relatively fine control over what is and is not removed at the API level.

4.2 Source-level Directives

Annotations used by this tool are specified via compiler directives:

```
#pragma skel [specific pragma text here]
```

For example,

```
#pragma skel loop iterate atmost(10)
```

Annotations are used to provide fine grained control of the skeletonizer at a finer level than that is captured in the API specification. Annotations also allow for targeted direction from the user at specific points in the program, versus program-wide guidance at the API level. The simplest annotations that we provide allow the user to preserve or remove program elements to override the decision made by the skeletonizer based on dependency analysis. These are placed above the corresponding program element:

```
#pragma skel preserve
x = y + z;
```

Directives are retained in the generated skeleton along with appropriate program structures accompanying them (including an empty block in the case of the remove directive). The interpretation of the directives by the skeleton generator is designed such that its application to an unmodified, auto-generated skeleton will result in exactly the same result being produced.

4.2.1 Loop Annotations

It is not uncommon for skeletonized code to no longer have the looping behavior of the original due to the removal of computations which provide the values that define a termination criterion. For example, say we have an iterative solver with the following structure:

```
do {
  // numerical computation
  for (i=0;i<n;i++) {
    prev[i] = current[i];
    current[i] = a_big_computation();
  }

  // compute delta based on computation
  for (i=0;i<n;i++) {
    delta += fabs(current[i] - prev[i]);
  }

  // do some message passing
  MPI_Send(...);
} while (delta > eps);
```

If the numerical computation is removed, we can be in a situation where delta will not ever change and will never drop below the threshold for termination—so the loop will iterate forever. Similarly, we may find that through some choice of initial values, the skeleton may initialize delta to be zero, so the loop will iterate only once (or never, depending on the type of loop used). In both cases, we would see behavior that is not representative of the real program. An annotation can be added to force the skeleton to contain a loop that iterates a certain number of times by having the skeleton generator introduce additional counters and code to increment and test their values.

Three loop annotations are available:

```
#pragma skel loop iterate exactly(n)
#pragma skel loop iterate atmost(n)
#pragma skel loop iterate atleast(n)
```

These correspond to forcing an exact, upper, and lower bound on the iteration count. The pragma must be placed immediately preceding the loop of interest. Loops constructed with 'for', 'while', or 'do while' are all supported as well as loops containing break and continue statements. We treat break statements as an exception that overrides the 'exactly' or 'atleast' annotations. If a break is reached in a loop before the n-th iteration, the loop is exited but a warning is printed to `stderr` indicating the violation of the pragma.

In the above annotations, `n` is a C expression that is interpreted in the current scope of the program.[1] This allows the programmer to specify program variables to be used in the stopping criteria that they are confident will contain meaningful values at skeleton execution.

Insertion of code to implement these loop control pragmas occurs after dependency analysis is performed and relevant code removed. This is implemented as an additional pass over the program AST seeking loop structures that have pragmas associated with them. These are guaranteed to be present if the loop body contains an API call that was invoked due to the presence of a control flow relation between the call and the loop. Code insertion is performed after code is flagged for removal to avoid the inserted loop control logic from itself being flagged for removal.

4.2.2 Data Declaration Annotations

If a program contains an array that should be preserved in the skeleton, it is useful to have control over how it is initialized since often the skeleton will not contain the computational code that populates the array elements. The initializer pragma allows these element values to be specified.

```
#pragma skel initializer repeat(x)
int myArray[14];
```

Where `x` is a C expression interpreted in the current scope of the program.

This will result in code being generated that iterates over the array elements assigning the value `x` to them. The variable initialization annotation supports arrays in the "auto" storage class (but not yet arrays in the "static" storage class). Future versions of the skeletonizer will support initialization of static arrays and dynamically allocated arrays. Future versions will also support initializing non-array variables.

4.3 Dependency Analysis

The core static analysis algorithm that we rely on is the computation of the Static Single Assignment (SSA) form of the program. This computation is provided as part of the ROSE framework. Once SSA form has been obtained for a program, def-use chains are available for relating uses of variables to their defining statements. For each call site of an API function to be included in the skeleton we obtain a set of variables corresponding to the contents of expressions that form the function call arguments. Each argument is tagged with the dependency type that is defined with the API specification, such as "payload" or "topology" in the MPI API discussed above.

The def-use chains for these expressions are then traversed, where each program element leading up to the call is labeled as a dependency along with the dependency type that is inherited from the API specification. The labeling process takes the union of dependency types that are derived for each program element. This labeling allows the user of the tool to have finer control over the transformation that removes code. Instead of preserving all code that an API call depends on, the transformation can preserve based on API-specific roles.

A current limitation of the skeleton generator is full support for whole program dependency propagation in programs containing multiple independently compiled program units. Program units (e.g., C++ source files) are analyzed and transformed independently. A result is that when one C++ file references code implemented in another, we lack information about any dependencies that should be propagated out to the caller. An elegant solution to this problem is to take an approach similar to languages like Fortran and Haskell, where processing of independent source files results in an additional file being created (such as a Fortran .MOD or Haskell .HI file) that contains metadata beyond the basic API types for use when compiling other program units that reference the corresponding file. An alternative approach is to modify our generator to be aware of the full set of source files that a project requires such that they can be loaded and processed at once (in an appropriate order). These engineering additions to our prototype are the subject of our ongoing development work, and do not affect the basic slicing concept at the core of the skeleton generator.

4.4 Code Transformation

After dependency analysis has been performed and AST nodes are annotated with their role in the skeleton, we perform a transformation on the AST before final code generation in the language of the original program. For a given program construct, there are three possible choices at transformation time: complete removal, complete preservation, or replacement. For code that is determined to not be in the dependency chain of API functions, removal is the default behavior. This must be overridden by using the `preserve` pragma described above. Code that is in the dependency chain is preserved by default unless the full set of roles associated with it appear in the `omit-deps` parameter of the API specification parameter file.

If a program element is flagged for omission, program statements are removed but variable declarations are preserved. This allows the API call to remain syntactically correct by having its full set of parameters available. A consequence of this is that initialization code may be removed, which can be particularly problematic in the case of variables with pointer types. The `initializer` directive can be used to provide initial values for declarations, as well as the use of the `preserve` to keep whatever amount of setup and initialization code that the user of the tool determines to be necessary. We also have additional directives that can be used by the user to replace conditional tests with probabilistic tests that can be driven by branch probability information obtained by dynamic analysis of the original program (e.g., via trace collection).

5. EXPERIMENTAL SETUP

Evaluation of the semi-automated skeleton extraction approach that we designed is approached by direct comparison under simulation to the original program. As discussed earlier, simulation of the original program is expected to be more time consuming than simulation of the skeleton. We

[1]Due to a limitation in current versions of ROSE, floating point constants cannot be specified directly within the pragmas. Constants must be expressed as rational numbers, such as 12345/100000 in place of 0.12345.

selected three simple programs for study that were small enough to enable manual examination of the generated skeletons.

5.1 Simulation Environment

Simulation was performed using the SST/macro simulator, which required minimal modifications to the skeletons that did not affect their functionality. The first change is including SST /macro-specific header files in place of the MPI header files, so that traffic is routed through the simulator and not the host machine. This code modification does not affect the skeleton code since the SST/macro's MPI interface is nearly identical to the original MPI interface [8]. The second change is renaming the *main* function to *user_skeleton_main*, which is called by the simulator after it has started up. The simulator provides a *makefile* which can be used to build the skeleton and generate an executable, linking against the simulator core. In addition, SST/macro provides a configuration file containing a set of basic simulation parameters such as network parameters, node parameters, and application parameters. These parameter choices allow for the tailoring of architecture characteristics and model approximations.

5.2 Target Applications

To demonstrate the practical use and accuracy of our approach we studied the following HPC proxy applications (implemented in C):

1. The HPCCG application [7] implementing the conjugate gradient method for solving a linear system.
2. A simple implementation of the Fast Fourier Transform (FFT) algorithm.
3. A 2D Jacobi iteration implementation.

MPI is used in all three applications to implement their communication model. The Jacobi iteration program that solves Laplace's equation is a simple representative of programs that utilize simple stencil-based iterative methods. The HPCCG program solves a more complex system based on a 3D diffusion problem using a 27 point implicit finite difference scheme. The FFT algorithm is a basic implementation in which a data set of size N where N is a power of two is decomposed into N/p element subproblems that are solved on p processors, with collective communication operators used to exchange their results before completing the computation. This set of test cases represents varying communication patterns (both point-to-point and collective), and exhibit different granularities of local computations that are performed between communication operations.

Each program is transformed by our skeleton generation tool after the introduction of annotations to aid the program slicing process. In some cases, preprocessor directives containing macros (`#define`) are replaced with static variables to prevent expansion during the skeleton creation. The original macros are restored before using the skeletons with SST/macro. This does not change the structure of the skeleton, and is a current workaround due to the expansion of preprocessor directives before analysis within ROSE. The code generator used by our current implementation is not aware of preprocessor directives and is therefore unable to replace their expansion in the AST with their original un-expanded form in the resulting skeleton code. Each program has been directly executed before skeletonization in SST/macro in order to collect runtime tracing information. We use the trace file execution logs to validate the accuracy of our skeleton-driven simulation approach.

Table 1: HPCCG - MPI event count

Function	Application	Skeleton
`MPI_Init`	128	128
`MPI_Send`	38862	38862
`MPI_Irecv`	38862	38862
`MPI_Wait`	38862	38862
`MPI_Allreduce`	38912	38912
`MPI_Finalize`	128	128

6. RESULTS

Here we present our experimental validation of the derived program skeletons' correctness against the application from which they are derived. The validation is done by comparing binary traces of both the application and the skeleton. We then explore the scalability of the skeletons under simulation with respect to the original applications via SST/macro.

6.1 Validation of Program Skeleton Correctness using DUMPI Traces

Skeleton correctness is of utmost importance in studying the scalability of an application using skeleton-driven approach. In order to use a skeleton in place of an application for scalability studies, the runtime behavior of the skeleton has to match the application's behavior both in terms of control flow and communication pattern.

Our approach relies on deriving this information from a binary trace that captures control flow and communication pattern in sufficient detail. However, the trace might vary according to the set of inputs the program receives and the network model setup on the simulator. This is due to the execution of branch statements that make program behavior depend on the set of inputs provided as well as the intermediate runtime values that the program calculates. As such, for each evaluation on the simulator, the inputs and hardware/network parameters are kept constant for both the application and the skeleton when trace files are generated.

The binary trace we generate is in DUMPI format, a custom MPI trace file format developed as part of the SST/macro simulator. The trace records MPI events with full signature of MPI calls, return values and MPI request information [4]. A trace is collected for each run of the full application and for the skeleton execution on the simulator. SST/macro also ships with a set of trace analysis tools, which produce an XML file that contain statistical MPI trace comparison information grouped together under different tags. In order to match the skeleton with the application, we compared DUMPI trace reports generated from trace files of both the skeleton and the application.

Tables 1, 2, and 3 show the number of times an MPI event occurs during the execution of the application and the skeleton. The results shown in the tables are derived from the DUMPI trace report. The MPI events are grouped by the function name and the count is shown for each function.

The number of MPI events that occur in an application are determined by the evaluation of different branch conditions and the number of iterations the loops undergo. For

Table 2: FFT - MPI event count

Function	Application	Skeleton
MPI_Init	16	16
MPI_Barrier	16	16
MPI_Gather	16	16
MPI_Scatter	16	16
MPI_Alltoall	16	16
MPI_Finalize	16	16

Table 3: Jacobi - MPI event count

Function	Application	Skeleton
MPI_Init	16	16
MPI_ISend	4800	4800
MPI_Irecv	4800	4800
MPI_Wait	9600	9600
MPI_Barrier	16	16
MPI_Finalize	16	16

a skeleton to match the application in terms of control flow and loop behavior, the number of MPI events (grouped by MPI function) that occur in both the program and its skeleton must be equal (or relatively close to equal). The trace files we derived in our experimental evaluation (as shown in Tables 1, 2, and 3) show that for each MPI function call, the number of events corresponding to the application and skeleton are essentially the same. This demonstrates the correctness of our skeleton extraction mechanism, with skeletons exhibiting the same behavior as that of the corresponding application. The communication pattern is determined by the point-to-point and collective MPI routines in the program. These MPI routines always occur in pairs with one process/rank sending the data and another process/rank receiving the data or all processes participating in the collective operations. One way to match the skeleton with the application in terms of communication patterns is to check whether the data transmitted by each rank match. The tables 4, 5, and 6 show the data transmitted in bytes by each rank and the total data transmitted in bytes both for the skeleton and the application. The results shown in the tables are derived from the DUMPI trace report.

Table 4: HPCCG - Bytes transmitted by each rank

Rank	Application	Skeleton
0	769020	769020
1 to 126	1.09772e+06	1.09772e+06
127	769020	769020
Total	1.39851e+08	1.39851e+08

Table 5: FFT - Bytes transmitted by each rank

Rank	Application	Skeleton
0	6.0398e+08	6.0398e+08
1 to 15	6.71089e+07	6.71089e+07
Total	1.61061e+09	1.61061e+09

The results shown in Tables 4, 5, and 6 demonstrate that skeletons exhibit similar communication patterns to the corresponding applications with each rank transmitting

Table 6: Jacobi - Bytes transmitted by each rank

Rank	Application	Skeleton
0,3,12,15	400000	400000
1,2,4,7,8,11,13,14	600000	600000
5,6,9,10	800000	800000
Total	9.6e+06	9.6e+06

the same number of bytes. The DUMPI trace report also contains a transmission matrix, which shows the amount of communication between all ranks. These were compared for the full application and skeleton, and for readability, Table 7 presents the results for 3 ranks (out of a total of 128 ranks). We found a one-to-one matching between each skeleton and the application transmission matrices, indicating that not only was the overall message count consistent but the pairwise message count between ranks was as well.

Table 7: Example transmission matrix for three ranks (out of 128) from the DUMPI trace report.

SrcDest	Rank_0	Rank_1	Rank_2...
Rank_0	3440	332140	3440
Rank_1	332140	3440	332140
Rank_2	3440	332140	3440

Examination of the transmission matrix is necessary to ensure that the skeleton did not exhibit a significantly altered messaging pattern. Failure to initialize variables correctly in the skeleton could cause this to occur, such as all ranks communicating to rank zero instead of their intended destination rank. In this case, the aggregate message count would be equal between the skeleton and the application, but the transmission matrix would indicate a significant deviation in the messaging pattern between the two at the rank pair level.

6.2 Scalability

In this section, we discuss how skeletons scale with respect to their corresponding applications. We compare the total execution time of a skeleton- driven simulation versus a simulation driven by the program's direct execution. In addition, we study the efficiency of our automatic skeletonization process by comparing the performance of our HPCCG automatically generated skeleton against an optimized handwritten skeleton of HPCCG developed during a previous study with SST/macro.

Figure 2 shows our experimental evaluation of both HPCCG skeletons. Careful inspection revealed that some routines in the auto- generated skeleton files remained unaltered with respect to the parent program because of statistical dependencies, leaving in some code that could have been removed. Both skeletons exhibit significant speedup over the full application, and the auto-generated one appears to scale well as the number of processors grows.

Figure 3 shows the speedup of the auto-generated FFT skeleton over its parent application. The implementation that we considered is a simple sequence of computations where each processor performs a local computation that is distributed via collective communications to other processors, followed by a final computation that combines the results computed locally with those computed remotely. Our

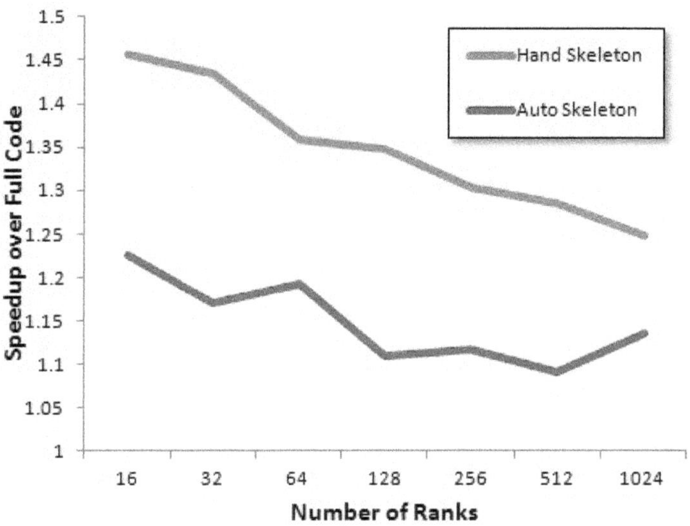

Figure 2: HPCCG - Speedup over application of hand written skeleton vs. autogenerated skeleton

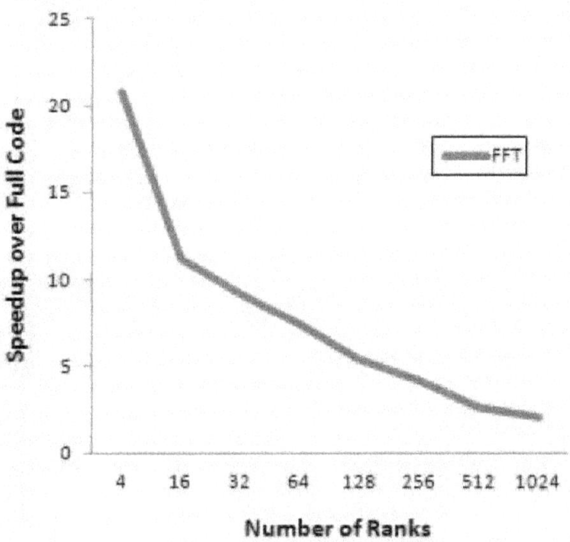

Figure 3: FFT - Speedup of autogenerated skeleton over application

skeleton generator was successful in removing all the computational steps, leaving only the collective communication operations, thus comparison to a hand-written version is not needed. As processor count grows, the cost of simulating collectives grows super-linearly, decreasing the savings we see from the skeletonization process. Also, the problem was strong-scaled, reducing the amount of computation per processor as processor count grows.

Figure 4 shows the speedup of the auto generated Jacobi skeleton over its parent application. The skeleton demonstrates a consistent speedup of about 2 over its parent program with a gradual increase in the speedup with the increase in the number of processes.

All skeletons we explored demonstrated performance gains

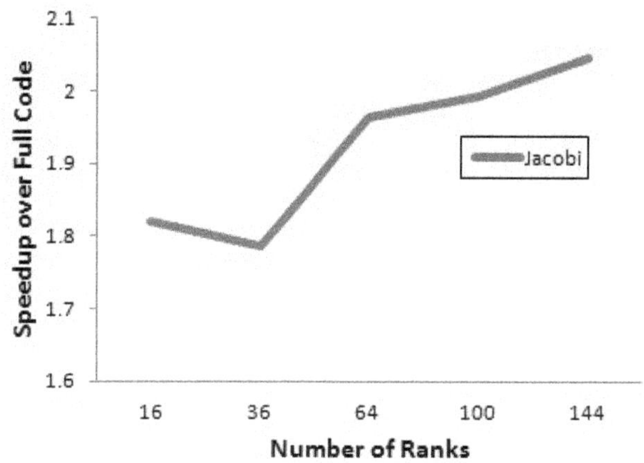

Figure 4: Jacobi - Speedup of autogenerated skeleton over application

when compared to their parent applications while at the same time preserving the application's behavior and correctness characteristics. The performance gain is the result of eliminating code that forms the computational part of the program and is not required to ensure that MPI operations execute correctly (e.g., buffer allocation code). If there is a significant reduction in the time spent in code unrelated to message passing in the skeleton, we observe significant performance gains in the skeleton relative to the parent program. In some cases where the computational load decreases as the processor count increases, we see scaling drop as the parent program performs less work per processor leading to less overhead in the parent application due to computation. This is true for our FFT example, in which a fixed problem size was decomposed across a set of processors such that as the processor count increases, the per-processor problem size decreases. In other cases where the problem size per processor is fixed regardless of the processor count (e.g., the Jacobi iteration example), the scaling of the skeleton versus the parent application would be a function of both this computational overhead along with the communication-specific scaling behavior.

Given that the canonical examples we studied in this work represent some of the core computational solver methods employed by many HPC applications, we expect that our automatic skeletonization tool can provide a direct benefit for the study of large-scale HPC codes. We also expect the results presented here to be a lower-bound on the savings achieved from skeletonization, given that these codes have relatively little computation to begin with.

7. CONCLUSIONS

In this paper we presented a methodology based on static analysis for generating program skeletons for large-scale performance analysis. We demonstrate that dependency analysis augmented with dependency role information allows slicing techniques to be controlled by the user of the skeleton generator. Compiler directives allow the tool user to convey information to the algorithm that cannot be inferred automatically (or, cannot be inferred easily). Our experiments show that an iterative process of skeleton generation and injection of directives provides a relatively straightforward approach to skeleton creation versus completely manual techniques.

Our results illustrate that under the SST/macro simulator, the program skeletons being small in size execute faster than the original applications that they were derived from, while still giving an accurate estimation of original application's behavior. The results strongly show that program analysis is an effective strategy to generate skeletons which can be used to evaluate the scalability of large-scale parallel applications. Our static analysis approach is effective in reducing the time to create the skeleton as well as reducing the likelihood of errors being accidentally introduced during manual skeleton creation. The skeleton driven simulation of applications can be extended to accurately study the effect of varying hardware design parameters such as number of nodes, processors per node, network topology, memory bandwidth and latency on the scalability of an application.

8. ACKNOWLEDGEMENTS

Sandia National Laboratories is a multiprogram laboratory operated by Sandia Corporation, a Lockheed Martin Company, for the United States Department of Energy's National Nuclear Security Administration under contract DE-AC04- 94AL85000.

9. REFERENCES

[1] V. S. Adve, R. Bagrodia, E. Deelman, and R. Sakellariou. Compiler-optimized simulation of large-scale applications on high performance architectures. *Journal of Parallel and Distributed Computing*, 62(3):393–426, March 2002.

[2] D. H. Bailey, E. Barszcz, J. T. Barton, D. S. Browning, R. L. Carter, L. Dagum, R. A. Fatoohi, P. O. Frederickson, T. A. Lasinski, R. S. Schreiber, H. D. Simon, V. Venkatakrishnan, and S. K. Weeratunga. The NAS parallel benchmarks–summary and preliminary results. In *Proceedings of the 1991 ACM/IEEE conference on Supercomputing* Supercomputing '91, pages 158–165, New York, NY, USA, 1991. ACM.

[3] J. Dongarra, T. Hey, and E. Strohmaier. PARKBENCH: Methodology, Relations and Results. In H. M. Liddell, A. Colbrook, L. O. Hertzberger, and P. M. A. Sloot, editors, *HPCN Europe*, volume 1067 of *Lecture Notes in Computer Science*, pages 770–777. Springer, 1996.

[4] C. L. Janssen, H. Adalsteinsson, S. Cranford, J. P. Kenny, A. Pinar, D. A. Evensky, and J. Mayo. A simulator for large-scale parallel architectures. *International Journal of Parallel and Distributed Systems*, 1(2):57–73, 2010.

[5] Lawrence Livermore National Laboratory. ROSE Compiler. `http://www.roseCompiler.org`

[6] R. Preissl, M. Schulz, D. Kranzlmüller, B. R. de Supinski, and D. J. Quinlan. Using MPI Communication Patterns to Guide Source Code Transformations. In *Proceedings of the 8th International Conference on Computational Science (ICCS)*, pages 253–260. Springer-Verlag, 2008.

[7] Sandia National Laboratories. HPCCG. `http://bec.syr.edu/hpccg.html`.

[8] Sandia National Laboratories. The Structural Simulation Toolkit. `http://sst.sandia.gov/`

[9] J. Shalf, D. Quinlan, and C. Janssen. Rethinking hardware-software codesign for exascale systems. *IEEE Computer*, 44(11):22–30, Nov. 2011.

[10] J. Subhlok and Q. Xu. Automatic construction of coordinated performance skeletons. In *Proceedings of the 2008 IEEE International Symposium on Parallel and Distributed Processing (IPDPS)*, pages 1–5, April 2008.

A Generic Adaptive Simulation Algorithm for Component-based Simulation Systems

Tobias Helms
Albert-Einstein-Str. 22
University of Rostock
18059 Rostock, Germany
tobias.helms@uni-rostock.de

Roland Ewald
Albert-Einstein-Str. 22
University of Rostock
18059 Rostock, Germany
roland.ewald@uni-rostock.de

Stefan Rybacki
Albert-Einstein-Str. 22
University of Rostock
18059 Rostock, Germany
stefan.rybacki@uni-rostock.de

Adelinde M. Uhrmacher
Albert-Einstein-Str. 22
University of Rostock
18059 Rostock, Germany
adelinde.uhrmacher@uni-rostock.de

ABSTRACT

The state of a model may strongly vary during simulation, and with it also the simulation's computational demands. Adapting the simulation algorithm to these demands at runtime can therefore improve the overall performance. Although this is a general and cross-cutting concern, only few simulation systems offer re-usable support for this kind of runtime adaptation. We present a flexible and generic mechanism for the runtime adaptation of component-based simulation algorithms. It encapsulates simulation algorithms applicable to a given problem and employs reinforcement learning to explore the algorithms' suitability during a simulation run. We evaluate the approach by executing models from two modeling formalisms used in computational biology.

Categories and Subject Descriptors

I.6.8 [**Simulation and Modeling**]: Types of Simulation—*Adaptive Simulation*; I.2.6 [**Artificial Intelligence**]: Learning—*Reinforcement Learning*

Keywords

Adaptive Algorithms, Component-based Simulation Software, Reinforcement Learning

1. INTRODUCTION

The performance of simulation algorithms (SAs) often varies over simulation runs. Consider the example in Figure 1, which shows the performance of two SAs during the execution of a sample model. While SA A exhibits a better performance during the first and the third quarter of the simulation, SA B achieves a better performance during the second and the fourth quarter of the simulation. This effect is due to changes in the computational load imposed by the model. This could be, for example, a changing number of model entities, other kinds of events to be processed, or structural changes within the model. Another reason could be changes in the execution environment, such as a change in the number of available processors, CPU load from other jobs, or changes in the network latency. Obviously, runtime adaption is required to reach peak performance in such situations.

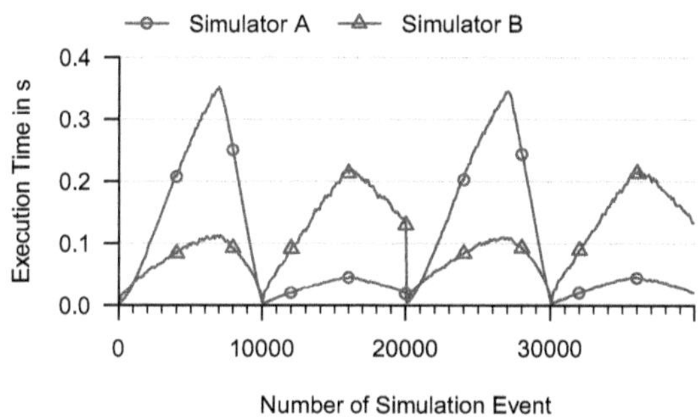

Figure 1: Execution times of two simulation algorithm setups for an ML-Rules benchmark model (see Sec. 5.4.1). Each data point shows the execution time summed over 100 simulation events.

Adaptation mechanisms are already widely used in the area of simulation, e.g., for continuous simulations or parallel discrete event simulations (PDES) [29, 8]. Yet, many of these adaptation mechanisms are tailored to a specific algorithm and merely adapt its parameters to improve the performance, e.g., Adaptive MTW [3]. Those algorithms are typically based on dividing a simulation into phases, i.e., sequences of simulation steps, where the optimal SA does not change and with which specific requirements are associated,

SIGSIM-PADS'13, May 19–22, 2013, Montréal, Québec, Canada.

e.g., [29]. The challenge of an adaptive mechanism is to determine such phases and to adapt the SA so that an optimal performance is achieved in each phase. An adaptive SA thus requires for each simulation phase performance estimates for all available SAs or heuristics to make an informed decision. Moreover, runtime adaptation also implies additional computational costs, so that the gains by adapting SAs have to be balanced with the increased effort.

To address these problems in a more general manner that allows the re-use of adaptation mechanisms across simulation domains, we present a generic adaptive SA called the adaptive simulator. It is neither restricted to a specific SA, nor is it restricted to adjusting algorithm parameters. Instead, it relies on configurations of existing SAs as a set of options to choose from. Such sets of options can also be generated automatically, so that the adaption at runtime is transparent to users and does not require additional configuration by them. With techniques from reinforcement learning [35], the adaptive simulator learns, based on a target function, which configuration of which SA suits which phase of the simulation best.

The next section discusses the concept of adaptive algorithms in general and reviews some adaptation mechanisms already applied in simulation. Section 3 develops our approach towards a generic adaptive simulator. After describing some implementation details (Sec. 4), we evaluate our implementation on two groups of SAs with customized benchmark models and realistic sample models (Sec. 5).

2. BACKGROUND AND RELATED WORK

Adaptation techniques can be used to change parameters and components of an algorithm so that it always suits the requirements of its environment [27]. Therefore, an adaptive algorithm can outperform the best available non-adaptive algorithm. Two types of adaptations are typically distinguished [27]: parameter adaptation and compositional adaptation. Whereas parameter adaptation allows to change algorithm parameters, compositional adaptation allows to change the structure of the algorithm. The latter often provides mechanisms to cope with a dynamic set of available components, which also requires to deal with erroneous or malicious components. Broadly speaking, compositional adaptation is more flexible, but also makes it more difficult to validate the behavior of the algorithm. However, the line between parametric and compositional adaptation is often blurry. For example, consider an adaptive sorting algorithm that uses an auxiliary algorithm to sort sub-lists. If the auxiliary algorithm is selected from a fixed set of options, we would regard it as a parameter of the adaptive sorting algorithm, while others may regard this as compositional adaptation.

Developers of adaptive algorithms often struggle to decide which adaptation action to choose in which situation. This problem can be addressed with techniques from machine learning. Reinforcement learning [35] is particularly well-suited to this task, as it operates in an incremental manner and does not require a training set that includes successful candidates of the concept to be learned. In the reinforcement learning setting, an agent perceives the state of a (non-deterministic) environment and then decides which action to execute for achieving some goal, e.g., to reach a specific state of the environment. The goal is encoded in numerical rewards the agent receives from the environment after each decision.[1] Then, the whole procedure is repeated, i.e., the new state of the environment is perceived and the agent has to decide upon its next action. The agent's task is to maximize the reward it receives overall, typically without any prior knowledge on the actions' effects, on the desirability of certain environment states (in terms of rewards), or on the transition probabilities between states. Thus, the agent has to *explore* the actions and the states of its environment, but it also has to *exploit* its (incrementally growing) knowledge to increase its reward, so that eventually the best action is chosen in any given situation. An adaptive SA based on this learning paradigm will therefore continuously re-configure itself to the computational problems it encounters and requires no intervention by the user.

Along these lines, Armstrong et al. [1] introduce a general scheme for adaptive algorithms that employs reinforcement learning in the same manner: an 'optimization system' collects sensor data (i.e., features of the input data), invokes a reinforcement learning algorithm, and executes its decisions (i.e., which algorithm to use). The (negated) execution time of the selected algorithm serves as reward. Their system relies on a mechanism to modify binary code at runtime. As a proof of concept, they let it switch dynamically between two auxiliary algorithms for a computational chemistry simulation and show how this improves the overall execution time. Lagoudakis et al. [23] presented a similar approach for sorting algorithms. While we follow the same basic approach, we strive to take it a step further. Firstly, we integrate it into a component-based simulation system that offers many more adaptation options. Even rather simple learning schemes may improve the performance when there are just two (as in [1]) or three (as in [23]) possible actions, but it is still unclear how well this scales to more actions. Secondly, our approach is tailored toward simulations. There are several simulation-specific aspects, such as the observation of simulation output or the repeatability of simulation runs, that need to be considered and for which our approach offers additional support.

Synchronization algorithms for parallel discrete event simulation (PDES) can be conservative, optimistic or hybrid (e.g., [5, 8]). Conservative algorithms only allow a logical process (LP) to process safe events and thus the parallelism may not be fully exploited. Optimistic algorithms also process unsafe events, but need rollback mechanisms to prevent incorrect results and thus may process many events unnecessarily. Hybrid protocols allow the LPs to compute unsafe events, but only if some additional conditions are satisfied. For example, the moving time window (MTW) protocol [34] limits the optimism of the LPs by only allowing to process events within the time interval $[GVT, GVT+\omega]$, where ω is a parameter and GVT is the global virtual time [11]. The performance of these algorithms depends on the phase the simulation is in [29]. Consequently, many adaptive algorithms have been implemented to cope with changing runtime environments and changing model characteristics. For example, the Adaptive MTW algorithm adapts ω to minimize the wall-clock time an LP is either blocking or processing rollbacks [3]. Another example is the Adaptive Bounded Time Windows protocol [31], which is also based on the MTW protocol and adapts the time window size ω for each LP, depending on its rate of committed events during the last

[1]Formally, this is a Markov decision process.

GVT cycle. Both adaptive algorithms realize a parameter adaptation, as they always adapt exactly one parameter.

Another important class of algorithms for PDES are load balancing algorithms (e.g., [5, 8]). Here, processor and communication load are two important metrics. Load balancing algorithms try to balance both values, but usually the more balanced the processor load is, the more unbalanced is the communication load (and vice versa). This is why load balancing algorithms must find a trade-off between a balanced processor and communication load. Which trade-off results in the best overall performance depends on the phase of the simulation, so that adaptive load balancing algorithms have been developed. For example, the adaptive load balancing algorithm in [28] realizes a selection mechanism that repeatedly chooses from two non-adaptive load-balancing algorithms: one balances the processor load and one balances the communication load. This approach in [28] uses reinforcement learning for the adaptation.

Various other adaptive schemes have been developed for specific PDES tasks (e.g., state saving [37]) or specific application areas (e.g., multi-agent systems [24]). Most adaptive PDES algorithms are tightly coupled to a particular SA (e.g., MTW [3])). While this allows them to exploit the full potential for performance improvement, it also requires considerable implementation and testing efforts. In contrast, we focus on a generic adaptation mechanism that shall be reusable *without* modifications of SA code, and with minimal additional work. Instead of being part of the logic of an SA to realize parametric adaptation, it works on top of an SA and realizes compositional adaptation. Consequently, it must be able to cope with a dynamic set of options. Finally, note that many PDES adaptation schemes work in a decentralized manner, whereas we assume a central point of decision-making.[2]

However, adaptations during single runs are not always beneficial. For example, adaptive algorithms are a well-known technique for continuous simulations [7, p. 101 ff.]. The step-size and the order of the integration method are the two most important parameters that influence the performance and accuracy of continuous simulations. Both parameters motivated the application of adaptive algorithms, namely step-size control algorithms and order-control algorithms. Whereas step-size control algorithms have shown to be efficient, order-control algorithms have not [7, p. 106].

3. A GENERIC ADAPTIVE SIMULATOR

The adaptive simulator is realized as a wrapper for other SAs, following the suggestion by McKinley et al. [27]. Consequently, it uses another SA to compute all state transitions of the model and at some times adapts this internal SA, i.e., changes its parameters or exchanges it completely with another SA. With the help of reinforcement learning techniques, the adaptive simulator learns which internal SA to use in which model state. The usage of reinforcement learning enables it to realize a form of compositional adaptation, because its decision process is not fixed to a static number of available internal SAs. Since a single simulation run may involve many individual events (or steps), it is also important to learn how often the adaptation should take place.

[2] This does not exclude PDES algorithms from our approach per se, since the decisions of the central agent may still be transferred to other physical processors.

Algorithm 1 Pseudo-code for the adaptive simulator (extended from [33, p. 776]).
Q: q-value matrix indexed by state $s \in S$ and action $a \in A$.
N: matrix of counters for visited (s, a) tuples.
$s, s' \in S$: previous and current state.
$a = (cs, ac) \in A$: action, consisting of internal SA (cs) and adaptation condition (ac).
$r \in \mathbb{R}$: reward.
$\sigma \in \Sigma$: current base state.
$\tau \in \Sigma^*$: current base state trajectory (seq. of base states).

```
1  s := s0
2  a := (cs0 ,ac0)
3  initialize(cs0)
4  repeat { //Adaptation loop
5          N[s,a] := N[s,a] + 1
6          τ := []
7          repeat { //Simulation loop
8                  simulate_next_event(a.cs)
9                  σ := observe_state(a.cs)
10                 τ := τ + σ
11         } until a.ac(τ)
12         r := R(τ) //Calculate reward
13         //Preprocess base state trajectory:
14         s' := p(τ)
15         //Q-learning:
16         Q[s,a] := Q[s,a] + alpha(N[s,a])·
17                   (r + γ · max_a' Q[s',a'] − Q[s,a])
18         s := s'
19         //Select next action based on s,Q,N:
20         a_next := f(s,Q,N)
21         //Adapt internal SA:
22         a := (adapt(a.cs, a_next.cs, σ),a_next.ac)
23 } until is_terminal(s)
```

Adapting an SA after every event, for example, may introduce a significant overhead, while adapting too rarely may waste computing time using sub-optimal SAs and may also slow down the exploration of potentially better alternatives.

Algorithm 1 shows the basic structure of the adaptive simulator's algorithm, which is based on the Q-learning algorithm [35]. Q-learning is a temporal-difference learning method, because it estimates the utility of a state s by also considering the estimated utility of the successor state s'. Temporal-difference learning is a model-free reinforcement learning strategy, i.e., it does not require any prior knowledge on the environment's state transitions. In contrast to Monte-Carlo approaches, which are also model-free, temporal-difference learning is not restricted to learning from episodes (i.e., sequences of states) and often converges faster in practice [35, p. 139]. Q-learning learns how valuable it is to take an action $a \in A$ in a state $s \in S$; these so-called q-values are given by a function $Q(s, a)$ that is unknown from the onset and gets refined step by step. In the simple case, $Q(s, a)$ is represented as an $|S| \times |A|$ matrix. The higher the q-value for a state and an action, the better it is to take this action in this state. For updating the q-value of the previous state and the selected action, Q-learning uses the old q-value, the received reward, and the best q-value of the current state, i.e., $max_{a' \in A} Q[s', a']$ multiplied by the discount factor γ (see line 14, Algorithm 1). The discount factor determines the influence of possible future utilities on the current q-value. The function $\alpha(N[s,a])$ (l. 14) determines the learning rate, i.e., the impact of new updates for the q-value, depending on how often action a has already been chosen in state s (which is stored in N). The result is typically a value between zero and one, and tends towards zero the more knowledge is available, i.e., the higher $N[s,a]$ is. The function $f : S \times \mathbb{R}^{|S|\times|A|} \times \mathbb{N}^{|S|\times|A|} \rightarrow A$ (l. 16) represents the policy (see [35]) responsible for action selection. Broadly speaking, it balances greed (based on Q, i.e., a preference to exploit the available knowledge and choose actions that promise a high utility) and curiosity (based on N, i.e., a preference to explore the effect of actions that have so far been chosen rarely in the current state).

To use this basic Q-Learning algorithm for the adaptive simulator, it has to be embedded in the context of SAs. The algorithm's outer loop (lines 4–18) covers the adaptive execution of a single simulation run, while the algorithm's inner loop (lines 7–11) covers the simulation between two adaptations, i.e., one step of reinforcement learning. The goal of the adaptive simulator is to maximize its received rewards, i.e., to maximize the performance of a single simulation run. During each execution of a simulation event, data of the model (e.g., values of state variables, the number of model components, or the coupling structure), data about the internal SA (e.g., the number of events triggered, the length of an event queue, or the usage of data structures), and the environment (e.g., the number of cores available or the memory load) can be collected. The tuple of all these data collected represents a so-called base state $\sigma \in \Sigma$. Clearly, Σ is high-dimensional and thus can hardly be used for reinforcement learning, in particular since all base states between two adaptation actions have to be considered as a whole. These base states hence define a base state trajectory $\tau \in \Sigma^*$:

$$\tau = \sigma_1\sigma_2 \ldots \sigma_n$$

Base state trajectories are used to derive states of a much smaller state space S, which represents the environment for the reinforcement learning. To do so, we follow [1] and introduce a preprocessor function $p : \Sigma^* \rightarrow S$ that aggregates a trajectory $\tau \in \Sigma^*$ to a state $s \in S$. As not all states of the environment are distinguishable anymore, we now deal with a partially observable Markov decision process.

To account for the task of learning not only *how* to adapt the simulation, but also *when*, we define an action $a \in A$ as a pair of a configuration of an SA, $cs \in CS$, and an adaptation condition, $ac \in AC$: $A = CS \times AC$. SA configurations $cs \in CS$ can be represented by trees. Each node corresponds to an algorithm, the node's children to its sub-algorithms, and so on. Algorithm parameters are defined via node labels, e.g., in form of (key, value) pairs. Adaptation conditions $ac \in AC$ can be defined as functions $ac : \Sigma^* \rightarrow \{true, false\}$. For example, the result of an adaptation condition could depend on the length of τ, a drastic change in model dynamics, or the amount of wall-clock time that has passed since the last adaptation (this could be encoded as environment data in Σ). Thus, choosing an action determines which configuration shall be used until the next adaptation, and also under which conditions the next adaptation is triggered. In some sense, an action therefore encodes a very simple adaptation policy in its own, which does nothing unless the adaptation condition ac is fulfilled and then hands over control to the adaptive simulator. This is similar to the notion of subroutines (or primitive operators) that are used in hierarchical reinforcement learning (e.g., see [4]). Rewards are computed with a function $R : \Sigma^* \rightarrow \mathbb{R}$, i.e., the reward calculation bases also on base state trajectories. This is done because the preprocessor might manipulate, aggregate or remove information that are required for reward computation. If the execution time or the used memory are integrated into the reward function, it should also consider the overhead caused by the `adapt` procedure, which executes an adaptation.

A major challenge for realizing the adaptive simulator as outlined in Algorithm 1 is that the correctness of the simulation results for all used SA configurations have to be warranted. Another potential source of errors is the adaptation process itself: a valid transition between old and new internal SAs has to be ensured. Therefore, section 3.2 discusses how the `adapt` procedure (l. 17) can be realized so that necessary state information is handed over from one internal SA to another. Besides this, the preprocessing (l. 13) is a crucial and application-dependent part of the algorithm.

3.1 Preprocessing

The set of collectible data for a base state σ may vary during a simulation. For example, if model components are created or removed, more or less data could be collected. Moreover, internal SAs may differ in their structure and hence may expose different statistics. Therefore, the preprocessor function $p : \Sigma^* \rightarrow S$ also has to deal with missing values in the base states $\sigma \in \Sigma$. Defining a suitable preprocessor function p is crucial for the success of the adaptive simulator: it has to aggregate data from the base state trajectories so that the state space S for reinforcement learning remains manageable. A large state space S is not desirable, as it increases the efforts required to learn a useful adaptation policy. Thus, the preprocessor p should remove any data that are unlikely to have a major impact on the decisions of the adaptive simulator. To identify such data, one could use methods for sensitivity analysis or feature selection [22]. Even relevant data should typically be preprocessed and merged, e.g., the preprocessor could calculate running averages or discretize numeric values into categories like {`small`, `medium`, `high`}. All in all, preprocessors can be used to reduce the state space and tailor it to the specific requirements of an experiment, so that the effort to learn the optimal policy is minimized as well as all phases of the simulation can be determined.

For example, a trivial preprocessor would map all possible trajectories to a single state, so that $|S| = 1$. Such a preprocessor would reduce the learning problem to a multi-armed bandit setting [2], which is a non-associative variant of the general reinforcement learning problem [35]. This problem is much easier to solve than reinforcement learning in general, since the state of the environment can be neglected when estimating the utility of an action. Nevertheless, different phases of the simulation cannot be distinguished any more.

3.2 Adaptation Actions

In general, the number of actions should be as small as possible: the more actions there are to choose from, the longer it takes the adaptive simulator to explore and exploit the most useful adaptations. One way to reduce the number of actions would be to select algorithm portfolios [16], i.e., subsets $P \subseteq CS$ of the available SA configurations. This may even be done at runtime by inspecting $Q(s, a)$, since a good portfolio should simply contain at least one well-performing SA configuration for each state $s \in S$. Alternatively, users may have additional knowledge regarding the model to be simulated or regarding certain SAs, so that the possibility to filter out elements of CS needs to be provided.

Besides the SA configuration $cs \in CS$, an action also defines an adaptation condition ac. As mentioned before, adaptation conditions enable the adaptive simulator to also adapt the adaptation frequency, e.g., to let it match the rate of simulation phase changes. In any case, adaptations should not be triggered too often. Besides the overhead of executing the outer loop in Algorithm 1, this may also bias learning: SAs can have warm-up phases, so that advantages of these algorithms are only noticeable after having processed several simulation events in a row. If adaptations are executed too often, the actual performance of such algorithms would never be noticed, although they might improve the overall performance significantly. However, with a set of suitable adaptation conditions, the adaptive simulator will automatically learn the optimal trade-off between minimizing the number of adaptations and using the optimal SA for each simulation phase.

Several mechanisms are possible to realize the `adapt` procedure in Algorithm 1. One way is to determine the differences between old and new internal SA, and to adapt the old SA only at those points (i.e., parameters, sub-algorithms) where it is necessary. This procedure is useful if the old and the new internal SA only differ in a few aspects that can be changed easily. On the other hand, this procedure must guarantee that the new internal SA has a valid state, i.e., new algorithms must be initialized properly and data structures must be checked and possibly adjusted if parameters are changed. To avoid these problems, another way to realize adaptation is to exchange the internal SA completely. Thus, the newly selected SA can simply use the current state of the model to initialize itself properly. While being more expensive, this approach does not burden developers with the additional complexity of dealing with differing state representations and formats. Instead, *any* SA can be used in this manner. Furthermore, the adaptive simulator does not need to determine the differences between old and new SA anymore, a process that may prove expensive (and error-prone) in itself.

4. IMPLEMENTATION

The adaptive simulator is integrated into the modeling and simulation framework JAMES II [20]. JAMES II is plug-in based, which means that all components are provided by plug-ins and the availability of plug-ins may vary over time. Plug-ins are organized by plug-in types: all plug-ins of a type generate the same kind of component (e.g., random number generators or event queues), which can be accessed via a common interface. A plug-in provides a description of its parameters and the types of plug-ins it requires to carry out sub-tasks. With this information, one can compute all possible SA configurations automatically, i.e., all combinations of available plug-ins and their parameter spaces (see [10]).

The adaptive simulator is implemented as a wrapper for SAs, i.e., it uses an SA to compute the next simulation event (line 8, Algorithm 1) and exchanges or adapts it as needed. With respect to the simulation system, however, it fulfills the same contract as all other SAs (e.g., regarding stopping criteria or observation components), and thus can be used transparently. The strict separation of model and simulator in JAMES II allows the adaptive simulator to implement the simple but robust `adapt` method described in section 3.2, i.e., to just replace the internal SA during an adaptation. Since models and SAs can be accessed via general interfaces specified by JAMES II, both the wrapping and the adaptation procedure are implemented in a formalism-independent way. This enables a loose coupling between the adaptive simulator and the SAs it works with.

Following the plug-in concept of JAMES II [20], most tasks of the adaptive simulator are delegated to plug-ins as well, so that it can be easily extended and configured to user requirements. Three plug-in types refer to the basic reinforcement learning scheme. Firstly, one plug-in type represents the learning algorithm as such (l. 14, Algorithm 1), i.e., the adaptive simulator is not restricted to Q-Learning. While the parameter γ of this plug-in can be set by the user, we set the parameter $\alpha = \frac{1}{N[s,a]}$, as suggested in [35]. Secondly, one plug-in type represents the function $f : S \times \mathbb{R}^{|S| \times |A|} \times \mathbb{N}^{|S| \times |A|} \rightarrow A$ (l. 16), which realizes the action selection (based on the matrix Q of q-values and the counter N of visited (s, a) tuples) and determines the trade-off between exploration and exploitation. Besides implementing some standard policies (see Sec. 5), we implemented a policy which selects an action based on a predefined sequence independently from the q-values. Such predefined sequence can be used to reproduce a simulation of the adaptive simulator. The third plug-in type was created to compute the reward function (l. 12). We have implemented two plug-ins for this type so far, one for computing the rate of simulated events per second and one computing the logarithm of this rate:

$$R(\tau) = ln(\frac{e_\tau}{wct_\tau}) \tag{1}$$

where wct_τ is the duration of the trajectory computation in wall-clock time in seconds and e_τ is the number of simulation events that have been computed in this time span. Previous experiments showed the logarithmic rate to be advantageous, as it pronounces the differences between small event rates over those between high rates [17]. However, both plug-ins consider the overhead caused by the execution of the `adapt` procedure by starting to measure the execution time before `adapt` is executed.

Data collection is realized by observing the model and the current internal SA, as well as all of its sub-algorithms that provide data for the base state. Another plug-in type was implemented to provide preprocessors (l. 13). So far, we have developed two general preprocessors: one which maps all trajectories to a single state (as discussed in Sec. 3.1) and one which implements a preprocessor which maps all trajectories to themselves, i.e., $p(\tau) = \tau$. As preprocessing is highly application-dependent, custom preprocessors should be implemented for each application domain of the adaptive simulator. Thus, we implemented specific preprocessors for the modeling formalisms we use for the evaluation (see Sec. 5). Another plug-in type represents adaptation conditions. Until now, we have implemented one plug-in of this type, which triggers a new adaptation after a fixed number of simulation events has been executed. Finally, there is a plug-in type that represents the `adapt` procedure (l. 17) and

Plug-in Type	Description
learning algorithm	Implements the specific learning algorithm of reinforcement learning.
policy	Implements the function $f : S \times \mathbb{R}^{\|S\|\times\|A\|} \times \mathbb{N}^{\|S\|\times\|A\|} \rightarrow A$.
reward	Computes the reward $R(\tau)$, e.g. the rate of computed events per second since the last adaptation.
preprocessor	Transforms a base state trajectory τ to a state s, $p(\tau) = s$, by aggregating the base states of τ and removing and merging data.
adaptation condition	Defines conditions for the adaptations.
internal SA handler	Manages the internal SA and implements the `adapt` method.

Table 1: The most important plug-in types of the adaptive simulator implementation.

thus provides methods to adapt (or exchange) the internal SA (see Sec. 3.2). So far, we again rely on a single plug-in, which completely exchanges the internal SA. The most relevant plug-in types for extending the adaptive simulator are summarized in Table 1.

5. EVALUATION

We evaluate the adaptive simulator by applying it to the simulation of two modeling formalisms from systems biology: species-reaction networks (SR) [14] and multi-level rules (ML-Rules) [26]. Sections 5.1 and 5.2 briefly describe the computational challenges of simulating SR and ML-Rules models. Section 5.3 discusses how the performance of the adaptive simulator can be evaluated. We then analyze its performance both on synthetic benchmark models (Sec. 5.4) and on realistic ML-Rules models (Sec. 5.5).

5.1 Species-Reaction (SR) Networks

Species-reaction networks represent populations of chemical species that are homogeneously distributed in space. Model dynamics are defined by reactions of the form

$$A + \ldots + B \xrightarrow{r_c} C + \ldots + D$$

between the species $A, \ldots, D$, where r_c is the rate constant, $A + \ldots + B$ are the reactants, and $C + \ldots + D$ are the products. The propensity of a reaction depends on the current state, as its computation involves the number of possible reactant combinations (see [14]). Since SR networks define continuous-time Markov chains (CTMCs), their trajectories can be computed with stochastic discrete-event simulation. The reaction that occurs next and the time of its occurrence are drawn from probability distributions that depend on the current state and the rate constants. Afterwards, the current state is updated, the probability distributions change accordingly, and the whole procedure is repeated.

The efficient simulation of SR networks is an important problem in its own right, as more complex modeling formalisms like ML-Rules (see Sec. 5.2) can be mapped to CTMCs and in principle are simulated similarly. Consequently, various approaches to improve simulation efficiency have been proposed over the years, e.g approximative algorithms [15]. For this evaluation, we focus on various variants of Gillespie's algorithm. These variants comprise the Direct Reaction Method, the First Reaction Method, the Next Reaction Method, the Logarithmic Direct Method, and the Optimized Direct Method [21, 25]. Furthermore, we focus on parameterizations of the Next-Reaction Method [13], which modifies the original algorithms (cf. [14]) by letting an event queue manage all reactions and by limiting the calculation of reaction propensities during a state update. We use five event queues for the experiments, `SimpleQueue`, `CalendarQueue`, `SimpleReBucketsQueue`, `MList`, and `PriorityQueue` (see [19]), as these had a strong impact on overall performance in previous experiments [21].

For SR, we define base states as $\sigma = (\sigma^s, \sigma^r)$, where σ^s is the number of species with amounts greater than zero and σ^r is the number of reactions with a propensity greater than zero, i.e., the number of reactions that may occur in the given state. These characteristics could be relevant, for example, to decide upon a suitable event queue implementation. We define a custom preprocessor for SR models that derives a state $s \in S$ from a base state trajectory $\tau = \sigma_1 \ldots \sigma_n$ as follows:

$$s = \left(\left\lfloor \frac{\frac{1}{|\tau|} \sum_{(\sigma^s,\sigma^r)\in\tau} \sigma^s}{species_{gen}} \right\rfloor, \left\lfloor \frac{\frac{1}{|\tau|} \sum_{(\sigma^s,\sigma^r)\in\tau} \sigma^r}{reactions_{gen}} \right\rfloor \right) \quad (2)$$

where $species_{gen}$ and $reaction_{gen}$ are positive integer parameters that determine the resolution with which the averaged base state variables σ^s and σ^r are aggregated. For example, for $\tau = ((10, 10), (15, 25))$, $species_{gen} = 10$, and $reaction_{gen} = 5$, the result of the preprocessor is $p(\tau) = (\lfloor \frac{12.5}{10} \rfloor, \lfloor \frac{17.5}{5} \rfloor) = (1, 3)$. Decreasing $species_{gen}$ and $reaction_{gen}$ thus allows to distinguish more simulation phases, but also makes the learning problem harder, because more states have to be explored. All in all, to use the adaptive simulator for SR, we extended the basic SA of SR, so that it provides a method to retrieve σ^s and σ^r and we implemented the explained preprocessor. Altogether three classes had to be implemented (two of them were simple factories [12]), and including all effort only about 250 lines of code (including whitespace and comments) were written.

5.2 ML-Rules

Biological systems are dynamic at different hierarchical levels, e.g., proteins, cells, and cell populations. ML-Rules [26] is a rule-based formalism which can be used to model a system and its dynamics at different levels of hierarchy. This includes nesting of model entities and explicit downward and upward causation across levels. Like SR, this formalism bases on CTMCs and thus it can also be simulated with stochastic discrete-event simulation. Models are described by rule schemata. A schema consists of a number of reactant patterns, a number of products, and a kinetic rate. A reactant pattern describes a species by its name (e.g., *A*, *Cell*, *Protein*), its desired attributes (e.g. *size*, *volume*, *age*), and further sub-species and their attributes. Such nested patterns can reach across an arbitrary number of levels. For example, the rule schema

$$A()[B()] : a + C() : c \xrightarrow{a \cdot c \cdot r_c} A() + B() + C()$$

describes reactions which move a species B that is nested in a species A to the outside of A, with the help of some catalyst species C and with the reaction propensity $a \cdot c \cdot r_c$, i.e., the propensity is computed with a constant reaction rate

r_c and the amounts of the species. Broadly speaking, a rule schema therefore stands for a (dynamically changing) *set* of reactions as they would be specified for species-reaction networks (see Sec. 5.1).

Rule schemata can be very complex and require an SA to deal with dynamic hierarchical structures and potentially infinite numbers of species, as the latter need to be distinguished based on their attribute values and sub-species etc. Due to the varying complexity of models and rules (e.g., with respect to the dynamics of the species hierarchy), different SAs should be used that are tailored to specific model requirements. We therefore realized the most important methods of the ML-Rules SA as JAMES II plug-in types (see [17]). For example, we developed three different mechanisms for species handling, which performances depend on the model state: the first mechanism saves all species in a list (**ListSpeciesHandling**), the second one saves them in a map indexed by the species name (**MapSpeciesHandling**), and the third one saves them in a grid-file [30], which is a multi-key index data structure (**GridSpeciesHandling**). The list implementation is efficient if the number of species to check for each reactant of each rule is always relatively small. The map can efficiently retrieve species by their name, but not by their attributes. Thus, the map can efficiently reduce a set of species by their name. In contrast, the grid-file can also efficiently retrieve species by their attributes, and thus is more suitable for matching species to reactant patterns that rely on this. Additionally, the number of different species of the model needs to be relatively small. Otherwise, a map-based solution might still be more efficient overall, because the overhead of maintaining a grid-file is relatively high. Eventually, at the beginning of a simulation run, it is typically unknown which species handling mechanism to select, because the relevant model properties may change during execution. The other most important methods of the ML-Rules simulation algorithm comprise the hashing computation of species and the creation, execution, and handling of reactions. For this evaluation, we use two plug-ins of the reaction handling, two plug-ins of the reaction execution, and the three plug-ins for the species handling explained earlier. This leads to $2 \cdot 2 \cdot 3 = 12$ plug-in combinations (i.e., SAs) to choose from.

Similarly to SR (see Sec. 5.1), the adaptive simulator collects the number of different species σ^s and the number of reactions σ^r for the base states of ML-Rules. In contrast to SR species, note that two ML-Rules species differ not only when their names differ, but also when they are nested in different species, their attributes differ, or their sub-species differ. Additionally, after each reaction execution, the adaptive simulator collects the number of new and removed species, σ^s_+ and σ^s_-, and the number of invalid and new possible reactions, σ^r_+ and σ^r_-. These values are useful to describe the effort to update and maintain used data structures. Altogether, a base state comprises six attributes:

$$\sigma = (\sigma^s, \sigma^s_+, \sigma^s_-, \sigma^r, \sigma^r_+, \sigma^r_-).$$

Our custom preprocessor for ML-Rules creates states $s \in S$ which have six attributes as well. The preprocessor aggregates the number of species and reactions like the preprocessor of SR (see Eq. 2). It does the same with the *ratio* of the other four attributes with respect to σ^s (σ^s_+, σ^s_-) and σ^r (σ^r_+, σ^r_-). The ratios are computed because the effort of update operations of data structures typically depends on the number of elements. The four values are aggregated by a parameter $\mu \in [0, 1)$, e.g., σ^s_+ is aggregated as follows:

$$\left\lfloor \frac{\frac{1}{|\tau|}\sum_{(\sigma^s,\sigma^s_+,\ldots)\in\tau}\frac{\sigma^s_+}{\sigma^s}}{\mu} \right\rfloor$$

For example, for $\tau = ((11, 3, 5, 22, 15, 4))$, $species_{gen} = 5$, $reaction_{gen} = 10$, and $\mu = 0.2$, the result of the preprocessor is $p(\tau) = (2, 1, 2, 2, 3, 0)$. The parameter μ behaves similar to the other parameters $species_{gen}$ and $reaction_{gen}$: the smaller it is selected, the more simulation phases can be distinguished by the computed states.

5.3 Measuring Adaptation Performance

We measure the performance of the adaptive simulator in terms of execution time. One way to measure its effectiveness and efficiency is to compare its results with the worst-, average- , and best-case results of non-adaptive SAs. To get these results, for each available SA, we execute 100 replications of the referring simulations. The performance of the adaptive simulator essentially depends on the quality of the q-values, i.e., how many explorations have been done to compute these values. To consider this issue, we sequentially execute several replications with the adaptive simulator, so that the q-values learned at the end of one replication are reused at the start of the next one: i.e., the adaptive simulator learns across all replications by successively improving its estimates of the true q-values. With this setup, we can analyze the impact of q-value quality on simulation performance. Execution time alone, however, gives little insights into the overall effectiveness of our approach, as it is unclear how much performance improvement we should expect. Therefore, we measure how useful it is to use the adaptive simulator for a specific number of replications, in relation to other approaches.

At first, we measure the static regret, sr_n, which is the relative execution time overhead of the adaptive simulator compared to a static selection of the best non-adaptive SA after n replications. It is defined as

$$sr_n = \frac{\sum_{i=1}^{n} runtime_i}{n \cdot runtime^{opt}_{static}} - 1 \tag{3}$$

with $runtime_i$ being the execution time of the adaptive simulator for the i-th replication and $runtime^{opt}_{static}$ being the execution time of the best non-adaptive SA. For example, the static regret allows to determine the number of (sequential) replications that are necessary to achieve a better overall performance than the best non-adaptive SA.

While the static regret allows a comparison to an ideal static SA selection, it gives no insights regarding the potential of dynamic adaptation. We hence also calculate the dynamic regret, dr_n, which is the relative execution time overhead of the adaptive simulator compared to its (hypothetical) execution with an ideal choice of adaptation actions:

$$dr_n = \frac{\sum_{i=1}^{n} runtime_i}{n \cdot runtime^{opt}_{adaptive}} - 1 \tag{4}$$

with all elements defined as in Equation (3) and $runtime^{opt}_{adaptive}$ being the best achievable execution time when using the same preprocessor and adaptation actions. Thus, dr_n represents the overhead induced by exploration, compared to a situation in which the true q-values are known and no exploration is necessary. The dynamic regret of the adaptive simulator should therefore approach zero for larger n.

Note that Equations (3) and (4) refer to quantities that need to be estimated, so that only estimates of sr_n and dr_n are reported in the following. The execution time of the best non-adaptive SA ($runtime^{opt}_{static}$) is approximated by averaging over 100 replications, the execution times of the adaptive simulator per replication ($runtime_i$) are approximated by an average over 100 replications. In particular, $runtime^{opt}_{adaptive}$ is hard to estimate, as it depends on the q-values, which in turn can only be approximated via learning. To make this explicit, we refer to the *approximately* optimal adaptive simulator and use a large number of replications ($n = 2,000$) to learn the q-values.

5.4 Benchmark Experiments

In this section, we describe the results of benchmark experiments, which enable us to analyze the effectiveness and the efficiency of the adaptive simulator. All these experiments share some configuration details of the adaptive simulator. They all use ϵ-decreasing [36] with $\epsilon = 5$ as policy:

$$f(s, Q, N) = \begin{cases} \text{random } a \in A, & \text{with prob. } \frac{\epsilon}{\sum_{a \in A} N[s,a]} \\ \underset{a \in A}{argmax}\ Q(s, a), & \text{otherwise} \end{cases}$$

It explores actions with a decreasing rate and has shown to be simple but efficient. Furthermore, we set the discount parameter γ of the Q-Learning rule to zero: previous experiments have shown that, in our case, a higher value of γ has no significant impact on the results [17]. This may be different when using SAs and data structures that exhibit longer warm-up phases. With $\gamma = 0$, the general reinforcement learning problem reduces to the associative search task, i.e., it is assumed that actions do not affect future situations and rewards [35]. The logarithmic reward function (see Eq. 1) is used throughout the experiments.

5.4.1 ML-Rules

At first, we have developed a cyclic ML-Rules model, which has two alternating phases [17]. Both phases describe degradation processes and need exactly 10,000 simulation events to be completed. Whereas the first phase degrades a subset of species which share an attribute value, the second phase degrades one species independently from all the others. Thus, to compute the first phase, an index data structure to select species, such as the grid-file, might be useful. After selecting the first species for a reaction, the attribute value of this reaction is assigned. Therefore, the other species can be selected efficiently by the grid-file (see Sec. 5.2). However, the overhead of the grid-file might be too high for the second phase of the model, because each species is selected independently from its attributes. Hence, for this experiment, we use two data structures for the ML-Rules SA to handle the species of the model: the list and the grid-file. One adaptation condition is used, which triggers an adaptation all 1000 simulation steps. Thus, the adaptive simulator can choose from only two actions. For the preprocessor, we use the ML-Rules preprocessor and set $species_{gen} = 10$, $reaction_{gen} = 10$, and $\mu = 0.1$ (see Sec. 5.2). We executed the model for 40,000 simulation events in each simulation run, which means that each model phase occurs twice. The introductory example in Figure 1

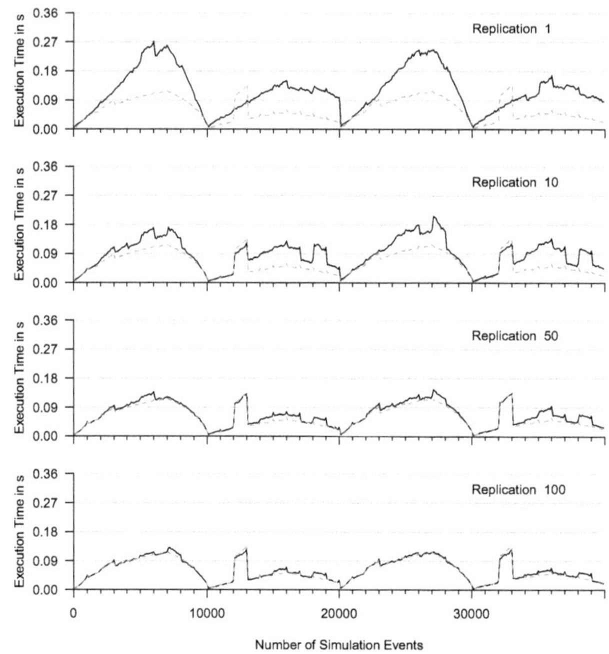

Figure 2: In-detail view on averaged execution times during specific replications of the ML-Rules synthetic benchmark model, using the adaptive simulator with two actions. Each data point shows the execution time summed over 100 simulation events. The dotted lines denote the average execution times of the approximatively optimal adaptive simulator.

shows the average detailed execution time values of the two ML-Rules simulation configurations: SA A uses a simple list to handle the species and SA B uses the grid-file to handle them. Both algorithms need ≈ 40 seconds to compute one simulation run. One can easily identify the phases of the simulation and — as expected — the grid-file performs better during the first phase, whereas the list performs better during the second phase. Next, we executed 100 replications with the adaptive simulator sequentially. Figure 2 shows the average detailed execution time values of the adaptive simulator for the first, the tenth, the 50th and the 100th replication. The dashed line shows the results of the approximatively optimal adaptive simulator, as discussed in section 5.3. The performance of the adaptive simulator converges to this approximately optimal performance during the first fifty replications, i.e., there are little differences between the optimal choice and the choices of replications $50, \ldots, 100$. More concretely, the average execution time with the optimal adaptive simulator is ≈ 24 seconds, which is almost achieved by the 50th replication of the adaptive simulator. Thus, after only 50 replications, the adaptive simulator outperforms both non-adaptive SAs by almost 40%.

However, there are large deviations in the average execution times at several points during the simulation runs (e.g., from the 13,000th event to the 14,000th event in Fig. 2), which are caused by a state space that is too coarse-grained, i.e., the preprocessor maps trajectories of both phases to the same state, although they require different SAs (cf. Fig. 1). Eventually, the adaptive simulator will learn to choose the

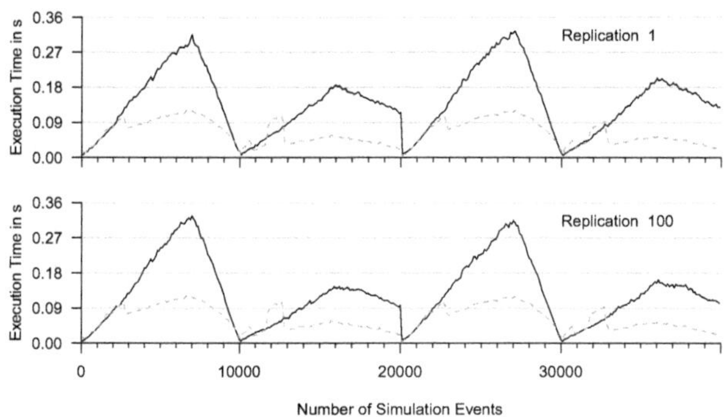

Figure 3: In-detail view on averages execution times during the first and the 100th replication of the ML-Rules synthetic benchmark model of the adaptive simulator with 36 actions.

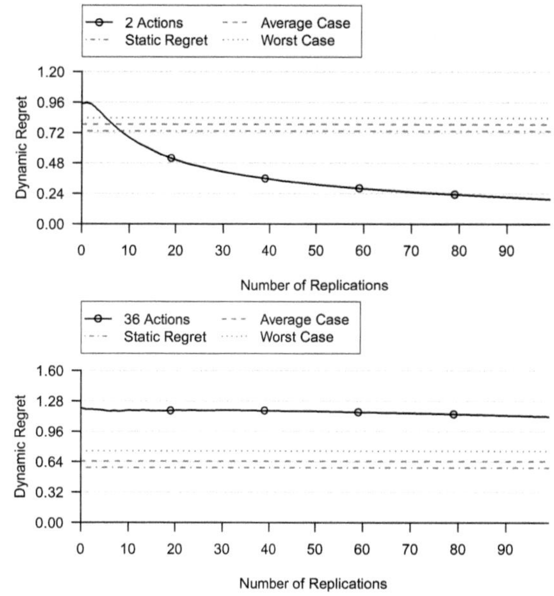

Figure 4: The dynamic regret of both adaptive simulator setups on the ML-Rules synthetic benchmark model.

action that yields the best performance *overall*, thus neglecting some (indistinguishable) situations in which indeed another action would be beneficial. As the approximatively optimal adaptive simulator uses the same preprocessor, it consequently does neither perform better at these points, because it cannot distinguish these situations, either. Clearly, a preprocessor that computes more fine-grained states would enable the adaptive simulator to distinguish these situations and thus would enable it to achieve a better overall performance. On the other hand, increasing the size of the state space also increases the effort to learn good policies, and additionally comes with other problems, e.g. it increases the overhead of the q-value management.

To examine the scalability of our approach, we repeated the same experiment setup (100 replications with 40,000 events each, each experiment repeated 100 times) with 36 instead of 2 actions and thus a larger q-value space (see Sec. 3). We used 12 configurations of the ML-Rules SA (see Sec. 5.2) and three adaptation conditions (adapt after 100, 1,000, or 10,000 events), which results in 36 actions. Figure 3 shows the average detailed execution time values of the adaptive simulator for the first and the 100th replication. Compared to the results with two actions, the adaptive simulator only achieves slight improvements over hundred replications, i.e., learning now takes much longer.

Figure 4 shows the average dynamic regret per replication for both the two-actions setup and the 36-actions setup. While the setup with two actions approaches the approximate optimum with a rather steep learning curve, the learning curve of the setup with 36 actions is quite gentle. This means that our current approach has to be carefully tuned to the number of available actions and may require a considerable amount of training before performing well. In our experiment, the number of adaptations during each replication with the 36-actions setup was relatively small (about 20 on average for the first 100 replications) compared to the number of different states (150) generated by the preprocessor for the benchmark model, and thus the overall number of q-values to be estimated ($150 \cdot 36 = 5,400$). Therefore, the ϵ-decreasing strategy with $\epsilon = 5$ might be too exploratory if one wants to achieve better results after *only* 100 replications. Additionally, consider the differences between the best and worst SA: in both cases, there is little difference in the overall performance of the best and the worst SA running in isolation. Since the optimal static choice is typically unknown, only the average performance of all actions can be expected in general. Compared to this, in the two-actions case, the adaptive simulator achieves an improvement after only 10 replications, whereas in the 36-actions case, the adaptive simulator does not even reach worst-case performance after 100 replications.

5.4.2 Species-Reaction Networks

The ML-Rules benchmark model lends itself well to an adaptive simulation, since it changes its phase after a fixed number of events. For species-reaction networks, we defined a more challenging benchmark model that changes its phase randomly instead. The model combines two existing benchmark models in their default parameter settings, the *cyclic chain system* (CCS) [21] and the *linear chain system* (LCS) [6]. At first, we introduce two new species, E_{CCS} and E_{LCS}, which are added to each CCS and LCS reaction, respectively, both as reactant and as product. Hence, a CCS (or LCS) reaction may only occur if the amount of E_{CCS} (or E_{LCS}) is greater than zero, and no reaction changes these amounts. Then, we define two reactions to switch between the phases ($E_{CCS} \xrightarrow{r_{LCS}} E_{LCS}$ and $E_{LCS} \xrightarrow{r_{CCS}} E_{CCS}$), and set the initial amounts of E_{LCS} and E_{CCS} to 1 and 0, respectively. This makes the model switch randomly between both phases. To consider the differing time scales of both benchmark models, we set the reaction rates $r_{LCS} = 10$ and $r_{CCS} = 1$, so that roughly the same amount of reaction events is simulated in each phase. Since CCS reactions are structurally different from LCS reactions (the former involve more reactants and products), the performance of simulation configurations on the individual benchmark models differs [21], and an adaptive simulation scheme should be able to exploit this. On the other hand, the points at which the model switches from one phase to the other are not pre-

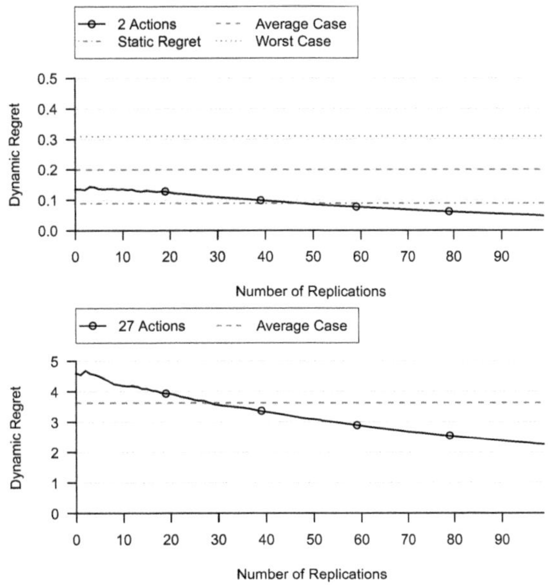

Figure 5: The dynamic regret of both adaptive simulator setups for the species-reaction network benchmark model.

dictable, so that a suitable algorithm can only be chosen after a switch occurred. This makes the benchmark model quite challenging for the adaptive simulator. Similarly to the previous experiments, once we use two actions for the adaptive simulator, containing the Next Reaction Method either using the `SimpleEventQueue` or the `MList` with one adaptation condition (adapt each 10,000 events), and once we use 27 actions containing nine SAs, including five parameterizations of the Next Reaction Method (see Sec. 5.1) and three adaptation conditions (adapt each 1,000, 10,000, or 50,000 events). Furthermore, we use the SR preprocessor with $species_{gen} = 10$ and $reaction_{gen} = 10$.

Figure 5 shows that adaptive simulation is effective for species-reaction networks. However, for the two-actions setup, there is less potential for performance gains, as the overall execution time with a static choice is only a little worse ($\approx 9\%$) than using an approximately optimal adaptive simulator. Still, the adaptive simulator is able to outperform a static selection after approximately 50 replications. The adaptive simulator's execution time is ≈ 25.59 seconds after 100 replications, while an approximatively optimal adaptive simulator would only need ≈ 24.21 seconds. As with the ML-Rules benchmark model, increasing the number of actions lets the performance of the adaptive simulator deteriorate dramatically. Again, this can be explained by the exploration of sub-optimal actions. Note that we left out worst case and static regret in the second plot of Figure 5. We omit the worst case because there is one SA that performs much worse than all others (its dynamic regret is > 24). The static regret is missing because the execution time of the referring SA is smaller than the execution time of the approximatively optimal adaptive simulator, i.e., its dynamic regret is negative (-0.5). This static SA needs about 3 seconds to execute a simulation run, whereas the approximatively optimal adaptive simulator needs about 6 seconds. As with the ML-Rules synthetic benchmark model, the adaptive simulator must explore too many state-action pairs, but in this case some states are visited very often while many other states are only visited rarely, so that our approximation of the true q-values, and thus dr_n, suffers (see Sec. 5.3). Due to the relatively high execution times of the poorly performing SAs, choosing such algorithms significantly increases the execution time and thus even the approximatively optimal adaptive simulator does not beat the best static SA. Nevertheless, in comparison with the average case (which is ≈ 3.6 times slower than the approximately optimal simulator, see Fig. 5), its results are still acceptable. After 100 replications, the adaptive simulator executes a simulation in ≈ 22.51 s on average, with a standard deviation of 2.1 s. While this is much better than the average case (≈ 31.78 s, std. dev. of ≈ 53 s), it is still much worse than simply selecting the best SA statically (with an execution time of ≈ 3.42 s). All in all, these experiments show that the adaptive simulator is able to exploit the performance potential of dynamic reconfiguration at runtime. As its performance may deteriorate when confronted with too many actions and states, a fine-tuning of the discretization via preprocessors and of the learning policy may lead to a faster convergence.

5.5 Evaluation on Realistic Models

Both benchmark models evaluated in section 5.4 exhibited only two different phases of constant (ML-Rules) or roughly similar (SR) length, in terms of simulation events. Realistic models, in contrast, exhibit an unknown (potentially large) number of (hard to distinguish) phases, between which they may switch rapidly. Consequently, we have conducted experiments with two realistic, complex ML-Rules models: the Cell Cycle model [26] for 100,000 simulation events and the Endocytosis model [18] for 50,000 simulation events. For both models, the adaptive simulator uses 36 actions as explained in section 5.4.1. To compare the results of the adaptive simulator, we also executed experiments with an adaptive task runner, which adaptively selects SAs for whole simulation runs. We used several configurations of the adaptive simulator and the adaptive task runner for both models, but the results of the configurations do not differ much. Therefore, only the best results are presented in Figure 6. Setting A represents the average overhead in relation to the best SA (overhead = 0) and the worst SA (overhead = 1) and its standard deviation of one simulation run after 100 replications. Ten threads are used to compute the simulation runs in parallel. For both models, the adaptive task runner performs better than the adaptive simulator after 100 replications (18.94 s compared to 21.49 s for Cell Cycle, and 24.06 s compared to 25.71 s for Endocytosis). For the Cell Cycle model, the adaptive task runner almost achieves the optimal performance (18.5 s). By contrast, the adaptive simulator only achieves slight improvements compared to the average execution time (21.69 s). Again, these results mean that the adaptive simulator must explore too many states, whereas the adaptive task runner only has to explore twelve SAs. However, in contrast to per-replication adaptation, the adaptive simulator gathers much more performance data and can act upon its new knowledge *immediately*. This is particularly helpful for longer-running simulations, so that we conducted another set of experiments for both models (Setting B). This time, we only executed three replications, but each with ten times more events (1,000,000 events for Cell Cycle and 500,000 events for Endocytosis), all executed

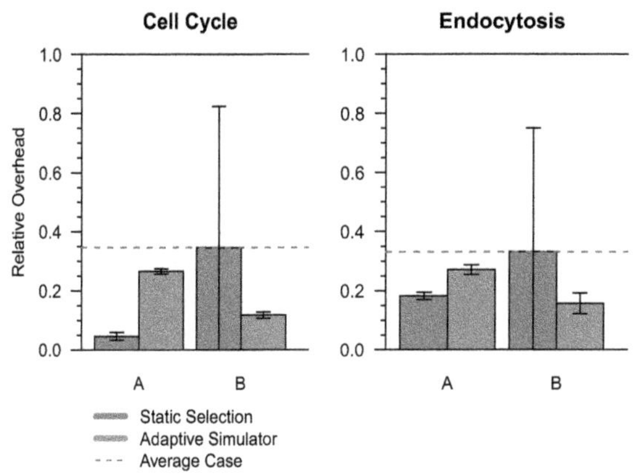

Figure 6: Relative overhead of the adaptive task runner and the adaptive simulator in relation to the best SA (overhead = 0) and the worst SA (overhead = 1) for the Cell Cycle and the Endocytosis model. The results of setting A refer to the performance after 100 replications, those of setting B refer to the performance after three replications (each containing ten times more events than those in A). Note that the adaptive simulator uses the trivial preprocessor in setting B.

in parallel. Furthermore, the adaptive simulator uses the trivial preprocessor in this setting, i.e., all trajectories are mapped to one state and consequently the adaptive simulator only has to explore one state for twelve actions. In this setting, the adaptive simulator performs much better than the adaptive task runner, which only achieves the average execution time. The adaptive simulator is able to perform better because it can use its learned knowledge at once. On average, it only needs 217 s for the Cell Cycle model and 170 s for the Endocytosis model, whereas the adaptive task runner needs 240 s and 194 s, respectively. In both cases, the adaptive simulator thus improves the performance compared to the adaptive task runner by more than 10%, and even by more than 30% compared to the worst-performing SA. Furthermore, the results of the adaptive simulator are very robust, because it is able to stop exploring the poor-performing SAs during a single run. Nevertheless, these benefits decrease with an increasing number of replications, so further experiments are needed to investigate this trade-off.

6. CONCLUSION

In this paper, we present a flexible and generic adaptive simulation algorithm. This so-called adaptive simulator (see Sec. 3) works on top of existing simulation algorithms (SAs), all of which are applicable to a given problem, and switches between them during a simulation run. It is generic in that it works with any set of SAs, and thus is not restricted to a particular modeling formalism (in contrast to the SAs, which typically are). It is flexible in that it can be reconfigured easily, by exchanging specific components of the overall adaptation mechanism (see Sec. 4). The adaptive simulator uses reinforcement learning (see Algorithm 1); it learns when to use which SA during a simulation run and without user intervention. Applying the adaptive simulator to existing algorithms requires little effort (see Sec. 5.1), provided that they are available as software components which can be instantiated and combined dynamically. Both the SAs and the model need to provide an interface to access (parts of) their states. This is particularly important for the model state, since it helps ensuring a consistent transition from one SA to another. Additionally, observations from the model, the SA, and the environment (all of which might be relevant for the next adaptation action) are collected and preprocessed into aggregate states for learning (see Sec. 3). One may therefore need to define a custom preprocessor to suit the task at hand, as we have done for our two sample applications (see Sec. 5.1 and 5.2).

As shown in our experiments (Sec. 5.4 and 5.5), the efficiency of the adaptive simulator depends on the size of the state space and the number of actions, i.e., the number of available SAs multiplied by the number of adaptation conditions. Thus, the preprocessor is crucial for the performance of the adaptive simulator, because it determines the size of the state space. Eventually, it must find a trade-off between the expressiveness of the state space and the effort to learn good policies. Until now, the user must define this trade-off manually, but there are also algorithms that dynamically change the discretization of (parts of) the state space [32]. Alternatively, algorithm portfolios could be selected to reduce the number of adaptation actions (e.g., [16]).

Although the adaptive simulator reduced the execution time of the ML-Rules benchmark model by $\approx$ 40% when compared to the best available SA, similar improvements could not be observed in the Cell Cycle and Endocytosis models. As the states of these models do not differ sufficiently during execution, our adaptive simulator simply chooses the best available SA (and hence cannot outperform it). However, the adaptive simulator can be applied successfully even under such conditions, when compared to our earlier approaches (e.g., see [10, p. 134 et sqq.]): due to the frequent feedback it receives, it is able to identify the most suitable SA much faster, i.e., within very few replications (see Sec. 5.5). As we are planning to develop cell biological models that are likely to exhibit bistability [9], we expect an even greater impact of the adaptive simulator on performance in these experiments.

Acknowledgments

This research was supported by the German research foundation (DFG), via research grants CoSA (UH 66/7-3), ALeSiA (EW 127/1-1), and VASSiB (part of SP 1335).

7. REFERENCES

[1] W. Armstrong, P. Christen, E. McCreath, and A. Rendell. Dynamic algorithm selection using reinforcement learning. In *Proc. International Workshop on Integrating AI and Data Mining (AIDM'06)*, pages 18–25, Dec. 2006.

[2] P. Auer, N. Cesa-Bianchi, and P. Fischer. Finite-time Analysis of the Multiarmed Bandit Problem. *Machine Learning*, 47(2–3):235–256, May 2002.

[3] D. M. Ball and S. M. Hoyt. The adaptive Time-Warp concurrency control algorithm. In *Proc. SCS Multiconference on Distributed Simulation*, pages 174–177, Jan. 1990.

[4] A. G. Barto and S. Mahadevan. Recent Advances in Hierarchical Reinforcement Learning. *Discrete Event Dynamic Systems*, 13(4):341–379, Oct. 2003.

[5] A. Boukerche and S. K. Das. Dynamic load balancing strategies for conservative parallel simulations. In *Proc. 11th Workshop on Parallel and Distributed Simulation (PADS'97)*, pages 20–28, July 1997.

[6] Y. Cao, H. Li, and L. Petzold. Efficient formulation of the stochastic simulation algorithm forchemically reacting systems. *The Journal of Chemical Physics*, 121(9):4059–4067, Sept. 2004.

[7] F. E. Cellier and E. Kofman. *Continuous System Simulation.* Springer, 2010.

[8] S. R. Das. Adaptive Protocols for Parallel Discrete-Event Simulation. In *Proc. Winter Simulation Conference (WSC'96)*, pages 186–193, Dec. 1996.

[9] O. Decroly and A. Goldbeter. Birhythmicity, chaos, and other patterns of temporal selforganization in a multiply regulated biochemical system. In *Proc. Natl. Acad. Sci. USA*, pages 6917–6921, July 1982.

[10] R. Ewald. *Automatic Algorithm Selection for Complex Simulation Problems.* PhD thesis, University of Rostock, 2010.

[11] R. M. Fujimoto and M. Hybinette. Computing global virtial time in shared-memory multiprocessors. *ACM Transactions on Modeling and Computer Simulation*, 7(4):425–446, Oct. 1997.

[12] E. Gamma, R. Helm, R. Johnson, and J. Vlissides. *Design Patterns: Elements of Reusable Software Components.* Addison-Wesley Professional, 1995.

[13] M. A. Gibson and J. Bruck. Efficient Exact Stochastic Simulation of Chemical Systems with Many Species and Many Channels. *The Journal of Chemical Physics*, 104(9):1876–1889, Feb. 2000.

[14] D. T. Gillespie. Exact stochastic simulation of coupled chemical reactions. *Journal of Physical Chemistry*, 81(25):2340–2361, Dec. 1977.

[15] D. T. Gillespie. Approximate accelerated stochastic simulation of chemically reacting systems. *Journal of Chemical Physics*, 115(4):1716–1733, July 2001.

[16] C. P. Gomes and B. Selman. Algorithm portfolios. *Artificial Intelligence*, 126(1–2):43–62, Feb. 2001.

[17] T. Helms. Adaptive Laufzeit-Konfiguration von ML-Rules Simulationen. Master's thesis, University of Rostock, 2012.

[18] T. Helms, J. Himmelspach, C. Maus, O. Röwer, J. Schützel, and A. M. Uhrmacher. Toward a language for the flexible observation of simulations. In *Proc. Winter Simulation Conference (WSC'12)*, Dec. 2012.

[19] J. Himmelspach and A. M. Uhrmacher. The event queue problem and PDEVS. In *Proc. of the SpringSim '07, DEVS Integrative M&S Symposium*, pages 257–264. SCS, 2007.

[20] J. Himmelspach and A. M. Uhrmacher. Plug'n simulate. In *Proc. 40th Annual Simulation Symposium (ANSS'07)*, pages 137–143, Mar. 2007.

[21] M. Jeschke and R. Ewald. Large-Scale Design Space Exploration of SSA. In *Proc. 6th International Conference on Computational Methods in Systems Biology (CMSB'08)*, pages 211–230, Oct. 2008.

[22] K. Kira and L. A. Rendell. The Feature Selection Problem: Traditional Methods and a New Algorithm. In *Proc. 10th National Conference on Artificial Intelligence (AAAI'92)*, pages 129–134, July 1992.

[23] M. G. Lagoudakis, M. L. Littman, and R. E. Parr. Selecting the Right Algorithm. In *Proc. 2001 AAAI Fall Symposium Series: Using Uncertainty within Computation (AAAI'01)*, Nov. 2001.

[24] M. Lees, B. Logan, C. Dan, and G. K. Oguara, Ton andTheodoropoulos. Decision-Theoretic Throttling for Optimistic Simulationsof Multi-Agent Systems. In *Proc. 9th Int'l Symp. on Distributed Simulation and Real Time Applications (DS-RT'05)*, pages 171–178, Oct. 2005.

[25] H. Li and L. Petzold. Logarithmic Direct Method for Discrete Stochastic Simulation of Chemically Reacting Systems. Technical report, Department of Computer Science, University of California: Santa Barbara, 2006.

[26] C. Maus, S. Rybacki, and A. M. Uhrmacher. Rule-based multi-level modeling of cell biological systems. *BMC Systems Biology*, 5(166), Oct. 2011.

[27] P. K. McKinley, S. M. Sadjadi, E. P. Kasten, and B. H. C. Cheng. Composing Adaptive Software. *Computer*, 37(7):56–64, July 2004.

[28] S. Meraji, C. Tropper, and W. Zang. A Multi-State Q-learning Approach for the Dynamic Load Balancingof Time Warp. In *Proc. 24th Workshop on Principles of Advanced and Distributed Simulation (PADS'10)*, pages 1–8, May 2010.

[29] D. M. Nicol and P. F. Reynolds Jr. Optimal Dynamic Remapping of Data Parallel Computations. *IEEE Transactions on Computers*, 39(2):206–219, Feb. 1990.

[30] J. Nievergelt, H. Hinterberger, and K. C. Sevcik. The Grid File: An Adaptable, Symmetric Multikey File Structure. *ACM Transactions on Database Systems*, 9(1):38–71, Mar. 1984.

[31] A. C. Palaniswamy and P. A. Wilsey. Adaptive bounded time windows in an optimistically synchronized simulator. In *Proc. 3rd Great Lakes Symposium on Design Automation of High Performance VLSI Systems*, pages 114–118, 1993.

[32] S. I. Reynolds. Decision boundary partitioning: Variable resolution model- free reinforcement learning. In *Proc. 17th International Conference on Machine Learning (ICML-2000)*, pages 783–790, 2000.

[33] S. J. Russell and P. Norvig. *Artificial Intelligence: A Modern Approach.* Prentice Hall, 2nd edition, 2002.

[34] L. M. Sokol and B. K. Stucky. MTW: Eperimental Results for a Constrained Optimistic Scheduling Paradigm. In *Distributed Simulation*, volume 22, pages 169–173. SCS, Jan. 1990.

[35] R. S. Sutton and A. G. Barto. *Reinforcement Learning: An Introduction.* MIT Press, 1998.

[36] J. Vermorel and M. Mohri. Multi-armed Bandit Algorithms and Empirical Evaluation. In *Proc. 16th European conference on Machine Learning (ECML'05)*, pages 437–448, Oct. 2005.

[37] R. Vitali, A. Pellegrini, and F. Quaglia. Autonomic Log/Restore for advanced optimistic simulation systems. In *Proc. Int'l Symp. on Modeling, Analysis and Simulation of Computer and Telecommunication Systems (MASCOTS)*, pages 319–327. IEEE CS, 2010.

Supporting Robust System Analysis with the Test Matrix Tool Framework

Edward Clarkson*^, Jennifer Hurt*, Jason Zutty*, Christopher Skeels#, Brian Parise* and Greg Rohling*

*Georgia Tech Research Institute
925 Dalney St., Atlanta GA 30332
^edward.clarkson@gtri.gatech.edu

#RAND Corporation
1776 Main St., Santa Monica, CA 90401
cskeels@rand.org

ABSTRACT
We present the Test Matrix Tool (TMT) framework, a simulation-agnostic framework providing end-to-end support for robust analysis of complex systems. The need to execute a large number of simulations is common to many problem environments, even those already reduced by Design of Experiments or similar methodologies. TMT addresses key end-user needs in easing the specification, execution and analysis of simulation workloads in ways that are consistent between specific applications of the framework. The TMT design contributes modular specifications for key data communicated between and within the specification, execution and analysis components. Our TMT implementation is an instantiation of those formats freely available for general use. TMT's data analysis component provides a variety of features—data filtering, comparison, transformation and visualization—for analytic tasks on any TMT-embedded model. We provide a brief case study as an example of its use in a real-world application.

Categories and Subject Descriptors
I.6.7 [**Simulation and Modeling**]: Simulation Support Systems.

General Terms
Design

Keywords
Simulation management; scientific intelligence; visualization

1. INTRODUCTION
Using simulation models to perform robust system performance analysis requires the specification, execution and analysis of a potentially large number of test cases. In the naïve full-factorial experimental design case, that number increases exponentially with the number of varied input parameters. As such, judging the global performance of even relatively simple systems can involve large amounts of computational capacity. The design of experiments (DOE) methodology reduces the number of cases in an experiment compared with more verbose classical designs (e.g., full factorial), but even so benefits from observing results from as many cases as possible.

The unfortunate reality is that a common approach (especially when application domain experts are doing the work) to conducting such simulation[1] workloads is to create an *ad hoc* framework: write a series of nested loops over each of the factors' parameter lists (forming what we call a *test matrix*), execute the model, collate the results, and write another set of ad hoc tools to parse the results, run statistical analyses and create visual representations (e.g., with Microsoft Excel).

The theoretical and pragmatic flaws of this approach are apparent. The *ad hoc* nature of such frameworks generally means they are not designed to minimize maintainability or extensibility costs. Similarly, when confronted with new system models, it can be as much or more effort to adapt an existing *ad hoc* framework as create a new one—leading to a modeling group with a whole suite of incompatible, hard-to-maintain frameworks. Finally, if a model is expensive to execute computationally, repeated executions of the same input parameters will waste considerable resources and wall-clock time unless efficient storage and retrieval mechanisms are implemented.

Theoretically, models of complex systems are often broken into a set of related subsystem models, which may have a variety of dependency relationships (i.e., if model A's output is an input to model B, B is *dependent* on A). Furthermore, subsystem models may themselves be reused in different high-level system models. Thus, the more fundamental problem with the *ad hoc* approach is that it does not ease composition of subsystem models or their reuse in new high-level system contexts. For example, models of an aircraft flight trajectory and a UV-spectrum sensor might be composed to examine the performance of that sensor in different flight conditions, and the sensor model might also be used in conjunction with a UV source model to examine how it responds to different UV-emitting objects.

These practical and theoretical issues drove our design of the Test Matrix Tool (TMT), a modular simulation management framework that simplifies the specification, execution and analysis of large-scale modeling and simulation workloads. It consists of three major components: an Input GUI, which collects information about what parameters to vary and how; the Run Manager, which enumerates the necessary computations from the parameter variations (forming a *test matrix*), submits and monitors simulation runs, and collates and records their results (without repeating runs already executed); and the Analysis GUI, which reads generic simulation data and generates a customized interface to filter, compare and visualize test matrix data.

TMT contributes freely available[2], simulation-agnostic XML schemata that support model chaining, reuse and extension and generic component implementations of the framework for the

[1] We use the term *simulation* as a general term for any executable process consuming input data and producing output data.

[2] http://tmt.gtri.gatech.edu

SIGSIM-PADS'13, May 19–22, 2013, Montréal, Québec, Canada.

input, execution and output of simulation data. In particular, the data analysis component of the framework has proven to be a valuable and robust tool for exploratory analysis activities. This work details these contributions and provides a case study illustrating the framework utility, and concludes with a discussion of future opportunities and directions.

2. RELATED WORK

A prominent approach to increasing throughput has been helping developers parallelize and decompose model implementations themselves. Discrete Event Systems Specification (DEVS) [22], Parallel Discrete Event Simulation (PDES) [9] and High-Level Architecture (HLA) [5] all provide formalisms for designing models that can be distributed and run in parallel. Other tools like PARSEC [1] and APOSTLE [19] provide direct programming and implementation support rather than architectural-level assistance.

In contrast, grid computing focuses on high-level external factors such as scheduler efficiency and resource contention [3] rather than issues internal to the simulations themselves. Other grid-level infrastructure work is often domain specific: computing networks [2], vehicular networks [8] and distributed computing itself [15] are just a few examples. Hadoop [17] and similar distributed storage and processing technologies are not specifically targeted at modeling and simulation activities, but could be used to address such needs at a large-scale.

If we can term these as "computing-driven" simulation frameworks, then "engineering-driven" frameworks tend to focus on systems engineering processes and optimization. General-purpose tools like Matlab and Simulink are commonly used to attack such problems, often driven by the well-known Design of Experiments methodology. Multidisciplinary Design Optimization (MDO) and Process Integration and Design Optimization (PIDO) also drive a large number of commercial tools for executing large sets of system models (e.g., ModelCenter/CenterLink [7], iSight/Simula, ModelFrontier, PIAnO and VisualDOC).

There are a few similar frameworks from the modeling and simulation academic literature as well. JAMES II [11] is a pluggable java-based system with a large number of available components. It is targeted both at methodological and application-oriented research. CoCoViLa [14] is another, and has chaining visualization component.

TMT differs from previous work in several ways. At the high level, much of the parallel grid-level work focuses on the processing efficiency of the computing infrastructure (e.g., scheduling and latency) or modeling and simulation methodological research questions. TMT explicitly layers on top of some existing grid manager, focusing on analyst-centric questions related to the ease of legacy model integration, run specification, and data analysis. The value of this focus is validated by recent work showing a substantial amount of data analyst time is spent simply wrangling data into desired input and output formats [13].

Similarly, TMT explicitly ignores issues of PDES-style intra-simulation parallelization by assuming only basic aspects of model characteristics: inputs and outputs that can be easily adapted to TMT data formats. Because the reality is that domain expert scientists and engineers—rather than modeling and simulation experts—develop many models (and thus may not have the expertise to implement PDES-style models, if they are even aware of that body of work), a framework that can integrate these legacy models is valuable. Some commercial tools are similar, but none to our knowledge (based on publicly-available literature) have the same combination of input, execution and analysis capabilities with the degree of flexibility as TMT. ModelCenter is among the most similar, but its analysis tool lacks the same degree of interactive filtering and configuration as TMT.

3. TMT DESIGN

The specification, execution and analysis of simulation workloads are the three tasks that drive TMT design. More specifically, we frame these tasks as the following high-level research questions:

- How does one efficiently and accurately specify how a parameter space should vary for a set of executions?
- For a specified set of executions, how can they be computed and stored efficiently?
- After execution, how can people make sense of and analyze the output data?

Key to how TMT answers these questions is its basic simulation abstraction, based on the adapter design pattern [10]. We term them *simulation wrappers*, and they are responsible for transforming TMT standard input and output data formats into whatever native formats the underlying simulation uses. Moreover, wrappers can be used to not just wrap legacy simulations, but to perform useful parallel computation on their own—for example, post-process common file formats (e.g., assemble a set of images into a movie)—in a composable, reusable manner.

Wrappers are then composed into *test matrix types*, which define simulation composition as well as the order and structure for how inputs are provided (e.g., whether TMT runs all combinations of values from different input variables, or whether some combinations are paired or grouped). Matrix types consist of a *matrix type transform*, which defines the simulation composition structure, and the *matrix type schema*, which defines the order and structure of the input XML. Users create that input XML—an instance of that matrix type (or *test matrix instance*)—either automatically via a TMT Input GUI (cf. §4.2) or manually by composing an XML document.

These matrix abstractions allow:

- Defining parameter variations that are customizable, yet have a consistent structure between disparate models.
- Updating existing or adding new system models to the framework by modifying/writing a lightweight adapter.
- Composing simulations in any acyclic manner—that is, feeding the output of one simulation to the input of any other that does not form a circular dependency.
- A single framework component (the TMT Run Manager framework component, cf. §4.3) that handles all of the common simulation execution overhead tasks: input/output validation, error checking, monitoring, result storage, etc.
- Unified input (cf. §4.2) and output (cf. §4.4) framework tools that require no customization to work with arbitrary simulation data.

Defining the architecture as we do is not without drawbacks. TMT has no native data types for network or time-series data—files (for arbitrary data formats) and statistical summaries of their content are the best proxy for such cases. Because TMT is not a PDES-oriented framework, small matrices will be relatively slower to complete than the equivalent PDE implementation of the same model. A tacit assumption is that wrapper execution results are deterministic.

```
<Executable name="ExampleWrapper">
  <Inputs>
    <Input name="WrapperVariableName" type="integer" required="false"/>
    <Input name="SourceX" type="integer" required="true"/>
    <Input name="SourceY" type="integer" required="true"/>
     <Input name="ReferenceFrame"type="string" required="true">
      <ValidValues>
       <Value>LLA</Value>
       <Value>NED</Value>
      </ValidValues>
    </Input>
    <Input name="LocationArray" type="array" required="true">
      <Input name="TargX" type="float" default="0" units="m" min="-500" max="500" required="true"/>
      <Input name="TargY" type="float" default="0" units="m" min="-500" max="500" required="true"/>
      <Input name="TargZ" type="float" default="0" units="m" min="0" max="500" required="true"/>
      <Input name="Label" type="string"/>
    </Input>
  </Inputs>
  <Outputs>
    <Output name="WrapperOutputEx" type="string" description="An example"/>
    <Output name="AnotherOutput" type="float" />
  </Outputs>
</Executable>
```

Listing 1. An example TMT wrapper spec.

We detail the XML-based core concepts of the framework before presenting their implementation in TMT. We do omit discussion of some minor features for reasons of simplicity and space.

3.1 Simulation Wrappers

Wrappers are divided into an XML *wrapper specification* (or *wrapper spec*) and the wrapper code itself, which may be any executable process (e.g., Perl, shell script, compiled code). The only requirement is that the wrapper take in the TMT input XML format and produce valid TMT output XML. Those XML formats are derived from the wrapper spec, which is itself an XML document.

The wrapper spec declares the wrapper inputs and outputs along with metadata about them—they can be thought of as a sort of Java interface or C/C++ header file for the executable wrapper. TMT uses the spec to validate wrapper input and output outside the wrapper itself. An XML schema document[3] (XSD) defines the full wrapper spec syntax. The wrapper spec syntax is relatively simple, an example of which is shown in Listing 1. Key rules illustrated there include:

- Valid attributes are `name`, `type`, `required`, `default`, `units`, `min`, `max`, `analyze` and `description` (only `name` and `type` are mandatory).
- A `ValidValues` element specifies an enumerated type.
- Valid type attribute values are `string`, `integer`, `float`, `boolean`, `filepath` and `array`.
  - The `array` type covers arrays of mixed-type data tuples in addition to a series of single same-type data elements.
  - The `array` type is not valid within an `array` element.

The wrapper itself can be any executable file type, but it must be called with a standard set of arguments, and use input and output XML files according to the XML wrapper spec. The argument syntax must be:

```
<wrapper> [input XML file] [input directory]
          [output XML file] [output directory]
          [wrapper spec XML]
```

There are also a standard set of diagnostic wrapper outputs that are not specified in the wrapper spec but that wrappers may provide: `SimulationError`, `WrapperError`, `OtherError`, `MachineName`, `TempDirectoryUsed`, `SimulationRunTime`, `WrapperStartTime` and `WrapperEndTime`.

A useful wrapper will, of course, read in the input XML file and use it to produce the correct output. A TMT input file conforming to the example wrapper spec in Listing 1 is shown in Listing 2.

A conformant wrapper will produce an output file with all required outputs plus the tacit diagnostic fields listed above. Note, however, that in normal TMT use, the end user never executes a wrapper directly—the Run Manager generates wrapper input files according to the test matrix instance parameters.

```
<Inputs>
    <SourceX>0</SourceX>
    <SourceY>0</SourceY>
    <ReferenceFrame>LLA</ReferenceFrame >
    <LocationArray>
      <Value>
        <TargX>-100</TargX>
        <TargY>-100</TargY>
        <TargZ>100</TargZ>
        <Label>Target 1</Label>
      </Value>
      <Value>
        <TargX>100</TargX>
        <TargY>100</TargY>
        <TargZ>100</TargZ>
        <Label>Target 2</Label>
      </Value>
    </LocationArray>
</Inputs>
```

Listing 2. Wrapper input XML file corresponding to the wrapper spec in Listing 1.

3.2 Matrix Types

TMT matrix types codify how one or more wrappers should be executed within the TMT framework, and are defined by a matrix transform and a matrix schema.

[3] See http://www.w3.org/XML/Schema

```
  <!-- Dimension Elements -->
  <xs:complexType name="dimensionsType">
    <xs:sequence>
      <xs:element name="ExampleDimension" minOccurs="1" maxOccurs="1"type="ExampleDimensionType" />
      <xs:element name="SourceLocations" minOccurs="1" maxOccurs="1" type="SourceLocationDimType" />
   </xs:sequence>
  </xs:complexType>

  <!-- Configuration/Attribute Elements -->
 <xs:complexType name="ExampleDimensionType">
    <xs:sequence>
      <xs:element name="ExampleConfig" minOccurs="0" maxOccurs="unbounded" type="ExampleCfgType" />
    </xs:sequence>
  </xs:complexType>
  <xs:complexType name="ExampleCfgType">
    <xs:sequence>
      <xs:element name="AnInput" type="xs:integer" />
    </xs:sequence>
  </xs:complexType>

  <xs:complexType name="SourceLocationDimType ">
    <xs:sequence>
      <xs:element name="SourceLocation" minOccurs="1" maxOccurs="unbounded" type="SourceLocCfg" />
    </xs:sequence>
  </xs:complexType>
  <xs:complexType name="SourceLocCfg">
    <xs:sequence>
      <xs:element name="X" type="xs:float" />
      <xs:element name="Y" type="xs:float" />
    </xs:sequence>
  </xs:complexType>
...
```

Listing 3. Sample excerpt of a test matrix schema that could be used with the wrapper in Listing 1 and the transform in Listing 4.

The transform can be thought of as a wrapper wiring diagram, specifying a matrix type as a set of simulation wrapper steps, where the output from one wrapper can be wired into the input of another. Transforms are XML documents.

If transforms are the internal wiring diagram for a matrix type, then matrix schemas are the schematics for the faceplate: they define the format of the XML document that end users submit to execute an instance of a particular matrix type (i.e., which parameters users need to specify, what they should be called, and the order in which they should appear). Schemas are XSDs.

Matrix schemas, transforms and wrappers are plugged into the TMT framework using an administrative tool; space limitations prevent its full discussion in this work.

3.2.1 Matrix Schemas

Matrix schemas are based on the TMT concepts of *dimensions*, *configurations* and *attributes.*[4] An *attribute* is a single unit of input data—a single wrapper input value, for example. A *configuration* is a collection of attributes, allowing settings to be grouped if necessary (e.g., X/Y coordinates). All configurations of the same type form a *dimension*. TMT forms a test matrix by taking the cross product of all configurations within each dimension. We refer to a single member of the test matrix set as a *test case*, and an individual subsystem model within a test case as a *test case node.*

The syntax of a schema must meet some basic criteria:

- The schema must define the root element as a node named "TestMatrix" whose last child node is a single complex node named "Dimensions".
- The schema must define simple string fields for a matrix's creator, name, type and description.
- The Dimensions node must be defined as a 3-tier hierarchy of tags representing a Dimension and its Configurations, and the Attributes they contain.
- Dimension schema elements define exactly one configuration schema element; configuration schema elements define at least one attribute element.

Listing 3 provides an excerpt of a schema that could be used with

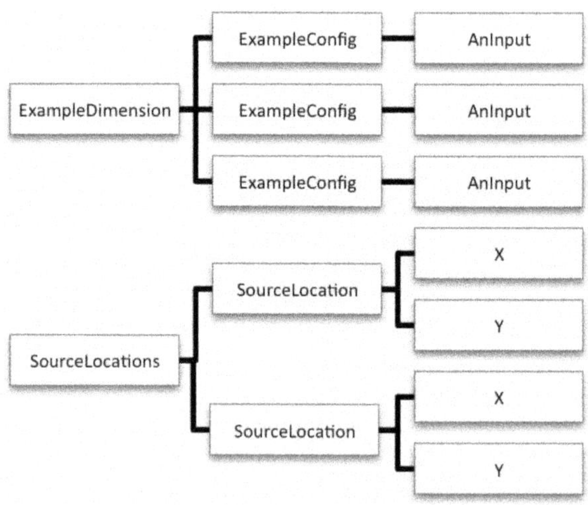

Figure 1. Diagram of the 3-tier XML matrix hierarchy architecture. The matrix schema defines the hierarchy with specific tag names; instances supply specific values that match the schema. This instance, matching Listing 3, consists of 6 test cases (3 example inputs and 2 pairs of X/Y coordinates).

[4] In addition to our usage, the term *attribute* is also used to refer to XML element properties; we attempt to be explicit or clear through context which sense of the term is meant in a given use.

```
<Transform>
<!--  STEP 1  -->
  <Executable name="ExampleWrapperStep"
              wrapperName="ExampleWrapper">
    <Input name="WrapperVariableName">
      ExampleConfig.InputName</Input>
    <Input name="SourceX">SourceLocation.X</Input>
    <Input name="SourceY">SourceLocation.Y</Input>
    <Input name="ReferenceFrame">@LLA</Input>
    <Input name="LocationArray">Targets.XYZ</Input>

    <Output name="WrapperOutputEx" />
  </Executable>

  <!--  STEP 2  -->
  <Executable name="ExampleStep2"
              wrapperName="AnotherWrapper">
    <Input name="AnExample">
      ExampleConfig.InputName</Input>
    <Input name="AltitudeASL">
      Trajectory.Altitude</Input>
    <Input name="SomeInput">
      $ExampleWrapperStep.WrapperOutputEx</Input>

    <Output name="SomeOutput" />
  </Executable>

<!--  STEP 3  -->
  <StopCondition>
    $ExampleStep2.SomeOutput eq 0
  </StopCondition>

<!--  STEP 4  -->
  <Executable name="SecondExampleWrapperStep"
              wrapperName="ExampleWrapper">
    <Input name="WrapperVariableName">
      $ExampleStep2.SomeOutput</Input>
  </Executable>
</Transform>
```

Listing 4. An example matrix transform using the wrapper given in Listing 1 and the schema in Listing 3.

the wrapper illustrated in Listing 1 and the transform in Listing 4.

3.2.2 Matrix Transform

Matrix transforms define which simulation wrappers are involved in a matrix type, how the schema elements are wired to the wrapper inputs, and how wrappers themselves are wired together (i.e., wrapper dependency information). Transforms identify which wrappers are used in a matrix type by an `Executable` tag and its `wrapperName` attribute. The `Executable name` attribute provides a unique *step name*. Inside the Executable element, wrapper inputs are connected to schema elements (i.e., user input from a matrix instance) or previous step outputs[5].

Schema elements are identified by joining configuration/attribute pairs[6] with a period: e.g., `ExampleConfig.AnInput`. Previous wrapper step output is referenced by joining step/output pairs with a period and prefixing the `$` symbol, as in `$ExampleWrapperStep.WrapperOutputEx`. Transforms only need specify necessary information—output variable tags for a wrapper step are only necessary if they are fed into other steps, for example, and input wiring for a wrapper step are required only for inputs required by the wrapper for which there is no default value given in the wrapper spec. However, any configuration/attribute pair defined in the schema must be used within the corresponding transform. Likewise, any Configuration/Attribute pair used in a transform must be defined in the schema.

Referencing previous step output forms wrapper dependency chains; the only restrictions on this chaining are type safety (i.e., data types of a step output must match that of the input) and acyclicity (i.e., wrapper chains must not form any circular dependencies).

Thus, if wrapper steps and the matrix schema are treated as nodes and input/output dependencies as directed edges, matrix types may define any connected directed acyclic graph (DAG). In fact, this fact is leveraged by the Run Manger to optimize model execution: it uses a topological sort algorithm to ensure models are executed as soon as possible after their dependencies have been satisfied.

Listing 4 shows an example of a transform illustrating a number of features of the design:

- **Input mapping:** Different wrappers may require the same information but use different variable names for that information. The transform allows the same piece of data from the matrix instance to be mapped to as many wrapper inputs as necessary. Here, the input data `ExampleConfig.InputName` goes to both `ExampleWrapper` and `AnotherWrapper` in the first and second steps, though each wrapper uses a different variable name (`WrapperVariableName` and `AnExample`, respectively).
- **Wrapper reuse**: Wrappers may be used more than once in the same matrix type in different steps. This is often used to create iterative simulations. In Listing 4, the wrapper `"ExampleWrapper"` will be executed twice, both in the first and fourth steps.
- **Stop conditions**: Wrapper output variables can be tested using comparison and boolean operators against constant values and halt execution of individual test cases that do not meet the criteria. Avoiding unnecessary computation is useful in optimization workloads when a subsystem model produces results that are unsatisfactory in some way and further modeling is not needed—for example, if a particular model of a factory assembly line produces results that are worse than some baseline, there may be no need to model further steps in the manufacturing chain. In Listing 4, if the output from `AnotherWrapper (SomeOutput)` is equal to zero, the test case is halted and the last step is not executed.

Matrix types can also group sets of wrapper outputs and process them as collections, but space limitations prevent details here.

3.3 Matrix Instances

The matrix instances are specific instantiations of a matrix type and in particular a type's matrix schema: a matrix schema is an XSD, so a valid instance is an XML document that passes standard XSD validation. Listing 5 shows an example instance excerpt. This document is what end users create either by hand or with the assistance of tools such as the Input GUI we describe in §4.2.

4. SYSTEM COMPONENTS

TMT is written in C++ using the open source Qt C++ libraries and tools. We have built a framework implementation around the TMT design concepts. It consists of three major components:

[5] …or constant values (prepended by the `@` symbol), as seen in Listing 3 for the variable `ReferenceFrame`.

[6] Because dimensions must have exactly one configuration element, instance data elements may omit the dimension name and still provide a one-to-one mapping.

```
<TestMatrix>
<!-- header information -->
<Creator>dknuth</Creator>
<Name>NameOfMatrixInstance</Name>
<Type>MatrixTypeName</Type>
<Description>Some comments/Description>

<Dimensions>
  <ExampleDimension>
    <ExampleConfig>
      <AnInput>0</AnInput>
    </ExampleConfig>
     <ExampleConfig>
      <AnInput>1</AnInput>
    </ExampleConfig>
    <ExampleConfig>
      <AnInput>99</AnInput>
    </ExampleConfig>
  </ExampleDimension>

  <SourceLocations>
    <SourceLocation>
      <X>1.1</X>
      <Y>1.2</Y>
    </SourceLocation>
    <SourceLocation>
      <X>1.1</X>
      <Y>1.2</Y>
    </SourceLocation>
  </SourceLocations>
                    (other input omitted...)
</Dimensions>
</TestMatrix>
```

Listing 5. An example test matrix instance with data matching the template shown in Listing 3.

- The Input GUI framework, which allows users to assemble a customized GUI from Qt Designer UI XML files and thus generate matrix instances.
- The Run Manager, which handles ingest, validation, execution and collations of matrix instances and their results.
- The Analysis GUI, which provides a flexible tool for filtering, comparing and visualizing data from any matrix instance.

TMT is designed as a high-level framework suitable for subject matter experts rather than modeling or parallel computing experts. As a result, it layers on top of a DRMAA-compatible[7] grid manager to perform core grid activities but takes care of the front- and back-end responsibilities for farming the runs to the grid and harvesting their results.

The following sections provide an overview of those components, their implementation and operation, before discussing a case study of their use.

4.1 Implementation Details

Individual TMT components use a variety of open source libraries: qwt[8], boost[9], etc., and the framework as a whole depends on the open source MySQL RDBMS[10] and a CORBA server of some kind (e.g., OmniORB[11]) for client/server communication.

Figure 2 depicts the high-level architecture of the TMT framework. All components are built for a RedHat Enterprise

[7] http://www.drmaa.org

[8] http://qwt.sourceforge.net/

[9] http://www.boost.org

[10] http://www.mysql.com

[11] http://omniorb.sourceforge.net

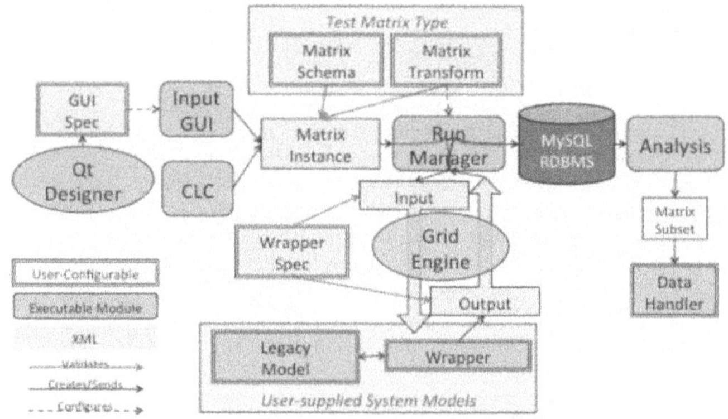

Figure 2. TMT architecture diagram.

Linux (RHEL) environment, though there are no technical barriers to building clients for Windows or OS/X, and the Run Manager for any platform for which a DRMAA-compatible grid manager is available (which consist of only linux and unix variants to the best of our knowledge).

Configurable parameters, such as the directories to store matrix type schemas and transforms, wrapper specs, output data are read from a `tmt.conf` configuration file. TMT XML files are loaded into those locations (along with other metadata in the database) through a Run Manager administrative tool.

4.2 Input GUI

The purpose of the Input GUI is to provide a graphical interface to the process of creating a matrix instance conforming to a given matrix type. A user can hand-edit instance XML and submit it via a command line client (which the TMT framework does provide), but that process lacks any inline error checking, validation or graphical illustration of input parameters prior to submission. The goal of the Input GUI is to decrease user errors by generating only submit valid matrix instances, but be flexible enough so that users can customize the GUI to their matrix types and wrappers without requiring recompilation of the entire framework.

The Qt Designer tool is a graphical GUI editor tool that integrates with the Qt UILoader infrastructure, which allows for the runtime specification and instantiation of arbitrary GUI widgets. It defines an XML format (`.ui` files) for specifying the value of public `Q_PROPERTIES` (i.e., public member variables) necessary to instantiate a widget. We have leveraged this infrastructure to allow end users to write a UI file and thus specify what Qt widgets to instantiate to form an appropriate GUI to specify matrix instance information.

We have created an `AbstractWidget` interface as an abstract Qt Designer plugin widget, which specifies the core properties and methods necessary to assemble a matrix instance from a set of GUI components. That interface (an excerpt of which is shown in Listing 6) requires derived widgets to indicate what dimension, configuration and attribute(s) they will provide; that data is instantiated by the end user, who edits a UI file (using the Qt Designer GUI editor) to specify which `AbstractWidget` implementations she would like to use for which matrix dimensions.

Widget implementations should ideally leverage the advantages of a graphical input modality vs. a textual one—for example, showing image content vs. a file name, or selecting a critical point on a 2D or 3D surface by clicking instead of specifying coordinates.

```
class AbstractWidget : public QWidget
{
   Q_OBJECT

   // Key global properties for this interface that that are defined in some containing
   // designer UI file by the user that determine what the instance XML should look like.
   Q_PROPERTY(QString dimension READ dimension WRITE setDimension DESIGNABLE true)
   Q_PROPERTY(QString configuration READ configuration WRITE setConfiguration DESIGNABLE true)
   Q_PROPERTY(QStringList attributes READ attributes WRITE setAttributes DESIGNABLE true)

   // Contains a set of object names to which this widget will QObject::connect() this
   // widget's widgetSignal to widgetSlot's of the other objects.
   // Implementing widgets are then responsible for deciding what data to emit
   // and handling data passed to them.  This is a very simple method of cross-widget communication.
   Q_PROPERTY(QStringList emitSignalTo READ emitSignalTo WRITE setEmitSignalTo DESIGNABLE true)

   /* Non-designable property that stores attribute properties */
   Q_PROPERTY(QList<Attribute> attrInfo READ attrInfo WRITE setAttrInfo)

public:
```

(constructor, getters/setters and members defined above omitted…)

```
   // Initialize is separate from the constructor and NOT called from there
   // to separate code that's needed by the widget but shouldn't be activated
   // when using the widgets from within Qt Designer (which does call the constructor)
   virtual void initialize();

   // ToXML is the raison d'etre of these widgets:  it produces valid XML
   // with tags named according to the dimension/configuration/attribute info
   // defined in the containing UI file with data as collected by whatever
   // kind of widget that implements this interface.
   virtual QDomDocument * toXML();

   virtual bool validate();

   // Loads a widget from XML that's been saved out
   virtual bool fromXML(QDomDocument * doc);

public slots:
    // Reimplement if a widget is expecting to receive data!
    virtual void widgetSlot(const QVariant & var);
}
```

Listing 6. `AbstractWidget` interface excerpt. The `Attribute` class encapsulates a field's data type, value constraints, etc. as derived from wrapper specifications.

This, of course, assumes that either the user or a 3rd party has implemented and compiled a shared library of such conforming widgets; we have developed sets of such widgets but only for proprietary matrix types.

At run time, the Input GUI first requests the installed matrix types from the TMT database. Users select which type they would like to create an instance of, and the Input GUI instantiates the widgets from UI files in a directory location specified in `tmt.conf`. The user then provides input to the widgets in whatever manner they specify (e.g., clicking on a 3D terrain to specify coordinates). The key advantage is that widgets collect the information that is both necessary and sufficient to form a valid instance, reducing the error possibilities vs. hand-editing XML. For example, the Input GUI can infer the data type of a given Attribute by parsing the matrix transform and looking at the data type of the wrapper variable(s) to which it is wired. Similar benefits accrue from the specification of wrapper variable defaults, min/max values, etc.

After interacting with each of the widgets, the Input GUI simply calls the `toXML()` method of each widget and assembles their outputs into a matrix instance, which it sends to the Run Manager via a CORBA method invocation.

4.3 Run Manager

The Run Manager's central purpose is to respond to input data requests from user matrix instances. As described in §3.2.1, taking the cross product of all configuration combinations within each dimension forms a test matrix comprising a series of test cases, which are in turn made up of a set of test case nodes representing individual wrapper executions. In the general case, the structure of each test case exactly matches the topology[12] of the test matrix transform, but because of individual run differences—i.e., errors and stop conditions—a test case may only contain a subset of the full matrix type graph structure.

As a result, the Run Manager must enumerate and monitor the execution of each node individually. Moreover, we want to avoid unnecessary recalculation of results for model wrappers that are computationally complex. To do that, when DRMAA notifies the Run Manager a test case node is finished, it stores the run results in a matching MySQL run table (there is one main table per wrapper[13]). An indexed key to that table is a `HashString`

[12] Used in the *network topology* sense of the term rather than the mathematical one.

[13] Array variable fields are normalized into tables linked with foreign keys the main wrapper table.

column, which is a SHA1 cryptographic hash of the wrapper name, input variables and values for a given case assembled into an input string like:

```
ExampleWrapper:
SourceX=0;SourceY=0;ReferenceFrame=LLA;
LocationArray=[TargX=-100;TargY=-100;TargZ=100];
[TargX=100;TargY=100;TargZ=100]
```

Thus, if different matrix instances (even of different matrix types!) result in a wrapper execution with matching inputs, we can avoid recomputing a potentially expensive result by simply querying the appropriate SQL table for the wrapper. Even though the hash maps an infinite set of possible inputs to a finite set of outputs, it is practically robust to collisions.[14]

A second challenge is linking generic TMT test case and test case node entries to wrappers that have been plugged into the framework by end users. It accomplishes this by recording test case and test case node data (and test case node linkages) in their own SQL tables; the test case node table has a field for the wrapper id and the corresponding row entry in that wrapper table corresponding to the node. While this allows nodes to reference arbitrary new wrappers, the major drawback is that these are semantic constraints, which SQL foreign keys cannot enforce. However, with domain-specific knowledge (i.e., that test case nodes have specific fields that identify a tuple in another table), TMT components (like the Analysis GUI) can generate SQL queries to extract the necessary data for a given matrix instance.

4.4 Analysis GUI

One of the key payoffs of TMT's consistent design structures is in the data analysis component: we can design a single, generic data analysis tool to support common analytic activities that exist across simulation application domains. There has been considerable work in the information visualization and visual analytic communities characterizing the nature of such high- and low-level activities (Yi et al. provide a recent survey [21]). But informally, such activities include data filtering, comparisons, transformation and visualization.

We accomplish this by adopting a faceted metadata design pattern, which originated in library science but has been replicated by information visualization [18], image browsing environments [20], and other general-purpose tools [4] (sometimes under different nomenclature, such as dimensional analysis in data warehousing). A number of current commercial business intelligence vendors (e.g., Tableau[15]) use faceted or similar design patterns; we think of TMT's data analysis component as a sort of scientific intelligence tool, with its features oriented towards high-dimensional simulation data for scientific and engineering applications. Other business intelligence tools applicable to these kinds of problems include TIBCO Spotfire[16] and SAS JMP[17].

Like many tools related to information visualization, much of its value comes not just from allowing users to answer specific questions, but from harder to quantify attributes such as allowing users to ask *better* questions, or prompting users to ask questions they did not know they had in the first place [6].

For any TMT matrix type, the analysis GUI forms a data cache by denormalizing all of the run data from a matrix into a single SQL table, trading space efficiency for speed, a common architecture for read-heavy database stores. Each column is then an input or an output of some wrapper step, and the analysis GUI forms a filter for each field. Each filter customizes its representation to the nature of the data in the field: high-variation scalar data use a slider GUI element; nominal and low-variation scalars have a series of checkboxes (cf. Figure 3 inset).

Figure 3 shows the high-level organization of the tool: filter widgets are grouped at left, with one of several data views (e.g., scatterplot visualization) at right. Data views always reflect the current data scope: initially, all data from a matrix is in scope, and filter choices successively narrow that scope (or enlarge it, if a filter limitation is removed). The current scope also affects filter widgets themselves: filters show how items currently in scope are distributed across a particular dimension. In the Figure 3 inset, the numbers next to each filter value represent the number of cases corresponding to each value. Here, there are many more right-handed (R) players than left-handed (L), and many more of either than those that use both hands (B).

The interaction design of the analysis tool is focused on minimizing actions necessary to accomplish major operations—filtering, comparing and visualizing—and removing opportunities to make unproductive choices. Streamlining these operations reduces the barriers to iterative investigation through visual hypothesis testing and analysis. Filtering operations are accomplished by single actions: clicking a checkbox or dragging a slider handle. Similarly, clicking the *Split* button (which is only shown for appropriate filters) triggers the data view to compare the data in scope by the different values of a filter; the current scope can be split along any number of dimensions.

Configuring the view is consistent across view types, and consists of making selections of data variables (which only show variables of an appropriate type) for each visual element *slot* in the given view. Variables are listed within combobox UI elements, so configuring a view consists of selecting the desired variable assignments for each slot via combobox choices.

The scatter chart in Figure 3 has slots for the X and Y axis as well as glyph color and size, but other views have fewer (e.g., line chart has only X and Y axis slots) or different (the parallel coordinates view [12] has a dynamic number of slots, all for parallel Y axes). Views implement the comparison action (triggered from the *Split* filter buttons) in different ways: scatterplots create one chart per value of the filter, while line charts create different color data series as shown in Figure 4.

There are currently five major view types: scatterplots, line charts, bar charts, parallel coordinates and a tabular data view. There are also polar variants of the scatter and line charts. Other analysis capabilities include data transformations (automatic unit

[14] There 2^{160} SHA1 hashes. Assume all SHA1 hashes are equally likely to be chosen. Let $sha1 = 2^{160}$. The probability of n runs not having the same hash is:

$$P(n) = 1 \times \left(1 - \frac{1}{sha1}\right) \times \left(1 - \frac{2}{sha1}\right) \times \ldots \times \left(1 - \frac{n-1}{sha1}\right).$$

From the first two terms of the Taylor series expansion of e^x, the probability of n runs not having the same hash is:

$$P(n) \approx e^{-\frac{1}{sha1} - \frac{2}{sha1} - \cdots - \frac{n-1}{sha1}} = e^{\frac{-n(n-1)}{2 \times sha1}} \approx e^{\frac{-n^2}{2^{161}}}.$$

While this approximation break down as $n \rightarrow sha1$, we can use it to find that for a small value like $5.5e + 21$, $P(n) = 0.99999$, which gives a probability of collision $1 - 0.99999 = 1e - 5$, or 0.001%. Thus, if a user makes a million runs per day after approximately $1.5e + 13$ years (15 trillion) there will be a 0.001% chance of having a collision.

[15] http://www.tableausoftware.com

[16] http://spotfire.tibco.com

[17] http://www.jmp.com

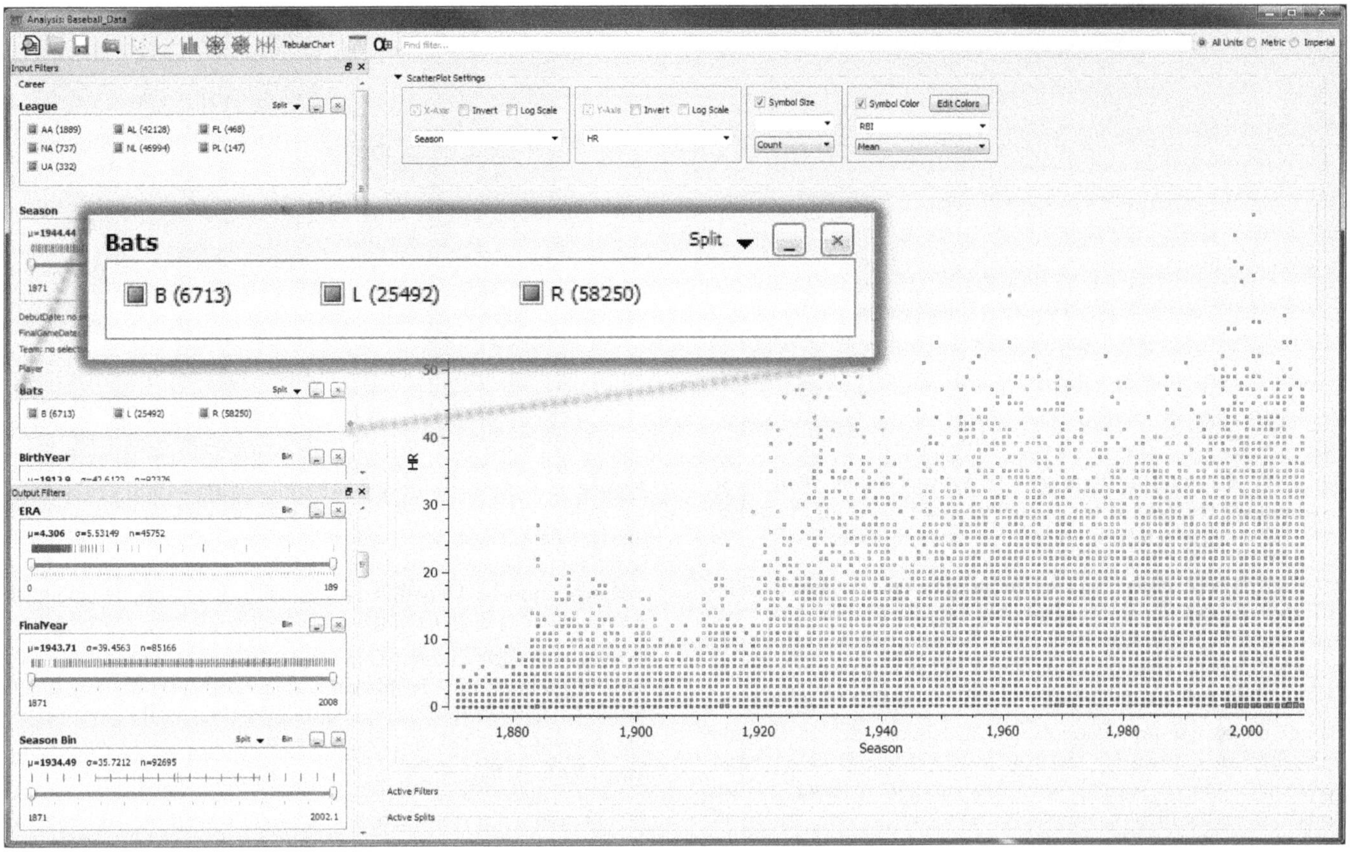

Figure 3. The TMT Analysis component, showing data from historical U.S. baseball statistics: data filters are assembled from the data at left; the active visualization is at right. Filter choices update the active visualization and the choices available in other filter widgets. Inset shows detail of a filter for the nominal variable *Bats* indicating a player's handedness. The view shows the number of home runs hit by players over time.

conversions, deriving new computed variables) and an external plugin API.

The scalability of the analysis component is limited by the memory and speed of the user's workstation as well as the nature of the test data (type and number of variables). On modern workstation-level hardware we have found practical limits to be between 100,000 and 1 million cases with up to about 300 dimensions.

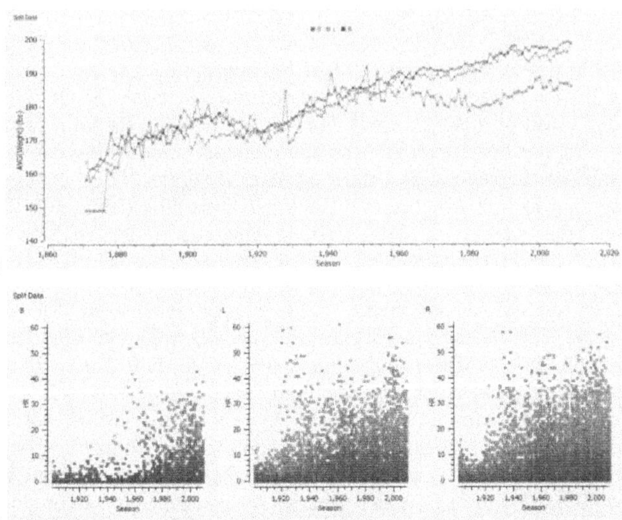

a)

b)

Figure 4. Differences between of split function between the a) line chart and b) scatterplot TMT Analysis view types.

5. CASE STUDY

We have used TMT in a variety of proprietary modeling applications over the past three years. Here we present a case study of a TMT application we conducted in collaboration with the Remote Sensing Group (RSG) at GTRI's Electro-Optical Systems Lab, who conducts research in bathymetric LIDAR applications (e.g., measuring laser reflections in water to determine seafloor depth and other environmental factors). In particular, there are a variety of ranging algorithms for calculating bathymetric LIDAR optical path length. Because of the vast numbers of parameters in both waveform generation and the ranging algorithms, large numbers of runs are necessary to adequately gauge the performance of various ranging algorithms under a variety of conditions. As such, it is well suited to TMT.

Our specific task was to conduct a robust evaluation of an interest point detection algorithm: given a set of synthesized LIDAR waveforms like the example in Figure 5, evaluate the performance of a specific feature detection approach to finding sea surface and floor ranges. With information about the LIDAR orientation, these measurements can be used to map sea floor depths over a large area.

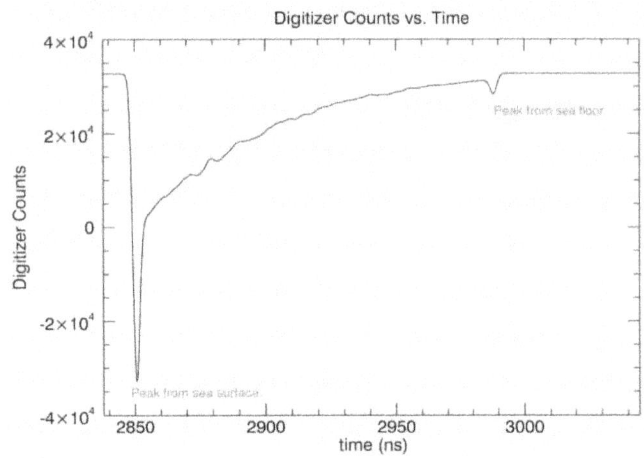

Figure 5. An example digitized LIDAR waveform. Note local extrema representing the sea surface and floor, and the noise between throughout the water column

Prior to this case study, the waveform generator was run through an Excelis ENVI/IDL[18] GUI that only supported making one run at a time. The waveforms were saved and run one at a time through various ranging algorithms. With this setup, it was difficult to execute, aggregate and analyze large sets of data.

Though it is not an experimental evaluation, the case study represents a real-world test of the end-to-end TMT user experience: write several wrappers around existing system models; combine them using one or more matrix types; form and execute appropriate test matrix instances; and analyze the results. Moreover, since RSG work was active in this area prior to the TMT application, the prior results are a kind of pseudo-control condition against the case study results.

5.1 Procedure

One expert and one novice TMT user (the second and third authors, respectively) conducted the work in the case study in January 2013. Neither author has developed any part of the TMT framework. The TMT matrix type includes three wrappers (and the matrix type schema and transform) arranged as in Figure 6. The first and second wrappers build on existing RSG implementations of the waveform generation and ranging algorithms, and are implemented in IDL. All wrapper run times are negligible, so the advantages of run reuse for more expensive computation are not leveraged.

The first wrapper runs a LIDAR waveform generator, which generates synthetic LIDAR signals based on 23 parameters that include environmental conditions and properties of the LIDAR hardware itself (e.g., water depth, noise level, and pulse power). For this evaluation, 10 of the 23 parameters were set to default values, leaving 13 parameters to be varied within the matrix type/instance. The output from this wrapper is a comma separated value (CSV) file containing the resulting LIDAR waveform.

The second wrapper runs the ranging algorithm. It smooths the raw waveform using a Savitzky-Golay smoothing filter [16], and detects the two extrema (valleys), which correspond to the initial return from the sea surface and the second return from the sea floor, and calculates an optical path length estimate. Aside from

[18] A popular commercial environment/language in the LIDAR community, see http://www.exelisvis.com/

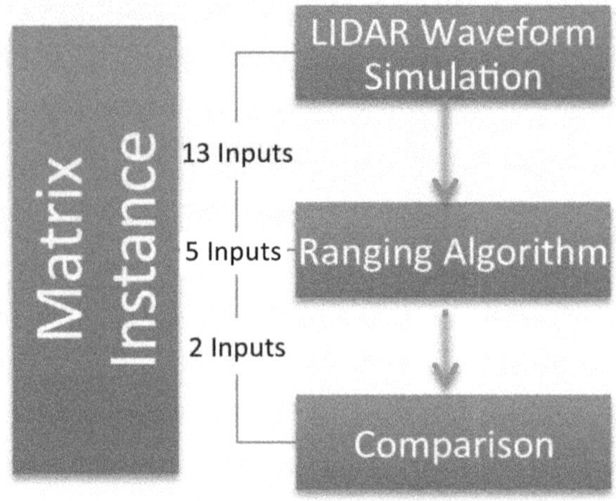

Figure 6. Transform design for ranging algorithm evaluation.

the raw data, there are 5 algorithm-related parameters as inputs (e.g., smoothing window, smoothing order, and search window), and in addition to the path length estimate, it outputs the smoothed waveform used in its calculations.

Finally, the third wrapper compares a generic estimate value to a generic ground truth (in this case, calculated from the raw inputs to the LIDAR waveform inputs) and provides evaluation metrics like percent error and raw distance error.

This matrix design illustrates several desirable properties:

- It allow for future reuse of both waveform and ranging algorithm data. For example, re-running a matrix after modifying or adding a new comparison metric output would only require rerunning the fast comparison wrapper.
- By separating the waveform generation and ranging steps, we allow for the future expansion of other ranging algorithm wrappers or the augmentation of the existing one with new variants.
- Implementing a generic Comparison wrapper means it can be reused in any context requiring simple comparative metrics.
- Separation of the IDL-dependent components means that only those steps will be rate limited by the IDL grid resource (since only a subset of our execution nodes have IDL licenses for cost considerations).

Table 1 provides an indicator of the approximate effort involved in the case study in terms of source lines of code (SLOC). The total effort of this case study (including data analysis not reflected in wrapper development) was approximately one man-week split between the second and third authors. Roughly 2/3 of that total devoted to infrastructure development (including debugging IDL and other integration issues) and the remainder to data analysis.

5.2 Equipment

Our internal development TMT cluster was used for this study. The cluster has six execution nodes, three with dual Xeon X5650 @2.67GHz (hex) cores, two with dual Xeon E5645 @2.4GHz (hex) cores, and one with dual Xeon E5620 @ 2.4GHz (quad) cores, for a total of 136 hyperthreaded cores. All the cluster machines run Red Hat Enterprise Linux 5.8 with virtualized servers providing TMT Run Manager, CORBA, MySQL, and Grid Engine services. A dedicated file server stores all run data and is NFS mounted to all server and execution nodes.

Table 1. Source lines of code (SLOC) for case study wrappers and matrix types; generated using David A. Wheeler's *SLOCCount.*

	Wrappers						Matrix Type			
	Waveform		Algorithm		Comparison				**Total**	
	Wrapper	Spec	Wrapper	Spec	Wrapper	Spec	Transform	Schema	**Perl**	**XML**
New	24	222	36	52	13	29	31	201	**73**	**535**
Boilerplate	71		71		71				**213**	**-**
Total	95	222	107	52	84	29	31	201	**286**	**535**

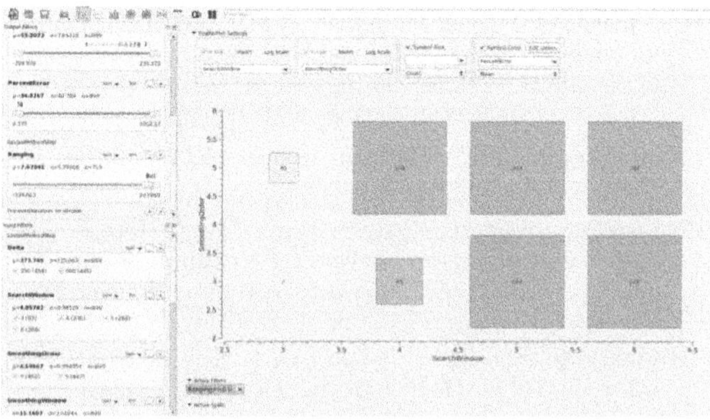

Figure 8. TMT Analysis scatterplot of smoothing order vs. search window size, with color indicating the algorithm error.

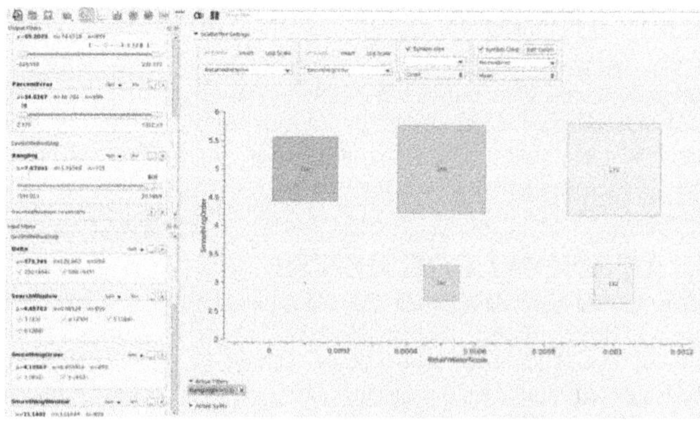

Figure 7. TMT Analysis scatterplot of smoothing order vs. noise values, with color indicating the algorithm error.

5.3 Results and Discussion

Over 13,000 runs over two calendar days were made with TMT during the specific duration of the case study. The runs were split over 22 instances, varying in size from 1 to 6,912 cases (with some overlap), and used to actively debug and analyze the ranging algorithm. As both the LIDAR simulation and the ranging algorithms are currently under development, TMT has identified both issues in the underlying simulations as well as trends to aid in optimizing the algorithm.

For example, Figure 8 shows the effects of varying the smoothing order[19] (Y axis) and search window[20] (X axis) parameters to the ranging algorithm wrapper. The figure scatterplot maps the ranging accuracy percent error to color (green/yellow/red stoplight pattern with green indicating a low error rate), and the size of each glyph indicating the count of runs made with a particular smoothing order/search window value combination.

In the figure, we have selected only ranging values greater than zero, which occurs when the algorithm is able to find an inflection point associated with each peak. A negative value represents a failure to detect the range. The visualization indicates that this occurs more often with lower search window sizes (3 or 4 vs. 5 or 6), but less often when the smoothing order is 5 vs. 3.

Figure 7 shows smoothing order (Y axis) vs. noise values (X axis). This example examines the robustness of an algorithm parameter against a simulation parameter. Here it is clear that a lower smoothing order results in fewer successful runs. The naïve explanation for this is that higher orders are inherently better, but based on further expert investigation using the Analysis GUI, we found this is most likely due to the fact that the higher order filter follows more of the noise, which allows it to return values—but ones which are noise artifacts and thus incorrect.

Apart from parameter tuning, TMT also helped evaluate some integration issues between pieces of the IDL code. After running the first matrix, it became immediately clear that the algorithm was not returning expected results. A small amount of investigation showed that in the IDL code we had been passing the waveform in units of Watts instead of digitizer counts, which the detection algorithm was expecting. TMT also illuminated some areas of the algorithm that needed revision, such as shallow water performance, in which we discovered that noise was even dominating the powerful sea floor returns. RSG is implementing a solution to this issue, and use of TMT has continued beyond the specific bounds of this case study.

Though brief, and involving authors of this work, this case study provides some validation of our belief that TMT can help improve the overall efficiency and efficacy of system performance analyses. In a matter of days, a 3rd party research group integrated its tool chain with the TMT infrastructure and—as envisioned—leveraged the framework to do more extensive testing and analysis than was previously expedient. In particular, the analysis tool provided several interesting insights and critically, led RSG personnel to generate new questions and new analytic goals.

6. FUTURE WORK AND CONCLUSIONS

The TMT framework is under active development with a variety of possibilities for future research. Because the framework defines a set of well-defined XML data interfaces, we can replace or provide alternatives to major components without affecting the overall system. For example, we could create an Input GUI

---

19 The degree of the polynomial used for local regression in the Savitzky-Golay filter.

20 The number of range bins prior to the peak to search for the inflection point.

infrastructure specifically for DOE methodologies, incorporating any number of structured or random input sampling techniques. Another approach under investigation is to integrate DOE sampling techniques within the Run Manager itself, creating an alternative to end users relying on factorial expansion or providing DOE-derived cases themselves.

The analysis component has proven to be a useful and flexible tool both in TMT context as well as for general-purpose data analysis. We are currently preparing a standalone version of the tool to use as a research testbed for information visualization and visual analytic research applications.

We have introduced the Test Matrix Tool, a framework for conducting large-scale performance analysis of complex system models. Its high-level design provides flexible ways of incorporating existing system and subsystem models, allowing for component and data reuse. Its implementation focuses on end-user ease of use for key tasks: run specification, execution, and analysis. We have presented a case study of its use on a new, real-world application and generated several useful insights that have generated an ongoing use of the tool for that user base.

7. ACKNOWLEDGMENTS

Many hands have developed TMT, past and present: thanks are due to Heyward Adams, Ethan Adler, Allison Aigner, Tom Aigner, David Bolding, Ray Decuir, Daniel Long, Daniel Luh, Ryan O'Neill and John Turgeson, Our appreciation also goes to the sponsors of TMT over the past several years.

8. REFERENCES

[1] Bagrodia, R., Meyer, R., Takai, M., Chen, Y. A., Zeng, X., Martin, J. and Song, H. Y. (1998). Parsec: A parallel simulation environment for complex systems. *IEEE Computer*, 31(10), pp. 77-85.

[2] Bagrodia, R., Yu-an Chen, Gerla, M., Kwan, B., Martin, J., Palnati, P., Walton, S. (1996). Parallel Simulation of a High-Speed Wormhole Routing Network. In *Proc. of the Tenth Workshop on Parallel and Distributed Simulation (PADS 96)*, pp. 47-56.

[3] Buyya, R. and Murshed, M. (2003). Gridsim: A toolkit for the modeling and simulation of distributed resource management and scheduling for grid computing. *Concurrency and Computation: Practice and Experience*, 14(13-15), pp. 1175-1220.

[4] Clarkson, E., Navathe, S. and Foley, J.D. (2009). Generalized formal models for faceted user interfaces. In *Proc. of the 9th ACM/IEEE Joint Conference on Digital Libraries (JCDL 09)*, pp. 125-134.

[5] Dahmann, J. S., Fujimoto, R. M. and Weatherly, R. M. (1997). The Department of Defense High Level Architecture. In *Proc. of the 29th Winter Simulation Conference,* pp. 142-149.

[6] Fekete, J. D., Van Wijk, J., Stasko, J. and North, C. (2008). The Value of Information Visualization. In *Information Visualization*, Andreas Kerren, John T. Stasko, Jean-Daniel Fekete, and Chris North (Eds.). Lecture Notes In Computer Science, Vol. 4950. Springer-Verlag pp. 1-18.

[7] Flager, F., Welle, B., Bansal, P., Soremekun, G., and Haymaker, J. (2009). Multidisciplinary Process Integration and Design Optimization of a Classroom Building. *Journal of Information Technology in Construction* (14), pp. 595-612.

[8] Fogue, M., Garrido, P., Martinez, F. J., Cano, J. C., Calafate, C. T. and Manzoni, P. (2012). A realistic simulation framework for vehicular networks. In *Proc. of the 5th International ICST Conference on Simulation Tools and Techniques,* pp. 37-46.

[9] Fujimoto, R. (1990). Parallel discrete event simulation. *Communications of the ACM* 33(10), pp. 30-53.

[10] Gamma, E., Helm, R., Johnson, R. and Vlissides, J. (1994). *Design Patterns - Elements of Reusable Object-Oriented Software*. Addison-Wesley.

[11] Himmelspach, J. and Uhrmacher, A.M. (2009) The JAMES II Framework for Modeling and Simulation. In *Proc. of the International Workshop on High Performance Computational Systems Biology (HIBI 09)*, pp.101-102.

[12] Inselberg, A. (1985). The plane with parallel coordinates. *The Visual Computer* 1(2), pp. 69-91.

[13] Kandel, S., Paepcke, A., Hellerstein, J. M. and Heer, J. (2012). Enterprise Data Analysis and Visualization: An Interview Study. *IEEE Transactions on Visualization and Computer Graphics*, 18(12), pp. 2917-2926.

[14] Kotkas, V., Ojamaa, A., Grigorenko, P., Maigre, R., Harf, M. and Tyugu, E. (2011). CoCoViLa as a Multifunctional Simulation Platform. In *Proc. of the 4th International ICST Conference on Simulation Tools and Techniques*, pp. 198-205.

[15] Rodrigues, A. F., Hemmert, K. S., Barrett, B. W., Kersey, C., Oldfield, R., Weston, M., Risen, R., Cook, J., Rosenfeld, P., CooperBalls, E. and Jacob, B. (2011). The Structural Simulation Toolkit. *ACM SIGMETRICS Performance Evaluation Review*, 38(4), pp. 37-42.

[16] Savitzky, A. and Golay, M.J.E. (1964). Smoothing and Differentiation of Data by Simplified Least Squares Procedures. *Analytical Chemistry* 36(8), pp. 1627–1639.

[17] Shvachko, K., Kuang, H., Radia, S. and Chansler, R. (2010). The Hadoop Distributed File System. In *Proc. of the IEEE Symposium on Mass Storage Systems and Technologies*, pp. 1-10.

[18] Spence, R. and Tweedie, L. (1998). The Attribute Explorer: Information Synthesis via Exploration. *Interacting with Computers*, 11(2), pp. 137-146.

[19] Wonnacott, P., Bruce, D. (1996). The APOSTLE simulation language: granularity control and performance data. In Proc. of the *Tenth Workshop on Parallel and Distributed Simulation (PADS 96)*, pp. 114-123.

[20] Yee, K. P., Swearingen, K., Li, K. and Hearst, M. (2003). Faceted Metadata for Image Search and Browsing. In *Proc. of the SIGCHI Conference on Human Factors in Computing Systems (CHI 03)*, pp. 401-408.

[21] Yi, J.S., Kang, Y., Stasko, J. and Jacko, J. (2007). Toward a Deeper Understanding of the Role of Interaction in Information Visualization, *IEEE Transactions on Visualization and Computer Graphics*, 13(6), pp. 1224-1231.

[22] Zeigler, B. P., Praehofer, H, and Kim, T.G. (2000) *Theory of modeling and simulation: Integrating Discrete Event and Continuous Complex Dynamic Systems*. Academic Press.

Can PDES Scale in Environments with Heterogeneous Delays?

Jingjing Wang, Ketan Bahulkar, Dmitry Ponomarev, and Nael Abu-Ghazaleh
Dept. of Computer Science, Binghamton University
Binghamton, NY, USA
jwang36@cs.binghamton.edu, kbahulkar@cs.binghamton.edu,
dima@cs.binghamton.edu, nael@cs.binghamton.edu

ABSTRACT

The performance and scalability of Parallel Discrete Event Simulation (PDES) is often limited by communication latencies and overheads. The emergence of multi-core processors and their expected evolution into many-cores offers the promise of low latency communication and tight memory integration between cores; these properties should significantly improve the performance of PDES in such environments. However, on clusters of multi-cores (CMs), the latency and processing overheads incurred when communicating between different machines (nodes) far outweigh those between cores on the same chip, especially when commodity networking fabrics and communication software are used. It is unclear if there is any benefit to the low latency among cores on the same node given that communication links across nodes are significantly worse. In this study, we examine the performance of a multi-threaded implementation of PDES on CMs. We demonstrate that the inter-node communication costs impose a substantial bottleneck on PDES and demonstrate that without optimizations addressing these long latencies, multi-threaded PDES does not significantly outperform the multiprocess version despite direct communication through shared memory on the individual nodes. We then propose three optimizations: message consolidation and routing, infrequent polling and latency-sensitive model partitioning. We show that with these optimizations in place, threaded implementation of PDES significantly outperforms process-based implementation even on CMs.

Categories and Subject Descriptors

I.6.8 [**Simulation and Modeling**]: Types of Simulation—*Discrete event, Parallel*

General Terms

Performance

Keywords

PDES, Cluster of Multi-cores, Multi-thread

1. INTRODUCTION

Communication latency represents one of the major challenges in scaling many important classes of parallel applications, especially those that exhibit fine-grained communication and synchronization patterns, such as Parallel Discrete Event Simulation (PDES). The emergence of multi-core processors and the trend of increasing the number of cores per processor offer a significant advantage for PDES applications: the low communication latency between cores allows for faster communication, and the tight memory integration allows for more efficient communication abstractions that reduce the software overheads of communication. Unfortunately, these advantages are limited to small scales: for large scale PDES applications that require more cores than is available on a single node[1], it is necessary to use a cluster of multi-cores (CMs). In such an environment, the communication delays and software overheads for communication across machines (inter-node communication) can be substantially higher than those between cores on the same machine (intra-node communication).

To understand and quantify this impact, we investigate the performance of PDES [16] on CMs. Specifically, the question that we address in this paper is the following: In the presence of heterogeneous delays, do fine-grained applications such as PDES benefit from the low latency available between some cores, or are they limited by the performance of the slowest links? To explore this question, we perform experiments on a cluster of multi-core nodes connected using Gigabit Ethernet and using MPI for communication across nodes. For cores on the same node, we explore the use of both MPI as well as more efficient communication exploiting the shared memory hierarchy between the cores on the same node. We show that the remote communication across nodes plays a critical role in determining the performance of PDES. The message processing delay on the communicating thread becomes a performance bottleneck of PDES. As a result, much of the available processing time is consumed in sending and receiving these events. Moreover, the high communication latency results in many messages arriving late, slowing down the simulation progress even further by causing rollbacks.

Therefore, we argue that the impact of the heterogeneous

[1] In this paper, we use node to mean a single multi-core machine.

delays must be considered as a first class design consideration when developing PDES algorithms to run on CMs. We demonstrate three techniques that significantly reduce the impact of the heterogeneous delays. The first technique we investigate is consolidated message routing between machines. In particular, to reduce the impact of message sending and receiving overheads, we combine messages originating from different cores on one machine to different cores on another machine to amortize the software overhead of processing them. Dedicated communication threads combine the messages on the sending side, without delaying messages. On the receiving side, the communication threads extract the individual messages and route them to the appropriate core using shared memory. We further improve the performance of the receiver communication thread by adjusting the frequency of polling for message arrival; with message consolidation, the number of messages is reduced, allowing us to reduce the frequency of the expensive polling operation. Combined, these two optimizations allow the threaded PDES implementation to achieve a 4.5X improvement in performance compared to the process-based implementation.

To further highlight the need for algorithmic awareness of the CM topology, we implement model partitioning in PDES in a way that is aware of the high cost of inter-node communication. In particular, we modified a recently proposed partitioning algorithm [1] to first partition across machines (minimizing the model communication between machines) and then partition the work across the cores on the same machine. We compare this strategy to one that partitions between the cores without consideration to the high communication latency between machines. Again, significant improvement in performance (up to 44% in some scenarios) is achieved by simply informing the partitioning tool of the communication cost hierarchy.

The remainder of the paper is organized as follows. Section 2 provides background information about the multi-core cluster environment we use, as well as PDES simulator. In this section, we also analyze the impact of the heterogeneous communication latencies on CMs for PDES. In Section 3, we focus on optimizations to help overcome this impact for PDES application. Section 4 presents an experimental evaluation of PDES performance. In Section 5, we overview some related work. Finally, in Section 6 we present some concluding remarks.

2. IMPACT OF HETEROGENEOUS CM LATENCIES ON PDES PERFORMANCE

In this section, we first present some background regarding clusters of multi-cores (CMs) used in our experiments. We follow this by evaluating PDES performance on CMs. The goal of these experiments is to show the large impact that the heterogeneous latencies present in these environments on PDES performance.

2.1 Multi-cores and Clusters of Multi-cores

In our experiments we use a cluster of 4-core Intel core i7 machines (Figure 1), running Debian 6.02 distribution for each node. Each core has private L1 and L2 caches, and shares the L3 cache with other cores. In addition, Simultaneous Multi-Threading (SMT) is employed on each node to increase the degree of available parallelism (SMT is called Hyper-Threading on Intel processors). More precisely, each core has two hardware threads which share most of the core pipeline structures, as well as the L1 and L2 caches. With 4 cores, each supporting two hardware threads, each node can execute up to 8 concurrent hardware threads. The nodes are connected using a Gigabit-Ethernet network.

We first use an MPI-based Ping-Pong benchmark to evaluate the communication latency in this environment. There are three types of communication in such CMs : intra-core, inter-core, and inter-node, as shown in Table 1. The intra-core communication occurs between two hardware threads on the same core, while inter-core communication happens among different cores on the same node. Inter-node communication is the communication over the network. Table 1 shows these three types of communication latency under different message sizes on the multi-core cluster connected through a Gigabit Ethernet switch. At any message size, the latency of inter-node communication is approximately two orders of magnitude larger than that of other two types of intra-node communication.

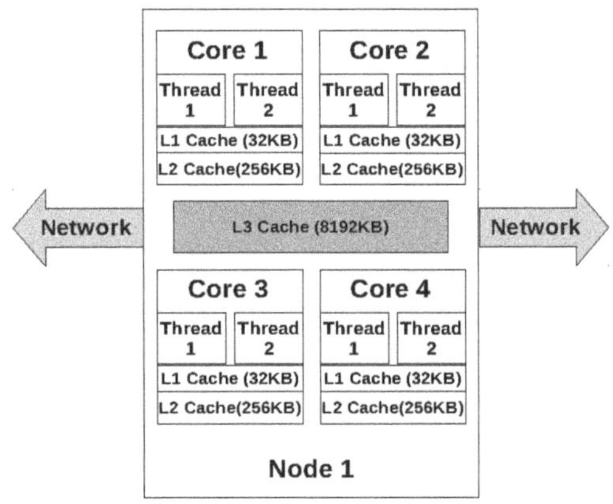

Figure 1: A cluster of Intel Core-i7 nodes

Message Size (Bytes)	intra-core	inter-core	inter-node
4	0.22	0.24	62.38
32	0.25	0.25	62.23
256	0.28	0.3	64.82
1024	0.35	0.38	78.06
8192	1.17	1.42	150.63
16K	2.37	2.88	268.61

Table 1: Heterogeneous Latency on the Cluster of Core-i7 Nodes (μSecs)

2.2 PDES Performance on CMs

We use a Parallel Discrete Event Simulation (PDES) engine to study the impact of heterogeneous latencies on CMs. PDES is an important application as it supports efficient simulation of large scale models in many domains including computing and telecommunication systems. In PDES, a simulation model is partitioned across multiple processing elements (PEs). Each PE processes the events destined to it in time-stamp order. For correct simulation, synchronization is needed to ensure that events generated from other PEs are also executed in the correct order [2, 16]. In conservative simulation, PEs must wait for assurance from other PEs that it is safe for them to process an event. In contrast,

	0% remote	20% remote	40% remote	60% remote	80% remote	100% remote
0% regional	7.3 sec	44.7 sec	70.3 sec	95.6 sec	117.5 sec	141 sec
20% regional	10.9 sec	44.4 sec	70.7 sec	95 sec	117.5 sec	N/A
40% regional	12.3 sec	44.9 sec	71.2 sec	95.4 sec	N/A	N/A
60% regional	12.8 sec	45.5 sec	71.9 sec	N/A	N/A	N/A
80% regional	14.3 sec	47.3 sec	N/A	N/A	N/A	N/A
100% regional	15.3 sec	N/A	N/A	N/A	N/A	N/A

Table 2: Effect of Heterogeneous Latency for baseline ROSS-CMT

	0% remote	20% remote	40% remote	60% remote	80% remote	100% remote
0% regional	N/A	100%	100%	100%	100%	100%
20% regional	0%	72.5%	82.3%	86%	87.3%	N/A
40% regional	0%	58.5%	70%	75.5%	N/A	N/A
60% regional	0%	48.9%	60.6%	N/A	N/A	N/A
80% regional	0%	41.9%	N/A	N/A	N/A	N/A
100% regional	0%	N/A	N/A	N/A	N/A	N/A

Table 3: The Rollback Percentage caused by remote events

optimistic simulation allows each PE to proceed without explicit synchronization. However, if an event is received with a time-stamp earlier than the current simulation time (a straggler event), the simulation is rolled back to a simulation time before that of the straggler event and re-executed. In both types of simulation, communication latency and software overheads play a critical role in determining performance. These overheads determine how fast event messages are communicated affecting simulation progress. The high latency also influences synchronization which has substantial effect on the progress rate and efficiency of the simulation.

We use the Rensselaer's Optimistic Simulation System (ROSS) as the simulation engine for our studies. ROSS is a highly efficient state-of-the-art simulator, that uses processes for each PE. Processes communicate with messages using the MPI library [6]. In the original ROSS simulator (ROSS-MPI), two message copy operations are needed for each message even when the PEs are on the same node, with access to shared memory. Message copies significantly increase the overhead of communication. In order to solve this performance bottleneck, a multi-threaded ROSS simulator (ROSS-MT) was implemented for a single multi-core shared memory node [19]. ROSS-MT uses message pointers to exchange messages and can avoid the message copying, forming, and other MPI overheads.

ROSS-MT is limited to a single node. To reach higher scales, an extended version of ROSS-MT, called ROSS-CMT, was recently developed to support CMs [33]. In ROSS-CMT, in order to avoid the overhead when multiple threads invoke MPI functions simultaneously, only one communication thread on each node performs communication across the network. The communication thread looks up the output queue of each thread in a round robin fashion, and sends remote events to the corresponding destination nodes. Once the communication thread at the receiver side probes (or polls) the event successfully, it then inserts the pointer of this event to the input queue of the destination thread. Generally speaking, ROSS-CMT performs better than ROSS-MPI on CMs, however, the delay of message processing at the side of communication thread imposes a performance bottleneck [33]. In this paper we use ROSS-CMT to study the impact of the heterogeneous latencies on CMs. Different from [33], this work provides three optimizations to hide high latency of inter-node communication for ROSS-CMT. Finally, we offer a detailed performance analysis of the optimized ROSS-CMT, by comparing it with both baseline ROSS-CMT and ROSS-MPI on CMs.

To characterize the impact of CMs on ROSS-CMT, we use the classical Phold benchmark [17]. Phold is a standard benchmark used in performance evaluation of PDES. It consists of a number of simulation objects distributed among multiple PEs. In our experiments, each PE is mapped to one thread in ROSS-CMT, or one process in ROSS-MPI. During execution each object randomly picks up a target and sends a time-stamped event message to the target. Upon receipt of the event, a new event may be generated to another target. Phold is controllable; allowing the percentage of communication between different objects to be specified to control the ratio between local, regional and remote events. Phold is a synthetic model with simple dependencies among objects, which allows us to study behavior under controlled conditions.

Table 2 shows the performance of ROSS-CMT with optimistic simulation, under different percentages of regional and remote communication on 4 nodes, with 8 threads each. Remote communication refers to traffic across nodes, while regional communication indicates the communication between cores on the same node. The rest of the communication is local and occurs within the same PE. Table 2 shows that the execution time increases substantially as the remote communication increases; at the case of 80% remote communication and 20% regional communication, the simulation runs approximately 10 times slower than 0% remote communication case with the same percentage of regional communication. Clearly, the impact of regional communication for ROSS-CMT is much less than that of remote communication. For example, at 0% remote communication, the performance drops only from 7.3 seconds to 15.3 seconds when regional communication increases from 0% to 100%.

Table 3 shows the percentage of rollbacks caused by remote communication. At the case of 20% remote communication and 20% regional communication, 72.5% of total rollbacks are caused by remote events. Rollbacks occur when events are arriving late and the local simulation time proceeds beyond their simulation time. It is considerably more likely for a rollback to be triggered by an incoming remote event, rather than regional event, because of the high latency on the slow communication link used to send the remote events. Thus, it is necessary to consider optimizations to reduce the cost of remote communication in PDES.

3. MANAGING HETEROGENEOUS COMMUNICATION LATENCY

In this section, we discuss the use of three optimizations to reduce the message communication overheads, and to hide the inter-node communication latency on CMs. The theme of these optimizations is to focus on the impact of the expensive communication links, by reducing the frequency of communication across them. We first describe the implementation of message consolidation on ROSS-CMT, where multiple messages are combined and routed through the slow links together. Next, we build up on the message consolidation technique by exploiting the observation that fewer messages now arrive from the distant links. To capitalize on this, we propose infrequent polling to reduce the frequency of the expensive operation to check for the incoming messages. Finally, we investigate making the high cost links visible to model partitioning in ROSS-CMT to better map the model around them.

3.1 Optimization 1: Message Consolidation and Routing

Message send operations across nodes incur significant overheads including multiple buffer copies and system calls/OS delays on both the sender and receiver sides. Therefore, when inter-node communication is frequent, these overheads can dominate, increasing the message processing latency, but also potentially delaying critical messages and slowing down overall application progress.

We address this limitation by employing an optimization called message consolidation and routing. Message consolidation creates designated communication threads on each node that act as consolidation points for communication. Instead of communicating directly, threads prepare their outgoing messages which are then collected by the communication threads and consolidated when possible to reduce communication overhead. More precisely, each thread maintains multiple output queues, and queues each remote event into the appropriate one based on which machine this event will be sent to. The communication thread looks up every output queue of each thread, and aggregates multiple events into one message before transmission. At the receiver side, the messages are deconsolidated and delivered to the appropriate thread.

A critical parameter for message consolidation is the number of messages consolidated in one send. In our approach, we set a threshold based on the cumulative size of the consolidated message. This approach allows us to match the sent message size to the underlying communication medium maximum payload size in order to avoid expensive MAC layer fragmentation. For Ethernet, the maximum payload size is 1500 bytes, which allows us to aggregate up to 10 event messages in ROSS-CMT. The use of Ethernet jumbo frames could offer room for higher degrees of consolidation, especially for applications that have large size messages.

This approach bears some similarity to traditional message consolidation (also known as message aggregation) [11]. In these approaches, messages from the same sender to the same receiver are consolidated to amortize overhead. Often, the sender artificially delays messages in hope of receiving additional messages to send to increase the opportunity for aggregation. In contrast, the proposed optimization combines messages from different senders to different receivers as long as these messages share the source and destination nodes. As such, it exposes significantly higher opportunities for consolidation and avoids the need for delaying messages in hopes of receiving later messages for consolidation. In other words, consolidation is not only carried out over time, it is also carried out across different senders and receivers sharing the same source and destination nodes. By focusing consolidation on the slow inter-node links–no consolidation is carried out between cores on the same node– we achieve the highest reduction in communication overheads.

3.2 Optimization 2: Infrequent Polling for Incoming Messages

In ROSS-CMT, each communication thread maintains a loop for sending and receiving remote messages. The next loop iteration will be processed if the communication thread sends or receives a remote message during the current loop iteration. In order to detect the incoming remote messages, each communication thread probes (or polls) the network every iteration. However, probing is an expensive operation, and probing too aggressively increases overhead, often discovering that no message is available. To avoid unnecessary expensive probes, we implemented infrequent polling in ROSS-CMT. In particular, the frequency of polling is controlled by a configurable parameter, called *polling frequency.* For example, a polling frequency of 4 indicates that a probe operation occurs after every fourth iterations processed. In addition, we investigated both static and dynamic polling strategies. For the static polling strategy, the polling frequency is fixed during the simulation. On the other hand, the polling frequency can be adjusted in the dynamic polling strategy based on the behavior of previous probes. It reaches an effective probing rate that balances the overhead of probing against the loss of efficiency that may result if some messages are received late. We also note that message consolidation can benefit probing because it reduces the message frequency, allowing us to probe less frequently.

Infrequent polling has been proposed before for optimizing the performance of asynchronous applications such as PDES [29]. However, when applying message consolidation in a CM environment the behavior is significantly different because a single thread polls for a group of simulation threads making the communication pattern different. The interplay between message consolidation (which reduces the number of overall messages) and infrequent polling has not been studied before.

3.3 Optimization 3: Exposing Heterogeneous Latencies to Model Partitioning

Partitioning can play a significant role in reducing the communication overhead for parallel applications [28, 23]; by keeping the most heavily communicating objects together, the overhead of communication can be controlled. A joint consideration of partitioning is maintaining load balancing between the processing elements by evenly distributing the work among them.

In an environment with heterogeneous delays, the higher delays between nodes can be exposed to the partitioning tool to allow it to make more informed partitioning deci-

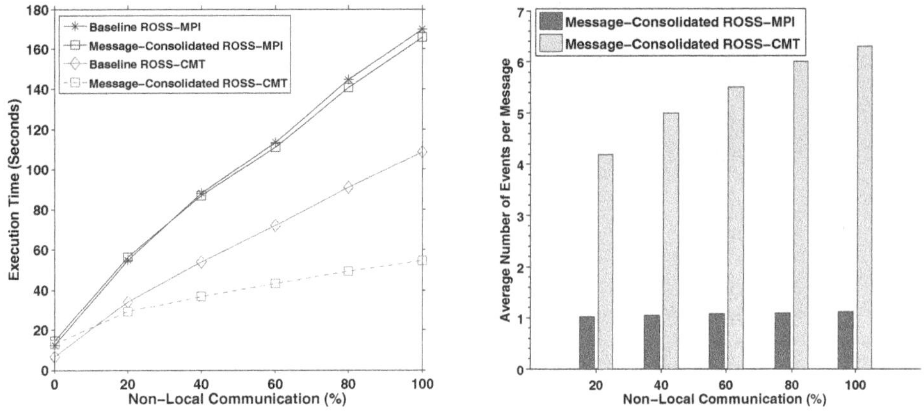

(a) Execution Time Comparison

(b) Average Number of Events per Consolidated Message

Figure 2: Performance of Message Consolidation on 32-Way PDES Simulation

sions. Without this information, the work would be simply partitioned between the cores without consideration to the heterogeneous delays between them.

As a target object of each event is randomly selected in the classical Phold model, there is no static communication structure in it. Thus, we use the hierarchical Phold model introduced in [1], to study the impact of partitioning on CMs. In this model, groups of objects are arranged in a hierarchical communication structure. Object groups closer to each other communicate more often while the farther groups have progressively less communication. Although this is still a synthetic model, it exhibits features of real models both in terms of topology and communication pattern. We use a partitioning algorithm that first profiles a short simulation using the hierarchical Phold model and then uses its behavior information (e.g., communication frequency of each pair of objects) to carry out partitioning [1]. The implementation uses a state of the art partitioning engine (*hMetis* [20]) to partition the simulation graph which is annotated with the profiling information. *hMetis* uses a multilevel partitioning algorithm for a weighted graph. It first coarsens the graph by collapsing edges and vertices. After multiple levels of coarsening, partitioning is started from the coarsest graph. Finally, a partition for the original graph is constructed and refined during the uncoarsening and refinement phase [20]. In our experiment, two types of partitioning strategies are compared. A latency heterogeneity-sensitive partitioning computes a node-level partition first and then each part is partitioned again at the core level. This strategy ensures that the groups of objects with most communication will be placed on the same node. It is compared with a latency-oblivious strategy introduced in [1] where the model is partitioned across cores, without differentiation between the heterogeneous latency among them.

4. EXPERIMENTAL RESULTS AND DISCUSSION

In this section, we study the effectiveness of the three proposed optimizations on the performance of PDES. Our results demonstrate that these optimizations allow us to mitigate the negative impact of slow communication links on PDES performance and scalability.

4.1 Message Consolidation

In our first experiment, we evaluate the performance of ROSS-CMT and ROSS-MPI with and without message consolidation, by using the classic Phold [17] benchmark, with 1000 objects for each PE. Figure 2 shows the impact of message consolidation on a 32-way optimistically synchronized simulation. In Figure 2(a), we see the run time as a function of the percentage of non-local messages (i.e., the percentage of Phold event targets that reside on another core; this includes cores on the same node, as well as cores on other nodes). As the non-local message percentage increases, message consolidation allows both versions of the simulation to improve their performance compared to the case without message consolidation. ROSS-CMT performs better than the MPI-based implementation with or without message consolidation. The benefits that ROSS-CMT obtains from message consolidation are significantly higher than those obtained by ROSS-MPI, because the CMT version can consolidate messages originating from any thread within the same node. In contrast, ROSS-MPI can only consolidate the messages from one process to another process, and as a result, it benefits from consolidation only slightly in the best case, and it is even harmed in some cases. These effects are shown in Figure 2(b), which depicts the average number of events that are consolidated into a message. Clearly, ROSS-CMT is able to consolidate a significantly higher number of messages eliminating the high per-message sending overhead. At 100% non-local communication, ROSS-CMT with the message consolidation is capable of providing a performance gain of 2X against the baseline ROSS-CMT, and 3X against ROSS-MPI.

In the next experiment, we show the impact of message consolidation on PDES scalability at 20% remote communication (Figure 3(a)), and 80% remote communication (Figure 3(b)) respectively. We fix the total number of objects (to 60480), and equally distribute them across the PEs. The simulation is performed on 2 nodes, 4 nodes, and 8 nodes respectively, with 8 hardware threads used for each node. Message consolidation achieves a performance gain of up to 2.2X against the baseline, and up to 2.5X against ROSS-MPI at 80% communication. We also discover that the message-consolidated ROSS-CMT performs worse than the baseline

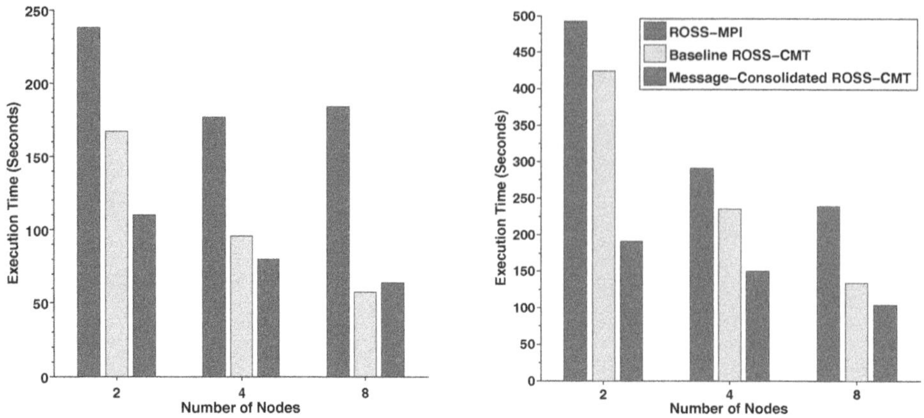

(a) 20% Remote Communication (b) 80% Remote Communication

Figure 3: Impact of Message Consolidation on PDES Simulation for Different Number of Nodes

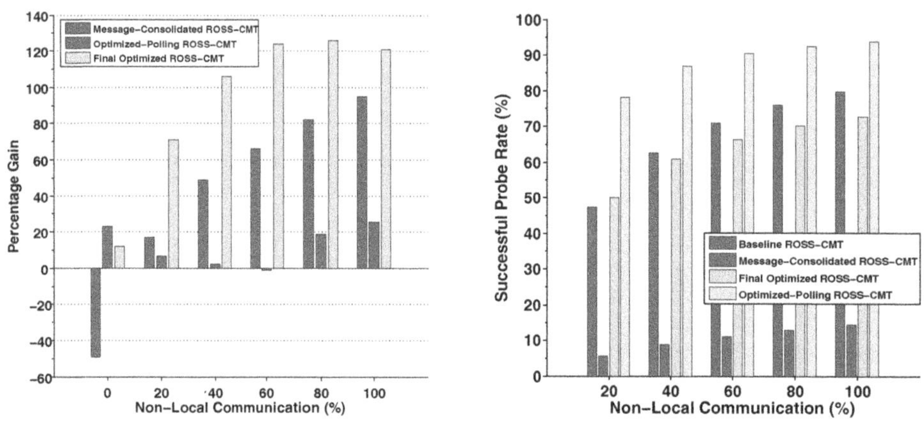

(a) Performance Improvement (against Baseline ROSS-CMT) (b) Polling Success

Figure 4: Infrequent Polling and Message Consolidation for 32-way PDES

ROSS-CMT with the case of 8 nodes at 20% remote communication. This is because of a large number of unsuccessful probe operations, leading to our next optimization.

4.2 Infrequent Polling

In asynchronous parallel applications, a receiver does not know when to expect communication from a sender, and has to resort to polling. Polling is an expensive operation on communication channels that are inter-node. In our next experiment, we study the performance impact of infrequent polling strategy applied to PDES, since it is an asynchronous application. We investigated several polling periods, and selected 4 (poll after processing every 4th iteration) because it works well across a range of communication frequencies and simulation scales. We also investigated adapting the polling frequency, but the effect was minor. Polling also interplays with message consolidation, since consolidation reduces the number of communication messages, increasing the chance of unsuccessful polls. Figure 4(a) shows the percentage gain in performance with infrequent polling on its own as well as when it is combined with message consolidation for a 32-way simulation. Somewhat surprisingly, there is a large performance drop of about 50% in message-consolidated ROSS-CMT at the non-local percentage of 0. We expected some performance loss since the message consolidation overhead is incurred, without finding opportunities for consolidation. While infrequent polling on its own results in modest improvements in performance (up to 20%), when combined with message consolidation it significantly improves performance (up to 120% relative to baseline). As message consolidation combines messages, they arrive less frequently, allowing infrequent polling to successfully eliminate message probes. Figure 4(b) shows the *successful probe rate* for each of the three simulator versions, as well as the baseline. We note that the baseline ROSS-CMT has a very good *successful probe rate* because of its frequent communication across the network as each communication point represents all the threads on that node. In contrast, ROSS-CMT with message consolidation only has much lower *successful probe rate* than the others, since message frequency is lower, but still has substantially shorter execution time (up to 90% improvement) than the baseline ROSS-CMT as shown in Figure 4(a). We repeated the experiment for a 64-way simulation (Figure 5(a) and Figure 5(b)), with similar results.

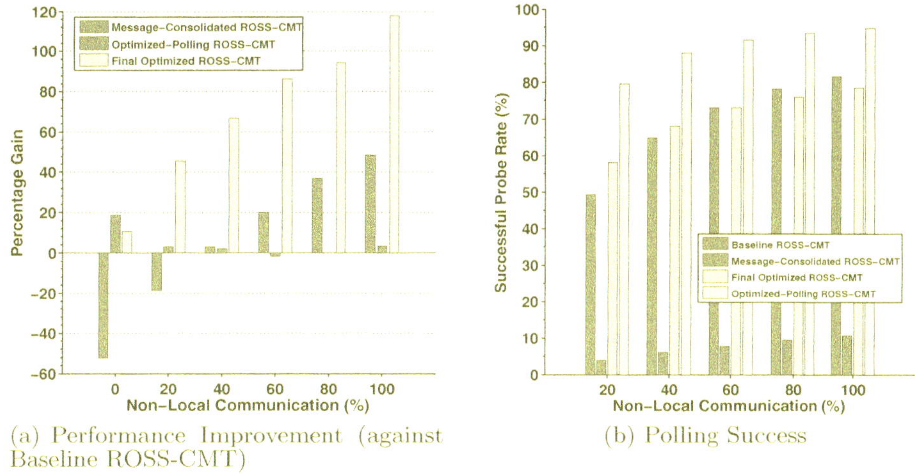

(a) Performance Improvement (against Baseline ROSS-CMT)

(b) Polling Success

Figure 5: Infrequent Polling and Message Consolidation for 64-way PDES

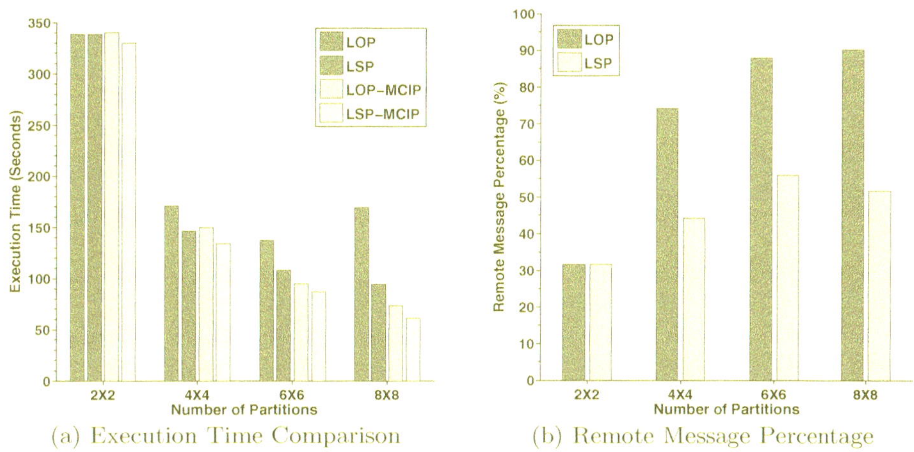

(a) Execution Time Comparison

(b) Remote Message Percentage

Figure 6: Performance Evaluation of Different Partitioning Strategies

4.3 Latency-Sensitive Model Partitioning

Figure 6 shows the impact of partitioning sensitive to heterogeneous latencies on CMs. In Figure 6, the number of partitions N x T indicates that N nodes are used with T threads per node. Each partition is mapped to one thread. This experiment uses a hierarchical Phold model [1]. The model is initialized with 4 initial events per object. In our experiment, four types of partitioning strategies are compared. A *Latency-Sensitive Partitioning (LSP)* computes a node-level partition first and then each part is partitioned again at the core level. This strategy ensures that the groups of objects with most communication are placed on the same node. It is compared with a *Latency-Oblivious Partitioning (LOP)* where the latency heterogeneity is ignored and the partitioning tool tries to minimize all communication between cores. The remaining two strategies combine the partitioning with both Message Consolidation and Infrequent Polling (MCIP).

Figure 6(a) demonstrates the impact of each of these strategies with the hierarchical model described above. It shows that the benefit of LSP increases as the number of partitions increases. LSP performs 15% better than LOP in the case of 16 partitions while up to 44% better in the case of 64 partitions. In addition, MCIP optimization is orthogonal to partitioning strategies and significantly improves the performance both in the case of LSP and LOP. Figure 6(a) also indicates that LSP and MCIP optimizations when used together (LSP-MCIP) provide the best performance of these 4 strategies compared here. Figure 6(b) shows the percentage of remote messages across nodes out of the total messages among partitions in the case of LSP and LOP. LSP places the most communicating object groups on the same node as indicated by the significant reduction in the percentage of remote messages.

4.4 Scalability Analysis of PDES

The next experiment shows the scalability of the simulator as the number of hardware threads per node is increased (Figure 7(a) with remote percentage of 20% and Figure 7(b) with remote percentage of 80%). In particular, the simulation is performed on 8 nodes, and each PE is mapped to one hardware thread. The total number of PEs used on the x-axis is increasing as we increase the number of hardware threads used on each node. In the case of 8 PEs on the x-axis, the three versions have a similar performance with each other because they each have a single thread or a pro-

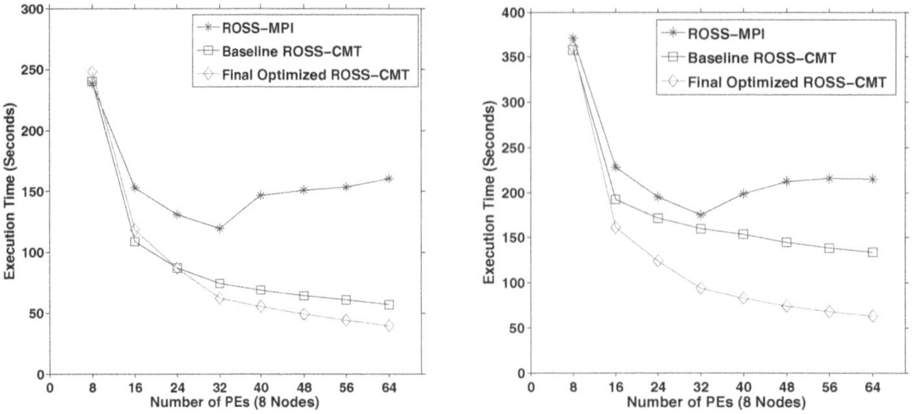

(a) 20% Remote Communication (b) 80% Remote Communication

Figure 7: PDES Scalability as Number of Hardware Threads per Node is Increased

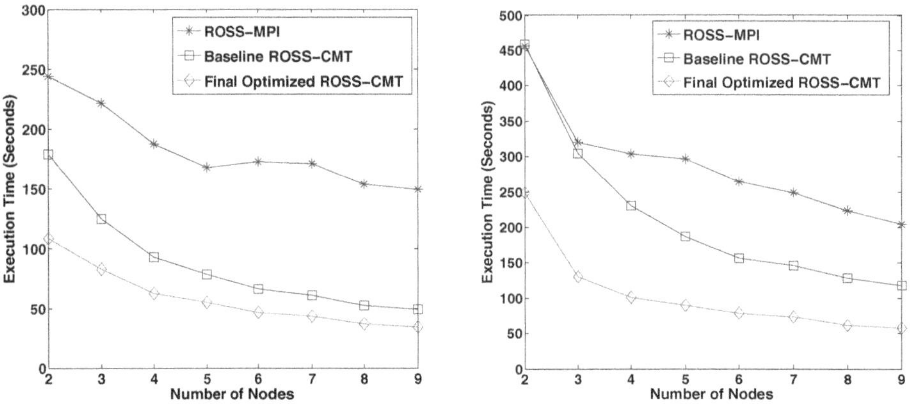

(a) 20% Remote Communication (b) 80% Remote Communication

Figure 8: PDES Scalability for Different Number of Nodes

cess on each node communicating through MPI. However, as the number of hardware threads per node is increased, ROSS-CMT is able to take advantage of the more efficient communication among threads on the same node avoiding the use of MPI, achieving over 2.8X speedup over ROSS-MPI for a 64 way simulation at 20% remote percentage (the improvement is a more modest 1.5X in the case of 80% remote percentage).

When message consolidation and infrequent polling are used, the optimized version of ROSS-CMT is able to scale much better, achieving about 4X improvement in performance over ROSS-MPI at both 20% and 80% remote event percentages. In addition, the performance of optimized ROSS-CMT exceeds that of baseline ROSS-CMT by a factor of 1.4X to 2X.

In the next experiment we show the scalability of the simulator as we increase the number of nodes used with a fixed number of hardware threads used per node (6 hardware threads). Figure 8(a) and Figure 8(b) show the scalability for optimistic simulation at 20% and 80% remote communication percentage respectively. We start with 2 nodes since it is impossible to create remote message traffic when only one node is used. Again, performance and scalability of the optimized ROSS-CMT are significantly better than the ROSS-MPI, achieving about 4X speedup at 80% remote message percentage and about 4.5X at 20% remote communication. In addition, in this experiment the performance of optimized ROSS-CMT exceeds that of baseline ROSS-CMT by a factor of up to 2X. Figure 9(a) and Figure 9(b) show the speedup of optimistic simulation against sequential simulation at both 20% and 80% remote communication percentages. Clearly, the optimized ROSS-CMT achieves better speedups than both baseline ROSS-CMT and ROSS-MPI. For example, at the case of 9 nodes, the speedup of optimized ROSS-CMT is 3.7X at 20% remote percentage, and 2.2 at 80% remote percentage.

In the next experiment we show the impact of Event Processing Granularity (EPG) for the scalability of PDES. EPG controls the amount of computation executed for each event. In our implementation the value of EPG determines the number of computation loops required for each event processing. A higher value of EPG makes the application more coarse-grained, and gives more computation load to the application. Note that most PDES models tend to require relatively small amounts of processing, typically to update state variables. However, it is possible to have models with significant event processing, and it is instructive to see how the ratio of computation to communication influences the per-

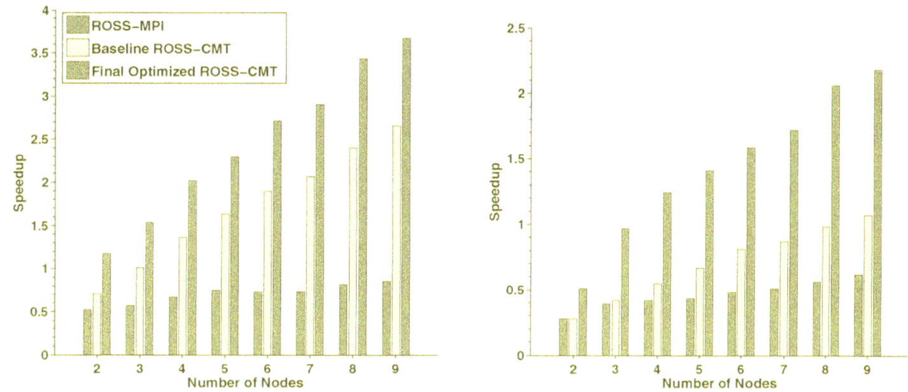

(a) 20% Remote Communication (b) 80% Remote Communication

Figure 9: Speedup of PDES Optimistic Simulation against Sequential Simulation

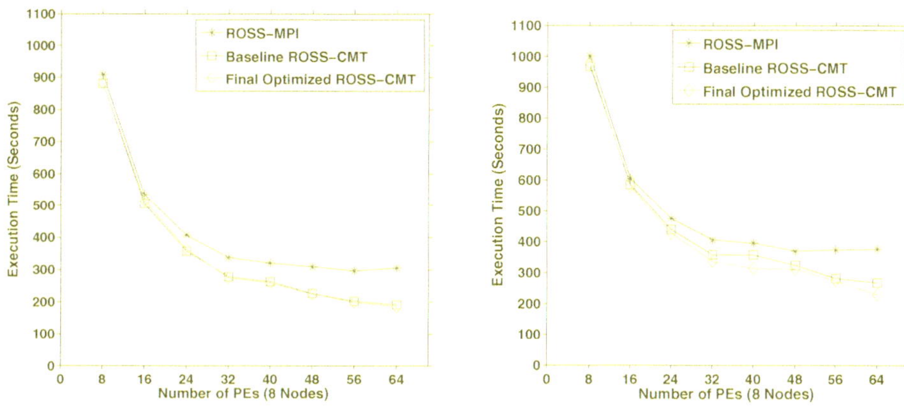

(a) 20% Remote Communication (b) 80% Remote Communication

Figure 10: Impact of Event Processing Granularity (EPG=3000)

formance of PDES on CMs. Figure 10(a) and Figure 10(b) show the three versions of ROSS with EPG value of 3000 under 20% and 80% remote communication respectively. We find that the baseline ROSS-CMT performs close to optimized ROSS-CMT. This indicates that with a high value for EPG, the performance of ROSS-CMT is not dominated by communication.

In the next experiment, we evaluate PDES on a real model of a Personal Communication Services (PCS) system [8]. In this model, a cellular provider infrastructure is simulated as a number of mobile customers use it. A mobile phone call is simulated as an event, moved from one cell phone tower to another. Upon receiving a phone call, the cell phone tower assigns an available channel to the call. Once this phone call ends, the allocated channel is released. In addition, another phone call or more may be generated. If all channels are busy, the call is blocked. Moreover, if a call's connected portable is leaving the cell's area, then the call is handed-off to the destination cell phone tower [8]. In our experiments, the PCS simulation consists of 57600 cell phone towers (LPs). In addition, the number of channels per cell phone tower is fixed at 10. Figure 11(a) shows the PCS scalability of three versions of ROSS simulator as the number of hardware threads per node is increased. In this experiment, the number of nodes is fixed at 8. At the case of 64-way simulation, the optimized ROSS-CMT exceeds the baseline ROSS-CMT by a factor of 1.7, and 2 over ROSS-MPI. Figure 11(b) shows PCS scalability as the number of nodes is increased, with a fixed number of hardware threads used per node (6 hardware threads). Clearly, the optimized ROSS-CMT outperforms both the baseline ROSS-CMT and ROSS-MPI.

4.5 Experimental Results Summary

In summary, we evaluated the performance of ROSS-CMT with proposed optimizations on CMs with highly heterogeneous delays. We discovered that:

1. Message consolidation significantly improves the performance of ROSS-CMT PDES simulator. It provides a performance gain of about 3X in ROSS-CMT against ROSS-MPI at high percentage of remote communication. However, the overhead of unsuccessful probes can't be ignored, especially in the case of low percentage of remote communication.

2. Infrequent polling is capable of providing up to another 20% gain in performance of ROSS-CMT.

3. Latency-sensitive partitioning without any of above optimizations provides up to 44% performance improve-

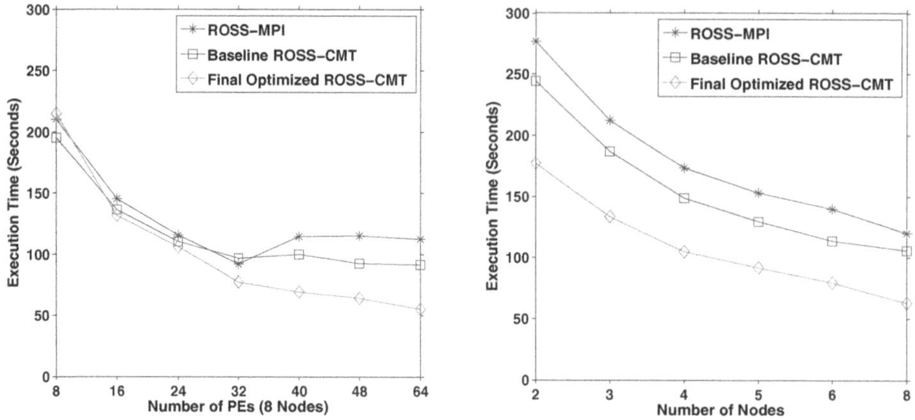

(a) Different Number of Hardware Threads per Node

(b) Different Number of Nodes

Figure 11: Scalability Study of PCS Model

ment over latency-oblivious partitioning in the model we considered.

4. With the proposed optimizations the performance of the optimized ROSS-CMT exceeds that of non-optimized ROSS-CMT by a factor of about 2X, and that of ROSS-MPI by a factor of about 4.5X.

5. RELATED WORK

Communication latency is one of the traditional challenges to the performance and scalability of parallel applications. One of the approaches to reduce the impact of this problem is to develop fast network interconnection fabrics [24]. Multi-threaded implementations of algorithms [27, 14] on multi-core systems are being increasingly used due to the fast thread-based communication through shared memory on such systems. To scale to large size applications using commodity processing nodes, clusters of multi-cores must be used; however, high latency on the network becomes a potential bottleneck for the performance in this environment, especially in some communication-bound applications such as Parallel Discrete Event Simulation (PDES).

5.1 Parallel Discrete Event Simulation

It has been long-recognized that PDES suffers from communication overheads due to its fine-grained nature [7]. As a result, significant PDES research exists on optimizing the communication of PDES applications to improve their performance. Partitioning [13] plays an important role in reducing the communication latencies, by placing the objects with frequent communication on the same processor before the execution of the simulation. In [1], both communication and object activity were profiled first, and then used for a partition tool [20] to make partitions. However, static partitioning may not be efficient because the behavior of some models may change dynamically. Therefore, run-time object migration [4, 26] has been proposed to adjust the partitions at run time and to balance the workload of each processor as well. El-Khatib et. al. [15] provide three metrics to monitor the behavior changes of the model for optimistic simulation. The workload of each processor is evaluated periodically, and the workload migration occurs once the condition of dynamic adjustments is satisfied.

5.2 Optimizing the communication cost

For PDES applications, several techniques have been proposed at the simulation kernel communication system level to reduce either the cost or frequency of communication. Sharma et. al. [29] argue that too aggressive polling strategy for message delivery in asynchronous applications may harm the performance due to the overhead of unsuccessful probes. However, it is difficult to predict the optimal polling frequency at compile-time. Thus, they studied three heuristics for infrequent polling. Message aggregation is often used to reduce the frequency of the communication by grouping multiple messages into a single one before transmission. For example, a dynamic message aggregation approach is proposed in [11], which defines an aggregation window whose value can be assigned statically or dynamically, with the objective of controlling the behavior of the message aggregation in a Time-Warp simulator. Sharma et. al. [30] proposed a multi-threaded based Time Warp simulator on Clusters of SMPs (Symmetric Multi-Processors). While, conceptually, clusters of SMPs are similar to clusters of multi-cores, the tighter integration on multi-cores makes the environment significantly different. Moreover, other advances in processor architectures, communication libraries, and network fabric over the past 15 years substantially influence the relative latencies and overheads on the two environments.

For other types of applications, message aggregation is also widely used. For example, in the Simulink application, message aggregation is used to combine forwarding of multiple values between two threads into a single message [5]. [9] presents an identity-based aggregate signature algorithm in a vehicular ad-hoc network application, which aggregates signatures of multiple messages into one, for the purpose of security as well as performance efficiency.

The main difference between our proposal and traditional message aggregation approaches is: In message aggregation, messages from the same sender to the same receiver are consolidated to amortize overhead. In contrast, our proposed optimization combines messages from different senders to different receivers as long as these messages share the source and destination nodes. Thus, it exposes significantly higher opportunities for consolidation, and can significantly improve the performance of application. Traditional message aggregation often requires delaying messages to improve opportunities for aggregation; in the proposed approach, since messages are aggregated across multiple senders, there are ample opportunities for aggregation without delaying messages.

5.3 Application Study on Multi-cores

The multi-core architecture can substantially reduce the latency of the intra-machine communication due to its tightly integrated cores on a single chip. Thus, some researchers study the performance of applications on emerging multi-cores and multi-core clusters. Scalability studies of PDES on a blue gene supercomputer demonstrate that scalability up to thousands of processors can be achieved due to the low communication latency [22, 3]. In [21], a multi-process based PDES kernel is used to evaluate the performance on both multi-core clusters and traditional clusters, and shows that a better performance can be achieved on CMs. Wilsey et al. [12] proposed an algorithm to allow dynamic core frequency adjustment during Time Warp simulations on multi-cores. This approach can improve the performance of simulation, by overclocking the cores containing LPs with smaller rollbacks, as well as underclocking the cores having LPs with larger rollbacks.

In order to achieve better performance on multi-cores, multi-threaded implementations of PDES simulation engines are widely used. [19, 18] developed a multi-threaded PDES kernel and optimized for a standalone multi-core node, where each thread worked for a different simulation kernel instance. Chen et al. [10] proposed a different multi-threaded PDES simulation engine that employed a global event scheduling mechanism, where each thread selected the smallest time-stamped event from a global queue shared by other threads. However, these studies are limited to a single multi-core node. To support CMs, a multi-threaded MPI simulator was recently developed, however, very small performance gain was achieved compared with multi-process based simulator due to the impact of inter-node communication [33][2]. Liu et al. [25] developed a multi threaded simulator, called *MiniSSF*, to support CMs. Different from our approach, two additional threads were created on each node to send and receive remote events respectively. In addition, a blocking receive operation was used to receive remote events. Vitali et al. [32, 31] proposed a load-sharing scheme developed in a multi-threaded PDES simulator, where the workloads of each simulation kernel instance were distributed across a dynamically changing set of threads.

6. CONCLUDING REMARKS

Parallel algorithms went through a phase where the impact of the communication topology was exposed to the programmer because of the high communication latency. Algorithms were developed in way specialized to the communication topology on the machine; it was common to have substantially different algorithms with different communication topologies. This situation changed substantially with the advent of high performance communication infrastructure where it became common to abstract communication as an ideal all-to-all medium, where messages were sent to destinations without regards to the underlying physical topology. In this paper, we argued that the high delay links necessitate a step back towards algorithms that are aware of the presence of these high delay links. We explored a set of such techniques and optimizations that can enable PDES application to tolerate the effect of high latency links.

In particular, our goal was to answer the following question: in the presence of highly heterogeneous delays on CMs, do fine-grained applications such as PDES benefit from the low latency between cores on a single machine, or are they limited by the communication across machines with relatively higher delay? We illustrate this problem by using ROSS-CMT PDES simulator. We find that on CMs, for ROSS-CMT, the network connections impact its performance and scalability significantly.

We proposed three optimizations to reduce the impact of communication across machines: consolidated message routing, infrequent polling, and partitioning aware of the heterogeneous latency. We discover that the performance of optimized ROSS-CMT with classical Phold model achieves a 2X speedup against non-optimized ROSS-CMT, and 4.5X speedup against the original multi-process ROSS simulator. Latency-sensitive partitioning can provide up to 44% performance improvement against latency-oblivious partitioning on CMs.

[2]Note that this is a poster that used a preliminary version of the simulator without characterizing PDES behavior on CMs, and without any of the optimizations discussed in this paper.

Acknowledgements

This material is based on research sponsored by Air Force Research Laboratory under agreement number FA8750-11-2-0004. The U.S. Government is authorized to reproduce and distribute reprints for Governmental purposes notwithstanding any copyright notation thereon. The views and conclusions contained herein are those of the authors and should not be interpreted as necessarily representing the official policies or endorsements, either expressed or implied, of Air Force Research Laboratory or the U.S. Government. We also gratefully acknowledge support from the National Science Foundation grants CNS-0916323 and CNS-0958501.

7. REFERENCES

[1] K. Bahulkar, J. Wang, N. Abu-Ghazaleh, and D. Ponomarev. Partitioning on dynamic behavior for parallel discrete event simulation. In *Principles of Advanced and Distributed Simulation (PADS)*, pages 221–230. IEEE, 2012.

[2] M. L. Bailey, J. V. Briner, Jr., and R. D. Chamberlain. Parallel logic simulation of VLSI systems. *ACM Computing Surveys*, 26(3):255–294, sep 1994.

[3] D. Bauer, C. Carothers, and A. Holder. Scalable time warp on bluegene supercomputer. In *Principles of Advanced and Distributed Simulation (PADS)*, pages 35–44, 2009.

[4] A. Boukerche and S. Das. Dynamic load balancing strategies for conservative parallel simulation. In *Principles of Advanced and Distributed Simulation (PADS)*, pages 32–37, 1997.

[5] A. Canedo, T. Yoshizawa, and H.Komatsu. Automatic

parallelization of simulink applications. In *Proc. of CGO*, pages 151–159, 2010.

[6] C. Carothers, D. Bauer, and S. Pearce. ROSS: A high-performance, low memory, modular time warp system. In *Principles of Advanced and Distributed Simulation (PADS)*, pages 53–60. IEEE, 2000.

[7] C. D. Carothers, R. M. Fujimoto, and P. England. Effect of communication overheads on Time Warp performance: An experimental study. In *Principles of Advanced and Distributed Simulation (PADS)*, pages 118–125, jul 1994.

[8] C. D. Carothers, R. M. Fujimoto, and Y.-B. Lin. A case study in simulating pcs networks using time warp. In *Principles of Advanced and Distributed Simulation (PADS)*, pages 87–94. IEEE, 1995.

[9] C. Chen, J. Zhang, R. Cohen, and P.Ho. Secure and efficient trust opinion aggregation for vehicular ad-hoc networks. In *Proc. of VTC*, pages 1–5, 2010.

[10] L. Chen, Y. Lu, Y. Yao, S. Peng, and L. Wu. A well-balanced time warp system on multi-core environments. In *Principles of Advanced and Distributed Simulation (PADS)*, pages 1–9. IEEE, 2011.

[11] M. Chetlur, N. Abu-Ghazaleh, R. Radhakrishnan, and P. A. Wilsey. Optimizing communication in Time-Warp simulators. In *Principles of Advanced and Distributed Simulation (PADS)*, pages 64–71. IEEE, 1998.

[12] R. Child and P. Wilsey. Dynamically adjusting core frequencies to accelerate time warp simulations in many-core processors. In *Principles of Advanced and Distributed Simulation (PADS)*, pages 35–43. IEEE, 2012.

[13] J. Cloutier. Model partitioning and the performance of distributed timewarp simulation of logic circuits. *Simulation Practice and Theory*, 5(1):83–99, 1997.

[14] J. Doi and Y. Negishi. Overlapping methods of all-to-all communication and FFT algorithms for torus-connected massively parallel supercomputers. In *Proc. of Int'l Conference on Supercomputing*, pages 1–9, 2010.

[15] K. El-Khatib and C. Tropper. On metrics for the dynamic load balancing of optimistic simulations. In *Proc. 32nd Hawaii International Conference on Systems Science (HICCS)*, 1999.

[16] R. Fujimoto. Parallel discrete event simulation. *Communications of the ACM*, 33(10):30–53, oct 1990.

[17] R. Fujimoto. Performance of time warp under synthetic workloads. *Proceedings of the SCS Multiconference on Distributed Simulation*, 22(1):23–28, 1990.

[18] D. Jagtap, K. Bahulkar, D.Ponomarev, and N.Abu-Ghazaleh. Characterizing and understanding pdes behavior on tilera architecture. In *Principles of Advanced and Distributed Simulation (PADS)*, pages 53–62. IEEE, 2012.

[19] D. Jagtap, N.Abu-Ghazaleh, and D.Ponomarev. Optimization of parallel discrete event simulator for multi-core systems. In *Parallel and Distributed Processing Symposium (IPDPS)*, pages 520–531. IEEE, 2012.

[20] G. Karypis and V. Kumar. hmetis: a hypergraph partitioning package. Available on WWW at URL: http://www.cs.umn.edu/ karypis/metis/hmetis.

[21] K.Bahulkar, N.Hofmann, D.Jagtap, N.Abu-Ghazaleh, and D.Ponomarev. Performance evaluation of pdes on multicore clusters. In *14th IEEE/ACM International Symposium on Distributed Simulation and Real-Time Applications (DS-RT)*, pages 131–140, 2010.

[22] K.S.Perumalla. Scaling time warp-based discrete event execution to 104 processors on a blue gene supercomputer. In *in Proceedings of the ACM Computing Frontiers*, pages 69–76, 2007.

[23] L. Li and C. Tropper. A design-driven partitioning algorithm for distributed verilog simulation. In *Principles of Advanced and Distributed Simulation (PADS)*, pages 211–218. IEEE, 2007.

[24] J. Liu, B. chandrasekaran, J. Wu, W. Jiang, S. Kini, W. Yu, D. Buntinas, P. Wyckoff, and D. Panda. Performance comparison of mpi implementations over infiniband, myrinet and quadrics. In *Proc. of ACM/IEEE conference on Supercomputing*, pages 58–71. IEEE, nov 2003.

[25] J. Liu and R. Rong. Hierarchical composite synchronization. In *Principles of Advanced and Distributed Simulation (PADS)*, pages 3–12. IEEE, 2012.

[26] P. Peschlow, T. Honecker, and P. Martini. A flexible dynamic partitioning algorithm for optimistic distributed simulation. In *Principles of Advanced and Distributed Simulation (PADS)*, pages 219–228. IEEE, 2007.

[27] R. Preissl, N. Wichmann, B. Long, J. Shalf, S. Ethier, and A. Koniges. Multithreaded global address space communication techniques for gyrokinetic fusion applications on ultra-scale platforms. In *Proc. of Int'l Conference on Supercomputing*, 2011.

[28] V. Sarkar and J. Hennessy. Compile-time partitioning and scheduling of parallel programs. In *Proc. of the SIGPLAN Symposium on Compiler construction*, pages 17–26, 1986.

[29] G. D. Sharma, N. B. Abu-Ghazaleh, U. V. Rajasekaran, and P. A. Wilsey. Optimizing message delivery in asynchronous distributed applications. In *Proc. of Euro-Par*, pages 1204–1208, 1998.

[30] G. D. Sharma, R. Radhakrishnan, U. V. Rajesekaran, N. B. Abu-Ghazaleh, and P. A. Wilsey. Time warp simulation on clumps. In *Principles of Advanced and Distributed Simulation (PADS)*, pages 174–181, may 1999.

[31] R. Vitali, A. Pellegrini, and F. Quaglia. Assessing load-sharing within optimistic simulation platforms. In *Proceedings of the 2012 Winter Simulation Conference*. IEEE, 2012.

[32] R. Vitali, A. Pellegrini, and F. Quaglia. Towards symmetric multi-threaded optimistic simulation kernels. In *Principles of Advanced and Distributed Simulation (PADS)*, pages 211–220. IEEE, 2012.

[33] J. Wang, D.Ponomarev, and N.Abu-Ghazaleh. Performance analysis of a multithreaded pdes simulator on multicore clusters. In *Principles of Advanced and Distributed Simulation (PADS) (Short Paper)*, pages 93–95. IEEE, 2012.

Hybrid Scheduling for Event-driven Simulation over Heterogeneous Computers

Bilel Ben Romdhanne
Mobile Communication
Eurecom
benromdh@eurecom.fr

Mohamed Said Mosli Bouksiaa
Mobile Communication
Eurecom
mosli@eurecom.fr

Navid Nikaein
Mobile Communication
Eurecom
nikaeinn@eurecom.fr

Christian Bonnet
Mobile Comminication
Eurecom
bonnet@eurecom.fr

ABSTRACT

In this work we propose a new scheduling approach designed from scratch to maximize heterogeneous computers usage and the event processing flow at the same time. The scheduler is built based on three fundamental concepts which introduces a new vision of discrete event simulation: 1) events are clustered according to their potential time parallelism on one hand and to their potential process and data similarity on the other hand. 2) events meta-data is enhanced with additional descriptor which simplifies and accelerates the scheduling decision. 3) the simulation is hybrid time-event driven rather than time- or event-driven. The concretization of our approach is denoted the H-scheduler which uses several processes to manage the event flow. Furthermore we propose a dynamic scheduling optimization which aims to further maximize the event flow. The combination of those features allows the H-scheduler to provide the highest efficiency rate compared to the majority of GPU and CPU schedulers. In particular it goes beyond the default Cunetsim Scheduler by 90% in average while it keeps a significant lead on existing simulators.

Categories and Subject Descriptors

I.6.0 [**Computing Methodologies**]: SIMULATION AND MODELING—*General*; C.4 [**Computer Systems Organization**]: PERFORMANCE OF SYSTEMS

Keywords

PADS, PDES, Large scale simulation, scheduling methodology, GPGPU, Heterogeneous computing

1. INTRODUCTION

Discrete event simulation (DES) is a tool used to model, analyze, and evaluate large and complex systems requiring continuous internal and external interactions, where formal analysis is difficult or non-deterministic. However, the efficiency and scalability of DES remains a challenge due to emerging heterogeneous computing node architecture. In particular, scheduling the execution of future events while maintaining a continuous load under large-scale conditions increases the scheduling cost, until becoming the bottleneck [12]. Most popular scheduling approaches rely on a centralized event scheduling model optimized mainly for the homogeneous computing node architecture. Such a model remains limited and does not exploit the full modern hardware potential. Hence, the parallel and distributed scheduling approaches used for parallel discrete event simulation (PDES) re-emerge as a candidate to increase the event generation rate over heterogeneous computing node architectures [25]. The objective is to exploit a multitude of parallel and interactive processors unified at the level of event scheduler to cooperate with each other. Examples include multi-core CPUs, multi-GPUs, multi processor system-on-chip, and accelerated processing unit introduced by INTEL.

Most of those architectures seem promising, but their ecosystems in some cases are either not fully developed or conflicting [5]. Benefits of GPU-enabled supercomputer have been highlighted in [21], where authors suggest revisiting and expanding the vision on DES. Nevertheless, most of the recent attempts assume the backward compatibility with the sequential scheduling concept [16, 27]. Such a methodology presents a conceptual weakness since it considers a multi-core computing node as a simple extension of a mono-core one. Furthermore, to remain backward compatible, the expected gain will be significantly reduced when compared to a dedicated software design which considers the parallel specificity of the current hardware as well as the communication latency [1].

In this work, we introduce a new parallel event scheduler for a heterogeneous computing node architecture, denoted as Hybrid scheduler (H-scheduler). The H-scheduler is designed to dynamically allocate events to the available computing resources while keeping the event rate and load stable. This is achieved as the scheduler is aware of the heap of processors and their capabilities and has a constant access to their instantaneous loads and execution time. The scheduler operates on all the available computing resources within the same addressable memory space. To increase the efficiency of the scheduler, the events are associated with metadata and organized in a 3-dimensional data structure. Furthermore, events are considered as different flows from the scheduler to each computing resources. The H-scheduler applies the conservative scheduling policy to avoid the overhead generated by the recovery mechanism and the state vector when considering optimistic policy in parallel and heterogeneous settings.

The H-scheduler is composed of four main processes: event dispatcher, event injector, GPU-scheduler, and CPU-scheduler, where event are flowing. The dispatcher fetches the newly generated events from different queues and adds them to a corresponding position within a 3-dimensional data structure optimized for the parallel execution while the injector directs a group of parallel events to the most adequate sub-scheduler based on the received feedback information. Each sub-scheduler is tailored and optimized for a specific hardware in order to maximize the activity rate of the corresponding computing resources.

Several optimizations are proposed to accelerate the scheduling decision as the bottleneck may change over time. To demonstrate, we adopt rapid and advanced scheduling policies for both the dispatcher and the injector processes, and enable switching dynamically between them based on feedback information. Comparative assessments have been demonstrated that the performance gain can be increased by a factor of 2 compared to centralized and conservative schedulers.

The reminder of this paper is organized as follows. Section 2 provides a related work on the scheduling in the event-driven simulation. Section 3 presents the H-scheduler in detail. The performance assessments and analysis are described in Section 4 followed by a discussion in Section 5. Finally, the conclusion is presented in Section 6.

2. RELATED WORK

Improving the efficiency and scalability of DES remains a challenging issue for the modern modeling approaches that require complex and sophisticated system representation. In such a context, PDES is commonly used as a scalable and efficient solution when compared to sequential approaches [7]. PDES relies on the partitioning of the model over several logical processes (LP)s collaborating with each other to perform the whole simulation [22, 13]. However respecting the simulation correctness while dealing with parallel execution makes event management extremely expensive. This is also acknowledged as one of the critical limitations of large parallel simulations, especially when dealing with heterogeneous resources, and raises two issues: data representation and event scheduling [20].

To store future events, most of the PDES use a sorted data structure. In the literature, the efficiency of central data structures was largely studied for both sequential and parallel execution, e.g. central event list (CEL) [23]. Nevertheless, under large parallelism conditions, such a data structure may present a bottleneck. Authors in [7] address the efficiency of three CEL implementations, namely the heap, the splay tree and the calendar, and they conclude that the performance of the CEL concept remains mitigated when thousands of concurrent processes access that structure. Therefore, the CEL implementation needs to be parallelized to cope with the parallel architecture of heterogeneous computing resources. The concurrent priority queue [24, 9] is a relevant solution to access and manage the CEL in parallel. An event list or message queue is usually distributed to each logical process in a PDES with its own local clock. The concurrent insertion and deletion of the priority queue, by involving mutual exclusion or atomic functions, leads to the improvement of the overall performance using a global event list [23]. In the same sense, Chen *et al.* propose a distributed queue which considers multi-core CPUs [6]. However, the above mentioned mechanisms, mutual exclusion and concurrent priority queue, are target-dependent and thus could not be directly applied to the GPU target. A different point of view was proposed by Park *et al.* [17], which relies on a hybrid time-event driven simulation based on a GPU-oriented CEL concept that uses a linked list implementation. Despite the fact that this approach has been developed with the goal of improving the GPU-based simulation, the overhead of managing a large number of parallel event remains an open issue due to a limited number of concurrent access to the same physical memory.

In the DES and PDES, a large portion of the overall simulation time is used for the event scheduling [18]. Specifically to PDES, the efficiency of the scheduler depends also on the synchronization method [14]. The conservative approaches prohibit out-of-order event execution, which in most cases is based on the lookahead concept to preserve the causality rule [11]. Parallel event scheduling is separately studied for a multi-core CPU target [27, 8] and GPUs [17]. Both approaches use a central event queue and several independent threads to fetch the next event from the queue. The multi-threading approach is also applied to reduce the scheduling cost and increase the simulation efficiency but only for a limited number of cores (4 and 8 respectively). Authors in [16] propose a dedicated GPU scheduling based on the SIMD programming model where the event queue is splitted into several sub-queues to avoid central bottlenecks. All the above mentioned approaches regard a GPU core as a CPU core, which in turn reduces the achievable gain.

The optimistic approach allows an out-of-order execution while ensuring the simulation correctness. Several optimizations were introduced recently to increase the efficiency of optimistic parallel simulations over multi-core CPUs while keeping a reasonable backward compatibility with standard software architecture [26, 15, 6]. Although such an approach increases the general efficiency by relaxing a substantial limitation of the conservative approach, it introduces memory overhead related to the state-vector saving mechanism, which becomes critical when targeting very large logical process.

In contrast with previous works, the H-scheduler design consider extremely large LPs while maximizing the simulation efficiency over heterogeneous computing architecture. In particular it outperforms prior works by considering events as flow and detecting the system bottleneck on the fly to adjust the behavior of the scheduler dynamically.

3. THE HYBRID SCHEDULER

To operate on a heterogeneous computing node, the hybrid scheduler relies on four fundamental concepts: (A) event descriptor, which associates metadata to an event when it is generated, (B) event structure, which organizes the events in an arraylist (AL) - namely cloned independent events (CIE) if the events differ only in data, independent foreign events (IFE) if events differ in both algorithm and data, and time interval - and (C) event flow, which considers the simulation process as a set of interconnected sub-processes producing and consuming events where the event rate stability across multiple computing resources has to be maintained. In the following paragraphs, we further explain each concept.

The event descriptor extends the traditional event metadata, namely timestamps, id, in/out data, to support additional information used to reduce the parallel event scheduling cost. In particular, it includes (i) event dependency information, (ii) event execution timestamp, (iii) I/O data access, (iv) event structure information, and (v) execution targets. Event dependency defines if an event has one or multiple dependencies (needs current output as input) that fall within the same time interval [3]. The event execution timestamp identifies which events can be scheduled in parallel for a given timestamp and is calculated based on the current timestamp and the safety lookahead. The I/O data access defines the permissions given to an event to read and/or write a shared memory area. The event structure information identifies an event as a CIE or a IFE for the given timestamp. Finally, the execution target defines where an event could be executed, CPU, GPU or both. It has to be mentioned that the scheduler can not infer the target without using system callback which is a costly procedure. Therefore including that information on the event descriptor accelerate the scheduling decision.

The event structure expands how the events are represented so as to increase the parallelism in a heterogeneous computing node architecture. For this purpose, events are dispatched over a 3-dimensional arraylist, where each element of the array represents the timestamp and the associated list represents the parallel event sets for a given timestamp interval. The parallel event set is composed of the CIE (SIMD-like) and IFE the (MIMD-like). It has to be mentioned that, the CIE are considered by the scheduler as an event set (ES) and processed by the scheduler as a unique entry while the IFE are considered as a heap of events and processed by the scheduler as multiple entries. If an IFE event has one or multiple dependencies that fall within the same time interval, they will be executed sequentially to preserve the correctness.

The event flow considers the simulation as a dynamic system where events are flowing between the producers and consumers. Depending on the simulation characteristics and the available resources, system bottleneck may change over time. Therefore, the event rate stability has to be dynamically maintained so as to maximize the simulation efficiency. Consequently, feedback information from each computing resource is needed to control the event rate through the scheduling. In the following sections, we detail the the scheduler design and algorithms.

3.1 Model and components

To perform an efficient parallel event scheduling in large scale conditions over a heterogeneous computing node, the scheduler is designed as a composition of several processes. It includes the future event list (FEL), the dispatcher, arraylists (AL), the injector, the GPU-scheduler, the CPU-scheduler, and feedback as shown in the Figure 2. The FEL is a standard FIFO providing reliable status flag used to collect and manage the produced events. There is one dedicated FEL per computing resources to gather the generated events and one FEL for all the incoming raw events. The dispatcher is the front-end of the scheduler, it first reads the events from the FEL following a given scheduling policy (e.g. weighted round robin). Then, it adds events into the global 3-dimensional AL data structure based on the event descriptor to ensure the simulation correctness. The injector proceeds on the per-interval basis and dynamically determines the target computing resource, i.e. GPU or CPU, as well as the subset of events to be allocated based on the event descriptor, received feedback information and the target capabilities.

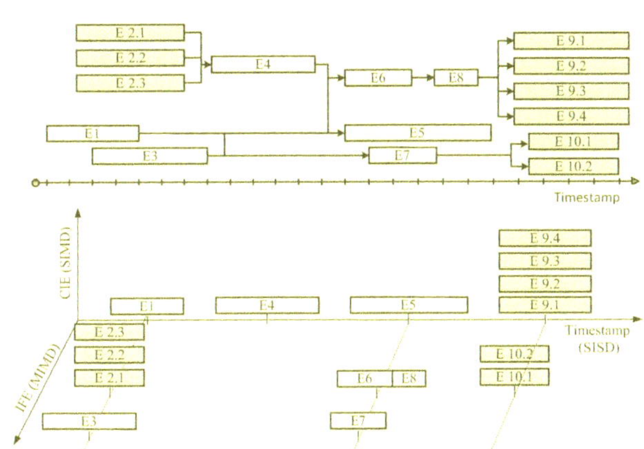

Figure 1: Event Structure

As a result, the subset of allocated events will be pushed to the local AL of a target. Please note that the injector starts the next interval only when all the events associated to the current interval are executed. Both the GPU and CPU scheduler receive events on a dedicated local AL buffer, where events are organized in the CIE and the IFE sets (see Figure 1). The dedicated GPU scheduler maps each entry of the AL to an asynchronous and non-blocking GPGPU calls. On the other hand, the dedicated CPU-scheduler will make use of multi-processing/threading technology (e.g. openMP). Upon the execution of an event, a new event might be generated (similar to producer-consumer processes) and pushed into the dedicated FEL. To dynamically adjust the event flow, each target sends feedback information about the instantaneous load and the execution time per event.

3.2 Scheduling Algorithms

In this part, we detail the different algorithms on which the H-scheduler is based, namely the advanced algorithm, the rapid algorithm and the hybrid algorithm.

3.2.1 *Advanced algorithm*

The advanced algorithm aims to thoroughly select the most adequate target for each event. The events flow starts from the FEL where all events are firstly inserted. The dispatcher is the first process which handles the event in order to push it on the correct place of the main AL. Based on the event timestamps, the dispatcher determines the correct sub-list where the event must be inserted. Then, it starts resolving its dependency using the event descriptor. If the

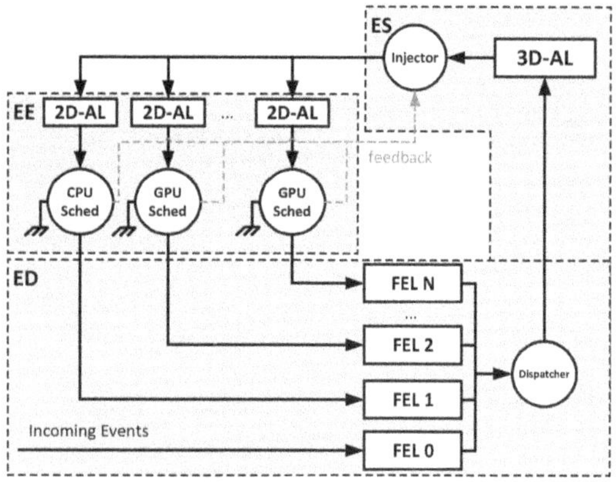

Figure 2: Event scheduler model

dispatcher detects a dependency between two events it has three choices: splitting the interval into two new ones, each of which includes independent events while respecting the timestamps correctness, creating a merged event including both or transforming the sub-list to a sequential one. Algo 1 presents the pseudo code of the dispatcher. There are two issues related to that process: detecting dependency and resolving it. To detect the dependency of two events, the dispatcher relies on their descriptors as follows: first it explores their explicit dependency descriptors. Second, it computes their durations, thus if both events are concurrent then they will be considered as independent. Third, if both events do not use the same data, the dispatcher concludes they are independent (this features must be explicitly enabled by the user). To resolve the dependency, the most adequate choice is to split the interval. However, if such a procedure induces a conflicting situation, the dispatcher creates a merged event. Finally, if dealing with the interval becomes complicated due to the large number of included events, then the sub-list will be transformed into a sorted list. The injector processes the AL sequentially, sub-list

```
for e ∈ FEL do
    if e.timestamps ∉ existing interval then
        createNewInterval(I, e.timestamps);
        insertEvent(I,e);
    end
    else
        for e1 ∈ I do
            if dependency(e1,e) then
                resolve(e1,e);
            end
        end
    end
end
```

Algorithm 1: Pseudo code of the dispatcher.

by sub-list. If the sub-list is sequential, then all events will be forwarded to one target. Otherwise, the injector considers each event individually based on the following routine: if the event is mono-compliant (CPU or GPU), then it is switched to the adequate sub-scheduler. If there are several instances of the target (several GPU or CPU scheduler then it will be switched to that having the lowest load currently. In what concerns grouped entries, the injector analyses the parallelism information to determine the target. If the number of parallel instances is reduced then the CPU is the most adequate target, and if that number is extremely large, the chosen target is the GPU. The boundaries of this decision are a function of the number of CPU & GPU cores. In the beginning of the simulation we use two arbitrary intervals where the decision is deterministic: $[1, 2 * core * 3 + 1] \Rightarrow$ CPU and $[200, +\infty] \Rightarrow$ GPU. Nevertheless, if the parallelism size is intermediate (number of instances greater than CPU's interval's upper boundary and lower than GPU's interval's lower boundary), then the injector inspects the load of each target and chooses the available one. Finally, it ensures the synchronization of all secondary ALs using a synchronization checkpoint at the end of each interval to maintain the correctness of the simulation.

```
for I ∈ MAL do
    for e ∈ I do
        if e.target=CPU then
            schedule(e,CPU);
        end
        else
            if e.target=GPU then
                schedule(e,GPU);
            end
            else
                if e.instance ∈ [1, NCPU] then
                    schedule(e,CPU);
                end
                else
                    if e.instance ∈ [NGPU, +∞] then
                        schedule(e,GPU);
                    end
                    else
                        balancedschedule(e,GPU,CPU);
                    end
                end
            end
        end
        Synchronize(I);
    end
end
```

Algorithm 2: Pseudo code of the injector.

The CPU-scheduler ensures event execution over available CPU cores. At the initialization phase, the CPU-scheduler starts by discovering available resources (asking the hardware and reading the configuration file); then it creates as many execution threads as available cores. Second, it feeds execution threads with events as soon as possible, without dependency control. Therefore, events of one sub-list are expected to be executed in parallel over available resources. Since the H-scheduler respects a conservative scheduling approach, it does not execute events of different sub-lists concurrently. The CPU-scheduler notifies the injector when finishing an interval and waits for its permission to consider the next one. The GPU-scheduler is slightly different, since it relies on a hybrid software-hardware scheduling mechanism. At the software level, sub-list includes always grouped entries that it translates to a CUDA call with predefined generic parameters. The CUDA driver ensures next steps, including generating threads and sending them to the GPU. At the hardware level, the embedded GPU GigaThread scheduler first distributes event thread blocks to various SMs, and second assigns each individual thread to an SP inside the corresponding SM.

3.2.2 Rapid algorithm

The rapid algorithm is a simplified version of the advanced one which aims to minimize the decision cost. It concerns particularly the dispatcher and the injector. It relies on a major simplification of the bottleneck of each process using a deterministic model.

As for the dispatcher, the most expensive routine is the dependency resolution; in particular, splitting an interval in two independent ones requires an expensive modification of the main AL structure. The rapid algorithm proposes to use always combined events if the dispatcher detects any dependency into one interval. We note however, that the dependency detection routine can not be simplified since it affects the correctness of the simulation.

Concerning the injector, the most expensive routine is the identification of the most suitable target. The rapid algorithm reduces its complexity by extending the borders of decision intervals for both CPU and GPU: the CPU interval becomes $[1, N]$, and the GPU one becomes $[N+1, +\infty]$, where N is a tuning parameter. The second critical routine is how to determine the most adequate target if we have multiple instances (multiple CPUs or GPUs). In that case, rather than evaluating resources loads, the injector uses a round robin assignment mechanism which aims to ensures a minimal load balancing based on the number of events.

3.2.3 Hybrid Algorithm

The hybrid algorithm aims to ensure the maximal stability for the system. It relies on two mechanisms: algorithm switching and the parameter recalibration. The switching mechanism changes the operating algorithm for both injector and dispatcher processes based on a bottleneck detection approach. Each process has one inbuffer which includes one filling rate attribute. The inbuffer of the injector is the main AL, and that of the dispatcher is the FEL. For each process, if the inbuffer is full, the hybrid mechanism supposes that the consumer process is the bottleneck and acts as follows: if the filling rate is between empty (E) and almost empty (AE) then the selected algorithm is the advanced. If that rate is between AE and almost full (AF) then the selected algorithm remains the advanced one, but the recalibration frequency is increased. Finally, if the inbuffer filling rate is between AF and full (F) then the selected algorithm is the rapid one. The switching decision occurs between two intervals and cannot be achieved during the execution of an interval.

The recalibration mechanism computes continuously the values of three parameters which define the behavior of both algorithms: the NCPU & NGPU of the advanced algorithm and the N of the rapid one. It maintains a statistical table which includes the average execution time of event sets in different targets. Figure 3 presents an example of a statistical table, where the recalibration process can assert that $NCPU = 24$, $NGPU = 192$ and $N = 48$. To compute the average execution time of a specific event set size, the recalibration mechanism considers the last M samples (which is a tuning parameter defined by the user), therefore the statistical table copes with the evolution of the simulation on one hand and the hardware characteristic on the other hand.

Target\ size	1	...	...	24	36	42	48	54	...	192	288	384
CPU	0.2	...	...	0.8	1	1	1	1.5	...	6.4	9.6	...
GPU	1	1	1	1	1	1	1	1	1	1	2	...

Figure 3: Statistical table used for recalibration

4. PERFORMANCE EVALUATION

To implement the H-scheduler, we rely on the network simulation framework Cunetsim [3, 4]. Both the H-scheduler and Cunetsim rely on five parallelization frameworks, namely CUDA, OpenMP, MPI, the thrust data management API [2], and the PGI development Kit [28], which are briefly explained below.

1. The Compute Unified Device Architecture (CUDA) is a software parallel computing platform and a programming model created by NVIDIA. In what concerns this work, the last CUDA release provides two main features: atomic operations and the GPUDirect technology which accelerates the communication between the GPU and the different components of the computer.

2. The Open Multiprocessing (OpenMP) is an API that supports multiprocessing in a shared memory context. We rely on the OpenMP to provide a compliant version with multi-core CPUs as explained later.

3. The Message Passing Interface (MPI) is a standardized and portable message-passing system designed to supply programmers with a standard for distributed programming.We rely on MPI to ensure the communication and the synchronization between different ELPs of the system.

4. Thrust is a parallel algorithm library which imitates the C++ Standard Template Library (STL). Thrust's interface enables performance portability between GPUs and multicore CPUs. Interoperability with established technologies (such as CUDA, TBB and OpenMP) facilitates integration with existing software. Due to these features we use thrust API to implement different data structures.

5. The PGI suite is a commercial C/C++ compiler which provides several automatic and semi-automatic parallelization features. Further it incorporates a full CUDA CC++ compiler for targeting X64 CPUs. Even more important, it introduces the unified binary technology (PUB), which consists on the creation of a multi-target binary (GPU, INTEL CPU and AMD CPU) from an initial native CUDA code.

Cunetsim is a distributed GPU-based framework designed for wireless mobile network simulation. It aims to achieve two main goals: enabling extra large-scale network simulation and providing a significant speedup compared to traditional CPU-based frameworks. It considers that the GPU architecture is adequate to hold the totality of a network simulation based on a CPU-GPU co-simulation [3]. It dedicates independent execution environments for each simulated node and uses the message passing approach through buffer exchange. The distributed design of Cunetsim is a fundamental cornerstone in support of heterogeneous computing architecture. In particular, the master-worker model was extended to a hierarchical architecture denoted as the coordinator-master-worker (CMW) model [4]. The default event scheduling policy handles the two types of event grouping described in section 3 but uses a centralized process and one data structure. Finally, synchronization and communication processes handle domain-specific operations between CM (Coordinator-Master) and MW (Master-Worker). As for the scheduling challenge, Cunetsim designers observe that its central event scheduler becomes the simulator bottleneck when the input event rate increases significantly. Moreover, they observe that a central event scheduler cannot handle several powerful GPUs. Therefore, a new scheduling approach becomes crucial to deal with those emerging architectures. Moreover, Cunetsim targets either CPU or GPU but not both at the same time; thus the H-scheduler concept presents a real asset to new frameworks generation.

In the remainder, we study the efficiency of the H-scheduler under extreme load and scalability conditions; therefore we use a very large scale network scenario which generates billions of events. First, we describe the evaluation scenario and setup and second we compare the efficiency of different scheduling policies under fair conditions. Finally, we analyze the performance of the H-scheduler where we detail the impact of each algorithm. In particular, we analyze the variation of the output event rate during the simulation, the decision path length and the variation of lookahead interval length during the simulation.

4.1 Scenario & Setup

We propose a large scale network experimentation scenario where we customize the benchmark methodology proposed in [3] by defining a static network topology composed of three independent activity areas (AA) each of which follows a grid configuration where the edge of an AA contains 750 nodes as illustrated in Figure 4; thus each AA includes 562.5K nodes[1]. The scenario includes one traffic source which generates 600 uniform 128-byte packets with 1 second of inter-departure time. All nodes forward unseen packets after a one-second delay to model the network latency whilst medium's reliability is reflected using dropping probability. Depending on the later, each node decides whether or not to relay a received packet. The drop probability (DP) is the parameter which allows us to introduce a random factor on the network behavior. To provide a valuable event rate while keeping a significant variation on the number of exchanged messages we use a DP of 0.1. The simulation duration is 5602 which ensures that the last generated message can reach the destination. In addition, we introduce a second scenario where we define for each node a randomly variable inter-departure-time in [0.1, 2] and a DP in [0, 0.28]. This scenario is used to study the robustness of the H-scheduler when the timestamp of different events present a significant entropy.

Even if these scenarios are outlying real networks and include major simplifications, we claim that they provide an important event number with a large rate variation as shown in Figure8. Moreover, they rely on a pool of simple events which did not require powerful computing resources individually, and use a simple implementation of both nodes and channels which provides a fair comparison later. Therefore, the main difference between considered approaches remains the scheduler efficiency. On the other hand, we use the Cunetsim framework, except for the NS3 case; thus all events are dual compliant with both CPU and GPU targets when we aim to use GPU. In what concerns the experimental context, the used frameworks are CUDA 5.0 and Open-MPI 1.4.1. The OS is Ubuntu Linux 11.10, the PGI compiler version is the 12.9 and the Nvidia driver version is 295.41. The hardware platform is one PC including an INTEL i7 3930k CPU (6 cores with hyper threading), 32 GB of DDR3 and three GeForce GTX860 2GB (1536 cores for GPGPU computing.

4.2 Comparative Evaluation

This section aims to highlight the efficiency of several scheduling approaches which differ by their execution targets and parallelism considerations. We distinguish three groups according to their execution targets respectively the CPU, the GPU and both, summarized in table 1. We use Cunetsim framework where we change solely the scheduler except for the NS3 simulator where we use the default scheduler. Moreover, we use the same implementation of nodes and channels; thus we guarantee a fair comparison. Based on the default scenario, we consider three metrics: the speedup with respect to a reference sequential execution, the hardware usage rate and the scheduling cost.

Table 1:

id	Target	Parallelism	Example
1	CPU	non	sequential
2	CPU	Op	NS3 scheduler [19]
3	CPU	Msv + Op	Cunetsim-CPU
4	GPU	Op	[17]
5	GPU	Msv	Cunetsim
6	GPU	Msv + distributed	D-Cunetsim
7	GPU+CPU	Msv + Op	H-scheduler

Table 2: List of different scheduling approaches, clustered their execution targets. Op =opportunistic and/or optimistic, Msv= Massive

Figure 5 shows the normalized speedup of each approach with respect to the sequential running time, computed using the average value of both sequential NS3 and Cunetsim. We observe that GPU-based approaches are extremely faster than all CPU-based ones. However we notify that the opportunistic approach on GPU (case 4) which presents an intermediate speedup (40x), did not consider the SIMD architecture of GPUs. In fact, its results are due to the efficiency of the hierarchical GPU memory and the existence of 24 independent SMX[2] in the used platform. On the other side, the GPU-based approach which relies on massive parallelism concepts(cases 5-6), presents an outstanding speedup which varies between 400x and 900x. Nevertheless, we observe that D-Cunetsim cannot reach the maximal expected

[1]That value represents the hardware limitation of the used GPU in term of memory space since each node needs 3.8 Ko

[2]The Kepler notation of the Streaming multi-processor

speedup (3*400x) while it uses 3 GPUs. Therefore we suspect that the scheduler is the main bottleneck since it cannot supply all GPUs with the correct rate. On the other hand, we observe that the H-scheduler is twice faster than the default scheduler while both use the same hardware. This considerable gain demonstrates that the hybrid scheduling approach reduces significantly the bottleneck impact.

Figure 6 presents the average hardware usage rate of each approach. It reflects the used resources to ensure the simulation. As expected, CPU-based schedulers ignore the GPU, however their CPU usage differs from one to the other. The sequential scheduler uses in average 20% of the CPU which represents the use of one CPU core. NS3 uses in average 84% of the CPU which means that the scheduler is not able to supply all available cores correctly while the third case (Cunetsim-CPU) ensures a full usage of the CPU. Therefore, we can assert that the event grouping policy presents a significant *added value*. The fourth case presents a mitigated score, it uses a small fraction of CPU and GPU resources but outperforms all CPU-based schedulers. This behavior confirms the previous observation.

In what concerns the dedicated GPU schedulers (5-7), we observe that the non distributed version of Cunetsim (case 5) uses efficiently one GPU and one core of the CPU; thus it does what it promises. We observe that the H-scheduler reaches the maximal CPU and GPU usage rate. In particular, it overcomes the default distributed scheduler which did not exceed 84% of the GPU usage rate while the H-scheduler approximates the 100%. These observations prove that the H-scheduler is able to maximize the usage of powerful solutions.

Figure 7 presents the average CPU usage rate of the scheduling process regardless of the simulation. Unsurprisingly, the H-scheduler needs in average between 6x and 8x more resources than CPU-based approaches and up to 3x more than GPU ones. This is due to the fact that it uses at least 4 different threads to achieve the scheduling process, in our case we use 6 threads distributed as follows: dispatcher, injector, one CPUscheduler and three GPUschedulers. Moreover, these threads work in parallel since the different data structures ensure the role of intermediate buffers. Therefore, the H-scheduler uses in average 30% of the CPU resources to ensure the maximal event flow.

We conclude that the H-scheduler is able to maximize the simulation efficiency, compared to a classical one; moreover it is able to deal natively with heterogeneous platforms if events are compliant. However, that efficiency requires additional dedicated resources compared to centralized approaches.

4.3 Performance Analysis

The H-scheduler is composed of several processes, and each process has two algorithms with the ability to switch between them autonomously, in addition, each algorithm reconfigures itself periodically based on a learning mechanism. In this section we propose to analyze the impact of each algorithm on the global behavior of the H-scheduler.

To analyze the impact of each algorithm we conduct the following experimentation series: First we measure the average event rate per simulated second, generated during the simulation across 100 runs. We realize so many runs because the shape of the curve of Figure 8 appears so perfect for a simulation including a random factor. Nevertheless we verify that the message propagation on the proposed network respects that shape. In particular, each peak of that curve reflects a maximal network activity in one AA. The second scenario which includes randomly variable connections between nodes, has a less regular curve[3]. Using the default scenario we process as follows: first we activate uniquely the advanced algorithm, second we activate the rapid one, third we activate the hybrid algorithm without any reconfiguration process or setting a timer and finally we consider the H-scheduler as described in section 3. The simulated time is 5602 seconds while the execution time varies between 413 and 670 seconds which complicates the comparison. To present an understandable representation, we normalize the output event rate with respect to the following formula $Outputrate = Nevents/Executionduration$. Corresponding results are shown in Figure 9. First of all, we observe that the advanced algorithm (red curve) is in general more efficient than the rapid one (green curve). However, the latter achieves punctually higher output rate, especially in the end of the simulation, characterized by a reduced number of messages. On the other hand, we observe that the hybrid algorithm provides better results while it introduces a large variability during the time as shown by the width of the curve (blue). We can assert that, when allowing each component to use the most adequate algorithm as a function of the situation, we reach a higher event rate with a risk of inefficient oscillation. Finally, the full H-scheduler which involves both hybrid algorithm and the continuous recalibration presents unquestionably the highest output rate but also the most variable behavior. In fact, we can distinguish four distinct and quasi-parallel sub-curves, each of which presents the maximal achievable rate of one of the available computing processors(1 CPU and 3 GPUs). We observe that the recalibration procedure allows the scheduler to match rapidly the typical hardware parameters which gives a significant gain of almost 30% compared to the hybrid algorithm only and about 90% compared to the default scheduler.

To illustrate the impact of the continuous re-calibration we propose to analyze the evolution of two parameters during the simulation: first we consider the average decision path length, computed as the average number of steps required to make the decision on where the event will be directed. Second, we consider the average scheduling interval length during one simulated second. As for the path length illustrated in Figure 10, we identify a first phase, where the length seems extremely variable, oscillating between 1 step (18%) and 5 steps (13 %). This presents a learning phase, which was arbitrary fixed to 500 simulated seconds. Afterwards, we observe a transition phase where the average decision path length decreases rapidly until reaching a steady state where the scheduling decision needs in average between one and two steps. We conclude that the continuous recalibration allows a significant gain in term of scheduling cost without compromising the decision quality. Regarding the scheduling interval length illustrated in Figure 11, we observe that the interval length is sensitive to the experimentation conditions; therefore its value decreases to 1-5 ms when messages number is high and increases to 10-15 ms when events are mixed. Considering that message events are na-

[3]We note that we vary the DP for that scenario between 0 and 0.28 because we loose the network activity beyond that threshold.

tively dependent, that behavior reflects in a faithful manner, the events relationship. Moreover, we observe that there is no learning phase since the unique rule during the whole simulation is to maximize event parallelism. Thus, an interval maximization phenomenon is observed in the beginning and the end of the simulation. This further confirms the bijective relation between the interval length and event dependency. Accordingly, we can conclude that the H-scheduler presents an interesting ability to deal with variable simulation rates under large scale conditions while maximizing the hardware usage rate even in heterogeneous context. Moreover, the re-calibration procedure and the dynamic behavior allow a significant support of the hardware characteristics without prerequisite knowledge.

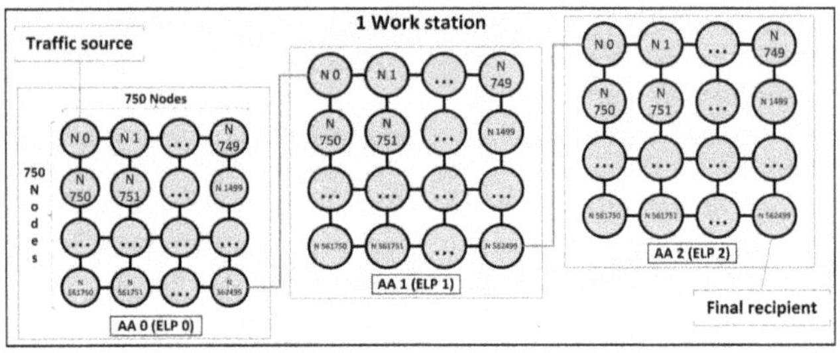

Figure 4: Topology of the benchmarking scenario

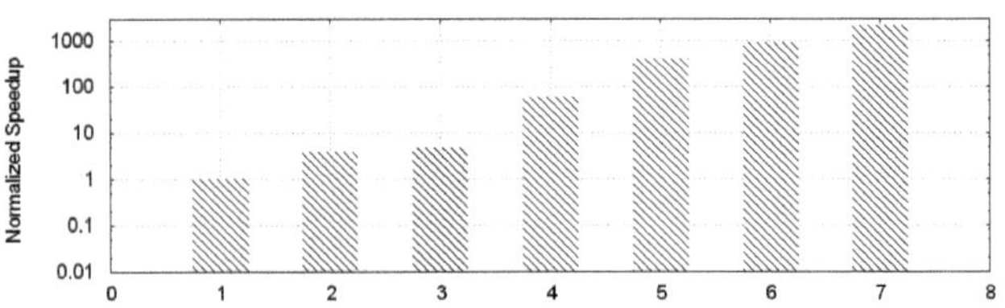

Figure 5: Normalized speedup with respect to the sequential runtime

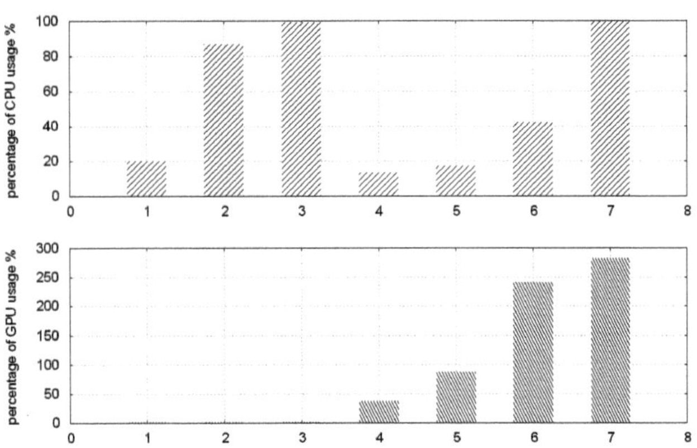

Figure 6: The hardware usage rate.

5. DISCUSSION

This paper presents a proof of concept where we aim to emphasis the potential of the H-scheduler. Thereby, we use an adequate machine including identical GPUs and well-designed scenario, suitable for high event rate. Nevertheless, we had identified five issues which need to be discussed: First, we did not consider the data structure filling issue. In fact, all events have the same importance whatever the status of the concerned buffer. An adaptive policy may use a RED [10] approach to manage different buffers. Second, the

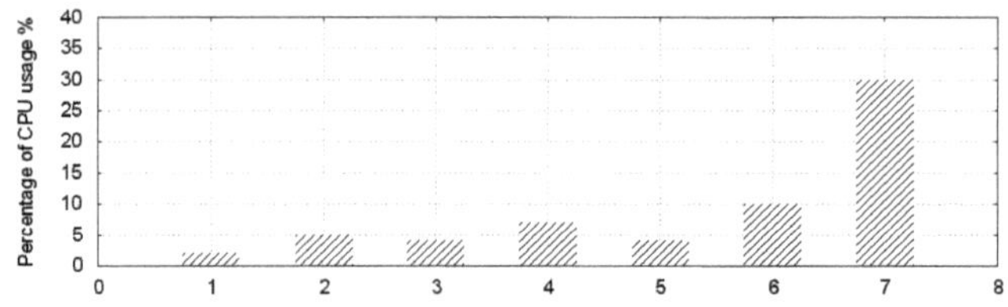

Figure 7: The scheduling cost.

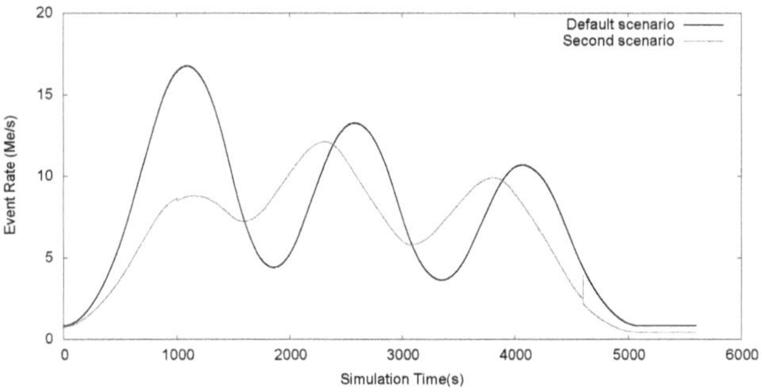

Figure 8: Variation of the input rate vs Time

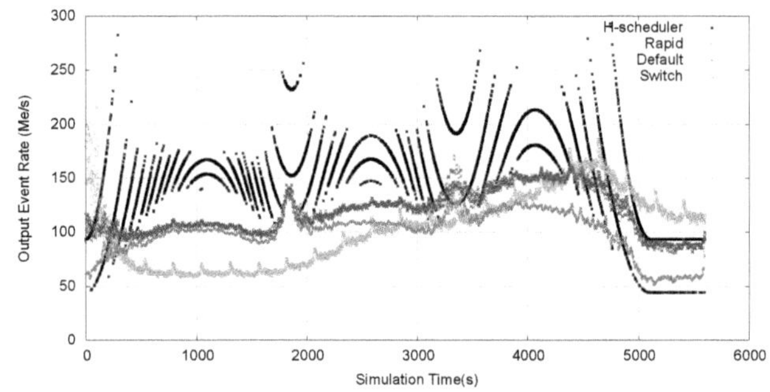

Figure 9: Output event rate of different algorithms.

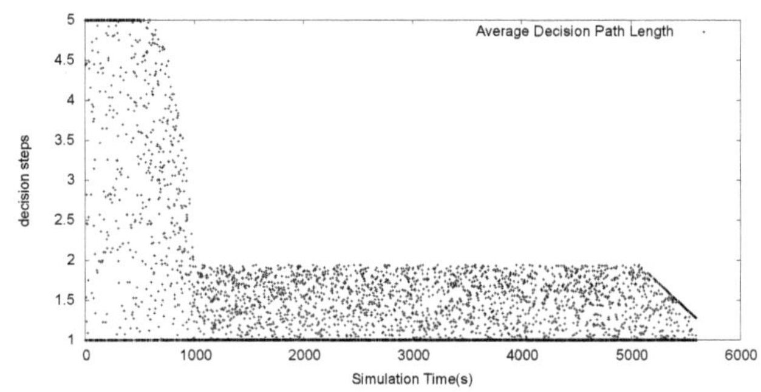

Figure 10: Average decision path length during the simulation.

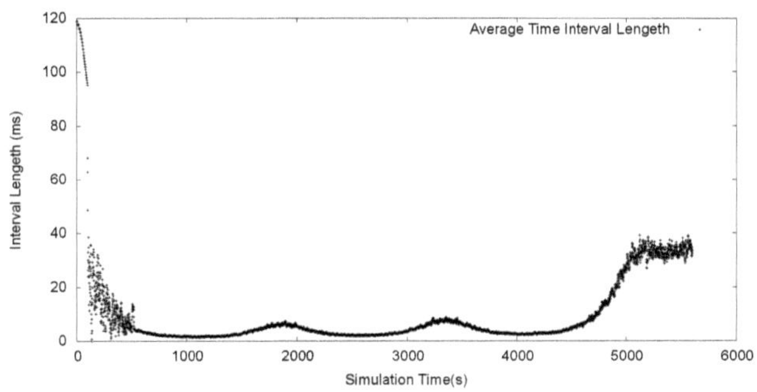

Figure 11: Average interval length during the simulation. It reflects closely the events dependency.

management of the algorithms switching relies on a loop-back mechanism which measures the load of each auxiliary resource. While this approach seems efficient to cope with very large scale simulations, analytical evaluation demonstrates that it may generate an instable system when the simulation pattern is unpredictable (such as the second scenario). Therefore, a weighted flow management appears as a reasonable stability compromise.

Third, we used in this work a limited range of computing hardware, including one GPU family and one Hexa-core CPU. We expect to evaluate the robustness of the H-scheduler under large heterogeneous conditions where we combine powerful CPUs (Xeon E5 2650) with professional GPUs and accelerators (Xeon Phi).

Fourth, we had observed that the brutal swing between both scheduling algorithm may be a source of instability; thus we had introduced a swing timer to stabilize the system. We expect that a smoothed transition between them may increases further the efficiency while providing enhanced stability. To conclude this discussion, we highlight that we rely on a data-abstraction mechanism which allows any event to access any data whatever its location. Therefore, the H-scheduler omits the data-access cost when computing the most suitable execution target. Nevertheless, we observe that the data locality is an emerging issue which may be considered on the event scheduling level, especially when targeting heterogeneous computer.

6. CONCLUSION

Discrete event simulation is widely recognized as an essential tool to analyze complex systems. Often, modern structures require sophisticated models while simulating a large number of entities in continuous interaction. However, the scalability of that simulation remains challenging, whatsoever in term of running time as well as in term of simulated entities. In that context, parallel (and distributed) discrete event simulation is actually the most relevant solution which allows a respectable scalability degree. However, event scheduling during the simulation over PDES requires optimized design to deal with emerging hardware innovation while respecting the simulation correctness. In particular, new computers are transformed into a heap of heterogeneous processors, each of which is more adequate for a specific task. Nonetheless, most of existing schedulers are derived from sequential concept which reduces their ability to cope with parallel hardware specifications. accordingly, the events flow is generally under expectation and the idle time is consequent.

We present in this work a new scheduling approach which aims to maximize the event throughput over heterogeneous computer while taking advantage of each processor specificity. Thereby, we rethought the event-driven simulation architecture to consider event flows rather than individual events. Therefore events are clustered as a function of their process and timestamps for the scheduling step while event flows are further directed to the adequate execution target. The implementation of our concept is denoted the H-scheduler referencing the heterogeneous computing; it considers particularly both GPU & multi-core CPU. In the current version, the H-scheduler is composed of four components: the dispatcher which computes the possible parallelization issues for events, the injector which determines the execution target of each parallel event group, the CPU-scheduler which ensures the execution of events on the corresponding CPU and the GPU-scheduler which ensures the execution of events on the corresponding GPU. Both injector and dispatcher present an abstraction layer which simplifies the user job. On the other side, both CPU-scheduler and GPU-scheduler are achieved according to a hardware/software co-design method; therefore we combine the simplicity of usage and efficiency of specific target-oriented solutions. Accordingly, experimental results demonstrate that the H-scheduler overcomes the majority of existing schedulers. In particular, it is able to achieve a reference simulation 1200x faster than the sequential one and 2x faster than the original Cunetsim scheduler while using the same workstation.

7. REFERENCES

[1] B. G. Aaby, K. S. Perumalla, and S. K. Seal. Efficient simulation of agent-based models on multi-gpu and multi-core clusters. In *Proceedings of the 3rd International ICST Conference on Simulation Tools and Techniques*, page 29. ICST (Institute for Computer Sciences, Social-Informatics and Telecommunications Engineering), 2010.

[2] N. Bell and J. Hoberock. Thrust: A productivity-oriented library for cuda. *GPU Computing Gems*, pages 359–371, 2011.

[3] B. Bilel, N. Navid, and M. Bouksiaa. Hybrid cpu-gpu distributed framework for large scale mobile networks simulation. In *Distributed Simulation and Real Time Applications (DS-RT), 2012 IEEE/ACM 16th International Symposium on*, pages 44–53. IEEE, 2012.

[4] B. Bilel, N. Navid, and B. C. Coordinator-master-worker model for efficient large scale network simulation. In *6th International ICST Conference on Simulation Tools and Techniques*, 2013.

[5] T. Braun, H. Siegel, N. Beck, L. Bölöni, M. Maheswaran, A. Reuther, J. Robertson, M. Theys, B. Yao, D. Hensgen, et al. A comparison of eleven static heuristics for mapping a class of independent tasks onto heterogeneous distributed computing systems. *Journal of Parallel and Distributed computing*, 61(6):810–837, 2001.

[6] L.-l. Chen, Y.-s. Lu, Y.-p. Yao, S.-l. Peng, et al. A well-balanced time warp system on multi-core environments. In *Principles of Advanced and Distributed Simulation (PADS), 2011 IEEE Workshop on*, pages 1–9. IEEE, 2011.

[7] R. Curry, C. Kiddle, R. Simmonds, and B. Unger. Sequential performance of asynchronous conservative pdes algorithms. In *Proceedings of the 19th Workshop on Principles of Advanced and Distributed Simulation*, pages 217–226. IEEE Computer Society, 2005.

[8] G. D'Angelo and M. Bracuto. Distributed simulation of large-scale and detailed models. *International Journal of Simulation and Process Modelling*, 5(2):120–131, 2009.

[9] K. Dragicevic and D. Bauer. A survey of concurrent priority queue algorithms. In *Parallel and Distributed Processing, 2008. IPDPS 2008. IEEE International Symposium on*, pages 1–6. IEEE, 2008.

[10] S. Floyd and V. Jacobson. Random early detection gateways for congestion avoidance. *Networking, IEEE/ACM Transactions on*, 1(4):397–413, 1993.

[11] R. Fujimoto. Lookahead in parallel discrete event simulation. Technical report, DTIC Document, 1988.

[12] R. Fujimoto, K. Perumalla, A. Park, H. Wu, M. Ammar, and G. Riley. Large-scale network simulation: how big? how fast? In *Modeling, Analysis and Simulation of Computer Telecommunications Systems, 2003. MASCOTS 2003. 11th IEEE/ACM International Symposium on*, pages 116–123. IEEE, 2003.

[13] M. Hybinette and R. Fujimoto. Cloning parallel simulations. *ACM Transactions on Modeling and Computer Simulation (TOMACS)*, 11(4):378–407, 2001.

[14] J. Liu and R. Rong. Hierarchical composite synchronization. In *Principles of Advanced and Distributed Simulation (PADS), 2012 ACM/IEEE/SCS 26th Workshop on*, pages 3–12. IEEE, 2012.

[15] H. Lv, Y. Cheng, L. Bai, M. Chen, D. Fan, and N. Sun. P-gas: Parallelizing a cycle-accurate event-driven many-core processor simulator using parallel discrete event simulation. In *Principles of Advanced and Distributed Simulation (PADS), 2010 IEEE Workshop on*, pages 1–8. IEEE, 2010.

[16] H. Park and P. Fishwick. A gpu-based application framework supporting fast discrete-event simulation. *Simulation*, 86(10):613–628, 2010.

[17] H. Park and P. Fishwick. An analysis of queuing network simulation using gpu-based hardware acceleration. *ACM Transactions on Modeling and Computer Simulation (TOMACS)*, 21(3):18, 2011.

[18] J. Parker and J. Epstein. A distributed platform for global-scale agent-based models of disease transmission. *ACM Transactions on Modeling and Computer Simulation (TOMACS)*, 22(1):2, 2011.

[19] J. Pelkey and G. Riley. Distributed simulation with mpi in ns-3. In *Proceedings of the 4th International ICST Conference on Simulation Tools and Techniques*, pages 410–414. ICST (Institute for Computer Sciences, Social-Informatics and Telecommunications Engineering), 2011.

[20] K. Perumalla. Parallel and distributed simulation: traditional techniques and recent advances. In *Proceedings of the 38th conference on Winter simulation*, pages 84–95. Winter Simulation Conference, 2006.

[21] K. S. Perumalla. Switching to high gear: Opportunities for grand-scale real-time parallel simulations. In *Proceedings of the 2009 13th IEEE/ACM International Symposium on Distributed Simulation and Real Time Applications*, pages 3–10. IEEE Computer Society, 2009.

[22] P. Peschlow, M. Geuer, and P. Martini. Logical process based sequential simulation cloning. In *Simulation Symposium, 2008. ANSS 2008. 41st Annual*, pages 237–244. IEEE, 2008.

[23] R. Rönngren and R. Ayani. A comparative study of parallel and sequential priority queue algorithms. *ACM Transactions on Modeling and Computer Simulation (TOMACS)*, 7(2):157–209, 1997.

[24] W. Tang, R. Goh, and I. Thng. Ladder queue: An o (1) priority queue structure for large-scale discrete event simulation. *ACM Transactions on Modeling and Computer Simulation (TOMACS)*, 15(3):175–204, 2005.

[25] H. Topcuoglu, S. Hariri, and M. Wu. Performance-effective and low-complexity task scheduling for heterogeneous computing. *Parallel and Distributed Systems, IEEE Transactions on*, 13(3):260–274, 2002.

[26] R. Vitali, A. Pellegrini, and F. Quaglia. Towards symmetric multi-threaded optimistic simulation kernels. In *Principles of Advanced and Distributed Simulation (PADS), 2012 ACM/IEEE/SCS 26th Workshop on*, pages 211–220. IEEE, 2012.

[27] S. Wang, C. Lin, Y. Tzeng, W. Huang, and T. Ho. Exploiting event-level parallelism for parallel network simulation on multicore systems. *Parallel and Distributed Systems, IEEE Transactions on*, 23(4):659–667, 2012.

[28] M. Wolfe. Implementing the pgi accelerator model. In *Proceedings of the 3rd Workshop on General-Purpose Computation on Graphics Processing Units*, pages 43–50. ACM, 2010.

GPU Accelerated Three-stage Execution Model for Event-parallel Simulation

Xiaosong Li, Wentong Cai and Stephen John Turner
Parallel and Distributed Computing Center
School of Computing Engineering
Nanyang Technological University, Singapore 639798
xli15@e.ntu.edu.sg, aswtcai@ntu.edu.sg, steve@pmail.ntu.edu.sg

ABSTRACT

This paper introduces the concept of event-parallel discrete event simulation (DES) and its corresponding implementation on the GPU platform. Inspired by the typical spatial-parallel DES and time-parallel DES, the event-parallel approach on GPU uses each thread to process one of the N events, where N is the total number of events. By taking advantage of the high parallelism of GPU threads, this approach achieves greater speedup. The GPU architecture is adopted in the execution of the event-parallel approach, so as to take advantage of the parallel processing capability provided by the massively large number of GPU threads. A three-stage execution model composing of generating events, sorting events and processing events in parallel is proposed. This execution model achieves good speedup. Compared with the event scheduling approach on CPU, we achieve up to 22.80 speedup in our case study.

Categories and Subject Descriptors

I.6.8 [**SIMULATION AND MODELING**]: Types of Simulation - Parallel; Discrete event; C.1.2 [**PROCESSOR ARCHITECTURES**]: Multiple Data Stream Architectures (Multiprocessors)– Single-instruction-stream, multiple-data-stream processors (SIMD)

Keywords

parallel discrete event simulation, GPU, algorithm

1. INTRODUCTION

Discrete event simulations (DES) are widely used and studied in the simulation area. One branch of the study focuses on designing protocols to run DES in a parallel fashion, by which the DES execution can be accelerated. A common method to convert a sequential DES into a parallel one is the spatial-parallel approach. A spatial-parallel DES has three components, namely, the state variables, the events and the logical processes. Respectively, the state variables are used to record the state of the simulated system. Each event occurs at a particular timestamp and makes changes of state in the system [17]. Between consecutive events, no change in the system is assumed to occur; thus the simulation can directly jump in time from one event to the next event. The LP (logical process) functions as an event processor. It advances the simulation clock and also communicates with other LPs. In spatial-parallel DES, the set of state variables of a simulation is decomposed into subsets [3]. Each of these subsets is assigned to an LP that manages the corresponding part of the global simulation state.

The time-parallel approach, inspecting the simulation execution from a different angle, is another way to convert a sequential DES into a parallel one. Instead of partitioning state variables into subsets in the spatial-parallel approach, the time-parallel approach partitions the whole simulation period into time intervals and assigns each LP an interval with the complete set of state variables. These time intervals can be processed concurrently. Then, the results of all time intervals are combined together to form the overall simulation results if state-mismatch does not happen [2]. State-mismatch is the major problem in the time-parallel approach, which will be explained in detail in Section 3.1. The time-parallel approach can achieve high concurrency if the time intervals are considerably short. The parallelism is determined by the granularity of time intervals defined by the modeler, however, the granularity is also restricted by the number of processing units the hardware can provide.

When investigating parallel discrete event simulation, it is always interesting to analyze how to achieve greater parallelism without losing the efficiency of execution. The time-parallel approach breaks the whole period of simulation into time intervals. The shorter the intervals are, the greater parallelism can be achieved as there will be more time intervals to be processed at the same time. By breaking the time intervals into the finest granularity, we have events. The parallel simulation with events to be concurrently processed is called event-parallel simulation. The terminology *event-level parallelism* defined here means that each of the N events is processed by one processing unit, where N is the total number of events.

The event-parallel simulation cannot be fulfilled without proper hardware to support it. In searching for the proper hardware platform, the GPU is found to be an ideal platform for executing event-parallel simulation. The GPU is capable of carrying out a huge number of simple workloads. Taking NVIDIA's GPU family as an example, the lowest level processing unit of the device is the SP (streaming processor, or core, short for CUDA core) with fully pipelined floating-point and integer arithmetic logic units. Multiple SPs form a SM (streaming multiprocessor). A multiprocessor is designed to execute hundreds of threads concurrently. To manage such a large number of threads, it employs an execution model called SIMT (Single-Instruction, Multiple-Thread). The multiprocessor creates, manages, schedules and executes in groups of 32 parallel threads called warps. Multiple warps form a block and multiple blocks form a kernel grid. When a CUDA program on the host CPU invokes a kernel grid, the blocks of the grid are enumerated and distributed to multiprocessors with available execution capacity. The threads of a thread block execute concurrently on a multiprocessor, and multiple thread blocks can execute concurrently on one multiprocessor. As thread blocks terminate, new blocks are launched on the vacated multiprocessors [11].

In this paper we present the idea of GPU accelerated event-parallel DES. Our approach leverages the massively parallel processing power of GPUs to concurrently process individual events. The overall goal of our work is to provide a cost-efficient alternative to the traditional approach of parallelizing discrete event simulations. The challenge here is to adapt an often unstructured DES with arbitrary dependencies to an architecture that is designed for executing regular array-like applications and in the meantime to maintain the logical correctness of the simulation. The main contribution of the paper is the three-stage strategy to realize DES on GPU. The key idea of the strategy is that the DES can be viewed as a series of events modifying the system state in timestamp order. It is executed in three stages: generating events, sorting events and processing events. To demonstrate and justify the strategy, a case study is conducted to test the correctness of the strategy and experiments are performed to show the performance advantages. Similar to the time-parallel approach, event-parallel simulation also faces the state-mismatch problem. It can only be implemented efficiently on GPU under certain assumptions (to be specified in detail in Section 4).

The rest of the paper is structured as follows: Section 2 talks about the related work. Section 3 discusses the challenges to support simulations in an event-parallel fashion. Section 4 introduces our three-stage execution strategy to execute simulations on GPU in an event-parallel fashion. Section 5 further elaborates our three-stage execution strategy by using a personal communication service (PCS) network simulation as an example. We describe the implementation details in length and give the performance statistics. Section 6 concludes the paper and points out some directions for the future work.

2. RELATED WORK

Parallel discrete event simulation has been studied for many years. Fujimoto [3] summarizes the fundamental concepts and techniques of parallel discrete event simulation. Two execution models, the conservative model and optimistic model, are described and compared for the spatial-parallel DES. Optimization of the two execution models are also discussed in the work.

The time-parallel approach is analyzed in a series of Kiesling's papers [6, 5, 4]. The state-mismatch problem is discussed in [6], and algorithms resolving this state-mismatch problem are also presented. One solution is to process time intervals in parallel and iteratively resolve the state-mismatch until the mismatch is limited to a tolerable range. The event-parallel approach proposed in this paper further extends this idea by processing the events in parallel.

The GPU serving as a generic computing platform facilitates simulations in many ways. Many works focus on the issues in adopting the GPU platform in the applications [1, 7, 16, 15, 14, 13]. The branch divergency of threads, memory hierarchy on GPU, host-device data transfer latency and global memory access pattern are mostly discussed in these works. Specifically for DES on GPU, the work of Kunzmulti [7] proposes algorithms to sort and group the events according to the event type to reduce the branch divergency. A strategy to pipeline data transfer between host and device and process the data on the device side is also discussed in the work.

In the work of Perumalla [16], the author argues that discrete event simulations are fit to be implemented with the GPU architecture, when the events have high density of computations. The DES on GPU in his work focuses more on the computation rather than the scheduling of the events. In other applications, e.g. the work of Pelechano et al. [15] and the work of Bleiweiss [1] on simulating agent movement in a crowd, the GPU threads are similarly utilized to perform independent computation with none or minimal inter-thread communication or concurrent modification to the global environment.

In the work of Park and Fishwick [14, 13], the authors propose more generic data structures to process parallel DES. The future event list (FEL) is decomposed into sub-FELs then assigned to GPU threads for concurrent processing. However, in their work, the iterative data transfer between host side and device side is a bottle neck.

3. CHALLENGES

3.1 The State-mismatch Problem

The state-mismatch problem comes from the decomposition of the simulation execution. Before explaining the state-mismatch problem, we begin with simulation decomposition. To illustrate simulation decomposition, we draw a graph to demonstrate as shown in Figure 1. In the graph, dashed vertical lines denote the occurrence of events and rows denote state variables, and consequently, a bold line segment represents that an event is impacting the corresponding state variable in the row. In spatial-parallel DES, we decompose the graph horizontally by partitioning the set of state variables then assigning subsets to LPs for parallel execution. Alternatively, the graph can be decomposed vertically by splitting the time axis evenly to form time-parallel DES (assuming the time interval is Δt).

Derived from the time-parallel DES, event-parallel DES divides the time axis according to events rather than time intervals to gain greater parallelism. Correspondingly, the parallel processing of each event independently inherits the state-mismatch problem, similar to the time-parallel approach [3, 6]. The state-mismatch problem is the situation where initial and final simulation states of adjacent events are inconsistent (as shown in Figure 2).

Let $ES=[e_1, e_2, e_3, \dots, e_N]$ be the *complete set of events* labeled according to the timestamp order. The e_i is the individual event, where i ranges from 1 to N and N is the total number of events. To perform the event-parallel DES,

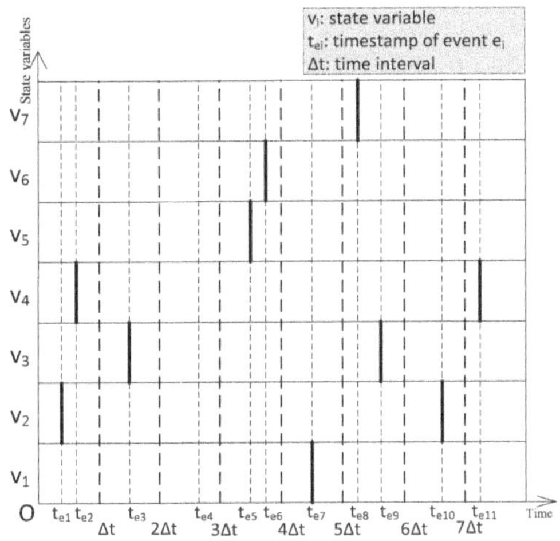

Figure 1: Comparisons among space-parallel, time-parallel and event-parallel simulation

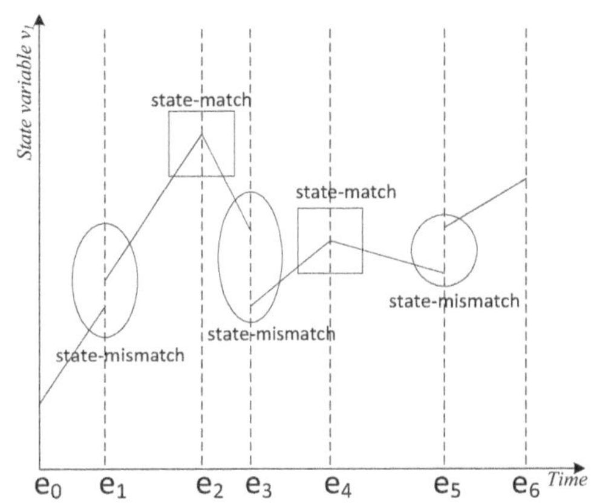

Figure 2: State-match and state-mismatch demonstrations

each event has to start the simulation from an initial state $\hat{s}_i$ and end with a final state $\check{s}_i$. At the beginning of the simulation only the initial state of e_1, (i.e., $\hat{s}_1$) is known, while the initial states of other events are unknown. As the simulation of different events are supposed to be executed in parallel, the mismatch of final and initial states of adjacent events is unavoidable, i.e., it is possible that $\check{s}_{k-1} \mathrel{!=} \hat{s}_k$ for event e_k.

Therefore, proper algorithms should be proposed to avoid this state-mismatch problem so as to maintain the logical correctness of the simulation. One intuitive way is to sequentially check the event set, then re-execute the simulation after detecting the event having the state-mismatch. A more sophisticated way is to take the mistakes under control within several iterations of re-execution, for example, the approach adopted in the time-parallel DES in [6]. In each iteration, the start-state and end-state for each interval will be modified to reduce the gap mismatch. This is done in parallel by processing units handling intervals. The iteration ends when mistakes are controlled within a tolerable range. Our approach is a hybrid of the above two methods: we correct the mistakes in several rounds of iterations and in each iteration multiple mistakes will be taken care of. A sequential check on a subset of the whole event set is needed to detect mistakes. The checking on different subsets can be processed in parallel. The detailed algorithms will be discussed in Section 4.

3.2 GPU Architecture

Supported by general purpose programming frameworks like OpenCL and NVIDIA's CUDA, GPUs have become a valuable tool for high-performance parallel computing. With hardware assisted thread scheduling, even greater numbers of threads can concurrently execute on a single GPU. In order to fully exploit the available processing power, two features of the GPU architecture need to be taken into account: i) a high degree of parallelism can only be achieved if careful programming is adopted to meet the GPU's architecture requirements, and ii) the dynamic memory allocation and collection, and dynamic data structures, such as tree, list and heap, are not well supported by the GPU architecture. In the following, we will illustrate how the above two points may impact the performance of executing event-parallel DES on GPU.

3.2.1 *Programming requirements*

As mentioned above, the warp is a basic scheduling unit in SM. Threads of a warp start together at the same program address, but they have their own instruction address counter and register state and are therefore free to branch and execute independently. A warp executes one common instruction at a time, so full efficiency is realized when all 32 threads of a warp agree on the same execution path. If threads of a warp diverge via a data-dependent conditional branch, the warp serially executes each branch path taken, disabling threads that are not on that path. Only when all branched paths complete, the threads converge back to the same execution path. Branch divergence occurs only within a warp; different warps execute independently regardless of whether they are executing common or disjoint code paths [11].

In event-parallel DES, event types may vary, which brings difficulties to achieve full parallelism in one warp. So it is possible that the threads process different types of events in one warp and follow different code paths, and branch divergences occur. As described above, different code paths belonging to one warp execute sequentially. In this case, the performance will suffer a degradation. A typical way to handle branch divergence is to group events of the same type together and assign them to the same warp. In [7], the authors propose a sorting-and-padding algorithm as an realization of this idea. In our approach, we redefine the concept of events so that they can be processed with the same instruction. The detailed description will be given in Section 4.

3.2.2 *Restrictions on memory manipulations*

Another restriction of GPU architecture is its deficiencies in supporting dynamic data structures and dynamic memory manipulation. Thus manipulations like insert and delete elements in a list or a tree are not supported. As a consequence, the functions executing on GPU need to operate on the array which is pre-allocated before the execution.

The restriction of memory manipulations on GPU can be easily dealt with, in general, for agent-based simulation. In agent based simulation, three aspects need to be specified: the set of agents, the agent relationships, and the agents' environment [8]. The agents and the environment need memory space to keep their information. Usually, the maximum number of agents in the environment, the number of obstacles in the environment, and the size of the environment will not change after the simulation starts, therefore the memory space for them can be pre-allocated. One example of this kind of simulations is the crowd simulations on GPU reported in [1]. In this work, agents move in an environment with obstacles. The environment is decomposed into nodes, each obstacle and agent keeps a vector recording its distance to each node. The navigation algorithm will access this information to direct agents to the exits. Since the agent number, obstacle number and number of nodes in the environment are fixed at runtime, the memory space on GPU can be easily allocated.

In discrete event simulation (DES), executing an event may schedule new events, which may cause the memory space used by the event list to be extended. To execute DES on GPU, in Park and Fishwick's work [14], at the end of each simulation loop, the future event list (FEL) on GPU will be copied back to the host side memory to either double the array size of the FEL or cut it in half, based on the number of elements in the FEL. By adjusting at the host side, the size of the FEL can be dynamic. Our approach does a one-time allocation by calculating the memory space required in the simulation. The requirement and procedure to achieve this will be discussed in length in later sections.

4. THE PROPOSED ALGORITHM

The overall goal of this paper is to provide a cost-efficient alternative for executing parallel discrete event simulation with the parallelism at the event level, in comparison with the traditional approaches executing on multi-core cluster architectures with the parallelism at the logical process level. Obviously, not all simulations can be implemented efficiently in an event-parallel manner on GPU. Simulations fit for the execution in an event-parallel fashion should satisfy two assumptions: i) the event generation and processing in the simulation should be separated into different phases; and ii) event processing can be transformed into merely simulation of state modifications, excluding operations like memory allocation and collection. The first assumption guarantees that the simulator has the knowledge of the total memory consumption so that the memory allocation on GPU can be done in advance, in order to provide enough space to place the generated events. The second assumption guarantees that events are efficiently executed on GPU hardware, to maximize the computing ability.

To begin with, the *event* will be redefined to accommodate our execution model. Each event e_i has three aspects to be specified. The first one is a collection of event attributes (e.g., the timestamp). The second aspect is a collection of simulation state variables $S(e_i)$ that will be affected by e_i. The third one is the effect vector $E(e_i)$ that defines to what extent the event e_i will affect $S(e_i)$. In the Personal Communication Service (PCS) simulation to be further described in Section 5, the simulation state can be represented by the set $\{C_{B_1}, C_{B_2}, \ldots, C_{B_{20}}\}$, where C_{B_i} is the number of occupied channels in base station i. Possible events in this simulation are call *Initiation*, call *Hand-over*, and call *Termination* events. Taking the ith *Initiation* event for base station j as an example (i.e., I_{i,B_j}), its corresponding $S(I_{i,B_j}) =< C_{B_j} >$ and $E(I_{i,B_j}) =< +1 >$. The effect vector for the ith *Termination* event for base station j (i.e., T_{i,B_j}) will be $< -1 >$ (i.e., $E(T_{i,B_j}) =< -1 >$).

To apply the effect of an event to the simulation state, an effect operation, $E(e_i) \bigoplus S(e_i)$, can be performed. The effect operation will change the value of state variables in $S(e_i)$ according to the effect specified in $E(e_i)$. For the *Initiation* event and the *Termination* event described above, the effect operation is simply the addition operation. That is, an *Initiation* event will effectively increase the number of occupied channels in the base station by one and a *Termination* event will decrease the number of occupied channels in the base station by one. Furthermore, an anti-effect vector $\widetilde{E}(e_i)$ can be used to cancel the effect caused by $E(e_i)$. Hence, events are transformed into effect vectors and processing events is transformed into the execution of effect vectors on the affected simulation state variables. These transformations are necessary to execute event-parallel DES on GPU because the branch divergences can be greatly avoided.

Based on the redefinition of event as described above, event e_i is executed correctly if the following two conditions are held:

1. All previous events having an effect on at least one of the state variables in $S(e_i)$ are correct, i.e., $\forall e_j$ where $e_j.timestamp < e_i.timestamp$ and $S(e_j) \bigcap S(e_i) \neq \emptyset$, e_j is correct;

2. The simulation state after executing $E(e_i) \bigoplus S(e_i)$ is correct.

Since we separate event generation from event processing and execute events in parallel, the execution of an event may or may not be correct. The effects of incorrectly executed events need to be cancelled and these events need to be re-executed.

In the following, we propose a three-stage execution model of event-parallel DES. The first stage, event generation stage, generates events and their effect vectors. A large number of events is important to the event-parallel DES simply because the capabilities of thousands of threads will not be fully exploited unless there are a commeasurable number of events ready for processing. The second stage, sorting stage, organizes the events according to the order required by the application (timestamp order in most cases). It also maps each event to an individual thread by placing the event in a specific location in memory to form the one to one event-thread relationship. The third stage, parallel processing stage which will be executed iteratively, invokes threads to process the events and modify the simulation states.

4.1 Generating Events

An initiation event represents the beginning of the life cycle of a simulation entity. The subsequent events can be generated according to the life cycle that the simulation entity may go through. The events related to one simulation entity form a chain starting from the initiation event, as shown in Figure 3. All the events of all the chains generated at this stage form a complete set of events. For example, in the PCS simulation, following the life cycle of a call, an event chain can be generated, which starts with an *Initiation* event, followed by possibly several *Hand-over* events, and finally ends with an *Termination* event. For trace-driven simulations,

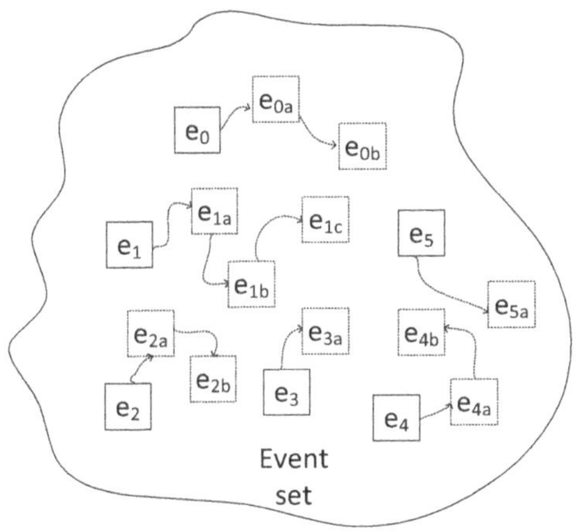

Figure 3: Initiation events and event chains in event generation step

event chains can be generated using the trace data directly. For distribution-driven simulations, event chains can be obtained by following the life cycles of simulation entities and sampling statistics distributions.

The effect vectors $E(e_i)$ of each e_i will be created correspondingly. The values of the elements in the vector are calculated according to the event type, attributes, etc.. Since each event chain is independent with each other, the generation of events in a chain and their respective effect vectors can be processed in parallel on GPU.

For now, it is assumed that all the events in the event set will be executed, however, events may not be generated correctly as the simulation state is not considered in event generation. Invalid events will be identified and discarded to guarantee the logical correctness of the simulation at a later stage. For example, in the PCS simulation, an *Initiation* event is an invalid event if the number of available channels of a base station becomes negative after executing the event.

4.2 Sorting

The second stage is to sort the event set into an ordered event list (*ordered_EL*). The ordering is based on application-dependent requirements. Recall the two conditions for correct execution of an event as specified in the beginning of this section. Without sorting, effects of events may not be applied to the simulation state variables accumulatively in a correct manner. So, the sorting stage can be considered as the pre-processing step for the next stage – parallel processing stage.

The most fundamental criterion for sorting is the timestamp of event. For instance, in the PCS simulation, the events are sorted first according to the base station IDs and then for all events belong to the same base station, they are further sorted according to the timestamps. More detail can be found in Section 5.

4.3 Parallel Processing

The third stage is the parallel processing of the events. Having all the events ordered and effect vectors generated, at this stage, we process the events by all the concurrent threads to achieve the maximum parallelism. Hence, the event processing is transformed into the execution of events' effect operations on simulation state variables. For each event, a GPU thread will be used to carry out this operation and all threads execute the same effect operation but using different effect vectors and possibly on a different set of state variables.

In the generic algorithm, *ordered_EL* denotes a data array that keeps the ordered events, and N is the total number of events in the *ordered_EL*. The *scan* operation is done by all the GPU threads in parallel for all e_i to apply the effects of events to the simulation state variables. Details of the algorithm that implements the parallel scan on GPU can be found in [10].

The parallel scan accumulates the impacts of events blindly, regardless of their correctness. To maintain the correctness of the simulation, one required task is to detect the events causing errors to the simulation state and correct these events. To achieve this, a parallel detection algorithm is necessary. One generic way of doing this is to let the GPU threads concurrently traverse event chains mentioned above. When detecting a wrong event in an event chain, the thread will mark it and its following events in the chain with a label *cancelable*. It is possible that performing deletion on an event may cause another *cancelable* event to be saved. So we repeat the scan and detection, until no more cancelable event is detected. An application dependent implementation can be found in the case study in Section 5.

Algorithm 1 Parallel processing

```
Input: ordered_EL
Output: statistics
  detect := TRUE;
  repeat
     scan(ordered_EL);
     detect := parallel_detecting_mistakes(ordered_EL);
     collect_statistics(statistics);
  until detect = FALSE
```

5. CASE STUDY: PCS SIMULATION

To further illustrate the proposed event-parallel simulation on GPU, here we demonstrate a real Personal Communication Service (PCS) [1] application implemented with this approach. This case study can be used to investigate, for example, how network configuration (specifically, the number of channels per base station) may affect the dropped and blocked call rates of phone calls.

5.1 Problem Description

Consider a one-way highway 40 km long, with 20 base stations along the highway with equal distance between any of the two adjacent stations (see Figure 4). Each station covers 2 km of the road. Cars travel along the highway from left to right. A call can be made at anytime and anywhere in the highway, and it is handled by the base station covering the road segment where the call is made. A call may need to be handed over to the next base station because of the movement of the car. The maximum capacity of each base station is 10 phone calls. A station will discard the phone calls if its capacity is full, causing call blocked when a call is attempted to be made, or call dropped if a call is attempted to be handed over. Cars are assumed to move

[1]http://bcf.usc.edu/~wdutton/comm533/PCS-STEW.htm

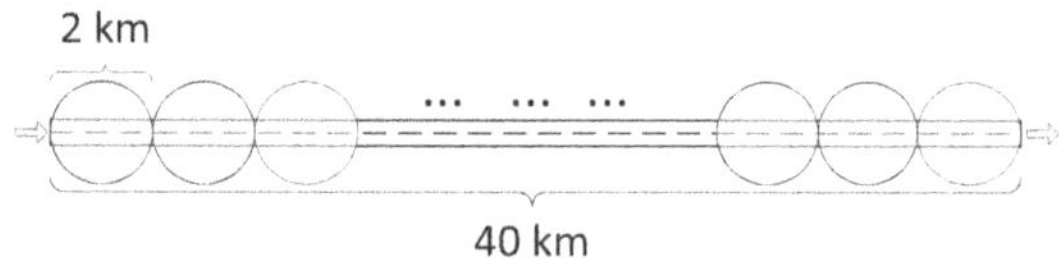

Figure 4: PCS problem illustration

at constant speed. All the parameters (e.g. inter-arriving time, call duration, etc.) of the simulation follow some specific distributions.

Let C_{B_i} represent the number of occupied channels of base station B_i. The simulation state can then be represented by the set of state variables $\{C_{B_1}, C_{B_2}, \ldots, C_{B_{20}}\}$. The following events can be identified for this simulation: *Initiation* – creating a call; *Hand-over* – passing a call to the next base station; and *Termination* – terminating a call. Depending on where a call is created, an *Initiation* event will affect only the state variable of a specific base station (e.g., B_i). The effect of this event on B_i is to increase C_{B_i} by 1. Similarly, a *Termination* event will also affect only the state variable of a specific base station (e.g., B_j). The effect of this event on B_j is to decrease C_{B_j} by 1. As for the *Hand-over* event, it will affect the state variables of two successive base stations (e.g., B_k and B_{k+1}). In fact, its effect on the simulation state variables can be emulated by executing a *Termination* event on B_k followed by an *Initiation* event on B_{k+1}.

5.2 Implementation

Having the problem description, now we apply the three-stage algorithm. The first step is to generate the *event_list* for further processing. Given the distributions, we can generate all call initiation events, say 10K initiation events, each of these events is composed of attributes such as *call_id*, *timestamp*, *call_duration*, *car_speed*, *car_position*, etc. Then we generate the consecutive hand-over and termination events for each of the call initiation events. To make the application compatible with GPU processing, we use SOA (struct-of-array) data structure to maintain the data in GPU memory [18]. For each call initiation event, it is possible to determine the number of consecutive hand-over and termination events using call duration and car speed. So, the starting and ending index of each event chain in the *event_list* and the total memory space needed for the *event_list* on the device side can be determined.

To generate the event chain in parallel on the device side, we use CUDA threads to process each initiation event. The initiation event and its consecutive events form a chain. The generation of events here is what we described previously, that is to determine events' attributes and effect vectors. The memory space for all the chains of events can be predetermined and allocated as described above. Each thread will then work on generating events in the chain belonging to the same call, that is to handle the initiation event and generate its corresponding hand-over and termination events, and put them in the *event_list* corresponding to its chain starting and ending index. The hand-over events are decomposed into two events as mentioned above. This procedure is depicted in Figure 5.

In the generation stage as described above, we generate all the possible events that might or might not be correct. It may happen that some initiation events or handover events

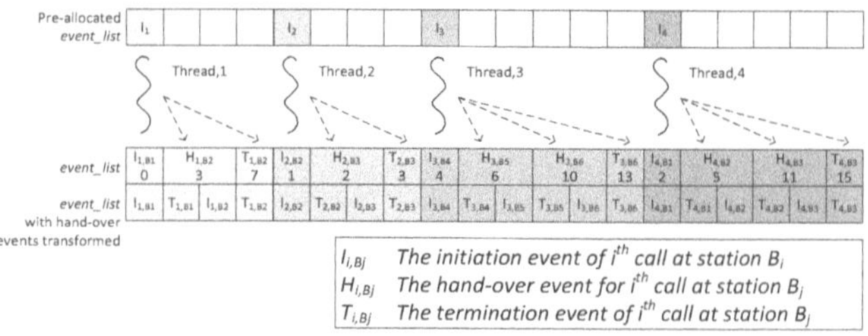

Figure 5: Generating event chains

cannot take place because of the full capacity of a base station. The detailed algorithm of event generation is shown in Algorithm 2.

Algorithm 2 Generate Event Chain

Input: *event_list* ▷ with initiation event only
Output: *event_list* ▷ full event list
for all $e \in event\_list$ **do in parallel**
  $call\_TTL := e.get\_call\_TTL()$;
  $speed := e.get\_car\_speed()$;
  repeat
    $pos := e.get\_car\_position()$;
    $time := time\_to\_next\_handover(pos, speed)$;
    $update\_car\_position(pos)$;
    if $time < call\_TTL$ **then**
      $generating\_handover\_event(time)$;
      $call\_TTL := call\_TTL - time$;
    else
      $generating\_termination\_event(time)$;
      $call\_TTL := 0$;
    end if
  until $call\_TTL = 0$;
end for

In the sorting stage, a *sorted_index* will be generated according to the *base_id* and the timestamps. The reason to use *sorted_index* is that the events in *event_list* are organized in the form of event chains. The data structure of *event_list* facilitates the access of neighboring events in a chain. The simulation state at a specific simulation time is determined by the accumulated effects of events till that time, if they are simulated in the correct logic order. The *sorted_index* will be used in the parallel processing step to get the effect vectors of events correctly accumulated on the simulation state. Figure 6 shows how the sorted index is generated. In the figure, the upper list is the *event_list*. The number below each event is the timestamp of the event. The lower list is the *sorted_index*, which keeps the index of events in the *event_list*. We use the sort API provided in the NVIDIA's Thrust Library [12] to do the parallel sort.

Recall previously, we mentioned that event-parallel simulation will suffer the state-mismatch problem. This is because the start state for simulating each event is unknown. Here we use the parallel scan to solve this problem, which is the first step for the parallel processing. This is done with the help of the *sorted_index* for keeping the logical correctness. The term scan here comes from the parallel prefix-sum algorithm, which uses parallel threads to calculate the sum of the prefix in an array. In our approach, the idea of scan is that the simulation state at the occurrence of one event

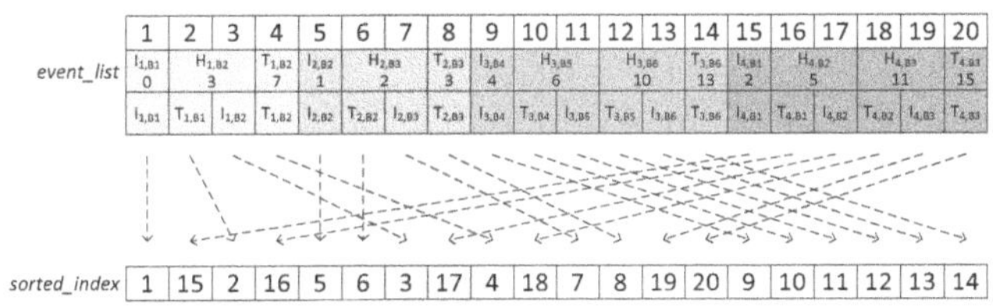

Figure 6: Sorting events

Algorithm 3 Cancelling wrong events

```
Input: event_list, chain_head_index
  flag = FALSE;
  for all idx ∈ chain_head_index do in parallel
      e0 := event_list[idx];
      e1 := event_list[idx + 1];
      while e0.chain_id = e1.chain_id do
          if flag = TRUE then
              e0.effect := 0;
              e0.mark := cancelable;
          end if
          if flag = FALSE and e0.state > 10 then
              flag := TRUE;
              e0.effect := 0;
              e0.mark := cancelable;
          end if
          idx + +;
          e0 := event_list[idx];
          e1 := event_list[idx + 1];
      end while
      if flag = TRUE then
          e0.effect := 0;
      end if
  end for
```

is determined by all the previous events. The realization of the algorithm is similar to the butterfly algorithm, which achieves the complexity of $O(logN)$ where N is the total number of events. A condition statement can be used to determine whether the influence of the current event is to be accumulated or not.

After obtaining the resulting states of all the events, we use parallel threads to check the correctness of events in each event chain concurrently. For each event chain, one thread will sequentially check the events and detect if any event produces a wrong simulation state. Once a mistake is detected, the event will be marked as *cancelable* and the following events in the chain will be marked as well. After an invalid simulation state is detected, we will do another round of scan and check. Besides marking active events to be cancelled, cancelable events can be revived. It is possible that some events generate wrong simulation results because of the influence of the previous cancelable events (the previous here is in terms of simulation time). Cancelling a previous wrong event may make the current wrong events correct.

All these procedures are illustrated in Figure 7. The first row in the figure represents a collection of effect values, one for each event. The second row represents a collection of state variable values after applying the corresponding effects, one for each state variable. Since there are 10 available channels in each base station, the criterion to cancel an

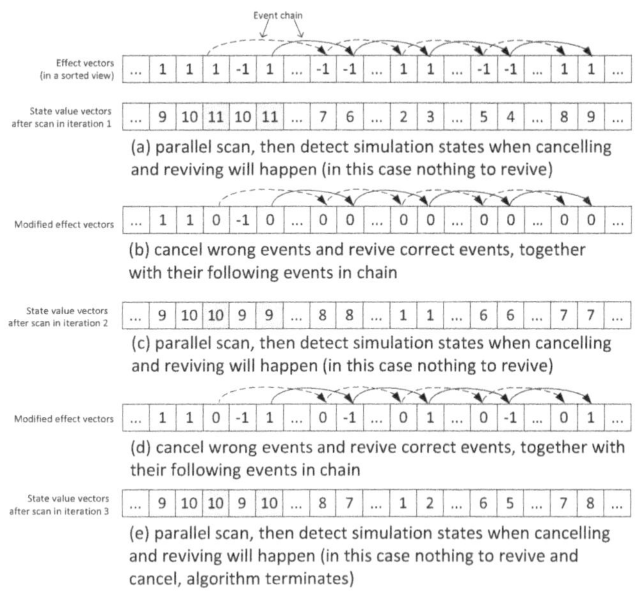

Figure 7: Parallel processing

event is that its effect operation causes the state of the corresponding base station to be greater than 10. The criterion to revive an event is that it is a previously cancelled event, and the resulting state of the corresponding base station becomes less than 10 in the current round of iteration.

In Figure 7-a, we begin the first iteration by applying the effect operation to the state variables using the parallel scan. Having the state values calculated, the next step is to detect events causing invalid system states and revive events which should be correct events. Then in Figure 7-b, we cancel the corresponding effects of wrong events and those of their following events in their chains. In this example in the first iteration, two wrong events (marked as grey in Figure 7-a) are detected but no events are revived. The effect of events causing invalid states is changed to 0 so that they will have no effect on the state variables in the next round of parallel scan (see Figure 7-b). In the next round of iteration, since effects have changed, the effect operation will be re-applied so as to obtain the simulation states with the modified effects (see Figure 7-c). Obtaining the states, detecting wrong events and reviving events will be done again. In Figure 7-d, one event chain is revived and no event is cancelled. As shown in Figure 7-e, a new round of iteration starts. In this round since there is nothing to cancel or revive, then the algorithm terminates.

Algorithm 3, cancelling wrong events, shows how the detection of wrong events works concurrently. Reviving cancelable events is similar to this algorithm. Recall after the sorting step, we have the *event_list* keeping events in the form of event chains, and an array *sorted_index* where event indexes are sorted and kept in that array according to the *base_id* and *timestamp* order of events. Besides, the position of each event-chain's head should also be acquired and kept in an array named *chain_head_index* in order to fetch the events according to the order in the chain. As described, the thread will iterate the events in one chain and terminate the iteration when the head of the next chain is detected. Different chains share different *call_arrival_no*.

Table 1: Mapping of CUDA Threads

Stages	Thread Mapping
generate_event_chain()	One per event-chain
sort()	One per event
parallel_scan()	One per event
cancel_wrong_events()	One per event-chain
revive_events()	One per event-chain

The overall procedure of the implementation is illustrated in Algorithm 4. In the event generation step, since the event in a chain is sequentially generated by each thread and the constructions of all the chains proceed simultaneously, how long this step takes depends on the number of events in the longest chain. In the sorting stage, the sorting primitive of Thrust Library [12] is adopted. The implementation strategy and complexity analysis of this primitive is reported in [9]. In the parallel processing step, in the worst case, we can correct only one event in each iteration. Then for K wrong events, we need K iterations, where $K \leq N$ and N is the total number of events. In each iteration, the parallel scan takes $log(N)$ steps. To perform *cancel_wrong_events* and *revive_events*, one thread is assigned to each event chain. Again, their execution time depends on the number of events in the longest event chain. Table 1 clearly indicates what a CUDA thread corresponds to at various stages of our proposed approach. The results of the PCS simulation can demonstrate the real execution of our algorithm. This will be given in the next subsection of experimental results.

Algorithm 4 Call Simulation

```
Input: data_file
Output: drop_rate, block_rate
  /*begin generating events, read file in host*/
  event_list := read_init_data(data_file);
  /*copy data to device, begin processing on device*/
  event_list := generate_event_chain(event_list);
  /*end generating events, begin sorting*/
  sorted_index := sort(event_list);
  /*end sorting, begin parallel processing*/
  repeat
    parallel_scan(event_list, sorted_index);
    detect := cancel_wrong_events(event_list);
    detect := revive_events(event_list);
  until detect = FALSE;
  /*end parallel processing*/
```

5.3 Experimental Results

On the device side, the PCS simulation with the three-stage execution model is implemented on NVIDIA Geforce GTX 580 graphic card. The GTX 580 card, manufactured by Palit Microsystems Ltd., is based on the Fermi architecture, equipped with 512 CUDA cores, 3GB of GDDR5 RAM over 384-bit width and 192.4GB/sec of memory bandwidth. The current price for this card is USD 575. In comparison with this device, we choose the Intel Xeon Processor X5450 with clock speed of 3.0 GHz. It is a quad-core CPU with 12 MB L2 cache and 45 nm manufacturing tech and it is priced at USD 852.

On CPU, we use two algorithms for comparison. One is the conventional algorithm based on event scheduling (denoted as *Scheduling*), whose performance is optimized by implementing the event list using an optimized priority queue. The other is the sequential counterpart of the event-parallel algorithm (denoted as *EP_Sequential*), which implements sequentially the steps of event generation, sorting of events, and event execution and correction. To be specific, we generate the event chains in the same way as we do for GPU (refer to Section 4 for detail) but sequentially, then sort all events according to timestamp only. After that, we sequentially process the sorted events to modify the simulation state.

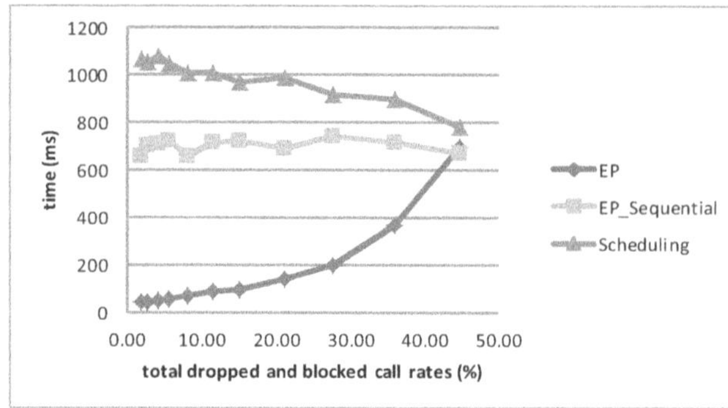

Figure 8: Time consumptions under different dropped and blocked call rates

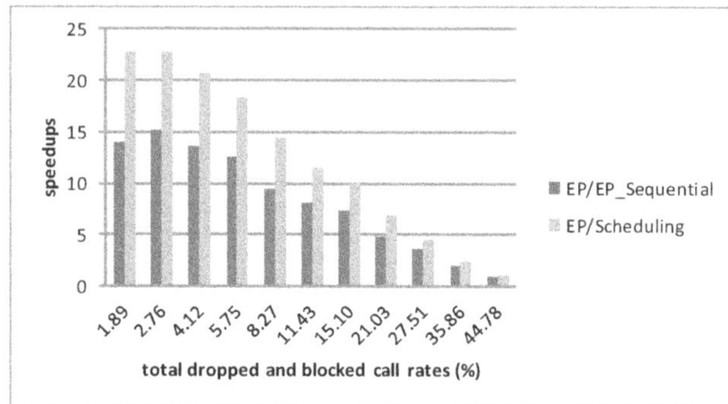

Figure 9: Speedups under different dropped and blocked call rates

Figure 8 shows the time consumption of the event-parallel approach on GPU, the event scheduling approach and the *EP_Sequential* algorithm on CPU. The time consumptions of all the three cases are collected from the start of the simulation including reading input files, memory allocation, and actual processing. In the experiments, we use the same input files for each approach. The total number of calls is 100K, and the number of events generated is about 600K. The time consumption is compared under different total percentages of blocked and dropped calls. Blocked and dropped rates are controlled by modifying the simulation parameters. With the increasing of dropped and blocked call rates, our event-parallel approach consumes more time. This is due to our design of iteratively correcting the wrong events. We try to correct multiple wrong events in an iteration, however, increasing dropped and blocked call rates causes more wrong events. Nonetheless, in a real system with QoS guarantee, a PCS network would not allow too many blocked

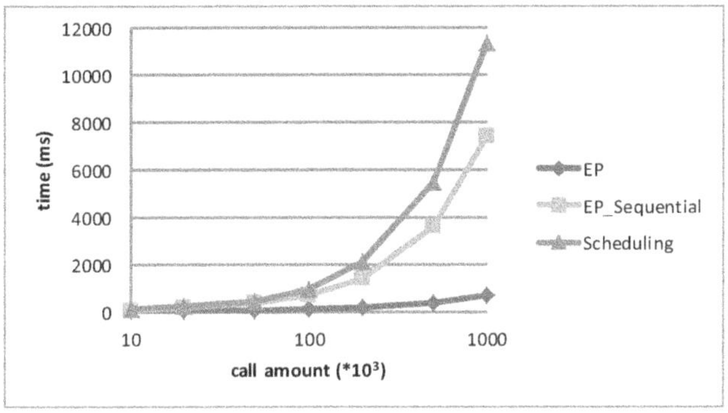

Figure 10: Time consumption under different call amounts

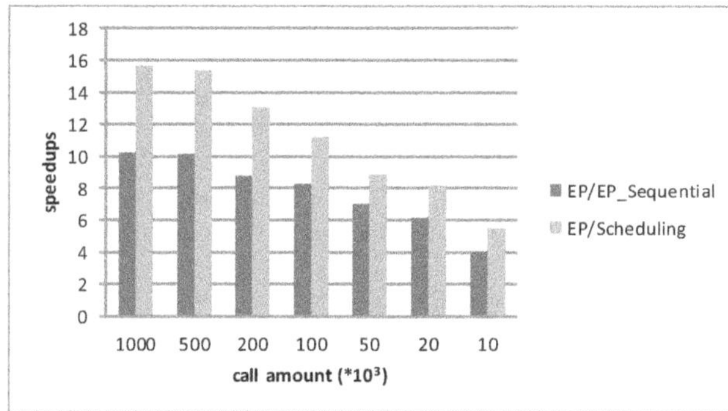

Figure 11: Speedup under different call amounts

or dropped calls. Thus practically, our approach achieves the goal of speeding up the simulation. As shown in Figure 8, the performance gap between the *Scheduling* and *EP_Sequential* narrows when the dropped and blocked call rates become large. Given the varied performance gap between the *Scheduling* and *EP_Sequential*, we therefore compute the speedup of the EP against both algorithms (as shown in Figure 9). The maximum achievable speedup, compared with the *Scheduling* and *EP_Sequential*, are 22.80 and 15.14 respectively.

The event scheduling approach consumes more time than the other two approaches. However, it has a trend of decreasing the time consumption when the dropped and blocked call rates increase, because there will be less events to be scheduled. The *EP_Sequential* approach consumes almost the same time in different situations because the memory space is pre-allocated and sorting is done for all the events in event chains. The *EP_Sequential* algorithm outperforms the event-scheduling approach possibly because the former allocates the memory space for all the events statically before processing them; whereas the latter allocates the memory for events dynamically. In other words, the event scheduling approach only allocates memory for an event when this event is sure to be executed.

Figure 10 compares the time consumption of the three approaches in the cases of different call amounts. In this experiment, we use the same total dropped and blocked call rates, which is 11.43%. The total events generated range from 60K to 6000K in 10K to 1000K calls cases. Overall, the execution time consumed by event-parallel DES does not increase a lot, however, the other two approaches increase their execution time drastically. This indicates that the event-parallel DES on GPU is insensitive to the data amounts. Figure 11 compares the speedups of event-parallel DES with the other two approaches. The maximum speedup achieved compared with the two CPU implementations are 10.25 and 15.66 respectively.

6. CONCLUSIONS

This paper introduces the concept of event-parallel DES and its corresponding implementation on the GPU platform. Compared with the typical spatial-parallel DES and the time-parallel DES, the event-parallel approach on GPU uses each thread to process one of the N events, where N is the total number of events. By taking advantage of the high parallelism of GPU threads, this approach achieves greater speedup. We use the GPU architecture to support the execution of the event-parallel approach, so as to take advantage of the parallel processing capacity of a massively large number of GPU threads. We propose a three-stage execution model consisting of generating events, sorting and parallel processing. For the parallel processing part, we design a multi-iteration algorithm to guarantee the correctness of the simulation. Compared with event scheduling approach on CPU, we achieve 22.80 speedup in our case study.

However, more effort is needed to make the event-parallel approach a more mature one. Further effort would target on three aspects. First of all, there is still room for the parallel processing algorithm to be improved. The second direction targets on widening the scope of simulations to be handled by our approach by proposing more generalized assumptions and algorithms. The third direction focuses on increasing the scalability of our execution model. Scalability means the ability to scale the simulation to larger scenarios, where the number of events cannot be processed by a single device and at the same time maintain reasonable performance.

7. REFERENCES

[1] A. Bleiweiss. Multi agent navigation on the GPU. *White paper, Game Developers Conference*, 9, 2009.

[2] K. Chandy and R. Sherman. Space-time and simulation. In *Proceedings of the SCS Multiconference on Distributed Simulation*, pages 53–57, 1989.

[3] R. M. Fujimoto. *Parallel and Distributed Simulation Systems*. John Wiley & Sons Inc, 2000.

[4] T. Kiesling. Progressive time-parallel simulation. In *Proceedings of the ACM/IEEE/SCS Workshop on Principles of Advanced and Distributed Simulation*, pages 82–91, 2006.

[5] T. Kiesling and J. Luthi. Towards time-parallel road traffic simulation. In *Proceedings of the ACM/IEEE/SCS Workshop on Principles of Advanced and Distributed Simulation*, pages 7–15, 2005.

[6] T. Kiesling and S. Pohl. Time-parallel simulation with approximative state matching. In *Proceedings of the ACM/IEEE/SCS Workshop on Parallel and Distributed Simulation*, pages 195–202, 2004.

[7] G. Kunz, D. Schemmel, J. Gross, and K. Wehrle. Multi-level parallelism for time-and cost-efficient parallel discrete event simulation on gpus. In *Proceedings of the ACM/IEEE/SCS Workshop on*

Principles of Advanced and Distributed Simulation, pages 23–32, 2012.

[8] C. Macal and M. North. Tutorial on agent-based modelling and simulation. *Journal of Simulation*, 4(3):151–162, 2010.

[9] D. Merrill and A. Grimshaw. High performance and scalable radix sorting: A case study of implementing dynamic parallelism for gpu computing. *Parallel Processing Letters*, 21(02):245–272, 2011.

[10] H. Nguyen. *GPU Gems 3*. Addison-Wesley Professional, 2007.

[11] NVIDIA. Nvidia cuda programming guide. `http://docs.nvidia.com/cuda/cuda-c-programming-guide/index.html`. [Online].

[12] NVIDIA. Thrust | nvidia developer zone. `https://developer.nvidia.com/thrust`. [Online].

[13] H. Park and P. Fishwick. A gpu-based application framework supporting fast discrete-event simulation. *Simulation*, 86(10):613–628, 2010.

[14] H. Park and P. Fishwick. An analysis of queuing network simulation using gpu-based hardware acceleration. *ACM Transactions on Modeling and Computer Simulation*, 21(3):18, 2011.

[15] N. Pelechano, J. Allbeck, and N. Badler. Controlling individual agents in high-density crowd simulation. In *Proceedings of the ACM SIGGRAPH/Eurographics symposium on Computer animation*, pages 99–108, 2007.

[16] K. Perumalla. Discrete-event execution alternatives on general purpose graphical processing units (gpgpus). In *Proceedings of the ACM/IEEE/SCS Workshop on Principles of Advanced and Distributed Simulation*, pages 74–81, 2006.

[17] S. Robinson. *Simulation: the Practice of Model Development and Use*. Wiley, 2004.

[18] D. Strippgen and K. Nagel. Multi-agent traffic simulation with cuda. In *Proceedings of the International Conference on High Performance Computing & Simulation*, pages 106–114, 2009.

Modeling Communication Software Execution for Accurate Simulation of Distributed Systems

Stein Kristiansen, Thomas Plagemann, Vera Goebel
Department of Informatics, University of Oslo
Oslo, Norway
[steikr, plageman, goebel]@ifi.uio.no

ABSTRACT

Network simulation is commonly used to evaluate the performance of distributed systems, but these approaches do not account for the performance impact that protocol execution on nodes has on performance, which may be significant. We propose a methodology to capture execution models from communication software running on real devices where the execution models can be integrated with discrete event network simulators to improve their accuracy. We provide a set of rules to instrument the software to obtain the events of importance, and present techniques to create executable models based on the obtained traces. To make the models scalable, processing stages are reduced to statistical distributions. When the resulting models are executed in a device model with a scheduler simulator, we are able to model the dynamics of multithreading and parallel execution. Our initial results from a proof-of-concept extension to Ns-3 show that our models are able to accurately model protocol execution on the Google Nexus One with low simulation overhead.

Categories and Subject Descriptors

I.6.5 [**Simulation and Modeling**]: Model Development—*Modeling methodologies*; D.4.8 [**Operating Systems**]: Performance—*Simulation*

General Terms

Design, Experimentation, Measurement, Performance

Keywords

Modeling, Methodology, Network, Simulation, Performance Evaluation, Operating Systems

1. INTRODUCTION

It is widely acknowledged that prediction of software performance is one of the core challenges in computer science [4]. This includes also communication software for networked and distributed systems. Even though discrete event network simulation is a broadly applied and adopted method to predict the performance of such systems, there is a fundamental lack in all applied network simulators, i.e., software running on nodes is basically neglected. This is because of the assumptions made about the network. The Internet has traditionally consisted of two classes of nodes: end-nodes and intermediate nodes, like routers and switches. The intermediate nodes are specialized devices and their performance can be basically captured through queuing models. However, recently we have seen a dramatic increase in the amount of mobile networks, both infrastructure-based, e.g., 3G, LTE and WiFi, and infrastructure-less, like MANET, VANET, WSN and DTN. In infrastructure-less networks the nodes must perform routing, forwarding and other communication tasks without dedicated hardware support. Therefore, these nodes can have a substantial impact on the network performance. Experiments with the Nokia N900 smartphone [8] show that it is not capable of forwarding more than 6 Mbps over a 54 Mbps network, and that the device introduces 10-40 ms forwarding delay with 2 Mbps traffic load. However, in the network simulator Ns-3, this delay is no more than 6.85 ms, and the throughput in the equivalent experiment is 10Mbps. So far all the well-known and most used network simulators ignore the fact that in these kinds of networks the nodes can have a substantial impact on performance which cannot be simply captured by queuing models. This means that in order to enable accurate simulations of such networks, the simulated nodes must be extended with realistic models of the execution of communication software.

In discrete event network simulators it is difficult to reproduce the impact of software execution in nodes. There is an increasing variety of devices that are able to run multithreaded operating systems (OS). It is challenging to model the complex, multithreaded deviceswhile at the same time preserving scalability. For models of communication software to be scalable, they must be simple enough to yield a low simulation overhead. Since simplification implies a reduction of detail, it also implies a loss of accuracy. To properly address the trade-off between accuracy and scalability, it is necessary to include in the models only those parts that are required to preserve an acceptable degree of accuracy, and to identify what can be simplified with a minimal loss of accuracy. The models must be easily understandable to help determine how performance is affected by varying configurations and workloads. This requires intuitive abstractions that expose central parameters to allow comparing the performance under different configurations. A challenge is to make the abstractions flexible enough to be able to model a range of different devices with varying characteristics. It is also important that the modeling effort is acceptably low. Finally, since network simulation is the most common approach to performance evaluation today, the models are only useful if they are integrated

Technique \ Requirement	Can Model Heterogeneous Devices	Can Model Multithreaded Devices	Accuracy	Scalability	Required Effort	Monetary Cost	Abstraction	Integration with Network Simulators
Real World Experimentation	Yes	Yes	High	Low	High	High	None	None
Machine Simulation	Yes	Yes	High	Low-High	High	Low	None-High	None
Emulation	Yes	Yes	*	Low	*	*	None	Inadequate
Analysis	Yes	No	High	High	Low	Low	High	None
Performance Prediction	Yes	No	High	High	Low	Low	High	None

Table 1: State-of-the-Art and Requirements, *: Acceptable for small-scale experiments.

in network simulators to enable the reuse of existing, well-tested protocol models.

These requirements are summarized in Table 1. The table presents an overview of the currently available techniques to evaluate the performance of mobile networks, and indicates the degree to which they satisfy the above-mentioned requirements. State-of-the-art in evaluating software performance can be classified into real world evaluation [20, 21, 24], machine simulation [17, 2, 23], emulation [9], analytical modeling [19, 18], and performance prediction techniques [22, 6]. Real world evaluation is often infeasible with large-scale networks, due to monetary cost and the difficulty of conducting controllable and repeatable experiments. The latter is especially difficult with mobile networks, even if they are small. These issues are solved by machine simulators, which can model hardware and OS in high enough detail to be able to execute real software. They provide accurate results, but the high level of detail compromises scalability and introduces a large modeling effort. This makes it difficult to obtain a high-level insight into system behavior and to easily make modifications in order to predict the performance of alternative configurations. Although existing modeling software such as System C [7] allows for higher abstraction levels, they still require all device components to be explicitly modeled at some abstraction level. This imposes a large modeling effort, especially for a network researcher that is often not well acquainted with the internals of the devices employed in the networks they investigate. Emulation aims to strike a compromise between simulative approaches and real world experimentation by combining real and virtual components across an emulation boundary. However, this suffers from scalability issues. First, when the number of nodes and traffic load grows, the inaccuracies introduced by the emulation boundary increases [9]. Second, the effort and cost increases rapidly with the scale of the experiment. Finally, although emulators are by definition a combination of simulators and real world components, they do not *integrate* the performance of the real components with the protocol models in the network simulator. Analytical models allow for scalability and promote understanding, but they are not suitable for modeling complex, dynamic and heterogeneous systems. Given an architectural description of a device, performance prediction techniques can estimate the number of CPU cycles spent on a given computational task. However, these techniques focus on predicting the behavior of individual computational tasks, and cannot be used for predicting the behavior of complete multithreaded systems.

Table 1 shows that (1) scalable techniques (analysis and performance prediction) are not able to model heterogeneous, multithreaded devices, and (2) none of thetechniques extends network simulators to increase their accuracy. Existing efforts that address the latter are limited to modeling specialized systems such as routers [5] or sensors [12], do not consider multi-threading [16] or parallel execution [15], or do not provide any method to relate the models to any real, existing system [15]. Extensions of network simulators that use machine simulators [13] suffer from scalability issues, large modeling effort and/or lack of abstractions.

In this work we address techniques to create models of multithreaded, heterogeneous devices that allows the models to be integrated into existing network simulators. We focus on discrete event simulation due to its popularity in network research. The contribution of this work consists of two parts: (1) a methodology that can be used to create scalable, configurable models of heterogeneous, multithreaded devices with a low modeling effort, and (2) an evaluation of our methodology using a proof-of-concept implementation in Ns-3 that executes models extracted from a modern smartphone, i.e., Google Nexus One (GN1). Our approach is distinguished from related work in that it provides a complete methodology to extract abstract *execution models* from real devices by means of software instrumentation and tracing, without the overhead of modeling device internals. The methodology is designed with integrability with existing discrete event network simulators in mind, and includes clear guidelines for how to perform the instrumentation and tracing. We furthermore adopt a modular approach to allow instrumentation to be distributed among protocol, OS and device developers, and to allow network researchers to focus on how to combine the execution models to construct a model of the network stack. There should be clear incentives for all groups of developers to perform this instrumentation, as it promotes the use of, and research on, the solutions they provide. Since an understanding of what impacts performance yields more efficient solutions, also service providers have incentives to promote this modeling. The results from our evaluation indicate that our methodology enables accurate modeling of the target system with low simulation overhead.

This paper is organized as follows: Section 2 presents an overview of our approach and methodology. Section 3 establishes central characteristics of the communication software we model, as well as an analysis to determine which elements must be captured in our models. Section 4 explains how to create these models. In Section 5, we present the proof-of-concept implementation for Ns-3, and an evaluation of our models based on this implementation. Section 6 presents our conclusions and elaborates on future work.

2. OVERALL APPROACH

Our approach follows the traditional scientific method to observe a system to collect reliable data about it. This data is used to create a model of the system, which in turn is used to predict the behavior of the modeled system under conditions of interest. To integrate the resulting model with network simulators, one of the two approaches presented in Figure 1 can be taken. In Approach 1, a specific network simulator is extended with models of specific device types. In Approach 2, modeling of devices and extension of network simulators are separated into two elements: (1) a methodology to create network simulator independent models of devices that can be stored in a device repository, and (2) design principles for how to extend general-purpose network simulators in order to utilize these models, with minimal modifications of the existing models.

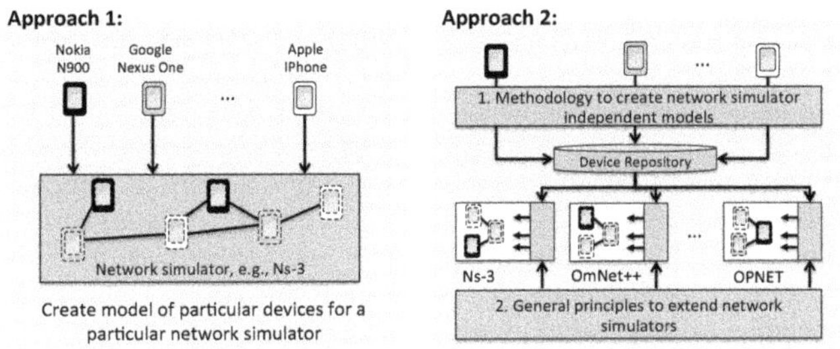

Figure 1: Two ways to approach problem.

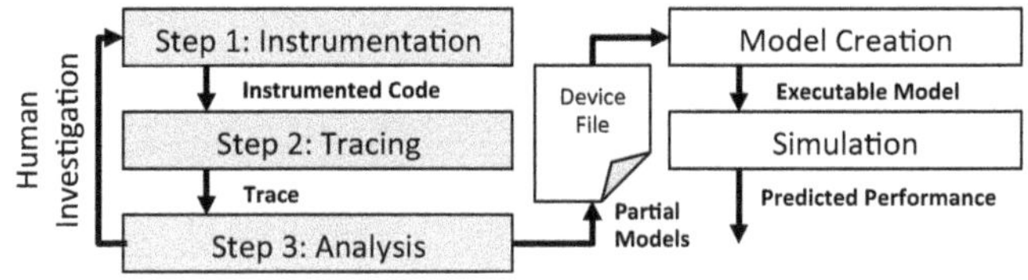

Figure 2: Overall approach.

Although Approach 2 is the most complex, it has several advantages over Approach 1. First, it allows one device model to be reused in multiple general-purpose network simulators. Since device modeling and network simulator extension must be performed only once per device and network simulator, the overall modeling effort is reduced. Second, there is a lower modeling effort per device due to the methodology that includes clear rules on how to perform modeling of arbitrary device types. Third, the decoupling of device modeling and integration with network simulators allows device modeling to be distributed among device developers. This reduces the effort required by the developers of network simulators, which is important with the current trend towards increasing heterogeneity among mobile devices. Consequently, our solution follows Approach 2. The remainder of this section presents a high-level description of our methodology, and the principles for extending network simulators. We describe the system we model, how to obtain reliable data to create device models, and how to use these models to predict the behavior of the modelled system.

We create models of the *execution behavior* of communication software that can be integrated with network simulators. We target systems where the majority of packet processing is performed in software, except for well-defined, predictable sub-tasks performed by specialized hardware such as e.g., network cards/chips (NIC) and direct memory access (DMA) controllers. We take a modular approach by modeling the behavior of individual protocol services handling individual packets. These models can be combined to reproduce the overall device behavior, with heterogeneous traffic and stacks. The benefit of a modular approach is the ability to capture the flexibility of software-based packet processing. The possibility to combine protocols in many different configurations makes it infeasible to model complete end-to-end packet paths through the device. The large amount of factors affecting performance, both related to traffic characteristics and stack composition, would cause the parameter space to grow too large. Since different packet streams traverse different subsets of protocols, a large amount of possible paths through the system would have to be modeled to properly cover the functionality of network simulators. This approach would also suffer from problems modeling the contention between multiple packet streams sharing subsets of these protocols. Finally, a holistic model of the system would prevent exploring alternative stack compositions, which is often a key element in performance prediction.

The data required to create execution models is a set of events that characterize execution behavior, including processing durations and interactions between services. The data must also describe how this behavior changes with execution conditions. The required events are presented in Section 3. To create reliable and realistic models, we observe individual protocol services running on real devices. This process consists of (1) instrumentation of the communication software, (2) traffic loading and tracing, and (3) semi-automatic analysis of the observed behavior. The outcome is a *device file* that can be used to create executable models for the network simulator (see Figure 2).

In Step 1, packet handling and OS software are instrumented to obtain a well-defined set of events. Instrumetation can be distributed among developers of protocols, OS and devices. This serves two main purposes. First, developers have intimate knowledge of protocol implementations. Since the task mainly consists of instrumenting code, a minimal amount of knowledge of the underlying computational machinery is required. Second, if execution modeling is mainly performed by developers, the effort required by the network researchers is minimized, allowing them to focus on selecting the proper execution models when constructing realistic network scenarios.

In Step 2, the instrumented software is executed on the target device. Traffic workload is generated while the behavior of the software is observed via tracing. The resulting trace constitutes the basis for creating models. To capture the effect of varying conditions, tracing must be performed while varying these conditions. Examples of conditions that can affect software behavior include packet characteristics (e.g., packet size or type), the state of queues and threads in the system (e.g., queues are full, not-empty or empty, threads are active or ready), and protocol state (e.g., the number of entries in the routing table, or the availability of the hardware resources at the driver). Since some of the conditions may be highly specific to the instrumented software, it is up to the instrumenter to generate suitable traffic to execute the software under all significant conditions.

In Step 3, the analyzer performs the initial work to create models of execution behavior. It creates individual descriptions under given conditions, which constitute partial models of the service. These are specified in high-level programs, where processing stages are represented as statistical distributions for scalability. This represents a key difference between our approach and that taken by many system simulators, where all machine instructions are explicitly executed. By investigating these programs, the modeler obtains an early insight into captured protocol behavior. If this shows that insufficient instrumentation has been performed in Step 1, instrumentation must be improved and Step 2 and Step 3 redone.

To create service execution models (SEM), all partial models are merged, and the components necessary to execute the models are instantiated in the target execution environment. Execution is performed within a discrete event network simulator. A key challenge is the inherent difference between protocol models in the network simulator and the corresponding real world implementations. Although protocol models in network simulators and real world implementations differ, the fact that one is a model of the other means that it is usually possible to find locations that correspond. In our approach, we leverage this high-level similarity to (1) create a mapping between functions in the network simulator and locations in real implementations, and (2) execute these functions when the models of the implementation state that they should be executed. Since network simulators lack execution models, they do not have

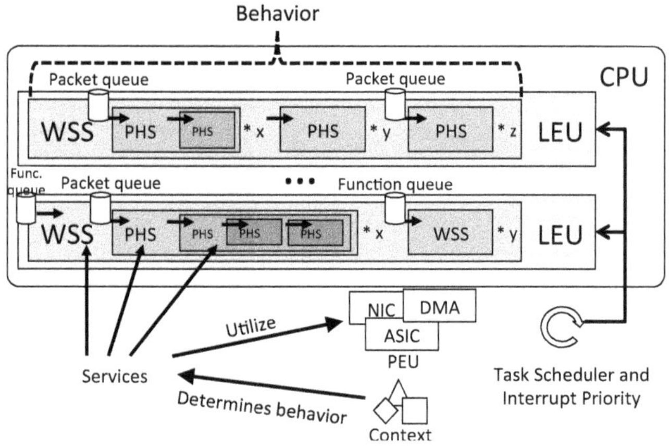

Figure 3: Relationships between the central abstractions.

the abstractions to model execution behavior. Thus, we extend existing node models in network simulators with execution environments that host models of queues, synchronization primitives and threads to run SEM. The threads are synchronized with those in a scheduler simulator to reproduce the dynamics of multithreading.

3. ANALYSIS OF THE TARGET SYSTEM

In this section, we analyze software-based communication systems to determine which data must be acquired to create the models. In this work we focus on *communication software*. We first describe the elements that affect performance, and then describe the events necessary to capture their impact on performance.

3.1 System Constituents

To model any system, it is first necessary to establish a set of abstractions by which to describe the elements of interest. Table 2 presents a set of general abstractions that we use to describe software-based communication systems. The relationships between the abstractions are illustrated in Figure 3, and a concrete instantiation is presented in Figure 4 (see Section). This section explains each abstraction.

Abstraction	Description
PEU	**P**hysical **E**xecution **U**nit: execution unit in addition to the CPU that can perform work on a packet in parallel with the CPU.
LEU	**L**ogical **E**xecution **U**nit: execution unit that shares CPU resources by means of timesharing.
PHS	**P**acket **H**andling **S**ervice: a function that performs well-defined operations on a packet.
WSS	**W**ork **S**cheduling **S**ervice: a function that schedules the execution of PHS and other WSS within a LEU.
Service	The modeling target. Refers to PHS and WSS collectively.
Behavior	The set of instructions executed within a service under a given context.
Context	A given set of values for all variables that affect the behavior of a service.

Table 2: Abstractions for software-based communication systems.

Execution units: Our primary focus is to model software running on computers that are small, portable and resource constrained, yet computationally powerful enough to run a multithreaded OS and complex protocols. We currently assume that this software is executed on a single CPU, but we support multiple, specialized processing units that can work in parallel, such as DMA controllers, NIC and other application specific integrated circuits (ASIC). Such execution units are referred to as *Physical Execution Units (PEU)*.

In multithreaded systems *threads* and *interrupts* share the CPU. We call these constructs *Logical Execution Units (LEU)*. The OS provides services to assign programs to run in a LEU, to schedule their execution according to specific rules, and to allow them to communicate. After being *activated*, i.e., marked as ready for execution, they are *dispatched* for execution at some later point in time depending on scheduling rules and concurrent workload. *Threads* are activated by LEU, and interrupts by PEU.

Services: We model the software running within LEU. This software is divided into *services*. These are separate modules dedicated to perform particular tasks, that are implemented by a particular function. A service consists of its function, as well as all functions called directly or indirectly from it, except for functions that implement other services. All communication software on a given device can be divided into services of two types: *Packet Handling Services (PHS)* and *Work Scheduling Services (WSS)*.

PHS are functions that act as entry points to protocol services. The task performed by a PHS is well-defined by the protocol specification it implements. This is the main reason why network simulators can be used to predict protocol performance. Examples include the receive and transmit functions of the driver, of the IP, UDP, ICMP and ARP protocols, and of sockets used by applications.

WSS schedule service execution *within* a LEU. The services they call are either hardcoded into the WSS or dequeued from a function queue. Examples of the former are functions executed first within newly forked threads, e.g., a WSS scheduling the execution of the PHS of the network driver. WSS of the latter type are usually found as OS services allowing one LEU to request work to be performed in a different LEU, including softirqs and tasklets in Linux that allow interrupt handlers to defer long-lasting work to a context where interrupts can occur. Other examples include timers and worker threads.

Behavior and Context: The sequence of instructions executed by a service at any given time may depend on the state of the OS and hardware. The part of this state that affects a service is referred to as a *context*, and the sequence of instructions executed by a service under a given context is referred to as a *behavior*. The number of different behaviors a service can exhibit is thus bounded by the number of contexts under which it may execute.

3.2 Required Events

This section determines which events are required to accurately describe the behavior of a given device, based on an analysis of how the components above impact performance. The analysis is performed by deep inspection of two generations of smartphones: the Nokia N900 and GN1. Both are based on the Linux kernel. Table 3 summarizes our findings and lists the events required to capture the different aspects of behavior. These events are described in the following sections.

What Affects Performance	Required Events
Separating Services	**Class 1**: CTXSwitch, HIRQStart/Stop, SRVStart/Stop
CPU processing delays	**Class 2**: CPU cycler (and/or hardware performance counters)
Interactions with the Task Scheduler	**Class 3**: Awake, Sleep, Synch
Work Scheduling within LEU	**Class 4**: SRVStart/Stop, Loop(Re)Start/Stop, En/Dequeue
Parallel Processing	**Class 5**: PEUStart, HIRQStart, Synch
Execution context	**Class 6**: CondRead/Write, De-queue, SRVEntry

Table 3: Events to capture the activities impacting performance.

3.2.1 *Separating Services*

As mentioned in Section 2, we follow a modular approach where each service is modeled independently. Since we base these models on events obtained from a running, multithreaded system, we need some way to determine which service each event belongs to. Most LEU execute more than one service, and it may be impossible to know a priori which services will execute within which LEU. A service is simply a function that can be called either directly from another service running within a LEU (intra-LEU request), or passed via a queue to a service running within another LEU that executes functions from this queue (inter-LEU request). An example of an intra-LEU request is when the IP send service is executed directly by the UDP send function within a user-space thread when traffic is transmitted from an application. The same function is called within a driver thread from the IP forward service when the device functions as a router. Examples of inter-LEU requests include when an interrupt requests a worker thread to perform work that is too long lasting to be performed in interrupt context. The same thread can be used for work offered by different interrupts.

In addition, events from different services are usually interleaved. In a scenario with an intra-LEU request involving a caller S_{caller} and a callee S_{callee}, events from one LEU will contain events from S_{caller} interspersed with events from S_{callee}. The reason for this is that S_{caller} will continue to execute once S_{callee} returns. Context switches may occur during the execution of any given service, causing an interleaving of events from services running within different LEU.

Required Events: It is necessary to distinguish between events generated in (1) different services, and (2) different LEU. By tracing switches between LEU it is possible to trace which LEU is executing at any given time. We must trace context switches (**CTXSwitch** events) and the beginning and end of hardware interrupts (**HIRQStart** and **HIRQStop** events). The events must include attributes identifying the LEU switch. To distinguish between services, it is necessary to trace the beginning (**SRVStart** events) and end (**SRVStop** events) of each service execution. These events must identify the related service. The above events enable the analyzer (Step 3 in Figure 2) to assign all events to the correct service models.

3.2.2 CPU Processing Delays

In general-purpose communication systems, packet processing is largely performed in software. It is clear that overall packet delays in the network are affected by processing delays in software on the nodes and that jitter is affected by variations in such delays. These delays also limit the number of packets that can be processed per time unit, i.e., throughput.

Processing delays on the nodes are determined by the number of CPU cycles spent per packet and the clock frequency of the CPU. The number of cycles spent is mostly determined by the number of executed instructions. The number of instructions executed within a service depends on its implementation complexity. In addition to per-packet and per-byte processing, there can be a significant per-service execution overhead. The cycles spent per instructions may vary between service executions due to pipeline flushing, branch misprediction and cache misses.

Required Events: Three approaches can be taken, with increasing accuracy: (1) measuring duration directly by means of timestamps, (2) sampling a cycle counter and calculating durations based on CPU clock frequency, or (3) sampling hardware performance counters to obtain events that together with an architectural model can be used to estimate the number of cycles spent. Approach 3 is commonly taken with performance prediction techniques. Since scalability is a key requirement in our context, we decide not to take this approach since using architectural models can reduce scalability. Among the two remaining alternatives we decide to measure the number of **CPU cycles** spent instead of durations because it is more accurate, efficient, and can be used to estimate processing durations under varying CPU frequencies. Samples of the CPU cycle counter are stored as an attribute in all events in order to calculate how much processing is performed between events.

3.2.3 Interactions with the Task Scheduler

When LEU_a requests LEU_b to handle a packet, LEU_b must be activated. This is performed via direct requests to the task scheduler or via synchronization primitives, and may be performed by LEU_a or by some other LEU (e.g., a timer). Any delays before LEU_b is activated, contribute to overall packet delays because the service in LEU_b cannot be executed before LEU_b is dispatched, which cannot happen before it is activated. Additional time elapses between LEU_b activation and dispatch. This duration depends on (1) the number of LEU using the CPU before LEU_b (including LEU_a), and (2) for how long each LEU uses the CPU. Each LEU can either yield the CPU voluntarily or be preempted. Yields are carried out via requests to the scheduler to sleep (or, in the case of interrupts, to terminate) or via synchronization primitives. Preemption is carried out when a thread exhausts its time quantum or upon the occurrence of an interrupt.

Required Events: The impact of scheduling is determined by (1) how services interact with the scheduler, (2) the workload in the system, and (3) the scheduling policies. As mentioned in Section 2, we predict overall system performance by executing service models in an environment that explicitly models how threads and interrupts are scheduled. Since the scheduler is explicitly modeled and the system workload depends on the simulation scenario, Points 2 and 3 above are covered by our extensions of the target simulator. To account for Point 1, we need to capture how services interact with the task scheduler to activate and deactivate threads. Interactions with the task scheduler are captured by **Awake** and **Sleep** events that identify the currently running LEU (interrupt or thread), and the target thread. It is important to capture the *attempt* to activate a thread, rather than an actual activation. Otherwise, the event will not be captured if the target thread is already active. Interactions via synchronization variables are captured by **Synch** events, that specify the type of the variable (e.g., a semaphore), the primitive used (e.g., "Up" or "Down") and an identifier of the variable.

3.2.4 Work Scheduling Within LEU

A LEU usually executes multiple different services. By the time a LEU is dispatched, multiple services may have packets waiting to be handled. Three elements determine how service execution and packet handling is serialized within a LEU. First, WSS schedules service execution using loops that serve one or more function queues or execute one or more hard-coded services per iteration. The number of iterations executed is determined by the availability of workload, an upper limit of iterations and/or protocol state. Second, loops are also utilized by PHS that obtain packets from queues instead of function arguments. The number of packets handled per execution impacts queue priority. Third, since services can execute other services, a chain of services is usually executed as a result of a call to one service within a loop. Any of these services may contain additional loops. The order of services within such chains contributes to the overall service execution order in the LEU.

Delay, jitter and throughput can be affected by the order in which services and packets are processed within a LEU. This is true even with a light workload. The reason for this is that realistic data traffic rarely is uniform, resulting in short periods of bursts. We illustrate the impact of work scheduling via an example. Consider the system outlined in Figure 4, showing how services are scheduled for exe-

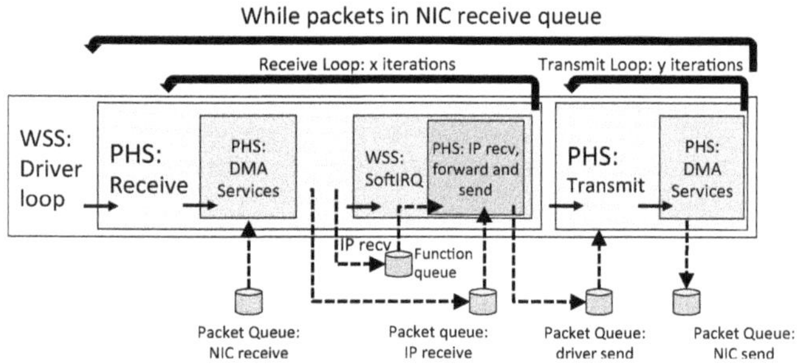

Figure 4: Structure of the GN1 driver thread.

cution during packet forwarding on the GN1 smartphone. Dashed lines illustrate packet and service queuing, and solid lines function calls. All services execute within one thread in which the *driver loop* WSS executes as the top-level function. It is hardcoded to alternate between the execution of the receive and send services of the driver. They transmit packets between the NIC and the main memory via DMA PHS. A loop in the *receive* service fetches up to x packets from the NIC, each of which is passed to the *IP receive* PHS via a function queue served by the *softirq* WSS. All packets end up in the driver transmit queue. A loop in the *send* PHS fetches y packets from this queue and transmits them back to the NIC. During high packet rates (e.g., bursts)the values of x and y determine how traffic is shaped. The larger the values, the larger the bursts in the forwarded traffic stream, i.e., the jitter increases. The *driver loop* performs long-lasting interactions with the NIC before each call to the receive PHS. Therefore, with low values of x and y, overall delay will increase as such interactions will occur more often, i.e., more cycles are spent per packet. Finally, the forwarding capacity of the system is affected by x, y and the queue sizes. If x is large relatively to y, most packets will be handled by the network stack, but lost in the driver send queue. This means that all computational resources on the system are consumed while only a fraction of the packets is forwarded. The mechanisms above are used also for services not explained here (e.g., DMA services, queue priority services provide by the OS, etc.).

Required Events: To capture how a service schedules the execution of other services, it is necessary to capture (1) which and when services are executed via direct function calls, (2) when packets and functions are inserted into queues, and (3) how loops are constructed. The first aspect is captured by the already mentioned **SRVEntry** and **SRVExit** events. To capture queue insertions, we need **EnQueue** events that specify the type of the queue (i.e., packet or service) and an identifier of the queue. **LoopStart** and **LoopEnd** events separate events obtained within the loop from those obtained in other parts of the service, and **LoopReStart** events separate between events obtained within different iterations. Finally, **DeQueue** events capture when packets are dequeued within loops.

3.2.5 Parallel Processing

PEU are specialized processing units that perform processing tasks in parallel with the CPU. Unlike the CPU, they do not perform complex timesharing of tasks. We can therefore assume that the duration of a given processing task is strongly correlated to well-known parameters. For instance, the duration of DMA transfers is strongly correlated with the number of bytes transferred.

Maximizing parallelism to maximize performance has its own challenges. How this is solved for a particular system can impact the overall system performance. If for instance the CPU busy-waits during a DMA transfer, fewer CPU cycles will be available for other threads. While the packet itself is usually fetched via DMA, the additional communication between the CPU and the PEU controllers usually consists of multiple smaller transfers performed via programmed IO. Both techniques are used in the network driver of the GN1 and N900, in addition to blocking IO. Due to PEU interactions, the total time spent per packet in the driver is much larger than the time spent in the network stack.

PEU are shared resources which under contention cause queuing delays. Contention can occur between different packet streams traversing the device in parallel, but also between different packets within the same traffic stream. For instance, during forwarding the handling of inbound packets may require DMA transfers while the DMA is occupied transferring outbound packets.

Required Events: Since the modeling target is the service, we only need *partial* models of PEU, capturing only the processing tasks used by the service. Since we only model temporal behavior, it is sufficient to measure the duration of PEU usage by capturing the beginning and end of the processing. Since we only instrument software, we rely on events obtainable at the CPU alone. PEU processing is initiated by software, captured by **PEUStart** events. Completion of processing is signaled from the PEU to the CPU via an interrupt, and is captured by **HIRQStart** events.

Due to PEU contention, interrupt sharing, and multiple PEU processing in parallel, it may be difficult or impossible to determine which HIRQStart results from which PEUStart event. This can be automatically discovered since threads on the CPU and tasks on the PEU need to be synchronized via a synchronization variable. By comparing the address of the synchronization variables used in the service activating the PEU and the one used in the interrupt handler, it is possible to couple HIRQStart events with PEUStart events. The PEU processing duration is calculated by deducting the cycle count in the PEUStart event from that in the HIRQStart event. Durations are measured in terms of CPU clock cycles, but a PEU often operates with frequencies that are either independent from or a constant ratio of the CPU frequency. In the former case, the calculated number of cycles must be converted to time before being included in the service model, in order to prevent PEU durations in the model to vary with CPU frequency.

3.2.6 Execution Context

Conditional statements that read context variables introduce variations in service behavior, which is reflected as multiple different event sequences from the same service. In communication systems, queue state (empty, not empty, full) and packet characteristics (e.g., size) usually constitute a major part of the service context. Protocol state may also impact behavior (e.g., dynamic queue priorities). In multithreaded systems, context may also include the state of threads (active or not active).

Required Events: When the variations in behavior are significant, it is important to capture events that link the behavior and the value of these variables. Events of type **StateRead** are captured to indicate which state yields which behavior, and the cycle counter determines when a conditional statement begins to affect the behavior of a service. These events indicate the type of the state variable, i.e., queue, thread or protocol state, and identify the variable accessed. Packet characteristics are stored within **DeQueue** or **SRVEntry** events, since a packet's impact on service behavior begins once a service obtains the packet from a queue or a function argument. StateRead, DeQueue and SRVEntry events identify the context under which an event sequence is obtained during a service execution. Executions under different contexts therefore result in differing event sequences that collectively describe how a service is affected by context. **CondWrite** events capture updates to state variables.

4. MODEL CREATION

In this section, we explain how to create models of services based on the events presented in the previous section. When executed in a target network simulator, these models extend existing protocol models in the simulated node with execution behavior. Section 4.1 explains the iterative process of Figure 2. Its first part, i.e., Steps 1 to 3, follows an iterative modeling methodology that is used to create scalable, partial models consisting of short event sequences and processing durations. Sections 4.2, 4.3 and 4.4 describe each step in this process. The second part is performed in the target network simulator, where the partial models are combined into the final model (Section 4.5).

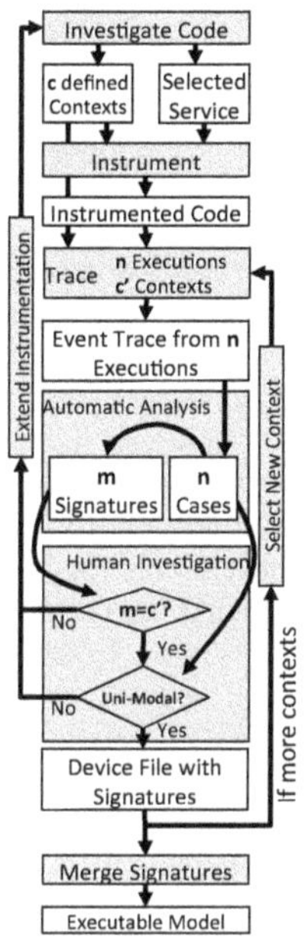

Figure 5: Iterative modeling.

Figure 5 expands the iterative process of model creation of Figure 2. It involves instrumentation, tracing, analysis, human investigation and creation of executable models. Tasks are represented as gray boxes and their results as white boxes. Before we explain these steps, we give an overview of the complete iterative process. The first step consists of instrumenting the selected service to capture all necessary events, where Class 6 events are determined by the parameters that have a non-negligible impact on its behavior. Identifying such parameters is an essential part of the modeling. The parameters are instantiated with values that are selected to sufficiently cover the complete parameter space, resulting in c different contexts.

4.1 Overview: Iterative Modeling Process

The iterative process focuses on obtaining accurate partial models of how the service behaves under each individual context, where multiple iterations are performed per partial model. The goal is to obtain models of the behavior of the service under a given context, represented as a sequence of events with intermediate distribution functions of processing duration. During tracing the instrumented service is executed n times while minimizing variations in context, to collect the necessary data for the processing distributions. Since certain contextual parameters can be difficult to fixate (e.g., the state of queues and threads), a service is usually executed under a subset c' of all the defined contexts c. Automatic analysis extracts from the trace n *cases*, describing each individual service execution, that are grouped to create m *signatures* describing each unique behavior among the cases. The resulting cases and signatures help to determine whether insufficient instrumentation is performed initially. This is important to avoid, since insufficient instrumentation leads to inaccurate models. The modeler must make sure that, (1) the number of signatures equals the number of contexts used during tracing (i.e., that m=c'), and (2) the same amount of processing is performed between equivalent events among cases within the same group (characterized by uni-modal empirical probability distributions of processing time). If not both requirements are met, the instrumentation must be extended. If Class 6 events are added, the number of parameters increases, in turn increasing the number of defined contexts c. Instrumentation, tracing and analysis are performed repeatedly until the modeler is satisfied with a given signature. At this point the next context among the defined contexts is selected, and the iterative process is repeated. When all signatures are obtained, they are stored in the device file for later use by network simulators, where they are combined to create the final executable models.

4.2 Instrumentation and Tracing

In this section, we explain the central and most difficult aspects of capturing the events in Section 3 (details are presented in [10]. Instrumentation is performed by placing into the code calls to special functions called *tracepoints*. When executed, they generate the events seen in Figure 6. Common attributes are: (1) the event type, (2) the value of the CPU cycle counter (or other Class 2 events), and (3) the memory address from which the tracepoint is called. The latter yields unique locations in the final models. Such unique locations can be associated with functions in network simulators and are useful when investigating the obtained models. The remaining fields are used to identify shared resources and to store the value of state variables. If the shared resources are accessible via global variables or functions, their addresses can be traced, and translated into unique symbols used during compilation. If they are not global (e.g., temporarily allocated on the stack), a central table of identifiers can be used and included in the final device file.

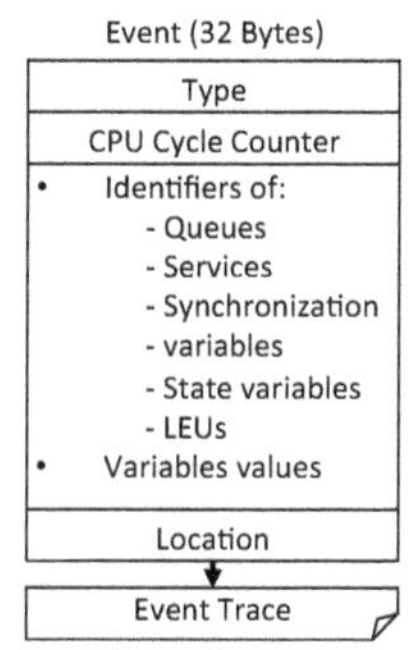

Figure 6: Traced events.

A large part of the instrumentation has to be performed in the kernel code, but it is sufficient to instrument each OS only once. Events from Class 1 and 3 are obtained to separate between LEU and capture interactions with the task scheduler, respectively. Class 1 events are obtained from the function that performs task switches (CTXSwitch events) and before and after the execution of interrupt handlers (HIRQStart and HIRQStop events), and Class 3 events from functions that manipulate the ready queue (Awake and Sleep events) and interact with synchronization variables (Synch events).

Events in Classes 1, 4, 5 and 6 are used to instrument services, some of which are general purpose WSS (e.g., timers) and standard networking protocols (e.g., IP, UDP, ICMP) in the OS. Their instrumentation is therefore part of the one-time OS instrumentation. The remaining software includes device-specific drivers and non-standard protocols (e.g., light-weight versions of sensors) or experimental protocols (e.g., delay tolerant streaming middleware) that are not yet established as part of the mainline kernel distribution. Of these, only the services provided by the protocols in the network simulators must be instrumented. SRVEntry and SRVExit events can be obtained at the beginning of the service function, and before its return statement(s). This can be captured using dynamic probes such as jprobes without recompilation [1]. Since dynamic probes have a relatively high tracing overhead compared to compiled-in, static tracepoints, they should not be used for frequently used OS services.

Events of Class 6 must be captured at the point where a state variable begins to affect the behavior of a service. For reasons explained below, they must include the value of the state variable(s). While De-Queue and SRVEntry events are placed at the beginning of queuing and service functions to capture relevant packet characteristics, CondRead events are placed as close as possible to the conditional brancing points to capture the value that determines the branching decision. To prevent the value from changing between event tracing and the branching decision (e.g., due to race conditions), the value should first be stored in a separate variable that is used for both tracing and branching.

Before tracing begins, a set of contexts must be defined by selecting different values of parameters to cover the parameter space. The finer the granularity of the selected values, the more accurate the final models will be, but the modeling effort and the complexity of the resulting models increase with the granularity. This allows the modeler to make a trade-off between required modeling effort, scalability and accuracy. Furthermore, if the parameter space grows impractically large for a particular service, the modeler can divide this service into multiple smaller services such that each is affected by a subset of the original parameters. During tracing, the context is fixed during n executions of the service. For instance, if packet size affects performance, a stream of n packets with the same size is injected into the system such that the target service handles each packet. This generates one event trace, which is used as input to a component performing automatic trace analysis.

4.3 Automatic Trace analysis

The analyzer transforms the trace file into a set of signatures, each of which describes one behavior of the traced service in terms of (1) the sequence of events generated, and (2) processing duration distributions between each event. This is performed in two phases. Since the trace file contains events generated in all parts of the kernel, Phase 1 filters out those events generated by the target service S. This yields one sequence of events per execution of S, where each sequence constitutes a high-level description of *one execution* of S. We refer to such sequences as **cases**. If S is executed n times during tracing, n cases are created. We also model loops as services, where each iteration yields one case.

In Phase 2, all n cases are sorted into m groups, where all cases in one group have the same event sequence and all attributes of the events have the same values. The cases in one group differ only in the execution times of the processing stages between the same events. This is due to the non-deterministic behavior of the CPU (e.g., memory caching) and minor variations in the number of executed instructions. To create for each group a single signature it is sufficient to calculate for each processing stage one probability function that fits the observed processing times for that processing stage. The analyzer stores all signatures, cases and processing durations in a human readable format, with information about which cases are used to create which signatures. This information is used in the subsequent step of human investigation.

4.4 Human Investigation

We propose two techniques to investigate whether the signatures constitute a good model of the target service or not. First, the automatic analysis above should yield one signature per context. Since context determines behavior, all parameter values are stored by Class 6 events, and the analyzer separates between signatures that have events with different attribute values. Therefore, multiple signatures per context implies that the service context is not properly captured. The number of cases covered by a given signature indicates whether some of the signatures describe highly unlikely behaviors that can be excluded from the models as outliers. The second technique involves plotting the empirical probability distribution of durations between events in a given signature. If sufficient instrumentation is performed, the durations are uni-modal,

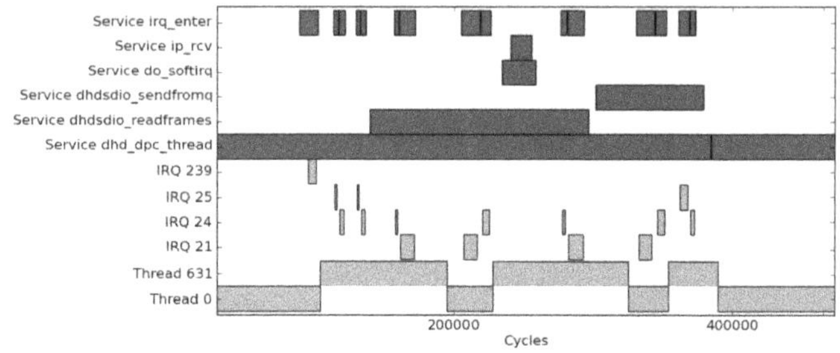

Figure 7: The LEU and service visualizer.

since approximately the same number of instructions is executed in each case. Multi-modal distributions indicate multiple entirely different tasks were performed between events, which also means that context (and potentially other events) is not properly captured.

In both cases, the instrumenter must return to Step 1 and refine the instrumentation. The location-attributes of the events provides valuable indications of where additional tracepoints are required. The analyzer implemented in our work provides further help by visualizing thread, interrupt and service execution over time. Figure 7 presents a screenshot[1]. Green and blue bars show the number of cycles spent in different LEU and services, respectively. By visualizing traces while varying workload and system parameters, the modeler gets indications of which parameters affect performance as well as which threads, interrupts and WSS are involved in packet handling.

4.5 Combining Signatures

All signatures produced for one service provide the information necessary to create its execution model. The final model is produced by merging these signatures to create what we refer to as a service execution model (SEM). This is performed by a parser in the target network simulator that takes as input the device file containing all signatures for all services for a given device (see Figure 8 where C is a state variable modeled by C_m). There is one signature per context, and context data is stored in Class 6 events. Therefore, different contexts result in different signatures. However, unless the first event in a signature is a Class 6 event, all signatures share a common subset of events and processing stages from their beginning. We therefore combine all signatures into a tree where events shared by different signatures follow the same path from the root. Conditional statements become branching points in the tree, such that one sub-tree is created per value of a state variable. When the service is executed, its statements are executed beginning at the root of the tree, and upon encountering a conditional statement, the value of the modeled state variable is read to select the proper subtree for further execution. The execution environment in the simulator contains a table of pointers to state extractor functions that provide the necessary values, and the identifier of the conditional statement (e.g., "IP::RTable::Size") is used as index into this table.

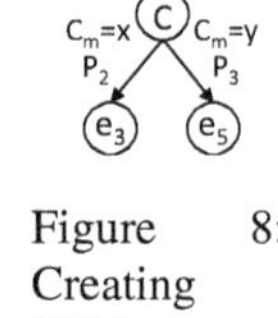

Figure 8: Creating SEM.

[1]Parts of the original screenshot are excluded due to space constraints.

5. EVALUATION

In this section, we evaluate the accuracy, scalability and the impact of our models on network simulation. A smartphone is chosen as the target device since it is configurable and powerful, and suitable for dynamic, mobile networks (e.g., MANETs) using complex protocols. This allows us to demonstrate that we can model rather complex device types as compared to wireless sensors. We analyze IP forwarding since this is a central task performed in networks such as MANETs, where the impact of forwarding delays increases with the number of hops. We instrument the GN1 smartphone to capture models of the software required for forwarding, including drivers, OS services and the IP protocol (see Figure 4). The context for all services includes the packet size and the state of threads (active/not active) and queues (empty, not empty, full). The complete instrumentation consists of 91 tracepoints, and the tracing overhead is found to be 289 cycles per obtained event. We account for this by deducting 289 cycles from all processing durations in the simulator.

The following sections present our results. To understand how we obtain the results, we first give a brief overview of our poof-of-concept implementation in the discrete event network simulator Ns-3 (the details are in [11]).

5.1 Proof-of-Concept Implementation in Ns-3

Figure 9 illustrates how we extend Ns-3 nodes with execution environments that can execute SEM within threads running on a CPU, and a separate scheduler simulator that schedules these threads. The execution environment is implemented as an Ns-3 *Object* that is aggregated in the node. Each thread has a call stack containing the location of execution within a SEM, the handled packet and temporary variables. Processing distributions are instantiated as Ns-3*RandomVariable* objects, which create random samples of processing durations. Delays are introduced by scheduling an event in the future that resumes execution at the statement following the processing stage. Upon preemption this event is cancelled and rescheduled according to remaining processing time when the thread is dispatched.

We use LinSched [3] as the scheduler simulator, which we extend to support synchronization primitives. LinSched is particularly realistic since it consists of real scheduler code from the Linux kernel. For efficiency we compile LinSched into the same binary as Ns-3. One LinSched instance can be loaded per node as a dynamically loaded library. Threads interact with the task scheduler via a generic task scheduler interface that calls LinSched functions via wrappers. Time in the scheduler simulators is synchronized with the network simulator time by continuously maintaining one event in the Ns-3 event queue that, when executed, resumes the event loop in a scheduler simulator at the time at which its next event is scheduled. The scheduler simulator returns once its next event has a scheduled time that exceeds that of the next event in the Ns-3 event queue.

The execution environment contains models of the PEU, queues and synchronization variables used by the SEM, as well as an interrupt controller (IC) capable of interrupt prioritization. The frequency of the CPU and PEU, the initial value of synchronization variables and the size and type of queues is provided in the device file along with the signatures. The device file also contains a table that associates selected services, queues or locations in SEM with *triggers* that have protocol independent service names (e.g., "IP::Forward"). When a protocol in Ns-3 wants to introduce execution delays, the packet is passed to the execution environment with (1) a name of a trigger and (2) a callback to an Ns-3 service function that is called upon executing a statement with that trigger. This

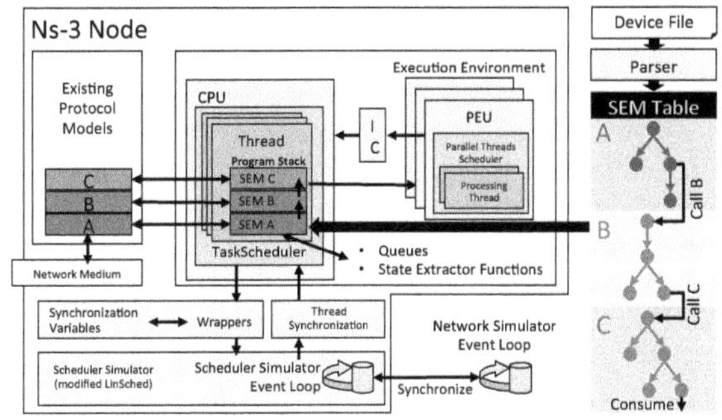

Figure 9: Ns-3 Extension.

mechanism synchronizes the execution of existing network protocols in Ns-3 with the execution of SEM.

5.2 Experiments and Results

We perform five experiments to evaluate (1) the accuracy of our models under light load, (2) the accuracy of our models in overload situations, (3) the impact of our models on network simulations, (4) the impact of blocking IO, and (5) the scalability of our models. Since we focus on the impact of forwarding, a simple three-node topology is sufficient to obtain significant insights into the performance of our models. In this topology, a source node S sends data to a forwarding node F, which forwards the data to the destination node D. In Experiments 1 and 2, we evaluate the accuracy of our models by performing the same experiment in a real world test bed and in the simulator, and comparing the results. In the real world test bed, S and D are laptops with dual-core 2.2Ghz CPUs. F is the GN1 with a CPU with a variable frequency between 245Mhz to 1Ghz. We fix its CPU at 245Mhz to investigate how our models perform in a worst-case scenario under resource constraints. In the simulation, F executes the SEM obtained from the GN1.

Experiment 1: We investigate whether our models introduce the same amount of intra-OS forwarding delays as the real device under light, non-uniform traffic loads. We select as the workload an RTP video stream, containing the *forman* video clip[2] encoded with H.264 (the main profile) at a target bitrate of 512 Kbps. This stream is bursty, and contains packets of various sizes. During the real world experiment, we monitor all packet arrivals at F via an additional laptop running tshark in monitoring mode. In this way the packet trace can be used to inject the identical traffic into our execution models in Ns-3. Since we are only interested in the accuracy of our own models, and not of the wireless channel, we measure processing delay *within the OS only*. We instrument the OS kernel at two points: (1) the time at which the driver begins to handle an inbound packet, and (2) the time at which the driver successfully transmits an outbound packet back onto the NIC. Similarly, in the Ns-3 simulationstraffic is injected directly into the execution models at F *without including the wireless medium*, and the measurements are made at equivalent locations in the execution models and the real implementations. Please note that standard Ns-3 does not have any models of protocol execution, i.e., its intra-node forwarding delay is always zero. It is therefore not meaningful to compare our results with those from standard Ns-3. The red (solid) and blue (dashed) lines in Figure 10(a) present the results from the real world experiments and the simulations, respectively. The x-axis denotes the RTP sequence number of the packets, and the y-axis the intra-OS delay for each packet in milliseconds. The nine periodic peaks

[2]Available from http://trace.eas.asu.edu

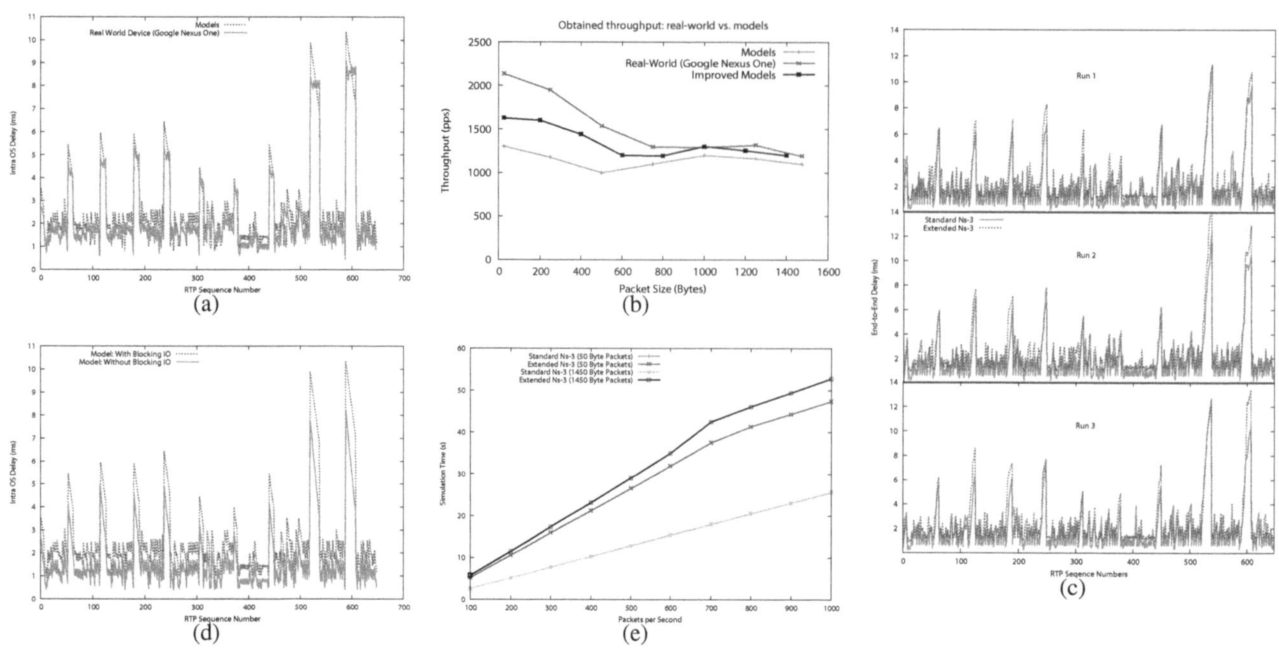

Figure 10: Results.

are caused by large bursts in the traffic stream, causing queuing delays in the node.

It is clear that our models are able to accurately approximate both the magnitude and variations in delay throughout the run. We nevertheless see that our models introduce a slightly higher delay than the real implementations. This is partly because we capture our models under minimal traffic loads, namely 25 packets per second (pps), while the average packet rate in the video traffic exceeds 50 pps. Under higher loads, memory caching reduces processing delays since instructions and data are more rarely evicted from the cache between packet handling. These models consequently estimate the worst-case performance of the services. We see that the delays introduced by the models drop rapidly during bursts. As shown in Figure 4, the driver alternates between calling its receive and transmit services, and both services have a loop that moves x packets from and y packets to the NIC, respectively. The delay discrepancies during bursts is due to insufficiently capturing the part of the context that controls x and y. In the real implementation, these are controlled by three constraints (1) x and y can never exceed 50 and 20, respectively, (2) x and y cannot exceed a variable quota set according to certain rules, and (3) after performing one iteration, the loop in the transmit service will only continue iterating if the previous execution of the receive service did not fetch all packets on the NIC with its provided quota. The context captured in our models includes Constraints 1 and 3, but does not account for the quota in Constraint 2. We find that during high-load conditions, i.e., during bursts, Constraint 3 is often ignored, and the quota causes x and y to become lower and more equal than in our models. When x and y decrease, this delay difference between packets in the bursts decrease. The transmit loop is less expensive than the receive loop, which imposes more queuing delays on packets in front of the bursts.

Experiment 2: We investigate how accurate the models are under overload conditions, by comparing the throughput of the real device and the models. We use uniform traffic streams with varying packet rates and sizes to determine the maximum number of packets handled per second. The traffic is generated using *pktgen* [14]. As in Experiment 1, in the simulations we inject traffic directly into the execution models at F to avoid the wireless medium. The results from the real world experiment are obtained by instrumenting the driver to capture the number of received and transmitted packets per second. A negligible amount of packets are lost in the wireless medium, which confirms that the device is the bottleneck. The results are presented in Figure 10(b), with packet sizes on the x-axis and the average throughput across three 30-second runs on the y-axis.

We find that our models are accurate for packet sizes larger than 500 bytes, but are too pessimistic with small packets. Three factors contribute to this. First, the benefit of memory caching is larger for small packets because more packets are handled per time-unit, resulting in lower probability of cache invalidation between iterations in loops. Second, our instrumentation does not sufficiently capture changes in the behavior of the receive and send services of the driver under high rates. By comparing signatures from high and low rates, we find that under high rates, fewer IO operations are carried out for a subset of the packets. For these packets, certain operations are omitted in the receive loop when multiple packets are available at the NIC. Finally, since our models do not account for the quota in Constraint 2 above, the transmit loop performs a single iteration more often in the models than in the real software during high rates. This results in more frequent iterations of the outer thread loop that executes the send and receive services, in turn causing an increased number of cycles spent per packet. We perform an additional experiment where the effect of Constraint 2 is reflected in the models. The results are presented as the black line in Figure 10(b). We see that throughput increases for all packet sizes, but that the increase is largest for small packets. A large portion of the remaining discrepancy is explained by the second factor above, and can therefore be accounted for by extending the instrumentation.

Experiment 3 We investigate how end-to-end performance is affected by our models when the nodes are connected via 802.11g links. The same traffic workload as in Experiment 1 is used, where

S transmits the data to D via F, including the wireless medium. Note that while Experiment 1 excluded the wireless medium by injecting traffic directly into F, in Experiment 3 all traffic passes the two wireless links from S to F and from F to D. We compare end-to-end delays with and without the execution models at F. The blue (dashed) and red (solid) lines in Figure 10(c) present results from simulations with and without our models, respectively. The x-axes denote the RTP sequence numbers of packets. We present results from three runs with identical workload, and with differing random seeds.

We first observe that the delays introduced by the models are non-negligible. The average end-to-end delay increases from 1.92 ± 0.02 to 2.45 ± 0.06 ms (i.e., by 27.6%). We find that $90.37 \pm 0.04\%$ of the execution delay is introduced by the NIC and DMA drivers. We only model the execution in F. If execution models from the GN1 are executed also on S and D, the overall amount of execution delay would increase by at least a factor of two. This is because more processing is required to pass packets between the NIC and the applications than between the NIC and the IP protocol, which includes copying packets between user and kernel space. We define jitter as the standard deviation of packet delays within runs. We find that jitter increases from 1.92 ± 0.07 to 2.04 ± 0.19 ms (i.e., by 6.13%) when introducing the execution models. Both jitter and the variations in jitter among runs increase, which can be seen by comparing the graphs from different runs. This is most easily seen during bursts, where the delays sometimes differ substantially. The reason for this is that the amount of delay introduced by the execution models is highly sensitive to the arrival rates of packets during bursts, which in turn is largely affected by random backoffs at the medium. Backoff delays differ between runs due to differing random seeds for different runs. This demonstrates that our models reproduce the unpredictability found in real systems. We finally observe that the delay using the execution models is occasionally lower than without them (e.g., around sequence number 400). Without the execution models, F attempts to retransmit packets immediately upon arrival, which causes a higher probability of contention among the links than when the packets are delayed due to execution. This means that with multi-hop transmissions, the lack of execution models causes unrealistically long-lasting backoff periods, especially during traffic bursts.

Experiment 4: We demonstrate how our models can be used to easily gain insight into how much a certain component affects forwarding performance. We redo Experiment 1 while ignoring durations spent waiting for blocking IO, and thereby quantify the impact of PEU models that are ignored in related work that extends network simulators with processing models. Figure 10(d) present intra-OS delays including (blue, dashed line) and excluding blocking IO (red, solid line). The x-axis denotes the RTP sequence numbers, and the y-axis the intra-OS delay in milliseconds.

Execution delay increases substantially when including the delays spent waiting for blocking IO. This consists of DMA transactions and interactions with the NIC initiated by the drivers. Of the time spent executing in the drivers, $40.30 \pm 0.09\%$ is spent waiting for PEU processing. $19.74 \pm 0.09\%$ of the time the driver thread goes to sleep, and during the remaining time the CPU performs busy waiting or programmed IO. Distinguishing between these is important, as it determines whether the CPU is free to execute work in other threads. These results also highlight the importance of accurate modeling of drivers, and accounting for time spent processing on PEU. To the best of our knowledge, no other efforts to extend network simulators with abstract execution models account for PEU processing.

Experiment 5: We investigate the scalability of our models by measuring how much additional simulation time they introduce. Simulation time is primarily affected by the number of packets handled per time unit. We therefore use as traffic uniform UDP traffic streams with varying packet size and rate, and measure simulation time with and without execution models running at F. The simulations are performed on one of two cores on a 2.4 Ghz Intel Xeon CPU. We use uniform traffic with small (25 bytes) and large (1475 bytes) packets. Figure 10(e) shows the time spent simulating 60 seconds, with and without the models. The x-axis denotes the packets per second transmitted from S to D, and the y-axis the number of seconds spent simulating. The green and red lines show the results from simulations without execution models, for 25 and 1474 byte packets, respectively, and the blue and black lines the simulation time including the execution models with 25 and 1474 byte packets, respectively. We present the averages across three runs.

The execution models increase simulation time with a factor between 1.85 and 2.35, depending on packet size and rate. More time is spent with large packets, because more statements are required to handle large packets. Fewer statements are executed per packet under high loads, since more packets are handled per service execution in loops. Simulation time does not change with packet size without execution models, since the existing protocol models perform the same amount of work for small and large packets. Most execution simulation time is spent in the NIC and DMA drivers. Depending on packet size and rate, between 89 and 108 statements are executed per packet in the driver models, and 47.07 to 54.16 in models of OS services, IP services and interrupts combined. The reason is that the drivers are the most complex software to model in the kernel. We therefore believe that introducing additional models of services further up in the network stack will not increase simulation time dramatically. We also conduct experiments to measure how much per-node overhead is introduced by LinSched, which executes 1-3000 events per second to handle scheduler ticks. We find that LinSched increases simulation time by no more than 2.09 to 13.46 seconds per node per simulated hour, depending on whether or not there are multiple simultaneously active threads in the node. The reason for the low overhead is that since the Linux scheduler code is highly optimized, each event performs very little work. Since our design allows simulations with multiple event queues, we further reduce simulation time significantly as it allows LinSched to use its native event scheduler instead of the much more complex and inefficient Ns-3 scheduler.

Summary: We demonstrate that our methodology can be used to obtain accurate models of complex, multithreaded systems (Experiments 1 and 2). The results deviate from real world results in certain situations, but that this can be improved by extending our instrumentation. We find that our models provide a significant improvement to the realism of network simulation (Experiment 3), without compromising scalability (Experiment 5). Finally, we show that our models can be used to quantify the impact of individual processing components, and demonstrate the importance of capturing blocking IO in processing models (Experiment 4).

6. CONCLUSIONS AND FUTURE WORK

Network simulators typically do not have models of protocol execution, which previous work have shown to be non-negligible if the devices are resource constrained and/or are executing complex protocols. We presented in this work a methodology to extract per-protocol service models from real, multithreaded OS by means of instrumentation and tracing, that when executed in an extended network simulator can account for such execution overhead. The methodology can be used to model various devices that impact network performance, e.g., in MANET, WSN or during tethering. We evaluated the accuracy and scalability of the models using a proof-of-concept implementation in Ns-3. The results show that our models can accurately reflect the behavior of real implementations under highly non-uniform, realistic traffic workloads, while preserving scalability for multiple-node network simulations.

We are currently extending our current models from the GN1 smartphone to improve their accuracy, and we are obtaining additional models from the Nokia N900 smartphone to demonstrate that our methodology can be used for other devices. Since the models are represented as simple programs, it is easy to determine which factors affect performance and to modify the models to predict performance under alternative configurations. As a next step, we plan to use our models to optimize the performance of the modeled software for different scenarios of interest. It is often desirable to determine that communication software performs *at least* as good as that predicted by models. We found that by extracting our models under conditions that negatively impact performance, the predicted performance is likely to be worse than that of the real software. More work is nevertheless needed to establish more reliable estimates on worst-case performance for time-critical applications. Our methodology is primarily designed to model uni-core architectures. A central part of future work is to investigate how our methodology must be extended to produce accurate results also for multi-core architectures.

7. REFERENCES

[1] Documentation/kprobes.txt. The Linux kernel sources.

[2] N. Binkert, R. Dreslinski, L. Hsu, K. Lim, A. Saidi, and S. Reinhardt. The m5 simulator: Modeling networked systems. *Micro, IEEE*, 26(4):52 –60, july-aug. 2006.

[3] J. M. Calandrino, D. P. Baumberger, Y. Li, Tong, J. C., and S. Hahn. Linsched: The linux scheduler simulator. PDCCS, 2008.

[4] V. G. Cerf. Where is the science in computer science? *Commun. ACM*, 55(10):5–5, Oct. 2012.

[5] R. Chertov, S. Fahmy, and N. B. Shroff. A device-independent router model. INFOCOM. IEEE, 2008.

[6] J. Cook, J. Cook, and W. Alkohlani. A statistical performance model of the opteron processor. *SIGMETRICS Perform. Eval. Rev.*, 38(4):75–80, Mar. 2011.

[7] T. Grotker. *System Design with SystemC*. Kluwer Academic Publishers, Norwell, MA, USA, 2002.

[8] S. Kristiansen, M. Lindeberg, D. Rodriguez-Fernandez, and T. Plagemann. On the forwarding capability of mobile handhelds for video streaming over manets. MobiHeld. ACM, 2010.

[9] S. Kristiansen and T. Plagemann. Accuracy and scalability of ns-2's distributed emulation extension. *Simulation*, 87(1-2):45–65, Jan. 2011.

[10] S. Kristiansen, T. Plagemann, and V. Goebel. Modelling communication software for accurate simulation of distributed systems. Technical report, University of Oslo, Department of Informatics, 2012.

[11] S. Kristiansen, T. Plagemann, and V. Goebel. Extending network simulators with communication software execution models. In *COMSNETS*. IEEE, 2013.

[12] O. Landsiedel, H. Alizai, and K. Wehrle. When timing matters: Enabling time accurate and scalable simulation of sensor network applications. In *IPSN*. IEEE, 2008.

[13] B. Muller-Rathgeber and H. Rauchfuss. A cosimulation framework for a distributed system of systems. In *VTC*. IEEE, 2008.

[14] R. Olsson. pktgen the linux packet generator. In *Proc. of the Linux Symposium*, 2005.

[15] P. Pagano, M. Chitnis, G. Lipari, C. Nastasi, and Y. Liang. Simulating real-time aspects of wireless sensor networks. *EURASIP Journal on Wireless Communication and Networking*, 2010:2:1–2:12, April 2010.

[16] R. Ramaswamy, N. Weng, and T. Wolf. Considering processing cost in network simulations. MoMeTools. ACM, 2003.

[17] M. Rosenblum, S. A. Herrod, E. Witchel, and A. Gupta. Complete computer system simulation: The simos approach. *IEEE Parallel Distrib. Technol.*, 3(4):34–43, Dec. 1995.

[18] K. Salah. Modeling and analysis of pc-based software routers. *Comp. Commun.*, 33(12):1462 – 1470, 2010.

[19] K. Salah and K. El-Badawi. Throughput-delay analysis of interrupt-driven kernels with dma enabled and disabled in high-speed networks. *J. High Speed Netw.*, 15(2):157–172, Jan. 2006.

[20] K. Salah and M. Hamawi. Comparative packet-forwarding measurement of three popular operating systems. *Jour. of Netw. and Comp. Applications*, 32(5):1039 – 1048, 2009.

[21] F. Trahay, E. Brunet, and A. Denis. An analysis of the impact of multi-threading on communication performance. In *IPDPS*. IEEE, 2009.

[22] R. Wilhelm, J. Engblom, A. Ermedahl, N. Holsti, S. Thesing, D. Whalley, G. Bernat, C. Ferdinand, R. Heckmann, T. Mitra, F. Mueller, I. Puaut, P. Puschner, J. Staschulat, and P. Stenström. The worst-case execution-time problem-overview of methods and survey of tools. *ACM Trans. Embed. Comput. Syst.*, 7(3):36:1–36:53, May 2008.

[23] E. Witchel and M. Rosenblum. Embra: fast and flexible machine simulation. SIGMETRICS. ACM, 1996.

[24] W. Wu, M. Crawford, and M. Bowden. The performance analysis of linux networking-packet receiving. *Comp. Commun.*, 30(5):1044 – 1057, 2007.

Leveraging Symbiotic Relationship Between Simulation and Emulation for Scalable Network Experimentation

Miguel A. Erazo
Florida International University
11200 S.W. 8th street
Miami, FL 33199
meraz001@cis.fiu.edu

Jason Liu
Florida International University
11200 S.W. 8th street
Miami, FL 33199
liux@cis.fiu.edu

ABSTRACT

A testbed capable of representing detailed operations of complex applications under diverse large-scale network conditions can be extremely helpful for investigating potential system design and implementation problems, and studying application performance issues, such as scalability and robustness, even before the applications are deployed in a real environment. We introduce a novel method that combines high-performance large-scale network simulation and high-fidelity network emulation, and thereby enables real instances of network applications and protocols to run in real operating environments, and be tested under large-scale simulated network settings. In our approach, network simulation and emulation form a symbiotic relationship, through which they are synchronized for an accurate representation of the large-scale traffic behavior. We introduce a model downscaling method, along with an efficient queuing model and a traffic reproduction technique, which can significantly reduce the synchronization overhead and improve computational efficiency, while maintaining the accuracy of the system. We validate our approach with extensive experiments via simulation and with a real-system prototype.

Categories and Subject Descriptors

C.4 [**Computer Systems Organization**]: Performance of systems—*modeling techniques*; I.6.5 [**Simulation and Modeling**]: Model development; I.6.3 [**Simulation and Modeling**]: Applications

General Terms

Algorithms; Experimentation

Keywords

Network simulation, emulation, modeling

SIGSIM-PADS'13, May 19–22, 2013, Montréal, Québec, Canada.

1. INTRODUCTION

The ability to conduct high-fidelity high-performance network experiments is crucial for studying future network systems and their complex behaviors. Existing network testbeds bring variable degree of satisfaction (or dissatisfaction) in fulfilling *controllability*, for creating diverse network scenarios, *scalability*, for capturing large-scale network operations, *realism*, for reproducing important system and network effects, and *performance*, for supporting high-throughput high-capacity data transport. A testbed capable of performing large-scale experiments over diverse network scenarios and network conditions, maintaining accurate representation of the target applications and network transactions, and supporting high-throughput high-capacity network traffic is ostensibly missing.

Physical testbeds (such as PlanetLab [23] and WAIL [3]) provide a realistic operational environment for testing network applications. They can directly test real applications *in-situ* with the needed operational realism and possibly even with live network traffic. However, physical testbeds lack controllability in testing applications under network conditions other than the prescribed setup of the physical platforms, which in general are also limited in scale. Such limitations make it impractical to use physical testbes for studying important design issues, such as application scaling issues and robustness under diverse environments and different hypothetical situations.

Simulation (e.g., *ns-2* [4] and OPNET [6]) is effective at capturing overall design issues, answering what-if questions, and revealing complex system behaviors (such as multi-scale interactions, self organizing characteristics, and emergent phenomena). Parallel simulation has also demonstrated its capability of dealing with large-scale detailed models by harnessing the collective power of parallel computing platforms. However, simulation often lacks a certain level of realism—reproducing realistic network traffic and operational conditions in simulation remains elusive. Emulation (e.g., ModelNet [30] and EmuLab [33]) provides a good balance between controllability and accuracy, whereas real applications can run directly in a native operating environment. However, like physical testbeds, its scale and capability is limited by the underlying platform, such as the processing speed, the bandwidth and latency of the supporting hardware.

Both simulation and emulation provide a good level of controllability and reproducibility necessary for conducting experiments under various network conditions. However, we observe that their expected capabilities differ significantly. In general, simulation offers great flexibility and scalability, but cannot provide the detailed behavior of the network and the execution environment. It is typically used to construct high-level network scenarios with protocols that may not be fully developed (such as those at the physical and link layers). A full-scale simulation is desirable for obtaining "the big picture", when a complete understanding of the system's complex behavior is absent. In contrast, emulation offers the important capability of being able to execute code directly on a real system that accepts application data as input and produces detailed responses as output. It provides the operational realism, but cannot handle all elements of a large-scale network experiment due to resource constraints.

To allow high-fidelity high-performance large-scale experiments, we propose to use separate systems to address the discrepancy between the macroscopic nature of simulation and the microscopic nature of emulation, and leverage the symbiotic relationship between simulation and emulation. We use *the simulation system* to run the full-scale network model with detailed network topology and protocols for a truthful representation of the global-scale network behavior. To simulate potentially massive-scale network system, we adopt parallel simulation and advanced traffic modeling techniques. We use *the emulation system* to inspect the detailed behavior of the target applications; we select a number of nodes on the virtual network as "emulated" to run unmodified software in a real operating environment, with the real operating system, network stack, and software tool chain.

Simulation and emulation forms a symbiotic relationship so that both can benefit from each other. The simulation system benefits from the emulation system by incorporating real network traffic generated by the unmodified software running on the real machines. The emulation system benefits from the simulation system by receiving up-to-date information of the global virtual network behavior and traffic conditions, and using it to calibrate the communication between the real applications. As a result, the symbiotic approach allows us to test and analyze applications by *embedding* them seamlessly in large-scale network settings and under diverse network conditions.

In this paper, we present the symbiotic approach to network experimentation that exploits the mutually beneficial relationship between a simulation system that studies the behavior of large-scale network models, and an emulation system that reproduces the distributed environment for running real applications. The specific contributions of this paper can be summarized as follows:

- We introduce a model-downscaling technique that can significantly reduce the complexity of large-scale network models, and therefore improve the computation efficiency of the emulation system, and reduce the synchronization overhead between the simulation and emulation systems.

- We propose a queuing model for the downscaled emulation system to efficiently and accurately synchronize with the large-scale traffic conditions at the simulated network.

- We propose a technique for reducing the synchronization overhead for the emulation system to update the simulation system on the state of the emulated traffic. Rather than measuring and transferring the detailed statistics at individual network devices, we collect the traffic demand at the transport layer and use the same transport-layer protocols implemented in simulation to reproduce the traffic flows.

The remainder of this paper is organized as follows. In section 2, we review related work. In section 3, we present an overview of the proposed symbiotic approach. In section 4, we present the model-downscaling technique. In section 5, we present the queuing model for effectively capturing the effect of simulated network conditions on the real applications running in the emulation system. In section 6, we introduce the technique for reproducing the emulated traffic in simulation. We conducted extensive experiments to validate our approach. In section 7, we describe the validation experiments for the queuing model using a simulator of the symbiotic system. In section 8, we describe a prototype implementation of the symbiotic system and the real-system validation results. Finally, in section 9, we provide our conclusions and outline future work.

2. RELATED WORK

In Biology, symbiosis is defined as the mutually beneficial relationship between two or more different organisms. A symbiotic system can be defined as "one that interacts with the physical system in a mutually beneficial way" [12].

There are two promising areas that combine network simulation and emulation. *On-line simulation* uses simulation as an integrated service for real-time network management with the goal of improving network performance, via network planning, monitoring, parameter tuning, and traffic engineering (e.g., [29, 34]). *Real-time simulation* performs simulation in real time so that the virtual network can interact with real network entities [9, 28, 36, 15, 1, 17, 19].

ROSENET [13] is an early attempt to promote the symbiotic relationship between simulation and emulation. It combines a high-performance simulator and a low-fidelity emulator running at separate locations. The simulator continuously updates the emulator with link statistics, including packet delay, jitter, and loss. The emulator also continuously updates the simulator with a summary of the real traffic. ROSENET has achieved limited success. However, it is only shown capable of emulating a single bottleneck link and dealing with applications that generate non-responsive traffic (i.e., UDP applications).

Network emulators, such as dummynet [26], test real applications with well orchestrated network conditions. They work by forwarding the network packets through a set of pipes that approximate the behavior of the corresponding network queues. Each pipe focuses only on a single link. Yet, most network studies are concerned with the end-to-end behavior; in this case, one has to compose the entire network path by chaining the pipes together. This approach obviously has a scalability issue.

Topology downscaling is based on the observation that only congested links introduce sizable queuing delays and packet losses [2, 10, 11, 22]. In other words, uncongested links, especially those with capacities large enough to simultaneously carry many flows, are somewhat transparent to the packets traversing them [8]. Papadopoulos et al. [21] proposed a method that aims at downscaling network topology by removing the uncongested links, retaining only the congested ones, and compensating for the removed links with additional delays. The problem with this approach is that the bottleneck links have to be known in advance. Although static analysis may help reveal the potential congestion points in the network, the selection is often too liberal to achieve an effective model reduction.

Sanaga et al. [27] proposed a method to approximate the entire network path with a single link, by modeling the link capacity and the available bandwidth separately. The method calculates the available bandwidth using non-responsive traffic (with constant bit rate). Although this approach gives a good approximation for an averaged behavior, it does not provide sufficient granularity to accurately capture the interaction between the simulated and emulated flows. Modeling the traffic intensity simply as non-responsive flows is obviously unfair to TCP.

3. SYMBIOTIC APPROACH

A network experiment consists of a virtual network with a detailed specification of the network topology, potentially connecting a large number of hosts and routers running various network protocols and distributed applications. Using the symbiotic approach, while it is expected that most of these protocols and applications are simulated, some hosts and routers can be designated to run unmodified distributed applications and real implementations of network protocols on real machines.

Directly running the applications and protocols on real machines brings at least two advantages. First, implementing complex distributed applications and network protocols in simulation can be time-consuming and error-prone. As such, the modelers typically implement in simulation only a subset of the functions of the applications considered as essential. However, in certain cases, it is not immediately clear which part of the applications shall be rendered in simulation with great accuracy. Second, directly running the applications in real systems offers a level of operational realism unavailable in simulation; for example, one can now investigate software configuration issues, system dependencies, deployment constraints, and other system-related artifacts.

We need to standardize the terminologies in order to describe our approach. Hereon we call the applications that are run in real as the *target applications*. To differentiate from the simulated components, we name the real machines that run the target applications as the *emulated hosts* or *emulated routers*, and we name the traffic between the emulated hosts and routers as either *emulated traffic* or *emulated flows*. Note that the emulated components, including the emulated hosts, routers, and emulated flows, are also represented in the simulated network. One should be able to distinguish between the physical realization and the simulated representation easily from the context.

Figure 1 shows an experiment with a virtual network consisting of both simulated and emulated components. In particular, the network contains four emulated hosts, H_1 to H_4, and two emulated routers, R_1 and R_2, all marked with solid circles. The rest of the hosts and routers on the virtual network will be simulated. The emulated hosts and routers will be instantiated and run as individual machines (either physical machines or virtual machines) in the emulation system. The emulated hosts will run target applications, such as web clients, web servers, and peer-to-peer applications. The emulated routers will typically run routing software as target applications, such as XORP [14] and Open vSwitch [20].

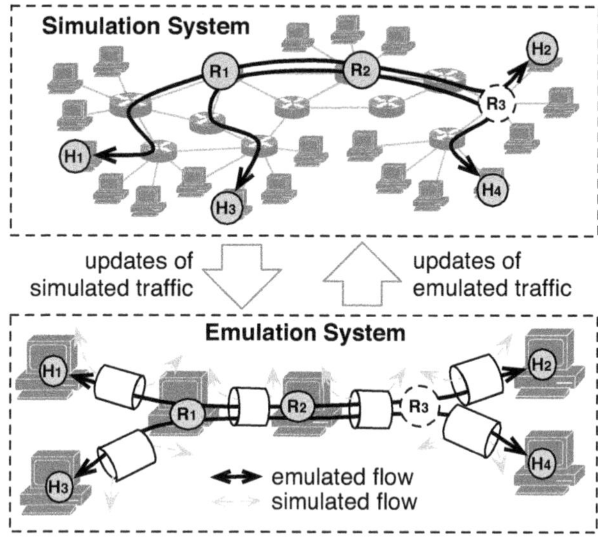

Figure 1: The symbiotic approach.

During the experiment, the target applications at the emulated hosts and routers may engage in communication with one another over the simulated network. As shown in this example, there are two emulated flows, one between H_1 and H_2, and the other between H_3 and H_4. Note that the two flows digress at R_1 and R_3, where R_1 is an emulated router and R_3 is a simulated router. Since the emulated flows are mixed with the simulated ones, one must be able to accurately capture the effect of the simulated flows on the emulated flows, and vice versa.

Figure 1 presents a schematic view of the architecture of the symbiotic system, which consists of a simulation system and an emulation system in a closed loop. The simulation system runs the full-scale network model with a detailed specification of the network topology, traffic and protocols. The network model can be partitioned and mapped onto a parallel computing platform for parallel simulation in order to represent detailed transactions of a large-scale network in real time. The emulation system consists of a set of emulated hosts and routers as physical or virtual machines that run the target applications. The emulated hosts and routers are connected via a set of active "pipes", which are responsible for modulating the emulated flows so that the traffic experiences the same delays and losses probabilistically as if the target applications were directly connected by the full-scale network.

The symbiotic approach allows us to run real network applications and protocols directly in the real machine environments. We can test these target applications by embedding them in a large-scale virtual network setting, and evaluating them using diverse network configurations and traffic conditions created by simulation. Of course, the effectiveness of the symbiotic approach lies in its ability to efficiently and accurately modulate emulated traffic in accordance with the simulated network conditions. Due to the interdependency of the simulation and emulation systems, the two systems must be effectively synchronized. We note that the emulated traffic (i.e., the flows of real packets sent between the target applications running on the real machines) will affect the simulated traffic (i.e., the traffic between the network entities in the simulation model). The reverse is also true. Both types of traffic compete for the network resources, including the buffer space at the network queues and the bandwidth of the communication links. For example, a sudden increase in emulated traffic may can create congestion at a bottleneck link on the virtual network. When the congestion happens, it can "strangle" the traffic traversing the link (including both simulated and emulated flows), which in turn would affect other parts of the virtual network traversed by other simulated and emulated flows.

It is important to note, however, unless the traffic is between a simulated host and an emulated host,[1] the simulation and emulation systems only need to consider the reciprocal effect of the simulated and emulated traffic—in this case, there is no need to exchange network packets between the two systems! The simulation system only needs to update the emulation system with the *effects* of the simulated traffic at the corresponding pipes. Similarly, the emulation system only needs to update the simulation system about the state of the emulated traffic between the target applications. In the subsequent sections, we address the individual challenges and solutions related to the symbiotic approach.

4. MODEL DOWNSCALING

As mentioned previously, the symbiotic approach aims to address the discrepancy in capabilities between simulation and emulation by combining them, using simulation to handle network models at scale and using emulation to directly test target applications. In order to improve the emulation performance, one cannot directly use the full-scale network model. Emulation only needs to render the same network behavior insofar the target applications are concerned. We can downscale the network models to reduce complexity. The downscaled model used by emulation needs to be functionally equivalent to the full-scale network model used in simulation for determining the end-to-end packet delays and packet losses. In particular, the downscaled model must be able to capture two important network effects:

1. *The cross-traffic effect.* The full-scale network will be populated with traffic originated from both simulated and emulated hosts. When calculating the end-to-end delays and packet losses between a pair of emulated hosts, we need to consider the effect of other traffic traversing the same segment of network links.

2. *The multi-bottleneck effect.* The emulated traffic may traverse several intermediate routers where congestion can happen. The effect of multiple bottlenecks is location-dependent and time-varying, and is highly dependent upon the simulated network conditions.

We propose a simple model downscaling algorithm. Since we need to run the algorithm before the experiment starts, network routing must be determined beforehand. This can be achieved using the spherical routing method, which conducts static routing hierarchically, by calculating the forwarding tables according to either shortest paths or simple policy specifications [32].

The modeling downscaling algorithm consists of two steps. Figure 2 shows an example with a simple network topology (with designated bandwidths and link delays), and illustrates the steps taken by the algorithm to obtain the final reduced model. In the first step, the algorithm takes the original network topology as input and prunes the topology by removing the network nodes and links not traversed by emulated flows. The simulated hosts and routers are not instantiated in the emulation system; therefore, the hosts and links that carry only simulated traffic are not needed in emulation for modulating emulated traffic.

The network topology can be further pruned if we have information *a priori* about the communication pattern between the emulated hosts. In particular, if we know that two emulated hosts will *never* contact each other during the experiment, we do not need to maintain the path between the two emulated hosts. In the worst case, we have to assume all emulated hosts are capable of contacting all other emulated hosts. Figure 2(a) shows the original model. Figure 2(b) shows the pruned topology with only emulated hosts, and links carrying emulated traffic between the emulated hosts.

In the second step, the algorithm takes the pruned topology as input and compresses the links traversed by the same emulated flows as a network segment. This is because the emulated flows traversing the same segment would experience the same network conditions at the segment (such as the processing delay, bandwidth, and congestion level), which eventually determine the packet delays and losses for the emulated flows going through the segment. Figure 2(c) shows the results of the path compression step. For example, the network path between the two emulated hosts A and B consists of two segments: one between host A and router R, and the other between router R and host B. Since the two segments carry different emulated flows, they cannot be combined further.[2]

The resulting downscaled topology will be mapped onto the emulation system. The emulated hosts and routers will be instantiated on individual machines and run designated target applications. The network segments will be mapped to the delay nodes and represented individually as "pipes", as shown in Figure 2(d). The emulated packets flowing through these pipes can be dropped or added with artificial delays to reflect the simulated network conditions. The state of the pipes will be updated constantly in real time by the simulation system using the statistics collected at the network interfaces that constitute the corresponding segments. In the next section, we describe the queuing model through which we can efficiently update the state of the pipes and ensure that the downscaled emulation model can accurately represent the simulated network conditions.

5. MODELING NETWORK SEGMENT

As mentioned in the previous section, a network segment consists of one or more links traversed by the same set of emulated flows. Here, we propose a queuing model to estimate the packet delays and packet losses for the emulated flows traversing through the network segment. It has been observed that traffic characteristics change little within a certain time interval; for packet loss, delay, and throughput, one can generally rely on their constancy at least at the

[1]The case for interactive simulation and emulation, which allows directly exchanging traffic between emulated hosts and simulated ones, has been explored extensively in our previous studies, e.g., [7] and [17].

[2]For the sake of simplicity, the example treats the path as bidirectional; in reality, there needs to be a separate path for each direction (which is not necessarily symmetric), and each path needs to be compressed separately following the algorithm.

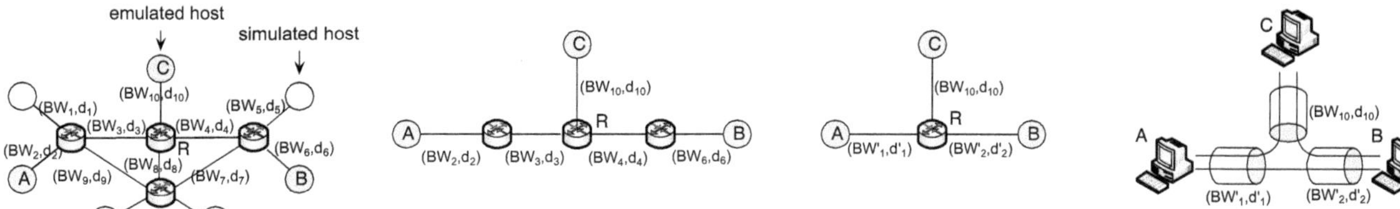

(a) Original topology

(b) Pruned topology with only hosts and links traversed by emulated traffic

(c) Downscaled topology with network paths compressed as segments.

(d) Actual model instantiated in emulation system.

Figure 2: An example for the model downscaling algorithm.

time scale of a minute [35]. As such, the queuing model we propose here can be updated at regular time intervals large enough to overcome the synchronization overhead.

We use a single M/D/1 queue to model the network effect at a segment in the emulation system. The service rate and the drop probability at the queue are calibrated periodically using measurements gathered from simulation. The details of the simulated traffic need not be propagated to emulation, since we model only the *effect* of the simulated traffic at the corresponding segments. We adopt the M/D/1 queuing model because it is simple and easy to manipulate in a closed form. We later show empirically that the model is not limited to Poisson arrivals; the model can generate good results for almost any type of traffic.

In the discussion to follow, we start with the situation that the network segment consists of only one link, and we assume that we deal only with the steady state. We then extend the model to handle multiple-link segments. After that, we complete the model to capture the transient network behavior.

5.1 Steady-State Queuing Model

Figure 3 depicts our queuing model for a segment with only one link. In simulation, a segment is traversed by both simulated flows and emulated flows. The emulated flows are regenerated in simulation; we discuss the detailed method in the next section.

Let λ_s be the arrival rate of the simulated flows entering the segment, and λ_p be the arrival rate of the emulated flows entering the segment. Let μ be the link bandwidth. Upon a packet arriving at a network queue (at a network interface), if the buffer is full, the packet will be dropped. Let p be the drop probability due to buffer overflow. Let λ_s^e and λ_p^e be effective arrival rate of the simulated flows and emulated flows, respectively. Surely, $\lambda_s^e = \lambda_s(1-p)$ and $\lambda_p^e = \lambda_p(1-p)$. Furthermore, we use W_1 to denote the average packet delay (for both simulated and emulated traffic) through the segment, which should be measured easily in simulation.

A segment in simulation is represented in emulation as a pipe and is modeled as an M/D/1 queue (with infinite buffer). We apply the packet drop probability before it enters the queue. In emulation, we have only emulated flows. We aim to set the service rate of the queue, μ^*, so that, once an emulated packet enters the queue, it will experience the same delay as it would in simulation.

According to the M/D/1 model, the average number of jobs in the system, L, can be obtained in a closed form as:

$$L = \rho + \frac{\rho^2}{2(1-\rho)} \tag{1}$$

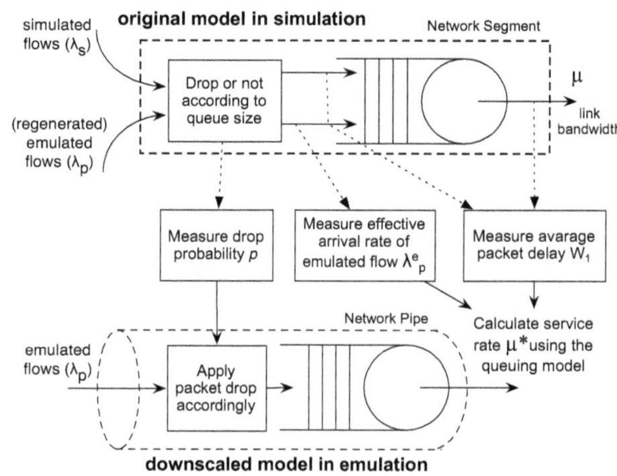

Figure 3: Queuing model for a single-link segment.

where ρ is the server utilization. We can then calculate W_2, the average time a job spent in the system:

$$W_2 = \frac{L}{\lambda_p^e} = \frac{\rho + \frac{\rho^2}{2(1-\rho)}}{\lambda_p^e} \tag{2}$$

We set $W_1 = W_2$, since it is expected that the original model and the downscaled model should generate the same average packet delay. We know that $\rho = \lambda_p^e/\mu^*$. We can so solve for the service rate of the queue:

$$\mu^* = \frac{\lambda_p^e}{1 + W_1\lambda_p^e - \sqrt{1 + W_1^2(\lambda_p^e)^2}} \tag{3}$$

Note that μ^* is simply a function of the average packet delay (W_1) and the effective arrival rate of the emulated flows (λ_p^e), both of which can be measured in simulation. We also measure the packet loss probability in simulation, and impose the same probability to drop the packets before they enter the queue.

The above queuing model can be readily extended to represent a network segment with multiple links. We can still use Eqn. (3) to calculate the service rate. In this case, W_1 is the average delay of packets traversing the whole segment, and λ_p^e is the minimum of the effective arrival rates at all network interfaces (i.e., the effective arrival rate at the bottleneck link). The latter is the same as the throughput achieved by the emulated traffic. We measure the packet drop probability at each network interface and calculate the packet drop probability as: $p = (1 - \prod_{i=1}^{n}(1-p_i))$, where

p_i is the drop probability at the ith link, assuming that the segment consists of n links.

5.2 Transient Effect

The previous model yields good results when the network congestion level is low. However, the model fails to provide accurate packet delays when congestions occur. This is because the model assumes that the physical system reaches the steady state during the update interval, which could be far from the truth if the congestion level is high when the packets experience significant queuing delays.

It is a non-trivial task to find a general closed form solution for the stochastic system. Our solution to this problem is a practical one. We observe that, during the network congestion, the packet delays measured in simulation will be different from the predicted values calculated by the steady-state queuing model due to the transient queuing effect. In order to remove such discrepancies, we can adjust the packet processing speed in emulation so that the delays match the simulation results.

Let ΔT be the interval at which the simulation system updates the emulation system with its measurements. At the end of each update interval, say, at time t, let $p(t)$ be the measured drop probability, let $\lambda_p^e(t)$ be the effective arrival rate of the emulated flows, and let $W_1(t)$ be the average packet delay through the network segment. All these measurements are collected during the last interval in simulation.

Let $W_2(t)$ be the average packet delay through the corresponding pipe in emulation, which we can measure during the same period. The difference between $W_1(t)$ and $W_2(t)$ indicates the transient effect. We can calculate such difference in the number of packets in the queuing system during this period:

$$\Delta L(t) = \mu^*(t)(W_2(t) - W_1(t)) \tag{4}$$

where $\mu^*(t)$ is the steady-state service rate calculated using Eqn (3). Now we can compute the excess (or deficit) service rate to compensate for the transient effect:

$$\Delta\mu^*(t) = \frac{\Delta L(t)}{\Delta T} = \frac{\mu^*(t)(W_2(t) - W_1(t))}{\Delta T} \tag{5}$$

Finally, we can add the adjustment to the steady-state service rate to derive the final service rate we use for the queue in emulation during the next update interval:

$$\begin{aligned}\hat{\mu}(t) &= \mu^*(t) + \Delta\mu^*(t) \\ &= \frac{\lambda_p^e(\Delta T + W_2(t) - W_1(t))}{\Delta T(1 + W_1(t)\lambda_p^e(t) - \sqrt{1 + W_1^2(t)\lambda_p^e(t)^2})}\end{aligned} \tag{6}$$

The adjustment effectually forces the emulation system to "track" the simulated network conditions at each update interval. Experiment results, which we show in section 7, confirm that using the adjusted service rate the emulation system is able to match with the simulated network behavior even during extremely heavy congestions.

6. REPRODUCING EMULATED FLOWS

Our queuing model is based on the assumption that the emulated flows—those between the target applications in the emulation system—can be faithfully reproduced in simulation. In Fig. 3 we show that the same arrival rate is used for the emulated flows entering the network segment in simulation and entering the corresponding pipe in emulation.

To do that, one approach is to directly "inject" the packets generated by the target applications into the simulator. That is, we generate a simulation event to represent the arrival of each emulated packet in emulation. Similarly, when a simulated packet reaches an emulated host or router, a real packet will be created in emulation. This is the approach taken by real-time simulation [16], which has demonstrated capable of achieving pretty accurate results. The problem with this approach is that the throughput of the emulated flows is bounded by the I/O capacity of the system; the accuracy of the model can be severely compromised if the emulated traffic load reaches its limitation [17].

We propose a different approach. Rather than directly injecting the emulated packets generated by the target applications into simulation, we make the emulated hosts only report the traffic demand of the target applications to simulation as metadata. In particular, the emulated hosts only need to capture the number of bytes (`appBytes`) requested by the target applications to be sent through the transport layer. In simulation, we implement the same transport layer to generate the simulated packets accordingly and recreate the same traffic load as in the emulation system.

This method can obviously scale better as it does not require exchanging individual network packets between the simulation and emulation systems; however, it depends on a careful implementation of the TCP/IP stack in simulation so that it can create the same traffic behavior as in the real systems. For example, the simulator needs to include various TCP flavors used commonly by the real systems. Previously, we implemented and validated fourteen TCP variants in our network simulator, which are found commonly in use today, including New Reno, BIC, CUBIC, among others. We ported code specific to the congestion control mechanism of of these TCP variants directly from the Linux TCP implementation [7].

There are several methods to capture the data size sent by the target applications. One way is to use `/proc` on Linux or similar facilities. This approach is most straightforward; however, it only supports polling, which would generate noticeable overhead if we use a small polling interval for accurate measurement. Another approach is to replace the transport-layer functions in the communication library with one added with a callback feature whenever the send functions are invoked. This can be achieved without modification to the application code, through either static or dynamic linking (e.g., [18]). It is also possible one can develop a separate kernel module to achieve the same function.

In our implementation, as a proof of concept, we simply rewrite the target applications, such as `iperf`, and let them report, through inter-process communication, to another program running on the same machine, which we call the "traffic sensor". The traffic sensor is then expected to update the simulator about the application data transfer request, which includes the transfer size, and the source and destination. Upon receiving the information, the simulator generates a series of packets accordingly using the same transport layer protocol.

7. MODEL VALIDATION

In this section we validate the queuing model. Here we use a simulator of the symbiotic system in order to conveniently explore different network settings, and stay clear from the potential system-related artifacts in a real implementation. We present real-system validation in the next section.

7.1 Single-Link Validation

Here we conduct experiment to validate the queuing model assuming that a network segment contains only one link. We examine whether the queuing model can be generalized and used for different packet arrivals with different mixture of simulated and emulated flows. In particular, we test the model with different packet inter-arrival time distributions: exponentially distributed, a combination of constant and exponentially distributed, and also from real packet traces. We test whether the model can reproduce the same packet delays in the downscaled system as those in the original system.

In the experiments, we designate two flows at a network interface: one as "simulated flow" and the other as "emulated flow", each with an independent input process. At each second (i.e., we set $\Delta T = 1$ second), we measure the drop probability, the effective arrival rate of the emulated flow, and the average packet delay of both emulated and simulated flows, at the network interface. The measurements are collected in a trace file and later used by a subsequent simulation of the emulation system that has only the "emulated flow" with exactly the same packet arrivals.

Poisson Arrivals. We first set the packet inter-arrival time of both simulated and emulated flows to be exponentially distributed. We set the bandwidth of the network interface to be 10 Mbps and the queue length to be 1.5 MB. We also fix the packet size to be 1500 bytes in this study. We vary the aggregate arrival rate of both simulated and emulated flows to be 10%, 50%, and 90% of the bandwidth for different service levels, and we vary the proportion of the emulated flow to be 20%, 50%, and 80%, respectively. We examine the accuracy of the model by comparing the packet delays between the original and the downscaled system.

Figures 4 shows the average packet delays measured at each second during the experiment for low, mid, and high service utilization scenarios. In all cases, both systems match quite well. The difference is almost negligible: around 10 μs for 10% utilization, 40 μs for 50% utilization, and below 1 μs for 90% utilization.

Mixed Poisson and Constant Arrivals. Next, we set the packet inter-arrival time of the emulated flow to be constant and that of the simulated flow to be exponentially distributed, and vice versa. We use the same experiment setting as that in the previous experiment. Again, we vary the aggregate arrival rate of both simulated and emulated flows to be 10%, 50%, and 90% of the total bandwidth, and we vary the proportion of the emulated flow to be 20%, 50%, and 80%, respectively.

Figures 5 shows the average packet delays for different service utilizations where the portion of the emulated flow is fixed at 20%. Similar results (not shown) are obtained for different mixture of the simulated and emulated flows. In all cases, the model matches well with differences below 1 μs.

Real Packet Traces. The simulator is able to read real packet traces generated by `tcpdump` so that it can reproduce similar traffic demand, with the same packet sizes and inter-arrival times as in the real system. We also add functions to either dilate or contract packet inter-arrival times by a constant factor in order to artificially adjust the traffic intensity if needed. For this experiment, we use a packet trace from *the CAIDA Anonymized Internet Traces 2011 Dataset* [5]. The trace is collected at an OC192 link (9953 Mbps), consisting of over twenty million packets.

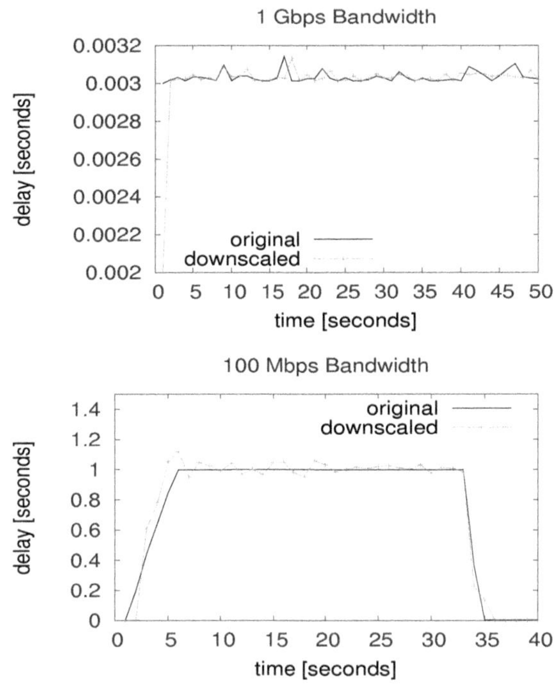

Figure 6: Results from using the CAIDA trace.

We replay the CAIDA trace as the simulated flow. To make it more interesting, we set up two experiments: one with a link bandwidth of 1 Gbps and the other with 100 Mbps. For the 1 Gbps experiment, we dilate the packet trace by a factor of 30; for the 100 Mbps experiment, we dilate the packet trace by a factor of 100. In this case, we get a lower traffic intensity for the first scenario than that for the second. In both scenarios, we limit the buffer size to be 12.5 MB and start the trace-driven simulated flow at the beginning and then cut it off at around 30 seconds. We also create an emulated flow with exponentially distributed inter-arrival time and set its traffic intensity at 50% of the bandwidth; the emulated flow lasts for the entire experiment.

Fig. 6 compares the average packet delays measured in the original system and the downscaled system. In the first scenario (with 1 Gbps bandwidth), there is rarely any congestion; there is no significant queuing delay, and the average end-to-end delay stays around 3 milliseconds. In the second scenario (with 100 Mbps bandwidth), during the first 5 seconds, the queue builds up quickly until packets start to get dropped. The congestion persists until 33 seconds before the average packet delay drops down resulting from the cutoff of the simulated flow. For both scenarios, the original and the downscaled model produce very similar results.

Exploring Various Network Settings. In order to quantitatively evaluate the effectiveness of our model in different situations, with and without congestion, we run a batch of experiments using different bandwidths and buffer sizes. For this experiment, we set the link bandwidth to be either 1, 10, or 100 Mbps, and the buffer size to be 100, 500, or 1000 packets. We fix the packet size to be 1500 bytes. For each distinct bandwidth and buffer size setting, we independently set the packet arrival rate of the emulated flow

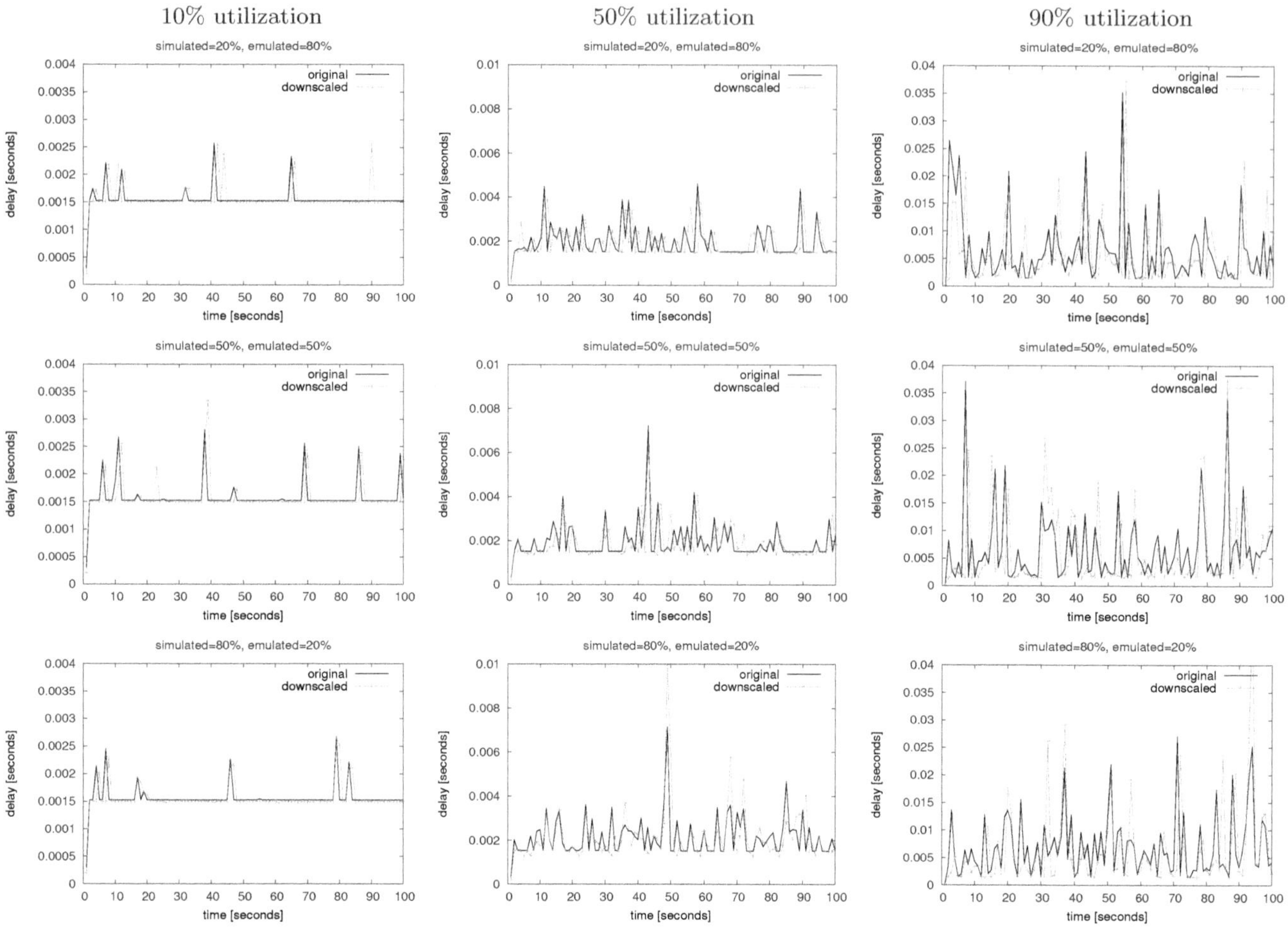

Figure 4: Packet delays for Poisson arrivals at different utilization levels.

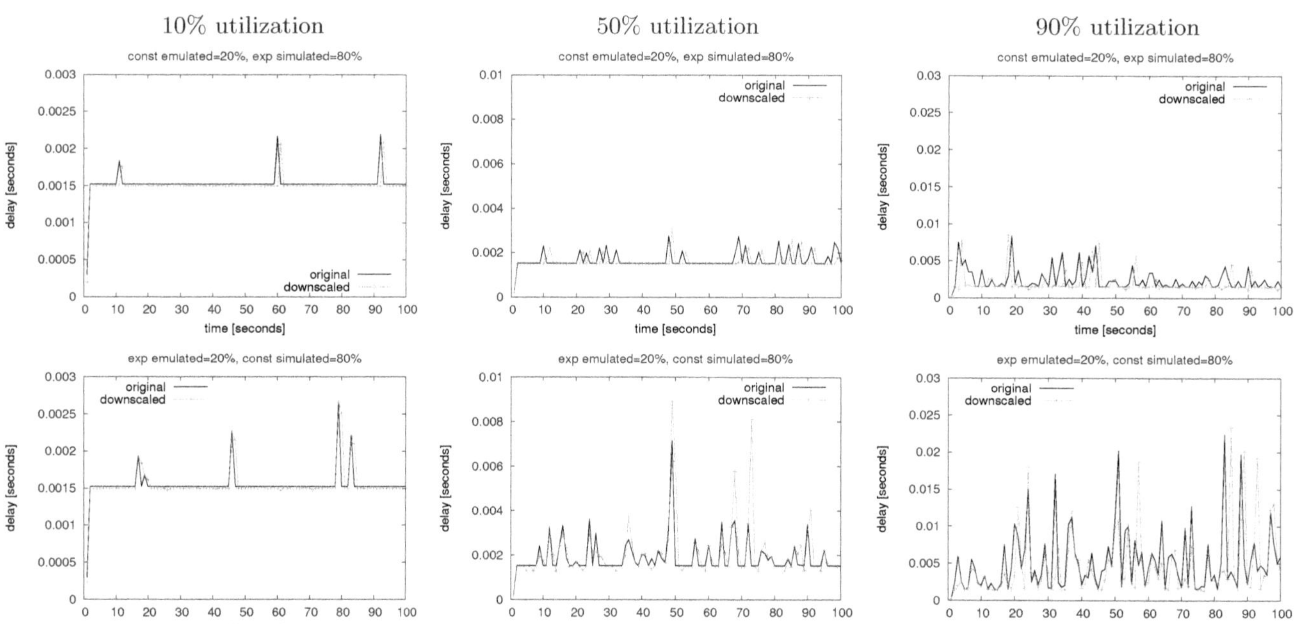

Figure 5: Packet delays for mixed Poisson and constant arrivals.

Table 1: Errors from a single-link segment

bandwidth (Mbps)	buffer (pkts)	delays *msec* (%)	lost packets	received packets
1	100	8.0 (7.96%)	0.22%	0.07%
1	500	8.0 (7.63%)	0.56%	0.16%
1	1000	7.0 (7.57%)	0.49%	0.07%
10	100	2.0 (8.83%)	0.13%	0.04%
10	500	2.0 (7.93%)	0.29%	0.07%
10	1000	2.0 (7.78%)	0.22%	0.04%
100	100	0.3 (5.04%)	0.62%	0.01%
100	500	0.4 (3.90%)	0.17%	0.02%
100	1000	0.4 (3.67%)	0.19%	0.02%

and that for the simulated flow to be 12, 25, 50, or 75% of the link bandwidth. Consequently we conduct a total of 16 experiments (with separate settings for the packet arrival rate for the emulated flow and for the simulated flow) for each distinct bandwidth and buffer size setting.

Each experiment is run for 100 seconds. Table 1 shows the differences in the average packet delays, the average number of dropped packets, and the average number of received packets between the original and the downscaled system—averaged across the 16 experiments for each combination of link bandwidth and buffer size.

The average percentage error (shown in the parentheses) for the number of dropped packets and the number of received packets is very small, indicating a good match between the two systems. For emulating a link with a bandwidth of 100 Mbps, the error in the packet delay is less than 1 millisecond. It goes up to 2 milliseconds for a 10 Mbps link, and 8 milliseconds for a 1 Mbps link. This is mainly due to the slower packet transmission time. The errors would be mostly imperceptible for high-bandwidth high-latency links. Overall, the results show conclusively that our queuing model provides a good approximation when emulating a single link regardless of the congestion levels.

7.2 Multiple-Link Validation

In the previous section, we show the validation results for a segment with a single link. In this section we examine the model behavior when the segment contains multiple links.

We use a network that consists of three nodes connected in tandem with distinct bandwidths. We designate an emulated flow to traverse all three network interfaces. We also direct three simulated flows, each entering at a different network interface, but all existing at the last one. The simulated and emulated flows have independent input sources with potentially different packet arrival rates.

Like before, we conduct two back-to-back simulations for each experiment setting—one for the original system and the other for the downscaled system. During the simulation of the original system, we measure the drop probability and the effective arrival rate of the emulated flow at each of the three interfaces. We also record the end-to-end delays through the network segment. These measurements are collected and stored in a trace file and used by a subsequent simulation of the downscaled system.

Staggered Arrivals. In this experiment, we set the bandwidth of the three links to be 1, 10, and 100 Mbps, respectively. We fix the packet size to be 1500 bytes. The buffer size of all network queues is set to be 200 packets. The packet arrival for all flows is Poisson. We set the arrival rate of the emulated flow to be 50 packets/s (i.e., 600 Kbps). We set the arrival rate of the simulated flows to be 600 Kbps, 9.6 Mbps, and 99.6 Mbps, respectively.

We start the emulated flow at the beginning of the experiment and let it persist through the whole experiment, which lasts for 120 seconds. We start the simulated flows in reverse order. The one entering the third network interface starts at the beginning of the experiment and lasts for 40 seconds. The one entering the second interface starts at 30 seconds and ends at 50 seconds. The one entering the first interface starts at 60 seconds and ends at 80 seconds. In this way, we manage to create three separate congestion points in the network segment.

Figure 7 shows the packet delay, the cumulative packet loss, and the throughput of the emulated flow over time. The delay and the throughput are average values measured at each second. We see clearly from the delay plot that congestion happens between 30 and 50 seconds, and between 60 and 100 seconds. And we see that it takes a while before a congestion is cleared up—the figure shows that the average delay waits until 106 seconds to come back to normal. The first link is the slowest; as expected, the longer packet transmission time at the first queue causes longer packet delays during the congestion (between time 60 and 106).

The packet loss is also significant between 60 and 100 seconds; this is because the emulated and simulated flows are mixed up with the same proportion at the first queue and therefore share the loss equally. At the other two queues the simulated flow dominates the emulated flow, the losses are there but much more insignificant. In all cases, the results from the original system and the downscaled system match very well. Our queuing model works correctly for the multiple links.

Exploring Various Network Settings. In order to quantitatively evaluate the effectiveness of our queuing model for emulating a segment with multiple links, we run a batch of experiments using different bandwidths for the links. To assess accuracy, we again compare the average packet delay, the number of dropped packets, and the number of received packets, between the original system and the downscaled system.

Like in the previous experiment, we fix the packet size to be 1500 bytes, the buffer size is 200 packets, and we use Poisson arrival for all flows. Unlike the previous experiment, here we independently set the bandwidth of the three links to be either 10 or 100 Mbps. We have three links, so there are eight combinations of the link bandwidth settings. For each of the eight settings, we conduct six separate experiments, by setting the packet arrival rate of all flows to be 12, 25, 50, 100, 125, or 150% of the link bandwidth where the respective flow is entering the system. For example, if we set the bandwidth of the first link (μ_1) to be 10 Mbps, and the bandwidth of the second and third link (μ_2 and μ_3) to be 100 Mbps, and if we set the arrival rate of all flows to be 50%, it means the packet arrival rate of the emulated flow and the first simulated flow would both be 5 Mbps, and the packet arrival rate of the second and the third simulated flow would be 50 Mbps.

We run the simulation for 500 seconds for each experiment. All flows start at time zero and last for the entire duration of the experiment. Table 2 shows the differences between the original and the downscaled systems, in packet

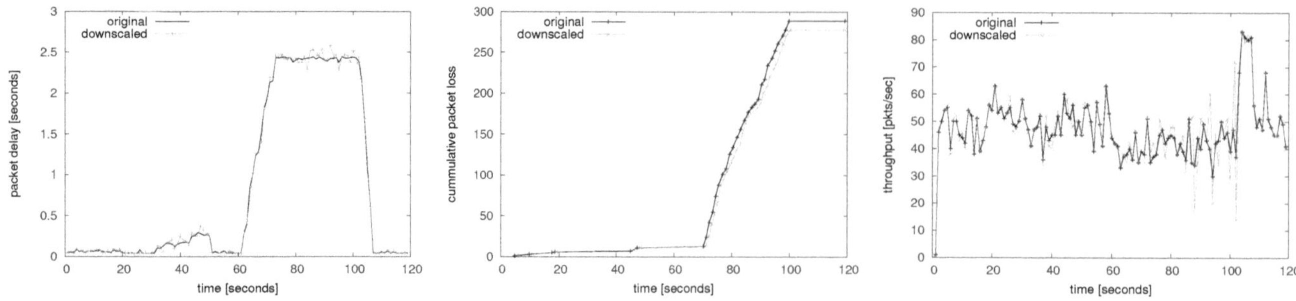

Figure 7: Experiment results from staggered arrivals.

Table 2: Errors from a multi-link segment

μ_1	μ_2	μ_3	delay	loss	throughput
10	10	10	1.72%	0.30%	0.28%
10	10	100	1.96%	0.59%	0.28%
10	100	10	1.91%	2.47%	0.21%
10	100	100	0.85%	0.40%	0.15%
100	10	10	0.54%	0.32%	0.99%
100	10	100	0.55%	0.18%	0.79%
100	100	10	0.19%	0.37%	0.97%
100	100	100	1.8%	0.23%	0.10%

delays, packet losses, and throughput of the emulated flow. Each row represents a different permutation of the link bandwidth setting and shows the average result of the six experiments with different traffic intensity. Again the two systems match well. The errors are all below 2%.

8. REAL SYSTEM VALIDATION

We implemented a network testbed, called *symbiosim*, for a prototype realization of the proposed symbiotic approach. In this section, we briefly describe design and implementation of the system, and present the results from preliminary experiments involving real applications and protocols.

8.1 Symbiosim Prototype

The prototype consists of several components, including a simulator, an emulator using physical machines for emulated hosts and delay nodes, and several utility programs for connecting the simulator and the emulator.

We use PRIME [24] for high-performance network simulation. PRIME can run the full-scale network model *in real time* as it can be executed on parallel platforms [16]. The simulator also has detailed models for various congestion control algorithms of all common TCP variants [7].

We use dummynet [26] as the the network emulator, which functions as the "delay node". The network is represented as a set of pipes with specific delay constraints. We apply our queuing model, and set the bandwidth and packet drop probability of the pipes using the statistics collected by the simulator to control the real network packets being pushed through them.

We instantiate PRIME, dummynet, and the emulated hosts and routers on individual physical machines using ProtoGENI [25]. ProtoGENI allows us to allocate an experiment slice, which can be configured to contain a set of machines with specific operating systems and network connections, on an EmuLab cluster [33].

We create three utility programs to facilitate communication between simulation and emulation. The first utility program is called the "data gatherer", which is expected to run side-by-side with the simulator instance.[3] The program takes as input the raw statistics exported by the simulator at the end of each update interval for all simulated network interfaces traversed by emulated flows. The program puts together the packet drop probabilities and calculates the service rates for the corresponding network segments, and then sends the update information to dummynet. The same program is also responsible for gathering information about the emulated traffic demand received from the emulated hosts, and informing the simulator to regenerate the emulated flows in simulation accordingly.

We run the second utility program, called the "actuator", at the machine which runs dummynet (i.e., the delay node). The program receives the state information from the data gatherer and then updates the parameters of the corresponding pipes in dummynet, including the drop probabilities and the service rates.

At each emulated host, we run third utility program, called the "traffic sensor", which collects the target applications' traffic demand (i.e., the `appBytes`). As a prototype, we simply rewrite the target applications and have them report to the collocated traffic sensor program through inter-process communication. The program collects the information and then sends an update to the "data gatherer" at the simulator site, which informs the simulator to regenerate the traffic in simulation.

8.2 Small-Scale Experiments

We conduct experiments to validate the accuracy of the symbiotic approach using real applications and real protocols. We compare the delay and throughput produced by the real applications running in *symbiosim* with those produced by simulated applications with similar characteristics running entirely in simulation. We make sure that simulated applications behaves the same as their real counterparts, such as using the same TCP variant with the same configurations.

We conduct this test using a network topology shown in Fig. 8. The network consists of six end hosts connected by four routers. We designate two end hosts (at the bottom) to be the emulated hosts. In the downscaled topology, the

[3]If the simulator is run in parallel, there will be one data gatherer associated with each parallel instance.

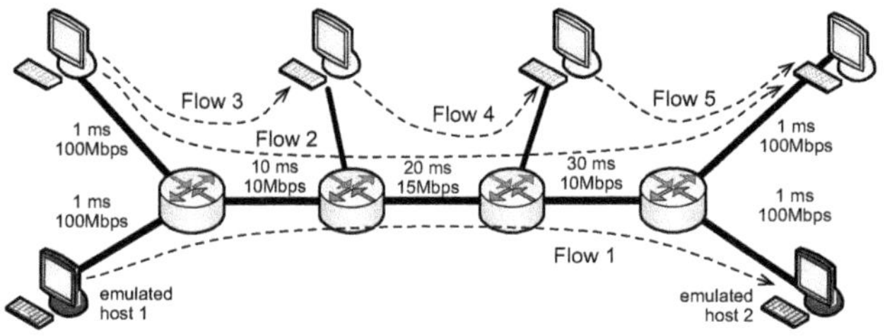

Figure 8: Baseline network for validation.

two emulated hosts will be connected by one network segment consisting of five links. The emulation system will be instantiated on three physical machines: one for each of the two emulated hosts, and a third for running dummynet connecting the two emulated hosts (i.e., as the delay node).

In the experiment, we direct five TCP flows, each containing multiple simultaneous TCP sessions. *Flow 1* is an emulated flow, which as only one TCP session generated by a pair of Java client/server applications that use HTTP to transfer a large data file over the network. The data transfer will span the entire experiment, which lasts for 60 seconds. The other four flows are all simulated flows. We carefully set the start time and the size of the data transfers so that we can create separate congestion points in the network throughout the experiment. *Flow 2* contains 5 simultaneous TCP sessions each transferring 0.5 MB of data and all starting at 10 seconds into the experiment. At 30 seconds, *Flow 3* starts with another 5 TCP sessions, each transferring 2 MB of data. Before the transfers finish, we start *Flow 4*, which contains 10 TCP sessions each transferring 1 MB of data. We intentionally make *Flow 3* and *Flow 4* overlap and thus create two bottlenecks in the network at the same time. Finally, at 50 seconds, *Flow 5* starts with another 5 TCP sessions each transferring 1MB of data.

The top plot of Figure 9 shows the measured round-trip times between the two emulated hosts, both from *symbiosim* and from pure simulation. For *symbiosim*, we run `ping` in parallel with the HTTP application, which provides us the measured round-trip time at each second during the experiment. The plot shows the results from running the same experiment fifteen times. In the figure we also plot the average round-trip time from the fifteen runs. For pure simulation, we extract the round-trip time from the trace files generated by the simulated TCP protocol. As shown in the figure, the delays from *symbiosim* closely follows what is expected from the simulation. The average round-trip time from simulation is 148 ms and that from *symbiosim* is 152 ms; the error is only about 3%. We also observe that, at the four congestion points we created in the simulation, *symbiosim* is able to react promptly as we can see the delays for the emulated flows jump accordingly due to the congestion.

The bottom plot of Figure 9 plots the sequence numbers of the received TCP segments over time. Again, we show the *symbiosim* results from the fifteen runs, along with the averages from both *symbiosim* and pure simulation. We see that the average sequence number history from *symbiosim* is almost indistinguishable from that of simulation. The maximum sequence number we collect at the end of the experiment in simulation is 20,843,961; *symbiosim* gets 20,748,458. The error is only 0.5%.

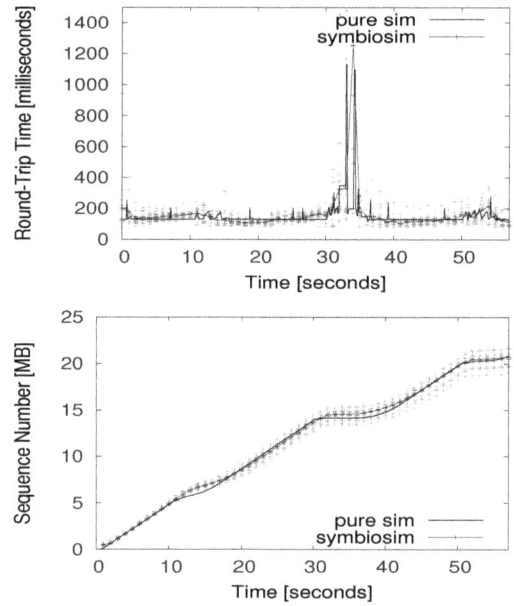

Figure 9: Results from real system experiments.

These results confirm that our symbiotic approach can accurately emulate the communication path between the target applications. The simulated network effect is handled promptly and accurately when *symbiosim* modulates the emulated traffic between target applications.

9. CONCLUSIONS AND FUTURE WORK

The proposed symbiotic approach provides a new way of evaluating complex networked systems, where large-scale network transactions can be modeled using simulation, while real application instances can run directly in real-machine environments and communicate through emulated paths reflecting the simulated traffic conditions of the large-scale network. We propose a model downscaling technique that can significantly reduce the computational complexity of the original large-scale model in order to enable high-capacity traffic emulation. In order for the full-scale simulated network model and the downscaled emulated network model to exhibit the same network behavior, we introduce a queuing model so that emulation can reproduce the same simulated traffic conditions between the target applications. We also introduce a technique for efficiently regenerating the same emulated traffic behavior in simulation, by capturing the target applications' traffic demand and then creating the traffic flows in simulation at the corresponding hosts. Extensive experiment results using simulation and with a prototype implementation of the symbiotic approach show that our approach is able to produce accurate results.

For future work, we are currently working on a full implementation of the symbiosim testbed. We will investigate methods for further scaling up the system, such as instantiating the emulation system on virtual machines, similar to what we have done for real-time network simulation [17, 31]. We will use the testbed to study real-world large-scale applications, such as peer-to-peer file sharing, content distribution multimedia streaming, and software-defined networking, to demonstrate the capability of our approach.

ACKNOWLEDGMENTS

This research is supported in part by NSF grants CNS-0836408, CCF-0937964, and HRD-0833093, and by a subcontract from the GENI Project Office at Raytheon BBN Technologies. We sincerely thank the anonymous reviewers for their constructive comments.

10. REFERENCES

[1] J. Ahrenholz, C. Danilov, T. Henderson, and J. Kim. CORE: A real-time network emulator. *MILCOM'08*, pages 1–7.

[2] C. Barakat, P. Thiran, G. Iannaccone, C. Diot, and P. Owezarski. A flow-based model for Internet backbone traffic. *IMW'02*, pages 35–47.

[3] P. Barford and L. Landweber. Bench-style network research in an Internet instance laboratory. *SIGCOMM Comput. Commun. Rev.*, 33(3):21–26, 2003.

[4] L. Breslau, D. Estrin, K. Fall, S. Floyd, J. Heidemann, A. Helmy, P. Huang, S. McCanne, K. Varadhan, Y. Xu, and H. Yu. Advances in network simulation. *IEEE Computer*, 33(5):59–67, 2000.

[5] CAIDA Anonymized Internet Traces 2011 Dataset. `http://www.caida.org/data/passive/passive_2011_dataset.xml`.

[6] X. Chang. Network simulations with OPNET. *WSC'99*, pages 307–314.

[7] M. A. Erazo, Y. Li, and J. Liu. SVEET! A scalable virtualized evaluation environment for TCP. *TRIDENTCOM'09*, pages 1–10.

[8] D. Eun and N. Shroff. Simplification of network analysis in large-bandwidth systems. *INFOCOM'03*.

[9] K. Fall. Network emulation in the Vint/NS simulator. *ISCC'99*, pages 244–250.

[10] C. Fraleigh, S. Moon, B. Lyles, C. Cotton, M. Khan, D. Moll, R. Rockell, T. Seely, and S. C. Diot. Packet-level traffic measurements from the Sprint IP backbone. *Netwrk. Mag. of Global Internetwkg.*, 17(6):6–16, 2003.

[11] C. Fraleigh, F. Tobagi, and C. Diot. Provisioning IP backbone networks to support latency sensitive traffic. *INFOCOM'03*.

[12] R. Fujimoto, D. Lunceford, E. Page, and A. M. Uhrmacher. Grand challenges for modeling and simulation. Technical Report 350, Schloss Dagstuhl, 2002.

[13] Y. Gu. *ROSENET: A remote server-based network emulation system.* PhD thesis, Georgia Institute of Technology, 2007.

[14] M. Handley, E. Kohler, A. Ghosh, O. Hodson, and P. Radoslavov. Designing extensible IP router software. *NSDI'05*, pages 189–202.

[15] M. Liljenstam, J. Liu, D. Nicol, Y. Yuan, G. Yan, and C. Grier. RINSE: the real-time immersive network simulation environment for network security exercises. *PADS'05*, pages 119–128.

[16] J. Liu. A primer for real-time simulation of large-scale networks. *ANSS'08*, pages 85–94.

[17] J. Liu, Y. Li, N. V. Vorst, S. Mann, and K. Hellman. A real-time network simulation infrastructure based on OpenVPN. *Journal of Systems and Software*, 82(3):473–485, 2009.

[18] X. Liu, H. Xia, and A. A. Chien. Network emulation tools for modeling grid behavior. *CCGrid'03*.

[19] D. M. Nicol, D. Jin, and Y. Zheng. S3F: the scalable simulation framework revisited. *WSC'11*, pages 3288–3299.

[20] Open vSwitch. `http://openvswitch.org/`.

[21] F. Papadopoulos, K. Psounis, and R. Govindan. Performance preserving topological downscaling of Internet-like networks. *IEEE J. Sel. Areas Commun.*, 24(12):2313–2326, 2006.

[22] K. Papagiannaki, S. Moon, C. Fraleigh, P. Thiran, F. Tobagi, and C. Diot. Analysis of measured single-hop delay from an operational backbone network. *INFOCOM'02*.

[23] L. Peterson, T. Anderson, D. Culler, and T. Roscoe. A blueprint for introducing disruptive technology into the Internet. *HotNets-I*, 2002.

[24] PRIME. `https://www.primessf.net/prime/`.

[25] ProtoGENI. `http://www.protogeni.net/`.

[26] L. Rizzo. Dummynet: a simple approach to the evaulation of network protocols. *SIGCOMM Comput. Commun. Rev.*, 27(1):31–41, 1997.

[27] P. Sanaga, J. Duerig, R. Ricci, and J. Lepreau. Modeling and emulation of Internet paths. *NSDI'09*, pages 199–212.

[28] R. Simmonds, R. Bradford, and B. Unger. Applying parallel discrete event simulation to network emulation. *PADS'00*, pages 15–22.

[29] B. K. Szymanski, A. Saifee, A. Sastry, Y. Liu, and K. Madnani. Genesis: a system for large-scale parallel network simulation. *PADS'02*, pages 89–96.

[30] A. Vahdat, K. Yocum, K. Walsh, P. Mahadevan, D. Kostić, J. Chase, and D. Becker. Scalability and accuracy in a large-scale network emulator. *SIGOPS Oper. Syst. Rev.*, 36(SI):271–284, 2002.

[31] N. Van Vorst, M. Erazo, and J. Liu. PrimoGENI: Integrating real-time network simulation and emulation in GENI. *PADS'11*, pages 1–9.

[32] N. Van Vorst, T. Li, and J. Liu. How low can you go? Spherical routing for scalable network simulations. *MASCOTS'11*, pages 259–268.

[33] B. White, J. Lepreau, L. Stoller, R. Ricci, S. Guruprasad, M. Newbold, M. Hibler, C. Barb, and A. Joglekar. An integrated experimental environment for distributed systems and networks. *OSDI'02*, pages 255–270.

[34] T. Ye, S. Kalyanaraman, D. Harrison, B. Sikdar, B. Mo, H. Tahilramani, K. Vastola, and B. Szymanski. Network management and control using collaborative on-line simulation. *ICC'01*.

[35] Y. Zhang and N. Duffield. On the constancy of Internet path properties. *IMW'01*, pages 197–211.

[36] J. Zhou, Z. Ji, M. Takai, and R. Bagrodia. MAYA: integrating hybrid network modeling to the physical world. *TOMACS*, 14(2):149–169, 2004.

Parallel Simulation of Software Defined Networks

Dong Jin
Department of Electrical and Computer Engineering
University of Illinois at Urbana-Champaign
Urbana, Illinois 61801
dongjin2@illinois.edu

David M. Nicol
Department of Electrical and Computer Engineering
University of Illinois at Urbana-Champaign
Urbana, Illinois 61801
dmnicol@illinois.edu

ABSTRACT

Existing network architectures fall short when handling networking trends, e.g., mobility, server virtualization, and cloud computing, as well as market requirements with rapid changes. Software-defined networking (SDN) is designed to transform network architectures by decoupling the control plane from the data plane. Intelligence is shifted to the logically centralized controller with direct programmability, and the underlying infrastructures are abstracted from applications. The wide adoption of SDN in network industries has motivated development of large-scale, high-fidelity testbeds for evaluation of systems that incorporate SDN. We leverage our prior work on a hybrid network testbed with a parallel network simulator and a virtual-machine-based emulation system. In this paper, we extend the testbed to support OpenFlow-based SDN simulation and emulation; show how to exploit typical SDN controller behavior to deal with potential performance issues caused by the centralized controller in parallel discrete-event simulation; and investigate methods for improving the model scalability, including an asynchronous synchronization algorithm for passive controllers and a two-level architecture for active controllers. The techniques not only improve the simulation performance, but also are valuable for designing scalable SDN controllers.

Categories and Subject Descriptors

I.6 [**Simulation and Modeling**]: Applications

Keywords

parallel discrete event simulation; software defined networking

1. INTRODUCTION

Complex networks with large numbers of vendor-dependent devices and inconsistent policies greatly limit network designers' options and ability to innovate. For example, to deploy a network-wide policy in a cloud platform, the network operators must (re)configure thousands of physical and virtual machines, including access control lists, VLANs, and other protocol-based mechanisms. Trends in networking, such as cloud services, mobile computing, and server virtualization, also impose requirements that are extremely difficult to meet in traditional network architectures. Software-defined networking (SDN) is designed to transform network architectures. In an SDN, the control plane is decoupled from the data plane in the network devices, such as switches, routers, access points, and gateways, and the underlying infrastructure is abstracted from the applications that use it. Therefore, SDN enables centralized control of a network with flexibility and direct programability. SDNs have been widely accepted and deployed in enterprise networks, campus networks, carriers, and data centers. For example, Google has deployed SDN in its largest production network: its data-center to data-center WAN [9].

OpenFlow [15] is the first standard communications interface defined between the control and forwarding layers of an SDN architecture. Existing OpenFlow-based SDN testbeds include MiniNet [13], MiniNet-HiFi [10], OFTest [3], OFlops [20], and NS-3 [2]. MiniNet probably is the most widely used SDN emulation testbed at present. It uses an OS-level virtualization technique called Linux container, and is able to emulate scenarios with 1000+ hosts and Open vSwitches [4]. However, MiniNet has not yet achieved performance fidelity, especially with limited resources, since resources are time-multiplexed by the kernel, and the overall bandwidth is limited by CPU and memory constraints. Execution of real programs in virtual machines exhibits high functional fidelity, and creation of multiple virtual machines on a single physical machine provides scalability and flexibility for running networking experiments, but low temporal fidelity is a major issue for virtual-machine-based network emulation systems. By default, all virtual machines use the same system clock of the physical machine. As a result, when a virtual machine is idle, its clock still advances. That raises the temporal fidelity issue when applications running on a virtual machine are expected to behave as if they were being executed on a real machine. All existing SDN emulation testbeds lack temporal fidelity. We have developed an emulation virtual time system in our prior work [22]. Freeing the emulation from real time enables us to run experiments slower or faster than real time. When resources are limited, we can always slow down experiments to ensure accuracy. On the other hand, experiments can be accelerated if system resources are sufficient. In this work, we extend the system to support OpenFlow-based SDN emulation with high functional fidelity and temporal fidelity.

While emulation testbeds offer fidelity, they are not suitable for large-scale network experiments. Simulation testbeds can provide scalability, but the accuracy degrades because of models' simplification and abstraction. Therefore, in prior work, we integrated a parallel network simulator with a virtual-machined-based emulation system based on virtual time [12]. When conducting network experiments, we can execute critical components in emulation and use simulation to provide a large-scale networking environment with background traffic. In this work, we also develop a framework to support OpenFlow-based SDN simulation, including models of an OpenFlow switch, controller, and protocol. The ns-3 network simulator also has an OpenFlow module [2] supporting both simulation and emulation, but, unlike our system, it does integrate virtual-time-based emulation and parallelized simulation. In addition, we have conducted extensive studies of application-level behaviors in our emulation system [21], and discovered that the errors introduced by the emulation system are bounded by one time slice, which is the system execution unit (e.g., 100 μs). However, the processing delay within a Gigabit switch is on the scale of one microsecond. If such a delay is critical to the SDN applications being tested, we can use simulation models instead, in which the time granularity is defined by the users to achieve the desired timing accuracy.

In this paper, we extend our network testbed with the capability to emulate and simulate OpenFlow-based SDNs. The extension is based on close analysis of how SDN controllers typically behave, which led to organizational and synchronization optimizations that deal with problems that might otherwise greatly limit scalability and performance. The testbed provides the following benefits and is a useful tool for SDN-based research in general:

- Temporal fidelity through a virtual time system, especially with limited system and networking resources, e.g., it can emulate 10 hosts, each with a gigabyte Ethernet interface, on a single physical machine with only one one-gigabyte Ethernet network card,
- More scalable network scenarios with simulated nodes,
- Background traffic at different levels of detail among the simulated nodes, and
- Sophisticated underlying network environments (e.g., wireless CSMA/CA).

An OpenFlow controller typically connects with a large number of OpenFlow switches. Not only is the centralized controller a potential communication bottleneck in the real networks, but also it gives rise to performance drawbacks in simulating such networks in the context of parallel discrete-event simulation. The large number of switch-controller links could potentially reduce the length of the synchronization window in barrier-based global synchronization, and could also negatively impact the channel scanning type of local synchronization. We investigate techniques to improve the scalability of the simulated OpenFlow controllers through analysis of a list of basic controller applications in POX, which is a popular OpenFlow controller written in Python [6]. We classify the controller applications into active controllers and passive controllers based on whether the controllers proactively insert rules into the switches, or the rule insertions are triggered by the switches. We design an asynchronous synchronization algorithm for the passive controllers, and a two-level architecture for the active controllers for use in building scalable OpenFlow controller models.

The main contributions of this paper are as follows: (1) We develop a network testbed for simulating and emulating OpenFlow-based SDNs. The testbed integrates a virtual-time embedded emulation system and a parallel network simulator to achieve both fidelity and scalability. (2) We explore and evaluate means to improve the performance of simulation of OpenFlow controllers in parallel discrete-event simulation, including an asynchronous synchronization algorithm for controllers that are "passive" (according to a definition given in Section 4), and a two-level architecture for controllers we classify as "active." (3) The two-level controller architecture is also a valuable reference for designing real scalable SDN controllers.

The remainder of the paper is organized as follows. Section 2 introduces background on software-defined networks. Section 3 describes the system design with emulation and simulation support for running of OpenFlow-based SDN experiments. Section 4 presents the performance issues caused by the simulated centralized controller and investigates various techniques to improve the scalability. Section 5 evaluates the performance of the proposed controller models. Section 6 concludes the paper with plans for future work.

2. OPENFLOW-BASED SOFTWARE-DEFINED NETWORKS

In a traditional network architecture, the control plane and the data plane cooperate within a device via internal protocols. By contrast, in an SDN, the control plane is separated from the data plane, and the control logic is moved to an external controller. The controller monitors and manages all of the states in the network from a central vantage point. The controller talks to the data plane using the OpenFlow protocol [1], which defines the communication between the controller and the data planes of all the forwarding elements. The controller can set rules about the data-forwarding behaviors of each forwarding device through the OpenFlow protocol, including rules such as drop, forward, modify, or enqueue.

Each OpenFlow switch has a chain of flow tables, and each table stores a collection of flow entries. A *flow* is defined as the set of packets that match the given properties, e.g., a particular pair of source and destination MAC addresses. A flow entry defines the forwarding/routing rules. It consists of a bit pattern that indicates the flow properties, a list of actions, and a set of counters. Each flow entry states "execute this set of actions on all packets in this flow," e.g., forward this packet out of port A. Figure 1 shows the main components of an OpenFlow-based SDN and the procedures by which an OpenFlow switch handles an incoming packet. When a packet arrives at a switch, the switch searches for matched flow entries in the flow tables and executes the corresponding lists of actions. If no match is found for the packet, the packet is queued, and an inquiry event is sent to the OpenFlow controller. The controller responds with a new flow entry for handling that queued packet. Subsequent packets in the same flow will be handled by the switch with-

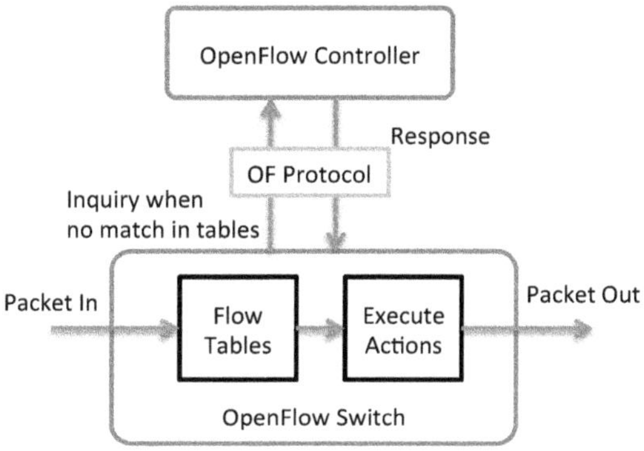

Figure 1: How an OpenFlow Switch Handles Incoming Packets

out contacting the controller, and will be forwarded at the switch's full line rate.

Some benefits of applying SDN in large-scale and complex networks include the following:

- The need to configure network devices individually is eliminated.
- Policies are enforced consistently across the network infrastructures, including policies for access control, traffic engineering, quality of service, and security.
- Functionality of the network can be defined and modified after the network has been deployed.
- Addition of new features does not require change of the software on every switch, whose APIs are generally not publicly available.

3. SYSTEM DESIGN

We have developed a large-scale, high-fidelity network testbed by integrating the OpenVZ network emulation into an S3F-based network simulation framework, and extended the testbed to support OpenFlow-based SDN simulation/emulation. Figure 2 shows the overall system architecture on a single physical Linux box. The system consists of three major components: OpenVZ, the network emulation system; S3F, the system kernel; and S3FNet, the parallel network simulator.

3.1 System Components

3.1.1 S3F – Parallel System Kernel

SSF (Scalable Simulation Framework) defines an API that supports modular construction of simulation models, with automated exploitation of parallelism [17]. Building on ten years of experience, we developed a second-generation API named *S3F* [19]. In both SSF and S3F, a simulation is composed of interactions among a number of *entity* objects. Entities interact by passing *events* through *channel* endpoints they own. Channel endpoints are described by *InChannels* and *OutChannels* depending on the message direction. Each entity is aligned to a *timeline*, which hosts an event list and is responsible for advancing all entities aligned to it. Interactions between co-aligned entities need no synchronization other than this event-list. Multiple timelines may run simultaneously to exploit parallelism, but they have to be carefully synchronized to guarantee global causality. The synchronization mechanism is built around explicitly expressed delays across channels whose end-points reside on entities that are not aligned. We call those *cross-timeline channels*. The concepts of entity, channel, timeline, and (non-)cross-timeline channel are depicted in the lower portion of Figure 2. The global synchronization algorithm in S3F creates synchronization windows, within which all timelines can safely advance without being affected by other timelines. More details about S3F are in [19].

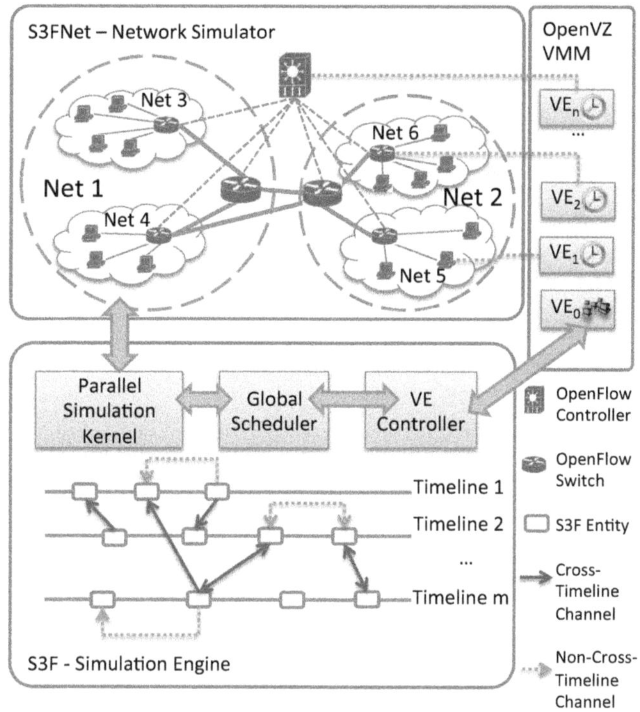

Figure 2: S3F System Architecture Design with OpenFlow Extension

One important feature of S3F is its support of OpenVZ-based emulation experiments based on the notion of virtual clocks. The VE controller and the global scheduler, shown in Figure 2, are responsible for managing the interaction between the simulation and the emulation systems.

The *VE controller* is designed to control all the emulation hosts according to S3F's command, and to provide necessary communications between VEs and their corresponding simulated nodes. The VE controller is a special API that offers three services: an advance emulation clock, the ability to transfer packets bidirectionally between simulation and emulation, and emulation lookahead. More details on the VE controller are in [12].

The *Global scheduler* coordinates safe and efficient advancement of the two systems. It ensures that the emulation runs ahead of the simulation, generating the network's offered load, but not so far ahead as to miss delivery of traffic. It also schedules the sequence and length of each emulation and simulation execution cycle to preserve causal relationships. Each VE has its own virtual clock, which is synchronized with the simulation clock in S3F. The complete synchronization algorithm used by the global scheduler is described in [12]. In addition, the global scheduler makes the emulation integration nearly transparent to the upper-layer network simulator.

3.1.2 S3FNet – Network Simulator

S3FNet is a network simulator built on top of the S3F kernel. While it is capable of creating models of network devices (e.g., host, switch, router) with layered protocols (e.g., IP, TCP, UDP) like other network simulators, the primary purposes of S3FNet for the entire system are to simulate a sophisticated underlying network environment (e.g., detailed CSMA/CD for traditional Ethernet, and/or CSMA/CA for wireless communication) and to efficiently model the extensive communication and computation in large-scale experiment settings (e.g., background traffic simulation models [18] [11]).

S3FNet has a global view of the network topology. Every VE in the OpenVZ emulation system is represented in the S3FNet as a host model within the modeled network, together with other simulated nodes. Within S3FNet, traffic that is generated by a VE emerges from its proxy host inside S3FNet, and, when directed to another VE, is delivered to the recipient's proxy host as shown in Figure 2. Only the global scheduler in S3F knows the distinction between an emulated host (VE-host) and a virtual host (non-VE host).

3.1.3 OpenVZ-based Network Emulation

OpenVZ is an OS-level virtualization technology that creates and manages multiple isolated Linux containers, also called *Virtual Environments (VEs)*, on a single physical server. Each VE performs exactly like a stand-alone host with its own root access, users and groups, IP and MAC address, memory, process tree, file system, system libraries, and configuration files. All VEs share a single instance of the Linux OS kernel for services such as TCP/IP. Compared with other virtualization technologies such as Xen (para-virtualization) and QEMU (full-virtualization), OpenVZ is lightweight (e.g., we are able to run more than 300 VEs on a commodity server with eight 2GHz cores and 16 GB memory), at the cost of diversity in the underlying operating system.

OpenVZ emulation allows users to execute real software in the VEs to achieve high functional fidelity. It also frees a modeler from developing complicated simulation models for network applications and the corresponding protocol stacks. In addition to functional fidelity, our version of OpenVZ also provides temporal fidelity through a virtual clock implementation [22], allowing integration with the simulation system.

In a real system, an application perceives time elapses when doing computation or when waiting for I/Os. Similarly, our system advances a VE's virtual clock between the time when the VE starts to execute and when the VE stops, and also between the time when the VE starts a blocking I/O, and when the VE finishes.

We used a timeslice-based mechanism to implement our virtual time system. A VE can run only after the VE controller has given it a timeslice and released it. Without being given a timeslice, a VE will remain suspended, and its clock will not advance. When an event occurs to unsuspend it (e.g., arrival of a message that had been blocked), the clock is advanced to the time of the event, leaping over an idle epoch. While a VE is suspended, the simulator can perform arbitrarily long simulation computation, as this will not affect the VE's state. That frees our emulation from having to run in real time; emulation can now run either faster or slower than real time, depending on the system load and the simulation model that is being used.

Another advantage is that the VE controller is able to control VE executions to prevent some VEs from running too far ahead (in terms of virtual time), potentially leading to causal violations. In regards to VE synchronization, we currently use a barrier-based mechanism. In particular, S3F computes a barrier (a virtual time value) to which all VEs can safely advance, and lets all VEs run to this barrier. Within two consecutive barriers, VEs are considered independent, and any VE interactions are postponed until arrival at the barrier. Details of the synchronization algorithm are provided in [12].

Our virtual time system introduces some timing errors via the timeslice-based mechanism. Once a VE has received a timeslice, the VE controller cannot interact or stop the VE until the timeslice has expired up on the hardware interrupt. In particular, the VE controller cannot deliver an event (i.e., a network packet arrival) to the VE at the exact same virtual time the packet leaves the simulation. Events occur at timeslice boundaries, so any error is bounded in magnitude by the length of the timeslice. We may reduce the error bound by setting a smaller hardware interrupt interval [22]. However, that interval cannot be arbitrarily small, because of efficiency concerns and hardware limits.

3.2 OpenFlow Integration

The design of SDN separates the control plane from the data plane in network forwarding devices (switches, routers, gateways, or access points). Users can design their own logically centralized controllers to define the behaviors of those forwarding elements via a standardized API, such as OpenFlow, which provides flexibility to define and modify the functionalities of a network after the network has been physically deployed. Many large-scale networks, such as data centers, carriers, and campus networks, have been deployed with SDNs. Network simulation/emulation is often used to facilitate the testing and evaluation of large-scale network designs and applications running on them. Therefore, we extend our existing network testbed to support OpenFlow, in particular, simulation and/or emulation of network experiments that contains OpenFlow switches and controllers, which communicate via the OpenFlow protocol.

To emulate OpenFlow-based networks, we can run unmodified OpenFlow switch and controller programs in the OpenVZ containers, and the network environment (such as wireless or wireline media) is simulated by S3FNet. Since the executables are run on the real network stacks within the containers, the prototype behaviors are close to the behaviors in real SDNs. Once an idea works on the testbed, it can be easily deployed to production networks. Other OpenFlow emulation testbeds, like MiniNet [13], have good functional fidelity too, but lack performance fidelity, especially with heavy loads. Imagine that one OpenFlow switch with ten fully loaded gigabit links is emulated on a commodity physical machine with only one physical gigabit network card. There is no guarantee that a switch ready to forward a packet will be scheduled promptly by the Linux scheduler in real time. Our system does not have such limitations, since the emulation system is virtual-time embedded. The experiments can run faster or slower depending on the workload. When load is high, performance fidelity is ensured by running the experiment slower than real time. On the other hand, when the load is low, we can reduce the execution time by quickly advancing the experiment.

However, experimental results show that errors introduced by the virtual time system at the application level are bounded by the size of one emulation timeslice. We may reduce the error bound by setting a smaller hardware interrupt interval [22]. Nevertheless, the interval cannot be arbitrarily small because of efficiency concerns and hardware limits. We typically use 100 μs as the smallest timeslice. If we want to simulate a gigabit switch whose processing delay is on the scale of a micro-second, a 100 μs error bound is simply too large. That motivated us to develop a simulated OpenFlow switch and an OpenFlow controller model; the simulation virtual time unit is defined by the users and can be arbitrarily small, typically a micro-second or nano-second.

Our OpenFlow simulation model has two components: the OpenFlow switch, and the OpenFlow controller. The switches and the controller communicate via the OpenFlow protocol [1], and the protocol library we use is the OpenFlow reference implementation at Stanford University [5], which has been used in many hardware-based and software-based SDN applications. The initial version of the switch and the controller models have been developed with reference to the ns-3 OpenFlow models [2]. Figure 3 depicts the model implementation details.

Our OpenFlow switch model can handle both simulated traffic and real traffic generated by the applications running in the containers. The switch model has multiple ports, and each port consists of a physical layer and a data link layer. Different physical and data link layer models allow us to simulate different types of network, such as wireless and wireline networks. A switch layer containing a chain of flow tables is located on top of the ports, as shown in Figure 3. It is responsible for matching flow entries in the tables and performing the corresponding predefined actions or sending an inquiry to the controller when no match is found in the tables. The controller model consists of a group of applications (e.g., learning switch, link discovery) as well as a list of connected OpenFlow switches. It is responsible for generating and modifying flow entries and sending them back to the switches.

Needless to say, running executables of OpenFlow components in the emulation mode has better functional fidelity than the simulation models do. We attempt to keep the high fidelity in the simulation models by using the original unmodified OpenFlow library, which has been used to design many real SDN applications. Also, the simulation models are not constrained by the 100 μs timeslice error bound in emulation. In addition, we can run experiments in the simulation mode with much larger network sizes. Finally, as a bonus effect of the OpenFlow design, we no longer have to preload a forwarding table at every network device, since where and how to forward the packets are decided on demand by the controller. Simulating a network with millions or even more network devices at the packet level is affordable in our system.

Figure 3 also shows the journey of a packet in our system. A packet is generated at the source end-host, either from the simulated application layer or from the real network application in a container. The packet is pushed down through the simulated network stacks of the host and then is popped up to the OpenFlow switch via the connected in-port. Depending on the emulation or simulation mode of the switch

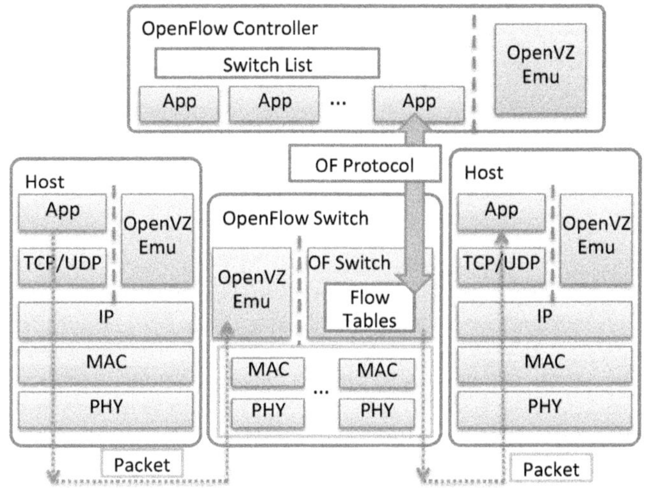

Figure 3: OpenFlow Implementation in S3F

(the OpenVZEmu module in Figure 3 is used to handle the case where the entity is associated with a virtual-machine container), the packet is searched within the simulated flow tables or the real flow tables in the container, and a set of actions are executed when matches are found. Otherwise, a new flow event is directed to the controller, meaning either the simulated controller model or the real controller program in the container. The controller generates new flow entries and installs the flow entries onto the switches via the OpenFlow protocol. Afterwards, the switch knows how to process the incoming packet (and subsequent additional packets of this type), and transmit it via the correct out-port. Eventually the packet is received by the application running on the destination end-host.

4. SCALABILITY OF SIMULATED OPENFLOW CONTROLLERS

SDN-based network designs have multiple OpenFlow switches communicating with a single OpenFlow controller. However, many-to-one network topologies not only create communication bottlenecks at the controllers in real networks, but also negatively impact the performance of conservative synchronization of parallel discrete-event simulations. The conservative synchronization approaches in parallel discrete-event simulation generally fall into two categories: synchronous approaches based on barriers [7] [14] [16], and asynchronous approaches, in which a submodel's advance is a function of the advances of other submodels that might affect it [8]. The single-controller-to-many-switch architecture can be bad for both types of synchronization.

We can view a network model as a direct graph: nodes are entities like hosts, switches, and routers; edges are the communication links among entities; and each link is weighted by a link delay. From S3F, the parallel simulation engine's viewpoint, the graph is further aggregated: a node represents a group of entities on the same timeline, and the simulation activity of all entities on a timeline is serialized; multiple links between timelines t_i and t_j are simplified into one link whose weight is the minimum (cross-timeline) delay between t_i and t_j.

A barrier-based synchronous approach is sensitive to the

Table 1: Basic Network Applications in the POX OpenFlow Controller

Controller Application	Description	Passive/ Active	State	Other Comments
openflow. keep_alive	The application sends periodic echo requests to connected switches. Some switches will assume that an idle connection indicates a loss of connectivity to the controller and will disconnect after some period of silence, and this application is used to prevent that.	Active	Distributed	The request-sending period is a good source of lookahead.
forwarding. l2_learning	The application makes an OpenFlow switch act as a type of L2 learning switch. While the component learns L2 addresses, the flows it installs are exact matches on as many fields as possible. For example, different TCP connections will result in installation of different flows.	Passive	Distributed	
forwarding. l2_pairs	The application also makes an OpenFlow switch act like a type of L2 learning switch. However, it installs rules based purely on MAC addresses, probably the simplest way to do a learning switch correctly.	Passive	Distributed	
forwarding. l2_learning	The application is not quite a router. It uses L3 information to perform data switching similar to a L2 switch.	Passive	Distributed	
openflow. link_discovery	The application sends specially crafted messages out of OpenFlow switches to discover link status, e.g., to discover the network topology. Switches raise events to the controller when links go up or down.	Active	Shared among the connected switches	The link status query period is a good source of lookahead.
forwarding. l2_multi	This application can still be seen as a learning switch, but it learns where a MAC address is by looking up the topology of the entire network.	Passive	Network-wide	
openflow. spanning_tree	This application constructs a spanning tree based on the network topology, and then disables flooding on switch ports that are not on the tree.	Active	Network-wide	

minimum incoming edge weight in the entire graph. If one of the OpenFlow switch-controller links has a very small link delay (e.g., a controller and a switch could be installed on the same physical machine in reality), even if there are few activities running on the link, the overall performance will be poor because of the small synchronization window. On the other hand, an asynchronous approach focuses on timeline interactions indicated by the topology, but is subject to significant overhead costs on timelines that are highly connected. The SDN-based architectures unfortunately always have a centralized controller with a large degree, which is not a desired property for asynchronous approaches either.

To improve the simulation performance with SDN architectures, we explore the properties of an OpenFlow controller with reference to a list of basic applications in POX, which is a widely used SDN controller written in Python [6]. The applications are summarized in Table 1. We have two key observations.

First, controllers can be classified as either passive or active. A controller is *passive* if the applications running on it never initiate communication to switches, but only passively respond to inquires from switches when no matches are found in switches' flow tables. The forwarding.l2_learning application is a good example of an application that runs on a passive controller. An *active* controller initiates communication to switches, e.g., detecting whether a switch or a link is working or broken. The openflow.link_discovery application is an example of an application that runs on an active controller.

Second, a controller is not simply a large single entity shared by all the connected switches. A controller actually has states that are shared by switches at different levels. Suppose there are N switches in a network, and m switches ($1 \leq m \leq N$) share a state.

- When $m = N$, the state is network-wide, i.e., the state is shared by all switches. For example, the openflow.spanning_tree application has a network-wide state, which is the global network topology.
- When $m = 1$, the state is distributed, i.e., no other switch shares the state with this switch. For example, the forwarding.l2_learning application has a distributed state, which is the individual learning table for each switch.
- When $1 < m < N$, the state is shared by a subset of switches of size m. For example, the openflow.link_discovery application has such a state, which is the link status shared among all the switches connected to that link.

Based on the above two observations, we revisit the controller design and investigate techniques to improve the performance of the simulation of OpenFlow-based SDNs with parallel discrete-event simulation. In particular, we design an efficient asynchronous algorithm for passive controllers; we also propose a two-level controller architecture for active controllers, and analyze performance improvement for three applications with different types of states. The proposed architecture is not only helpful with respect to simulation performance, but also a useful reference for designing scalable OpenFlow controller applications.

4.1 Passive Controller Design

A passive controller indicates that applications running on the controller do not proactively talk to switches, a feature we can use in designing a controller whose functionality is known to be passive. A new design is also motivated by another observation: when a switch receives an incoming packet, the switch can handle the packet without consulting the controller if a matched rule is found in the switch's flow table; and, for some applications, the number of times the controller must be consulted (e.g., first time the flow is seen, or when the flow expires) is far lower than the number of packets being processed locally. All the learning switch applications in the POX controller have this property.

Therefore, our idea is that for a passive controller, switches are free to advance their model states without constraint, until the switches have to communicate with the controller. If multiple switches share a state, then the controller needs to refrain from answering the inquiring switch until all its cross-timeline dependent switches have advanced to the time of the inquiring switch. The algorithm is presented as follows:

Let A be the set of applications running in the OpenFlow controller, and R be the set of OpenFlow switches in a network model. We define $TL(r)$ to be the timeline to which switch r is aligned. For each $a \in A$ and $r \in R$, we define $f(r, a)$ to be the subset of OpenFlow switches that share at least one state with switch r for application a. For example, $f(r_1, a_1) = \{r_2, r_3\}$ means that switches r_1, r_2, r_3 are dependent on (sharing states with) application a_1. Causality is ensured only if the controller responds to the inquiry from switch r_1 with timestamp t_1, after all the dependent cross-timeline switches r_i, i.e., $r_i \in f(r_1, a)$ and $TL(r_i) \neq TL(r_1)$, have advanced their times to at least t_1. For an application with network-wide states, $f(r, a) = R - \{r\}$; for a fully distributed application, $f(r, a) = \phi$.

Algorithm 1 is designed for efficient synchronization among switches and fast simulation advancement with correct causality in the case of a passive controller. The algorithm is divided into two parts: one at the controller side and another at the switch side. Since the controller cannot actively affect a switch's state, it is safe for a switch to advance independent of the controller until a switch-controller event happens (e.g., a packet is received that has no match in the switch's flow tables). The delays between the controller and the switches thus do not affect the global synchronization. The causality check is performed at the controller, since it has the global dependency information of all the connected switches. Upon receiving an OpenFlow inquiry, the controller is responsible for making sure no response will be sent back to the switch (thus, the switch will not advance its clock further) until all its dependent switches have caught up with it in simulation time. In addition, this design does **not** require that the controller be modeled as an S3F entity, which means that the controller does not have to align with any timeline. All the interactions can be done through function calls instead of via message passing through S3F channels. This design works only for a passive controller and can greatly reduce the communication overhead between the controller and switches. As a result, a passive controller is not a bottleneck in conservatively synchronized parallel simulation, as low latency to switches and high fan-out might otherwise cause it to be.

Algorithm 1 Synchronization Algorithm with Passive Controller

```
Controller Side
/* Upon receiving an OpenFlow inquiry from switch r_i
with timestamp t_i */
for each application a_j related to the inquiry do
  for each switch r_k ∈ f(r_i, a_j) AND TL(r_k) ≠ TL(r_i)
  do
    get the current simulation time, t_k, of r_k
    if t_k < t_i then
      schedule a timing report event at time t_i on the
      timeline of r_k
      increase dcts[i] by 1
      /* dcts[i] is the counter of unresolved dependent
      cross-timeline switches for switch r_i */
    end if
  end for
end for

pthread_mutex_lock()
while dcts[i] > 0 do
  pthread_cond_wait()
end while
pthread_mutex_unlock()

process the inquiry (i.e., generate rules to handle packets)
send an OpenFlow response to switch r_i

Switch Side
/* Upon receiving a packet at an ingress port */
check flow tables
if found matched rule(s) then
  process the packet accordingly
else
  send an OpenFlow inquiry to the controller
end if

/* On reception of an OpenFLOW response */
store the rule(s) in the local flow table(s)
process the packet accordingly

/* Scheduled timing report event for switch r_i fires */
pthread_mutex_lock()
decrease dcts[i] by 1
if dcts[i] = 0 then
  pthread_cond_signal()
end if
pthread_mutex_unlock()
```

Figure 4 illustrates our synchronization algorithm with an example. The steps are as follows.

1. Switch r_1 sends an inquiry to the controller with $t_1(now)$

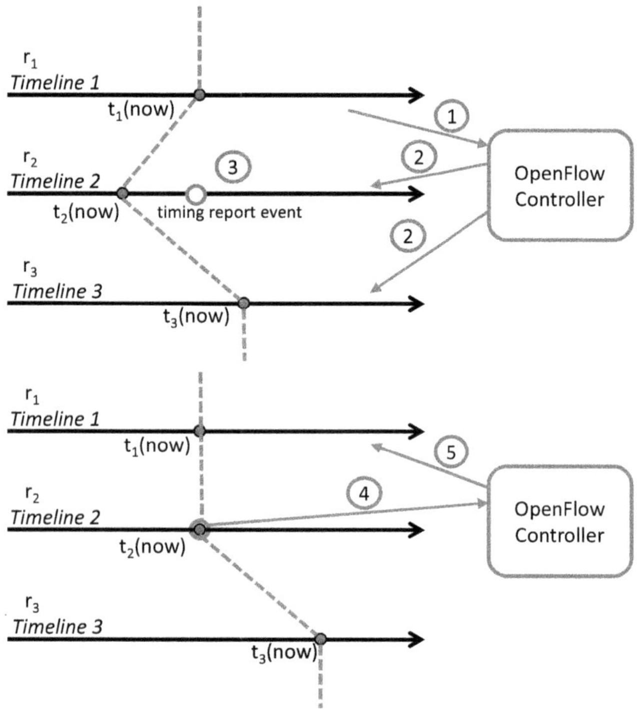

Figure 4: Sample Communication Patterns between the OpenFlow Switch and the Passive OpenFlow Controller Using Our Synchronization Algorithm

2. The controller gets the current times of all dependent cross-timeline switches, e.g., $t_2(now)$, $t_3(now)$

3. Because $t_2(now) < t_1(now)$, the controller schedules a timing report event at $t_1(now)$ on timeline 2; no event is scheduled on timeline 3 since $t_3(now) > t_1(now)$

4. At $t_1(now)$ on Timeline 2, r_2 signals the controller

5. The controller generates rule(s) based on the up-to-date states and sends a response back to r_1

The algorithm works for all passive controllers, whether the state is distributed (e.g., forwarding.l2_learning) or network-wide (e.g., forwarding.l2_multi). The state property plays an important role in the active controller design, which will be discussed in Section 4.2. However, the performance of passive controllers does benefit from use of distributed states as well as the smaller number of cross-timeline dependent switches.

4.2 Active Controller Design

Active OpenFlow controllers proactively send events to the connected OpenFlow switches, and those events can potentially affect the states of switches. Therefore, the switches do not have the freedom to advance the model states like those switches that connect to passive controllers, but are subject to the minimum link latency between the controller and the switches. However, the question we have is: are the assumptions about connectivity in SDNs overly pessimistic? For example, can any timeline generate an event at any instant that might affect every other timeline?

We make the following observations about the active controller applications. First, not all controllers have only network-wide states. Some have fully distributed states, e.g., a switch's on/off state (openflow.keep_alive application); some have states that are shared among a number of switches, e.g., a link's on/off state is shared among switches connected to the same link (openflow.link_discovery application). Second, not all events will result in global state changes, and quite often a large number of events are handled locally, and only influence switches' local states. For instance, only when a communication link fails, or when a link is recovered from failure or when some new switches join or leave the network, a link status change event is generated for the openflow.link_discovery application, so that it updates its global view; during the remaining (most of the) time, the network-wide state, i.e., the global topology, remains unchanged. Therefore, for such applications, instead of having a centralized controller frequently send messages to all the connected switches and wait for responses, we can first determine which events affect network-wide states and which do not, and then off-load those events, which only cause local state changes, towards the switch side. Thus, we relieve the pressure at the controller.

Based on our observations of active controller applications, we propose a two-level active controller architecture as depicted in Figure 5. Local states are separated from network-wide states in a controller, and the controller is divided into a top-controller and a number of local controllers. The top controller communicates only with the local controllers, not with the switches, to handle events that potentially affect the network-wide states. The local controllers run applications that can function using the local states in switches, e.g., the local policy enforcer, or link discovery. There are no links among local controllers. With the two-level controller design, we aim to improve the overall scalability, especially at the top controller, as follows:

- The top controller has a smaller degree, which is good for local synchronization approaches.
- Fewer messages are expected to occur among local controllers and the top controller for many applications, since the heavy communication is kept between the switches and local controllers. That is good for local synchronization approaches as well.
- If we align the switches that share the same local controller to the same timeline, the local controllers actually do not have to be modeled as an entity. Message passing through channels is not needed, as function calls are sufficient.

Conversion of a controller into a two-level architecture requires that modelers carefully analyze the states in the controller applications. That process is not only useful in creating a scalable simulation model, but also helpful in designing a high-performance real SDN controller, because it offloads local-events processing to local resources. In the remainder of this section, we will inspect three active controller applications with our two-level controller design: openflow.keep_alive with fully distributed states, openflow.link_discovery with shared states, and openflow.spanning_tree with network-wide states.

The **openflow.keep_alive** application is designed to send periodic echo requests to all connected switches to prevent loss of connections, since some switch firmware by default treats an idle link as a link failure. Meanwhile, the controller also maintains a complete list of the running switches in the network. Since the on/off state of a switch is independent of other switches, the openflow.keep_alive is an example of applications with fully distributed states. In the two-level controller design, one local controller is created for each switch. Let us now compute the total number of simulation events (e.g., message-sending events, message-receiving events, and time-out events) within one echo request period with the single controller and the two-level controller.

Assume that the network has n switches, and let p be the probability that a switch fails during one request period. In the single-controller case, the controller needs one timer event to enable the echo request sending process, and then sends one request to each switch. If a switch is working, the request is received at it, and it replies with a response; finally, the controller receives the response. If a switch fails, a timeout event occurs at the controller. Therefore, for the single-controller case, the total number of events within one period is $M_1 = 1 + n + (1 - p) * n * (1 + 1 + 1) + p * n = 1 + 4n - 2pn$. In the two-level controller case, we have n local controllers, and each local controller fires one timer event to start the request-sending process. Since the communication with the local controllers and the switches is modeled by function calls instead of by message passing, no event occurs as long as a switch is working. If a switch fails, the local controller reports the state change to the global controller, and the global controller receives the report. Therefore, for the two-level controller case, the total number of events within one period is $M_2 = n + p * n * (1 + 1) = n + 2pn$.

Assume $n \gg 1$; when the fail rate of a switch, p, is 0.75, the single-controller and the two-level controller have approximately the same total number of events. If $p < 0.75$, the two-level controller has fewer events to simulate. If p is close to 0, which means that switches rarely fail during experiments, $M_2 \approx n$ events, and $M_1 \approx 4n$ events. Also, let us count the total number of events processed at the top controller within one period. The single controller has the total number of events $C_1 = 1+n+n*(1-p)+n*p = 1+2n$, and the two-level controller has the total number of events $C_2 = np$. The latter is always smaller than the former, and thus the two-level controller for the openflow.keep_alive application results in a more scalable controller. Actually, it is possible to remove the top controller as long as all the applications running in the controller are fully distributed, like openflow.keep_alive. If so, we can prevent a single global controller from becoming a potential system bottleneck.

The **openflow.link_discovery** application periodically requests messages from switches in order to discover the link status, and switches raise events to the controller when links go up or down. Potentially, this application could be used to discover the network topology. The states of this application are the links' on/off states shared among all the switches connecting to the link. With the two-level controller design, we assign one local controller to each switch, and let the top controller manage the shared states.

Let us calculate the total number of simulation events within one link discovery period for both cases; the switch-switch and switch-host interactions are not counted, since they are the same for both cases. Assume that the network has n switches, and that the probability that a switch has at least one link state change is q. For the single-controller case, the controller fires one timer event to start the link discovery process, and then sends each switch a link discovery request. Upon receipt of the request at every switch, the switch sends back a response if at least one of its links has a state change. Finally, the response is received at the controller to update the global topology. Therefore, the total number of events within one period is $M_1 = 1+n+n+q*(n+n) = 1+2n+2qn$. For the two-level controller case, n local controllers fire one timer event each to start the link discovery process locally. Since the interaction between the local controller and the switch is modeled by function calls instead of by message passing, no event is generated if no link state change is detected. If a link change is discovered by the switch, the local controller then reports the change to the global controller, and the global controller receives the report. Therefore, the total number of events within one period for the two-level controller is $M_2 = n + q * n(1 + 1) = n + 2qn$. We can see that there are $2n$ fewer events than in the single-controller scenario. Let us count the number of events processed at the top controller within one period. The single controller has $1 + n + qn$ events, while the two-level controller has qn events. Therefore, the two-level controller always has better scalability, especially when the network has a relatively steady topology. The two-level controller is also a good reference design for the real link discovery application in the SDN controller. The number of packets being processed at the top controller is greatly reduced to achieve good scalability.

Good lookahead can improve performance in simulating networks with either the single controller or the two-level controller. We notice that the link discovery request is sent to the switch periodically. The period is often quite long compared with the time to transmit a packet, and the period can serve as a good source of lookahead. In addition, another optimization we could do is to model the top controller as a passive controller since the requests are now initiated at the local controllers.

The **openflow.spanning_tree** application establishes a spanning tree based on the network topology, and then it disables flooding on switch ports that are not on the tree. The application has only one state, the global network topology. The state is a network-wide state. Therefore, it is hard to convert this application to a two-level controller. However, the openflow.spanning_tree application still has invariants that we could utilize to improve the system performance.

S3F synchronizes its timelines at two levels. The inner level uses the barrier-synchronization and the channel-scanning-synchronization for parallel discrete-event simulation. At the outer level, timelines are left to run during an epoch, which could terminate either after a specified length of simulation time, or when the global state meets some specified conditions. Between epochs S3F allows a modeler to do computations that affect the global simulation state, without concern for interference by timelines. A spanning tree algorithm is often running at the beginning of an experiment and then is triggered by topology changes or a global timer. In the scenarios in which a network topology does not change frequently, it is reasonable to assume that the topology is invariant for a certain minimum length of time, and we can use that time length as the length of an epoch. Between two epochs, a spanning tree is recomputed. States (particular spanning trees) created by those computations

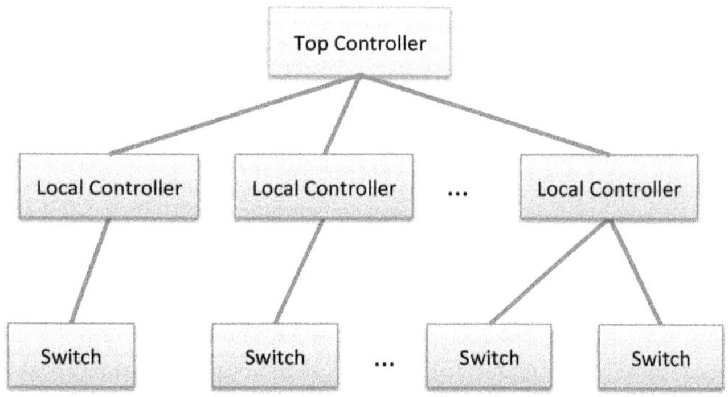

Figure 5: Two-level Controller Architecture

are otherwise taken to be constant when the simulation is running.

We have studied three active applications in the POX controller. Through careful application state analysis, we can often convert applications with local states into two-level controller architectures for simulation performance gain. The analysis not only helps modelers to create scalable SDN network models, but also helps in the design of scalable real SDN controllers. Many SDN applications can be far more complicated than the basic applications in POX. They could be a combination of passive and active applications, with both distributed and network-wide states, and the states may change dynamically with time and network conditions. Even so, it is still useful to divide a complex controller into small building-block applications, classify them according to the state type as well as passiveness/activeness, and then apply the corresponding performance optimization techniques.

5. EVALUATION

We first study the performance improvement with the asynchronous synchronization algorithm for the passive controllers. We created a network model with 16 timelines. The backbone of the network model consisted of 32 OpenFlow switches, and each switch connected 10 hosts. Half of the hosts ran client applications, and the other half ran server applications. File transfers between clients and servers were on UDP. The minimum communication link delay among switches and hosts was set to be 1 ms. During the experiments, each client randomly chose a server from across the entire network, and started to download a 10 KB file. Once the file transfer was complete, the client picked another server and started the downloading process again. All the OpenFlow switches connected to an OpenFlow controller, and the controller ran the openflow.learning_multi application, which is essentially a learning switch, but learns where a MAC address is by looking up the topology of the entire network. In the first case, we modeled the controller as a normal S3F entity, and it connected to switches through channels. In the second case, we used the passive controller design described in Section 4.1 . Since all switches shared the global network topology, they were dependent on one another. We ran the experiments on a machine with 16 2GHz-processors and 64 GB memory.

In the first set of experiments, we varied the link delay between the switches and the controller with values of 1 μs, 10 μs, 100 μs and 1 ms. Each experiment was executed for 100 seconds in simulation time for both cases. We observed 12,810 completed file transfers for both cases. Figure 6 shows the event-processing rates for both cases. In the first case, the traditional barrier-type global synchronization was used. Since the minimal controller-switch link delay was set to be no larger than other link delays within the network, that delay dominated the synchronization window calculation with the global synchronization algorithm in S3F. Therefore, the performance degraded as the minimum link latency decreased because of more frequent synchronization overheads. In the second case, synchronization was actually two-level: the global synchronization was used to simulate activities among switches and hosts, and within a synchronization window, the asynchronous synchronization algorithm was used to simulate interactions between the switches and the passive controller. Therefore, the controller-switch delay did not affect the global synchronization window size. For the passive controller case, the event-processing rate remained almost unchanged, and the performance was 2 to 3 times better than in the first case, when the controller-switch delay was small. The performance was still better in the second case even when the controller-switch link delay was set to 1 ms (equal to the minimal delay of the other links). The reason is that the interactions between the passive controller and the switches were through function calls instead of event-passings with S3F channels, which we explored further in the next set of experiments.

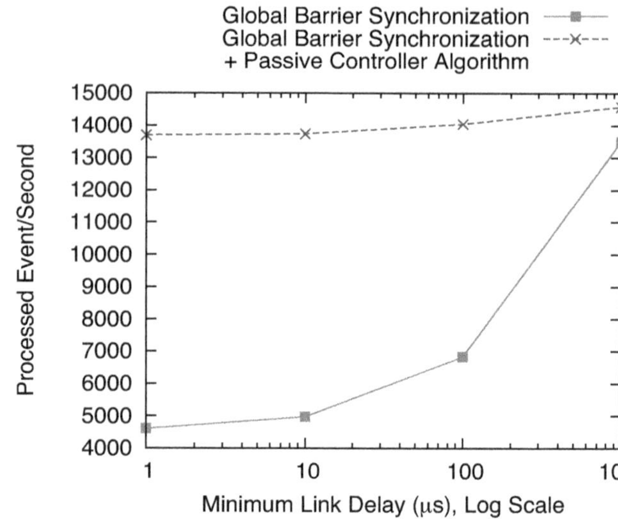

Figure 6: Performance Improvement with the Passive Controller Asynchronous Synchronization Algorithm: Minimal Controller-Switch Link Latency

In the second set of experiments, we increased the number of OpenFlow switches connected to the controller, and the size of the network was thus increased proportionally. Every client application performed the same actions as in the first experiment set. The model still used 16 timelines, and each experiment was simulated for 100 seconds with the two types of controller. Let λ be the event-processing rate of a model using the passive controller algorithm over the event-processing rate of the same model with the S3F entity controller. λ indicates the performance improvement of asynchronous synchronization designed for passive controllers. As shown in Figure 7, λ grows as the number of switches

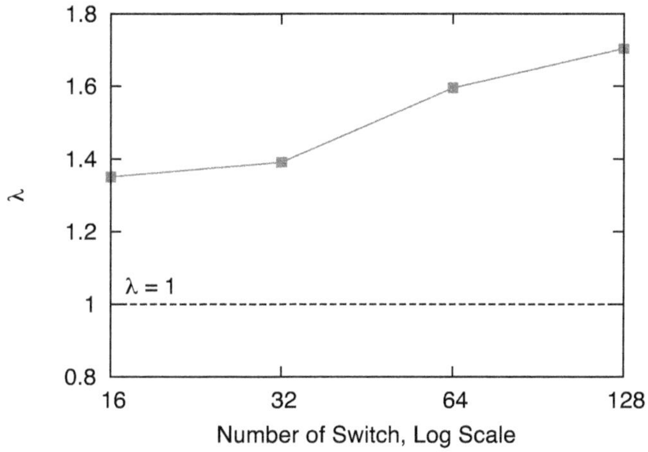

Figure 7: Performance Improvement with the Passive Controller Asynchronous Synchronization Algorithm: Number of OpenFlow Switches in the Network

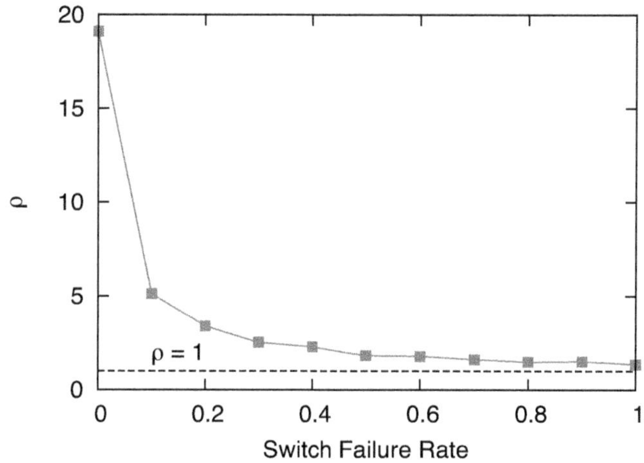

Figure 8: Performance Improvement for the openflow.keep_alive Application with a Two-level Controller Architecture

increases. Since each switch needs a larger flow table as the size of the network increases, switches have more interactions with the controller. As a result, the performance gain of replacing the message-passing mechanism with function calls for the controller-switch interactions is more prominent. In addition, the modeled controller application has a network-wide state, resulting in a fully dependent switch list in the passive controller. More performance improvement is expected for modeling controller applications with distributed states.

We also investigated the performance improvement with the two-level architecture for active controllers. The openflow. keep_alive application was developed with the two designs as discussed in Section 4.2: (1) a single centralized controller, and (2) a two-level controller in which the local controllers are responsible for querying switch states and reporting to the top controller when switch failures are discovered. The network model had 80 OpenFlow switches with a minimal link delay of 1 ms, running with 16 timelines. The switch state inquiry period was set to be 1 second. Let us define the performance indicator ρ to be the event-processing rate of a model using the two-level controller architecture over the event-processing rate of the same model using the single controller. We varied the switch failure rate, and the results are shown in Figure 8.

The model with the two-level controller performed better than the model with the single controller under all switch failure rates. The reasons are that (1) switches and their local controller were in the same timeline, and the switch state inquiry activities were well-parallelized; and (2) the switch state responses were sent back to the top controller only when switch failures were detected, resulting in less data communication with the top controller. Simulating a network with smaller switch failure rates had better performance, e.g., 19 times faster with a zero failure rate, and 5 times faster with a 10% failure rate, as shown in Figure 8.

6. CONCLUSION AND FUTURE WORK

In this paper, we described how we extended our network testbed, consisting of virtual-machine-based emulation and parallel simulation, to support OpenFlow-based SDNs. Users can conduct SDN-based network experiments with real OpenFlow switch and controller programs in virtual-time-embedded emulations for high functional and temporal fidelity, or with OpenFlow switch and controller simulation models for scalability, or with both. We also explore ways to improve the scalability of the centralized simulated controllers, including an asynchronous synchronization algorithm for passive controllers and a two-level architecture design for active controllers, which also serves as a useful guideline for real SDN controller design.

We plan to evaluate the network-level and application-level behaviors for different SDN applications under various network scenarios (e.g., long delay, or lossy link). We would also like to conduct a performance comparison with ground truth data collected from a real physical SDN testbed as well as data collected from other testbeds, like MiniNet. In addition, we plan to utilize the testbed to design and evaluate SDN applications, especially in the context of the smart grid; an example would be design of efficient quality-of-service mechanisms in substation routers, where all types of smart grid traffic aggregate.

7. ACKNOWLEDGMENTS

This material is based upon work supported in part by the Department of Energy under Award Number DE-OE0000097, and by the Boeing Corporation [1].

[1]Disclaimer: This report was prepared as an account of work sponsored by an agency of the United States Government. Neither the United States Government nor any agency thereof, nor any of their employees, makes any warranty, express or implied, or assumes any legal liability or responsibility for the accuracy, completeness, or usefulness of any information, apparatus, product, or process disclosed, or represents that its use would not infringe privately owned rights. Reference herein to any specific commercial product, process, or service by trade name, trademark, manufacturer, or otherwise does not necessarily constitute or imply its endorsement, recommendation, or favoring by the United States Government or any agency thereof. The views and opinions of authors expressed herein do not necessarily

8. REFERENCES

[1] Openflow switch specification version 1.1.0. http://www.openflow.org/documents/openflow-spec-v1.1.0.pdf, 2011.

[2] ns-3 OpenFlow switch support. http://www.nsnam.org/docs/release/3.13/models/html/openflow-switch.html, Accessed 2012.

[3] OFTest, a Python based OpenFlow switch test framework. http://www.openflow.org/wk/index.php/OFTestTutorial, Accessed 2012.

[4] Open vSwitch. http://openvswitch.org/, Accessed 2012.

[5] OpenFlow Switching Reference System. http://www.openflow.org/wp/downloads/, Accessed 2012.

[6] POX. http://www.noxrepo.org/pox/about-pox/, Accessed 2012.

[7] R. Ayani. *A parallel simulation scheme based on distances between objects*. Royal Institute of Technology, Department of Telecommunication Systems-Computer Systems, 1988.

[8] K. Chandy and J. Misra. Distributed simulation: A case study in design and verification of distributed programs. *IEEE Transactions on Software Engineering*, (5):440–452, 1979.

[9] Google. Inter-Datacenter WAN with centralized TE using SDN and OpenFlow. https://www.opennetworking.org/images/stories/downloads/misc/googlesdn.pdf, Accessed 2012.

[10] N. Handigol, B. Heller, V. Jeyakumar, B. Lantz, and N. McKeown. Reproducible network experiments using container-based emulation. In *Proceedings of the 8th international conference on Emerging networking experiments and technologies*, pages 253–264. ACM, 2012.

[11] D. Jin and D. Nicol. Fast simulation of background traffic through fair queueing networks. In *Proceedings of the 2010 Winter Simulation Conference (WSC)*, pages 2935–2946, Baltimore, MD, December 2010.

[12] D. Jin, Y. Zheng, H. Zhu, D. Nicol, and L. Winterrowd. Virtual time integration of emulation and parallel simulation. In *Proceedings of the 2012 Workshop on Principles of Advanced and Distributed Simulation (PADS)*, pages 120–130, Zhangjiajie, China, July 2012.

[13] B. Lantz, B. Heller, and N. McKeown. A network in a laptop: rapid prototyping for software-defined networks. In *Proceedings of the Ninth ACM SIGCOMM Workshop on Hot Topics in Networks*, page 19. ACM, 2010.

[14] B. Lubachevsky. Efficient distributed event-driven simulations of multiple-loop networks. *Communications of the ACM*, 32(1):111–123, 1989.

[15] N. McKeown, T. Anderson, H. Balakrishnan, G. Parulkar, L. Peterson, J. Rexford, S. Shenker, and J. Turner. OpenFlow: Enabling innovation in campus networks. *ACM SIGCOMM Computer Communication Review*, 38(2):69–74, 2008.

[16] D. Nicol. The cost of conservative synchronization in parallel discrete event simulations. *Journal of the ACM (JACM)*, 40(2):304–333, 1993.

[17] D. Nicol, J. Liu, M. Liljenstam, and G. Yan. Simulation of large scale networks using SSF. In *Proceedings of the 2003 IEEE Winter Simulation Conference*, volume 1, pages 650–657, 2003.

[18] D. Nicol and G. Yan. High-performance simulation of low-resolution network flows. *Journal of Simulation*, 82(1):21–42, 2006.

[19] D. M. Nicol, D. Jin, and Y. Zheng. S3F: The Scalable Simulation Framework revisited. In *Proceedings of the 2011 Winter Simulation Conference (WSC)*, pages 3283–3294, Phoenix, AZ, December 2011.

[20] R.Sherwood. OFlops. http://www.openflow.org/wk/index.php/Oflops, Accessed 2012.

[21] Y. Zheng, D. Jin, and D. M. Nicol. Validation of application behavior on a virtual time integrated network emulation testbed. In *Proceedings of the Winter Simulation Conference*, page 246, 2012.

[22] Y. Zheng, D. M. Nicol, D. Jin, and N. Tanaka. A virtual time system for virtualization-based network emulations and simulations. *Journal of Simulation*, 6(3):205–213, August 2012.

state or reflect those of the United States Government or any agency thereof.

Event Pool Structures for PDES on Many-Core Beowulf Clusters

Tom Dickman
School of Electronic and Computing Systems
Cincinnati, OH 45221-0030
tdickman@gmail.com

Sounak Gupta
School of Electronic and Computing Systems
Cincinnati, OH 45221-0030
sounak.besu@gmail.com

Philip A. Wilsey
School of Electronic and Computing Systems
Cincinnati, OH 45221-0030
wilseypa@gmail.com

ABSTRACT

Multi-core and many-core processing chips are becoming widespread and are now being widely integrated into Beowulf clusters. This poses a challenging problem for distributed simulation as it now becomes necessary to extend the algorithms to operate on a platform that includes both shared memory and distributed memory hardware. Furthermore, as the number of on-chip cores grows, the challenges for developing solutions without significant contention for shared data structures grows. This is especially true for the pending event list data structures where multiple execution threads attempt to schedule the next event for execution. This problem is especially aggravated in parallel simulation, where event executions are generally fine-grained leading quickly to non-trivial contention for the pending event list.

This manuscript explores the design of the software architecture and several data structures to manage the pending event sets for execution in a Time Warp synchronized parallel simulation engine. The experiments are especially targeting multi-core and many-core Beowulf clusters containing 8-core to 48-core processors. These studies include a two-level structure for holding the pending event sets using three different data structures, namely: splay trees, the STL multiset, and ladder queues. Performance comparisons of the three data structures using two architectures for the pending event sets are presented.

Categories and Subject Descriptors

D.1.3 [**Programming Techniques**]: Concurrent Programming—*parallel programming, distributed programming*
; I.6.8 [**Simulation and Modeling**]: Types of Simulation—*parallel, distributed, discrete event*

General Terms

Algorithms, Performance

Keywords

Time Warp, pending event lists, multi-core, threads, Beowulf clusters

1. INTRODUCTION

Trends in desktop microprocessors have shown that the shift from multi-core to many-core is on the horizon. The road maps of all the major processor providers (Intel, AMD, and IBM) clearly show this progression. Both Intel and AMD have commodity multi-core processors with hardware support for up to 16 simultaneous threads. These can be configured in multi-chip motherboards for a hardware SMP configuration supporting as many as 64 simultaneous threads. IBM's Power7 product is expected to support up to 32 threads per chip [9]. Intel has demonstrated a 48 core Single-Chip Cloud computer (SCC) [8] and a 50-core Knights Corner (both implementing x86 compatible cores). Following these patterns, it is clear that desktop processors may soon contain hardware support providing capabilities for hundreds of simultaneously executing threads.

As the number of cores increases, it is increasingly challenging for application software to take advantage of the additional parallel processing capabilities. The key to successfully harnessing this power lies with new advances to better introduce parallelism into the practice of computer system and software development [6]. From the standpoint of parallel discrete event driven simulation (PDES), one of the key challenge areas lies in the need for solutions providing effective, contention-free pending event list management. This is especially true since many discrete event simulation models tend to have relatively fine-grained computational requirements making frequent access to the pending event set necessary.

In this manuscript, we examine the design of a software architecture and data structures to hold the pending event sets on each node of a many-core Beowulf cluster executing Time Warp synchronized parallel simulations. In particular, we examine a two-level structure to manage the pending event sets and evaluate three different data structures (splay tree, STL multiset, and ladder queues) within the two-level structure. The two-level structure explores a multiple-worker-thread/multiple-event-pool model that is ultimately designed for many-core processors with lightweight on-chip load balancing. In this paper the preliminary implementation using various configurations of the event-pool model without dynamic load balancing is examined. Explorations with the ladder queue are especially significant as we have future plans to exploit its bucketing of events to build a shared event pool that is fully managable with atomic move instructions — implementing a wait-free pending event list. This concept is more fully discussed in Section 6.

The remainder of this manuscript is organized as follows. Section 2 reviews the previous literature on pending event list management in Time Warp simulation. Section 3 provides a brief background review of the ladder queue data structure. Section 4 reviews the software architecture of the Time Warp simulation kernel (WARPED) that is used in this work. Section 5 presents the results of our experimental analysis. Section 6 contains a discussion on some possible extensions of the event pool structures studied in this work. Finally, Section 7 presents some concluding remarks.

2. RELATED WORK

Events in WARPED are organized into two event pools, namely: `Unprocessed` and `Processed` [18]. The incoming events, waiting to be executed, are stored in the `Unprocessed` pool. To a certain degree, the WARPED design inherently incorporates tolerance towards the execution order of events in their causal order. The existing `Unprocessed` events are optimistically executed and since the processed events may be required for later reexecution, they are moved to a holding list called the `Processed` queue [12]. This model is used elsewhere in other time warp synchronized simulators. For example, Ronngren *et al* [18] discuss the use of `Linear List` which is essentially a doubly linked list structure that can hold all events (processed and unprocessed) along with information about the execution status of each event. This design allows for simple implementation, quick and efficient rollback as well as efficient `fossil` collection. The effectiveness of this structure is questioned in [18] because of inefficient insertion into a significantly large `Unprocessed` event pool. They suggest the use of an improved skew heap as a possible data structure for storing the events to be executed.

Prasad *et al* [14] explored parallelized Calendar Queues [3] for medium to coarse-grained optimistic simulators. Separate calender queues are allocated to each processor. They observed from a comparative study between the global-queue-based and local-queue-based simulators that both achieved excellent load balancing with the former being faster with fewer rollbacks. They also exploited the property of *grain packing* in parallel heap for fine-grained simulation.

Santoro *et al* [20] explored a version of a Least-TimeStamp-First (LTSF) Scheduler that is somewhat similar to the Calendar Queue, except it is created using an array and a hierarchical bitmap. The main advantage that this data structure provides versus the Calendar Queue is that access to it is in constant-time, and it has low-overhead.

3. LADDER QUEUE

The ladder queue data structure [22] is a bucket based priority queue that shares many characteristics with calendar queues [3]. The chief advantage of a ladder queue is that the buckets (months) storing events are dynamically split when the number of stored events exceed some threshold. Thus, instead of resizing the entire data structure as is done in calendar queues, ladder queues simply break the bucket in question up into another collection of buckets. An illustration of the principle components of a ladder queue is shown in Figure 1. A brief description of the operation of a ladder queue is presented below.

Initially the ladder is empty and incoming events are linked (unsorted) together in the `Top` component. As they arrive, the minimum and maximum timestamps on the events in `Top` are recorded. When the first "dequeue event" operation occurs, all of the events in `Top` are transferred to the buckets in `Rung[1]`. The number of buckets in `Rung[1]` is a dynamically configurable parameter. Each bucket in `Rung[1]` is defined to hold events for a time range that equally subdivides the range between the minimum and maximum timestamps of all events that were originally in `Top`. The events from `Top` are placed (unsorted) into the bucket in `Rung[1]` corresponding to its timestamp.

The buckets in the ladder queue are defined to hold a maximum number of events. Whenever the number of events in a bucket exceed this maximum, a new lower `Rung` in the ladder is defined and those events are redistributed into it, and so on. An example of this redistribution is shown in Figure 1. Note the redistribution of the events from the 5th bucket in `Rung[1]` into `Rung[2]`).

To complete the dequeue event, all events from the leftmost non-empty time bucket (containing events with the smallest timestamps) are sorted and placed in `Bottom`. The dequeue operation then pulls the first event out of `Bottom`. Successive dequeue event operations pull from `Bottom` until it is empty which then triggers another pull of events from the leftmost non-empty bucket in the ladder. Once all of the buckets in the rungs of the ladder are empty, events are once again pulled down into the rungs of the ladder from `Top`.

After the initial ladder is constructed, incoming events are distributed into the ladder according to their timestamp. Those falling into the time window for the rungs in the ladder are placed into the corresponding rung/bucket location (including being sorted into `Bottom` if that is where it falls). Incoming events with a timestamp greater than the maximum timestamp used to create the ladder rungs are placed in `Top` (where new minimum/maximum timestamps are recorded).

Conceptually, the ladder queue is organized into epochs where the `Bottom` and `Rung` elements hold events with timestamps between t and $t + \Delta t$ while the `Top` element holds events with timestamps above $t + \Delta t$. Incoming events populate the ladder queue elements accordingly and once the dequeue operations empty the `Bottom` and `Rung` elements, another ladder queue epoch occurs and the events in `Top` repopulate the ladder `Rungs` and `Bottom`. Coincident with a new epoch, the time range of the ladder (t to $t + \Delta t$) is redefined by the minimum and maximum timestamps of events pulled from `Top`. There are a few additional special case situations that are more fully described in [22].

4. WARPED: A TIME WARP SIMULATION KERNEL

WARPED is a discrete event simulation kernel that implements the Time Warp synchronization protocol [10]. It was originally designed and optimized for executing parallel simulations on a Beowulf Cluster containing single core processors. It is highly configurable and incorporates many different sub-algorithms (*e.g.,* periodic checkpointing [5], and lazy, aggressive, and dynamic cancellation [16]) of the Time

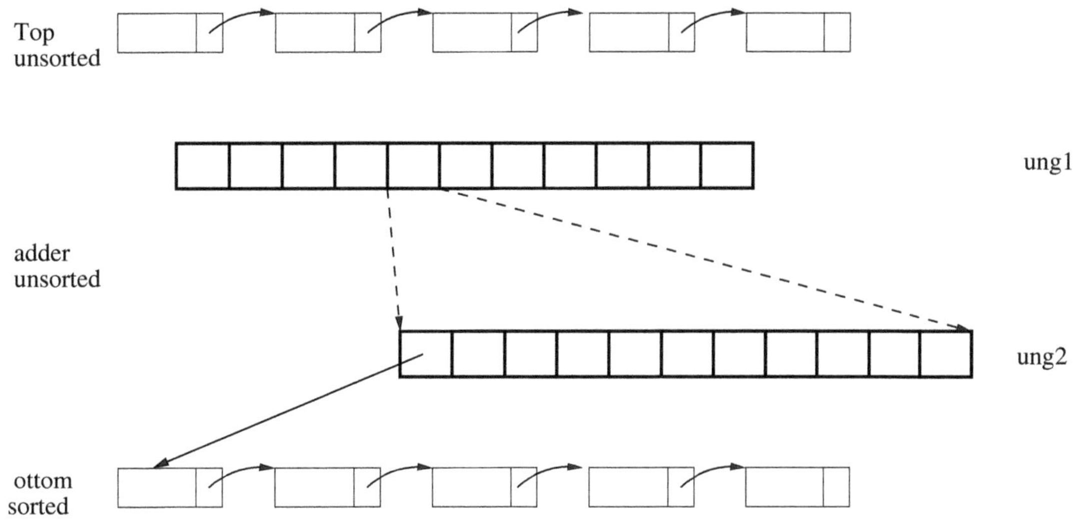

Figure 1: Illustration of the Ladder Queue Structure

Warp mechanism [5]. Structurally, the Logical Processes (LPs) of a simulation are grouped together on each processing node where the LPs are scheduled according to a Least-Timestamp-First (LTSF) event scheduling policy. The node architecture reduces the Time Warp housekeeping functions such as GVT estimation, termination detection, and fossil collection into a set of common services for the entire population of LPs on that node. This architecture is similar to that reported in [1] and [15].

Most recently several attempts to build a threaded extension of WARPED have been pursued [11, 12]. These studies have produced a solution that works reasonably well for smaller multi-core processors. The overall design structure depicting the main pending event pool and the executing threads is shown in Figure 2. A threaded instance of WARPED contains a manager thread and one or more worker threads. The *manager thread* (labeled `M` in Figure 2) processes the Time Warp housekeeping functions and also processes the receipt and transmission of event messages exchanged with remote nodes in the cluster (local event insertion is performed by the worker threads). Additional details on the operation of the manager thread are available in [12]. The *worker threads* (depicted as `W0` and `Wn` in Figure 2) are responsible for dequeueing and executing pending events and generating new events accordingly. The pending event sets are organized into a two level structure as described below.

The pending event lists for each LP are maintained as independent sorted[1] lists that are independently locked. The lowest timestamped event from each LP event list is placed in a common LTSF pending event queue. The (locked) LTSF queue is sorted and used by the *worker threads* to schedule the next event for execution. After dequeuing and processing an event from the LTSF, each worker thread will then access the pending event set of the LP corresponding to the event just executed and remove the next least-timestamped event for insertion back into the LTSF queue. An abstract representation of the general event processing algorithm performed by the worker threads is shown in Figure 3.

[1]Although the prospect of using a partially sorted data structure such as calendar queues [3], lazy queues [19], or ladder queues [22] is possible.

```
worker_thread()

  lock LTSF queue
  dequeue smallest event from LTSF
  unlock LTSF queue

  while !done loop

    process event (assume from LPi)

    lock LPi queue

    dequeue smallest event from LPi

    lock LTSF queue

    insert event from LPi
    dequeue smallest event from LTSF

    unlock LTSF queue
    unlock LPi queue
  end loop
```

Figure 3: Generalized event execution loop for the worker threads. Many details have been omitted for the sake of clarity.

While the above described design works well when the system is configured with only a few worker threads, once the number of worker threads exceeds 5-6, contention for the LTSF queue begins to negatively impact performance. Since the LP event pools are independently locked and since only one worker thread and the manager thread will simultaneously access the same LP event pool, contention to these structures is minimized. The principle point of contention for pending events in this architecture are at the LTSF queue. Thus, this study examines alternate designs

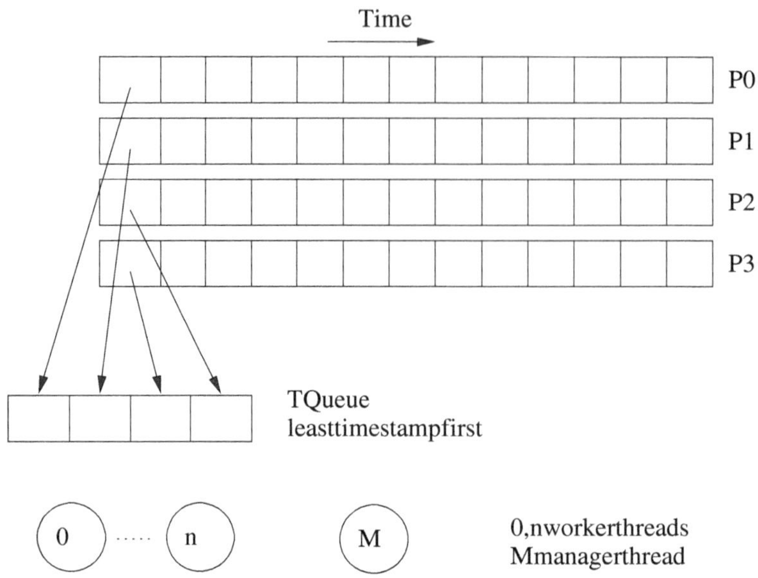

Figure 2: The principle input queues in warped.

for organizing the pending event list and especially the LTSF queue.

5. EXPERIMENTAL ANALYSIS

This study pursues two main issues with the pending event lists in the above described implementation of threaded WARPED. The first part of this study is to address the contention issue to the LTSF queue. We address this problem by creating multiple instances of the LTSF queue and partitioning the worker threads and the LPs to one of the LTSF queues. The second part of this study is the use of alternate data structures underlying the implementation of the LTSF queue. In particular, we study replacing the multiset from the C++ standard template library (STL) with two alternates, namely: (i) splay trees [21] and (ii) ladder queues [22]. These experiments are described in details below.

The following experiments are all performed on the same machine to ease comparison between different simulation configurations, and to keep results consistent. All simulations were performed on a machine with 48 cores with different configurations for the number of executing threads. The machine has four 12-core AMD Opteron 6168 processors, with each core running at a clock rate of 1.9GHz. The machine is configured with 64 GB of RAM.

The following simulation models are used for the experimental analysis:

RAID-5: This simulation model represents a Level 5 RAID (Redundant Array of Inexpensive Disks) setup as seen in Figure 4. The simulation model is composed of 136 logical processes (LPs) that simulate 32 disks, 8 forks and 96 sources. The sources generate requests for data from the array, and these requests pass through the respective forks, which divide each request to the necessary disks. Each disk then responds to this request for data after a predetermined amount of time that simulates the access time to that sector of the disk. This simulation is performed until the global execution time reaches one hundred thousand seconds.

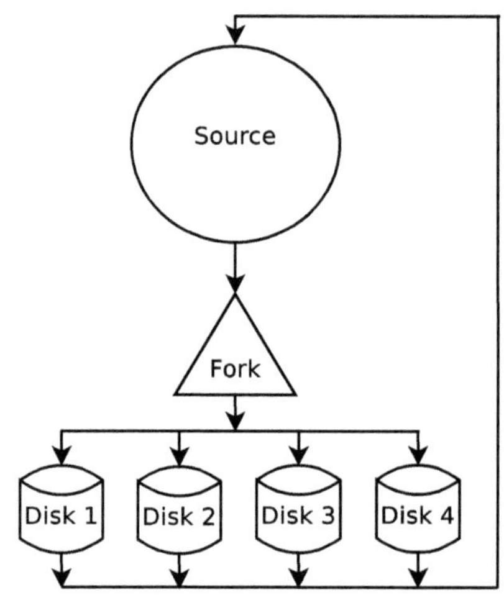

Figure 4: RAID-5 Simulation Model

High-level ISCAS-85 benchmark circuits: The ISCAS-85 benchmarks are comprised of several different combinational logic circuits [7]. Our experiments are performed using two of these circuits, namely: C2670 and C7552. The C2670 circuit emulates a 12-bit ALU and controller. The circuit consists of an ALU with a comparator, an equality checker and several parity trees. The circuit has 157 input lines, 64 output lines, 1193 logic gates and 7 major functional blocks. These specifications translate to 1414 logical processes (LPs) for the simulation model. The second circuit, C7552, emulates a 32-bit adder/comparator. The circuit consists of a 32-bit adder, a 32-bit magnitude comparator using another 32-bit adder and a parity checker. The circuit has 207 input lines, 108 output lines, 3512 logic gates and 8 major functional blocks. These specifications translate to 3827 LPs for the simulation model.

5.1 Experiments with Multiple LTSF Queues

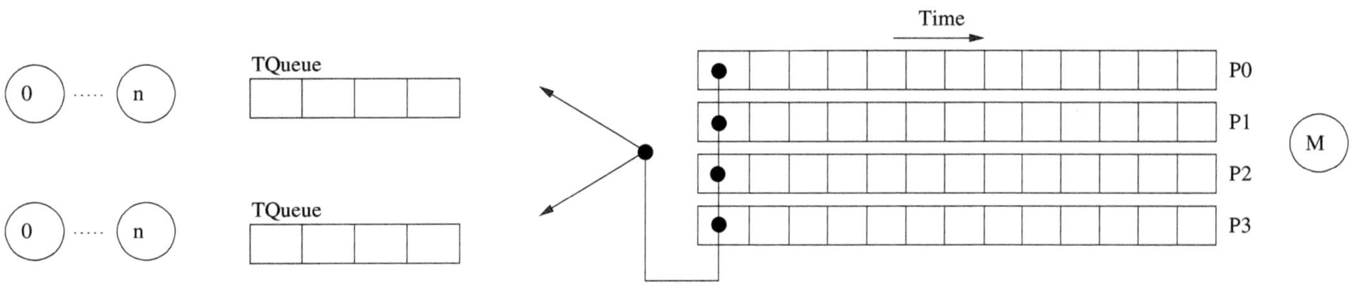

Figure 5: The principle input queues in warped.

As previous mentioned, the shared LTSF queue in WARPED (Figure 2) starts to become a bottleneck when the number of worker threads is increased beyond approximately 5 or 6. To address this contention, we have modified the WARPED kernel to support multiple LTSF queues (Figure 5). In our preliminary implementation of multiple LTSF queues, the worker threads are divided into independent groups that are statically (and permanently) assigned to an LTSF queue (in Figure 5, the two groups of worker threads denoted W0· · · Wn, represent independent sets). Likewise, the LPs are divided and statically assigned to LTSF queues. The LTSF queues are then populated with events from their assigned LPs as outlined above in the single LTSF implementation.

In our preliminary studies with multiple LTSF queues, we experienced wide variations in runtimes from run to run of the same configuration of the RAID model. Due to this instability, we started examining the partitioning of LPs to LTSF queues. As a result, several different approaches were explored for binding LPs to LTSF queues in an attempt to stabilize the system. In particular, we attempted to follow the source dependency chain of event flow between the LPs of the simulation model to guide the partitioning. However, this contributed no noticeable performance gain or stability improvement and thus, none of these results are included in this paper. For the results in this manuscript, the partitioning was a simple round robin assignment of LPs to LTSF queues. Further analysis and discussion of this performance variance issue is provided at the end of this section.

Simulations were performed with several different configurations that varied the numbers of worker threads. In particular, configurations of 4, 8, 16, 32, and 48 worker threads were studied. We also explored several different configurations of LTSF queues. Specifically we ran experiments with 1, 2, 4, and 8 LTSF queues. The number of LTSF queues was increased by a power of two so the number of threads was evenly divisible by the LTSF queues in an attempt to keep the simulations balanced. All results were obtained by taking the median of ten simulation runs. These results from these LTSF queue experiments are described below.

5.1.1 RAID-5

As shown in Figure 6, increasing the number of LTSF queues causes a decrease in execution time. In all cases, going from one LTSF queue to two queues causes a substantial decrease in the execution time. This occurs due to the decrease in contention as the number of LTSF queues increases. This decrease in simulation time continues for all thread configurations up to 4 LTSF queues. The simulation results in Figure 6 show a slight decrease in simulation time when moving from 4 to 8 LTSF queues for the 48 threaded version. This decrease can likely be attributed to the further decrease in contention when moving from 12 threads per LTSF queue to 6 threads per LTSF queue. All other simulations see an increase in simulation time when moving to 8 LTSF queues, due to the low number of threads bound to each LTSF queue.

5.1.2 ISCAS-85

As shown in Figure 7, all configurations show a decrease in simulation time when going from one to two LTSF queues. The simulations with a larger number of threads continue to show a decrease in simulation time as the number of LTSF queues is increased. All simulations have the minimum simulation time when the number of threads assigned to each LTSF queue is between four and eight. As shown in Figure 8, the c7552 simulation shows similar results, except the simulation time decreases in a more linear manner as the number of threads is increased. It also shows that the optimal number of threads per LTSF queue is between four and eight.

In previous studies with a single LTSF queue, Muthalagu [12] reports that simulation times start to increase when more than 6 threads are used in a simulation model. We arrived at a similar ratio (between four and eight threads per LTSF queue) when using the ISCAS-85 benchmark circuits as explained in the section above. By using multiple LTSF queues, we are able to reduce this contention by assigning fewer threads to each LTSF queue.

When more than eight LTSF queues are used, the simulation time is highly variant. This variance can likely be linked to the increase in the number of rollbacks that occur due to the unbalanced nature of having a large number of LTSF queues. For example, when using a single LTSF queue, the number of rollbacks was very low, almost zero. When multiple LTSF queues were used, the number of rollbacks increased significantly. An increase was expected, but this is likely due to an instability caused by the large number of LTSF queues. For example, if the LPs assigned to one LTSF queue contain fewer events, this may result in a large number of rollbacks when the LPs in one LTSF queue get too far ahead of the events in the other LTSF queue. One potential solution for this is some sort of load balancing algorithm to reassign LPs to keep any one LTSF queue from containing events with timestamps too different from the other LTSF queue.

5.2 Experiments with Ladder Queues

In this section, we present a comparative study of performance of threaded WARPED based on manipulation of the

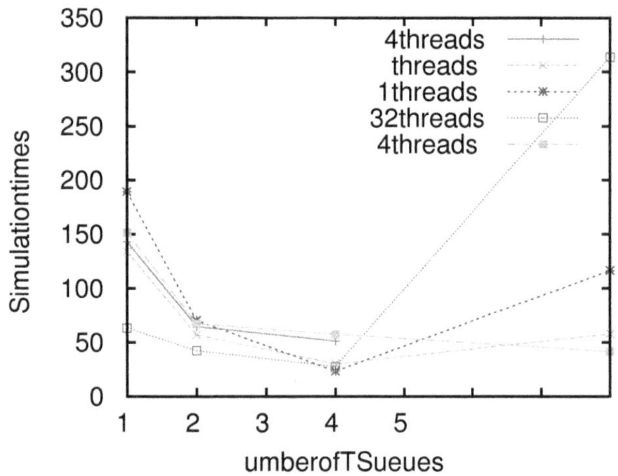

Figure 6: Performance of Multiple LTSF Queues using STL Multiset on RAID-5

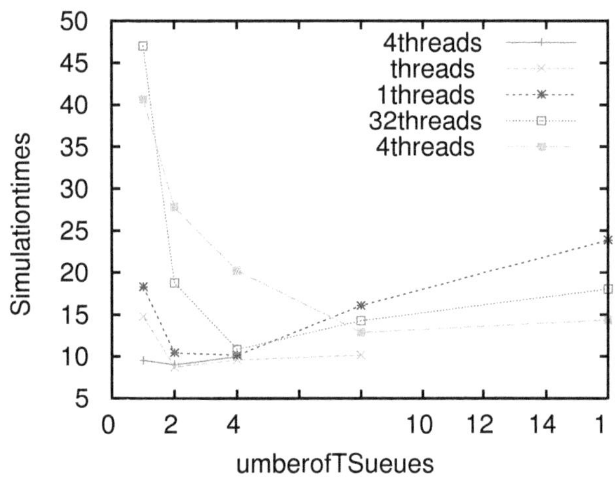

Figure 7: Performance of Multiple LTSF Queues using STL Multiset on ISCAS c2670

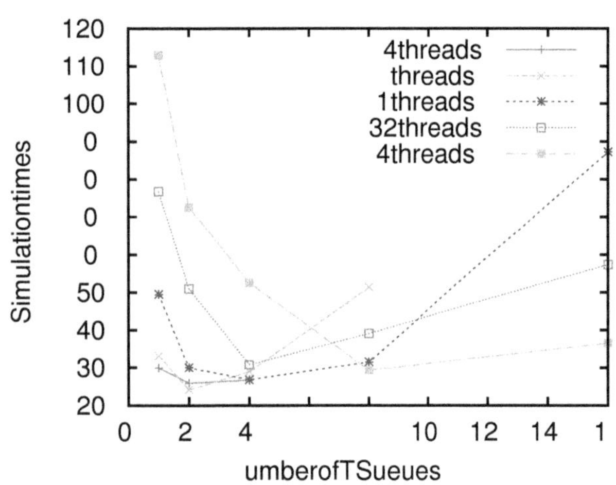

Figure 8: Performance of Multiple LTSF Queues using STL Multiset on ISCAS c7552

underlying data structure of LTSF queue. Prior to this study, the LTSF queues in threaded WARPED were based on the multiset object from the C++ Standard Template Library (STL). The STL multiset is an implementation of red-black tree, a type of balanced binary search tree. The asymptotic run time for insertion, deletion and lookup in a red-black tree is O(log n) [2]. We replaced the STL multiset data structure used for the LTSF queue with the Splay tree data structure. Splay tree is a self-adjusting binary search tree where recently accessed elements can be accessed again quickly. Insertion, look-up and deletion can be performed in O(log n) *amortized* [23] time. The splay tree library used in threaded WARPED is a faithful implementation of the splay tree algorithm [21].

The ladder queue data structure has already been introduced in Section 3 with a brief discussion about the potential benefits of its use as the underlying data structure for the LTSF queues. The empirical evidence presented by Tang *et al* [22] illustrates that Ladder queue exhibits O(1) *amortized* [23] complexity.

While implementing and testing the ladder queue data structure, an issue with the original algorithm [22] arose. In particular, a problem arises when, during a redistribution event, the time window of the bucket is smaller than the number of buckets in a new lower rung. More precisely, recall that a redistribution of events in a bucket occurs when the number of events in that bucket exceeds some (configurable, but static) `threshold`. The events are redistributed into a new lower rung that has a number of buckets equal to the `threshold`. Thus, let t to $t + \Delta t$ be the size of the time window for event timestamps stored in a bucket in Rung[i]. If Δt is less than `threshold`, then a new rung cannot be defined (the time cannot be decomposed into `threshold` subparts). In this case, if the bucket in question is not the first non-empty bucket of the last rung, our algorithm simply allows the bucket size to grow beyond the `threshold` and a redistribution event does not occur.

When the number of events in the first non-empty bucket of the last rung exceeds the `threshold`, we allow the events of that bucket to be moved to the `Bottom` structure of the ladder queue. Figure 9 provides the pseudo-code for our implementation of the Ladder Queue.

This deviation from the original ladder design calls for handling of the situation where the number of events in `Bottom` exceeds a certain `threshold`. Under this circumstance, as a design compromise, we allow the algorithm to ignore the specified `threshold` for number of events in `Bottom`.

The results from the tests we performed in threaded WARPED using Ladder Queue, STL Multiset and Splay Tree on a single LTSF queue respectively are presented in Figures 10, 15 and 20. Figures 10 and 15 clearly point towards superior performance of Ladder Queue for most configurations of the simulation. However, Figure 20 does not point in the same direction as the other two figures. Here the Ladder Queue seems to perform on par with Splay Tree and STL multiset until the number of worker threads reaches 32, after which its performance degrades. The degradation in Ladder Queue's performance on transition of the number of worker threads from 32 to 48 is likely due to thread swapping on one or more of the processor cores. The threaded WARPED kernel requires a manager thread in addition to the configured number of worker threads(here 48). The hardware platform in use has 48-cores only. The ISCAS-85 benchmark circuits are a re-

```
if (new event insertion location is first non-empty bucket of last rung) then

  if (first non-empty bucket of last rung exceeds threshold) then

    /* trigger for new rung creation */
    if (bucket width of last rung equals 1) then
      transfer events from that bucket to bottom
      insert the new event directly into bottom

    else

      /* calculate bucket width of new rung */
      bucket width of new rung =
        bucket width of previous rung / max bucket length
      transfer events from that bucket to the new rung

      /* new rung now becomes the last rung */
      insert the new event in the appropriate bucket of new rung

    end if

  else /* first non-empty bucket of last rung does not exceed threshold */

    insert new event into the bucket

  end if

else /* new event insertion location somewhere else */
  continue with faithful implementation

end if
```

Figure 9: Ladder Queue with the modifications introduced for threaded warped. Many details have been omitted for sake of clarity.

cent addition to our inventory of simulation models. We are still in the process of understanding the nature of event sets that are being generated by these circuits. We suspect that Ladder queue's performance might be getting affected by improper distribution of events in the rung structure. Locking individual rungs, rather than the entire Ladder Queue data structure, is one promising approach for performance enhancement we plan to incorporate in our future work.

5.3 Experiments Combining Ladder and Multi-LTSF Queues

This section combines the work from the previous two sections and explores various configurations using the different data structures underlying the LTSF queue with multiple instances of the LTSF queue. Throughout the remainder of this section, each performance plot shows the simulation time for a fixed number of LTSF queues, and varies the number of threads to show the performance as the number of threads is increased. The number of LTSF queues used is given in the figure caption.

Figures 10, 11 and 15 show that the ladder queue is faster under most circumstances. This can likely be attributed to the proper distribution of events in the `rung` structure and O(1) complexity of the ladder queue.

Figures 12, 16, 17, 20 and 21 show the ladder queue as being only slightly faster or similar in performance. This is likely due to thread-level contention or uneven distribution of events in the `rung` structure during one or more `epochs`. We suspect that migrating the locking mechanism in Ladder Queue to the individual `rungs` would lead to superior performance of Ladder queue for these simulations. This is one avenue we plan to explore further.

Figure 22 shows the Splay tree outperforming Ladder Queue when the number of worker threads is set to 16. This sudden poor performance of the Ladder Queue might well be another example of contention issues.

Figures 13, 14, 18, 19, 23 and 24 display somewhat erratic performance for 8 and 16 LTSF queues. This is likely due to the upper limit for the ideal number of LTSF queues. Dynamic load balancing between the LTSF queues, as explained in sections 5.1 and 6, could partially reduce the effects of this. Further analysis will be necessary to fully understand what is occurring.

Many plots show an interesting simulation time convergence at 32 threads and subsequent divergence for 48 threads. As explained at the end of section 5.2, it is likely due to thread swapping on one or more of the processor cores.

6. DISCUSSION

This study pursues two main issues with the pending event lists in the above described implementation of threaded WARPED. The first part of this study is to address the contention when accessing the LTSF queue. We address this problem by repli-

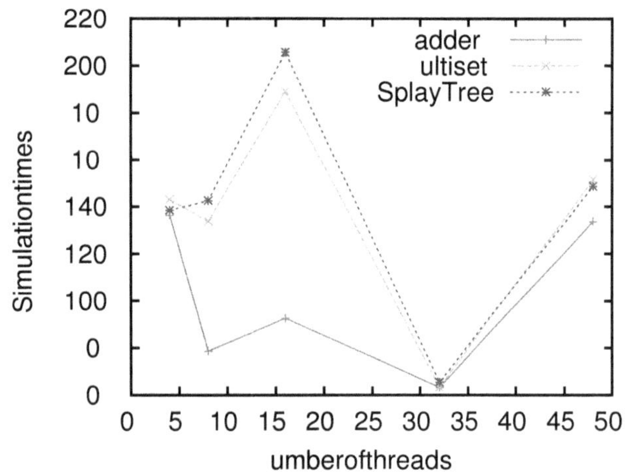

Figure 10: Performance of Different LTSF Data Structures using 1 LTSF Queue with RAID-5

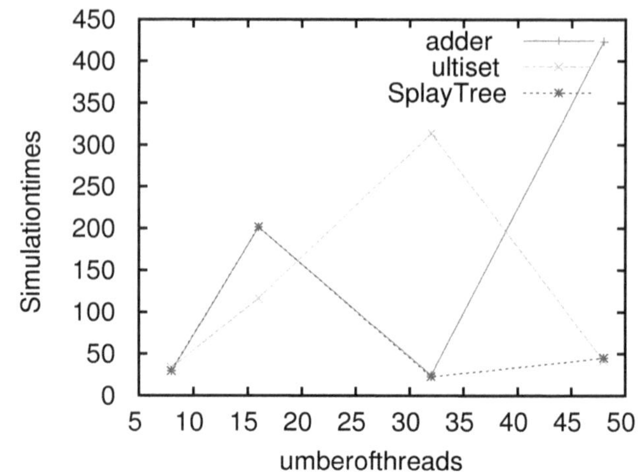

Figure 13: Performance of Different LTSF Data Structures using 8 LTSF Queues with RAID-5

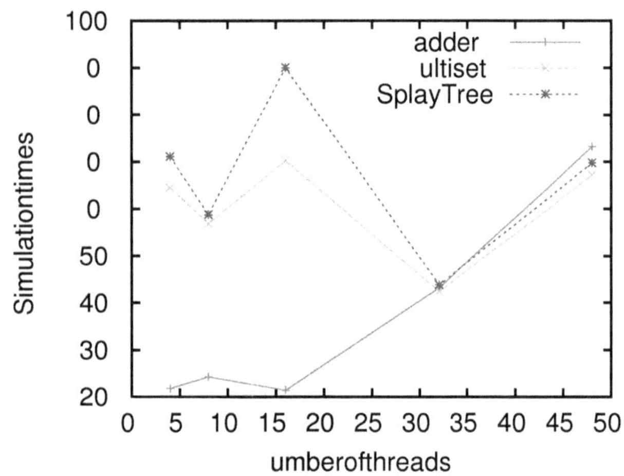

Figure 11: Performance of Different LTSF Data Structures using 2 LTSF Queues with RAID-5

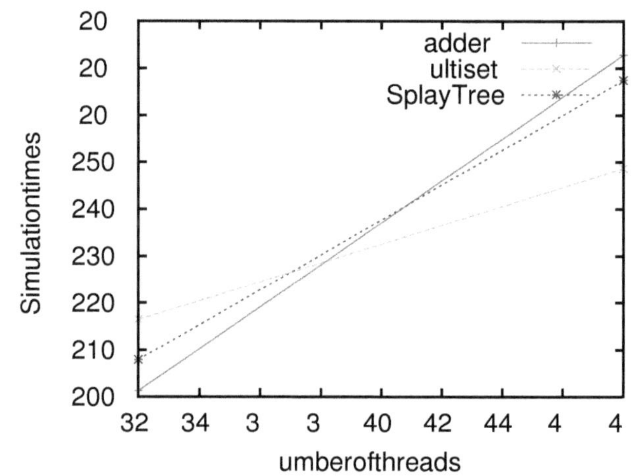

Figure 14: Performance of Different LTSF Data Structures using 16 LTSF Queues with RAID-5

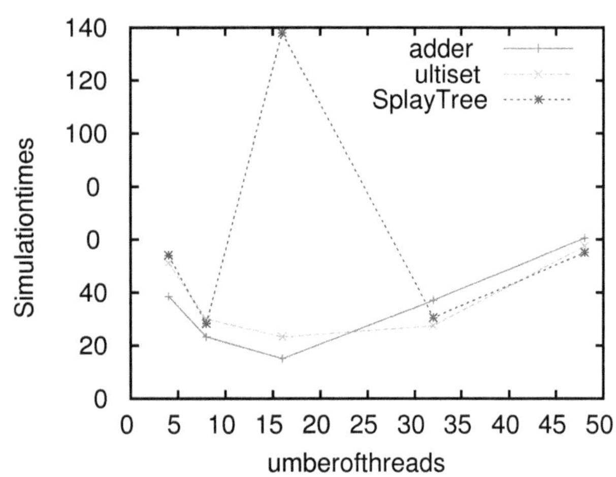

Figure 12: Performance of Different LTSF Data Structures using 4 LTSF Queues with RAID-5

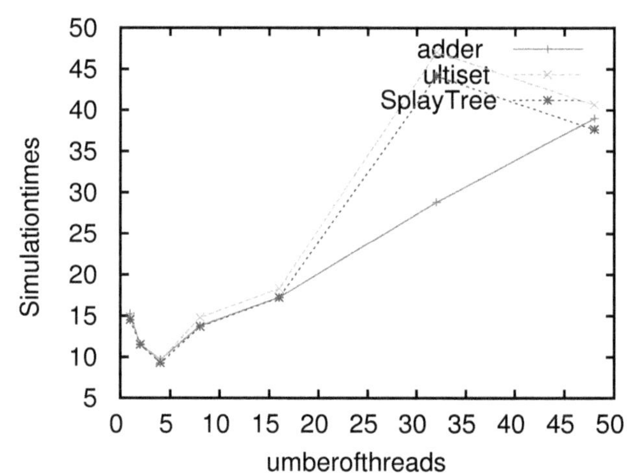

Figure 15: Performance of Different LTSF Data Structures using 1 LTSF Queue with c2670

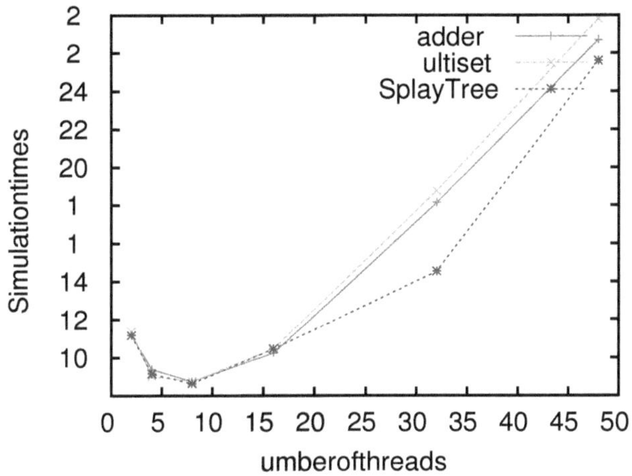

Figure 16: Performance of Different LTSF Data Structures using 2 LTSF Queues with c2670

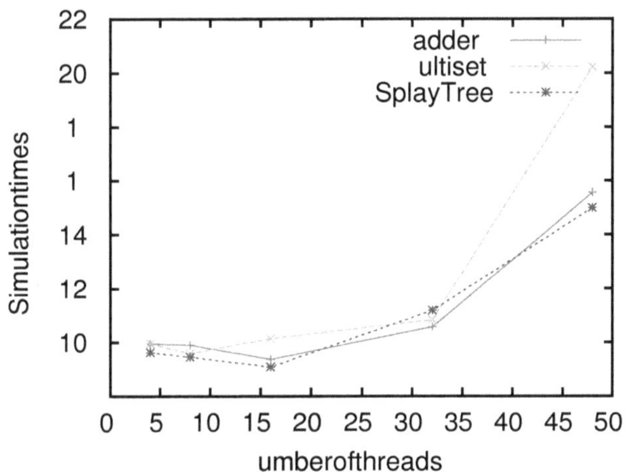

Figure 17: Performance of Different LTSF Data Structures using 4 LTSF Queues with c2670

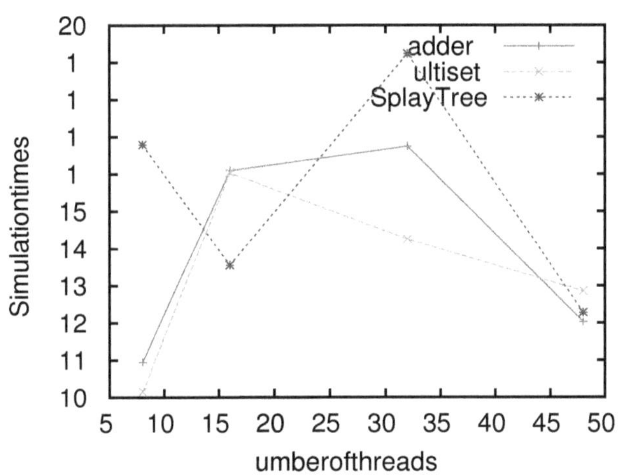

Figure 18: Performance of Different LTSF Data Structures using 8 LTSF Queues with c2670

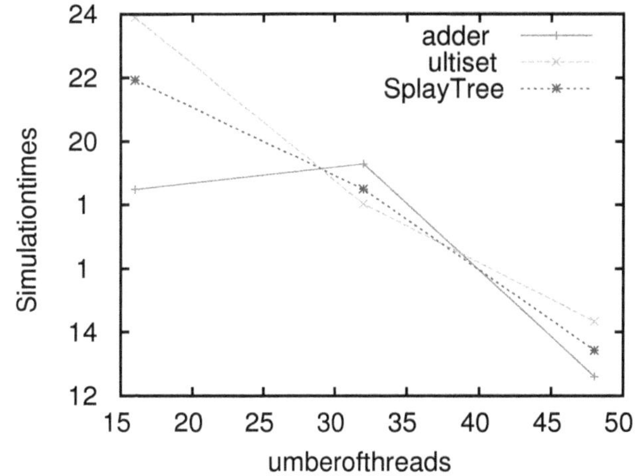

Figure 19: Performance of Different LTSF Data Structures using 16 LTSF Queues with c2670

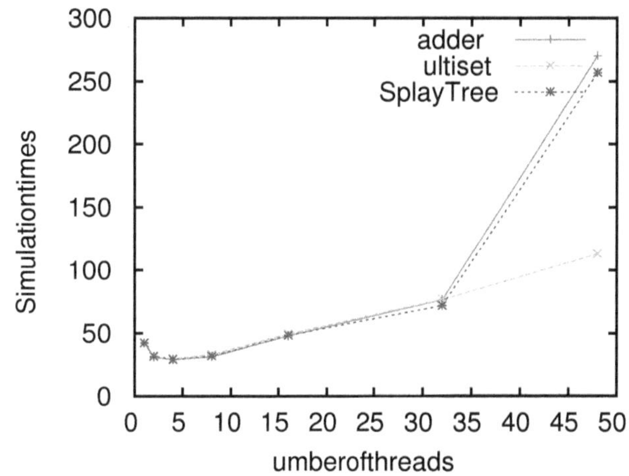

Figure 20: Performance of Different LTSF Data Structures using 1 LTSF Queue with c7552

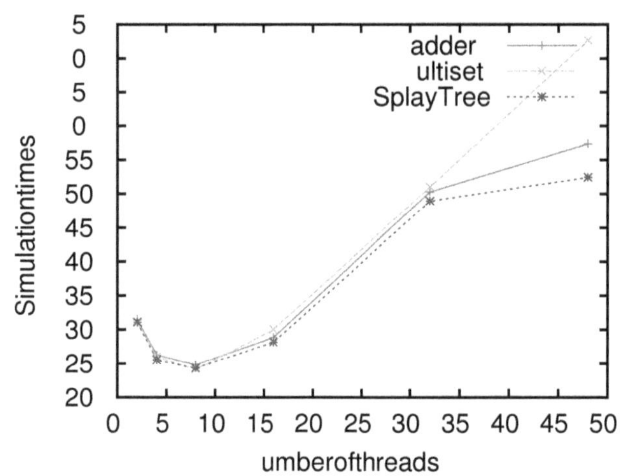

Figure 21: Performance of Different LTSF Data Structures using 2 LTSF Queues with c7552

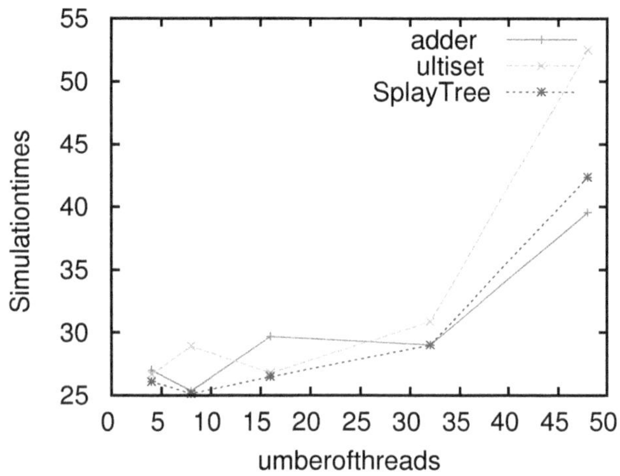

Figure 22: Performance of Different LTSF Data Structures using 4 LTSF Queues with c7552

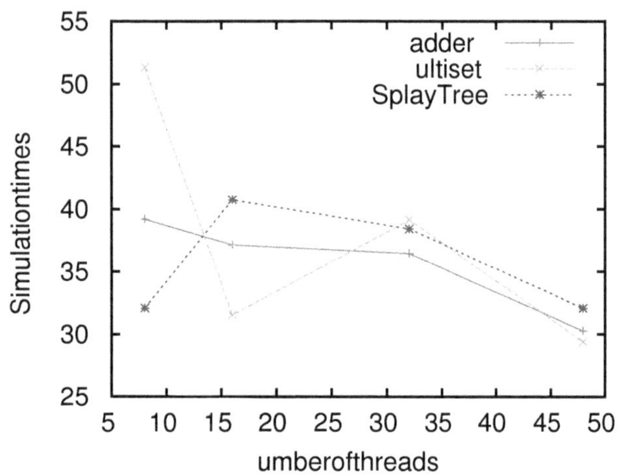

Figure 23: Performance of Different LTSF Data Structures using 8 LTSF Queues with c7552

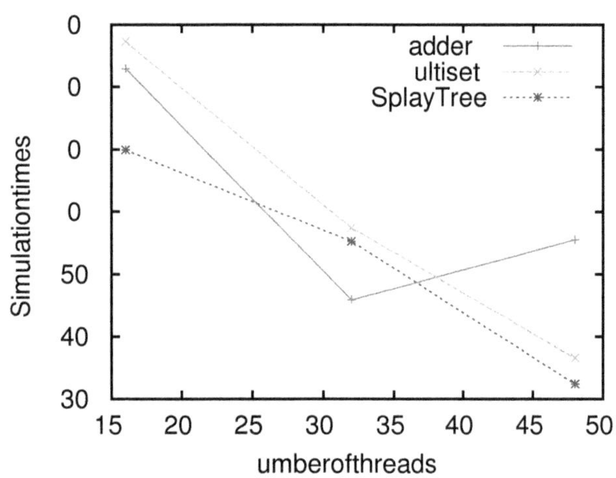

Figure 24: Performance of Different LTSF Data Structures using 16 LTSF Queues with c7552

```
worker_thread_at_LTSFi()
    lock LTSFi queue
    dequeue smallest event from LTSFi
    unlock LTSFi queue
  while !done loop
    process event (assume from LPk)
    lock LPk queue
    dequeue smallest event from LPk
    if loadBalanceRequested then
      lock LTSFj (new target) queue
      insert event from LPk
      unlock LTSFj queue
      unlock LPk queue
      lock LTSFi queue (get next event)
      dequeue smallest event from LTSFi
      unlock LTSFi queue
    else
      lock LTSFi queue
      insert event from LPk
      dequeue smallest event from LTSFi
      unlock LTSFi queue
    end if
  end loop
```

Figure 25: The addition of load balancing/sharing into the worker threads.

cating the LTSF queue and partitioning the worker threads and the LPs to one of the LTSF queues (Figure 5). This proposed design solution is setup so that the pending event lists for each LP are maintained as independent lists with individual locks. The lowest timestamped event from each LP event list is placed in one of multiple LTSF pending event queues. The (locked) LTSF queues are sorted and used by the *worker threads* to schedule the next event for execution. The worker threads are assigned to a specific LTSF queue and only retrieve work from that LTSF queue. After dequeuing and processing an event from the LTSF, each worker thread then accesses the pending event set of the LP corresponding to the event just executed and removes the next least-timestamped event for insertion back into the LTSF queue. While this approach helps the problem, the challenge of partitioning the work so that the entire system stays in balance and processes events along the critical path of time becomes more problematic. Fortunately, the software architecture used in this study should setup a streamlined mechanism to implement a lightweight load balancing algorithm as described below.

6.1 Load Balancing between LTSF Queues

Conceptually, the manager thread will monitor the system progress and balance to determine if and when a load balance event occurs. The Time Warp mechanism is unique in that events are aggressively processed which complicates the issue of determining which processes are working effectively and which are not. Fortunately the problem of identifying a "useful work" metric for the LPs of a Time Warp simulation has been previously studied [4] [13] [17]. We anticipate exploring these and other metrics to determine the effective work being done from a load balancing perspective. The worker threads can then be triggered by the manager to move LPs from one LTSF queue to another as shown in

Figure 25. This mechanism of load balancing is somewhat similar to the top/bottom-halves based kernel-level synchronization discussed in [24]. In addition to these ideas with LTSF queues, we also believe that the ladder queue data structure presents some key opportunities. This is outlined below.

6.2 Ladder Queue Possibilities

Much like lazy queues [19], ladder queues [22] are related to the calendar queue data structure [3]. While the ladder queue presents some interesting properties that can be readily exploited for further optimizing parallel simulation (described below), all of the calendar queue mechanisms present an opportunity for implementing a finer-grained locking mechanism that is suitable for use on many-core processing systems. In particular, all of these mechanism present a hierarchical structure of buckets that can be independently locked for the insertion and deletion of events. The key advantage of ladder queues are the dynamic sizing of the time windows for the buckets used to hold events.

While these bucket queue data structures have an O(1) average access time and have been proposed for use in managing the pending event lists in discrete event simulation, the ladder queue has some interesting advantages that we propose are highly desirable for implementing the pending event lists in Time Warp synchronized parallel simulation. In both calendar queues and lazy queues, the bucket size is set to a specific size that may occasional require a resizing operation to manage the time windows sizes. In contrast, the ladder queue has a builtin structure to manage the bucket sizes as per the time density of the incoming events.

We believe that we can further relax the definition of the `Bottom` component of the ladder queue so that it becomes an unsorted list of elements that are accessed using a fully wait-free mechanism achieved through atomic move instructions. Briefly elements are appended and removed in a queue structure without regard to a strict enforcement of time order. The principle idea is that the events in any one bucket are causally independent and therefore a full sorting of these events is unnecessary. Furthermore, because Time Warp maintains the ability to rollback and recover whenever a causal violation occurs, the assumption of causal independence is not catastrophic to the simulation when it fails to hold. The system would simply rollback and reprocess the event after the causally dependent parent event is processed. Of course this solution may not work for simulation models with tight causal relations. That said, this failure will occur only for simulation models where the Time Warp mechanism would not generally succeed anyway and thus, no loss of generality in the use of a Time Warp synchronized parallel simulation solution occurs.

The key advantage of the ladder queue is that the structure is relatively independent on the time granularity of the simulation model operating on top of the simulation kernel. Ideally, the dynamic range of event timestamps for the limited range of local events that define each epoch of the ladder should help ensure that the events within any bucket of the ladder queue are causally independent. This idea is related to the lookahead property of conservatively synchronized parallel simulation [5]. The lookahead concept results from a static analysis of the simulation model that guarantees a time window ahead of any source timestamp in which no additional events will be generated (effectively a minimum time delay guarantee on the event processing latency). While not as strong as lookahead, a key hypothesis for our work is that *the bucket size for the ladder queue will typically encompass a range of event timestamps that are causally independent.* This hypothesis falls from the observation that time ladder queue is reasonably stationary in the time window, t to $t+\Delta t$, for incoming events that arrive in the epochs when events are pulled from `Top` into the ladder (`Rungs` and `Bottom`) of the ladder queue. This causal independence is the principle rationale for the proposed unsorted, wait-free, generalization of the ladder queue proposed herein.

7. CONCLUSIONS

The work described in this paper introduces the ability to use multiple LTSF queues in an attempt to reduce the contention when large numbers of threads are used for the threaded WARPED simulation kernel. Preliminary results show definite improvements for all numbers of threads when moving from one to two LTSF queues, and slight improvements as the number of queues is increased up to some maximum depending on the number of threads used. The ISCAS-85 simulation results show that the optimal configuration contains between four and eight threads assigned to each LTSF queue, which confirms the value found by Muthalagu [12].

The use of Ladder Queues for the LTSF queues shows an increase in simulation performance for most configurations, performing at least as well, and even significantly better in some circumstances. Splay trees show performance that closely matches that of multiset, and even performs slightly worse in some situations. Based on the results from these simulations, Ladder Queues are an interesting option, especially if we take advantage of the ability to relax the definition of the BOTTOM data structure to make it unsorted.

Once this kernel is further stabilized, we hope to run further experiments using other simulation models to see the effects of these new data structures, and the introduction of multiple LTSF queues. These results show that both Ladder Queues and multiple LTSF queues have performance benefits, but further research needs to be performed into how best to exploit these benefits.

8. ACKNOWLEDGMENTS

Support for this work was provided in part by the National Science Foundation under grant CNS–0915337. We also extend our thanks to Xinyu Guo for implementing the `ISCAS-85` benchmark circuit simulation models.

9. REFERENCES

[1] H. Avril and C. Tropper. Clustered time warp and logic simulation. In *Proceedings of the Ninth Workshop on Parallel and Distributed Simulation (PADS'95)*, pages 112–119, June 1995.

[2] P. D. R. Bayer. Symmetric binary b-trees: Data structure and maintenance algorithms. *Acta Informatica*, 1(4):290–306, Dec. 1972.

[3] R. Brown. Calendar queues: A fast O(1) priority queue implementation for the simulation event set problem. *Communications of the ACM*, 31(10):1220–1227, Oct. 1988.

[4] R. Child and P. A. Wilsey. Using DVFS to optimize time warp simulations. In *Proceedings of the 2012 Winter Simulation Conference*, July 2012.

[5] R. Fujimoto. Parallel discrete event simulation. *Communications of the ACM*, 33(10):30–53, Oct. 1990.

[6] A. Ghuloum. Face the inevitable, embrace parallelism. *Communications of the ACM*, 52(9):36–38, Sept. 2009.

[7] M. Hansen, H. Yalcin, and J. P. Hayes. Unveiling the iscas-85 benchmarks: A case study in reverse engineering. *IEEE Design and Test*, 16(3):72–80, July-Sept 1999. (benchmarks available online at: `http://web.eecs.umich.edu/~jhayes/iscas.restore/`).

[8] Intel Press Release, Intel Corporation. Futuristic intel chip could reshape how computers are built, consumers interact with their pcs and personal devices. Technical report, Intel Press Release, Intel Corporation, Dec. 2009.

[9] R. Kalla. Power7: Ibm's next generation power microprocessor. In *Hot Chips 21*, Aug. 2009.

[10] D. E. Martin, T. J. McBrayer, and P. A. Wilsey. WARPED: A Time Warp simulation kernel for analysis and application development. In H. El-Rewini and B. D. Shriver, editors, *29th Hawaii International Conference on System Sciences (HICSS-29)*, volume Volume I, pages 383–386, Jan. 1996.

[11] R. Miller. Optimistic parallel discrete event simulation on a beowulf cluster of multi-core machines. Master's thesis, University of Cincinnati, 2010.

[12] K. Muthalagu. Threaded warped: An optimistic parallel discrete event simulator for clusters fo multi-core machines. Master's thesis, School of Electronic and Computing Systems, University of Cincinnati, Cincinnati, OH, Nov. 2012.

[13] A. Palaniswamy and P. A. Wilsey. Parameterized Time Warp: An integrated adaptive solution to optimistic pdes. *Journal of Parallel and Distributed Computing*, 37(2):134–145, Sept. 1996.

[14] S. K. Prasad, S. I. Sawant, and B. Naqib. Using parallel data structures in optimistic discrete event simulation of varying granularity on shared-memory computers. In *IEEE First International Conference on Algorithms and Architectures for Parallel Processing*, pages 365–374, Apr. 1995.

[15] R. Radhakrishnan, L. Moore, and P. A. Wilsey. External adjustment of runtime parameters in Time Warp synchronized parallel simulators. In *11th International Parallel Processing Symposium, (IPPS'97)*. IEEE Computer Society Press, Apr. 1997.

[16] R. Rajan and P. A. Wilsey. Dynamically switching between lazy and aggressive cancellation in a Time Warp parallel simulator. In *Proc. of the 28th Annual Simulation Symposium*, pages 22–30. IEEE Computer Society Press, Apr. 1995.

[17] P. L. Reiher and D. Jefferson. Dynamic load management in the time warp operating system. *Transactions of the Society for Computer Simulation*, 7(2):91–120, 1990.

[18] R. Rönngren, R. Ayani, R. M. Fujimoto, and S. R. Das. Efficient implementation of event sets in time warp. In *Proceedings of the 1993 workshop on Parallel and distributed simulation*, pages 101–108, May 1993.

[19] R. Rönngren, J. Riboe, and R. Ayani. Lazy queue: An efficient implementation of the pending-event set. In *Proc. of the 24th Annual Simulation Symposium*, pages 194–204, Apr. 1991.

[20] T. Santoro and F. Quaglia. A low-overhead constant-time ltf scheduler for optimistic simulation systems. In *Proceedings of the The IEEE symposium on Computers and Communications*, pages 948–953, June 2010.

[21] D. Sleator and R. Tarjan. Self adjusting binary search trees. *Journal of the ACM*, 32(3):652–686, July 1985.

[22] W. T. Tang, R. S. M. Goh, and I. L.-J. Thng. Ladder queue: An o(1) priority queue structure for large-scale discrete event simulation. *ACM Transactions on Modeling and Computer Simulation*, 15(3):175–204, July 2005.

[23] R. E. Tarjan. Amortized computational complexity. *SIAM J. Alg. Disc. Meth.*, 6(2):306–318, Apr. 1985.

[24] R. Vitali, A. Pellegrini, and F. Quaglia. Towards symmetric multi-threaded optimistic simulation kernels. In *Proceedings of the 2012 ACM/IEEE/SCS 26th Workshop on Principles of Advanced and Distributed Simulation*, pages 211–220, July 2012.

Interference Resilient PDES on Multi-core Systems: Towards Proportional Slowdown

Jingjing Wang, Nael Abu-Ghazaleh, and Dmitry Ponomarev
Dept. of Computer Science, Binghamton University
Binghamton, NY, USA
jwang36@cs.binghamton.edu, nael@cs.binghamton.edu, dima@cs.binghamton.edu

ABSTRACT

Parallel Discrete Event Simulation (PDES) harnesses the power of parallel processing to improve the performance and capacity of simulation, supporting bigger models, in more details and for more scenarios. PDES engines are typically designed and evaluated assuming a homogeneous parallel computing system that is dedicated to the simulation application. In this paper, we first show that the presence of interference from other users, even a single process in an arbitrarily large parallel environment, can lead to dramatic slowdown in the performance of the simulation. We define a new metric, which we call proportional slowdown, that represents the idealized target for graceful slowdown in the presence of interference. We identify some of the reasons why simulators fall far short of proportional slowdown. Based on these observations, we design alternative simulation scheduling and mapping algorithms that are better able to tolerate interference. More precisely, the most resilient simulators will allow dynamic mapping of simulation event execution to processing resources (a work pool model). However, this model has significant overhead and can substantially impact locality. Thus, we propose a locality-aware adaptive dynamic-mapping (LADM) algorithm for PDES on multi-core systems. LADM reduces the number of active threads in the presence of interference, avoiding having threads disabled due to context switching. We show that LADM can substantially reduce the impact of interference while maintaining memory locality reducing the gap with proportional slowdown. LADM and similar techniques can also help in situations where there is load imbalance or processor heterogeneity.

Categories and Subject Descriptors

I.6.8 [**Simulation and Modeling**]: Types of Simulation—*Discrete event, Parallel*

General Terms

Design

Keywords

PDES, Multi-cores, Proportional Slowdown, Interference

1. INTRODUCTION

Discrete Event Simulation (DES) is an efficient simulation methodology used in domains where changes of state occur at discrete times. It is widely used in a range of application domains such as the simulation of computer and telecommunication systems, war-gaming, transport systems, operational planning and biological simulations. Parallel Discrete Event Simulation (PDES) [12] harnesses the computational power and resources of parallel computing to improve the performance and capacity of DES, allowing the simulation of larger models, in more details, and for more scenarios.

PDES simulators have traditionally been designed under the assumption of a homogeneous environment with no interference from other co-located applications. Interference from other applications as well as other noise in the system creates competition for the available resources leading to potential slow downs in parallel applications [20, 31, 27, 22]. In the presence of interference, we expect an application to slow down proportionately to the reduction in its share of the resources: a metric introduced in this paper which we call *proportional slowdown*. Surprisingly, we found the impact of interference on PDES to far exceed proportional slowdown, even when the amount of interference is small. For example, when evaluating a multi-threaded fixed-mapping PDES engine, we discover that even 1 external load can result in a performance slowdown of a factor of up to 3.9 for an 8-way simulation on the core i7 platform, and up to 2.8 for a 48-way simulation on an AMD Magny-Cours platform.

A primary reason for the disproportionately high cost of interference is related to the granularity of the operating system (OS) scheduler. In particular, when the OS schedules an interfering process on a core, it has to context switch one of the simulation threads out, making it inactive. As a result, this thread is stalled, while, assuming optimistic simulation, other simulation processes surge forward. Eventually, when the OS schedules the process again, its late events cause rollbacks throughout the simulation: thus, most of the time on all processes is lost, and additional inefficiency results from the overhead of rollbacks. The problem continues to occur whenever the noise process is scheduled. Describing and characterizing this behavior in the presence of noise is one of the contributions of this paper.

It is important to note that this problem differs significantly from load-balancing problem that can be solved with dynamic object migration [23, 15]: unless all objects are migrated away from a context switched thread, the problem persists. Moreover, the problem happens at the granularity of the OS scheduler: a thread stops execution completely while it is context switched out, only to return to normal execution later. The victim thread typically changes based on affinity settings and OS scheduler decisions.

Carothers et al. noted that interference from external loads can pose significant performance slowdown [7], but did not elaborate on the reasons, or propose solutions to this problem. More recently, Malik et al. [19] studied the problem of executing PDES in a cloud environment where many applications are scheduled on the same infrastructure and co-interfere with each other. The impact of the problem was extensive, and they proposed the use of a master-worker model to provide flexibility of assigning available computational threads to execute the available simulation events. Flexible mapping of workers to work can provide resilience to interference as well as load imbalance, but could result in poor locality as simulation state moves frequently between hardware threads, rather than staying with one thread, and reaping the benefits of caching. To the best of our knowledge, no prior work in PDES has analyzed the impact of interference on PDES, explained the slowdown, or proposed solutions to it.

The goal of this paper is to develop alternative organizations to PDES simulation that are more resilient to the impact of external interference. In conventional PDES implementations a simulation model is partitioned across multiple processing elements (PEs). Each PE (a group of LPs) is executed by a process (or thread). In many existing PDES simulators such as ROSS [3] and WarpIV [30], the mapping between PEs and processes (or threads) is established at the initialization of simulation, and does not change during the simulation (the so called fixed-mapping, or FM, scheme). FM can achieve optimal performance in a load balanced simulation in the absence of external interference, primarily because it promotes locality of memory references, and because it incurs little overhead for scheduling [14]. However, FM suffers in the presence of interference because a stalled thread remains responsible for simulating its objects leading to poor performance.

In this paper, we explore interference-resilient execution of PDES on two multi-core platforms: a quad-core Intel core i7 system, and a 48-core AMD Opteron Magny-Cours platform with Non-Uniform Memory Access (NUMA) latencies. We first propose a dynamic-mapping (DM) scheme that is capable of dynamically changing the mapping between PEs and threads during the simulation. In particular, each thread attempts to work on a PE in a round-robin fashion. For correctness, each PE can only be mapped to one thread at a time. As a result, DM has limited opportunities to solve the problem: a thread is often switched out while in the middle of processing events on a PE. Other threads thus cannot assist and execute the PE until the thread gets scheduled again and releases the lock, causing the PE to lag far behind of others. Thus, although some performance benefit can be obtained, we discovered that the baseline DM cannot effectively solve the interference problem.

To address this problem, we propose an adaptive DM scheme that reduces the number of active threads when interference is detected. As a result, the number of threads is again matched to the available hardware contexts, and the simulation does not have to suffer extended periods when one of its threads is switched out. In this context, the remaining threads have to service a number of PEs that is larger than them. Having the threads switch in round robin fashion among the PEs, promotes load balanced operation but leads to poor locality as PEs move among threads causing cache interrogation. More precisely, the Locality Aware Adaptive DM (LADM) scheme creates a schedule where each thread is primarily associated with one PE, but spends a portion of its time helping one other PE. The proportion of time is chosen so that the total active time each PE receives remains balanced, avoiding straggler objects. Since each thread works on a limited number of PEs (two under reasonable interference conditions), locality is kept high.

LADM has the following key characteristics:

1. In the absence of external loads, LADM incurs small performance loss (less than 5%) compared with the optimal FM implementation on both the Intel core i7 and AMD Magny-Cours machines. The loss includes the overhead of detecting interference, but also the cost of rate misprediction of interference; a problem we hope to address with more careful design of the detector.
2. LADM can substantially reduce the impact of interference, thus reducing the gap with proportional slowdown.
3. LADM can successfully detect performance anomalies caused by external loads during the simulation without user interaction.
4. LADM exhibits good locality of memory references on both multi-core platforms.

As a result, LADM is able to achieve 2-4X improvement in performance in the presence of interference on both a 4-core (8 hardware threads) Intel core i7 and a 48-core AMD Magny-cours machine.

The remainder of the paper is organized as follows. Section 2 provides background information regarding both PDES simulator and two multi-core platforms we used in our experiments. We then define *proportional slowdown* to quantify the PDES performance in the presence of external loads in Section 3. In Section 4, we show the actual impact of external loads on the performance of fixed-mapping PDES simulators. We then explain why the performance of PDES simulator with FM implementation suffers considerably when the simulation is interfered by external loads. In Section 5, we provide a design overview of the baseline DM mechanism. In Section 6, we provide the details of our LADM scheme that can address the limitations in the baseline DM implementation. Section 7 presents an experimental evaluation. In Section 8, we overview some related work. Finally, in Section 9 we present some concluding remarks.

2. BACKGROUND

In this section, we first overview the multi-threaded simulator used in this paper. We follow by providing an overview of the two multi-core platforms used in the experiments: a quad-core Intel core i7 system, and a 48-core AMD Opteron Magny-Cours.

2.1 ROSS-MT: A state-of-the-art Multi-thread PDES Simulator

We use a recently developed multi-threaded version [17] of the Rensselaer's Optimistic Simulation System (ROSS) [3]. ROSS is a state-of-the-art PDES simulation engine which supports both conservative and optimistic simulations. The multi-threaded ROSS (ROSS-MT) encapsulates each group of objects as a PE and assigns each PE to a thread (i.e., it uses Fixed Mapping). The thread-based implementation allows optimizing communication using fast shared memory operations.

In ROSS-MT, a simulation model is partitioned across multiple PEs. Each PE processes the events in time-stamp order, and communicates with others via time-stamped events. In the optimistic simulation, ROSS-MT leverages efficient reverse computation [4], instead of the more conventional state saving [21], to undo incorrectly processed events in case of rollbacks. The events for each PE are executed repeatedly within a simulation loop until the simulation time of the PE reaches the simulation completion time. During each iteration, a designated number of events (batch size) can be processed before moving to the next iteration. Global virtual time (GVT) is computed every GVT interval, which is a configurable variable.

2.2 Multi-core Platforms

We use two multi-core platforms with significantly different CPU and memory organizations. The first is a quad-core Intel core i7 system. In this platform, each core has private 32 KB L1 and 256 KB L2 caches, and shares 8MB L3 cache with other cores. With Hyper-Threading enabled, each core can simultaneously execute two hardware threads which share both L1 and L2 caches. The second architecture we use is an AMD 48-core machine. It consists of four AMD Opteron 12-core chips, connected with Hyper-Transport links. Each chip has two dies, with each die holding six cores. Each core has private 64 KB L1 and 512 KB L2 caches, and shares 6MB L3 cache with other cores on the same die. In addition, the memory accesses to different memory regions on this platform have non-uniform memory access (NUMA) latencies [9].

3. IDEAL SLOWDOWN UNDER INTERFERENCE

Consider a PDES simulation running with N_p threads on a multi-core platform. Let N_c be the total count of hardware threads such that all these threads can execute at the same time; hardware threads refers to cores, or hardware contexts in the case of Simultaneous Multi-Threaded (SMT) processors. Suppose that an external interfering load can start and terminate at any time during the simulation. Thus, to measure performance more accurately, we divide the simulation into n small intervals $[X_{j-1}, X_j]$ indexed by j. In addition, let N_{total} be the total number of software threads executing on the machine (i.e., the number of PDES threads, as well as the number of external loads running concurrently) during the interval j. We assume that the operating system scheduler fairly allocates its CPU resources to each thread. In other words, each load obtains $(\frac{N_c}{N_{total}})$ of the available CPU time on average during the interval j, assuming that N_{total} loads compete for N_c CPUs. Therefore, the expected PDES slowdown under such conditions during the interval j is approximated by:

$$S_j = \frac{N_{total}}{N_c} = \frac{N_p + N_e}{N_c} \qquad (1)$$

where N_e is the number of external loads running concurrently with PDES during the interval j. Note that the above reasoning assumes that threads are computation bound and are therefore available to run whenever the scheduler schedules them. We call S_j the *proportional slowdown* during the interval j, since S_j increases proportionately to the number of interfering load processes. We assume that N_{total} is always greater than or equal to N_c, and the interference from external loads on PDES performance occur if $N_{total} > N_c$.

The run time of the entire PDES simulation in the presence of external loads can be approximated by adding up the expected run time across all intervals. Let T_j be the execution time required for the interval j of a FM simulation without interference. By multiplying T_j by the corresponding S_j, we obtain $T_j^{'}$, defined as the execution time required for the interval j of the simulation in the presence of external loads. Therefore,

$$T_{ideal} = \sum_{j=1}^{n} T_j^{'} = \sum_{j=1}^{n} T_j \times S_j \qquad (2)$$

denotes the ideal runtime of the entire simulation in the presence of external loads. T_{ideal} represents a best case scenario where the presence of interference merely reduces the amount of available resources and results in a slowdown proportional to this reduction. We will show that in practice, the impact is significantly worse than T_{ideal} because of the dependencies between the threads belonging to one application.

4. MEASURED IMPACT OF INTERFERENCE

In the previous section, we defined *proportional slowdown* as a metric that expresses the ideal slowdown of an application in the presence of interference from external processes. In this section, we evaluate the slowdown experienced by both the ROSS-MT and WarpIV PDES simulators, showing that both far exceed proportional slowdown. In the next section, we start exploring approaches to improve the performance of simulation in the presence of interference.

4.1 PDES Slowdown Under Interference

For most of the experiments, we use the Phold simulation model [13], which equally distributes a number of simulation objects among PEs. We use a controllable version of Phold that allows specifying the communication percentage between different objects on different cores. The simulation consists of 8 PEs running on the Intel core i7 platform, and 48 PEs running on the AMD 48-core machine, with 1000 objects per PE. Each PE was also mapped to a different thread, thus all CPU resources were used by ROSS-MT threads in the absence of external loads. In addition, we selected a GVT interval of 128 on both platforms, with a batch size of 24 events. Although the results are somewhat sensitive to the GVT interval (as a small GVT interval acts as a throttle to the simulation [26]), these values are in the range where ROSS-MT is most efficient across a range of models.

We use a CPU-intensive process as the external load; the process repeatedly performs computation within a tight loop. Thus, the process when active competes continuously

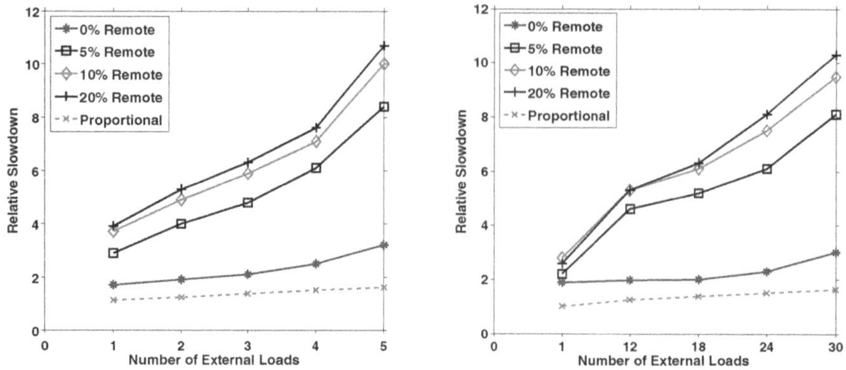

(a) Intel Core i7 System (b) AMD Magny-Cours System

Figure 1: The Relative Slowdown of ROSS-MT caused by External Loads

for CPU cycles with the ROSS-MT threads. In the experiments, the external load is started with ROSS-MT, and executes for the duration of the simulation. Thus, *proportional slowdown* from 1 external load can be calculated by Equation 1 to be $\frac{9}{8}$ for the core i7 and $\frac{49}{48}$ for the AMD Magny-cours. In these experiments, we do not set the CPU affinity for either ROSS-MT or the noise process, providing the OS scheduler complete freedom in scheduling the processing threads to the hardware resources.

Figure 1(a) and Figure 1(b) show the relative slowdown experienced by ROSS-MT as the number of external loads increases, on the Intel core i7 system and AMD Magny-Cours machine respectively. The relative slowdown is calculated by dividing the execution time of simulation in the presence of interference by the one without interference. We show these results as the percentage of remote communication is increased, which increases the dependencies among the different PEs. ROSS-MT with 0% remote communication performs close to proportional slowdown: since there are no dependencies between PEs, if a PE is delayed it does not affect the progress at other PEs. The OS scheduler does not always context switch out the same thread; thus, all threads make progress with their computation. In contrast, the interference from external loads dramatically degrades the performance of ROSS-MT even when a small amount of remote communication exists, far beyond proportional slowdown. For example, even 1 external load can result in a performance slowdown in ROSS-MT of a factor of up to 3.9 on the Intel core i7 machine, and up to 2.8 on the AMD Magny-Cours machine; these values far exceed the ideal slowdown of 1.125 and 1.02 for the core i7 and the Magny-cours respectively.

The problem is not specific to ROSS: we were able to demonstrate similar trends, and even worse slowdown, on the WarpIV PDES simulator [30]. Table 1 shows 4-way optimistic and conservative simulations interfered by 1 external load on a quad-core processor; due to export control restrictions on WarpIV, we had to run this experiment on a quad-core Xeon machine. Somewhat surprisingly, the simulation almost stops when the external load takes 100% of the time on one core (a situation which occurred some times, a decision that the linux scheduler makes). We believe this situation is due to the fuzzy barrier used in GVT computation in WarpIV [16]. At any given time, one thread is not executing and the fuzzy barrier condition is not met. However, even when the external load gets a lower scheduling priority and shares one of the CPU cores with a PDES process, the WarpIV simulation still experiences a performance slowdown of a factor of about 2. The situation was the same for both conservative and optimistic simulation.

Table 1: Execution Time of a 4-way Simulation on a Quad-core Processor using WarpIV Simulator

	Optimistic	Conservative
No External Load	6 sec	10 sec
1 External Load takes 50% CPU of a core	12 sec	19 sec
1 External Load takes 100% CPU of a core	> 4.7 hours	> 40 hours

4.2 Explaining the Impact of Interference

Table 2 and Table 3 show the efficiency of ROSS-MT achieved on the two multi-core platforms. The interferences from even one external load substantially reduces the efficiency of the simulation (from around 95% to around 61% on the Intel core i7 platform). Additional interfering processes further degrade efficiency.

To understand the drop in efficiency and the resulting slowdown, we first explain the event processing mechanism within ROSS-MT. As is typical with most PDES simulators, each thread is assigned a unit of work comprising of a group of objects (PE). The groups of objects assigned to each thread are selected, often via a partitioning algorithm (e.g., [2]), to minimize costly communication and to load balance computation. Each thread is responsible for processing all events whose destination is an object in its PE group. Thus, the mapping of work to threads is fixed.

Consider a 2-way simulation of ROSS-MT, with 1 LP per PE, as seen in Figure 2. PE 1 and PE 2 are executed by thread 1 and thread 2 respectively. Suppose an external load starts and interferes with thread 2 at wall clock time t_1, after a GVT computation phase (which requires barrier synchronization in ROSS). Once the interfering noise process is scheduled, thread 2 is context switched out and stops execution, while thread 1 continues. Thread 2 does not get scheduled again until the noise process exhausts its OS quantum (or otherwise, some other hardware context becomes available); the OS quantum is typically in the 10s of

Table 2: **Efficiency of 8-way Simulation on the Intel Core i7 machine**

Remote Communication (%)	Number of External Loads					
	0	1	2	3	4	5
0	100%	100%	100%	100%	100%	100%
5	94.6%	61.0%	51.4%	48.0%	45.3%	42.3%
10	96.3%	51.6%	46.0%	42.9%	40.8%	38.3%
20	96.8%	49.8%	43.6%	40.9%	38.8%	36.8%

Table 3: Efficiency of 48-way Simulation on the AMD Magny-Cours machine

Remote Communication (%)	Number of External Loads					
	0	1	12	18	24	30
0	100%	100%	100%	100%	100%	100%
5	95.9%	78.5%	47.0%	44.5%	45.4%	42.1%
10	96.4%	65.7%	41.7%	39.5%	39.0%	38.0%
20	96.9%	66.5%	41.5%	39.0%	36.6%	35.9%

milliseconds, sufficient for Thread 1 to execute several million CPU cycles. At a wall clock time t_2 ($t_2 > t_1$), thread 2 resumes execution, and PE 2 sends an event e_1 to PE 1. Due to the large pause in execution, this event is most likely a straggler as PE 1 has executed far ahead of PE 2 limited only in the ROSS case by the GVT computation interval; in other simulators, the degree of optimism can be unbounded.

Upon receiving e_1, PE 1 is rolled back to a simulation time before that of e_1, and then is re-executed. Thus, not only is processing time lost at PE 2 while it is context switched out, but most of the time available to PE 1 is also wasted, which explains why the slowdown exceeds proportional slowdown. The overhead of large rollbacks in terms of state restoration (or reverse computation), sending anti-messages, and other data structure restoration exacerbates the inefficiency. This effect exists whenever any of the simulation threads is context switched out, leading to the type of slowdown that we observe.

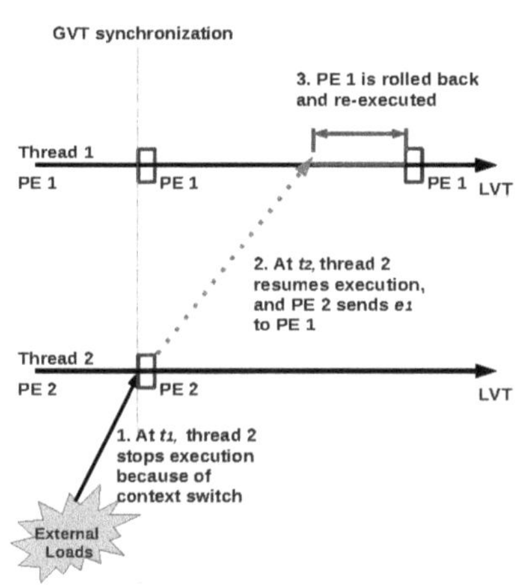

Figure 2: A Rollback caused by Interferences from External Loads

Note that the effect also holds if we use conservative simulation. A thread that is context switched out is not able to update the lookahead at other LPs, preventing them from proceeding. In fact, this problem generalizes to any parallel application with dependencies.

5. CAN DYNAMIC MAPPING HELP?

To address the destructive behavior that occurs in the presence of interference, we first attempt *dynamic mapping* (DM) of threads to PEs. More specifically, in this scheme, we periodically remap the threads to different PEs (recall that each PE encapsulates a group of objects in the simulation). The intuition behind DM is that it allows active threads to rotate across the different PEs, avoiding having a PE lag far behind the others.

Recall that each thread in ROSS-MT executes a loop that repeatedly performs the simulation tasks such as sending and receiving events and event processing. To implement DM, we add a new step at the beginning of the loop where a thread determines which PE to associate itself with; the base implementation simply rotates threads in a round-robin fashion across the PEs. Consider the example as shown in Figure 2. After thread 2 finishes the execution of PE 2 for an iteration, it then switches to PE 1. Thus, in principle, the active thread alternates working on PE 1 and PE 2, reducing the LVT difference between them. Alternative basis for scheduling PEs to threads are possible (for example, attempting to work on the PE with the lowest LVT).

Note that a side-effect of remapping threads to PEs is a loss of data locality: FM permanently maps a hardware thread to a unit of work, and the caches for the core are populated with the data relevant to it. As DM remaps work across cores, the PE data must be brought to each new core (from shared lower level caches or main memory).

A second, more serious, limitation of DM is its limited opportunity for assisting performance. More precisely, for correctness, two threads cannot be attached to the same PE concurrently, which prevents remapping from being able to assist if the context switched thread happens to hold the lock on the PE. We implemented efficient synchronization using a condition variable and a spin lock for each PE. More precisely, a PE status is checked (without locking); if the status is busy, the thread moves on to the next PE. If the status is free, the thread acquires the spin lock for the PE, and checks if it is still free. If it is, the thread sets the PE to busy, and is admitted to work on the PE. Once the iteration is over, it sets the PE status to free and moves on again to the next PE.

Thus, DM is limited if the first thread is switched out while in the middle of processing a batch since the PE will

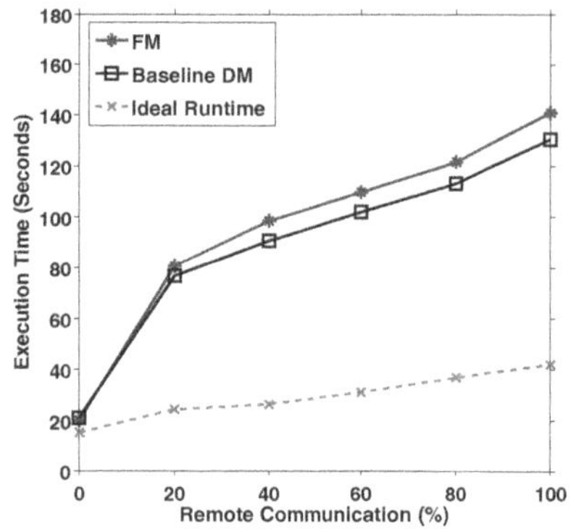

(a) Intel Core i7 System

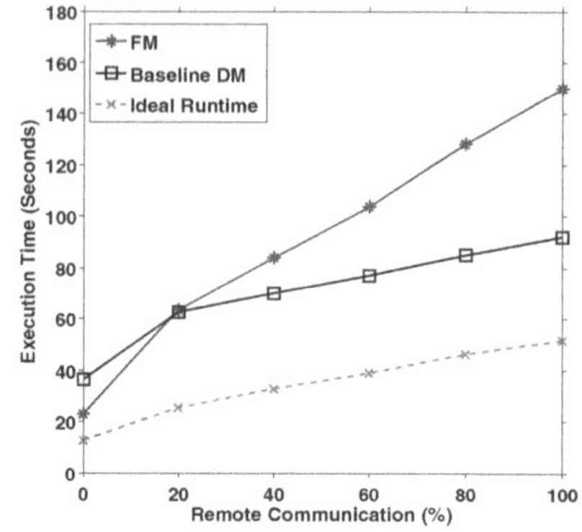

(b) AMD Magny-Cours System

Figure 3: Performance of FM vs. Baseline DM (Interfered by 1 External Load)

be marked as busy until the thread is scheduled again. Since this is the common case, DM cannot effectively solve the problem. Figure 3 shows the performance of original FM ROSS-MT in comparison to the baseline DM version for both the Intel core i7 (Figure 3(a)) and the AMD Magny-Cours (Figure 3(b)) platforms. In particular, the entire simulation is interfered by 1 external load. We find that DM achieves up to 10% performance improvement over FM on the Intel core i7 platform. Moreover, DM can achieve better performance than FM on the Magny-cours only under high remote communication (> 20%). The gap remains substantial with respect to ideal runtime (Equation 2).

Table 4: Efficiency of FM vs. Baseline DM on the Intel Core i7 System (Interfered by 1 External Load)

Remote Comm (%)	20	40	60	80	100
FM	49.9%	47.1%	47.8%	48.6%	46.7%
Baseline DM	50.7%	49.5%	49.8%	51.2%	49.7%

Table 5: Efficiency of FM vs. Baseline DM on the AMD Magny-Cours System (Interfered by 1 External Load)

Remote Comm (%)	20	40	60	80	100
FM	67.0%	62.9%	61.1%	58.5%	56.8%
Baseline DM	87.3%	87.9%	88.5%	88.3%	88.3%

The efficiency of a simulation interfered by 1 external load is shown for both the Intel core i7 (Table 4) and the AMD Magny-Cours (Table 5) platforms. While the results of AMD Magny-Cours system show improvements in efficiency of the baseline DM in comparison to the FM version are observed, the efficiency remains low especially for the core i7. In most cases, DM was not able to help because the context switched thread held the PE lock.

6. LOCALITY AWARE ADAPTIVE DM

DM offers only limited relief from the slowdown experienced in the presence of interference. In addition, DM experiences poor cache locality, because of transient short term association between threads and PEs. In this section, we propose a locality-aware adaptive DM (LADM) scheduler that is capable of addressing limitations of DM.

6.1 Adapting the Number of Threads

The first improvement to DM, which we call adaptive DM (ADM), adjusts the number of work threads to the available hardware contexts: when a noise process is detected, the number of active threads is reduced to avoid experiencing expensive context switches. Thus, only active threads are allowed to execute PEs. Supporting ADM requires two main mechanisms: one to detect the presence of interference, and another to adjust the number of active threads. Finally, a third mechanism is required to check if the interference is no longer there and to reactivate idle threads. We discuss these mechanisms in the remainder of this subsection.

The presence of noise is detected as follows. During execution, each active thread periodically monitors its total event processing time (the period is set to $\frac{T_{gvt}}{4}$ simulation loop iterations in our implementation, where T_{gvt} is the GVT interval). The *average processing time per event* (APTE) of each active thread is calculated by dividing the total event processing time by the corresponding number of processed events. A performance anomaly is decided if the rate of maximum APTE to minimum APTE is beyond a user-defined threshold. After the mechanism decides a performance anomaly, the status of the thread with maximum APTE will be configured as "inactive". Each thread checks its status at the beginning of the simulation loop, and inactive threads idle. We discover that the threshold plays an important role in the performance of simulation. If the value of the threshold is too large, then the performance anomaly is not reliably detected when interference from external loads exist. On the other hand, too small a value can cause ADM to incorrectly inactivate a PDES thread in an interference-free environment. We use a threshold of 1.8, which we empirically found to work effectively on both platforms.

The final mechanism checks if the noise has disappeared, and hardware contexts are again available. One inactive thread is re-activated periodically. If noise remains present, then the deactivation logic detects that and deactivates the thread. Thus, the reactivation period must be significantly larger than the detection period to avoid too frequent testing: (we use $10 \times T_{gvt}$, 40 times larger than the detection period).

ADM can reduce the effect of interferences from external loads, and thus significantly improves the performance of the

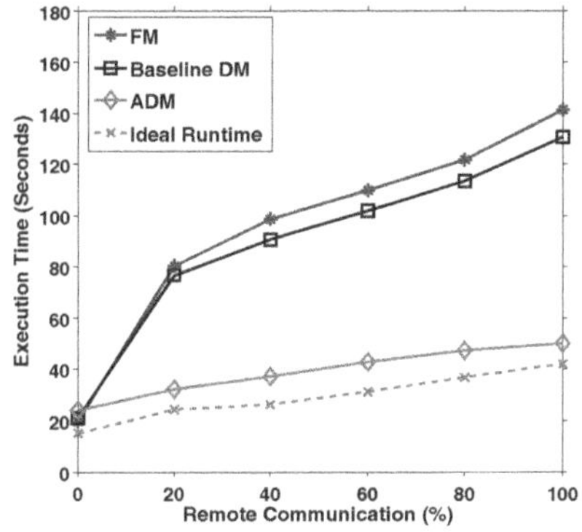

(a) Execution Time

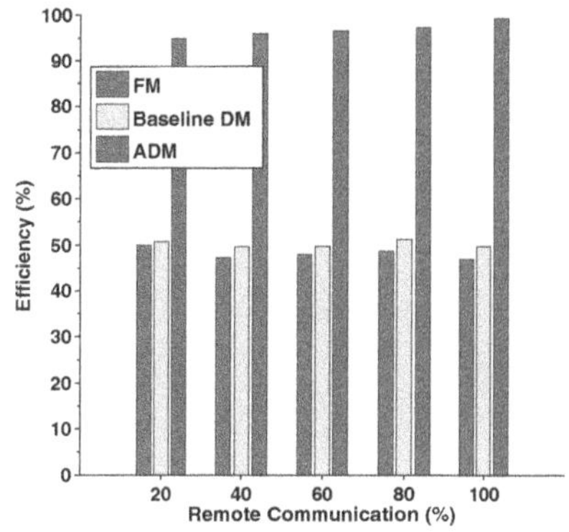

(b) Efficiency

Figure 4: Performance of ADM on the Intel Core i7 System (Interfered by 1 External Load)

simulation in the presence of external loads. Consider an 48-way simulation interfered by 1 external load on the 48-core AMD Magny-Cours machine, for example. Once a performance anomaly is successfully detected, the simulation is then executed by 47 active threads. The OS scheduler will later assign each thread to a different core, thus reducing interferences between PDES threads and the external load.

6.2 Improving the Data Locality

To improve the data locality, we modified the ADM scheduler to increase locality: we call this implementation locality-aware adaptive dynamic-mapping (LADM). Similar to FM, at the initialization of simulation, each thread is assigned to a primary PE, and maintains this assignment in the absence of interference to maximize locality. Once interference is detected and a thread (or more) is deactivated, the PE assigned to the inactive thread is marked as an orphan until such a time where its thread is reactivated. The remaining active threads divide their time between their primary PEs and orphan PEs.

In particular, after each event processing iteration on its primary PE, each active thread checks PEs on the orphan list in a round-robin fashion; it selects an orphan that is currently behind its primary PE in the number of processing iterations (alternatively, LVT may be used). The status of the selected PE is then checked, and the spin lock for it is acquired if its status is free. Once the thread is admitted to work on the PE, it executes N_{batch} iterations before switching back to its primary PE. We set N_{batch} to 10 in our simulations. The thread returns to its primary PE if all the orphan PEs have caught up with it. Unlike ADM, the PE whose primary thread is active remains exclusively processed by that thread, and only orphan PEs experience a loss of locality.

6.3 The Expected Runtime of LADM

Suppose that the simulator is configured with N_p threads at the initialization of simulation, where N_p equals with the total count of hardware threads on the multi-core platform. In addition, we divide the simulation into n small intervals $[X_{j-1}, X_j]$ indexed by j. Let N_j be the number of external loads running concurrently with PDES during the interval j of the simulation. Once LADM detects N_j ($N_j < N_p$) external loads, the simulation is then executed by (N_p - N_j) active threads during the interval j. The expected runtime of the entire simulation is thus approximated by:

$$T_{expected} = \sum_{j=1}^{n} \frac{N_p}{N_p - N_j} \times T_j \qquad (3)$$

where T_j is the execution time required for the interval j of a FM simulation without interference. Moreover, LADM allows at least 1 active thread to execute the simulation if $N_j \geq N_p$.

It is important to note that LADM does not achieve proportional slowdown. ADM schedulers simply give up hardware contexts that are in contention to avoid a situation where they are context switched. Because of this conservative behavior, it is possible for interference loads to crowd-out the simulation threads resulting in significant slowdown under high interference. However, the OS scheduling policy will cause inefficient operation if more threads are running than there are available hardware contexts. To approach proportional slowdown, alternative OS scheduling policies are needed.

7. PERFORMANCE EVALUATION

This section presents a performance evaluation of ADM and LADM in comparison to FM. Most of the experiments use the Phold benchmark [13], with 1000 objects per PE. For some experiments, we use Personal Communication Services (PCS) system to show that the technique transitions to real models [6].

7.1 Evaluation of ADM

In the first experiment, we evaluate the performance of ADM without the data locality optimization. Figure 4 and Figure 5 show the performance of ADM compared to FM and baseline DM on the core i7 and Magny-Cours platforms respectively. In this experiment, we introduce the interfering load at the start of the simulation, and it runs for the duration. In Figure 4(a) and Figure 5(a), we see the execution time as a function of the percentage of remote communication (the communication between PEs). ADM achieves better performance than FM on the core i7, but only outperforms FM at high remote communication ($\geq$ 20%) percentages.

The behavior can be partially explained by the high cost of lower level cache accesses on the Magny-cours relative

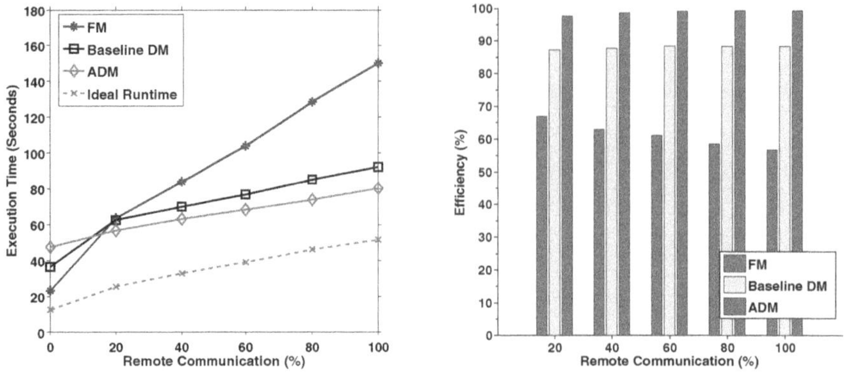

(a) Execution Time (b) Efficiency

Figure 5: Performance of ADM on the AMD Magny-Cours System (Interfered by 1 External Load)

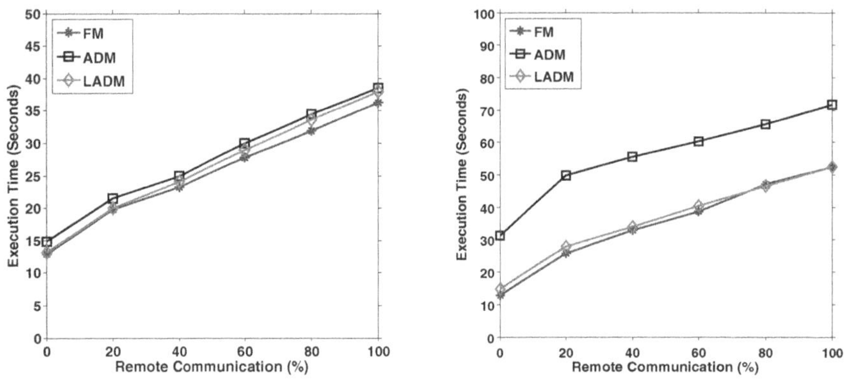

(a) Intel Core i7 System (b) AMD Magny-Cours System

Figure 6: Performance of Locality-aware Adaptive Dynamic-Mapping Scheme (No External Load)

to the core i7. At 100% remote communication, for example, ADM can achieve a speedup of 2.8X against FM on the core i7 machine, and 1.8X on the Magny-Cours platform. ADM performs closer to the ideal runtime (predicted by proportional slowdown) on the core i7 platform than on the Magny-Cours machine. Thus, the benefit from ADM is offset somewhat by the increased cache misses and the poorer locality that results from continuous re-mapping of the work. The locality aware version of ADM attempts to address this issue.

As described in Section 6, the baseline DM will experience poor efficiency when contention becomes heavy, while ADM can reduce such contention by inactivating some threads. To demonstrate this, we present efficiency of corresponding simulations (as shown in Figure 4(b) and Figure 5(b)). Clearly, the baseline DM exhibits a poor efficiency similar with FM on the core i7 machine, but can achieve relatively better efficiency on the Magny-Cours machine. In contrast, ADM can achieve efficiency of over 90% on both platforms.

7.2 The Impact of Data Locality

In ADM, each active thread moves to the next free PE in a round-robin fashion at the beginning of the simulation loop, even when there is no interference. Thus, ADM can lead to poor cache locality, as each thread accesses different PEs causing their state to be interrogated between caches. LADM improves data locality by associating threads with primary PEs. Only orphan PEs (those whose primary thread is inactive) experience a loss of locality as their events are processed by the other active threads.

The next experiment evaluates the performance of FM, ADM and LADM in the absence of external loads to measure the overhead of the mechanisms when they are not needed. As seen in Figure 6, LADM performs up to 11% better than ADM on the core i7 machine, and up to 53% on the Magny-Cours machine. In addition, LADM incurs small performance loss (less than 5%) relative to the FM version. The overhead is partially due to the extra checking that LADM does; however, we also noticed that rarely, LADM incorrectly detects the presence of interference. We believe that there is room for improving the interference detection algorithm in future work.

In the next experiment, we consider a scenario with 1 external interfering process (Figure 7). At high remote communication ($\geq$ 20%), LADM outperforms the original FM by a factor of up to 2.8X on the core i7 machine, and up to 2.2X on the Magny-Cours machine. In addition, LADM performs up to 43% better than ADM on the Magny-Cours machine, due to the fact that LADM can achieve better data locality. Figure 8 shows the cache miss rates, demonstrating how LADM has substantially lower cache miss rates than ADM.

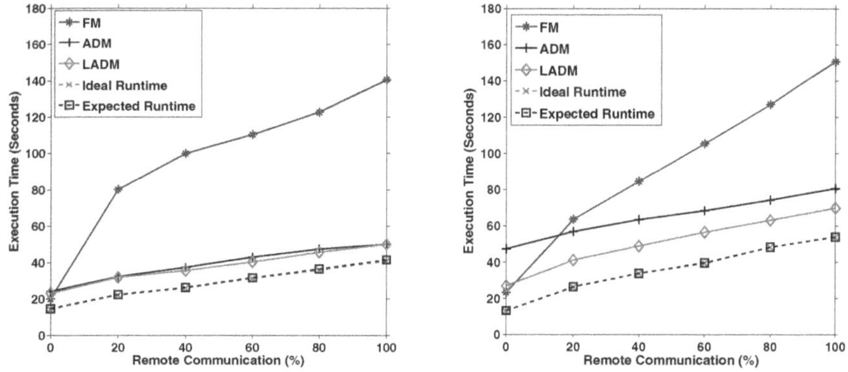

(a) Intel Core i7 System (b) AMD Magny-Cours System

Figure 7: Performance of Locality-aware Adaptive Dynamic-Mapping Scheme (1 External Load)

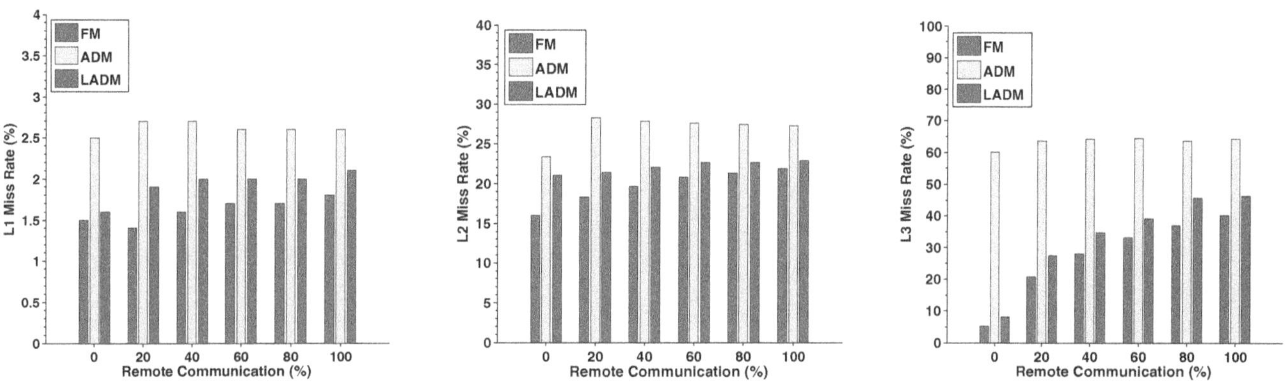

(a) L1 Cache Miss Rate (b) L2 Cache Miss Rate (c) L3 Cache Miss Rate

Figure 8: Cache Performance of 48-way Simulation on the AMD Magny-Cours System

7.3 Impact of Event Processing Granularity

In the next experiment we modify the Phold model to increase the granularity of event processing time. In particular, a new parameter, called *EPC*, is defined to control the amount of computation for each event processing in Phold. A higher value of EPC gives more computation load increasing the ratio of computation to communication.

We evaluate the performance of FM and LADM as the number of external loads is increased, for both the Intel (Figure 9) and AMD Magny-Cours (Figure 10) platforms at remote communication percentage of 40%. As seen in Figure 9 and Figure 10, LADM performs better than FM on both platforms when the simulation is interfered by external loads. In addition, the gap with the ideal performance is decreased as EPC increases. Moreover, the gap between LADM and the ideal performance on the Magny-Cours machine is larger than that on the core i7 machine. We believe that the penalty of a cache miss on the AMD Magny-Cours machine is high, due to its NUMA characteristics.

Another interesting observation is that FM performs closer to LADM as EPC increases. We discover that FM is capable of achieving relatively better efficiency at higher EPCs. As each event requires more time for processing in the case of higher EPC, the advance rate of each PE in FM is more balanced than that in the case of lower EPC.

7.4 Performance Evaluation of PCS Model

In this experiment, we study a model of a Personal Communication Services (PCS) system [6]. The PCS model simulates how a cellular provider infrastructure handles a number of mobile phone calls. In this model, an event represents a mobile phone call, sent from one cell phone tower to another. Each cell phone tower has a fixed number of channels. Upon receiving a call, the cell phone tower assigns an available channel to the call, and later releases the allocated channel when the call completes. If all channels are busy, the call is blocked. In addition, the call is handed-off to the destination cell phone tower if the call's connected portable is leaving the area of the cell phone tower [6, 5].

The PCS simulation consists of 36864 cells (LPs) distributed among 8 PEs on the Intel core i7 machine, and 48 PEs on the AMD Magny-Cours machine. Moreover, we fixed the number of channels per cell phone tower at 10. Figure 11(a) and Figure 11(b) show the performance of PCS model in the presence of external loads on the core i7 machine and the AMD Magny-Cours machine respectively. Clearly, LADM performs better than FM on both platforms. At the case of 5 external loads, for example, the performance of LADM exceeds that of FM by a factor of 3.7X on the core i7 machine. In addition, LADM outperforms FM by a factor of about 2.5X at the case of 30 external loads on the Magny-Cours machine.

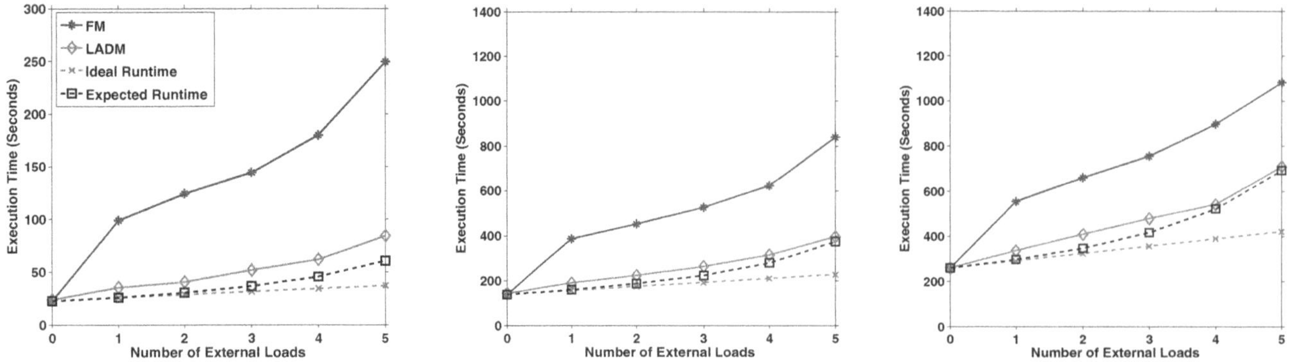

(a) EPC=0 (b) EPC=500 (c) EPC=1000

Figure 9: Impact of Event Processing Granularity on the Intel Core i7 Machine

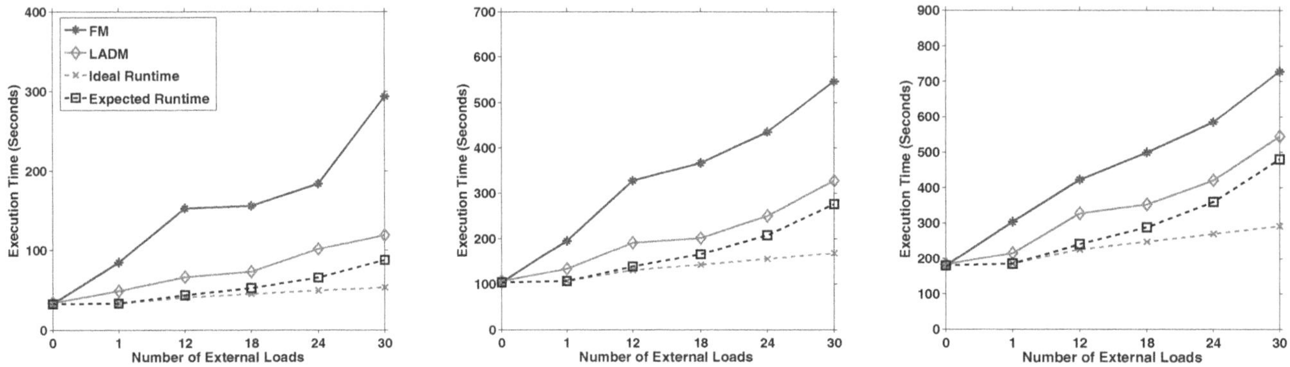

(a) EPC=0 (b) EPC=500 (c) EPC=1000

Figure 10: Impact of Event Processing Granularity on the AMD Magny-Cours System

8. RELATED WORK

In this section, we first overview some prior works in the context of PDES. We follow this by describing the interference problem in the general parallel processing community.

8.1 Dynamic load-balancing Approaches for PDES

Dynamic load-balancing approaches rely on a monitoring scheme to detect load imbalance, and make dynamic adjustment to improve the performance of simulation. These approaches differ in metrics of detecting load imbalance, and balancing schemes.

Vitali et al. [29, 28] present a load-sharing scheme developed for a symmetric multi-threaded optimistic PDES simulator. Each PE is executed by multiple worker threads, in order to improve parallelism of the simulation. The approach works by allowing a PE that is lagging behind to acquire additional threads to assist with its computation. Thus, the approach is on the face of it similar to our approach in that threads can be redirected to work on lagging PEs. The approach can effectively foster load balanced simulation, but cannot effectively solve the interference problem, as other threads cannot assist when threads keep getting context switched in the middle of event processing.

Wilsey et al. [8] proposed a different approach to support run-time core frequency adjustment on many-core systems, with the goal of accelerating the critical path of execution of the Time Warp simulation. To balance workloads of LPs, the cores containing LPs with larger rollbacks are underclocked, while the cores having LPs with smaller rollbacks are overclocked. Though this approach may reduce rollbacks caused by external loads, the performance issue caused by the interference still exists as LPs can't advance if their executing thread is switched out.

Carothers et al. [5, 7] designed a scheme to support background execution of Time Warp. A background central process periodically monitors the workload of each processor, and dynamically determines the set of processors to be used for the Time Warp Simulation. LPs are then distributed across these processors, by using object migration which is widely used in many existing dynamic load-balancing approaches [24, 10, 18]. Dynamic object migration cannot solve the interference problem as well unless all objects are migrated away from a context switched thread.

8.2 Other Approaches to Reduce the Effect of Interference on PDES

In this paper, we demonstrate that the optimistic fixed-mapping PDES simulation kernel can suffer considerably in the presence of interference on the multi-core platforms, due to excessive rollbacks being generated. Malik et al. [19] observed the same behavior present in the cloud environment. To reduce excessive rollbacks caused by interference, they developed a protocol, called *TW-SMIP*, with the goal of

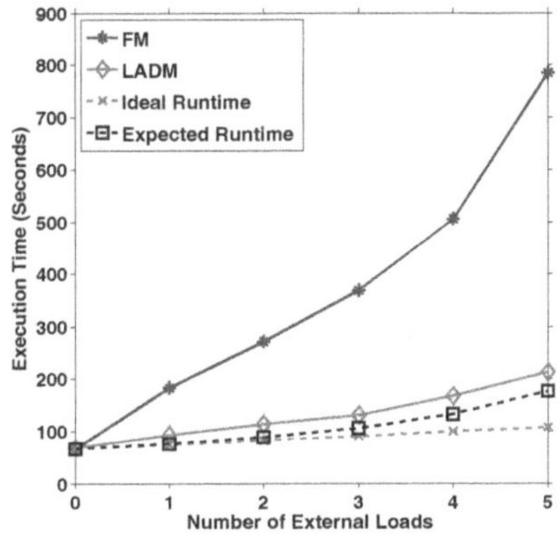

(a) Intel Core i7 System

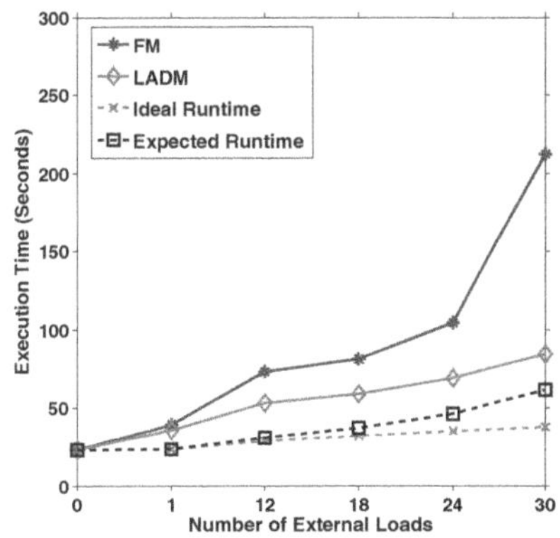

(b) AMD Magny-Cours System

Figure 11: Performance of PCS Model

identifying straggler messages early and thus avoiding frequent rollbacks.

Replication is another approach that is capable of reducing the effect of interference. As presented in [25], multiple copies of PDES simulation are executed simultaneously on heterogeneous workstation cluster. It allows the runtime reconfiguration in terms of runtime resource availability, and thus this approach can adapt to interferences from external loads.

8.3 Interference in General Parallel Processing

Similar to PDES, most parallel applications have dependencies between executing threads. Thus, when the interference occurs, active threads have to wait for context switched ones before continuing to execute and the pace of the execution is determined by the slowest thread. As a result, the performance of these applications can be substantially harmed [20, 27, 22]. Two approaches are widely used to balance workloads of threads at run-time: *work-sharing* and *work-stealing*. In work-sharing, when a thread completes its task, it grabs a new one from a central work pool shared across all threads [1]. In contrast, in work-stealing scheme, once a thread finishes its tasks, it steals other threads' tasks [11]. However, neither approach can solve the interference problem unless a context switched thread does not hold any task.

9. CONCLUSIONS

In this paper, we demonstrated the sometimes dramatic slowdown that can result in the presence of external interference. We presented a new metric, called *proportional slowdown*, to measure the idealized slowdown of PDES in the presence of interference and showed that in practice the observed slowdowns far exceed it. We proposed to use dynamic mapping to allow active threads to work on the PEs in a fair way, allowing the simulation to continue to proceed even if one or more threads are context switched. We then proposed a locality-aware dynamic-mapping (LADM) scheme that improves the locality of the proposed adaptive scheme by attempting to keep PEs assigned to their primary threads. Our experimental results showed that LADM is significantly better able to tolerate interference than fixed-mapping implementation, thus reducing the gap with proportional slowdown.

Our future work targets effective approaches for improving the algorithm of scheduling between PEs and threads. In the current study, each active thread looks up a PE on the orphan list in a round-robin fashion. We believe that a better locality can be achieved if the workloads of PEs on the orphan list are equally divided, and each workload is assigned to a specific active thread. We also plan to improve the accuracy of the interference detection algorithm.

Acknowledgements

This material is based on research sponsored by Air Force Research Laboratory under agreement number FA8750-11-2-0004. The U.S. Government is authorized to reproduce and distribute reprints for Governmental purposes notwithstanding any copyright notation thereon. The views and conclusions contained herein are those of the authors and should not be interpreted as necessarily representing the official policies or endorsements, either expressed or implied, of Air Force Research Laboratory or the U.S. Government. We also gratefully acknowledge support from the National Science Foundation grants CNS-0916323 and CNS-0958501.

10. REFERENCES

[1] G. R. Andrews. *Foundations of Multithreaded, Parallel, and Distributed Programming.* Addison-Wesley, Nov. 1999.

[2] K. Bahulkar, J. Wang, N. Abu-Ghazaleh, and D. Ponomarev. Partitioning on dynamic behavior for parallel discrete event simulation. In *Principles of Advanced and Distributed Simulation (PADS)*, pages 221–230. IEEE, 2012.

[3] C. Carothers, D. Bauer, and S. Pearce. ROSS: A high-performance, low memory, modular time warp system. In *Principles of Advanced and Distributed Simulation (PADS)*, pages 53–60. IEEE, 2000.

[4] C. Carothers, K. Perumalla, and R. Fujimoto. Efficient optimistic parallel simulations using reverse computation. *ACM TOMACS*, 1999.

[5] C. D. Carothers and R. M. Fujimoto. Background execution of time warp programs. In *Principles of Advanced and Distributed Simulation (PADS)*, pages 12–19. IEEE, 1996.

[6] C. D. Carothers, R. M. Fujimoto, and Y.-B. Lin. A case study in simulating pcs networks using time warp. In *Principles of Advanced and Distributed Simulation (PADS)*, pages 87–94. IEEE, 1995.
[7] C.D.Carothers and R. M. Fujimoto. Efficient execution of time warp programs on heterogeneous, now platforms. *IEEE Transactions on Parallel and Distributed Systems*, 11:299–317, 2000.
[8] R. Child and P. Wilsey. Dynamically adjusting core frequencies to accelerate time warp simulations in many-core processors. In *Principles of Advanced and Distributed Simulation (PADS)*, pages 35–43. IEEE, 2012.
[9] P. Conway, N. Kalyanasundharam, G. Donley, K. Lepak, and B. Hughes. Cache hierarchy and memory subsystem of the amd opteron processor. *IEEE Micro*, 30(2):16–29, 2010.
[10] R. Eduardo, D. Grande, and A. Boukerche. Dynamic load redistribution based on migration latency analysis for distributed virtual simulations. In *Haptic Audio Visual Environments and Games (HAVE)*. IEEE, 2011.
[11] M. Frigo, C. E. Leiserson, and K. H. Randall. The implementation of the cilk-5 multithreaded language. In *Proceedings of the ACM SIGPLAN 1998 conference on Programming language design and implementation*, pages 212–223, 1998.
[12] R. Fujimoto. Parallel discrete event simulation. *Communications of the ACM*, 33(10):30–53, oct 1990.
[13] R. Fujimoto. Performance of time warp under synthetic workloads. *Proceedings of the SCS Multiconference on Distributed Simulation*, 22(1):23–28, 1990.
[14] R. M. Fujimoto. *Parallel and Distributed Simulation Systems*. Wiley Interscience, Jan. 2000.
[15] D. Glazer and C. Tropper. On process migration and load balancing in time warp. *IEEE Transactions on Parallel and Distributed Systems*, 4(3):318–327, 1993.
[16] R. Gupta. The fuzzy barrier: a mechanism for high speed synchronization of processors. In *Proc. ASPLOS*, pages 54–63, 1989.
[17] D. Jagtap, N.Abu-Ghazaleh, and D.Ponomarev. Optimization of parallel discrete event simulator for multi-core systems. In *Proc. International Parallel and Distributed Processing Symposium (IPDPS)*, pages 520–531. IEEE, 2012.
[18] M. Y. H. Low. Managing external workload with bsp time warp. In *Proceedings of the 2002 Winter Simulation Conference*. IEEE, 2002.
[19] A. W. Malik, A.J.Park, and R. Fujimoto. Optimistic synchronization of parallel simulations in cloud computing environments. In *Proceedings of the International Conference on Cloud Computing*, pages 49–56. IEEE, 2009.
[20] A. Nataraj, A. Morris, A. Malony, M. Sottile, and P. Beckman. The ghost in the machine: observing the effects of kernel operation on parallel application performance. In *Proc. of ACM/IEEE Confernece on Supercomputing*, pages 1–12. IEEE, 2007.
[21] A. Palaniswamy and P. A. Wilsey. An analytical comparison of periodic checkpointing and incremental state saving. In *Proc. of the 7th Workshop on Parallel and Distributed Simulation (PADS 93)*, pages 127–134. Society for Computer Simulation, July 1993.
[22] F. Petrini, D. J. Kerbyson, and S. Pakin. The case of the missing supercomputer performance: Achieving optimal performance on the 8,192 processors of asci q. In *Proc. of ACM/IEEE Confernece on Supercomputing*, page 55. ACM, 2003.
[23] P. Reiher and D. Jefferson. Virtual time based dynamic load management in the time warp operating system. In *Proceedings of the SCS Multiconference on Distributed Simulation*, pages 103–111, 1990.
[24] V. Sachdev, M. Hybinette, and E. Kraemer. Controlling over-optimism in time-warp via cpu-based flow control. In *Proceedings of the 2004 Winter Simulation Conference*. IEEE, 2004.
[25] K. H. Shum. Replicating parallel simulation on heterogeneous clusters. *Journal of Systems Architecture*, 44:273–292, 1998.
[26] S. C. Tay, Y. M. Teo, and S. T. Kong. Speculative parallel simulation with an adaptive throttle scheme. In *Principles of Advanced and Distributed Simulation (PADS)*, pages 116–123. IEEE, 1997.
[27] D. Tsafrir, Y. Etsion, D. Feitelson, and S. Kirkpatrick. System noise, os clock ticks, and fine-grained parallel applications. In *Proc. of ACM/IEEE Confernece on Supercomputing*, pages 303–312. ACM, 2005.
[28] R. Vitali, A. Pellegrini, and F. Quaglia. Assessing load-sharing within optimistic simulation platforms. In *Proceedings of the 2012 Winter Simulation Conference*. IEEE, 2012.
[29] R. Vitali, A. Pellegrini, and F. Quaglia. Towards symmetric multi-threaded optimistic simulation kernels. In *Principles of Advanced and Distributed Simulation (PADS)*, pages 211–220. IEEE, 2012.
[30] WarpIV Technologies (J. Steinman et al). The warpiv parallel simulation kernel version 1.5.2, 2008. Software available from `http://www.warpiv.com/`.
[31] S. Zhuravlev, S. Blagodurov, and A. Fedorova. Addressing shared resource contention in multicore processors via scheduling. In *Proc. of ASPLOS*, pages 129–142. ACM, 2010.

Optimizing Parallel Simulation of Multicore Systems Using Domain-Specific Knowledge

Jun Wang, Zhenjiang Dong, Sudhakar Yalamanchili, and George Riley
School of Electrical and Computer Engineering
Georgia Institute of Technology
Atlanta, Georgia, USA 30332-0250
{jun.wang, zdong30, sudha, riley}@ece.gatech.edu

ABSTRACT

This paper presents two optimization techniques for the basic Null-message algorithm in the context of parallel simulation of multicore computer architectures. Unlike the general, application-independent optimization methods, these are application-specific optimizations that make use of system properties of the simulation application. We demonstrate in two aspects that the domain-specific knowledge offers great potential for optimization. First, it allows us to send Null-messages much less eagerly, thus greatly reducing the amount of Null-messages. Second, the internal state of the simulation application allows us to make conservative forecast of future outgoing events. This leads to the creation of an enhanced synchronization algorithm called Forecast Null-message algorithm, which, by combining the forecast from both sides of a link, can greatly improve the simulation look-ahead. Compared with the basic Null-message algorithm, our optimizations greatly reduce the number of Null-messages and increase simulation performance significantly as a result. On a subset of the PARSEC benchmarks, a maximum speedup of about 6 is achieved with 17 LPs.

Categories and Subject Descriptors

I.6.8 [**SIMULATION AND MODELING**]: Types of Simulation—*Parallel; Discrete event*

General Terms

Algorithms, Performance

Keywords

Null-message algorithm, domain-specific knowledge, optimization, multicore systems, parallel discrete event simulation

1. INTRODUCTION

The current trend in CPU design is moving increasingly toward multicore systems [10], where multiple processing cores are integrated in the same physical chip. Multicore systems bring an extra dimension of complexity, i.e., core-level concurrency and related issues. As always, simulation is playing an important role in helping designers to explore the design space and meet the new challenges. As system complexity increases, researchers have turned to parallel discrete event simulation (PDES) [8] in order to achieve better simulation performance.

The most important difference between PDES and sequential simulation is that events are processed in a distributed manner and the simulation processes, called logical processes (LPs), send messages to each other. To ensure global order of the events, various synchronization algorithms have been created. These are broadly classified as conservative or optimistic algorithms. The *Null-message algorithm*, or the *CMB algorithm* after its inventors [2], is the first synchronization algorithm for PDES. It is a conservative algorithm that maintains correct event order and avoids deadlock by sending the so-called Null-messages. The advantages of the Null-message algorithm are its conceptual simplicity and ease of implementation. However, a commonly faced problem with this algorithm is low performance due to the large amount of Null-messages. Various optimizations of the basic algorithm have been proposed [15][17][6]. Generally speaking, these are general, application-independent optimizations that focus on the algorithmic aspect of the basic scheme. An important fact about the Null-message algorithm is that it depends on a system property called *look-ahead* in order to function. Look-ahead quantifies the simulation process' ability to predict its future and is highly application dependent. Poor look-ahead generally leads to poor performance for the Null-message algorithm. Based on this, we believe that, while general, application-independent optimizations are useful and should be adopted if applicable, optimizations that take advantage of problem-domain knowledge are more effective, particularly if inter-process communication is not heavy. Simulation models of multicore computer systems are just this kind of systems.

This paper presents two optimizations we have created with Manifold [13], our parallel simulation framework for multicore computer architectures. The first optimization differs from the basic scheme in determining when Null-messages are to be sent, and greatly reduces the number of Null-messages and improves performance significantly as a result. In the second optimization, we look inside the data structures of the simulation application and attempt to pre-determine the time-stamp of the next output event over an inter-LP link. Through a simulation kernel API, this information is passed to the synchronization algorithm, which in turn improves its look-ahead when sending out Null-messages. Based on this idea, an enhanced synchronization algorithm called *Forecast Null-message algorithm* is created, where the Null-message carries an LP's forecast of future output events in addition to its time-stamp. By combining the forecast information from both sides of an inter-LP link, the Forecast Null-message algorithm can greatly improve an LP's lookahead. This enhanced algorithm further reduces the number of Null-messages. Although the reduction of the number of Null-messages only produces limited performance improvement when all of the LPs are running on a single physical node, in the more likely and more scalable simulation environment that involves multiple physical nodes, the performance improvement is substantial.

2. BACKGROUND AND RELATED WORK

The Null-message, or CMB, algorithm [2] is the first algorithm created to address the synchronization problem in PDES. The purposes of the algorithm are to avoid deadlocks that may arise because of the conservative principle of event processing, and to insure correct total ordering of events leading to correct event causality. While the algorithm does achieve its goal of guaranteeing causality correctness and preventing deadlocks, it has the potential problem of poor performance due to the excessive number of Null-messages exchanged among the LPs. A number of variations of the basic algorithm have been proposed to address this problem. Two schemes are discussed in [15]. One is to use a time-out such that Null-messages are only sent after a time-out, and another is demand-driven where Null-messages are only sent when requested. In [17], a few variants of a central theme are presented, namely, deferring sending of either Null-messages, or simulation event messages, or both, and combining the messages so as to reduce the messaging overhead. In [6] the author explored ways to reduce the number of Null-messages by predicting the time-stamp of future messages for incoming channels that are current empty. The prediction is based on the underlying network topology, specifically, the feedforward and feedback topologies. These are all optimizations aimed at reducing of the Null-message overhead of the basic algorithm. They are general in nature and independent of the simulation applications. It should be noted that, if the look-ahead of the system can somehow be improved, the number of Null-messages will also be reduced because the simulation time can advance more before an LP needs to send Null-messages. Since look-ahead is heavily dependent on the application, making use of problem-domain knowledge to improve look-ahead can potentially be more effective than the general methods.

The computer architecture community has been using simulation as an effective design and research tool. However, traditionally the simulators being developed and used are sequential. In recent years, a few parallel simulation frameworks have appeared in the computer architecture literature.

SST [16] is an open-source, parallel simulation framework designed for the research of new technologies in the area of supercomputing. It takes a modular approach that allows system models to be built using the components in its repository. For parallel simulation, it uses barriers to address the synchronization problem. For each inter-LP link, a *sync object* is created and is scheduled periodically. When the action associated with the sync object is processed, a global synchronization is performed. Unlike the Null-message algorithm, this is a barrier-based conservative algorithm.

In [4] the authors explore the design space for parallel simulation of chip-multiprocessors and evaluate the impact of a few design choices, including distributed vs. centralized L2 cache, blocking vs. non-blocking cache access, and Null-message vs. barrier-based algorithm. An abstract of the full-fledged simulator is used in the evaluation, and with the Null-message algorithm a speedup of about 2 is achieved with 16 LPs. Apparently the Null-message algorithm used is the basic algorithm without optimizations. We are not aware of any parallel simulators for multicore systems that have explored optimizations of the Null-message algorithm.

Two other parallel simulation systems for computer architectures can be classified as optimistic simulation because they allow violations of the local causality constraint. In other words, they allow external events to arrive in an LP's past. *SlackSim* [3] defines a quantity called *slack* which basically specifies how far in the simulation time an LP can go from its current local time. A separate thread monitors the smallest local time of all LPs, i.e, the global virtual time (GVT). As the GVT moves, the upper bound for event execution also moves. This makes it different from quantum simulation, which uses explicit barrier synchronization. *Graphite* [14] is similar to SlackSim in that it allows causality violations. It supports three simulation schemes: *Lax*, *Lax-Barrier*, and *Lax-P2P*. *Lax* is essentially unlimited optimism. *Lax-Barrier* is like a quantum simulation, and in *Lax-P2P* an LP periodically chooses a random peer with which to synchronize. These methods are fundamentally different from the Null-message algorithm, which executes events in a conservative manner and does not allow simulation errors.

3. THE MANIFOLD SIMULATION SYSTEM

Manifold [13] is a scalable parallel discrete event simulation framework designed for the research of modern multicore computer architectures. Manifold adopts a component-based open software architecture, which, coupled with standardized inter-component interfaces, allows easy integration of third party components. The software package is composed of a parallel simulation kernel and a set of computer architecture models, such as processor, cache, interconnection network, and DRAM controller models. Users use the kernel and the models to build system models for parallel simulations. A typical architecture that Manifold is designed to simulate is the tiled multicore system as discussed in [10]. This architecture is made up of a number of identical processor nodes connected with an interconnection network. The system model is shown in Figure 1. As can be seen, the system model consists of a few processor nodes and one or more memory controller nodes, interconnected through the underlying interconnection network. The processor nodes each consist of a processor core and one or more level of cache. The dashed lines in Figure 1 shows the partitioning scheme used by our simulator, which will be explained later.

Manifold adopts a layered software architecture [5], separating the simulation kernel and the computer architecture components into two different layers. The simulation kernel layer encapsulates all the PDES services. For parallel simulation, two conservative synchronization algorithms are supported, Null-message and lower bound time-stamp (LBTS)

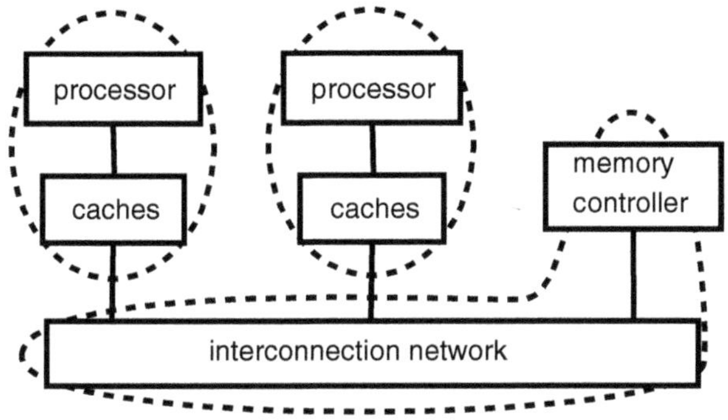

Figure 1: Manifold's example system model and partitioning scheme.

[8]. Quantum simulation is also supported, for users who can allow a small percentage of inaccuracy in exchange for faster simulation speed.

4. OPTIMIZING THE NULL-MESSAGE ALGORITHM IN MANIFOLD

Manifold does not use automatic partitioning, mainly because the number of components in a system model is relatively small. Instead, components are assigned to different LPs in the simulator program. A typical partitioning scheme we have been using is shown in Figure 1 with dashed lines denoting LP boundaries. As can be seen, in this partitioning scheme, the entire interconnection network and the memory controller(s) are in one LP, and each processor node is in a separate LP. In the following we shall assume this partitioning choice.

Another important characteristics of Manifold that should be mentioned in advance is that the system model represents a clock based digital system. Although Manifold allows link delays to be specified in seconds, in this paper we confine our discussion to the cases where link delays are specified in clock ticks. Therefore, all events occur at discrete clock ticks, and the simulation moves from one clock tick to the next.

4.1 Baseline algorithm

We start with a basic implementation of the Null-message algorithm, as shown in Algorithm 1. This is the Null-message algorithm in its most general form. It is application-independent, therefore, does not make use of any characteristics of the simulation application.

In this baseline algorithm, the LP first receives messages in a non-blocking fashion. It then finds out the clock whose next edge is the earliest (There may be multiple clocks). The simulation time of this particular clock edge is kept in the variable `nextClockTime`. Next, the minimum time-stamp of Null-messages from all of the input channels is determined and kept in `min_null`. If `nextClockTime` is less than `min_null`, then all of the events scheduled for the clock edge are safe to process and therefore are processed. Finally, Null-messages are sent to all successors of the LP with time-stamp set to the smaller of `nextClockTime` and `min_null`, plus the look-ahead value. Of course, Null-messages are only sent if the time-stamp is larger than that of the last Null-messages. The look-ahead is set to a value that is slightly smaller than the minimum link delay in the system model.

Algorithm 1 Baseline Null-message algorithm.

while simulation not terminated **do**
  receive messages
  nextClock := clock whose next edge has smallest time-stamp among all clocks
  nextClockTime := simulation time of next edge of *nextClock*
  receive Null-messages
  min_null := minimum time-stamp of Null-msgs from all input links
  if $nextClockTime < min\_null$ **then**
    process all events scheduled for the clock edge
  end if
  $null\_ts := min(nextClockTime, min\_null) + Lookahead$
  Send Null-messages to all successors with time-stamp set to *null_ts* if *null_ts* is larger than time-stamp of the previous Null-message
end while

4.2 Optimization 1: When To Send Null-Messages

The baseline algorithm in Algorithm 1 does achieve its basic design goals, namely, to avoid deadlock and to prevent causality errors. Its drawback is that a lot of Null-messages are sent, most likely more than necessary. This has a big impact on the overall simulation performance, particularly when the messages have to go through a network.

Therefore, we start our optimization of the baseline algorithms by exploring ways to reduce the sending of Null-messages. Two optimization algorithms have been tested with success. It should be pointed out that both these algorithms make use of features of the simulation application, i.e., the multicore computer architecture. Therefore, these are application-specific optimizations.

The first algorithm shall be referred to as Send-When-Safe, or *SWS*. In this algorithm, shown in Algorithm 2, Null-messages are only sent when the clock edge is safe to process.

Algorithm 2 SWS: send Null-message when clock edge is safe.

while simulation not terminated **do**
  receive messages, determine nextClock and nextClockTime, receive Null-messages, determine min_null
  if $nextClockTime < min\_null$ **then**
    process all events scheduled for the clock edge
    send Null-message with time-stamp set to $nextClockTime + Lookahead$
  end if
end while

SWS is possible because of the following properties of the simulation application:

SYSTEM PROPERTY 1. *Each LP moves in the fixed step of half clock tick.*

SYSTEM PROPERTY 2. *The look-ahead is bigger than half clock tick.*

To see the simulation can progress without deadlock, we can simply look at one LP. Assume the minimum link delay in the system is 1 tick and the look-ahead is set to 0.9 ticks, and denote by $Null(ts)$ the Null-message with time-stamp set to ts. First, the LP processes tick 0, which is safe, and sends out $Null(0.9)$. Next, tick 0.5 cannot be processed until the minimum time-stamp of all the Null-messages it gets from the input links is greater than 0.5. This is guaranteed because, with the properties above, all of its fan-ins would process tick 0 and send $Null(0.9)$ to it. When that occurs, it processes tick 0.5 and sends $Null(1.4)$. Then it moves on to tick 1. Eventually it will receive $Null(1.4)$ from all its fan-ins and be able to process tick 1, and so forth.

The second optimization algorithm, Send-When-Block, or *SWB*, does the opposite of *SWS*. It sends Null-messages only when it is blocked, as shown in Algorithm 3.

Algorithm 3 SWB: send Null-message when clock edge is blocked.

```
1: while simulation not terminated do
2:     receive messages, determine nextClock and nextClock-
       Time, receive Null-messages, determine min_null
3:     if nextClockTime < min_null then
4:         process all events scheduled for the clock edge
5:     else
6:         send Null-message with time-stamp set to min_null +
           Lookahead
7:     end if
8: end while
```

It can be easily verified that this algorithm is correct in general, independent of the simulation application. However, this algorithm forces a certain degree of sequential execution. For any LP, once it is blocked, it can only make progress after all of its fan-ins have made progress, and its fan-outs can only make progress after it has made progress.

This, however, is not a serious problem for our simulation model. With the star topology shown in Figure 1. the *SWB* algorithm causes the simulation to progress in lock-step between two groups of LPs. On the one hand is the center of the star, or the network+memory controller, and on the other hand is the rest of the system, i.e,. the processor nodes. Since the processor nodes are much more complex and perform most of the simulation work, and they still do the work in parallel, this lock-step execution between the two groups has only limited impact. Of course, if the workload of the star center is much heavier, it may be necessary to send more Null-messages if parallelism can be improved.

4.3 Optimization 2: Improving Look-ahead

Look-ahead plays a critical role in the Null-message algorithm. Generally speaking, the bigger the look-ahead, the better the parallelism, and hence the better the performance. Therefore, our next optimization focuses on improving look-ahead in our simulation.

As mentioned above, we set our look-ahead to a value that is close to the minimum link delay in the system. To be precise, it is set to $(d_{min} - 0.1)$ ticks, where d_{min} is the minimum link delay. This can be improved if we look a little deeper into the LPs. In the following, we explain how we improve the look-ahead for *Iris*, our interconnection network model, and *MCP-cache*, our coherence cache model.

Iris consists of a number of routers connected in a ring or torus topology. Each router is connected to one network interface (NI), and vice versa. An NI is connected to a single *terminal*, such as a cache component or a memory controller.

In the partitioning scheme in Figure 1 the link between the network interface and MCP-cache crosses LP boundary. We can make two improvements for the look-ahead for this link.

First, we observe that a component in our system models sends out messages at the rising clock edges. This is a system-wide property and applies to both Iris and MCP-cache.

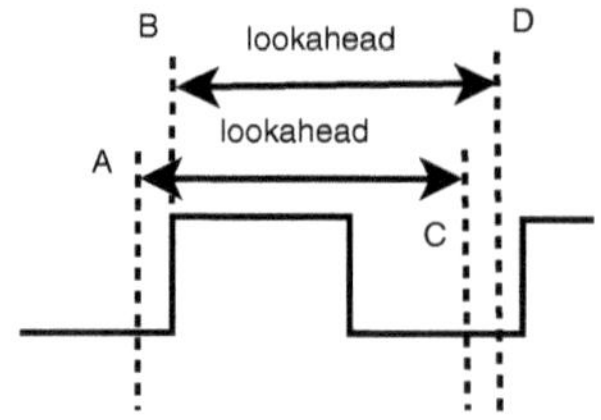

Figure 2: Look-ahead improvement due to synchronous output.

System Property 3. *A component only sends out messages at the rising clock edges.*

This means that the time-stamp for the Null-messages in line 6 in *SWB* in Algorithm 3 can be set to $\lceil t \rceil + Lookahead$ instead of $(min\_null + Lookahead)$, where the meaning of $\lceil t \rceil$ is:

$$\lceil t \rceil = \begin{cases} \text{current edge} & \text{if t is rising edge} \\ \text{next rising edge} & \text{if t is falling edge} \end{cases}$$

This is further illustrated in Figure 2 which shows four points in time: A is *min_null*, or the minimum Null-message time-stamp from all input links, B is the current edge for which the safety of processing is being determined, $C = A + Lookahead$ is the time-stamp of the Null-messages to be sent, based on *SWB* in Algorithm 3, and D is the improved time-stamp for the Null-messages based on the fact that the earliest event to be sent will be sent at the clock edge B. If B is a falling edge, then the Null-message time-stamp would be set to the next rising edge plus the look-ahead.

Note that this improvement cannot be made in the general Null-messages-based simulation, because an event could occur between A and B and cause another event that is earlier than B. So, in the general case, when B is not safe to process, the time-stamp of the Null-messages can only be $A + Lookahead$.

This improvement is shown in Algorithm 4.

Algorithm 4 Improvement of SWB: using next rising edge.

```
while simulation not terminated do
    receive messages, determine nextClock and nextClock-
    Time, receive Null-messages, determine min_null
    if nextClockTime < min_null then
        process all events scheduled for the clock edge
    else
        if nextClockTime is rising edge then
            null_ts := nextClockTime + Lookahead
        else
            null_ts := next rising edge +Lookahead
        end if
        send Null-message with time-stamp set to null_ts
    end if
end while
```

The second improvement of look-ahead makes use of the knowledge of the internal state of Iris and MCP-cache. Based on the internal state, we can forecast *conservatively* the earliest time when Iris or MCP-cache will send out a message and

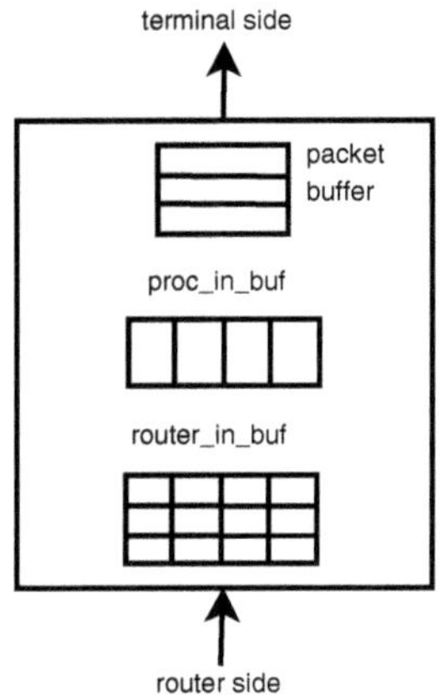

Figure 3: Iris network interface.

use this information to improve look-ahead. In the following, we first describe how the conservative forecast is achieved in Iris and MCP-cache without considering flow control messages. Then we describe the complications caused by flow control, and how the forecast is made in the presence of flow control messages. And finally we present the improved algorithm that uses the forecast.

Iris' routers operate at the flit level [7]. When a packet is received for delivery, at the source NI, the packet is broken up into flits and passed to the router one flit at a time. For each packet, there is one head flit, zero or more body flits, and zero or one tail flits. At the receiving NI, the flits for the packet are assembled. When the entire packet has been received, it is put in the output buffer before being delivered to the terminal. Figure 3 shows the internal structure of the Iris NI for the router-to-terminal direction of traffic. The other direction has a similar structure. As can be seen, there are three buffers. The *router_in_buf* holds individual flits for each of the virtual channels. The *proc_in_buf* is where the flits are assembled into packets. It has one slot for each virtual channel. Finally the *packet buffer* holds the assembled packets before delivery.

The system properties of Iris that we use to forecast its output messages are summarized as follows:

System Property 4. *If the packet buffer of an Iris NI is empty, then the earliest time it will send out a packet is the next tick.*

System Property 5. *If the last flit of a packet arrives at the NI's proc_in_buf at tick t, then the earliest time when the packet is moved to the packet buffer is $t+1$.*

System Property 6. *The router sends at most one flit per tick to the NI.*

System Property 7. *The router has a 3-stage pipeline. Therefore, it takes at least three ticks for a head flit to go through the router.*

Using these properties, Iris NI can make conservative forecast of the earliest possible tick when it will send out a message to its terminal.

On the MCP-cache side it is much simpler. The cache has a parameter called *lookup time* that represents the number of ticks it takes for the cache to send out a message as a result of an incoming request. Furthermore, we can know L ticks in advance if there is an outgoing message, where L is the lookup time. This is summarized below.

System Property 8. *When a request is received by the MCP-cache at tick t, the earliest time when a message is sent out as a result of the request is $t+L$, where L is the lookup time. And if there is a message, it is known at t.*

Although the above system properties of Iris and MCP-cache allow us to forecast outgoing messages, this information cannot be used right away to improve the look-ahead. This is because both Iris and MCP-cache implement a credit-based flow control mechanism. In addition to normal event messages, both Iris and MCP-cache send credit messages, which could violate our forecast of outgoing event messages. The credit message has the following property.

System Property 9. *For each received event message, a credit message is sent.*

The difficulty lies in predicting when a credit is sent, which is component dependent. MCP-cache sends a credit one tick after a message is received, while Iris sends a credit only after a packet is moved from the terminal-side input packet buffer to the router-bound middle buffer. For simplicity we assume the worst case, namely, a credit can be sent any time after a message is received.

Algorithms 5 and 6 show the outgoing message forecast algorithm for Iris and MCP-cache respectively. Both functions return 0 if an outgoing message could occur at the current tick, otherwise, they return the earliest possible tick for the next outgoing message.

In Algorithm 5, lines 2-7 are self-explanatory. Lines 9-14 deal with the problem of making forecast in the presence of un-credited incoming messages, which require credits to be sent. To handle outstanding credits, we use a FIFO queue. Every time there is an incoming message, its scheduled time is entered into the queue. When a credit is sent, the first element in the queue is removed. When there is an un-credited incoming message scheduled at *m_ts*, if its already past, then the credit could be sent at any moment, therefore, we return 0. Otherwise, since the credit for the message could be sent at *m_ts*, we make the conservative forecast that the earliest possible time for an outgoing message is *m_ts* (line 13).

Lines 16-26 handle the case where there are no outstanding credits to be sent. In this situation, we don't have to worry about sending out credits. Therefore we look at the NI's buffers to forecast the next outgoing event message. For each virtual channel, we first look at *proc_in_buf*, where the packet is assembled. If *proc_in_buf* is not empty (line 18), since the head flit carries the packet length in terms of the number of flits, we know how many more flits are yet to come, and since we can only receive one flit per tick, that is the lower bound of the remaining ticks it takes before we have a complete packet. If *proc_in_buf* is empty, we check the *router_in_buf*. If it is not empty (line 21), then it must holds the head flit because *proc_in_buf* is empty. Therefore, it takes at least $packetlen - 1 + 1$ before all the flits for the packet enters *proc_in_buf*. If *router_in_buf* is also empty (line 23), then we consult the router for the earliest possible time when it could forward a head flit to the NI on the

Algorithm 5 Iris' algorithm for forecasting outgoing message.

```
1: function IRIS_FORECAST_NEXT_OUTPUT
2:     if outgoing credit scheduled for this tick then
3:         return 0                                  ▷ this tick

4:     if output packet buffer not empty then
5:         return 0                                  ▷ this tick

6:     if an output packet will be assembled this tick then
7:         return 0                                  ▷ this tick

8:     if there is an input message then
9:         m_ts := input message scheduled time
10:        if (m_ts < now) then
11:            return 0              ▷ credit could be sent any time
12:        else
13:            forecast := m_ts − now
14:        end if
15:    else                      ▷ no un-credited incoming messages
16:        for each virtual channel v do
17:            if (proc_in_buf[v] has flits) then
18:                forecasts[v] := packet len - received flits
19:            else                          ▷ proc_in_buf[v] is empty
20:                if (router_in_buf[v] has flits) then
21:                    forecasts[v] := packet len
22:                else                     ▷ router_in_buf[v] empty
23:                    forecasts[v] := router → earliest() + 2
24:                end if
25:            end if
26:        end for
27:    end if
28:    forecast := min(forecasts[ ])
29:    return now + forecast
30: end function

31: function ROUTER::EARLIEST
32:     if there is one in-transit packet bound for NI then
33:         return 0
34:     else
35:         return 3
36:     end if
37: end function
```

Algorithm 6 MCP's algorithm for forecasting outgoing message.

```
function MCP_FORECAST_NEXT_OUTPUT
    if L1's output buffer not empty OR L2's output buffer not
empty then
        return 0                                  ▷ this tick

    forecast := 0
    if there is msg or credit scheduled then
        forecast := earliest msg or credit time-stamp

    if (forecast == now) then
        return 0                                  ▷ this tick

    if no msg or credit scheduled then
        forecast := min(L1's lookup time, L2's lookup time)
    return now + forecast
end function
```

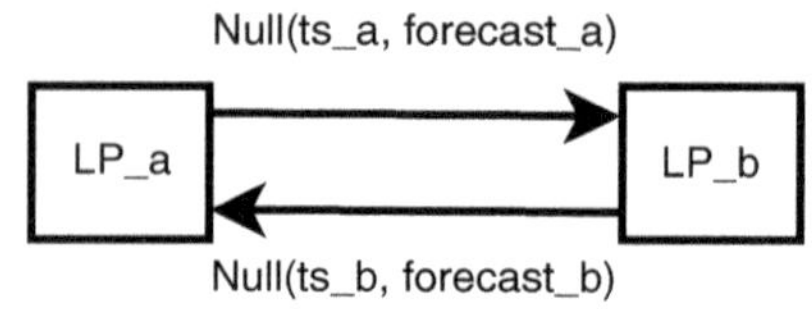

Figure 4: Null-message with event forecast.

given virtual channel. We add two ticks to the router's forecast (one for entering *router_in_buf*, and one for entering *proc_in_buf*). Finally, in line 28, we find out the minimum forecast value from all of the virtual channels and use that as our forecast for the Iris NI.

The forecast algorithm for MCP-cache is much simpler because: (1) its internal structure is simpler, and (2) it always sends out a credit one tick after receiving a message. We use a priority queue to hold the ticks of future outgoing event messages and credits. If this queue is not empty, the first element is used as the forecast. Otherwise, the smaller of L1 and L2 caches' lookup time is used as the forecast.

We now present the improved Null-message algorithm that uses the event forecast as described above to improve look-ahead. For this purpose the Null message itself is slightly enhanced such that it carries a pair $Null(ts, forecast)$, where the meaning of the time-stamp ts is as usual, and $forecast$ means the sender will not send a message before $forecast$ unless it receives a message between ts and $forecast$. The enhanced Null-message is shown in Figure 4. The basic idea of the algorithm is to use the minimum of the forecast values from both sides of a link as the basis for the time-stamp of the next Null-message.

The Forecast Null-message algorithm is shown in Algorithm 7.

As can be seen, Algorithm 7 is a modification of *SWB*. It also sends Null-messages only when it is blocked.

Lines 6-8 are where the forecast is made. Each component that is interested in making forecast should register its forecast function with the clock object. At a rising edge of the clock when the LP's execution is blocked, the registered functions are called.

In the loop in lines 10-26 we find out the time-stamp for the next Null message for each successor LP. The forecast is used as follows. The LP sending the Null-messages will compare its forecast for the successor ($out\_forecast$) and the successor's forecast carried in the received Null-message ($in\_forecast$). If $out\_forecast > in\_forecast$, then we can guarantee we will not send out a message before $in\_forecast + 1$, assuming the minimum inter-LP delay is 1. Otherwise, the earliest time when we are going to send a message is simply $out\_forecast$.

We find out the minimum time-stamp for the Null-message for all of the successors, and then in the loop in lines 27-29, we send out the Null-messages. Using the minimum is because experiments have shown this gives better performance results.

4.4 Section Summary

This section has presented two optimizations for the Null-message algorithm, particularly, an enhanced Null-message algorithm called Forecast Null-message algorithm. A few important points should be noted regarding the applicability of the methods.

Algorithm 7 The Forecast Null-message algorithm.

```
while simulation not terminated do
    receive messages, determine nextClock and nextClock-
    Time, receive Null-messages, determine min_null
    if nextClockTime < min_null then
        process all events scheduled for the clock edge
    else
        for each registered component c do
            c → forecast_next_output() to determine the next
            possible cross-LP output event
        end for
        min_null_ts := 0
        for each successor do
            out_forecast := time of next possible output
            in_forecast := forecast of next possible input from
            successor
            if out_forecast > in_forecast then
                forecast := in_forecast + 1          ▷ assuming
                                                     ▷ LP-to-LP delay is 1
            else
                forecast := out_forecast
            end if
            null_ts := nextClockTime + Lookahead
            if forecast > nextClockTime then
                null_ts := forecast + Lookahead
            end if
            if (min_null_ts==0 || min_null_ts > null_ts) then
                min_null_ts := null_ts
            end if
        end for

        for each successor do
            send Null-message with time-stamp set to
            min_null_ts
        end for
    end if
end while
```

- The optimization methods use domain-specific knowledge. It should be pointed out that the knowledge used is generally available in the application domain, namely, multicore system models. For example, a simulator for multicore systems is generally clock-cycle-based, a cache model usually has an access latency, and a router of an interconnection network is generally pipelined. Therefore, the methods are by no means limited to the particular components or simulation system that we used and are applicable to other similar systems.

- The methods are not dependent on the partitioning scheme shown in Figure 1. This partitioning scheme is based on the observation that, because cache hit rate is generally well over 95%, only a small amount of messages are exchanged between the caches and the network. If, for example, a different way of partitioning puts two neighboring routers in two different LPs, the optimizations presented are still applicable, except that we need to look inside the routers to in order to use the Forecast Null-message algorithm.

- The domain-specific optimizations do not preclude the general optimization methods such as the idea of deferring the sending of Null-messages as presented in [17]. However, how well the two kinds of optimizations work together in a single simulation system is yet to be studied.

5. EXPERIMENTAL RESULTS

We have implemented the four algorithms described above: *Baseline*, *SWS*, *SWB*, and *Forecast*. This section describes the experimental results obtained with the four algorithms, and presents our analysis of the results.

5.1 Experiment Environment

Tests are conducted on a standalone machine and on a Linux cluster. The standalone machine has two Intel Xeon E5-2620 6-core CPUs with hyperthreading, for a total of 24 hardware threads. The operating system is Debian Wheezy and the MPI package used is OpenMPI 1.4.3. The two nodes that we use on the cluster each have two Intel Xeon X5670 6-core CPUs with a total of 24 hardware threads. The operating system is RHEL release 6.3, and the MPI package is OpenMPI 1.5.4.

We randomly selected five programs from the PARSEC 2.0 benchmark suite [1] for our testing. These are widely used parallel benchmark programs. A program that uses Intel's Pin API [9] was used to generate trace files from the binaries of the benchmark programs. The trace files are fed to the simulator as input.

The simulation system model consists of 16 processor nodes, a memory controller node, and a torus interconnection network, like the model shown in Figure 1. Each processor node has a processor component, a private L1 cache, and a shared L2 cache slice. The processor component is a cycle-accurate out-of-order x86 model called Zesto [12]. The caches implement a directory-based MESI (Modified-Exclusive-Shared-Invalid) coherence protocol to maintain cache coherence. The lookup time is set to 5 ticks for both L1 and L2 caches. For simplicity, there is one clock used by all of the components.

For each tested benchmark, 16 trace files are used as input, one for each processor component. A multicore shared-memory machine emulator called QSim [11] was used in generating the trace files.

As shown in Figure 1 the network and the memory controller are assigned to one LP, and the processor nodes are each assigned to a separate LP, for a total of 17 LPs.

5.2 Results

Two sets of tests have been conducted. In the first set, all of the LPs are allocated to the same machine. And in the second set, the LPs are allocated to two machines.

5.2.1 Test Set 1

This Test Set is run on the standalone machine. Results for the Test Set are given in Tables 1 - 3 and Figure 5. We run the simulation for 10 million simulated clock cycles. Each data item in the table is the average value of three runs.

Table 1 shows the number of Null-messages sent/received by the interconnection network component, Iris, per link. Each entry has two numbers, for sent and received Null-messages respectively. With the baseline algorithm, a large number of Null-messages are exchanged. In fact, the average interval between Null-messages is less than 0.2 ticks, even though the look-ahead is 0.9 ticks. The number of Null-messages in *SWS* can be predicted. It sends two every tick per link. The interval between two Null-messages is half a tick. Compared with the baseline algorithm, this is a big improvement. *SWB* reduces the number of Null-messages even further. The lock-step execution between the network component and the processor nodes results in the fixed interval of 1.8 ticks between two successive Null-messages. This is twice the look-ahead. Finally, *Forecast*, by dynamically improving the look-ahead of both sides of the cross-LP links, achieves an additional 29 to 61% reduction of the number of Null-messages compared with *SWB*. On the Iris side, the Null-message frequency is reduced to one in 3.5 to 3.9 ticks, with the exception of *bodytrack*. On the cache side, the frequency is one in 3.9 to 5.8 ticks.

Table 1: Number of Null-messages per link.

Benchmarks	Baseline	SWS	SWB	Forecast
bodytrack	81,462,560	20M	5,555,559	5,298,071
	78,362,448	20M	5,555,560	2,554,396
facesim	73,753,704	20M	5,555,557	2,832,306
	66,864,855	20M	5,555,557	1,748,367
freqmine	67,549,584	20M	5,555,557	2,833,459
	60,451,605	20M	5,555,557	1,760,523
streamcluster	68,659,786	20M	5,555,557	2,558,872
	61,198,045	20M	5,555,557	1,704,793
vips	82,331,880	20M	5,555,557	2,571,159
	75,666,786	20M	5,555,557	1,715,470

Table 2 shows the simulation running time of the tests. Table 3 shows the performance improvements of the Forecast Null-message algorithm over SWB, and the speedup numbers relative to the sequential simulation. The table shows a maximum speedup of 6.3. In Figure 5 we show the running time of the three optimization algorithms, normalized with respect to the running time of SWB.

As we can see, compared with the baseline algorithm, all of *SWS*, *SWB*, and *Forecast* reduce the simulation time by more than 60%. However, among the three optimization algorithms, the situation looks more complex. For example, compared with *SWS*, *SWB* has significantly fewer Null-messages, but this does not translate into reduction in running time. On the contrary, *SWS* outperforms *SWB* in 4 cases. On the other hand, *Forecast* outperforms *SWB* by 8-12%, while the Null-message reduction is much bigger, in the range of 29 - 61% In the case of *freqmine*, *Forecast* only outperforms *SWS* by 2.3% while we have an 88% reduction in the amount of Null-messages. In this test setting, all of the LPs are running on the same shared-memory machine. The overhead of inter-process messaging is very low to start with. The results suggest two conclusions. First, in this environment, reducing the number of Null-messages has diminishing returns. Second, the results show *SWS* outperforms *SWB* in 4 cases even though its Null-message count is 3-4 times higher. This indicates some other factor may play a more important role than the number of Null-messages. One possibility is that, because *SWS* sends Null-messages more frequently than *SWB*, it may have better run-time parallelism. We leave to our future work the study of the tradeoff between the number of Null-messages and parallelism.

5.2.2 Test Set 2

This Test Set is run on the cluster. In this Test Set, we allocate the 17 LPs roughly evenly to the two test machines, with 9 LPs on one machine and 8 on another. This makes half of inter-LP links cross the machine boundary, therefore, messages on these links, including Null-messages, will go

Table 2: Simulation running time in seconds.

Benchmarks	Seq.	Baseline	SWS	SWB	Forecast
bodytrack	2410	2592	856	868	769
facesim	4323	2154	869	825	722
freqmine	4457	2099	764	814	746
streamcluster	4630	1957	761	815	733
vips	4508	2446	769	807	719

Table 3: Forecast Null-message: improvements over SWB and speedup.

Benchmarks	Improvement	Speedup
bodytrack	11.4%	3.1
facesim	12.5%	6.0
freqmine	8.4%	6.0
streamcluster	10.1%	6.3
vips	10.9%	6.3

through the physical network. We expect the number of Null-messages has a much bigger impact on the simulation performance than in Test Set 1.

Results are shown in Tables 4 - 6, and Figure 6. We run the simulation for 10 million simulated clock cycles. Each data item in the tables is the average value of three runs. Results for the baseline Null-message algorithm are not collected simply because it takes too long (over 24 hours) to finish one run, making it an unviable choice in this testing environment.

Table 4 shows the number of Null-messages sent/received by Iris, Table 5 shows the simulation running time, Table 6 shows the performance improvements of the Forecast Null-message algorithm over SWB, and its speedup numbers relative to the sequential simulation, and Figure 6 shows the running time normalized with respect to SWB. Compared with Test Set 1, it seems the number of Null-messages has a much bigger impact on the performance. For example, in Test Set 1, the running times of *SWS* and *SWB* are close, with *SWS* outperforms *SWB* in a few cases. Here we see *SWB* outperforms *SWS* consistently by a significant amount: 26-36%. Comparing *Forecast* with *SWB*, we see a reduction in simulation time of 14-38%. Therefore, we can state that reducing the number of Null-messages is very important in the case where inter-LP links cross physical machine boundaries.

6. CONCLUSIONS AND FUTURE WORK

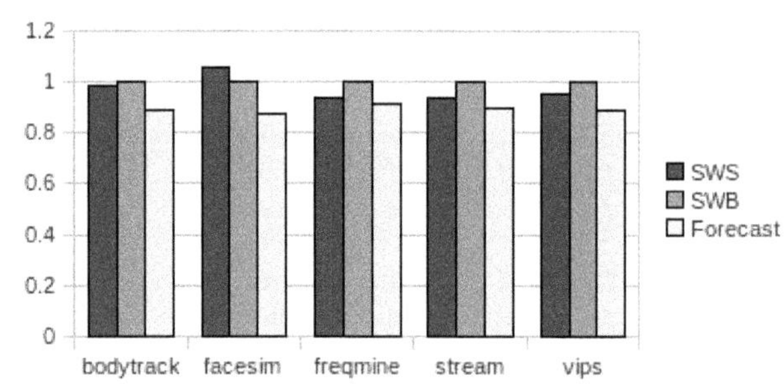

Figure 5: Test Set 1 normalized running time.

Table 4: Number of Null-messages per link.

Benchmarks	SWS	SWB	Forecast
bodytrack	20M	5,555,559	5,824,030
	20M	5,555,558	2,622,173
facesim	20M	5,555,559	2,737,507
	20M	5,555,558	1,730,305
freqmine	20M	5,555,989	2,841,734
	20M	5,555,989	1,736,944
streamcluster	20M	5,555,558	2,553,496
	20M	5,555,558	1,679,566
vips	20M	5,555,560	2,586,544
	20M	5,555,559	1,669,547

Table 5: Simulation running time in seconds.

Benchmarks	Seq.	SWS	SWB	Forecast
bodytrack	2326	1915	1304	934
facesim	4340	1658	1178	1006
freqmine	4210	2091	1321	913
streamcluster	4080	1963	1297	811
vips	4023	1592	1179	723

Two optimizations of the Null-message algorithm using domain-specific knowledge are presented in the context of parallel simulation of multicore systems. Because of the characteristics of the simulation application, we can send Null-messages much less eagerly than the baseline algorithm. In addition, the internal state of the LP together with the partitioning topology allows us to make conservative forecast of future events. Based on this, an enhanced algorithm called Forecast Null-message algorithm is created, in which the Null-message is enhanced to carry the forecast information. And with the forecast from both sides of the inter-LP link we can achieve a dynamic look-ahead that is much greater than what can be obtained statically from the inter-LP delays. The optimizations greatly reduce the number of Null-messages compared with the baseline algorithm. When the simulation is run on multiple physical machines, the reduced number of Null-messages has a great impact on the performance. However, if all the LPs run on the same machine, the reduction of Null-messages has diminishing returns. For our future work, we intend to investigate the scalability of the methods, the impact of different partitioning schemes, and other possible factors that could play an important role in improving simulation performance.

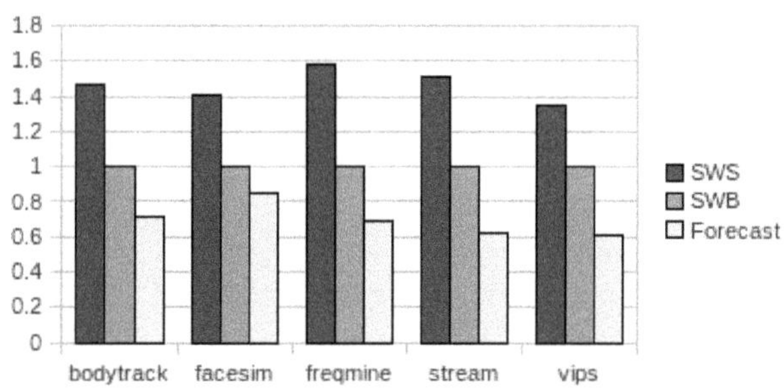

Figure 6: Test Set 2 normalized running time.

Table 6: Forecast Null-message: improvements over SWB and speedup.

Benchmarks	Improvement	Speedup
bodytrack	28.4%	2.5
facesim	14.6%	4.3
freqmine	30.9%	4.6
streamcluster	37.5%	5.0
vips	38.7%	5.6

7. REFERENCES

[1] C. Bienia and K. Li. Parsec 2.0: A new benchmark suite for chip-multiprocessors. *Proceedings of the 5th Annual Workshop on Modeling, Benchmarking and Simulation*, 2009.

[2] K. Chandy and J. Misra. Distributed simulation: a case study in design and verification of distributed programs. *IEEE Transactions on Software Engineering*, SE-5(5):440–452, 1979.

[3] J. Chen, L. Dabbiru, D. Wong, M. Annavaram, and M. Dubois. Adaptive and speculative slack simulations of cmps on cmps. *Proceedings of the 43rd Annual IEEE/ACM International Symposium on Microarchitecture*, pages 523–534, 2010.

[4] M. Chidester and A. George. Parallel simulation of chip-multiprocessor architectures. *ACM Transactions on Modeling and Computer Simulation*, 12(3):176–200, July 2002.

[5] P. Clements, F. Bachmann, L. Bass, D. Garlan, J. Ivers, R. Little, P. Merson, R. Nord, and J. Stafford. *Documenting Software Architectures: Views and Beyond.* Addison-Wesley, 2nd edition, 2011.

[6] R. DeVries. Reducing null messages in misra's distributed discrete event simulation method. *IEEE Transactions on Software Engineering*, 16(1):82–91, January 1990.

[7] J. Duato, S. Yalamanchili, and L. Ni. *Interconnection Networks, an Engineering Approach.* Morgan Kaufmann, 2003.

[8] R. Fujimoto. *Parallel and Distributed Simulation Systems.* John Wiley & Sons, 2000.

[9] Intel. Pin - a dynamic binary instrumentation tool. `http://software.intel.com/en-us/articles/pin-a-dynamic-binary-instrumentation-tool`.

[10] S. Keckler, K. Olukotun, and H. Hofstee, editors. *Multicore Processors and Systems.* Springer, 2009.

[11] C. Kersey, A. Rodrigues, and S. Yalamanchili. A universal parallel front-end for execution driven microarchitecture simulation. *Proceedings of the 2012 Workshop on Rapid Simulation and Performance Evaluation Methods and Tools*, pages 25–32, 2012.

[12] G. Loh, S. Subramaniam, and Y. Xie. Zesto: A cycle-level simulator for highly detailed microarchitecture exploration. *International Symposium on Performance Analysis of Software and Systems*, pages 53–64, 2009.

[13] manifold.gatech.edu. Manifold. `http://manifold.gatech.edu`.

[14] J. Miller, H. Kasture, G.Kurian, C. Gruenwald, N. Beckmann, C. Celio, J. Eastep, and A. Agarwal. Graphite: A distributed parallel simulator for

multicores. *Proceedings of the 16th International Symposium on High-Performance Computer Architecture*, pages 1–12, 2010.

[15] J. Misra. Distributed discrete event simulation. *ACM Computing Surveys*, 18(1):39–65, March 1986.

[16] A. Rodrigues, K. Hemmert, B. Barrett, C. Kersey, R. Oldfield, M. Weston, R. Risen, J. Cook, P. Rosenfeld, E. CooperBalls, and B.Jacob. The structural simulation toolkit. *ACM SIGMETRICS Performance Evaluation Review*, 38(4):37–42, March 2011.

[17] W.-K. Su and C. Seitz. Variants of the chandy-misra-bryant distributed discrete-event simulation algorithm. Technical Report Caltech-CS-TR-88-22, California Institute of Technology, 1988.

Hierarchical Interest Management for Distributed Virtual Environments

Ke Pan
School of Computer Eng.
Nanyang Technological Univ.
Singapore
pank0001@ntu.edu.sg

Xueyan Tang
School of Computer Eng.
Nanyang Technological Univ.
Singapore
asxytang@ntu.edu.sg

Wentong Cai
School of Computer Eng.
Nanyang Technological Univ.
Singapore
aswtcai@ntu.edu.sg

Suiping Zhou
School of Computing
Teesside University
United Kingdom
s.zhou@tees.ac.uk

Hanying Zheng
School of Computer Eng.
Nanyang Technological Univ.
Singapore
zhen0084@ntu.edu.sg

ABSTRACT

An Interest Management (IM) mechanism eliminates irrelevant status updates transmitted in Distributed Virtual Environments (DVE). This paper proposes a new hierarchical IM mechanism for DVEs. The hierarchical mechanism divides the virtual world into multiple levels of cells and keeps the relationship between an entity and an Area-Of-Interest (AOI) at a particular cell level according to their relative position. As their relative position changes, the relationship level is updated accordingly. Compared with the traditional area-based and cell-based mechanisms, the proposed hierarchical mechanism significantly reduces the communication bandwidth consumption of IM and thus considerably improves the scalability of DVEs. In addition, the proposed mechanism also has much lower computation cost than the traditional mechanisms and very acceptable storage requirement for its data structures.

Categories and Subject Descriptors

C.2.4 [**Computer - Communication Networks**]: Distributed Systems—*Distributed applications*

General Terms

Algorithms, Design, Performance

Keywords

Distributed Virtual Environment, Interest Management

1. INTRODUCTION

Distributed Virtual Environments (DVE) allow multiple participants to interact with each other in shared virtual worlds. A prominent application of DVEs is today's popular Massively Multiplayer Online Games (MMOG) [7]. In a typical DVE, a set of inter-connected computers work together to simulate the behavior of many entities in the shared virtual world [31]. Traditionally, DVEs follow a client-server architecture [7, 35] in which one or multiple servers are responsible for maintaining all entity status and disseminating status updates to clients. This creates both computation and communication bottlenecks at the server site. Recently, many Peer-to-Peer (P2P) DVEs emerge [4, 16, 18]. In a P2P architecture, each peer is responsible for maintaining a subset of entities and disseminating their status updates to the other peers. The P2P architecture distributes the computation demand for maintaining entity status among peers. However, since each peer has to send status updates to many other peers, the P2P architecture creates higher communication demand at the peers compared to that at the clients in a client-server architecture [26, 29]. This limits the scalability of a P2P DVE because the peers often have Internet connections of restricted bandwidth.

Interest Management (IM) is an important mechanism for reducing the communication demand in DVEs. It is realized by defining an Area-Of-Interest (AOI) for each entity that describes a region in the virtual world which an entity is interested in. An entity only needs to receive status updates of the other entities which are located inside its AOI. These status updates are called *relevant status updates*. In this way, the number of status updates that need to be transmitted can be significantly reduced.

This paper focuses on the performance of IM mechanisms for DVEs. Traditionally, there are two IM mechanisms, namely an area-based mechanism [6, 12] and a cell-based mechanism [18, 22]. As shall be discussed in Section 2, both mechanisms introduce regular IM-control communication among all entities, irrespective of their relative positions. This gives rise to considerable amount of IM-control communication overhead, particularly in large-scale DVEs. To reduce the communication overhead, in this paper, we propose a new hierarchical IM mechanism that divides the virtual world into multiple levels of cells and keeps the relationship between an entity and the AOI of another entity at a particular cell level according to their relative position. As their relative position changes, the relationship level is updated accordingly. The IM-control communication demand self-adapts to the relative positions between entities: less frequent communication is required between entities that are further apart. A wide range of experiments are conducted to compare the proposed mechanism against the traditional mechanisms in a P2P multiplayer game scenario. The results show that the proposed mechanism significantly reduces the communication bandwidth consumption of IM and thus considerably improves the scalability of DVEs. In addition, the proposed mechanism also has much lower computation cost than the traditional mechanisms and very acceptable storage requirement for its data structures.

The rest of this paper is organized as follows. Section 2 outlines the two traditional IM mechanisms. Section 3 presents the proposed hierarchical IM mechanism. The experimental setup and results are discussed in Section 4. Section 5 summarizes the related work. Finally, Section 6 concludes the paper.

2. TRADITIONAL IM MECHANISMS

The area-based and cell-based mechanisms are two traditional IM mechanisms. In the area-based IM mechanism [6, 12], each entity keeps updating its AOI position with all other entities. Upon receiving an AOI update of another entity, the receiving entity checks whether it falls in the AOI and this process is known as *matching*. Based on the matching results, an entity is able to send its status updates to the other entities which are interested in it. However, it is not affordable for an entity to continuously send out its AOI updates in every frame as this causes too much communication overhead as well as computation cost for matching [25]. A simple practical strategy is to send AOI updates periodically [2, 21, 25]. Another strategy is to perform AOI updates in a space-driven manner [2], where an entity sends a new AOI update only when its AOI position has changed over a distance threshold since the last AOI update. The matching results maintained by these strategies may be inaccurate since the entities are not aware of the changes in AOI positions between successive updates. In order not to miss out any relevant status update, both strategies require an entity to artificially expand the AOI sent out in its AOI update to enclose all its possible AOI positions before the next AOI update [6, 25]. This expansion causes *irrelevant status updates* between entities in that an entity may receive status updates of other entities that are outside its real AOI. The tradeoff between the AOI update overhead and irrelevant status updates requires the updating period or distance threshold to be carefully chosen in order to optimize the communication efficiency of the area-based IM mechanism.

The cell-based IM mechanism divides the virtual world into disjoint cells generally in squares [1, 30], or hexagons [14, 22]. Without IP multicast support in the Internet, the IM mechanism of a DVE needs to manage the entity-in-cell information by itself. Each entity maps its AOI to the cells and sends out updates about the set of cells overlapping with its AOI to all other entities. As a result, every entity is able to maintain the list of entities whose AOIs overlap with each individual cell. Based on this information, each entity always sends its status updates to all entities in the list of its current residing cell. Similar to the area-based mechanism, there is a tradeoff between the IM-control communication overhead and irrelevant status updates in the cell-based mechanism. The IM-control overhead includes the updates sent by entities about their AOIs when their AOIs move across cell borders. Irrelevant status updates, on the other hand, are caused by imperfect matching: as long as an entity B's AOI overlaps with another entity A's residing cell, A sends its status updates to B even if A's position is not really located inside B's AOI. Both the IM-control overhead and the volume of irrelevant status updates are dependent on the cell size. In order to optimize the communication efficiency of the cell-based IM mechanism, the cell size needs to be carefully chosen to strike a balance between the IM-control overhead and irrelevant status updates.

In both the area-based and cell-based mechanisms, each entity regularly updates its AOI information with all other entities irrespective of its relative position to the other entities. This leads to significant IM-control communication overhead. In the next section, we propose a new hierarchical IM mechanism for reducing the IM-control communication overhead.

3. HIERARCHICAL IM MECHANISM

Without loss of generality, we consider a set of interconnected computers that host entities moving around in a shared Virtual World (VW). These computers can be either the servers in a distributed server architecture [3, 27] or the peers in a P2P architecture. Each computer periodically refreshes the status of its hosted entities based on their kinetics and user actions. The period between two successive refreshes is called a frame. Each entity has an associated AOI that moves along with the entity. The entity position is represented by a single point in the VW, and the AOI is a region of any shape in the VW. The hierarchical IM mechanism proposed in this paper is applicable to VWs with any number of dimensions. For the simplicity of presentation, we shall focus our discussion on two-dimensional VWs.

3.1 Relationship between an Entity and an AOI

As shown in Figure 1, we recursively partition the VW into a hierarchy of cells in which each cell at an intermediate level is divided into a 2×2 grid of four equal-size cells at the next lower level. The partition proceeds until the cell size at the bottom level is within the minimum distinguishable unit of the VW. Suppose the maximum size of the VW along all dimensions is D and the smallest unit of the coordinate system is σ, then the depth of the cell hierarchy is given by $\lceil \lg(D/\sigma) \rceil$. For example, if the VW is a two-dimensional space of 1000×1000 distance units and the smallest unit of the coordinate system is 0.001 distance unit, there are $\lceil \lg(1000/0.001) \rceil = 20$ levels in the hierarchy.

To simplify our discussion, we shall assume that the VW size is $2^K \cdot \sigma$ distance units by $2^K \cdot \sigma$ distance units, where σ is the smallest unit of the coordinate system, K is the depth of the cell hierarchy, and each cell at the bottom level of the hierarchy is a minimum distinguishable unit of the VW. As shown in Figure 1, we label the levels in the cell hierarchy with increasing numbers from the root to the bottom. At each level m $(1 \leq m \leq K)$, there are a total of $2^m \times 2^m$ cells, each of which is denoted as $C_{m,(x,y)}$, where x is the cell index numbered from 0 to $2^m - 1$ along the horizontal dimension, and y is the cell index numbered from 0 to $2^m - 1$ along the vertical dimension. Figure 1 also shows that each cell border has an associated level that represents the highest level of cells (i.e., the largest cells) of which it is the border.

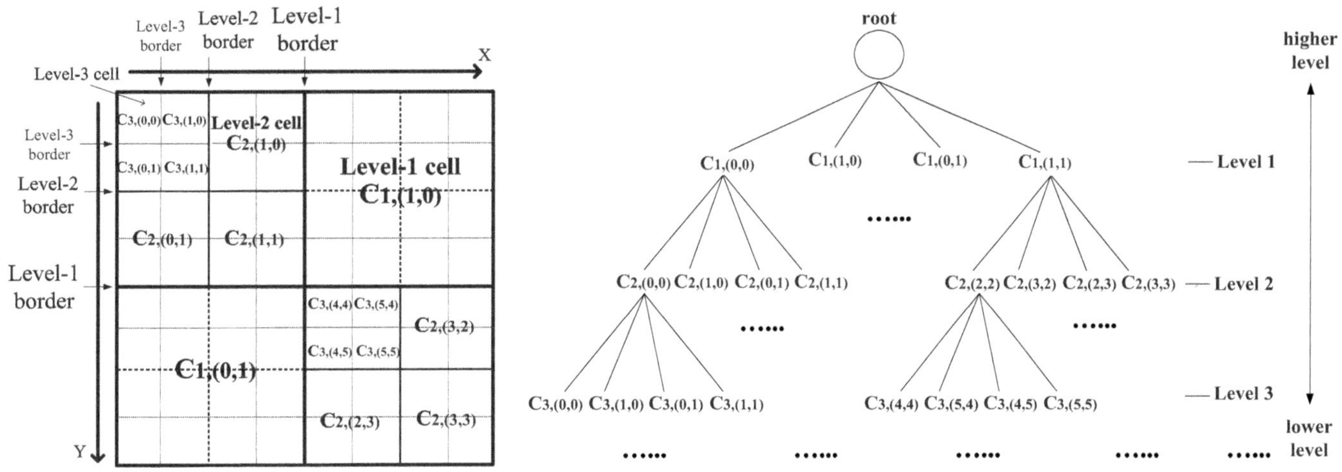

Figure 1: The Cell Hierarchy of a Virtual World

We define the level-m residing cell of an entity as the cell at level m in which the entity is located. With a total of K levels in the cell hierarchy, at any time, an entity has K residing cells, one at each level. A larger residing cell at a higher level completely covers a smaller residing cell at a lower level. We denote the level-m residing cell of an entity E by $RC_m(E)$. Figure 2(a) shows the top three levels of the cell hierarchy in an example VW that contains six entities A, B, C, D, F and G, all of which have rectangle-shaped AOIs. In this example, the residing cells of entity G are $RC_1(G)=C_{1,(0,0)}$, $RC_2(G)=C_{2,(1,1)}$, $RC_3(G)=C_{3,(3,2)}$.

We denote the AOI of an entity E by AOI(E). We classify the relationship between an entity E and the AOI of another entity E' into the following two types.

- **Enclosing**: AOI(E') encloses entity E. That is, AOI(E') covers the minimum distinguishable unit in which entity E is located (i.e., entity E's level-K residing cell). In this case, entity E is required to send its status updates to entity E'. For example, in Figure 2(a), AOI(C) encloses entity G, so it has an enclosing relationship with G.
- **Apart**: AOI(E') does not enclose entity E, so entity E does not need to send its status updates to entity E'. In this case, AOI(E') does not cover E's level-K residing cell. We describe the apart relationship between entity E and AOI(E') by the highest-level residing cell (i.e., the largest residing cell) of E that AOI(E') does not overlap. For example, in Figure 2(a), AOI(B) overlaps with $RC_2(G)$ but does not overlap with $RC_3(G)$, so its apart relationship with G is described by $RC_3(G)=C_{3,(3,2)}$. AOI(D) and AOI(F) overlap with $RC_1(G)$ but do not overlap with $RC_2(G)$, so their apart relationships with G are described by $RC_2(G)=C_{2,(1,1)}$. AOI(A) does not overlap with $RC_1(G)$, so its apart relationships with G is described by $RC_1(G)$ $=C_{1,(0,0)}$. In general, if an entity is located further away from an AOI, their apart relationship is described by a higher-level cell (i.e., a larger cell).

3.2 Overview of the Hierarchical Mechanism

In our hierarchical IM mechanism, the relationship between entity E and AOI(E') (including the cell describing the apart-type relationship) is remembered by both entities E and E'. When entity E or AOI(E') moves, their relationship may change. If the original relationship between E and AOI(E') is enclosing, entity E keeps sending its status update to entity E' at every frame. Since an entity's current position is normally included in its status update, entity E' is able to check whether its AOI still encloses entity E whenever it receives a status update from E. If a received status update indicates that E is located outside AOI(E'), their relationship should be changed to apart. In this case, based on the received position of E and the position of AOI(E'), entity E' calculates the cell describing the new apart relationship between E and AOI(E'), and then notifies entity E of the new relationship.

If entity E and AOI(E') originally have an apart relationship described by E's level-m residing cell $RC_m(E)$, then the relationship changes only if any of the following situations arises: (1) entity E moves out of $RC_m(E)$; (2) AOI(E') moves to become overlapping with $RC_m(E)$; and (3) AOI(E') moves to become not overlapping with $RC_{m-1}(E)$.

Situation (1) is detected by entity E based on its position and knowledge of $RC_m(E)$. On observing situation (1), entity E sends its position to entity E' for E' to calculate the new relationship. Then, E' informs E of the new relationship. For example, in Figure 2(a), entity G has an apart relationship with AOI(D) that is described by $RC_2(G) = C_{2,(1,1)}$. If entity G moves to its new position as shown in Figure 2(b), G moves out of $RC_2(G)$. Thus, G sends its new position to entity D. Then, entity D calculates the new relationship between AOI(D) and entity G (which is described by $RC_3(\text{new } G) = C_{3,(3,1)}$), and notifies entity G of the new relationship.

Situations (2) and (3) are detected by entity E' based on its AOI position and knowledge of $RC_m(E)$. On observing situation (2), entity E' sends its AOI position to entity E for E to calculate the new relationship. Then, E informs E' of the new relationship. For example, in Figure 2(a), the apart relationship between entity G and AOI(A) is described by $RC_1(G)=C_{1,(0,0)}$. If entity A moves to its new position as shown in Figure 2(c), AOI(A) becomes overlapping with $RC_1(G)$. Thus, A sends its new AOI position to entity G. Then, entity G calculates its new relationship with AOI(A)

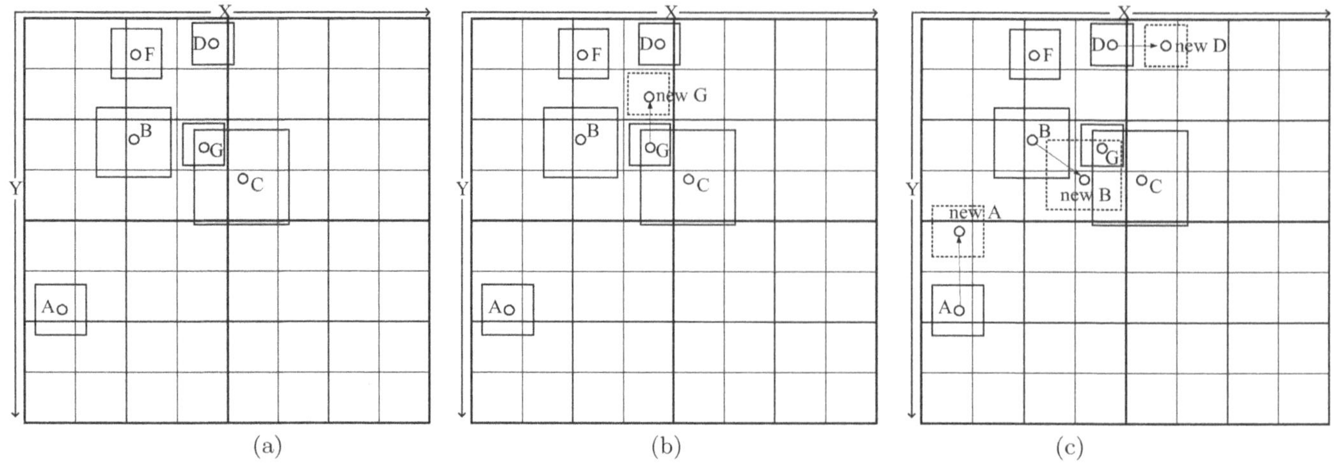

Figure 2: An Example of Relationships between Entities and AOIs

as an apart relationship described by $RC_2(G)=C_{2,(1,1)}$ and informs entity A of the new relationship. Similarly, in Figure 2(a), the apart relationship between G and AOI(B) is described by $RC_3(G)=C_{3,(3,2)}$. If entity B moves to its new position as shown in Figure 2(c), AOI(B) becomes overlapping with $RC_3(G)$. Thus, B sends its new AOI position to entity G. Then, entity G calculates its new relationship with AOI(B) as an enclosing relationship and informs entity B of the new relationship.

On observing situation (3), entity E' is capable of locally calculating the new relationship based on its AOI position and the knowledge that entity E is located in $RC_m(E)$. After the calculation, entity E' notifies entity E of the new relationship. For example, in Figure 2(a), the apart relationship between entity G and AOI(D) is described by $RC_2(G)=C_{2,(1,1)}$. If entity D moves to its new position as shown in Figure 2(c), AOI(D) becomes not overlapping with $RC_1(G)$. Thus, D locally calculates the new relationship between G and AOI(D) as an apart relationship described by $RC_1(G)=C_{1,(0,0)}$. Then, entity D notifies entity G of the new relationship.

In summary, the IM-control communication between entities E and E' for maintaining the relationship between E and AOI(E') occurs only when the relationship changes. The IM-control communication demand self-adapts to the relative position between E and AOI(E') due to the hierarchical partitioning of the VW. If E and AOI(E') are further away from each other, the cell describing their apart relationship is larger (i.e., at a higher level) and the IM-control communication is less frequent. In this way, the IM-control communication overhead is significantly reduced compared with the traditional mechanisms. Meanwhile, since an entity sends its status updates to an AOI only when their relationship is enclosing, irrelevant status updates are also reduced to minimum.

We remark that the aforementioned operations are meant for maintaining the relationship between entity E and AOI(E'). Since each entity has its own AOI, the relationship between entity E' and AOI(E) should also be maintained.[1] This can be done symmetrically to what is described above. In the next section, we present the data structures used by each entity for maintaining its relationship with the AOIs of all other entities and its AOI's relationship with all other entities.

[1]Different entities may have AOIs of different sizes. So, entity E being located in AOI(E') does not necessarily imply that entity E' is located in AOI(E).

3.3 Per Entity Data Structure

The data structures in this section and the algorithm in the next section are presented on a per entity basis in the sense that each entity maintains its own copy of the data structures and executes the same algorithm in parallel. This is consistent with the feature of many P2P DVE applications as in most of today's multiplayer online games, each player controls only one entity, i.e., its avatar. For DVEs where a computer is responsible for a set of entities (e.g., a server in a distributed server architecture), the per entity data structures and algorithm can be adapted in a straightforward manner for each computer to manage all of its hosted entities.

A local entity records its relationships with the AOIs of all remote entities in an array of $K+1$ lists, `RemoteAOIList[0, ..., K]`, where K is the depth of the cell hierarchy. The first list `RemoteAOIList[0]` records the remote entities whose AOIs have enclosing relationships with the local entity. For each $1 \leq m \leq K$, the list `RemoteAOIList[m]` records the remote entities whose AOIs have apart relationships with the local entity that are described by the local entity's level-m residing cell. The elements in each list are simply the identifiers of remote entities. In the example of Figure 2(a), entity G's `RemoteAOIList[0]` records entity C; entity G's `RemoteAOIList[1]` records entity A; entity G's `RemoteAOIList[2]` records entities D and F; and entity G's `RemoteAOIList[3]` records entity B.

The relationships between the local entity's AOI and all remote entities are recorded by a list called `EnclosingEntityList`, and a tree called `ApartEntityTree`. `EnclosingEntityList` records the remote entities that the local entity's AOI encloses. Each element in the list is simply the identifier of a remote entity.

`ApartEntityTree` records all remote entities that have apart relationships with the local entity's AOI in a tree structure that follows the cell hierarchy. Each tree node corresponds to a cell in the hierarchy and records the identifiers of remote entities which have apart relationships with the local

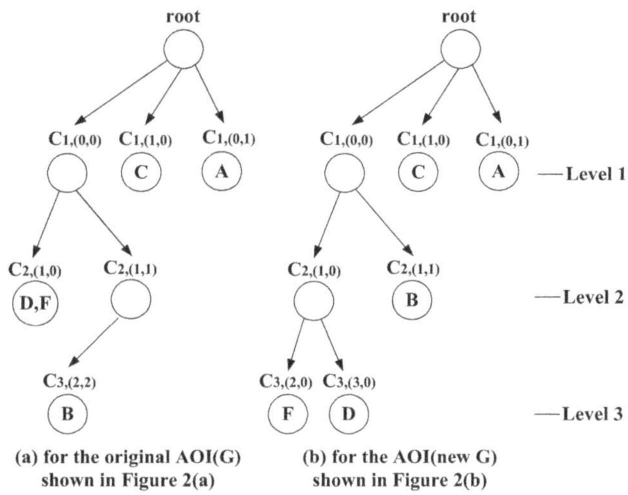

Figure 3: Entity G's `ApartEntityTree` recording the relationships between AOI(G) and other entities

entity's AOI described by the cell. Note that at any given time, only a subset of the cells in the hierarchy are eligible to describe the apart relationships involving the local entity's AOI. For example, consider entity G in Figure 2(a). Since AOI(G) does not overlap with cell $C_{1,(1,0)}$ (the upper-right level-1 cell in the VW), any entity located in cell $C_{1,(1,0)}$ has an apart relationship with AOI(G) described by $C_{1,(1,0)}$. As a result, no descendant cell of $C_{1,(1,0)}$ in the hierarchy is eligible to describe any apart relationship involving AOI(G). In addition, among the eligible cells, some cells may not be actually used to describe any apart relationship because there is no remote entity located in these cells. Therefore, to make `ApartEntityTree` as space efficient as possible, we include in `ApartEntityTree` only a subtree of the full cell hierarchy induced by the cells that are actually used to describe the apart relationship between the local entity's AOI and at least one remote entity. In the example of Figure 2(a), entities A, B, C, D and F's apart relationships with AOI(G) are described by cells $C_{1,(0,1)}$, $C_{3,(2,2)}$, $C_{1,(1,0)}$, $C_{2,(1,0)}$ and $C_{2,(1,0)}$ respectively. Thus, the `ApartEntityTree` maintained by entity E is as shown in Figure 3(a).

In general, each leaf node in `ApartEntityTree` records at least one remote entity, and the cell associated with each leaf node does not overlap with the local entity's AOI. Each internal node in `ApartEntityTree` does not record any remote entity, and the cell associated with each internal node overlaps with the local entity's AOI.

Suppose that there are a total of N entities in the VW. Then, for each entity, at most $N-1$ cells in the hierarchy are actually used to describe the relationships between the local entity's AOI and the $N-1$ remote entities. So, there are at most $K \cdot (N-1)$ tree nodes in the `ApartEntityTree` maintained by the local entity, where K is the depth of the cell hierarchy. Therefore, the worst case space complexity of `ApartEntityTree` is $O(KN)$. In practice, as shall be shown by our experimental results in Section 4, the space complexity of `ApartEntityTree` is orders of magnitude lower than the worst case because a leaf node at a high level (i.e., close to the root and corresponding to a large cell) normally records many remote entities.

Next, we present the algorithm for updating the above data structures when the entities and their AOIs move.

3.4 Per Entity Algorithm

When the local entity moves, its relationships with the AOIs of remote entities and its AOI's relationships with remote entities may change. Which remote entities are affected by the movement is dependent on the extent of the movement. Recall that each cell border has an associated level that represents the highest level of cells (i.e., the largest cells) of which it is the border. We characterize the extent of an entity movement by its Highest Level of Crossed Cell Borders ($HLCCB_{entity}$), which is defined as the highest level of all cell borders crossed by the entity movement.[2] For example, when entity G moves as shown in Figure 2(b), the $HLCCB_{entity}$ is 2 because G has moved across a level-2 cell border but does not move across any level-1 cell border.

At each frame, when the local entity moves, we first calculate the $HLCCB_{entity}$ of the entity movement. If the AOI of a remote entity has an apart relationship with the local entity that is described by its residing cell at level $1, 2, ...,$ or $HLCCB_{entity}-1$, their relationship is not affected by the local entity's movement because the local entity has not moved out of that residing cell. Therefore, the local entity sends its new position to only the remote entities recorded in lists `RemoteAOIList[`$HLCCB_{entity}, ..., K$`]` for relationship calculation, i.e., the remote entities whose AOIs have apart relationships with the local entity described by its residing cells at levels $HLCCB_{entity}$, $HLCCB_{entity}+1$, ..., K. When the local entity receives the new relationships calculated by the remote entities, it updates its `RemoteAOIList` accordingly and starts sending its status updates to the remote entity if the new relationship is enclosing.

For example, in Figure 2(a), entity E has apart relationships with AOI(A), AOI(B), AOI(D) and AOI(F) described by $RC_1(G)$, $RC_3(G)$, $RC_2(G)$ and $RC_2(G)$ respectively. If entity E moves to its new position as shown in Figure 2(b), $HLCCB_{entity} = 2$. So, entity G sends its new position to entities B, D and F only. Entities B, D and F then calculate the new relationships between their respective AOIs and entity G as apart relationships all described by $RC_3(\text{new } G) = C_{3,(3,1)}$, and inform entity G of the new relationships.

The movement of the local entity normally results in the movement of its AOI as well. Now, we describe how to update the relationships between the local entity's AOI and remote entities. Similarly, we define the Highest Level of Crossed Cell Borders for an AOI movement ($HLCCB_{AOI}$) as the highest level of all cell borders crossed by the AOI movement. For example, when entity E moves as shown in Figure 2(b), the $HLCCB_{AOI}$ of its AOI movement is 2.

At each frame, when the local entity's AOI moves, we first calculate the $HLCCB_{AOI}$ of the AOI movement. If a remote entity has an apart relationship with the local AOI at level $1, 2, ...,$ or $HLCCB_{AOI}-1$, their relationship is not affected by the local AOI's movement because the local AOI has not moved to become overlapping with the cell or to become not overlapping with its parent cell. For example, when entity G moves as shown in Figure 2(b), $HLCCB_{AOI} = 2$. Since AOI(G)'s apart relationships with entities A and C

[2]Any movement of an entity must cause it to cross some cell borders, since the cells at the bottom level of the hierarchy are minimum distinguishable units of the VW.

before the movement are described by the level-1 residing cells of A and C respectively, these relationships remain unchanged after the movement of AOI(G). For relationship update, only the remote entities whose apart relationships with the local AOI are described by cells at levels $HLCCB_{AOI}$, $HLCCB_{AOI}+1$, ..., K are required to be checked. To do so, we traverse the tree nodes in `ApartEntityTree` level-by-level down the tree starting from level $HLCCB_{AOI}$.[3]

Recall that the cell associated with each internal node in `ApartEntityTree` overlaps with the local entity's AOI before the AOI moves. For each internal node encountered in the traversal, if the local AOI becomes not overlapping with the cell of the internal node, the apart relationships between the local AOI and all remote entities recorded in the subtree rooted at the internal node should now be described by the cell of the internal node. In this case, the internal node is updated to record these remote entities and all descendant nodes of the internal node are removed from `ApartEntityTree`. In addition, these remote entities are notified of the new relationships. If the cell of an encountered internal node remains overlapping with the local AOI, the internal node does not need to be updated. For example, if entity G moves as shown in Figure 2(b), the `ApartEntityTree` of AOI(G) before and after its movement are shown in Figures 3(a) and 3(b) respectively. In this case, since the movement of AOI(G) has $HLCCB_{AOI} = 2$, the `ApartEntityTree` is traversed level-by-level down the tree starting from level 2. When the internal tree node of $C_{2,(1,1)}$ in Figure 3(a) is visited, it is found that AOI(new G) does not overlap with $C_{2,(1,1)}$. Therefore, the subtree rooted at the tree node of $C_{2,(1,1)}$ is compressed into a single node and the relationships between AOI(G) and all the remote entities recorded in the subtree (i.e., entity B) are upgraded to be described by cell $C_{2,(1,1)}$ as shown in Figure 3(b).

Remember that the cell associated with each leaf node in `ApartEntityTree` does not overlap with the local entity's AOI before the AOI moves. For each level-K leaf node encountered in the traversal (i.e., whose cell is a bottom-level cell in the hierarchy representing a minimum distinguishable unit of the VW), if the local AOI now covers the cell of the level-K node, the remote entities recorded in the level-K node become enclosed in the local AOI. In this case, the `EnclosingEntityList` is updated to include these remote entities, and the level-K node is removed from `ApartEntityTree`. In addition, these remote entities are notified of the new enclosing relationships for them to start sending their status updates to the local entity. If the local AOI remains not overlapping with the cell of an encountered level-K leaf node, the node does not need to be updated.

For each non-level-K leaf node encountered in the traversal, if the local AOI becomes overlapping with the cell of the leaf node, the apart relationship between the local AOI and the remote entities recorded in the node should now be described by lower-level cells (i.e., smaller cells). In this case, the local entity sends its AOI's new position to these remote entities for relationship calculation. When the local entity receives the new relationships calculated by the remote entities, it updates its `ApartEntityTree` and `EnclosingEntityList` accordingly. For example, in Figure 2(a), AOI(G) does not overlap with cell $C_{2,(1,0)}$ and AOI(G)'s apart relationships with entities D and F are both described by cell $C_{2,(1,0)}$ as shown in Figure 3(a). If entity G moves as shown in Figure 2(b), AOI(new G) becomes overlapping with cell $C_{2,(1,0)}$. So, entity G sends its new AOI position to entities D and F for relationship calculation. Entities D and F compute their new apart relationships with AOI(G) which are described by cells $C_{3,(3,0)}$ and $C_{3,(2,0)}$ respectively. Then, entities D and F reply to G with the new relationships. On receiving the replies, entity G updates its `ApartEntityTree` accordingly as shown in Figure 3(b). Now, the node of $C_{2,(1,0)}$ in G's `ApartEntityTree` has two child nodes $C_{3,(3,0)}$ and $C_{3,(2,0)}$ which record entities D and F respectively.

Determining the cell that describes the apart relationship between an entity and an AOI is an operation widely performed in our proposed IM mechanism. Recall that the cell describing the apart relationship is the highest-level residing cell (i.e., the largest residing cell) of the entity that the AOI does not overlap. So, a binary search can be used to efficiently calculate the cell. With a total of K levels in the cell hierarchy, the computational complexity of the binary search is only $O(\lg(K)) = O(\lg(\lg(D/\sigma)))$, where D is the maximum size of the VW along all dimensions and σ is the smallest unit of the coordinate system. Similarly, the $HLCCB_{entity}$ of an entity movement or the $HLCCB_{AOI}$ of an AOI movement can also be computed using binary search with a computational complexity of $O(\lg(K))$.

4. EXPERIMENTAL EVALUATION

4.1 Experimental Setup

To evaluate the performance of the proposed hierarchical IM mechanism, we simulated a P2P multiplayer game scenario with a two-dimensional VW of 1000×1000 distance units. The smallest unit of the coordinate system was set to $1000/2^{20} \approx 0.001$ distance unit so that there were 20 levels in the cell hierarchy. Each player controls one entity, i.e. its avatar, and the avatar is associated with a square AOI whose per dimension size was randomly generated from a uniform distribution between 50 and 150 distance units. So, the average AOI size per dimension is 100 distance units. The AOI is centered at the position of the player's avatar and moves along with the avatar. The moving speed of an avatar was randomly generated from a uniform distribution between 0 and 0.4 distance units per frame. Thus, the average moving speed is 0.2 distance units per frame. The random direction mobility model (also called the random walk model) [20] was used to simulate the movement of one half of all avatars, and the random waypoint mobility model [20] was used to simulate the movement of the other half of avatars. In the random direction model, an avatar repeatedly chooses a random direction to travel for a random duration. A uniform distribution between 0 and 2π radian is used to generate the random travel direction and a uniform distribution between 0 and 100 frames is used to generate the random travel duration. In the random waypoint model, an avatar chooses a random destination point in the VW and moves towards it. Upon arrival, the avatar chooses another random destination point and repeats the process.

In addition to the proposed hierarchical IM mechanism, we also implemented the traditional area-based and cell-based IM mechanisms for performance comparison. For the area-based mechanism, we implemented both the periodical

[3]To facilitate level-by-level traversal, all tree nodes at the same level in `ApartEntityTree` can be linked together and maintained as a double-linked list.

strategy and the space-driven strategy. In our experiments, we simulated these traditional mechanisms over wide ranges of their algorithm parameter values, namely the Period (P), the Distance Threshold (DT) and the Cell Size (CS). For each experimental setting, the best communication performance (i.e., the minimum upload bandwidth usage) achieved by each traditional mechanism is presented in this paper and used for comparison with our proposed hierarchical mechanism. The algorithm parameter values producing the best communication performance are also given in the figures.

All simulation experiments were carried out on a machine with Intel dual-core CPU 6700, 2 GB RAM and Windows XP OS. All avatars were initially placed at random in the VW. Each run simulated the game execution for a period of 10000 frames. The upload bandwidth used by various mechanisms is measured and compared. We assume that the network packet has a header size of 28 bytes. Each data value transmitted, such as a coordinate on a dimension or an entity identifier, accounts for 4 bytes. The payload size of a status update was set at 100 bytes so that a status update packet including its header has 128 bytes in total, similar to empirical observations [8, 13]. In addition to the communication performance, we also compare the computation cost of different mechanisms.

4.2 Scalability with respect to Number of Players

To evaluate the scalability of various mechanisms, we varied the number of players from 1000 to 5000 while keeping the other settings the same as the default. Figure 4 shows the average upload bandwidth used by a player (in bytes per frame) and the breakdown of the usage including relevant status updates, irrelevant status updates and IM-control messages. As seen from Figure 4, the hierarchical mechanism uses significantly lower bandwidth than the other mechanisms. Note that among different types of messages, only relevant status updates are really interested by the players and the rest are overheads. Figure 4 shows that the hierarchical mechanism uses an order of magnitude lower bandwidth for irrelevant status updates and IM-control messages than the other mechanisms whereas the bandwidth used for relevant status updates is the same for all mechanisms.

Typical frame rates for various game genres range from 1 to 20 frames per second [16]. Suppose that the experimental game scenario has a frame rate of 10 frames per second. With today's broadband connection, a player normally has an upload capacity not exceeding 1Mbps [4, 32]. Assume that each player has an upload capacity of 512Kbps. Then, the upload bandwidth consumption of a player should be smaller than or equal to 6400 bytes per frame. With this limit, Figure 4 shows that all the traditional mechanisms can only support around 2000 players in the same game. In contrast, the proposed hierarchical mechanism is able to support more than 4000 players and is therefore much more scalable than the traditional mechanisms.

In the hierarchical mechanism, the `ApartEntityTree` maintained at a player site changes dynamically over time. In our experiments, we recorded the average and largest numbers of tree nodes in the `ApartEntityTree` at each player site over the simulation run. Then, we calculated the average tree size of all player sites, and the average and the maximum of the largest encountered tree sizes of all player sites.

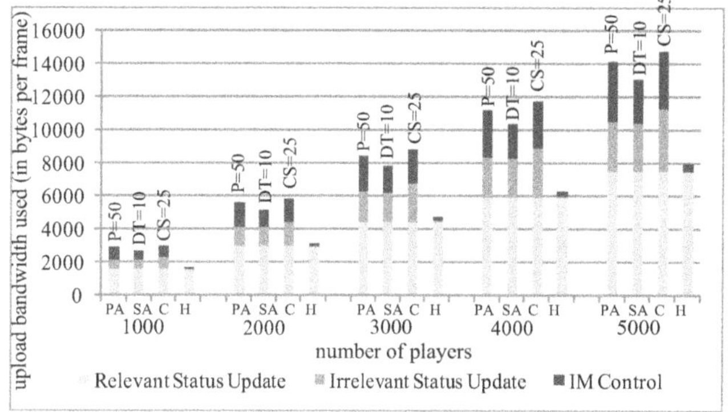

Figure 4: Average Upload Bandwidth Used by a Player vs. Number of Players

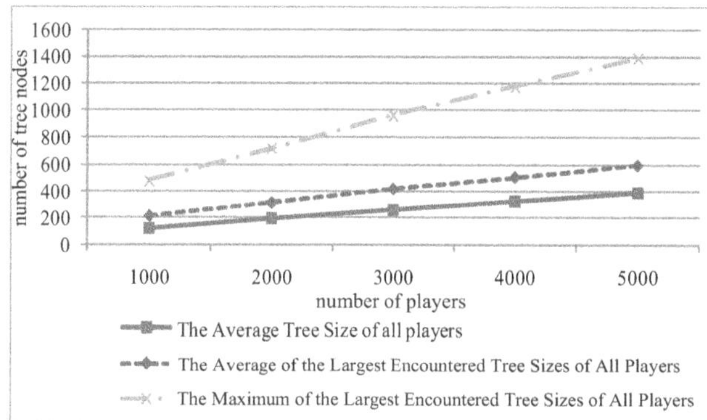

Figure 5: `ApartEntityTree` Size vs. Number of Players

As shown in Figure 5, the tree size is much smaller than the worse case complexity analyzed in Section 3.3 (with 20 levels in the cell hierachy and 5000 avatars, the worst case space complexity is $20 \times 5000 = 100,000$ nodes) and the tree size grows slowly with increasing number of players. This is because most avatars tend to be recorded by leaf nodes at high levels in `ApartEntityTree` and each of these leaf nodes normally records a large number of avatars. The tree sizes observed in the subsequent experiments are all well below 1000 nodes. Thus, the results of tree size will not be further presented in this paper.

Figure 6 shows the computation cost of different mechanisms. The computation cost is measured in terms of the average CPU time spent by a player site for IM in a frame. The computation time includes all the updates made to the data structures maintained by each mechanism (e.g., the `ApartEntityTree` in the hierarchical mechanism). The results show that the IM computation times of the two area-based mechanisms are very close to each other. Our proposed hierarchical mechanism significantly outperforms all the traditional mechanisms in that it has much shorter IM computation time and its IM computation time grows much slower than the other mechanisms with increasing number of players. With a frame rate of 10 frames per second, the frame time is 100 milliseconds. Figure 6 shows that, with 5000 players, the per player site per frame IM computation time of the

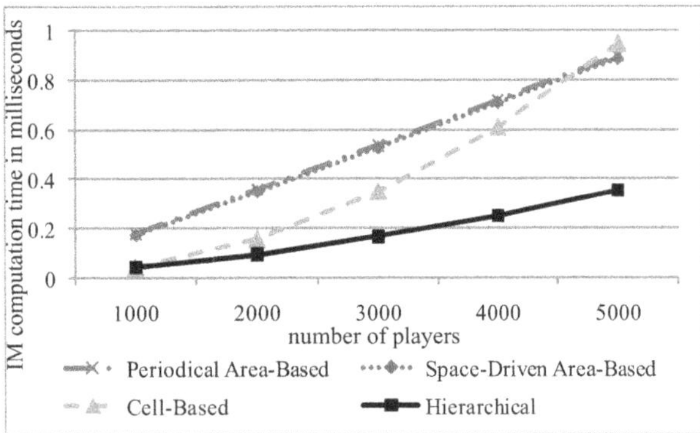

Figure 6: Per Player Site Per Frame IM Computation Time vs. Number of Players

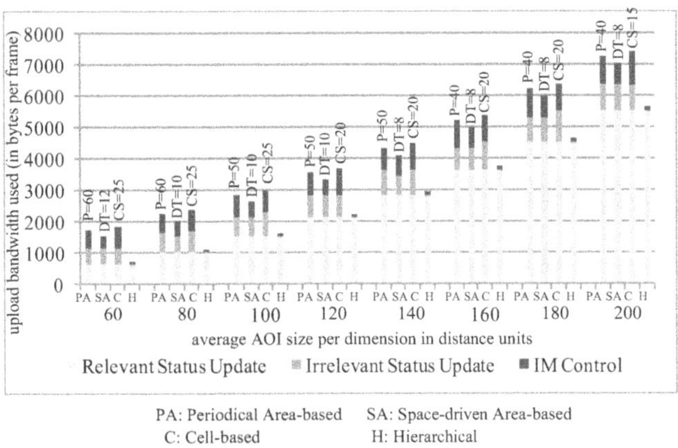

Figure 7: Average Upload Bandwidth Used by a Player vs. AOI Size per Dimension

hierarchical mechanism is just 0.35 milliseconds. Therefore, in a frame, each node spends only 0.35 percent computation power on IM, which is very acceptable. Similar observations about the low computation cost of the hierarchical mechanism have been made in all the subsequent experiments. Thus, the experimental results of IM computation time will not be further presented in this paper.

4.3 Performance for Different AOI Sizes

In this experiment, the average AOI size per dimension was varied from 60 to 200 distance units. Given an average AOI size of ℓ, each avatar was associated with a square AOI whose per dimension size was randomly generated from a uniform distribution between $\ell-50$ and $\ell+50$ distance units. The other settings were kept the same as the default. Figure 7 shows the performance results of upload bandwidth. In general, larger AOIs enclose more avatars and thus increase the bandwidth used for relevant status updates. The hierarchical mechanism consistently uses much lower bandwidth than the traditional mechanisms throughout the range of AOI size tested. The bandwidth used by the hierarchical mechanism for irrelevant status updates and IM-control messages is always an order of magnitude lower than all the traditional mechanisms.

4.4 Performance for Different Avatar Moving Speeds

In this experiment, the average avatar moving speed was varied from 0.2 to 1 distance units per frame. Given an average moving speed, each avatar's moving speed was randomly generated from a uniform distribution between 0 and twice the average moving speed. The other settings were kept the same as the default. As shown in Figure 8, the avatar moving speeds hardly affect the bandwidth used for relevant status updates because the number of relevant status updates is primarily determined by the AOI size and the density of avatars in the VW. On the other hand, the bandwidth used for IM-control messages increases with avatar moving speeds because a fast moving avatar changes its relationships with the AOIs of other avatars more frequently. The relative performance of different mechanisms remains similar for different avatar moving speeds. The hierarchical mechanism significantly and consistently outperforms the traditional mechanisms in terms of communication performance.

4.5 Remarks

Note that for the traditional IM mechanisms, we only report their best achievable communication performance in the figures. Figures 7 and 8 show that, the optimal algorithm parameter settings for the traditional mechanisms to achieve their best communication performance vary with the AOI size and avatar moving speed. Extensive experiments need to be carried out to find the optimal parameter setting of a traditional IM mechanism for a specific scenario. In addition, it is also difficult to dynamically change algorithm parameters in a running system where the AOI size and avatar moving speed evolve over time. If the algorithm parameters are not carefully chosen in the traditional mechanisms, their performance can be much worse than that shown in the figures. In contrast, our proposed hierarchical IM mechanism does not require parameter tuning based on factors like the AOI size and avatar moving speed, and it works well for a wide range of system configurations.

In order not to miss out any relevant status update, AOIs sometimes need be expanded to account for the communication latencies between players [6, 25]. In this paper, we have

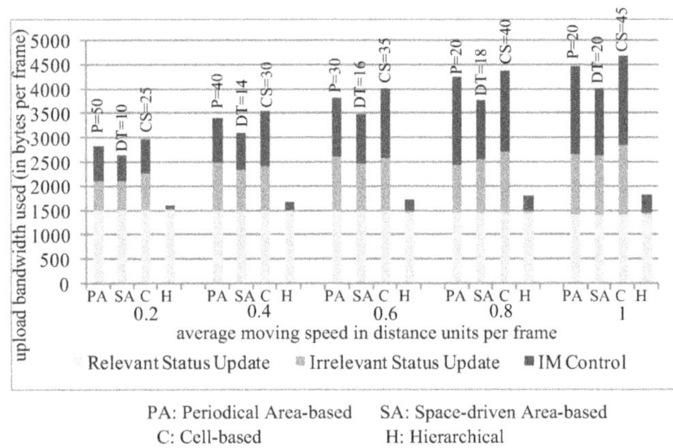

Figure 8: Average Upload Bandwidth Used by a Player vs. Avatar Moving Speed

not taken into consideration the AOI expansion due to the communication latency because such expansion is insignificant. The King[4] dataset shows that most inter-node round trip times in the Internet are shorter than 500 ms and thus inter-node latencies are normally shorter than 250 ms [23]. With a frame rate of 10 frames per second, the latencies are generally shorter than 2.5 frames. Therefore, the AOI expansion due to the latency should be much smaller than the AOI size and would not qualitatively affect our experimental observations.

5. RELATED WORK

There has been extensive research on interest management in distributed virtual environments and the Data Distribution Management (DDM) service of the High Level Architecture (HLA) [19, 24, 33]. Some works have combined the traditional area-based and cell-based mechanisms together for IM [10, 28, 34]. Tan et al. [34] proposed a hybrid approach for the DDM service of HLA-RTI, in which a central DDM coordinator maps the update and subscription regions into grid cells and then matches each update region against only the subscription regions that overlap with common cells. While this approach reduces the number of matches performed, it does not reduce communication cost since the coordinator still needs to collect all update and subscription regions for matching. Boukerche et al. [10] proposed a similar grid-filtered region-based mechanism and further reduced the number of matches by considering an update region to overlap with all subscription regions in a cell if the proportion of the cell covered by the update region exceeds a threshold. As a result, its matching results are less accurate. In an earlier work [28], we proposed a hybrid IM mechanism that utilizes a cell-based algorithm to reduce the AOI updates in the area-based algorithm. However, only with carefully chosen cell size and AOI updating period or distance threshold does the hybrid mechanism reduce communication overhead compared to the traditional area-based and cell-based mechanisms. Thus, the hybrid mechanism suffers from the same parameter tuning problem as the traditional mechanisms. Furthermore, the hybrid mechanism still requires regular residing cell updates among all entities irrespective of their relative positions.

Boukerche et al. [9, 11] proposed an optimized dynamic grid-based mechanism that performs area-based matching in each cell for reducing the total number of multicast groups used by the cell-based algorithm. Abrams et al. [1] proposed a multi-tiered mechanism in which the first tier uses the cell-based algorithm to roughly filter low fidelity data of entities and then the second tier uses the low fidelity data to do matching using the area-based algorithm. Both of the above works assumed that the underlying network has IP multicast support, which is unfortunately not available between most computers in the Internet. Our proposed hybrid IM mechanism does not rely on the network support for multicast communication and is more flexible for DVEs in the Internet.

In addition, there are some studies on building structured P2P overlays for networked games [5, 18]. However, they were based on either the traditional area-based IM mechanism [5] or the traditional cell-based IM mechanism [18]. Some recent works reduce the communication demand of relevant status updates in the case when there are many entities in the AOI by differentiating the frequency of status updates for different entities in the AOI based on factors like proximity [4, 17]. Our work complements the above studies in that we propose a new hierarchical mechanism for reducing the communication overhead in determining which entities are located in the AOIs.

[4]King is a tool that estimates the latency between arbitrary Internet end hosts [15].

6. CONCLUSIONS AND FUTURE WORK

In this paper, we have proposed a new hierarchical IM mechanism for DVEs. In this mechanism, the VW is divided into multiple levels of cells for describing the relationship between an entity and an AOI according to their relative position. We have elaborated how to maintain the relationships between entities and AOIs when their relative positions change. Compared with the traditional area-based and cell-based mechanisms, the proposed hierarchical mechanism significantly reduces the communication bandwidth consumption of IM and thus considerably increases the scalability of DVEs. The experimental results also show that the proposed mechanism has much lower computation cost than the traditional mechanisms and very acceptable storage requirement for its data structures. In addition, unlike the traditional mechanisms, the proposed mechanism does not require parameter tuning based on factors like the AOI size and avatar moving speed, and it works well for a wide range of system configurations. In the future work, we plan to build an analytical model for the proposed hierarchical IM mechanism in order to theoretically analyze its performance.

7. ACKNOWLEDGMENTS

This research is supported by Multi-plAtform Game Innovation Centre (MAGIC) in Nanyang Technological University. MAGIC is funded by the Interactive Digital Media Programme Office (IDMPO) hosted by the Media Development Authority of Singapore.

8. REFERENCES

[1] H. Abrams, K. Watsen, and M. Zyda. Three-tiered interest management for large-scale virtual environments. In *Proc. 5th ACM Symposium on Virtual Reality Software and Technology*, pages 125–129, 1998.

[2] M. Bassiouni, M. H. Chiu, M. Loper, and M. Garnsey. Relevance filtering for distributed interactive simulation. *Computer Systems Science and Engineering*, 13(1):39–47, 1998.

[3] D. Bauer, S. Rooney, and P. Scotton. Network infrastructure for massively distributed games. In *Proc. ACM NetGames'02*, pages 36–43, 2002.

[4] A. Bharambe, J. R. Douceur, J. R. Douceur, J. R. Lorch, T. Moscibroda, J. Pang, S. Seshan, and X. Zhuang. Donnybrook: Enabling large-scale, high-speed, peer-to-peer games. In *Proc. ACM SIGCOMM'08*, pages 389–400, 2008.

[5] A. R. Bharambe, M. Agrawal, and S. Seshan. Mercury: Supporting scalable multi-attribute range queries. In *Proc. ACM SIGCOMM'04*, pages 353–366, 2004.

[6] A. Bharamebe, J. Pang, and S. Seshan. Colyseus: A distributed architecture for interactive multiplayer games. In *Proc. NSDI'06*, pages 155–168, 2006.

[7] Blizzard Entertainment. World of Warcraft, available via `http://www.worldofwarcraft.com/index.xml`.

[8] M. S. Borella. Source models of network game traffic, available via `http://eprints.kfupm.edu.sa/65974/1/65974.pdf`, 2000.

[9] A. Boukerche and K. Lu. Optimized dynamic grid-based ddm protocol for large-scale distributed simulation systems. In *Proc. IEEE IPDPS'05*, 2005.

[10] A. Boukerche, N. J. Mcgraw, and R. B. Araujo. A grid-filtered region-based approach to support synchronization in large-scale distributed interactive virtual environments. In *Proc. 2005 International Conference on Parallel Processing Workshops*, pages 525–530, 2005.

[11] A. Boukerche and A. Roy. Dynamic grid-based approach to data distribution management. *Journal of Parallel and Distributed Computing*, 62(3):366–392, 2002.

[12] D. J. Van Hook and J. O. Calvin. Data distribution management in RTI 1.3. In *Proc. 1998 Spring Simulation Interoperability Workshop*, 1998.

[13] J. Farber. Network game traffic modelling. In *Proc. ACM NetGames'02*, pages 53–57, 2002.

[14] S. Fiedler, M. Wallner, and M. Weber. A communication architecture for massive multiplayer games. In *Proc. ACM NetGames'02*, pages 14–22, 2002.

[15] K. P. Gummadi, S. Saroiu, and S. D. Gribble. King: Estimating latency between arbitrary internet end hosts. In *Proc. 2nd ACM SIGCOMM Internet Measurement Workshop*, pages 5–18, 2002.

[16] S. Hu, J. Chen, and T. Chen. VON: a scalable peer-to-peer network for virtual environments. *IEEE Network*, 20(4):22–31, 2006.

[17] J.-R. Jiang, Y.-L. Huang, and S.-Y. Hu. Scalable aoi-cast for peer-to-peer networked virtual environments. In *Proc. IEEE ICDCS'08 Workshops*, pages 447–452, 2008.

[18] B. Knutsson, H. Lu, W. Xu, and B. Hopkins. Peer-to-peer support for massively multiplayer games. In *Proc. IEEE INFOCOM'04*, pages 96–107, 2004.

[19] B. Kumova. Dynamically adaptive partition-based data distribution management. In *Proc. PADS'05*, pages 292–300, 2005.

[20] J. Le Boudec and M. Vojnovic. Perfect simulation and stationarity of a class of mobility models. In *Proc. IEEE INFOCOM'05*, pages 2743–2754, 2005.

[21] J. Lui. Constructing communication subgraphs and deriving an optimal synchronization interval for distributed virtual environment systems. *IEEE Transactions on Knowledge and Data Engineering*, 13(5):778–792, 2001.

[22] M. R. Macedonia, M. J. Zyda, D. R. Pratt, D. P. Brutzman, and P. Barham. Exploiting reality with multicast groups. *IEEE Computer Graphics and Applications*, 15(5):38–45, 1995.

[23] MIT King Data. `http://www.pdos.lcs.mit.edu/p2psim/kingdata`.

[24] K. L. Morse, R. Brunton, J. M. Pullen, P. McAndrews, A. Tolk, and J. Muguira. An architecture for web services based interest management in real time distributed simulation. In *Proc. IEEE DS-RT'04*, pages 108–115, 2004.

[25] K. L. Morse and J. S. Steinman. Data distribution management in the HLA - multidimensional regions and physically correct filtering. In *Proc. 1997 Spring Simulation Interoperability Workshop*, 1997.

[26] J. Muller and S. Gorlatch. Gsm: A game scalability model for multiplayer real-time games. In *Proc. IEEE INFOCOM'05*, 2005.

[27] B. Ng, R. Lau, A. Si, and F. Li. Multiserver support for large-scale distributed virtual environments. *IEEE Transactions on Multimedia*, 7(6):1054–1065, 2005.

[28] K. Pan, W. Cai, X. Tang, S. Zhou, and S. J. Turner. A hybrid interest management mechanism for peer-to-peer networked virtual environments. In *Proc. IEEE IPDPS'10*, 2010.

[29] J. D. Pellegrino and C. Dovrolis. Bandwidth requirement and state consistency in three multiplayer game architectures. In *Proc. ACM NetGames'03*, pages 52–59, 2003.

[30] S. J. Rak and D. J. Van Hook. Evaluation of grid-based relevance filtering for multicast group assignment. In *Proc. 14th Distributed Interactive Simulation Workshop*, pages 739–747, 1996.

[31] S. Singhal and M. Zyda. *Networked Virtual Environments: Design and Implementation.* ACM Press, 1999.

[32] SingTel. SingTel broadband service, available via `http://www.singnet.com.sg/plans_and_services/broadband/snbb.asp?snbb=15Matl`, 2009.

[33] I. Tacic and R. M. Fujimoto. Synchronized data distribution management in distributed simulations. In *Proc. PADS'98*, pages 108–115, 1998.

[34] G. Tan, Y. Zhang, and R. Ayani. A hybrid approach to data distribution management. In *Proc. 4th IEEE/ACM International Workshop on Distributed Simulation and Real-Time Applications*, pages 55–61, 2000.

[35] Valve Software. Counter Strike, available via `http://www.counter-strike.com/`.

Bayesian-based Scenario Generation Method for Human Activities

Yunsick Sung
Dept. of CISE
University of Florida
Gainesville, FL 32611
United States
sung@cise.ufl.edu

Abdelsalam Helal
Dept. of CISE
University of Florida
Gainesville, FL 32611
United States
helal@cise.ufl.edu

Jae Woong Lee
Dept. of CISE
University of Florida
Gainesville, FL 32611
United States
jwlee@cise.ufl.edu

Kyungeun Cho
Dept. of Multimedia Eng.
Dongguk University
Seoul 100-715, Republic of Korea
cke@dongguk.edu

ABSTRACT
Emerging smart space applications are increasingly relying on capabilities for recognizing human activities. Activity recognition research is however challenged and slowed by the lack of data necessary for testing and validation. Collecting data through live-in trials in real world deployments is often very expensive and complicated. Legitimate limitations on the use of human subjects also renders a much smaller dataset than desired to be collected. To address this challenge, we propose a scenario generation approach in which a small set of scenarios is used to generate new relevant and realistic scenarios, and hence increase the base of testing data needed for activity recognition validation. Unlike existing methods for generating scenarios, which usually focus on scenario structure and complexity, we propose a Bayesian-based approach that learns the stochastic characteristics of a small number of collected datasets to generate additional scenarios of similar characteristics. Our approach is prolific and can generate enormous datasets with high degree of realism at affordable cost. The proposed approach is validated using a Viterbi-based algorithm and a real dataset case study. The validation experiment confirms that the generated dataset has highly similar stochastic characteristics as that of the real dataset.

Categories and Subject Descriptors
I.6.4 [**SIMULATION AND MODELING**]: Model Validation and Analysis – generate *test dataset*.

General Terms
Algorithms, Measurement, Performance, Design, Reliability, Experimentation, Standardization, Theory, Verification.

Keywords
Scenario generation, Bayesian probability, human activity, activity recognition.

1. INTRODUCTION
The goal of a smart space is to learn user needs and provide the most appropriate services to the human user. It is required to recognize human activities to decide what services are needed the most, or to help a user complete an activity (e.g., patients with dementia). Many researchers have proposed various algorithms for human activity recognitions [1][11]. However, it is difficult for them to test and validate their algorithms in an actual smart space due to the cost and time spent in deploying and utilizing sensors and collecting datasets in real time. To avoid these challenging costs, some researchers utilize activity datasets collected from other smart spaces [3,4]. However, activity datasets remain to be very scarce and limited in their scope and applicability to a range of rising applications. Therefore, testing activity recognition algorithms remains to be a very challenging task.

In response to this problem, dataset generation methods have been looked at as alternative to provide the needed supply of datasets. Some methods utilize a scenario that consists of multiple possible and expected paths [7-9]. Scenario generation research usually focuses on how to express a scenario [6] and how to reduce the complexity of a scenario [5].

The reality of the generated scenarios is however questionable in existing approaches. The overhead of generating the scenarios is also questionable. More realistic and efficient scenario generation methods are needed. First, only the dataset that can occur in the target smart space should be generated. If a dataset which cannot occur in the target smart space is generated, the whole dataset is useless. Secondly, a dataset that can test all functions of the activity recognition algorithms should be generated. To do this, diverse kinds of datasets need to be generated. Third, the cost and time to generate the scenarios should be reasonable, meaning that the cost and time for generating such scenarios should be much lower than that for collecting datasets in an actual smart space. Moreover, the human effort needed to configure and administer the generation process should be minimized.

In this paper, we propose a Bayesian-based scenario generation method for producing datasets for activity recognition researchers to test their algorithms. Our method addresses the following concerns. First, only the scenarios collected in a smart space are utilized to increase the reality of generated scenarios. Instead of generating a new dataset to increase the number of generated scenarios, the collected dataset is divided and the divided datasets are combined with each other. Secondly, only minimum constraints to divide and combine dataset are defined. The more constraints there are, the more accurate generated scenarios becomes. However, constraints in our approach are limited for generic scenario generation processes.

This paper is organized as follows. Section 2 introduces related approaches for testing activity recognition algorithms. Section 3 describes our approach. Section 4 proposes algorithms for scenario generation in detail. Section 5 evaluates the performance of our approach and validates our approach by utilizing collected dataset. Finally, in Section 6, we conclude the paper and discuss the future work..

SIGSIM-PADS'13, May 19–22, 2013, Montréal, Québec, Canada.

2. RELATED WORK

Research for testing activity recognition algorithms can be divided into two approaches. The first entails using simulation. For instance, the Persim simulator provides user interfaces for setting activities and scenarios and generating synthesized datasets [2][14]. After scenarios are configured based on the activities set, activity recognition algorithms are validated. Persim is implemented based on SDDL to share dataset among researchers [12][13]. Persim is currently being extended to Persim 3D, which allows 3D user interfaces to validate activity recognition algorithms within 3D environments [10]. The disadvantage of the simulation approach is that the simulator of a smart space should be implemented to capture the real smart space. If there are differences between the real smart space and the simulator, the activity recognition algorithms cannot be tested accurately. While the simulation approach is feasible, it entails human efforts in designing the simulation project.

The other approach is validating activity recognition algorithms using a sensory dataset that is collected in a smart space [3][4]. By using the sensory data, activity recognition algorithm can be validated more accurately compared to simulations. However, the cost of collecting a real sensory dataset is expensive. Therefore, it limits the range of validation.

To overcome the cost problem of collecting real sensory dataset, scenario generation methods can be applied. Research in scenario generation originally aims at predicting all possible situations and helping to make a decision or predict adverse situations. For example, to solve a long-term planning problem, there is a method that generates a scenario tree to predict all possible paths by using a small number of sample scenarios [5]. This method focuses on ways to reduce the complexity of a scenario tree by using a cluster algorithm. To reduce the number of nodes in a scenario tree, there is another method that combines the nodes in the same level [8]. In the case of training systems for crisis management, there is a Noisy-Or Bayesian networks (NOBN)-based scenario generation method [7]. By utilizing the NOBN-based method, human experts and instructors design scenarios that are composed of serial crisis events, and then an automated scenario generation system generates scenarios by imitating the process of the human experts and instructors. At last, a method to express uncertainty of scenarios by using random variables was introduced [9]. The random variables are generated according to the stochastic characteristics of sample scenarios.

These scenario generation approaches have the limit of being unable to generate enormous scenarios because a scenario tree is only composed of events according to the linearly invoked time. Given that the number of nodes in a scenario tree is increased as the size of the scenario tree is increased, space for the nodes becomes a problem. Therefore, a scenario generation method requires solving the space problem and increasing the number of generated scenarios. In this paper, we propose a prolific scenario generation method that solves these problems found in traditional scenario generation approaches.

3. SCENARIO GENERATION METHOD

3.1 Scenario Generation Approach

We define scenario as serial sensory values that happened monolithically over time. A single actual scenario can be used by our method to generate other scenarios but, to generate more scenarios, few scenarios, which are reasonable to collect, are utilized in our approach.

Our approach divides and combines the collected scenarios to generate new scenarios. Formatting scenarios is necessary in our approach which allows us to utilize scenarios collected from diverse sources. As a result, the process of generating new scenarios is divided into four stages, as shown in Figure 1.

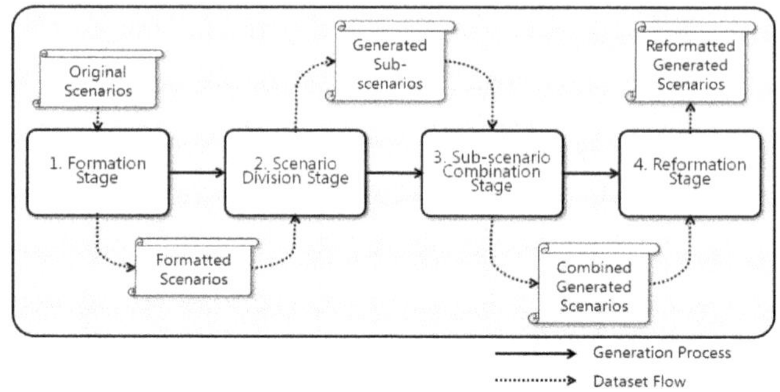

Figure 1. Scenario Generation Procedure

Scenario division and sub-scenario combination stages are for scenario generation procedures, and formation and reformation stages are for scenario conversion procedures. Each stage generates its own formatted scenarios. The scenarios of one stage are used as the input of the other stages. We call the data collected in a smart space *original scenario*, which is the input of our approach. In the formation stage, the original scenarios (e.g., publically available datasets) are transferred to the format required by our approach. We call transferred scenario *formatted scenario*. The scenario division stage divides formatted scenarios into *generated sub-scenarios*, and the sub-scenario combination stage combines generated sub-scenarios into *combined generated scenarios*. Finally, in the reformation stage, the combined generated scenarios are transferred back to the format of the original scenarios to generate the *reformatted generated scenarios*.

3.2 Formation and Reformation Stages

There are diverse kinds of formats of existing original scenarios. Therefore, we do not provide a general algorithm for formatting original scenarios to our required format or for reformatting formatted scenarios to original format, but we do define constraints of the required format for original scenarios and formatted scenarios.

We assume that original scenarios contain information about time, sensory IDs and sensory values and pertain to the same smart space, over mostly the same set of sensors and over similar timelines (e.g., hours, days, weeks, months). Sensory values that are not common to all original scenarios are eliminated.

In formatted scenarios, all sensory values are required to be expressed numerically (no labels). For example, Boolean values, true or false, are transformed into 0 or 1, respectively. All sensory values are time-stamped using monolithically increased timestamp values. Each entry contains only one sensor value change. Time is described by seconds.

Each original scenario is formatted according to the above requirements prior to scenario generation. After generating combined scenarios, the scenarios are formatted back to the format of the original scenarios by extracting and including the information of the original scenarios.

3.3 Scenario Division Stage

To describe the structure of a scenario, we define the following terms first. Sensory value (SV) is a measured value from a sensor. Sensory value tuple (SVT) is a tuple of all of SVs measured at the same time. Therefore, a scenario is a set of SVTs measured at monolithically increasing time, which contains sensory data of the same lifestyle.

In our approach, formatted scenarios are divided and utilized to generate new combined scenarios, increasing the reality of the scenarios. Therefore, the way to divide formatted scenarios is required in advance. Given that SVs are invoked by performing serial activities of humans, it is ideal that one serial SVTs, a sub-scenario, corresponds to the dataset invoked by one meaningful human activity. Therefore, formatted scenarios are divided by grouping co-related serial SVTs.

We expect that a specific SVT would occur many times right after the other SVT if both SVTs were interrelated. Therefore, all correlations of occurrence between all pairs of two consecutive SVTs are analyzed, based the number of occurrences of the SVTs in advance. The relationship among more than two consecutive SVTs can be analyzed, however, it would be more complex than that of two consecutive SVTs and could be based on that of two consecutive SVTs. Therefore, our approach focuses on the essential parts, two consecutive SVTs, and then we will handle more than two SVTs in future work.

In our approach, Bayesian probability is applied to reveal the relation of two consecutive SVTs in all formatted scenarios, which calculates each conditional probability of the next SVT occurrence with respect to the current SVT. By using Bayesian probability, the relation can be obtained from all formatted scenarios. In other words, the formatted scenarios are utilized not only to generate new scenarios by combining divided formatted scenarios but also to reveal the relation of two SVTs. Then the formatted scenarios are divided according to the calculated Bayesian probabilities. Through the scenario division stage, various sub-scenarios are generated.

3.4 Sub-scenario Combination Stage

To combine generated sub-scenarios, the realism of combined generated scenarios should first be considered. Some scenarios, which never happen in a smart space, should not be generated. To prohibit such scenarios, we define some combination constraints for combination. Therefore, each generated sub-scenario is combined with various other generated sub-scenarios one by one by connecting the ending part of one generated sub-scenario with the starting part of another generated sub-scenario, considering the constraints. Then the connected sub-scenarios of the starting part are also connected to other sub-scenarios by the same way recursively. One serial connected sub-scenarios represent one scenario. Therefore, with the connected sub-scenarios, a new combined scenario is generated.

To describe combinations, we define the following terms. First SVT is the first SVT in any formatted scenario. Last SVT is the last SVT in any formatted scenario. First sub-scenario is a generated sub-scenario that includes any first SVT. Last sub-scenario is a generated sub-scenario that includes any last SVT. Starting SVT is the first SVT in any generated sub-scenario. Ending SVT is the last SVT in any generated sub-scenario. First SVT is one of starting SVTs and last SVT is one of ending SVTs.

Starting from the first sub-scenario, each ending SVT of any generated sub-scenario is combined with all possible starting SVTs of other generated sub-scenarios, one by one, recursively, considering the combination constraints until all possible last sub-scenarios are combined instantly, as shown in Figure 2. Any path from a first sub-scenario to any last sub-scenario represents a combined generated scenario. When any last sub-scenario is combined, a new combined scenario is generated by copying and outputting the SVTs of this path.

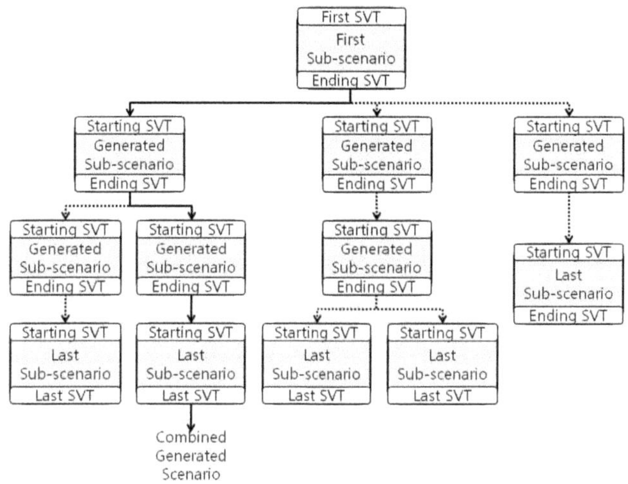

Figure 2. An Example of Combined Generated Scenarios

We apply dynamic programming (DP) to combine generated sub-scenarios. DP is proper to process the same routine recursively. Combination is started from the first sub-scenario in the first formatted scenario. After generating new combined scenarios, which start from the first sub-scenario, other new combined scenarios are also generated, starting from other first sub-scenarios, sequentially. Therefore, DP is executed N times, which is the number of formatted scenarios.

The key to combining generated sub-scenarios is the combination constraints. The probabilities of two consecutive SVTs were already calculated during the scenario division stage and represent the unique relation of SVTs in collected original scenarios well. Therefore, we define the combination constraints based on these probabilities.

4. SCENARIO GENERATION ALGORITHMS

4.1 Count and Probability Matrix Generation Algorithm

The first step before dividing and combining scenarios is analyzing the relation of two SVTs by calculating Bayesian probability. To describe the relation of two SVTs, we define the following notations. $v_{j,n,i}$ is the *ith* sensory value of the *nth* SVT in the *jth* formatted scenario. If $v_{j,n,i}$ is not measured, $v_{j,n,i}$ is set to null but the sensory value could be assigned by the estimated value considering the previous value. ξ is the number of sensors without considering types of sensors. $V_{j,n}$ is the ordered set of SVs of the *nth* SVT in the *jth* formatted scenario, $V_{j,n}=\{v_{j,n,1}, v_{j,n,2}, \ldots, v_{j,n,\xi}\}$. Therefore, $v_{j,n,i}$ is an element of $V_{j,n}$, $v_{j,n,i} \in V_{j,n}$. $t_{j,n}$ is the measured time of $V_{j,n}$. N_j is the number of SVTs of the *jth* formatted scenario. V_j is the ordered set of the SVTs collected in the *jth* formatted scenario, $V_j=\{V_{j,1}, V_{j,2}, ..., V_{j,N_j}\}$. $V_{j,n}$ is an element of V_j, $V_{j,n}\in V_j$. T_j is the ordered set of times of V_j. $t_{j,n}$ is an element of T_j, $t_{j,n}\in T_j$. N is the total number of formatted scenarios. V is the set of all formatted scenarios, $V=\{V_1, V_2, ..., V_N\}$. V_j is an element of V. Figure 3 shows a visual relationship among all notations.

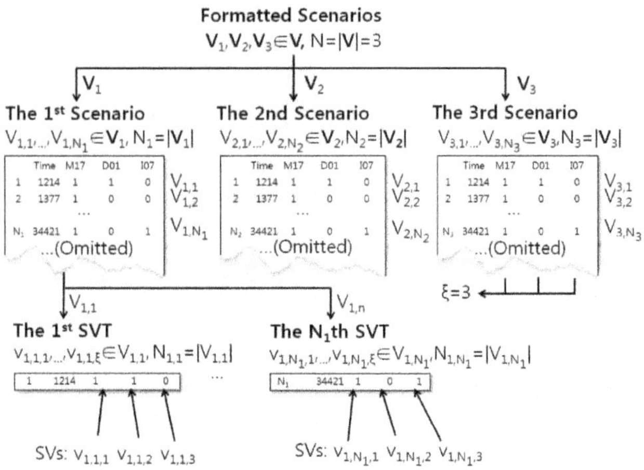

Figure 3. Structure of Formatted Scenarios

To apply Bayesian probability to reveal the correlation between two consecutive SVTs in all formatted scenarios, each $V_{j,n}$ is paired with the next occurring $V_{j,n+1}$, as shown in Figure 4. For example, $V_{1,1}$ is paired with $V_{1,2}$, and $V_{1,2}$ is paired with $V_{1,3}$. We call these two SVTs ($V_{j,n}$ and $V_{j,n+1}$) in any formatted scenario 2-SVT ($2V_{j,n}$). $V_{j,n}$ in $2V_{j,n}$ is called the anterior SVT. $V_{j,n+1}$ in $2V_{j,n}$ is called the posterior SVT.

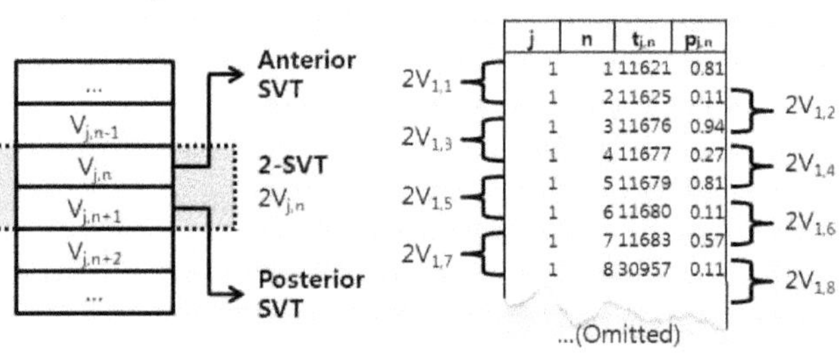

Figure 4. 2-SVTs in Each Formatted Scenario

To calculate conditional probabilities of 2-SVTs, each number of occurrences of 2-SVT is counted in advance. We invert all formatted scenarios by first identifying all unique SVTs of the formatted scenarios in a separate search. Then these SVTs are used as indices to a Count Matrix and a Sum Set. Count Matrix stores all counts of 2-SVTs in which a particular posterior SVT is followed by another anterior SVT, and Sum Set stores all counts of each occurrence of anterior SVTs. Therefore, we calculate the counts of 2-SVTs and then the counts are stored in Count Matrix. Then, we count each number of types of anterior SVTs and then the numbers are stored in Sum Set. Count Matrix and Sum Set are created only once during the entire generation process and are only used for calculating conditional probabilities of 2-SVTs.

For Count Matrix and Sum Set, we define the following notations. M is the ordered set of all identified unique SVTs in all formatted scenarios, whose elements are used for indices for matrixes. M_k is the *kth* unique SVT that denotes an anterior SVT of 2-SVT and is an element of M, $M_k\in M$. M_m is the *mth* unique SVT that denotes a posterior SVT of 2-SVT and an element of M, $M_m\in M$. C is the Count Matrix. $c_{k,m}$ is the count that M_m is followed right after M_k in all formatted scenarios and is an element of C, $c_{k,m}\in C$. S is the ordered sum set of all sums. s_k is the sum from $c_{k,1}$ to $c_{k,|M|}$ and is an element of S, $s_k\in S$.

Count Matrix and Sum Set are calculated as shown in Figure 5. The function GetIndex returns the order of a SVT in M. As a result, the function GenerateCountMatrixAndSumSet calculates the counts and sums of all 2-SVTs by getting indices of $V_{j,n}$ and $V_{j,n+1}$ and increasing one of the counts and sums corresponding to both SVTs.

```
function GenerateCountMatrixAndSumSet(V, M)
  set C, S←0
  for j←1 to N
    for n←1 to Nj-1
      k←GetIndex(M, Vj,n)
      m←GetIndex(M, Vj,n+1)
      ck,m←ck,m+1
      sk←sk+1
    end for
  end for
  return C, S
end function
```

Figure 5. Generating Count Matrix and Sum Set

We use the Count Matrix and Sum Set to calculate a Probability Matrix. The Probability Matrix is a matrix of conditional probabilities of all kinds of 2-SVTs and is also created only once during an entire generation.

We define that P is the Probability Matrix and $p_{k,m}$ is the conditional probability of M_m right after M_k, $p_{k,m}=P(m_m|m_k)=c_{k,m}\div s_k$ where $p_{k,m}\in P$. The Probability Matrix is calculated as shown in Figure 6.

```
function GenerateProbabilityMatrix(M, C, S)
  P←0
  for k←1 to |M|
    for m←1 to |M|
      pk,m←ck,m÷sk,m
    end for
  end for
  return P
end function
```

Figure 6. Generating Probability Matrix

Each $p_{k,m}$ is calculated by the pre-calculated $c_{k,m}$ and $s_{k,m}$. The Probability Matrix is generated for reducing the amount of repeated calculation of each $p_{k,m}$ when the $p_{k,m}$ is referenced. All conditional probabilities can be obtained on demand by calculating them each time they are needed based on the Count Matrix with Sum Set and without having to have a generated Probability Matrix. This is because the space for Probability Matrix can be too large to store all conditional probabilities.

Therefore, the generation of Probability Matrix must be avoided in practice, even though conceptually and for explanation clarity, we refer to it as a materialized Probability Matrix.

4.2 The 2-SVT Division Algorithm

After generating Probability Matrix, we will choose some conditional probabilities in the Probability Matrix to select the 2-SVTs that will be split to divide the formatted scenarios. We are going to choose the probabilities that are high or low compared to other probabilities: high means the 2-SVTs are connected strongly because their pairing happens frequently, and low means the 2-SVTs are connected loosely because their pairing happens rarely. When 2-SVTs are connected strongly, the anterior in the 2-SVT has the opportunity for meaning full and acceptable generation through *permutation* over all occurrences of the anterior SVTs and posterior SVTs. In the other case when 2-SVTs are connected loosely, the anterior in the 2-SVT has a very good opportunity for meaningful and acceptable generation through *combination* of the two elements of the SVT.

Conditional probabilities are selected by defining the certain periods of probabilities. We define two thresholds: θ_f is a frequent occurrence threshold, and θ_r is a rare occurrence threshold. We call the probability that is bigger than or equal to θ_f, frequent probability, and we call the probability that is smaller than or equal to θ_r and is not 0 rare probability.

When we define that $q_{j,n}$ is the conditional probability of $2V_{j,n}$, Q_j is the ordered set of probabilities of 2-SVTs of V_j and $q_{j,n}$ is an element of Q_j, $q_{j,n} \in Q_j$. Therefore, $q_{j,n}$ is $p_{k,m}$ where $V_{j,n}$ is equal to M_k and $V_{j,n+1}$ is equal to M_m. All probabilities of 2-SVTs in all formatted scenarios are obtained as shown in Figure 7. By using the function GetIndex, the orders, k and m, of $V_{j,n}$ and $V_{j,n+1}$ are inquired. Then the probability of the orders in the Probability Matrix, $p_{k,m}$, is assigned to $q_{j,n}$.

```
function GenerateSVTProbabilities(V, M, P)
  Q←0
  for j←1 to N
    for n←1 to N_j-1
      k←GetIndex(M, V_j,n)
      m←GetIndex(M, V_j,n+1)
      q_j,n←p_k,m
    end for
  end for
  return Q
end function
```

Figure 7. Setting SVTs' Probabilities

We call 2-SVTs with frequent probability frequent 2-SVTs, and we call 2-SVTs with rare probability rare 2-SVTs. By referencing the selected probabilities in Probability Matrix, all frequent and rare 2-SVTs in all formatted scenarios that correspond to the selected probabilities are selected. Then the middles of all frequent and rare 2-SVTs are split conceptually. Therefore, all formatted scenarios are divided into sub-scenarios by cutting the middle of the 2-SVTs of the selected probabilities. In other words, generated sub-scenarios do not exist in reality but exist conceptually. To figure out generated sub-scenarios, each conditional probability of all SVTs in the formatted scenario is checked. Then if the conditional probability of the SVT is rare probability or frequent probability, the anterior SVT is used as an ending part of a sub-scenario, and the posterior SVT is used as a starting part of a sub-scenario. Therefore, SVTs between a starting part and an ending part are grouped as a generated sub-scenario.

4.3 Scenario Division and Combination Algorithms

To reduce time complexity, division and combination can be executed concurrently. Based on two approaches, a new scenario generation algorithm is proposed.

4.3.1 Four Sub-stage Overview

In the division and combination, there are two types of combinations of SVTs: One for grouping SVTs in the same generated sub-scenario during the scenario division stage and the other for combining ending SVTs with starting SVTs during the sub-scenario combination stage. We call the former inner combination and the latter inter combination. Even though both combinations handle SVTs differently, both can be handled concurrently to reduce the amount of calculation.

In the case of inner combination, if any 2-SVT is not a rare or frequent 2-SVT, two SVTs in the 2-SVT are inside the same sub-scenario as shown in Figure 8(a). The anterior SVT of the 2-SVT is only combined with the posterior SVT of the same 2-SVT to group SVTs in the same sub-scenario. For the inner combination, we add the constraint that $V_{j,n}$ is combined with $V_{j,n+1}$ to the set of combination constraints to handle inner combination and inter combination consistently.

In the case of inter combination, if any 2-SVTs is rare or frequent 2-SVTs, the two SVTs in the 2-SVT are not inside the same generated sub-scenario after the scenario division stage. The anterior SVT is an ending SVT trying to combine with other starting SVTs to combine two generated sub-scenarios as shown in Figure 8(b). If there are available starting SVTs by checking combination constraints, the anterior SVT and starting SVTs are combined.

As a result, the process of dividing formatted scenarios and combining generated sub-scenarios amounts to combining two SVTs repeatedly from the first SVT to any last SVTs considering the combination constraints.

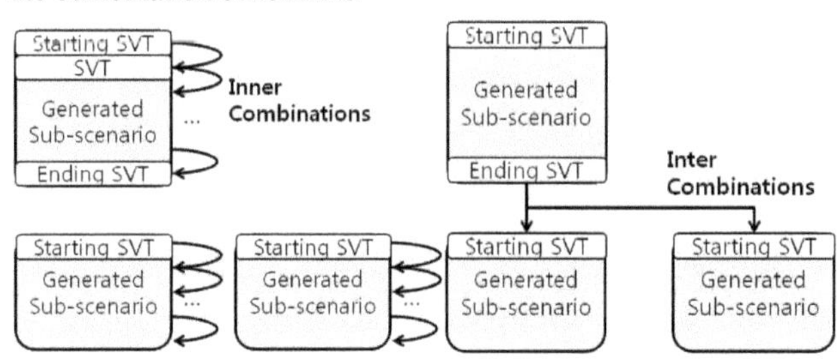

(a) Inner Combinations (b) Inter Combinations

Figure 8. Inner and Inter Combinations

To describe the sequence of generation, we define the following terms. Level is a distance from a first SVT to a specific SVT in a new combined scenario. Current SVT is the first SVT or the last combined SVT with previously combined serial SVTs until now. Next SVTs are the SVTs that will be combined with current SVT. Previous SVT is the SVT that was combined right before combining the current SVT. Sibling SVTs are the SVTs with the same previous SVT at the same level.

SVTs are combined according to the depth first search (DFS) approach from any first SVT. In other words, next SVTs are combined before combining other sibling SVTs at a current SVT. The size of a stack can be reduced if the DFS approach is applied compared to the breath first search (BFS) approach.

Current SVT is changed to one of the next SVTs after being combined with the next SVT. The next SVT is combined with the next SVTs of the next SVT recursively. Whenever each current SVT finishes to combine with all next SVTs, the current SVT is also changed back to the previous SVT of the current SVT. Then the changed current SVT is combined with uncombined others repeatedly. When all SVTs are combined with each other, the combination is complete.

4.3.2 Four Sub-stage Procedures

Whenever current SVT starts to be combined, four sub-stages are always processed alternately for inter and inner combination as shown in Figure 9. The current SVT are stored with time for a new SVT in a new combined scenario. Next, if the current SVT is not any last SVT, it is combined with any next SVTs one by one that qualify the combination constraints. Each next SVT is set as a current SVT, performs four sub-stages and then the previous SVT of next SVT is set back as a current SVT. Whenever any last SVT is combined, a new combined scenario is generated with the stored SVTs and time. Finally, the stored SVT and time are erased. The reason for erasing the stored SVTs will be discussed later.

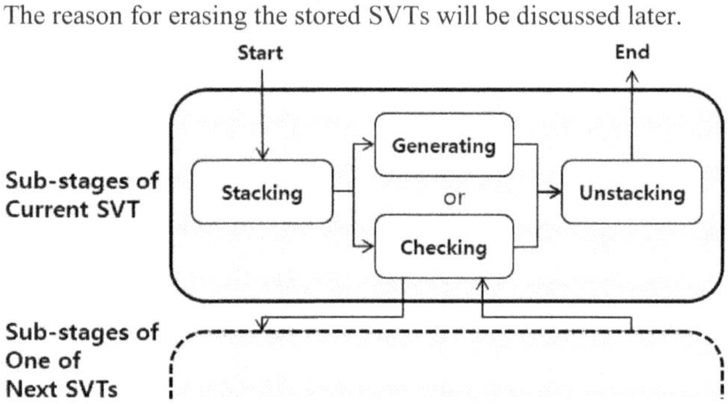

Figure 9. Four Sub-stages

There are enormous number of SVTs. Storing all SVTs in formatted scenarios requires much space to generate combined scenarios, which could make space problems. Therefore, we use and share one stack to store SVTs of one path from a first SVT to any last SVT. Because of using a stack, the pairs of SVT and time are stored sequentially and removed inversely.

Whenever each first SVT starts, the SVT and its time for a new SVT in a new combined generated scenario are pushed as a pair in the stack firstly. Whenever each SVT except first SVTs is combined with previously combined serial SVTs, the SVT and newly calculated time for a new SVT in a new combined generated scenario are also pushed as a pair in the stack. In this case, time denotes when the last combined SVT is invoked in a new combined scenario. In other words, time marks when the previous SVT of the last combined SVT was invoked in a new scenario and the difference between the time of the last combined SVT and the time since the previous SVT passed. Therefore, time for a new SVT is calculated by adding the time of the previous SVT to the difference time between the time of the last combined SVT and the time of the previous SVT of the last combined SVT. SVTs and time in the stack are an intermediate result of a new combined scenario.

During the checking sub-stage, each SVT tries to find all possible SVTs that can be combined together among all SVTs in all formatted scenarios, considering combination constraints one by one.

When the current SVT is any last SVT, a new combined scenario is generated by copying the SVTs and the time in the stack sequentially during the generating sub-stage in any formatted scenario. In other words, the stack is not cleared after generation.

After generation or check, during the unstacking sub-stage, the current SVT is changed back to the previous SVT by popping the stack. Then the changed current SVT starts to combine with other uncombined next SVTs in all formatted scenarios continuously.

4.3.3 Four Sub-stage Algorithms

As shown in Figure 10, the combination process from a first SVT is performed N times, which is the number of first SVTs in formatted scenarios.

```
function GenerateScenarios()
  for j←1 to N
    n←1
    t←t_{j,1}
    d←t_{j,1}
    CombineSVT(j, n, t, d)
  end for
end function
```

Figure 10. Generating Scenarios

The function CombineSVT processes the four sub-stages and is implemented by DP as shown in Figure 11. Whenever the function CombineSVT is called, $V_{j,n}$ and t are stored at first, and in the end of the function CombineSVT the function Unstack is called to pop the stored $V_{j,n}$ and t. If $V_{j,n}$ is the last SVT, the function GenerateOneScenario is called to generate combined scenarios. If not, the function CombineSVT is called to combined other next SVTs after checking combination constraints.

```
function CombineSVT(j, n, t, d)
  Stack(V_{j,n}, t)
  if V_{j,n} is any last SVT then
    GenerateOneScenario()
  else
    for each (j', n') in all SVTs in all formatted Scenarios
      if CheckCombinationConstraints(j,n,j',n',t,d)=true then
        if V_{j',n'} is any starting SVT then
          d = 0
        end if
        CombineSVT(j', n', t+(t_{j',n'}-t_{j',n'-1}), d+(t_{j',n'}-t_{j',n'-1}))
      end if
    end for
  end if
  Unstack()
end function
```

Figure 11. Combining SVTs

In our approach, enormous combined scenarios are generated. The number of generated combined scenarios can be controlled by θ_f and θ_r. However, it still takes too much time to generate the combined scenarios. Therefore, another approach is required. We reduce the number of inter combinations by limiting the duration of sub-scenarios. Therefore, the generated sub-scenarios with a duration shorter than ζ will be eliminated. This constraint is also included in combination constraints. As shown in Figure 11, when $V_{j',n'}$ is combined as inter combination, the duration of the current generated sub-scenario is initialized by 0, and when $V_{j',n'}$ is combined as an inner or inter combination, the duration is increased by the difference between $t_{j',n'}$ and $t_{j',n'-1}$. Then, the calculated duration is utilized within combination constraints.

We also define some terms for the description of a stack as follows. $V''_{j'',n''}$ is the n''*th* SVT in a j''*th* new combined scenario, $t''_{j'',n''}$ is the n''*th* time in the j''*th* new combined scenario, $V'_{n''}$ is the n''*th* pushed SVT in the stack, and $t'_{n''}$ is the n''*th* pushed time in the stack. $V'_{n''}$ and $t'_{n''}$ is copied to $V''_{j'',n''}$ and $t_{n''}$ where j'' is initialized by 1 and increased by 1 after each combined scenario generation. All SVTs and time in the stack are copied to SVTs and time in the new combined scenario, as shown in Figure 12.

set **j''←0**
function **GenerateOneScenario**()
  j''←j''+1
  for n''←1 to |**V'**|
    $\mathbf{V''_{j'',n''} \leftarrow V'_{n''}}$
    $\mathbf{t''_{j'',n''} \leftarrow t'_{n''}}$
  end for
end function

Figure 12. Procedure of Generating One Scenario

We assume that V, T, Q, V'', T'', V' and T' are referenced directly by the function GenerateScenarios, GenerateOneScenario, CheckCombinationConstraints and CombineSVT without receiving those sets as parameters.

4.4 Defining Combination Constraints

To check whether a $V_{j,n}$ can be combined with any $V_{j',n'}$, we define combination constraints. When a $V_{j,n}$ tries to be combined with $V_{j',n'}$ which is actually $V_{j,n+1}$, both are combined as an inner combination.

For an inter combination, there are four constraints. First, there are combination constraints based on the conditional probabilities: one for frequent 2-SVTs and the other for rare 2-SVTs. For these constraints, when any ending SVT $V_{j,n}$ is trying to combine with the starting SVT $V_{j',n'}$, four SVTs ($V_{j,n}$, $V_{j,n+1}$, $V_{j',n'}$, and $V_{j',n'-1}$) are compared with each other, as shown in Figure 13. When the ending SVT $V_{j,n}$ and the ending SVT $V_{j',n'-1}$ of the proceeding sub-scenario of the starting SVT $V_{j',n'}$ are anterior SVTs of frequent 2-SVTs, both should be equal and the starting SVT $V_{j',n'}$ and the starting $V_{j,n+1}$ of the following sub-scenario of the ending SVT $V_{j,n}$ should be equal. When both ending SVTs $V_{j,n}$ and $V_{j',n'-1}$ are anterior SVTs of rare 2-SVTs, the ending SVT $V_{j,n}$ and the starting SVT $V_{j',n'}$ should have only one sensor value difference. The ending SVT $V_{j,n}$ has the opportunity to be combined with any starting SVTs, but if there are different sensory values more than one, the ending SVT $V_{j,n}$ and the starting SVT $V_{j',n'}$ cannot be combined because it is against the required format. In other cases, $V_{j,n}$ cannot be combined with $V_{j',n'}$.

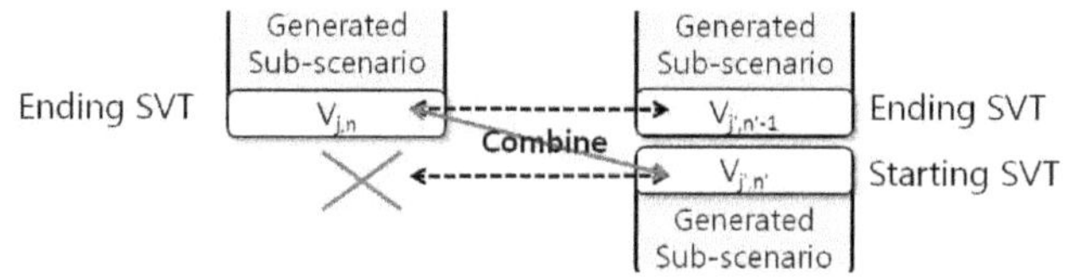

Figure 13. The Comparison of SVTs in Combination Constraints

Second, if the duration of the sub-scenario to the ending SVT $V_{j,n}$ is smaller than ζ, the ending SVT $V_{j,n}$ cannot be combined with any starting SVTs. This constraint limits the duration of the generated sub-scenarios to control the number of combined generated scenarios.

Third, when any ending SVT $V_{j,n}$ is combined with starting SVT $V_{j',n'}$, if there is any SVT of the j'*th* scenario in a stack, the serial SVTs from the SVT of the j'*th* scenario in the stack to the ending SVT $V_{j,n}$ are compared with the serial SVTs to the staring SVT $V_{j',n'-1}$ considering the same number of SVTs. If both serial SVTs are equal, the ending SVT $V_{j,n}$ cannot be combined with the starting SVT $V_{j',n'}$ to eliminate redundant reformatted generated scenarios.

Fourth, any ending SVT $V_{j,n}$ cannot be combined with starting SVT $V_{j',n'}$ where the starting SVT $V_{j',n'}$ is not invoked at the time when the starting SVT $V_{j',n'}$ will occur in a new combined generated scenario to increase the reality of the combined generated scenario. To make the starting SVT $V_{j',n'}$ be combined more, we define δ to make the period of the time where the starting SVT $V_{j',n'}$ can be combined.

For both combinations, the maximum time t_{max} of a combined scenario is limited to prevent generating new combined scenarios with periods over t_{max}. If the period of the combined scenario is compared with the maximum time t_{max} whenever the new combined scenarios are generated, it is too late to check because of the amount of calculation. Having a combined scenario period over the maximum time t_{max} occurs often during combinations. Therefore, to reduce useless combinations of SVTs, the period of the combined scenario is checked whenever any SVT is combined.

4.5 Space and Time Complexity Analysis

To analyze our approach, the space and time complexities of our approach are analyzed. Space complexity is calculated by counting the number of all SVs and all numeric values that need to be stored. Time complexity is calculated by counting the number of all references to SVs and all other numeric values that are referenced or changed.

When the maximum number of the possible numbers of sensors is defined by ω, there are ω^{ξ} unique SVTs maximally. Usually t_{max}, ξ and ω are predefined according to the environment of a smart space. Therefore, these parameters are handled as constants when space or time complexity is calculated.

4.5.1 The Complexity of the Formation Stage

All SVs need to be stored to combined generated scenarios. There are N formatted scenarios. The *jth* scenario has N_j SVTs. Each SVT has ξ SVs.

We define κ as the number of all SVTs in the formatted scenarios. Therefore, κ is the sum from N_1 to N_N. There are $\xi \times \kappa$ SVs in all formatted scenarios. κ space is also required for storing times of SVTs. As a result, the space complexity $g_f(\xi, \kappa)$ of the formation stage is $O(\kappa)$, as shown in Eq(1).

$$g_f(\xi, \kappa)=\xi\times\kappa+\kappa+c=(\xi+1)\kappa+c\approx O((\xi+1)\kappa)\approx O(\kappa) \quad (1)$$

We don't calculate the time complexity for the formation stage because the algorithm of the stage is not our concern.

4.5.2 The Complexity of the Count and Probability Matrix Generation Algorithms

The number of counts in the Count Matrix is $\omega^{2\xi}$. Therefore, the space complexity g_m of Count Matrix is $O(\omega^{2\xi})$. We also need the space g_s of Sum Set. There are ω^{ξ} sums maximally which is equal to the number of unique SVTs. Therefore, the space g_s is $O(\omega^{\xi})$. When generating Probability Matrix, the space complexity $g_p(\omega)$ for probability matrix is the same as Count Matrix. Therefore, all space complexity $g_d(\omega)$ for generating the Count Matrix, the Sum Set and the Probability Matrix is O(1), as shown in Eq(2).

$$\begin{aligned} g_d(\omega)&=g_m(\omega)+g_s(\omega)+g_p(\omega) \quad (2)\\ &=(\omega^{2\xi})+(\omega^{\xi})+(\omega^{2\xi})+c=2\omega^{2\xi}+\omega^{\xi}+c\\ &\approx O(\omega^{2\xi})\approx O(1) \end{aligned}$$

When Count Matrix is generated, we reference $\xi\times\kappa$ SVs to look up all formatted scenarios once and also change counts $\xi\times\kappa$ times. Therefore, we need $2\times\kappa\times\xi$ time SV references and changes. the time complexity f_m for generating Count Matrix is $O(\xi\kappa)$. To calculate sums, all counts are added to each sum, which need $\omega^{2\xi}$ sum changes. The time complexity f_s of sums is $O(\omega^{2\xi})$. To generate Probability Matrix, we calculate probabilities $\omega^{2\xi}$ times. Each probability is calculated by referencing one count and one sum. Therefore, we need $3\times\omega^{2\xi}$ times. Therefore, the time complexity f_p is $O(\omega^{2\xi})$. As a result, the time complexity $f_d(\xi, \kappa, \omega)$ of generating the Count Matrix, the Sum Set and the Probability Matrix is $O(\kappa)$, as shown in Eq(3)

$$\begin{aligned} &f_d(\xi, \kappa, \omega) \quad (3)\\ &=f_m(\xi, \kappa, \omega)+f_s(\xi, \kappa, \omega)+f_p(\xi, \kappa, \omega)\\ &=(2\times\xi\times\kappa)+(\omega^{2\xi})+(3\times\omega^{2\xi})+c=2\xi\kappa+4\omega^{2\xi}+c\\ &\approx O(\xi\kappa+\omega^{2\xi}))\approx O(\kappa) \end{aligned}$$

4.5.3 The Complexity of the Scenario Division and Combination Algorithms

The worst case for the space complexity and time complexity of the scenario division and generation algorithms is the case as follows. The period of every SVT is one second, which increases the number of SVTs in each combined generated scenario. All SVTs in all formatted scenarios are equal, which means all SVTs can be combined each other. δ is equal to or bigger than t_{max}. As δ increases, each SVT can combine with more other SVTs. Given that the number of scenarios is in proportion to the number of calling the function CombineSVT, all scenarios have t_{max} SVTs.

The required space is only for storing combined SVTs in a stack. The minimum period of SVTs is 1 ms, and the maximum period of combined generated scenarios is t_{max}. Therefore, the maximum number of SVTs in the stack is t_{max}. The space complexity $g_c(t_{max})$ of the scenario division and combination algorithms is $O(t_{max})$, as shown in Eq(4).

$$g_c(t_{max})=t_{max}\approx O(t_{max})\approx O(1) \quad (4)$$

Four sub-stages are implemented by DP by calling the function CombineSVT, recursively. Therefore, the time complexity f_c of the scenario division and combination algorithms is equal to the time complexity f_g of the function GenerateScenarios. This function calls the function CombineSVT N times. When we define σ as shown in Eq(5), the function CombineSVT calls itself σ times recursively during the worst case.

$$\sigma=\sum_{p=1}^{((t^{max}-1)\div\zeta-1)} N^p \quad (5)$$

There are two functions inside the function CombineSVT. The time complexity of combination constraints is $O(3\xi)$ because three pairs of SVTs are compared for inter combinations. The time complexity of the function GenerateOneScenario is $O(\xi t_{max})$ maximally, which is called N times, which is the number of all last SVTs. Therefore, time complexity of the function GenerateScenarios is:

$O(N^{tmax-1}+N^2)$.

$$\begin{aligned} f_c(\xi, N, \sigma, t_{max})&=f_g(\xi, N, \sigma, t_{max})= N\times f_s(\xi, N, \sigma, t_{max}) \quad (6)\\ &=N\times(3\xi\times\sigma+\xi t_{max}\times N+c)=\sigma3\xi N+\xi t_{max}N^2+c\\ &\approx O(\sigma\xi N+\xi t_{max}N^2)=O(\xi N^{tmax-1}+\xi t_{max}N^2)\approx O(N^{tmax-1}+N^2) \end{aligned}$$

4.5.4 The Complexity of the Reformation Stage

To transfer SVs to the original format, additional space is required. However, its size depends on the original format. We assume that its size will not be big enough to consider.

We don't also calculate the time complexity for the reformation stage because the algorithm of this stage is not our concern.

4.5.5 The Complexity of Our Approach

Our approach has four stages. Therefore, the space complexity and time complexity of the proposed method are the maximum value among all complexities. Space is required maximally when the space for SVs is stored ($O(\kappa)$).

$$\begin{aligned} g(\xi, \kappa, \omega)&=g_f(\xi, \kappa)+g_d(\omega)+g_c(t_{max})) \quad (7)\\ &\approx max(O(\kappa), O(1), O(1))=O(\kappa) \end{aligned}$$

Time complexity has the maximum value when function CombineSVT is called recursively σ times or Count Matrix is generated. Therefore, the final time complexity is:

$O(max(\kappa, N^{tmax-1}+N^{2}))$.

$$\begin{aligned} f(\xi, \kappa, \omega)&=f_d(\xi, \kappa, \omega)+f_c(\xi, \kappa, \sigma, t_{max}) \quad (8)\\ &\approx max(O(\kappa),O(N^{tmax-1}+N^2)=O(max(\kappa, N^{tmax-1}+N^2)) \end{aligned}$$

5. VALIDATION

5.1 Initial Scenario Dataset

To generate scenarios by using our approach, original data from a smart space is required. For validation, we utilized *Kasteren* dataset [4], because multiple original scenarios can be obtained easily by dividing the dataset by each day. The dataset is collected from an apartment occupied by a 26-year-old man for 28 days, but only data of 24 days are available for our approach. One single file is separated into 24 original scenarios, excluding four scenarios. 17 original scenarios are used for scenario generation as shown in Figure 14. Each day is represented by a separate, original scenario.

Mon	Tue	Wen	Thr	Fri	Sat	Sun
2/25	**26**	**27**	**28**	29		**3/2**
3	4	**5**	**6**	**7**	8	
10	**11**	12	**13**	**14**	**15**	16
17	**18**	**19**	20	**21**		
~~23~~						

Figure 14. Used Original Scenarios

Each original scenario has values of 14 proximity sensors. Each row of the dataset contains starting time, ending time, and sensory ID.

We observed in the dataset that the human subject sometimes sleeps after midnight (0:00AM). Therefore, we assumed each day to start from 2:00AM, where there are no sensory value changes for about one hour. This represented a clearer beginning of day for scenario generation purposes.

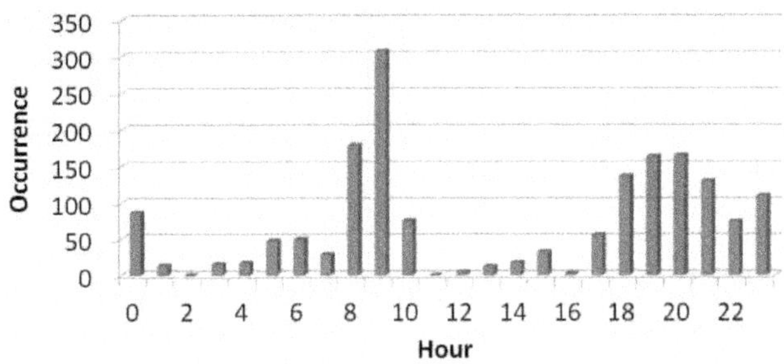

Figure 15. Event Occurrence Count

To convert the dataset to our required format, each event is split into two events: one for the starting event and the other for the ending event. The sensory values of starting events are assigned to 1, because of proximity sensors. The sensory values of ending events are assigned to 0. Moreover, in our formatted scenarios, each row includes all sensor values in each entry. As a consequence of augmenting the table with all sensors, in addition to the single sensor with value change, we had to use "null" value as the sensor value that is not changed and previously unknown. However, by analyzing the table, we can use value changes to a given sensor to estimate previous values of the same sensor. Furthermore, given that only proximity sensors are used in the dataset, we can further assume that sensors with all "null" values in the table can be estimated to have 0 values, as the human subject could not possibly be in proximity of all "null" value sensors all the time.

5.2 Scenario Generation Analysis

5.2.1 The Result of Reformatted Scenarios

To generate two matrices and one set, ξ and t_{max} are set depending on the configuration of the smart space of the Kasteren dataset and other parameters are set considering the number of generated sub-scenarios, as shown in Table 1. The bigger θ_r is or the smaller θ_f is, the more the number of reformatted scenarios increases.

Table 1. Parameters for Generating Reformatted Scenarios

	ξ	θ_r	θ_f	t_{max}
Values	14	0.01	1.00	24×60×60

By merging all SVTs of formatted scenarios, M is defined by 109 unique SVTs. Then Count Matrix, Sum Set and Probability Matrix are generated based on M. In the Count Matrix, there are only 249 counts, about 2% of all ccounts, bigger than 0. In the Probability Matrix, 11 rare probabilities and 67 frequent probabilities are defined among 249 probabilities. Then in formatted scenarios, 18 rare probabilities and 258 frequent probabilities are defined by reflecting the Probability Matrix. Therefore, 293 sub-scenarios are generated.

As a result, by using the Kasteren dataset as original scenarios and our approach, 546,383 reformatted scenarios were generated maximally, as shown in Table 2.

Table 2. Reformatted Generated Scenarios

	ζ	δ	*Generated Scenarios*	*Redundant Scenarios*	*Consumed Time*
1		900 sec	408	0	1 min
2		1,800 sec	5,257	0	5 min
3	60 sec	2,700 sec	48,994	-	65 min
4		3,600 sec	185,782	-	6 hours
5		4,500 sec	546,383	-	1 day
6	45 sec	900 sec	1763	-	4 min
7		1,800 sec	284,829	-	8 hours

5.2.2 The Redundancy of Reformatted Scenarios

Enormous reformatted scenarios can be generated by the proposed method. However, if many redundant reformatted scenarios are generated, it would be difficult to use the reformatted scenarios. Therefore, we compare the reformatted generated scenarios one by one.

When ζ is set to 60 sec and δ is set to 900 or 1,800 sec, no redundant reformatted scenarios are generated, as shown in Table 2. However, this doesn't mean that our approach doesn't generate any redundant reformatted scenarios. Fortunately, no redundant sub-scenarios are generated after the formatted scenarios of Kasteren dataset is divided. If there are any redundant generated sub-scenarios, redundant reformatted scenarios may be generated. In addition, if there are same original scenarios, redundant reformatted scenarios can be generated because the same original scenarios make a lot of the same sub-scenarios.

5.2.3 The Complexity of Reformatted Scenarios

We expect that the 5,257 reformatted generated scenarios are adequate to test activity recognition algorithms - they amount to 14-year scenarios! The space complexity of 5,257 reformatted generated scenarios from the Kasteren dataset is calculated. Given that there are 14 sensors with only Boolean values, each scenario defines 24 hours maximally, the number of unique SVT ω^{ξ} is 109, the total number of SVT κ is 1,710 and SVTs are stored in a stack not up to t_{max} but up to 286 times maximally, it requires 49,833 spaces. When reformatted scenarios are generated, only 2% of the space of the Count Matrix and Probability Matrix is used. The space complexity can be lowered if other algorithms such as hash functions are applied.

$$\begin{aligned} g(\xi, \kappa, \omega, t_{max}) &= g_f(\xi, \kappa) + g_d(\omega) + g_c(t_{max}) \\ &= ((\xi+1)\kappa) + (2\omega^{2\xi} + \omega^{\xi}) + (t_{max}) + c \\ &\geq 25{,}650 + 23{,}871 + 312 \\ &\approx 49{,}833 \end{aligned} \quad (9)$$

The time complexity of the proposed method is $O(\max(2\xi\kappa+4\omega^{2\xi}, \sigma 3\xi N+\xi t_{max}N^2))$, which is very high. The weakness of the proposed method is that the scenario generation process consumes too much time, depending on parameters such as ζ and δ. Therefore, it is very important to set those parameters. When ζ and δ are set by 60 seconds and 1,800 seconds as shown in Table 2, σ is 998,737 calculated by counting the number of calling the function CombineSVT directly and SVs are changed and updated 714 million times, as shown in Eq(10).

The time complexity is not low by all means but practically only minutes are needed to generate scenarios significantly larger than the original scenarios. In the above example, about five minutes were all it took to generate 5,257 scenarios.

$$f(\xi, \kappa, N, \omega)=f_d(\xi, \kappa, \omega)+f_c(\xi, N, \sigma, t_{max}) \quad (10)$$

$$=(2\xi\kappa+4\omega^{2\xi})+(\sigma 3\xi N+\xi t_{max} N^2)+c$$

$$\geq 95{,}404+(998{,}737\times 3\times 14\times 17+14\times 286\times 289)$$

$$=95{,}404+713{,}098{,}218+1{,}157{,}156$$

$$\approx 714 \text{ million}$$

5.3 Viterbi-based Validation Analysis

By using the proposed method, enormous reformatted scenarios can be generated. Increasing the number of the reformatted scenarios is one of our goals, but the reality of those scenarios is more important. It is therefore crucial that we validate the reality of our reformatted scenarios.

Our approach to validate the reality of the reformatted scenarios is to check whether the reformatted scenarios have the same stochastic characteristics as the original scenarios. The Count Matrix, Sum Set and Probability Matrix from the original scenarios represent the stochastic characteristics of the original scenarios. The Count Matrix, Sum Set and Probability Matrix of the reformatted generated scenarios also represent the stochastic characteristics of the reformatted generated scenarios. Therefore, we will compare both Probability Matrix in both scenarios to validate the reality of the reformatted scenarios.

Serial SVTs can be generated by transferring SVTs from a first SVT to any last SVTs by only using Probability Matrix. However, such serial SVTs would not be invoked in a smart space. As we proposed combination constraints, there must be some constraints to transfer SVTs.

We utilize dynamic Bayesian network (DBN) to represent the flow of time by combining the concepts of Probability Matrix and combination constraints as shown in Figure 16.

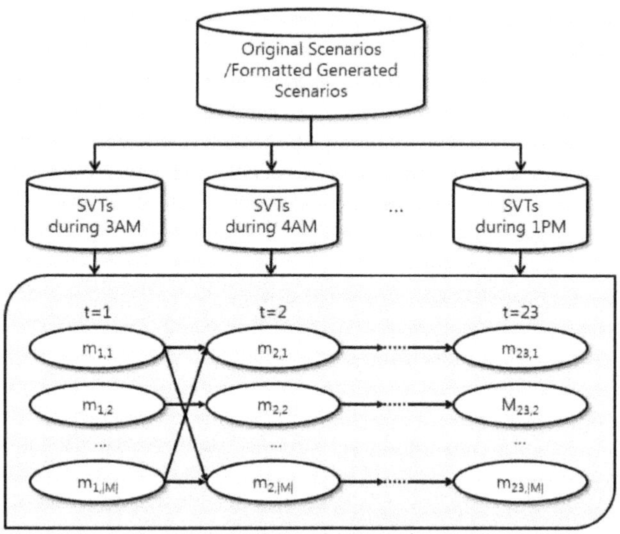

Figure 16. Dynamic Bayesian Network Generation Process

First, all SVTs from original scenarios or reformatted generated scenarios are divided into 23 sets according to invoked hours. Each set of SVTs is utilized by being classified into subsets by SVs for the SVTs of each hour in DBN. In figure 16, $m_{1,2}$ denotes the second subset in the first hour (2:00AM). The transition probability between two subsets in different sets is calculated by Bayesian probability by utilizing SVTs of each subset. The subsets are linked, except those subsets of 0% conditional probability. Finally, serial SVTs are generated by transferring from subsets of each first SVT to subsets of any last SVTs in DBN. In the original scenarios, there were 17 first SVTs and 17 last SVTs, but some are redundant. Therefore, only 13 first SVTs and 14 last SVTs are utilized.

The optimal serial SVTs from a first SVT to any last SVTs are chosen by Viterbi algorithm [16] to compare the results of both DBNs, as shown in Figure 17. First, a DBN is generated based on original scenarios, and then the sets of optimal serial SVTs are generated using the DBN and a Viterbi algorithm. Second, reformatted scenarios are generated based on original scenarios through Count and Probability Matrics. Then another DBN is generated based on the reformatted generated scenarios, and other sets of optimal serial SVTs are generated using the second DBN and a Viterbi algorithm. Each set of the optimal serial SVTs by original and reformatted generated scenarios is divided by first SVTs. Finally, the divided set is compared with the other set, which starts from the same first SVT in other types of scenarios.

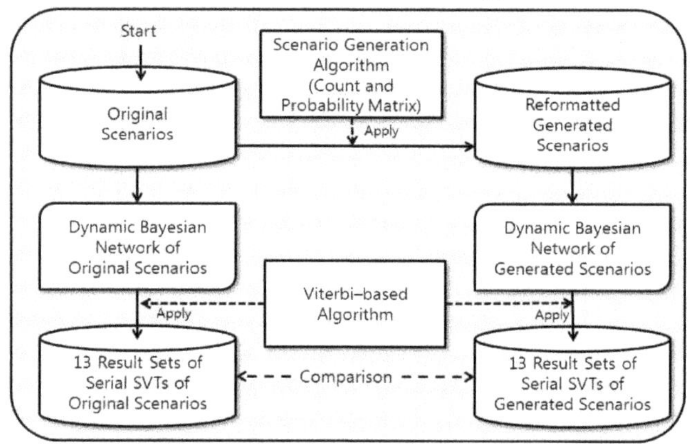

Figure 17. Validation Process

Given that there are 14 last SVTs, the possible maximum number of serial SVTs is 14. Figure 18 shows the numbers of serial SVTs of sets according to first SVTs. Both scenarios generate the same number of serial SVTs.

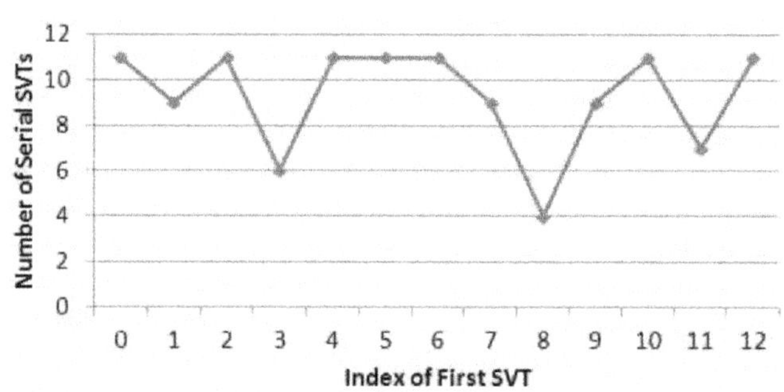

Figure 18. Number of Serial SVTs according to First SVT

Then we measured exactly how many times the same serial SVTs, or the same serial SVTs except one SVT, are generated by both scenarios. Figure 19 shows the result of comparison. The average of the percent of the same serial SVTs was 80.07%, and that of the same serial SVTs except one SVT was 86.25%. Conditional probability is very sensitive. Because of the slight difference of the probabilities of SVTs, totally different serial SVTs could be generated. 80.07% means each probability of reformatted generated scenarios maintains the similar difference among the probabilities of the same anterior SVTs. Therefore, reformatted generated scenarios have stochastic characteristics very similar to those of the original scenarios.

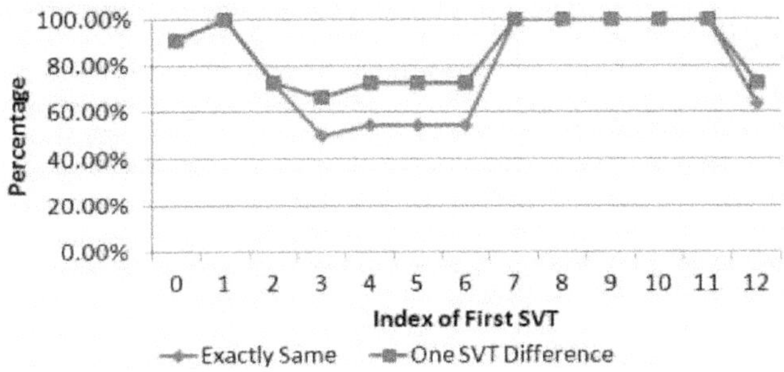

Figure 19. 13 Results of Serial SVTs

6. CONCLUSION AND FUTURE WORK

We introduced a Bayesian probability-based scenario generation method. To increase the reality of generated scenarios, original scenarios are utilized by dividing and combining according to carefully designed and justified combination constraints. By using a small number of original scenarios, an enormous amount of reformatted scenarios was generated.

We showed that 546,383 reformatted scenarios could be generated based on only 17 original scenarios. By setting parameters properly we can generate more scenarios, but much more time will be required. Although we validated the viability of the proposed method in terms of the reality of its generated scenarios, further enhancements are needed to further enhance realism but at reduced time and space complexities.

Another issue that needs to be addressed is redundantly reformatted scenarios. They could be generated because when each reformatted scenario is generated, the existence of the same sub-scenarios is not checked.

Finally, further enhancements to the reality of the reformatted scenarios could be achieved through more sophisticated combination constraints, other than the ones we proposed in this paper. We plan to further research combination constraints.

7. REFERENCES

[1] Helal, S., Kim, E., and Hossain, S. 2010. Scalable approaches to activity recognition research. *Proceedings of the Workshop titled "How to do good activity recognition research? Experimental methodologies, evaluation metrics, and reproducibility issues".* (Helsinki, Finland, May 17-20, 2010)

[2] Helal, S., Lee, J. W., Hossain, S., Kim, E., Hagras, H. and Cook, D. 2011. Persim - Simulator for human activities in pervasive spaces. *Proceedings of the 7th International Conference on Intelligent Environments*, (Nottingham, UK, July, 2011), 192-199.

[3] Singla, G., Cook, D. J., and Schmitter-edgecombe, M. 2008. Incorporating temporal reasoning into activity recognition for smart home residents. *Proceedings of the AAAI Workshop on Spatial and Temporal Reasoning.*

[4] Kasteren, T. V., Noulas, A. Englebienne, G. and Kröse, B. 2008. Accurate activity recognition in a home setting. *Proceedings of the Tenth International Conference on Ubiquitous Computing.* (Seoul, Korea, Sep. 21-24, 2008), 1-9.

[5] Pranevicius, H., Sutiene, K. 2007. Scenario tree generation by clustering the simulated data paths. *Proceeding of the 21st European Conference on Modelling and Simulation.* (Prague, Czech Republic, June 4-6, 2007).

[6] Pham-Nguyen, C., and Garlatti, S. 2008. Context-aware scenarios for pervasive long-life learning. *IEEE/WIC/ACM International Conference on Web Intelligence and Intelligent Agent Technology.* 1 (Dec. 9-12, 2008), 824-827.

[7] Grois, E., Hsu, W. H., Voloshin, M., and Wilkins, D. C. Bayesian network models for generation of crisis management training scenarios. *Proceedings of The Fifteenth National/Tenth Conference on Artificial Intelligence/Innovative Applications of Artificial Intelligence.* 1113-1120.

[8] Kuchler, C. and Vigerske, S. 2007. Decomposition of multistage stochastic programs with recombining scenario trees.

[9] Høyland, K., Kaut, M., Wallace, S. W. 2001. Generating scenario trees for multistage decision problems. *Management Science.* 47, 2, 295-307.

[10] Helal, A., Cho, K., Lee, W., Sung, Y., Lee, J.W., Kim, E. 2012. 3D Modeling and Simulation of Human Activities in Smart Spaces. *Proceeding of Nineth International Conference on Ubiquitous Intelligence & Computing and Nineth International Conference on Autonomic & Trusted Computing.* (Fukuoka, Japan, Sept. 4-7, 2012), 112-119. doi: 10.1109/UIC-ATC.2012.35.

[11] Nazerfard, E., Das, B., Holder, L. B. and Cook, D. 2010. Conditional Random Fields for Activity Recognition in Smart Environments. *Proceedings of ACM International Health Informatics Symposium.* (Nov. 2010).

[12] Helal, A., Mendez-Vazquez, A., Hossain, S. 2009. Specification and synthesis of sensory datasets in pervasive spaces. *IEEE Symposium on Computers and Communications.* (Sousse, Tunisia, July 5-8, 2009).

[13] SDDL: Sensory dataset description language - specifications and resources web site: http:// www.icta.ufl.edu/persim/sddl

[14] Persim: A Simulator for pervasive spaces - project official web site:http://www.icta.ufl.edu/projects_persim.htm.

[15] Cameron, K., Hughes, K., and Doughty, K. 1997. Reducing fall incidence in community elders by telecare using predictive systems. *Proceedings of the International IEEE-EMBS Conference.* (Oct. 1997), 1036-1039.

[16] Viterbi, A.J. 1967. Error bounds for convolutional codes and an asymptotically optimum decoding algorithm. *IEEE Transactions on Information Theory.* 13, 2, 260–269. doi:10.1109/TIT.1967.1054010.

Modeling and Simulation of Crowd using Cellular Discrete Event Systems Theory

Ronnie Farrell, Mohammad Moallemi, Sixuan Wang, Wang Xiang, Gabriel Wainer
Dept. of Systems and Computer Engineering
Carleton University, Ottawa, ON, Canada
Centre of Visualization and Simulation (V-SIM)
{ronnie;moallemi;swang;wxiang;gwainer}@sce.carleton.ca

ABSTRACT
In this paper, we discuss how Cellular Discrete Event System Specification (Cell-DEVS) theory can be used in modeling and simulation of the crowd. We will show that the efficient cell update mechanism of Cell-DEVS allows for more efficient entity-based simulation of the crowd compared to cellular automata. On the other hand the formal interfacing mechanisms provided by this theory allows for integration of other components such as DEVS atomic processing component or visualization and building information modeling components with the Cell-DEVS model. Finally, we describe in details of the design and development of several pedestrian models and present the results.

Categories and Subject Descriptors
I.6.5 **[MODEL DEVELOPMENT]**: Modeling methodologies;
I.6.8 **[SIMULATION AND MODELING]**: Types of Simulation –Discrete event, Visual.
J.6 **[COMPUTER-AIDED ENGINEERING]**: Computer-aided design (CAD)

General Terms
Algorithms, Human Factors.

Keywords
Cellular Discrete Event Systems; Pedestrian; Crowd.

1. INTRODUCTION
Human society is a diverse yet cooperative environment in which each member decides and acts independently while the action of the entire members can converge to a single and workforce. This outcome can be constructive or destructive and it depends on various physiological, psychological and social factors. Modeling such kind of behavior can provide insight in learning about human behavior. In particular, Modeling and Simulation (M&S) of crowd behavior can be used for predicting the impact of the behavior of a group of people in different situations. This topic has been of interest in many different fields such as safety, Architectural design, Industrial design, computer games, and transportation.

Crowd behavior simulation has been studied to investigate possible risks in architectural designs and emergency management systems. These include physics-inspired models such as Helbing's social force model [1], cellular automata models based on predefined rules [2], and agent-based models that use multiple agents to simulate a crowd where each agent has its own behavior and interacts with other nearby agents [3]. Computer-based simulation of the crowd can be categorized based on the size of the model (large, medium, small) and also duration of the simulation (long-term and short-term) [4]. In small-size crowds the modeler can implement the behavior of each individual in the crowd as a separate entity; while in a huge size crowd, the focus is usually on the emergent behavior. From this perspective, crowd modeling approaches are divided to three categories: *flow-based*, *entity-system*, and *agent-based* approaches [4]. Flow-based approaches (e.g. [5]) consider the crowd as a flow of movement that is focused on the overall physical aspects of the crowd with low granularity, which is suitable for large-size simulations due to its light computational demands. Entity-system approaches attack the problem in a more detailed perspective, considering each individual as a separate entity that can render social and physical behavioral aspects. The particles are homogeneous entities that form a crowd in which the movement, speed and social behavior of the individuals are controlled by a set of laws. Hence, this approach demands higher computation and presents more details of the interactions between the particles. Examples of this approach are presented in [6] and [7]. The agent-based approach reflects each individual as an independent and autonomous entity that can behave based on specific rules defined for that entity. The local phenomena can affect the decision-making process of each individual, while the entire crowd can produce an emerging pattern that is deducted by the social and physical aspects of each individual. Due to customized and independent decision-making processes performed by each individual, this approach requires heavy computational resources to be implemented and it is usually not suitable for large-size or long-term simulations. On the other hand, with the rapid advancement of processing resources and sophisticated flexibility and accuracy offered by this approach, it is gaining significant scientific attention. In general, the agent-based models are independent individuals governed by local rules, while entity-based models are homogeneous entities governed by global rules that are semi-independent and reply to local events.

There are different behavioral factors that the modelers capitalize on when modeling crowds. Physical factors consist of position, size, speed, direction, power, etc. Psychological factors involve stress level, courage, etc. Finally, the social factors include family ties, culture, leadership, laws and regulations, etc. Crowd models can be evaluated based on flexibility, extensibility, execution performance, and scalability.

As discussed earlier, M&S has been used as a tool for efficient analysis, design, and verification of crowd behavior. It provides a hierarchical design scheme in which higher abstract levels are branched into levels that contain more details. In particular, the use of a formal M&S methodology would allow one to express groups of people using mathematical notations in which the details of the behavior of the crowd are accurately modeled. Other advantages of formal M&S include applying formal model checking techniques at design time, the incremental refinement of the initial simulation models, simulation-based validation, and reuse of the existing models.

One of the promising theoretical approaches towards resolving crowd modeling specific problems is Cellular automata (CA) theory [10]. In this branch of discrete dynamic systems, which space is represented by a regular grid, with each cell being a state machine. The time advances in a discrete manner, triggering state changes in the cells, based on the value of their neighbor cells. This theory is used in physics, complexity science, theoretical biology, microstructure modeling, and spatial modeling. The Cell-DEVS formalism [9] is derived from both CA and Discrete-EVent System Specification (DEVS) [8]. The Cell-DEVS formalism solves the problem of unnecessary processing burden in quiescent cells, and it allows for a more efficient asynchronous execution.

DEVS is a well-known formal discrete-event M&S methodology, which is based on generic dynamic systems theory. Discrete-event approaches provide event-driven response to external stimuli, which can represent human reaction to the environment. On the other hand, discrete-event methodologies provide continuous timing of the events. In particular, DEVS includes well-defined coupling of components, hierarchical, modular construction, support for discrete event approximation of continuous systems and support for repository reuse. Based on these ideas, Cell-DEVS uses a continuous time base, and provides advanced timing constructions for the cellular models. In this methodology, each cell is represented as a DEVS atomic model that changes state in response to the occurrence of events in an event-driven fashion. Cell-DEVS was originally introduced for modeling and simulation of spatial systems and, as it will be shown in this article, it can be seamlessly adapted for crowd modeling.

We used the DEVS and the Cell-DEVS formalisms for the following reasons:

- DEVS provides a formal foundation to M&S that proved to be successful in different complex applications [9].

- It integrates a simulation approach with the benefits of a formal modeling technique, which provides fast prototyping and incremental development while allowing for reuse of previously existing models.

In the remaining sections of the paper, we discuss the advantages of using Cell-DEVS formalism and show how it can be used to model the crowd in an entity-based approach. The rule-driven nature of cell behavior definition provides a platform for particle-based decision-making definition, leading to easier and faster adoption and implementation of entity-based crowd modeling algorithms. The other advantage of this method is its fast computing apparatus working asynchronously on the cellular grid, increasing the execution speed compared to CA, hence allowing for long-term crowd simulation. Finally, the formal I/O port definitions in the formalism, allows for interfacing variety of environment models with different occupants, and data transfer between different spatial components. The idea is to convert urban environments or architectural spaces into cellular models and provide diverse sceneries to be simulated in 2D and even in 3D cellular models.

2. RELATED WORK

Research on flow-based crowd modeling assumes a crowd of people as a flow of liquid and tries to solve the problem using differential equations. This continuous modeling approach has been investigated in [11], where the authors include a "thinking" factor that is added to the fluid dynamics to assimilate the flow of humans. Another example is the EVACNET4 [12] software, which provides a M&S environment for building evacuation. The tool allows for modeling the buildings and rooms as nodes in a network whose arcs represent the corridors and pass-ways. The modeler assigns capacities to the nodes and arcs, and travel-time to each of these components. Then, the model is computed using a linear programming approach to find the shortest path during the evacuation of the building. A recent application of this software for evacuation M&S in high-rise buildings has been presented in [13].

As mentioned earlier, these approaches do not provide high-resolution details of the behavior of the individuals in the simulation and are somewhat difficult to model. Instead, other research in this area has focused on visualization aspects of the crowd modeling. In [14] flow tiles have been introduced, in order to model the flow of crowd concentrating on the visual and physical aspects of the crowd movement rather than the social and psychological aspects. Therefore, this technique does not render an accurate simulation of the crowd, but it provides a suitable augmented reality representation of the crowd flow to be used in computer game development.

Other existing long-term crowd models can be categorized as flow-based models that tackle the problem from a higher abstract level. Examples of these models are the social life and neighborhood evolution models presented in [15].

There has been a series of models investigating the spread of extremist opinion and beliefs among people in long-term. In [16], the authors investigated the spread of extremism in four different networks of people in which different patterns have emerged based on factors such as uncertainty, influence of other peoples' words and the learning process of each individual. The uncertainty factor in each individual represents the chances that an individual can give up his/her opinion and accept extremist ideologies. The decision-making of an individual is modeled by a mathematical equation representing the evolution strategy of opinion. It is observed that the single extreme convergence is favored by small shortest paths between all pairs of nodes in the network.

Another agent-based simulation of opinion spread among crowd has been done in [17]. The model is a continuous dynamic opinion spread system where self-organizing agents carry out the simulation based on the principle of meta-contrast. The model considers factors such as network interactions on the evolvement of people's opinions, and indicates that consensus, polarization or extremism can be produced even without interaction with an extremist agent.

An entity-based model of pedestrian reaction in panic situation has been proposed in [18] in which the factors such a s distance, velocity, mass, and forces are incorporated to quantitatively assess the panic. Each individual is represented as an entity containing mass and power which affects the socio-psychological factors in decision making.

A similar work to ours has been introduced in [19] in which a cellular automata-based small-size model of the environment and the crowd of people as agents is integrated with virtual reality engine to render a 3D representation of the simulation. In this model, spatial representation of the sources of fields that are signals that diffuse in the environment interact with crowd agents with a "perception of signal" factor that is the state of the agent. This perception can lead to the behavioral reactions of the agents in the environment turning the agent to an autonomous or controlled agent. Other factors also can be introduced to the field such as emission-diffusion-perception mechanism that can affect the behavior of the agents.

Another very similar and motivating pedestrian movement M&S approach has been introduced in [20]. In this research, bi-directional pedestrian flow has been modeled using Cellular Automata considering different behavioral factors such as position exchange, lateral-move and step back. As an entity-based model, it defines a Moore neighborhood for each entity and applied sophisticated rules to achieve a realistic pedestrian movement in urban walkways. The position exchange and lateral movement allowed for investigating and increasing the speed of movement in low-density areas and provided a high-resolution simulation of the crowd however, the collision is not managed very well.

Nevertheless, as mentioned earlier the efficient and intelligent computation of cell-state variations in Cell-DEVS (compared to CA) and the interfacing mechanisms provided by this technique allows for developing larger models and faster execution of models as well as straightforward integration of these models with other visualization or modeling tools. We will present different models developed using Cell-DEVS and capitalize on these advantages.

On the other hand, most modeling and simulation methods listed above run on single-user workstations, which normally require too much time for installation and configuration of all the software and dependencies needed for simulation. It is more efficient to access simulation resources remotely by web services, improving scalability (e.g. accessibility, availability and interoperability). In this way, users can reuse and share simulation resources on-site without worrying about the limitations of their local workstations in terms of processing power or memory capacity. SOAP-based Web Services use the Remote Procedure Call (RPC) to allow two distributed heterogeneous systems to call the functions of each other; but it exposes the implementation details and lacks scalability [21]. Another better way is to use RESTful Web Services. Its purpose is to transfer messages of Web resources using a set of uniform operations. Access to RESTful Web Services is through Web resources (URIs) and XML messages using HTTP methods (GET, PUT, POST and DELETE). Based on these ideas proposed in [21], the authors presented the RESTful Interoperability Simulation Environment (RISE) middleware. The main objective of RISE is to support interoperability and mash-ups of distributed simulations regardless of the modeling formalism, programming language, or simulation engine.

3. Crowd Modeling using Cell-DEVS

Cell-DEVS [9] is an extension to DEVS [8] that allows defining cellular models with explicit timing delays. A Cell-DEVS model is a lattice of cells holding state variables and a computing apparatus, which is in charge of updating the cell states according to a local rule. This is done using the current cell state and those of a finite set of nearby cells (called its neighborhood). Cell-DEVS improves execution performance of cellular models by using a discrete-event approach. It also enhances the cell's timing definition by making it more expressive. Each cell is defined as a DEVS atomic model, and it can be later integrated to a coupled model representing the cell space. Cell-DEVS models are informally defined as shown in Figure 1.

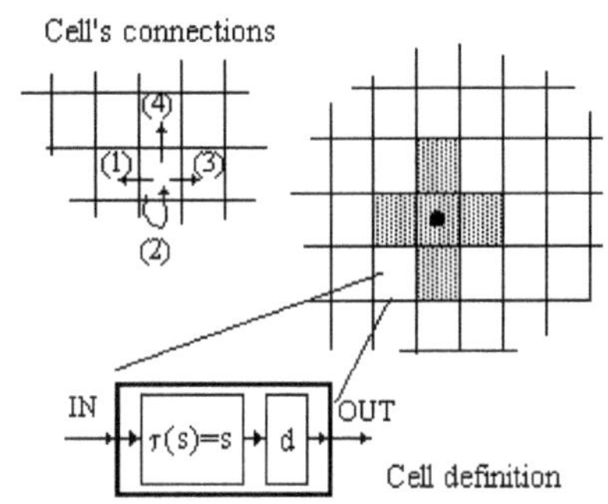

Figure 1. Cell-DEVS model [9].

CD++ [9] is a M&S tool that provides a development environment for implementing DEVS and Cell-DEVS models. DEVS atomic models can be developed and incorporated into a class hierarchy programmed in C++. Coupled models can be defined using a built-in specification language. Cell-DEVS models are built following the formal specifications for DEVS, and a built-in language is provided to describe the behavior rules. The language is based on the formal specifications of Cell-DEVS. The model specification includes the definition of the size and dimension of the cell space, the shape of the neighborhood and borders. The cell's local computing function is defined using a set of rules with the form POSTCONDITION DELAY {PRECONDITION}. These indicate that when the PRECONDITION is satisfied, the state of the cell will change to the designated POSTCONDITION, whose computed values will be transmitted to other components after consuming the DELAY. If the precondition is false, the next rule in the list is evaluated until a rule is satisfied or there are no more rules.

3.1 Building Information Modeling

In our previous research presented in [22], Cell-DEVS has been used in modeling evacuation of the crowd and detecting bottlenecks and congestion points in the buildings. Cell-DEVS models developed in CD++ were interfaced with Building Information Modeling (BIM) [23] models developed in Autodesk Revit™ Architecture [24] in order to export the building information from BIM and feed it to Cell-DEVS model to compute the crowd evacuation procedure. The results of the simulation in the Cell-DEVS model are then transported back to Autodesk 3D Max™ [25] to visualize of the simulation steps.

Figure 2 illustrates the three components used in the simulation of the crowd evacuation, where the BIM model data are extracted from Autodesk Revit™ tool using the APIs and the BIM add-in, and stored in CD++ initial value file. This file contains the initial coordinates of the BIM elements extracted from BIM model by the Parameter Extractor component from *Coordinate Loader*. Some other rule-construction data are also extracted and stored in CD++ *include* files. After this, a 2D cellular model of the BIM system is constructed in CD++ based on the dimensions and initial values extracted from BIM model. The multi-level cellular evacuation model defined in CD++ is declared using a set of rules indicating the output value for the cell's state after satisfying a precondition. A neighborhood consisting of down, left, up and then right cells that are adjacent to the central cell is declared. The model performs the following five rules wherever they apply, in order to simulate the evacuation in the building: 1) someone enters the current cell; 2) someone moves from the current cell to another one, 3) someone exits the floor, 4) someone enters a stairwell, and 5) someone exits a stairwell. After the Cell-DEVS model is executed in CD++ and the results are stored in a log file, they are then imported to the 3D Max™ to be visualized in 3D. Finally, the produced log file is parsed by looking for simulation times, cells locations and values and then the simulation scenario is visualized in the already created 3D visualization of the initial BIM model, imported from Revit™ to 3D Max™ by the *Data Loader*.

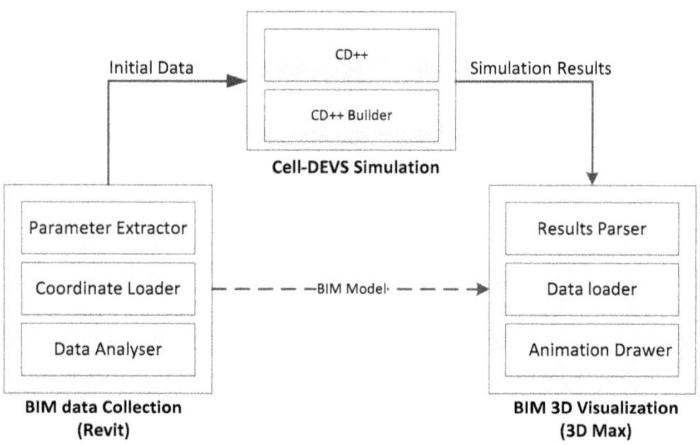

Figure 2. Interactive simulation system architecture [22].

3.2 Bi-directional Pedestrian Flow

Pedestrian movement M&S tries to render the intelligent, physical, and social behavior of the people in which the resultant movement of the crowd in different situations is calculated based on predefined rules. We modeled three different situation 1) Pedestrian walkway 2) Advanced pedestrian walkway 3) Pedestrian movement at doorway.

3.2.1 Pedestrian Movement on Walkway

Figure 3 shows the DEVS model definition diagram of this project. The *Pedestrian Gen* blocks are atomic DEVS components producing random sequence. The *Walkway* is a 2D Cell-DEVS coupled component of size 8×20 cells with the top-most and the bottom-most rows representing the walls of the walkway. Pedestrians are generated at the left and right ends of the walkway. The DEVS random generators are interfaced with the Cell-DEVS *Walkway* coupled component through the I/O definitions provided by DEVS formal structure. The goal of the project is to program the "pedestrians" to travel to the opposite end of the walkway without collision. The speeds of all "pedestrians" are modeled at a constant rate, and everyone travels at that same speed.

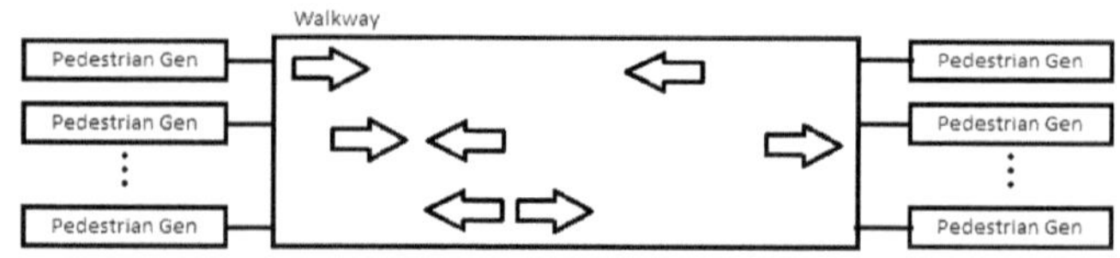

Figure 3. Bi-direction pedestrian Cell-DEVS model.

The rules that are used to regulate the behaviors of the pedestrians are explained below in detail.

Rule 1: Moving forward rule: If the cell in front of a "pedestrian" cell from either direction is empty, and no other "pedestrian" from the opposite direction is located two cells ahead, move forward. This is the highest priority rule. No action from other rules can take the empty square of moving forward rule (See Figure 4).

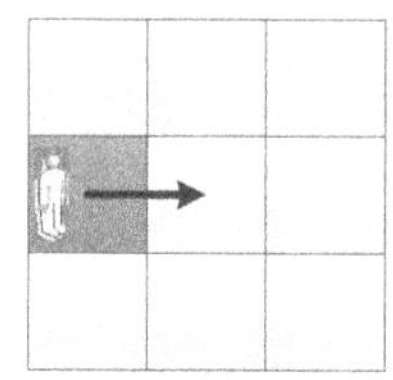

Figure 4. Rule 1.

Rule 2: Side stepping when straight movement is blocked: If a "pedestrian" is blocked by the opposite side "pedestrian", both "pedestrians" try to step to the right if that cell is empty (Figure 5.a). If the "pedestrian" is blocked by another one traveling to the same direction, simply do nothing but wait the other one to move first (Figure 5.b). This is the second highest priority rule.

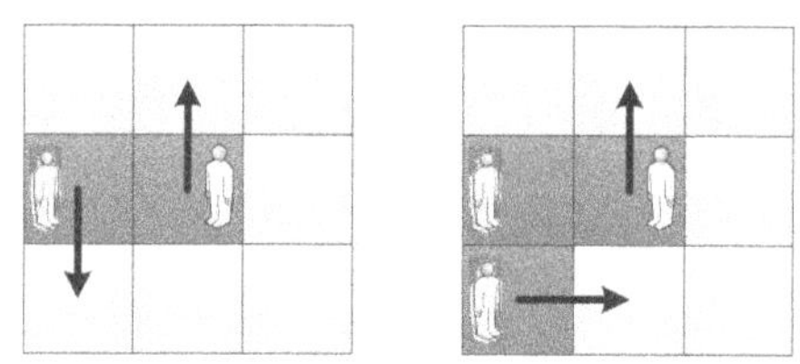

a) b)

Figure 5. Rule 2.

Rule 3: Side stepping when trying to take the same cell for straight movement: If two "pedestrians" from opposite side trying to take the same empty cell, both step to the right (Figure 6). If they are travelling in the same direction, Rule 1 takes care of it. This is the third highest priority rule.

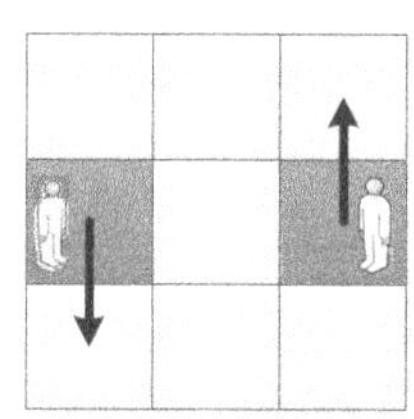

Figure 6. Rule 3.

Rule 4: Side step to the left if the right side is a wall: For the cases where side step to the right blocked by a wall (borders of the model), the "pedestrians" try to step to the left if there is an empty cell. This rule applies to both side-stepping when blocked or trying to take the same cell (Figure 7).

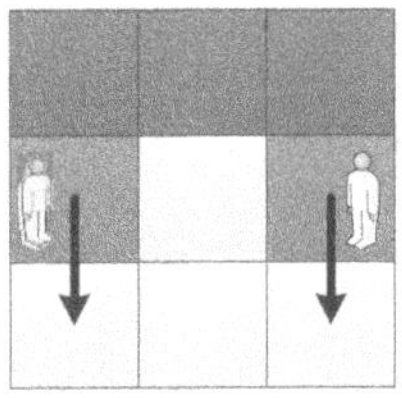

Figure 7. Rule 4.

These rules are a subset or a generalization of the 8 rules provided in [20] according to human natural way of walking. Moving straight forward is the most fundamental and most important form of traveling. Pedestrians change lane only when necessary. Also, people tend to step to the right when encountering another pedestrian traveling the opposite direction. Given everyone travel at same speed, it does not make sense to make a side step when encounter someone with the same direction as the pedestrian. Aside from these basic rules, other rules to control the entrance and exiting of the pedestrians have been implemented.

A customized neighborhood is defined for the cells based on the aforementioned rules. Cell (0,0) represents the core cell which is the pedestrian and it can move to the adjacent cell either north, south, east or west based on the rules specified above. In this neighborhood definition, each cell must watch 2 cells ahead of itself. Because cells move to either direction, therefore we need to include 2 cells from each side. Each cell also needs to watch 2 cells on its right and left side.

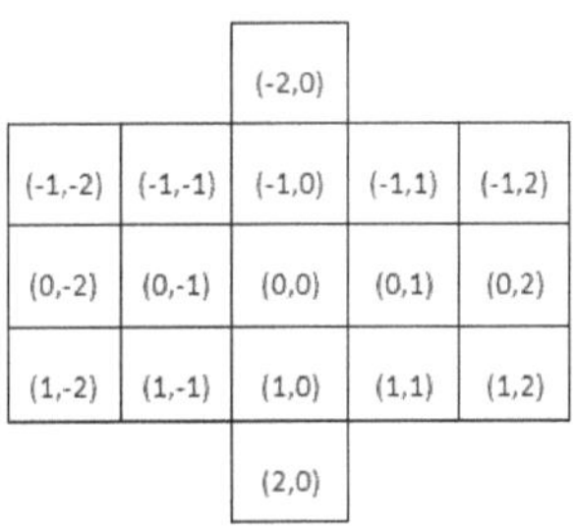

Figure 8. Neighborhood for pedestrian walkway.

This model has been implemented on CD++ with the following assumptions:

Assign a value of 2 to the pedestrians who are walking towards left. Assign a value of 1 to the pedestrians who are walking towards. Empty cells have a value of 0 and walls are 3. If cells with value of 2 attempt to step to the cell above and found out the above row is the "wall", the cell then try to move to the cell below. The opposite rule applies to the cells with value of 1.

The results of this model were visualized using CD++ Animation tool. The blue cells are pedestrians moving to right direction and the red cells move to left. Black cells are walls. In Figure 9 and Figure 10 the side stepping event is extracted from the animation where in left the first step shows that cells that are blocked turn right to avoid collision. In Figure 9 the red cell on the top turns left to avoid the oncoming blue cell and the wall on the right.

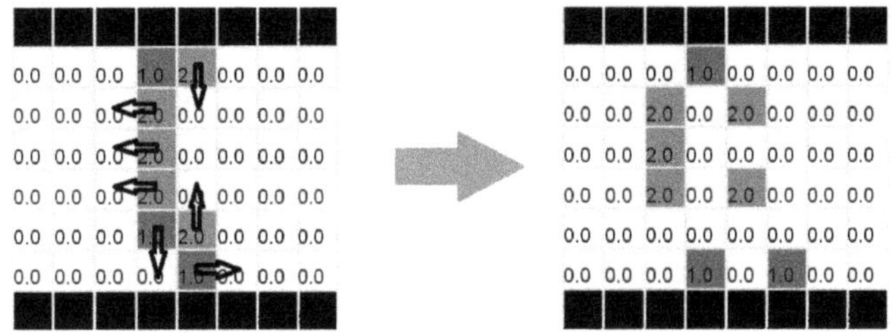

Figure 9. Side stepping rule when blocked 1.

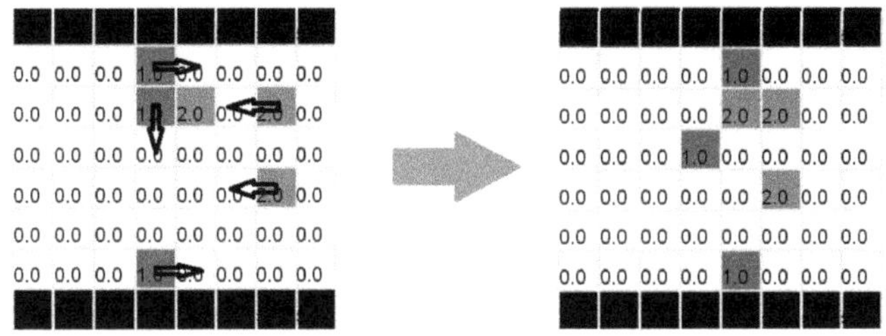

Figure 10. Side stepping rule when blocked 2.

The indicated cells in Figure 11 try to avoid entering the same cell, thus the blue cell turns right. However the red cell freezes in this step because its right neighboring cell is already occupied. In Figure 12, the indicated cells avoid entering the same cell thus the blue cell turns right while the red cell turns left because its right neighbor is a wall. Therefore, they encounter the same situation in the next step, however this time both turn right and continue their movement.

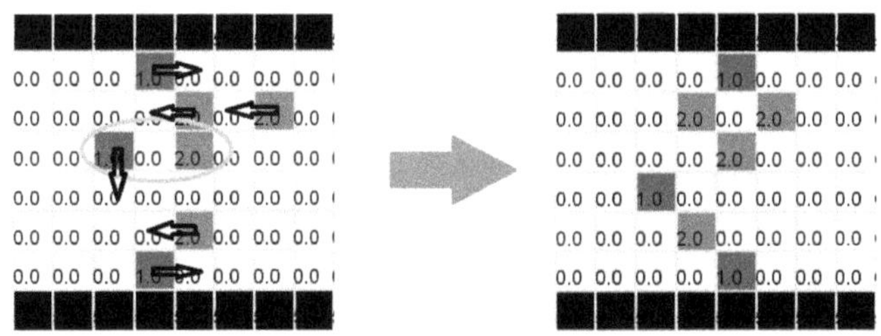

Figure 11. Side stepping due to heading to the same cell.

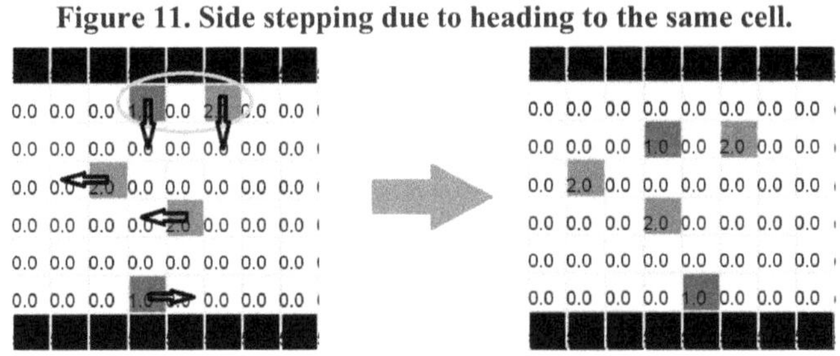

Figure 12. Boarder behavior.

3.2.2 Advanced pedestrian walkway

Observed from the previous approach, the priority scheme is basically an order of sequence in which the rules should be executed in TIME. The basic idea is that after higher priority rules made the changes, the lower priority rules only need to check if the cell it attempts to move to is empty. This is because all other higher level priority rules have already been executed, and thus the only empty cells left are for the current level of priority rule to use. After many implementation experiments performed, the following is the final design of this approach. In this approach we aim at avoiding any collision which was not supported in the previous model.

The fundamental conflict of sidestepping is due to two cells try to sidestep into the same empty cell from the opposite side. One of the cells has to step upwards, while the other one has to step downwards to result in the conflict. Then instead of applying the priority scheme to the time of execution, apply priorities with respect to the directions of pedestrian movements. For example, the highest priority is assigned to horizontal movements or the straight movements from both directions. For this level of priority, Cell-DEVS only needs to check if the cell they are going to move in is empty, and there is no other cell attempting to move into the same cell from the other direction. Then assign the second priority to the rules that would result in sidesteps upwards. These rules includes sidestepping to the right if the pedestrian is traveling to the left; also includes sidestepping to the left if the pedestrian is travelling to the right and there is a wall to the right of the pedestrian. This level of priority rules not only need to check if they need to perform a sidestep possibly due to blocked by another cell, they also need to check if level 1 priority rules can happen to the cell they attempt to move to. Lastly, the lowest priority is assigned to the rules that would result in sidesteps downwards. These rules basically are composed of the opposite rules as priority 2 rule set. However, this lowest priority rule set need to check all higher priority rules. If there is another cell that can step upwards into the target cell, then the testing cell cannot step downwards to that same cell. It seems the check procedure grows exponentially towards lower priority levels. However, there are only 3 levels in the system, so this design is promising.

With the new priority scheme developed, the implementation of the scheme was surprisingly simple and successful. No 3D cell space is needed, nor multiple state variable are required. Only changes required to make was to regroup the rules and develop a few more precondition checks for level 3 priority rules. With this approach, there are only 5 more cells added to the neighborhood (see Figure 13) comparing to the implementation of the previous model. This is an acceptable sacrifice to achieve conflict free simulation.

		(-2,0)		
(-1,-2)	(-1,-1)	(-1,0)	(-1,1)	(-1,2)
(0,-2)	(0,-1)	(0,0)	(0,1)	(0,2)
(1,-2)	(1,-1)	(1,0)	(1,1)	(1,2)
(2,-2)	(2,-1)	(2,0)	(2,1)	(2,2)
		(3,0)		

Figure 13. Neighborhood for advanced pedestrian walkway.

Figure 14 shows the new behavior after the implementation of the sidestep checks. As shown in the green circle, the cell with value of 1 is blocked for moving straight to the right; and the cell with value of 2 is blocked for moving straight to the left. This is the situation where the conflict of sidestepping would occur. In the implementation of the previous model, the cell with value of 1 would step downwards, and the cells with a value of 2 would step upwards. Thus, one cell will overlap another and thus "kill" one pedestrian. Now, after the implementation of sidestep check with priority scheme, this conflict does not occur anymore. After those two cells in the green circle discover that they are blocked towards moving straight forward, the second level priority rule tells the cell with value of 2 to check if the cell above is empty. If it is empty, step upward. Then the third level priority rule tells the cell with value of 1 to check whether the cell below is empty or there is another cell moving into it. Since there is indeed a cell moving into the empty cell, the cell with value of 1 waits in this cycle. One more thing worth to mention is that the priority scheme makes the pedestrian flow very naturally. Imagine that there was no priority scheme applied to the model, but all rules need to check all other rules. Those two cells in the green circle will both detect that the other one is potentially moving into the empty cell. Thus both cells will just wait in that cycle. This is not very desirable and might cause a traffic jam in some situation. Figure 14 does not really illustrate this situation, but it is definitely desirable to have one cell to move to ease the traffic.

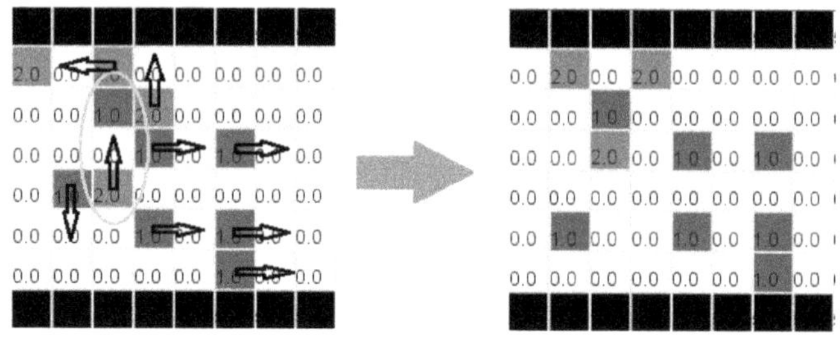

Figure 14. Conflicting sidestep rules.

3.2.3 Pedestrian movement at doorway

A new simulation model using the pedestrian rules from the previous models is proposed that involves taking two room components and allowing pedestrians to walk between them through a doorway. The purpose of this project is to simulate the effect that pedestrians have while walking in a doorway. In order to cover all cases of pedestrian behavior, new rules will need to be implemented, aside from the existing rules. This new model involves creating two different Cell-DEVS components; one to represent the room, and the other to represent the hall. These two components both use the pedestrian behavior rules mentioned earlier. In order to get pedestrians to walk from one component to the other, a DEVS model is created and interfaced to both cell-DEVS models, which connect the two components together. In addition, in order to obtain proper behavior of the pedestrians when they reach the door, a new zone was implemented.

Figure 15 shows the coupled model definition of the project. The *Pedestrian Gen* blocks are DEVS atomic random sequence generator components. The *Hall* is a Cell-DEVS model with a cell space of 10×6 cells. The *Room* is also a Cell-DEVS model with a cell space of 10×10 cells. The *Door Controller* block is a DEVS atomic component that has two input ports, and two output ports (one for the hall and one for the room).

When the Door Controller receives a message on an input port, it sends the value of the message to the associated output port after a specific time. For example, when port *inHall* receives a value of 2, port *outHall* will generate a value of 2 after 50msec. In this model there are two *Door Controller* components representing a doorway with two doors.

The doorway which connects the room and hall components is represented by dotted lines in the coupled model. It consists of cells (0,2) and (0,3) in the *Hall*, and cells (9,4) and (9,5) in the *Room*. The doorway cells have both input and output ports associated with them, as pedestrians can both enter and exit the areas through the door. The output ports of the hall and room components are connected to the input ports of the *Door Controller* component respectively. The output ports of the *Door Controller* component is connected to the input ports of the *Hall* and *Room* components respectively.

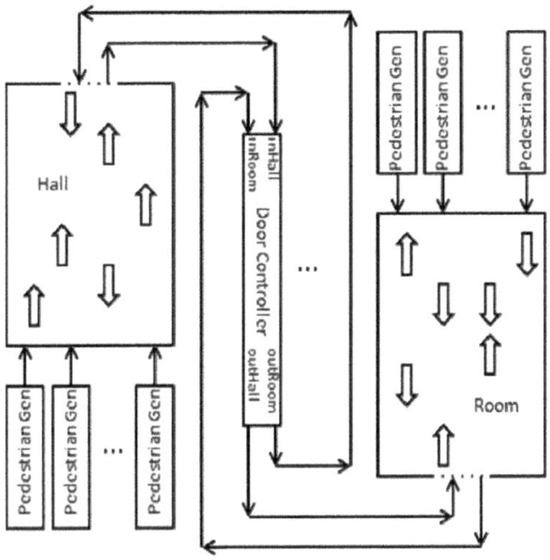

Figure 15. Cell-DEVS Coupled Model.

Pedestrians are generated at the bottom of the hall, and at the top of the room. Once the pedestrians reach the doorway, they leave their current area through the door, and enter the other area through the door. The goal of this project is to program the pedestrians to walk from one room to the other via the door, and see the effects that result from the doorway. The speed of all the pedestrians are modeled as a constant speed and everyone travels at this rate. To do this, some rules are used to regulate the behaviors of the pedestrians.

Figure 16 is a graphical representation of the neighborhood. The neighborhood has been increased to avoid collisions.

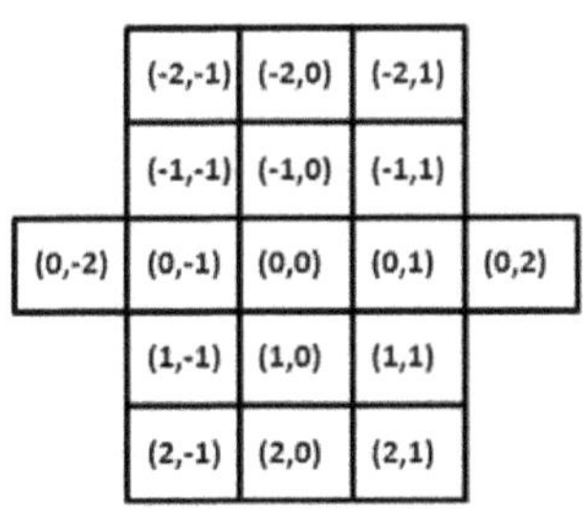

Figure 16. Neighborhood for pedestrian doorway.

As mentioned earlier, to manage the pedestrian movement at the boundary of the *Room* or the *Hall* components, extra rules are needed. In order to have the pedestrians walk towards the door (and not to step to the right to avoid a collision) a new zone was implemented at the boundary. The followings are the rules for pedestrians at the boundary of the *Hall*. The same logic applies to the rules for the *Room*.

Rule 1: Up walker at the door, exit Hall: The up walker enters one of the door cells (i.e. value of 1 on cell (0,2) or (0,3)). To represent the walker exiting the *Hall*, in the next time step the cell will become empty. This rule also sends a value of 1 to the doors output port which is connected to the input port of the Door Controller DEVS model. This rule has the highest priority.

Rule 2: Enter boundary: There is an up walker at the boundary, have them walk forward one cell into the boundary in the next time-step, if the intended cell in the boundary is empty. This rule has the second highest priority.

Rule 3: Up walker in boundary to the right of the Door walk left if possible: There is a walker in the boundary, and they are on the right side of the Door, move to the left adjacent cell if that cell is unoccupied, and another walker is not going to take that cell in the next time-step. This rule has the third highest priority.

Rule 4: Up walker in boundary to the left of the Door, walk right if possible: There is a walker in the boundary, and they are on the left side of the door, move to the right adjacent cell if that cell is unoccupied, and another walker is not going to take that cell in the next time-step. This rule has the fourth highest priority.

Rule 5: Down walker that entered Hall from Door, leave boundary: A down walker that has entered the hall boundary from the room through the door, they leave the boundary in the next time step if the adjacent cell below them is empty.

Rule 6: Default: If none of the other rules execute, the walker does nothing and waits where they are. This rule also contains the behavior for the obstacles, as they never move.

After implementing the model on CD++, we show some of the results generated by CD++ Animation tool that are related to the door entrance and exit, to emphasize on the new features of this model. Figure 17 demonstrates that the up walkers are in fact able to enter the boundary of the hall, and that down walkers are able to enter the boundary of the room. The boundary is represented by a blue rectangle. The larger rectangle is the boundary of the room, whereas the smaller rectangle is the boundary of the hall. It also demonstrates how the walkers leave the boundary.

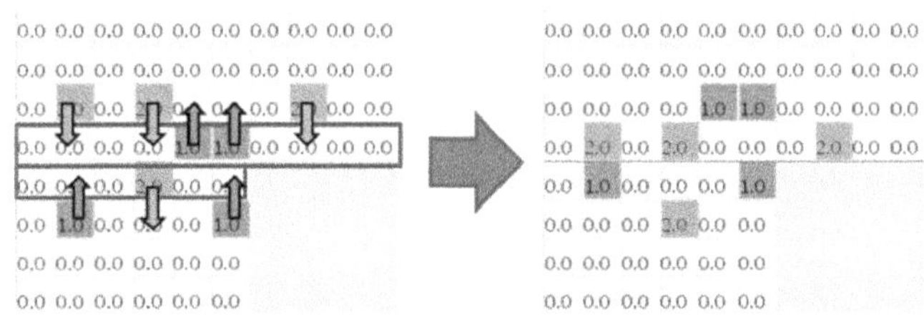

Figure 17. Entering Boundary.

Figure 18 demonstrates how pedestrians in the hall, who are trying to walk to the room (orange), walk towards the door (red boxes) in the hall. The same is true for the pedestrians in the room trying to walk to the hall. More videos of this model can be watched here: http://www.youtube.com/watch?v=I77-zLCRpS4

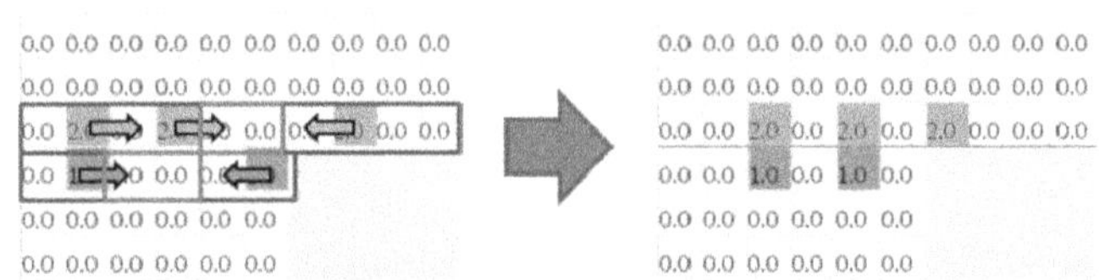

Figure 18. Move towards door.

4. INTEGRATED FRAMEWORK

After modeling the details of pedestrian movement, we are interested in integrating this cellular simulation framework with Computer-Aided Design (CAD) tools. Figure 19 illustrates the integrated Modeling, Simulation and Visualization Framework. The overall approach includes four subsystems: Data Collection, Cell-DEVS modeling, Remote Simulation and 3D Visualization. This framework relies on the CAD file/databases supported by different CAD tools as an information repository for different transportation facilities projects. These CAD files are object-oriented, attribute-driven with 3D geometric information.

The main four steps in the integrated framework are:

1) Data Collection: it is done automatically, generating initial data files from CAD files into the Cell-DEVS model. This includes an *Element Filter* for selective properties, and a *Coordinate Extractor* for getting *(x, y, z)* coordinates of filtered elements. The generated files are used for pedestrian movement model inputs explained earlier.

2) Cell-DEVS Modeling: it builds a Cell-DEVS pedestrian movement model according to the collected data and models the pedestrian behaviors.

3) DEVS Simulation: it submits Cell-DEVS model to RISE Web Services URI, executes the simulation remotely, and then gets the simulation results.

4) BIM 3D Visualization: it visualizes the simulation results in 3D, based on transportation facilities CAD file, providing an intuitive mean for analysis. It parses the simulation log files, and loads it using *GUI Script*. The results are generated by the *Models Animation*.

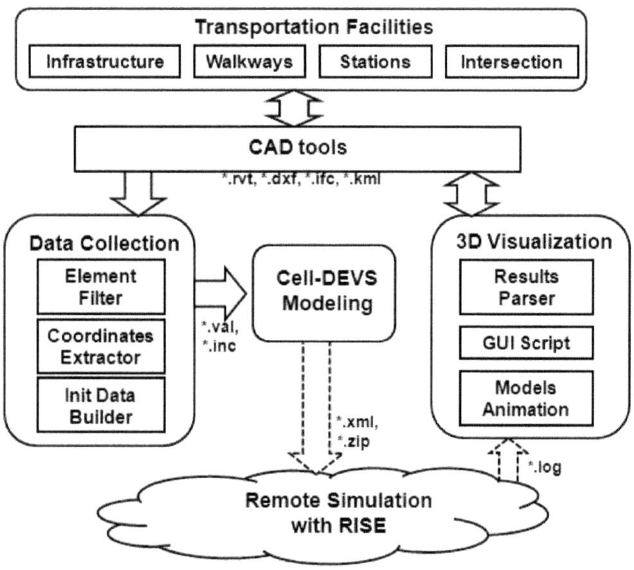

Figure 19. Integrated Modeling, Simulation and Visualization Framework.

4.1 CAD Data Collection

With the development of digital technology, CAD has gained with excellent capability to support management of graphical and geometric information. Such information has been used in object-oriented modeling and building information modeling (BIM) to evaluation of the designs. Therefore, pedestrian movement analysis can benefit from CAD tools from which information of transportation facility can be extracted. In current implementation, we chose Autodesk Revit Architecture for this purpose, as it includes a well-defined parametric API and a BIM add-in. Revit can be used to build 3D models and 2D drawings, and the Revit API can be used to find and manipulate different model elements (walls, doors, obstacles, etc.).

As seen from Figure 19, for getting information from CAD for initial date to our Cell-DEVS model, we need three main steps: 1) Filtering elements; 2) Extracting Coordinates; 3) Building Initial files.

For the first step, we use Revit build-in API to filter needed element type (e.g. wall, obstacles), then extract parameter properties that we need (e.g. length, width). For the second step, based on the filtered elements ID, we extract their coordinates according to the coordinates system. Figure 20 shows a segment after these two phases, in which each line represents wall (Element ID, coordinates, width, length and area scale).

--Filter Elements & Extract Coordinates
180921: x(-524") y(314") z(0") width(8") length(600") area(480.00 SF)
180922: x(24") y(314") z(0") width(4") length(600") area(240.00 SF)
180923: x(-524") y(914") z(0") width(8") length(600") area(480.00 SF)
180924: x(24") y(914") z(0") width(4") length(600") area(240.00 SF)

Figure 20. Result segment of Data Collection.

For the third step, based on the extracted data, we can generate initialization data files for the Cell-DEVS model. For example, in this occupancy models, we firstly calculate the scale of the space, converting it to a unified size: *XMIN* (the horizontal ordinate of the left-most point) and *XMAX* (the horizontal ordinate of the right-most point). Similarly, we get *YMIN* and *YMAX* for the vertical ordinates. Then, knowing the size of each cell, we can compute the number of cells in the three dimensions, and next generate initial **.val* file which contain initial value of the grid. The basic idea of initializing state of each cell is to "pave" all needed elements according to the extracted info (starting points, width, length, and so on). For the pedestrian model, we got (30×30) size of space and the related initial **.val* file.

4.2 RISE Remote Simulation

As discussed in section 2, RESTful Web Services can further increase the scalability in terms of the plug-and-play interoperability and availability. In [21], the authors presented the first existing RESTful Interoperability Simulation Environment (RISE) middleware. RISE is accessed through Web resources (URIs) and XML messages using HTTP methods. Implementations can be hidden in resources, which are represented only via URIs. Users can run multiple instances as needed, which are persistent and repeatable by specific URIs. The HTTP methods are typical four types: *GET* (to read a resource), *PUT* (to create or update a resource), *POST* (to append data to a resource), and *DELETE* (to remove a resource). An interface between RISE and CD++ (supporting DEVS and Cell-DEVS) allows running DEVS/Cell-DEVS distributed simulations. RISE API likes URL http://www.example.com/cdpp/sim/workspaces, attached by the following services:

- ***../{userworkspace}*** contains of all simulation services for a given user.
- ***../{userworkspace}/{servicetype}*** contains of all frameworks for a given user and simulation service type (e.g. a simulation engine CD++).
- ***../{userworkspace}/{servicetype}/{framework}*** allows interacting with a framework (including the simulation's initial files, configuration and src code).

- ***../{userworkspace}/{servicetype}{framework}/simulation*** interacts with the simulator execution.
- ***../{userworkspace}/{servicetype}/{framework}/results*** contains of the simulation outputs.
- ***../{userworkspace}/{servicetype}/{framework}/debug*** contains of the model-debugging files.

For a specific simulation, we can realize the remote simulation by using these URIs with HTTP methods. For example, after getting initial model and configuration files for simulation, we use *PUT* to create a framework with the configuration file and *POST* to upload these initial model files to this framework. Then, this newly created simulation environment can be executed by using PUT to *{framework}/simulation*, then we wait for the simulation to finish and *GET* the simulation results files from *{framework}/results*.

4.3 3D Visualization

3D visualization provides a more intuitive and attractive way to obtain visual simulation results in CAD tools, enabling the designers to check the building performance and people behaviors under different properties. Most CAD tools support full-featured 3D visualization of building. Among them, Autodesk 3ds Max is a powerful option for its animation and rendering ability for 3D visualization. In [26], we have developed an advanced visualization tool in 3ds MAX, which is upgraded based on our existing version. This new tool expanded new functionalities for reusability and scalability, including a parser program using Python script (to parse simulation results log file), expanded GUI in 3ds Max with extendable script. The GUI provides several options of hiding different building floors for visibility and filtering models in a small area for the optimization purpose. We then added new animation features of models: 1) arrow models with key framing ability and 2) realistic models to animate real body movement using Motion Mixer. This work brings better visualization of simulation results, enabling the designers to check the simulation results, find the flaws and plan for improvement. Figure **21** shows its UML class diagram, which is based on the Model-View-Controller design pattern. The controller is *CDVizController*. The simulation grid is represented by an array of *GridCell* objects, which keep track of which person is in that cell, and each person in the simulation is represented by an instance of *PersonModel*.

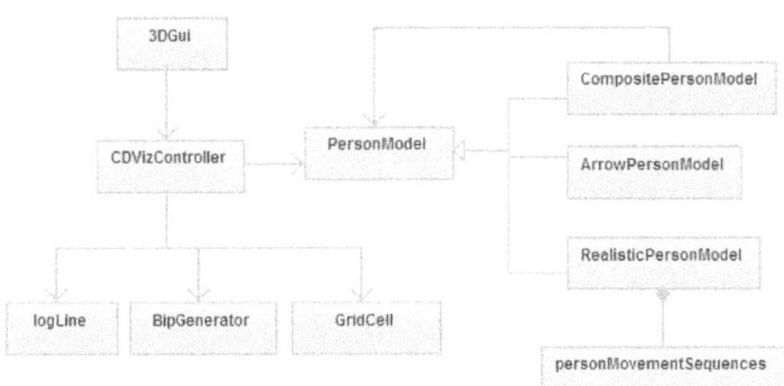

Figure 21. Class diagram of the visualization plug-in [26].

5. CASE STUDY

Now, let us see how to use the integrated framework proposed in this paper to increase scalability and interoperability. Firstly, we use the developed CAD data collection tool in Revit to get the layout of the studying area of bi-directional pedestrian walkway. We modeled a 30×30 cellular space and the related initial *pedestrian.val* file for walls and obstacles. Then, we upload the initialized files with our Cell-DEVS model (*pedestrian.ma*) for remote simulation. With the RISE server, we can use the PUT method to create a framework *.../PedestrianMovement* for simulation, and the POST method to upload the initial model files. We can run this simulation by using PUT to *.../PedestrianMovement/simulation.* We wait until the simulation finishes, then by using GET method simulation results are fetched from *.../PedestrianMovement/results.* The configuration XML file for this *.../PedestrianMovement* framework in RISE looks like the following:


```
<?xml version="1.0" encoding="UTF-8" standalone="no"?>
<ConfigFramework>
  <Doc>This model Simulates bi-directional pedestrian movement using Cell-Devs.</Doc>
    <Files>
      <File ftype="sup">pedestrian.val</File>
      <File ftype="inc">pedestrian.inc</File>
      <File ftype="ma">pedestrian.ma</File>
    </Files>
  <Options>
    <TimeOp>00:00:10:000</TimeOp>
    <ParsingOp>false</ParsingOp>
  </Options>
  <DCDpp>
    <Servers>
      <Server IP="134.117.53.66" PORT="8080">
          <ZONE>pedestrian(0,0)..(29,29)</ZONE>
      </Server>
    </Servers>
  </DCDpp>
</ConfigFramework>
```


Finally, after parsing the simulation log file for the specific 3D visualization, we can load the same version of the CAD file in 3d MAX and visualize the simulation animations with the help of its GUI. Figure **22** shows how the 3D visualization would look like. This tool helps the designers to observe different animation features of pedestrians: the realistic model for real pedestrian movement (a, b and c) and the arrow model for pointing the moving direction (d). According to the performance (occupancy level or bottlenecks analysis) observed from this 3D visualization, all steps can be reused for the next design iteration.

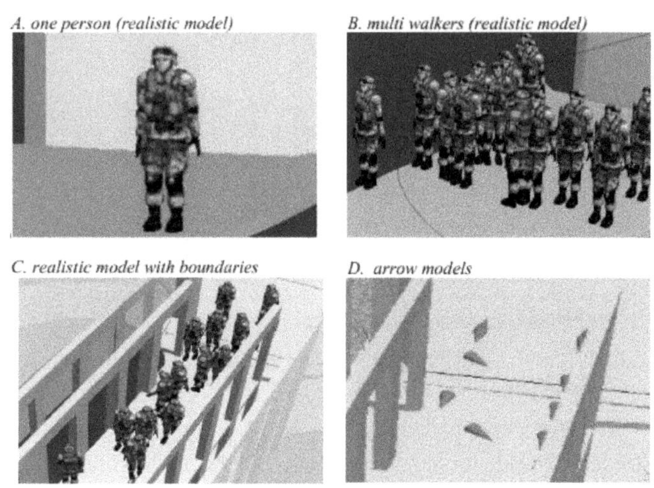

Figure 22. 3D Visualization Results.

6. CONCLUSIONS

We showed how Cell-DEVS can be used in M&S of the crowd by using its cellular structure to render crowd entities, obstacle, or empty space. Multiple simulations were performed, and different techniques were discussed. We showed how Cell-DEVS can be integrated with BIM tools to model building evacuation simulation, thanks to the formal structure of DEVS. In the next series of models, we demonstrated pedestrian movement flow M&S and collisions management. Multiple simulations were also performed while varying the pedestrian's generator values. Based on the experiments it was concluded that Cell-DEVS is very suitable for entity-based simulation of the crowd, capable of simulating small to medium size models. However, large-size models can also be simulated using the flattened coordinator version of the CD++ tool in which the initial cell creation processing is dramatically faster. We showed how to extract information from CAD tool, run simulation remotely on RISE server using Cell-DEVS and view advanced 3D visualization in 3D Max. This system allows designers to analyze the pedestrian movement behaviors more comprehensively, check the performance of the design, and plan for improvements.

7. REFERENCES

[1] Helbing D., Farkás I.J., Molnár P., Vicsek T. 2002 Simulation of pedestrian crowds in normal and evacuation situations, in: M. Schreckenberg, S.D. Sharma (Eds.), Pedestrian and Evacuation Dynamics, *Springer, Berlin,* (2002), 21–58.

[2] Blue V.J., Adler J.L. 2001 Cellular automata microsimulation for modeling bi-directional pedestrian walkways, *Transportation Research Part B 35* (3) (2001) 293–312.

[3] Penn A., Turner A., Space syntax based agent simulation, in: M. Schreckenberg, S.D. Sharma (Eds.), Pedestrian and Evacuation Dynamics, *Springer, Berlin,* (2002), 99–114.

[4] Zhou, S., Chen, D., Cai, W., Luo, L., Low, M. Y. H., Tian, F., ... & Hamilton, B. D. (2010). Crowd modeling and simulation technologies. *ACM Transactions on Modeling and Computer Simulation (TOMACS)*, 20(4), 20.

[5] Hughes, R. L. (2003). The flow of human crowds. *Annual Review on Fluid Mechanics* 35, 169–182.

[6] Helbing, D., Farkas, I., and Vicsek, T. (2000). Simulating dynamical features of escape panic. *Letters to Nature* 407, 487–490.

[7] Castonguay, P., & Wainer, G. (2009, March). Aircraft evacuation DEVS implementation & visualization. *In Proceedings of the 2009 Spring Simulation Multiconference. San Diego, CA.* 144.

[8] Zeigler, B. P., Praehofer, H., & Kim, T. G. (2000) Theory of modeling and simulation. 2000.

[9] Wainer, G. A. (2009). Discrete-event modeling and simulation: a practitioner's approach. CRC.

[10] Wolfram, S. (1986). Theory and applications of cellular automata.

[11] Hughes, R. L. (2003). The flow of human crowds. *Annual Review on Fluid Mechanics* 35, 169–182.

[12] Kisko, T. M., Francis, R. L., & Nobel, C. R. (1998). EVACNET4 User's Guide. *University of Florida.*

[13] Zhang, W. M., Huang, L., & Wang, B. (2009). Application of the EVACNET4 model to evacuation in high-rise building [J]. *Fire Science and Technology*, 3, 014.

[14] Chenney, S. (2004). Flow tiles. *In Proceedings of the 2004 ACM SIGGRAPH/Eurographics symposium on Computer animation* (pp. 233-242). Eurographics Association.

[15] Miller, J. H., & Page, S. E. (2007). Complex adaptive systems: An introduction to computational models of social life. *Princeton University Press.*

[16] Deffuant, G. (2006). Comparing extremism propagation patterns in continuous opinion models. *Journal of Artificial Societies and Social Simulation*, 9(3).

[17] Salzarulo, L. (2006). A continuous opinion dynamics model based on the principle of meta-contrast. *Journal of Artificial Societies and Social Simulation*, 9(1).

[18] Helbing, D., Farkas, I., & Vicsek, T. (2000). Simulating dynamical features of escape panic. *Nature*, 407(6803), 487-490.

[19] Bandini, S., Manzoni, S., & Vizzari, G. (2006). Crowd Modeling and Simulation. *Innovations in Design & Decision Support Systems in Architecture and Urban Planning*, 105-120.

[20] Tao, W., & Jun, C. (2009). An Improved Cellular Automaton Model for Urban Walkway Bi-directional Pedestrian Flow. *In Measuring Technology and Mechatronics Automation, 2009. ICMTMA'09. International Conference* Vol. 3, pp. 458-461.

[21] Al-Zoubi, K. and Wainer, G. (2010). Distributed Simulation Using Restful Interoperability Simulation Environment (RISE) Middleware. *Intelligence-Based Systems Engineering*, Pages 129–157.

[22] Wang, S., Van Schyndel, M., Wainer, G., Rajus, V. S., & Woodbury, R. (2012). DEVS-based building information modeling and simulation for emergency evacuation. *In Proceedings of the Winter Simulation Conference* (p. 60). Winter Simulation Conference.

[23] Wright, F. L. (2009). Building Information Modeling.

[24] AutoDesk. (2013). "Autodesk Revit Architecture." Accessed Feb. 15. http://usa.autodesk.com/revit-architecture/.

[25] AutoDesk. (2013). "Autodesk 3ds Max." Accessed Feb. 15. http://usa.autodesk.com/3ds-max/.

[26] Freire, V., Wang, S., and Wainer, G. (2013). Visualization In 3ds Max For Cell-DEVS Models Based On Moving Entities. *Symposium on Simulation for Architecture and Urban Design (SimAUD'13)*. San Diego, USA.

Parallel Stepwise Stochastic Simulation: Harnessing GPUs to Explore Possible Futures States of a Chromosome Folding Model Thanks to the Possible Futures Algorithm (PFA)

Jonathan Passerat-Palmbach*
ISIMA
Blaise Pascal University, Clermont-Ferrand, France
LIMOS - UMR CNRS 6158
passerat@isima.fr

Jonathan Caux
ISIMA
Blaise Pascal University, Clermont-Ferrand, France
LIMOS - UMR CNRS 6158
Murex S.A.S.
caux@isima.fr

Yannick Le Pennec
INSA - Rennes
LIMOS - UMR CNRS 6158
yannick.lepennec@insa-rennes.fr

Romain Reuillon
Institute of Complex Systems, Paris Ile de France
reuillon@iscpif.fr

Ivan Junier†
Centre for Genomic Regulation (CRG), Dr. Aiguader 88, 08003 Barcelona, Spain
i.junier@gmail.com

François Kepes
Epigenomics Project and Institute of Systems and Synthetic Biology Genopole®, CNRS, University of Evry
francois.kepes@epigenomique.genopole.fr

David R.C. Hill
ISIMA
Blaise Pascal University, Clermont-Ferrand, France
LIMOS - UMR CNRS 6158
david.hill@univ-bpclermont.fr

ABSTRACT

For the sake of software compatibility, simulations are often parallelized without much code rewriting. Performances can be further improved by optimizing codes so that to use the maximum power offered by parallel architectures. While this approach can provide some speed-up, performance of parallelized codes can be strongly limited *a priori* because traditional algorithms have been designed for sequential technologies. Thus, additional increase of performance should ultimately rely on some redesign of algorithms.

Here, we redesign an algorithm that has traditionally been used to simulate the folding properties of polymers. We address the issue of performance in the context of biological applications, more particularly in the active field of chromosome modelling. Due to the strong confinement of chromosomes in the cells, simulation of their motion is slowed down by the laborious search for the next valid states to progress. Our redesign, that we call the Possible Futures Algorithm (PFA), relies on the parallel computation of possible evolutions of the same state, which effectively increases the probability to obtain a valid state at each step. We apply PFA on a GPU-based architecture, allowing us to optimally reduce the latency induced by the computation overhead of possible futures. We show that compared to the initial sequential model the acceptance rate of new states significantly increases without impacting the execution time. In particular, the stronger the confinement of the chromosome, the more efficient PFA becomes, making our approach appealing for biological applications.

While most of our results were obtained using Fermi architecture GPUs from NVIDIA, we highlight improved performance on the cutting-edge Kepler architecture K20 GPUs.

*corresponding author
†corresponding author

Categories and Subject Descriptors

I.6.3 [Applications]; D.1.3 [Concurrent Programming: Parallel programming]

Keywords

GPU; parallel simulation; chromosome folding; Possible Futures Algorithm; PFA; stochastic simulation; stepwise simulation

1. INTRODUCTION

Two major design choices are available for code parallelization. One possibility is to adapt the existing application to fit a parallel template, which mainly consists in breaking loops to spread their workload across several parallel computing elements, be they threads or processors. This approach tends to be limited by the so called Amdahl's law [1, 8] that computes the maximum speed-up of an application, taking into account the part of it that can effectively be parallelized. Another possibility consists in redesigning the application from scratch, to use the most possibility of the target parallel platform. In this case, the application is more likely to benefit from performance gain laid down by the Gustafson's law [6]. Both situations present advantages: adapting an existing application will make it easier to write; redesigning an application from scratch often opens new parallelization perspectives.

For instance, when dealing with particular hardware accelerators such as GPUs, which are constrained by their underlying architecture, it is usually more efficient to provide a dedicated parallel implementation. Such an approach allows this implementation to better fit the platform's requirements. In the case of GPUs, applications are expected to favour computing intensive algorithms rather than those containing a high number of branches instructions.

Parallelization of an existing code, even from scratch, can be severely limited by the sequential nature of the underlying algorithms, which have been originally thought for Turing-like architectures. In this context, it may be useful to redesign the algorithmic principles themselves, just as new algorithmic schemes have emerged from the possibility of quantum computing. In this article, we present the redesign of a traditional model of polymer folding, which has been extensively used in the field of chromosome modelling [11]. These models are known to suffer from poor efficiency when considered in situations that are similar to *in vivo* becaue of the strong confinement of chromosomes. So far, "simple" code parallelization has mainly been set up using tools such as OpenMP [2] or MPI [13]. More recently, parallelization of dynamical models have been realized on GPU architecture, demonstrating the usefulness of such technology for the modeling of long polymers [15]. In the same spirit, our algorithm is mainly meant to exploit massively parallel processors, more particularly NVIDIA CUDA-enabled GPUs.

Our algorithm is based on a two-step procedure: i) generation of several potential future states, and ii) selection of the next state as a random choice amongst the set of valid futures. We hence call this approach the "Possible Futures Algorithm" (PFA). PFA can be compared to the branch prediction feature available in modern CPUs, which enables CPUs to load the instructions following the branches of a conditional statement, prior to knowing the result of this statement. This avoids offloading the pipeline mechanism, and consequently waste precious instruction cycles [12, 17]. As a result, we show that PFA highly increases the acceptance rate of the new model. While the initial algorithm only accepts $\sim 5\%$ of the proposed states in certain configurations, our solution maintains a satisfying acceptance rate over 60% in the same conditions, regardless of the input parameters of the model.

The paper is organized as follows. First, we describe the initial chromosome folding model on which our parallel declination is based. Next, we point out the limitations that led us to design a new model. We then introduce our new parallel chromosome folding model and the PFA approach. Finally, we discuss some implementation choices and study the performances of our algorithm.

2. A CLASSICAL MONTE-CARLO SIMULATION OF POLYMER MODELS

Large-scale properties of polymers have been efficiently captured thanks to simplified models that ignore the details of both the polymer composition and the exact nature of the surrounding solvent [3]. In biology, various models have been used to model the behavior of DNA molecules and of chromosomes [18]. Chromosomes have been modeled as simple flexible chains that cannot overlap with themselves (self-avoidance effect) – see Figure 1. These so-called worm-like chains provide a coarse-grained description of protein-coated DNA that is simple enough so that, using Monte-Carlo simulations, they can be used to investigate the folding properties of rather long biomolecules [11]. Thus, they have been used to adress both the problem of the structuration of chromosomes *in vivo* [5] and, more recently, the interplay between structuring and function [9].

The worm-like chain is a continuous polymer model that needs to be discretized to be simulated on a computer. To this end, the polymer chain is divided into contiguous cylinders. Two consecutive cylinders are jointed together so that they can rotate freely around their joint (Figure 1), which is used to make the polymer conformations evolve dynamically. To mimic the persistence of the directional order of the polymer chain (see Figure 1), the junctions between each cylinder (hereafter called joints) carry an energy called "bending energy". This energy is exchanged with the solvent using a Monte-Carlo algorithm (see below) and depends on the angle between the two cylinders connecting the joint. We further consider chromosomes that are confined into cells that are more or less narrow, so that our approach can address the computational properties of chromosomes in confined geometries [3]. In the following, we call "cell" the embedding volume of the chromosomes during the simulations, *i.e. in silico*. In the most general case, this may not correspond to the nucleus in which chromosomes are embedded *in vivo*.

In summary, a chromosome *in silico* can be viewed as a long string of contiguous "cylinders". The chromosome can be circular (as in bacteria) or linear (as in human). Its statistical properties are the result of its jiggling motion due to the interaction with the surrounding solvent. In these models, the solvent is not taken explicitly. Instead, we used a standard stochastic algorithm, also called a Monte-Carlo procedure, to make the chain move step by step. Each of these steps is conceptually simple, and altogether, they form Algorithm 1.

We used the standard Metropolis rate for accepting the rotation depending on its energy, *i.e.* if the new bending energy is lower, the transition is accepted; otherwise, the transition is accepted with probability $e^{-\Delta E/k_B T}$ where ΔE stands for the increase of energy and $k_B T$ for the thermal energy characterizing the solvent (k_B is the Boltzmann constant and T is the temperature). This dynamics is known to satisfy the required properties to simulated the thermodynamic behaviour of polymer models. In practice, it favours movements whose energy variation is dictated by the value of the temperature T. As a result, the chromosome is prompted

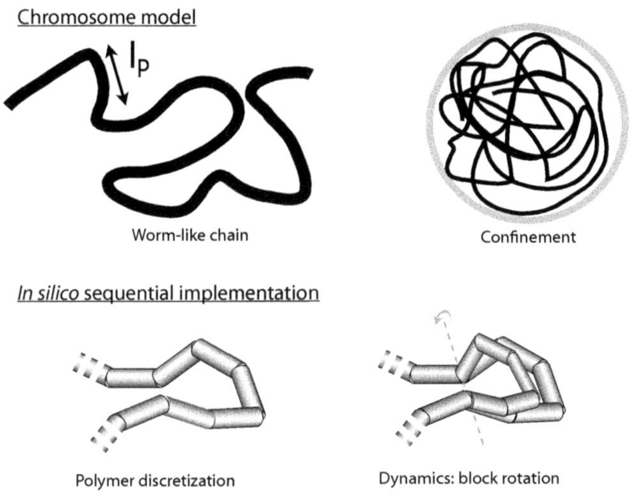

Figure 1: Worm-like chain model of chromosomes. On the top is indicated the original continuous model, which is characterized by the length beyond which the chromosome looses the memory of its directional order (persistence length l_p). The actual situation to be modelled is a situation where the chromosome is confined to a small volume (on the right). To be simulated on a computer, this model is discretized into cylinders (bottom). In this discretized version, two consecutive cylinders can rotate around their common joint but have to pay some energy to do so because as they are semi-flexible (captured by the persistence length). In the simulations, we use five cylinders per persistence length (figures adapted from [10]).

to a state of equilibrium between the energies of the conformations and the number of equivalent conformations at a given energy, also called entropy.

This stochastic algorithm slowly makes the chromosomes evolve following a combination of random and physical constraints, over hundreds of millions of runs. The limiting factor for this evolution happens when most rotations are rejected due to the overlapping conditions, which occurs very often when the embedding cell is small, as in biological situations. In particular, simulations of large chromosomes become extremely time-consuming, which make this type of algorithms poorly efficient to tackle in detail the folding problems of multiple chromosomes *in vivo*.

Algorithm 1 Monte Carlo procedure involved in the simulation process

Select a section of consecutive cylinders of random size (called "block" in the following);
Perform a rotation of the block by a random angle around the axis that intercepts the first and last joint of the block;
if The rotated block does not overlap with the rest of the polymer **then**
  Compute the new bending energy of the joints at the edges of the block;
  Accept the rotation with some probability depending on the variation of the bending energy;
end if
Increase time +1;

3. LIMITATIONS OF THE SEQUENTIAL MODEL

3.1 The collisions bottleneck

The original algorithm picks up a "block" at random on the chromosome, and randomly rotated it around an axis. And so on. By definition, it is therefore sequential. As a consequence, for string confinement constraints, *i.e.* for small cell sizes, it is difficult for the algorithm to find valid configurations towards which to evolve. Thus, because valid configurations are hard to find through random attempts, a large number of (wasted) steps is required to provide a new valid configuration. In situation of string confinement, 95% of the generated rotations can produce collisions (see below). It is consequently a major bottleneck that needed to be tackled in order for the model to scale up with chromosomes sizes. A first possibility would be to reduce the amplitude of the rotations. However, in this case, motions of the polymer are very small and both a large number of blocks and a large number of tries are necessary to thermalize the system (*i.e.* to make it visit all most likely conformations). Thus, in any case, the use of parallel motions can facilitate the dynamical evolution of the polymer.

3.2 The Possible Futures Algorithm (PFA)

We propose a parallel simulation model which considers two parallel optimizations. The first one consists in handling several blocks in parallel, instead of only one block as in the sequential algorithm. Processing blocks in parallel is possible in our case because it does not break any physical law at the heart of the model. In particular, it does not break the so-called ergodicity, *i.e.* the unbiased sampling of the configuration space. This new parallel rotation step is presented in Figure 2.

The second optimization consists in considering for each single block a set of several possible rotations to maximize the chances of producing a correct rotation. We call each of these rotations a "possible future" of a block. In Figure 3, we can see a chain of cylinders called "Base". It represents the chromosome as it is at the beginning of an iteration. Yellow cylinders belong to different blocks labelled Block 0 through Block 2. Starting from blocks defined on the base chromosome, the algorithm will generate several possible futures for each block, applying each time a different rotation angle to the block. In Figure 3, three futures are generated for each of the three blocks defined.

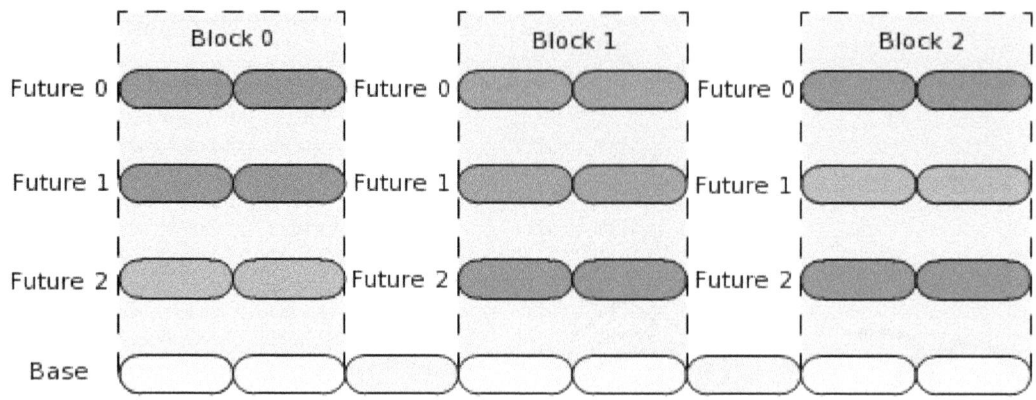

Figure 3: Example of generation of three possible futures for three different blocks

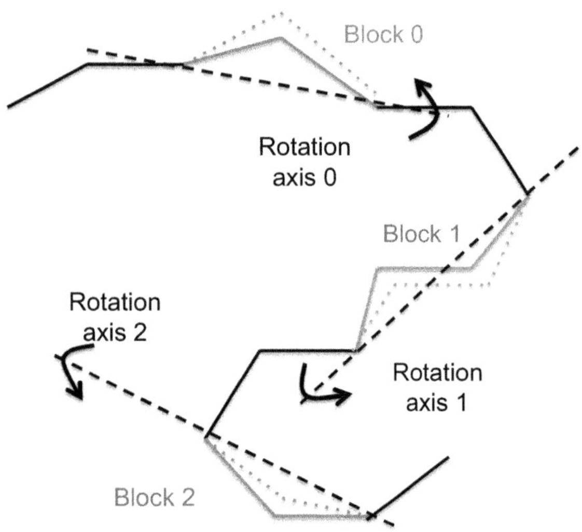

Figure 2: A parallel rotation step

Cylinders in grey do not belong to any block, and therefore remain static during this iteration. It is important to note that at each step, the current state of a given block is also viewed as a possible future. Consequently, the fact of not rotating a block is valid, and is always a possible solution for the dynamical evolution of the polymer (which is here a no-motion).

4. PARALLEL MODEL

The Possible Futures Algorithm induces extra computation time, since futures need to be created before each step of the simulation, and merged as a complete new state for the whole chromosome at the end of each simulation step. However, such an organization reminds of a frequently used pattern in parallel computing: map/reduce [4]. This pattern is particularly adapted to GPU computing and some frameworks can even simplify its implementation on GPU [7]. In our case, the map stage consists in generating and processing new futures; this stage is processed in parallel, while the reduce stage is performed sequentially to build the resulting state of the chromosome at the end of the current simulation step. Next section will detail the stages of our parallel simulation model.

We describe now the consecutive steps allowing the parallel algorithm to generate and transform possible futures, before combining them as a whole new state for the chromosome. In view of the massive number of repeated parallel tasks that result from the possible future approach, we have chosen to exploit GPU accelerators to run this algorithm.

4.1 Generate possible futures

First, the map stage must be initiated sequentially by generating random blocks in the chromosome. Blocks are equally sized arrays of consecutive joints from the chromosome. Each block owns a different, non-overlapping chain of joints. Blocks also differ from the random angle describing the rotation which will be applied to them. Blocks cannot overlap to prevent the same cylinder from being involved in two different rotations.

To generate futures, a "master" thread runs alone on the GPU to define random blocks and to generate random rotation angles. Then, a burst of threads is launched to clone the original blocks and change their rotation angles, thus making them into possible futures of the original block. Upon completion, possible future blocks are ready to be processed in parallel by thousands of GPU threads.

Calling F the number of possible futures per block and N the number of blocks, one can see that this stage operates in parallel the equivalent of what the sequential algorithm used to do over $F \times N$ time step. The potential performance gain is hence on the order of $F \times N$ since while the sequential simulation checks after each step that the block can be moved, the parallel implementation fully transforms each possible future without wasting time on intermediate verifications.

4.2 Select valid futures

Once all the futures have been transformed and represent a potential future state of their base block, it is necessary to filter them: *i.e.* dismiss those that are not valid. The algorithm calculates the bending energy carried by the joints at the edges of a future block. To be stated as valid the resulting bending energy of a future must be lower than the one of its original block. Should the new bending energy be greater than the original one, then the considered future has gained energy. In this case, there is a probability that the future may be valid, determined by a random draw according to the physical properties of chromosomes. In any other case, the physical properties of the future make it unsatisfying, and it is consequently withdrawn. The remaining futures must still meet two other requirements, referred to as static and dynamic conditions, to be compatible with their environment and to be potentially included in the global solution.

Static conditions are met when all cylinders of the future are within the virtual cell in which the chromosome must remain confined. Moreover, none of the cylinders of the future can collide with parts of the chromosome that did not evolve during this simulation step. By doing so, we eliminate all futures that are not physically possible.

For dynamic conditions to be valid, a second evaluation determines which futures are suitable with respect to the other futures. A future is suitable as long as it does not collide with any of the other valid future generated at this step of the simulation.

Futures acceptance tables are displayed in green in Figure 3, while dismissed futures appear in red.

To sum up, we have introduced extra operations when delaying the selection of valid futures, but this stage offers many potential solutions to increase the acceptance rate of rotations that make the chromosome evolve. This stage justifies on its own the use of a massively parallel architecture such as GPUs to speed-up the computation of the algorithm. Let's now study the operations which compose the reduction stage of a simulation step.

4.3 Determine compatible futures

We consider a two-round reduction in our algorithm. The first round models the problem as a graph to determine the compatible futures. The vertices of the graph represent possible futures, and the presence of an edge between two vertices represents the compatibility between two possible futures.

4.4 Compose the global result

The second reduction step now aims at composing a global result from the compatible futures identified by the graph. From this graph hundreds of random cliques are built from the whole set of possible futures at hand. A constant number of vertices is simply picked at random in the graph to build equally-sized cliques, with the particular care to always draw a vertex from each group of possible futures.

We now compose a global result by finding one maximum clique from the set of cliques issued previously. A maximum clique owns as many possible block futures as there are blocks in the original chromosome. Thus, any maximum clique forms a solution to our problem and its nodes are the new state of each block defined at the beginning of the simulation step. Please note: should several maximum cliques be found during the first round of the reduction, one would be chosen at random, since they all represent equivalent satisfying solutions to make the chromosome evolve.

The elements from Figure 3 are displayed as a graph in Figure 4. It shows that the possible future 0 from Block 1 is suitable in terms of physics criteria, but is not compatible with any possible future from Block 2 (Although this future is compatible with the current state of the chromosome, for the sake of simplicity, it is not shown in Figure 4).

In Figure 4, we see a clique compounded of 3 vertices: $\{$*Block0.Future2, Block1.Future1, Block2.Future1*$\}$.
This means these three are inter-compatible futures, and together form a global consistent future for the chromosome.

To validate the whole operation, each possible future block is stored in the base chromosome, replacing its original counterpart.

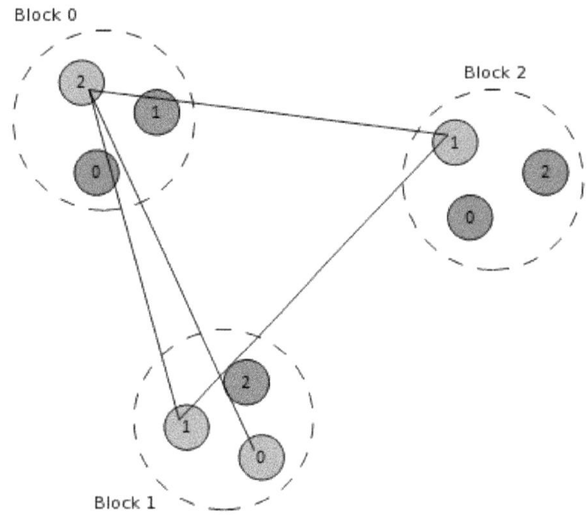

Figure 4: Compatibility graph of the possible futures

5. GPU IMPLEMENTATION CHOICES

5.1 GPUContext: avoid memory transfers between host and device

GPU applications often suffer from the excessive latency induced by memory accesses. It is strategic to optimize them as much as possible in order to obtain the best performance (memory transfers from the host to the device, or memory accesses from threads on the device) [16].

In our case, we have decided to cut any communication between the host and the device, except synchronizations. Indeed, GPUs cannot have all their threads synchronized at one point, at the time of writing, due to hardware constraints. On the other hand, some stages of the simulation need the data to be in a particular state before they can achieve their part of the computation. The only way to synchronize all the threads on a GPU is to wait for the completion of the kernel that has launched them. Each simulation step is consequently divided into several parallel stages, launched consecutively on the GPU. Such a design enables us to finely tune the parallelism grain of the simulation: at each stage the parallelism grain is the most adapted to the kernel that is to be launched.

As a result, communications are shrunk to their utter minimum from the host to the device. Simulations data are transferred back to the host from the GPU only when a checkpoint of the state of the simulation is reached.

5.2 Approximate cylinders to avoid branch divergence

In the original model, the elements that compose the chromosomes are represented by cylinders with rounded edges, as shown in Figure 5. In this diagram, the point *mid* is the middle of the cylinder, and *e1* the direction vector that indicates the orientation of the cylinder. *rin* and *rfin* are two points which denote the edges of the cylinder.

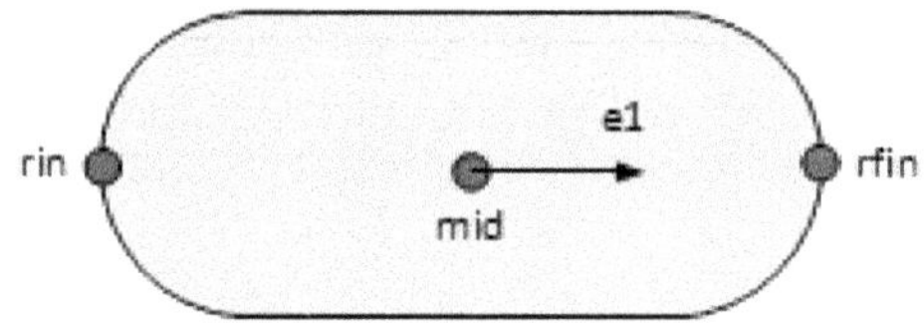

Figure 5: Cylindrical element that is part of the chromosome

This representation has the advantage of being accurate according to the observed physics, but on the other side, it highly complicates the calculation of collisions. Indeed, computing an intersection between two cylinders is rather slow: the corresponding code is about 200 lines and contains many conditions, which makes it less suitable for execution on GPUs.

Instead, cylinders can be approximated by groups of spheres, as illustrated in Figure 6. Points *sphere0*, *sphere1* and, *sphere2* are the centres of the three spheres composing the cylinder. Points *joint0* and *joint1* are the edges of the cylinder.

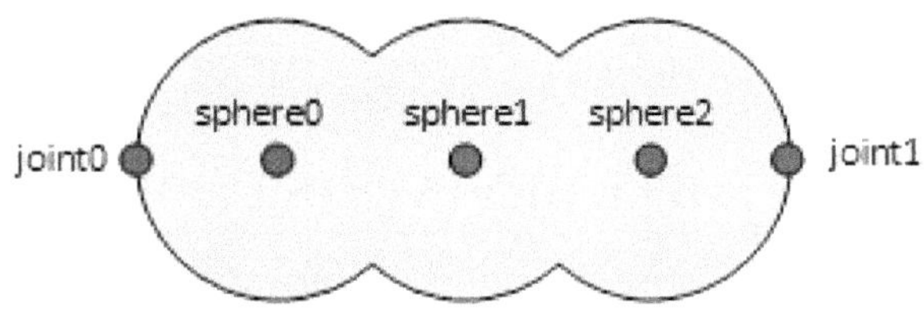

Figure 6: Pseudo-cylindrical approximation of a segment

Thanks to this representation, calculating the presence of a collision between two cylinders consists in calculating the collisions between the three spheres of the first cylinder and the three spheres of the second cylinder. Furthermore calculating collisions between two spheres is a trivial operation, as shown in Listing 1:

Listing 1: Calculation of collisions between spheres

```
bool Sphere::collision (
        const Sphere & otherSphere)
{
  Vector3 vector = this->Position -
              otherSphere.position;
  // All spheres have a radius RADIUS.
  // We compare the squared lengths
  // to avoid an expensive square root.
  return vector.squaredLength() -
        (RADIUS * RADIUS);
}
```

Three spheres (rather than two or four) were chosen because it allows a very good approximation of the original cylinders and collisions observed. Moreover, using more than three spheres does not increase the accuracy of the approximation in a significant way.

6. RESULTS

Thanks to the log files generated by the application, which contain the 3D coordinates of each joint, we can obtain a 3D representation of chromosomes using third-party software such as *gnuplot*. Figure 7 is the output drawing generated by *gnuplot* for a circular chromosome after 100 million iterations.

All the results presented in this section have been obtained through simulations run on homogeneous machines equipped with the following configuration: Intel Core i7-2600k 3.40GHz CPUs and NVIDIA GeForce GTX590 GPUs.

6.1 Efficiency of the parallelization approach

The first metric that is interesting to study from the new parallel model is the efficiency of the possible futures approach regarding the acceptance rate. Figure 8, shows the efficiency of the PFA approach in increasing the acceptance rate. As we can see, the acceptance rate increases with the number of possible futures involved in each simulation step.

For clarity's sake, the acceptance rate depicted in Figure 8 is obtained by averaging the acceptance rates of several configurations benefiting successively from 4, 8, 64 and 128 possible futures per block. The configuration test set is as follows:

- number of blocks $\rightarrow \{1; 3; 7; 15\}$
- maximal block size $\rightarrow \{32; 64; 256; 510\}$

Eventually, it appears that the acceptance rate becomes trickier to improve when the number of blocks increases. Indeed, the number of cliques grows exponentially with the number of blocks. Thus, it is more and more difficult for the algorithm to find a maximal clique amongst the set of randomly generated cliques.

6.2 Performance on the cutting-edge Kepler architecture K20 GPU

Parallel architectures and especially GPUs evolve very quickly. In the particular case of NVIDIA GPUs, a new generation is shipped every two years. Thus, an application running on this architecture must take advantage of these evolutions and display improved performance when run on the forefront GPUs. Having run our benchmark on Fermi architecture GTX 590 GPUs, we have tested some identical configurations on a recent Kepler architecture K20 GPU [14]. Figure 9 depicts the speed-up obtained at no cost, only by switching from the GTX to the K20 GPU.

7. CONCLUSION

In this paper, we have described a parallel model of chromosome folding and its implementation on GPU, using the NVIDIA CUDA technology.

The purpose of this model is to make chromosomes evolve in the confined space of a cell, by applying successive rotations on random chunks of the chromosome. This new parallel model is based on an initial sequential one, which encounters difficulties when the cell space becomes more confined. The acceptance rate of the simulated rotations then quickly falls, making the sequential model evolve slower.

In order to increase the acceptance rate of simulated rotations, especially when the space becomes more and more confined, we designed a Possible Futures Algorithm (PFA). This approach proposes different new configurations for each

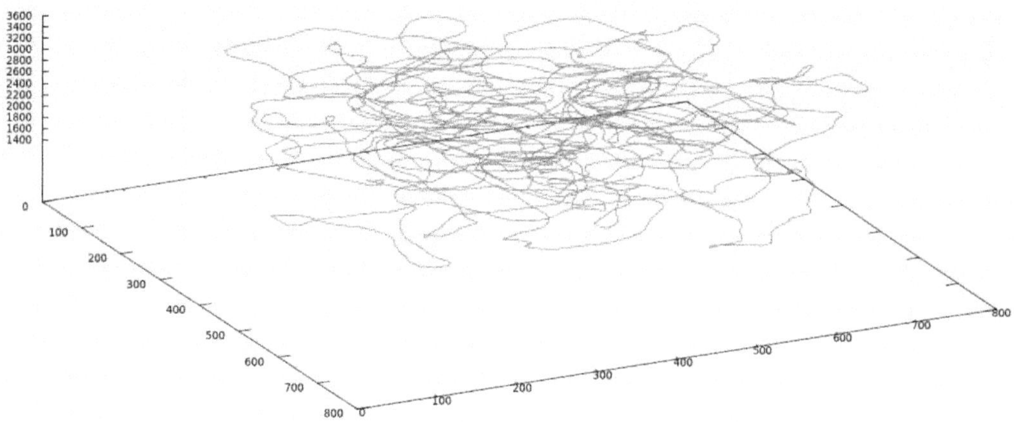

Figure 7: Gnuplot 3D representation of a chromosome

block at each step, which have to be checked for inter-compatibility. All the futures can be generated and processed in parallel, thus inducing a massively parallel workload of repetitive tasks.

This approach has shown satisfying results in terms of acceptance rate. While the original model was likely to dismiss about 95% of the rotations, the possible future approach displays a satisfying acceptance rate of more than 60%. Such an acceptance rate enables the chromosome to evolve to a new configuration after almost each simulation step.

We now plan to challenge this parallel model with an implementation of the sequential one. Such a benchmark will have to be conceived very carefully, as long as the two models operate in two different ways and the same metrics cannot be easily compared between the two models. For instance, a simulation step does not perform the same actions in the two models. That is why we focused on the acceptance rate in this study. Still, the parallel implementation should display far better performance than the sequential one thanks to its possible futures approach. The more the chromosome becomes confined within the cell space, the more the parallel algorithm will be efficient. In fact, the efficiency of the parallel implementation is due to its ability to maintain a high acceptance rate throughout the execution, whereas the sequential model will see its acceptance rate decrease with the various stages and the confinement.

The interested reader will find a free version of both sequential and parallel implementations in the git repository of the French Institute of Complex Systems[1].

8. ACKNOWLEDGMENTS

Ivan Junier is supported by a Novartis grant (CRG). This work is also partly funded by the Auvergne Regional Council and the FEDER. The authors would like to thank Alice Chalet for her careful reading and useful suggestions on the draft.

9. REFERENCES

[1] G. M. Amdahl. Validity of the single processor approach to achieving large scale computing capabilities. In *Proceedings of the April 18-20, 1967, spring joint computer conference*, pages 483–485. ACM, 1967.

[2] L. Dagum and R. Menon. Openmp: an industry standard api for shared-memory programming. *Computational Science & Engineering, IEEE*, 5(1):46–55, 1998.

[3] P.-G. de Gennes. *Scaling concept in polymer physics.* IthacaNY: Cornell University Press, third edition, 1988.

[4] J. Dean and S. Ghemawat. Mapreduce: simplified data processing on large clusters. *Communications of the ACM*, 51(1):107–113, 2008.

[5] G. Fudenberg and L. A. Mirny. Higher-order chromatin structure: bridging physics and biology. *Current Opinion in Genetics & Development*, 22(2):115–124, 2012.

[6] J. L. Gustafson. Reevaluating amdahl's law. *Communications of the ACM*, 31(5):532–533, 1988.

[7] B. He, W. Fang, Q. Luo, N. K. Govindaraju, and T. Wang. Mars: a mapreduce framework on graphics processors. In *Proceedings of the 17th international conference on Parallel architectures and compilation techniques*, pages 260–269. ACM, 2008.

[8] M. D. Hill and M. R. Marty. Amdahl's law in the multicore era. *Computer*, 41(7):33–38, 2008.

[9] I. Junier, R. K. Dale, C. Hou, F. Képès, and A. Dean. CTCF-mediated transcriptional regulation through cell type-specific chromosome organization in the Îš-globin locus. *Nucleic Acids Research*, 2012.

[10] I. Junier, O. Martin, and F. Képès. Spatial and topological organization of dna chains induced by gene co-localization. *PLoS computational biology*, 6(2):e1000678, 2010.

[11] J. Langowski and D. Heermann. Computational modeling of the chromatin fiber. *Seminars in Cell & Developmental Biology*, 18(5):659–667, 2007.

[12] J. K. Lee and A. J. Smith. Branch prediction strategies and branch target buffer design. *Computer*, 17(1):6–22, 1984.

[13] Message Passing Interface Forum. Document for a standard message-passing interface. Technical report, University of Tennessee, 1993.

[14] NVIDIA. Nvidia's next generation cuda compute architecture: Kepler gk110. Technical report, 2012.

[15] D. Reith, L. Mirny, and P. Virnau. Gpu based

[1] `https://forge.iscpif.fr/projects/dna/repository`

molecular dynamics simulations of polymer rings in concentrated solution: Structure and scaling. *Progress of Theoretical Physics Supplement*, 191:135–145, 2011.

[16] S. Ryoo, C. I. Rodrigues, S. S. Baghsorkhi, S. S. Stone, D. B. Kirk, and W.-m. W. Hwu. Optimization principles and application performance evaluation of a multithreaded gpu using cuda. In *Proceedings of the 13th ACM SIGPLAN Symposium on Principles and practice of parallel programming*, pages 73–82. ACM, 2008.

[17] J. E. Smith. A study of branch prediction strategies. In *25 years of the international symposia on Computer architecture (selected papers)*, pages 202–215. ACM, 1998.

[18] T. R. Strick, M.-N. Dessinges, G. Charvin, N. H. Dekker, J.-F. Allemand, D. Bensimon, and V. Croquette. Stretching of macromolecules and proteins. *Reports on Progress in Physics*, 66:1, 2003.

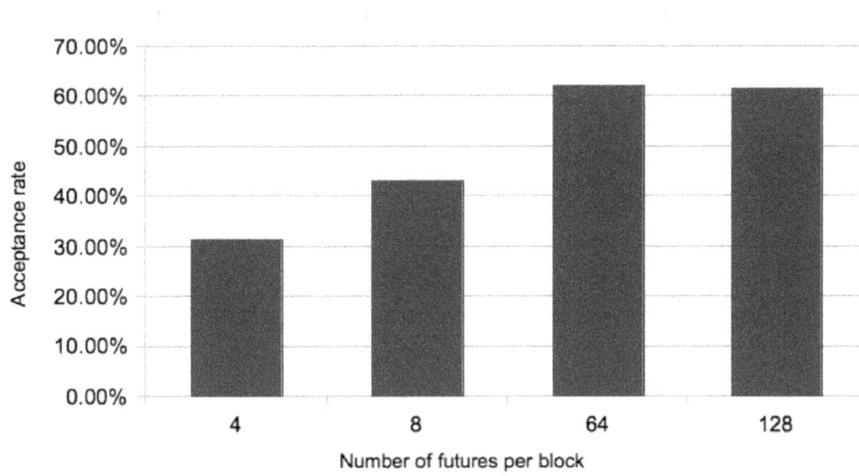

Figure 8: Increase in the acceptance rate with the number of possible futures

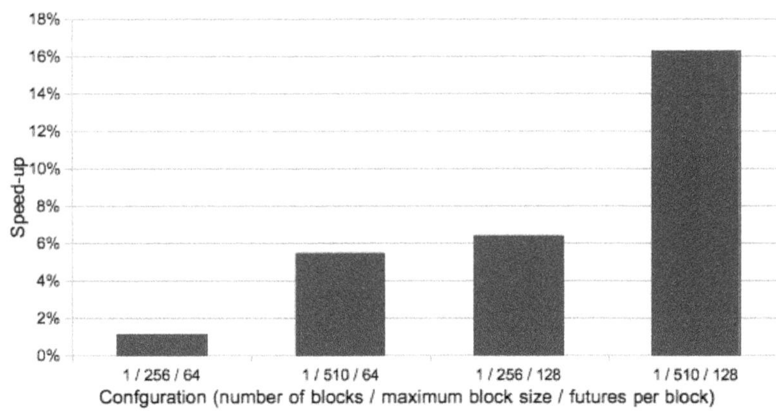

Figure 9: Model improved performance when run on a Kepler architecture K20 GPU

On the Parallel Simulation of Scale-Free Networks

Robert Pienta and Richard M. Fujimoto
School of Computational Science & Engineering
Georgia Institute of Technology
pientars@gatech.edu,
fujimoto@cc.gatech.edu

ABSTRACT

Scale-free networks have received much attention in recent years due to their prevalence in many important applications such as social networks, biological systems, and the Internet. We consider the use of conservative parallel discrete event simulation techniques in network simulation applications involving scale-free networks. An analytical model is developed to study the parallelism available in simulations using a conservative time window synchronization algorithm. The performance of scale-free network simulations using two variants of the Chandy/Misra/Bryant synchronization algorithm are evaluated. These results demonstrate the importance of topology in the performance of synchronization protocols when developing parallel discrete event simulations involving scale-free networks, and highlight important challenges such as performance bottlenecks that must be addressed to achieve efficient parallel execution. These results suggest that new approaches to parallel simulation of scale-free networks may offer significant benefit.

Categories and Subject Descriptors

I.6 [**Computing Methodologies**]: Simulation and Modeling

Keywords

conservative synchronization; discrete event simulation; parallelism; power law degree distribution; scale-free; scale-free degree distribution; scale-free network simulation; simulation synchronization

1. INTRODUCTION

Parallel discrete event simulation (PDES) offers a means to accelerate, and/or enable large-scale simulations by distributing the execution of a simulation program over multiple processors. It has been applied to a wide variety of applications such as simulating telecommunication networks [24], surface and air transportation systems [29, 31], and disease spread [23], to mention a few. A PDES program consists of a collection of logical processes (LPs) that communicate by exchanging timestamped messages, or events.

A synchronization mechanism is needed to ensure the parallel execution of the simulation produces exactly the same results as the corresponding sequential execution. Synchronization algorithms are broadly classified as conservative mechanisms that rely on blocking logical processes in order to ensure events within each LP are always processed in non-decreasing timestamp order, and optimistic algorithms that allow out-of-order event processing to occur, but utilize a rollback mechanism to recover when events have not been processed in timestamp order. A critical factor impacting parallel performance is the amount of overhead, e.g., additional messages or rolled back computation, that must be introduced by the synchronization mechanism. Managing this overhead is critical to achieving efficient executions.

The PDES topology is a graph with each node representing an LP, and each link connecting two LPs indicating those LPs may communicate by sending a message between them. Here, we assume undirected arcs, and do not distinguish between the sending and receiving LP except to clarify the presentation.

We are concerned with one important class of network topologies that have become known as *scale-free networks* [4]. A scale-free network is one where the node degree follows a power law distribution. A distinguishing characteristic of scale-free networks is a significant number of nodes referred to as *hub* nodes contain a large node degree, while most nodes, often referred to as *leaf nodes*, contain relatively small degree. Scale-free networks are known to exhibit "small world" properties, meaning, the minimum path length between any pair of nodes in the network is small relative to the number of nodes in the network. As will be seen later, these properties have important ramifications for parallel discrete event simulation.

Scale-free networks have received a considerable amount of attention in recent years because it has been observed that many real-world systems contain networks that exhibit the scale-free property [30]. For example, it is widely believed that the autonomous system (AS) level topology of the Internet is scale-free [11, 25, 13, 33]. In the broad area of systems biology, the study of complex biological systems, protein-protein interaction networks have been demonstrated to follow scale-free distributions [16]. Some financial networks such as the interbank payment network exhibit scale-free behavior [27] Social networks, the world-wide-web, the internal structuring of superconductors, the airline transportation network, and human interaction networks such as those characterizing the spread of diseases have been observed to exhibit the scale-free property.

Other networks, while not following a power-law distribution, do appear to have heavy skew in their node degree distribution. For example, initial studies suggested that the router-level topology of the Internet followed a power law, but more recent work reports the topology is driven by engineering and economic considerations as well as physical node and link capacity constraints, resulting in a node degree distribution that is skewed, but does not follow a power law [32]. The router-level topology contains many high-degree routers at the edge of the network designed to aggregate traffic from many low-bandwidth connections coupled with a mesh-like core of high capacity routers with a smaller number of high bandwidth links. Although the work described here focuses on networks with a power law degree distribution, we conjecture that many of the results derived in this study also have applicability to networks with heavily skewed degree distribution.

We are concerned with the efficiency of parallel simulation techniques in terms of parallelism and overhead of synchronization protocols for scale-free networks. It seems clear that topology will have strong implications regarding performance. For example, it has been observed empirically that the distribution of event-level parallelism in simulations of communication networks can lead to severe load imbalances [19]. In [9] load distribution issues in scale-free network simulations are examined. However, to our knowledge, the relationship between power law topology and parallel simulator performance has not been previously studied at a foundational level.

The remainder of this paper is organized as follows. The next section describes qualitatively the relationship between scale-free network topologies and overhead of PDES synchronization protocols. While an exhaustive examination of all synchronization protocols is beyond the scope of this work, this section discusses examples from major classes of synchronization protocols. Section 3 reviews the power law degree distribution that characterizes scale-free networks. Section 4 develops an analytical model to assess the parallelism available in parallel simulations of scale-free networks using a simple, synchronous window-based PDES protocol. This is followed by results from simulation studies that consider parallelism and overhead using two variations of the well-known Chandy/Misra/Bryant protocol. Finally we present conclusions and areas of future research.

2. PDES SYNCHRONIZATION

Most PDES synchronization protocols were designed to be used to simulate networks of arbitrary topology. One exception is the protocol described in [17], that was designed for feedforward networks. Conservative synchronization algorithms broadly fall into two general categories. Synchronous algorithms utilize global synchronization points, e.g., barriers, to synchronize the computation. By contrast, asynchronous algorithms use only local synchronization mechanisms. One well-known example of the latter is the Chandy-Misra-Bryant (CMB) [6] algorithm.

Briefly, CMB sends a *null message* to another LP to indicate a lower bound on the timestamp of any message it might send in the future. The receiver uses this information to determine a lower bound on the time stamp (LBTS) of all future messages it might receive. Events with timestamp smaller than this LBTS value may be safely processed. In its simplest form, each LP broadcasts a null message on each of its outgoing links after processing each event. We refer to this approach as naïve CMB.

The number of links connected to an LP, i.e., the node degree, impacts the performance of the algorithm in two ways. First, an updated LBTS must be computed by each LP. In the worst case the number of comparisons is $O(logN_L)$, where N_L is the node degree of LP L. This calculation takes little time, but must be repeated often, as much as once for each received message. More importantly, however, an LP must send a null message to each of its neighbors, as often as after each message that it processes. This overhead is clearly proportional to node degree. This overhead is problematic for scale-free networks because high degree nodes will incur a significant overhead to send, receive, and process null messages. As will be seen later, hub nodes tend to have a disproportionately large amount of event computation that can cause them to become bottlenecks. The aforementioned overheads clearly aggravate this situation.

An alternative version of CMB uses a demand-driven approach [28]. Rather than broadcasting a null message at each message send, an LP L requests a null message from each LP when it must block to wait on an empty message queue. This will significantly reduce the number of null messages that are required. However, even with this optimization, one would expect the hub nodes to have to request more null messages than leaf nodes due to the large number of incoming links. Later, we use simulations to evaluate this question further.

Synchronous algorithms typically repeat the following steps: (1) compute LBTS values to determine which events are safe to process, (2) process those events with timestamp less than the LP's LBTS value and send any messages produced in processing these messages, (3) perform a barrier synchronization. Each iteration through these steps is referred to as an *epoch*. One of the simplest algorithms is YAWNS [22] that completes the first step by computing a global minimum that specifies the smallest timestamped message that could be generated, and uses this value as the LBTS. The performance of the YAWNS protocol for scale-free networks will be examined in much greater detail later.

Other synchronous algorithms put greater effort into computing the LBTS values. A common approach is to use the *distance between objects* [3] to determine the minimum amount of simulation time that must elapse for an event in one LP to affect an event in a different LP. To accomplish this, an LP must consider the smallest timestamp event within each other LP, and use the precomputed distance to compute an LP's LBTS value. This may require examining many other LPs to determine which events are safe. The bounded lag approach uses a simulation time window to limit the scope of this search, thereby arguing that the protocol scales to large numbers of processors [20]. The events within the window are considered *near future* events while those outside the window are considered *far future* events. The width of the window is important to ensure runtime efficiency; too small a window and the LP's won't be able to process very many events per epoch. Too large a window and the events that should be far future are included in the the calculations, again decreasing the runtime efficiency of the simulation.

Scale-free networks are a challenging test case for these synchronization algorithms. This is because scale-free networks possess the so-called *small world* property. Popularized in the media, small world networks have the property that the average minimum path length between two randomly selected nodes in the network tends to be very small, even for networks containing a large number of nodes. As discussed momentarily, power law distributio'ns are characterized by the parameter λ that determines the number of high degree nodes that will occur. In cases with $2 \leq \lambda \leq 3$, a common range for natural scale-free networks, the average path length grows even slower ($\log \log N$) [8]. Stated another way, the number of nodes (LPs) reachable from a given node increases exponentially with the number of hops. This suggests that algorithms that require examination of other LPs to determine what events are safe to process are doomed to failure because a very large number of nodes will have to be examined to determine what events are safe. Windowing schemes such as that used in bounded lag are unlikely to solve this problem because the relevant "neighborhood" of nodes that must be examined grows too rapidly.

Network topology may also impact the performance of optimistic synchronization algorithms [5]. Approaches such as the well-known Time Warp algorithm [15] utilize a rollback propagation mechanism that can severely degrade performance. Analysis of time warp systems has been carefully studied through a number of different approaches. Overall parallel performance bounds have been studied through modeling the critical path within simulations [18]. The general performance of time warp systems has also been rigorously investigated assuming a fully connected network topology [14, 1]. The propagation of rollbacks through the network is dependent on network topology; however, the relationship of the rollback propagation mechanism to topology is complex, and not well understood. Our focus here is to explore parallelism in scale-free network simulations and to elucidate the behavior of conservative synchronization approaches on scale-free topologies. Here, we focus exclusively on conservative synchronization algorithms.

3. SCALE-FREE NETWORKS

For the examination of scale-free networks it is generally assumed that the node degree probability is [7]:

$$P(k) \sim ck^{-\lambda}$$

Where k is the node degree, c is a scalar normalization constant, and λ is a parameter. Intuitively, smaller values of λ indicate the network will contain more nodes with large degree. Typical values of λ for networks that appear in practice generally fall in the range $\lambda \in (1, 3]$ [4, 7]. Early investigations of natural systems by Italian economist Vilfredo Pareto found that many observable phenomena follow a Pareto distribution [2].

The Pareto cumulative distribution function follows:

$$F(x) = \begin{cases} 1 - \left(\frac{m}{x}\right)^{\alpha} & \text{for } x \geq m, \\ 0 & \text{for } x < m \end{cases}$$

where m is the positive, minimum degree across all vertices in the network. The Pareto distribution is a reformation of the general power-law distribution shown above:

$$\left(\frac{m}{x}\right)^{\alpha} = m^{\alpha}\left(\frac{1}{x}\right)^{\alpha} = m^{\alpha}(x)^{-\alpha}$$

In this case $c = m$ and $\alpha = \lambda$. This leads to to the probability mass function:

$$F(x)' = f(x) = \begin{cases} \alpha\left(\frac{m^{\alpha}}{x^{\alpha+1}}\right) & \text{for } x \geq m, \\ 0 & \text{for } x < m \end{cases}$$

From this the expectation can be formulated:

$$E(X) = \int x f_X(x) dx = \frac{\alpha m}{\alpha - 1}, \text{ for } \alpha > 1$$

These definitions will be called upon later during the analysis of scale-free network behavior to yield quantitative information about the network.

4. CONSERVATIVE PDES ANALYSIS

4.1 Application Model and Execution

We have developed a general model of synchronous simulation using the YAWNs protocol described earlier. The system utilizes an event processing paradigm based on the well-known PHOLD model [12] adapted for scale-free networks. The system initially contains a fixed set of messages that are uniformly distributed across all LPs in the system. When an event is processed, exactly one new event is created and sent to a destination LP that is chosen at random from a uniform distribution among the LP's neighboring nodes. We assume each LP has a lookahead of L, and the timestamp increment for each newly created event is L plus a value drawn from an exponential distribution. We assume each LP is mapped to a separate processor. It is assumed that each event requires one unit of wall clock time to process that event.

In the synchronous YAWNS protocol a fixed sized window is used whose size is equal to the lookahead L of each LP. All events with timestamp in the window $[Min, Min + L)$ are processed in each epoch, where Min is the minimum timestamp event among those that have not yet been processed. We assume the time to compute LBTS values and communication overheads, e.g., to send and receive events, are negligible, and event computations are not preempted once the processing of an event begins. Therefore, the time to complete an epoch is proportional to the maximum number of events among the LPs whose timestamp reside within the current window.

4.2 Analytical Model

The main goal of the analytical model is to analyze the affects of the underlying topology on the amount of parallelism in the simulation. To aid this investigation we created a stochastic analytical model to estimate the steady state arrival of events within an epoch of width L. In window-based synchronous approaches, the LP with the longest runtime will become the bottleneck. When the number of events within each time window among the different LPs vary widely, the underutilized LPs will become idle, waiting for the LP containing the largest number of events. This results in a loss of parallelism and reduces the efficiency of the distributed simulation. In order to empirically measure the parallelism in the model, our approach calculates the available parallelism as follows: Let the number of events per LP_i for a single epoch be n_i. The bottleneck LP, or longest running LP in wallclock time, (LP-4 in fig. 1) is:

$$\arg\max\{n_i\}$$

Since the processing time of each event is 1 unit of wallclock time, the amount of time to complete the epoch is e_{max} (see fig. 1) where:

$$e_{max} = \max\{n_i\}$$

The total amount of work, i.e., the number of events within the epoch is W (represented as the events inside the shaded region) can then be calculated:

$$W = \sum_i n_i$$

The amount of parallelism, P, is:

$$P = \frac{W}{e_{max}}$$

In other words, P is the maximum speedup that can be obtained by a parallel execution of the simulation.

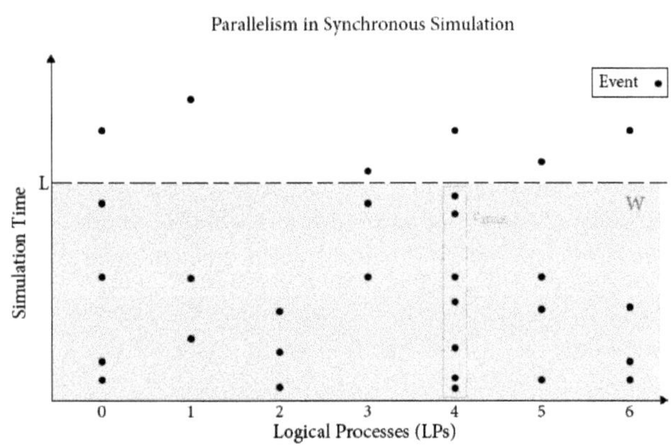

Figure 1: The measure of parallelism, P, is based on the LP with the largest number of events and the total amount of time spent processing events in the epoch. In this example the shaded region denotes a single epoch with 7 LPs. LP-4 determines the value of $e_{max} = 7$ and the total number of events $W = 24$ is the number of events in the shaded region.

The exact arrival time distribution for a message is complex, so we have adopted a number of approximations and simplifications for its form. Many of the approximations are common when attempting to analytically model a simulation system [10, 22]. Numerical sample estimates can then be computed for each of the parameters. This is predicated on the notion that the arrival time, t, of a particular event can be viewed as the sum of some number of past service events. This analysis is novel in that it considers the effect of a scale-free or power-law degree distribution within the simulation network topology. In the following analysis we taxonomize nodes in the simulation network as either "leaf" or "hub" nodes. Leaf nodes are nodes of relatively low degree while the hub nodes are those of high degree. Let the top f fraction of nodes be hubs while the remaining $1 - f$ fraction of nodes are leaves.

With the message arrival times following an approximate distributional form, it is possible to compute a new probability distribution of the number of events executed within a known period of simulation time. Similar to Dickens et al. the analysis presented in this work focuses on epochs or generations of messages across a known period of simulation time [10]. Each generation is a window of simulation time $[t, t + L)$. All events with timestamp $e_t \in [t, t + L)$ are considered to be members of that generation. As events are processed within the first generation some number of the new events will fall within the next or subsequent generations and are not counted among the events in the current generation.

The number of service events that an LP starts in $[t, t+L)$ is a random variable e_{serv} that follows a Poisson distribution with mean determined by the previous epoch. Because the routing of an event in a scale-free network is not uniform, the number of job arrival events is a random variable J, conditioned on the type of node, i.e., hub or leaf.

Given N messages at generation k the number arriving at an LP is a binomial distribution conditioned on the node type. Because the connectivity between nodes is by definition not uniform, this conditioning is used to model the average case hub and leaf nodes. Let u_i and v_i be the number of events at a hub and leaf at generation i respectively. The values V_h and V_l are the expected number of edges for each type of node. The resulting binomial for hubs is then $B(u_i, 1/V_h)$ and $B(v_i, 1/V_l)$ for leaves. Because the hubs are picked as some fraction, f, of the most highly connected nodes, there exists a well defined point x_f after which lies a fraction f of the measurements.

$$\int_{x_f}^{\infty} cx^{-\lambda}\, dx = f \int_{x_{min}}^{\infty} cx^{-\lambda}\, dx$$

Given $\lambda > 1$, x_f exists and can be solved for; yielding:

$$x_f = \left(\frac{1}{f}\right)^{1/\lambda - 1} x_{min}.$$

With the boundary point x_f, it is possible to separately calculate the expected degree in the points up to x_f (leaves) and after it (hubs). In the case of hubs with $\lambda > 2$:

$$V_h = \int_{x_f}^{\infty} xcx^{-\lambda}\, dx = -\frac{c}{-\lambda + 2} x_f^{-\lambda+2}$$

The expected the degree for the leaves is similar:

$$V_l = \int_{x_{min}}^{x_f} xcx^{-\lambda}\, dx = \frac{c}{-\lambda + 2}\left[x_f^{-\lambda+2} - x_{min}^{-\lambda+2}\right]$$

For a power-law distributed network a similar derivation as the one above can be used to show the fraction of edges going to some fixed fraction of the most highly connected nodes. Consider a scale-free network where E denotes the fraction of the edges connected to some fraction f of the highest degree nodes, then the following equation relates E to f:

$$E = f^{\frac{\lambda - 2}{\lambda - 1}}$$

This solution, derived first in [21], yields an important measure of the probability that a randomly selected edge will lead to either a hub or a leaf, determined entirely by the parameters of the scale-free distribution. For example, if we take the top 50% of nodes to be the hubs on a scale-free network with $\lambda = 2.1$, we can say that $0.5^{\frac{0.1}{1.1}} \approx 0.938$ or that approximately 93% of all edges will go to hubs while only 7% will go to leaves. Considering the equation above, the number of hub edges per leaf edge increases heavily as

$\lambda \rightarrow 2$. The imbalance of edges may cause disproportionate amounts of communication with the hubs and therefore decrease the overall load balance.

The expected number of arrival events a leaf expects to see, R_l, is modeled by the expected number of edges for a leaf, split into fN hubs and $(1-f)N$ leaves for a network with N nodes, each scaled by the average case probability of receiving a message on that edge. We use f to partition the nodes into two sets for the analysis. With the approximate number of total edges, we must separate the expected number of edges from hubs and leaves and then scale by the probability that a message was sent down those channels. By calculating leaves and hubs separately, the total number of incoming messages can be calculated. First for a leaf:

$$Rl_i = V_l(1-f) \cdot E[B(v_{i-1}, 1/V_l)] + V_l f \cdot E[B(u_{i-1}, 1/V_h)]$$

and for a hub:

$$Rh_i = V_h(1-f) \cdot E[B(v_{i-1}, 1/V_l)] + V_h f \cdot E[B(u_{i-1}, 1/V_h)]$$

Often such binomial distributions are approximated with Poisson random variables of matched mean. Because $1/V_l$ may be relatively large, our approach cannot safely make this substitution. Here we make use of the expectation of a binomial $E[\,B(N,p)\,] = Np$ resulting in:

$$Rl_i = V_l(1-f)\frac{v_{i-1}}{V_l} + V_l f \frac{u_{i-1}}{V_h}$$

for the average leaf node and,

$$Rh_i = V_h(1-f)\frac{v_{i-1}}{V_l} + V_h f \frac{u_{i-1}}{V_h}$$

for the average hub node.

Let the service time of events be an exponential random variable, with rate μ_s. We are interested in determining the expected number of messages that are scheduled in the ith subsequent generation. If the current time is t, the ith subsequent generation is the period in simulation time for which the events timestamps are $[t+(i+1)L, t+(i+2)L)$.

$$P\{Service\ entry\ arrival\ time \in ith\ generation\}$$

$$= \int_{t+(i+1)L}^{t+(i+2)L} e^{-\mu_s u} du$$

$$= \frac{1}{\mu_s}\left(e^{-\mu_s(t+iL+L)} - e^{-\mu_s(t+iL+2L)}\right)$$

With the above probability, the mean number of events that fall outside of the first generation into each of the ith subsequent generations can be calculated. This value is added to the expeceted number of messages in that generation. This calculation must be done at each iteration to mimic the effects of scheduling future events.

Leaf:

$$E[Gl_0] = Gl_{init}$$

Hub:

$$E[Gh_0] = Gh_{init}$$

Initial values for the number of events in the first generation, Gh_{init} and Gl_{init} are required. The next generation is a recurrence based on the previous value, because the number of messages received at generation i dictates the number of messages to be dealt with in the next and subsequent generations. Given the first generation expected values, later generations within this model may be determined.

Leaf:

$$E[Gl_i] \mathrel{+}= Rl_i$$

Hub:

$$E[Gh_i] \mathrel{+}= Rh_i$$

The recurrence lies within the calculations of Rl_i and Rh_i and the number of events already scheduled in the current generation. Given initial conditions to determine the first generation, subsequent generations can be solved in an interative manner. This iterative analysis steps generation by generation over the course of a simulation. From these results the expected number of messages per epoch as well as some of the scale-free network behavior can be gleaned.

4.3 Largest Node Degree

In order to investigate the workload of the largest hub, an estimate of that node's degree is needed.

Given n samples drawn from a power-law distribution, we first compute the probability that the largest value, x_{max}, lies in the interval between x and $x + dx$. Let $P(x)$ be the probability that $x \geq X$, then:

$$P(x) = \int_x^\infty p(x')dx' = \left(\frac{x}{x_{min}}\right)^{-\lambda+1}$$

We are concerned with the total proportion of nodes with degree greater than or equal to x_{max}. Consider the following heuristic argument:

$$\frac{P(x \geq x_{max})}{P(x \geq x_{min})} \approx \frac{1}{n},$$

for some x, then there will be on average a single sample in the range x to ∞. This single sample will be the largest value. Given that

$$\frac{\int_{x_{max}}^\infty cx^{-\lambda}dx}{\int_{x_{min}}^\infty c'x^{-\lambda}dx} \approx \frac{1}{n},$$

solving for x_{max}:

$$x_{max} \approx x_{min} \cdot n^{\frac{1}{\lambda-1}}.$$

In the case where the minimum out-degree across all nodes is one ($x_{min} = 1$), the equation above simplifies further to

$$x_{max} \approx n^{\frac{1}{\lambda-1}}.$$

For a more rigorous derivation that arrives at the same approximation see the appendix of [21].

This result is important because the hub with the largest degree will likely form the bottleneck when using the synchronous simulation protocol. For $\lambda > 2$ the largest hub grows at a fractional power of the hubs. However when $\lambda = 2$ the largest degree grows linearly with the number of vertices and when $\lambda < 2$ the rate of growth is superlinear. For example let $\lambda = 1.8$ the maximum degree grows at a rate approximately $n^{1.25}$ [21, 26]. Although in a real network the maximum degree reaches a hard limit of the number of vertices in the graph, the value of λ determines how quickly x_{max} reaches this point.

4.4 Numerical Experiments and Results

For illustrative purposes, consider the analytical model introduced previously assuming the top 25% of nodes are hubs in a scale-free network with $\lambda = 2.5$. Let $x_{min} = 1$, such that all nodes have at least one edge connecting them in the network. Initially, each node has the same initial number of events. In the following experiments an initial set of 10 events per LP was used. As mentioned in the previous section, each event that is processed produces exactly one new event with timestamp increment drawn from an exponential distribution. The model is iterated until a steady-state is reached.

This iteration is repeated for leaf, hub, and the largest (highest degree) hub expected for a particular network size N. The steady state expected number of messages per node type is calculated, with an estimate of the number of messages the largest hub would receive. The minimum time for completion, e_{max}, as determined by the longest running LP is calculated. In all cases tested e_{max} was determined by the largest hub. The total number of messages processed W is calculated. From these values P emerges. This process is repeated for scale-free distributions with varied λ's.

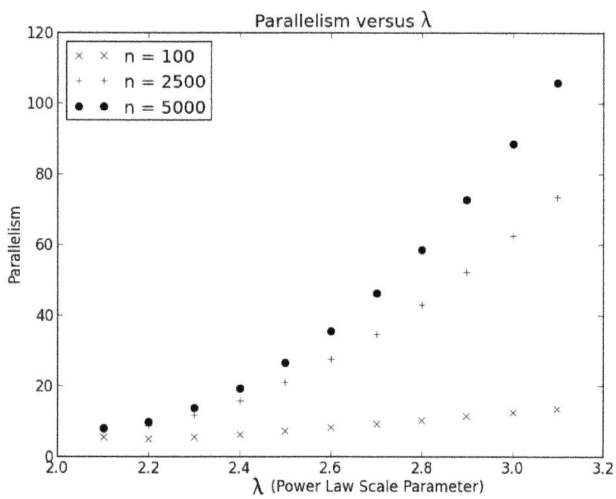

Figure 2: The model's potential parallelism given varied λ and network size.

Consider the behavior shown in figure 2. As expected, the potential parallelism increases with the number of nodes, however it is seen to be strongly dependent on λ. Because the derivation of the analytical model requires that $\lambda > 2$, the experiments focused on values larger than 2. While the analytical model cannot be used to for networks where $\lambda < 2$, the behavior of those scale-free networks will be more imbalanced than the networks tested here. This arises from the fact that as $\lambda \to 1$ the distribution becomes more tail-heavy, with the bulk of edges being pushed toward the hubs.

Given the analytical synchronous model above, one is naturally interested in the relevant λ's for networks that arise in practice. We have calculated the available parallelism for a telecommunications dataset. The dataset represents the collection of phone calls made during a single day among a large group of entities who made or received at least one call. The calculation of P utilizes several summary parameters from the dataset; network size (number of entities), minimum number of connections or calls (one call) and approximations of empirical λ for the dataset. For $\lambda = 2.22$ [21] and a network containing 1.1 million nodes the empirical data yielded a potential parallelism of only $P = 55.21$. As an approximate upper bound of the potential parallel improvement for simulating this network in a distributed setting, this value suggests that the scale-free nature of the network topology will significantly limit the amount of speedup that can be obtained using parallel simulation. The parallelism was limited largely by the low λ value which was caused by a few hub-entities making a large numbers of calls; likely these originated from businesses or telemarketing groups.

4.5 Discussion

The analytical model for synchronous approaches makes some assumptions that increase it's sensitivity to changes in λ. For example, the system utilizes the aforementioned relation, $E = f^{\frac{\lambda-2}{\lambda-1}}$, to calculate the proportion of edges connected to hubs. This relation is derived from a set of integrals that diverge when $\lambda \leq 2$. This does not necessarily mean that the averages themselves will all be infinite, but rather that individual measurements may be so large and varied that the average never converges. What happens analytically as $\lambda \to 1$ is that the tail of the distribution becomes heavier and heavier. In terms of a network topology this means that the number of edges going to the hubs increases until the point of saturation, wherein every edge is connected to a node in the set of hubs.

As expected, parallelism increases with the number of LPs (see fig. 4). However the amount of parallelism increases at only a modest rate. This is because the hub nodes become a bottleneck, limiting parallelism increases as more LPs are added. The parallelism increases more slowly for lower values of λ because these networks have more heavily loaded hub nodes. The higher the degree of the hubs nodes, the more events they receive and the longer it takes to process these events in a given epoch. Because the calculation of parallelism is determined by the longest epoch runtime (realized by the highest degree hub), there is less parallelism available in these networks. This suggests that the λ value of a scale-free network has significant implications on the amount of speedup that can be obtained.

5. SIMULATION RESULTS

We now describe the results of simulation experiments using the naïve and demand-driven CMB protocol to evaluate performance and overhead in simulating scale-free networks. A graph with an approximate power-law degree distribution of fixed λ was created via the Barabasi-Albert method implemented using a stochastic algorithm [4]. The experiments covered in this section were run on various sizes of scale-free networks. The simulated CMB algorithm begins by queuing simulated events with timestamp drawn from an exponential distribution. We assume that when each event is processed, a single new event is scheduled with timestamp increment drawn from an exponential distribution. We assume a finite, nonzero lookahead. A neighboring LP is then selected from a uniform distribution and the event is sent to that LP. This approach maintains a constant number of messages. A steady state behavior can be observed after an initial transient period. The number of null messages are counted as a measure of simulation overhead.

5.1 CMB Results

We calculate the parallelism for the CMB methods. Let e_{sim} be the number of simulation-relevant events–events that are not null messages–and e_{null} be the total number of null messages. Assume that each message, null or simulation-relevant, requires only 1 unit of wallclock time. The parallelism of the entire simulations can then be calculated as:

$$P = \frac{e_{sim}}{e_{sim} + e_{null}}$$

The following data were collected with experimental $\lambda = 2.5$. The top 25% of the most connected nodes were considered as the hubs. The mean null and event message counts were taken once the system reached steady state.

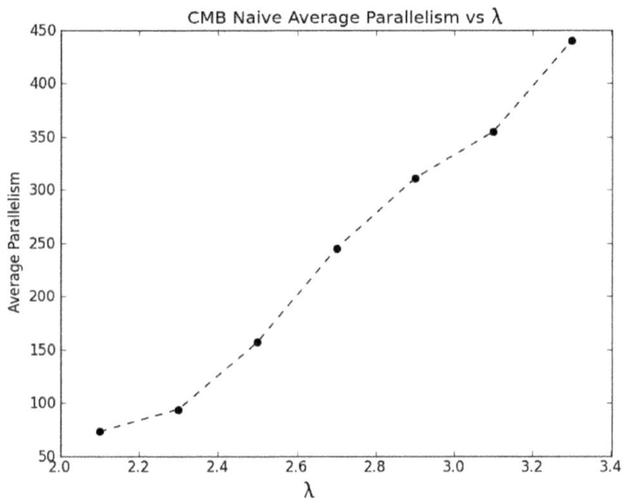

Figure 3: The average parallelism for the naïve CMB algorithm versus λ.

Experimental results for naïve CMB are presented in figure 3. The average parallelism as λ is varied is shown, and indicates that parallelism with asynchronous approaches is also driven by λ. The average parallelism for the naïve CMB algorithm increases as the value of λ increases. This agrees with the intuition that low values of λ cause a large amount of null message traffic to and from hub nodes.

The same experimental experimental conditions were used in the demand driven approach to assure experimental consistency. Even the parallelism of the CMB algorithm with the previously discussed optimizations is still susceptible to changes in λ; see figure 4. The demand driven CMB exhibited similar results to its naïve predecessor, albeit with significantly less overhead. Because this optimization reduces the amount of null message passing, it reduces the strain on the hubs when broadcasting null messages considerably; allowing for more parallelism than the naïve approach.

Figure 5 illustrates the number of null messages received by each distinct set of nodes. The hubs receive a constant factor more null messages than the leaves as the network size increases. Both asynchronous synchronization algorithms exhibited this behavior; again the demand driven CMB used fewer total null messages.

The mapping of LPs to processors in order to balance the workload is an important issue in any distributed simulation program. Given the rich get richer nature of heavy tailed degree distributions, the amount of work and number of messages going to hubs can be wildly disproportionate.

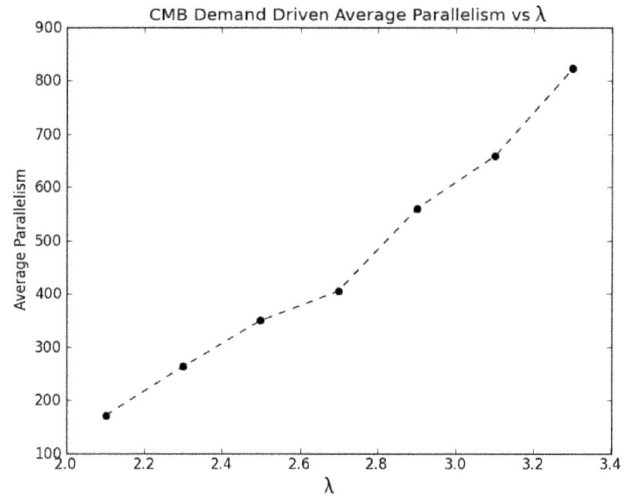

Figure 4: The average parallelism for the demand driven CMB algorithm versus λ.

5.2 Discussion

Both CMB parallelism experiments resulted in an increase in average parallelism as the value of λ increases. This is consistent with the observation that the heavy tails of scale-free networks lead to limited parallelism.

Both CMB experiments show an increasing number of overhead messages as the network grows. For the naïve case, we expect that the growth in null messages will scale superlinearly with the number of nodes. This growth arises from the naïve choice to broadcast the null messages to each neighbor. See figure 5.

This highlights potential issues regarding the scalability of these synchronization protocols for large scale-free networks. These experiments indicate that the difference in the load received and processed by LPs is a constant factor scaled by the size of the network and the particular λ value. The hubs become increasingly more severe bottlenecks as the size of the topology is increased. As both CMB experiments require a stochastically generated network sampled from a power-law degree distribution, they are less reliant on the edge-wealth relation and therefore more resilient to perturbations in λ.

6. CONCLUSIONS AND FUTURE WORK

Both the analytical model and simulation experiments highlight the highly unbalanced nature of parallel simulations of scale-free networks. The analytical model shows that hub nodes quickly become severe bottlenecks in parallel simulations. The exponent of the power-law distribution, λ plays an important role in determining the severity of the resulting hub node bottleneck. As λ decreases toward 1, the tail of the degree distribution becomes heavier, increasing the magnitude of the bottleneck. This results in the degree of the largest hub growing extremely quickly as network size is increased, especially when λ is near 2 or smaller. Our analytic model as well as the empirical simulation results

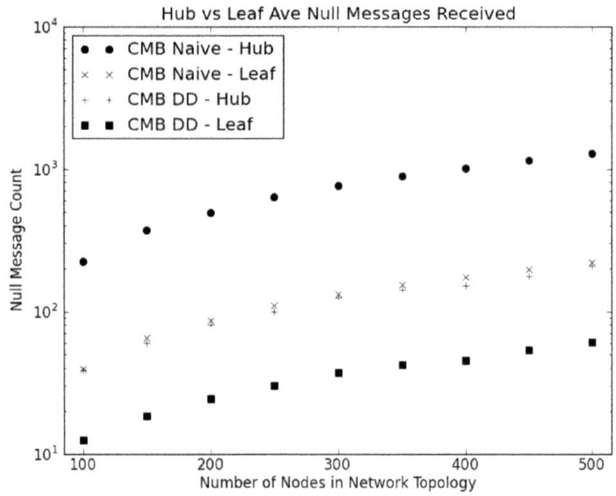

Figure 5: The overhead for both CMB approaches broken down by hub and leaf nodes.

showed that the value of λ has a strong influence on parallelism, and the potential speedup that may be obtained.

Networks with power law degree distribution appear in many natural and human-made systems. These studies illustrate that achieving efficient parallel execution of simulations of scale-free networks is a challenging task. There are many avenues of future research. The analytic models described here require further refinement and generalization for different classes of workload models. There are two important extensions to the analytical model; the first in the distribution of events across the LP's and the second to investigate the potential costs of LP-LP link delays. The impact of non-uniform event distributions across the LPs have not been deeply investigated and will help generalize the results to more realistic systems. The second extension to the model will allow us to model realistic synchronous distributed simulations with higher granularity by controlling the link delay distribution.

Models of other synchronization protocols are needed, e.g., other conservative protocols and optimistic synchronization mechanisms. More extensive experiments with real-world applications are needed to verify the observations reported in this paper appear in practice. Because scale-free and approximately power-law distributions appear in many important natural systems, a key facet of the future work will be spent examining distributed simulations running scale-free models.

Finally, many challenges exist to achieve efficient parallel simulation of large, scale-free networks. Additional research is required to identify effective synchronization methods for scale-free network simulations. Effective means to addressing the bottleneck issues of scale-free networks are needed. Scale-free networks have the potential to reveal interesting behaviors in complex systems. More real world data are needed relating the performance of new systems to their underlying topology.

7. REFERENCES

[1] I. F. Akyildiz, L. Chen, S. R. Das, R. M. Fujimoto, and R. Serfozo. The effect of memory capacity on time warp performance. *International Journal of Parallel and Distributed Computing*, 18(4):411–422, August 1993.

[2] B. C. Arnold. Pareto and generalized pareto distributions. 5:119–145, 2008.

[3] R. Ayani. *A Parallel Simulation Scheme Based on Distances Between Objects.* Technical report (Kungl. Tekniska högskolan. Dept. of Telecommunication Systems-Computer Systems). Royal Institute of Technology, Department of Telecommunication Systems-Computer Systems, 1988.

[4] A. L. Barabasi and R. Albert. Emergence of scaling in random networks. *Science (New York, N.Y.)*, 286:509–512, Oct. 1999.

[5] D. Bauer, G. Yaun, C. Carothers, M. Yuksel, and S. Kalyanaraman. Ross.net: optimistic parallel simulation framework for large-scale internet models. In *Simulation Conference, 2003. Proceedings of the 2003 Winter*, volume 1, pages 703 – 711 Vol.1, dec. 2003.

[6] K. Chandy and J. Misra. Distributed simulation: A case study in design and verification of distributed programs. *Software Engineering, IEEE Transactions on*, (5):440 – 452, sept. 1979.

[7] A. Clauset, C. R. Shalizi, and M. E. J. Newman. Power-law distributions in empirical data. *SIAM Rev.*, 51(4):661–703, Nov. 2009.

[8] R. Cohen and S. Havlin. Scale-free networks are ultrasmall. *Phys. Rev. Lett.*, 90, 2003.

[9] G. D'Angelo and S. Ferretti. Simulation of scale-free networks. In *Proceedings of the 2nd International Conference on Simulation Tools and Techniques*, Simutools '09, pages 20:1–20:10, ICST, Brussels, Belgium, Belgium, 2009. ICST (Institute for Computer Sciences, Social-Informatics and Telecommunications Engineering).

[10] P. M. Dickens, D. M. Nicol, P. F. Reynolds, Jr., and J. M. Duva. Analysis of bounded time warp and comparison with yawns. *ACM Trans. Model. Comput. Simul.*, 6(4):297–320, Oct. 1996.

[11] M. Faloutsos, P. Faloutsos, and C. Faloutsos. On power-law relationships of the internet topology. *SIGCOMM Comput. Commun. Rev.*, 29(4):251–262, Aug. 1999.

[12] R. M. Fujimoto. Parallel discrete event simulation. *Commun. ACM*, 33(10):30–53, Oct. 1990.

[13] R. Govindan and H. Tangmunarunkit. Heuristics for internet map discovery, 2000.

[14] A. Gupta, I. F. Akyildiz, and R. M. Fujimoto. Performance analysis of time warp with multiple homogeneous processors. *IEEE Trans. Softw. Eng.*, 17(10):1013–1027, Oct. 1991.

[15] D. Jefferson and H. Sowizral. Fast concurrent simulation using the time warp mechanism. 1982.

[16] H. Kitano. Systems biology: A brief overview. *Science*, 295(5560):1662–1664, 2002.

[17] D. Kumar. Simulating feedforward systems using a network of processors. In *Proceedings of the 19th annual symposium on Simulation*, ANSS '86, pages 127–144, Los Alamitos, CA, USA, 1986. IEEE Computer Society Press.

[18] Y.-B. Lin. Parallelism analyzers for parallel discrete event simulation. *ACM Trans. Model. Comput. Simul.*, 2(3):239–264, July 1992.

[19] X. Liu and A. A. Chien. Realistic large-scale online network simulation, 2004.

[20] B. D. Lubachevsky. Efficient distributed event-driven simulations of multiple-loop networks. *Commun. ACM*, 32(1):111–123, Jan. 1989.

[21] M. E. J. Newman. Power laws, pareto distributions and zipf's law. *Contemporary Physics*, pages 323–351, 2005.

[22] D. M. Nicol. The cost of conservative synchronization in parallel discrete event simulations. *J. ACM*, 40(2):304–333, Apr. 1993.

[23] D. Rao and A. Chernyakhovsky. Parallel simulation of the global epidemiology of avian influenza. In *Simulation Conference, 2008. WSC 2008. Winter*, pages 1583 –1591, dec. 2008.

[24] G. F. Riley, M. H. Ammar, R. M. Fujimoto, A. Park, K. Perumalla, and D. Xu. A federated approach to distributed network simulation. *ACM Trans. Model. Comput. Simul.*, 14(2):116–148, Apr. 2004.

[25] G. Siganos, M. Faloutsos, P. Faloutsos, and C. Faloutsos. Power laws and the as-level internet topology. *IEEE/ACM Transactions on Networking*, 11(4):514–524, 2003.

[26] W. Small and J. D. Singer. Resort to arms: International and civil wars, 1816-1980. *Notices of the American Mathematical Society*, 1982.

[27] K. Soramaki, M. L. Bech, J. Arnold, R. J. Glass, and W. E. Beyeler. The topology of interbank payment flows. *Physica A: Statistical Mechanics and its Applications*, 379(1):317 – 333, 2007.

[28] W. Su and C. L. Seitz. Variants of the chandy-misra-bryant distributed discrete-event simulation algorithm. Technical report, Pasadena, CA, USA, 1988.

[29] S. Thulasidasan and S. Eidenbenz. Accelerating traffic microsimulations: A parallel discrete-event queue-based approach for speed and scale. In *Simulation Conference (WSC), Proceedings of the 2009 Winter*, pages 2457 –2466, dec. 2009.

[30] X. F. Wang and G. Chen. Complex networks: small-world, scale-free and beyond. *Circuits and Systems Magazine, IEEE*, 3(1):6 – 20, 2003.

[31] F. Wieland. Practical parallel simulation applied to aviation modeling. In *Proceedings of the fifteenth workshop on Parallel and distributed simulation*, PADS '01, pages 109–116, Washington, DC, USA, 2001. IEEE Computer Society.

[32] W. Willinger, D. Alderson, and J. C. Doyle. Mathematics and the internet: A source of enormous confusion and great potential, 2009.

[33] L. Zhang, X. Deng, J. Yu, and X. Wu. The degree and connectivity of internet's scale-free topology. *CoRR*, abs/1101.4285, 2011.

Approximate Parallel Simulation of Web Search Engines

Mauricio Marin[1,2] Veronica Gil-Costa[1,3] Carolina Bonacic[2] Roberto Solar[1]

[1]Yahoo! Labs Santiago, Chile
[2]DIINF, University of Santiago, Chile
[3]CONICET, University of San Luis, Argentina

ABSTRACT

Large scale Web search engines are complex and highly optimized systems devised to operate on dedicated clusters of processors. Any, even a small, gain in performance is beneficial to economical operation given the large amount of hardware resources deployed in the respective data centers. Performance is fully dependent on users behavior which is featured by unpredictable and drastic variations in trending topics and arrival rate intensity. In this context, discrete-event simulation is a powerful tool either to predict performance of new optimizations introduced in search engine components or to evaluate different scenarios under which alternative component configurations are able to process demanding workloads. These simulators must be fast, memory efficient and parallel to cope with the execution of millions of events in small running time on few processors. In this paper we propose achieving this objective at the expense of performing approximate parallel simulation.

Categories and Subject Descriptors

I.6 [**SIMULATION AND MODELING**]: General

General Terms

Algorithms, Design, Performance

Keywords

Discrete Event Simulation, Parallel Computation.

1. INTRODUCTION

Web search engines are usually built as a collection of services hosted in large clusters of processors wherein each service is deployed on a set of processors. Services are software components executing operations such as (a) calculation of the top-k documents that best match an user query; (b) routing queries to the appropriate services and blending of results coming from them; (c) construction of the result Web page for queries; (d) advertising related to query terms; (e) query suggestions, among many other operations. Services are assembled to meet specific application requirements. For instance, the design of a vertical search engine dedicated to retrieve advertisement pertinent to user queries is quite different from the design of a search engine dedicated to retrieve Web documents relevant to user queries. Consequently, the realization of each service may involve the use of different algorithms and data structures devised to support efficient query processing. Discrete-event simulation is a suitable tool for assisting the development cycles associated with the algorithm engineering required to achieve efficient and scalable search engines [10].

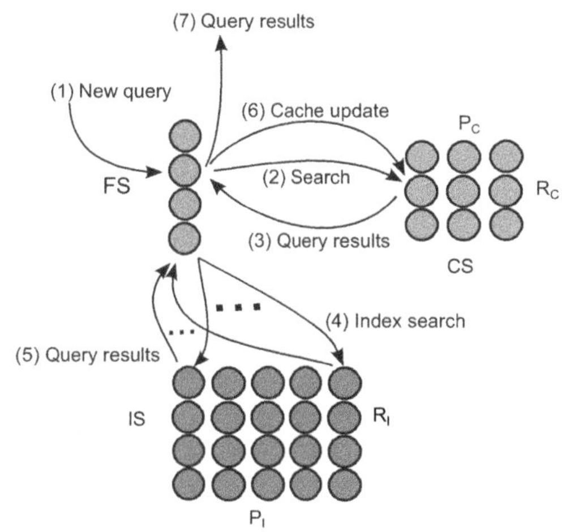

Figure 1: A typical query processing scheme

Figure 1 shows an example of an organization of services for a vertical search engine [1, 12]. The Front-end Service (FS) is composed of several nodes where each node is hosted by a dedicated cluster processor. Each FS node receives user queries and sends back the top-k results for each query to the users. After a query arrives to a FS node, it selects a caching service (CS) node. These nodes keep the top-k results for frequent queries previously issued by users so that response time for these queries is made very small. The query-results set for this service is kept partitioned into P_C disjoint subsets and each partition is replicated R_C times to increase query throughput. A simple LRU strategy can be used [12] to implement the CS nodes. A hash function on the query terms is used to select a CS partition whereas a respective replica (i.e., a CS node allocated in a cluster processor) can be selected in a round-robin manner.

SIGSIM-PADS'13, May 19-22, 2013, Montréal, Québec, Canada.

If the query is not cached, it is sent to the index service (IS) cluster. The IS contains a distributed index built from the document collection held by the search engine (e.g. HTML documents from a big sample of the Web). This index is used to speed up the determination of what documents contain the query terms and calculate scores for them. The k documents with the highest scores are selected as the query answer. The index and respective document collection is partitioned into P_I partitions and each partition is kept replicated R_I times to enable high query throughput. Partitions help to reduce response time for individual queries since time is proportional to the number of documents that contains the query terms. Queries are sent to all partitions and the results are merged to obtain the global top-k results.

Figure 1 also shows an overall description of the message traffic among processors in a cluster of computers. These messages must pass through a number of communication switches to reach their destinations. Switches are usually organized in a fat-tree topology. On the other hand, each processor is expected to be a multi-core cluster node capable of concurrently executing a number of threads. Thus search engine service nodes are multithreaded components where it is necessary to take into consideration the effects in performance of concurrency control strategies.

The above description sets the level of detail at which simulators can be constructed to predict performance. We refer to simulators representing a good compromise between precision of performance metrics as compared against the ones obtained with the actual implementation of search engine components, and efficient running time of simulations.

Practice and experience tell us that such simulators can be achieved by considering the following guidelines:

- Include user behavior by feeding simulators with queries submitted by actual users from search engines. This implies executing large query logs with millions of queries containing different query arrival rates and topic trends expressed in the query terms.

- Hide complexities of simulating data center hardware by using models of parallel computation devised to represent key features of hardware cost. The model drives the construction of benchmark programs used to measure costs on the actual hardware.

- Determine the cost of relevant query processing operations by executing benchmark programs on actual samples of the Web. Typically there are available unithread implementations of query processing methods, or it is fairly simple to prototype them, and the aim is to study performance of very large systems.

- Organize the simulation of individual queries as directed graphs where arcs indicate the order in which query operations take place and vertices represent the cost of executing these operations on the hardware resources (threads, processors, shared memory and communication layer). Each operation competes for using the resources with co-resident queries.

In this paper we present two use cases of the above guidelines and propose their respective approximate parallelizations. The first one applies process oriented simulation to model query processing at multi-core architecture level where it is relevant to study how to efficiently organize threads in index service nodes supporting real time search. The second one applies event driven simulation of timed colored Petri nets to model the system described in Figure 1. These techniques, as applied following the guidelines we suggest above, are capable of predicting quite well performance of real search engines (error is less than 10%).

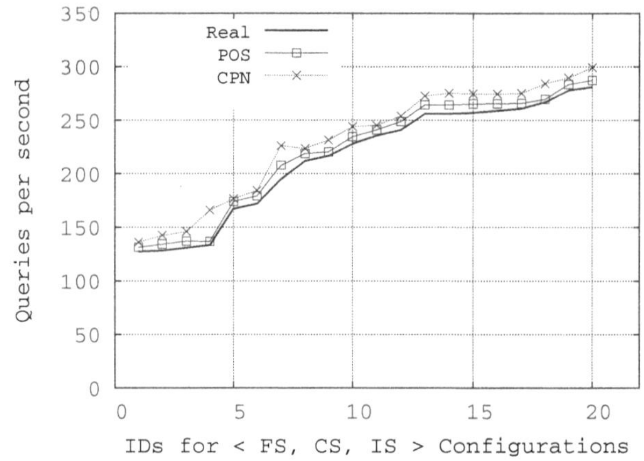

Figure 2: Simulation versus real implementations

For instance, Figure 2 shows results from sequential simulations of the system described in Figure 1. The curves labeled POS and CPN stand for process-oriented simulation and timed colored Petri nets respectively. The curve labeled "Real" shows results from an actual implementation of the same system. The figure shows query throughput results for different configurations given by specific values for the number of replicas of the FS, and the number of partitions and replicas of the CS and IS. In total, these configurations range from 115 to 240 processors. Overall, the results clearly indicate that simulations are able to predict performance trend of the service configurations. POS achieves better precision than CPN as it simulates the fat-tree communication infrastructure whereas CPN models it stochastically. However, a typical POS execution takes more than 4 hours to complete whereas running times for CPN are of the order of 15 minutes. Even for stochastic modelling of communication, we observed that POS running times are much larger than CPN running times since POS must cope with costly elements such as co-routine management.

Our parallelization proposal for the POS and CPN sequential simulators is generic and follows a standard late 90's trend for distributed discrete event simulation. Computations are organized in a bulk synchronous manner and there exists a rule to prevent processors from going too far into the simulation future without considering the state of event causality related processors. Ours are like optimistic distributed simulations where no rollback mechanism is employed and thereby they approximate sequential simulations of the same systems. Simulation objects are expected to be uniformly distributed at random on the processors.

In this paper we suggest that, given the nature of our application, a properly restrained bulk synchronous parallel simulation is capable of efficiently producing statistical results which are very similar to the results produced by a respective sequential simulation. We illustrate this point for process oriented and event driven simulation by means of our two use cases. We propose specific methods to parallelize the respective sequential simulators.

2. BACKGROUND AND RELATED WORK

Sequential discrete-event simulation techniques for performance evaluation studies in Web search engines and related systems are being applied by the information retrieval research community (c.f. [10]). To our knowledge, parallelization of these simulators have not been mentioned in the technical literature. Note that parallel simulators can be used not only in the context of research and development but also rutinarely in production systems operating as auxiliary components for search engines. An use case is as a capacity planning tool for data centers where engineers must periodically determine the amount of hardware resources assigned to search engine services in accordance with the observed query traffic. A challenging use case in terms of running time is as an automatic control support component in which the effects of user driven events in overall performance are simulated in real-time in order to tune the operation of the actual search engine.

Efficient strategies for parallel discrete-event simulation (PDES) have been widely studied in the late 90's and early 2000's literature [11, 25]. This topic has deserved recent attention in the context of clusters of multi-core processors [19, 15]. The work in [20] proposes a multi-grained parallelism technique based on the discrete Event System Specification (DEVS) methodology. The work in [6] presented a global schedule mechanism approach for improving the effectiveness based on a distributed event queue. In [8] the authors presented a distributed approach based on the migration of simulated entities. The work presented in [29] evaluated symmetric optimistic simulation kernels for a multi-core cluster which allows dynamic reassignment of cores to kernel instances.

In PDES, parallelism is introduced by partitioning the system into a set of concurrent simulation objects called logical processes (LPs). Events take place within LPs, their effect is the change of LP states, and LPs may schedule the occurrence of events in other LPs by sending event messages to them. Once the LPs are placed onto the processors, one is faced with the non-trivial problem of synchronizing the occurrence of events that take place in parallel so that the final outcome is equivalent to that of a sequential simulation of the same events. The Time Warp (TW) strategy [11] solves this problem by optimistically processing the occurrence of events as soon as they are available at the LPs and locally re-executing events whenever the simulation of earlier events is missed in one or more LPs.

In TW, the simulation time may advance at differing time intervals in each LP. Whenever a LP receives a "straggler" message carrying an event e with timestamp in the "past", the LP is "rolled back" into the state just before the occurrence of e and the simulation of the LP is resumed from this point onwards. That is, all the events with timestamps later than e's timestamp are re-simulated. The LPs save periodically their states to support roll-backs. In addition, any change propagated to other LPs as a result of processing erroneous events is corrected with similar roll-back method. To this end, special (anti-)messages are sent to the affected LPs in order to notify them of the previous sending of erroneous messages. During simulation, a quantity called global virtual time (GVT) is calculated periodically. Its value is such that no LP can be rolled-back earlier than it, and thereby the processed events and anti-messages with timestamps less than GVT are discarded to release memory. GVT steadily advances forward regardless the amount of roll-backs. When the rate of roll-backs is kept small, performance becomes very efficient.

In contrast, to achieve competitive performance, conservative synchronization [3] requires developers to enhance model definition with additional constructs such as lower bounds on the time the effects of events are propagated across the model. Instead, optimistic simulation makes it transparent for the developer to execute the simulation model either in parallel or sequentially. Another important advantage of optimistic simulation is that it does not impose any restriction on the communication topology among the simulation objects. That is, model developers are not required to be aware of parallelization details.

There are also recent works on parallel simulation of Petri nets models. A parallel simulator tailored to GPUs is presented in [13]. The work in [17] presents a strategy for distributed timed colored Petri net simulation. This scheme introduces a logical time and a priority vector to decide the exact ordering of all incoming and local events in an atomic unit of time.

A timed colored Petri Net (CPN) [16] is a high-level formalism that provides primitives to model latency, concurrency and synchronization of complex systems. It introduces the notion of token types (colors) which may be arbitrary data values. CPNs are represented as directed graphs with nodes containing places and transitions, and connecting arcs to indicate how tokens may flow through places and transitions. Places are graphically represented as ovals and transitions as rectangles. A place may have an initial set of tokens (initial marking). Arcs may contain expressions on token types/values used to indicate the condition by which one or more tokens may move from one transition to one place, and viceversa. Tokens passing through transition nodes may suffer time delays. There can also be expressions signaling tokens movement from several places (transitions) to several transitions (places). An expression is evaluated to true when all input places contain the required tokens.

Parallelization of process-oriented simulators has been considered in the literature as an involved task. Work in this topic has been presented in [21]. In our case, parallelization is simplified as we do not consider the execution of rollbacks to correct erroneous computations.

3. PARALLELIZATION METHOD

We use a bulk-synchronous multi-threading and message-passing strategy to automatically conduct simulation time advance. The practical implementation of these ideas comes from combining open-source software such as MPI [31], OpenMP [32], BSPonMPI [30], and LibCppSim [24] operating on top of the `C++` programming language.

To explain the parallelization method we resort to BSP parlance [28]. In BSP the computation is organized as a sequence of *supersteps*. During a superstep, the processors (master threads) may perform computations on local data and/or send messages to other processors. The messages are available for processing at their destinations by the next superstep, and each superstep is ended with the barrier synchronization of the processors. The underlying communication library ensures that all messages are available at their destinations before starting the next superstep.

We assume a cluster of P processors where each processor contains T threads so that simulation objects are evenly distributed on the $T \times P$ threads. Each thread has its own instance of a sequential simulation kernel (e.g., LibCppSim for process-oriented simulation) which includes a local event list and functions related to event processing and message handling. In each processor there is one master thread that synchronizes with all other $P-1$ master threads to execute the BSP supersteps and exchange messages. In each processor and superstep, the remaining $T-1$ threads synchronize with the master thread to start the next superstep, though they may immediately exchange messages during the current superstep as they share the same processor main memory.

As it is well-known, processing events in parallel during periods of time where no messages from other processors are received can lead to the problem of missing the arrival of event messages at the right simulation time. We simply ignore such situations though (when possible) proper care is taken to correct measures such as response time of individual queries. The challenge is to limit the extent in simulation time of these straggler messages [11] by making no assumptions on the event time increments and communication topology among the simulation objects run by the $T \times P$ sequential kernels. We achieve this by means of a windowing strategy.

3.1 Sliding time window strategy

In each superstep the simulation time is advanced W units of time. A new value for W is obtained every n supersteps to follow variations in the evolution of the simulation model. The method extends ideas from [22]. Each processor stores tuples (t, s, d) for each message sent to other processor, where t is the occurrence time of the event, s is the source processor and d is the destination processor. At the end of the n-est superstep, all processors send their arrays of tuples (t, s, d) to one master processor. The master contains an array C holding P supersteps counters initialized to zero and an event list that is initialized with the incoming tuples (t, s, d). This allows the master to determine the minimum number of supersteps S required to process the (t, s, d) tuples. To this end, the master processor extracts them from event list in chronological order and for each tuple (t, s, d) it sets $C[d] = \max\{C[s]+1, C[d]\}$ where $s \neq d$. Once all tuples have been extracted, the total number of supersteps S is the maximum value in the array C. Therefore, if Δ is the total simulation time increment from the first to the last (t, s, d) tuple, the window W is defined by $W = \Delta/S$.

In each superstep, all threads process events with time less than or equal to B and the time barrier B is increased by $B = B + W$ in the next superstep, and so on. The global virtual time (GVT) of the distributed simulation is defined as the event with the least time across all threads [11]. This value is calculated at the end of any superstep after all messages have been delivered and inserted in their respective kernel event lists. Thus assuming that a new value of GVT is produced every n_g supersteps, the time barrier B is periodically re-initialized to $B = \text{GVT} + (n_g + 1) \cdot W$.

3.2 Self-increment of supersteps

The above windowing scheme may be prone to pathological cases in which the minimum number of supersteps S actually degenerates event processing into something similar to a sequential simulation. For instance, assume a two processor system where in one processor we place simulation objects that only send messages to be consumed by simulation objects located in the second processor. In this case, the values of S calculated by the master processor is just 2 and the simulation becomes sequential. Namely, in the first superstep, processor 1 generates all messages, and in the second superstep, processor 2 causes the occurrence of all events caused by those messages whilst processor 1 performs no event processing. Patterns similar to this could randomly take place in a very large simulation model during unpredictable periods of simulation time.

To solve this problem, during the chronological processing of tuples (t, s, d) we impose an upper limit to the number of tuples processed in each superstep and processor. This forces the self-increment of the superstep counters $C[s]$ for processors that have not received messages during a long period of simulation time. We define a processor global event list as the union of the event lists of all threads co-located in the same processor. We use the average size L_E of the global event list maintained in each processor to assume that in each superstep, each processor should consume no more than one of its respective global event list. The time elapsed in the consumption of these events indicates the average size of an auxiliary sliding time window W_2. This window is used to force the self-increment of the counters $C[s]$ when required in the master processor and it can be calculated locally in each processor. In particular, for a processor s that has simulated $N_E[s]$ events in the period of n supersteps, the value of its window $W_2[s]$ can be calculated as $W_2[s] = f \cdot (\Delta/N_E[s]) \cdot L_E[s]$ where $f \geq 1$ is a slackness factor like 1.3. The window $W_2[s]$ along with tuples (t, s, d) is sent to the master processor.

The average value of L_E observed during the n supersteps is calculated as in [26], that is, it is efficiently calculated by modelling the problem as a G/G/∞ queuing system. In this case the average number of active servers is L_E, which is defined as the ratio of the arrival rate of events λ to the service rate of events μ, namely $L_E = \lambda/\mu$. At steady state, for n large enough, N_E events are inserted in and N_E events are extracted from the event list. Thus the arrival rate is given by $\lambda = N_E/\Delta$. In addition, in this model, each event e_i requires a "service time" δ_i that is given by $\delta_i = t_a - t_b$, where t_b is the simulation clock at the time in which e_i is inserted in the event list, and t_a is the simulation time at which the event is scheduled to take place. Thus the average service rate μ is given by $\mu = N_E / \sum_{i=1}^{N_E} \delta_i$, and thereby $L_E = \sum_{i=1}^{N_E} \delta_i/\Delta$. The simulation kernels calculate these statistics as they process events during the n supersteps.

4. USE CASE 1: APPLICATION FOR PROCESS ORIENTED SIMULATION

The index services of current search engines are expected to be designed to accept concurrent updates to support real time search. The objective is to include in the query results Web documents published in the very recent past. This leads to the problem of efficiently organizing multi-threading so that read and write conflicts are prevented from happening as query processing (read only transactions) and index updates (write only transactions) take place concurrently in each multi-core processor. A number of concurrency control strategies can be borrowed from the OS and DB literature, and the problem is to determine which of them are more efficient and scalable in the search engine domain [2].

Web search engines use inverted indexes to determine the top-k results for queries. The index is composed of a vocabulary table and a set of inverted or posting lists. The vocabulary contains the set of relevant terms found in the text collection. Each of these terms is associated with an inverted list which contains the document identifiers where the term appears in the collection along with the term frequency in the document. Frequencies are used to calculate document scores. To solve a query, it is necessary to get from the inverted lists the set of documents associated with the query terms and then to perform a ranking of these documents based on their score values. Updates in the index take place when a new document is stored in the respective processor. This implies modifying the posting lists associated with the terms present in the new document.

People tend to favor reduced subsets of terms both in queries and documents, which means that some terms are much more popular than others in the inverted index. This has the potential of causing R/W conflicts among running threads in search engines serving workloads of hundred thousand queries per second.

To illustrate modelling and simulation of this use case we focus on a simple concurrency control strategy. There exists a processor input queue that contains the arriving read and write transactions, and any thread requesting a transaction (1) locks the queue, (2) removes the transaction, (3) requests locks for all terms involved in the transaction, (4) when all locks are granted it releases the lock on the input queue, (5) then it safely starts processing the transaction, and (6) once processing is completed, it releases all locks.

The simulation model uses a processes and resources approach. Processes represent threads in charge of transaction processing. Resources are artifacts such as inverted lists and global variables like exclusive access locks. The simulation program is implemented using LibCppSim [24], where each process is implemented by a co-routine that can be blocked and unblocked at will during simulation. The operations *passivate()* and *activate()* are used for this purpose. Co-routines execute the relevant operations of threads/transactions. The operation *hold(t)* blocks the co-routine during t units of simulation time. This is used to simulate the different costs of transactions and the cost of the different tasks performed by the simulated multi-core processor. The dominant costs come from operations related to ranking of documents, intersection of inverted lists and update of inverted lists. These costs are determined by benchmark programs implementing the same operations. Figure 3 illustrates the main ideas where we placed the *rank()* operation to emphasize that these simulations can also be driven by the outcome of the actual process being simulated.

To include the effects of the processor architecture in performance we use the Multi-BSP model of parallel computation [27] proposed recently for multi-core processors. Using process oriented simulation we extend the model with processor caches and special lock variables. The processor cache entries (cache lines) are managed with the LRU replacement policy, where each entry is a memory block of 64 bytes like Intel processors, and we use a directory based coherence protocol for cache entries.

In the Multi-BSP model a multi-core processor is seen as a hierarchy of memories (caches and main memory) that form a tree with root being the main memory and leaves being pairs (core, cache L1). To simply description let us assume

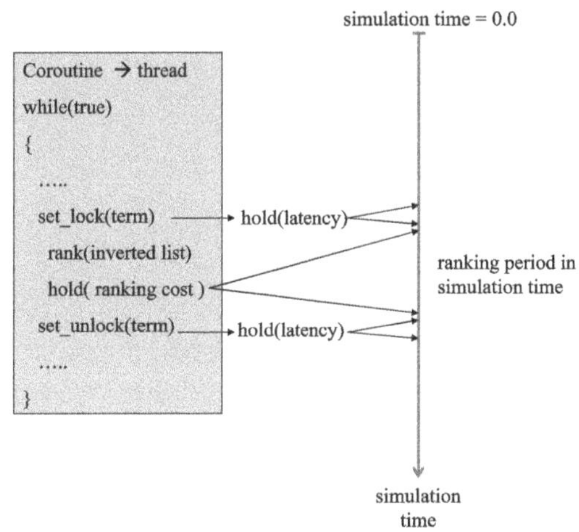

Figure 3: Concurrent routines simulating the steps taken by a thread to process a query (read-only transaction) and generating cost in simulation time.

a processor composed of eight cores, where four pairs (core, L1 cache) are connected to a single L2 cache, and two L2 caches are connected to the main memory. Cores (CPUs) can only work on local data stored in their respective L1 caches. When a core references data out of its L1 cache, the data is look at the respective cache L2. If found, a cache line transfer (or several lines if data pre-fetching is enabled) is performed between caches L2 and L1. The cost of this transfer is given by a parameter g_1. If not found, a cache line sized piece of the data is transfered from main memory to cache L2 at cost g_2, and then from L2 to L1 at cost g_1.

Computations in Multi-BSP are organized as sequences of three supersteps where each superstep is ended with a synchronization barrier. During the first superstep, all data transfers take place between main memory and the two L2 caches. During the second superstep, all data transfers take place between the L2 and L1 caches. During the third superstep, all cores are allowed to perform computations on the data stored in their respective L1 caches. Certainly this bulk-synchronous structure of computations is intended to make mathematically tractable the analysis of algorithms. We do not require this structure but it helps during (1) simulation program debugging, (2) benchmark program construction to measure g_1 and g_2, and (3) understanding performance. Process oriented simulation enables us to simulate these actions asynchronously. In addition, the LRU policy and the read/write coherence protocol on caches provide a more realistic setting to our processor model.

Lock variables are forced to be global by keeping them updated in main memory at all time. This accounts for its fairly larger ($g_1 + g_2$) cost than standard local and global program variables.

Figure 4 shows the steps followed during the simulation of a thread that executes a cost dominating transaction operation that takes `time_cpu` units of simulation time and works on a piece of data whose space address is given by `[base_address:offset_bytes]`. To this end, the respective simulator co-routine executes the function `run( time_cpu, base_address, offset_bytes )`. The cost of data transfers and computation performed by cores is simulated by calls to functions of the form `thread->causeCost*(...)`, which con-

```
Core::run(  double time_cpu,
            string base_address, int offset_bytes )
{
   int nblocks = offset_bytes / cache_block_size;
   time_cpu = time_cpu / nblocks;

   for( int i= 0; i < nblocks; i= i+1 )
   {
      sprintf(str,"%s %d", base_address.c_str(), i);
      if ( cacheL1->hit( str ) == true )
      {
         cacheL1->update( str );
         thread->causeCost_CPU( time_cpu );
      }
      else
      if ( cacheL2->hit( str ) == true )
      {
         cacheL2->update( str );
         thread->causeCost_TransferL1L2( Latency_g1 );
         cacheL1->insert( str );
         thread->causeCost_CPU( time_cpu );
      }
      else
      {
         thread->causeCost_TransferL2Mem( Latency_g2 );
         cacheL2->insert( str );
         thread->causeCost_TransferL1L2( Latency_g1 );
         cacheL1->insert( str );
         thread->causeCost_CPU( time_cpu );
      }
   }
}
```

Figure 4: Simulating the execution of a cost dominating operation defined by *run(...)*, which is executed by a simulator co-routine.

tain corresponding hold(t) operations. Cache entries that get replaced by the LRU policy and have been modified by threads, are copied to the lower memory in the hierarchy (L1 $\rightarrow$ L2, L2 $\rightarrow$ main memory). The coherence protocol maintains track of cache entries that contain copies of the same data so that when a thread modifies an instance of a replicated data, the remaining copies are invalidated.

The implementation of exclusive locks associates a name string with a lock variable along with a queue for co-routines (threads) waiting to get access. Lock administration takes a latency $g_1 + g_2$ in simulation time, as they are always read and written in main memory.

4.1 Parallelization

The LibCppSim library ensures that the simulation kernel grants execution control to co-routines in a mode of one co-routine at a time. Co-routines are activated following the sequential occurrence of events in chronological order. The co-routines implement simulation object (called processes in LibCppSim) and we communicate each other through message passing. When an object x places a message in object z the object x can activate z if z has been passivated earlier in the simulation.

Assuming that every time a simulation object is executing code no other simulation object is allowed to execute code, then we define an auxiliary BSP simulation object (co-routine) to make it in charge of communicating and synchronizing with other LibCppSim instances running in other processors or even running in other cores of the same processor. Each LibCppSim instance is a separate Unix process and BSPonMPI enables them to communicate and synchronize each other in determined points of the simulation time.

To this end, we use the BSPonMPI library that provides primitives to send and receive messages among Unix processes deployed on different processors or cores, and it provides a primitive to barrier synchronize Unix processes so that after the synchronization point all messages are delivered at their destinations (i.e., there are no messages in transit after the synchronization point). The Unix processes can be executed on different physical processors by means of the MPI library. Thus the auxiliary BSP object running in each LibCppSim instance can execute the following steps:

```
void inner_body( void )
{
   while( time() <= END_SIM_TIME )
   {
      hold( Sim_Time_Window );

      Send all messages buffered during the period.

      bsp_sync();// synchronize all Unix processes.

      Receive all messages from Unix processes and
      place them in their destination objects.
   }
}
```

The value of `Sim_Time_Window` is periodically adjusted to fit with the automatic windowing scheme described in Section 3. A new superstep starts after the `bsp_sync()` operation finishes. This operation (1) waits for all Unix processes to reach a synchronization point, (2) causes the sending and reception of all messages, and (3) let each Unix process continue computations. In the BSP simulation object the associated co-routine retains control of the execution until the call to the next hold(t) operation.

The relevant part of the cost in running time comes from the execution of the operation run(...) presented in the Figure 4. This operation acts on a set of L1 and L2 cache objects, and simulation objects representing threads cause cost in the simulation time depending on the contents of these cache objects. Thus for object distribution, a straightforward approach is to store related simulation objects (threads and caches) in the same processor to exploit locality.

5. USE CASE 2: A FRAMEWORK FOR CPN EVENT DRIVEN SIMULATION

The parallelization strategy of the process oriented simulation application presented in the previous section was specific to the problem at hand. To this end, it was necessary to define (1) a BSP simulation object and related housekeeping for message passing, (2) a particular distribution of simulation objects among processors, and (3) a strategy for approximating the sequential simulation. In addition, no shared memory was exploited in each processor due to the single process design of LibCppSim. That is, cores in processors are treated as individual processors by placing LibCppSim Unix process on them by means of BSPonMPI and communication is through message passing.

In this section we present a framework to model and simulate general Web search engines using timed colored Petri nets. This illustrates the fact that the parallelization strategy proposed in Section 3 used in combination with the *key* based approach and framework described in this section enable to hide the complex details of parallelization to the user.

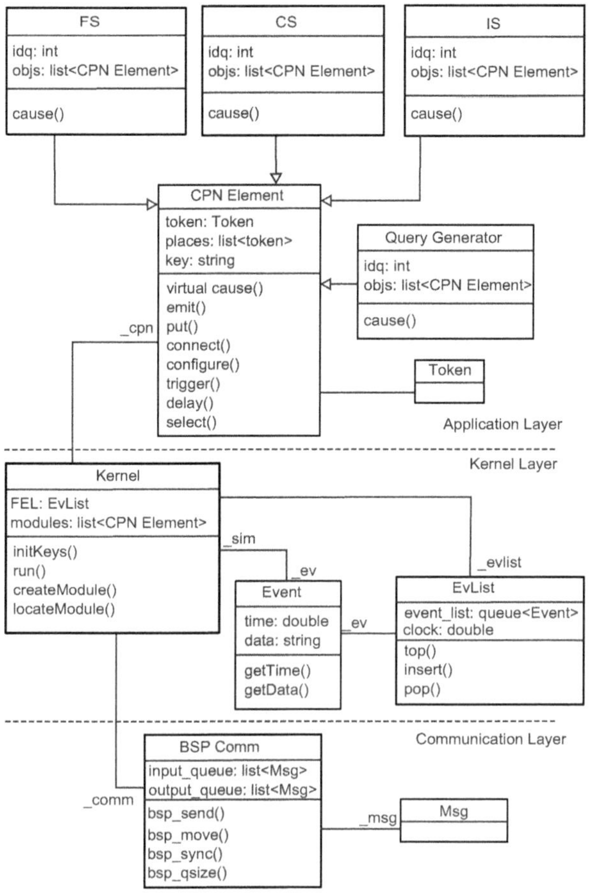

Figure 5: Abbreviated class diagram.

Figure 5 shows a class hierarchy for our software framework applied to the example of Figure 1.

The communication layer (at the bottom) uses the *BSP comm* class. Messages move Petri net tokens from one processor to the another so that tokens can be circulated through the distributed graph composed of transitions and places. The kernel layer defines the simulation kernel classes used to sequence events and administer simulation objects belonging to classes derived from the class *CPN element*. There is one simulation kernel per running thread, and one thread per processor core. One master thread per processor has access to the BSP communication layer and the remaining threads are barrier synchronized to wait for the start of the next superstep. During supersteps co-resident kernels may exchange tokens by using exclusive locks to prevent from R/W conflicts. We use OpenMP to administer the set of threads deployed in each processor.

The application layer consists of a set classes used to specify the user model. To this end, there is a *CPN Element* class with a set of pre-defined attributes and methods required to implement a timed colored Petri net (CPN) model. Figure 6 shows an example for a simple CPN Element named A. It is composed by one place P_0 and one transition T_0 with two out-links. This is specified by *configure("Places=1; Transitions=1; Ports=2")*. The *connect("Port=0; Place=0" ,A)* operation connects the first out-link of the transition T_0 to the place P_0. The function *connect()* is used to set connections between pairs of CPN elements. Namely, *connect()*

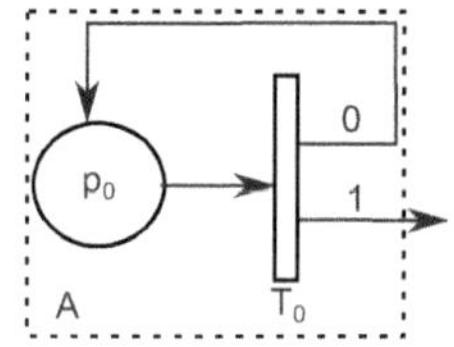


```
cpnElement *A= new cpnElement();
A->configure("Places=1;
             Transitions=1;
             Ports=2");
A->connect("Port=0;Place=1",A);

A->transition( Delay(),
               Trigger(),
               Select() );
```

Figure 6: CPN Element configuration code.

defines which out-link of transition i is connected to which in-link of a place j, so that tokens can flow from i to j. The C++ template binary functions *Trigger()*, *Delay()* and *Select()* are defined by the user to specify the behavior of the transition. In general, these functions perform the following: (1) *Trigger* determines if the corresponding transition must be fired, (2) *Delay* returns the duration of the transition in simulation time units, and (3) *Select* defines the out-link to be followed by a token after the transition delay has finished. The framework provides pre-defined version of these functions with standard behavior for CPN elements.

In general, the idea is that the user defines CPN modules which are composed of one or more objects of class *CPN Element*. Each simulation kernel simulates sequentially the occurrence of events in the CPN modules hosted by the kernel. The *cause()* operation is defined by the user to handle the events received and internally generated by the respective module. These events may indicate the arrival and departure of tokens. The user has to explicitly define the route followed by those tokens as shown in the C++ fragment code located in the bottom part of Figure 7. In this case, the *put()* operation is used to place the token in one of the CPN elements of the module whereas the *emit()* operation is used to send a token to another module. The destination module may be located in the same simulation kernel, or it may be located in a co-resident simulation kernel or located in a remote simulation kernel hosted by other processor.

To make CPN module location transparent to the user and also to enable scaling to a very large number of modules, we use a *key* based approach. Each CPN module is associated with an unique *key*. Any departing token must specify the module destination key. The concept is that the token is *emitted* to the "outside" of the module so that it is left to the kernel the responsibility of routing the token to the right destination module. Keys are strings and thereby char arrays can be defined to assign identifiers to modules in a flexible manner. Modules are automatically instantiated and deployed on processors by the simulation framework upon the emission of a new key during simulation.

The typical content of a *key* is a string like "class= *ClassName*; instance=*ID*", say "class= FrontService; replica=128", or a more convenient definition for a search engine such as "class= IndexService; partitionID=22; replicaID=133". The only requirement is to specify the class identification field to let the simulation framework instantiate the right object. The whole simulation is started by emitting one or more keys which identify the class names of the modules in charge of generating the initial tokens of the simulation. The simulation framework applies a hash function on the keys to decide in what processors and threads are the respective modules deployed and subsequently located.

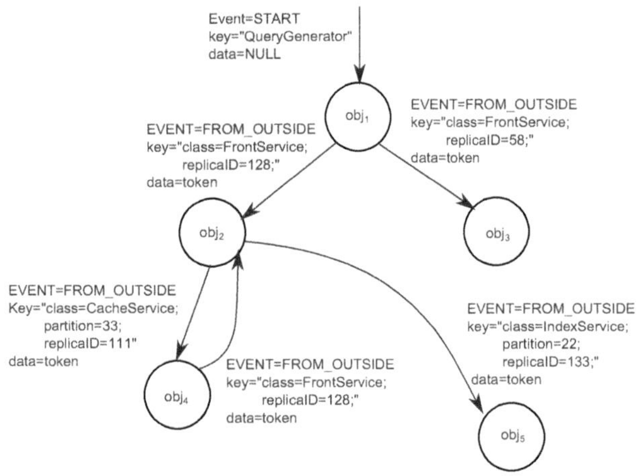


```
cause( Token token ) // token arrival
{
    switch( token->type() )
    {
      case FROM_OUTSIDE:
           A->put("Place=0",token);
           break;
      case FROM_INSIDE:
           emit(key,token); // token departure
           break;
    }
}
```

Figure 7: ***Key*** **based approach example.**

The upper part of Figure 7 shows an example where the initial key is generated with the *START* event which creates a *Query Generator* object. The other objects are created as soon as the query generator sends tokens to them. In the figure, obj_1 contains the query generator module, objects obj_2 and obj_3 are front-service modules, and obj_4 is a cache service node whereas obj_5 is an index service node. All these objects are expected to be complex CPN modules as they must also simulate the cost of executing service operations in the respective cluster processor. They stand for timed CPN models specifically designed to represent the cost of query processing in search engines as described in [7].

5.1 CPN modelling example

For lack of space we are not able to provide more details on CPN modelling. Nevertheless, to provide an idea of how a CPN module, with all its CPN element members, might look like, we present in Figure 8 a model of the multi-threading strategy presented in Section 4 for process oriented simulation. The diagram uses CPN tools notation [33]. For an index node operating on a processor with T threads, the input place in element A accepts arriving tokens representing read and write operations which we identify as tokens of type "RWtype". The place *Lock A* is used to lock the input queue so that a new RWtype token can be removed from the queue. Then, for each term i contained in the R/W operation, the *ContainTerm(i)* function triggers a copy of the token be stored in place PB_i of element B_i. The place *Lock B* in each element B_i is used to lock the associated posting list so that one token at a time is sent to the place PD_i of the succeeding element D_i. Thus for each term i, a pair (B_i, D_i) is involved in token displacement. In total there are n pairs (B_i, D_i), one per term i in the inverted index. Elements D_i represent either the cost of performing document ranking in

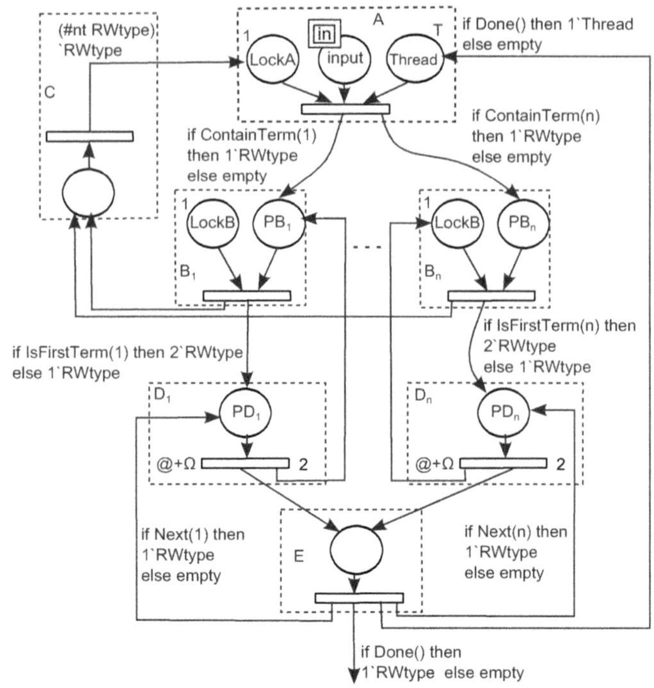

Figure 8: CPN module for an index service node.

the posting list (read operation), or the cost of updating the posting list (write operation). The service time required by these operations is denoted by $@+\Omega$.

Notice that the elements D_i must be visited sequentially and the lock on each element B_i must be released immediately after visiting each D_i. To this end, the transition in D_i is triggered with two tokens which occurs when either (1) the value i refers to the first term in the operation as determined by the *IsFirstTerm(i)* function or (2) the second token arrives from another D_j (through element E) that contains a term located just before term i in the R/W operation being solved. Element E is used to decide the next D_i to be visited as determined by the *Next(i)* function or to finish the token movements when the *Done()* function returns true.

Consider as an example a query operation with two terms 1 and 2. One token of type query enters into the place PD_2 of D_2 and two tokens of type query enter into the place PD_1 of D_1 which triggers the transition of D_1. After the first query term 1 has been processed by the pair of elements (B_1,D_1) a token of type query enters into the place of the element E. The next term to be visited is set to 2. Then, only the arc connecting element E with element D_2 is evaluated to true, and a second token of type query enters into the place PD_2 of D_2. This last action triggers the transition of D_2. After this, the token enters into the place of element E. Now the *Done()* function returns true and the token of type query is sent to the remitting FS processor.

At all time, at most T R/W operations may go beyond element A. This is solved with place *Thread* in A so that each time a RWtype token departs from element E, a token of type "Thread" is returned to place *Thread* in A. The variable *#nt* contains the number of terms in each R/W operation and element C is used to release the input queue when the current R/W operation has obtained all posting list locks for its terms.

6. EXPERIMENTS

We performed experiments with a log of 36,389,567 queries submitted to the AOL search service between March 1 and May 31, 2006. This query log exposes typical patterns present in user queries [1, 12]. We pre-processed the query log following the rules applied in [12]. The resulting query log has 16,900,873 queries, where 6,614,176 are unique queries and the vocabulary consists of 1,069,700 distinct query terms. We also used a sample (1.5TB) of the UK Web obtained in 2005 by the Yahoo! search engine, over which a 26,000,000 terms and 56,153,990 documents inverted index was constructed. We executed the queries against this index to get the cost of the query processing operations. The document ranking method used was WAND [4] (index service) and the cache policy used was LRU (caching service). All benchmarks were run with all data in main memory to avoid access to disk. Results were obtained on a cluster with 256 nodes composed of 32-cores AMD Opteron 2.1GHz Magny Cours processors with 16GB of main memory per node. Simulations are driven by query traces containing information such as query terms, ranking cost, and posting lists size.

We have conducted experiments with three different CPN models in order to test the behavior of our approximate parallel discrete-event simulation under different scenarios:

Log: This model describes a Web search engine composed of a set of front-end (FS) nodes, index service (IS) nodes and caching service (CS) nodes (6,047 nodes in total). Queries are injected in the FS nodes by using the above AOL query log. Queries are not actually stored in the caches of the CS service. Instead, each CS node uses a probabilistic function where 15% of queries processed are signaled as cache hits (i.e., they are found in the cache). The CPN models for FS and IS are described in Figure 9. The model for CS is similar to IS but with different cost for query processing operations. The model for the multi-threaded processor module is a simplified version of the model presented in Figure 8 since in this case it is not necessary to lock posting lists as all transactions are read only.

LogCache: This model is similar to the above Log model but it includes actual implementations of two levels of caches in the CS. The first level consists of a results cache which stores the most frequent queries with their top-k results. In the second level we include a location cache which stores the partition IDs of the index service capable of placing documents in the top-k results for frequent queries. The idea is that when a query is not found in the results cache, a second look-up is performed in the location cache to decide whether to send the query to all partitions of the IS or to a subset of them. The memory space used by location cache entries is less than 1% of the result cache entries. Frequent queries requiring a small number of partitions to be solved are good candidates to be kept in the location cache. The total number of cache entries in the results cache is adjusted to achieve a similar hit ratio than in the Log simulator (15%).

AsyncRW: This is the multi-threading model described in Figure 8. The model represents a single multi-core processor that must process read and write transactions given by user query and index update operations respectively. We simulate the CPN model described in Figure 8 and the process oriented simulation model described in Section 4. Read transactions are user queries whose answers must be calculated by reading all items of the posting lists associated with the query terms. Write operations insert new items in the posting lists. We perform experiments with 100,000 terms. That is, the model contains CPN elements $B_1 \dots B_n$ and $D_1 \dots D_n$ with $n = 100,000$ in Figure 8. It simulates $T = 128$ threads which means instantiate the model with 128 tokens in place *Thread* of the CPN element labeled A in Figure 8. No processor caches are considered in the CPN model. On the other hand, the process oriented model is also simulated for 128 threads and it contains the organization of processor caches L1 and L2 described in Section 4 (Figure 4).

6.1 Evaluation of Performance

Figure 10 shows how the window size W dynamically adapts it-self as the simulation time advances forward. With a larger number of processors the window size tends to be smaller since simulation objects are distributed in more processors and thereby message passing among them increases the minimum number of supersteps S required to process the (t, s, d) tuples (Subsection 3.1). However, the figure shows curves in which the number of processors P is doubled and the window size grows in a much smaller proportion. This is independent of the number of threads (simulation kernels) executed in each processor. The reason is that the minimum number of supersteps does not grow linearly with the number of processors. This is observed in Figure 11 for different number of processed events in the simulations. In these experiments the number of processed events ranges from one million to eight millions and the relative increase in S with P remains fairly stable. In general, the total number of real supersteps executed by the simulator is about 30% larger than the minimum number of supersteps required to simulate the same period of simulation time.

In Figure 12 we show results for the percentage of events that should be re-simulated if our parallelization strategy were implemented with a roll-back mechanism. In some cases the fraction of events that must be re-simulated reaches 30%, though it could be reduced by reducing the size of the window W. As expected this is correlated with the number of simulation objects hit by queries. In the case of the Log simulator after each cache miss the respective query is sent to all index service partitions whereas in the LogCache simulator the number of partitions is reduced due to use of the location cache. Thus in the LogCache simulator less simulation objects are hit by queries than in the Log simulator.

In Figure 13 we show speed-up results for the CPN models of the search engine described in Figure 1. The results show some advantage of performing asynchronous multithreading in each processor during supersteps. For instance, the speed-up for (P=1, T= 32) is better than for (P=8, T= 4) where P is the number of processors and T the number of running threads in each processor.

In Figure 14 we show speed-up results for the AsyncRW model simulated using the CPN model described in Figure 8 and the process-oriented (PO) model described in Section 4. The results show that PO simulations scale up better than CPN simulations. However, PO simulations are much more demanding in running time than CPN simulations. Granu-

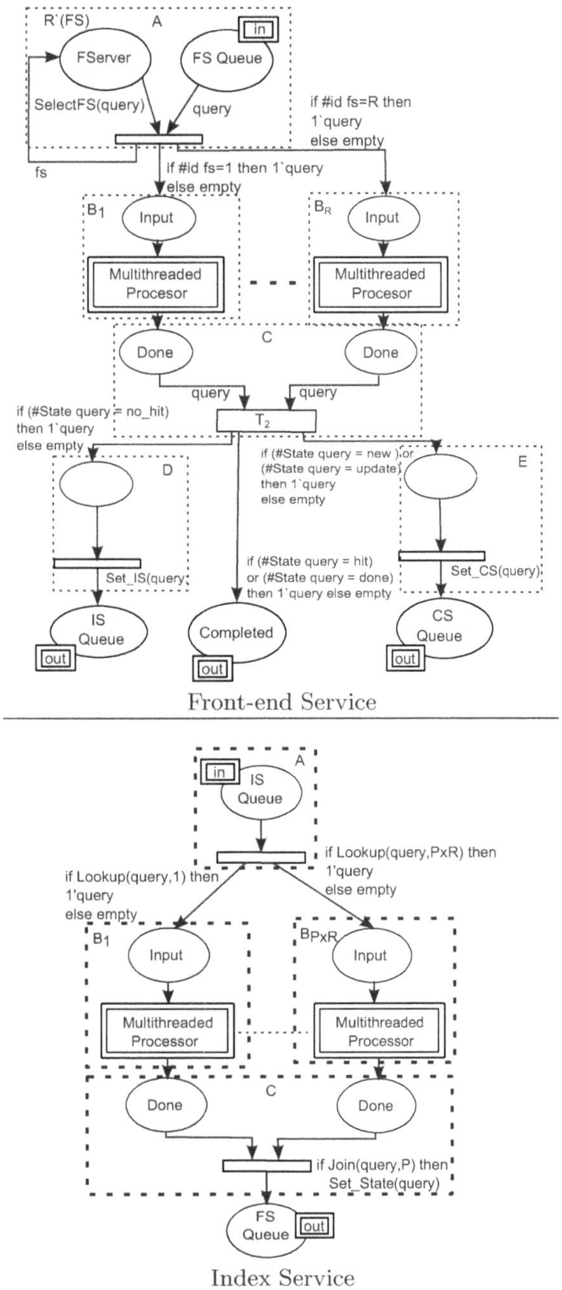

Figure 9: CPN models of services.

larity of computation per event is large and load balance is near perfect and thereby speed-ups are better in PO simulations. The LibCppSim library is not thread safe so only Unix processes were distributed on the processor cores.

6.2 Evaluation of Accuracy

In this section we evaluate the accuracy of our approximate parallel simulations. That is, how well they approximate the performance metrics determined by the sequential simulation of the same systems. Regarding global metrics such as query throughput there is no relevant differences, just small fluctuations less than 1%. Therefore we first focus on a much more demanding case. We compare the relative values of the response time of individual queries. To this end, we compute the Pearson correlation among query

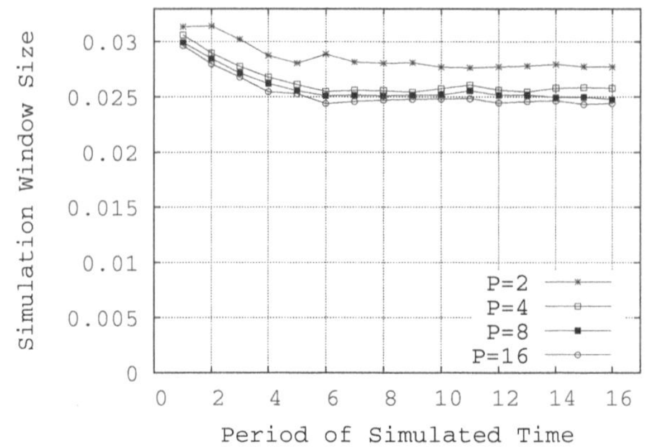

Figure 10: Window size along simulation time.

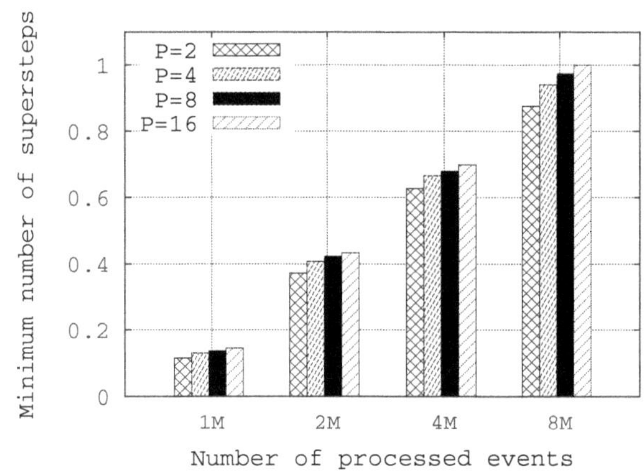

Figure 11: Minimum number of supersteps.

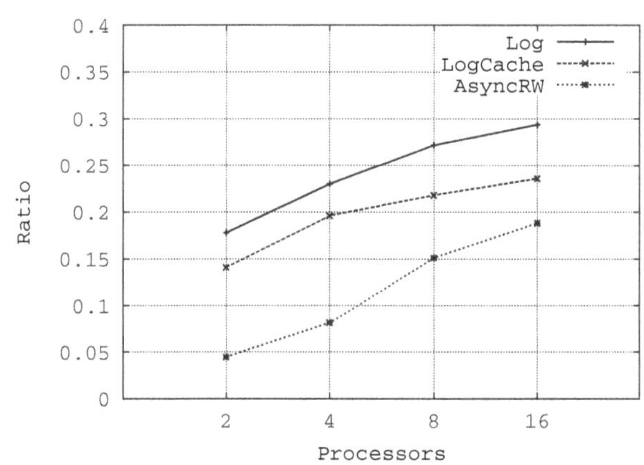

Figure 12: Ratio of number of events that should be re-simulated to total number of processed events.

response times reported by the sequential simulation and the response times for the same queries as reported by our approximate parallel simulations.

In Figure 15 we show the Pearson correlation ($y-$axis values) achieved for different random samples of queries ($x-$axis values) and curves for different number of queries N included in the samples. Each sample is composed by N pairs $< id\_query, response\ time >$ obtained as follows. We identify a query q_i which produces a straggler event in a

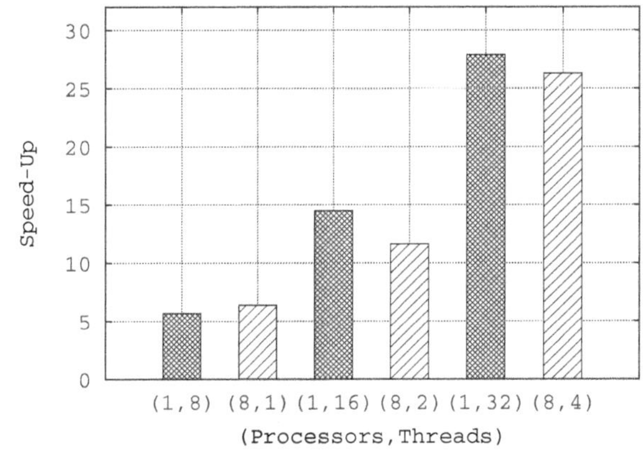

Figure 13: Speed-up for the Log simulator (similar results are obtained for the LogCache simulator).

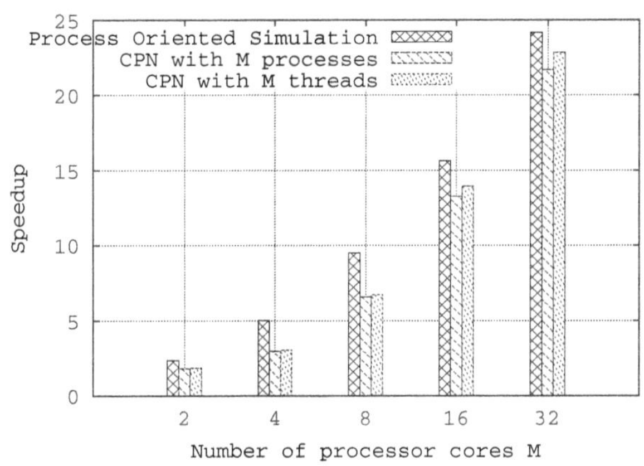

Figure 14: Speed-ups for the CPN and process-oriented AsyncRW models.

CPN module and we build the sample by taking $N/2$ queries whose events take place before and $N/2-1$ queries whose events take place after q_i in the simulation time in the same CPN module. Namely, each sample contains the neighborhood of a query that would have caused a roll-back in an equivalent Time Warp simulation of the same system. The results shown are for the Log simulator as it is the simulator that achieves the largest number of potential roll-backs as compared with the LogCache and AsyncRW simulators.

Figure 15 shows that even with a small sample size of $N = 10$ the parallel simulations have a Pearson correlation of almost 0.9 (with 1.0 meaning perfect correlation). In other words, there is a strongly positive correlation among the results from the sequential and approximate parallel simulations. We expanded these results for a single sample containing the whole set of 16,900,873 queries, for different number of processors and threads per processor, and for the Log, LogCache and AsyncRW CPN simulators. All of the results were above 0.998.

We also executed the Kolmogorov–Smirnov (KS) test over the query response time data which is a non-parametric test that allows comparing the cumulative distributions of two samples. It is used for verifying whether two samples are drawn from the same distribution. Like in the Pearson test, one sample is given by the query response times obtained

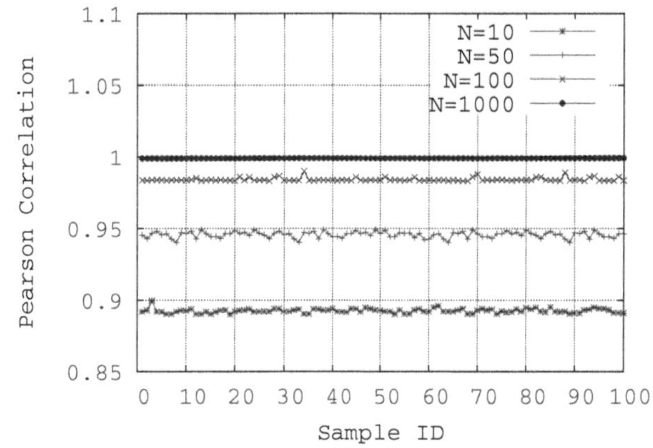

Figure 15: Pearson correlation obtained with different sample sizes.

with sequential simulations and the second sample is given by the query response times obtained with approximate parallel simulations for different values of the pairs (processors, threads per processor). In Figure 16 we show the ρ-value of the KS test which reports if the samples differ significantly (ρ= 1 means no discrepancy). As the ρ-values close to 1 we cannot reject the hypothesis that the two samples come from the same distribution. Only the Log simulator reports a few ρ values less than 1 but they are above 0.8 which is a value large enough to claim that both distributions are very similar. The values are for the whole query log (N=16M) and the average taking small samples of 100 queries (N=100).

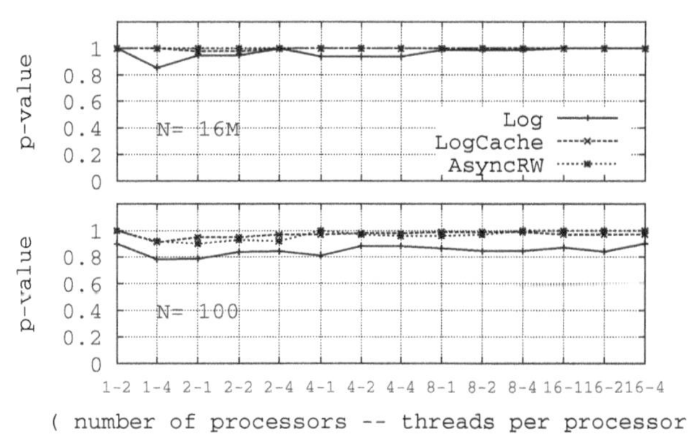

Figure 16: Kolmogorov-Smirnov test.

Finally we calculated the root mean square error of the deviation which is a measure of the differences between values obtained by the sequential simulation and the values reported by the parallel simulations. It is defined as $\epsilon_m = \sqrt{(\sum(x_i - \overline{x})^2/(n \cdot (n-1))}$ and we calculated the relative error (e_r) as $\epsilon_m/\overline{x}$.

In Table 1 we show the relative errors achieved by the parallel simulation for the following global metrics: query throughput, query response time (minimum, maximum and average over all queries) and hit ratio observed in the query caches. The row for query response time shows the biggest error among the minimum, maximum and average response times. In general, the error values reported in the table for the global performance metrics are very small.

Table 1: Relative error for global metrics.

	AsyncRW	Log	LogCache
Throughput (e_r)	0.03%	0.1%	0.3%
Response Time (e_r)	Min. 0.4%	Max. 0.6%	Max. 0.9%
Hits R. Cache (e_r)	-	-	0.2%
Hits L. Cache (e_r)	-	-	0.05%

7. CONCLUDING REMARKS

We have presented approximate parallel discrete event simulation strategies for performance evaluation of search engines. The proposed methods are generic and can be used to evaluate alternative designs for search engine components and support capacity planning studies for data centers.

The experimental evaluation shows that our approximate parallel simulation methods achieve good statistic agreement with results from sequential simulations of the same search engine realizations. The nature of this application makes it suitable for relaxed synchronization of events in the simulation time across processors. These simulations are driven by the processing of individual queries where each query competes for using the hardware resources with other many thousand queries competing for the same resources. As long as queries in the parallel simulation compete against similar number of queries than in the sequential simulation, their simulated processing costs tend to be weakly affected by eventual straggler events with timestamps in the past arriving at the processors.

Overall, the benefits of our proposals are efficient parallel simulations in running time and memory usage, and the possibility of preventing the user from getting involved in the complex details of parallelization. We demonstrated these features by presenting a C++ framework for event driven simulation of timed colored Petri net models for search engines. We also showed that process oriented simulation models can be efficiently parallelized. Our proposal consisted of combining a sliding time window strategy with bulk-synchronous parallel processing at thread and processor levels.

8. REFERENCES

[1] C. S. Badue, J. M. Almeida, V. Almeida, R. A. Baeza-Yates, B. A. Ribeiro-Neto, A. Ziviani, and N. Ziviani. Capacity planning for vertical search engines. *CoRR*, abs/1006.5059, 2010.

[2] C. Bonacic, C. García, M. Marín, M. Prieto-Matías, and F. Tirado. Building efficient multi-threaded search nodes. In *CIKM*, 2010.

[3] A. Boukerche and S. K. Das. Dynamic load balancing strategies for conservative parallel simulations. *SIGSIM Simul. Dig.*, 27(1):20–28, 1997.

[4] A. Z. Broder, D. Carmel, M. Herscovici, A. Soffer, and J. Y. Zien. Efficient query evaluation using a two-level retrieval process. In *CIKM*, 2003.

[5] C. D. Carothers and R. M. Fujimoto. Efficient execution of time warp programs on heterogeneous, now platforms. *TPDS*, 11(3) 2000.

[6] L.-l. Chen, Y.-s. Lu, Y.-p. Yao, S.-l. Peng, and L.-d. Wu. A well-balanced time warp system on multi-core environments. In *PADS*, 2011.

[7] V. Gil-Costa, J. Lobos, A. Inostrosa and M. Marin. Capacity planning for search engines: An approach based on coloured Petri nets. In *ICATPN*, 2012.

[8] G. DAngelo and M. Bracuto. Distributed simulation of large-scale and detailed models. *IJSPM*, 5(2) 2009.

[9] B. Fitzpatrick. Distributed caching with memcached. *J. of Linux*, 2004:72–76, 2004.

[10] A. Freire, F. Cacheda, V. Formoso and V. Carneiro. Analysis of performance evaluation techniques for Large Scale Information Retrieval. In *LSDS-IR*, 2013.

[11] R. Fujimoto. Parallel discrete event simulation. *Comm. ACM*, 33(10):30–53, Oct. 1990.

[12] Q. Gan and T. Suel. Improved techniques for result caching in web search engines. In *WWW*, 2009.

[13] R. Geist, J. Hicks, M. Smotherman, and J. Westall. Parallel simulation of petri nets on desktop pc hardware. In *WSC*, 2005.

[14] D. W. Glazer and C. Tropper. On process migration and load balancing in time warp. *TPDS*, 4(3) 1993.

[15] S. Jafer and G. A. Wainer. A performance evaluation of the conservative devs protocol in parallel simulation of devs-based models. In *SpringSim (TMS-DEVS)*, 2011.

[16] K. Jensen and L. Kristensen. *Coloured Petri Nets.* Springer-Verlag Berlin Heidelberg, 2009.

[17] M. Knoke and G. Hommel. Dealing with global guards in a distributed simulation of colored petri nets. In *DS-RT*, 2005.

[18] M. Knoke, F. Kühling, A. Zimmermann, and G. Hommel. Towards correct distributed simulation of high-level petri nets with fine-grained partitioning. In *ISPA*, 2004.

[19] J. Liu and R. Rong. Hierarchical composite synchronization. In *PADS*, 2012.

[20] Q. Liu and G. A. Wainer. Multicore acceleration of discrete event system specification systems. *Simulation*, 88(7) 2012.

[21] M. L. Loper and R. Fujimoto. Exploiting temporal uncertainty in process-oriented distributed simulations. In *WSC*, 2004.

[22] M. Marin. Time Warp on BSP. In *ESM*, 1998.

[23] L. Mellon and D. West. Architectural optimizations to advanced distributed simulation. In *WSC*, 1995.

[24] M. Marzolla. LibCppSim: A SIMULA-like, Portable Process-Oriented Simulation Library in C++. In *ESM*, 2004.

[25] D. M. Nicol: Discrete-Event Simulation in Performance Evaluation. Performance Evaluation 2000: 443-457.

[26] K.S. Panesar and R.M. Fujimoto. Adaptive flow control in Time Warp. In *PADS*, 1997.

[27] L. G. Valiant. A bridging model for multi-core computing. J. Comput. Syst. Sci. 1(77), 2011.

[28] L. G. Valiant. A bridging model for parallel computation. *Comm. ACM*, 33(8) 1990.

[29] R. Vitali, A. Pellegrini, and F. Quaglia. Towards symmetric multi-threaded optimistic simulation kernels. In *PADS*, 2012.

[30] BSPonMPI. http://bsponmpi.sourceforge.net/

[31] MPI. http://www.mcs.anl.gov/research/projects/mpi/

[32] OpenMP. http://openmp.org/

[33] CPN Tools. http://cpntools.org/

Empirical Evaluation of Conservative and Optimistic Discrete Event Execution on Cloud and VM Platforms

Srikanth B. Yoginath and Kalyan S. Perumalla
Computational Sciences and Engineering Division,
Oak Ridge National Laboratory, USA
yoginathsb@ornl.gov, perumallaks@ornl.gov

ABSTRACT

Virtual machine (VM) technologies, especially those offered via Cloud platforms, present new dimensions with respect to performance and cost in executing parallel discrete event simulation (PDES) applications. Due to the introduction of overall cost as a metric, the choice of the highest-end computing configuration is no longer the most economical one. Moreover, runtime dynamics unique to VM platforms introduce new performance characteristics, and the variety of possible VM configurations give rise to a range of choices for hosting a PDES run. Here, an empirical study of these issues is undertaken to guide an understanding of the dynamics, trends and trade-offs in executing PDES on VM/Cloud platforms. Performance results and cost measures are obtained from actual execution of a range of scenarios in two PDES benchmark applications on the Amazon Cloud offerings and on a high-end VM host machine. The data reveals interesting insights into the new VM-PDES dynamics that come into play and also leads to counter-intuitive guidelines with respect to choosing the best and second-best configurations when overall cost of execution is considered. In particular, it is found that choosing the highest-end VM configuration guarantees neither the best runtime nor the least cost. Interestingly, choosing a (suitably scaled) low-end VM configuration provides the least overall cost without adversely affecting the total runtime.

Categories and Subject Descriptors

I.6.1 [**Computing Methodologies**]: Simulation and Modeling – *Discrete*; I.6.8 [**Computing Methodologies**]: Simulation and Modeling – *Types of Simulation (Discrete Event, Parallel)*

General Terms

Algorithms, Measurement, Performance, Design, Experimentation

Keywords

Virtual Machines, Cloud Computing, Parallel Discrete Event Simulation, Optimistic and Conservative Synchronization, Performance, Performance Study

1. INTRODUCTION

Historically, PDES has largely assumed the luxury of picking the highest-end among the set of computer configuration choices one could access, and proceeding to achieve the highest possible speeds on the chosen high-end system. However, with the introduction of the Cloud platforms, the new dimension of *price* is introduced into consideration. Since there is a price one must pay for all compute cycles used by the application, a "dollar value" is now attached to each PDES run. The most interesting aspect about this new dimension is that the price variation is non-linear. The user might have to pay more than double the price for double the performance. Alternatively, doubling the cost does not guarantee double the performance. In this new milieu, little is known about the price-performance features of PDES execution on Cloud platforms, and about the configuration choices of PDES over VM platforms in general.

There are several questions that arise. What, if any, is the level of performance penalty taken by a PDES application when moving from a traditional native execution to a VM? Is there any performance gain obtained by insisting that the VM be a privileged one versus the default, unprivileged mode of VMs? Does the highest-end VM/Cloud hardware configuration always deliver the least total execution time, and at what overall cost? If the highest-end VM configuration is too expensive for the user, what is the next best configuration to choose, considering overall cost? How well does a Cloud platform designed primarily for embarrassingly parallel jobs execute tightly coupled PDES applications? Are runtime and dollar value largely opposed to each other as one might expect? In general, how do the total execution time and total cost vary with different VM/Cloud instance configuration options?

Here, an empirical approach is undertaken to help answer such questions. Results and findings are reported to understand the new configuration space for PDES enabled by the introduction of new, Cloud-specific concepts such as abstracted speeds of virtual processors, normalized units of processors and memories, price per packaged compute-unit, and overall "bottom-line" cost. Using actual PDES application runs executed on a Cloud platform and on high-end VM hosts, we study the configuration space to uncover new insights, trends, and guidelines on the problem of economically executing PDES applications in Cloud environments. For experimentation purposes, we chose the popular Amazon AWS (EC2) [1] Cloud computing platform, and gathered data from a variety of configurations with varying price-performance characteristics. The empirical study makes use of two benchmarks: one is the popular synthetic PHOLD benchmark, and the other is a complex disease spread model at the individual level in a large population. Both optimistic and conservative synchronization schemes are exercised, with varying levels of locality of events.

The rest of the article is organized as follows. Section 2 briefly introduces virtual machine systems, Cloud infrastructure, and PDES execution. Section 3 introduces the PDES applications, their scenario configurations, and the hardware used for the performance study. This is followed by the performance results

SIGSIM-PADS'13, May 19–22, 2013, Montréal, Québec, Canada.
Copyright © 2013 ACM 978-1-4503-1920-1/13/05...$15.00.

and their analyses in Section 4. The work is summarized and future work identified in Section 5.

2. BACKGROUND

2.1 Virtual Machines and Cloud Computing

Virtual Machine (VM) technology moves the traditional operating system (OS) away from the actual hardware interface and transplants it to work over a software interface. The decoupling enables entirely new modes of execution from a user's point of view, and provides many benefits such as flexibility, multiplexed use, fault tolerance, dynamic migration, automated load balancing, and cost sharing. Anyone can exploit the benefits of VM technology by deploying the VM implementations on their own hardware. Cloud computing is a term generally used to refer to such installations that provide the advantages of virtualized computing (and storage) interfaces. Due to economies of scale, only large commercial, dedicated installations provide the most cost-effective provisioning of VM technologies and make them accessible over the Internet via Web-based interfaces for very attractive prices. They provide on-demand access to compute resources without the burden of housing, installation, maintenance, and upgrading needs.

Since commercial offerings of Cloud computing are profitable mostly due to the ability to multiplex many smaller units of virtual hardware on larger units of physical hardware, one can expect a price structure that permits the most flexibility for multiplexing. In particular, the price structure favors smaller virtual units, and, more importantly for PDES, charges a non-linearly larger price for the highest-end virtual units. Thus, virtual machines whose resources (e.g., speeds and numbers of virtual processors) are close to the capacity of the underlying physical hardware can be expected to be the most expensive.

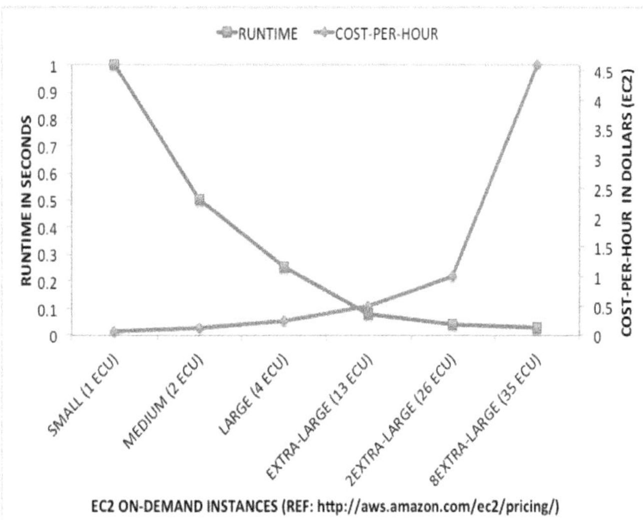

Figure 1 EC2 cost-value model

Figure 1 illustrates the cost model for the Amazon AWS-based EC2 Cloud service that is based on the allotted hardware resource sizes. Suppose the user requires the Cloud for executing a parallel job, and further suppose the user's application enjoys an ideal parallel execution by which the runtime decreases in proportion to the number of processors. The runtime for a parallel job is plotted against different computational units offered by the Cloud platform. Along the abscissa, the size of each indivisible virtual computational unit increases moving from left to right. On the left ordinate, the ideal parallel runtime is plotted. On the right ordinate, the cost for the computational unit is plotted. The non-linear aspect of the price is notable. Also, additional non-linear effects can be expected due to shared-memory effects, shared network effects, scheduling effects, and inter-VM communication effects. Thus, unless the parallel job is embarrassingly parallel in nature, it is rather difficult to predict the trends of runtime and overall cost of parallel jobs, and an empirical study is inevitable for properly understanding the overall tradeoffs.

2.2 Hypervisor

The VM technology relies on a component called the *hypervisor* that replaces the OS to be the lowest-level software running directly over the hardware. By doing so it the segregates the hardware and the OS by virtualizing the hardware components to the OS, and relieves the tight hardware-OS coupling. As an important consequence, OS instances from different vendors co-exist and run on a same physical resource, interacting with the virtual counterparts of the physical hardware. In general there are two different types of virtualization: full-virtualization, and para-virtualization. In full-virtualization, the hypervisor supports any unmodified guest OS to run. In para-virtualization, the hypervisor provides *hypercalls* to the OS for accessing hardware services; this requires the modification of a guest OS. In the empirical study here, we use the Xen® hypervisor platforms for our performance evaluation. The Amazon's EC2 Cloud infrastructure also uses the Xen hypervisor.

Xen Hypervisor

The Xen [2] hypervisor is a popular open source industry standard for virtualization, supporting a wide range of architectures including x86, x86-64, IA64, and ARM, and guest OS types including Windows®, Linux®, Solaris® and various versions of BSD OS. A VM in Xen terminology is referred to as Guest Domain or simply DOM. Each DOM has a unique identifier called its Domain ID (DOM ID). The first DOM called DOM0 is a privileged one with special management rights. System administrative tasks such as suspension, resumption, and migration of DOMs are managed via DOM0. Any other VM is called a DOMU.

Each DOM has its own set of virtual devices, including virtual multi-processors called virtual CPUs (VCPUs). The hypervisor's scheduling functionality mainly deals with the efficient mapping (multiplexing) of all the VCPUs of multiple VMs onto the available physical processor cores (PCPUs). The *credit-based scheduler* is the default Xen scheduler, which schedules VCPUs on to PCPUs based on the principle of fair sharing of computational cycles. This scheduler is very widely used, and works excellently for a very large variety of virtualization users.

2.3 Parallel Discrete Event Simulation

A discrete event simulation model of a system emulates the system's behavior over time in terms of events and state changes. An event is a discrete point on the virtual timeline that corresponds to a change in the evolution of the physical system state. A parallel execution of the discrete event model involves a coordinated evolution of several serial discrete event timelines in parallel. The modeled system state is divided into a set of encapsulated states; each encapsulated state with its own simulation timeline is generally referred to as Logical Process (LP) in the PDES literature. The timelines are synchronized according to the timestamps of the events spanning all the timelines, guaranteeing a global timestamp-ordered execution. Two distinct synchronization mechanisms namely, conservative and optimistic synchronizations are popularly used in the PDES literature. In conservative synchronization, no timestamp order violation is allowed. In contrast, in optimistic synchronization, LPs are allowed to incur transient violations of timestamp order, which are detected at runtime and corrected on the fly using various algorithms. More details on PDES and its synchronization mechanisms can be found in [3]. In our experiments, we use a parallel/distributed simulation engine that is optimized for very fast execution on native hardware. The engine supports the notion of a Federate that hosts one or more LPs. Each Federate is essentially a UNIX process with its own simulation loop that processes the events of all LPs mapped to that Federate. There is exactly one Federate launched per virtual core in each VM.

2.4 Related Work

Evaluating the HPC applications performance on Cloud infrastructure has been reported in [4], but these applications are largely high-performance scientific applications such as Community Atmospheric Model (CAM), and are not PDES applications. Network performance on Amazon EC2 data-centers has been studied and an evaluation of the impact of virtualization on network parameters such as latency, throughput, and packet-loss was discussed in [5], again in non-PDES context. There is a good overview and discussion of generic utilization of Cloud infrastructures for PDES applications focusing on the advantages and challenges it poses [6], which also serves as a good motivation and background for PDES on Cloud platforms. The Master-Worker approach to distributed (and fault tolerant) PDES has been explored in multiple places [7][8][9], and is somewhat related, although it is different from the traditional PDES execution view in which all processors are equal. Recently, an evaluation of a set of conservative synchronization protocols on EC2 was reported [10]. Overall, the area is nascent, and much additional research in PDES execution is needed to explore the space opened by the new metrics of VM/Cloud computing beyond the raw speed execution.

3. EMPIRICAL STUDY SETUP

3.1 Synchronization Protocols

Our empirical study uses an optimized implementation of parallel discrete event simulation that provides the option of conservative as well as optimistic synchronization. The synchronization protocols are the blocking-based variant of the set of highly scalable global virtual time (GVT) algorithms recently tested at very large scale on supercomputers [11]. The algorithms are implemented using the blocking collective call `MPI_Allreduce()` inside the iterations of the GVT algorithm to account for all transient messages. Since this is a Mattern-style [12][13] epoch-based framework that colors messages and uses reduction-based counting of transient messages, no NULL messages are needed. The parallel implementation is competitive with sequential execution, with a high efficiency.

3.2 Benchmark Applications

PHOLD

The de-facto standard PHOLD [14] benchmark application is used as one of the applications for our performance evaluation. In all our experiments we utilize the following variants for performance evaluation.

- Synchronization: Type of synchronization used [OPT=optimistic, CONS= conservative]
- Number of LPs per Federate (NLP): [NLP=100 means the Federate hosts100 LPs]
- Number of messages (NMSG): [NMSG=1000 means 1000 messages/LP]
- Locality of the LP generated message destination (LOC): In terms of intra-processor event communication [LOC=50, or LOC=90]. Values of 50 and 90 suggest respectively that 50% and 90% of the messages generated by an LP are local to its Federate. Hence, a value of 50% for LOC involves more LP message exchanges across the network and results in increased network traffic.

Disease Spread Simulation

For the second application, we use an epidemiological disease spread model [16] that defines a discrete event model for the propagation of a disease in a population of individuals in groups called locations and aggregates of locations called regions. Each region is mapped to a Federate. Multiple locations are contained in each region. Each location is housed in an LP. Multiple individuals are instantiated at each location, and they not only interact with individuals within the same location but also periodically (conforming to an individual-specific time distribution function) move from one location to another. Similar to PHOLD, the number of individuals per location are varied (e.g., 1000 individuals/location), and the number of locations per region (e.g., 10 locations/region).

3.3 Benchmark Configurations

Using the PDES applications listed in the previous section, four benchmark applications, namely, conservative and optimistic executions for each of *PHOLD Simulation Benchmark* (PSB) and *Disease Spread Benchmark* (DSB) were designed. In all the benchmarks using PHOLD a *lookahead* of 1 was used.

PHOLD Scenarios (PSB)

With PHOLD, we used scenarios with 100 LPs/Federate, 100 and 1000 messages/LP, with 32 Federates for 50% and 90% LOC values. With performance data gathered for both optimistic and conservative synchronization scenarios, a total of 8 sets of readings are gathered for this benchmark.

For 100 LPs/Federate and 100 messages/LP on 32 Federates, 3200 LPs are hosted on 32 DOMs to simulate exchanges of 320,000 PHOLD messages over 100 units of simulation time. Similarly, for 100 LPs/Federate and 1000 messages/LP on 32 Federates, 3200 LPs are hosted on 32 DOMs to simulate exchanges of 3,200,000 PHOLD messages over 100 seconds of simulation time. With a locality value LOC of 50% half of the messages generated are destined to LPs on remote Federates (outside the VCPU). With a locality value LOC of 90%, only 10% are destined to LPs on remote Federates. Thus, LOC 50 is much more taxing on the network than LOC 90.

Disease Spread Benchmark (DSB)

DSB simulates the disease spread across regions. Each Federate is mapped to a region, which are formed of number of locations that are mapped to LPs. In the experiments 32 Federates and 10 locations per Federate are instantiated (representative of a small city sized scenario for disease propagation) and each such location has a population of 1000 people. Hence the benchmark involves simulation of spread of disease across 320 locations across a population of 320,000 for a simulation time of 7 days. The mobility of the population can be set to a certain percentage, similar to PHOLD. In the DSB we experiment with 50% and 90%. The LOC 50 mobility suggests that 50% of the trips tend to travel across regions, while LOC 90 suggests only 10% of the trips travel across regions. DSB is slightly I/O intensive generating around 32M of output data compared to less than 200 KB of output data of PSB.

3.4 Test Platforms

We utilize two platforms for the VM-based experiments. One is a local high-end machine in our laboratory, and the other is a commercial Cloud offering. The details of these two platforms are provided next.

Local Test Platform (LTP)

LTP is our custom-built machine with a Supermicro® H8DG6-F motherboard supporting two 16-core (32 cores in total) AMD® Opteron 6276 processors at 2.3 GHz, sharing 256GB of memory, Intel Solid State Drive 240GB and a 6TB Seagate constellation comprising 2 SAS drives configured as RAID-0. Ubuntu-12.10 runs with Linux® 3.7.1 kernel runs as DOM0 and DOMUs, over Xen 4.2.0 hypervisor.

All DOMUs are para-virtual and networked using a software bridge in DOM-0. DOM-0 is configured to use 10GB of memory and the guest DOMs were configured to use at least 1GB memories each, which were increased as necessitated by the application benchmarks. Each guest DOM uses 2GB of LVM-based hard disk created over SAS drives, while the DOM-0 uses an entire Solid State Drive (SSD). OpenMPI-1.6.3 (built using gcc-4.7.2) was used to build the simulation engine and its applications. A machine-file listing the IP addresses of the VMs was used along with *mpirun* utility of OpenMPI to launch the MPI-based PDES applications onto VMs.

EC2 Cloud Platform

We also ran our benchmarks on Amazon's EC2 Cloud platform. We built a cluster of para-virtual VM instances of Ubuntu 12.04 LTS. The following are the VM clusters used to run the benchmarks (typical offerings available to Amazon EC2 users).

- *m1.small* is a single-core VM with compute power of 1-ECU and has a memory of 1.7 GB.
- *m1.medium* is a single-core VM with compute power of 2-ECUs and has a memory of 3.7 GB.
- *m1.large* is a 2-core VM with compute power of 4 ECUs and has a memory of 7.5 GB.
- *m1.xlarge* is a 4-core VM with compute power of 8 ECUs and has a memory of 1.5 GB.
- *m3.2xlarge* is an 8-core VM with compute power of 26 ECUs and has a memory of 30 GB.
- *hs.8xlarge* is a 16-core VM with compute power equivalent to 35 ECUs and has a memory of 117 GB.

The term ECU here refers to a "EC2 Compute Unit" which is an abstraction defined and supported by Amazon as a normalization mechanism to provide a variety of virtual computation units independent of the actual physical hardware support that they use/maintain/upgrade without user intervention. OpenMPI-1.6.3 was built on the virtual instance, which was used to build the simulation engine and all the PDES applications. A machine-file listing the DNS names of the allotted instances was used to launch the MPI-based PDES applications using *mpirun*.

4. PERFORMANCE STUDY

4.1 Results from Local Test Platform (LTP)

PDES being a parallel computing application, two important factors, namely, computation and communication, determine the overall application performance. The hypervisor essentially virtualizes the hardware resources and hence a VM running over hypervisor uses a virtual CPU (VCPU) and a virtual network interface for computation and communication, respectively. The hypervisor essentially maps the VCPUs onto the available CPUs, while networking is performed using front-end and back-end virtual interfaces. Hence, the hypervisor essentially introduces some overhead due to its presence.

Virtual Computational Performance

We know that the hypervisor is a necessity to realize Cloud computing. However, this implies that native execution of PDES is not possible in the presence of a hypervisor, which may introduce overheads such as context switching costs and system call (and hypercall) trap costs. Hence, a performance comparison between the native and VM runs is essential to determine the amount of degradation, if any, that PDES suffers simply for the fact that the execution is moved from native to VM platforms.

In Figure 2, the performance results of both PSB and DSB benchmarks runs are presented from *Native*, *DOM0* and a single *DOMU*. The *Native* readings correspond to a setup where Linux® runs directly over the hardware as usual, without the hypervisor. The *DOM0* readings correspond to a setup where the control-DOM with Linux® runs over the Xen hypervisor as the only running instance and is configured to use all 32 CPUs. A single DOMU readings correspond to a setup where a user-DOM with Linux® runs in the presence of control-DOM (dOM0); however DOM0 is not loaded with any load during performance runs. These results demonstrate how the presence of the hypervisor affects the compute-performance of a PDES application. As seen from Figure 2, somewhat surprisingly, the results from all the three setups are almost identical across all the runs, suggesting that the overhead of the Xen® hypervisor in delegating the CPU resources is almost negligible.

This data is helpful in addressing the issue of native *vs.* VM-based performance of PDES execution, and may encourage the community to move towards a Cloud environment by allaying uninformed fears of incurring a significant performance penalty.

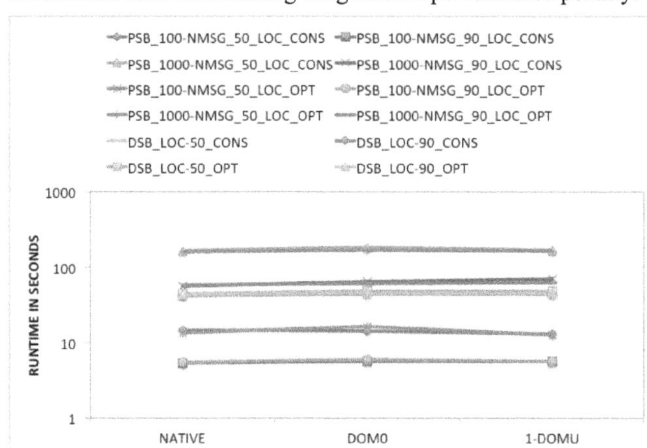

Figure 2 Native, DOM-0 and single DOMU performance comparison on LTP

Effects of Virtual Communication and I/O via DOM0

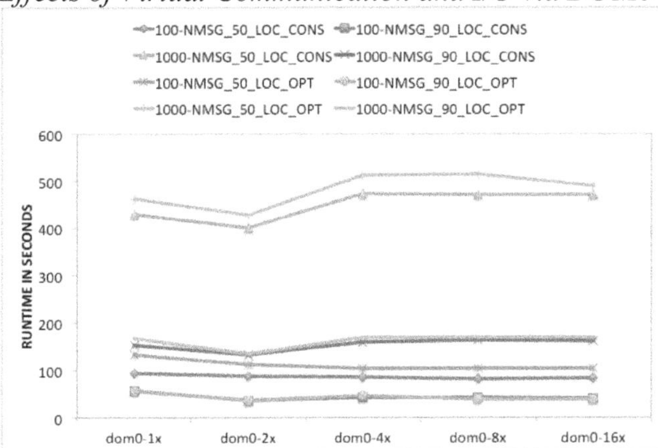

Figure 3 PSB runtime performance in 32 VM setup scenario for varying weights of DOM0 on LTP

Since DOM0 is partially involved in servicing the network communication and input/output (I/O) for all DOMU, DOM0 may need to receive sufficient number of CPU cycles (or a higher priority weight). The need for higher DOM0 weights for better performance was demonstrated in [17] using an older version (3.4.2) of the Xen distribution. To understand such requirements in the current version, the weight assigned to DOM0 relative to all DOMU is varied from 1 to 16. For example, a factor of 4 implies that DOM0 has four times more credits than any DOMU. This provides an overburdened DOM0 more CPU cycles compared to DOMUs.

The runtimes with varying weights are plotted in Figure 3 for the PSB, and in Figure 4 for the DSB. The seemingly flat curves of Figure 3 suggest very slight or no impact of higher weights for DOM0 on the runtime performance with the newer version of Xen contrary to the observation in [17]. This change can be attributed to the incorporation of Netchannel2 [18] in Xen networking, which transfers the burden of copying network data from DOM0 to the DOMUs. However, for DSB, a good improvement in the performance as the weight of DOM0 is doubled is seen in Figure 4. DSB being I/O intensive and also due to the fact that DOM0 services the I/O, the additional weight provided for DOM0 helps significantly in speeding up the I/O functionality during DSB runs.

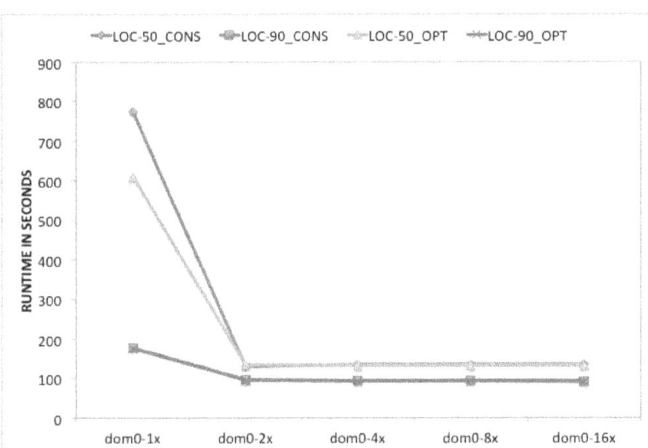

Figure 4 DSB runtime performance in 32 VM setup scenario for varying weights of DOM0 on LTP

Virtual Computation and Communication Performance

To study the impact of combined virtual computation and communication effects on PDES applications, we ran the benchmarks on our LTP, varying the number of VMs in the experiments from a single DOMU with 32 VCPUs to 32 DOMUs with 1 VCPU, keeping the total number of VCPUs constant.

Figure 5 and Figure 6 show the benchmark results obtained from varying the number of DOMs hosted on LTP using PSB and DSB, respectively. For the same benchmark the figures show how the performance varies with the increase in the number of DOMs. Note that as the number of DOMs running the benchmark increases, the number of VCPUs within each DOM also decreases. Also note that in each of these benchmark runs, the number of Federates is equal to the number VCPUs, i.e., Federates have a 1:1 mapping to the VCPUs. Hence, in a fast network environment, we expect the runtime across all types of DOM configurations to be largely identical, since the same number of VCPUs are involved in the computation.

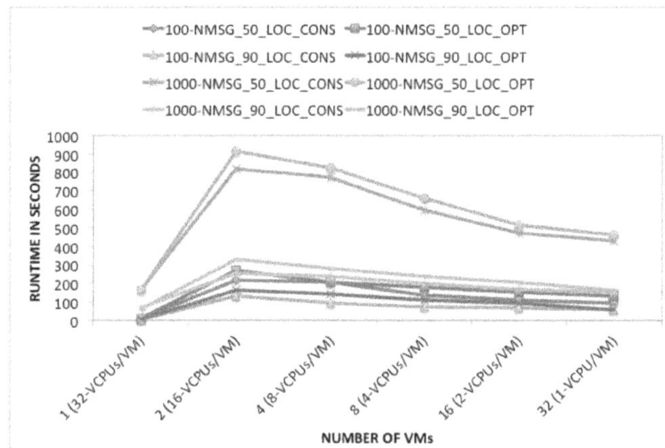

Figure 5 Performance comparison with increase in number of DOMs using PSB on LTP

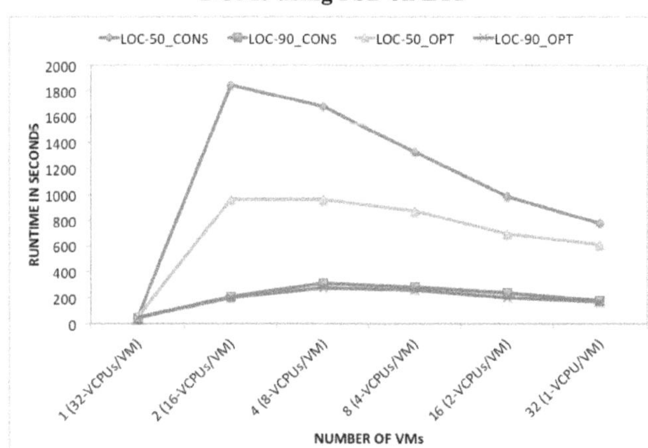

Figure 6 Performance comparison with increase in DOMs using DSB on LTP

A very interesting and common trend across all the benchmark runs is the degradation of performance with fewer numbers of VMs beyond 1, and its betterment with the increase in number of VMs hosted. In other words, there is a steep rise in runtime when moving from 1 VM to 2 VMs but a gradual drop from 2 to 32 VMs. The effect is predominant in the cases where the network traffic is high (LOC=50), as seen in both Figure 5 and Figure 6, for PSB and DSB, respectively.

This trend is counterintuitive to a general parallel-computing user because a better performance is expected in scenarios involving VMs with more VCPUs. The intuition is that the parallel processing libraries like MPI generally use shared-memory to communicate across processes within the same VM. Hence, one expects to observe better performance by increasing the communication across Federates within a DOM (shared memory) and reducing the inter-DOM messages by reducing number of DOMs.

The underlying reason for the counterintuitive trend is as follows. When a VM contains many VCPUs, a bottleneck is created at the virtual network interface card (NIC) because of serialization. Further, DOMUs doing most of the networking work as observed in the Figure 3 in previous section adds on to this performance degradation.

In real hardware, the communication is often highly optimized via direct memory accesses, cache coherence mechanisms between NIC and CPU, and so on. However, in the case of VMs, the NIC is a software implementation, and all synchronization is performed in software, which significantly reduces the network speed. This degradation increases in a quadratic nature with the number of VCPUs sharing the virtual NIC. Unfortunately, there is little that can be done regarding this issue other than reduce the network traffic generated per VCPU or reduce the number of VCPUs per VM.

As observed earlier in Figure 1, the Cloud operators charge a lower price for low-end machines and higher cost for high-end machines. The benchmark performance results suggest that PDES applications can in fact take very good advantage of the lower cost of smaller sized VMs *and* gain lower execution time simply by moving to the other extreme of 1 VCPU/VM, and greatly benefit from the existing cost model offered by the Cloud infrastructures, like EC2.

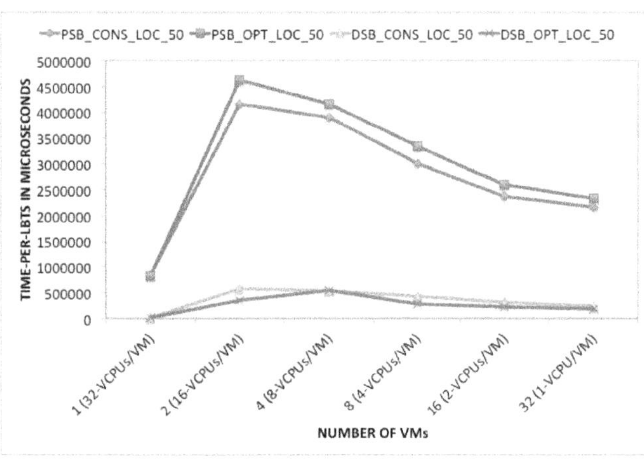

Figure 7 Time taken per LBTS computation with increase in the number of VMs on LTP

In Figure 7, we show the time that the simulator takes to compute a lower bound on incoming timestamps (LBTS) for the most-affected PSB runs namely, 1000-NMSG_50_LOC_CONS and 1000-NMSG_50_LOC_OPT runs along with LOC-50_CONS and LOC_50_OPT DSB runs. However, the number of LBTS computations remained the same across the same benchmark runs even while the number of VMs is changed. Hence, within PDES, it is the prolonged LBTS computation that affects the overall runtime of the simulation application.

4.2 Results from EC2 Cloud

To deal with possible variance of performance in the Cloud due to periodicity of loads and other uncontrollable phenomena, each data point in the results is derived as an average from three runs executed on three different days and times. Note that each request for VMs from Cloud assigns a different set of machines and hence, the virtual cluster built for every run is different from the other. This averaging for variance applies to the Cloud performance results in Figure 8 through Figure 12.

Note also that all the machines that the EC2 provides are VMs. This provides the Cloud operator an ability to multiplex multiple VMs more numerous than the available hardware resources. However, by overloading the host machine, the compute cycles of the physical machine are shared among the VM instances. By defining the Elastic Compute Unit (ECU) that is always lesser or equal to the compute cycles offered by physical CPU-core, the Amazon EC2 is able to overload the host machine and still guarantee the provision of the assured ECU worth of computational service.

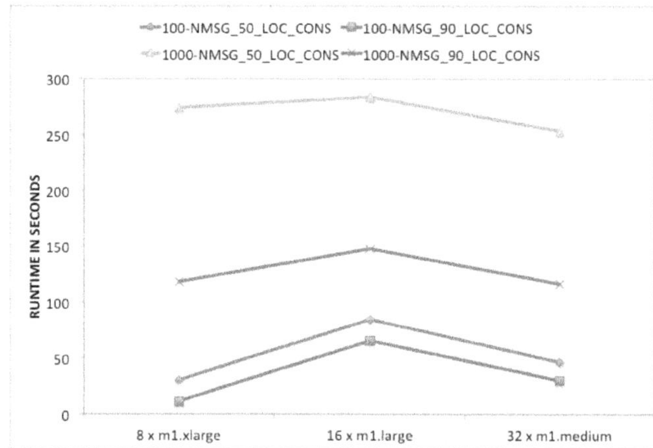

Figure 8 Runtime performance of PSB with conservative synchronization on EC2 Cloud

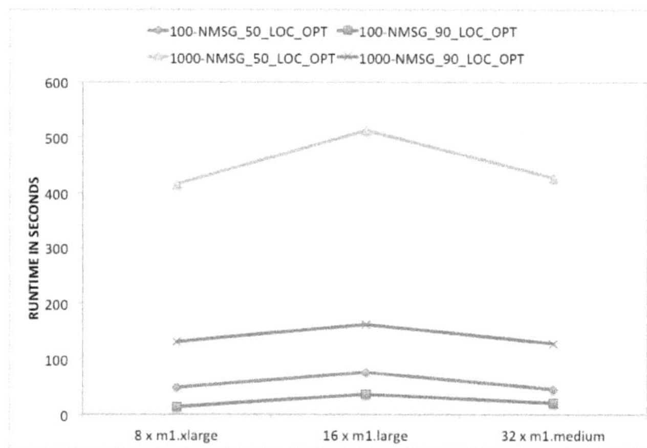

Figure 9 Runtime performance of PSB with optimistic synchronization on EC2 Cloud

With a Cloud infrastructure, the user is not guaranteed in advance specific details of the physical hardware. The user is only assured of the ECU, number of cores and amount of memory for an instance created. The performance unit of the CPU-core is provided in terms of ECUs. For example: *m1.small* and *m1.average* are both single-core VMs but with compute units of 1 ECU and 2 ECUs, respectively. The *m1.small* instance's assured compute cycles (in ECUs) can be compared to a low priority task that can be migrated across physical nodes or multiplexed flexibly at the Cloud runtime's discretion. Hence, a good performance from *m1.small* instances is not guaranteed. Since, we would not be able to characteristically determine *a priori* the hardware-specific details of a physical CPU-core from the Cloud, the next best option is to choose the VM configuration with a single core with high number of ECUs and use it as a baseline for selecting multi-core machines, if needed.

To observe the performance trend observed with PSB and DSB benchmarks on our LTP we use *m1* set of machines comprising *m1.small*, *m1.medium*, *m1.large* and *m1.xlarge*. Of this set the *m1.medium*, *m1.large* and *m1.xlarge* VMs are *single*, *dual* and *quad* support VCPUs, respectively. Further, the compute cycles of these increase by a factor of 2; i.e., 2 ECUs, 4 ECUs and 8 ECUs in the same specified order. The *m1.small* that provides 1ECU worth of compute cycles is not considered for this set of runs because it is difficult to use it for a fair comparison with other configurations. We built three virtual clusters using these VM instances. *32×m1.medium*, *16×m1.large* and *8×m1.xlarge* are the 3 virtual clusters built using 32, 16 and 8 instances of *m1.medium*, *m1.large* and *m1.xlarge* VMs, respectively.

The conservative and optimistic synchronization-based PSB runtimes from EC2 runs are plotted in Figure 8 and Figure 9, respectively. Figure 10 presents the results for DSB runs on EC2. Interestingly, similar to LTP results, we observe a consistent trend across all the plots. The runtime in most of the cases is at its best with *8×m1.xlarge* virtual cluster, which worsens with *16×m1.large* virtual cluster and gets better with *32×m1.medium* virtual cluster runs. Note that in each of these benchmark runs the number of Federates is equal to number VCPUs.

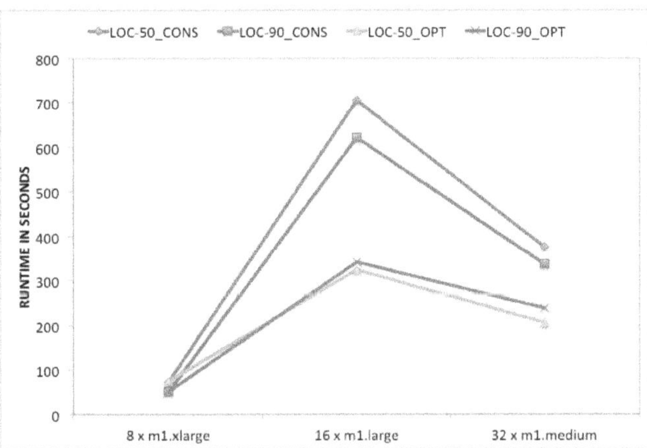

Figure 10 Runtime performance of DSB on EC2 Cloud

VM *m1.xlarge* is the most powerful among all the other offered VMs in the *m1* set. The observed counterintuitive behavior on the Cloud can be reasoned using our prior understanding of the benchmark behavior on LTP, with *m1.xlarge* considered as the physical node capacity on which the all VMs belonging to *m1* can run. Given, the lack of *a priori* guarantees about the physical hardware properties of machinery that hosts EC2 VMs, this is a fair assumption for all *m1* set of VMs. In this case, the runtime reduction in the *8×m1.xlarge* virtual cluster can be attributed to the very low involvement of the virtual network as the quad-core VMs occupying entire physical node mainly use the high-speed physical inter-connect during parallel computation. The increase in runtime in *16×m1.large* setup (instead of decrease as observed in LTP runs) can be attributed to the presence and active utilization virtual-networking as more than one *m1.large* could have been hosted on a physical node. The reduction in the runtime with increase in number of VMs in the *32×m1.medium* setup is consistent with our observations on our LTP.

4.3 LTP and EC2 Results Comparison

In comparing the results from LTP and EC2, note that all VMs running on LTP use the virtual network, whereas an indeterminate combination of real and virtual-network is typical of EC2 environment. While the LTP uses 32 CPU-cores of AMD Opteron at 2.3 GHz, the *m1* set of EC2 is perceived to use Intel Xeon CPU-cores at 2.6 GHz (*cpuinfo* of Cloud instance).

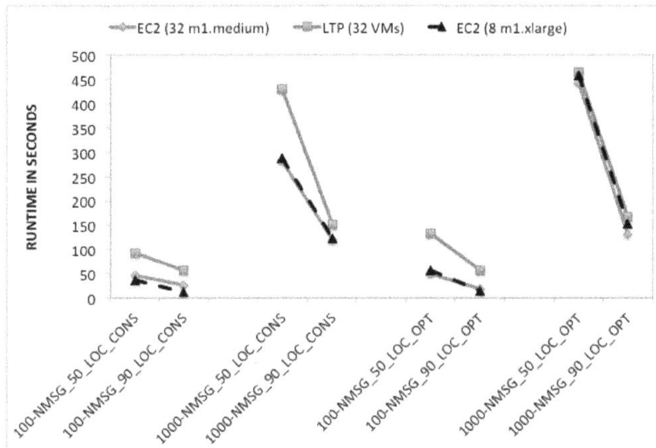

Figure 11 LTP and EC2 Cloud runtime comparison for PSB

The PSB's LTP and EC2 runtime comparisons using 32 VM scenarios are shown in Figure 11; similar runtime comparisons for DSB are shown in Figure 12. An important aspect of PSB plots in Figure 11 is the close similarities for the LTP and EC2 trends.

However, the DSB runtime plot comparisons in Figure 12 differ from this view, especially in 32 VM runs. Note that LTP runs are highly affected by network load as suggested by huge drop in runtimes as LOC value changes from 50 to 90. However, the corresponding 32 *m1.medium* EC2 runs seem unaffected, essentially suggesting the absence or minimal utility of virtual network. Further, 32 *m1.medium* EC2 runtime during LOC 90 is greater than its LTP peer, suggesting EC2 performance being effected by distribute I/O. The 8 *m1.xlarge* EC2 runtimes provide the best runtimes on EC2, suggesting that distribute I/O affects VM dispersed across many nodes more than on fewer nodes. This observation seems to be consistent with LTP, where runtimes are more affected by network performance than I/O.

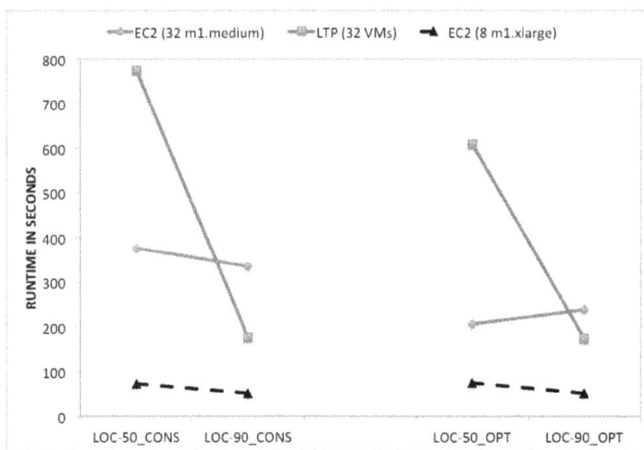

Figure 12 LTP and EC2 Cloud runtime comparison for DSB

Finally, we note that these observations can be helpful in determining an upper bound runtime on the Cloud environments utilizing processors of similar clock speeds.

4.4 Cost-Value Evaluation on EC2

In Table 1, the relevant details of on-demand VMs provided by the Amazon EC2 service are tabulated. For cost-value evaluation we selected set of VMs based on the specified ECU value. To run the PSB and DSB, we built 4 clusters of VM instances. The cheapest VM instance for the least compute unit of 1-ECU is *m1.small* and a VM cluster formed using 32 such instances is called *32×m1.small.* Similarly, VM clusters of *16×m1.medium, 8×m1.large and 2×m3.2xlarge,* are formed using 16, 8 and 2 instances of *m1.medium, m1.large, m3.2xlarge* VMs, each of these VMs have an ECU of 2, 4 and 26, respectively. The *hs1.8xlarge* is the most powerful and most expensive VM that EC2 offers and, it assures an ECU of 35.

Table 1 Details of EC2 on-demand instances

EC2 Instances	Cost/hour in Dollars	Number of VCPUs	Assured Performance in ECUs
m1.small	0.06	1	1
m1.medium	0.12	1	2
m1.large	0.24	2	4
m1.xlarge	0.48	4	8
m3.2xlarge	1.00	8	26
hs.8xlarge	4.60	16	35

PSB and DSB Runtime Performance

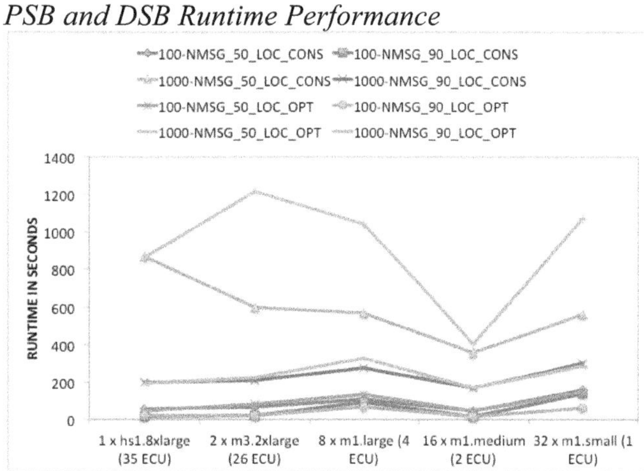

Figure 13 PSB runtime performance on EC2 Cloud

Figure 13 plots the runtimes of various PSB scenarios. While the runs with lower network traffic are almost flat, the optimistic and conservative curves vary significantly across different VM clusters. Three significant observations can be made from the 1000_NMSG-50_LOC_CONS and 1000_NMSG-50_LOC_OPT runtime plots. They are (a) contrary to the trend observed in the LTP runs the runtime of both OPT and CONS curves worsen on *32×m1.small*, (b) the runtime on high-end *hs1.8xlarge* VM, where the Federates are hosted on a single node and in the absence of network utilization during parallel computing, the runtime is the worst among all (c) the best performance across almost all runs is obtained with *16×m1.medium* cluster setup, where 32 Federates are hosted on 16 instances of single-core VMs.

A VM with ECU 1 on a hypervisor running on CPU-cores whose compute capacity is often multiple of ECUs, can be realized either in scenarios where *m1.small* VMs are overloaded on the hypervisor or on nodes where it's often run as VM with lower weight and are generally capped so that they do not exceed their provision. Either of these cases is detrimental for highly asynchronous parallel computing PDES applications. Hence, the poor performance with *32×m1.small* is expected.

Regarding the poor performance on *hs1.8xlarge* runs, note that the *hs1.8xlarge* is a 16-core VM and is loaded with 32 Federates. In overloaded scenarios such as these the hypervisor VCPU scheduler in quest of ensuring fairness in physical CPU utilization among all VCPUs affects the performance. This is a known problem [17].

Further, good runtime performance can be expected from *16×m1.medium* virtual cluster runs based on our previous observations both on LTP and EC2.

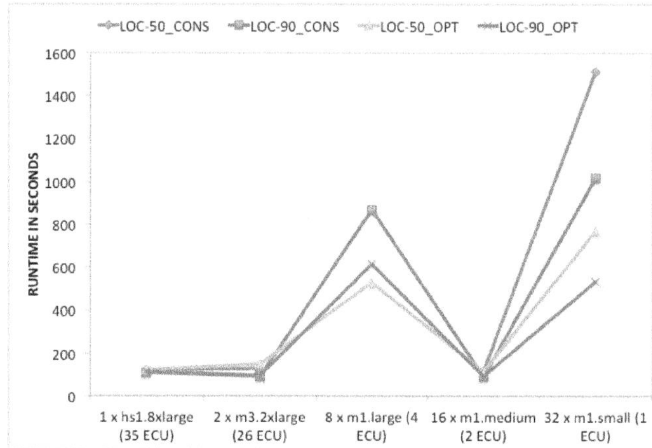

Figure 14 DSB runtime performance on EC2 Cloud

Figure 14 plots the runtimes of various DSB scenarios. Here, the runtimes are almost same on *hs1.8xlarge*, *2×m3.2xlarge* and *16×m1.medium* virtual clusters. Same reason as stated for PSB explains the bad performance of DSB on *32×m1.small.* The readings for *8×m1.large* are consistent with the observations seen with *16×m1.large* virtual cluster runs shown in Figure 10 and the performance degradation can be attributed to virtual-networking.

Cost factoring to PSB and DSB Scenarios

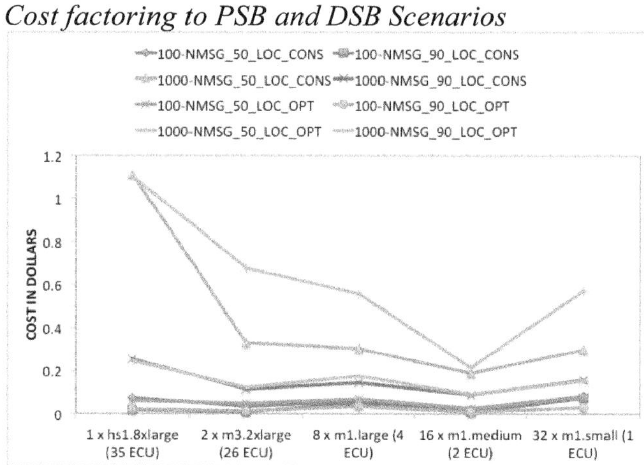

Figure 15 Overall cost of PSB on EC2 Cloud

After obtaining the runtime from the PSB and DSB runs and the cost-per-hour from the EC2 specifications, we computed the overall cost for the PSB and DSB scenarios. Figure 15 and Figure 16 plot the cost of execution in terms of dollars on various virtual clusters. For most of the runs it was found that the *16×m1.medium* virtual cluster provided the best cost-value across almost all runs for both PSB and DSB scenarios.

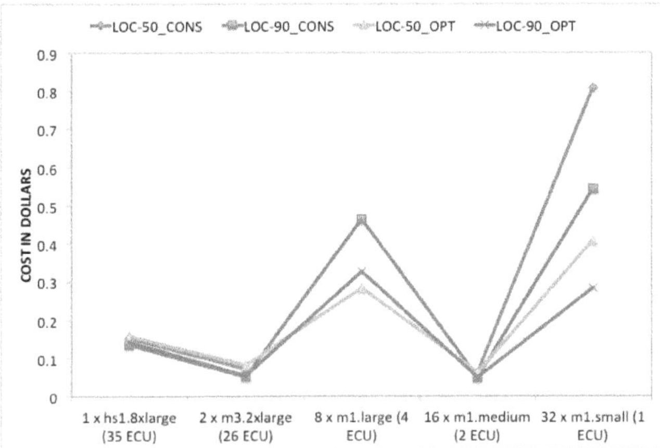

Figure 16 Overall cost for DSB on EC2 Cloud

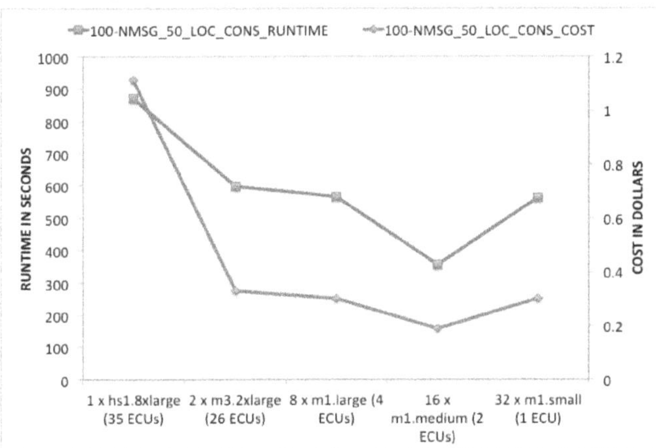

Figure 17 Cost and runtime plots of PSB 1000-NMSG 50-LOC scenario with conservative synchronization on EC2 Cloud

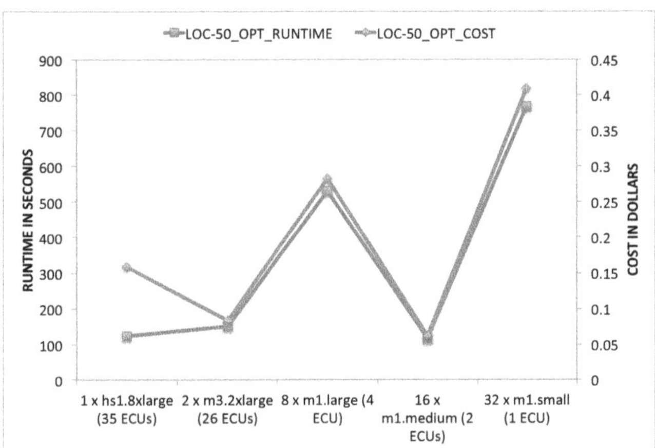

Figure 18 Cost and Runtime plots of DSB with LOC-50 using optimistic synchronization on EC2 Cloud

To compare the runtime and costs, we pick the better-performing large-scale scenarios with high-network traffic from PSB (100-NLP_1000-NMSG_50-LOC_CONS) scenario and DSB (LOC-50_OPT) scenario, as shown in Figure 17 and Figure 18, respectively. The PSB plot in Figure 17 shows best runtime and best cost associated with virtual cluster of decently compute-intensive instances of VM, i.e. *16×m1.medium*, which is against popular belief. The cost and runtime on the expensive high-end resource is far higher than that on the *16×m1.medium* cluster.

Similar to PSB, the DSB plot shown in Figure 18 also provides better runtime performance and cost at *16×m1.medium*. Even though the runtime provided by the expensive high-end compute resource compares well with runtime, the cost of computation is higher than that of *16×m1.medium*.

4.5 Performance Summary

From the benchmarks and scenarios, we find that VM-based execution can be as fast as native execution, with little perceivable performance degradation. Also, privileged and unprivileged VMs deliver the same runtime, indicating that it is not worthwhile to elevate privileges with the goal of increasing performance for PDES runs.

On dedicated machines in which the number of virtual cores is exactly the same as the number of physical cores, the fastest execution is obtained by using only a single VM that contains all the virtual cores. However, such a dedicated allocation of virtual to real cores is almost impossible to ensure in a typical Cloud environment because the underlying physical machine is opaque and also subject to change. Thus, the fastest execution that is competitive with native execution cannot be obtained on the Cloud. In fact, due to complex scheduler artifacts that arise due to a fundamental mismatch between virtual time order and fair scheduling order, the PDES execution on the highest end VM configuration in the Cloud suffers from degraded performance. To make matters worse, since the computational cycles on the highest-end configuration also cost significantly more than other lower end configurations, the overall cost can be much higher, hence less competitive, than execution on lower end configurations. Thus, on the Cloud, it seems to be more economical to choose some of the least expensive configurations (which have only one or two virtual cores per VM), which deliver a dramatic reduction in cost coupled with good runtime relative to the high-end configurations.

On dedicated VM hosts outside the Cloud, there is also an interesting tendency towards the extremes: while the best runtime is obtained on one VM with all the virtual cores, the next best is obtained on the other extreme of the spectrum in which each VM has only one virtual core. In other words, to obtain the best performance, either 1xN or Nx1 should be chosen (N is the number of physical cores), but all other configurations in between should be avoided as they suffer from worse performance.

Recommendations to Cloud users

We find that an analogy to automobiles is appropriate here. An automobile engine may be designed for speed (e.g., 0-60mph time) and/or gas mileage (miles per gallon, mpg). While racecars may exclusively focus on speed, consumer market automobiles have to find a good tradeoff between speed and mileage. Similarly, while PDES has largely focused so far on speed, it may be time to visit the counter part of miles per gallon, namely, the dollar value, when the PDES applications are executed in a Cloud environment.

Taking the preceding observations into account, it is clear that low cost and small runtime are not always opposed to each other, and that trade-offs exist.

- On a node with N physical processor cores, the overheads of the virtual network interface should be avoided either by using the entire physical node with a single-VM using N VCPUs or or by using N VMs each with only one VCPU.
- When a PDES simulation is executed using a single VM (that uses the entire physical node), the host node must avoid not be overloaded with more VCPUs than physical cores; i.e., the number of federates per VM should equal the number of VCPUs (not the number of ECUs). This avoids the undesired effects of VM scheduling on PDES performance.

5. CONCLUSIONS AND FUTURE WORK

Virtual Machine-based systems form an appealing computational platform that is a strong alternative to high-end native execution that has been the traditional focus of PDES. However, due to the introduction of new dimensions such as configuration options and corresponding price points, a PDES user is faced with a new problem of having to decide on the most cost-effective configuration. Overall, the dollar-value of PDES runs has now become an important metric. In this context, relatively few studies exist as guidance to help contemplate, understand and decide on the various factors and effects for effective use of VM-based platforms such as commercial Cloud offerings. To help bridge this gap, an empirical study was conducted on a wide range of VM configurations, PDES applications, and scenarios. The results helped uncover counter-intuitive effects, the significant among which being that it may be not only economical but also faster to split the simulation into fine units; dividing the simulation into many VMs may in fact provide a better overall dollar-value than using the highest-end or second-to-highest VM configurations. Also, PDES runs may benefit from the inclusion of a network metric in the specification of the abstract computational unit, the absence of which seems to leave the computation to be highly sensitive to the vagaries of virtual network devices. The study and results presented here are among the first to evaluate the characteristics of PDES in detail. The results are also timely due to the great appeal of commercial Cloud offerings that many find to be very user-friendly and convenient to access and manage. Additional work is needed to evaluate even larger VM configurations, and more PDES applications with a wider variety of event granularity and event loads. Also, Cloud-specific synchronization algorithms may also be needed to be resilient to variations in virtual network latencies.

ACKNOWLEDGMENTS

This research was performed as part of a project sponsored by the U.S. Army Research Laboratory. This paper has been authored by UT-Battelle, LLC, under contract DE-AC05-00OR22725 with the U.S. Department of Energy. Accordingly, the United States Government retains and the publisher, by accepting the article for publication, acknowledges that the United States Government retains a non-exclusive, paid-up, irrevocable, worldwide license to publish or reproduce the published form of this manuscript, or allow others to do so, for United States Government purposes.

REFERENCES

[1] *Amazon Elastic Compute Cloud User Guide* http://docs.aws.amazon.com/AWSEC2/latest/UserGuide/Welcome.html

[2] D. Chisnall, "The Definitive Guide to the Xen Hypervisor," ISBN 978-013-234971-0, Prentice Hall, 2008

[3] R. M. Fujimoto, "Parallel and Distributed Simulation Systems," Wiley Interscience, 2000

[4] K. R. Jackson, L. Ramakrishnan, K. Muriki, S. Canon, S. Cholia, J. Shalf, H. J. Wasserman, and N. J. Wright, "Performance Analysis of High Performance Computing Applications on the Amazon Web Services Cloud," *IEEE 2nd International Conference on Cloud Computing Technology and Science (CloudCom),* pages 159-168, December 2010

[5] G. Wang and T.S.E. Ng, "The Impact of Virtualization on Network Performance of Amazon EC2 Data Center," *IEEE INFOCOM*, pages 1-9, March 2010

[6] G. D'Angelo, "Parallel and distributed simulation from many cores to the public cloud," *High Performance Computing and Simulation (HPCS),* pages14-23, July 2011

[7] R. M. Fujimoto, A. W. Malik, and A. J. Park, "Parallel and Distributed Simulation in the Cloud," *SCS Modeling and Simulation Magazine*, Vol. 1, No. 3, July 2010

[8] A. Malik, A. Park, and R. M. Fujimoto, "Optimistic Synchronization of Parallel Simulations in Cloud Computing Environments," *IEEE International Conference on Cloud Computing,* pages 49-56, September 2009

[9] A. J. Park, "Master/Worker Parallel Discrete Event Simulation" in College of Computing. PhD thesis, *Georgia Institute of Technology*, 2008

[10] K. Vanmechelen, S. De Munck, and J. Broeckhove, "Conservative Distributed Discrete Event Simulation on Amazon EC2," *12th International Symposium on Cluster, Cloud and Grid Computing (CCGrid)*, pages 853-860, May 2012

[11] K. S. Perumalla, A. J. Park, and V. Tipparaju, "GVT Algorithms and Discrete Event Dynamics on 129K+ Processor Cores," *International Conference on High Performance Computing (HiPC)*, December 2011

[12] A. O. Holder, and C. D. Carothers, "Analysis of Time Warp on a 32,768 Processor IBM Blue Gene/L Supercomputer," *European Modeling and Simulation Symposium (EMSS)*, 2008

[13] F. Mattern, "Efficient Algorithms for Distributed Snapshots and Global Virtual Time Approximation," *Journal of Parallel and Distributed Computing*, Vol. 18, No. 4, 1993.

[14] R. M. Fujimoto, "Performance of Time Warp Under Synthetic Workloads," *Distributed Simulation Conference*, pages 23-28, 1990

[15] K. S. Perumalla, "µsik - A Micro-Kernel for Parallel and Distributed Simulation Systems," *Workshop on Principles of Advanced and Distributed Simulation (PADS)*, 2005

[16] K. S. Perumalla, and S. K. Seal, "Discrete event modeling and Massively Parallel Execution of Epidemic Outbreak Phenomena," *Simulation*, Vol. 88, No. 7, pages 768-783, 2012

[17] S. B. Yoginath, and K. S. Perumalla, "Optimized Hypervisor Scheduler for Parallel Discrete Event Simulations on Virtual Machine Platforms," *International ICST Conference on Simulation Tools and Techniques (SIMUTools)*, 2013

[18] S. J. Renato, G. Janakiraman, Y. Turner, and I. Pratt. "Netchannel 2: Optimizing network performance." *Proceedings of the XenSource/Citrix Xen Summit,* 2007.

Accelerating Optimistic HLA-based Simulations in Virtual Execution Environments

ZengXiang Li, Xiaorong Li, TA Nguyen Binh Duong
Institute of High Performance Computing
Agency for Science, Technology and Research (A*STAR) Singapore
{liz,lixr,tanbd}@ihpc.a-star.edu.sg

Wentong Cai, Stephen John Turner
School of Computer Engineering
Nanyang Technological University Singapore
{aswtcai,assjturner}@ntu.edu.sg

ABSTRACT

High Level Architecture (HLA)-based simulations employing optimistic synchronization allows federates to process event and to advance simulation time freely at the risk of over-optimistic execution and execution rollbacks. In this paper, an adaptive resource provisioning system is proposed to accelerate optimistic HLA-based simulations in *Virtual Execution Environment* (VEE). A performance monitor is introduced using a middleware approach to measure the performance of individual federates transparently to the simulation application. Based on the performance measurements, a resource manager distributes the available computational resources to the federates, making them advance simulation time with comparable speeds. Our proposed approach is evaluated using a real-world simulation model with various workload inputs and different parameter settings. The experimental results show that, compared with distributing resources evenly among federates, our proposed approach can accelerate the simulation execution significantly using the same amount of computational resources.

Categories and Subject Descriptors

I.6 [**Computing Methodologies**]: SIMULATION AND MODELING

Keywords

HLA-based Simulations, Optimistic Synchronization, Virtual Execution Environment, VM Scheduling, Cloud Computing

1. INTRODUCTION

Parallel and distributed simulations are usually built to study large-scale and complex systems in desired detail and fidelity. The *High Level Architecture* (HLA), IEEE 1516 standard [11], provides a general framework to build a parallel and distributed simulation (*federation*) by integrating various simulation models (*federates*). Most work to date has focused on conducting HLA-based simulations on a traditional execution platform composed of a group of dedicated computing nodes. Recently, we have witnessed an increasing interest of moving data and computation to the Cloud. Large amount of resources can be obtained on the Cloud for the purpose of executing compute- and data-intensive HLA-based simulations [6]. Furthermore, resources can be provisioned elastically according to the simulation workload. Different from traditional execution platforms, most of the Infrastructure as a Service (IaaS) Cloud providers [1] adopt *Virtual Execution Environment* (VEE) relying on virtualization technologies [2]. In this paper, we investigate how to accelerate HLA-based simulations in VEE.

One of the greatest challenges in HLA-based simulations is the time synchronization among federates, which ensures that all events are processed in *time stamp* (TS) order. In this paper, we focus on the optimistic synchronization approach [13], which allows a federate to process events and to advance simulation time freely at the risk of over-optimistic executions and execution rollbacks. It has good performance when all federates can advance their simulation time with comparable speed [6]. This usually requires that federates should have homogeneous simulation workload and should execute on homogeneous computational resources. Unfortunately, it is very difficult to meet such requirement in practice. Federates which simulate different parts of an unsymmetric system have probably different workloads. Furthermore, the workload of each federate might change during the simulation execution. In the traditional execution platform, federates might execute on heterogenous computing nodes. In VEE, federates may share resources with other federates or even other applications.

In this paper, each federate is encapsulated and executed on a *virtual machine* (VM). VMs consolidated on a computing node are scheduled by a hypervisor to share the underlying resources. By setting relevant parameters of the

VM scheduling algorithm, VMs can be constrained to use a desired share of computational resources, i.e., CPU compute cycles (to be explained in Section 3.2). Consequently, the performance of federates can be controlled. Inspired to this, we propose an adaptive resource provisioning system for the purpose of accelerating optimistic HLA-based simulations in VEE. A performance monitor is introduced using a middleware approach to measure the execution performance of federates transparently to the simulation application. A resource manager is developed as a bridge between the performance monitor and hypervisor. It periodically retrieves performance measurements of federates from the performance monitor and the amount of available resources from the hypervisor. Based on the performance measurements, the resource manager can predict workload of the federates and then distribute the available resources to the federates accordingly. As a result, federates are able to advance their simulation time with comparable speed, avoiding over-optimistic executions and execution rollbacks. Hence, the simulation execution can be accelerated using the same amount of computational resources.

The rest of the paper is organized as follows: Section 2 discusses the related work. Section 3 introduces some background knowledge including HLA-based simulations and VM scheduling in VEE. Section 4 illustrates the details of our proposed adaptive resource provisioning system. Section 5 describes the experiment design and discusses the experimental results. Finally, Section 6 concludes the paper and outlines the future work.

2. RELATED WORK

A number of research work have been done on accelerating parallel and distributed simulations on traditional execution platforms. Federate migration protocols [15] were proposed to achieve workload balance in the federation execution. Different synchronization approaches are mixed [25] or replicated [16] for the purpose of taking their advantages in the same simulation execution. The *Adaptive Time Warp* protocol [24] improves performance of optimistic synchronization by reactively blocking the optimistic execution of simulation components. Specifically, a simulation component is blocked if it has executed far beyond others in the same simulation execution. The protocol is most closely related to our proposed approach. However, its performance is sensitive to the frequency of global synchronization, which is time-consuming in the Cloud due to the unstable network performance [30].

Recently, researchers have tried to tackle the technical challenges that arise in moving parallel and distributed simulations to the Cloud [26, 6]. Malik et. al [17] have proposed a novel protocol to enhance optimistic synchronization efficiency on the Cloud in the presence of high network latency and jitters. Similar to the *Adaptive Time Warp* protocol [24], the protocol proposed in [17] reactively blocking the execution of fast simulation components. In contrast, we propose to proactively make federates advance simulation time with comparable speed, and thus, avoids execution rollbacks.

In addition, researchers have also tried to accelerate parallel and distributed simulations on modern many-core processors [7, 4]. Similar to our proposed approach, Child and Wilsey [4] have explored the features of Dynamic Voltage and Frequency Scaling (DVFS) for the purpose of reducing the execution rollbacks in optimistic simulations. The performance of individual simulation components are controlled by adjusting the frequency and voltage of their corresponding CPU cores. However, due to the hardware limit, only four to six discrete frequency-voltage pairs are made possible. To the best of our knowledge, we are the first to consider accelerating HLA-based simulations by harnessing virtualization technologies which are commonly used in the Cloud. Different from DVFS, the virtualization technologies leveraged in this paper enable fine-grained adjustment of CPU resources (to be explained in Section 3.2).

In Cloud computing, under-provisioning resources will cause *Service Level Objective* (SLO) violation, resulting in financial penalties; while over-provisioning resources will increase cost and waste resources that could be assigned to other users. To avoid these problems, several elastic resource allocation systems [10, 28, 14, 22] have been proposed. In [10, 28], signature-driven and state-driven approaches are used to predict application workload. According to the workload prediction, resources are automatically allocated to the corresponding VMs. In [14, 22], the amount of resources necessary to achieve application SLO is automatically determined using a control theory-based estimator. Unfortunately, these resource allocation systems are targeted at web server applications and cannot be directly applied on optimistic HLA-based simulations. For instance, the workload of web server applications can be predicted according to historical CPU utilization rate [10, 28], as the CPU is put to idle when the workload is light. In contrast, optimistic federates consume allocated CPU resource on optimistic executions which might be rolled back in the future. Hence, the CPU utilization rate does not represent the useful workload of federates. In addition, the performance target of server applications are well defined in SLO and their real performance can be measured easily [14, 22]. In contrast, the performance of an HLA-based simulation is concerned with the performance of individual federates, as well as the time synchronization among them. It is also non-trivial to measure federate performance transparently to the simulation applications.

3. BACKGROUND

3.1 HLA-based Simulations

In an HLA-based simulation, federates might be developed by different participants from different organizations. They are executed in a parallel and distributed manner. The HLA interface specification implemented by a *Runtime Infrastructure* (RTI) defines how a federate interacts with other federates in the federation. Usually, an RTI component is provided by the RTI to connect each joined federate to the federation. It keeps part of the RTI state concerned with the federate and takes care of the federate's need to exchange messages and to request time advancement. The bidirectional interface between the federate and its RTI component is usually implemented via ambassadors. Federates invoke services provided by the RTI ambassador, while the RTI delivers callbacks to the federate through its federate ambassador. For instance, a federate sends messages by invoking the corresponding RTI services (e.g., *SendInteraction*). These messages are delivered to receiving federates in the form of callbacks (e. g., *ReceiveInteraction*).

An optimistic federate invokes *Flush Queue Request* (FQR)

service iteratively during the simulation execution. It forces the RTI to deliver all buffered messages to the federate. In the mean time, the FQR request might trigger a federation-wide time synchronization. The time granted by the RTI after FQR service is referred to as *logical time* of the federate. It defines the lower bound of future execution rollbacks. It can be used for fossil collection in the federate, e.g., the storage space containing checkpointed states with TS smaller than the granted time can be reclaimed. Since the federate is allowed to process events freely, its *simulation time* (i.e., TS of the event being processed) might be greater than its logical time. However, it might receive a straggler message whose TS is smaller than its simulation time. If so, a causality error happens and the federate needs to rollback its execution by discarding the *over-optimistic execution* (i.e., the execution of those events with TS greater than the TS of the straggler message). It must undo the modification on federate state relying on federate state saving and restoration mechanism [13, 9]. Additionally, it needs to invoke *Retract* services to unsend those incorrect messages which were sent during the over-optimistic execution. In the case that the messages have already been delivered to the receiving federates, the RTI informs those federates to remove the effect of the incorrect messages through *Request Retraction* (RR) callbacks. This may cause secondary execution rollbacks in the receiving federates.

3.2 VM Scheduling

In VEE, the hypervisor monitors the underlying resources and performs VM scheduling. Credit scheduler [33], the default CPU scheduler in Xen, is a proportional share scheduler. The credit allocation for VMs is managed by two parameters: a weight and an optional cap. By default, only weight is defined for each VM. In this case, the credit scheduler is work-conserving, which means that a VM that has expended all of its credit will be allocated additional CPU share if no other VM is using its allocated share. Optionally, we can use cap to specify the maximum CPU share the VM is allowed to consume. In this case, the credit scheduler is non-work-conserving, which means that a VM never consumes CPU share beyond the cap even if the rest of CPU share is left idle. Compared with work-conserving, non-work-conserving provides better performance isolation among VMs [3, 27]. The cap value, rather than the weight value, precisely specifies the CPU share allocated to a VM. It can be any integer value (denoted as c) between 1 and 100, indicating that c% time of one CPU core is scheduled for the VM [1]. In this paper, the computational resources allocated to federates are controlled through the fine-grained adjustment of the CPU caps of their resident VMs.

4. ADAPTIVE RESOURCE PROVISIONING SYSTEM

4.1 Architecture Overview

The architecture of our proposed adaptive resource provisioning system is illustrated in Figure 1. Each federate is executed on its individual resident VM. Similar to the solutions in [31], a performance monitor can be inserted between the federate and its RTI component as a middleware. By intercepting the RTI services and callbacks, the performance monitor is able to measure the performance of the federate transparently to the simulation application. More details will be provided in Section 4.2.

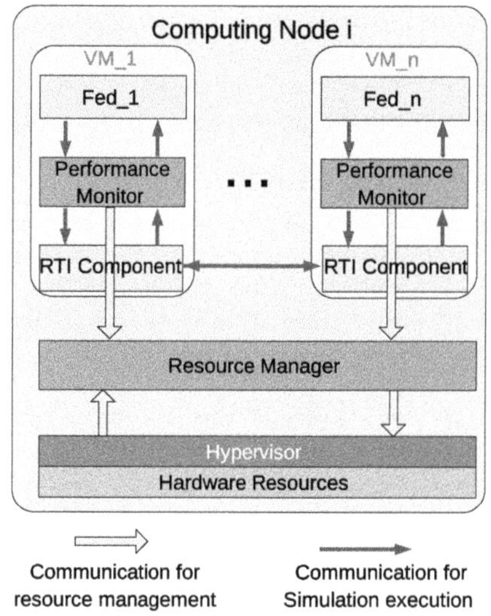

Figure 1: Overview of the adaptive resource provisioning system

A resource manager is developed as a bridge between the performance monitor and the hypervisor of the computing node. It periodically adjusts the resource shares for federates in the federation for the purpose of making them have the same performance. The simulation execution is divided into a number of successive control intervals. The control interval length is a parameter used in the adaptive resource provisioning system. In each control interval, the resource manager retrieves performance of federates through their performance monitors. In the meantime, it retrieves the available resources of the computing node through its hypervisor. An algorithm is developed to distribute the available resources among federates. Finally, the resource manager sends resource shares of federates (i.e., caps of their resident VMs) to the hypervisor, and the latter schedules VMs accordingly (as described in Section 3.2). By allocating appropriate computational resource shares, the federates with different workloads are able to achieve comparable performance. Compared with the scheme that evenly distributes computational sources among federates, the adaptive resource provisioning system allocates less computational resources to federates with low workload. Hence, they can avoid over-optimistic executions and execution rollbacks. On the other hand, the adaptive resource provisioning system allocates more computational resources to federates with high workload. Hence, the overall federation execution can be accelerated. More details will be provided in Section 4.3.

Although only one computing node is illustrated in Figure 1, the adaptive resource provisioning system can be easily extended to multiple computing nodes for large-scale HLA-based simulations. In this case, the resource managers deployed at different computing nodes should coordinate with each other for the purpose of making all federates in

[1]The cap value can also be greater than 100, indicating that more the one CPU core is scheduled for the VM

the federation have the same performance. In addition, the resident VMs should be migrated among computing nodes if necessary to achieve workload balance and/or to reduce communication overhead [5].

4.2 Performance Monitor

In HLA-based simulations, the performance of a federate is measured by its execution speed, i.e., how fast the federate can advance its simulation time. Intuitively, it can be measured as the advanced simulation time in a control interval divided by the control interval length. However, execution rollbacks might happen during the control interval. If so, the simulation time decreases and the federate wastes time on over-optimistic executions and execution rollbacks. Hence, the execution speed measured in this manner may not accurately characterize the useful workload of the federate. In some extreme cases, the measured execution speed might even be a negative value. To solve this problem, the simulation execution is partitioned into epochs, which is usually much smaller than the control interval. Only the epochs without over-optimistic executions and execution rollbacks are taken into account for performance measurement.

As shown in Figure 1, the performance monitor in the middleware is able to intercept FQR services invoked by federates. By default, the argument (i.e., the *requested time*) of a FQR service is the TS of the next internal event in the federate. Usually, it is quite close to the simulation time of the federate. Hence, we can use the requested time to estimate the progress of federates approximately[2]. In this way, federate execution can be partitioned into epochs, each of which is defined as the requested time interval between two subsequent FQR requests. Usually, federates are not required to invoke a FQR service before processing every event. Hence, an epoch is likely to include multiple processed events.

Algorithm 1 Intercept FQR service

1: Let **E** be the list of epochs in each control interval
2: **if** $RollbackFlag == true$ **then**
3: $\quad RollbackFlag = false$
4: **else**
5: $\quad$ Append a new epoch (E_k) at the end of **E**
6: $\quad E_k \rightarrow begTS = ReqTime(k-1)$
7: $\quad E_k \rightarrow endTS = ReqTime(k)$
8: $\quad E_k \rightarrow advTS = ReqTime(k) - ReqTime(k-1)$
9: $\quad E_k \rightarrow exeTime = Clock(k) - Clock(k-1)$
10: **end if**

As shown in Algorithm 1, the epochs in the control interval are kept in a list denoted as **E**. On intercepting the kth FQR invocation, the performance monitor creates a new epoch E_k (Lines 5), except that an execution rollback is detected (to be discussed later) before the FQR invocation (Lines 2 and 3). In the meantime, it also records the requested time denoted as $ReqTime(k)$ and the wall time clock denoted as $Clock(k)$. Then, $ReqTime(k-1)$ and $ReqTime(k)$ respectively defines the beginning and the end of E_k (Lines 6 and 7). The advanced simulation time and execution time of E_k is $ReqTime(k) - ReqTime(k-1)$ and $Clock(k) - Clock(k-1)$ respectively (Lines 8 and 9).

As mentioned in Section 3.1, messages and RR callbacks

Algorithm 2 Intercept messages and RR callbacks

1: Let **M** be the list of delivered messages and RR callbacks after each FQR service
2: $minMsgTS = \min_{M_i \in \mathbf{M}} M_i \rightarrow TS$
3: **for** Each $E_i \in \mathbf{E}$ **do**
4: $\quad$ **if** $minMsgTS < E_i \rightarrow endTS$ **then**
5: $\quad\quad$ Remove E_i from **E**
6: $\quad\quad RollbackFlag = true$
7: $\quad$ **end if**
8: **end for**

are delivered to federates after each FQR invocation. In order to detect the execution rollbacks, the performance monitor intercepts the delivered messages and RR callbacks, as shown in Algorithm 2. Firstly, it calculates $minMsgTS$, i.e., the minimum TS of those messages and RR callbacks (Line 2). In the case that the $minMsgTS$ is smaller than the $endTS$ of an epoch in **E**, the epoch includes over-optimistic execution which will be rolled back. Therefore, it should not be considered for performance measurement (Lines 3 to 5). Once an execution rollback is detected, the $rollbackFlag$ is set to true. This will prevent the performance monitor from creating an epoch on intercepting the subsequent FQR invocation (Lines 2 and 3 in Algorithm 1).

At the end of each control interval, the performance monitor is required to measure the execution speed of the federate during the control interval, as shown in Algorithm 3. It is possible that the control interval might not include any epoch, especially when the control interval is too short and/or when the federate encounters an execution rollback. In this case, the performance monitor simply reports an invalid execution speed, i.e., NaN (Not a Number). Otherwise, the execution speed of the federate is calculated as the sum of advanced simulation time of all epochs in the control interval divided by the sum of execution time of those epochs. After the performance is measured, the list **E** is able to be cleared up for keeping epochs in the subsequent control interval.

Algorithm 3 Measure performance

1: **if E** is empty **then**
2: $\quad exeSpeed = NaN$ //NaN: Not a Number
3: **else**
4: $\quad exeSpeed = \frac{\sum_{E_i \in \mathbf{E}} E_i \rightarrow advTS}{\sum_{E_i \in \mathbf{E}} E_i \rightarrow exeTime}$
5: **end if**
6: Remove all elements from **E**
7: **return** $exeSpeed$

4.3 Resource Manager

Since the workload prediction is not the main focus of this paper, we simply use the simulation workload in the current control interval to predict that in the subsequent control interval. It is also assumed that federate performance increases proportionally with increasing VM Cap [27]. Take the ith federate as an example, at the end of kth control interval, the resource manager retrieves the *measured execution speed* denoted as $MES_i(k)$ from the performance monitor.

[2]For better accuracy, the performance monitor can provide federate with a modified FQR interface including both simulation time and requested time arguments. However, such modified interface is not compliant to the HLA standard.

Suppose that the caps of its resident VM at k^{th} and $(k+1)^{th}$ control intervals are set to $Cap_i(k)$ and $Cap_i(k+1)$ respectively, we can get the *predicted execution speed* (PES) at the $(k+1)^{th}$ control interval as:

$$PES_i(k+1) = \frac{MES_i(k)}{Cap_i(k)} \times Cap_i(k+1) \quad (1)$$

To accelerate the simulation execution, the PES of all federates should be maximized at every control interval. However, some constraints should be satisfied in the meantime. Firstly, the federates can only consume the available resource. Suppose that the federation scale is N; the simulation execution time is T; the control interval length is t; the number of available CPU cores is M, we can get

$$\sum_{i=1}^{N} Cap_i(k) \leq M * 100 \quad (2)$$

for each $k \in \{1, 2, ..., \frac{T}{t}\}$. Secondly, each federate cannot consume more than one CPU core, because the federate, as a simulation component, is usually single-threaded [18]. That is,

$$Cap_i(k) \leq 100 \quad (3)$$

for each $i \in \{1, 2, ..., N\}$ and $k \in \{1, 2, ..., \frac{T}{t}\}$. Thirdly, to avoid execution rollbacks, federates should have the same PES in the same control interval. That is,

$$PES_i(k) = PES_j(k) \quad (4)$$

where i and $j \in \{1, 2, ..., N\}$ and $k \in \{1, 2, ..., \frac{T}{t}\}$.

The functionality of the resource manager is illustrated in Algorithm 4. $\mathbf{F}$ denotes the set of all federates in the federation. At the end of each control interval, the resource manager retrieves MES from the performance monitor of all federates in the federation (Lines 5 to 10). In the case that the retrieved MES is NaN (Not a Number), the MES is approximately set as the PES of the federate in the control interval. After that, the resource manager distributes available resources to federates in the federation for the purpose of maximizing PES of all federates while satisfying aforementioned constraints.

According to Equation 1, the federate with smaller $\frac{MES(k)}{Cap(k)}$ should have greater $Cap(k+1)$ to meet the third constraint (Equation 4) in the next control interval. In other words, F_m with the minimum $\frac{MES(k)}{Cap(k)}$ should have the maximum $Cap(k+1)$ in the federation. Due to the second constraint (Equation 3), $Cap_m(k+1)$ can be set to 100 at the most. Without considering the first constraint (Equation 2), we can initially set $Cap_m(k+1) = 100$. Then, $PES_m(k+1)$ can be calculated according to Equation 1 (Line 13). According to the third constraint, other federates should have the same PES as F_m (Line 15). Then, $Cap(k+1)$ for other federates can be calculated by rewriting Equation 1 (Line 16).

However, the first constraint (Equation 2) will not be satisfied if the ratio of $M \times 100$ to $\sum_{F_i \in \mathbf{F}} Cap_i(k+1)$, denoted as φ, is smaller than one. To make it satisfied, the caps of all federates should be reduced by φ times. Obviously, the second constraint will be satisfied as well. Since the PES of all federates will be reduced by φ times, they will remain the same, making the third constraint satisfied. In the case that $\varphi > 1$, the federates in the federation cannot consume all the available CPU resources. F_m becomes the bottleneck that holds back the simulation execution.

Algorithm 4 Resource Manager

1: $\mathbf{F} = \{F_1, F_2, \cdots, F_N\}$;
2: $k = 0$;
3: **while** $k < \frac{T}{t}$ **do**
4: Thread.sleep(t);
5: **for** each $F_i \in \mathbf{F}$ **do**
6: $MES_i(k) = F_i \rightarrow measurePerformance()$;
7: **if** $MES_i(k) == NaN$ **then**
8: $MES_i(k) = PES_i(k)$;
9: **end if**
10: **end for**
11: Choose $F_m \in \mathbf{F}$ where $\frac{MES_m(k)}{Cap_m(k)} = \min_{F_i \in \mathbf{F}} \frac{MES_i(k)}{Cap_i(k)}$;
12: $Cap_m(k+1) = 100$;
13: $PES_m(k+1) = \frac{MES_m(k)}{Cap_m(k)} \times Cap_m(k+1)$;
14: **for** each $F_i \in \mathbf{F} - \{F_m\}$ **do**
15: $PES_i(k+1) = PES_m(k+1)$;
16: $Cap_i(k+1) = \frac{PES_i(k+1)}{MES_i(k)} \times Cap_i(k)$;
17: **end for**
18: $\varphi = \frac{M \times 100}{\sum_{F_i \in \mathbf{F}} Cap_i(k+1)}$;
19: **if** $\varphi < 1$ **then**
20: **for** each $F_i \in \mathbf{F}$ **do**
21: $Cap_i(k+1) = \varphi \times Cap_i(k+1)$;
22: $PES_i(k+1) = \varphi \times PES_i(k+1)$;
23: **end for**
24: **end if**
25: $k++$;
26: **end while**

5. EXPERIMENTS AND RESULTS

5.1 Experiment Design

A *Massively Multiplayer Online Games* (MMOGs) ecosystem simulation model is used in our experiments to evaluate our proposed adaptive resource provisioning system. Nae et. al [21] have proposed a dynamic resource provisioning method and introduced the concepts of MMOGs ecosystem. In the MMOGs ecosystem, game operators rent resources (CPU, Network and Memory) from data centers for running the MMOG servers. They are able to dynamically adjust the amount of renting resources according to the workload of MMOGs (e.g., the number of players and their interactions). We develop an HLA-based simulation to simulate the MMOGs ecosystem. It can be used to study the effect of dynamic resource provisioning schemes using different workload prediction algorithms and different resource hosting policies.

In our HLA-based simulation, each federate simulates the game servers in a data center. It generates a local event to simulate the performance and resource provisioning of the game servers in each time step (i.e., 10 seconds) of the MMOGs execution [21]. That is, the difference of simulation time between any two successive local event is 10. Each local event calculates the response time of each interaction initialized by players connected to the data center and measures the quality of game experience from the perspective of those players, using the resources rented from the data center in the corresponding time step. Therefore, the simulation model can be used to evaluate resource provisioning schemes using performance metrics such as resource over-allocation and resource under-allocation [21]. In addition, we can also get that the computational resource required for processing a local event increases proportionally with the increasing number of players connected to the data center in the corresponding time step. In our experiments, the number of players connected to the data centers are retrieved from the trace of RuneScape [21]. They have strong diurnal pattern. Therefore, the simulation workload of the corresponding federates also have strong diurnal pattern. In the case that the data centers locate at regions in different time zones, the corresponding federates may have different simulation workloads at the same simulation time. For simplicity, the federation scale is set to two in our experiments. Various cases of simulation workloads (specifically, the number of players connected to the corresponding data centers) are introduced in the two federates. In Case 1, the data centers locate in the regions within the same time zone. In Cases 2 and 3, the time difference between the data centers is around 6 and 12 hours, respectively. For instance, the number of players during a day in Case 3 is illustrated in Figure 2.

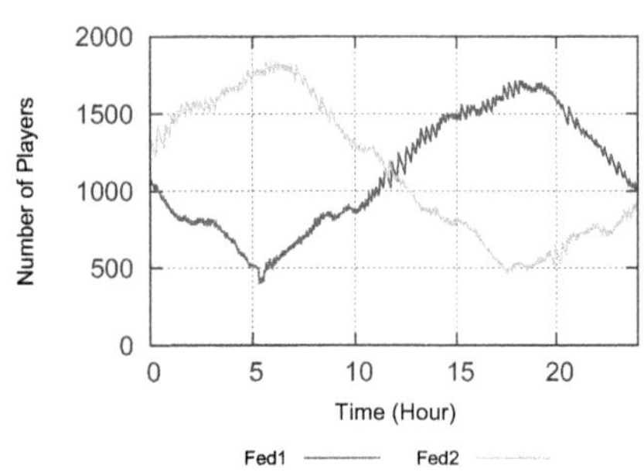

Figure 2: Simulation workload of federate (Case3)

In addition, federates might send external events to each other to simulate the communication between servers located at different data centers. For instance, servers may replicate some parts of their game state in different data centers to tolerate unpredictable failures [19]. Depending on different strategies, state replications might be triggered at different situations and the replication frequency might vary in a large range. For simplicity, we assume each external event is triggered by an internal event. The probability of generating external events is denoted as $P_{ExternEvent}$. The TS of an external event equal to TS of the processing internal event plus a *lookahead* (LA) [9], indicating that the external event will affect the receiving federate after LA simulation time. $P_{ExternEvent}$ and LA are used as parameters in our HLA-based simulation. In our experiments, we will evaluate the performance of a number of simulation executions with different parameter inputs, i.e., different values of $P_{ExternEvent}$ and LA.

Optimistic synchronization is employed in the MMOGs ecosystem simulation model. Federates are allowed to process three events before invoking the next FQR service. In addition, the infrequent state saving approach described in [8] is adopted. Federates save their state after processing 15 events. When a causality error happens, the federate must roll back to a previous saved state and coast-forward execution to recreate the desired execution state.

The simulation executes on an RTI implemented by reusing the code in SOHR [23]. For efficiency consideration, RTI components are implemented as the libraries of their corresponding federates; the communication among RTI components use JAVA socket instead of the heavy Grid service invocation. Experiments are carried out on a computing node installed with 12 Intel Xeon 2.67GHz CPU cores, 24 GB RAM, CentOS 6.2 and Xen 4.1.2. Each federate executes on a VM with one VCPU core, 2 GB RAM and CentOS 6.2.

Two execution scenarios are studied. In the *Fixed* scenario, the caps of VMs are fixed at 50, i.e., two federates share one CPU core evenly. In the *Adaptive* scenario, the caps of the resident VMs are dynamically adjusted using our proposed adaptive resource provisioning system. However, the sum of their caps is always equal to 100. The simulation length is 2 days, including the first day as the warm up period.

5.2 Experiment Results

In the first series of experiments, we compare the simulation execution performance in *Fixed* and *Adaptive* scenarios with aforementioned workload cases. The experimental results are illustrated in Figure 3, including the simulation execution time, the number of execution rollbacks and the execution efficiency. The execution efficiency is defined as the ratio of useful events to total events processed [17]. Besides the useful events, federate might process events in the over-optimistic execution and the coast-forward execution. The *Fixed* scenario (*Adaptive* scenario) for workload cases 1, 2 and 3 are respectively denoted as $F(1)$, $F(2)$ and $F(3)$ ($A(1)$, $A(2)$ and $A(3)$) in the figure. The control interval length as the parameter in the adaptive resource provisioning system ranges from 80 to 5 seconds. Obviously, it is meaningful for the *Adaptive* scenario, but not the *Fixed* scenario. For simplicity, the parameters of the simulation model are set as follows: $P_{ExternEvent} = 1\%$ and $LA = 45$. Different parameter inputs of the simulation model will be studied latter.

In Case 1, federates have similar workload during the simulation execution. Therefore, federates executed in both *Fixed* and *Adaptive* scenarios are able to advance simulation time with comparable speed. Hence, federates encounters a small number of execution rollbacks (Figure 3(b)); and they have high execution efficiency (Figure 3(c)). Therefore, we can observe from Figure 3(a) that the *Fixed* and *Adaptive* scenarios have similar execution performance. In Cases 2 and 3, federates have different workload. For the *Fixed* scenario, compared with Case 1, the numbers of execution rollbacks are much greater (Figure 3(b)). Furthermore, the over-optimistic execution discarded in each execution rollback can be very huge due to the different execution speed of federates. As a result, the execution efficiency are much lower (Figure 3(c)). Therefore, we can observe from Figure 3(a) that the execution time of $F(2)$ and $F(3)$ are much greater than that of $F(1)$. Different from the *Fixed* scenario, federates in the *Adaptive* scenario have comparable execution speed. They encounter less execution rollbacks (Figure 3(b)) and have higher execution efficiency (Figure 3(c)). Therefore, our proposed adaptive resource provisioning system is able to reduce the simulation execution time significantly (Figure 3(a)).

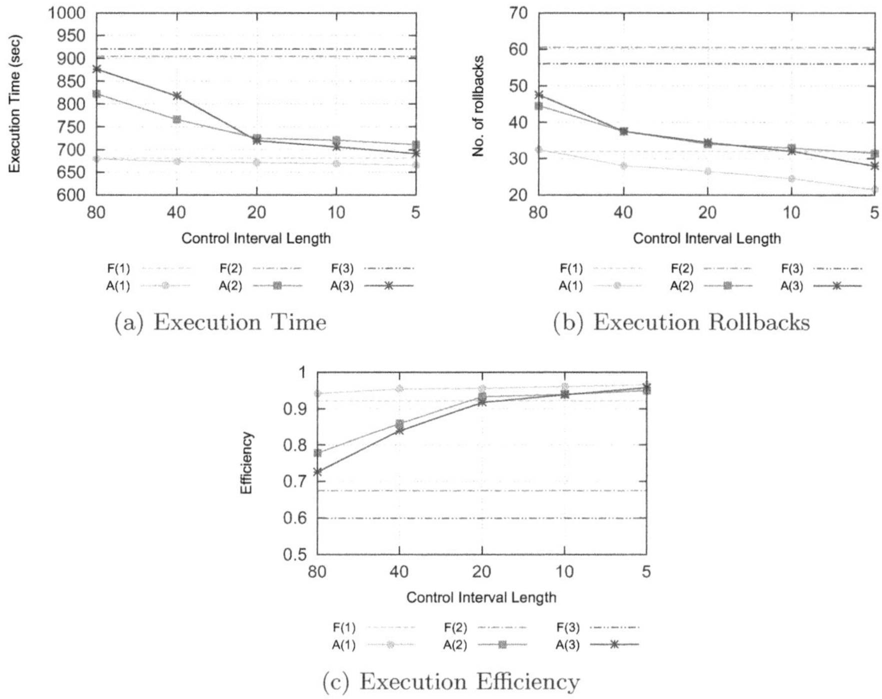

Figure 3: Performance comparison with different workload cases and decreasing control interval length

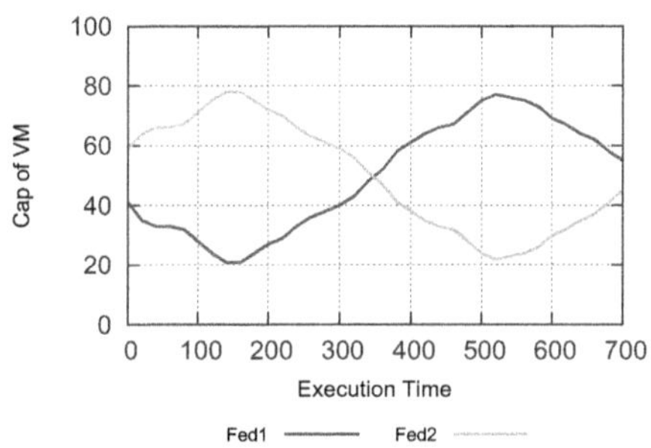

Figure 4: Caps of the resident VMs (Case3)

Generally speaking, the smaller the control interval length, the more accurately the resource manager is able to adjust the resource provisioning according to simulation workload. As a result, federates encounter less execution rollbacks (Figure 3(b)) and have higher execution efficiency (Figure 3(c)). Therefore, we can observe from Figure 3(a) that the simulation execution time in *Adaptive* scenario decreases with the decreasing control interval length. When the control interval length is equal to 5 seconds, the adaptive resource provisioning system can obtain 22% and 25% *performance enhancement* (i.e., the difference in execution time between *Fixed* and *Adaptive* scenarios divided by the execution time in *Fixed* scenario) for Cases 2 and 3 respectively. It is worth to point out that federates executed in the *Adaptive* scenario cannot avoid all execution rollbacks. This is because that they cannot advance their simulation time with the same speed in practice, due to the accuracy of workload prediction and performance overhead in VEE [20]. Figure 4 illustrates the caps of resident VMs of federates during the simulation execution when the control interval length is 20 seconds. By comparing Figure 2, we can observe that the CPU resource is proportionally distributed to federates according to their simulation workloads.

The second series of experiments are carried out to compare the simulation execution performance in *Fixed* and *Adaptive* scenarios with different parameter inputs of the simulation model. Due to the space limit, we only report the experimental results for Case 3 simulation workload, which is quite common in the MMOGs ecosystem, as the data centers usually locate at different places around the world. In addition, the control interval length is set to 20 seconds. Figure 5 illustrates the simulation execution, number of execution rollbacks and execution efficiency with $P_{ExternEvent}$ increasing from 1% to 10%. Three different LA values (i.e., 15, 45 and 105) are taken into account. The *Adaptive* and *Fixed* scenarios for $LA = l$ are denoted as $A - l$ and $F - l$ respectively.

As aforementioned, our proposed adaptive resource provisioning system does not ensure that federates advance their simulation time with the same speed in practice. Hence, we can observe from Figure 5(b) that, federates in the *Fixed* and *Adaptive* scenarios encounter similar number of execution rollbacks when LA is too small (e.g., $LA = 15$). In the case that $P_{ExternEvent}$ is small, the over-optimistic execution discarded in each execution rollback is much longer in the *Fixed* scenario than that in the *Adaptive* scenario. For this reason, the *Adaptive* scenario has much higher execution efficiency (Figure 5(c)) and outperforms the *Fixed* scenario significantly (Figure 5(a)). With the increasing $P_{ExternEvent}$, the over-optimistic execution decreases as the faster federate is frequently rolled back by the slower federate due to the straggler messages. As a result, the differ-

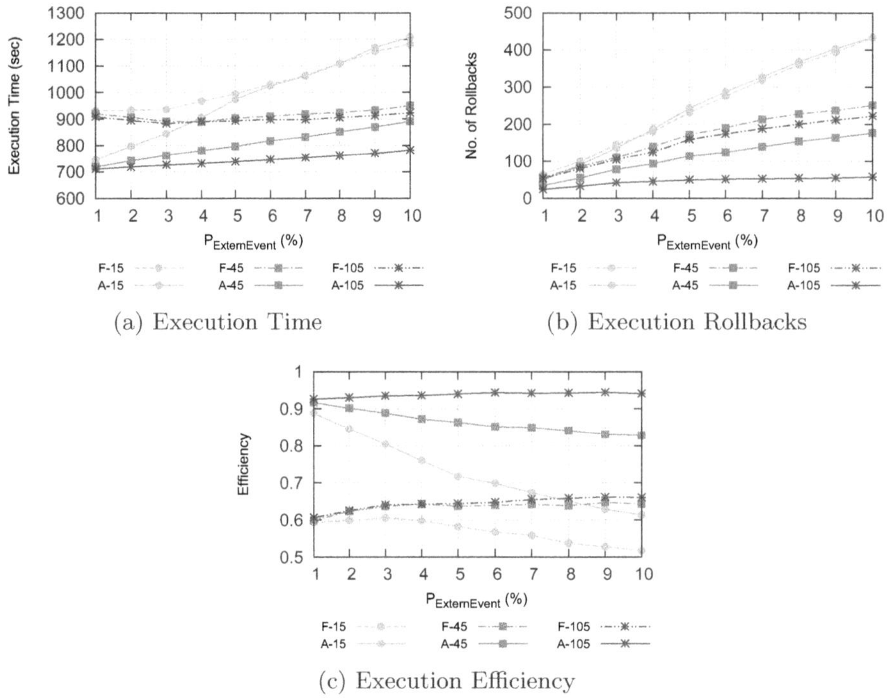

(a) Execution Time (b) Execution Rollbacks

(c) Execution Efficiency

Figure 5: Performance comparison with different LA and increasing $P_{ExternEvent}$

ence in the execution efficiency and execution time between *Adaptive* and *Fixed* scenarios decreases.

When LA is large (e.g., $LA = 105$), federates in the *Adaptive* scenario with comparable execution speed are able to avoid almost all rollbacks (Figure 5(b)). As a result, the execution efficiency in *Adaptive* scenario is close to one and is much higher than that in the *Fixed* scenario. Furthermore, the number of execution rollbacks and execution efficiency are almost the same regardless of the increasing $P_{ExternEvent}$. Therefore, we can observe from Figure 5(a) that the adaptive resource provisioning system can always achieve significant performance enhancement. When $LA = 45$, the *Adaptive* scenario can still outperform the *Fixed* scenario. However, the performance enhancement significantly decreases with the increasing $P_{ExternEvent}$, as the number of execution rollbacks increases and the execution efficiency decreases in the *Adaptive* scenario.

Figure 6 illustrates the performance enhancement of the adaptive resource provisioning system with respect to various parameter inputs of the simulation model. As we can see, the adaptive resource provisioning system can achieve significant performance enhancement except for those parameter inputs $LA = 15$ and $P_{ExternEvent} > 6\%$. This is because that the number of execution rollbacks and over-optimistic executions discarded in execution rollbacks are similar in *Adaptive* and *Fixed* scenarios. With the decreasing $P_{ExternEvent}$, the performance enhancement increases as the over-optimistic execution in the *Fixed* scenario increases. With the increasing LA, the performance enhancement increases as the number of execution rollbacks in the *Adaptive* scenario decreases.

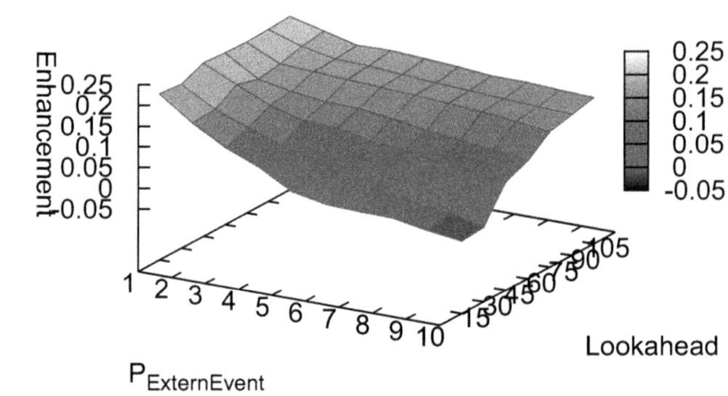

Figure 6: Performance enhancement of the adaptive resource provisioning system

6. CONCLUSION AND FUTURE WORK

In this paper, we have proposed an adaptive resource provisioning system for the purpose of accelerating optimistic HLA-based simulations in VEE. Using a middleware approach, the performance monitor is able to measure the performance of individual federates transparently. Based on the performance measurements, the resource manager can predict the workload of federates, and then, adjust their resource allocations accordingly by changing the resource shares of their VMs. In this way, federates in the same federation can advance their simulation time with comparable speeds, and thus, avoid wasting resources on over-optimistic executions and execution rollbacks. Experiments are carried out using a MMOGs ecosystem simulation model where federates are likely to have dynamic and imbalanced simulation workload. Furthermore, different parameter inputs of the simulation model are investigated. As experimental results have shown, the adaptive resource provisioning system can significantly accelerate the simulation executions with most of the investigated parameter inputs.

For simplicity, we have assumed that federates are single-threaded in this paper. However, in order to exploit the computational potential of multi-core processors, a federate can be a group of concurrent and tightly dependent threads [12]. In the future, we will extend our proposed adaptive resource provisioning system to support the executions of multi-threaded federates. Their corresponding VMs will have multiple virtual CPU cores and the cap values can be greater than 100. In addition, co-scheduling solutions [32, 29] where virtual CPU cores of the same VM are scheduled simultaneously will be adopted to reduce the synchronization latency among the threads in the same federate. In the meantime, we will also evaluate the scalability of our system using large scale simulations on large execution environments with many computing nodes. With the increasing simulation scale, the communication and computation overhead of our system increase, as shown in algorithm 4. However, on the other hand, the problem of workload imbalance become more critical. As for future work, we also plan to extend our proposed adaptive resource provisioning system by adopting more accurate workload prediction algorithms [10, 14, 22, 28]. Besides HLA-based simulations, our system will also be applied and integrated to other parallel and distributed applications.

7. ACKNOWLEDGMENTS

This work is supported under future data center technology thematic strategic research programme by Singapore Agency for Science, Technology and Research (A*STAR) with grant number 112 172 0015.

8. REFERENCES

[1] Amazon. Amazon Elastic Compute Cloud. http://aws.amazon.com/ec2/.

[2] P. Barham, B. Dragovic, K. Fraser, S. Hand, T. Harris, A. Ho, R. Neugebauer, I. Pratt, and A. Warfield. Xen and the art of virtualization. *SIGOPS Oper. Syst. Rev.*, 37(5):164–177, Oct. 2003.

[3] S. K. Barker and P. Shenoy. Empirical evaluation of latency-sensitive application performance in the cloud. In *Procs of conference on Multimedia systems (MMSys'10)*, pages 35–46, 2010.

[4] R. Child and P. A. Wilsey. Using DVFS to optimize time warp simulations. In *Procs of the 44th Conference on Winter Simulation (WSC '12)*, 2012.

[5] C. Clark, K. Fraser, S. Hand, J. G. Hansen, E. Jul, C. Limpach, I. Pratt, and A. Warfield. Live migration of virtual machines. In *Procs of conference on Symposium on Networked Systems Design & Implementation - Volume 2 (NSDI'05)*, pages 273–286, 2005.

[6] G. D'Angelo. Parallel and distributed simulation from many cores to the public cloud. In *Procs of the International Conference on High Performance Computing and Simulation (HPCS'11)*, pages 14–23, 2011.

[7] G. D'Angelo, S. Ferretti, and M. Marzolla. Time warp on the go. In *Procs of the 5th International ICST Conference on Simulation Tools and Techniques*, SIMUTOOLS '12, pages 242–248, 2012.

[8] J. Fleischmann and P. A. Wilsey. Comparative analysis of periodic state saving techniques in time warp simulators. In *Procs of workshop on Parallel and distributed simulation(PADS '95)*, pages 50–58, 1995.

[9] R. M. Fujimoto. *Parallel and Distributed Simulation Systems*. Wiley Interscience, 2000.

[10] Z. Gong, X. Gu, and J. Wilkes. Press: Predictive elastic resource scaling for cloud systems. In *Procs of International Conference on Network and Service Management (CNSM'10)*, pages 9–16, 2010.

[11] IEEE. *1516-2010 IEEE Standard for Modeling and Simulation (M&S) High Level Architecture (HLA)– Framework and Rules*, August 2010.

[12] D. Jagtap, N. Abu-Ghazaleh, and D. Ponomarev. Optimization of parallel discrete event simulator for multi-core systems. In *Procs of the 26th International Parallel and Distributed Processing Symposium (IPDPS'12)*, pages 520–531, 2012.

[13] D. R. Jefferson. Virtual time. *ACM Transactions on Programming Languages and System*, 7(3):404–425, 1985.

[14] E. Kalyvianaki, T. Charalambous, and S. Hand. Self-adaptive and self-configured cpu resource provisioning for virtualized servers using kalman filters. In *Procs of international conference on Autonomic computing (ICAC'09)*, pages 117–126, 2009.

[15] Z. Li, W. Cai, S. J. Turner, and K. Pan. Federate migration in a service oriented HLA RTI. *Procs of Symposium on Distributed Simulation and Real-Time Applications (DS-RT '07)*, pages 113–121, 2007.

[16] Z. Li, W. Cai, S. J. Turner, and K. Pan. Improving performance by replicating simulations with alternative synchronization approaches. In *Procs of the 40th Conference on Winter Simulation (WSC '08)*, pages 1112–1120, 2008.

[17] A. Malik, A. Park, and R. Fujimoto. Optimistic synchronization of parallel simulations in cloud computing environments. In *Procs of the Conference on Cloud Computing (CLOUD'09)*, pages 49–56, 2009.

[18] D. E. Martin, T. J. McBrayer, and P. A. Wilsey. Warped: A time warp simulation kernel for analysis and application development. In *Procs of the 29th Hawaii International Conference on System Sciences Volume 1: Software Technology and Architecture (HICSS'96)*, pages 383–386, 1996.

[19] J. Mason. A detailed look at data replication options for disaster recovery planning. White Paper, June 2009.

[20] A. Menon, J. R. Santos, Y. Turner, G. J. Janakiraman, and W. Zwaenepoel. Diagnosing performance overheads in the xen virtual machine environment. In *Procs of the 1st ACM/USENIX international conference on Virtual execution environments (VEE'05)*, pages 13–23, 2005.

[21] V. Nae, A. Iosup, S. Podlipnig, R. Prodan, D. Epema,

and T. Fahringer. Efficient management of data center resources for massively multiplayer online games. In *Procs of the conference on Supercomputing (SC'08)*, pages 10:1–10:12, 2008.

[22] P. Padala, K.-Y. Hou, K. G. Shin, X. Zhu, M. Uysal, Z. Wang, S. Singhal, and A. Merchant. Automated control of multiple virtualized resources. In *Procs of European conference on Computer systems (EuroSys'09)*, pages 13–26, 2009.

[23] K. Pan, S. J. Turner, W. Cai, and Z. Li. A service oriented HLA RTI on the Grid. In *Procs of Conference on Web Services (ICWS 2007)*, pages 984–992, 2007.

[24] K. S. Panesar and R. M. Fujimoto. Adaptive flow control in time warp. In *Procs of workshop on Parallel and distributed simulation (PADS '97)*, pages 108–115, 1997.

[25] K. S. Perumalla. μsik - a micro-kernel for parallel/distributed simulation systems. In *Procs of Workshop on Principles of Advanced and Distributed Simulation (PADS '05)*, pages 59–68, 2005.

[26] A. J. P. R. M. Fujimoto, A. W. Malik. Parallel and distributed simulation in the Cloud. *SCS Modeling and Simulation Magazine, Society for Modeling and Simulation, Intl.*, 1, July 2010.

[27] D. Schanzenbach and H. Casanova. Accuracy and responsiveness of cpu sharing using xenâĂŹs cap values. Technical report, 2008.

[28] Z. Shen, S. Subbiah, X. Gu, and J. Wilkes. Cloudscale: elastic resource scaling for multi-tenant cloud systems. In *Procs of Symposium on Cloud Computing (SOCC'11)*, pages 5:1–5:14, 2011.

[29] O. Sukwong and H. S. Kim. Is co-scheduling too expensive for smp vms? In *Procs of the sixth conference on Computer systems (EuroSys'11)*, pages 257–272, 2011.

[30] G. Wang and T. S. E. Ng. The impact of virtualization on network performance of amazon ec2 data center. In *Procs of conference on Information communications (INFOCOM'10)*, pages 1163–1171, 2010.

[31] X. Wang, S. J. Turner, M. Y. H. Low, and B. P. Gan. Optimistic synchronization in HLA-based distributed simulation. *Simulation*, 81:279–291, April 2005.

[32] C. Weng, Q. Liu, L. Yu, and M. Li. Dynamic adaptive scheduling for virtual machines. In *Procs of the 20th international symposium on High performance distributed computing (HPDC'11)*, pages 239–250, 2011.

[33] Xen. Xen Credit Scheduler. http://wiki.xen.org/wiki/Credit_Scheduler.

Towards Performance Evaluation of Conservative Distributed Discrete-Event Network Simulations Using Second-Order Simulation

Philipp Andelfinger and Hannes Hartenstein
Steinbuch Centre for Computing and Institute of Telematics
Karlsruhe Institute of Technology
76131 Karlsruhe, Germany
{philipp.andelfinger, hannes.hartenstein}@kit.edu

ABSTRACT

Whether a given simulation model of a computer network will benefit from parallelization is difficult to determine in advance, complicated by the fact that hardware properties of the simulation execution environment can substantially affect the execution time of a given simulation. We describe SONSim, an approach to predict the execution time based on a *simulation of an envisioned distributed network simulation* (second-order simulation). SONSim takes into account both network model characteristics and hardware properties of the simulation execution environment. To show that a SONSim prototype is able to predict distributed performance with acceptable accuracy, we study three reference network simulation models differing fundamentally in topology and levels of model detail – simple topologies comprised of interconnected subnetworks, peer-to-peer networks and wireless networks. We evaluate the performance predictions for multiple configurations by comparing predictions for the three reference network models to execution time measurements of distributed simulations on physical hardware using both Ethernet and InfiniBand interconnects. In addition, utilizing the freedom to vary simulation hardware and model parameters in the second-order simulation, we demonstrate how SONSim can be used to identify general model characteristics that determine distributed simulation performance.

Categories and Subject Descriptors

C.4 [**Computer Systems Organization**]: Performance of Systems—*Modeling Techniques*; I.6.1 [**Computing Methodology**]: Simulation Theory—*Model Classification*; I.6.5 [**Computing Methodology**]: Model Development—*Modeling Methodology*; I.6.8 [**Computing Methodology**]: Types of Simulation—*Parallel, Distributed, Discrete Event*

Keywords

performance prediction, simulation, parallel, distributed, discrete-event, network simulation, network models

1. INTRODUCTION

Simulation is used to investigate computer networks that are both difficult to model analytically and that cannot be examined physically. However, accurate simulation of complex and large networks is time-consuming, creating the need for performance improvements. Parallel and distributed simulation can potentially reduce runtime by distributing the computational load to multiple processors connected by a network or by shared memory. However, the benefit of parallelization of network simulations described in the literature varies: in some cases, a substantial reduction of runtime and near-linear scaling with the number of processors was achieved [12, 24]. In other cases, only limited speedup was observed compared to sequential simulation, or performance gains did not scale beyond modest numbers of processors [16, 22]. Development of an efficient parallel implementation of a simulation is both time-intensive and error-prone [3]. Therefore, to avoid unnecessary effort, the benefit obtained by parallelization of a simulation should be evaluated prior to implementation. Additionally, there is a need to reconsider the performance of distributed simulations with respect to modern elastic execution environments exemplified by infrastructure-as-a-service offerings [31]. Particularly when considering usage-based billing, the issue of choosing an efficient scale for distributed simulations becomes a critical one. Furthermore, a general classification of network models according to their parallelization potential would be helpful.

In this paper, we describe *SONSim* (second-**o**rder **n**etwork **sim**ulation), an approach to predict the benefit gained through parallelization of simulations of computer networks. Based on information gathered during the runtime of an existing sequential simulator, SONSim simulates distributed execution on sets of interconnected processors, factoring in both properties of the simulated network and the hardware to be used for simulation. We refer to simulation of a simulation as *second-order simulation*.

The SONSim approach is a first step to attack the problem of deciding whether the effort for parallelization of a discrete-event network simulation is justified, based solely on properties of an existing sequential simulator and measurements of the network the simulation is to be executed in. Additionally, if a sufficient benefit cannot be expected for a given model, SONSim predicts the impact of modifications to the network model and to the hardware used on distributed simulation performance. More generally, by allowing modelers to vary properties of a network model and the hardware, SONSim will help determining not only *whether* a given simulation will benefit from parallelization, but can also give hints towards *why* this is the case.

Utilizing SONSim's performance predictions and the ability to vary key model parameters, we present examples on how SONSim can enable more general statements on the potential of classes of network models for parallelization.

The rest of the paper is structured as follows. In Section 2, we discuss related work. Section 3 describes the methodology underlying SONSim's operation and specifies the steps required to obtain performance predictions as a basis for investigating performance characteristics of computer network models. Section 4 characterizes the experiments conducted. Section 5 discusses the results and the prediction accuracy. In Section 6, we investigate the distributed performance of simulations under varying model detail, lookahead and simulation scale, demonstrating the usage of SONSim for making more general statements about the distributed performance of network simulations. Finally, Section 7 gives a summary of our work.

2. RELATED WORK

The performance of parallel and distributed simulations has been the focus of intensive research for over twenty years. In the past few years, there has been a renewed interest in performance investigation of parallel applications in general [14, 27] and parallel and distributed simulations in particular [10, 31], as current multi-core and many-core architectures make parallel processing not a preference, but a requirement for steady increases in computational performance [29]. Our focus is on *discrete-event* simulations characterized by system state which is manipulated by events scheduled at discrete points in simulated time, focusing on conservative synchronization where simulation correctness is ensured at all times by a synchronization algorithm.

Existing works in the field of performance prediction for parallel and distributed simulations can be grouped into three categories: *measurements*, *analytical modeling* and *simulation*. As we focus on the performance resulting from interactions between properties of the simulated networks and the hardware used to run the simulation, we disregard the wide range of work studying the performance of specific synchronization algorithms and simulator implementations for this overview.

First, *measurements* have been widely used to determine the potential and real-world benefits of parallel discrete-event simulations [5, 18, 23] with respect to specific hardware, simulator implementations and synchronization algorithms. Bagrodia et al. [2] described a performance evaluation method for comparing synchronization algorithms. An execution trace is generated during runtime of a sequential simulator and subsequently used to guide a parallel simulation. The execution trace allows for global knowledge of the simulation progress and enables perfect synchronization. In a recent work, De Munck et al. [10] studied the performance of parallel and distributed simulations in modern multi-core environments using traditional synchronization algorithms and proposed hybrid and adaptive algorithms to reduce synchronization overheads. The algorithms were evaluated with reference to simulation runs based on execution traces. In our work, guided parallel runs on physical hardware are also used for the evaluation of SONSim's prediction accuracy. However, for the performance prediction itself, instead of executing a simulation using physical hardware, SONSim simulates the execution. Therefore, a parallel implementation of the simulator is not required and properties of the simulation model and the hardware used for the simulation can be varied easily.

Second, ideally, the system under study can be accurately modeled *analytically*, allowing for mathematical predictions of distributed performance. Critical path analysis [7] is a common analytical approach which determines the parallelism inherent in a simulation based on an event precedence graph representing event interdependencies. Critical path analysis determines an upper bound for the speedup achievable for a given simulation model using conservative synchronization, but in contrast to SONSim does not explicitly consider the hardware in use.

Some works combine measurements and analytical considerations to perform performance predictions. Gianni et al. [13] utilize knowledge of the hardware to be used and design-time information about the model to conduct predictions based on queuing networks. In 1999, Liu et al. [19] used microbenchmarks performed on physical hardware as a basis for back-of-the-envelope calculations to give surprisingly accurate predictions of parallel performance. In general, due to the complex interactions between real-world models and the used hardware, mathematical performance analysis is only feasible with reasonable effort when applying simplifications, resulting in a trade-off to be made between performance prediction accuracy and analytical effort. Like critical path analysis, SONSim employs simplifications to help understand a model's inherent parallelism without being closely tied to hardware specifics. However, as the hardware used for the distributed simulation does have substantial impact on performance, we consider it explicitly.

Third, *simulative* approaches base their predictions on measurements performed during simulator runs on physical hardware in combination with subsequent simulations of the parallel simulation under study. These approaches are similar in nature to performance prediction methods for general applications [6]. However, the discrete-event paradigm limits the entities and activities involved in modeling parallel simulations, allowing for less complex models. As in the existing works using simulative approaches for performance prediction of parallel simulations, we use traces of sequential simulation runs to guide the predictions. Using this approach, both hardware and system model characteristics are reflected in performance predictions and can be varied easily, enabling an exploration of the parameter space. In [15] and [26], toolkits for performance predictions of high-performance parallel scientific codes are presented. While closely related to our work methodically, the authors focus on highly detailed modeling of the hardware and do not share our goal of a more generalized comprehension of performance potentials of computer network models which is reflected by SONSim's more abstract hardware model. Ewald et al. [11] presented another approach to performance prediction of parallel simulations, not relying on traces. Their goal, however, is the performance evaluation of parallel simulators and of the synchronization algorithms used instead of investigating model characteristics relevant to parallel per-

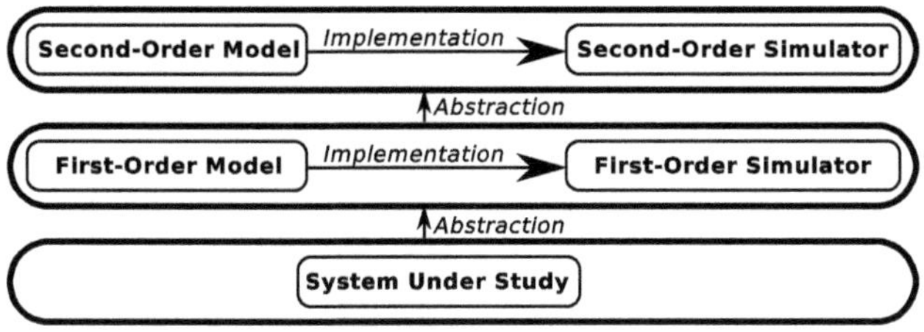

Figure 1: Levels of abstraction in modeling of simulations.

formance. Existing works with intents and abstraction levels closer to ours seem to lack a thorough evaluation for multiple simulation models and hardware environments. While Swope et al. [30] give no evaluation of prediction accuracy, both Perumalla et al. [21] and Juhasz et al. [17] compare performance predictions to physical simulator performance for a single specific simulation model and hardware platform. We evaluate SONSim's predictions with reference to measurements made for three fundamentally differing distributed network simulations running on physical hardware linked by two modern and commonly used interconnects: Ethernet and InfiniBand. With respect to modeling detail and intent, SONSim lies between performance models with coarse abstractions such as critical path analysis and highly detailed simulative models.

In summary, our performance model *considers the simulation execution hardware more closely than analytical methods*, yet in contrast to related work using measurements or simulative approaches employing detailed hardware models *is not tied to specific simulator implementations or low-level hardware specifics*. Therefore, we argue that SONSim enables reasonably accurate predictions, but at the same time is abstract enough to allow us to focus on identifying fundamental performance characteristics arising from properties of the investigated network simulation models.

3. PERFORMANCE PREDICTION METHODOLOGY

In this section, we describe the methodology used by SONSim to obtain performance predictions. Based solely on information gathered from an existing sequential simulator and simple network measurements, SONSim predicts the performance of a distributed implementation of the simulator, enabling decisions on whether parallelization of a simulation will give a performance benefit. In addition, we discuss the effort required to apply our prototypical implementation to existing simulators.

3.1 Levels of Abstraction

Figure 1 illustrates the levels of abstraction involved in simulating a distributed simulation. The original existing or envisioned system under study (e.g. a network of computers) is abstracted from by means of a *first-order model.* The executable implementation of the first-order model is the *first-order simulator* whose performance we intend to investigate. To this end, a model of the state and behavior of the first-order simulator is created. The resulting *second-order model* is implemented in a corresponding *second-order simulator.*

As we are concerned with network simulation, for us the original system under study is a network of computers which we will refer to as the ***network under study***. We contrast the ***network under study*** with the network a distributed first-order simulator is executed in, which in the following we will refer to as the ***execution network***.

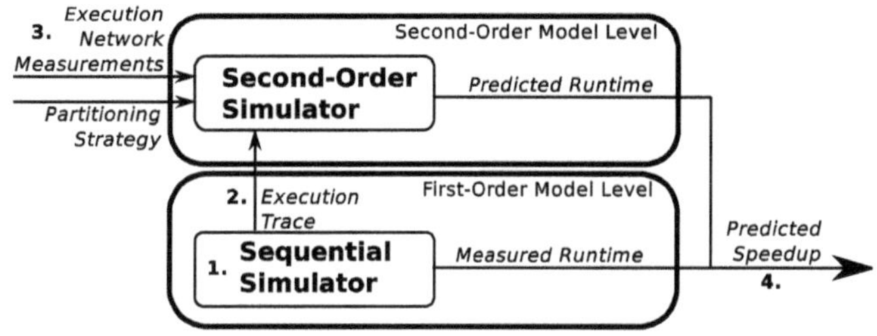

Figure 2: Data flow during performance prediction.

3.2 Prediction Process

We will now describe the concrete sequence of activities performed to obtain performance predictions (cf. Figure 2).

1. The existing sequential first-order simulator is executed multiple times for a given scenario to determine the average sequential runtime as a reference for speedup calculation.
2. The sequential first-order simulator is instrumented to perform time measurements for execution of individual event types and to generate an *execution trace.* The execution trace contains the sequence of event executions including event timestamps and the mapping of individual events to nodes of the network under study in the first-order simulation, as well as the sequence of events being created during simulation. The instrumented sequential simulator is executed to obtain the execution trace. Note that the sequential run in step 1. is performed without tracing to avoid overheads.
3. As a basis for predicting the network overhead involved in the distributed simulation, we measure the average time required for individual message transfers in the execution network.
4. Finally, after supplying the execution network measurements, a partitioning of the first-order network model and the execution trace to the SONSim implementation, a performance prediction for the distributed first-order simulation is obtained.

3.3 Deployment

Our approach can be applied to existing discrete-event simulators easily if the simulator source code is available. Step 2. of the prediction process (cf. 3.2) requires instrumentation of the event handling code in the simulator with simple timing calls. In a discrete-event simulator, event handlers are usually implemented as a separate procedure per event type. Hence, the placement of timing calls poses no substantial difficulty. All subsequent steps are simulator-agnostic. Our prototypical implementation of SONSim with the code used for validation is available from our web site[1].

3.4 First-Order and Second-Order Model

In this section, we describe the entities constituting the first-order and second-order models used by SONSim. Both first-order and second-order model are based on the familiar discrete-event modeling paradigm. Discrete-event models are composed of two types of entities: system objects

[1]http://dsn.tm.kit.edu/english/3367.php

describing the system state and timestamped events modeling state changes at set points in simulated time [4]. In a distributed simulation, system objects are distributed to multiple interconnected machines. The simulator instances handling a subset of all system objects are called *logical processes* (LPs). Consistent with this modeling approach, networks under study are commonly reflected by first-order models as follows.

- **System objects** represent the nodes in the network under study.
- **Events** model transmissions and receptions of packets by individual nodes.
- **Logical processes** run on nodes of the execution network, each storing a number of system objects and executing events pertaining to these system objects.

Applying the same modeling pattern again, we represent state and behavior of the distributed simulation in a sequential *second-order* simulation as follows.

- **System objects** represent the logical processes of the first-order simulation.
- **Events** model activities performed by individual logical processes in the distributed simulation: execution network operations and execution of first-order events.
- As the second-order simulator itself is executed sequentially, only a single **logical process** is executed on the physical hardware.

To be able to predict the runtime of first-order simulations, a model of the operations executed by each logical process of a first-order simulator is required. A sequential discrete-event simulator operates in a simple loop: all events to be executed are stored in a queue. In each step, the event with the lowest timestamp is executed and removed from the queue. If the execution of the event triggers the creation of further events, the newly created events are added to the queue. With the addition of the execution network operations, we model each logical process' behavior as illustrated by the execution loop listed in pseudo code in Algorithm 1.

Algorithm 1 Model of the execution of each logical process as a basis for runtime prediction.

```
repeat
  repeat
    if event incoming then
      receive event
      enqueue event
    end if
  until no event received
  execute next event
  if new events created then
    enqueue locally or transfer to remote logical process
  end if
until no events left
```

The distributed execution loop extends the basic sequential discrete-event logic in two ways: first, before proceeding with execution of the next local event, logical processes probe for incoming events sent by other logical processes. Second, if a newly created event pertains to a system object handled by a remote logical process, the event is transferred to the remote logical process. Reception, execution and transfer are each associated with a runtime cost, which is added to simulation runtime for the corresponding logical process. The sum of these costs corresponds to the predicted runtime for the logical process. The maximum of the predicted runtimes among all logical processes is SONSim's prediction for the total distributed simulation runtime.

3.5 Second-Order Simulator Operation

In this section, we describe SONSim's operation, detailing the mapping of first-order to second-order simulation events. When supplied with an execution trace of a first-order simulation, measurements of the execution network and a partitioning of the model, the second-order simulator loads the execution trace and translates all initial first-order events to second-order events. There are three types of second-order events, corresponding to the operations performed in the first-order simulator execution loop: *Execution* of an event by a logical process, *Transfer* of an event to another logical process and *Reception* of an event via the execution network. SONSim operates by executing second-order events in timestamp order until no events are left in the queue. Each second-order event extends the position in simulated time according to the time measurements used as input to SONSim. On termination of the second-order simulation, the final position in simulated time represents SONSim's prediction of the first-order simulation runtime. In the second-order simulation, the second-order events are associated with the following operations.

- **Execution**: simulate creation of additional first-order events, if triggered by the event modeled. If a newly created event is associated with a system object handled by a remote logical process, a second-order *Transfer* event is scheduled for the remote first-order logical process.
- **Transfer**: respecting the target first-order logical process' state, find the arrival time of the first-order event at the target logical process and schedule a second-order *Reception* event at this point in simulated time.
- **Reception**: schedule an *Execution* event for the first-order logical process associated with the *Reception* event, respecting the remaining time required for all *Reception* and *Execution* events already scheduled.

All idle times between second-order events are considered to be spent on probing for incoming messages.

Since each logical process can receive events with arbitrary timestamps from other logical processes, explicit synchronization using an appropriate algorithm is required to maintain timestamp order. A common synchronization algorithm for parallel and distributed discrete-event simulations is the Chandy-Misra-Bryant algorithm [8, 9]. The algorithm is based on the notion of the *lookahead*, which we will use to denote the distance in simulated time from the last executed event of a logical process to the timestamp of the earliest new event that may be transferred to a remote logical process. The lookahead can be used to identify which events can be executed safely without violating timestamp order. After a second-order simulation run, SONSim returns two pieces of information: First, the *runtime of the envisioned distributed simulation* using the configured execution network hardware, simulation model and partitioning. Comparing this value to the measured sequential runtime, we can predict the benefit of parallelization. Second, a *distributed simulation schedule* allowing for examination of the first-order logical processes' interactions during execution.

3.6 Step-by-Step Analysis

In this section, we discuss the aspects of the performance of distributed simulations we will focus on in turn, motivating which performance-related characteristics need to be investigated in each of our experiments. The most important questions about a simulation model that can be answered using SONSim can be summarized as follows: **1.** Does the simulation model in itself exhibit a sufficient level of parallelism? **2.** How well must the parallelism in the model be understood at simulation runtime to achieve a speedup? **3.** What is an efficient simulation scale with respect to the number of logical processes to distribute the simulation to?

To address question 1., we need to determine upper performance bounds enabled by the parallelism in the simulation model without considering specific synchronization algorithms. Therefore, we will first assume infinite lookahead. As in [2], for experiments with infinite lookahead, synchronization is achieved by providing knowledge of all events in the simulation to all logical processes based on an execution trace created by the sequential first-order simulator, allowing logical processes to execute events as soon as possible without violating timestamp order per system object. In Section 6.2, we will proceed to demonstrate how SONSim is used to answer question 2. by investigating the performance of simulation models with synchronization under various amounts of lookahead. We demonstrate how to address simulation scale (question 3.) in Section 6.3.

4. EXPERIMENTS

The accuracy of the predictions made using SONSim was evaluated by comparing performance predictions to measurements of distributed simulation runs on physical hardware. We implemented three network models in a basic discrete-event simulation engine built from scratch, supporting sequential and distributed runs in an execution network.

The evaluation process is comprised of the following steps (cf. Section 3.2): **1.** We measure the *sequential runtime* of a simulation executed on physical hardware. **2.** An *execution trace* is gathered during a sequential simulation run on physical hardware. **3.** The time required for individual network operations is measured in the execution network. **4.** Supplied with the information from the previous steps, SONSim predicts the distributed performance. Finally, we supply the execution trace to the distributed implementation of the simulator created for evaluation to obtain a measurement of the simulation performance on physical hardware in the execution network. By comparing predicted and measured simulation performance, the prediction accuracy is evaluated.

We perform evaluation in two different execution networks, using up to six nodes for simulation: first, a cluster equipped with Intel Xeon E5504 processors operating at 2.00GHz interconnected using GBit/s Ethernet. Communication is performed using TCP. Second, a high performance computing cluster equipped with Intel Xeon E5540 processors at 2.53GHz interconnected using InfiniBand 4X QDR.

4.1 Considered Network Models

We base our experiments on three specific models of networks under study. The models are characterized by three properties: the simulated network topologies, the communication patterns between nodes and the level of detail in the modeling of the networking stack. *Packet-level* network models use packets as the smallest unit of consideration, modeling packet loss using probabilistic methods. In contrast, *signal-level* network models accurately consider effects of the physical channel on packet transmissions. In general, more detailed modeling of the networking stack translates to events that are more computationally intensive and associated with larger amounts of data. As even for small simulations, it is not clear to what extent specific types of network models benefit from parallelization, we limit our experiments in this work to distributed simulations using up to six logical processes simulating up to 1000 nodes.

Of course, the topologies of the considered networks under study display high degrees of symmetry with obvious partitionings of the models to logical processes. For more asymmetrical topologies and communication patterns, it is necessary to seek workload distributions tailored to the given topology and communication patterns, which for large simulation is a non-trivial problem. While out of scope for this paper, SONSim can already be used to guide efficient partitioning of models by repeating performance predictions for multiple candidate partitionings generated manually or using existing graph partitioning toolkits.

The following three network models were implemented in the first-order simulator to be run on physical hardware sequentially and in parallel.

1. **Interconnected Campus Networks:** As a baseline with respect to event sizes and computational demands, we study a packet-level model with a simple topology composed of a set of so-called campus networks, which can be used as building blocks to construct larger and more complex topologies [12]. A campus network is comprised of a set of nodes, each connected to a shared router. Larger networks are constructed by interconnecting multiple campus network routers. The communication patterns in the network can be influenced by configuring the amount of traffic *between* campus networks (*cross-traffic*) in relation to traffic *within* campus networks.

2. **Peer-to-Peer Networks:** Models of peer-to-peer networks are regarded as benefitting particularly little from parallel simulation [22]. We base our investigation of peer-to-peer models on the packet-level model used for the interconnected campus networks. However, in contrast to the clearly defined communication patterns given by the structure of the campus network topology, we simulate a worst case scenario with respect to simulation partitioning: as must be assumed by any parallel simulator without far-reaching knowledge of the peer-to-peer protocol and simulation model in use, a node can send a packet to any other node at arbitrary points in simulated time. The scenario is close in behavior to simulations of peer-to-peer networks with low-traffic node interactions such as distributed hash tables.

3. **Wireless Networks:** The substantial computational demands induced by the signal processing required to emulate the physical layer render signal-level wireless network simulation an obvious target for efforts to reduce runtime through parallelization [1]. Due to the demanding signal processing required, signal-level models can be considered extreme cases with respect to event data sizes and processing times in network simulations. In contrast to the previous network models, the broadcast nature of the wireless channel requires all nodes in the proximity of a sender to process each transmitted frame. For our experiments, we extracted the signal processing procedures from PhySimWifi [20], an

Table 1: **Execution network measurements and event execution times from sequential simulation runs with 95% confidence intervals for the three networks under study.**

Operation	Ethernet			InfiniBand		
	Campus	Peer-to-Peer	Wireless	Campus	Peer-to-Peer	Wireless
MPI Transfer	*fit function*		*fit function*	1.72±0.05μs		85.08±4.11μs
MPI Reception	0.36±0.01μs		12.97±0.12μs	0.39±0.01μs		72.07±3.53μs
MPI Probing	0.61±0.02μs		0.60±0.00μs	0.37±0.00μs		0.39±0.03μs
Send Event	3.08±0.00μs	3.26±0.02μs	997.25±13.87μs	3.07±0.03μs	3.25±0.02μs	933.17±64.60μs
Receive Event	0.91±0.00μs	0.87±0.01μs	8085.21±7.67μs	1.07±0.01μs	1.09±0.03μs	12291.92±538.51μs

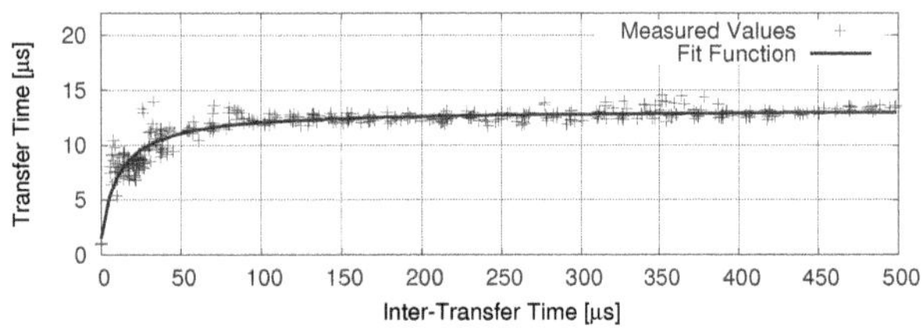

Figure 3: Time used per MPI transfer operation for 24 bytes of data depending on inter-transfer time in the Ethernet environment.

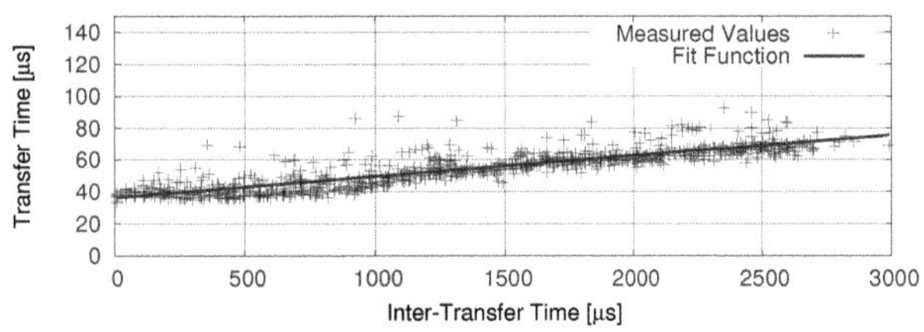

Figure 4: Time used per MPI transfer operation for 51204 bytes of data depending on inter-transfer time in the Ethernet environment.

IEEE 802.11 physical layer extension to the popular network simulator NS-3 [25].

4.2 Measuring Execution Network Overhead

For communication within the execution network, our distributed simulator implementation uses the Message Passing Interface (MPI) [28]. In the Ethernet environment, OpenMPI 1.4.1 was used, the InfiniBand experiments used HP MPI 02.03.01.00.

In order to measure the time required for MPI calls in the distributed simulator (MPI_Send, MPI_Recv, MPI_Iprobe), we implemented a simple MPI benchmark. The benchmark transfers a number of messages between a single sender and receiver, measuring the time used for each library call. Table 1 lists the time required for individual reception and probing operations for the packet-level and signal-level models with 24 and 51204 bytes of data per event, respectively.

In the Ethernet environment, we observed a substantial dependence of MPI transfer operation times on the delay between individual transfers between a given sender and receiver pair (*inter-transfer time*). To generate a basic model for the time required for transfer operations in our SONSim prototype, we applied simple curve fitting between inter-transfer times and MPI transfer operation durations in the Ethernet environment. Figures 3 and 4 depict the transfer times measured for the packet-level and signal-level models, varying inter-transfer times and the fit functions approximating the relationship between the two metrics. Given the inter-transfer time x, we get a close fit to the transfer time per message for the packet-level models using a function of the form $a/bx + c$ with $a = -131.235$, $b = 11.1845$ and $c = 13.2387$. For the signal-level model we approximate the transfer times using the fit function $mx + c$ with $m = 0.0131651$ and $c = 36.2832$. SONSim is supplied with the fit functions to predict execution network overheads depending on the inter-transfer time for each individual transfer operation. In the InfiniBand environment, transfer times did not vary significantly depending on inter-transfer times, allowing us to use averaged measured transfer times.

Table 2: Deviation of speedup predictions from measurements for the campus network (CN), peer-to-peer (P2P) and wireless network (WN) models.

	Ethernet			InfiniBand		
	CN	P2P	WN	CN	P2P	WN
Min.	3.2%	12.8%	18.3%	10.7%	34.8%	15.0%
Max.	17.1%	24.8%	19.6%	38.6%	38.6%	18.9%
Avg.	9.5%	18.0%	19.0%	21.5%	37.3%	16.3%

5. RESULTS AND DISCUSSION

We contrast the predicted speedup of distributed simulations compared to sequential runs with the speedup for distributed simulations performed in the execution networks. Table 2 lists the deviations between predictions and measured runtimes averaging over ten runs for each configuration. 95%-confidence intervals corresponded to 1.72% of total runtime on average.

Figures 5 and 6 depict the prediction and measurement results from physical simulation runs in the Ethernet and InfiniBand environments of the campus network model for two up to six logical processes. As distributed performance for the campus network model depends strongly on the proportion of cross-traffic between campus networks, we choose two levels: 10% and 50%. In the Ethernet environment, there is a close match between predicted speedup and measurement results, with an average deviation of 9.5% and a maximum deviation of 17.1% over all parameterizations. In the InfiniBand environment, we observed an average deviation of 21.5% and a maximum deviation of 38.6%. We measured a speedup factor of up to 3.18 using Ethernet and 4.27 for the InfiniBand interconnect. Given the predicted speedups of 3.68 and 4.78, a user would likely, and correctly, decide upon parallelization of the simulation.

For the peer-to-peer model (cf. Figure 7), we observed average prediction errors of 18.0% and 37.3%, respectively. The maximum deviation in the Ethernet environment was 24.8%, compared to 38.6% for InfiniBand. Parallel simulations using the InfiniBand interconnect achieve speedups of up to 2.55 compared to 1.16 for Ethernet, suggesting that parallelization in the InfiniBand environment would give some benefit. In the Ethernet environment, however, dis-

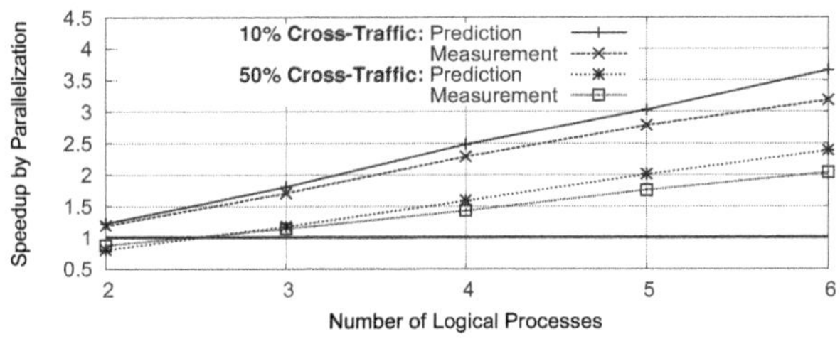

Figure 5: Evaluation of prediction accuracy for the campus network model depending on the number of logical processes and campus networks for two levels of cross-traffic in the Ethernet environment.

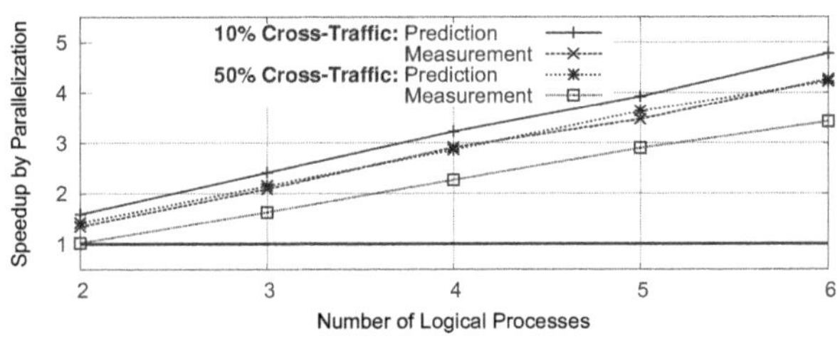

Figure 6: Evaluation of prediction accuracy for the campus network model depending on the number of logical processes and campus networks for two levels of cross-traffic in the InfiniBand environment.

tributed simulation with up to six logical processes is barely worthwhile, even assuming infinite lookahead. Based on speedup predictions of 3.51 and 1.44, we assume that a user of SONSim would come to the same conclusions.

In contrast to the results for the campus network and peer-to-peer network models, prediction accuracy for distributed simulations of the wireless network model (cf. Figure 8) is comparable between Ethernet and InfiniBand interconnects. We observed average deviations of 19.0% and 16.3%, and maximum deviations of 19.6% and 18.9%, respectively. The higher prediction accuracy compared for the wireless model is explained by its high computational demands. As network overheads make up a substantially lower proportion of the runtime, the impact of inaccuracies in the prediction of network overheads is less pronounced. Measured speedups are slightly lower for Ethernet, with a maximum speedup of 4.25 compared to 4.77 for InfiniBand. Again, given predicted speedups of 5.06 and 5.67, a user would likely decide upon parallelization and achieve performance gains as expected.

Considering all experiments, we observe that predictions are consistently overly optimistic. The limitation in prediction accuracy is caused by an underestimation of execution network overheads by SONSim which reduces predicted runtime. As increasing the number of logical processes reduces the event execution time for each logical process, inaccuracies in the predictions for the network overhead gain in impact. Therefore, for larger numbers of logical processes, final prediction accuracy decreases. In future work, we will integrate an existing and more detailed execution network model in SONSim, which we hope will further improve prediction accuracy.

As a basis for discussing the sufficiency of SONSim's prediction accuracy, we compare our results to the related work discussed in Section 2 with comparable intent and level of modeling detail to SONSim. Juhasz et al. [17] evaluated their performance prediction tool with respect to a single unspecified simulation model and in a single execution network,

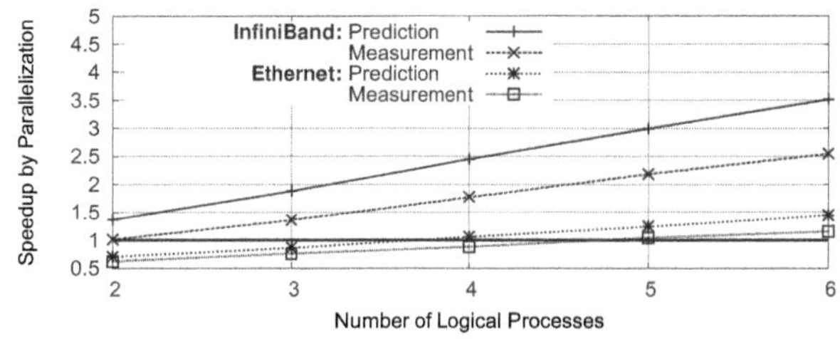

Figure 7: Evaluation of prediction accuracy for the peer-to-peer network model depending on the number of logical processes.

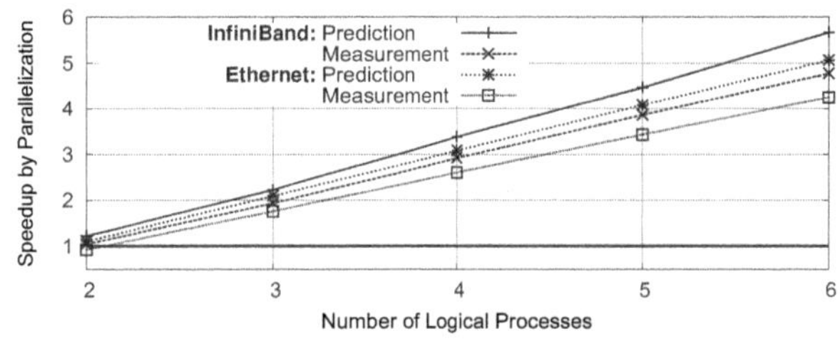

Figure 8: Evaluation of prediction accuracy for the wireless network model depending on the numbers of logical processes and nodes.

noting that for low event processing times, diminishing prediction accuracy was observed. Prediction errors were below 15% for five or less logical processes, with deviations of up to 66% for six and seven logical processes. In [21], Perumalla et al. evaluate performance predictions for a physics simulation model in a single execution network, achieving prediction errors of about 10% to 20%. Perumalla et al. point out that for the purpose of performance predictions, some deviation can be tolerated. As substantial performance gains are required to justify the implementation effort for parallelization of a model, even SONSim's maximum observed prediction error of 38.6% in the InfiniBand environment might still be acceptable for making informed decisions on parallelization. Hence, we consider SONSim's prediction accuracy an acceptable starting point for its intended purpose. Nevertheless, especially with regard to large execution networks, integrating an established and more accurate model of the execution network is a focus of our ongoing work.

6. UNDERSTANDING SPEEDUP POTENTIALS

Having evaluated strengths and limitations of SONSim's predictions, we demonstrate the performance statements that can be made using SONSim. As model and hardware parameters can be varied easily in the second-order simulation, general statements about a network models potential for parallelization depending on the parameters can be made. We show this usage of SONSim by varying the degree of modeling detail, the lookahead and the simulation scale and examine the effects on distributed simulation performance.

6.1 Impact of Modeling Detail

As a first example, based on the observation that higher levels of modeling detail are typically reflected by more computationally intensive events, we vary the execution time per event for the three reference network models to investigate the impact of the level of detail in the model of the network under study on the distributed simulation performance.

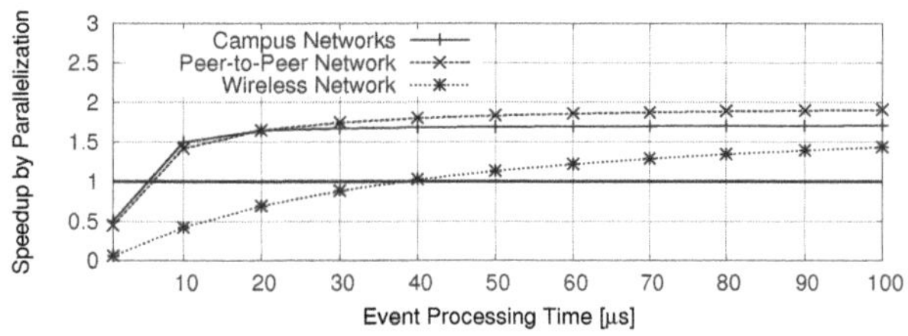

Figure 9: Predictions for the speedup by distributed simulation of the three network models using two logical processes in the Ethernet environment, varying processing times per event.

Figure 9 shows SONSim's speedup predictions for distributed simulations using two logical processes in the Ethernet environment. For the campus network model with 50% of cross-traffic, a performance gain is achieved for events associated with processing times larger than about $4\mu s$, not adjusting for SONSim's current overestimation of speedups.

Similar to the predictions for the campus network model, a modest increase in processing time for each event suffices to make distributed simulation of the peer-to-peer model worthwhile even for only two logical processes. This indicates that with sufficient lookahead, distributed simulation of peer-to-peer networks could have a substantial benefit. However, achieving large lookahead can be difficult depending on the network protocols modeled. In 6.2, we will demonstrate how SONSim can be used to examine how much lookahead is required for specific types of network models.

Even for the wireless model, where events are associated with 51204 bytes of data each compared to 24 bytes for the packet-level models, considerable speedup is achieved for comparatively low processing times per event. This is remarkable considering that for every frame transmitted in the wireless network under study, an event is transferred in the execution network.

Based on the prediction results, we note the clear difference in event processing times required for performance gains through parallelization between the packet-level and signal-level network models and identify event processing times as an obvious influencing factor to distributed performance. In our future work, we intend to conduct a systematic study of the influencing factors to establish a classification of computer network models according to their parallelization potential.

6.2 Impact of Model Lookahead

It is well-known that distributed simulation performance is highly dependent on the amount of lookahead available in the given model. As discussed briefly in Section 3.5, lookahead describes the amount of simulated time for which a logical process will not send any new events to remote logical processes, which for all other logical processes is closely related to the amount of simulated time for which it is safe to execute events from the local queue. The upper bound for the amount of lookahead that can be extracted from a network model depends on properties such as the topology of the simulated network, link latencies, communication patterns and the considered network protocols. Some amount of lookahead can be extracted statically based on knowledge of the model of the network under study, e.g. using the known minimum message latency between nodes simulated on different machines of the execution network. If more lookahead is required for reasonable performance, the simulator can dynamically calculate the lookahead depending on the state of the simulated system at a given point in time. This calculation may be quite expensive depending on how deeply the system state must be examined. Hence, dynamic calculation of the lookahead carries a tradeoff between the amount of processing time spent on lookahead maximization and the performance gains resulting from larger lookahead values. Besides guiding decisions on how much computational and developmental effort should be expended on determining the maximum lookahead value, SONSim can help answering the more general question *"How much lookahead is required for a distributed simulation of the given model to perform well?"*.

In our description of the lookahead experiments we loosely follow the terminology of Bagrodia et al. [2].

- *Lookahead*: the lowest possible delta between the timestamp of the event currently executed by a logical process and the timestamp of any locally created event to be executed on another logical process.
- *Earliest Conditional Output Time (ECOT)*: for each logical process, the ECOT is the earliest possible timestamp of a locally created event to be executed on another logical process.
- *Earliest Input Time (EIT)*: for each logical process, the EIT is the earliest possible timestamp of an event which will be received from another logical process. A lower bound for the EIT can be determined from the minimum of all other logical processes' ECOTs.

To perform lookahead experiments, SONSim's behavior was extended as follows.

- After a logical process has executed an event, the logical process determines its ECOT and stores it in a variable accessible to all other logical processes. For the example presented here, the ECOT is chosen as the sum of the timestamp of the event executed in this step and a fixed lookahead value.
- Before executing an event, a logical process determines the EIT, which is the minimum of all remote ECOTs. All events with timestamps lower than the minimum ECOT are considered safe to execute. If no such event exists, the logical process waits.
- If all logical processes are waiting for the EIT to advance beyond the timestamp of any of the events in the local queue, the simulation is deadlocked. Deadlocks are resolved using a simple policy: all logical processes advance their ECOT to the timestamp of the earliest event in the queue, allowing the simulation to proceed.

In effect, SONSim's behavior simulates an idealized version of the Chandy-Misra-Bryant protocol disregarding overheads for signaling of ECOTs. We can now study the effects of various quantities of lookahead in given network models by varying the lookahead and predicting the performance of the resulting distributed simulations.

Figure 10 shows the predicted performance of distributed simulations for the campus network model in the Ethernet execution network using two logical processes. We investigated the performance for setups with very low lookahead ($5\mu s$) up to very large lookahead (1s). The predicted speedup by distributed simulation varies from 0.961 to 1.163 for 10% of cross-traffic and from 0.469 to 0.689 for 50% of

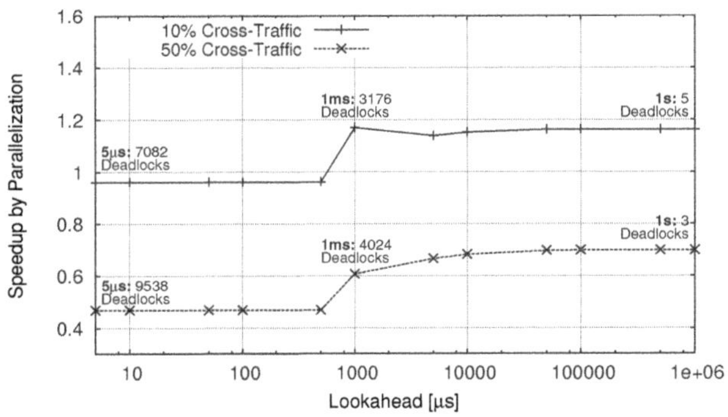

Figure 10: Predictions for the speedup by distributed simulation of the three network models using two logical processes in the Ethernet environment, varying the amount of lookahead.

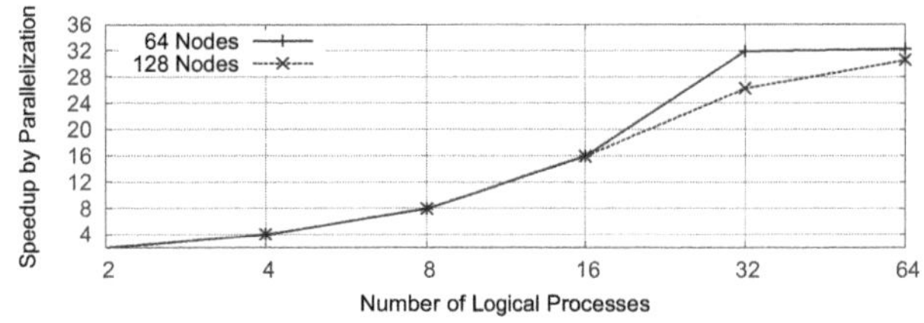

Figure 11: Predictions for the speedup by distributed simulation of the wireless network model in the Ethernet environment, varying the number of logical processes.

cross-traffic. For 1s of lookahead, the predicted speedups closely approach the results measured under the assumption of infinite lookahead in our validation (cf. Figure 5). There is no discernible difference in the speedup between 5 and 500μs of lookahead. The reason is that for these low amounts of lookahead, the simulation advances almost solely due to deadlock resolution. The large increase in speedup for 1000μs of lookahead is explained by the spacing of 1000μs between initial send events in our example simulation model. As in many cases, the earliest next event to be executed by a logical process lies 1000 μs in the future, lower lookahead values tend to not allow us to be sure about the next event being safe to execute, increasing the probability for waiting and for deadlocks. Nevertheless, as there is no runtime penalty for deadlock resolution in this experiment, speedup values remain relatively large even for large numbers of deadlocks. As can be seen by comparing the speedup for 1000 μs and 5000μs of lookahead and 10% of cross-traffic, larger numbers of deadlocks can actually be beneficial to the predicted speedup if there is no overhead involved, as during deadlock resolution, ECOTs are increased for all logical processes. As an example, if we were to introduce a penalty of 10 μs for deadlock detection and resolution, the predicted speedup for 5μs of lookahead would drop to 0.367 for 10% of cross-traffic and to 0.256 for 50% of cross traffic.

In summary, we note that – as expected – speedup predictions vary substantially with varying amounts of lookahead, especially when factoring in overheads for deadlock resolution. Of course, the largest investigated lookahead value of 1s cannot be expected for most real-world simulations without deep insight into the simulation model during runtime, and gaining this insight might be associated with high computational demands in itself. However, knowledge about what level of performance is to be expected for large lookahead values can guide decisions on how much computational and developmental effort should be expended on dynamic lookahead maximization. Additionally, when investigating classes of network models, the results might show that performance would require unattainably large amounts of lookahead, rendering parallelization of these classes of networks models a futile endeavor.

6.3 Determining Simulation Scale

Given a simulation model which is known to lend itself to parallelization, an appropriate simulation scale has to be selected, as simulation performance may stagnate or degrade beyond a certain number of logical processes. Particularly considering today's highly scalable execution environments such as cloud services employing usage-based billing, maximizing efficiency becomes an important issue. By varying the number of logical processes in a simulation, we demonstrate how SONSim can help determining scalability limits of network models for given hardware environments. As an example, Figure 11 shows the predicted speedup by parallelization of simulations of the wireless network model in the Ethernet environment for simulations of 64 and 128 nodes. As we can see, for 64 nodes, predicted speedups scale close to linearly for up to 32 logical processes, with a predicted speedup of 31.85. Beyond 32 logical processes, diminishing returns are observed due to the increasing influence of execution network overheads. As the speedup for 64 logical processes is only 32.21, more than 32 logical processes are not useful in this scenario. For simulations of 128 nodes, performance scales slightly worse, with a speedup of 26.20 for 32 logical processes. Using 64 logical processes, the predicted speedup increases only slightly to 30.52. As the predictions are based on the basic model of the execution network implemented in the SONSim prototype, we assume the results shown to only give rough estimates for large and congested execution networks. Reliable prediction of optimal simulation scale will be addressed based on the more detailed modeling of the execution network overheads as part of our future work, which will allow for simulation scale to be included in our model classification.

7. CONCLUSION

We presented SONSim, an approach towards performance evaluation of distributed simulations of computer networks. SONSim predicts the performance of distributed discrete-event network simulations to determine whether parallelization of an existing sequential simulator is worth the required development effort. In addition, by varying model parameters, SONSim's predictions can help identifying the network model and hardware characteristics limiting simulation performance. We demonstrated this usage by varying the computational intensity, the available lookahead and the simulation scale for three models and predicting the effect on distributed performance. The prediction accuracy of our prototypical implementation was evaluated for three common network topologies simulated on two hardware platforms.

In our future work, we will extend and improve our prototypical implementation, in particular with respect to performance prediction accuracy. We expect that building upon an existing accurate model of the execution network will result in closer performance estimates for large simulations. Our intention is to utilize SONSim to get a clear understanding on which conditions are required for high performance in distributed simulations of various simulated network types and considering characteristics of existing model implementations in common simulators. Ideally, the gained understanding will enable us to establish a classification of computer network models with respect to their potential for parallelization.

8. ACKNOWLEDGEMENTS

The authors would like to thank the anonymous reviewers for their insights and helpful comments.

9. REFERENCES

[1] P. Andelfinger, J. Mittag, and H. Hartenstein. GPU-Based Architectures and Their Benefit for Accurate and Efficient Wireless Network Simulations. In *19th Int'l Symp. on Modeling, Analysis and Simulation of Comp. and Telecomm. Systems*, pages 421–424, 2011.

[2] R. Bagrodia and M. Takai. Performance Evaluation of Conservative Algorithms in Parallel Simulation Languages. *IEEE Transactions on Parallel and Distributed Systems*, pages 395–411, 2000.

[3] R. L. Bagrodia. Perils and Pitfalls of Parallel Discrete-Event Simulation. In *Proc. of the 28th Winter Simulation Conference*, pages 136–143. IEEE Computer Society, 1996.

[4] O. Balci. The Implementation of Four Conceptual Frameworks for Simulation Modeling in High-Level Languages. In *Proceedings of the Winter Simulation Conference*, pages 287–295, 1988.

[5] L. Barriga, R. Ronngren, and R. Ayani. Benchmarking Parallel Simulation Algorithms. In *Proceedings of the IEEE First International Conference on Algorithms and Architectures for Parallel Processing*, 1995.

[6] S. Becker, H. Koziolek, and R. Reussner. Model-Based Performance Prediction with the Palladio Component Model. In *Proceedings of the 6th International Workshop on Software and Performance*, pages 54–65. ACM, 2007.

[7] O. Berry and D. Jefferson. Critical Path Analysis of Distributed Simulation. In *Proceedings of the 1985 SCS Multiconference on Distributed Simulation.*

[8] R. E. Bryant. Simulation of Packet Communication Architecture Computer Systems. Technical report, 1977.

[9] K. Chandy and J. Misra. Distributed Simulation: A Case Study in Design and Verification of Distributed Programs. *IEEE Transactions on Software Engineering*, SE-5(5):440–452, 1979.

[10] S. De Munck, K. Vanmechelen, and J. Broeckhove. Revisiting Conservative Time Synchronization Protocols in Parallel and Distributed Simulation. *Concurrency and Computation: Practice and Experience*, 2013.

[11] R. Ewald, J. Himmelspach, A. Uhrmacher, D. Chen, and G. Theodoropoulos. A Simulation Approach to Facilitate Parallel and Distributed Discrete-Event Simulator Development. In *IEEE Int'l Symposium on Distr. Simulation and Real-Time Applications*, pages 209–218, 2006.

[12] R. Fujimoto, K. Perumalla, A. Park, H. Wu, M. Ammar, and G. Riley. Large-Scale Network Simulation: How Big? How Fast? In *11th IEEE/ACM Int'l Symposium on Modeling, Analysis and Simulation of Computer Telecommun. Systems*, pages 116–123, 2003.

[13] D. Gianni, G. Iazeolla, and A. D'Ambrogio. A Methodology to Predict the Performance of Distributed Simulations. In *Workshop on Principles of Advanced and Distributed Simulation (PADS)*, pages 31–39, 2010.

[14] A. Gupta, L. V. Kalé, D. S. Milojicic, P. Faraboschi, R. Kaufmann, V. March, F. Gioachin, C. H. Suen, and B.-S. Lee. Exploring the Performance and Mapping of HPC Applications to Platforms in the Cloud. In *Proceedings of the 21st International Symposium on High-Performance Parallel and Distributed Computing*, HPDC, pages 121–122, 2012.

[15] S. D. Hammond, G. R. Mudalige, J. A. Smith, S. A. Jarvis, J. A. Herdman, and A. Vadgama. WARPP: a Toolkit for Simulating High-Performance Parallel Scientific Codes. In *Proc. of the 2nd Int'l Conference on Simulation Tools and Techniques*, pages 19:1–19:10, 2009.

[16] Q. He, M. Ammar, G. Riley, H. Raj, and R. Fujimoto. Mapping Peer Behavior to Packet-Level Details: a Framework for Packet-Level Simulation of Peer-to-Peer Systems. In *11th IEEE/ACM Int'l Symposium on Modeling, Analysis and Simulation of Computer Telecommunications Systems*, pages 71–78, 2003.

[17] Z. Juhasz, S. Turner, K. Kuntner, and M. Gerzson. A Performance Analyser and Prediction Tool for Parallel Discrete Event Simulation. In *UKSIM 2001: Conference On Computer Simulation*, pages 148–155, 2001.

[18] P. Konas and P.-C. Yew. Parallel Discrete Event Simulation on Shared-Memory Multiprocessors. In *Proc. of the 24th Annual Simulation Symposium*, pages 134–148, 1991.

[19] J. Liu, D. Nicol, B. Premore, and A. Poplawski. Performance Prediction of a Parallel Simulator. In *Thirteenth Workshop on Parallel and Distributed Simulation*, pages 156–164, 1999.

[20] J. Mittag, S. Papanastasiou, H. Hartenstein, and E. Ström. Enabling Accurate Cross-Layer PHY/MAC/NET Simulation Studies of Vehicular Communication Networks. *Proceedings of the IEEE*, 99(7):1311–1326, 2011.

[21] K. Perumalla, R. Fujimoto, P. Thakare, S. Pande, H. Karimabadi, Y. Omelchenko, and J. Driscoll. Performance Prediction of Large-Scale Parallel Discrete Event Models of Physical Systems. In *Proc. of the Winter Simulation Conference*, pages 356–364, 2005.

[22] M. Quinson, C. Rosa, and C. Thiery. Parallel Simulation of Peer-to-Peer Systems. In *CCGrid 2012 - The 12th IEEE/ACM Int'l Symposium on Cluster, Cloud and Grid Computing*, pages 668–675, 2012.

[23] P. F. Reynolds, Jr., and P. M. Dickens. SPECTRUM: A Parallel Simulation Testbed. In *Proceedings of the Hypercube Conference*, 1989.

[24] G. F. Riley, M. H. Ammar, R. M. Fujimoto, A. Park, K. Perumalla, and D. Xu. A Federated Approach to Distributed Network Simulation. *ACM Transactions on Modeling and Computer Simulation*, pages 116–148, 2004.

[25] G. F. Riley and T. R. Henderson. The NS-3 Network Simulator. In *Modeling and Tools for Network Simulation*, pages 15–34. Springer Berlin Heidelberg, 2010.

[26] A. F. Rodrigues, K. S. Hemmert, B. W. Barrett, C. Kersey, R. Oldfield, M. Weston, R. Risen, J. Cook, P. Rosenfeld, E. Cooper-Balls, and B. Jacob. The Structural Simulation Toolkit. *SIGMETRICS Performance Evaluation Review*, 38(4):37–42, 2011.

[27] C. A. Schaefer, V. Pankratius, and W. F. Tichy. Engineering Parallel Applications with Tunable Architectures. In *Proc. of the 32nd ACM/IEEE Int'l Conference on Software Engineering - Volume 1*, pages 405–414, 2010.

[28] M. Snir, S. W. Otto, D. W. Walker, J. Dongarra, and S. Huss-Lederman. *MPI: The Complete Reference.* MIT Press, 1995.

[29] H. Sutter and J. Larus. Software and the Concurrency Revolution. *Queue*, 3(7):54–62, 2005.

[30] S. M. Swope and R. M. Fujimoto. Optimal Performance of Distributed Simulation Programs. In *Proc. of the 19th Winter Simulation Conference*, 1987.

[31] K. Vanmechelen, S. De Munck, and J. Broeckhove. Conservative Distributed Discrete Event Simulation on Amazon EC2. In *Proceedings of the 2012 12th IEEE/ACM International Symposium on Cluster, Cloud and Grid Computing*, CCGRID, pages 853–860, 2012.

Formalization of Emergence in Multi-agent Systems

Yong Meng Teo and Ba Linh Luong
Department of Computer Science
National University of Singapore
13 Computing Drive
Singapore 117417
{teoym,luongbal}@comp.nus.edu.sg

Claudia Szabo
Department of Computer Science
The University of Adelaide
North Terrace
Adelaide 5005, Australia
claudia.szabo@adelaide.edu.au

ABSTRACT

Emergence is a distinguishing feature in systems, especially when complexity grows with the number of components, interactions, and connectivity. There is immense interest in emergence, and a plethora of definitions from philosophy to sciences. Despite this, there is a lack of consensus on the definition of emergence and this hinders the development of a formal approach to understand and predict emergent behavior in multi-agent systems. This paper proposes a grammar-based set-theoretic approach to formalize and verify the existence and extent of emergence without prior knowledge or definition of emergent properties. Our approach is based on weak (basic) emergence that is both generated and autonomous from the underlying agents. In contrast with current work, our approach has two main advantages. By focusing only on system interactions of interest and feasible combinations of individual agent behavior, state-space explosion is reduced. In formalizing emergence, our extended grammar is designed to model agents of diverse types, mobile agents, and open systems. Theoretical and experimental studies using the boids model demonstrate the complexity of our formal approach.

Categories and Subject Descriptors

D.2.4 [**Software Engineering**]: Software/Program Verification—*validation*; I.6.5 [**Simulation and Modeling**]: Model Development—*modeling methodologies*

General Terms

Verification, Theory

Keywords

Emergent behavior, multi-agent system, simulation

1. INTRODUCTION

Systems with a large number of components and complex interconnection are ubiquitous [33, 40]. If components interact with other components and make decisions individually based on internal logic, the system can be modeled as a multi-agent system where agents play the role of components [19]. A system is said to be complex if it exhibits designed (expected) properties that can be derived from the system specification, as well as properties that are irreducible from knowledge of the interconnected components [12, 13, 23]. These irreducible properties are defined as *emergent properties* or *emergence*. For example, flocking is an emergent property of a group of birds [33]. Having attributes and behavior rules of the birds does not enable us to identify the flocking patterns or how they avoid obstacles.

Originating from philosophy [6, 20, 30], emergence has become of interest for studying complex systems and multi-agent systems. Emergence study provides great potential to understand the interactions of agents and their environment [9, 10], and to explain how natural systems work [35]. Furthermore, it is important to know whether emergent properties are beneficial or harmful so that we can exploit the positive impacts of the beneficial properties and minimize, or even prevent negative consequences due to the harmful properties. On the one hand, emergence is beneficial because it confers additional functionalities to the systems. For instance, users adapt software products to support tasks that the designer never intended. On the other hand, emergence may be harmful, such as unforeseeable failures make a system harder to design, analyze, and control [27]. As a result, emergence in a system should be predicted and verified. Unfortunately, it is difficult to *predict* emergence [34]. According to Dyson [14], emergent phenomena cannot be predicted through analysis at any level simpler than that of the system as a whole. Even worse, *verifying* that emergence exists is also difficult [32]. Although in some cases, emergent properties can be regular, which is recurring and recognizable, it does not imply that they are easily recognized [20]. Most studies focus only on post-mortem observation of emergence when a tangible representation of the system is available to examine [17, 25], rather than on verifying that emergence exists.

Kubik [22] proposed a method for formalizing weak emergence without prior knowledge of emergence. The approach adopts a set-based view on the world, where emergence is seen as the difference between a calculated and an observed behavior. However, like other work, the definition of emergence is too broad because emergence is any kind of system states that cannot be obtained from summing individual agents' behaviors. Moreover, the calculation of the expected behavior suffers from state explosion and renders the

SIGSIM-PADS'13, May 19–22, 2013, Montréal, Québec, Canada.

method infeasible for practical use [38, 39]. Our contribution is twofold. First, based on Kubik's approach, we propose a grammar-based framework with a new definition of emergence that distinguishes possible system states and emergent properties of interest, from the larger set of all combinations of system states. Second, in contrast to Kubik's approach, our grammar allows for different agent types, includes mobile agents, and permits the study of open systems where the number of agents varies over time.

The remainder of the paper is organized as follows. Section 2 reviews different perspectives, classifications, and formal studies of emergence. Our emergence definition and proposed approach are presented in Section 3. Using the boids model [33], we show how to apply our approach to detect flocking behavior in a group of birds. Section 4 presents a theoretical and experimental analysis of our work. Section 5 concludes this paper and discusses future work.

2. RELATED WORK

Despite a long history of complex systems research [28], there is no consensus on the definition of emergence. Emergence can be considered in three main perspectives, namely, philosophy, natural and social sciences, and computer science. From a *philosophical* perspective, emergent properties are subjectively a product of both the unexpected behavior of complex systems and the *limitations* of the *observer's knowledge* [21] and the tools employed. Other limitations come from the scale and level of abstraction under which the system is observed [7]. *Scientific perspectives* [1, 22] criticize the idea of temporary lack of knowledge of the observer because it implies that we are unable to study emergence scientifically. Therefore, emergent properties are defined as intrinsic to a system and independent from the eye of the beholder [11]. *Natural and social sciences* explain emergence via theories, mainly in physics, biology, chemistry, and human behavior. Two concepts of emergence in this perspective are self-organization and hierarchy. First, emergence is the formation of order from disorder based on *self-organization* [16]. Second, a property is emergent if it is discontinuous from the properties of the components at the lower levels in the *hierarchy* [2]. *Computer science* aims to predict, verify, validate, and reason about emergence. Prediction is done before the observation of emergence, while verification is done only when emergence is observed. Verification of emergent properties is a complex task because it may lead to combinatorial explosion in terms of the system states. More importantly, emergent properties should be defined first before verifying which is typically not straightforward. Verifying emergence without prior knowledge of emergence is a research challenge. Validation allows us to determine whether an emergent property is beneficial or harmful[37]. Finally, reasoning enables the understanding of the cause-and-effect of emergence. The most frequent studied type of emergence in computer science is *weak* (or *basic*) emergence [4, 6, 8, 16, 22].

A macro level property characterizing the system as a whole is defined to be *weakly* emergent if it can be derived from the micro level dynamics but only by a finitely long simulation [5]. Other definitions see weak emergence in the case whereby the whole is constrained or influenced by the parts through *upward causation* (UC), but at the same time the parts are influenced by the whole through *downward causation* (DC) [6, 30]. DC can be either positive or negative. First, positive DC amplifies UC and leads the system to unstable states [31]. For example, when the general price level of goods and services raises, the cost of living increases. Higher living cost demands higher income, that in turn results in higher prices of goods and services. The cycle continues until a policy to decrease the inflation rate is introduced. Second, negative DC weakens the UC and keeps the system in stable states. There is a balance between autonomy through UC and self-organization through DC. Birds fly in different directions to avoid collision. At the same time, they stay close to each other, try to match the neighbors' speed, and steer to the center of the flock.

Scientific study of emergence requires a formal specification of the system, system components, and even emergent properties. Emergence formalisms can be mainly classified into three categories, namely, variable-based [15, 26, 35], event-based [10], and grammar-based [22]. Each has advantages and disadvantages. In *variable-based* methods, a variable is chosen to represent emergence [29]. Changes in the center of mass of a group of birds, for example, can be used for identifying flocking behavior. Usually, emergence is measured numerically, i.e. quantitative emergence, based on information theory and probability theory. Many variable-based studies deploy Shannon entropy [36] to measure the uncertainty and unpredictability of a system with regard to a particular attribute [15, 26]. The more structural a system is, the lower entropy it has. Entropy is, however, not suitable for systems with continuous attributes. Although differential (continuous) entropy can be defined [31], it lacks some important characteristics, and usually is not a good measure of uncertainty. For example, the differential entropy can be negative because probability density functions could be greater than one; also it is not invariant under continuous linear transformations of variables [31]. Fisch et al. [15] regard emergence as an unexpected or unpredictable change of the distribution underlying the observed samples. However, the computation is costly and user intervention is required. Seth [35] defines G-emergence as a measure of emergence based on G-causality and G-autonomy, which compute the dependence and the autonomy of a variable with respect to a set of other variables respectively. However, a set of variables must be defined and the computations of G-causality, G-autonomy, and G-emergence are expensive. Variable-based approach limits describing details of components, so it gives little understanding of the causes of emergent properties. In addition, defining the abstraction level at which the variable is measured is non-trivial.

In *event-based* methods, component behavior is defined as a sequence of events at some level of abstraction [10]. A *simple event* is a state transition that results from the execution of a single state transition rule. A *complex event* is either a simple event or two complex events satisfying a set of constraints with respect to each other. Emergence is complex events that can be reduced to a sequence of simple events. As with the variable-based approach, event types and emergent behavior have to be formalized beforehand. Identifying and defining the proxy event is not trivial.

To overcome the challenging problem of a prior definition of emergence, Kubik [22] proposes a *grammar-based* approach. An extended cooperating array grammar system is used to formalize the environment, agents, and cooperation among them. Behavior of the system is therefore the language, i.e. a set of words, resulting from derivations of grammars (agents) on the tape (two-dimensional array of symbols). The approach is based on an intuition of emergence that "the whole is more than the sum of its parts". An emergent property is defined as a system state that results from the interactions of agents and cannot be produced by summing their individual states. Given an initial system state, two languages L_{WHOLE} and L_{PARTS} are calculated, using two grammar systems that define the execution of agents together and individually respectively. L_{WHOLE} defines a set of system states produced by the system agents acting together and interacting as a whole. L_{PARTS}, on the other hand, presents the sum of the agents' behaviors without considering the interactions among them. As a result, emergence is defined as $L_{WHOLE} - L_{PARTS}$. The approach is exemplified using a small game of life example. The grammar-based approach does not require a priori definition of emergence. This approach, however, has four main limitations: (1) there is no explicit provision for agent type, (2) it is unclear how to deal with mobile agents, (3) in the game of life example, agents are stationary, the number of agents is always equal to the number of cells, and (4) the state spaces of L_{WHOLE} and L_{PARTS} are unnecessarily large.

3. PROPOSED APPROACH

Our approach for the verification of emergent properties extends Kubik's grammar-based approach [22] to derive emergent property states. The set of emergent property states is defined as the difference:

$$L_\xi = L_{whole} - L_{sum} \tag{1}$$

where L_{whole} describes all possible system states due to agent-to-agent and agent-environment interaction, and L_{sum} is the sum of all individual agents' behaviors, without considering agent interactions. L_ξ contains the set of system states that are in L_{whole} but not in L_{sum}. This broad perspective of emergence, as in Kubik's approach, leads to state explosion when determining L_{sum} and L_{whole}. This is because all possible combinations of individual agent states are considered following a defined superimposition operator, without including system-defined rules.

We propose a new perspective that significantly reduces the state space for L_ξ. Firstly, it is important to highlight here that while Kubik refers to the difference $L_{whole} - L_{sum}$ as emergence, we refer to this set as the emergent states set, because it is the set from which emergent properties can be deduced. Secondly, we observe that the size of L_{whole} is dependent of the number of interactions and state transition rules defined by a modeler, and a subset of interest (to the modeler) from all the rules in a given system. This would be the case, for example, when we consider different kinds of rules in the modeling a flock of birds: the entire rule set, or some rules of interest while ignoring others. As shown in Figure 1, L_{whole} can be redefined as:

$$L_{whole} = L^{I}_{whole} \cup L^{NI}_{whole} \tag{2}$$

where L^{I}_{whole} is bounded by the number of interaction rules that are of interest to the user for the particular study, and L^{NI}_{whole} represents the set of all possible system states that are not of interest.

The size of L_{sum} increases exponentially with the increase in the number of agents as all possible combinations of agent states are considered. Similarly, L_{sum} can be also redefined

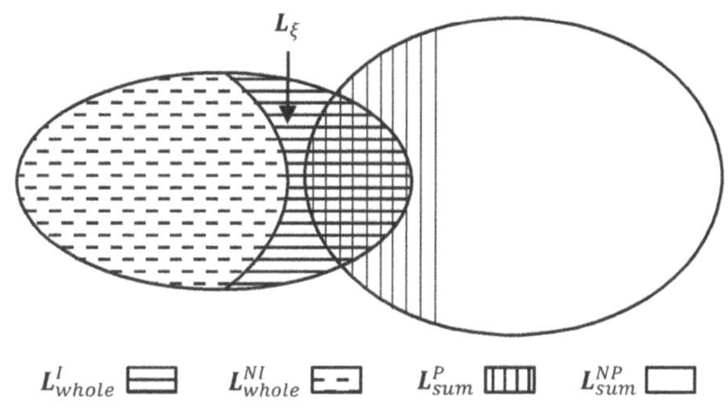

Figure 1: Set of Emergent Property States

as follows:

$$L_{sum} = L^{P}_{sum} \cup L^{NP}_{sum} \tag{3}$$

Although it is mathematically possible to derive L_{sum}, in practice there is a subset of feasible combinations of agents' behaviors (L^{P}_{sum}), and the remaining are combinations of agents' behaviors that will not exist in practice (L^{NP}_{sum}).

Given the above, the set of emergent property states L_ξ is redefined as:

$$L_\xi = L^{I}_{whole} - L^{P}_{sum} \tag{4}$$

Emergent property states, with respect to a model of interest, are due to non-trivial interactions among agents, and cannot be derived by summing individual agents' states. As shown in Figure 1, there are states in L^{I}_{whole} that can be found in L^{P}_{sum}, in other words,

$$L^{I}_{whole} \cap L^{P}_{sum} \neq \emptyset \tag{5}$$

Intuitively, these states are resultant from agent computation that do not require interactions, or from the interactions of agents that has no effect on agent behavior. For example, in the flock of birds model detailed in Section 3.2, two individuals can be very far apart and as such interaction rules between them have no effect.

Contrary to Kubik's approach, which regards emergent properties as system states, we do not consider that L_ξ contains the emergent behavior but only states that together, following particular criteria, can form an emergent property. In the next step, we propose to determine whether L_ξ contains emergent properties that have been seen before, or that are beneficial or harmful to the system. Towards this, we propose to use emergent properties criteria derived from the system expert, as well as information obtained from L^{NI}_{whole}. In this paper, we show the process of calculating the set of emergent property states L_ξ.

Next, we enhance the grammar-based approach with three main extensions: (1) introduce agent type (A_{ij} denotes an agent instance j of type i), (2) introduce mobile agents by defining mobility as attributes of agents $P_i = P_{i\_mobile} \cup P_{i\_others}$ where P_i denotes the set of attributes of agents of type i, (3) model open systems where agents can enter and leave system. As a result, the proposed approach has a wide variety of applications in which components belong to different types, can move in space, and have multiple attributes. These kinds of systems are ubiquitous in practice such as traffic networks [24], social networks [18], and flock of birds [33], among others. Our proposed approach consists of two major steps, namely, modeling the system as a multi-agent system, and the application of our extended grammar-based formalism for different types of mobile agents.

3.1 Emergence Formalism

A multi-agent system consists of m different types of n agents (A) interacting in an environment (E). The environment E is a part of the system that lies outside the agents and can be regarded as a platform for agent interactions. For simplicity, we assume that E has no behavior rules and changes only as a result of agent actions. Changes of the environment, in turn, impact the agent behavior. E is modeled as a 2D grid[1] that is subdivided into c units called cells (e). Changes of the environment are therefore changes of the states of the cells. For example, a cell turns from "occupied" to "free" when the agent that occupies the cell moves to another cell. V_e denotes the set of possible states of the cell e. Similarly, V_E denotes the set of possible cell states. In addition, the environment state is made up of the states of all cells in the environment. $s_e(t)$ and $S_E(t)$ denote the state of cell e and the environment E at time t respectively. Table 1 provides a glossary of notations used for formalizing the system. Agents are classified into m different types in which all agents of the same type have the same attributes and behavior rules. A_{ij} denotes an agent of type i ($1 \leq i \leq m$) and instance j ($1 \leq j \leq n_i$), where n_i is the number of agent instances of type i, and $n_1 + n_2 + ... + n_m = n$. An agent of type i is characterized by three factors: a set of attributes for agents of type i (P_i), a set of behavior rules for agents of type i (R_i), and an initial state ($s_{ij}(0)$). It is important to distinguish agent attributes from their values. For instance, attribute color has several values, such as red, yellow, and green. Only the initial state $s_{ij}(0)$ is specific to the agent, while P_i and R_i are common to all agents of type i. P_i consists of two main subsets: P_{i_mobile} modeling the mobility of agents of type i and P_{i_others} modeling other attributes.

Agent behavior (L) is characterized by behavior rules (R) that define how agents interact with other agents and the environment. We assume that no evolutionary processes are involved in the system, i.e. behavior rules do not change over time. R_i denotes the set of behavior rules of agents of type i. R_i consists of R_{i_mobile} that impacts agent mobility, i.e. changes values of attributes of P_{i_mobile}, and R_{i_others} for the rest. An agent changes its state because it is triggered by a rule that affects the agent itself or one of its neighbors changes state. The state of A_{ij} at time t, denoted by $s_{ij}(t)$, is defined by values of its attributes at time t. V_{A_i} denotes the set of possible agent states for agents of type i.

3.1.1 *System Formalism*

A multi-agent system consisting of an environment and a set of agents is formalized as an extended cooperating array grammar system where context-free grammars represent agents, and a two-dimensional array of symbols represents the environment. Each grammar has its own rewriting rules defining how the grammar cooperates with the other grammars and with the array, i.e. rewrite the symbols on the array. A system of m agent types and a total of n agents $A_{11}, \ldots, A_{1n_1}, \ldots, A_{mn_m}$ interacting in a 2D grid environment of c cells is defined as follows:

$$GBS = (V_A, V_E, A_{11}, \ldots, A_{1n_1}, \ldots, A_{mn_m}, S(0)) \quad (6)$$

where V_A denotes the set of possible agent states for all agent types, V_E denotes the set of possible cell states, A_{ij} denotes an agent of type i ($1 \leq i \leq m$) and instance j ($1 \leq j \leq n_i$), and $S(0)$ denotes the initial system state. A system state is composed of the state of the environment and the states of all agents.

For the environment (E),

$$V_E = \bigcup_{e=1}^{c} V_e \quad (7)$$

where V_e denotes the set of possible states of cell e. The state of the entire environment is made up of the states of all its cells. The states of cell e and the environment E at time t are $s_e(t) \in V_e$ and $S_E(t) \in V_E^c$ respectively.

For the agents (A),

$$V_A = \bigcup_{i=1}^{m} V_{A_i} \quad (8)$$

where V_{A_i} denotes the set of possible states for agents of type i.

Agent of type i ($1 \leq i \leq m$) and instance j ($1 \leq j \leq n_i$), A_{ij}, is defined as follows:

$$A_{ij} = (P_i, R_i, s_{ij}(0)) \quad (9)$$

where P_i denotes the set of attributes for agents of type i, R_i denotes the set of behavior rules for agents of type i, and $s_{ij}(0)$ denotes the initial state of the agent. P_i is defined as:

$P_i = P_{i\_mobile} \bigcup P_{i\_others}$ where

$P_{i\_mobile} = \{\text{x} \mid \text{x is an attribute that models mobility}\}$

$P_{i\_others} = P_i \setminus P_{i\_mobile}$

Agents change their states according to behavior rules that are regarded as functions from a set of agent states to the set itself. Some of these rules that affect the mobility of agents, for example change location or speed, are defined as mobile rules.

$R_i : V_{A_i} \rightarrow V_{A_i}$

$R_i = R_{i\_mobile} \bigcup R_{i\_others}$

A_{ij} has an initial state $s_{ij}(0) \in V_{A_i}$. The system state at time t ($S(t)$), is composed of state of the environment ($S_E(t)$) and states of agents ($s_{ij}(t)$) at time t. Hence,

$$S(t) = S_E(t) \bigcup_{\forall i \forall j} s_{ij}(t) \quad (10)$$

3.1.2 *Verification of Emergence*

Our approach for the verification of emergence computes two sets of system states corresponding to the two levels of abstraction defined above, namely, the macro level when regarding the system as a whole and the micro level when regarding the system as an aggregation of its individual agents. The set of emergent system states is defined as:

$$L_\xi = L_{whole}^I - L_{sum}^P$$

L_{sum}^P can be determined by adding agent constraints among others but is not straightforward. We leave this as future work and for simplicity we use L_{sum} for the rest of this paper.

Taking the interactions of agents (denoted as *GROUP*) into account, the system behavior of interest (L_{whole}^I) returns a set of words (w) that represents the set of system

[1]E can be easily extended to model other topologies.

	Notation	Description
System	$S(t)$	state of system at time t
Environment	V_E	set of possible cell states
	V_e	set of possible states of cell e
	$S_E(t)$	state of environment at time t
	$s_e(t)$	state of cell e at time t
Agent Type	m	number of agent types
	n_i	number of agents of type i $(1 \leq i \leq m)$
	V_{A_i}	set of possible states for agents of type i
Agent	n	number of agents
	A_{ij}	agent of type i $(1 \leq i \leq m)$ and instance j $(1 \leq j \leq n_i)$
	V_A	set of possible agent states for all agent types
	P_i	set of attributes for agents of type i
	R_i	set of behavior rules for agents of type i
	$s_{ij}(t)$	state of agent A_{ij} at time t
	$L_(A_{ij})$	set of system states representing the behavior of agent A_{ij}
Emergence	$\oplus$	superimpose operator
	L^I_{whole}	set of system states representing behaviors of interest due to agent interactions
	L^P_{sum}	set of possible system states representing all combinations of agents' behaviors
	L_ξ	set of emergent property states

Table 1: Glossary of Notations

states reachable from the initial system state. Given an initial state, the system is simulated until it reaches a state that has already appeared before. We stop the simulation when the system state repeats itself. Complex adaptive and non-linear systems with strange attractors where system states vary continuously are not considered in this study. L^I_{whole} with respect to the initial state is therefore the set of all distinct states obtained as follows:

$$L^I_{whole} = \{w \in V^{c+n} \mid S(0) \Rightarrow^*_{GROUP} w\} \quad (11)$$

The sum of agents' behaviors (L_{sum}) is defined as the set of words resulting from superimposing behaviors of individual agents.

$$L_{sum} = \oplus(L(A_{11}), \ldots, L(A_{1n_1}), \ldots, L(A_{mn_m})) \quad (12)$$

where $L(A_{ij})$ denotes the behavior of agent A_{ij} and $\oplus$ is the superimpose operator defined in [22]. The superimpose operator $\oplus$ does a sum of the individual agents' behaviors when they do not interact with each other. Let $w_1 = a_1a_2 \ldots a_x, w_2 = b_1b_2 \ldots b_y$ be words of symbols $a_i, b_j, 1 \leq i \leq x, 1 \leq j \leq y$ over an alphabet $(V_A \cup V_E)^+$, and ϵ denotes the empty symbol. Hence, the superimposition of the word w_1 on the word w_2 is a function $\oplus : V^* \times V^* \rightarrow V^*$ that results in $w_{supimp} = c_1c_2 \ldots c_z$ of symbols $c_k, 1 \leq k \leq z$, defined as follows:

1. $z = max(x, y)$;
2. if $a_i \in V_A$ then $c_k = a_i$;
3. if $a_i = \epsilon$ then $c_k = b_j$;
4. if $b_j = \epsilon$ then $c_k = a_i$;
5. if $a_i \in V_E$ and $b_i \in V_E$ then $c_k = a_i$;
6. if $a_i \in V_E$ and $b_j \in V_A$ then $c_k = b_j$.

The superimposition is done over all permutations of n behaviors of agents. It is important to note that ordering is important in the process of calculating the superimposition. The expression below shows the superimposition of three languages L_1, L_2, and L_3.

$$\begin{aligned}\oplus(L_1, L_2, L_3) = {} & L_1 \oplus (L_2 \oplus (L_3)) \cup L_1 \oplus (L_3 \oplus (L_2)) \\ & \cup L_2 \oplus (L_1 \oplus (L_3)) \cup L_2 \oplus (L_3 \oplus (L_1)) \\ & \cup L_3 \oplus (L_1 \oplus (L_2)) \cup L_3 \oplus (L_2 \oplus (L_1))\end{aligned}$$

Defining the sum of the individual agents' behaviors is difficult. Ideally, the result should contain exactly all designed system states that can be derived from the system specification. Unfortunately, this is only true if agents are independent from the others in the system. Given the initial system state, we obtain n states where each consists of one agent. Considering only the agent in the system, the agent's behavior returns a set of words (w) that represents the set of system states reachable from the corresponding system state. $L(A_{ij})$ is defined as follows:

$$L(A_{ij}) = \{w \in V^{c+1} \mid (S_E(0) \cup s_{ij}(0)) \Rightarrow^* w\} \quad (13)$$

Agent symbols have priority over environmental symbols. Any non-empty symbol has priority over the empty symbol ϵ. For example, consider $V_A = \{a_1, a_2, a_3\}, V_E = \{o, f\}$, $L_1 = \{fa_1of\}, L_2 = \{oa_2ff\}, L_3 = \{foffa_3\}$. Then the superimposition of the agents' behaviors will be the language $L_{sum} = \{fa_1ofa_3, oa_2ffa_3, fa_1ffa_3, fa_2ffa_3\}$.

3.2 Example: Flock of Birds Model

The boids model [33] captures the motion of bird flocking and is a seminal example for studying emergence [9]. At the macro level, a group of birds tends to move in a V-like formation, which has aerodynamic advantages, obstacle avoidance, and predator protection, regardless of the initial positions of the birds. At the micro level, three simple rules define how each bird flies: (1) separation - steer to avoid crowding neighbors, (2) alignment - steer towards the average heading of neighbors, and (3) cohesion - steer towards the average position of neighbors [33].

To demonstrate our proposed approach, we extended the boids model to include two types of birds, ducks and geese. For ease of discussion, we model a multi-agent system with ten birds with equal numbers of ducks and geese interacting in an environment represented as a 2D grid of 8×8 cells. Each cell is *occupied* by a bird or *free*, and two birds cannot be located at the same cell at the same time. Birds have two attributes: position and velocity. Position and velocity model birds' mobility. The *position* of a bird is location of the cell occupied. The *velocity* is a vector that contains moving direction and speed. Ducks can fly zero, one, or two cells per time step in one of eight directions: north, north-east, east, south-east, south, south-west, west, and north-west. Similarly, geese can fly at the maximum speed of three cells per time step. The vector representation for velocity of ducks is shown in Table 2. Birds behave according to three

Direction	Speed		
	0	1	2
North	(0,0)	(0,1)	(0,2)
North-East	(0,0)	(1,1)	(1,2), (2,1), (2,2)
East	(0,0)	(1,0)	(2,0)
South-East	(0,0)	(1,-1)	(1,-2) (2,-1), (2,-2)
South	(0,0)	(0,-1)	(0,-2)
South-West	(0,0)	(-1,-1)	(-1,-2), (-2,-1), (-2,-2)
West	(0,0)	(-1,0)	(-2,0)
North-West	(0,0)	(-1,1)	(-1,2), (-2,1), (-2,2)

Table 2: Vector Representation for Velocity of Ducks

rules: (1) separation: avoid collision with nearby birds, (2) alignment: fly as fast as nearby birds of the same type, and (3) cohesion: stay close to nearby birds of the same type.

3.2.1 System Formalism

The boids model is formalized as:

$$GBS_{boid} = (V_A, V_E, A_{11}, \ldots, A_{15}, A_{21}, \ldots, A_{25}, S(0))$$

where A_{1j} denotes a duck instance j ($1 \leq j \leq 5$), and A_{2j} denotes a goose instance j ($1 \leq j \leq 5$), $V_A = V_{A_1} \cup V_{A_2}$ denotes the set of possible states for the ducks (V_{A_1}) and the geese (V_{A_2}), V_E denotes the set of possible cell states. $S(t) \in (V_A \cup V_E)^+$ denotes system state at time t, and $S(0)$ denotes the initial system state at time zero.

For cell e, $V_e = \{o, f\}$ where o means occupied and f means free, and $s_e(t) \in V_e$. For the entire environment E, $V_E = \bigcup_{e=1}^{64} V_e = \{o, f\}$, and $S_E(t) \in V_E^{64}$, where $64 = 8{\times}8$ is the number of cells.

A duck instance $A_{1j} (1 \leq j \leq 5)$ is defined as follows:

$$A_{1j} = (P_1, R_1, s_{1j}(0))$$

where

$P_1 = P_{1\_mobile} \cup P_{1\_others}$

$P_{1\_mobile} = \{position(g_{1j}), velocity(v_{1j})\}$

$P_{1\_others} = \varnothing$

$V_{A_1} = \{(x, y) | 1 \leq x \leq 8, 1 \leq y \leq 8\} \times \{(\alpha, \beta) | -2 \leq \alpha \leq 2, -2 \leq \beta \leq 2\}$

$R_1 = R_{1\_mobile} \cup R_{1\_others}, R_{1\_others} = \varnothing$

$s_{1j}(t) \in V_{A_1}$

R_{1_mobile} defines the update of the position $g_{1j}(t)$ and the velocity $v_{1j}(t)$ of duck A_{1j} over time. We limit the speed of ducks to two cells per time step so that they cannot fly arbitrarily fast. Consequently, absolute values of the horizontal component (α) and the vertical component (β) of the velocity vector are bounded to two cells. Let $sign(\alpha)$ and $sign(\beta)$ return signs of α and β, i.e. 1 for positive and -1 for negative, respectively. Both position and velocity of birds are represented as 2D vectors; the update is therefore simply vector additions.

$(\alpha, \beta) = v_{1j}(t) + separation(A_{1j}) + align(A_{1j}) + cohesion(A_{1j})$

$v_{1j}(t+1) = (sign(\alpha)min(|\alpha|, 2), sign(\beta)min(|\beta|, 2))$

$g_{1j}(t+1) = g_{1j}(t) + v_{1j}(t+1)$

Separation: If duck a is close to another duck or goose b, i.e. within ϵ cells, then a flies away from b

$$separation(a) = \sum_{distance(a,b) \leq \epsilon} a.position - b.position$$

Alignment: Duck a changes its velocity by λ% towards the average velocity of its neighboring ducks

$$align(a) = (\frac{\sum_{\substack{duck(b)\\ neighbor(a,b)}}^{k} b.velocity}{k} - a.velocity) \times \frac{1}{\lambda}$$

Cohesion: Duck a moves by γ% towards the center of its neighboring ducks

$$cohesion(a) = (\frac{\sum_{\substack{duck(b)\\ neighbor(a,b)}}^{k} b.position}{k} - a.position) \times \frac{1}{\gamma}$$

The model for geese follows in a similar manner except that their maximum speed is three cells per time step.

3.2.2 Emergence Verification

Our proposed approach returns only a set of emergent property states. To verify that these states contain emergent properties, we show how the well-known flocking of birds emegence is derived from L_ξ. The initial system state is given as the state at time t = 0 in Figure 2. For ease of visualization, we distinguish ducks from geese using a star (*) symbol and bolded cell. <$j, (\alpha, \beta)$> denotes a bird instance j, with velocity (α, β). Figure 2 shows a simulation of the system when $\epsilon = 2$, $\lambda = 10$, and $\beta = 8$. We observe that the birds keep flying in the same pattern since t = 4. Moreover, the system gets back to the system state $S(4)$ at time t = 12: $S(12) = S(4)$. Hence, $L^I_{whole} = \{S(0), S(1), \ldots, S(11)\}$.

L_{sum} is calculated using the superimpose operator as $L_{sum} = \oplus(L(A_{11}), \ldots, L(A_{25}))$. By definition and following our discussion above, L_{sum} tends to be very large, even for small problem sizes. As such, we consider for illustration two geese A_{23} and A_{25}. For simplicity, the superimposition of two birds, $L(A_{23})$ and $L(A_{25})$, is shown in Figure 3. Formally,

$$\begin{aligned} &\oplus (L(A_{23}), L(A_{25})) \\ &= L(A_{23}) \oplus (L(A_{25})) \cup L(A_{25}) \oplus (L(A_{23})) \\ &= \{((2, (1, 1), (1, 1))fff \ldots (2, (1, 2), (1, 0))fff \ldots), \\ &\quad (fff \ldots (2, (2, 2), (1, 0))fff \ldots), \\ &\quad (fff \ldots (2, (8, 2), (1, 0))fff \ldots (2, (8, 8), (1, 1))\} \end{aligned}$$

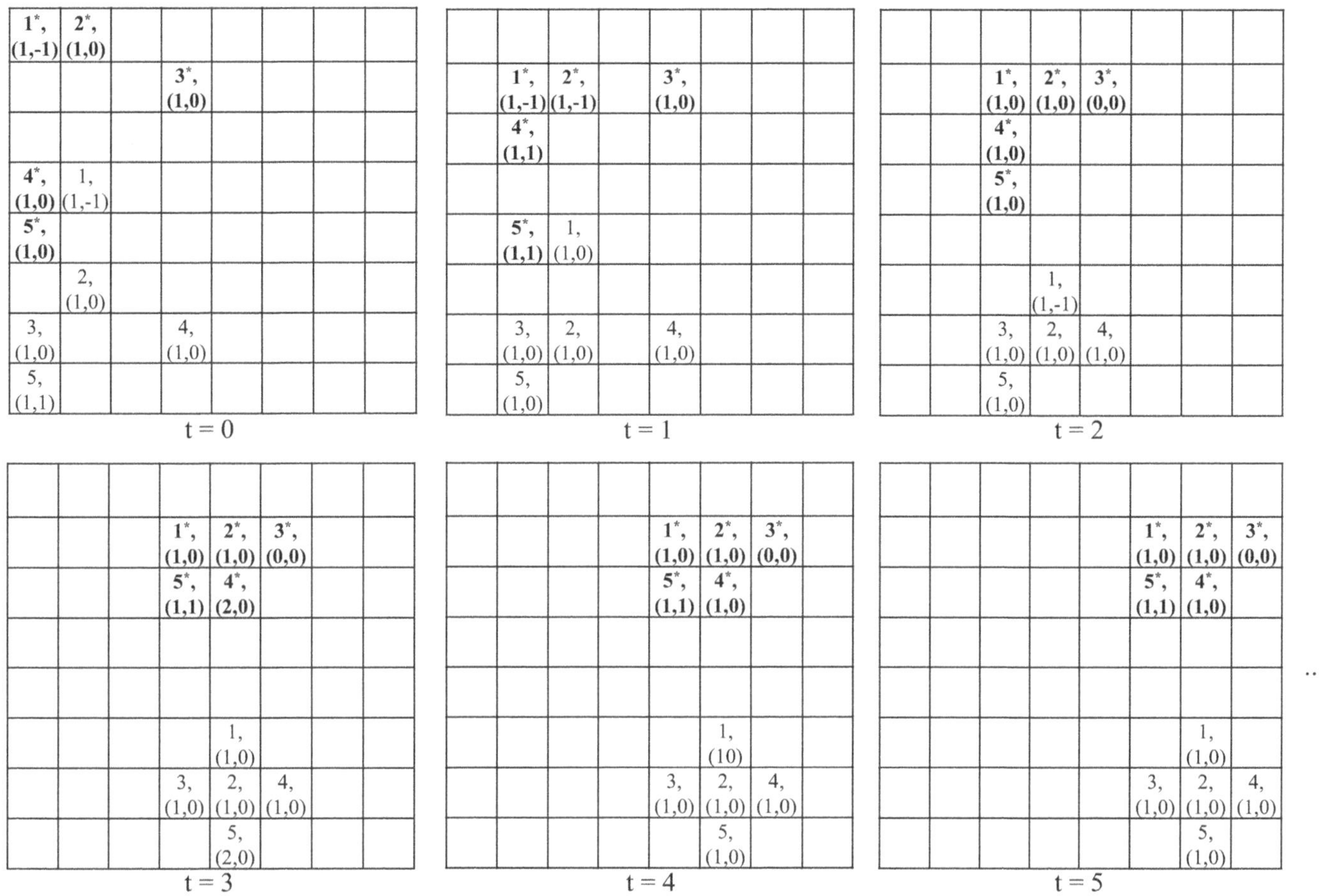

Figure 2: Snapshot of Emergent Property States

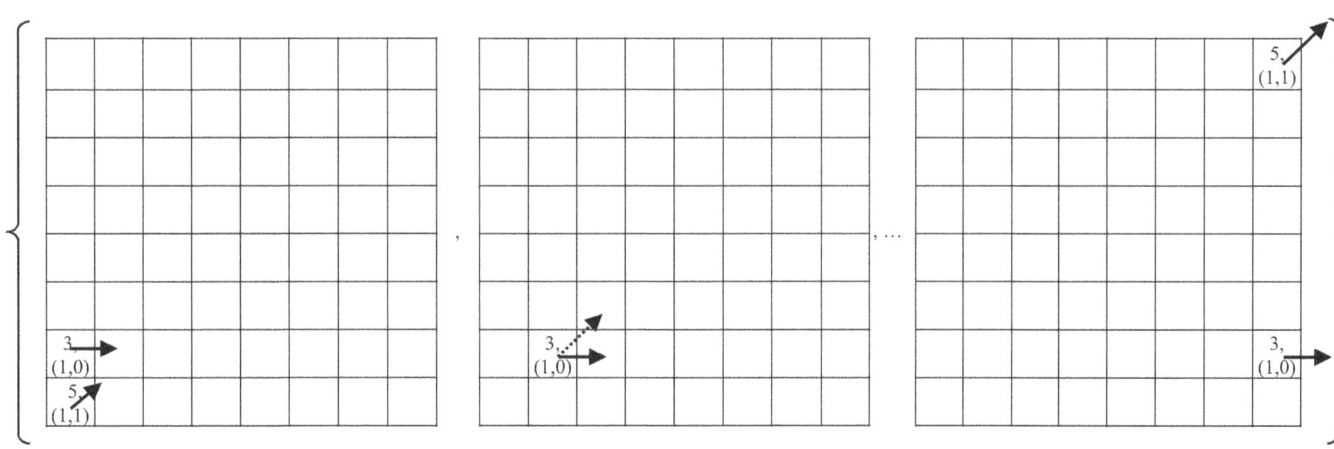

Figure 3: Example of $\mathbf{L}(\mathbf{A_{23}}) \oplus (\mathbf{L}(\mathbf{A_{25}}))$

$L_(A_{23})$ and $L_(A_{25})$ are behaviors of agent A_{23} and A_{25} respectively. f represents an empty cell and a tuple $<i, (x, y), (\alpha, \beta)>$ represents the state of a bird of type i at cell (x, y) with velocity (α, β). For example, $<2, (1, 2), (1, 0)>$ represents a goose locating at cell $(1, 2)$ with velocity $(1, 0)$. Note that the x-axis is horizontal and oriented from left to right, and the y-axis is vertical and oriented from bottom to top. In the example of ten birds, L_{sum} contains one common state, S(0), with L^I_{whole}. Therefore, $L_\xi = \{S(1), S(2), \ldots, S(11)\}$. Furthermore, we assume that a group of birds form a flock if at least five birds of the same type fly *together*, with each bird has at least one immediate neighbor of the same type. Ten emergent property states from $S(2)$ to $S(11)$ therefore have flocking emergent property. In addition, flocking patterns in $S(3), \ldots, S(11)$ are identical, regardless of different positions of the birds forming the flock. In other words, we have two types of the known flocking emergent property: one type in $S(2)$ and one type in $S(3), \ldots, S(11)$. We leave the unknown emergent property state $S(1)$ for the future work.

4. EVALUATION

In this section, we present the theoretical and experimental analysis of our approach. Since we derived the sets of states for L^I_{whole}, L_{sum}, and L_ξ, we present the complexity in terms of the number of states. We implemented our approach using a Java program, and our experimental analysis quantifies the state size, by varying the number of birds.

4.1 Theoretical Analysis

The complexity of deriving L_ξ ($O(L_\xi)$) consists of two parts: complexity of L^I_{whole} ($O(L^I_{whole})$) and complexity of L_{sum} ($O(L_{sum})$) .

$$O(L_\xi) = O(L^I_{whole}) + O(L_{sum}) \tag{14}$$

Because detecting emergence is to differentiate system states that appear when taking into account interactions of agents, but not when regarding them separately, it is reasonable to use the number of system states as a complexity measure. Key complexity factors include: the environment size (2D grid of size x by y), the number of agent types (m), the number of agents (n), and the number of possible states an agent can take (s). We derive $O(L^I_{whole})$ and $O(L_{sum})$ in the *worst case*. Let $n = n' + n''$ where n' is the number of mobile agents, and n'' is the number of stationary agents.

$\boldsymbol{O(L^I_{whole})}$: Given a position, an agent can take one of s states. Moreover, stationary agents are fixed in n'' positions. There are $\binom{xy-n''}{n'}$ possibilities for allocating n' mobile agents into the remaining $xy - n''$ positions. Hence,

$$O(L^I_{whole}) = O(\binom{xy - n''}{n'} s^n) \tag{15}$$

$\boldsymbol{O(L_{sum})}$: Without considering the interactions of agents, a mobile agent, in the worst case, can arbitrarily move to any position (cell) in the environment. Hence, the upper bound complexity of superimposing individual behaviors for all agents is:

$$O(L_{sum}) = O((xy)^{n'} s^n) \tag{16}$$

For example in the game of life, agents are stationary, i.e. $n' = 0$ and $n'' = n$, and $O(L^I_{whole}) = O(L_{sum}) = O(s^n)$). If all agents are mobile, i.e. $n' = n$ and $n'' = 0$, then $O(L_{sum}) = O((xy)^n s^n)$, which is much larger than $O(L^I_{whole})$ $= O(\binom{xy}{n} s^n)$. This is because the summing operation involves all combinations of individual agents' behaviors, including those that could never happen in practice, as discussed above.

To reduce $O(L_{sum})$, we consider the fact that some results from the superimposition cannot be possible due to system wide rules, so we eliminate these from the calculation. For example, in a traffic junction model, car A following car B in a one-lane road cannot move ahead of B at any point in time. Adding system constraints that can be obtained from the system specification to the superimposition process to reduce L_{sum} to L^P_{sum} is part of our future work. The more known constraints we add, the smaller L_{sum} is.

4.2 Experimental Results

We implemented the boids model as a Java simulator to further understand the relationship among L^I_{whole}, L_{sum}, and L_ξ. We also analyzed how interactions of agents affect the size of L_ξ with respect to the size of L^I_{whole}. As L_{sum} suffers from state-space explosion, we varied the number of birds from four to ten, with equal numbers of ducks and geese. A difference between ducks and geese is maximum speed, which is two cells per time step for ducks and three cells per time step for geese. Position and velocity of birds are initialized randomly. Both ducks and geese follow three behavior rules defined in Section 3.2. Given an initial system state, at some point of time t, the system will arrive in a state that has already happened at time $t' < t$ because the number of possible system states is finite, even if it can be very large. Due to the assumption that agents' behavior rules do not change over time, the simulation loops afterwards. As a result, the size of L^I_{whole} is the number of distinct system states obtained from the beginning until time t. L_{sum}, on the other hand, is computed over all possible combinations of isolated agents' behaviors with respect to the initial system state. The initial system state belongs to both L^I_{whole} and L_{sum}.

For every experiment, we ran the simulation ten times and took the average number of states as shown in Table 3. As

number of birds	number of states			$\frac{L_\xi}{L^I_{whole}}$
	L^I_{whole}	L_{sum}	L_ξ	
4	13	767	6	0.46
6	18	70,118	12	0.67
8	13	509,103	9	0.69
10	26	13,314,066	23	0.88

Table 3: Sizes of L^I_{whole}, L_{sum}, and L_ξ

expected, the size of L_{sum} is large and increases exponentially with the number of birds. For instance, L_{sum} grows by 90 times when the number of birds changes from four to six. Another interesting observation is that L_ξ / L^I_{whole} tends to increase with the number of birds. In other words, more interactions (interdependences) among birds lead to more emergent property states that cannot be derived by summing the independent agents' behaviors. Furthermore, the number of common elements between L^I_{whole} and L_{sum} is small. Consequently, computation is wasted on calculating L^{NP}_{sum} states that are not feasible in practice. However, when the impact of neighboring agents on an agent is not strong, then L^{NP}_{sum} tends to be small. For example, agents do not interact frequently because they are far from each other, such as when the number of agents is much smaller than the number of cells in the environment.

5. CONCLUSION

In this paper, we formalized emergence using an extended cooperating array grammar system so as to verify the existence and the size of emergent property states in multi-agent systems. In weak emergence, the set of emergent property states for a given system (L_ξ) is derived by taking the difference between the set of observed system states due to agent interactions (L_{whole}), and the set of system states obtained by combining the behaviors of individual agents (L_{sum}). However, this broad definition suffers from state explosion. As a first contribution, we introduced a tighter definition of weak emergence to reduce the size of the system state space. In studying a system, users focus only on modeling agent interactions of interest ($L^I_{whole} < L_{whole}$). Though all combinations of L_{sum} are mathematically possible, a large number of these system states may not be feasible because of system constraints. Thus, L_{sum} can be reduced to L^P_{sum}, i.e. set of possible combinations of agents' behaviors.

In the second contribution, we proposed a grammar-based formalism of emergence that models agents of different types, mobile and static agents, as well as open systems with agents arriving and departing over time. Theoretical analysis reveals a number of observations, e.g. the complexity of L_{sum} increases exponentially with the number of agents. These observations were also verified experimentally using a boids model with two types of birds. In addition, we showed how a known emergent property such as bird flocking can be extracted from the emergent property states. In terms of system state-space size, our approach is comparable with model checking. State-of-the-art model checkers can address state space of about 10^9 states with explicit state-space enumeration, and over 10^{20} with techniques for alleviating state explosion [3]. Preliminary experimental results show that our simulator can handle L_{sum} of about 10^8 states. L_{sum} can be further reduced by identifying system-specific constraints that eliminate impossible states when summing individual agents' behaviors.

This paper provides a first step towards advancing our understanding of emergence but much work remains to be done. New techniques are needed to extract *known* emergent properties, and to identify new (or *unknown*) emergent properties from the set of emergent property states. For example, if emergent properties are known, our formalism facilitates post-mortem emergence analysis to determine the causes of emergence. As our approach is both compute and memory intensive, more efficient state representations, such as bit state hashing and state vector compression used in model checking, are required. We are exploring the application of this approach to study emergence in concurrent program verification. Given a program and its specification, the cause-and-effect of both known and unknown properties, such as deadlock, can be analyzed by examining the corresponding system states. This approach compliments model checking where the main goal is to verify predetermined behavioral properties of a given system.

6. ACKNOWLEDGMENTS

This work is supported by the National University of Singapore under grant number R-252-000-470-112.

7. REFERENCES

[1] R. Abbott, Emergence Explained: Abstractions Getting Epiphenomena to Do Real Work, Complexity, 12(1):13-26, 2006.
[2] N. A. Baas and C. Emmeche, On Emergence and Explanation, Intellectica, pages 67-83, 1997.
[3] C. Baier and J. Katoen, Principles of Model Checking, The MIT Press, 2008.
[4] Y. Bar-Yam, A Mathematical Theory of Strong Emergence Using Multiscale Variety, Complexity, 9(6):15-24, 2004.
[5] M. A. Bedau, Weak Emergence, Philosophical Perspectives: Mind, Causation, and World, 1997.
[6] M. A. Bedau, Downward Causation and the Autonomy of Weak Emergence, Principia 3, 3:5-50, 2003.
[7] E. Bonabeau and J. Dessalles, Detection and Emergence, Intellectica, 25(2), 1997.
[8] D. J. Chalmers, Strong and Weak Emergence, The Re-emergence of Emergence, Oxford University Press, 2006.
[9] W. K. V. Chan, Interaction Metric of Emergent Behaviors in Agent-based Simulation, Proc of Winter Simulation Conference, pages 357-368, 2011.
[10] C. C. Chen, Complex Event Types for Agent-based Simulation, PhD thesis, University College London, 2009.
[11] J. P. Crutchfield, Is Anything Ever New? Considering Emergence, Complexity: Metaphors, Models, and Reality, G. Cowan, D. Pines, and D. Melzner (eds.), SFI Series in the Sciences of Complexity XIX:479-497. Addison-Wesley, 1994.
[12] V. Darley, Emergent Phenomena and Complexity, Artificial Life IV, pages 411-416, 1994.
[13] J. Deguet, L. Magnin, and Y. Demazeau, Elements about the Emergence Issue: A Survey of Emergence Definitions, ComPlexUs, 3:24-31, 2006.
[14] G. B. Dyson, Darwin Among the Machines: The Evolution of Global Intelligence, Perseus Books Group, 1998.
[15] D. Fisch, M. Janicke, B. Sick, and C. Muller-Schloer, Quantitative Emergence - A Refined Approach Based on Divergence Measures, Proc of 4th IEEE International Conference on Self-adaptive and Self-organizing Systems, pages 94-103, 2010.
[16] J. Fromm, Types and Forms of Emergence, Complexity Digest, vol. 25(3), 2005.
[17] R. Gore and P. F. Reynolds, Applying Causal Inference to Understand Emergent Behavior, Proc of Winter Simulation Conference, pages 712-721, 2008.
[18] P. Haglich, C. Rou, and L. Pullum, Detecting Emergence in Social Networks, Proc of 2nd IEEE International Conference on Social Computing, pages 693-696, Minneapolis, MN, USA, 2010.
[19] B. Heath, R. Hill, and F. Ciarallo, A Survey of Agent-based Modeling Practices (January 1998 to July 2008), Journal of Artificial Societies and Social Simulation, 12(4):9, 2009.

[20] J. H. Holland, Emergence: From Chaos to Order, Addison Wesley, 1997.

[21] C. W. Johnson, What are Emergent Properties and How Do They Affect the Engineering of Complex Systems? Reliability Engineering and System Safety, 12:1475-1481, 2006.

[22] A. Kubik, Toward a Formalization of Emergence, Artificial Life IX, 9(1):41-65, 2003.

[23] Z. Li, C. H. Sim, and M. Y. H. Low, A Survey of Emergent Behavior and Its Impacts in Agent-based Systems. Proc of IEEE International Conference on Industrial Informatics, pages 1295-1300, 2006.

[24] E. J. Manley and T. Cheng, Understanding Road Congestion as an Emergent Property of Traffic Networks, Proc of 14th World Multi-conference on Systemics, Cybernetics and Informatics, pages 25-34, 2010.

[25] T. Moncion, P. Amar, and G. Hutzler, Automatic Characterization of Emergent Phenomena in Complex Systems, Journal of Biological Physics and Chemistry, 10:16-23, 2010.

[26] M. Mnif and C. Muller-Schloer, Quantitative Emergence, Proc of IEEE Mountain Workshop on Adaptive and Learning Systems, pages 78-84, Logan, UT, USA, 2006.

[27] J. C. Mogul, Emergent (Mis)Behavior vs. Complex Software Systems, Proc of 1st ACM SIGOPS/EuroSys European Conference on Computer Systems, volume 40, pages 293-304, New York, USA, 2006.

[28] M. E. J. Newman, Complex Systems: A Survey, American Journal of Physics, 79:800-810, 2011.

[29] I. Norros, B. J. Prabhu, and H. Reittu, Flash Crowd in a File Sharing System Based on Random Encounters, Proc of Workshop on Interdisciplinary Systems Approach in Performance Evaluation and Design of Computer & Communications Systems, New York, USA, 2006.

[30] T. O'Conner, Emergent Properties, American Philosophical Quarterly, 31(2):91-104, 1994.

[31] D. T. Pele and A. M. Tepus, Information Entropy and Efficient Market Hypothesis, Proc International Conference on Applied Economics, 2011.

[32] M. Randles, H. Zhu, and A. Taleb-Bendiab, A Formal Approach to the Engineering of Emergence and its Recurrence, Proc of 2nd International Workshop on Engineering Emergence in Decentralized Autonomic Systems, 2007.

[33] C. W. Reynolds. Flocks, Herds and Schools: A Distributed Behavioral Model, Proc of 14th Annual Conference on Computer Graphics and Interactive Techniques, pages 25-34, New York, NY, USA, 1987.

[34] C. Rou, A. Vanderbilt, M. Hinchey, W. Truszkowski, and J. Rash, Properties of a Formal Method for Prediction of Emergent Behaviors in Swarm-based Systems, Proc of 2nd IEEE International Conference on Software Engineering and Formal Methods, September 2004.

[35] A. K. Seth, Measuring Emergence via Nonlinear Granger Causality, Artificial Life XI, pages 545-552, 2008.

[36] C. E. Shannon, A Mathematical Theory of Communication, Bell System Technical Journal, 27(3):379-423, 2000.

[37] C. Szabo and Y. M. Teo, An Integrated Approach for the Validation of Emergence in Component-based Simulation Models, Proc of Winter Simulation Conference, pages 242:1-242:12, 2012.

[38] C. Szabo and Y. M. Teo, An Objective-based Approach for Semantic Validation of Emergence in Component-based Simulation Models, Proc of 26th ACM/IEEE/SCS Workshop on Principles of Advanced and Distributed Simulation, pages 155-162, ZhangJiaJie, China, July 15-19, 2012.

[39] Y. M. Teo and C. Szabo, Semantic Validation of Emergent Properties in Component-based Simulation Models, Book Chapter in Ontology, Epistemology, and Teleology of Modeling and Simulation - Philosophical Foundations for Intelligent M&S Applications, edited by Andreas Tolk, pages 319-333, Springer-Verlag, 2013.

[40] B. Zhan, D. N. Monekosso, P. Remagnino, S. A. Velastin, and L. Q. Xu, Crowd Analysis: A Survey. Machine Vision and Application, 19(5-6):345-357, September 2008.

Post-mortem Analysis of Emergent Behavior in Complex Simulation Models

Claudia Szabo
Department of Computer Science
The University of Adelaide
North Terrace
Adelaide 5005
claudia.szabo@adelaide.edu.au

Yong Meng Teo
Department of Computer Science
National University of Singapore
Computing 1, 13 Computing Drive
Singapore 117417
teoym@comp.nus.edu.sg

ABSTRACT

Analyzing and validating emergent behavior in component-based models is increasingly challenging as models grow in size and complexity. Despite increasing research interest, there is a lack of automated, formalized approaches to identify emergent behavior and its causes. As part of our integrated framework for understanding emergent behavior, we propose a post-mortem emergence analysis approach that identifies the causes of emergent behavior in terms of properties of the composed model and properties of the individual model components, and their interactions. In this paper, we detail the use of reconstructability analysis for post-mortem analysis of known emergent behavior. The two-step process first identifies model components that are most likely to have caused emergent behavior, and then analyzes their interaction. Our case study using small and large examples demonstrates the applicability of our approach.

Categories and Subject Descriptors

D.2.4 [**Software Engineering**]: Software/Program Verification—*validation*; I/6.5 [**Simulation and Modeling**]: Model Development—*modeling methodologies*

Keywords

Emergent behavior, emergence, simulation, reconstructability analysis

1. INTRODUCTION

The behavior of complex systems cannot often be reduced only to the behavior of their individual components and systems require thorough analysis once unexpected properties have been observed [8, 17, 20]. These properties, called *emergent properties*, are increasingly becoming important as software systems grow in complexity, coupling, and geographic distribution [1, 15, 17, 20]. Examples of emergent properties include connection patterns in data extracted from social networks [6], trends in big data analytics [9], and power supply variation in smart grids due to provider competition [3]. More malign examples of emergent properties in computer systems include the Ethernet capture effect [24], router synchronization problems [10], and load-balancer failures in a multi-tiered distributed system [20]. Because emergent properties may have undesired and unpredictable effects and consequences, and unpredictable systems are less credible and difficult to manage, techniques for the identification and validation of emergent properties are becoming of crucial importance.

Despite ongoing research since the 1970s [1, 7, 11, 15, 26], very few methods for identifying, classifying, and explaining emergent properties exist [5, 18, 26, 27], and they are usually employed only on simplified examples that are not often found in real life [27]. These approaches can be classified broadly from two orthogonal perspectives, namely live analysis and post-mortem analysis [27]. *Live emergence analysis* proposes to identify emergence as it happens, using meta-models of calculated composed model states [27], or representations of system interaction [4]. *Post-mortem* emergence analysis starts from a definition of a known or observed emergent property and aims to identify its cause, in terms of model components and their interaction [5, 26].

A key challenge remains in the definition and identification of variables or attributes that describe the system sub-components, or the *micro-level*, and the system as a whole, or the *macro-level*, and the relationships between these two levels. Next, *weak emergence* [1, 15] results from the interaction between the model components at the micro-level but current approaches to identify weak emergence have only considered models with a small number of components. Current approaches [5, 18, 26] are demonstrated using simple models such as flocks of birds, and have limiting assumptions and constraints when applied to more complex systems. For example, most approaches do not consider mobile agents [18], or assume unfeasible a-priori specifications and definitions of emergent properties [27].

Simulation has been identified as a suitable means of analyzing complex systems [1], especially through the use of component-based models, that permit the study of increasingly large systems, both in size and complexity. To this extent, Page and Opper proposed a formal framework for analyzing the complexity of composition and the emergence of new behavior [22]. Other approaches compare well-known examples of emergence, such as simulations of flocks of birds, to simulations that exhibit no emergence at all, such as brownian movement, and establish interaction measures [4]. The emergence of a particular variable value can be identified in the simulation code using static and dynamic program analysis [14]. These approaches can be classified as post-mortem emergence analysis, because an emergent property is previously

SIGSIM-PADS'13, May 19–22, 2013, Montréal, Québec, Canada.

observed and defined, and the system is analyzed to identify its causes. Despite employing knowledge of the emergent behavior, the post-mortem analysis of emergence still has important issues [27]. Challenges lie in the lack of formalisms for the definition of the emergent property as a function of the composed model states and of the states of the model components of interest [27]. Moreover, existing approaches have only been applied to simplified models such as models of flocks of birds [5, 26] and predator-prey [26], with a small number of components. In our previous work, we have proposed an integrated approach for the identification and validation of emergence, looking at both live emergence analysis and post-mortem analysis [27]. Our previous work focussed on detailing live emergence analysis and how it could be applied to a simple model of flocks of birds.

This work enhances the discussion of post-mortem analysis and presents how it can be applied to more complex examples such as the game of life and traffic junction models. In this paper, we detail the use of reconstructability analysis (RA) [2] to facilitate post-mortem emergent behavior identification. Given a data model defined as a set of input/output variables and their values, reconstructability analysis can help to identify relations and interactions between input variables that cause particular output values. RA has considerable value for analyzing quantitative variables linked by non-linear relations [2], which makes it appealing for the study of emergent behavior as non-linearity has been shown to be one of the fundamental characteristics of complexity [7], and, inherently, of emergence [1]. The use of RA provides a simple and straightforward method to formalize the definition of micro and macro properties.

We propose an experimental study of post-mortem emergence analysis using examples of emergent behavior that have not been studied before in this context. The purpose of our case study is three fold. Firstly, current work analyzed the causes of emergent behavior using approaches similar to our proposed post-mortem analysis but only focusing on simple, small-scale examples such as flocks of birds or predator-prey models. Our case study starts from the game of life model and introduces larger models such as flocks of birds and traffic junctions. Secondly, while reconstructability analysis has been proposed to study complex systems, its suitability for understanding emergence has yet to be analyzed, in particular for systems with a large number of model components that are observed for a long period of time. Thirdly, while post-mortem analysis seems more straightforward than live emergence analysis, our examples show that post-mortem analysis is nevertheless a challenging task. For example, a key challenges is representing emergent behavior as a measurable macro property, and identifying the micro properties that might facilitate analysis.

This paper is organized as follows. We compare and contrast current work to the validation and identification of emergence in Section 2. Section 3 presents an overview of our proposed approach to the identification of emergence and discusses important concepts. Section 4 presents our experimental analysis, and Section 5 concludes this paper and presents future work.

2. RELATED WORK

An emergent property can be defined as "a property of an assemblage that could not be predicted by examining the components individually" [1]. Many characteristics of emergence have been identified in various works [1, 7, 15] and include: radical novelty (features not previously observed in systems); coherence or correlation (meaning integrated wholes that maintain themselves over some period of time); self-organization (individual model components organize into systems without pre-defined rules); a global or macro "level" (i.e. there is some property of "wholeness"); it is the product of a dynamical process (it evolves); and it is "ostensive" (it can be perceived); it is the result of rich interaction, but this interaction is short range (information is received primarily from neighbours). An important perspective for understanding emergence is the separation between *micro* and *macro* levels, that refer to abstraction at each individual level and at the level of the composed model as a whole respectively. Of interest to our approach is that the micro-level properties are usually measured by observing the component states, e.g. the collection of all variables and their values, of each system component. In contrast, the macro-level properties can be measured either as an aggregation of all the states of the system sub-components, or by observing the overall system behavior and trends.

In this paper we focus on *weak emergence* [1], a fundamental type of emergence that states that the properties of the whole, or the macro level, are resulted from the properties of the parts, or the micro level, and the interaction at the micro level, but that it is not trivial to infer the properties of the whole, and that extensive simulation studies are required to analyze and understand emergent behavior [15]. Approaches to identifying and understanding emergent behavior can be classified in three main categories, namely, *grammar-based*, *event-based* and *variable-based*, and further into live emergence analysis methods, where emergent behavior is not known beforehand, and post-mortem emergence analysis methods, that employ some specification or definition of emergence.

Grammar-based methods are live emergence analysis methods which aim to identify emergence in agent-based systems using two grammars, L_{WHOLE} to describe the properties of the system as a whole, and L_{PARTS} to describe the properties obtained from the reunion of the parts, and a definition of emergence as the difference between L_{WHOLE} and L_{PARTS} [18]. The behavior of an agent in a multi-agent system can be represented as a *grammar*, which is a set of rules that governs the formation of *words* using a set of *symbols*. L_{WHOLE} and L_{PARTS} can be easily calculated as sets of words that are constructed following agent behavior descriptions. This method does not require a prior observation of the system to identify possible emergent properties or behaviors, which makes it suitable for large-scale composed models where such observations are almost impossible. However, the nature of the formalism and the computation of the composed model states make it difficult to scale. *Event-based methods* are post-mortem analysis approaches in which behavior is defined as a series of simple and complex events that change the system state state [5]. Complex events are defined as compositions of simple, atomic events. Emergence is defined by a system expert as a complex event, and the approach focuses on determining the causes of emergence in terms of the sequence of complex and simple events in the system. In *variable-based methods*, a specific variable or metric is chosen to describe emergence. Changes in the values of this variable are said to signify the presence of emergence properties [26]. For example, the centre of mass of a bird flock could be used as an example of emergence in bird flocking behavior, as shown in [26]. The approach uses Granger causality to establish the relationships between a macro-variable, representing a system property, and micro-variables, representing properties of the system sub-components. This has the advantage of providing a clear process to identify emergence, that can be easily implemented. However, the approach requires system expert knowledge. Other approaches use metrics such as Shannon entropy [12, 23] and variety [16, 31] to measure emergence in a system. These approaches do not require system expert knowledge because they use general definitions rooted in complex systems the-

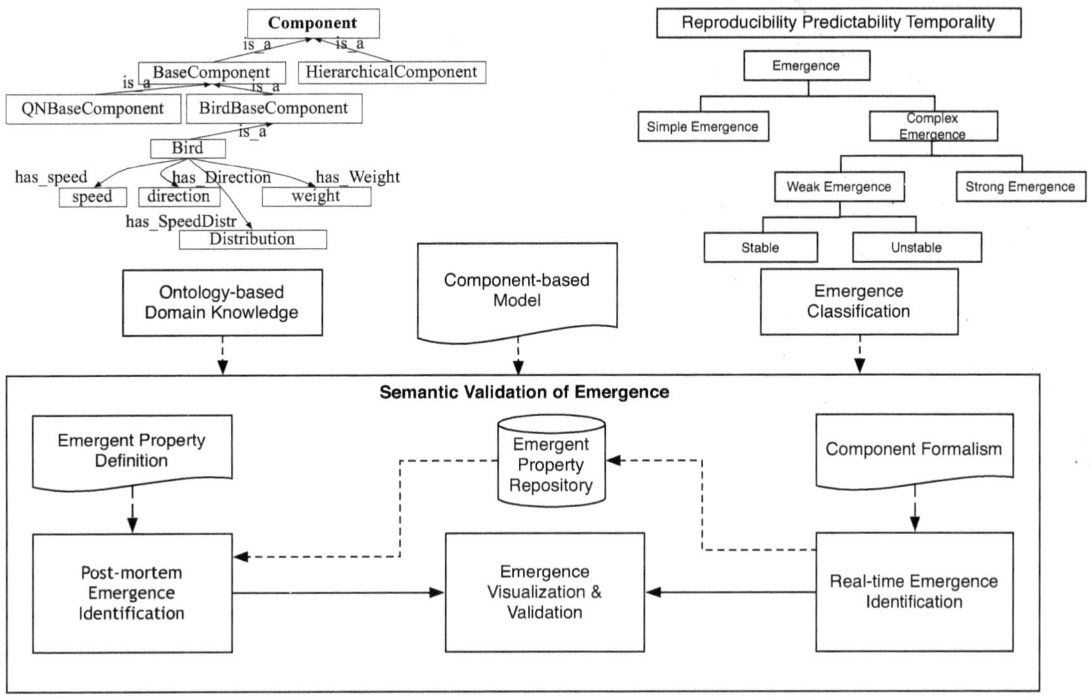

Figure 1: Integrating Orthogonal Perspectives in Emergence Validation

ory. However, to date they have only been applied to simple toy examples.

Page and Opper [22] propose a formal framework for analyzing the complexity of composition and emergence. They propose a definition emergent behavior consisting of the components a and b i a composition $a \diamond b$, an objective o, and the "satisfies" operator $\models$. If $a \models o$, then a satisfies objective o. If $a \not\models o$ and $b \not\models o$, but $(a \diamond b) \models o$, then we can say that the composition is *emergent*. Similar to variable-based methods, Gore and Reynolds denote emergence as a specific variable value and propose to highlight the lines in the simulation source code that cause that particular value [14]. They further propose a taxonomy for analyzing emergent behavior based on reproducibility, predictability, and temporality [13], but the identification of emergent behavior as well as its validation are not addressed. Another measure of emergence is the interaction between agents in an agent-based model [4], which is defined as an agent-specific counter that increases as the agent interacts in terms of direct message passing with other agents in the environment. Emergence is said to appear if the interaction measure deviates from normality. This approach provides a straightforward measure of emergence. However, cases where emergence is a result of indirect interaction between agents, such as in flocks of birds [25] and in Conway's Game of Life [11] are not addressed.

3. ANALYZING EMERGENT BEHAVIOR

This section presents an overview of our post-mortem emergence analysis within our proposed integrated framework for the identification and validation of emergent behavior. We present an overview of our framework, discuss the steps for our proposed post-mortem analysis and highlight the use of reconstructability analysis within our approach.

3.1 Overview

In our previous work [27], we proposed an integrated approach for the identification and validation of emergent behavior. As shown in Figure 1, we identify two orthogonal perspectives to understand emergent properties, namely, live and post-mortem. Firstly, *live emergence analysis* identifies emergence as it happens, without requiring prior knowledge of emergent properties. The approach relies on a representation of model components in terms of *what* they achieve rather than *how*, using an objective-based meta model component. A composed model state, or the *macro* is constructed from the states of its model components. The constructed state is then compared with the observed simulation state and significant differences are highlighted to the system expert. Live emergence relies on an ontology-based representation of specific domain knowledge represented in the figure as COSMO, our proposed ontology for component-based simulation [29]. Subsequently, properties identified as emergent are saved into the emergent property repository. Despite its appeal, live emergence analysis requires model components to be specified formally in terms of their objective, which may be difficult to obtain in practice.

Secondly, if emergent behaviors are identified beforehand, *post-mortem emergence analysis* can be applied to cause in terms of interaction between model components, their attributes and values. This assumes that emergent behaviors have been identified at the macro or system level, and that the model component properties, or the micro properties, can be measured. The information obtained from the analysis is saved into the emergent property repository, which is a collection of properly specified and defined emergence properties that leverage on existing work in the classification of emergence with respect to type, application domain, and specific occurrence among others [1, 13].

Arguably the more straightforward of the two perspectives, post-mortem emergence analysis remains challenging. Firstly, as discussed above, existing approaches have studied models with a small number of components and a low level of detail in the component representation. This affects the number of micro properties that can be considered in the analysis. Secondly, it is difficult to formally define the observed emergent behavior as a system-wide property at the macro level and a collection of component attributes at a micro level. Next, defining a formal process for identifying the relationships between micro and macro levels in a manner that is independent from the system under study to facilitate automated emergence identification remains a key challenge. Towards this, we propose the use of reconstructability analysis (RA) [2, 32] for the post-mortem analysis of emergent behavior. RA facilitates the study of systems with a large number of micro properties and can help to identify specific interactions between model components that lead to the emergence of a macro property.

3.2 Post-mortem Emergence Analysis

Post-mortem emergence analysis aims to identify the causes that lead to the identified emergent properties. Our approach relies on a representation of model components that captures component attributes and behavior. More formally, model components are represented by *meta-components*, $C_i = \langle R, A_i, B_i \rangle$, which describe the component *required attributes R*, *specific attributes*, *A*, and *behavior*, *B*. The required attributes are common to all components and are generally employed for version control, e.g. `author`, `location`, `lastUsed`. Examples of specific attributes include `interArrivalTime`, `speed`, `direction` etc. Component behavior describes the data that it receives and outputs as a set of states. The transitions between states are defined as a set of triggers expressed in terms of input, time and conditions.

Post-mortem emergence analysis is divided in three main steps as shown in Figure 2. Firstly, an emergent property, EP, for a composed model is defined based on previous knowledge extracted from the system expert or from observations of the system. Secondly, to identify the causes of EP, the composed model simulation is executed and the model components, representing the *micro* level, are observed throughout the simulation run and recorded as a set of values μP. The values of EP, or the *macro* level, are also recorded. Thirdly, we employ reconstructability analysis to determine the relationship between μP and EP. For a set of recorded values for the micro properties μP_{ij} at every simulation time step j, and the set of recorded macro properties EP_j, we construct a system in which the inputs are μP_i and the output is EP, and the observations are μP_{ij} and EP_j at every simulation step j. We divide our application of RA into two steps, namely, the identification of predicting micro properties $\mu P_{predict}$ that are most probable to generate EP, and the detection of interaction between model components.

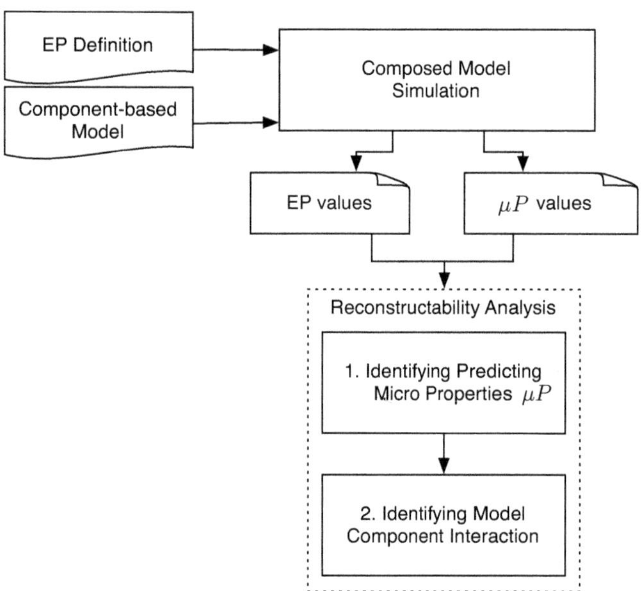

Figure 2: Post-mortem Emergence Analysis

3.2.1 *Reconstructability Analysis*

RA decomposes a system expressed as data in the form of set theoretic relations or multivariate probability distributions, into parts, namely relations or distributions involving subsets of variables [2, 32]. Of interest to our approach is the fact that observational data can be modeled and compressed by variable-based decomposition. RA models, which specify the inter-dependencies and interactions among the variables, are selected to minimize error and complexity. RA has considerable value for analyzing quantitative variables linked by non-linear relations [2], which, as discussed above, makes it appealing for studying emergent behavior where non-linearity is frequent [1, 7].

Two types of systems can be analyzed using RA, namely, direct and neutral [32]. In a *direct* system, a number of input variables are analyzed for their capability of predicting one or more output variables. In a *neutral* system, there is no distinction between input and output variables. Given a system represented by a number of variables, a reconstructability analysis tool such as Occam3 [32, 21] searches through a lattice of possible model component or model inter-dependencies structures. These structures are analyzed based on observed data, and goodness measures, such as information entropy, type 1 errors, structure complexity, model confidence, etc. are calculated.

For example, given three variables A, B, C the possible structures to be considered for a directed system are shown in grey in Figure 3 and in white for neutral systems (Figure adapted from [32]). In a directed system, for inputs A, B, and output C, five model structures will be considered, namely, ABC, AB:AC:BC, AB:AC, AB:BC, AB:C. In model ABC, A and B interact in their joint effect on C. Structure AB:C signifies that the output is independent of the input. Structure AB:AC signifies that variable A best predicts output variable C, and structure AB:AC:BC signifies that output variable C depends separately on A and on C, and so on. Structure A:B:C is called an independence model for the neutral system. For a directed system with output C, the independence model is AB:C. definition of a parent-child relationship. Given a particular structure, each child structure is created by removal of a relation and reinsertion of all the embedded relations within that relation which are not already present in other relations of the structure. A search through this lattice analyzes each model based on the measures defined above.

Reconstructability analysis promises to scale well in terms of the number of properties and their observations, with RA tools such as Occam3 being proven to analyze systems with up to 2^{16} observations of micro variables [32]. Moreover, in contrast to existing work, it also permits the formal and statistical analysis of the influence of component interaction on the emerging behavior, which increases the insight into the system execution.

In this paper, we employ the Occam3 reconstructability analysis tool proposed by the Systems Science group at the Portland State University. Occam3 [21] provides a web-based interface that allows users to upload a data file with variable observations, performs the required analysis, and permits the viewing and downloading of results. For directed systems, Occam3 reports measures such as Shannon entropy, the probability of Type 1 errors, and the uncertainty reduction. Alpha (α), the probability of making a Type 1

Model	Problem Size	Micro Property (μP) & Macro Property (EP)
Game of life	10 x 10 grid size	μP: $state(i,j)$ - state of cell (i,j): alive/dead EP: Δe - rate of expansion of alive cells
Flock of birds	10 / 20 / 50 birds	μP: $d(b_i, CP)$ - distance from *bird i* to the center of the drawing panel EP: $d(CM, CP)$ - distance from center of mass of flock to the center of the drawing panel
Traffic junction	10 / 50 / 100 cars	μP: v_i - velocity of car i EP: Δc - rate of growth of traffic congestion
		μP: p_i - politeness of car i EP: Δc - rate of growth of traffic congestion
		μP: (v_i, p_i) - velocity and politeness of car i EP: Δc - rate of growth of traffic congestion

Table 1: Experiments Overview

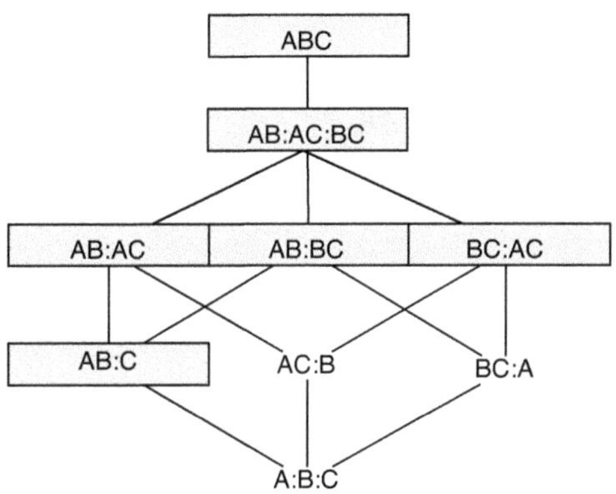

Figure 3: Lattice of Specific Structures for a 3-variable System

error, is the probability of being in error if one rejects the null hypothesis that the model is the same as the reference model. The uncertainty reduction refers to the percent reduction in the uncertainty of the output variable given the independent variables in the predicting components. When employing reconstructability analysis for directed systems, a model is considered good if it has a high information content, a small complexity (i.e., a small number of structures), and a low α.

3.2.2 Post-mortem Analysis using RA

Reconstructability Analysis is helpful in the study of complex systems because it can determine the model components and their interaction that best describe the system. In post-mortem analysis, the system expert highlights the *macro* property that best characterizes the emergent property, and thus in some sense there is some understanding of what component attributes, i.e., *micro* properties, cause it. With the help of RA, we propose to determine the model components whose interaction, direct or indirect, with the greatest influence on the emergent property. Furthermore, we aim to determine the component interaction that best causes emergence. In the following, we view the composed model as a *directed* system from the RA perspective, with the output being the macro property, and the input being the observer values of the micro properties, i.e., the component attributes and their values. Using the Occam3 reconstructability analysis tool, we follow a two-step process to determine model component interaction that causes emergent behavior, as shown below.

Step 1. Identifying Predicting Micro Properties
In the first step, the model components that are most likely to cause the emergent property EP are identified. This is done by performing an upwards search in the lattice using the independence model containing all micro properties as reference. We stop the search when adding a new independent variable to the search is not statistically significant, and construct the set of predicting micro properties $\{\mu P_{predict}\} \subseteq \{\mu P_i\}$ For this upward search, we are looking for models with low α. For example, if four micro properties and one macro property exist, namely, A, B, C, D, and Z respectively, the independence model is *ABCD*:*Z*, which says that each micro property can predict the macro property equally.

Step 2. Identifying Model Component Interaction
In the second step, we aim to determine the interaction between the micro properties in $\mu P_{predict}$ that is most significant to determine EP. This is done by performing an upwards search in the lattice using a disjoint reference model, where components are formed from the predicting micro properties $\mu P_{predict}$. For example, if two predicting micro properties A, B have been identified in step 1 from the set $\{A, B, C, D\}$, the search would start from the disjoint reference model *AB*:*AZ*:*BZ*. The result would indicate interaction between A and B if alpha is small for the model *ABZ* and if it reduces the uncertainty of Z by more than the reference model. For three variables A, B, C, and output Z, the reference model *ABC*:*ABZ*:*ACZ*:*BCZ* is better than *ABC*:*AZ*:*BZ*:*CZ* because it ascertains that the interaction involves all three variables.

4. EXPERIMENTAL ANALYSIS

Our experimental analysis considers a case study of post-mortem emergence analysis of three composed models, namely, the game of life, flocks of birds, and traffic junctions. To better highlight the suitability of our approach and reconstructability analysis, our experiments present small and large models, with respect to the number of components and the number of attributes included in the analysis, as summarized in Table 1. For the game of life model, we attempt to use a previously published definition of a macro property, namely, the rate of expansion of live cells, but find it lacking for the particular example under study, and as such propose a new definition. On the other hand, using our proposed approach, we were able to confirm annecdotal and CCTV-camera studies [19] that suggest that driver politeness causes traffic jam. Moreover, we study models for which the micro property, μP, is expressed in terms of more than one attribute, as in the case of the traffic junction model.

We implemented the flocks of birds and game of life models, and the traffic junction model is adapted from a microsimulation of road traffic flow [30]. The source code includes observations of micro and macro properties and the output is in a format suitable for our chosen reconstructability analysis tool. We employ the web-based implementation of Occam3 [32]. Experiments are executed on a 2.7GHz Intel Core i5, 16GB RAM desktop machine, and, except

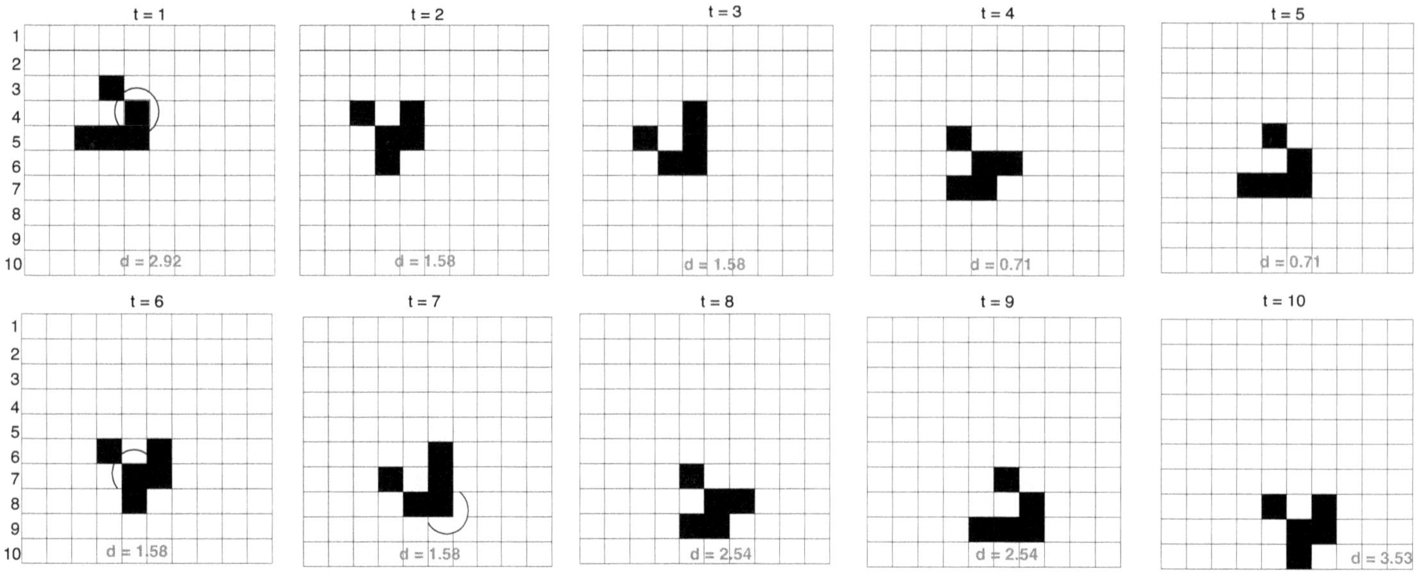

Figure 4: Glider in the Game of Life

for the game of life implementation, the simulation output values represent averages of 10 runs.

4.1 Game of Life Model

The Game of Life is a well-known cellular automaton in which the world is represented as a two-dimensional grid of cells and each cell has two possible states, alive or dead [11]. Every cell interacts with its neighbors and at each step, the cells may change state from alive to dead and vice-versa according to the game of life rules [11]:

- *under-population*: a live cell with fewer than two live neighbours will die
- *normal life*: a live cell with two or three live neighbours remains alive
- *over-crowding*: a live cell with more than three live neighbours will die
- *reproduction*: a dead cell with exactly three live neighbours will become a live cell

An initial pattern represents the seed of the system. In our experiment we look at the well-known glider pattern, which is a moving, recurring pattern of an spaceship-like arrow, as shown in Figure 4. In our experiment, we abstract the cell as a model component with two attributes, `position` and `state`. Our automaton is executed for the first ten steps, data is collected and an input file for Occam3 is generated. At each step, we record the state of each cell i (alive or dead) as the micro property μP_i. In the literature, the rate of expansion of live cells has been suggested as a possible macro property for the Game of Life [1, 7]. This is not however possible in the case of the glider pattern, because the number of alive cells remains constant. As such, we record the distance between the center of the smallest bounding box that surrounds the glider and the center of the grid as the macro property EP. These distance values are shown in Figure 4. A part of the input file is shown in Figure 5. Each data row has 101 values, representing the cell states (μP_i) and the distance (EP) respectively, with the last value representing the distance.

An Occam3 input file first starts with the definition of the subcomponent variables, which are defined as `name, cardinality, input/output, short_name`. For example, for variable `Cell1`, representing the first top-left cell in the grid, there are two possible values (alive or dead), hence a cardinality of 2, and the variable is an input value, hence value 1. Observations about the values of the specified variables follow after the `data:` token. Because the size of the input data is large, we show in Figure 5 the alive cells as line 5 in the grid for the first five observations, and line 7 in the grid for the last five observations.

```
:nominal               :data
Cell1,2,1,Cell1        0 0 0 ...0 0 1 1 1 0 0 0 0 0 ...4
Cell2,2,1,Cell2        0 0 0 ...0 0 0 1 1 0 0 0 0 0 ...2
Cell3,2,1,Cell3        0 0 0 ...0 0 1 0 1 0 0 0 0 0 ...2
Cell4,2,1,Cell4        0 0 0 ...0 0 0 1 0 0 0 0 0 0 ...1
Cell5,2,1,Cell5        0 0 0 ...0 0 0 0 1 0 0 0 0 0 ...1
Cell6,2,1,Cell6        0 0 0 ...0 0 0 0 1 0 0 0 0 0 ...2
Cell7,2,1,Cell7        0 0 0 ...0 0 0 0 1 1 0 0 0 0 ...2
Cell8,2,1,Cell8        0 0 0 ...0 0 0 0 0 1 1 0 0 0 ...3
Cell9,2,1,Cell9        0 0 0 ...0 0 0 0 0 0 1 0 0 0 ...3
Cell10,2,1,Cell10     0 0 0 ...0 0 0 0 1 0 1 0 0 0 ...5
...
D,5,2,D
```

Figure 5: Occam3 Input File for the Game of Life Model

Step 1. Identifying Predicting Micro Properties
As discussed above, the first step in our method identifies model components that are most likely to cause the emergent property EP by performing an upwards search in the lattice using the independence model containing all micro properties μP_i as the reference. The cells are numbered starting with cell one, in the top left corner of the grid, and proceeding from left to right until cell 100, in the bottom right of the grid. The independence model for the game of life model is

$$Cell1Cell2\ldots Cell100 : D \text{ or } IV : D$$

where IV means *independed variables*. Table 2 presents the results. As discussed above, a good set of predicting micro proper-

Model	Entropy	Complexity	α
IV : D	5.45	0	0.00
IV : Cell65Cell77D	4.13	12	0.11
IV : Cell75Cell77D	4.09	12	< 0.01
IV : Cell75Cell86D	4.09	12	< 0.01
IV : Cell56Cell75Cell77D	3.59	28	0.59
IV : Cell56Cell75Cell86D	3.59	28	0.59
IV : Cell35Cell75Cell86D	3.59	28	0.59

Table 2: Predicting Micro-Properties using RA

ties achieves in a reconstructability analysis search a small value for the measure of complexity in terms of the number of structures, and a low α. From the results in Table 2 it can be seen that micro properties *Cell*75 and *Cell*86, highlighted in Figure 4 using a circle, are the best predictors and generators for the macro property *D*. They are the cells that stay alive and interact the most in the second glider pattern that is formed from iteration 6 to 9. In a similar manner, *Cell*75 and *Cell*77 are equally good candidates. It is important to highlight here that, if a larger number of predicting micro properties were to be considered, the set containing *Cell*35, *Cell*75, and *Cell*86 would also be a good candidate. *Cell*35 is also highlighted in Figure 4, and represents one of the cells in the first glider pattern that remains alive the longest. We define set $\mu P_{predict}$ as $\mu P_{predict} = \{Cell75, Cell86\}$.

Step 2. Identifying Model Component Interaction
The next step proposes to determine if the interaction between the micro properties in set $\mu P_{predict}$ is the cause of the values of the macro property EP. The reconstructability search starts from a disjoint reference model that is constructed from the micro properties in $\mu P_{predict} = \{Cell75, Cell86\}$ as

$$IV : Cell75Cell86 : Cell75D : Cell86D$$

The results in Table 3 show that *Cell75Cell86D* has an $\alpha = 0.00$ and reduces the uncertainty of output macro variable *D* by more than the disjoint reference model. This analysis shows that the interaction between the micro properties of *Cell*75 and *Cell*86 is responsible for the emergence of property *EP* represented by the distance between the center of the bounding box that surrounds the glider and the center of the grid. Using reconstructability analysis, we are able to identify indirect interactions and the influences between micro properties. This would not be possible using current direct measures of interaction.

Model	Entropy	Complexity	α	Uncertainty Reduction (%)
Cell75Cell86D	2.13	4	0.00	64.60
IV : Cell75D : Cell86D	19.13	0	1.0	56.23

Table 3: Identifying Interaction in the Game of Life

4.2 Flocks of Birds Model

Our flock of birds experiment looks at the well-known boid model [25], in which each component abstracts a moving bird whose position changes based on a set of simple rules that define its current position and the position of other birds in the flock. These rules are

- *separation* - individual bird steer to avoid crowding the other birds in the flock
- *alignment* - individual steer towards the average herding of local flock mates
- *cohesion* - individual moves towards the average position of local flock mates

The boid model has been shown to exhibit emergent behavior of flocking and of flocking after encountering an obstacle, when the flock splits and reunites.

In our experiment we abstract a bird as a model component with `position` and `speed` as attributes, among others.We define the emergent macro property as the trajectory of the center of mass (CM) of the flock of birds. This is in accordance with previous studies that looked as emergence in the flock of birds model [26].

The simulation of the flock of birds is executed, and data is collected, pre-processed, and collated into a file that is then supplied to Occam3. As an example we employ ten birds that go through a sequence of 20 position changes according to the rules specified above, starting from random positions on the drawing panel. At each simulation step, each bird changes position according to the rules specified above; we log each bird position, as well as that of the center of mass of the flock. We reduce the number of variables by computing the distance d_i from the center of the environment, i.e. the center of the drawing panel. The values of d_i are saved into an output file, similar to that shown in Table 4 for the first ten steps.

Bird 1	Bird 2	Bird 3	Bird 4	Bird 5	Bird 6	Bird 7	Bird 8	Bird 9	Bird 10	CM
53	209	128	67	43	104	121	130	118	95	69
45	174	112	65	44	91	104	111	103	81	65
40	129	88	60	43	72	81	84	80	61	61
39	76	59	51	38	49	52	53	55	38	62
38	27	42	34	37	31	19	30	31	23	69
54	32	48	11	57	9	31	53	42	36	80
59	71	69	13	75	18	70	102	81	69	101
56	113	100	42	94	51	111	153	125	109	131
58	154	136	79	118	92	155	202	171	153	169
82	195	175	125	151	140	200	247	213	202	213

Table 4: Distance from the Center of Drawing Panel

To further reduce the number and values of the variables, we discretize the distance values, as $floor(d_i/100) + 1$. The results are then transformed into an Occam3 input file, as shown in Figure 6.

```
:nominal      :data
b1,4,1,a      1 3 2 1 1 2 2 2 2 1 1
b2,4,1,b      1 2 2 1 1 1 2 2 2 1 1
b3,4,1,c      1 2 1 1 1 1 1 1 1 1 1
b4,4,1,d      1 1 1 1 1 1 1 1 1 1 1
b5,4,1,e      1 1 1 1 1 1 1 1 1 1 1
b6,4,1,f      1 1 1 1 1 1 1 1 1 1 1
b7,4,1,g      1 1 1 1 1 1 1 2 1 1 2
b8,4,1,h      1 2 1 1 1 1 2 2 2 2 2
b9,4,1,i      1 2 2 1 2 1 2 3 2 2 2
b10,5,1,j     1 2 2 2 2 2 3 3 3 3 3
cm,4,2,k        ...
```

Figure 6: Occam3 Input File for the Boid Model

Step 1. Identifying Predicting Micro Properties
The first step identifies the model components that are most likely to cause the emergent property *EP* by performing an upwards search in the lattice using the independence model containing all micro properties μP_i as the reference. The independence model for the boid model observed above is

$$ABCDEDFGHIJ : K \text{ or } IV : K$$

Table 5 shows the results of the search. As discussed above, we

Model	Entropy	Complexity	α
IV : K	5.85	0	1.00
IV : HK	4.83	9	< 0.01
IV : GK	4.78	9	< 0.01
IV : FGK	4.02	45	0.68
IV : GJK	4.36	57	0.94
IV : GHK	4.32	45	0.58
IV : GHJK	4.18	237	0.46

Table 5: Predicting Micro-Properties using RA for the Game of Life

are looking for a structure from a set of predicting micro properties that has a small value for the measure of complexity in terms of the number of structures, and a low alpha. The results presented in Table 5 show that micro properties F, G, H are the best predictors and generators for the macro property K. As such, the set $\mu P_{predict}$ is defined as $\mu P_{predict} = \{b7, b8, b9\}$. It is important to highlight here that sets $\{b7, b8\}$, $\{b7, b9\}$ and $\{b5, b6\}$ are also good candidates for $\mu P_{predict}$, but include a smaller number of micro properties.

Step 2. Identifying Model Component Interaction
We next attempt to determine if the interaction between the micro properties in $\mu P_{predict}$ is the cause of the values of the macro property EP. As discussed above, we start the reconstructability search from a disjoint reference model. For set $\mu P_{predict} = \{b7, b8, b9\}$, we use the disjoint reference model

$$IV : GHJ : GHK : GJK : HJK$$

As shown in Table 6, model $GHJK$ has an $\alpha = 0.00$ and reduces the uncertainty of output macro variable K by more than the disjoint reference model.

Model	Entropy	Complexity	α	Uncertainty Reduction (%)
GHJK	3.48	108	0.00	72.12
IV : GHJ : GHK :GJK:HJK	17.48	0	1.0	61.24

Table 6: Identifying Interaction using RA

In a similar manner, we execute post-mortem analysis for a flock of birds model with 20 and 50 individuals respectively. A summary of the results is shown in Table 10. As it can be seen, a large number of individuals interact to generate EP for the model of size 50. We believe that a reason for this is that the initial condition of the simulation caused by the size of the drawing panel, causes the individuals to be in an already flocked initial position as shown in Figure 7.

4.3 Traffic Junction Model

In this experiment we employ a traffic simulation model adapted from [30]. For simplicity, we simulate only two types of vehicles, cars and trucks, that are distinguished based on their speed. Another parameter of interest is driver politeness, which reflects an intelligent driver model that allows other vehicles to change lanes ahead of it. In our analysis, we employ models of 10, 50, and 100 vehicles respectively, and at every time step record the driver speed as a micro property, and the size of the congested area as a macro property. A congested area is shown in red in Figure 8 on the north-west side of the ring road. An additional micro property recorded is driver politeness. Recent studies of driver behavior used CCTV camera videos from a UK highway [19] to prove that driver politeness is the cause of the emergence of traffic jams. We arrive at the same conclusion using reconstructability analysis as shown below.

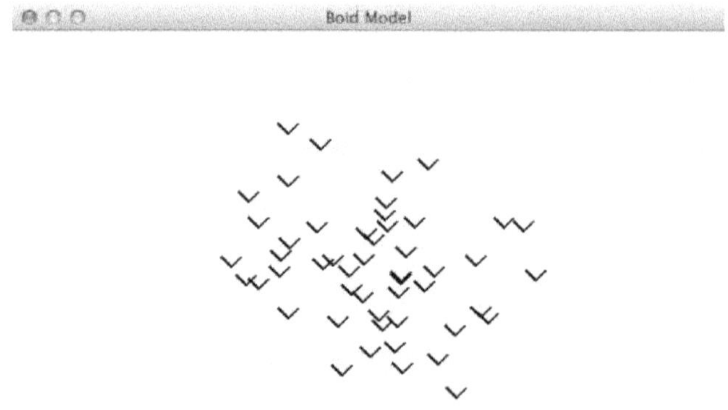

Figure 7: Flock of Birds Model

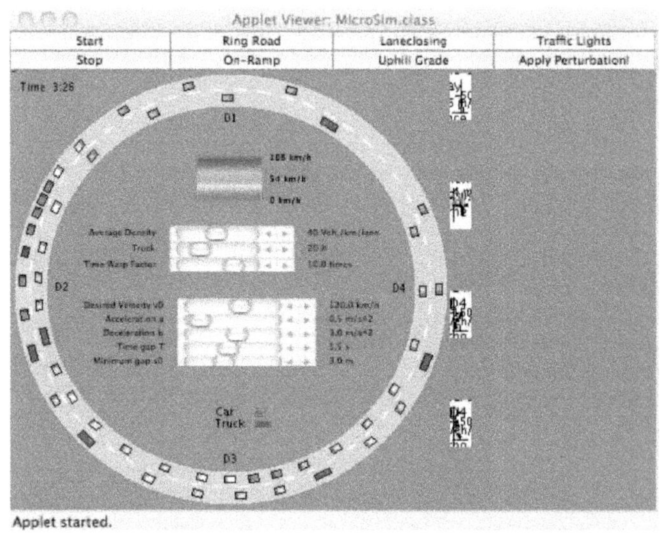

Figure 8: Emergence of Traffic Jam

A model with ten vehicles exhibits no emergence of traffic jam as the number of vehicles in the ring road is too small for the traffic to become congested. For a model with 50 cars, we introduce three impolite drivers, driving vehicles with id `Car4`, `Car16`, and `Car23` respectively. Our first experiment records vehicle speeds as the micro property. In a similar manner to the flocks of birds model, we execute the simulation for two minutes and record vehicle speed and size of the congested area. In all experiments, the drivers of the above vehicles are polite for the 30 seconds, impolite for a minute, and revert to politeness for the last 30 seconds. An analysis of the data shown in Table 7 reveals that no predicting variables can be identified, and that the independence model is the most trustworthy for these observations.

In the second experiment we record the politeness of each driver as a micro property.

Step 1. Identifying Predicting Micro Properties
As it can be seen in Table 8, the vehicles with impolite drivers are identified as predicting micro-properties for the macro property

Model	Entropy	Complexity	α
IV : Car28Car6Road	10.02	11594	1.00
IV : Car28Road	11.41	612	1.00
IV : Car24Road	11.43	612	1.00
IV : Road	13.57	0	0.00

Table 7: Vehicle Speed as Prediction for Congestion

`Road`. It is important to notice here that all impolite drivers have been identified as individually predicting the traffic congestion, and that all structures with up to three components are equivalent in terms of complexity and entropy. This is also the case when the drivers are impolite for the entire duration of the simulation run. Looking for a larger structure in terms of the micro properties, we define $\mu P_{predict}$ as $\mu P_{predict} = \{Car0, Car1, Car23\}$.

Model	Entropy	Complexity	α
IV : Car0Car1Car23Road	4.74	31	< 0.01
IV : Car0Car23Road	4.74	31	< 0.01
IV : Car10Car16Road	4.74	31	< 0.01
IV : Car10Car23Road	4.74	31	< 0.01
IV : Car10Car4Road	4.74	31	< 0.01
IV : Car4Road	4.74	31	< 0.01
IV : Car16Road	4.74	31	< 0.01
IV : Car23Road	4.74	31	< 0.01

Table 8: Predicting Micro-Properties for Impolite Drivers

Step 2. Identifying Model Component Interaction
We analyze whether the interaction between impolite drivers and the other drivers on the ring road can be captured by RA. Towards this, we look at the disjoint model

$$Car0Car1Car23 : Car0Car1Road : Car0Car23Road : Car1Car23Road$$

As shown in Table 9, model *Car0Car1Car23Road* has an $\alpha = 0.00$ and reduces the uncertainty of output macro variable *Road* by more than the disjoint reference model, as shown by the last column in the table.

Model	Entropy	α	Uncertainty Reduction (%)
Car0Car1Car23Road	4.74	0.00	28.75
IV:Car0Car1Car23:Car0Car1Road	6.74	1.0	20.56

Table 9: Identifying Driver Interaction

In our third experiment, we combine the two micro properties, velocity and politeness, into a single variable (v_i, p_i) defined as their product, $v_i * p_i$. The results are similar to those presented above, in that the interaction between impolite drivers and other cars are deemed to be the cause of emerging traffic jams.

4.4 Discussion

Table 10 summarizes our key results. Our runtime analysis highlights that our approach scales well even for large models. This is important when considering that other emergence identification approaches proposed in the literature can only be applied to small models [28]. Our proposed post-mortem analysis highlights to the system experts the entities whose interaction is most likely to generate particular behaviors. This information can be used to improve future simulation runs in two ways. Firstly, interactions between entities that are similar to those that have generated emergent behaviors can be highlighted to the user, to increase insight into the simulation results. Secondly, an analysis of these interactions can be used in the model validation.

4.4.1 Micro and Macro Properties

Our experimental analysis also shows that the success of our approach depends on how well the micro and the macro properties are chosen. For example, in our analysis of the game of life model, we did not use the *EP* suggested by literature, i.e., the rate of expansion of live cells because it was not appropriate to the glider pattern under study. Instead, we employed a definition of *EP* that captured the semantics of the glider, i.e., its movement, by looking at the distance between the surrounding bounding box of the glider and the center of the grid. Moreover, our analysis of the traffic junction model confirmed that, counter-intuitively, the driver speed cannot be shown to be the cause of the emergence of traffic jams, whereas driver politeness has been shown to cause traffic jams. These observations only show that post-mortem analysis, despite being more straightforward than live emergence analysis, remains challenging.

4.4.2 Scalability

Our experiments show that our approach can be applied to large-scale models. Occam3, the tool we employ for reconstructability analysis, can analyze very large state spaces with up to 2^{16} states, and as such the scalability of our approach is limited to models for which the state space generated by the model entities and their attributes does not exceed this size. For the traffic junction model, we have applied reconstructability analysis to models of up to 500 entities. From a practical perspective, difficulties arise from the specification of micro and macro properties, as a large and complex model is difficult to observe, and some micro or macro properties might be missed by the system expert. Towards this, a visualization tool that highlights behaviors and systems states that might be of interest to the system expert is needed.

4.4.3 Multi-dimensional Variables

Besides the main challenge in identifying system-specific definitions of micro and macro properties to facilitate analysis, another important issue remains the analysis of multi-dimensional micro-properties. For example, in the traffic junction model, while we have shown that the driver politeness causes the emergence of traffic jams, more insight could be obtained by analyzing the impact of driver politeness and driver speed together on the emergence of traffic jams. A limitation of the RA tool used is that it can only analyze single-dimension variables. Formulae can be devised to transform these micro-properties into single-dimension variables, but with a loss of meaning in the analysis.

5. CONCLUSION

Identifying and analyzing the causes of emergent behavior remains a challenging task even when system expert knowledge about emergence is available. In this paper, we propose a two-step approach for the post-mortem analysis of the causes of known emergence, in terms of model component attributes and values, as well as model component interaction. Firstly, we propose to use reconstructability analysis (RA) to identify micro properties that contribute to the cause of emergent macro properties identified by a system expert. Secondly, from the set of predicting micro properties, we identify using RA if the interaction between the respective model components causes the emergent property.

In contrast with current approaches, we apply our approach to both small and large examples defined in terms of the number of model components in the model, as well as the number of micro properties considered. Our experimental analysis of the game of

Model	Size	EP	μP	EP Identified	EP causes	Runtime (s)
Game of life - glider	10 x 10	Δe	$state(i,j)$	Yes	Indirect interaction between two cells	4.6
Flock of birds	10	$d(CM,CP)$	$d(b_i,CP)$	Yes	Interaction between 3 birds	6.73
	20			Yes	Interaction between 5 birds	17.97
	50			Yes	Interaction between 38 birds	4.02
Traffic junction	10	Δc	v_i p_i (v_i,p_i)	No	No traffic jam.	-
	50	Δc	v_i	No	Traffic jam present - no relevant results	3.28
			p_i	Yes	Interaction between impolite drivers and other cars	2.01
			(v_i,p_i)	Yes	Interaction between impolite drivers and other cars	3.32
	100	Δc	v_i	No	Traffic jam present - no relevant results	3.31
			p_i	Yes	Interaction between impolite drivers and other cars	2.56
			(v_i,p_i)	Yes	Interaction between impolite drivers and other cars	4.78

Table 10: Summary of Results

life, flock of birds, and traffic junction models identifies interaction between specific model components in the model as the cause of emergence. For traffic junction models, reconstructability analysis is able to identify driver politeness as one of the direct causes of the emergence of traffic jam, to support both anecdotal evidence as well as previous studies using CCTV camera observations.

Our approach proposes a first step towards a formal method to determine the causes of emergence due to the model component interactions. Our case study shows the applicability of our approach but also highlights important avenues for future work. Firstly, the interaction information related to a particular emergent property can be saved into the repository and used it to augment live emergence analysis. This could help to identify emergence as it happens, if the model under study exhibits an interaction pattern similar to one encountered before. Next, techniques have to be developed to determine the attributes of interest for each model component, and the grouping attributes to allow for multi-dimensional analysis.

6. REFERENCES

[1] M. Bedau. Weak Emergence. *Philosophical Perspectives*, 11:375–399, 1997.

[2] R. Cavallo and G. Klir. Reconstructability Analysis of Multi-dimensional Relations: A Theoretical Basis for Computer-aided Determination of Acceptable System Models. *Int. Journal of General Systems*, 5:143–171, 1979.

[3] W. Chan, Y. S. Son, and C. M. Macal. Simulation of Emergent Behavior and Differences Between Agent-Based Simulation and Discrete-Event Simulation. In *Proceedings of the Winter Simulation Conference*, pages 135–150, 2010.

[4] W. K. V. Chan. Interaction Metric of Emergent Behaviors in Agent-based Simulation. In *Proceedings of the Winter Simulation Conference*, pages 357–368, Phoenix, USA, 2011.

[5] C. Chen, S. B. Nagl, and C. D. Clack. Specifying, Detecting and Analysing Emergent Behaviours in Multi-Level Agent-Based Simulations. In *Proceedings of the Summer Computer Simulation Conference*, 2007.

[6] L. Chi. Transplating Social Capital to the Online World: Insights from Two Experimental Studies. *Journal of Organizational Computing and Electronic Commerce*, 19:214–236, 2009.

[7] P. Cilliers. *Complexity & Postmodernism*. Routledge, 1998.

[8] P. Davis. New Paradigms and Challenges. In *Proceedings of the Winter Simulation Conference*, Orlando , USA, 2005.

[9] U. Fayyad and R. Uthurusamy. Evolving Data Into Mining Solutions for Insights. *Communications of the ACM*, 45, 2002.

[10] S. Floyd and V. Jacobson. The synchronization of Periodic Routing Messages. In *Proceedings of SIGCOMM*, pages 33–44, 1993.

[11] M. Gardner. *The Fantastic Combinations of John Conway's New Solitaire Games*. Mathematical Games, 1970.

[12] C. Gershenson and N. Fernandez. Complexity and Information: Measuring Emergence, Self-organization, and Homeostatis at Multiple Scales. *Complexity*, 2012.

[13] R. Gore and P. Reynolds. An Exploration-based Taxonomy for Emergent Behavior Analysis in Simulation. In *Proceedings of the Winter Simulation Conference*, pages 1232–1240, Miami, USA, 2007.

[14] R. Gore and P. Reynolds. Applying Causal Inference to Understand Emergent Behavior. In *Proceedings of the Winter Simulation Conference*, pages 712–721, Miami, USA, 2008.

[15] J. Holland. *Emergence, From Chaos to Order*. Basic Books, 1999.

[16] O. T. Holland. Taxonomy for the Modeling and Simulation of Emergent Behavior Systems. In *Proceedings of the 2007 Spring Simulation Multiconference*, pages 28–35, 2007.

[17] C. W. Johnson. What are Emergent Properties and How Do They Affect the Engineering of Complex Systems? *Reliability Engineering and System Safety*, 12:1475–1481, 2006.

[18] A. Kubik. Towards a Formalization of Emergence. *Journal of Artificial Life*, 9:41–65, 2003.

[19] E. Manley and T. Cheng. Understanding Road Congestion as an Emergent Property of Traffic Networks. In *Proceedings of International Multiconference on Complexity, Informatics and Cybernetics*, pages 109–114, 2010.

[20] J. C. Mogul. Emergent (mis)behavior vs. Complex Software Systems. In *Proceedings of the 1st ACM SIGOPS/EuroSys European Conference on Computer Systems*, pages 293–304, New York, USA, 2006.

[21] Occam. Occam reconstructability analysis: http://dmm.sysc.pdx.edu/, Last retrieved Feb. 2013.

[22] E. Page and J. Opper. Observations on the Complexity of Composable Simulations. In *Proceedings of the Winter Simulation Conference*, volume 1, pages 553–560, Phoenix, USA, 1999.

[23] M. Prokopenko, F. Boschetti, and A. J. Ryan. An Information-theoretic Primer of Complexity, Self-organization and Emergence. *Complexity*, 15:11–28, 2009.

[24] K. K. Ramakrishnan and H. Yang. The Ethernet Capture Effect: Analysis and Solution. In *Proceedings of the IEEE Local Computer Networks Conference*, Minneapolis, USA, 1994.

[25] C. Reynolds. Flocks, Herds, and Schools: A Distributed Behavioral Model. In *Proceedings of ACM SIGGRAPH*, pages 25–34, 1987.

[26] A. K. Seth. Measuring Emergence via Nonlinear Granger Causality. In *Proceedings of the Eleventh International Conference on the Simulation and Synthesis of Living Systems*, pages 545–553, 2008.

[27] C. Szabo, Y. Teo, and S. See. An Integrated Approach for the Validation of Emergence in Component-based Simulation Models. In *Proceedings of the Winter Simulation Conference*, pages 2412–2423, 2012.

[28] C. Szabo and Y. M. Teo. Semantic Validation of Emergent Properties in Component-based Simulation Models. *Ontology, Epistemology, and Teleology of Modeling and Simulation Ð Philosophical Foundations for Intelligent MS Applications*, pages 319–333, 2012.

[29] Y. Teo and C. Szabo. CODES: An Integrated Approach to Composable Modeling and Simulation. In *Proceedings of the 41st Annual Simulation Symposium*, pages 103–110, Ottawa, Canada, 2008.

[30] M. Treiber and A. Kesting. *Traffic Flow Dynamics*. Springer, 2013.

[31] B.-Y. Yaneer. A Mathematical Theory of Strong Emergence using Multiscale Variety. *Complexity*, 9:15–24, 2004.

[32] M. Zwick. An Overview of Reconstructability Analysis. *Kybernetes*, 33:877–905, 2004.

Simulation-based Verification of Hybrid Automata Stochastic Logic Formulas for Stochastic Symmetric Nets

Elvio Gilberto Amparore
Università di Torino,
Dipartimento di Informatica
Torino, Italy
amparore@di.unito.it

Benoît Barbot
ENS Cachan, CNRS & INRIA
LSV
Cachan, France
barbot@lsv.ens-cachan.fr

Marco Beccuti
Università di Torino,
Dipartimento di Informatica
Torino, Italy
beccuti@di.unito.it

Susanna Donatelli
Università di Torino,
Dipartimento di Informatica
Torino, Italy
susi@di.unito.it

Giuliana Franceschinis
Università Piemonte Orientale,
DiSIT
Alessandria, Italy
giuliana.franceschinis@di.unipmn.it

ABSTRACT

The Hybrid Automata Stochastic Logic (HASL) has been recently defined as a flexible way to express classical performance measures as well as more complex, path-based ones (generically called "HASL formulas"). The considered paths are executions of Generalized Stochastic Petri Nets (GSPN), which are an extension of the basic Petri net formalism to define discrete event stochastic processes. The computation of the HASL formulas for a GSPN model is demanded to the COSMOS tool, that applies simulation techniques to the formula computation. Stochastic Symmetric Nets (SSN) are a high level Petri net formalism, of the *colored* type, in which tokens can have an identity, and it is well known that colored Petri nets allow one to describe systems in a more compact and parametric form than basic (uncolored) Petri nets. In this paper we propose to extend HASL and COSMOS to support colors, so that performance formulas for SSN can be easily defined and evaluated. This requires a new definition of the logic, to ensure that colors are taken into account in a correct and useful manner, and a significant extension of the COSMOS tool.

Keywords

Generalized Stochastic Petri Nets, Hybrid Automata Stochastic Logic, Simulation-based Verification, Stochastic Symmetric Nets

Categories and Subject Descriptors

I.6 [**Computing Methodologies**]: Simulation and Modeling

General Terms

Performance, Measurement

1. INTRODUCTION

Simulation of Discrete Event Stochastic Processes (DESP) is one of the most widespread techniques for evaluation of several types of quantitative (e.g. performance or reliability) measures. Although in a number of cases it can be combined with analytical or numerical analysis techniques, stochastic simulation is the preferred technique when the system is very complex and large, and/or its state space is very large or potentially infinite, or when some of the system characteristics (e.g. delay probability distributions, complex scheduling policies) prevent the application of other mathematical methods.

On the other hand, a class of performance measures that has drawn significant attention in the last years is that of path-based formulas: formulas that take into account a subset of the behaviors of the system. Path formulas may prove useful, for example, to compute the probability of the set of paths that lead to a safe final state in a reliability model, or the time to complete a production in a flexible manufacturing system when no machine breaks down during the production phase. Examples of path-based languages are the Extended Stochastic Probes (XSP [10], that define passage time over a subset of the behaviors of a PEPA model [14]), or the formalism of Path Automata (PA, operating on Stochastic Activity Networks [16]). Both XSP and PA have been devised as an extension of classical performance evaluation measures.

Another set of languages that allows to "deal with paths" comes from the community of temporal logics (logics that define path-based qualitative properties, like CTL [12] or LTL [17]) and of the associated stochastic extension, like Continuous Stochastic Logic (CSL)[1] and CSLTA [11, 8]. Here the paths considered are timed executions of a Continuous Time Markov Chain (CTMC). Paths in CSL are identified through two path operators, the time-bounded neXt and the time-bounded Until, while, to allow more flexibility, CSLTA identifies paths through a timed automata that "reads" timed execution traces. As usual in stochastic model checking the "target measure" is the computation of the probability of the set of timed paths that satisfies the path formula or, for CSLTA, the probability of the set of timed paths that are accepted by the timed automata. To be precise the logic formula being evaluated is the following "is the probability of accepted paths greater or equal (or less than) a given threshold?", which obviously requires the computation of the path probabilities. For the desire to stay within analytical solution methods CSL and CSLTA only deal with CTMCs, although the size of the models has led to the use of statistical model checkers, that compute path probabilities via discrete event simulation. Examples of statistical model checking tools for CSL are: YMER [21] and VESTA [18]. VESTA is a Java-based tool for statistical analysis of probabilistic systems. It implements statistical methods based on Monte-Carlo simulation and statistical hypothesis testing. YMER is instead a command-line tool, written in C/C++, for verifying transient properties of CTMCs and generalizations. It implements statistical CSL model checking techniques, based on discrete event simulation and acceptance sampling.

A language that subsumes path-based performance measures as defined in Path Automata or in XSP, as well as the stochastic logics of CSL and CSLTA is the one defined for the Hybrid Automata Stochastic Logic (HASL) which has been recently introduced in [5]. HASL addresses Generalized Stochastic Petri Nets (GSPN) [15] models with general distributions (thus going beyond the CTMC limits) and defines paths through the Linear Hybrid Automata (LHA) that allows a richer definition of paths than CSL and CSLTA. The COSMOS tool [4] has been developed to evaluate HASL formulas on GSPNs. COSMOS evaluates the HASL formulas using simulation techniques, it is therefore considered a tool in the family of statistical model checkers.

This paper proposes an extension of HASL to deal with a colored extension of GSPN known as Stochastic Symmetric Nets (SSN) [9]. The HASL language has been redefined to work with the "colored" tokens and transition instances of SSN, leading to a more parametric and compact language for large systems with symmetric structure and behavior. The COSMOS tool has been extended consequently.

The expressiveness of SSNs and of the extension of HASL to handle *colors*, allows to build compact models (and compact and parametric formulas) for complex systems comprising several similarly behaving components. Colors in SSNs allow to both represent (discrete) data structures and to uniquely identify "customers" or "resources", a feature that is particularly useful when defining path properties that refer to a sequence of steps through which a given customer or resource must undergo (e.g. average processing time of a part entering a pipeline, conditioned on the occurrence of a limited number of breakdowns along the path).

The paper is organized as follows: Section 2 introduces background material on the GSPN formalism and on HASL, and introduces a number of small LHA to exemplify the specification of basic performance indices.The COSMOS tool is also briefly reviewed. Section 3 presents SSN and the extension of HASL to account for colors. The extension proposed is the discussed and evaluated on three main examples in Section 4. Planned future works are discussed in the last section, concluding the paper.

2. BACKGROUND: THE GSPN FORMALISM AND HASL

In this section we shall present the background material, in particular the formalism of GSPN and the logic HASL. We shall also briefly recall the main features of the tool COSMOS, that evaluates HASL properties over GSPN models.

2.1 The GSPN formalism

Generalized Stochastic Petri Nets[15] (GSPN) are a formalism to describe discrete event dynamic systems. They have widely been used in the past to describe and evaluate systems, and we recall them briefly in the following. A GSPN is a bipartite directed graph with weighted arcs in which nodes are split into places (circles) and transitions (bars). Each place may contain zero or more tokens, and the state of the GSPN is determined by the number of tokens in each place. The state change is an effect of the firing of a transition: the direct arcs connecting places to transitions define the conditions under which the transition may fire (enabling) while the whole set of arcs to and from a transition defines the state change induced by the firing of the transition. Figure 1(a), top, shows a simple example of a GSPN model of a processor sharing open queue in which jobs are served at batches of 2, and there are 3 servers attending the queue, were each server may go idle for a while after having provided service. Transition T_1 describes the arrival process, T_2 the service time, T_3 the idle time, and t_1 and t_2 the decision of going idle (t_2) or not (t_1).

The enabling of a transition t requires that there are at least n_p tokens in each input place p of t, where n_p is the weight of the arc from p to t. If no weight is indicated, the weight is 1 by default. The firing of t removes n_p tokens from each input place p and adds $n_{p'}$ tokens to each output place p'. For the GSPN in the figure, $T1$ is always enabled, T_2 requires two jobs in the queue (place P_1) and a server available (place P_3), and its firing removes two tokens from P_1 and one from P_3, while adding two tokens into the output buffer (place P_2) and a token into the server decision place P_4. From P_4 the server may either choose to go idle (place P_5) or to go directly back to work (place P_3).

Box transitions describe a timed event with an associated delay probability distribution, the exponential distribution being the default, while thin transitions describe events that require no time (typically a decision, as in the case of t_1 and t_2). A GSPN describes therefore a stochastic process, and if all transitions are exponential or immediate this process is a CTMC, and analytical techniques can be applied to compute performance indices. When either the discrete state space is potentially infinite (as in our example) or the transitions are not exponential, simulation becomes the most widespread analysis technique. Classical performance indices includes the distribution (or mean value) of tokens in a place and the throughput of a transition. More elaborate performance indices, like the distribution of the passage time over a subnet, may not be directly computed upon the basic performance indicators [2] hence more elaborate ways of defining performance indices for a GSPN are needed. In this paper we concentrate on the computation of performance indices based on timed paths, where a path is a net execution (an (in)finite sequence of transitions and associated delays), in other words, a simulation trace of the GSPN. With reference to the GSPN of Figure 1, we might be interested in the probability that a customer, that arrives in the queue

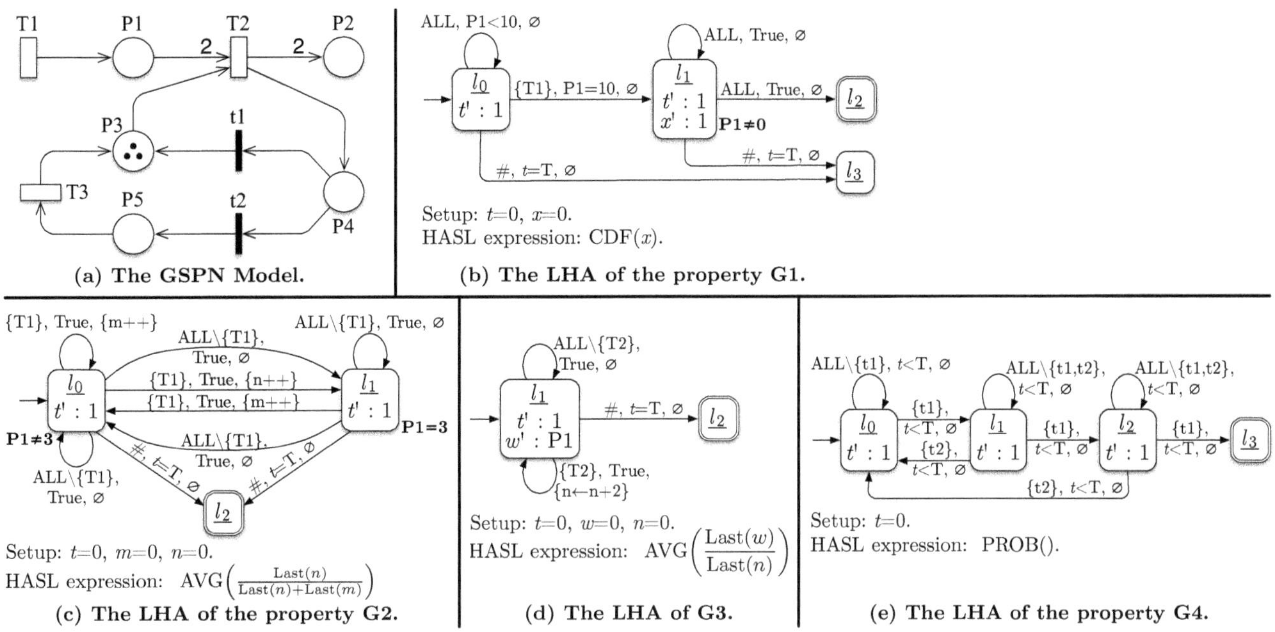

Figure 1: A simple GSPN model and a set of properties written as LHAs.

P_1 while there are already k tokens in there, experiences a time to reach the output buffer P_2 greater than a threshold value T_{max}.

It has been already observed by many authors (for example [11, 16]) that automata can be a good way to specify properties that depend on a subset of the possible executions, since an automaton defines the language of "accepted paths" (paths of the GSPN recognized by the automaton), and that, in particular, timed automata can be used when the executions to be considered include some timing constraints. As explained in the introduction, the performance indices we consider are the ones that can be specified using the HASL language.

2.2 Hybrid Automata Stochastic Logic

A specification in HASL is composed of a Linear Hybrid Automaton (LHA) and one or more formulas for the performance indicators. LHA are automata (composed of a set of locations and a set of edges) enriched with a set of variables. The state of an LHA is therefore a pair (location, variables' evaluation). The purpose of an LHA is to recognize (accept or reject) simulation traces of a GSPN (also called timed executions in the model checking community) and perform measures on the accepted paths by properly updating its variables. Figure 1(b) is an example of LHA with four locations: with the common graphical notation, l_0 is identified as an initial location (incoming arrow) and l_2 as a final one (double border). LHA variables come in two flavors: stable variables, which are discrete variables that can be updated only when an edge is taken, and flow variables, which are continuous variables that are continuously increased or decreased linearly according to a derivative that is specified in each location of the automaton. Also edges come in two flavors: synchronized edges that are taken when one of the GSPN transitions in its "synchronization set" fires in the simulation trace, and autonomous edges that can be taken by the LHA as soon as a condition on the LHA variables and/or the GSPN marking evaluates to true. Every edge may have an associated condition on the variables and on the marking (for the edge to be taken) and an update of the LHA variables (to be executed when the edge is taken). Autonomous edges are taken as soon as the associated condition is verified, with priority over other arcs.

An example of synchronized edge in the LHA of Figure 1(b) is that from l_0 to l_1, which synchronizes with the firing of transition T_1 in the trace under the condition that the GSPN marking reached after firing T_1 has 10 tokens in place P_1; this edge does not update any variable. An example of autonomous edge is that from l_0 to l_3; The sharp sign indicates that the edge is of the autonomous type, and condition $t = T$ indicates that the edge can be taken as soon as the LHA flow variable t is equal to the constant value T. Locations can have an associated condition, that may involve both the stable variables of the LHA and the marking of the GSPN. An example is shown in the LHA of Figure 1(c): location l_1 has an associated condition $P_1 = 3$, meaning that, while recognizing a GSPN trace, the LHA can stay in location l_1, or can reach this location, only if the marking reached in the trace has 3 tokens in place P_1.

Formulas in HASL allow one to define the following performance indicators to be computed on the observed traces: the probability that a GSPN trace lead the automaton to a final state, i.e. that the trace is accepted by the automaton (operator PROB), the cumulative distribution of a trace expression (operator CDF), the average over all accepted traces of a trace expression (operator AVG). If ve is a variable expression (arithmetic expression of the value of LHA variables and of the number of tokens in the net places), then a trace expression has the form last(ve), min(ve), max(ve), mean(ve), integral(ve) which define, for a given trace, respectively the last value of ve, the min/max value of ve, the time-weighted average of ve, and the integral of ve.

The LHA describes which simulation traces are of interest: while simulating a GSPN execution trace, each transition firing of the GSPN has to be matched by a corresponding synchronized edge, otherwise the trace is discarded. In addition, autonomous edges provide an "internal" behavior of the LHA that is independent from the GSPN model execution (e.g. to represent timeouts or to detect a given condition). Hence, the GSPN and LHA evolve in parallel until the LHA reaches either an accepting final state or a state where there are no autonomous edges enabled and no edges that can synchronize with the GSPN next transition (in the former case the trace is accepted, in the latter it is immediately discarded). Along the trace, the LHS cannot influence the GSPN behavior; note that one has to specify self-loops labeled with all GSPN transitions that do not cause a LHA location change, but should not cause the trace to be discarded (e.g. the self loop on l_1 in Figure 1(c) with synchronization set ALL$\setminus\{T_1\}$ is needed, otherwise the path would be rejected if a transition different from T_1 were fired in the GSPN).

The HASL measures are computed only from the set of accepted traces (i.e. execution paths that reach a final state in the LHA). When the LHA moves to a final location, the simulation ends, and the HASL measures are updated. Simulations are run (in parallel on multi-core systems) until all the estimators reach the specified accuracy. The measure PROB gives the fraction of simulations accepted by the LHA.

To better illustrate the use of HASL for the definition of performance indices, we shall consider a few examples. The reader may refer to [5] for a formal definition of HASL.

Figure 1(c) is an LHA, whose objective is to compute, for the time interval $[0, T]$, the probability that an arriving customer (token increase in place P_1 due to the firing of T_1) "sees" 2 customers already in P_1 (property **G2**). The LHA has two stable, discrete variables, n and m, to account for the number of arrivals that see (or do not see) two tokens in P_1, and a flow variable t, that is continuously and linearly incremented with derivative 1 in both locations: variable t plays the role of a timer that counts the time elapsed in the path being recognized by the LHA. There are two non-final locations, characterized by the conditions $P_1 \neq 3$ (location l_0) and $P_1 = 3$ (location l_1) on the marking of the GSPN, and a final one (location l_2, identified by a double border) that is reached when the time elapsed along the considered path is greater than a threshold value T.

For a path that starts in the initial marking of the GSPN, the automaton stays in location l_0, accepting all transitions. When the transition that fires is T_1 the behavior of the automaton depends on the marking of the net *after* the firing of T_1: if the number of tokens is different from 3 it stays in l_0 and increments the variable m, if it is equal to 3 it increments variable n, since this firing of T_1 has taken place when there were 2 customers in P_1. When variable t reaches the threshold T, the automaton moves to the final location l_2. Note that the automaton is deterministic: given a marking and a transition there is a single arc of the automaton that can be taken. This is a specific requirement of HASL, otherwise the resulting stochastic process would be partially undefined (or better, underspecified). The formula computed is AVG(last(n)/(last(n)+last(m)), which gives precisely the estimation of the probability that an arriving customer sees exactly two tokens in the queue.

The LHA of Figure 1(d) allows one to compute the average waiting time in $P1$, in the $[0, T]$ interval (property **G3**). The waiting time is computed as the total of the waiting times experienced by each single token in P_1 (accumulated in the LHA variable w), divided by the total number of customers that have left the system (accumulated in the discrete variable n). Note that n is incremented by 2 at each firing of T_2, due to the batch service type, while variable w is used to accumulate the time spent in P_1, and it is linearly incremented as time elapses, with a derivative equal to the number of tokens in P_1. The waiting time is then estimated by AVG(last(w)/(last(n)). Using variable w we can also compute the mean number of tokens in P_1, as AVG(last(w)/(last(t)) (considering that t counts the time elapsed along the accepted trace, this formula can also be expressed using the timed weighted average mean, as AVG(mean(w)).

The LHA of Figure 1(b) shows instead an example of computation of the distribution of the time it takes to empty a queue starting from an arrival that "sees" 9 tokens upon arrival, on the interval $[0, T]$ (property **G1**). The LHA uses two flow variables: t to accumulate the elapsed time along the path, as in the previous examples, and x to accumulate the time from when the queue goes to 10 to when it goes to zero. Note the use of two locations without any outgoing arc: l_2 is final (the corresponding path will be taken into account in the performance computation), while l_3 is not (and therefore the paths ending up in l_3 will not be considered). Location l_0 is used to accept all the traces until there is a firing of T_1 that leads to a queue (P_1) of 10 customers, which takes the automaton to location l_1. Note that x is incremented only when the automaton is in location l_1. The CDF is then estimated using the formula CDF(last(x)).

The last LHA considered, depicted in Figure 1(e), shows an example of the use of the automaton to recognize paths with specific conditions upon the transitions that fire along the path. The performance index considered is the probability of the executions that, up to time T, encounter three consecutive services in which the server does not go idle after having provided service (property **G4**). A server goes idle when transition t_2 is executed, while it goes immediately back to service when t_1 is executed, therefore the automaton accepts only paths that see 3 firing of t_1 without any firing in t_2 in between. The performance indicator is then PROB() which "counts" the percentage of GSPN executions that are accepted by the automaton.

2.3 The COSMOS tool

The performance indicators specified in HASL may be very difficult to compute analytically, and indeed the most promising performance evaluation technique in this case is simulation. The COSMOS simulator [4] computes the estimation of the PROB(), CDF(), and AVG() expressions in a HASL specification for a given GSPN model.

COSMOS is a statistical model checker which takes as input a GSPN model and an HASL formula, and computes the estimated value of the performance indices specified as HASL formulas, together with the associated confidence intervals for the required confidence level and accuracy. A classical batch estimator is used to decide when the simulator has collected enough samples to reach the requested accuracy for the target HASL formulas. The language of GSPN accepted by COSMOS is extended to support transitions with both exponential distributions and general distribution. The latter are chosen from a predefined set of statistical distributions with positive support.

To speed up the simulation COSMOS transforms the GSPN model and the LHA into C++ code, and then builds and runs the compiled C++ application. Parallel simulation is supported, using multiple instances of the compiled application that run over multiple cores of the same machine, or multiple machines. In this case, the COSMOS application itself coordinates the parallel simulators. Recently COSMOS has been extended to support rare events handling with importance sampling [7, 6]. COSMOS is integrated into the CosyVerif [19] platform and uses its file format GrML both for GSPN and LHA. It also allows to use the graphical editor Coloane for drawing GSPN and LHA.

3. EXTENSION TO COLORED NETS

In the previous section we have presented HASL as a rich language to specify path-related performance indices of GSPN models, but HASL for GSPNs has also some limitations, for example the time needed for a token to complete a task described by a subnet (the so-called "passage time") is not easily specifiable. This is actually true also in more classical performance approaches: when the goal is the mean passage time computation we can apply Little's law, but when the goal is to compute the passage time distribution, things gets more complicated. It has been already recognized in the literature [2] that the distribution of the passage time requires the identification of the elements that circulate in a subnet. This is the main motivation for the extension of HASL, and of the associated tool COSMOS, to colored Petri nets presented in this section, since colored nets are nets in which each single token can have a unique identity. By extending HASL and COSMOS to work with colored nets we also gain the possibility of using HASL in some more realistic settings, where colored nets are typically used for their ability of representing complex models in a more compact and modular manner.

3.1 The colored formalism of Stochastic Symmetric Nets

The colored formalism considered for the extension of HASL is that of Stochastic Symmetric Nets (SSN)[1]. SSN are here introduced by means of the example in Fig. 2, representing a distributed database update protocol: a number of sites host processes that may update a shared distributed database, this must be done in mutual exclusion, and once an update has been performed by a process at one site it must notify the change to all the other sites, and wait until it receives an acknowledge message from each of them to then release the mutually exclusive access to the updated piece of information. The main difference of the SSN formalism with respect to GSPNs is the possibility to associate information to tokens (so that tokens are said to have *different colors*, instead of being all black and indistinguishable). Each place $p \in P$ has an associated color domain (a data type) denoted *cd*(*p*) and each token in a given place has an associated value from *cd*(*p*). Color domains are built from elementary types called *color classes* ($\{C_1, C_2, C_3, \ldots, C_n\}$), so that $cd(p) = C_1^{e_1} \times C_2^{e_2} \times \ldots \times C_n^{e_n}$, where e_j is the number of times C_j appears in *cd*(*p*). Color classes are finite, non empty and disjoint sets, they may be ordered (in this case a successor function is defined on the class, inducing a circular order among the elements in the class), and may be partitioned into (static) subclasses. In the database example of Fig. 2 there are two classes called S (for *site*) and F (for *file*), and the places have either color domain S, or F or $S \times F$. Also transitions have an associated color domain specified as a set of *typed variables* plus a *guard*, the variable types are color classes. A valid *transition binding* is an assignment of values to its variables, satisfying the predicate expressed by the *guard*. A pair *(transition,binding)* is called *transition instance*. All transitions in the example net have color domain $\{s : S, f : F\}$ and the guards are all set to *true* (which is the default and is omitted in the picture). Each arc connecting a place p and a transition t is labeled with an expression denoting a function $arcf : cd(t) \to Bag(cd(p))$ where $Bag(A)$ is the set of all possible multisets that may be built on set A. The valuation of $arcf$ given a legal binding of t gives the multiset of *colored tokens* to be withdrawn from (in case of input arc) or to be added to (in case of output arc) the place connected to that arc upon firing of such *transition instance*. The arc expressions in SSNs are built upon a limited set of primitive functions whose domains must be color classes. A typical arc expression takes the form of a linear combination of *function tuples* (denoted $\langle f_1, \ldots, f_n \rangle$), and each element of a tuple is either a *projection function*, denoted by a variable in the transition color domain (e.g. s and f appearing in the arc expression $\langle s, f \rangle$ labeling several arcs in the example net), a *successor function*, denoted $x{+}{+}$ were x is a variable in the transition color domain whose type is an ordered class; a constant function returning all elements in a class (or subclass) denoted *classname.All*; a complement function denoted *classname.All*$-x$ where x is a variable of type *classname* in the transition color domain. Transition guards are boolean expressions whose terms take the form of *basic predicates*: $x = y$, $x \in subclass$, $d(x) = d(y)$ where x and y are variables of the transition with same type, and $d(x)$ denotes the static subclass x belongs to. The dynamic behavior of a SSN model is defined in terms of transition instances enabling and firing: the initial marking of the net in Fig. 2 enables $|S| \cdot |F|$ instances of transition *Start*, with binding $s = s_i, f = f_j, \forall s_i \in S, f_j \in F$ (the only condition for the enabling of such bindings is the presence of a token with color s_i in the input place *all_active*). Upon

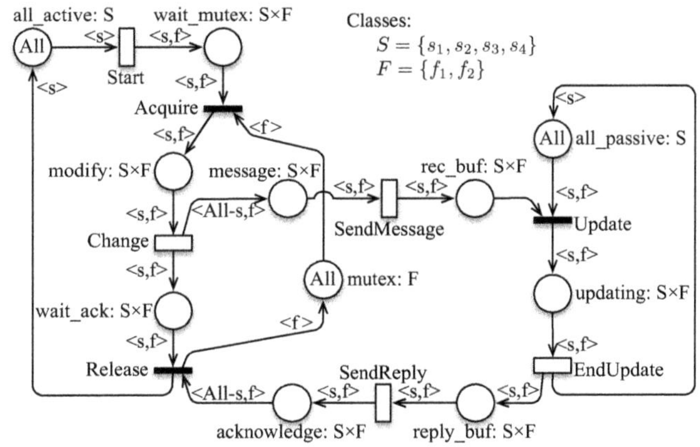

Figure 2: SSN model of a distributed database.

[1]SSN were previously known as *Stochastic Well-formed Nets*[9]; recently the untimed version of such formalism has been included in the High Level Petri Nets ISO standard **ISO/IEC 15909**, under the new name of Symmetric Nets (part 1, annex B.2).

firing of one enabled instance a token of color $\langle s_i \rangle$ is withdrawn from place *all_active* and a token of color $\langle s_i, f_j \rangle$ in place *wait_mutex*. The new reached marking enables only one instance of immediate transition *Acquire* with binding $s{=}s_i, f{=}f_j$: it is enabled because there is a token of color $\langle s_i, f_j \rangle$ in place *wait_mutex* and a token of color $\langle f_j \rangle$ in place *mutex* which are removed when the transition fires, while a token of color $\langle s_i, f_j \rangle$ is put into place *modify*. This enables the instance of transition *Change* with binding $\langle s_i, f_j \rangle$, which upon firing withdraws one token of color $\langle s_i, f_j \rangle$ from place *modify* and puts a similar token in place *wait_ack*, and $|S| - 1$ tokens $\langle s_k, f_j \rangle, s_k \in S, s_k \neq s_i$ in place *message*. A simulation trace of a SSN model consists of a sequence $m_i, ((t_i, b_i), \tau_i), m_{i+1}, ((t_{i+1}, b_{i+1}), \tau_{i+1}), \ldots$ of marking and transition instances (t_i, b_i) with the corresponding firing times τ_i.

3.2 Extending HASL to SSNs

The extension of HASL to support SSN models focuses on the definition of colored variables, of condition on colored markings, and on transition instances. Variables should be extended to be able to store colors as well, and edges should be able to discriminate between instances of the same transition with different bindings. The extension should be rich enough to allow also a reference to "coarser" quantities, for example, with reference to the place *modify* in the Database SSN, of color domain $S \times F$, we may want to refer to the total number of tokens, independently of the sites and files identities, or to the number of tokens with first color component equal to a specific site s_i.

To reach this goal each variable x of the LHA is indexed by a *color domain*, denoted as $cd(x)$. A *flow variable* x has a valuation $\bar{x}$ in $\mathbb{R}^{|cd(x)|}$. This implies that x is actually a (multidimensional) array of variables. Stable variables are further partitioned into *discrete* variables, whose valuation $\bar{x}$ is in $\mathbb{N}^{|cd(x)|}$ (and again this in general results in an array of variables), and *color* variables that represent just a color in a specified color class. Plain real and integer variables as in classical HASL are obtained by taking as colored domain the *neutral* one, which leads to *scalar* real (or integer) variables.

Transition names over edges should now be enriched to refer to transition instances, or to more coarser information about transition firings, although we should not forget that transition firing that synchronize with the automaton are the ones of the colored traces, that is to say, colored transition instances. To illustrate this aspect let us consider the three LHAs of Figure 3, in particular the self loops on l_0 that synchronize with the *Release* transition and increments variable x. In the leftmost LHA the transition is referred to simply as *Release*, and x is an integer variable, therefore x counts the number of occurrences of the transition *independently* from the binding. In the central LHA the transition is referred to as *Release*$\langle s, f \rangle [s, f = \langle s1, f1 \rangle]$, which synchronizes only with the firing of *Release* for an instantiation of the SSN variables s and f equal to the colors *s1* and *f1* respectively, therefore variable x only counts the firings for that specific binding in the $S \times F$ domain of *Release*. Finally, the rightmost LHA considers colored transition instances, and counts the number of firings "per color", since now variable x is declared over the color domain $S \times F$, and the increment is for $x[s, f]$.

Expressions to be used in boolean conditions associated to locations may now refer to LHA colored variables and to

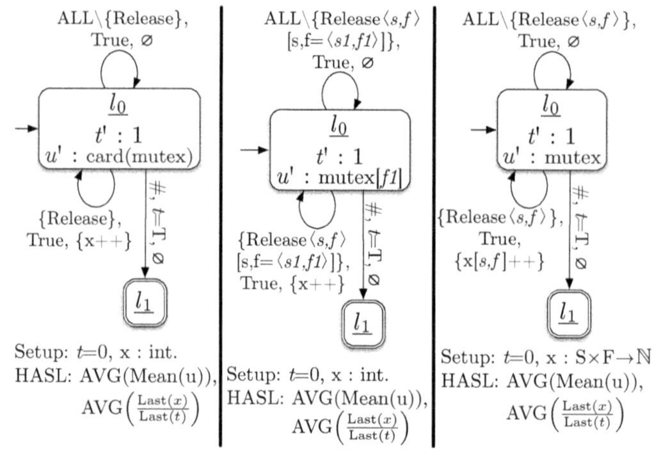

Figure 3: Three LHAs to compute the average number of tokens in place *mutex* and the throughput of *Release* at different granularity levels.

SSN markings, therefore they are typed with the color of the variable or of the SSN place. An expression typed with the neutral color is a scalar expression, while expressions in a color domain are vector expressions. Different types are incompatible, and cannot be mixed together. The language of *marking-dependent colored expressions* is then defined as:

$$exp ::= \alpha \mid p \mid x \mid exp\{+,-,*\}exp \mid (exp) \mid exp[color] \mid \mathrm{card}(exp)$$

where $\alpha \in \mathbb{R}$ is a scalar constant, $p \in P$ is a place, x is a variable. Algebraic operators follow the usual scalar/vector semantics. The product between a scalar and a colored expression is allowed, and is interpreted as a scalar product with the same type of the colored operand. The *color* term is a colored token or a color variable. The *selection operator* $exp[color]$ gives the number of tokens of the specified color, as a scalar expression. The function card() gives the scalar cardinality of an expression (the total number of tokens, independently of their colors). When the color domain of a place or of a variable is the neutral domain, the selection operator $[color]$ may be omitted, since variables in the neutral domain are scalar variables.

Boolean conditions are defined over the marking-dependent colored expressions, according to the following grammar:

$$lg ::= \text{true} \mid \neg lg \mid lg \wedge lg \mid exp \bowtie exp$$

where $\bowtie$ is a comparison operator. Comparisons on colored expressions are interpreted with the usual semantics of vectors comparison.

Color variables (stable variables that store a color) allows instead to store a color from a transition binding that synchronizes with an edge. Since color variables can be used to replace a color constant in an expression or in a transition specification, this allows to "match" transitions firing along a trace. To better illustrate this concept, let us consider the LHA of Figure 4, which has two color variables xs and xf of domain S and F respectively. The edge from l_1 to l_2 updates the color variables with the valuation of the variables s and f *of the SSN* as instantiated in the transition instance which synchronizes with the edge. Considering that location l_1 is entered when the time elapsed is equal to T, then

xs and xf store the identity of the first firing of transition *Start* after time T, the same identity is then used to select the "matched" firing of the *Release* transition.

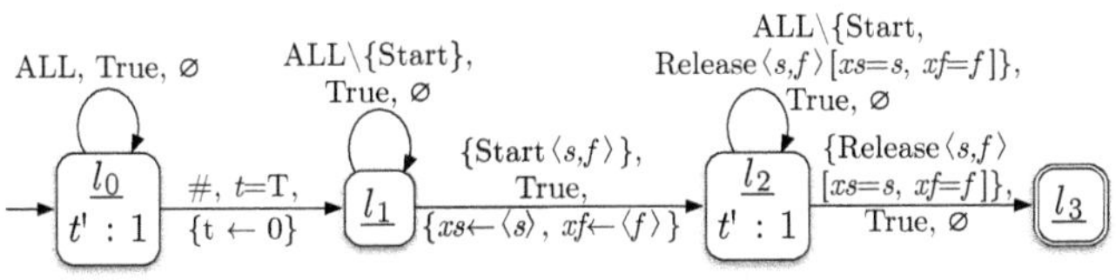

Figure 4: An LHA to compute the probability that the first update starting after a period [0,T] ends before any other update can start.

To conclude the description of the colored extension of LHA we explain the properties specified by the four LHAs of Figure 3 and 4. The formulas for the leftmost LHA in Figure 3 compute, for the $[0, T]$ period, the throughput of transition *Release*, independently of the specific transition binding, as AVG(last(x)/last(t)), and the mean number of tokens in place mutex, independently of the color, with the formula AVG(mean(u)). Note that u is a flow variable of neutral color, that accumulates the cardinality of place *mutex* independently from the color of the tokens. The formulas for the central LHA compute two similar quantities, but, as explained before, the throughput is now accumulated for a single specific color, $s1, f1$, and the average number of tokens in place *mutex* only considers tokens of color $f1$. The rightmost LHA computes instead, for each formula, *a vector of performance indices*. Indeed the throughput is computed for each pair of s, f colors (combination of sites and files) and the number of tokens is computed "per file".

The formula PROB() in the LHA of Figure 4 computes the probability that the first update that starts after a period $[0, T]$ it will be able to terminate its update with a release of the mutex, before any other update starts. As explained before a color variable is used to match the firing of the considered *Start* transition with the corresponding firing of *Release*. Note the use of the flow variable t to compute the passage time distribution from the first *Start* after time T, until its *Release*, for those paths in which the matching *Release* happens before any other *Start*, this computation is correct because, thanks to colors, we are able to match exactly a *Start* instance with the corresponding instance of *Release*.

Color support in COSMOS.

Colors changes the way COSMOS manages markings and tokens. Colored places and bindings are supported by generating the proper C++ code that declares, for each domain d, its container data structure that represent a multiset. These multisets may have a co-domain as *double* (for flow variables) or *int* (for stable variables). The SSN support is heavily influenced by the design of the CosyVerif platform [19]. CosyVerif is a software environment made of several software tools, including the graphical interface *Coloane* for drawing SSN models and LHA automata, and COSMOS for the statistical model checking. This platform already have support for stochastic nets (which was the input format for COSMOS) and symmetric nets. COSMOS now takes as input an extension of the file format for the symmetric nets formalism of CosyVerif.

4. EXAMPLES

In this sections three examples are presented: they are taken from the literature and are used to illustrate the possibilities offered by the colored extension of COSMOS.

The hospital model.

In Fig. 5 we show our second SSN example modeling a hospital Emergency Department (ED) [3]. According to the description provided by [20], the ED patients are divided in three categories: patients requiring resuscitation (high priority), patients with major illnesses or injuries (medium priority) and patients with minor illnesses or injuries (low priority). This is modeled in the SSN model partitioning the color class P, representing the patients, in three static subclasses P_H, P_M and P_L; so that each static subclass identifies a different level of urgency of treatment (and hence of priority) of the corresponding patients.

All the healthy patients are in the place *Healthy*, while the sick patients heading towards the hospital are in place *Ill*. An healthy patient that falls sick is represented by the firing of (an instance of) transition *FallIll*, while the evaluation of sick patient reaching the hospital is modeled by the guards associated with transitions *HighPrio*, *MediumPrio* and *LowPrio*. All the high priority patients are immediately move into the resuscitation room (place *ResuscRoom*) to be stabilized: the stabilization process can start (transition *BtoStabilize*) iff there is at least one trauma team available (place *TraumaTeam* marked). When a patient is stabilized (transition *EtoStabilize*) then he/she is moved into the monitored room (place *MonitoredRoom*).

All the patients with medium priority, since they do not need for being stabilized, are immediately admitted (transition *MediumPrio*) into the monitored room where they are constantly monitored until the results of the blood and X-ray exams become available (transitions *EBloodExam* and *EX-Ray*); then the patient is treated or operated by a doctor according to the outcomes of his/her tests (transitions *ToDoctorM* and *ToSurgery*). A medical examination requires at least one doctor available (place *Doctors* marked), while a surgical operation at least one doctor and one operating room (place *OperatingRoom* marked) available.

Patients with low priority are moved in the waiting room (place *WaitingRoom*) and they are examined by a doctor only when no more higher priority patients need to be treated or operated (inhibitor arc from *ReadyT* to *ToDoctorL*).

Finally, transitions *DischargeL*, *DischargeM* and *DischargeRec* model the discharge of a patient from the ED.

LHA for computing passage time.

Now we describe how LHA extended with color can be used to compute passage time of selected paths.

The passage time distribution is an example of performance measure which is not straightforward to define on a PN model since it expresses the probability of the time required for a (specific) token to pass through a given subnet. However, it is a more informative measure than the average response time measures when we study the service level agreements or the safety-related requirements of a system.

Exploiting the expressiveness of LHA it is possible to de-

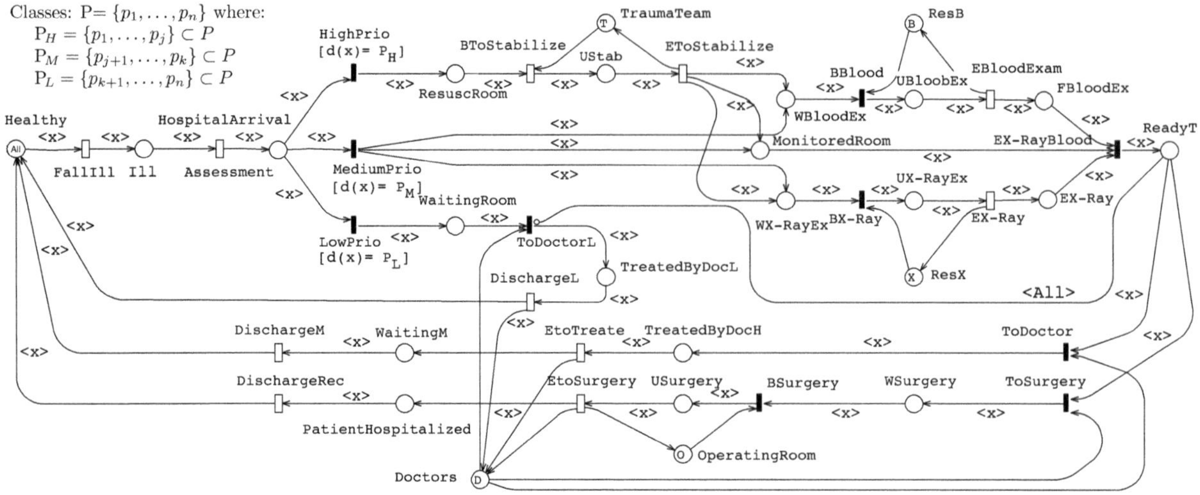

Figure 5: SSN model of patients flow in a hospital Emergency Department.

fine passage-time measures with quite complex constraints which may involve state conditions, transition firings, and performance characteristics of the model; it is also possible to decide in a very flexible way when the time count should be started and stopped on each path, including the possibility to interrupt the count in between the first start and final stop. This is much more powerful than classical state based specifications of passage time measures (which in their simplest form require to define the sets of entry, exit and forbidden states).

Hereafter, we describe two examples of passage-time measures:

H1: the CDF of the passage-time from arrival to discharge of a high priority patient given that at most n medium priority patients were in the hospital during his/her stay in the hospital;

H2: the CDF of the passage-time from arrival to discharge of a high priority patient given that the *average number* of medium priority patients has been less then n during his/her stay in the hospital.

The corresponding Colored LHAs are shown in Figs 6 and 7. In these two automata, the initial location l_0 is used only to skip an initial transient phase, so that a random trajectory of duration *initT* is simulated before starting the measure computation. After this initial phase the automata remains in l_1 until the first occurrence of the transition *HighPrio*, whose firing moves the automaton into the location l_2. On the edge connecting l_1 to l_2 the notation $px \leftarrow \langle x \rangle$ is used to "tag" a specific high priority patient assigning its specific color to the color variable x. Then, in the first automaton a path from l_2 is accepted by reaching final location l_3 as soon as the tagged patient is discharged from the hospital (i.e. transition *DischargeH* firing for the some colored assigned to px). Moreover, the condition $C1$ associated with l_2 assures that in all the accepted paths the number of medium priority patients in the hospital cannot be greater than n until the tagged patient is not discharged. Finally, the continuous flow variable pt is used to compute the time spent by the tagged patient inside the hospital.

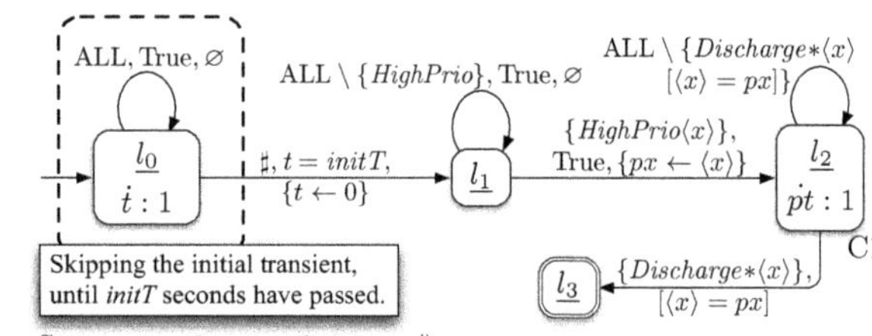

Setup: $t = 0,\ pt = 0,\ px = \langle\rangle$
HASL expression: CDF(pt)
Condition C1: $card(\text{P.All} \setminus \{Healthy, Ill\}) \leq n$
Discharge∗ is the set {*DischargeM*, *DischargeRec*}.

Figure 6: Colored LHA for the H1 property.

Instead, in the second automaton a path from l_2 is accepted as soon as the tagged patient is discharged from the hospital provided that the average number of medium priority patients in the hospital has not been greater than n (i.e. edge notation $\frac{navg}{pt} \leq n$) during the patient stay.

In Fig.8 the CDF of passage time (with related confidence intervals) is plot for the properties H1 and H2 considering 20 patients (i.e. 4 high priority patients, 8 medium priority patients and 8 low priority patients). Note that the state space of this model becomes quite large increasing the number of patients (for instance, with 2 high priority patients, 3 medium priority patients and 6 low priority patients it has more than 1.5 billion states), so that the simulation approach becomes virtually the only applicable method. The time required to compute the data for Fig.8 with 20 patients is about 1.5 seconds on a laptop computer. The tool simulates approximatively 100,000 trajectories to ensure confidence intervals smaller than 0.001.

The Client-Server model.

The SSN model in Fig. 9(left) represents a client-server architecture where several similar clients whose identities are modeled by color class C, can require remote services to a server. When a client decides to send a request (transition *SendReq*), its message is queued in the server buffer to be pre-processed (place *pre_proc*); then it is served iff at

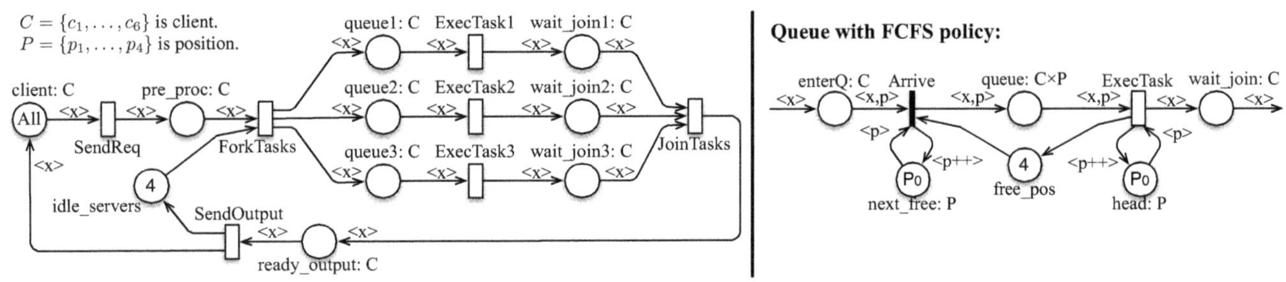

Figure 9: Client-server model.

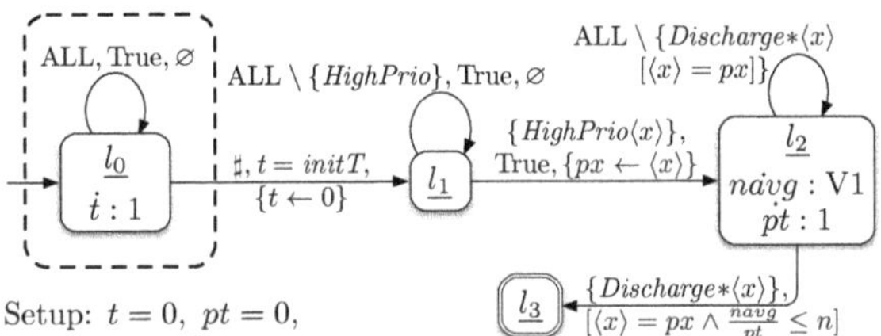

Setup: $t = 0$, $pt = 0$, $px = \langle\rangle$, $navg = 0$

HASL expression: CDF(pt)

Value V1: $card$(P.All \ {*Healthy*, *Ill*})

Discharge∗ is the set {*DischargeM*, *DischargeRec*}.

Figure 7: Colored LHA for the H2 property.

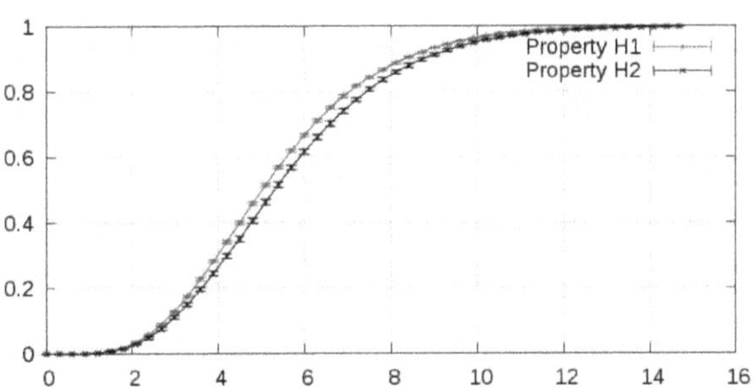

Figure 8: Passage time for the Hospital properties H1 and H2. For each point the related confidence interval is reported.

least one server is available (marking of place *idle_servers* greater than 0). Hence, three threads are generated (transition *ForkTask*) and executed in parallel (places $queue_i$ and transitions $ExecTask_i$). The computation result is sent back to the client (transiton *SendOutput*), only after all three threads end (transition *JoinTasks*).

The threads in places $queue_i$ are served using a Processor Sharing (PS) queueing policy (realized through a marking-dependent rate); while if we want to model a First-Come-First-Served (FCFS) queueing policy we have to replace the place $queue_i$ and its corresponding transitions $ExecTask_i$ with the submodel in Fig. 9 (right). In this submodel the place *queue*, with color domain $C \times P$, represents a circular array where the ordered color class P is used to encode the array indices. Places *head* and *next_free* encode the pointers to the first element in queue and to the first empty element, respectively.

The immediate transition *Arrive* assigns to a new thread in place *enterQ* the first empty position in the queue (i.e. marking of place *next_free*) if the queue limit is not reached (i.e. place *free_pos* is marked); and it updates the color of token in *next_Free* to the successor of p (i.e. denoted with the arc function $p++$). Instead, the firing of the transition *ExecTask* removes from place *queue* the token $\langle x, p\rangle$ with p equal to the color of the (unique) token in place *head*, then the color of the token in this place is updated to the successor of p.

LHA specification some performance indices.

The properties considered for this example are:

C1: throughput of *SendRequest* in transient and steady state;

C2: mean number of tokens in places *client* and *pre_proc* in transient and steady state;

C3: the CDF of the passage-time for the first client request processed by the server (from transition *ForkTask* to transition *JoinTask*) after the initial transient.

Observe that $C1$ and $C2$ are quite "standard" measures specified by means of reward function.

The Colored LHAs for these measures are shown in Figs 10, 11 and 12.

In details, the two automata for property $C1$ in Fig. 10 are different as regards to the dashed part used to skip an initial transient during the property computation. Then, the stable variable n is updated when transition *SendRequest* fires (independently by its colored binding). The computed formula is $AVG\frac{Last(n)}{Last(t)}$ where t is used to measure the time. For instance, considering 6 clients and 4 servers the throughput of the transition *SendRequest* assuming $initT = 100$ is 0.88629 ± 0.00019 when the threads in $queue_i$ are scheduled according to a PS policy, and 0.77278 ± 0.00017 when the threads in $queue_1$ are served using FCFS and the threads in $queue_2$ and $queue_3$ are served using PS.

In Fig. 11 the two automata show how to define the property $C2$ in transient and steady state. The flow variable p is used to store the number of tokens in places *client* and *pre_proc*. Hence, the computed formula is $AVG\frac{Last(p)}{Last(t)}$. For instance, the average number of tokens in these places with $initT$ equal to 100 time units, 6 clients and 4 servers is 0.89240 ± 0.00049 when the threads in $queue_i$ are served using PS, and 0.78369 ± 0.0003 when the threads in $queue_1$ are served using FCFS and the threads in $queue_2$ and $queue_3$ are served using PS.

Finally, the last automaton in Fig.12 is an example of CDF of the passage-time in which a color variable (i.e. c)

1) *Throughput of* SendRequest *in transient* [0, T].

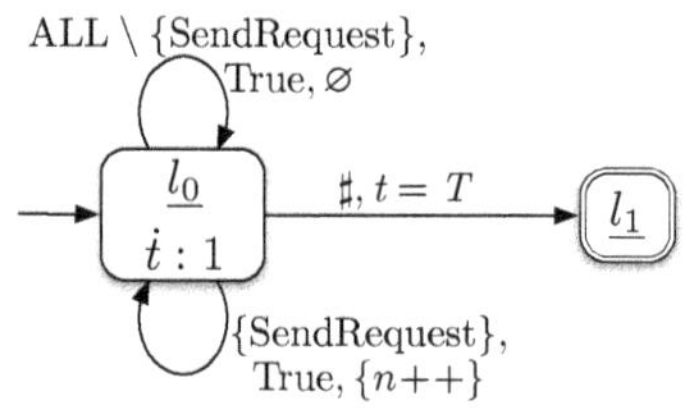

Setup: $t = 0$, $n = 0$.
HASL expression: $\text{AVG}\left(\frac{\text{Last}(n)}{\text{Last}(t)}\right)$

2) *Throughput of* SendRequest *in steady-state.*

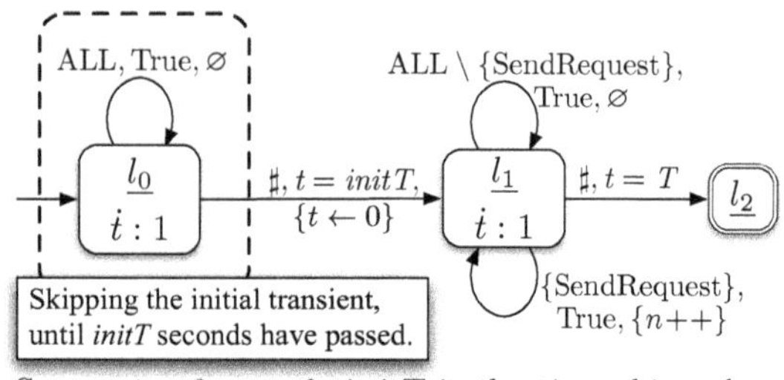

Setup: $t = 0$, $n = 0$, $initT$ is the time skipped for the initial transient, T is the total sample time for each path.
HASL expression: $\text{AVG}\left(\frac{\text{Last}(n)}{\text{Last}(t)}\right)$

Figure 10: C1: throughput of SendRequest.

1) *Mean number of tokens in P in transient* [0, T].

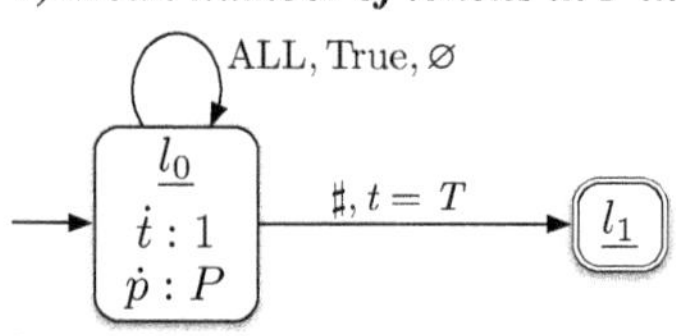

Setup: $t = 0$, $p = 0$. The variable p accumulates in l_0 the token count of P.
P is the sum of tokens in *client* and *pre proc*
HASL expression: $\text{AVG}\left(\frac{\text{Last}(p)}{\text{Last}(t)}\right)$

2) *Mean number of tokens in P in steady-state.*

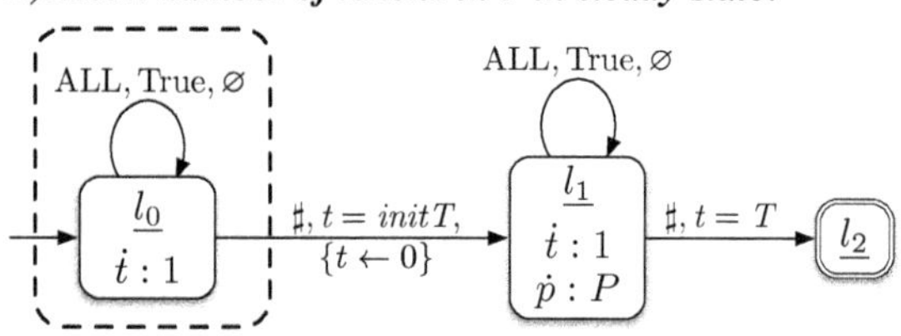

Setup: $t = 0$, $p = 0$.
HASL expression: $\text{AVG}\left(\frac{\text{Last}(p)}{\text{Last}(t)}\right)$

Figure 11: C2: the mean number of tokens in P.

is used to tagged a generic client request (i.e. $c \leftarrow \langle x \rangle$), and shows another pattern for letting the initial transient to elapse. Indeed, the automaton moves from l_0 to l_1 only when the initial transient is elapsed ($t \geq initT$) and the transition *ForkTask* fires. The color associated with this

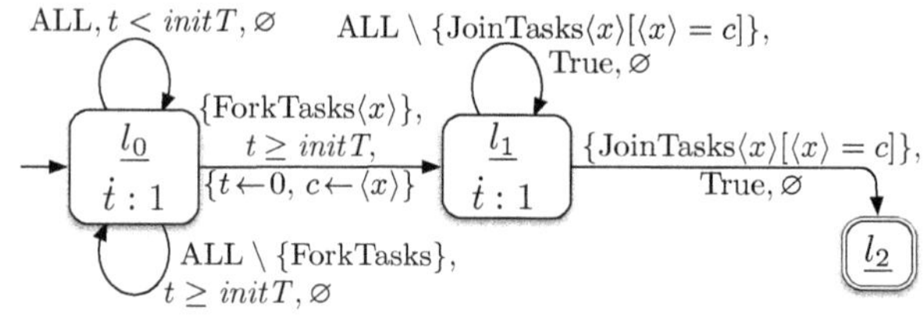

Setup: $t = 0$, $c = \langle\rangle$. c *is a color variable.*
HASL expression: CDF(t)

Figure 12: C3: passage time of the first observed client.

firing is stored in c, so that the corresponding client request is tagged. Then, the automaton reaches the final location l_2 iff the transition *JointTask* fires for the same tagged client request (*JointTask*$[\langle x \rangle = c]$).

In Fig. 13 the CDF of passage time computed by this automaton is shown considering: 1) PS queueing policy associated with places $queue_i$; 2)FCFS queueing policy associated with place $queue_1$ and PS to the others two places $queue_2$ and $queue_3$.

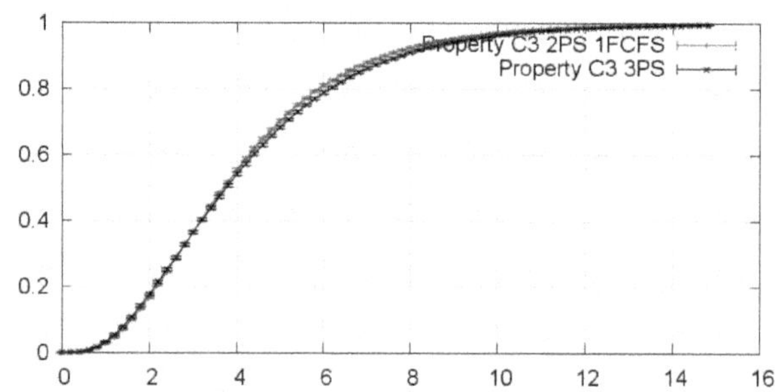

Figure 13: Passage time CDF of the first client request processed by the server after the initial transient for different task scheduling policies.

The Database model.

In this section the model in Fig. 2, already introduced in Section 3.1, is analyzed by means of COSMOS.

Two measures of interest are defined and computed:

D1: CDF of the time required for a change request to complete, under the condition that the time to acquire the mutex on the file to be changed does not exceed a given threshold and the time to send all the messages from the active site who modified the file and the passive sites is below a given threshold;

D2: the probability that a request for change, arriving when there are no other submitted requests, is the first to complete (i.e. no other request arriving later will overcome it)

The automata for D1 and D2 are shown in Figs. 14 and 16, respectively.

The automaton in Fig. 14 includes the usual pattern for letting the initial transient to elapse (from l_0 to l_1), after which the first occurrence of *Start* makes the automaton move to location l_2 while storing the binding in the two

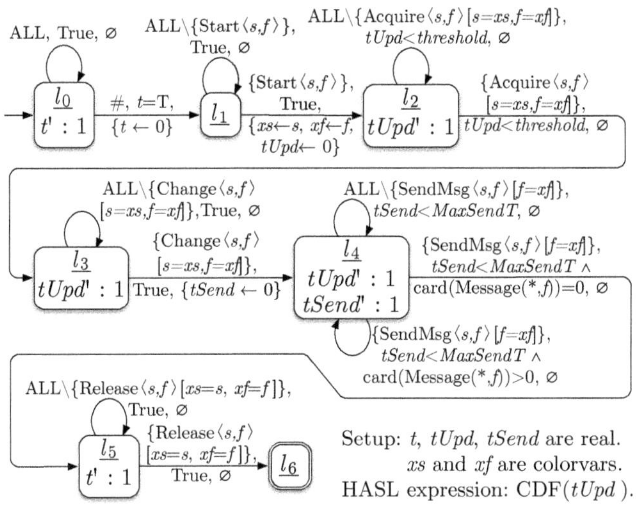

Figure 14: D1: passage time of a distributed update conditioned on a time thresholds on mutex acquisition and on update messages transmission.

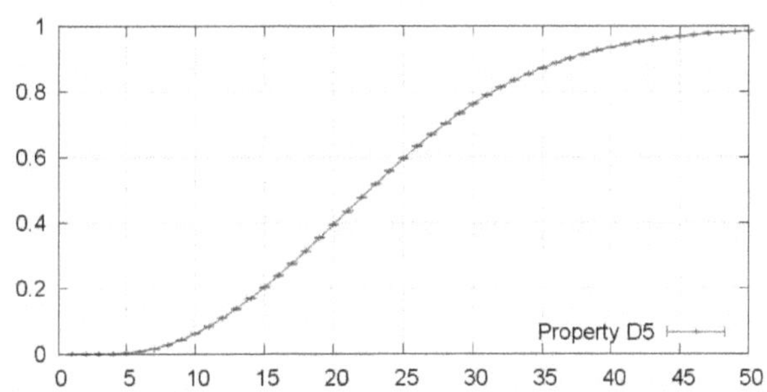

Figure 15: D1: CDF of the passage time of a distributed update conditioned on two time thresholds on intermediate steps.

color variables xs and xf. When entering l_2 the timer *tUpd* is started and the control on the time elapsed until the firing of transition *Acquire* for the same binding is checked: if it exceeds the threshold the trace is discarded (condition *tUpd* < *threshold* on all outgoing arcs). The firing of *Acquire* within the threshold brings the LHA to location l_3 where it remains until transition *Change* fires for the binding $\langle xs, xf\rangle$: this event starts the new timer *tSend* and causes the LHA to move into location l_4. The purpose of location l_4 is to check that all messages from site xs to the other sites arrive to their destination within $MaxSendT$ time units (condition *tSend* < $MaxSendT$ on all outgoing arcs). The LHA moves on to location l_5 when an instance of transition *SendMsg* fires with variable f bound to xf which moves the last update message for file xf out of place *Message* (condition $card(Message(*, f)) = 0$) on the arc from l_4 to l_5. From l_5 the trace is accepted when transition *Release* fires with binding $\langle xs, xf\rangle$: timer *tUpd* grows with rate 1 in all locations from l_2 to l_5 so that when the final location is reached it contains the time required to complete the update.

In Fig.15 the CDF computed for this property is reported.

The automaton in Fig. 16 has two initial locations to account for the possibility of different initial markings. Proposition Φ identifies a state where there are no ongoing updates (which is the case for the initial marking of the database example in Fig. 2). Hence the initial marking is matched with the appropriate initial location, l_0 or l_1; if it matches l_0 then the automaton remains in such state until a state is reached which satisfies Φ (that causes the automaton to move on to l_1), then at the first firing of transition *Start* the path recognition starts, recording the binding of s in the color variable c and moving on to location l_2. In l_2 the first occurrence of *Release* makes the automaton to either accept the path (if the binding of variable s is equal to c, moving to the final location l_3) or discard it (if s is bound to a value different from that stored in c). The measure is defined simply using the expression PROB(). This gives us the result of $0.5681588 \pm 9.02441 \cdot 10^{-4}$, computed with COSMOS using a confidence level of 99% on a total of 1.991.043 paths.

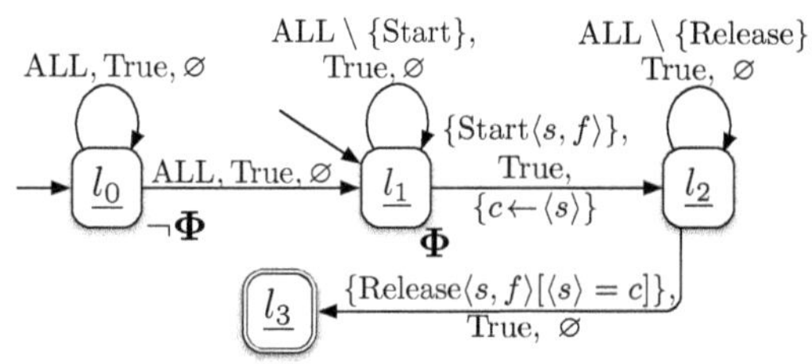

Setup: $t = 0$, OK $= 0$, $c = \langle\rangle$.
Condition $\mathbf{\Phi}$ is: all_active = All.
HASL expression: PROB()

Figure 16: D2: LHA for the probability of proper serialization in mutex acquisition.

5. CONCLUSIONS AND FUTURE WORK.

This paper presents an extension of the automata based language HASL, to express complex performance properties of SSN models in the COSMOS tool. The use of an High Level (Stochastic) Petri Net formalism allows to describe realistic systems, on the other hand the possibility to use LHA extended with color-indexed variables and propositions involving colored markings provides a rich and powerful language for property specification, increasing the practical applicability of the COSMOS simulator. This has been demonstrated on three examples (taken from the literature).

The current implementation of the COSMOS extension to SSNs and HASL does not embed a number of optimizations that could be implemented taking advantage of the specific symmetric properties of the SSN models. The type of arc functions that characterize the formalism naturally leads to several possibilities for the optimization of the future event list updating and handling. The approach proposed in [13] and implemented in the GreatSPN software tool can be adapted and improved in COSMOS: this includes methods to efficiently determine which transition instances are newly enabled or disabled, based on a preliminary analysis of the net structure; the techniques must be adapted to take into account the COSMOS architecture, which is based on the generation of model specific code to be compiled with the simulator engine core.

6. REFERENCES

[1] A. Aziz, K. Sanwal, V. Singhal, and R. Brayton. Model-checking continuous-time Markov chains. *ACM Trans. Comput. Logic*, 1(1):162–170, 2000.

[2] G. Balbo, M. Beccuti, M. De Pierro, and G. Franceschinis. First Passage Time Computation in Tagged GSPNs with Queue Places. *The Computer Journal*, 2010. First published online July 22, 2010.

[3] G. Balbo, M. Beccuti, M. D. Pierro, and G. Franceschinis. Computing first passage time distributions in stochastic well-formed nets. In *ICPE'11 - Second Joint WOSP/SIPEW International Conference on Performance Engineering*, pages 7–18, Karlsruhe, Germany, March 2011.

[4] P. Ballarini, H. Djafri, M. Duflot, S. Haddad, and N. Pekergin. COSMOS: a statistical model checker for the hybrid automata stochastic logic. In *Proceedings of the 8th International Conference on Quantitative Evaluation of Systems (QEST'11)*, pages 143–144, Aachen, Germany, Sept. 2011. IEEE Computer Society Press.

[5] P. Ballarini, H. Djafri, M. Duflot, S. Haddad, and N. Pekergin. HASL: An expressive language for statistical verification of stochastic models. In *Proceedings of the 5th International Conference on Performance Evaluation Methodologies and Tools (VALUETOOLS'11)*, pages 306–315, Cachan, France, May 2011.

[6] B. Barbot, S. Haddad, and C. Picaronny. Coupling and importance sampling for statistical model checking. In C. Flanagan and B. König, editors, *TACAS*, volume 7214 of *Lecture Notes in Computer Science*, pages 331–346. Springer, 2012.

[7] B. Barbot, S. Haddad, and C. Picaronny. Importance sampling for model checking of continuous time markov chains. In P. Dini and P. Lorenz, editors, *SIMUL 2012*, pages 30–35, Lisbon, Portugal, Novembre 2012. IARIA.

[8] T. Chen, T. Han, J.-P. Katoen, and A. Mereacre. Quantitative Model Checking of Continuous-Time Markov Chains Against Timed Automata Specifications. *Logic in Computer Science, Symposium on*, 0:309–318, 2009.

[9] G. Chiola, C. Dutheillet, G. Franceschinis, and S. Haddad. Stochastic well-formed coloured nets for symmetric modelling applications. *IEEE Trans. on Computers*, 42(11):1343–1360, nov 1993.

[10] A. Clark and S. Gilmore. State-aware performance analysis with extended stochastic probes. In *Proceedings of the 5th European Performance Engineering Workshop on Computer Performance Engineering*, EPEW '08, pages 125–140, Berlin, Heidelberg, 2008. Springer-Verlag.

[11] S. Donatelli, S. Haddad, and J. Sproston. Model checking timed and stochastic properties with CSL^{TA}. *IEEE Trans. Softw. Eng.*, 35(2):224–240, 2009.

[12] E. Emerson and E. M. Clarke. Using branching time temporal logic to synthesize synchronization skeletons. *Science of Computer Programming*, 2(3):241 – 266, 1982.

[13] R. Gaeta. Efficient discrete-event simulation of colored petri nets. *IEEE Trans. Softw. Eng.*, 22(9):629–639, Sept. 1996.

[14] J. Hillston. Process algebras for quantitative analysis. In *Proceedings of the 20th Annual IEEE Symposium on Logic in Computer Science*, pages 239–248, Washington, DC, USA, 2005. IEEE Computer Society.

[15] M. A. Marsan, G. Balbo, G. Conte, S. Donatelli, and G. Franceschinis. *Modeling with Generalized Stochastic Petri Nets*. J. Wiley, New York, NY, USA, 1995.

[16] W. D. Obal, II and W. H. Sanders. State-space support for path-based reward variables. *Perform. Eval.*, 35:233–251, May 1999.

[17] A. Pnueli. The temporal logic of programs. In *FOCS*, pages 46–57. IEEE Computer Society, 1977.

[18] K. Sen, M. Viswanathan, and G. Agha. Statistical model checking of black-box probabilistic systems. In *In 16th conference on Computer Aided Verification (CAVÕ04), volume 3114 of LNCS*, pages 202–215. Springer, 2004.

[19] The CosyVerif Group. Cosyverif. `http://www.cosyverif.org`.

[20] S. Wau Men Au-Yeung. *Response Times in Healthcare Systems*. PhD thesis, Imperial College, London, 2008. `pubs.doc.ic.ac.uk/response-times-in-healthcare`.

[21] H. L. S. Younes. Ymer: A statistical model checker. In *COMPUTER AIDED VERIFICATION. LNCS*, pages 429–433. Springer, 2005.

A Time Management Optimization Framework for Large-Scale Distributed Hardware-In-The-Loop Simulation

Wei Dong
Tsinghua National Laboratory for Information Science and Technology
Department of Automation, Tsinghua University, Beijing 100084, China
86-10-62796411
weidong@tsinghua.edu.cn

ABSTRACT

Large-scale distributed HIL(Hardware-In-The-Loop) simulation is an important and indispensable method for testing and verifying complex engineering systems. An important necessary condition for realizing HIL simulation is that the speedup ratio of full-speed simulation must be greater than 1, and satisfying this condition becomes more and more difficult with the ceaselessly increasing scale of simulation. Aiming at the problem how to maximizing the speedup ratio, a time management optimization framework for large-scale distributed HIL simulation is proposed in this paper. Different from other works on performance optimization of HIL simulation, in this paper, the problem is focused on simulation speedup ratio and is considered in the range of analysis simulation, which means causal abnormity is intolerable. According to this goal, a new formal description framework of distributed simulation is given based on the automata theory. Then the basic objective and condition of distributed simulation are formally analyzed, which results in the conclusion that the classical Local Causality Constraint for distributed simulation is only a sufficient condition rather than sufficient and necessary condition. Based on this, the optimization problem for simulation speedup ratio is radically analyzed and the overall strategy for this problem is given. Considering different conditions, two different levels of optimization mechanisms respectively for time advance and task partition are given. And finally, the application and experiment result shows the effectiveness of the proposed method.

Categories and Subject Descriptors

I.6.8 [**SIMULATION AND MODELING**]: Types of Simulation *–Discrete event, Distributed, Parallel.*

General Terms

Algorithms, Performance, Design, Theory.

Keywords

Large-scale distributed simulation, Hardware-In-The-Loop simulation, time management, speedup ratio of simulation, optimization framework.

1. INTRODUCTION

With the rapid development of engineering technology, artificial engineering systems become more and more complex and large-scale. Nowadays, these systems play more and more important roles in many fields, and many of them, such as train control system for high-speed railway and process control system in chemical plant and so on, have direct relationship with safety, which means functional defects of these artificial engineering systems may result in catastrophes. So, these systems must be tested enough before being put into use. HIL(Hardware-In-The-Loop) simulation is an important technology aiming at this requirement. It embeds the SUT(system under test) in a simulation environment which interacts with the SUT in the same way as the real working environment. Compared to site test, HIL simulation test has a lot of advantages such as low cost, repeatability, controllability and safety.

However, existing HIL simulation systems mainly aim at small-scale test for single device and are not suitable for large-scale system test. Since large-scale system is more difficult for analyze and verify, HIL simulation for large-scale system is more valuable and significant, and becomes an important and challenging problem in this field. The main difficulty for large-scale HIL simulation lies in time advance efficiency of simulation (i.e., with increasing simulation scale, how to advance the simulation time as fast as possible so that it can be faster than real time). This is because, in HIL simulation, the simulation environment must run in real time for interacting with real devices normally. This can be done only if the simulation environment has the ability to run faster than real devices, i.e. when the simulation environment runs with full speed, the ratio of simulation time to wall-clock time (known as speedup ratio of simulation system) must be higher than 1. However, satisfying this requirement is becoming more and more challenging with the growth of simulation system's complexity and scale.

Due to limitation of computing power, simulation in single computer is not a promising direction for solving this problem and distributed simulation becomes an inevitable method for large-scale HIL simulation. Considering large-scale distributed HIL simulation, the key to the problem becomes as follows: Given specific simulation task and enough simulation nodes (i.e. single computer) with specific computing power, how to advance the simulation time as fast as possible? Or, in other words, how to make the speedup ratio of simulation system as high as possible? The complication of this problem mainly lies in time management of distributed simulation. Time management is used to ensure correct causal logic among different simulation nodes of distributed simulation system. And at the same time, time management becomes a constraint that don't allow one simulation node to advance simulation time freely. It is just because of this constraint, when we increase the number of simulation nodes to N times of the original number, the speedup ratio can't be increased to N times of the original value. So, instead of increasing the number of simulation nodes drastically, optimizing time management and task partition becomes a more important way to boost simulation efficiency. Based on this idea, the problem evolves as follows:

1) If the simulation task, computing power of single computer and the number of simulation nodes are given, how can we make the speedup ratio of simulation system as high as possible?

2) In the problem 1), if the number of simulation nodes is not given and can be increased arbitrarily, how will the optimized speedup ratio change with the number of simulation nodes? And how can we determine the optimized number of simulation nodes so that we can gain the highest speedup ratio?

3) In the problem 2), if the amount of simulation task is increased due to the increasing scale and complexity of the target system, how will the optimized speedup ratio change? And when the scale and complexity of the target system increase persistently, can we always make the speedup ratio of simulation system higher than 1 by increasing the number of simulation nodes, so that the HIL simulation condition can be met?

Time management of distributed simulation is not a fresh topic yet. Many researchers have contributed to this area since 1970s [1]. However, the previous research mainly focuses on how to design effective time management protocol to ensure correct causal logic, how to avoid the deadlock problem and how to optimize the amount of messages used for time management, not involving how to maximize the speedup ratio of distributed simulation. The main difference between previous research and this paper is rooted in the special requirement of HIL simulation. Since the previous research on time management of distributed simulation does not aim at HIL simulation, the speedup ratio is not the primary concern.

The performance aspects of previous research concentrate on the comprehensive performance including both message throughput and execution efficiency. However, the optimization objectives of these two aspects may be contradictory, which means the promotion of simulation execution efficiency may be at the cost of increasing the time-management message throughput. So, almost none of previous research focuses on how to maximize the simulation execution efficiency (i.e. speedup ratio of distributed simulation). Consideration for message throughput is necessary for previous research, since the corresponding network environment may be Wide Area Network(WAN), for which network bandwidth is an expensive resource. However, in this paper, the situation changes when considering HIL simulation. For implementation convenience, HIL distributed simulation is always built on Local Area Network(LAN), for which network bandwidth is no longer an expensive resource (with rapid development of network technology, nowadays the network throughput of new LAN has reached to 10Gbps). In addition, and more importantly, how to promote the speedup ratio to ensure it is higher than 1 is crucial for HIL simulation, especially for large-scale distributed HIL simulation. So, how to purely maximize the speedup ratio of distributed simulation becomes a new important problem when the scale of HIL simulation is persistently increasing.

In order to analyze and solve the above problem theoretically, a time management optimization framework for large-scale distributed HIL simulation is proposed in this paper. In this framework, the above problem is formalized by automata theory and related formal methods, so that the problem, as well as the influencing factors and the solution channels, can be analyzed roundly and radically. By this framework, a foundation will be established to solve the three problems mentioned above. However, since all the three problems are unlikely to be solved in one paper, this paper only addresses the first problem, but the fundamental framework will also serve the follow-up work. Because time wrap is not suitable for real device in HIL simulation, only conservative time management is considered in this paper. Besides, this paper has no direct relationship with the concrete mechanisms of HIL simulation (such as real-time synchronization, etc.), however, since the problem focused by this paper is rooted in the requirement of HIL simulation and is a premise for HIL simulation, the inclusion of "HIL simulation" in this paper's title is reasonable.

This paper is organized as follows: Section 1 gives an overall background and introduces the problem; section 2 gives the related research status; section 3 gives the formal description framework of distributed simulation, which is a basis for subsequent content; section 4 gives the time management optimization framework for large-scale distributed HIL simulation; section 5 gives the application example and experimental result; finally, section 6 gives the conclusion.

2. RESEARCH STATUS

Since the concept of parallel and distributed simulation was proposed, time management has been all along a hot topic in this area [1]. In respect of conservative time synchronization, Bryant [2] gave the standard description on the time synchronization problem of parallel simulation for the first time, and proposed the basic time synchronization algorithm based on conservative strategy. Aiming at the deadlock problem which may happen in [2], Chandy and Misra [3] proposed an improved scheme, introducing null message and lookahead to avoid deadlock. [2] and [3] together formed the classical CMB synchronization algorithm for distributed simulation. Aiming at performance shortage of basic conservative synchronization algorithm, Chandy and Misra [4], as well as Fujimoto [5], proposed a series of improved strategy and alternative models, introducing the concepts of LBTS(lower bound on the timestamp) and logical process distance and so on, which overcame the shortage to a certain extent. Deelman [6] adopted improved lookahead mechanism to promote simulation performance. M.Kyoung [7] adopted a kind of software execution path prediction method to improve the computation of lookahead. Zhao [8] proposed a method named MCTS(multi-node coordination time synchronization), which adopted multicast to promote the protocol efficiency of time management. Adltyavijay [9] proposed a time synchronization method based on time interval in order to reduce the message throughput for time management. Park [10] proposed a performance evaluation model for CMB null message algorithm. Lin [11] proposed a micro-synchronization method in order to excavate the degree of parallelism inside logical process. Pan [12] proposed a hybrid time management algorithm based on both conditional and unconditional information. The main problems of the research in this aspect are as follows: Early synchronization algorithms focused on solving problems of abnormal sequential logic and deadlock, not considering performance problem; the subsequent researchers proposed a lot of improved schemes for performance, but mainly involving protocol design and communication load, not involving degree of parallelism and speedup ratio; some other research aiming at lookahead and task decoupling did improve the degree of parallelism, but didn't consider how to maximize the degree of parallelism and speedup ratio of simulation.

Aiming at how to relax the synchronization constraint for time management, some research has been done. Some researchers (Sokol [13], Rao [14]) just ignored the sequential relationship of events, which may result in abnormal causal logic and is not suitable for analysis simulation. Some researchers (Fujimoto [15], Beraldi [16]) took time interval as a substitute for precise time stamp, and took full advantage of uncertainty about time information to improve the performance of time management. Some other researchers (Lee [17], Cai [18]) adopted causal sequential relationship to substitute time-stamp sequential relationship so as to reduce task coupling and promote simulation performance. Chen [19] proposed a hierarchical federation structure based on causal sequential relationship to promote simulation performance. However, the methods based on time interval or causal sequential relationship can't guarantee enough simulation precision or completely correct causal logic. In addition to this, the above research didn't take maximizing simulation speedup ratio as an objective.

In respect of distributed simulation standards, SIMNET project [20] adopted distributed simulation for the first time to establish virtual battlefield environments used for soldier training. Beginning from this project, a series of distributed simulation protocols and standards have been developed. SIMNET project directly led to the forming of DIS(Distributed Interactive Simulation) standard(IEEE1278.1). Subsequently developed ALSP(Aggregate Level Simulation Protocol) standard used the SIMNET's concepts of model reusing and interoperation for distributed simulation applications(e.g. war game, etc.). DIS and ALSP are finally replaced by HLA(High Level Architecture) standard(IEEE1516), which was established by United States Department of Defense. HLA is now widely used for many distributed simulation applications such as training, analysis, test and evaluation. However, HLA is mainly established for system interoperation and reusing, not aiming at maximizing simulation efficiency and speedup ratio.

Aiming at real-time simulation and HIL simulation, there has also been a lot of research. Wuerfel [21] researched the performance problem of HLA for the first time, and pointed out its shortcoming in performance. McLean and Fujimoto [22] designed a real-time distributed simulation middleware for HIL simulation application. Brutzman and Zyda [23, 24] designed VRTP(virtual reality transfer protocol) in order to overcome the shortcoming of TCP and UDP and adapt to the requirement of distributed real-time interaction. Beginning with real-time object library, Gill and Ryan [25, 26] designed related method for real-time simulation. Fujimoto [27] and Ferenci [28] adopted shared-memory multiprocessor and cluster computing platform to implement high-performance simulation computing. Zhao [29] introduced QoS feature into RTI(Runtime Infrastructure), so as to make a real-time extension for HLA RTI. Azzedine [30, 31, 32] proposed a design method for real-time RTI based on RT-DEVS(real-time discrete event system specification), and adopted dynamic-thread-pool based load balancing strategy to improve RTI's performance. The problem is, the above research mainly focused on network performance, OS(operating system) performance, basic-level software performance and QoS features of RTI, but didn't aim at problems related to parallelism such as task decoupling and speedup ratio. RTI' QoS mechanism is important for real-time distributed simulation, however, if the speedup ratio of simulation can't be higher than 1, RTI' QoS mechanism can't take effect and real-time simulation can't be achieved. So, optimization problem of simulation speedup ratio is another fundamental problem for realizing large-scale HIL simulation. This paper mainly addresses this problem.

3. THE FORMAL DESCRIPTION FRAMEWORK OF DISTRIBUTED SIMULATION

3.1 Overall Description

In order to give a formal analysis for optimization problem of distributed simulation's speedup ratio, we must first establish a formal description framework of distributed simulation. In this framework, the target and pivotal structure of distributed simulation will be defined formally, so that the basic requirements for time management of distributed simulation can be concluded.

The formal description framework of distributed simulation is defined in the way as follows: First, the formal description method of target system should be considered. Second, the formal description of single simulator is given as a basis for distributed simulator. Finally, the formal description of distributed simulator is given based on single simulator. The relationship of target system, single simulator and distributed simulator can be shown as follows:

$$\text{Target System} \backsim \text{Single Simulator} \backsim \text{Distributed Simulator} \quad (1)$$

The above symbol "$\backsim$" means some similarity relationship, which embodies simulation effect and objective. The key point here is that the formal description of single simulator is taken as an intermediary between target system and distributed simulator.

3.2 Formal Description of Single Simulator

When considering discrete-event simulation, target system is essentially a discrete-event system. Since automata theory is a basic and general theory for describing and analyzing discrete-event systems, target system as well as single simulator and distributed simulator will be formally described in the framework of automata theory.

Mealy automaton is the basic and standard form for automaton with output, so it is taken as a fundamental element in the formal description framework. The definition of Mealy automaton is first given as follows:

DEFINITION 1(Mealy automaton): A **Mealy automaton** is a six-tuple as follows:

$$M = (X, E^{in}, E^{out}, \delta, \lambda, x_0) \quad (2)$$

where

(i) X is a finite nonempty set of states;
(ii) E^{in} is a finite nonempty set of input events;
(iii) E^{out} is a finite nonempty set of output events;

(iv) $\delta : (E^{in} \times X) \to X$ is called the transition function;

(v) $\lambda : (E^{in} \times X) \to E^{out}$ is called the output function;

(vi) x_0 is the initial state.

□

Based on Mealy automaton, a target system is defined formally as follows:

DEFINITION 2(target system): A **target system** of distributed simulation is formally described as a Mealy automaton:

$$M_t = (X_t, E^{in}{}_t, E^{out}{}_t, \delta_t, \lambda_t, x_{t0}) \quad (3)$$

□

A single simulator can also be directly described by a Mealy automaton. However, since single simulator has more in-depth general structure, we will not only simply describe a single simulator as a Mealy automaton, but use Mealy automaton as a core element for formal description of single simulator.

DEFINITION 3(single simulator): A **single simulator** is a quintuple as follows:

$$SIM_s = (M_s, t_s, g_s, h_s, Q_s) \quad (4)$$

Where

(i) M_s is a Mealy automaton used to implement the core behavior of the single simulator:

$$M_s = (X_s, E^{in}{}_s, E^{out}{}_s, \delta_s, \lambda_s, x_{s0}) \quad (5)$$

(ii) t_s is the current timestamp of the single simulator SIM_s. Compared to Mealy automaton, the main extension of single simulator is that it adds timestamp mechanism to the formal model. For this goal, every input or output event will be added a timestamp. A timestamp is a real number with the unit "second". t_s is defined as the timestamp of the latest input event:

$$t_s = e^{in}{}_{latest}.TimeStamp \quad (6)$$

(iii) $g_s : (E^{in} \times X) \to R$ is a function to add timestamp information to the output events. For output event $e^{out} = \lambda_s(e^{in}, x)$, $e^{out}.TimeStamp = t_s + g_s(e^{in}, x)$. In other words, $g_s(e^{in}, x)$ is the increment from current timestamp to the timestamp of output event $e^{out} = \lambda_s(e^{in}, x)$.

(iv) $h_s : (E^{in} \times X) \to \{inner, outer\}$ is an indicator function to indicate whether an output event $e^{out} = \lambda_s(e^{in}, x)$ of the Mealy automaton M_s is an output event of the single simulator SIM_s. If $h_s(e^{in}, x) = inner$, then the event $e^{out} = \lambda_s(e^{in}, x)$ will be forwarded to the internal queue Q_s of the single simulator. If $h_s(e^{in}, x) = outer$, then the event $e^{out} = \lambda_s(e^{in}, x)$ will be forwarded to outside of the single simulator.

(v) Q_s is a queue for events with timestamps. Events in this queue will be sorted according to the events' timestamps. And when the single simulator runs, the event with the earliest timestamp can be popped out and sent to the Mealy automaton. Events with timestamps earlier than the current timestamp t_s can't be inserted to the queue.

□

The structure of single simulator can be shown in Fig.1.

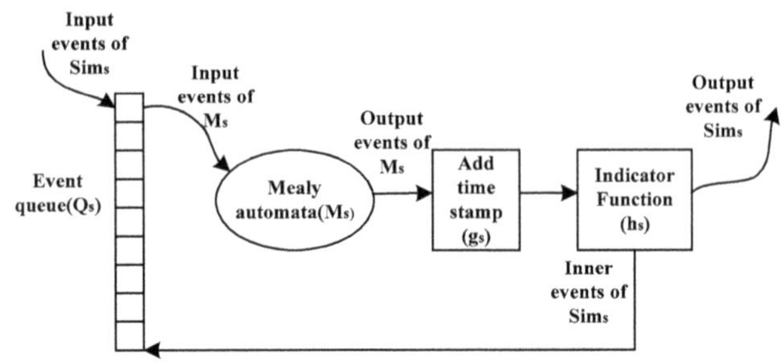

Figure 1. Structure of single simulator.

3.3 Formal Description of Distributed Simulator

Based on the formal description of single simulator, we can establish the formal description of distributed simulator. First of all, the constraint condition of distributed simulator which will be established should be clarified. In section 3.1, the relationship between target system, single simulator and distributed simulator has been mentioned. Here, the similarity relationship "∽" can be defined more clearly.

DEFINITION 4(simulation similarity relationship): In the range of analysis simulation, a **simulation similarity relationship** "∽" can be defined as follows: For specific input-output level, if when arbitrary sequence of events is input to system A and system B, we can get the same sequence of output events from system A and system B, then we say system A and system B have a simulation similarity relationship, shown as:

A ∽ B

□

Base on the above definition, the constraint conditions of distributed simulator which will be established can be given as follows:

(a) The distributed simulator should have a simulation similarity relationship with the corresponding single simulator, which means they should have the same input-output behavior.

(b) The distributed simulator should be deployed on multiple computers, so the single Mealy automaton in single simulator should be split into multiple Mealy automatons in distributed simulator.

In order to establish the formal description of distributed simulator under the above two constraint conditions, in the remaining part of this section, the single Mealy automaton in single simulator will be split into multiple Mealy automatons under the constraint condition(a). In this way, the structure of basic distributed simulator can be shown in Fig.2.

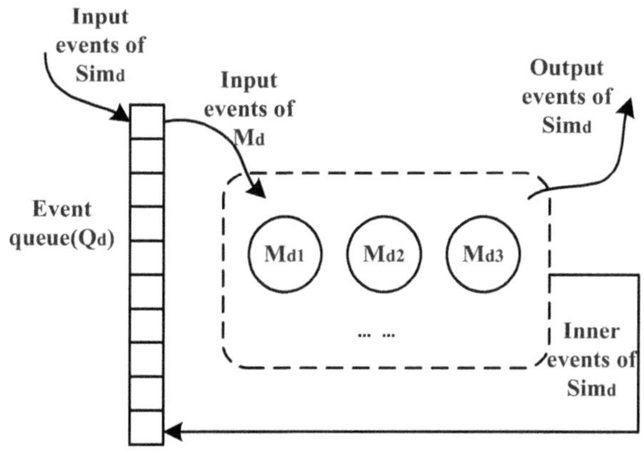

Figure 2. Structure of basic distributed simulator.

The steps for establishing the distributed simulator are stated as follows:

Step 1(state space splitting): For single simulator, suppose there is a memory to store the Mealy automaton's state. For distributed simulator, this memory must be split into multiple memories, each of which is used to store one Mealy automaton's state of the distributed simulator. In this way, the state of single simulator can be stored in a distributed pattern. That is, the state space of single Mealy automaton M_s is split into multiple state spaces corresponding multiple Mealy automatons $M_{di}(i=1,2,...,n)$. Here, n is the number of Mealy automatons in the distributed simulator (i.e. the number of simulation nodes in the distributed simulation system). This problem can be formally described as follows:

DEFINITION 5(state space splitting): State space splitting of a Mealy automaton M_s means there are multiple surjections $f_i : X_s \to X_{di}(i=1,2,...,n)$ which map single state space into multiple state spaces(X_{di} is the state space of Mealy automaton M_{di}), satisfying the following condition: there exists a bijection $f : X_s \to X_{d1} \otimes X_{d2} \otimes \cdots \otimes X_{dn}$ ($\otimes$ means cartesian product) s.t. $\forall x \in X_s$, $f(x) = (f_1(x), f_2(x),..., f_n(x))$. A state space which can be split is named as separable state space.

□

Step 2(input event splitting): After state space splitting, the next important step is to split each input event of single Mealy automaton M_s into multiple input events for Mealy automatons $M_{di}(i=1,2,...,n)$, so that they have the same effect. This problem can be formally described as follows:

DEFINITION 6(local event): An input event $e^{in}{}_j$ of M_s is a **local event** in M_{dj} if the following conditions are satisfied:

$$\Pi = \{1,2,...,n\} \tag{7}$$

$$\Omega = \{i \mid \forall x \in X_s, x' = \delta_s(e^{in}{}_j, x), s.t. f_i(x) = f_i(x'), i \in \Pi\} \tag{8}$$

$$\Omega' = \Pi / \Omega \tag{9}$$

$$\Omega' = \{j\} \tag{10}$$

The intuitive meaning of the above conditions is: if an input event $e^{in}{}_j$ of M_s is a local event in M_{dj}, then this event will only affect M_{dj} 's state space and will not affect other Mealy automatons' state spaces.

□

DEFINITION 7(separable input event): An input event e^{in} of M_s is a **separable input event** if $|\Omega'| \neq 1$ (so e^{in} is not a local event), but the following condition is satisfied:

$$\text{for } \forall x_1, x_2 \in X_s,\ \delta_s(e^{in}, x_1) = x_1', \delta_s(e^{in}, x_2) = x_2'$$

$$f_j(x_1) = f_j(x_2) \Rightarrow f_j(x_1') = f_j(x_2'), \forall j \in \Omega' \tag{11}$$

This condition means: under the impact of input event e^{in}, the consequent sub state in X_{dj} is only determined by the original sub state in X_{dj}.

□

For separable input event, we have the following theorem.

Theorem 1: A separable input event e^{in} of single Mealy automaton M_s can be split into multiple input events for Mealy automatons $M_{dj}(j=1,2,...,n)$, so that they have the same effect.

Prove:

For a separable input event e^{in} of single Mealy automaton M_s, suppose $j \in \Omega'$, then the sub event $e^{in}{}_j$ can be defined as follows:

$$\delta_j(e^{in}{}_j, f_j(x)) = f_j(\delta_s(e^{in}, x)) \tag{12}$$

Since the condition in formula(11) is satisfied, the above formula(12) can uniquely define the sub event $e^{in}{}_j$, which is a local event.

In this way, if we see e^{in} as a function defined on X_s, shown as $e^{in} : X_s \to X_s$, then e^{in} can be seen as a composite function of $e^{in}{}_j(j \in \Omega')$, shown as $e^{in} = e^{in}{}_{j_1} \circ e^{in}{}_{j_2} \circ ... \circ e^{in}{}_{j_m} (\Omega' = \{j_1, j_2, ..., j_m\})$. This is because:

Since there exists a bijection $f : X_s \to X_{d1} \otimes X_{d2} \otimes \cdots \otimes X_{dn}$, X_s and $X_{d1} \otimes X_{d2} \otimes \cdots \otimes X_{dn}$ is isomorphic. So, e^{in} can be seen as a function defined on $X_{d1} \otimes X_{d2} \otimes \cdots \otimes X_{dn}$, shown as $e^{in} : X_{d1} \otimes X_{d2} \otimes \cdots \otimes X_{dn} \to X_{d1} \otimes X_{d2} \otimes \cdots \otimes X_{dn}$. $e^{in}{}_j$ is a function defined on X_{dj}, which can be extended to a function defined on $X_{d1} \otimes X_{d2} \otimes \cdots \otimes X_{dn}$, shown as $e^{in}{}_j : X_{d1} \otimes X_{d2} \otimes \cdots \otimes X_{dn} \to X_{d1} \otimes X_{d2} \otimes \cdots \otimes X_{dn}$. Based on the above definitions, it can be seen that e^{in} will only affect the sub state spaces $X_{dj}(j \in \Omega')$.

Because the condition in formula(11) is satisfied, the consequent state in X_{dj} is only determined by the original state in X_{dj}. Thus, when the event e^{in} is executed, the state's change can be divided into multiple stages: state change in X_{dj_1}, state change in X_{dj_2},..., state change in X_{dj_m}, which corresponds to the event splitting $e^{in} = e^{in}_{j_1} \circ e^{in}_{j_2} \circ ... \circ e^{in}_{j_m} (\Omega' = \{j_1, j_2, ..., j_m\})$. So, e^{in} and $e^{in}_{j_1} \circ e^{in}_{j_2} \circ ... \circ e^{in}_{j_m}$ have the same effect on the state space $X_{d1} \otimes X_{d2} \otimes \cdots \otimes X_{dn}$.

□

In step 2, the proving process of theorem 1 actually gives a method for input event splitting, which is indeed the splitting of transition function δ_s.

Step 3(output function splitting): The third step should be to split the output function λ_s, which is used to determine the output events. Suppose $\lambda_s(e^{in}, x) = e^{out}$, in order to split λ_s into multiple output functions for Mealy automatons $M_{dj}(j = 1, 2, ..., n)$, e^{out} must be first split into $e^{out}_{ij}(i, j = 1, 2, ..., n)$ using the method in step2. Here, i means e^{out}_{ij} is generated from M_{di}, and j means e^{out}_{ij} will affect M_{dj}. Then, in this way, the output function λ_s can be split into $\lambda_{ij}(i, j = 1, 2, ..., n) : \lambda_{ij}(e^{in}, x) = e^{out}_{ij}$, satisfying the following condition:

$$\forall e^{in}_1, e^{in}_2 \in E^{in}_s, \forall x_1, x_2 \in X_s$$

$$\text{if } \lambda_{ij}(e^{in}_1, x_1) = e^{out}_{ij1}, \lambda_{ij}(e^{in}_2, x_2) = e^{out}_{ij2}$$

$$(\eta_i(e^{in}_1) = \eta_i(e^{in}_2) \text{AND} f_i(x_1) = f_i(x_2)) \Rightarrow e^{out}_{ij1} = e^{out}_{ij2} \quad (13)$$

In the above formula, $\eta_i(e^{in})$ means getting e^{in}'s sub event for Mealy automaton M_{di} by input event splitting. The intuitive meaning of the above conditions is: the result of λ_{ij} will only be affected by the sub event and the sub state space for the Mealy automaton M_{di}. In this way, $\lambda_{ij}(e^{in}, x) = e^{out}_{ij}$ represents that the output event is generated from M_{di} and will be forwarded to M_{dj}. Based on λ_{ij}, g_s and h_s can be split correspondingly.

Step 4(event queue splitting): Through the above three steps, the events in the global event queue have been split into local events. Since a local event only has relation with the corresponding local Mealy automaton and has no relation with other Mealy automatons, the global event queue can be split into multiple local event queues and the execution effect of the simulator will not change.

DEFINITION 8(distributed simulator): A **distributed simulator** can be established from a single simulator by the above four steps. A distributed simulator can be formally described as follows:

$$SIM_d = (SIM_1, SIM_2, ..., SIM_n) \quad (14)$$

$$SIM_i = (M_{di}, t_{di}, g_{di}, h_{di}, Q_{di}) \quad (15)$$

$$M_{di} = (X_{di}, E^{in}_{di}, E^{out}_{di}, \delta_{di}, \lambda_{di}, x_{di0}) \quad (16)$$

$$\lambda_{di} = \{\lambda_{i1}, \lambda_{i2}, ..., \lambda_{in}\} \quad (17)$$

Here, SIM_i means the i th local simulator of the distributed simulator SIM_d. The structure of final distributed simulator is shown in Fig.3.

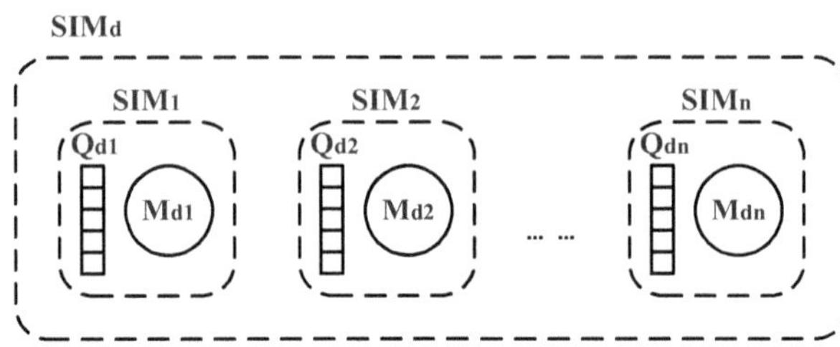

Figure 3. Structure of final distributed simulator.

□

Theorem 2: Under the Local Causality Constraint(LCC), the distributed simulator established by the above four steps will have the same input-output behavior as the corresponding single simulator.

Local Causality Constraint(LCC) can be stated as follows [5]:

"A discrete-event simulation, consisting of logical processes(LPs) that interact exclusively by exchanging time stamped messages obeys the local causality constraint if and only if each LP process events in non-decreasing timestamp order."

Prove:

When establishing distributed simulator SIM_d from SIM_s through the above four steps, each step guarantees that there is no change in simulator's external characteristics(see also step1-4 in the above), so the distributed simulator SIM_d will have the same input-output behavior as the corresponding single simulator SIM_s.

The reason that the LCC is needed is as follows:

In single simulator SIM_s, the event queue Q_s's operating mechanism guarantees that the events are processed in non-decreasing timestamp order, which corresponds to the real situation in physical world and is a sufficient condition for correct causal logic. After event queue splitting, though the events in different local event queues can be processed in arbitrary order, the events in the same local event must still be processed in non-decreasing timestamp order. So, LCC is a natural condition for distributed simulator SIM_d.

In addition, because there are output events with specific timestamps from one local simulator to another local simulator, LCC indeed contains the synchronization condition between different local simulators. So, from this perspective, LCC is also a basic condition for time management of distributed simulation.

□

4. TIME MANAGEMENT OPTIMIZATION FRAMEWORK FOR LARGE-SCALE DISTRIBUTED HIL SIMULATION

4.1 Non-Necessity Analysis for Local Causality Constraint(LCC)

Based on the formal description framework of distributed simulation, the basic condition for time management of distributed simulation (i.e. LCC) is concluded, which is the same as the previous research. However, the main contribution of this formal description framework is that it provides a channel for in-depth analysis of LCC.

In order to analyze the necessity of LCC, the process for establishing the distributed simulator should be reviewed, shown as Fig.4.

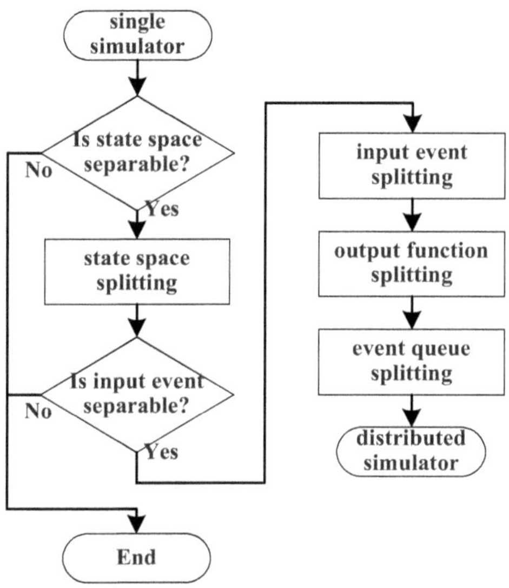

Figure 4. Flow chart for establishing distributed simulator.

In Fig.4, the most pivotal step is state space splitting, which determines the subsequent steps and the structure of distributed simulator. Once state space splitting is given, following the subsequent steps, the finally gained distributed simulator will have the same input-output behavior as the original single simulator. This condition is only a sufficient condition rather than sufficient and necessary condition. This problem can be analyzed from two aspects as follows:

a) Since the scheme of state space splitting determines the structure of distributed simulator, with different schemes of state space splitting, we will get different structures of distributed simulators. If the state space is firstly split into two sub state spaces, then a distributed simulator with two local simulators will be gained. This distributed simulator satisfies the condition of LCC and has the same input-output behavior as the original single simulator. But, obviously, it is not promising that a distributed simulation system with only two simulation nodes will have good performance. If we take the local simulator as single simulator and continue to split its state space, we will get distributed simulator with more refined structure, which is hopeful to have better performance. So, LCC is not a necessary condition for distributed simulation.

b) From another point of view, in single simulator, because events in the event queue must be processed one by one, serial processing of events is the main obstacle to improve performance. However, since some events are exchangeable, which means exchanging the processing order of the events will not change the execution results of the simulator, these events can be processed concurrently. This kind of parallelization is the main contribution point for performance improvement. If a distributed simulator with multiple local simulators is established, then most events in different local event queues are exchangeable. So, the degree of parallelism is excavated to a certain extent by event queue splitting. However, we can't determine whether there is still remaining degree of parallelism which can be excavated in local event queue. In other words, there may be still exchangeable events in local event queue, and these events needn't to be processed in timestamp order. So, LCC is only a sufficient condition rather than sufficient and necessary condition for time management of distributed simulation.

The non-necessity of LCC indicates that if we want to maximize the speedup ratio of distributed simulation, we can't only consider the problem inside the framework of LCC.

4.2 Optimization Method for Speedup Ratio of Distributed HIL Simulation

In order to give an overall analysis for the optimization problem of simulation speedup ratio, the establishment of a distributed simulation system should be divided into several stages:

a) Determine the structure of the target system, which is the basis for determining the structure of the distributed simulator.

b) Determine the number of simulation nodes and the partition method of the distributed simulator. Then establish the abstract structure of the distributed simulator. In this stage, there are two kinds of cases:

1) Suppose all the simulation nodes have the same computing power, and all the events have the same processing time.

2) Consider different simulation nodes have different computing power, and different events have different processing time.

In this paper, only the first kind of cases are considered.

c) Determine the time management strategy of the distributed simulator.

d) Considering the computing power of real computers, realize the abstract distributed simulator on real computers and networks.

The above four stages do cover every aspect of establishing a distributed simulation system, so we only need to consider things in these four stages. In addition, these stages are mutually independent, so they can be considered respectively. In the following part of this section, these stages will be respectively considered to maximize the speedup ratio of distributed simulation.

First, stage a) is only about the target system, so suppose stage a) as well as the total simulation time is determined in advance.

Then maximizing the speedup ratio is equal to minimizing the execution time of simulation task.

Second, since stage d) has no relation with simulation algorithm, it will not be considered in this paper.

Stage c) and b) will be considered as follows:

4.2.1 Optimized Strategy for Time Management of Distributed HIL Simulation

Suppose stage a) and b) have already been determined, and the case 1) in stage b) is considered. Under this condition, an optimized strategy for time management of distributed HIL simulation should be designed to maximizing the speedup ratio in stage c).

According to the above analysis, in stage c), LCC is the only requirement for time management. (The non-necessity of LCC will be considered in stage b), but not here.) Under LCC, a local event queue only needs to guarantee that no external event from other event queues has earlier timestamp than current timestamp. To achieve this goal, each local event queue should know the earliest timestamp of events from other local event queues. Suppose $OutputTS(i,j)$ denotes the earliest timestamp of output events from the j th local event queue to the i th local event queue, $GALT(i)$ denotes the Greatest Available Logical Time of i th local event queue. $GALT(i)$ can be calculated as follows:

$$GALT(i) = \min_{j \neq i}(OutputTS(i,j)) \tag{18}$$

The i th local event queue is not allowed to process events whose timestamps are greater than $GALT(i)$, and $GALT$ is the only constraint for local event queue to process events. Since the goal is to minimize the execution time of simulation task, each local event queue should process events as soon as possible, and the $GALT(i)$ should be advanced as fast as possible. To achieve this, according to formula(18), $OutputTS(i,j)$ should be advanced as fast as possible. $OutputTS(i,j)$ is transmitted from the j th local event queue to the i th local event queue by OTP(Output Time Promise) messages, so the following theorem can be concluded:

Theorem 3: The sufficient and necessary condition for maximizing the speedup ratio in stage c) is: each local event queue must send OTP messages as soon as possible.

Remark (1): This theorem means OTP messages is the only kind of messages used for time management. And sending OTP messages is the only action needed for local event queue to realize time management. So the time management mechanism is very simple.

Remark (2): "send OTP messages as soon as possible" means once local event queue has ability to give a better $OutputTS(i,j)$, it should send the OTP message immediately. So, the opportunity for sending OTP messages is very important.

□

The main differences between this time management strategy and traditional time management strategies such as HLA are as follows:

a) There is no mechanism for "time advance request". Since the simulation time need to be advanced as fast as possible, a local event queue needn't tell others that it wants to advance the simulation time. Instead, it only needs to relax its constraint on time advance of other local event queues as soon as possible. This is an "I for everyone, everyone for me" running strategy.

b) There is no explicit lookahead concept. The lookahead concept is indeed implicitly contained by the OTP messages. However, the OTP message directly gives the final output time rather than current time plus lookahead. This mechanism provides enough flexibility for advancing GALT as fast as possible.

c) In order to achieve higher speedup ratio, the amount of time management messages will be larger than that of traditional methods. However, for HIL simulation in LAN, this is not a problem.

4.2.2 Sub-Optimized Strategy for Task Partition of Distributed HIL Simulation

Because complete optimization for task partition of distributed simulation is a very hard and complex problem, in this section of this paper, we only consider a sub-optimized strategy as a preliminary scheme.

Suppose the number of simulation nodes (denoted as n) is given. The goal considered here is to divide the simulation task into n parts to achieve a good overall performance. In this case, the distributed simulator will have n local simulators.

Considering from engineering practice, the target system for simulation always has a natural partition. In this natural partition, a sub system commonly corresponds to a device, an object or a module etc., which has obvious boundary in physical space or logical function. In general, the number of parts under this natural partition (denoted as m) is larger than the given number of simulation nodes (i.e. n). So, the problem is translated into the following one: How to divide the m natural parts of target system into n sub systems (m>n) to form a distributed simulator, so as to achieve a good overall performance? This problem can be shown in schematic Fig.5.

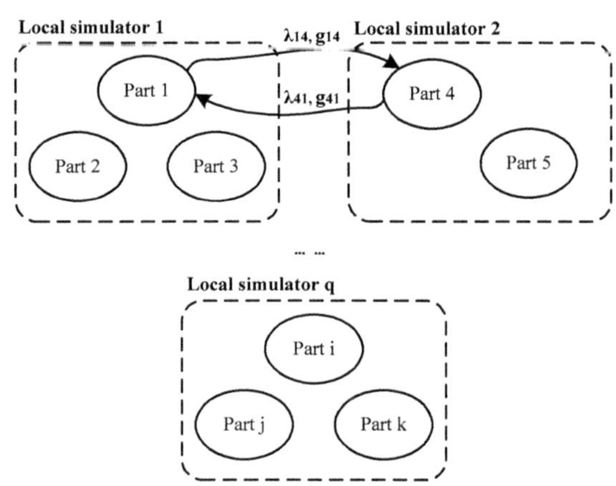

Figure 5. Problem description of simulation task partition.

In the situation of natural partition, we can see the target system as a distributed simulator with m local simulators. Thus, the only connection between different natural parts is λ_{ij} and g_{ij} mentioned in section 3.3. If g_{ij} is small, it means part i has a strong constraint on part j's time advancing. Oppositely, if g_{ij} is large, it means part i has a weak constraint on part j's time advancing. So, we can define minimum value of g_{ij} and g_{ji} as a measurement of coupling between part i and part j, shown as follows:

$$c_{ij} = c_{ji} = \min(\min(g_{ij}), \min(g_{ji})) \quad (19)$$

Based on this concept, the sub-optimized strategy for task partition of distributed HIL simulation can be stated as follows:

Task partition strategy for distributed simulation:

In order to get "n+1" partition from "n" partition, select the maximal $c_i = \min_{j \neq i}(c_{ij})$,(j and i are in the same local simulator) and separate the part i from others to form a new simulator.

Remark: This strategy does not consider the problem of load balancing. For engineering practice, the final partition result should be adjusted considering the factor of load balancing.

□

5. APPLICATION EXAMPLE

In order to verify the effect of the method proposed in this paper, we adopt the distributed HIL simulation system for CTCS-3 (Chinese Train Control System Level 3) as an application example. And the method proposed in this paper is compared to the time management mechanism of HLA.

CTCS-3 is a computer-based control system used to ensure the running safety of high-speed railway. CTCS-3 consists of ground devices, on-board devices, track-side devices and train-ground communication devices, which has the typical features of large-scale complex engineering system. The CTCS-3 HIL simulation system has been built as a basic environment for line-level CTCS-3 integration testing, which is a typical application of large-scale distributed HIL simulation. In this application example, we adopt data from a test line, and the structure and parameters of the simulation environment are shown in Table 1. The parameters of simulation node are shown in Table 2, and the algorithms of time advance are shown in Fig.6.

Table 1. Structure and parameters of the simulation environment

Node No.	Model Type	Model Number
Node 1~5	Rail line information model	5
	Track circuit model	406
	Balise model	188
	Point switch model	32
	Signaler model	117
Node 6~9	Train model	20
Node 10	Simulation interface	1
	Train factory	1
	Train scheduler	1

Table 2. Parameters of simulation node

Type	Parameters
CPU	Intel Core^{TM}, 2.01GHz (dual core)
Memory	DDR3 2GB
Network Interface	Ethernet 100Mbps
Development Environment	Java, JDK1.6
Initial Heap of JVM	2048MB

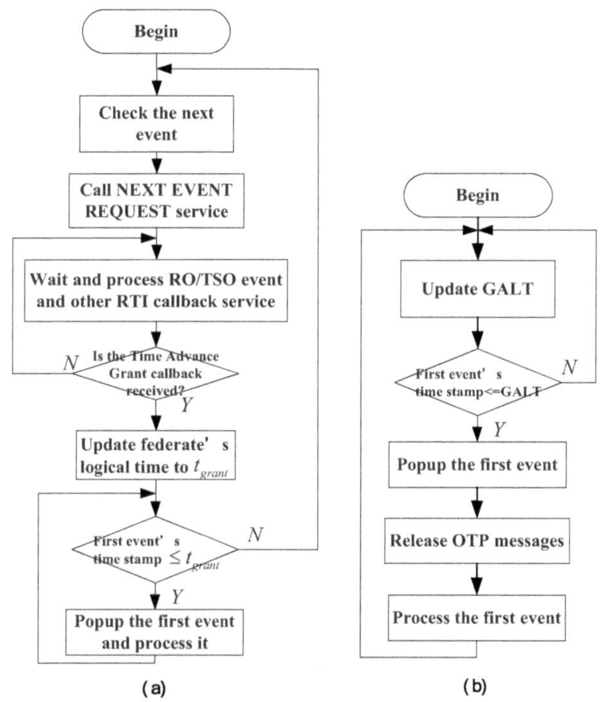

Figure 6. Time advance algorithms of HLA(a) and this paper(b)

In the comparison experiment, the CTCS-3 simulation platform runs in full speed and the simulation experiment lasts for about 160 seconds with two methods respectively. According to the recorded experimental data, the experimental results are shown in Fig.7.

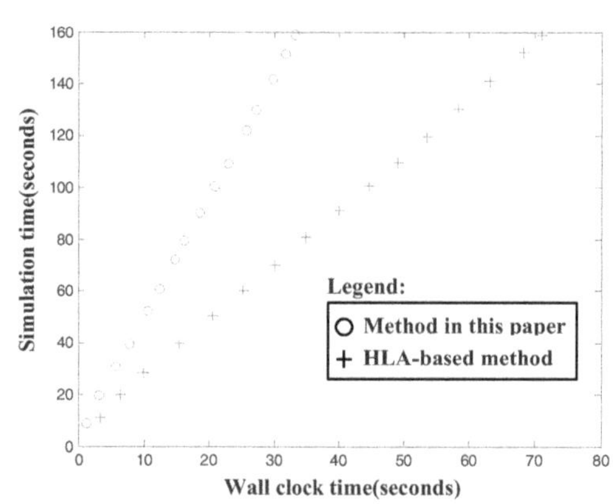

Figure 7. Experimental results for performance comparison.

The above figure shows the relationship between simulation time and wall-clock time, so the slope of the line represents the speedup ratio of simulation. In Fig.7, it can be seen that, compared to traditional HLA-based method, the method proposed in this paper has a much better performance.

6. CONCLUSION

Aiming at the application of large-scale distributed HIL simulation and the problem how to maximizing the speedup ratio, a time management optimization framework for large-scale distributed HIL simulation is proposed in this paper. The problem is focused on simulation speedup ratio, because an important necessary condition for realizing HIL simulation is that the speedup ratio of full-speed simulation must be greater than 1, and satisfying this condition becomes more and more difficult with the ceaselessly increasing scale of simulation. In order to formally analyze this problem, a new formal description framework of distributed simulation is given based on the automata theory. Then the basic objective and condition of distributed simulation is analyzed, which results in the conclusion that the classical Local Causality Constraint(LCC) for distributed simulation is only a sufficient condition rather than sufficient and necessary condition. Based on this, the optimization problem for simulation speedup ratio is radically analyzed and the overall strategy for this problem is given. Considering different conditions, two different levels of optimization mechanisms respectively for time advance and task partition are given. And finally, the application and experiment result shows the effectiveness of the proposed method. Further optimization of task partition, formal analysis of event's partial order relationship and system's scalability will be the future work.

7. ACKNOWLEDGMENTS

This work was partly supported by the NSFC under Grants 61104019 and 61004070, the National Key Technology R&D Program under Grant 2009BAG12A08 and Tsinghua University Initiative Scientific Research Program.

8. REFERENCES

[1] Richard M.Fujimoto. Parallel and Distributed Simulation System. Proceedings of the 33nd Winter Simulation Conference. Arlington, USA, 2001. pp.147-157.

[2] Bryant, R. E. Simulation of Packet Communication Architecture Computer Systems. Technical Report(TR-188) from Computer Science Laboratory, Massachusetts Institute of Technology, 1977.

[3] Chandy, K. M. and J. Misra. Distributed Simulation: A Case Study in Design and Verification of Distributed Programs. IEEE Transactions on Software Engineering 1978, 5(5), pp.440-452.

[4] Chandy, K. M. and J. Misra. Asynchronous Distributed Simulation via a Sequence of Parallel Computations. Communications of the ACM, 1981, 24(4), pp.198-205.

[5] Fujimoto, R. M. Parallel and Distributed Simulation Systems, Wiley Interscience, 2000.

[6] Deelman, E., et al. Improving Lookahead in Parallel Discrete Event Simulations of Large-Scale Applications using Compiler Analysis. Proceedings of the 15th Workshop on Parallel and Distributed Simulation. California, USA, 2001. pp.5-13.

[7] M.Kyoung Chung, C.Min Kyung. Improving Lookahead in Parallel Multiprocessor Simulation Using Dynamic Execution Path Prediction. Proceedings of the 20th Workshop on Principles of Advanced and Distributed Simulation (PADS'06). 2006. pp.11-18.

[8] ZHAO QinPing, ZHOU Zhong, LÜ Fang. Algorithm of simulation time synchronization over large-scale nodes. Science in China Series F: Information Sciences, 2008, 51(9), pp.1239-1255.

[9] Adltyavijay Rathore, Balaji Balaraman, Xlaobing Zhao, et al. Development and Benchmarking of an Epoch Time Synchronization Method for Distributed Simulation. Journal of Manufacturing Systems. 2005, 24(2), pp.69-78.

[10] Alfred Park, Richard M. Fujimoto, Kalyan S. Perumalla. Conservative Synchronization of Large-Scale Network Simulations. Proceedings of the 18th Workshop on Parallel and Distributed Simulation (PADS'04). Kufstein, Austria, 2004. pp.153-161.

[11] Siming Lin, Xueqi Cheng, Jianming Lv. Micro-synchronization in Conservative Parallel Network Simulation. Proceedings of 22nd Workshop on Principles of Advanced and Distributed Simulation. 2008. pp.195-202.

[12] Ke Pan, Stephen John Turner, Wentong Cai, Zengxiang Li. A Hybrid HLA Time Management Algorithm Based on Both Conditional and Unconditional Information. SIMULATION. 2009, 85(9), pp.559–573.

[13] Sokol, L. M. and B. K. Stucky. MTW: Experimental Results for a Constrained Optimistic Scheduling Paradigm. Proceedings of the SCS Multiconference on Distributed Simulation. 1990, pp.169-173.

[14] Rao, D. M., et al. Unsynchronized Parallel Discrete Event Simulation. Proceedings of the Winter Simulation Conference. 1998, pp.1563-1570.

[15] Fujimoto, R. M. Exploiting Temporal Uncertainty in Parallel and Distributed Simulations. Proceedings of the 13th Workshop on Parallel and Distributed Simulation. 1999, pp.46-53.

[16] Beraldi, R. and L. Nigro. Exploiting Temporal Uncertainty in Time Warp Simulations. Proceedings of the 4th Workshop on Distributed Simulation and Real-Time Applications. 2000, pp.39-46.

[17] Lee, B.S., et al. A Causality Based Time Management Mechanism for Federated Simulations. Proceedings of the 15th Workshop on Parallel and Distributed Simulation. 2001, pp.83-90.

[18] Wentong Cai, Stephen J. Turner, Bu-Sung Lee. An Alternative Time Management Mechanism for Distributed Simulations. ACM Transactions on Modeling and Computer Simulation, 2005, 15(2), pp.109–137.

[19] Chunpeng Chen,Yiping Yao,Huaimin Wang. Hierarchical Federation Community and Time Management. SIMULATION. 2008, 84(7), pp.373–383.

[20] Miller, D. C. and J. A. Thorpe. SIMNET: The Advent of Simulator Networking. Proceedings of the IEEE, 1995, 83(8), pp.1114-1123.

[21] Wuerfel, Roger. A comparison of HLA and DIS Real-Time Performance. Proceedings of the Spring Simulation Interoperability Workshop. Orlando FL, 1998,

[22] Thom McLean, Richard Fujimoto, Brad Fitzgibbons. Middleware for Real-Time Distributed Simulations. Journal of Concurrency and Computation, 2004.

[23] Brutzman, Don, Zyda, Michael, Watsen, Kent, Macedonia, M. Virtual reality transfer protocol (vrtp) Design Rationale. Proceedings of the IEEE Sixth International Workshop on Enabling Technologies: Infrastructure for Collaborative Enterprises (WET ICE '97), Distributed System Aspects of Sharing a Virtual Reality workshop. Massachusetts, USA, 1997, pp.179-186.

[24] Watsen. Kent, Zyda. Michael. Bamboo - A Portable System for Dynamically Extensible, Networked, Real-Time, Virtual Environments. Proceedings of VRAIS 98, Atlanta, GA, 1998, pp.252-259.

[25] Gill, C., D. L. Levine, and D. C. Schmidt. The Design and Performance of a Real-Time CORBA Scheduling Service. The International Journal of Time-Critical Computing Systems, special issue on Real-Time Middleware, March 2001, 20(2).

[26] O'Ryan, C., D. C. Schmidt and J. R. Noseworthy. Patterns and Performance of a CORBA Event Service for Largescale Distributed Interactive Simulations. International Journal of Computer Systems Science and Engineering, 2001.

[27] Fujimoto, R.M. and P. Hoare. HLA RTI Performance in High Speed LAN Environments. Proceedings of the Fall Simulation Interoperability Workshop. Orlando, FL. 1998.

[28] Ferenci, S. and R.M. Fujimoto. RTI Performance on Shared Memory and Message Passing Architectures. Proceedings of the 1999 Spring Simulation Interoperability Workshop. Orlando, FL, 1999.

[29] Zhao, H. and N. D. Georganas. HLA Real-Time Extension. Proceedings of 5th IEEE International Workshop on Distributed Simulation and Real Time Applications. Cincinnati, Ohio, 2001.

[30] Azzedine Boukerche, Kaiyuan Lu. A Novel Approach to Real-Time RTI based Distributed Simulation System. Proceedings of the 38th Annual Simulation Symposium (ANSS'05), 2005.

[31] Azzedine Boukerche, Ahmad Shadid, Ming Zhang. A Formal Approach to RT-RTI Design Using Real Time DEVS. IEEE International Workshop on Haptic Audio Visual Environments and their Applications (HAVE 2007). Ottawa, Canada, 2007.

[32] Azzedine Boukerche, Ming Zhang, Ahmad Shadid. DEVS Approach to Real-time RTI Design for Large-scale Distributed Simulation Systems. SIMULATION, 2008, 84(5), pp.231–238.

Dynamic Resolution in Distributed Cyber-Physical System Simulation

Dylan Pfeifer
The University of Texas at Austin
2501 Speedway, Stop C0803
Austin, TX 78712, USA
011-512-232-4297
dcpfeifer@ieee.org

Andreas Gerstlauer
The University of Texas at Austin
2501 Speedway, Stop C0803
Austin, TX 78712, USA
011-512-232-8294
gerstl@ece.utexas.edu

Jonathan Valvano
The University of Texas at Austin
2501 Speedway, Stop C0803
Austin, TX 78712, USA
011-512-471-5141
valvano@mail.utexas.edu

ABSTRACT
Cyber-physical systems challenge distributed simulation techniques for reasons of the heterogeneous tools used to model system components at different levels of abstraction, each with potentially different notions of time. The SimConnect and SimTalk distributed cyber-physical system simulation tools meet the synchronization challenge of distributed simulation, but also offer dynamic resolution among coordinated simulators for tradeoffs in simulation speed versus accuracy. This paper discusses the dynamic resolution capabilities of SimConnect and SimTalk, and evaluates the tools in distributed simulation of a closed-loop motor control system. Results show selectable tradeoffs in speedup versus accuracy over non-dynamic coordination.

Categories and Subject Descriptors
I.6.8 [**Modeling and Simulation**]: Types of Simulation – *Combined, Distributed, Parallel.*

General Terms
Experimentation

Keywords
Kahn Process Networks, dynamic distributed hybrid co-simulation, heterogeneous co-simulation, co-simulation backplanes, cyber-physical system simulation, DC motor PID/PWM simulation

1. INTRODUCTION
Cyber-physical systems (CPS) are engineered systems that integrate computation and physical processes [1]. They inherit the field of real-time embedded systems and challenge modern electronic design automation [2] as computation elements continue to proliferate in quantity, decrease in area and power, and increase in system-on-chip (SOC) complexity. Heterogeneous by definition, cyber-physical systems are a challenge to simulate at the system level because a design may include hardware, software, mechanical, or even biological components [1]. While individual simulators may specialize in modeling some of these components, no single simulator yet performs superlatively in modeling all of them, especially as the complexity of components continues to grow in the diverse range of CPS [3][4][5]. For example, while a Spice 3.0-based simulator solution [6] may excel in modeling cyber-physical system analog electronics, it may not excel in modeling a microcontroller at an instruction-set accurate level of abstraction such as the TExaS [7] Freescale 9S12 simulator does. Therefore, cyber-physical system simulation can benefit from coordinating multiple different simulators, each specializing in an engineering domain required by the system.

Heterogeneous simulator coordination brings a range of challenges, principally the synchronization and causality challenge of independent simulators running with local time and independent state. Solutions to this challenge are given in the field of parallel and distributed simulation (PADS) [8][9][10][11]. Once the coordination challenge is overcome, a remaining challenge is to reduce the simulation time required, since some simulators can increase in simulation time exponentially as model complexity increases [12].

One means of PADS simulated time reduction is through dynamic time resolution, a service offered by the SimConnect and SimTalk distributed cyber-physical system tools [13][14]. In applying dynamic resolution to the distributed simulation of a closed-loop motor control system, we find speed up offered with the tools with a configurable tradeoff in speed versus accuracy.

2. RELATED WORK
SimConnect and SimTalk present a backplane based [15][16][17] solution to the distributed cyber-physical system challenges. The architecture of the tools, how they relate to previous backplane techniques, and how they perform among both multiple homogenous and heterogeneous simulators is covered in [13][14]. One benefit of the tools is the reduction of the backplane control structure to the properties of a Kahn Process Network (KPN) [18], simplifying implementation and enforcing simulation causality by limiting the tokens of the backplane KPN to a type defined as "interpolated events" (IEs). Interpolated events, covered in [14], provide compliance to the *local causality constraint* [8] in distributed simulation, but also enable dynamic time management during the simulation.

Previous results with SimConnect and SimTalk achieved distributed simulation speed up by increasing spatial distribution, increasing parallelism in the simulation model [12], or relaxing IE resolutions *statically* configured. In results of this paper, however, new speed-ups are obtained by *dynamic* resolution of the IE duration as the simulation proceeds.

SIGSIM-PADS'13, May 19-22, 2013, Montréal, Québec, Canada.

Infrastructure and support is added to the SimConnect/SimTalk tools achieve this capability. With dynamic resolution, time segments during the simulation can be "zoomed in" in event resolution or "zoomed out" at demand. A higher resolution means more synchronization traffic, for increased simulation time. Lower resolution means less synchronization traffic, so simulators achieve a faster local speed.

The potential speedup benefit of dynamic time management in distributed simulation is discussed in [19], with application specific solutions offered in [20][21][22]. However, for cyber-physical systems, the High Level Architecture (HLA)-based [23] techniques discussed in [19] require HLA support among cyber-physical system simulators, a development yet to be evaluated for the challenges discussed [14]. The SimConnect/SimTalk based solution to dynamic time management, by contrast, is straightforward through the interpolated event data type. Implementation of the service added less than 500 lines of C code to the tools from their code size given in [14].

In regard to interoperating with real-time distributed simulation systems (a feature supported by HLA [23] and former DIS-like solutions [25]), while SimConnect/SimTalk can support real-time interoperability and scaled wall-clock time execution, on the other hand, the domain challenge of cyber-physical system simulation state complexity currently prohibits simulating at speeds anywhere close to real-time or wall-clock time. That is, the micro-event focus of CPS engineering design, focusing on events and signals in the simulation space with kilohertz, megahertz or gigahertz frequencies results in simulation times that must run at "as fast as possible" speeds. Even simulating as fast as possible on current workstation-grade machines, the execution time of seconds of simulation time in the systems hosted by SimConnect/SimTalk still can take minutes of wall-clock time due to the computation time of connected CPS simulators (see Figure 16). Therefore, interoperability with real-time distributed simulations or systems with "humans in the loop" [25] is not yet a feature demanded of SimConnect/SimTalk CPS simulations. When the simulation can execute simulation time faster than wall-clock time, real-time wall-clock scaling can be enforced by the SimConnect backplane. This is a difference in domain focus required by CPS engineering design, even though it is still a PADS application. Further discussion of this domain challenge of CPS in regard to event focus is given in [14].

3. DYNAMIC RESOLUTION WITH INTERPOLATED EVENTS

The interpolated event type is defined in [13]. IEs are 3-tuple set elements (v, t_m, t_n) from the product set $V \times T \times T$, where $\{ V \}$ is a set of values, and $\{ T \}$ is a set of tags. This extends the value/tag "(v, t)" definition of an event covered in [24]. For a given interpolated event (v, t_m, t_n), the value v is defined to be constant on the interval $[t_m, t_n)$ specified in the IE, such that the tag set $\{ T \}$ is ordered. $\{ T \}$ is conventionally the real number set $\boldsymbol{R}^1$ in timed, event driven simulations, representing the simulation time stamp when an event occurs. For an interpolated event (v, t_m, t_n), the range $[t_m, t_n)$ assigns a "stable" time to the signal value v for producers and consumers.

If a simulator consumes an interpolated event (v, t_m, t_n), it may assume the value v is constant on the tag range $[t_m, t_n)$, and not need to input the value again until expiration time t_n. So, an interpolated event encapsulates both communication (the signal value) and synchronization (the start and end time). In terms of PADS synchronization, the expiration t_n value can be seen as a look ahead value [9] and lower bound on the t_m value on all future IEs posted on a FIFO. It can also be considered the *lower-bound time stamp* (LBTS) value [19] for input signal IEs in the HLA RTI conservative synchronization terminology [25]. An IE (v, t_m, t_n) can also be considered as the union of event (v, t_m) and the set of all Chandy/Misra/Bryant NULL messages [9][10] $\{ (t_i, \text{NULL}) \}$ such that $t_m < t_i < t_n$. Discussions of deadlock, synchrony, and blocking with IEs are given in [14].

The SimConnect backplane routes interpolated events from producer to consumers in a publish/subscribe client/server architecture. Signal producers and consumers are independently running simulators. Simulators connect to the SimConnect server through TCP/IP sockets and publish or subscribe interpolated events as they proceed in simulation. Mapped to nodes in a Kahn Process Network, simulators consume IEs, run, and produce IEs until the expiration tag of the last consumed IE. At this time point simulators sample their FIFOs again for a new IE. If their input FIFOs are empty, simulators block, enforcing the *local causality constraint* [8] because each simulator cannot advance in time beyond the expiration tags of IEs on its input FIFOs. Simulators may be distributed across any compute/network topology with TCP/IP services, and they share no run-time variables or state with each other. They only connect to the backplane through the SimTalk protocol and produce IEs to the backplane, or consume IEs from it, agnostic to other simulators in the distribution.

Selection of services to implement the networking and interoperability requirements of this hierarchy are flexible, but TCP/IP and BSD sockets were chosen for simulators offering an OS-level programming interface for familiarity and facility. The Message Passing Interface (MPI), for example, could be used to transport SimTalk IE messages, and the backplane could store IEs in a relational database such as MySQL, but implementation with socket programming and minimal library dependencies in the SimConnect backplane was desired. More examples and details of SimConnect and SimTalk backplane/simulator based configurations are given in [12][13][14].

Dynamic resolution can be achieved with interpolated events through two means. First, a signal producer has complete write authority over a posted t_n value, the expiration time of an IE (v, t_m, t_n). Therefore, a signal producer may vary this value anytime during the simulation based on internal knowledge of the signal's change frequency or some other application criteria. Changing the IE t_n value will change the time the consuming simulator of the IE next queries the backplane, there by changing the time of next synchronization. As t_n increases beyond t_m, the IE duration increases, and therefore the event resolution relaxes (the time between synchronizations on the IE signal increases). As t_n approaches, but yet is still greater than t_m, the IE duration decreases, so the event resolution increases (more synchronization events). This is similar to dynamically varying an HLA-based LBTS values [19], but with implementation simplicity.

A second method to achieve dynamic resolution with IEs is for the backplane, simulation operator, or another simulator to *command* a signal producer to change its $(t_n - t_m)$ duration for future IEs. In this way an agent may externally vary the IE duration of a signal producer, there by even throttling the rate of its incoming signals. External IE resolution change requests are registered to the backplane in the form of (*signal_name, time, resolution*) 3-tuples stored in the backplane. These can be entered at any time during the simulation through the SimTalk protocol to the backplane by any connected simulation participant.

For a backplane resolution change tuple (*signal_name, time, resolution*), the tuple specifies that for the signal specified by string *signal_name*, all IEs posted by the signal producer for which the IE t_n value is greater than or equal the tuple *time* value must have a duration value of $(t_n - t_m) = resolution$. If a series of resolution tuples is entered for a signal, such as the series (*signal_name*, t_0, r_0), (*signal_name*, t_1, r_1), (*signal_name*, t_2, r_2), (*signal_name*, t_3, r_3), such that $t_0 < t_1 < t_2 < t_3$, then for all IEs (v, t_m, t_n) of *signal_name* with $t_0 < t_n < t_1$, the duration of the IE, $(t_n - t_m)$ shall be value r_0. For all IEs (v, t_m, t_n) on *signal_name* such that $t_1 < t_n < t_2$, the duration of the IE, $(t_n - t_m)$ shall be value r_1, for all $t_2 < t_n < t_3$, the resolution shall be r_2, and so on. Therefore, a string of resolution tuples may be registered in the backplane for arbitrary IE resolution adjustment.

Because a signal producer has no idea what resolution tuples have been registered in the backplane, the backplane notifies the signal producer of a resolution change when its broadcasted local time (indicated an IE posted t_n value) reaches a time greater than or equal to resolution tuple time entry. The backplane then sends notification of a resolution change through a SimTalk "res" request message in response to the posted IE, a SimTalk "res [*signal_name*] [*value*]" message. Receipt of this message by any agent in the backplane indicates that the agent shall adjust the resolution $(t_n - t_m)$ of future IEs it is posting on *signal_name* to the value given in the [*value*] field of the message until further notice from the backplane. The simulator proceeds to post IEs at the new resolution value until its local time reaches another resolution tuple point, indicated by an IE t_n value. SimTalk "res" messages only occur at points of IE resolution change, so "res" messages are infrequent relative to IE "get" and "set" messages [13].

If a simulator itself posts a "res" message *to* the backplane, versus receiving one, it logs a new resolution tuple. In this way simulators may post resolution change requests to signal producers (or any broadcasted signal in the simulation), as well as adjust resolution on their own outgoing signals.

4. EXPERIMENT

4.1 Background and Purpose

In [14], a means was needed to evaluate the accuracy of a SimConnect/SimTalk hosted distributed simulation against a truth condition. The microcontroller-based, software PID/PWM controlled DC motor was chosen as the system to simulate because it contained sufficient model diversity (a microcontroller model, Spice electrical model, and Matlab/Simulink electro-mechanical model) to demonstrate SimConnect and SimTalk facility with heterogeneous simulation while also being a system with known behavior. The Matlab/Simulink-only simulation of the PID/PWM control system served as a single-simulator truth condition to evaluate the accuracy of the more realistic 3-simulator based simulation. However, the studies of [14] used static IE resolution. For this experiment, dynamic resolution is employed. The same system (DC motor control system) is chosen as the simulation target to have a means to evaluate accuracy. The 2-simulator representation of the system (TExaS and Matlab/Simulink) was selected for simplicity, and could be evaluated for accuracy against the statically controlled 2-simulator based system in [14].

To support dynamic resolution messaging, source code was added to the SimConnect backplane to implement resolution tuple storage and new SimTalk "res" message passing. Support for SimTalk "res" messages was also added to each SimTalk software plugin for the TExaS [7] and Matlab/Simulink simulators [26].

The PID/PWM microcontroller-based DC motor controller system in [14] was re-simulated in the 2-simulator case but with dynamic resolution. The setup of the model is repeated for illustration. For a control condition, the system is first modeled in a 1-simulator case with Matlab/Simulink.

4.2 1-Simulator setup

The DC motor is modeled in Simulink block-diagram form with summing, integrating, and gain blocks in Figure 1.

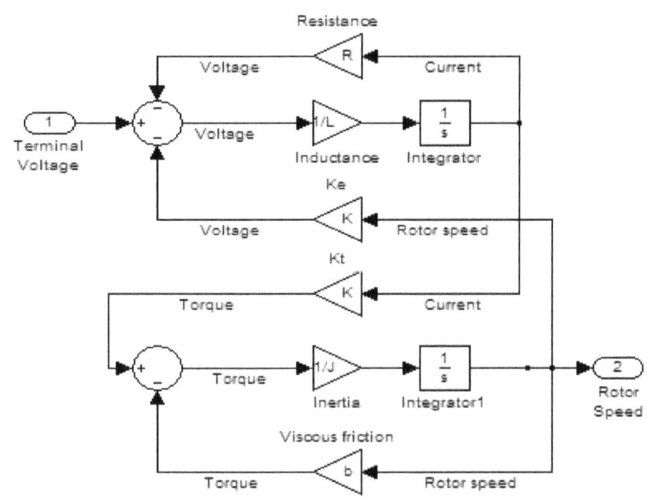

Figure 1. Simulink DC motor electro-mechanical model

The model is parameterized for the simulation as follows:

R	motor terminal electrical resistance	$1.0\ \Omega$
L	motor terminal inductance	0.001 H
K_t	torque constant	0.1 Nm/A
K_e	electrical constant	0.1 Nm/A
b	rotor viscous friction coefficient	$0.001\ \mathrm{Nm} \cdot \mathrm{s}$
J	rotor moment of inertia	$0.01\ \mathrm{kg} \cdot (\mathrm{m/s})^2$

Figure 2. DC motor model parameters

The model is driven with the Simulink PID continuous controller block in Figure 3, configured to a set point of half-speed 23.44 radians/s, 5 Volt output ceiling, with K_p, K_i, and K_d coefficients of 8, 2, and 1 respectively, with clamping anti-integrator windup. The closed-loop transient response is plotted in Figure 6.

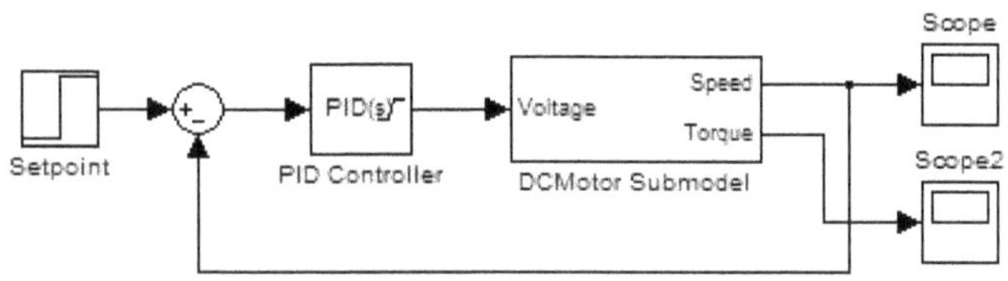

Figure 3. Simulink continuous PID controller

4.3 2-Simulator setup

For distributed modeling and increased realism, the controller is refined to a software-based PID difference-equation algorithm with PWM actuators hosted on the 9S12 microcontroller, simulated with TExaS at the cycle-estimating, instruction-set architecture (ISA) level. The SimConnect/SimTalk signal structure is given in Figure 4.

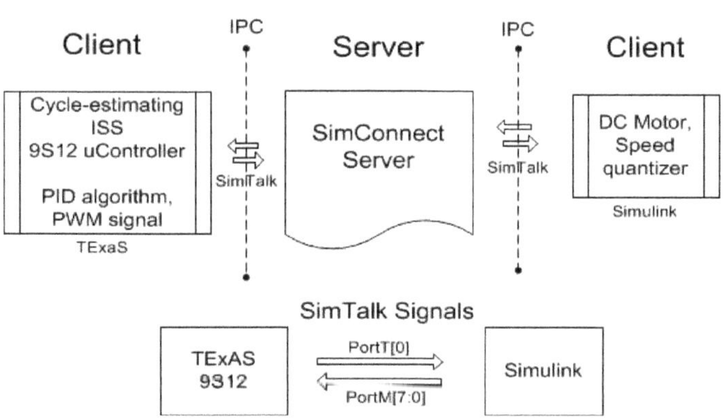

Figure 4. 2-Simulator configuration

The software-based PID algorithm in 9S12 assembly is adapted from [7]. Conversion of a continuous-time frequency-domain specified controller to a digital controller is covered in [27]. This refinement uses a free-running 1 kHz sampling rate PID main loop of 63 9S12 assembly instructions, and a total code length of 158 instructions. The algorithm also incorporates anti-integrator windup and output limit checking. The refined Simulink model is given in Figure 5. The "socket_input" and "socket_output" S-Functions register SimTalk signals PortT[0] and PortM[7:0] for exchange with the SimConnect server. The PortT[0] digital signal is the PWM wave generated by TExaS. The 0/1 signal is amplified to 5 Volts for application to the motor terminals. The PWM wave and voltage in this configuration is modeled as ideal (zero rise/fall time).

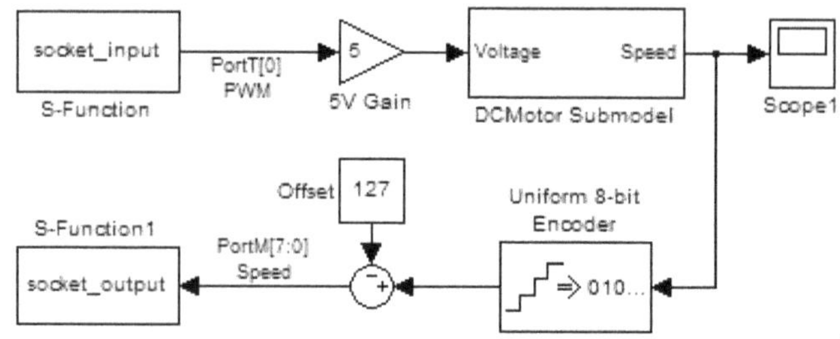

Figure 5. Simulink DC motor model with SimTalk I/O interface

5. RESULTS

The 2-simulator model is conducted first at a static 100 µs IE ($t_n - t_m$) resolution on signals PortT[0] and PortM[7:0]. The transient response is plotted against the Simulink-only classical continuous and cases in Figure 6 to verify the functionality of the distributed modeling of the digital PID/PWM microcontroller-based simulation versus the Simulink continuous-time 1-simulator controller.

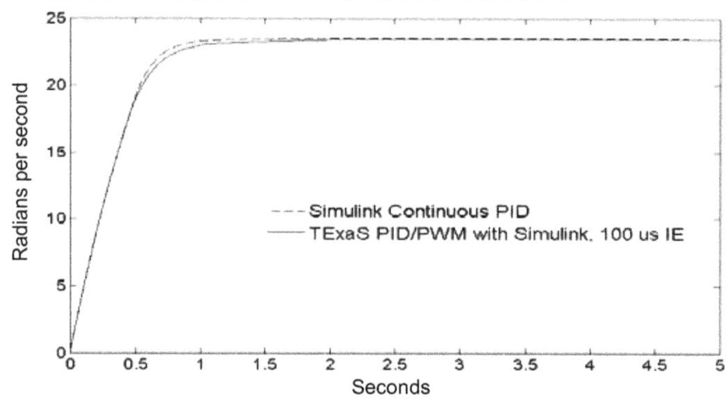

Figure 6. Model output speed versus time with Simulink-only and 2-simulator PID control model cases

In Figure 6, there is some departure from the continuous model because the applied terminal signal is a PWM wave from the 9S12 microcontroller in a software PID loop. However, the control profile shows set point agreement. The static 100 µs 2-simulator Case A is used as a baseline for checking dynamic resolution experiments, with simulation times given in Figure 16. In Case B, the static simulation localized to one machine to demonstrate the effect of network latency as a distribution cost. In Case C, the IE resolution is dynamically changed early in the simulation. The resolution begins at 100 µs IE resolution to set initial conditions, and is relaxed to 10 ms at simulation time 1 ms.

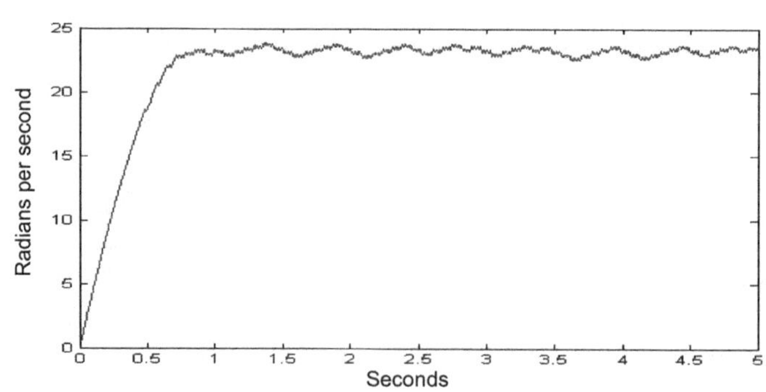

Figure 7. Case C model output speed versus time

Figure 7 shows set point approach, but steady state instability as Simulink and TExaS only receive signal updates every 10 ms (the relaxed IE duration). However, the simulation time decreases significantly, as shown in Figure 16.

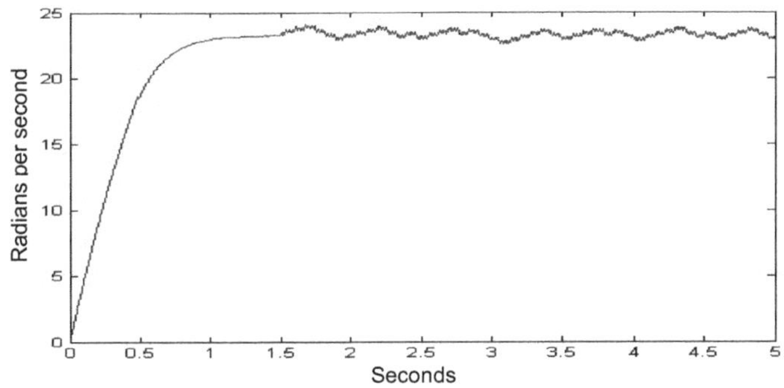

Figure 8. Case D model output speed versus time

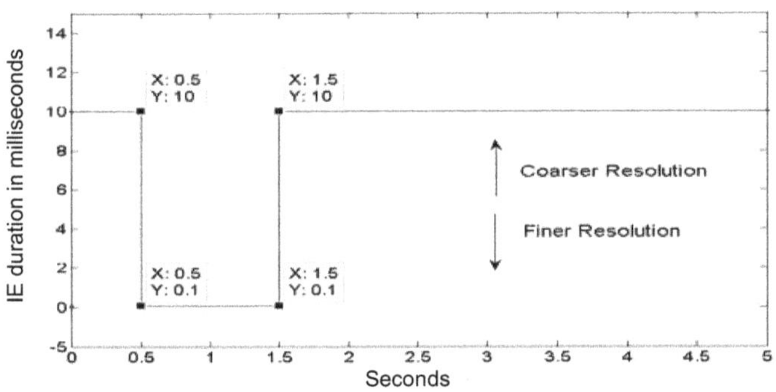

Figure 9. Case D dynamic IE duration change

In Case D, coarse resolution (10 ms IE) is used in the motor run-up phase (0 to 0.5) seconds, then finer resolution (100 μs IE) during the set point approach phase (0.5 to 1.5 seconds), then coarse resolution again in the steady state phase (1.5 to 5 seconds). The control profile matches the static high-resolution case up to 1.5 seconds, where the controller is unstable again in the error due to relaxed resolution (10 ms IE signals). The simulation time is still decreased (Figure 16).

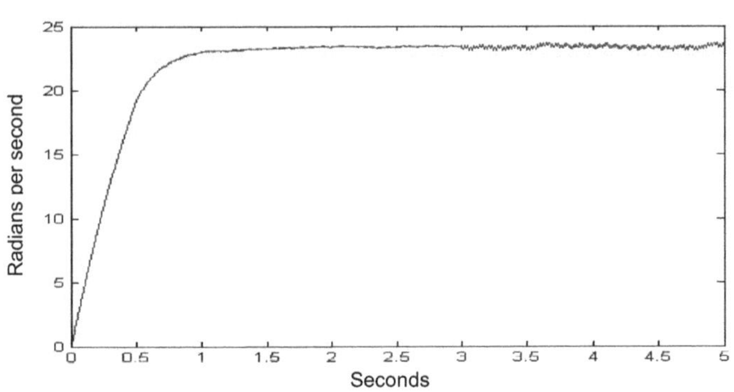

Figure 10. Case E model output speed versus time

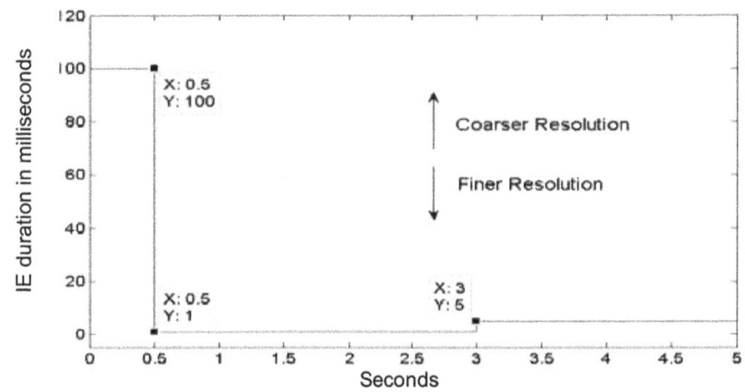

Figure 11. Case E dynamic IE duration change

In Case E, coarse resolution IE (100 ms) is used to 0.5 seconds in the simulation, then finer resolution (1 ms IE) as the set point approaches, and then 5 ms IE resolution in the steady state after 3 seconds. The instability around the set point is reduced over the Case D 10 ms IE resolution after 3 seconds, but variance persists due to controller only getting samples once in every five PID loops (5 ms IE with a 1 kHz PID loop).

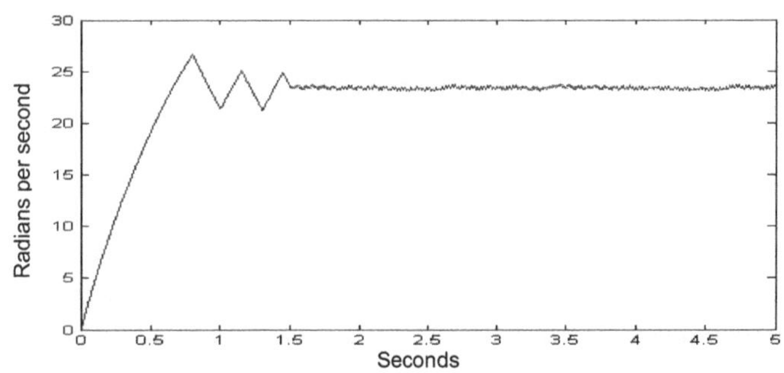

Figure 12. Case F model output speed versus time

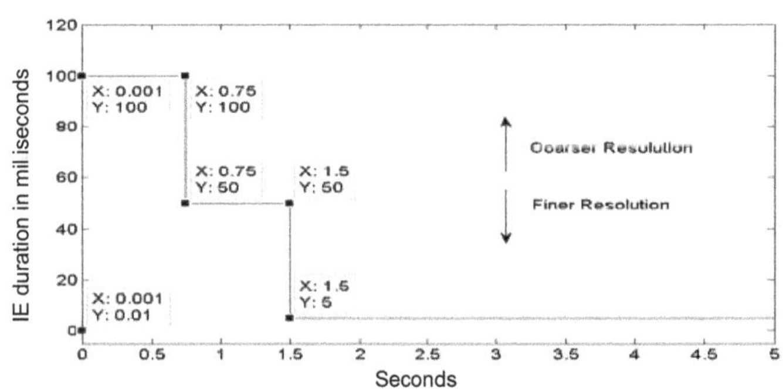

Figure 13. Case F dynamic IE duration change

In Case F, we suppose coarse resolution might apply during the run-up and set point approach phases. Coarse resolution IE (100 ms) from 0 to 0.75 seconds is applied, medium resolution (50 ms IE) from 0.75 to 1.5 seconds, and then 5 ms IE resolution after 1.5 seconds. Figure 12 shows that although the control oscillates coarsely under low resolution, the oscillation decreases significantly when the resolution increases around controller steady state set point.

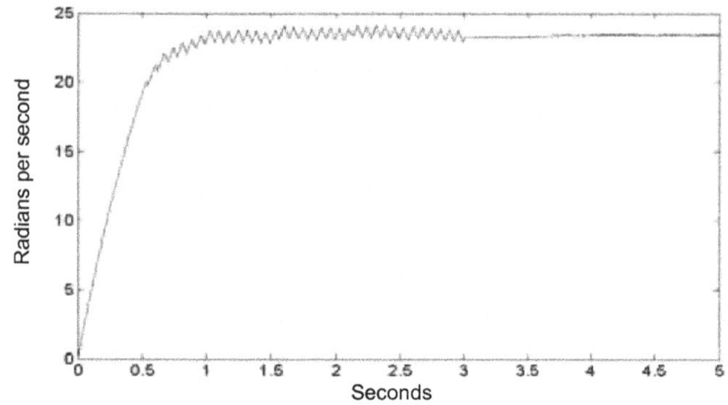

Figure 14. Case G model output speed versus time

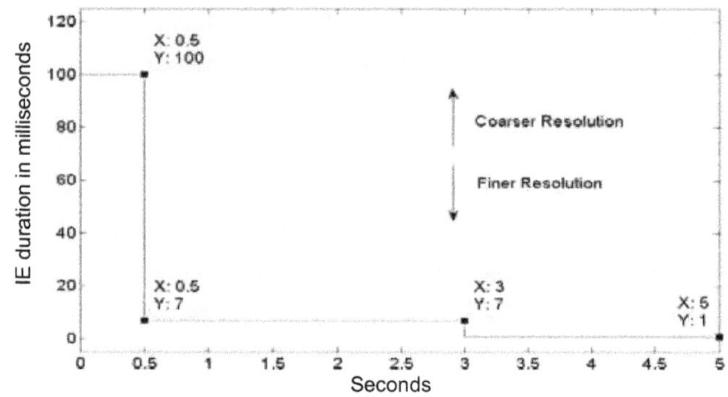

Figure 15. Case G dynamic IE duration change

In Case G, coarse resolution IE (100 ms) is used from 0 to 0.5 seconds, finer resolution IE (7 ms) approaching the set point, and then 1 ms IE resolution after 3 seconds. The steady state oscillation decreases significantly as the PID controller receives IE updates ever 1 ms. Noise still exists due to 1 ms IE sampling of the PortT[0] PWM wave that has a higher duty cycle resolution than 1 ms. However, Case F shows that we can *arbitrarily* bring down the error term around the set point by increasing the resolution, while using coarse resolution in the run-up and approach phases.

In Figure 16, simulation runtime counters and the speed up multiplier of each experiment (A through G) is plotted against the static resolution simulation time of Case A. The maximum percent error of measurement around the set point value after 3 seconds for each experiment is also plotted, with Cases A and B considered the truth condition. Figure 16 shows that percent error of around the set point can be reduced arbitrarily while decreasing simulation time by dynamic resolution. In the best trial, Case G, there is a maximum 0.21 percent error of measurement around the set point but with a 6.14 times faster simulation time than the static resolution Case A.

In regard to IE token communication cost, Figure 16 shows that distribution (2 machines versus 1 machine in Cases A and B) affects simulation time, since IEs must travel over a local area network. However, even with this cost, dynamic resolution still decreases simulation time in Cases C through G over the static resolution cases. The SimConnect server in all cases but B ran on GNU/Linux 2.6.16 kernel Intel Xeon 2.93 GHz machine. The TExaS and Matlab/Simulink simulators ran on a Windows 8 OS Intel Core i5 2.50 GHz laptop computer.

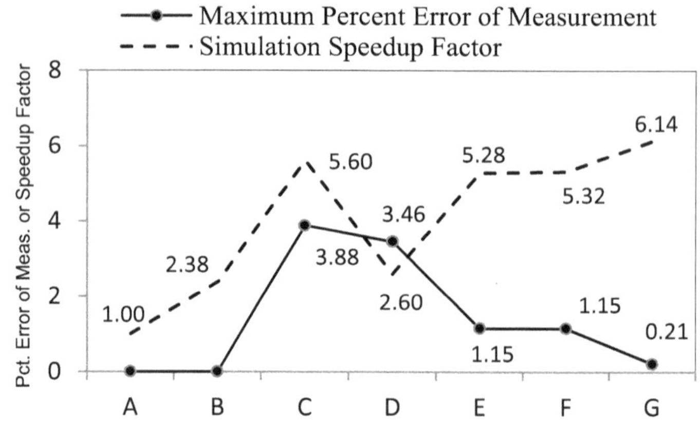

A	B	C	D	E	F	G	H	I
A. S,T,I	100 μs	3	4000	20	11.8	5.0	13:35	2
B. S,T,I	100 μs	3	4000	20	11.8	5.0	5:51	1
C. S,T,I	(dyn)	3	4.8	20	11.8	5.0	2:29	2
D. S,T,I	(dyn)	3	800	20	11.8	5.0	5:21	2
E. S, T,I	(dyn)	3	24	20	11.8	5.0	2:38	2
F. S,T,I	(dyn)	3	6.5	20	11.8	5.0	2:37	2
G. S, T,I	(dyn)	3	19.7	20	11.8	5.0	2:16	2

Column Legend

A Experiment case and distributed simulators : Simulink(S), TExaS(T), SimConnect server(I)
B Static IE resolution, or (dyn) if dynamic resolution
C Number of instantiated SimTalk connectors
D Number of SimTalk messages (times 10^3)
E Number of 9S12 cycles (times 10^6)
F Number of 9S12 instructions (times 10^6, rounded 10^5)
G Simulated Time (seconds)
H Simulation Execution Time (minutes: seconds)
I Number of host machines

Figure 16. Simulation times, configurations and traffic

In regard to scaling, generally, SimConnect can service connections from simulators hosted anywhere on the Internet. As the number of connected, coordinated simulators increases, the latency of servicing SimTalk messages in the SimConnect backplane increases, since it must maintain and service more socket connections. SimConnect presently services socket states in a serial, cyclic loop. This latency does not include SimTalk message delivery latencies, which depend on the network. The scaling profiles of simulation time versus number of connected simulators is under study, but in the experiments of [13], which coordinated up to 128 independent Ngspice simulators, the latency of simulation was dominated by the execute time of individual simulators as they ran in each time slice specified in an IE. In [12], the message servicing and delivery cost of the simulation latency was still less than one percent of the total latency from one IE consumption to the next measured in a consuming simulator. Therefore, scaling is presently a function of the compute time of individual simulators. We have not yet found an inflection point where the backplane message servicing latency dominates the simulation, but from the results of [13] we anticipate it will require many hundreds of simulators. This estimate does not include pathological cases where a network fault or distribution abnormality introduces an asymmetrical message delivery delay.

5.1 Interpretation of Results

Figure 16 emphasizes the simulation speed up potential offered by dynamic resolution, essentially relaxing resolution during periods of infrequent inter-simulator signaling, and increasing resolution during frequent signaling. While speed up with dynamic resolution control is not unique to this study, the benefit of the SimConnect/SimTalk approach is that dynamic resolution is straightforward to implement using the KPN/IE dataflow dynamics that SimConnect/SimTalk strictly adheres to, as long as a blocking-API can be applied to connected simulators through a SimTalk connector.

A limitation, however, is that the interpolated event (IE) data token incurs similar limitations and accuracy tradeoffs of an ideal sample-and-hold based analog-to-digital converter. That is, the IE is a sample-and-hold, piecewise-constant based representation of the underlying signal. Primarily this results in delay of signal change information that is at minimum the duration of the IE. The cost of delay inaccuracies are seen in [12]. The cost of quantization error in control systems with sample-and-hold signal converters is covered in [27]. Therefore, whether IEs are varied statically with repeated simulations, or varied dynamically in one simulation per this study, there is an unavoidable, inversely proportional speed-versus-accuracy tradeoff with the KPN/IE approach. The effect of this may be negligible for some systems, particularly if the IE resolution is on the order of the minimum clock period of the simulated system, or it may be completely determinable based on bandwidth and gain parameters for control systems [27]. However, the approach currently does not have a means to guarantee a metric of accuracy that is independent of the system being simulated. That is, the accuracy effects of IE resolution are highly tied to the coupling interface of the system under simulation where the signal couple is represented by an IE. Fortunately, analog-to-digital converters are a common coupling point in CPSs, lending to IE representation. However, if a clocked digital gate or storage element is represented by an IE, the IE duration can introduce a delay of the circuit change state, or completely mask the change state. So, speed-versus-accuracy tradeoffs are presently system-by-system determined.

Another limitation is that the system requires connectable simulators to offer an OS-level programming interface for the SimTalk connector. Fortunately, preeminent simulators in CPS simulation offer this.

6. SUMMARY AND CONCLUSIONS

Two independent simulators, TExaS and Matlab/Simulink, were coordinated with the SimConnect/SimTalk tools to model a closed loop, software-based PID/PWM control system with Freescale 9S12 microcontroller ISA and 2nd order DC motor model realism. Dynamic resolution demonstrated up to 6.14 times speed up over the non-dynamic case, with configurable tradeoffs in speed up versus accuracy. Dynamic resolution implementation in the SimConnect/SimTalk tools was straight forward with the interpolated event (IE) data type and SimTalk "res" messages. In the space of simulated software-based PID control, these results show that more coarse resolution is tolerable while the PID error value is high, while a higher resolution is required as the controller settles around the set point. As an application specific result, this can speed up PID/PWM-based simulations in cyber-physical systems by relaxing resolution when a new controller set point is ordered, then increasing resolution through steady state of the simulated controller.

For future work, adaptive control of the simulation resolution is being developed for the SimConnect backplane. Because the backplane services all SimTalk messages in the system, it can monitor any signal or groups of signals consting of streams of IEs. Any numerical metric can be applied to these, such as finite differences applied to the { v } values of IEs evaluated at their { t_m } time points, for numerical differentiation of the IE signal. Similarly the IEs can be integrated at their { v, t_m } values using standard numerical integration techniques. The backplane can calculate combinations of metrics on IE signals and adjust the simulation resolution (through *res* messages described here) based on preset thresholds. The most simple adaptive control would be to relax resolution as an IE signal stream stabilizes (measured by a such as a numerical derivative applied the IE stream), and to increase resolution dynamically as the signal changes more frequently. Alternatively, resolution can change when the backplane moniters an event on a specific signal, such as an interrupt pin in the system represented as SimTalk singal stream, causing the backplane to employ high resolution during the interrupt service routine in the simulated software. There are many possibilities for adaptive control in the SimConnect backplane, and work is underway on these features.

7. REFERENCES

[1] Lee, E.A., "Cyber-Physical Systems: Design Challenges," *The University of California at Berkeley Center for Hybrid and Embedded Software Systems,* Technical Report No.UCB/EECS-2008-8, Jan. 2008.

[2] Sangiovanni-Vincentelli, A., "Quo Vadis, SLD? Reasoning about the Trends and Challenges of System Level Design," *Proceedings of the IEEE*, vol.95, no.3, pp.467-506, March 2007.

[3] National Science Foundation (NSF), "Cyber-Pysical Systems," http://www.nsf.gov/pubs/2012/nsf12520/nsf12520.htm, 2006.

[4] Klesh, A.T., Cutler, J.W., and E.M. Atkins, "Cyber-Physical Challenges for Space Systems," *The 2012 IEEE/ACM Third International Conference Cyber-Physical Systems (ICCPS),* pp. 45-52, 17-19 April 2012.

[5] Rajkumar, R., Lee, I., Sha, L., and J. Stankovic, "Cyber-Physical Systems: The Next Computing Revolution," *The 2010 ACM/IEEE 47th Design Automation Conference (DAC),* pp.731-736, 13-18 June 2010

[6] Nenzi, P., and V. Holger, "Ngspice Users Manual." V. 22, Sep 2010, ngspice.sourceforge.net.

[7] Valvano, J., Embedded Microcomputer Systems: Real Time Interfacing, 3rd ed. Stamford, CT: Cengage Learning, 2011.

[8] Fujimoto, R.M., "Parallel and Distributed Simulation," *Proceedings of the 1995 Winter Simulation Conference*, pp. 118-125, 3-6 Dec 1995.

[9] Fujimoto. R.M. "Parallel Discrete Event Simulation," *Proceedings of the 1989 Winter Simulation Conference*, pp. 19-28, 4-6 Dec 1989.

[10] Chandy, K.M., and J. Misra, "Distributed Simulation: A Case Study in Design and Verification of Distributed Programs," *IEEE Transactions on Software Engineering,* vol. SE-5, no. 5, Sep 1979.

[11] Jefferson, D.R., "Virtual Time," *ACM Transactions on Programming Languages and Systems*, vol. 7, no. 3, 1985.

[12] Pfeifer, D. and A. Gerstlauer, "Expression-level Parallelism for Distributed Spice Circuit Simulation," *The 15th IEEE/ACM International Symposium on Distributed Simulation and Real Time Applications, DS-RT 2011.* 4-7 September, 2011.

[13] Pfeifer, D. and J. Valvano, "Kahn Process Networks Applied to Distributed Heterogeneous HW/SW Cosimulation," *The 2011 Electronic System Level Synthesis Conference, ECSI.* 5-6 June 2011.

[14] Pfeifer, D., J. Valvano, and A. Gerstlauer. "SimConnect and SimTalk for Distributed Cyber-Physical System Simulation." *Simulation: Transactions of the Society for Modeling and Simulation International.* OnlineFirst, DOI: 10.1177/0037549712472755. 5 March 2013.

[15] Schmerler, S., Tanurhan, Y., and K.D. Muller-Glaser, "A Backplane Approach for Cosimulation in High-level System Specification Environments," *Proceedings of the European Design Automation Conference, EURO-DAC '95 with EURO-VHDL*, pp. 262-267, 18-22 Sep 1995.

[16] Atef, D., Salem, A., and H. Baraka, "An Architecture of Distributed Cosimulation Backplane," *The 42nd Midwest Symposium on Circuits and Systems*, vol. 2, pp.855-858, 1999.

[17] Sung, W., and S. Ha, "A Hardware Software Cosimulation Backplane with Automatic Interface Generation," *Proceedings of the Asia and South Pacific Design Automation Conference, ASP-DAC '98,* pp.177-182, 10-13 Feb 1998.

[18] Kahn, G., "The Semantics of a Simple Language for Parallel Programming," *Information Processing*, pp. 471-475, Stockholm, Sweden, Aug 1974.

[19] Dou Zhiwu; Li Yanfeng; , "Dynamic Time Management Algorithms Research in Simulation System HLA-Based," *Computer Science and Engineering, 2009. WCSE '09. Second International Workshop on* , vol.1, no., pp.580-583, 28-30 Oct. 2009

[20] Lungeanu, D.; Shi, C.-J.R.; , "Distributed simulation of VLSI systems via lookahead-free self-adaptive optimistic and conservative synchronization," *Computer-Aided Design, 1999. Digest of Technical Papers. 1999 IEEE/ACM International Conference on* , vol., no., pp.500-504, 1999

[21] Lee, C.; Coe, E.; Clark, J.M.; Stepanek, J.; Raghavendra, C.; Bhatia, S.; Puri, R.; , "Scalable time management algorithms using active networks for distributed simulation," *DARPA Active NEtworks Conference and Exposition, 2002. Proceedings* , vol., no., pp. 366- 378, 2002

[22] Moo-Kyoung Chung; Chong-Min Kyung; , "Improving Lookahead in Parallel Multiprocessor Simulation Using Dynamic Execution Path Prediction," *Principles of Advanced and Distributed Simulation, 2006. PADS 2006. 20th Workshop on* , vol., no., pp.11-18, 2006

[23] "IEEE Standard for Modeling and Simulation (M&S) High Level Architecture (HLA)-- Framework and Rules," *IEEE Std 1516-2010*, vol., no., pp.1-38, Aug. 18 2010.

[24] Lee, E.A., and A. Sangiovanni-Vincentelli, "Comparing Models of Computation," *The IEEE/ACM International Conference on Computer-Aided Design Digest of Technical Paper,s ICCAD-96*, pp.234-241, 10-14 Nov 1996.

[25] Fujimoto, R.M. and R.M Weatherly, "Time Management in the DoD High Level Architecture," *The Proceedings of the 1996 10th Workshop on Parallel and Distributed Simulation*, pp. 60-67, 1996.

[26] The MathWorks Corp. www.mathworks.com. 2012.

[27] Franklin, G., J.D. Powell, and A. Emami-Naeini. Feedback Control of Dynamic Systems, 4th ed. Upper Saddle River, NJ: Prentice Hall, 2002.

CoAP-Mediated Hybrid Simulation and Visualisation Environment for Specknets

Diana Alexandra Crisan
School of Informatics
The University of Edinburgh
Edinburgh, United Kingdom
dcrisan7@gmail.com

Ion Emilian Radoi
School of Informatics
The University of Edinburgh
Edinburgh, United Kingdom
emilian.radoi@gmail.com

D K Arvind
School of Informatics
The University of Edinburgh
Edinburgh, United Kingdom
dka@inf.ed.ac.uk

ABSTRACT
This paper describes an integrated hybrid simulation environment in which physical electronic devices interact in real-time with a discrete-event simulator and a 3D visualisation engine, where the communication between the real devices and the virtual world is mediated by CoAP. The resulting simulation framework is a powerful tool for designers of Internet of Things (IoT) applications to assess design decisions ahead of deployment, based on realistic data from sensors and typical movement of people within built spaces. A motivating example is used to illustrate the capabilities of hybrid simulations based on a multi-residence housing facility intended for elderly people, each wearing an on-body speck with one or more sensors, to monitor their condition such as breathing, heart-rate, and activity, and which transmits this information via a mesh network of base-stations to a central hub. The results demonstrate that design decisions can be made on the choice of routing protocols based on real-time transmission of data from people, which captures their typical movement in a built environment and based on actual data transmitted by on-body devices.

Categories and Subject Descriptors
D4.8 [**Performance**]: Simulation;
I.6 [**Simulation and Modelling**]: Types of Simulation – *animation, combined, discrete event.*

General Terms
Algorithms, Measurement, Performance, Human Factors.

Keywords
Specknets, SpeckSim, discrete-event simulator, hybrid simulation, wireless sensor networks, CoAP, routing protocols, RPL, CTP, AODV, DSR, Californium, Unity.

1. INTRODUCTION
A specknet is a wireless network of miniature autonomous specks, which provides one or more services: each speck is capable of sensing and is programmed to process this data, and a collection of specks that collaborate to extract information from the sensed data in a distributed manner. Specknets link the physical world of sensory data with the virtual world of networks of computers, and are designed to form the fabric of the emerging Internet of Things (IoT) [21]. A specknet on the person with the appropriate sensors can, for example, monitor movement and physiological conditions, and in turn infer the state of his/her well-being, which is transmitted over the internet. Computation with specknets affords new modes of interaction with the digital world, in which the physical world is the primary site of interaction. It is precisely for this reason that simulating specknets in one of the many network simulators such as ns-2/-3 [23, 31], COOJA [22], TOSSIM [24], ATEMU [25], Avrora [26], OMNet++ [27], and OPNET [28], is inadequate, as they do not capture the rich sources of interactions in the physical world involving people and their movements.

Consider the following scenario of a multi-residence housing facility intended for elderly people, each wearing an on-body speck with one or more sensors to monitor their condition such as breathing, heart-rate, and activity, and which transmits this information via a mesh network of base-stations to a central hub, where an overseer can monitor and respond to events such as falls, and out-of-range physiological parameters, or anomalous behaviour such as extended periods of inactivity. The performance of the mesh network of base-stations will be influenced by a number of factors such as the frequency of sensing and wireless bandwidth, the transmission rate of the sensed data, and patterns of movement of people within the building. The coverage of each on-body speck is limited to a few meters in built environments, and the sensed data is transmitted to the nearest in-range base-station for onward transmission. The movement of people would result in crowding around particular base-stations creating communication hot-spots, which will in turn impact on the quality of service of the mesh network. Timely arrival of information may be critical for prompt responses to emergency events. The motivation for hybrid simulation is to provide more realistic simulation of the testing scenario. Simulating the performance of the wireless network of base-stations, which captures both realistic movement patterns of people and the actual sensor data, should provide results of greater fidelity. Current simulators offer cyclic or probabilistic models for the movement of crowds of people. However, data generated based on heuristics or algorithms cannot model precisely the traffic bursts and noise of real-world activities of people. The thesis is that hybrid simulations inject realistic input, which better reflects the chosen scenario and enhances the fidelity of the simulation results.

The paper describes an integrated hybrid discrete-event behavioural simulation and visualisation environment; it is hybrid in the sense that the real physical specks on people, each collecting sensory data, interact via CoAP with their respective virtual base-stations modelled in the simulator, determined by the physical location of the person; the discrete-event simulation environment models the behaviour of the protocol stack (CoAP application layer, a selection of routing algorithms and MAC protocols) running on the base-stations connected as a mesh network; the results of the simulation are visualised in 3D in the application captured in the UNITY game engine.

Hybrid simulations [18] have been used in the past in combining finite element simulation models of engineering structures with physical testing in the laboratory, which is more cost-effective compared to shaking table tests for applications in earthquake engineering. The terminology co-simulation is often used for combining digital and analogue simulators also known as mixed-signal simulations, or combining hardware simulators and software emulators for co-design and co-simulation of embedded systems. Our notion is more in tune with the former, i.e. hybrid simulations environment combining both behavioural simulation and the 3D visualisation of the applications and the integration of real sensor hardware on crowds of people whose data is routed in real-time to the simulation models.

The simulation environment also has resonances with other paradigms such as real-time, human-in-the-loop simulation [17], although the humans in our case are providers of real-time data, of actual positional and sensor values.

In the rest of this paper, Section 2 gives a brief overview of the protocols either used or modelled in the simulator: CoAP, the four routing protocols for wireless mesh network, and the UNITY game engine for 3D visualisation. Section 3 presents other existing simulators for WSNs, Section 4 describes the architecture and modules of the SpeckSim simulator and Section 5 outlines the motivating example with the results of experiments described in Section 6.

2. BACKGROUND

2.1 CoAP

Constrained Application Protocol (CoAP) [1] is currently being developed by the Constrained RESTful Environments (CoRE) working group for use in resource-constrained networks. It aims to minimise the need for message fragmentation by utilising a low header overhead. CoAP was designed according to the REST architecture [20], and thus exhibits functionality similar to that of Hyper Text Transfer Protocol (HTTP). It easily translates to HTTP to provide a generic web protocol suitable for use in constrained environments, while also providing machine-to-machine (M2M) application features such as multicast support, built-in discovery and asynchronous message exchanges. The scope of this protocol is not only to bridge HTTP, but also to include constraints of the REST architecture: statelessness, cacheability, layered system and uniform interface.

HTTP, which is based on the REST architecture, is designed for port-oriented, stable connections and deemed unsuitable for constrained devices. Unlike HTTP-based protocols, CoAP binds to UDP and uses a simple retransmission mechanism, as opposed to the congestion control provided by TCP. Despite operating on top of UDP, CoAP provides optional reliability measures through multicast and unicast support, URI and content-type support and stateless HTTP mapping, which allow simple proxy and caching capabilities.

The CoAP interaction model can be considered similar to that of HTTP because it provides four request methods corresponding to the HTTP variants: POST, PUT, GET and DELETE. However, unlike HTTP, CoAP supports M2M interactions by allowing a node to act both as a server and as a client (commonly referred to as an endpoint).

The CoAP layer interoperates with RESTful applications and systems on the Web via the Californium framework [5], which offers intuitive interaction with CoAP endpoints and also provides specific services.

The CoAP implementation modelled in SpeckSim uses UDP over an ID-based addressing scheme for the nodes (each node is allocated a node ID) for local simulations. CoAP addresses the unreliable nature of UDP messaging using the reliability measures mentioned previously.

2.2 Routing Protocols

Four routing protocols, including standards-based ones, have been modelled in SpeckSim, which can be used in a spectrum of applications ranging from static networks to dynamic ad-hoc ones.

2.2.1 RPL

IPv6 Routing Protocol for Low power and Lossy Networks (RPL) [2] is the IETF standard for routing in wireless sensor networks deployed in environments including urban, industrial, building or home networks. RPL provides multipoint-to-point (MP2P), point-to-multipoint (P2MP), and occasionally point-to-point (P2P) traffic. The distinction between the traffic models is that MP2P is used for collection networks and P2MP for propagating configuration information from sink nodes to the rest of the nodes in the topology.

RPL is a tree-based protocol that can have multiple root nodes. It uses several types of messages for building a rank-based topology. (The neighbour with the smallest rank is preferred when selecting a route to the root node.)

2.2.2 CTP

Collection Tree Protocol (CTP) [15] is a tree-based address-free routing protocol designed for wireless sensor networks. A topology running CTP can have multiple root nodes, and all other nodes implicitly choose a root by selecting a next hop.

2.2.3 AODV

Ad hoc On-Demand Distance Vector (AODV) [8] was proposed by the IETF for mobile and ad hoc networks and it uses multi-hop routing. The "counting to infinity" problem is avoided by using destination sequence numbers for the routing table entries, thus offering loop-free routes. The sequence number represents a distance metric, so in case of multiple possible routes, the one with the largest number is chosen.

AODV nodes do not keep routing tables to reduce storage overhead, and they perform a route request process when a route is needed, which is cached for subsequent use. However, it does keep an up-to-date neighbour table by periodically generating hello messages.

2.2.4 DSR

Similar to AODV, Dynamic Source Routing (DSR) [7] is designed for use in ad hoc mobile networks, by offering multi-hop routing and does not maintain routing tables. For acquiring a path to a desired destination and retaining it in a cache table, DSR also uses route discovery and route maintenance processes, but unlike AODV, DSR nodes do not maintain neighbour tables.

2.3 Californium, JCoAP and Copper

2.3.1 Californium

Californium [5] is a modular and extensible CoAP implementation written in Java using a flexible, layered architecture which provides an intuitive, easy-to-use framework to interact with CoAP endpoints or provide specific services. Even though it eases the users' use of CoAP by providing a layer of abstraction, it allows complex configurations of protocol components in order to suit extended requirements.

2.3.2 JCoAP

JCoAP [16] is an early-stage open-source Java library implementing the main features of CoAP with both reliable and unreliable messaging. This library was used for the main message formats such as the header and options.

Besides CoAP-to-CoAP interfacing, JCoAP provides CoAP-HTTP and HTTP-CoAP proxy interfacing, along with a simple API, which was used to integrate it within SpeckSim. JCoAP recently released the piggy-backed responses, representing an alternative to sending separate acknowledgement and data messages.

2.3.3 Copper

Copper [3] is a generic browser for the Internet of Things (IoT) based on CoAP. It is a user-agent developed for the Firefox web browser allowing user interaction via the CoAP URI scheme to the IoT devices. It provides the GET, POST, PUT and DELETE functionalities of CoAP, which allow the user to interact with the CoAP server.

2.4 Unity

Unity [4] is an open-source cross-platform game engine and IDE developed by Unity Technologies. It is a powerful 3D rendering visualisation tool used in gaming industries as a game development ecosystem. Unity enables the user to create interactive 3D content and it has the ability to dynamically display movement or actions in a plane. For our purposes, it can be used for visualising applications.

3. RELATED WORK

This section SpeckSim with other simulation environments for wireless sensor networks.

COOJA [22], a simulator for networks of sensors running the Contiki sensor node operating system, is also Java-based and capable of offering cross-level sensor network simulation.

The NS-2 [23] network simulator has the capability to run the same source code on simulated nodes as on real hardware devices. Since NS-2 is widely known and used, other simulators, such as SensorSim, were built on top of it to extend its functionality. NS-3 [31] is a new version of NS-2, which integrates newly developed models and patches on a refactored simulation core.

Just as COOJA is a simulator for the Contiki sensor node operating system, TOSSIM [24] is a simulator for the TinyOS operating system [30]. The two simulators differ in how they represent multiple node instances in simulations. In TOSSIM the source code is different for every node instance, and in COOJA there are different instances executing the same source code.

ATEMU [25] and Avrora [26] are cycle-accurate simulators which operate at the instruction/ machine code level. The Avrora simulator overcomes the scalability limitations introduced by its predecessor ATEMU, and offers faster performance while preserving the same level of accuracy.

OMNet++ [27] is a simulation platform which allows the building of different simulation frameworks on top of it. It is open-source and designed to support simulations of parallel and distributed systems.

The OPNET [28] simulator comes with a large selection of protocol models such as IPv6, MPLS, and OSPFv3. However, it is not open-source and is not designed specifically for wireless sensor network simulations.

SensorSim [29] is a hybrid simulator for wireless sensor networks, by enabling real nodes to interact with simulated ones. SensorSim extends the NS-2 simulator core to use SensorWare [19] as a middleware platform, which provides mobile code support. The protocol stack provided in the simulator consists of a Radio and MAC layers, with an optional Routing layer (consisting of the DSR routing protocol).

Of all the simulators considered, only SensorSim has the capability to provide hybrid simulations. But SensorSim adopts a tightly-coupled approach and requires much effort, as the interaction between real and simulated nodes takes place on top of the MAC layer. SpeckSim adopts a more loosely-coupled and distributed approach, and the physical devices can potentially be located in different geographic locations connected using CoAP. The 3D visualisation was made available by bridging the SpeckSim simulator with the Unity game engine. This offers visual inspection of the results of simulations of complex scenarios especially involving mobile entities.

In summary, SpeckSim offers web-enabled hybrid simulation, external 3D visualisation capabilities and a full protocol stack with multiple protocol choices for the MAC and Routing layers.

4. SPECKSIM SIMULATOR

SpeckSim was developed at the Centre for Speckled Computing, University of Edinburgh, for algorithmic-level simulations of network behaviour, for different hardware and protocol configurations of mobile computing devices.

4.1 Simulator Description

SpeckSim is a discrete-event behavioural simulator for modelling computation on networks of specks. It is written in the Java programming language and includes models of devices, networks and deployment environments described at different levels of abstraction, ranging from algorithms to faithful representation of standards-based protocols.

The simulator was originally developed as a behavioural level network simulator for use as a tool in development and analysis of distributed algorithms for localisation and routing in wireless sensor networks. Further development has incorporated lower layer communication protocols, radio channel models and modelling of hardware for analysis of power consumption and resource usage.

The current version of SpeckSim contains a full protocol stack implementation: MAC, Network, Transport and Application Layers.

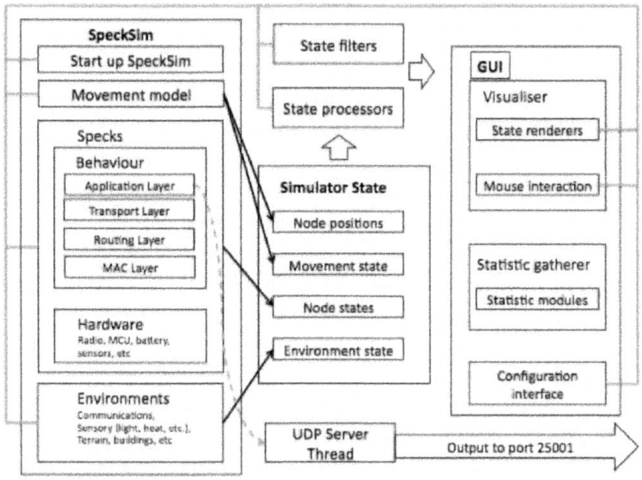

Figure 1. SpeckSim Architecture

4.2 Architecture

The core of the simulator is the event queue and any model-related activity is initiated by an event and the global simulation time progresses as events are popped from the queue. All the activities of the simulated devices are therefore asynchronous.

The architecture of the SpeckSim simulator, as shown in Figure 1, has four main components:

• Simulation Core - The Simulation Core contains the core functionality of the simulator and the three top-level categories of simulation models: Devices (Specks), Environments and Movement models.

• Simulation State: The Simulation State is a snapshot of the state of the Simulation Core at specific instants, containing the current state of the models being used in the simulation. The state of the simulation is extracted to produce visualisations and statistics of an executing simulation within the GUI.

• Statistics and Data Processing: The simulator includes a number of statistical and data analysis modules to extract the results of interest in a simulation. These modules execute analysis algorithms on the state of the simulation either as the simulation is running or after completion. The simulator provides analysis of device power consumption and battery lifetimes, MAC and routing protocol performances (delivery ratio, latency and throughput), communication channel performances (collisions, packet loss and contention levels). Higher level and application specific behaviour can also be analysed by extending existing classes.

• Graphical User Interface (GUI): The SpeckSim user interface is automatically generated from annotations made to the Java simulation models and allows users to configure any variable parameter of a simulation model as specified in the implementation. An OpenGL 3D visualisation of the simulation is also provided. Renderer classes provide visualisations; existing renderers include those displaying devices, terrain, communication links and device's positional estimations. Additional visualisations may be added to display interesting aspects of the simulation state such as 3D visualisation of the scenario, log viewers and configuration panes showing menus for configuration of the simulation models.

4.3 Simulation Models

4.3.1 Hardware and Device Modelling

Devices are the top layer of simulated entities and essentially model wireless sensor devices. The simulator may be extended to model the behaviour of other types of devices, such as application servers and mechanical or actuation devices. Each device object contains an instance of models of the hardware, software and communication protocols required by the simulated physical device. There is no operating system for devices within the simulator; high level application specific operation is termed as Behaviour and may be implemented directly within the class describing a device type or within Behaviour classes. The main purpose of hardware component models is to simulate the energy usage of battery-operated sensor devices.

Bridging SpeckSim with Unity is achieved by using a localhost UDP client-server connection. Thus, SpeckSim and the external 3D visualisation platform are required to run on the same machine, which ensures that no packets can be lost.

4.3.2 Battery Model

Battery models simulate the effect of drawing current from a battery over periods of time. The simulator includes models for several specific batteries and a cell that can be configured for any desired capacity and voltage.

4.3.3 Micro-controller and Clock Models

The simulator includes models for a micro-controller and clock system. The MCU model provides current consumption figures for typical MCU states such as *sleep*, *power down* and *active* and is used in current consumption analysis.

The clock model simulates the real-time clock aspects of a typical micro-controller and allows for the effects of clock frequency drift to be simulated. The clock also provides a real-time scheduling interface for simulated software components to use to schedule events.

4.3.4 Radio Model

Radio models provide devices with access to communication channels and also simulate radio device hardware. There are several models in the simulator:

• CC2420 - A model of the Texas Instruments CC2420 2.4 GHz radio transceiver

• CC1000 - A model of the Texas Instruments CC2420 sub-1 GHz radio transceiver

• Selectable Transmission Shell Radio - A simple radio model that enables simulation of range- and shape-controlled transmissions. Using this model, users can specify the range and 3D shape of a transmission made by the radio (devices lying within the shell may receive transmissions). This can be configured with many different shells modelling different antenna designs and orientations.

The simulator is extensible and additional radio models can be included in the future.

4.3.5 Protocol Models

Devices may use a communication stack made up of different protocol models. Protocol models are stacked to pass transmissions and receptions from application level behaviour to a radio via routing and mac protocols and vice versa.

4.3.6 Application Behavioural Models

A device may have many top-level behaviours allowing for simulation of multi-purpose devices. A device's behaviour has access to all the components of the device such as protocols and radios for communications, the device clock for real-time scheduling and the battery model for power-aware behaviour.

4.3.7 Communication Models

Communication Models simulate the properties of wireless and wired communication channels, of which there are several in the simulator. The model used in a simulation is dependant on the hardware models configured in the simulated devices. For example, the transmissions of a wireless device configured with a transmission shell-based radio will be passed via the simulation mode for calculating interference and reception of such radio models whereas the communications of a device configured with a model of a real radio such as a CC2420 or CC1000 will be handled via the communications model of free space path loss and transmission power based contention.

4.3.8 Movement Models

Movement models specify the position and orientation of devices within the simulation environment. The simulation environment uses a floating point, 3-dimensional position system, movement models are required to provide 3D positions and if required velocity vectors for each simulated device.

Multiple movement models may be used within a single simulation to allow for different devices to use different models. All movement models also share some common configuration functionality such as 2D/3D modes, fixed and randomised orientations, maximum device velocity control and interaction with Environment models such as those modelling ground terrain and buildings to position devices according to the topology of the ground or a building within the simulation environment.

4.3.9 Environments

Environment models are used to simulate any global parameters within a simulation; the variety of models and parameters are diverse and include:

• World: provides configuration of the simulation world such as the scaling factor applied to the simulators floating-point positional reference frame.

• Failure: controls the failure rate of devices within the simulation, allowing for specific, randomised or position based failure of individuals of groups of devices.

• Radio Impediments: allows impediments and interference sources to radio transmissions to be positioned within the simulation environment.

• Terrain: a model of the terrain of the environment that can take height map data from image or standard *csv* formats.

• Building: models buildings that are specified by inputting architectural drawings showing wall positions. The walls are added as radio impediments and can be used in a specific communication model for indoor environments.

• Environmental conditions: Conditions such as Water Level, Humidity, Temperature and Gravity are modelled in individual environments. These models can be configured to simulate the effects of changes to such conditions.

4.4 Hybrid Simulations and External 3D Visualisation

SpeckSim has recently been extended to support hybrid simulations by enabling physical external nodes to communicate with the virtual ones at the CoAP layer.

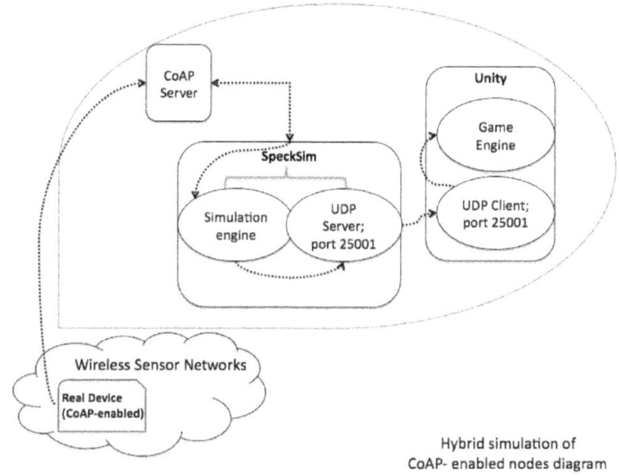

Figure 2. Communication Flow

Furthermore, 3D visualisation is made possible by providing a bridge between the SpeckSim simulator and the Unity game engine. This allows users to take advantage of all of Unity's functionality for the 3D visualisations of their simulations.

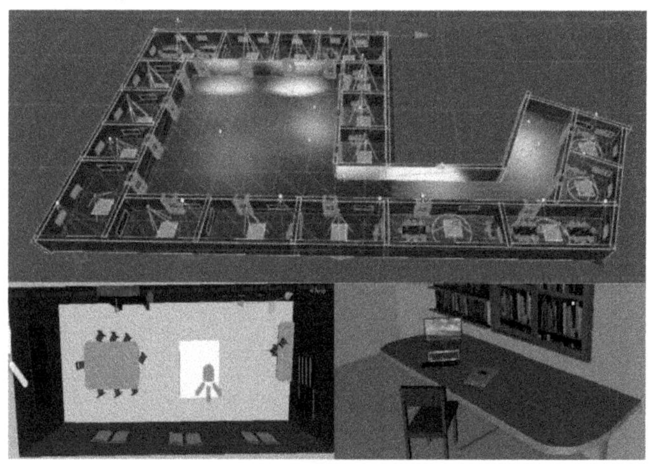

Figure 3. 3D Visualisation of a building in Unity

5. MOTIVATING SCENARIO

The chosen application was inspired by a healthcare scenario. On-body specks can be used to measure people's vital signs such as breathing and heart-rate, and social signals such as their activity. This type of application is emerging in sheltered homes and hospitals, where patients wear these devices for long periods of time for continuous monitoring. The data collected is transmitted via radio to base-stations, installed in individual rooms and public spaces such as corridors, stairwells, and reception and dining areas. The data from the ambulatory patient is routed via the in-range base-station to a central hub through a wireless mesh network of base-stations.

This scenario was implemented using the hybrid capabilities of SpeckSim and experiments were conducted using three physical on-body nodes, three real base-station nodes connected to PCs and an 18-node virtual mesh network of base-station nodes. The on-body nodes send packets at a rate of 12.5 Hz to the base-stations, which further transmit the data via CoAP to CoAP-enabled base-station nodes in the simulator. The topology used in the simulator mimics the floor plan of our test building as shown in Figure 3, and the CoAP-enabled server nodes are placed in the simulated topology in the rooms corresponding to the rooms containing the base-stations in reality. Once the packets reach the nodes in the simulator, they are routed to a central hub over different routing protocols (AODV, DSR, RPL, CTP).

The performance of each routing protocol is measured in order to determine its suitability for this application and the movement of people is captured by the hybrid simulation.

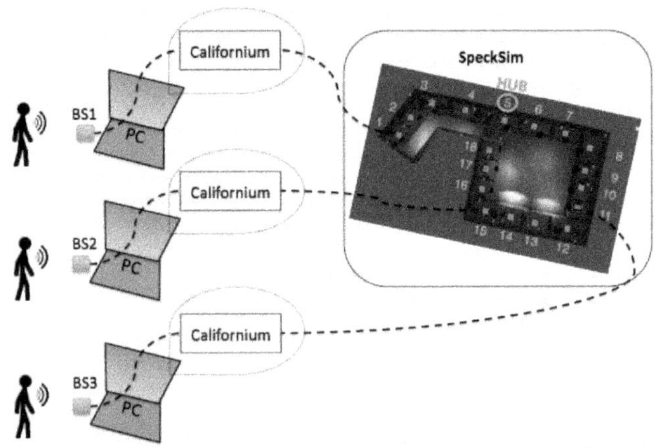

Figure 4. Scenario Diagram

The hardware platform used as base-station nodes is the Prospeckz-5 programmable prototyping platform developed at the Centre for Speckled Computing, University of Edinburgh, which was designed for developing IoT applications.

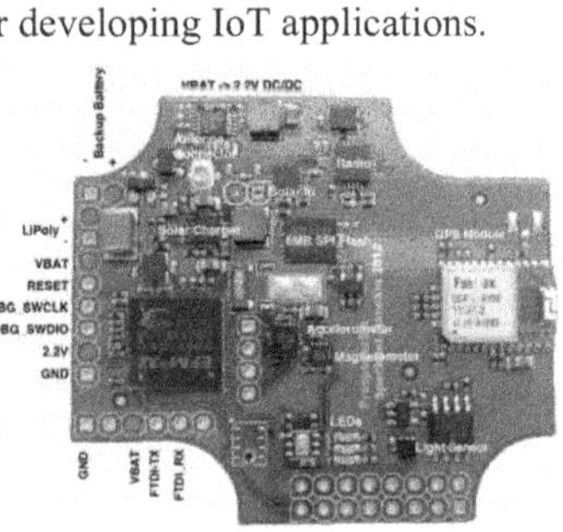

Figure 5. Prospeckz-5 Platform

The board is equipped with GPS, accelerometer, magnetometer and light sensors, and allows the possibility of connecting others.

6. EXPERIMENTS AND RESULTS

This section describes the experiments conducted, the metrics chosen for evaluation and presents the results that were obtained. The scenario exercises the choice of one of four possible routing protocols for the wireless mesh network of base-stations, which connect to a central hub for collecting all the sensor data of ambulatory patients. The virtual base-station nodes were running a full protocol stack having fixed protocols at each layer except routing: CoAP at the application layer, UDP at transport layer and SpeckMAC-D [32] at the MAC layer.

Each experiments was repeated five times to eliminate exceptional behaviour, and the results presented are the average of these values.

6.1 Performance of Routing Protocols

The performance of the routing protocols was evaluated on the basis of five metrics deemed relevant for the chosen scenario. As can be seen in Figure 4, the three physical base-station nodes send CoAP messages to nodes 1, 15 and 11 in the simulator, which route the data to the central hub, node 5. The nodes in the virtual topology are configured to have a limited radio range, so that they can only reach their neighbours (e.g. node 5 is in range of node 4, 6 and 18).

6.1.1 Delivery Ratio

The delivery ratio is one of the main metrics taken into account for network communication protocols. The routing layer does not discard packets but tries to find a route. Thus, if a packet has not turned up at the destination, it means that either a route to that destination was not found or it was dropped at the MAC layer. This metric can also be used for evaluating fault tolerance capabilities of routing protocols.

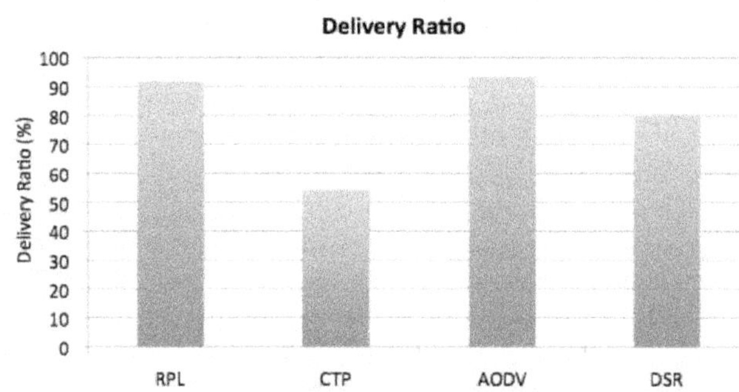

Figure 6. Delivery Ratio

Figure 6 compares the delivery ratio for the four protocols for the data packets routed to the collection hub. It can be seen that the best performances are achieved by RPL and AODV with a delivery ratio percentage of over 90%.

6.1.2 Latency

The importance of the latency metric depends on the type of deployment, i.e. it is a critical metric in emergency management scenarios that require low latency to ensure quick response.

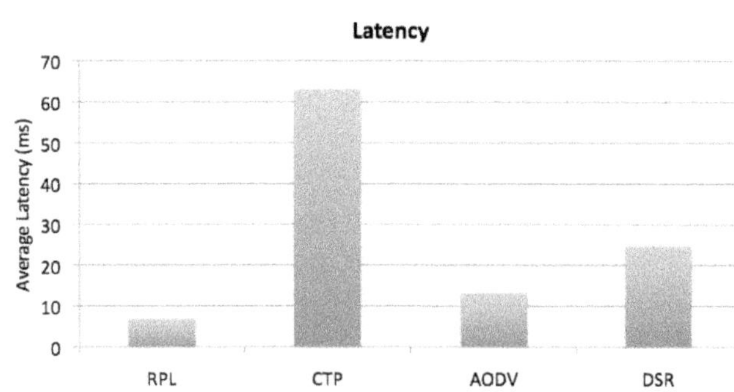

Figure 7. Latency

Figure 7 presents the average latency in the network for the choice of routing layers. RPL has the best performance, with an average latency lower than 10ms.

6.1.3 *Overhead*

The overhead of the routing protocols is relevant since it can place a burden on the network and also influences its overall power consumption. This metric is measured in terms of the number of control packets exchanged by the network during its lifetime.

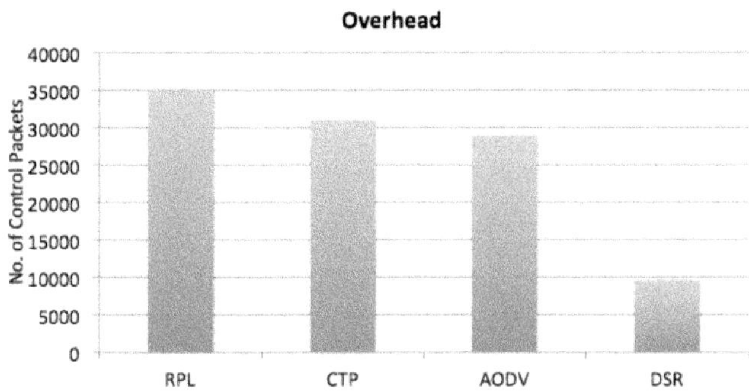

Figure 8. Overhead

Figure 8 presents the overhead of the routing protocols measured in terms of the number of control packets generated during the deployment. The best performance belongs to DSR, followed by AODV. This was expected, as nodes running these two protocols send control packets only when requiring routing information, as opposed to RPL and CTP, which have the nodes generate routing tables and periodically exchange control packets for maintaining them. The difference between AODV's and DSR's overhead is due to AODV's maintenance of neighbour tables which are kept up-to-date by periodically exchanging "hello" messages.

6.1.4 *Energy Consumption*

Energy consumption is a major concern in the case of battery-operated autonomous wireless sensor networks, as this metric determines the lifetime of a deployment or the mean time between charging the batteries.

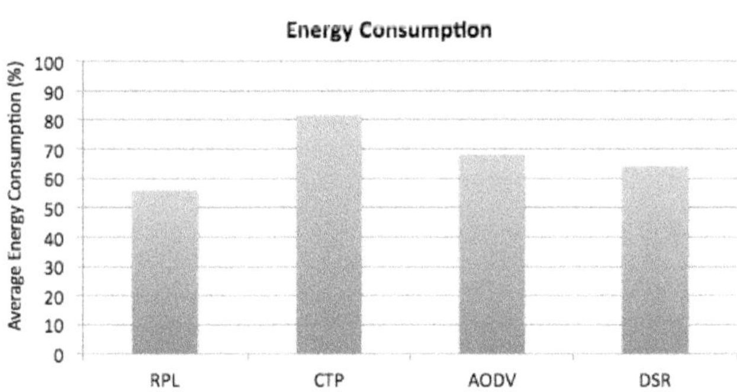

Figure 9. Energy Consumption

Figure 9 compares the average energy consumption of the nodes in the topology expressed in the percentage of depleted battery life during the deployment. The batteries selected for the simulated nodes have the capacity of 25 milliampere-hour. Even though it was expected that RPL would have the highest energy consumption due to its high overhead, it turned out that the overhead has less influence over the average energy consumption of the network for this scenario. However, for CTP, AODV and DSR, in Figure 9 it can be observed that the energy consumption reflects the overhead pattern presented in Figure 8.

6.1.5 *Fault Tolerance*

The fault tolerance of the network is worth considering, as it highlights the capabilities of protocols to react to topology changes due to the vagaries of wireless communication in built environments or due to node failures. For testing the fault tolerance capabilities of the protocols, a forced node failure was injected in the topology, making sure to affect a node from the path chosen by the routing protocol and that an alternative path towards the hub exists. Thus, the fault tolerance was tested on the communication between node 15 and 5 (hub), by causing the failure of node 17.

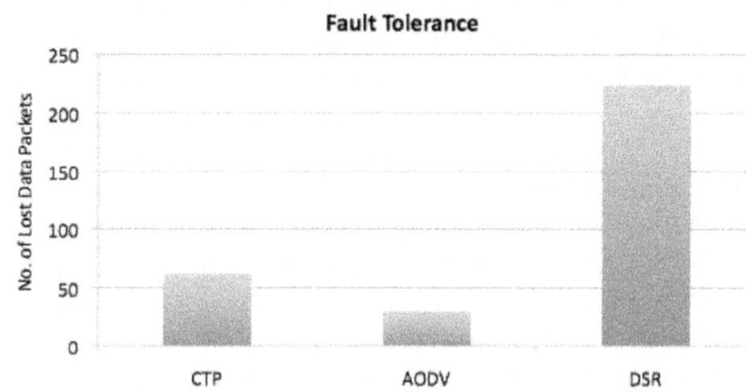

Figure 10. Fault Tolerance

Figure 10 compares the fault tolerance capabilities of the protocols expressed in terms of the number of lost data packets since a node failure occurred until the topology re-converged. RPL was not included in these tests, as the current implementation of the protocol in the SpeckSim simulator does not include a fault tolerance mechanism. The protocol with the best performance in this case was AODV, with a significantly lower number of packets lost before network re-convergence, compared to CTP and DSR.

The big difference between AODV's and DSR's down time is probably due to two implementation aspects of the protocols. Firstly, in case of packet loss, AODV has up to 5 retransmissions, whereas DSR has up to 15. This should offer more reliability in terms of reducing packet loss for DSR but it will also enlarge the time it takes to detect node failures or topology changes. Secondly, AODV is implemented to use only bidirectional links, thus *Route Reply* messages will use the backward route of the *Route Request* messages, while DSR can also make use of unidirectional links, meaning that a *Route Reply* message can reach the initiator of the *Route Request* message through a different path. Thus the route discovery process for DSR can be twice as long.

6.2 SpeckSim Resource Utilisation

Both CPU and memory usage are relevant when simulating large networks or performing network scalability exercises. The CPU used to run the simulator is a 2.53 GHz Intel Core 2 Duo, with a 3MB L2 cache.

The graphs presented in Figures 12 and 13 show the CPU and memory usage for both cases: running SpeckSim with and without the external 3D visualisation. The overhead added by the Unity 3D visualisation is displayed in red. It seems to have a minor variation in terms of CPU usage, with a standard deviation of 1.3, and a slightly higher one, of 18.62, for memory consumption.

6.2.1 CPU Usage

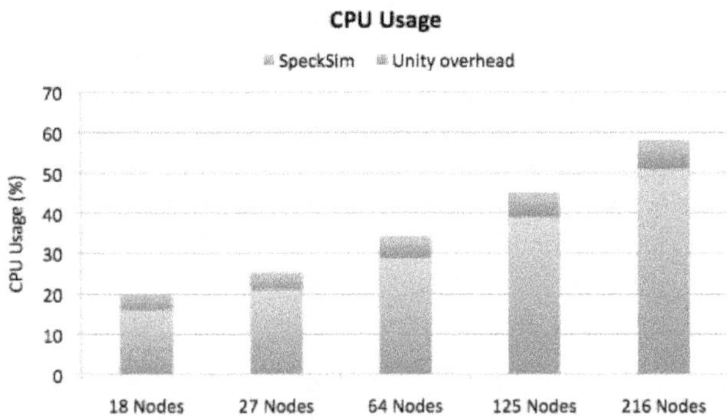

Figure 12. CPU Usage

6.2.2 Memory Usage

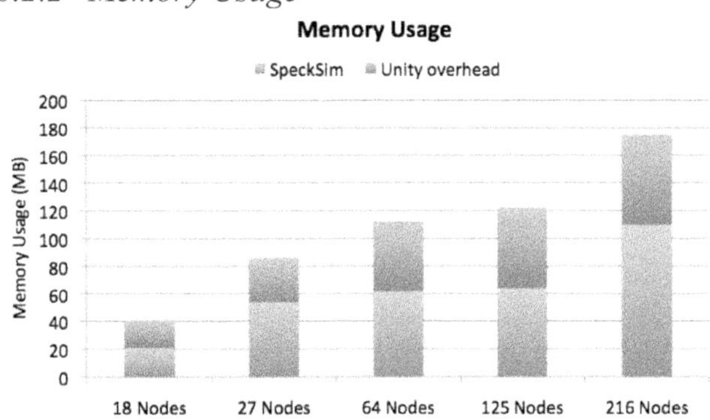

Figure 13. Memory Usage

In both cases, the simulation complexity is considered to be the number of nodes simulated in the network. Both CPU and memory usage seem to increase linearly with the number of nodes in the simulator.

7. CONCLUSIONS

The paper describes the hybrid simulation capability and external 3D visualisation environment of the SpeckSim simulator. It enables the integration of physical devices, such as on-body sensors worn by people, which capture both their movement and their physiological data, which is routed in real-time via CoAP to virtual instantiations of base-stations in the simulator. This data is used to exercise the performance of different protocols to route the data over the wireless mesh network of base-stations to a central hub. A number of observations can be highlighted in this exercise. The metrics that should matter most in this scenario are delivery ratio followed by latency. It can also be observed that the overhead metric is not the main factor that influences energy consumption; the obvious example is RPL, which in spite of having the highest overhead also has the lowest energy consumption.

8. ACKNOWLEDGMENTS

The authors wish to thank partial support from HOBNET ICT FP7 project (257466) and PLANET ICT FP7 project (257649).

9. REFERENCES

[1] Z. Shelby, K. Hartke, and B. Frank, "Constrained Application Protocol (CoAP) draft-ietf-core-coap-08", Dec. 6, 2012.

[2] T. Winter, P. Thubert, and the ROLL Team, "RPL: IPv6 Routing Protocol for Low power and Lossy Networks draft-ietf-roll-rpl-19", March 13, 2011.

[3] http://people.inf.ethz.ch/mkovatsc/copper.php, [Feb 2013].

[4] http://unity3d.com/unity/, [Feb 2013].

[5] D. Pauli and D. I. Obersteg, "Californium", Lab Project at the Institute for Pervasive Computing, Department of Computer Science, ETH Zurich, December 2011.

[6] I.E. Radoi, "Evaluation of Routing Protocols in WSN", MSc Dissertation, School of Informatics, University of Edinburgh, 2011.

[7] D.B. Johnson, D.A. Maltz, and J. Broch. "DSR: The Dynamic Source Routing Protocol for Multi-Hop Wireless Ad Hoc Networks", Ad Hoc Networking, chapter 5: pp. 139 - 172. Addison-Wesley, 2001.

[8] C. Perkins, E. Belding-Royer, and S. Das, "Ad hoc On-Demand Distance Vector (AODV) Routing", rfc 3561, July 2003.

[9] B.C. Villaverde, and D. PESCH, "Constrained Application Protocol for Low Power Embedded Networks: A Survey", in Innovative Mobile and Internet Services in Ubiquitous Computing (IMIS), 2012 Sixth International Conference, Palermo, Italy, ISBN: 978-1-4673-1328-5.

[10] A. P. Castellani, et al. "Architecture and Protocols for the Internet of Things: A Case Study", in Proceedings of First International Workshop on the Web of Things (WoT), 2010.

[11] K. Kuladinithi, O. Bergmann, T. Ptsch, M. Becker, and C. Gorg, "Implementation of CoAP and its Application", in Transport Logistics. In Proc. IP+SN, Chicago, IL, USA, 2011.

[12] M. Kovatsch, M. Weiss, and D. Guinard, "Embedding internet technology for home automation", in Proc. of ETFA 2010 (IEEE Conference on Emerging Technologies and Factory Automation), 2010.

[13] I. E. Radoi, A. Shenoy and D. K. Arvind, "Evaluation of Routing Protocols for Internet-Enabled Wireless Sensor Networks", The Eighth International Conference on Wireless and Mobile Communications – ICWMC, June 24-29, 2012 - Venice, Italy.

[14] M. Kovatsch, S. Duquennoy, and A. Dunkels, "A low-power coap for Contiki", in Mobile Adhoc and Sensor Systems (MASS), 2011 IEEE 8th International Conference on, oct. 2011, pp. 855 –860.

[15] R. Fonseca, O. Gnawali, K. Jamieson, S. Kim, P. Levis, and A. Woo, The Collection Tree Protocol (CTP), TEP 123, TinyOS Network Working Group, 2006.

[16] http://code.google.com/p/jcoap/, [Feb 2013].

[17] L. Rothrock and S. Narayanan (eds.), Human-in-the-Loop Simulations, DOI: 10.1007/978-0-85729-883-6_2, Springer-Verlag, 2011.

[18] V. E. Saouma and M. E. Sivaselvan (eds.), Hybrid Simulation – Theory, Implementations and Applications, Taylor and Francis, 2008.

[19] A. Boulis, C. Han, and M. B. Srivastava, "Design and implementation of a framework for efficient and programmable sensor networks", in International Conference on Mobile Systems, Applications and Services (MobiSys), pages 187–200. ACM Press, 2003.

[20] R.T. Fielding, "Architectural Styles and the Design of Network-based Software Architectures", PhD Dissertation, Chapter 5, Dept. of Computer Science, University of California, Irvine, CA, USA, 2000.

[21] L. Atzori, A. Lera, and G. Morabito, "The Internet of Things: A Survey", Computer Networks vol. 54, no. 15, pages 2787-2805, Oct 2010.

[22] F. Osterlind, A. Dunkels, J. Eriksson, N. Finne, and T. Voigt, "Cross-Level Sensor Network Simulation with COOJA", in Proceedings of the First IEEE International Workshop on Practical Issues in Building Sensor Network Applications (SenseApp 2006), Tampa, Florida, USA, Nov. 2006.

[23] The network simulator - ns-2, http://www.isi.edu/nsnam/ns/, [March 2013].

[24] P. Levis, N. Lee, M. Welsh, and D. Culler, "TOSSIM: accurate and scalable simulation of entire tinyos applications", in Proceedings of the first international conference on Embedded networked sensor systems, pages 126–137, 2003.

[25] M. Karir, "Atemu - sensor network emulator / simulator / debugger", Technical report, Centre for Satellite and Communication Networks, Univ. of Maryland, 2003.

[26] B.L. Titzer, D.K. Lee, and J. Palsberg, "Avrora: scalable sensor network simulation with precise timing", in Proceedings of the 4th international symposium on Information processing in sensor networks (IPSN), April 2005.

[27] A. Varga and R. Hornig. "An overview of the OMNeT++ simulation environment", in Proceedings of the First International Conference on Simulation Tools and Techniques for Communications, Networks and Systems (SIMUTools 2008'), March 2008.

[28] OPNET, http://www.opnet.com/solutions/network_rd/modeler.html, [March 2013].

[29] S. Park, A. Savvides, and M. B. Srivastava. Sensorsim: A simulation framework for sensor networks. In International Workshop on Modeling, Analysis and Simulation of Wireless and Mobile Systems, Boston, MA, USA, Aug. 2000.

[30] J. Hill, R. Szewczyk, A. Woo, S. Hollar, D. Culler, and K. Pister, "System architecture directions for networked sensors", in Proceedings of the 9th International Conference on Architectural Support for Programming Languages and Operating Systems, November 2000.

[31] The NS-3 network simulator, http://www.nsnam.org/, [March 2013].

[32] Wong, K. J., Arvind, D. K., 2006 "SpeckMAC: Low-power Decentralised MAC Protocols for Low data-rate Transmissions in Specknets'", in Proc. 2nd ACM Int. Workshop on Multi-hop Ad-hoc Networks, Florence, Italy, May 2006, ACM.

A Marine Traffic Simulation System for Hub Ports

Shell Ying Huang, Wen Jing Hsu, Hui Fang
School of Computer Engineering
Nanyang Technological University
Block N4, Nanyang Avenue
Singapore 639798
{assyhuang, hsu, hfang}@ntu.edu.sg

Tiancheng Song
Maritime and Port Authority of Singapore
460 Alexandra Road
PSA Building
Singapore 119963
Tiancheng_SONG@mpa.gov.sg

ABSTRACT
Ensuring congestion-free marine traffic is crucial for hub ports in the world. For these hub ports, there has been increasing demand in marine transport. Therefore a capacity-assessment tool that models and simulates the navigational network, the traffic flows and complex navigational behaviors of vessels is needed. The simulation model presented in this paper is unique in the scale and complexity of the waterway networks covered, the flexibility in defining the traffic flow patterns, and the degree of accuracy demanded of navigational behaviors. As such, none of the existing models and simulation tools is adequate for assessing the waterway capacity. The model was calibrated based on detailed analysis of historical records and consultations with domain experts. The model was used in the study of several future scenarios of a hob port. The simulation system built has laid a useful foundation for planning future marine traffic for hub ports.

Categories and Subject Descriptors
I.6[**Simulation and Modelling**]: Model development, Model Validation and Analysis.

General Terms
Algorithms, Management, Measurement, Verification.

Keywords
Capacity assessment, marine traffic simulation, hub ports.

1. INTRODUCTION
Marine traffic has increased rapidly in many parts of the world over the past decades, for example, the size of the world merchant fleet has grown from 672,000 in 1980 to 1,276,000 in 2010 [23]. This trend is expected to continue into the foreseeable future. A busy hub port usually offers a number of different types of marine services to various types of vessels, for example, cargo loading/unloading service, ship supply service and ship repair and maintenance service. There is often a network of interconnecting waterways leading to a multitude of terminals from sea in such a hub port. The waterways may have narrow passages at certain spots, sections with heavy traffic and 'junction' areas with multiple crossing traffic flows. Vessels may enter/leave a waterway at any points from/for a terminal or an anchorage. Increasing traffic volumes could result in congestions in parts of the port waters or in waterways leading to the port, resulting in longer delays in vessel schedules to reach or leave port facilities and greater navigational risks. Therefore, it is crucial to assess the capacity of the waterway network and plan ahead for possible future traffic scenarios.

To assess the capacity of such a waterway network is a challenging task. Presently there is no universally accepted definition of capacity [2] that captures the intuitive notion of the maximum traffic a waterway network can sustain. Conventionally, the capacity of a waterway is considered from two respects: physical dimensions and navigational throughput. The physical dimensions of a waterway, i.e., its width, length and depth, define a capacity threshold for admitting individual vessels. In contrast, *throughput* is a dynamic measure of waterway capacity and can be considered in terms of (a) the number of vessels passing though per unit time, (b) the vessel waiting time, and (c) vessel turnaround time [3]. This throughput-linked definition of capacity is suggested in the Permanent International Association of Navigation Congresses (PIANC) channel design guidelines, as well as International Maritime Organization (IMO) [1] and International Association of Lighthouse Authorities (IALA) [4] risk management initiatives.

Intuitively, when a traffic network reaches its capacity limit, any further increment of traffic, such as higher rate of vessel arrivals, will drastically increase the travel delays (cf. Little's Theorem for queuing systems). Obviously, under such a scenario, the risk level, as measured in terms of, e.g. number of actions required to avoid incidents, will also increase drastically. For the port administration, in order to ensure the quality of service, both the average delays (optionally, maximum delay) and the risk level must be maintained below an acceptable level, a level which is termed as a service guarantee (or service target). Thus we define the capacity of a marine traffic network N as the maximum throughput that may be sustained on N without breaking a given service guarantee.

However, it is a very difficult (if not impossible) task to analytically derive the capacity of a network of waterways. To date, there is no analytical model that captures the navigational rules and dynamics among the vessels, which depend on numerous variables such as the traffic conditions, physical environment of the locale, physical characteristics of the vessel, interactions among the vessels and others. As such, computer simulation is the only hope and proven approach for assessing the throughput and capacity, as well as for other marine traffic planning and management purposes [5-6, 12]. Nevertheless, it is also nontrivial to develop simulation models that essentially emulate the vessels' behaviors for a large-scale marine traffic system. Due to the complexities of navigation, apart from the general collision guidelines such as COLREGS, no explicit rules exist to date for making optimal decisions for each situation. Much depends on the captain's seamanship, experience and judgment [22]. Compared to the land-based traffic, marine traffic dynamics are quite different, as vessels are much heavier objects with great inertia, and water is a fundamentally different medium to operate in. As such, there are major differences between the two systems, e.g., vessels are much harder to accelerate/decelerate and, unlike the marked lanes on highways and roads, there is no fixed lane in the waterways.

There is no existing simulation model that can adequately model the vessel behaviors and their interactions at a large scale. The known simulation systems [9-11, 13, 14, 16, 21] assume that each vessel generally moves at a predefined speed and take collision-avoidance measures only when there is imminent danger. However, type specific, location and situation specific behaviors are observed in historical data. These behaviors do affect other vessels in the area and hence the overall traffic flow. Similarly, analysis of historical radar records also reveals other intricate behaviors. For instance, certain types of vessels but not all types are more likely to speed up when they are leaving the port waters and approaching the sea. The existing simulation models do not capture such location-aware and situation-dependent behaviors. As a result, the traffic flow rate simulated by using a conventional system is less realistic. Therefore, to obtain accurate capacity of a marine traffic network, it is essential to accurately model the navigational behavior of vessels and their interactions within the network.

We have thus designed and built a sophisticated marine traffic simulation system (MTSS) which is unique in terms of the scale *and* complexity of the traffic system involved. We accurately capture the intricate behaviors mentioned above. Our simulation of marine traffic in a network of waterways is different from the previous mainly in three aspects: (1) the complexity of the navigation network; (2) collision-free control of a large number of active vessels and differentiated speed modeling; (3) extensive calibration and validation. The resulting simulation system proves to be suitable for evaluating various aspects of the overall traffic system, e.g., assessing the throughput, delays, density, bottlenecks, etc. It is also very flexible, and it may be reconfigured to simulate different traffic scenarios on different networks of waterways. Using this tool we have successfully generated traffic flows under several identified scenarios and conducted traffic capacity studies for these scenarios. The model records the vessel speeds during their journeys, the travel times taken to complete their trips, and the number of instances they are compelled to take actions (other than cruising at the same speed) to resolve potential conflicts with the other vessels throughout the navigational network. These findings have helped identify waterways and traffic conditions that are likely to incur congestions and risk of collisions.

In the rest of the paper, we present the related literature in section 2. The design of the simulation system is discussed in section 3. The calibration and validation techniques and results are described in section 4. Section 5 describes how the simulation system is used for a capacity study for a hub port. Section 6 concludes the paper.

2. RELATED WORK

Marine traffic simulation has been an active research topic in the past decade [7, 10, 11, 13] for various objectives, including mainly evaluating channel capacity, risks of navigation and forecasting vessel activities.

Golkar et al. [10, 16] presented a simulation model for Panama Canal. They stressed in detail how a comprehensive simulation system was constructed by different model components. The simulator was used mainly to evaluate the pilot working conditions.

Osaka University's SMARTS (Ship-with-a-captain MARine Traffic Simulation system) [11, 15, 20] is a multi-agent model to simulate marine traffic in Osaka Bay and Tokyo Bay of Japan. It can automatically create marine traffic flow according to the statistical data to drive the simulation runs. Hasegawa et al., the system inventors, applied a fuzzy expert system to navigate vessels through waterways. This model was used for marine risk assessment and navigation rule evaluation.

Kose et al. [13] presented the simulation of marine traffic in Istanbul Strait. Because of the physical conditions, they used First-In-First-Out policy to model the traffic inside the Strait. In this model vessels travel in only two directions in a "tunnel" channel. Accordingly, their simulator made several assumptions: vessel arrival time is uniformly distributed; vessels are forbidden to overtake each other; constant separation distance between vessels is maintained; the designed speed for vessel is 10 knots; all vessels are transiting (i.e., no dwelling). Their simulation was used to assess the impact on the waiting times at the two particular entrances with increasing Strait traffic.

BMT's Dymitri [7] is a time-stepping model in which a number of vessels in the simulated area move along prescribed routes and maneuver according to a set of rules. Their model is able to provide an enhancement to the operator's decision-making abilities: the risks are evaluated at every time step; then avoidance maneuvers (slowing and/or steering) are suggested to operator for human decision.

Fan and Cao [8] modeled a sea space as a directed graph, and proposed a method to compute the capacity for both links and nodes. A link refers to a section of a fairway, while a node refers to a boundary point of sea space, a junction, a boarding point for port pilots, a separation point which divides a fairway into two sections, a berthing area, or an anchorage area. The link capacity was defined as the maximum number of vessels passing through the link in a given time interval. The node capacity was computed based on the average dwell time. They then extended this computation method for capacity to multiple lanes, by dividing link width using the average width of vessel domain. However, *this approach obviously did not consider the overtaking scenario for vessels*, i.e., a vessel may or may not switch to another lane in the middle of its voyage. Thus, the capacity of a multi-lane link cannot be derived by multiplying single lane capacity, since this formulation ignores the constant dynamic interactions among vessels in multiple lanes.

Huang et al. [12] conducted a simulation study of the capacity of multiple anchorages by reproducing realistic mix of arriving vessels, dwelling time and the current practices in choosing anchoring spots within an anchorage. They show that it is important to simulate details of the system behaviours when evaluating capacities and detecting bottlenecks of a system.

Maritime navigation is a process that depends heavily and crucially on the navigator's experience and judgement [21]. There is no rule about the optimal decision for each situation apart from the general collision regulations COLREGS. The dynamics of vessels are very complex and depend on many factors due to a vessel's own physical characteristics, physical conditions of the local environment and the captain's practice of seamanship. Up to now, all reported simulation studies have either disregarded the regulations or employed specific databases to emulate COLREGS while abstracting dynamic navigation behaviours by average speeds. Average speed is not a realistic model of vessel navigation behavior. Our analysis of historical radar records brings us to use a distribution of vessel speed for each type of vessels. It is also not realistic to just simulate average behavior for collision avoidance actions. Because there are no fixed lanes in the waterways, the collision avoidance behavior and the overtaking behavior will need to be flexible.

For a simulation model of a complex system, calibration and validation is a task that requires careful planning and execution. Brockfeld et al. [17-19] presented a procedure for the calibration and validation of microscopic simulation models. Specifically, their calibration procedure consists of four steps: (1) calibration of driving behavior models; (2) calibration of route choice model; (3) OD (Origin-Destination) estimation; (4) model fine-tuning. Their validation was done by computing objective functions of the calibration. Two objective functions were provided: one is to minimize the deviation between the observed and corresponding simulated traffic counts at selected locations for peak hours, and another one is to minimize the traffic counts at selected locations in five-minute interval. It can be seen that calibration of microscopic simulation models involves numerous parameters for tuning, resulting in a very time consuming process for validation.

3. THE SIMULATION SYSTEM

3.1 System Components

We design our simulation system to achieve flexibility in the following aspects.

1) The simulation system should be able to simulate different waterway configurations, for example, changes to waterway lengths, widths and shapes or changes to the locations of terminals/shipyards. This means that in future, if a certain waterway is widened in order to cater for heavier traffic, or is made narrower by land reclamation, or a terminal is relocated, the change can be put into effects by changing some input files to the current simulation system. New fairways, new terminals/shipyards may also be specified in the input files.

2) The simulation system should be able to simulate different vessel traffic volumes, different percentages of various types of vessels using the waterways, or different vessel calling patterns to the various port facilities.

3) The simulation system should allow changes to routing policies that determine which path a vessel follows from its origin to its destination.

4) To modify or extend the vessel's navigational behaviours, such as the distributions of vessel speeds for one or more types of vessels, only the input to the simulation model should need changing. Changes to other navigational behaviours such as how collisions are avoided should be limited to certain parts of the simulation model without affecting most of the other components.

To satisfy these requirements, the Marine Traffic Simulation System (MTSS) includes the following sub-models:

- Navigational Network Model
- Traffic Flow Model
- Vessel Movement Model
- Vessel Navigational Behavior Model

Each of the four sub-models is independent and can run with changes incorporated in the other sub-model(s) of the simulation system. We will present these models in the following sections.

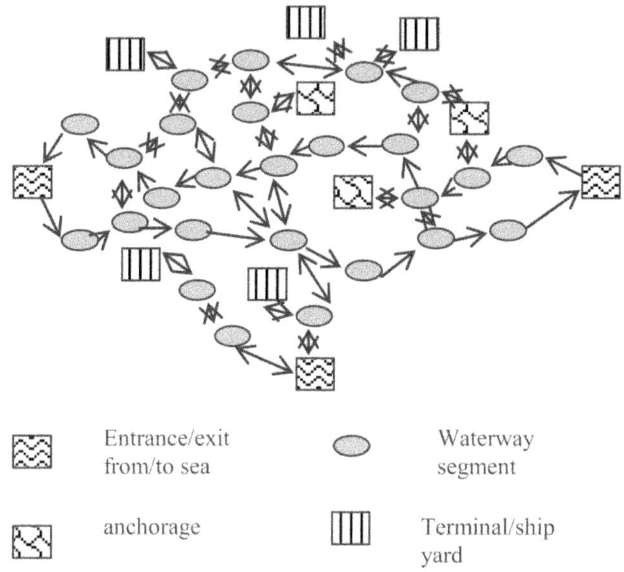

Figure 1. The navigational network.

3.2 The Navigational Network Model

The navigational network model represents the network of waterways used by the simulated traffic flows. Conceptually, as shown in Figure 1, the whole network consists of nodes and links. Nodes are either the starting or ending points of vessel trips or sections of waterways that vessels travel through. Links represent possible directions of navigation from one section to another section along a waterway. Note that some links are uni-directional and others are bidirectional, depending on whether there is uni-directional or bidirectional traffic between the two sections. Figure 1 shows that some segments have traffic coming in from multiple neighbouring segments and/or have traffic going out to multiple neighbouring segments. These are the busy traffic junctions in the network. In each segment, depending on the width, usually two or more vessels may move in parallel in the same direction, sometimes overtaking each other if they want.

We use the concept of *waterway segment* (or, simply, segment) in the representation of a waterway channel. Each fairway or channel is represented by a sequence of segments as shown in Figure 2. Note that each segment is a node in the navigation network. Each segment is a convex polygon with three or four corner points representing one section of a fairway or channel. Each segment is small enough such that a straight line at the side of the segment is a good approximation of the side of that section of the waterway. Each corner of a segment is defined by its latitude and longitude. An input file to the simulation system contains the lists of waterway channels to be simulated. Each waterway channel is defined by a list of (latitude, longitude) pairs which are the corner points of the segments of the waterway channel. This input file may be modified or replaced if a different network of waterway channels is to be simulated.

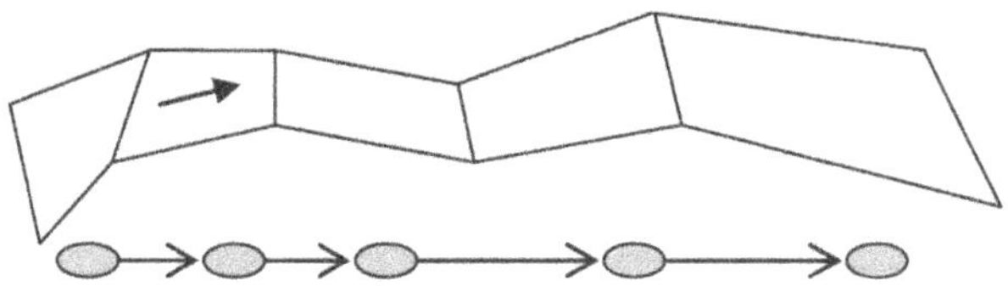

Figure 2. Waterway segments and their conceptual representation using nodes and links.

Each edge of a segment in Figure 2 is assigned a mode which allows or forbids vessels to pass through this edge. Specifically, mode 0 disables vessel entry or exit, mode 1 enables entry but disables exit, mode 2 enables exit but disables entry, and mode 3 enables both entry and exit. This means traffic within the segment consists of vessels going from an edge with mode 1 or 3 to an edge with mode 2 or 3. When enabling both entry and exit, an edge will generally split traffic into halves to separate incoming vessels and outgoing vessels that cross this edge to go from one segment to the next. An edge that allows vessels to come in but is not shared by two segments represents a starting point (an origin) of vessels trips in the simulated navigational network. An edge that allows vessels to go out but is not shared by two segments represents an ending point (a destination) of vessels trips. A vessel may start or end her trip in the waterway network at any point along such edges. The starting and ending points of a vessel journey may be a terminal, a shipyard, an anchorage, an entry point or an exit point of the navigational network.

The set of all segments defines the movement area of all the vessels in our simulation. The set of segment edges with their modes defines the permissible directions of traffic flows. Vessels are supposed to keep within the segments during their entire journeys, including the time they maneuver to overtake other vessels.

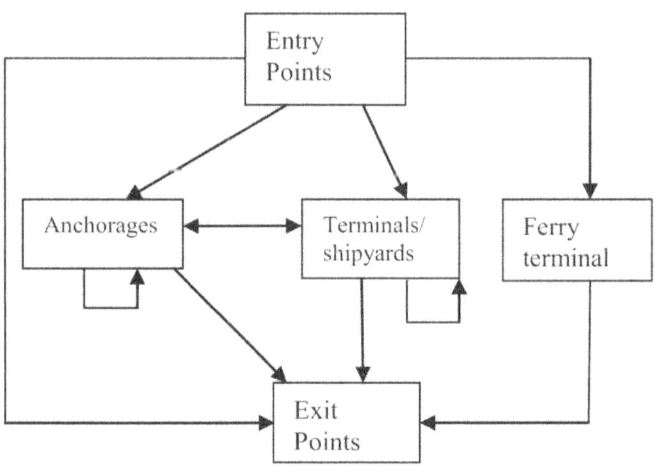

Figure 3. The different types of vessel trips in the traffic flow model.

3.3 The Traffic Flow Model

The traffic flow model generates the traffic flows. A traffic flow is formed by a set of trips to be made by vessels. A vessel trip is represented by an origin-destination pair. Figure 3 shows a graphical representation of the different types of vessel trips in the traffic flow model. Each box in the figure represents one type of the origins or destinations of vessel trips. In the figure, the box "Anchorages" actually represents all the anchorages in the navigational network and the box "terminals/shipyards" also represents all the terminals of different types (oil terminals, chemical terminals, container terminals) and shipyards. Each directed arrow with one box at each end represents one type of origin-destination pair. For example, the link from "Entry Points" to "Anchorages" represents all trips from one of the entry points on the navigational network to an anchorage. The simulation system is driven by the generated traffic flow, or, in other words, by the generated vessel trips.

Vessel visits to the port are not a set of independent vessel trips. For example, if a vessel comes to the port just to unload and load cargo at a terminal, she will at least take one trip from an entry point to the terminal and another trip from the terminal to an exit point. If this vessel needs to wait at an anchorage before berthing at the terminal, there will be three trips: entry point -> an anchorage -> terminal -> exit point. If an oil tanker needs to visit three oil terminals when coming to the port, the visit will consist of four trips: entry point -> oil terminal 1 -> oil terminal 2 -> oil terminal 3 -> exit point. Such travel patterns and their probabilities can be obtained from analyzing historical data of the port. Travel patterns depend on the vessel type and whether the vessel is a calling vessel, transiting vessel or intra-port transiting vessel. Each travel pattern starts from an origin followed by one or more destination nodes that this vessel will visit before exiting from the navigational network. When a vessel is generated (along with its physical attributes based on the statistics obtained from the analyses of historical data), it is at one of the entry points of the navigational network. The vessel is then assigned a travel pattern according to the probability table of travel patterns. According to this travel pattern, a number of vessel trips will be generated for this vessel.

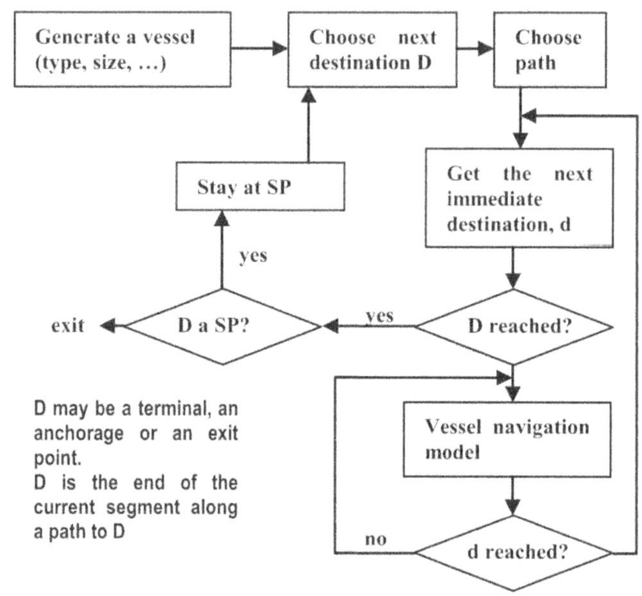

Figure 4. A vessel follows a path defined by the vessel movement model to move from an origin to a destination.

3.4 The Vessel Movement Model

This is a model of the routing choices of vessels during a voyage in the navigational network from its origin to its destination. For each vessel trip, the path a vessel will take is determined by the vessel movement model.

From the time a vessel enters the navigational network to the time of its exit, a vessel may go through one or more trips. Each trip is a voyage specified by an origin-destination pair. Each origin or destination may be an entry/exit point of the simulated area, a service point (SP) which may be a terminal, a shipyard or an anchorage. Figure 4 shows that after a vessel's arrival at an entry point of the navigational network it will have a trip generated which specifies which destination this vessel will travel to. This is denoted as D in Figure 4. A sequence of Ds is generated for the vessel by the traffic flow model described in the last section. To go to the next D, a path consisting of a sequence of segments will be generated by the vessel movement model at the step "Choose path". Then the vessel will travel through this sequence of segments one by one by moving to the end point d of each segment. The last d in this sequence will be the destination of the current vessel trip, D. On reaching D, if this D is a SP, the vessel will stay in the SP for a period of time before the next trip (the next D) is generated for the vessel. The modeling of dwell times at SPs are done according to historical data. If there is no more D, the vessel exits the navigational network.

3.5 The Vessel Navigational Behaviour Model

The vessel navigational behaviour model consists of four components including three sub-models, the free travel model, the overtaking model and the slow down/speed up model, as shown in Figure 5. It is a time-stepped model such that detailed navigational and collision avoidance behaviors of vessels can be simulated. At each time step till a vessel reaches its destination, it will try to detect potential conflicts with other vessels and plan for its movement.

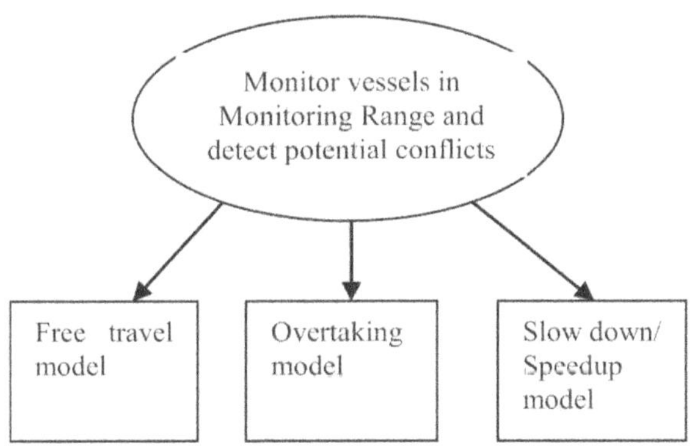

Figure 5. Navigational behaviour model

3.5.1 Detection of potential conflicts

Possible collision scenarios include: catch-up, head-on, and crossing conflicts.

Each vessel has a domain which is a rectangle defined by its length and beam width. A *vessel domain* is usually used to separate this vessel from others with safe distance. We use a rectangle with the size of 3 (configurable) times of vessel length and 3 times of beam width to represent its domain. Other definitions of vessel domain have also been proposed, for example half circle in [7]. However, for computational simplicity, a rectangle is chosen. At all times, a vessel should make sure that necessary actions are taken so that its domain does not overlap with the domain of another vessel.

In a medium or large size simulation model, there may be hundreds or even thousands of vessels navigating through the waterways at any time. In order to save computational time, not all vessels will be checked against all other vessels for potential conflicts. Only vessels that will be in the same segment or in two neighbouring segments for a same period of time may incur potential conflicts. So checks are performed on all pairs of vessels satisfying this condition. A two stage test is done. The first is a closest point of approach test to filter out vessels that will not be getting close to each other. Vessels failing the first test will go through the second test to confirm whether there is a potential collision.

A closest point of approach between two vessels is the minimum distance between them. We first compute the time interval during which two vessels V_1 and V_2 will be both in the same segment (or two neighbouring segments). Given this time interval, the minimum distance of these two moving vessels' centre points is computed as follows. Let $[t_a, t_b]$ be the time interval. Let $v = v_1 - v_2$ be the relative velocity for one vessel to the second vessel. Let $z = z_1 - z_2$ be the relative displacement vector at the initial time t_a. Then the function of distance between two vessels is $d(t) = \| z + v*t \|$. Its minimum value d* can be obtained by choosing

$$t^* = \arg\min_t d(t) = -\frac{z \cdot v}{\|v\|^2}$$

$$d^* = \|z + v \cdot t^*\|$$

Comparing three values of d(t) at time 0, t* and $t_b - t_a$, and checking if t* is in $[0, t_b - t_a]$, we obtain the minimum distance between two vessels for the time interval $[t_a, t_b]$. Also, we obtain the precise time when two vessels reach this minimum distance. This algorithm as shown in Figure 6 enables us to quickly judge if it is possible that the two vessels may get into each other's domain.

D = Inf;

$[t_a, t_b]$ = intersection of two vessels' time intervals in the segment;

Compute the relative speed v, and relative displacement z;
Compute the minimum distance d, and denote the time t*;*
If t not in $[t_a, t_b]$:*

Let d = min(distance at time t_a, distance at time t_b);*

D = min(D, d);*

*Return D>= 3*the length of the smaller of the two vessels.*

Figure 6. Distance Test.

The second test in the detection for potential collision is to pre-determine if two vessels' domains would overlap if they continue on their current tracks, given the time interval to look ahead and the current speeds of the vessels. Our algorithm is derived from Separating Axis Theorem [16]. The Separating Axis Theorem determines whether or not two static convex polygons intersect. It projects two polygons onto every axis of both polygons. If these projections intersect on all axes, then the polygons are intersecting. Otherwise, they are not intersecting. In our context, it is not enough to check whether the two domains of the two vessels overlap at the beginning and at the end of the time interval where they are in the same area (the same segment or two neighbouring segments). This is because during this interval, the two vessels may 'go through' each other. So we extend this theorem to the cases with two moving convex polygons: each convex polygon is given an initial speed and acceleration. The algorithm to determine if two moving convex polygons overlap or not is presented in Figure 7.

For each edge vector of both polygons:

1. *Determine the separating axis, which is the normal of the unit vector of the edge.*
2. *For each polygon: find the dot product between each corner point (with two positions respectively at time t0 and t2) in that polygon and the separating axis; the projection of that polygon onto the separating axis spans between the smallest of those projected points and the largest of them.*
3. *If the projections do not intersect, terminate. That means the polygons are not intersecting. If step 2 was completed, the polygons must be intersecting.*

Figure 7. Detecting potential collision between two moving vessels.

3.5.2 Free travel model

Each vessel is supposed to follow its designated voyage until it reaches its destination by moving through the segments given in its path. To move through a segment, the vessel travels from the entry edge to the exit edge of the segment directly. In fact, a vessel moves towards one point on the exit edge. Choosing this point on the exit edge is part of the segment planning process.

Usually a segment's width is wide enough to allow multiple vessels to move in parallel. The streams of traffic in a segment can be from the simplest with one direction only, to the most complicated with 12 directions as shown in Figure 8. The stream of traffic in each direction may have vessels moving in parallel. To simulate this, the point on the exit edge is chosen carefully for use of multiple-way traffic. If an edge of the segment allows two directional traffic streams, that is, vessels cross the edge to come in and out of the segment, the exit points will be on half of the edge, leaving the other half for vessels to come in. For example, in Figure 8(b), all in-coming traffic crosses the left half of the edge while the out-going traffic crosses the right half of the edge. Each half of an edge (or the whole edge for single direction of traffic) is further divided into multiple intervals for exit points to allow vessels to travel in parallel.

We simulate a common behavior in which vessels intending to turn left (right) soon tend to move along the left (right) side of the waterway. On the other hand, if the vessel's path in the near future is to go straight, the vessel tends to move along the middle of the waterway. The simulation of this behavior is by assigning a leftmost exit point to the vessel if it is going to turn left in the next segment and a right most exit point if it is going to turn right in the next segment. An exit point in the middle interval(s) of the exit edge will be given to the vessel if it is going straight. With this, the chances of vessels crossing each other in the segment are reduced and congestion at a cross junction is also alleviated. Figure 8(b) illustrates this.

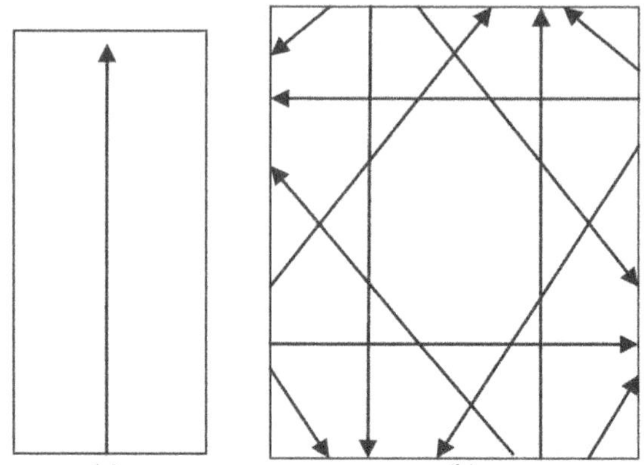

(a) (b)

Figure 8. (a) A segment with a single direction of traffic; (b) A segment with 12 directions of traffic. Each direction may have vessels traveling in parallel.

During the movement in the navigational channel, a vessel will normally follow a constant speed, called *normal speed*, if there is no potential collision. Based on our analysis of historical radar data, we find that normal speeds for different types of vessels are different. Normal speeds in a wider waterway compared with those in narrower waterways for the same type of vessels are also quite different. To simulate realistic behaviour, the normal speed of vessels will form a distribution. The distributions of speeds for different types of vessels in different parts of the navigational network are simulation parameters.

A vessel will gradually pick up speed when it is starting a journey. Similarly it gradually reduces speed when it is ending a journey. If a vessel needs to pick up a pilot in a boarding segment, it will slow down to an appropriate speed and later on resume its normal speed after the boarding segment.

Usually a waterway is wide enough, multiple vessels may move in parallel.

3.5.3 Resolution of potential conflicts

When a potential crossing conflict is detected, the rule of right-of-way applies. This rule says a vessel should give way to another vessel on its right at the point of conflict. This rule specifies which vessel will take action to resolve the potential conflict. The actions to take include adjusting its speed, either to slow down or speed up. It can only do so between a minimum speed and a maximum speed. The values of the minimum and maximum speeds depend on the vessel type and where the vessel is. We use a location-aware scheme to specify a vessel's permissible speed range. These simulated speed ranges are statistically calculated based on historical radar data. The vessel may also change course or change speed and course.

Overtaking at the current speed is the first choice if a vessel is catching up with another vessel in front except in certain waterways. If overtaking at the current speed is perceived to lead to conflicts, i.e., no safe path is found, the vessel will slow down or choose a combination of changing course and changing speed. The vessel needs to decide how much to change course and how much to slow down. These means a number of alternatives are possible. We treat the alternatives by a priority rule starting with minimum change of course and minimum change of speed. For example, a vessel will firstly try keeping its original speed but possibly changing directions, to avoid collision. If all alternatives fail due to severe congestion, we will try to find a solution at an earlier time moment in the real time path planning for the vessel. After overtaking another vessel, a vessel will turn back to the original path when it can. After a slow down, if the vessel in front is not there anymore, a vessel will return to its normal speed.

A potential head-on conflict is resolved by vessel(s) changing course. The possible actions are similar to perform an overtaking maneuver.

4. CALIBRATION AND VALIDATION

Our simulation model is calibrated and validated based on real historical data at a hub port. In this hub port, there is a main waterway outside port waters. Vessels passing the hub port without visiting a port facility will transit through it without stopping. There is also not less than 15 smaller waterways in port waters, inter-connected with each other and some connected to the main waterway. The input to the simulation model during calibration and validation are the actual vessel arrivals in historical data. We also have the radar data recording vessels' positions and speeds as they move through the waterways.

First, for the calibration of navigational behaviours, there are two types of parameters to tune. The first type is the normal speeds for vessels travelling through the various waterways in the network. The second is how much effort a vessel will try when it attempts to overtake another vessel before deciding to slow down. This means how much deviation from its current course a vessel is willing to take when overtaking. Parameter values are set such that the difference between the simulation results and radar data is minimized.

For the normal speeds of vessels, we treat vessels according to a number of categories: (i) vessels transiting through the main waterway without visiting any port facilities, referred to as transiting vessels; (2) vessels traveling through the main waterway on their way to reach/leave port facilities, referred to as calling vessels; (3) vessels travelling through the smaller waterways in port waters on their way to reach a port facility or on their way to leave the port after visiting a port facility. This cauterization is to catch the different behaviours of the vessels due to the purpose of a vessel's trip. Transiting vessels generally travel at a higher speed than calling vessels in the same waterway. Vessels traveling in port waters have to observe the regulations of speed of the port. We also group vessels in the main waterway according to the vessel types like container vessels, tankers, chemical vessels, general cargo ships, etc. From historical data analysis, we observe different speed profiles for different types of vessels. Vessels in the various smaller waterways in port waters are treated as one group. We do not differentiate among different vessel types, because (a) limited types of vessels use each of these smaller waterways; (b) among the several types of vessels that use a certain waterway, one or two types dominate the traffic.

We first tune the model on

1) vessel speeds of each type of transiting vessels, in the two opposite directions respectively, when they travel in the main waterway outside port waters;
2) vessel speeds of each type of calling vessels, in the two opposite directions respectively, when they travel in the main waterway outside port waters;
3) vessel speeds, in the two opposite directions respectively, in different waterways in port waters;

The objective is that the vessel travel times through the various waterways match the travel times in the historical data. This is to make sure the simulated vessels will use realistic amount of the waterway resources in our capacity study. The travel time in a waterway is also an indicator of the degree of congestion in that waterway. When the tuning of vessel speeds cannot get the travel times closer to the historical results any more, minor adjustments are done to how much deviation from its current course a vessel is willing to take when overtaking. This two-step tuning produced very good calibration results.

As two examples of the results of calibration for transiting vessels, Figures 9 and 10 show the speed curves of two types of vessels travelling through the main waterway outside port waters from radar records and from simulated vessels. The waterway is divided into 120 intervals and the curves show the average vessel speeds recorded in each interval. Table 1 shows the percentage differences in average travel times for different types of vessels through the main waterways simulated. For each type of vessels,

Percentage Difference =
(average travel time in simulation – average travel time in radar data)/average travel time in radar*100%

It can be seen that the differences are very small. After the calibration, a different set of data is used for validation and we see the percentage differences only increase by about 2% from the results in Table 1. To avoid "over-fitting" of the simulation model to one set of data, historical radar data from three periods of time are used. All produced acceptable results.

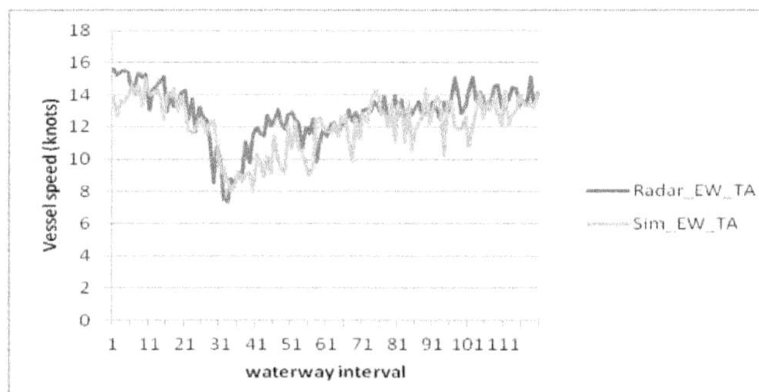

Figure 9a. Average speed of transiting tankers along the main waterway outside port waters in the east-west direction from radar records and from simulation.

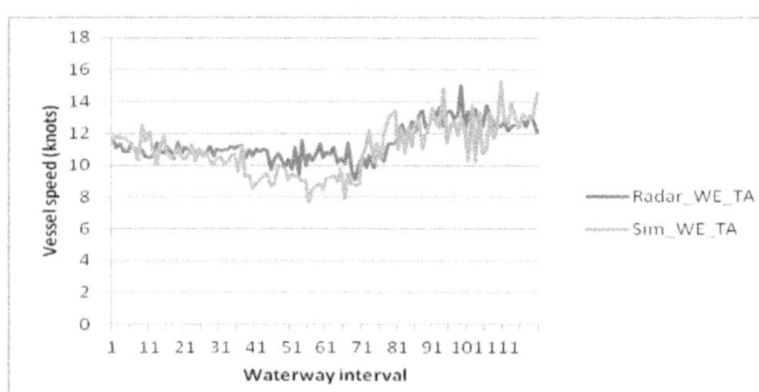

Figure 9b. Average speed of transiting tankers along the main waterway outside port waters in the west-east direction from radar records and from simulation.

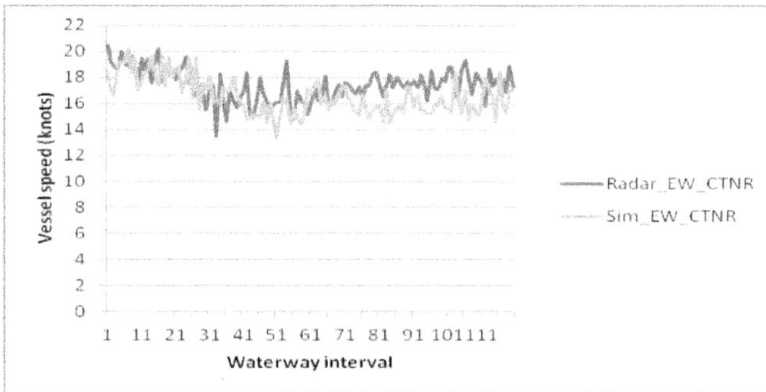

Figure 10a. Average speed of transiting containerships along the main waterway outside port waters in the east-west direction from radar records and from simulation.

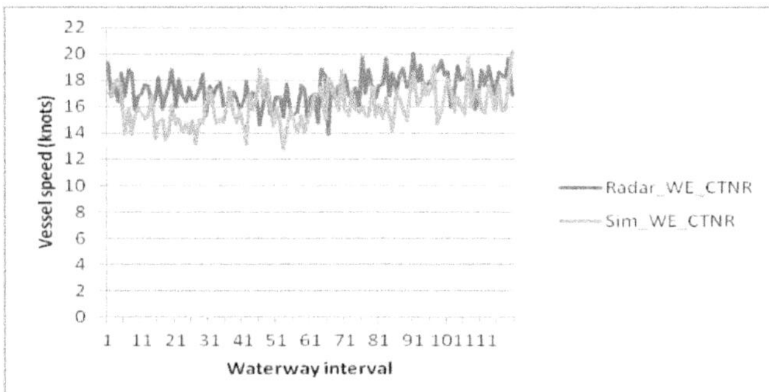

Figure 10b. Average speed of transiting containerships along the main waterway outside port waters in the west-east direction from radar records and from simulation.

Table 1. Percentage differences of average travel times of transiting vessels in the main waterway outside port waters.

Direction	Vessel Type	Percentage Difference
westbound	Bulk carrier	-0.24%
westbound	Chemical tanker	0.01%
westbound	Containership	0.63%
westbound	Freighter	-2.88%
westbound	Oil tanker	0.80%
eastbound	Bulk carrier	-3.73%
eastbound	Chemical tanker	4.75%
eastbound	Containership	-0.67%
eastbound	Freighter	-3.45%
eastbound	Oil tanker	-1.30%

Table 2 shows the calibration results for calling vessels in the main waterway outside port waters. Calling vessels refer to those vessels that are visiting port facilities such as terminals, shipyards and/or anchorages. They only travel part of the main waterway. The distances of the voyages of calling vessels in the main waterway depend on where they enter or exit from it. There are smaller waterways that connect to the main waterway. Hence a vessel may enter or leave the main waterway at various points. Unfortunately, the radar records are not fine-grained enough to catch the exact times vessels cross between a small waterway and the main waterway. Therefore for calling vessels, the travel times in the main waterway are a random variable whose distribution is hard to capture. We instead compare the average speeds of different types of calling vessels in the two opposite directions respectively and Table 2 shows the percentage differences in average speeds of calling vessels between the radar records and the simulated vessels. Compared with transiting vessels, there are more types of calling vessels using the main waterway. All the percentage differences are smaller than 5%.

Table 2. Percentage differences of average speed of calling vessels in the main waterway outside port waters.

Direction	Vessel type	Percentage Difference
westbound	Barges	4.79%
westbound	Bulk carrier	0.16%
westbound	Chemical tanker	-1.94%
westbound	Coasters	0.95%
westbound	Containership	-0.65%
westbound	Ferries/Cruises	-3.95%
westbound	Freighter	1.97%
westbound	Passenger Vessels	3.74%
westbound	Oil tanker	-3.42%
eastbound	Barges	2.47%
eastbound	Bulk carrier	0.21%
eastbound	Chemical tanker	-1.04%
eastbound	Coasters	-4.28%
eastbound	Containership	-1.12%
eastbound	Ferries/Cruises	-4.77%
eastbound	Freighter	-0.20%
eastbound	Passenger Vessels	3.43%
eastbound	Oil tanker	-1.13%

Table 3. Differences of average travel times of vessels in some of the smaller waterways in port waters.

Waterway	Percentage Difference	Absolute Difference (in minutes)
Fairway1_in	7.74%	2.11
Fairway1_out	-0.15%	0.01
Fairway2_in	4.04%	1.41
Fairway2_out	-3.19%	-1.26
Fairway3_in	NA	NA
Fairway3_out	1.51%	0.43
Fairway4_in	-6.13%	-1.72
Fairway4_out	1.76%	0.20
Fairway5_toEast	-4.13%	-0.97
Fairway5_toWest	-6.20%	-1.55
Fairway6_in	-6.34%	-0.68
Fairway6_out	3.76%	0.27
Fairway7	6.09%	0.65
Fairway8_in	2.39%	0.65
Fairway8_out	3.66%	0.97
Fairway9_in	-0.11%	-0.08
Fairway9_out	8.37%	2.04

Table 3 shows the calibration results for vessels in some of the smaller waterways in port waters. These waterways are much shorter than the main waterway. Normally a vessel traverses such a waterway within half hour or less. Therefore we also provide the absolute difference in travel time in units of minutes for comparison.

The suffix in the name of each waterway "in" or "out" indicates whether this is a direction going towards a port facility or leaving from a port facility. Table 3 shows that all percentage differences are below ±10% while the maximum absolute difference is about 2 minutes. These results show that our simulated vessels' use of the navigational space in various waterways in port waters is very close to the results as recorded by the radar.

After the navigational behaviours of vessels are validated, we still need to make sure that the simulated vessels will use the waterway resources in the right parts of the navigational network. In other words, we need to look at the distribution of the traffic in various parts of the whole navigational network: whether the distribution is correct. It is also a verification of correct implementation of the routing policies and the distribution of traffic arriving at various entry points of anchorages. Because if the routing policies implemented in the simulation model are very different from what the vessels actually do, vessels will be using the wrong waterways. Then when we simulate future scenarios with higher traffic expected, we will be creating traffic congestion at the wrong place. If the distribution of traffic arriving at various entry points of anchorages is not right, we would be creating traffic congestion at the wrong place as well.

This step of the validation is done by comparing the averages of the instantaneous number of vessels in the main waterway and various smaller waterways between simulation results and historical records. The routes vessels use when traveling in port waters and the entrance and exit points the vessels use when they visit the anchorages will affect the distributions of traffic flows in the network. A number of anchorages are bordering two or more waterways in port waters. So where vessels go in and get out will affect the vessel counts in these waterways. The routes vessels use in the simulation are obtained from domain experts largely according to regulations and shortest paths. During calibration, some changes to the vessel routing and the distribution of the choices of the entrance/exit points for some anchorages by domain experts are made. Table 4 shows the differences in the average instantaneous number of vessels in the various waterways in port waters and in the main waterway outside port waters.

Table 4. Differences in the average instantaneous number of vessels in various parts of the navigational network.

Location	Difference	Location	Difference
Fairway1	0.001	Fairway10	0.017
Fairway2	-0.021	Fairway11	0.103
Fairway3	0.112	Fairway12	0.097
Fairway4	0.771	Fairway13	0.387
Fairway5	0.463	Fairway14	0.61
Fairway6	0.601	Fairway15	0.104
Fairway7	0.627	Fairway16	0.105
Fairway8	0.26	Fairway17	0.309
Fairway9	-0.015		
Main waterway_EW	-3.92	Main waterway_WE	0.02
All locations	0.61		

5. A TOOL FOR CAPACITY STUDY

The simulation system as a capacity assessment tool takes in several categories of data. The input of the simulation model includes

a) The configuration of the waterways, locations of the various terminals, shipyards and anchorages.

b) The proportions, volumes and arrival patterns of the various types of vessels using the sea space of the hub port.

c) The patterns of the service demand on various port facilities by vessels and the dwell times of vessels at these port facilities are part of the input.

d) The distributions of the speeds of transiting and calling vessels of different types in the various waterways.

The three main categories of output data reported by the simulation system are

a) The average instantaneous number of vessels per square kilometers in various waterways.

b) The number of times vessels need to change course and/or speed to avoid potential collision per square kilometers.

c) The travelling times between specified source-destination locations.

The average instantaneous number of vessels per square kilometer is used as an indicator of congestion. The number of times vessels need to change course and/or speed to avoid potential collision per square kilometers is an indicator of risk. The travelling time is an important indicator of efficiency and service level of the waterways in a port.

The simulation model is used to simulate some predicted future scenarios of a hub port. This includes alternative configurations of the navigational network and predicted traffic flows. The simulation experiments show the usefulness of the simulation system as a capacity assessment tool.

6. CONCLUSIONS

We have presented the design of a capacity-assessment tool for a network of waterways for hub ports. The carefully calibrated simulation system proves to be suitable for evaluating various aspects of the overall traffic system, for example, assessing the throughput, travel delays, waterway densities, bottlenecks. This system is the first of its kind, capable of covering a complex waterway network with hundreds of vessel access points, handling hundreds of vessels simultaneously with detailed navigational behaviors, and producing the most accurate traffic flows known to date. It is also very flexible, and it may be reconfigured to simulate different traffic scenarios on different networks of waterways. Using this tool we can generate traffic flows under identified scenarios and conduct traffic capacity studies. The model can record the vessel speeds during their journeys, the travel times taken to complete their trips, and the number of instances they are compelled to take special actions (other than cruising at the same speed) to resolve potential conflicts with the other vessels throughout the navigational network. This last statistics is an indicator of the risk of travelling through a certain waterway.

With the tools, future research can develop and evaluate provably-efficient *strategies* to better distribute the vessels among various waterways and anchorages, leading to more robust services for the calling vessels and productive use of sea space.

7. ACKNOWLEDGMENTS

Our thanks go to the Maritime and Port Authority of Singapore for funding the project. We would also like to express our appreciation for Captain Charles De Souza and Captain Daknashamoorthy Ganasen for the helpful discussions about marine traffic rules.

8. REFERENCES

[1] International Maritime Organization (1997): Interim Guideline for the Application of Formal Safety Assessment for the IMO Rule-Making Process, MSC/Circ.829 & MEPC/Circ.335.

[2] CDR S.M. Neill (2001): A Survey of Waterway Capacity and Policy Issues. Web Access: http://gulliver.trb.org/conferences/2001Waterway&Harbor/Neill.pdf

[3] Permanent International Association of Navigation Congresses (1995): Approach Channels: A Guide for Design.

[4] International Association of Lighthouse Authorities (2000): IALA Guidelines on Risk Management.

[5] T. Huet, T. Osman, and C. Ray. Modeling traffic navigation network with a multi-agent platform. In *Proceedings of 17th European Simulation Multi-conference* - SCS Europe, pages 111–117, Nottingham, UK, June 2003.

[6] A. N. Ince and E. Topuz. Modeling and simulation for safe and efficient navigation in narrow waterways. *Journal of navigation*, 57(1), 53–71, 2004.

[7] R. D. Colwill, D. Wignall, and I. Dand. The applications of marine risk simulation to the nearcasting and prevention of collision incidents. In VTS 2004 - *the 10th Int'l Symposium on Vessel Traffic Services*, 2004.

[8] H. Fan and J.-M. Cao. Sea space capacity and operation strategy analysis system. *Transportation Planning and Technology*, 24(1), 49–63, January 2000.

[9] A. Frima. Capacity study for the rio de la plata waterway, Argentina. Master's thesis, Delft University of Technology, October 2004.

[10] J. Golkar, A. Shekhar, and S. Buddhavarapu. Panama canal simulation model. In WSC '98: *Proceedings of the 30th conference on Winter Simulation*, pages 1229–1238. IEEE Computer Society Press, 1998.

[11] K. Hasegawa, G. Tashiro, S. Kiritani, and K. Tachikawa. Intelligent marine traffic simulator for congested waterways. In *Proceedings of International Symposium for Young Researchers on Modeling and their Applications*, pages 181–186, October 2002.

[12] Shell Ying Huang, Wen Jing Hsu and Yuxiong He. (2011). Assessing capacity and improving utilization of anchorages. *Transportation Research Part E: Logistics and Transportation Review, 47*(2), 216-227.

[13] E. Kose, E. Basar, E. Demirci, A. Guneroglu, and S. Erkebay. Simulation of marine traffic in Istanbul strait. *Simulation Modeling Practice and Theory*, 11, 597–608, October 2003.

[14] J. R. van Dorp, J. R. W. Merrick, J. R. Harrald,T. A. Mazzuchi, and M. Grabowski. (2001). A risk management procedure for the Washington state ferries. *Risk Analysis*, 21(1), 127-142.

[15] K. Hasegawa, Some Recent Developments of Next Generation's Marine Traffic Systems, *CAMS* 2004.

[16] L.A.G. Franzese, L.O. Abdenur, R.C. Botter, D. Starks, and A.R. Cano. Simulating the Panama Canal: Present and Future. In *Proc. of the 2004 Winter Simulation Conference*.

[17] B. Park and J.D. Schneeberger, Microscopic Simulation Model Calibration and Validation: Case Study of VISSIM Simulation Model for a Coordinated Actuated Signal System, *Transportation Research Record (TRB)* 2003 Annual Meeting.

[18] E. Brockfeld, R.D. Kuhne, and P. Wagner, Calibration and Validation of Microscopic Traffic Flow MOdels, *Transportation Research Record (TRB)* 2004 Annual Meeting.

[19] L. Chu, H.X. Liu, J. Oh, and W. Recker. A Calibration Procedure for Microscopic Traffic Simulation. *Transportation Research Record (TRB)* 2004 Annual Meeting.

[20] K. Hasegawa. 1993. Knowledge-based Automatic Navigation System for Harbour Maneuvering. *Proc. Of 10th Ship Control Systems Symposium*, pp.67-90.

[21] CheeKuang Tam, Richard Bucknall and Alistair Greig. 2009. Review of Collision Avoidance and Path Planning Methods for Ships in Close Range Encounters. *The Journal of Navigation*, 62, 455–476.

[22] Davis, P. V., M. J. Dove & C. T. Stockel. 1980. A computer simulation of marine traffic using domains and arenas, *The Journal of Navigation*, 33, 215–222.

[23]UNCTAD. 2010. Merchant fleet by flag of registration and by type of ship, annual, 1980-2010. http://unctadstat.unctad.org/TableViewer/tableView.aspx?ReportId=93

Reducing Simulation Costs of Embedded Simulation in Yard Crane Dispatching in Container Terminals

Shell Ying Huang and Xi Guo
School of Computer Engineering
Nanyang Technological University
Block N4, Nanyang Avenue
Singapore 639798
{assyhuang, guox0006}@ntu.edu.sg

ABSTRACT

Embedding simulation in optimization algorithms will incur computational costs. For NP-hard problems the computational costs of the embedded simulation in the optimization algorithm are likely to be substantial. YC dispatching is NP-hard. So it is very important to be able to minimize simulation costs in YC dispatching algorithms. In the optimization algorithm for yard crane dispatching published, simulation of YC operations of the entire (partial) sequence of YC jobs are carried out each time the tardiness of a (partial) sequence needs to be evaluated. In this paper we study two approaches to reduce simulation costs in these embedded simulations in the optimization algorithm. Experimental results show that one approach significantly reduces the computational time of the optimization algorithm. We also analyze the reasons for the other approach which fails to reduce the computational time.

Categories and Subject Descriptors

F.2.2 [**Analysis of Algorithms and Problem Complexity**]: Nonnumerical Algorithms and Problems – *Sequencing and scheduling*

General Terms

Algorithms, Management, Measurement, Performance.

Keywords

Optimization, embedded simulation, computational costs.

1. INTRODUCTION

Container terminals serve as crucial hubs in the global transportation chain of the ever increasing cargo flows. When a vessel berths at a terminal, a number of Quay Cranes (QCs) are allocated to serve the vessel. QCs first unload containers from the vessel onto in-terminal vehicles. Vehicles take the containers to specific job locations at various yard blocks in the storage yard. Yard Cranes (YCs) pick up the containers from the vehicles and temporarily store them in the yard blocks. The operation of loading containers onto a vessel is carried out in the reverse order. External trucks come into the storage yard through terminal gates to the yard blocks to get export containers unloaded or import containers loaded by YCs.

One of the most important objectives of terminal operations is to reduce vessel turnaround time [15]. Previous studies have pointed out that YC operations are of great importance and are likely to be a potential bottleneck to the overall terminal performance [12]. This is because when vehicles are delayed in the storage yard, they will not be able to reach their QCs on time. As a result, the loading/unloading operations of QCs will be delayed and vessel turnaround time lengthened. In YC operation management there are two main problems: (i) deciding job sequence for a YC which we refer to as the YC dispatching problem; (ii) allocating YCs to different parts of the yard which we refer to as the YC deployment problem. This paper is concerned with the efficiency of algorithms to solve the YC dispatching problem.

The YC dispatching problem was studied by Kim and Kim [9] where they considered the loading operations only for a single YC with a given load plan and a given bay plan. A Mixed Integer Programming (MIP) model is proposed to minimize the total gantry time of the YC. Later, Kim and Kim [10] and Kim *et al.* [8] extended the study of this problem by comparing exact optimization, a beam search heuristic and a Genetic Algorithm (GA). Ng and Mak [14] developed a heuristic to solve the single YC dispatching problem with different ready times to minimize the total job waiting time. It is known that for large problems, the MIP model has limited applicability due to the excessive computational times. On the other hand, heuristics cannot guarantee optimal solutions. Guo *et al.* [3] applied A* search to compute optimal single YC dispatching sequence based on vehicle arrival times to minimize vehicle waiting times.

In many works presented in the past, the objective of the YC dispatching algorithm is to minimize the total (average) vehicle waiting time or to minimize the make-span. A more effective way to help reduce vessel turnaround time is to help minimize QC waiting time for a vehicle. In order to avoid the situation where a QC has to wait for a vehicle, the vehicle has to reach the QC by a certain scheduled time. In order to be on time, the vehicle has to finish the transfer of a container at a yard block at a specified time. This time is referred to as the deadline of the vehicle job. Given the deadlines of the vehicle jobs and their predicted arrival times at the yard block, Huang *et al.* [4][5] computes an optimal serving sequence to minimize the average (total) job tardiness. This will be more effective in reducing vessel turnaround time.

When designing a YC dispatching algorithm, many previous works assume that the YC service times for vehicle jobs are constant ([1], [3], [7], [11]). This is correct when the container to be retrieved or stored is on the top of the container stack in the yard. The scenarios where the containers are not on top of the stack are not considered and thus the times to reshuffle some containers are ignored. This assumption simplifies the logic of the algorithms but reduces the applicability of the algorithms in real operations. When a container is not on top of the stack, YC service time for this job is sequence dependent [5]. When a YC dispatching algorithm searches for an optimal job sequence, the sequence dependent service times need to be used to evaluate the quality of a sequence among the alternatives. Simulation of YC job sequence will enable accurate estimation of YC job service times which leads to accurate evaluation of total job tardiness of a sequence. Huang *et al.* [5] embed simulation to estimate the sequence dependent YC services times for jobs in their algorithm to compute total job tardiness of a sequence.

Embedding simulation in optimization algorithms will incur computational costs. For NP-hard problems the computational costs of the embedded simulation in the optimization algorithm are likely to be substantial. YC dispatching is NP-hard [13]. So it is very important to be able to minimize simulation costs in YC dispatching algorithms. In the optimization algorithm for yard crane dispatching published in [5], simulation of YC operations of the entire (partial) sequence of YC jobs are carried out each time the tardiness of a (partial) sequence needs to be evaluated. In this paper we study two approaches to reduce simulation costs of these embedded simulations in the optimization algorithm. The idea is to save the changed yard block states by the YC jobs to avoid repeated simulations. As our experiments show, the method to save the changed states plays a critical role to whether computational time is reduced.

In the remaining parts of the paper, we present the YC dispatching problem and the optimization algorithm which employs embedded simulation [5] in Section 2. Section 3 describes the two approaches with the objective to reduce the costs of the embedded simulation in the optimization algorithm. Then the computational times of using these two approaches are compared with that of the original algorithm in Section 4. Section 5 concludes the paper.

2. THE DISPATCHING PROBLEM AND THE OPTIMAL ALGORITHM

2.1 The Dispatching Problem

In our formulation, the following notations are used:

$J = \{1, 2, \ldots, n\}$,	the set of job identifiers in a YC's working zone for a planning window
a_i	the arrival time of job *i*.
p_i	the service time of job *i* by a YC.
d_i	the deadline of job *i*
m_{ij}	the time for YC gantry from the position of job *i* to that of job *j*.
S_i	the time a YC starts processing job *i*.
C_i	the time a YC completes processing job *i*.

J is the set of in-coming jobs to be sequenced for a YC. m_{0j} is the YC gantry time from its position at the start of the time window to the position of job j. C_0 is the time the YC is available to start to move from its current position to the position of its first job in the YC dispatching sequence.

For a set *J* of *n* vehicle jobs with predicted job arrival times a_i ($i = 1, 2, \ldots, n$), deadlines d_i ($i = 1, 2, \ldots, n$) and YC gantry times m_{ij} ($i = 0, 2, \ldots, n; j = 1, 2, \ldots, n$), the tardiness of a job J_i is defined as $T_i = max\ (0, C_i - d_i)$, where C_i is the completion time of J_i. The objective of YC dispatching is to find a sequence so as to

$$\text{Minimize } \frac{1}{n}\sum_{i \in J} T_i$$

The completion time for job *i* is equal to its start time + service time, that is, $C_i = S_i + p_i$.

We believe that solving the YC dispatching problem by the integer programming approach will not be feasible for practical applications. Given a YC dispatching problem of *n* jobs, there are *n*! possible dispatching solutions in total. The solution space can be transformed into a tree-search problem as shown in Figure 1. The root of the tree is the start node before the first job is selected. Each path from the start node to a leaf node in the tree represents a complete dispatching sequence of height *n*. The edge weight from node *i* to node *j* has a value equal to the tardiness of job *j* if the YC is to do job *j* immediately after finishing job *i*. This edge weight is given by

$$W_{ij} = \max\ \{0, \max\ (C_i + m_{ij}, a_j) + p_j - d_j\} \qquad (1)$$

$C_i + m_{ij}$ is the time the yard crane will arrive at the position of job *j* after finishing job *i*. Therefore max $(C_i + m_{ij}, a_j)$ is the start time of job *j* and max $(C_i + m_{ij}, a_j) + p_j$ is the completion time of job *j*. The task is to find a path of minimum total distance (i.e. minimum total tardiness for a given *n*) from the start node to a leaf node that visits each job exactly once. From (1), it can be seen that each edge weight is not pre-defined and depend on *i*. In addition, the YC service time p_j depends on not only *i* but also all other predecessor jobs in the path from s to *j*. The YC service time depends on whether this job is at the top of the stack *when YC comes to serve this job*. A job which is not at the top of the stack at the beginning of the job sequence may become top of the stack if the containers above it are loaded onto vehicles in the early part of the job sequence. The number of containers to be reshuffled depends on how many containers are on top *at the time when YC comes to serve this job*. So p_j needs to be dynamically computed by the embedded simulation in the process of searching for the optimal job sequence.

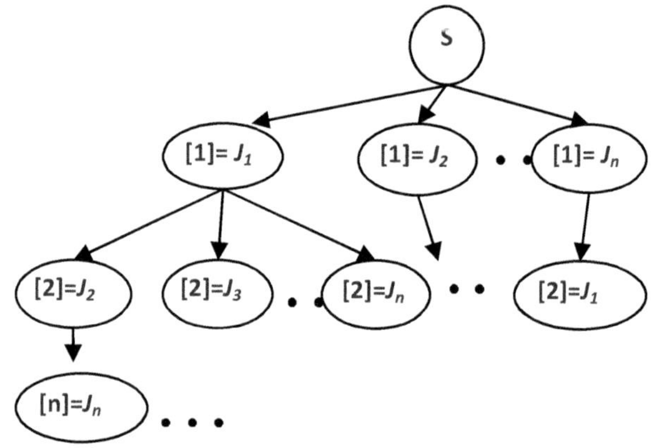

Figure 1. Search Space of the Problem.

At the beginning of the planning window for the YC operations, the number of containers in each stack of the yard block is given. The slot, row and tier numbers of the container of each vehicle job are also given (ref. Figure 2). To determine the service time p_j of a job [*j*] in a path in the search tree in Figure 1, simulation of the YC operations starting from the initial yard block status and the first job in the path is employed in Huang *et al.* [5]. Each job in the path will change the yard block status which may affect the service times of jobs later in the path. We assume that containers at the top of a stack at the beginning of the job sequence will not be blocked by other containers during reshuffling in the early part of the job sequence. This can be guaranteed by the reshuffling policy that will not put a reshuffled container on top of a container stack involved in the job sequence.

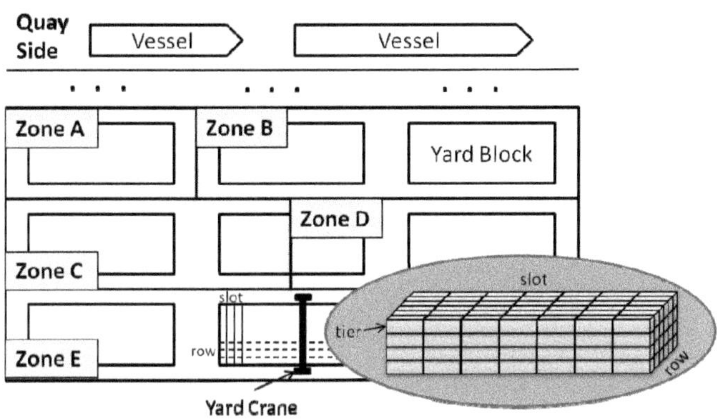

Figure 2. Container Storage yard with yard crane working zones

2.2 The Optimal Algorithm with Embedded Simulation: MT-RBA*

In finding the least-cost path of the YC dispatching problem, we need to traverse the tree to search for the optimal solution. As the problem is strongly NP-hard, exhaustive search would be time-consuming to perform. A Recursive Backtracking (RB) algorithm is therefore used. RB is complete and optimal if the depth of a search tree is finite and there is no time constraint. However, it needs to traverse the entire tree to find the optimal solution, which is time-consuming. An evaluation function $f(i) = g(i) + h(i)$ is used to prune the search space without missing the optimal solution. At any time when expanding the current partial job sequence, if $f(i) = g(i) + h(i)$ is not smaller than the total tardiness of the current best solution, the search path will be pruned.

A YC's dispatching sequence is built by adding jobs to a partial job sequence one at a time. A partial job sequence with job i as the last job is chosen to be expanded if the value of $f(i) = g(i) + h(i)$ is the minimum among all partial sequences. $g(i)$ is the total tardiness from the start node to i and $h(i)$ is the estimated lowest total tardiness from i to a leaf node in the search tree in Figure 1. When a job j is added to a partial sequence, $f(j)$ is computed. The algorithm terminates when the $f(i)$ for all partial sequences is not better than the total tardiness of the current best solution. The current best solution is guaranteed to be the optimal job sequence.

2.2.1 The Total Tardiness of a Partial Sequence, g(i)

The total tardiness of a partial sequence $g(i)$ is the sum of the tardiness of each job as defined by (1). This is obtained by the simulation of the YC operations following the job sequence. The following assumptions about the YC operations are made.

- When storing a container, the YC will put the container at the top of the allocated container stack.
- When retrieving a container, the YC will simply take the container if it is on the top tier of the stack.
- When retrieving a container that is not on the top tier of the stack, the YC will move the container(s) above the wanted container to the top of a stack of a different row in the same slot (bay). In doing so, the YC will not choose a stack which has reached the maximum stack height or it will block the container of a job later in the job sequence. If a suitable stack cannot be identified, a stack in the neighbouring slot will be used. The container(s) moved will have their locations updated. If a moved container is one for a job later in the job sequence, the new location will also be reflected in the job information.
- The time to unload a container from a vehicle and put it on top of a stack, the time to take a container from the top of a stack and load it on a vehicle and the time to move a container from the top of one stack to the top of another stack are assumed to be approximately the same. Let this time be T_p.

Figure 3 shows the pseudocode for the simulation of the YC operations in following the job sequence. The function sequenceTardiness() simulates the YC operations when following a (partial) job sequence JobList and computes the total job tardiness of this sequence. A (partial) job sequence is a path starting from node s and ending at a certain node in the tree in Figure 1. The total tardiness is the sum of W_{ij} as defined by Equation (1) where (i, j) is an edge in the path. The sequence dependent p_j is obtained dynamically by simulating the YC operations in the job sequence. Note that since YC operations change the yard block status, the block status has to be restored to its initial state before the simulation of a job sequence is done each time (first line in sequenceTardiness() in Figure 3).

Simulating YC operations for each (partial) job sequence has a cost. For each sequence, the computation time is $O(n^2)$ where n is the number of jobs in the sequence. It is $O(n^2)$ because for each loading job simulated, the job sequence needs to be searched to see whether a reshuffled container is a future job.

2.2.2 Lower Bound of Total Tardiness, h(i), of Jobs Not Sequenced Yet

An admissible heuristic $h(i)$ is designed to estimate the lower bound of the total tardiness of jobs not included in the job sequence to help evaluate a partial sequence and guide the search for an optimal one.

$$h(i) = [\sum_{j \in F_{later}} (\max(C_i + m_{ij}, a_j) + T_p - d_j)] + [1 + 2 + \ldots + (|F_{later}| - 1)] * T_p + \sum_{k \in F_{earlier}} Max\ \{0, \max(C_i + m_{ik}, a_k) + T_p - d_k\} \quad (2)$$

$h(i)$ computes the lower bound in total job tardiness of jobs not yet included in the YC dispatching sequence if job i is chosen to be the next job in a partial job sequence. F_{later} is the set of jobs that will definitely miss their deadlines. These are the jobs such that even if they are processed immediately after the completion of job i, their completion time will be after their own deadlines. The other group $F_{earlier}$ is the rest of the jobs. In other words, a job j is in F_{later} if its completion time would be after d_j even when it is the immediate next job to be served after job i. For each job j in F_{later}, the minimum tardiness is

```
sequenceTardiness(JobList)    // JobList with job [i] as the last job
{ ReInititalizeYardBlock; //start simulation with initial yard block status
  FOR each job k in JobList    {
       serveJob(JobList,k);
       Calculate job_tardiness;
       update Cummulative Tardiness of Joblist
  }
}

serveJob(JobList, k)       // called from sequenceTardiness()
{ YC moves to JobList[k].slot;    // YC gantry move
  IF JobList[k].isLoading  {
       //Check for reshuffle and update the process time and ContainerLoc
       IF container not at top tier      // reshuffle
              FOR each container above the job  {
                     Set this container's location to unoccupied
                     moveContainer(container's slot, container's row, container's tier)
              }
       Load JobList[k] to vehicle;
       Set container's location to unoccupied;
  } ELSE  {    // unloading
       Unload from vehicle to store in stack;
       Increment the stack height;
       Set container's location to occupied
  }
  pk = number of containers moved * Tp;
}

moveContainer(s,r,t)     //Called from serveJob()
{   FOR each yard bay b starting from s
    FOR each neighbouring row of r  //Shifting to a neighbouring row
        IF height of stack(b, row)< maximum and this stack has no future job {
          Move the container to the stack;
          Set the location to occupied;
              IF container at (s, r, t) is a future job
                   Update job location in JobList;
                  Return;
        }
}
```

Figure 3. Pseudocode for simulation to compute $g(i)$.

$\max(C_i + m_{ij}, a_j) + p_j - d_j$, because the earliest time job j may be started after i is $\max(C_i + m_{ij}, a_j)$. Since p_i for each future job not included in the partial sequence is unknown, T_p is used in its place so that we will never overestimate the tardiness. T_p is The minimum service time of a job (time to load or unload one container without the need to reshuffle other container(s)).

In addition to the above minimum tardiness just explained, the second job to be handled in F_{later} has an additional tardiness of at least one T_p, the minimum service time of the first job handled in F_{later}. The third job to be handled in F_{later} has an additional tardiness of at least $2*T_p$, the sum of minimum job service times of the first and the second job handled in F_{later}. Likewise, the last job to be handled in F_{later} will have an additional tardiness of at least $(|F_{later}|-1)*T_p$, the sum of the job service times for the previous $(|F_{later}|-1)$ jobs in F_{later}. To sum up these minimum tardiness, we have $(1 + 2 + \ldots + (|F_{later}|-1))*T_p$.

Jobs in $F_{earlier}$ are the ones for which $C_i + m_{ik} + T_p \leq d_k$. However, tardiness for a job k in this set will happen if a_k is after $C_i + m_{ik}$ and its completion time $a_k + T_p > d_k$. Note that $a_k + T_p$ is a very conservative estimation of the job completion time since the actual job service time may be longer than T_p if reshuffling of containers is required. The minimum tardiness for such a job is $\max(0, \max(C_i + m_{ik}, a_k) + T_p - d_k)$. The optimality of the job sequence found is guaranteed by the admissible heuristic $h(i)$.

<u>Proof: *h(i)* is admissible</u>

a) The tardiness as expressed by the first two terms in (2) is the very minimum for jobs in F_{later} because (i) each job has at least to wait until Job J_i is complete and move to its location; (ii) it is the total tardiness for these jobs when no job in $F_{earlier}$ would be served before any job in F_{later} and the YC gantry time between jobs is not considered except the first job after J_i.

b) The tardiness as expressed by the last term in (2) is the very minimum for each of the jobs in $F_{earlier}$ as if it were the first job to be served after job J_i.

The three terms in (2) do not overlap with each other, h(i) can never overestimate the total tardiness for the remaining jobs. Thus h(i) can never overestimate the cost to the leaf node and is hence admissible.

2.2.3 *Prioritized Recursive Backtracking with Heuristics*

The algorithm MT-RBA* will not miss the optimal solution and will greatly reduce the computation time of RB. At any time when expanding the current partial job sequence, if $f(i) = g(i) + h(i)$ is not smaller than the total tardiness of the current best solution, the search path will be pruned. Therefore, discovery of a good path which has near-optimal total tardiness at the early stage of the tree search is crucial to the performance of MT-RBA*. For this purpose, a technique called prioritized search order is used which is more likely to discover a good dispatching sequence early in the planning process, instead of choosing the next job randomly. The prioritized search order used is the ascending order of the job deadlines. Intuitively, if the YC serves a job with an earlier deadline first, it will contribute to the minimization of total job tardiness.

3. REDUCING SIMULATION COSTS

3.1 The Issue of Simulation Costs

In general, an optimization problem can be expressed as finding the best solution x to a problem (P), i.e. minimizing or maximizing a function $f(x)$. A solution x fits problem (P) if it satisfies a set of constraints that defines the space X of feasible solutions.

$$Problem\ (P)\ \begin{cases} optimize & f(x) \\ subject\ to & x \in X \end{cases}$$

A general illustration of simulation-based optimization is shown in Figure 4. The main process consists of two components (modules): the *optimization module* and the *simulation module.* The *optimization module* is responsible for (i) generating candidate decision-making solutions; (ii) analyzing and evaluating the prediction of performance λ and (iii) selecting the final solution. The *simulation module* is responsible for conducting what-if simulation experiments according to candidate decision-making solution as requested by the optimization module to predict the performance of these solutions. Simulation-based optimization explores the set of finite solutions $X = \{x_1, x_2, \ldots, x_n\}$ to optimize f. For each candidate solution $x \in X$, the simulation module estimates its performance vector λ. One Challenge in simulation-based optimization is that optimization problems are usually NP-Hard. The number of candidate solutions is increasing exponentially or faster than exponentially with the size of the problem. So reducing computational costs in both the optimization module and the simulation module is very important.

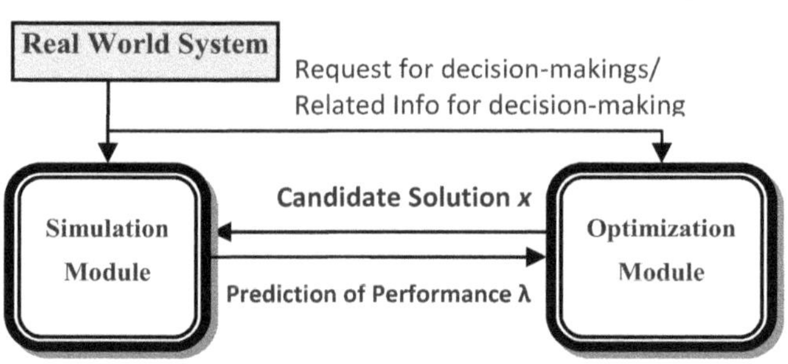

Figure 4. Simulation-based optimization.

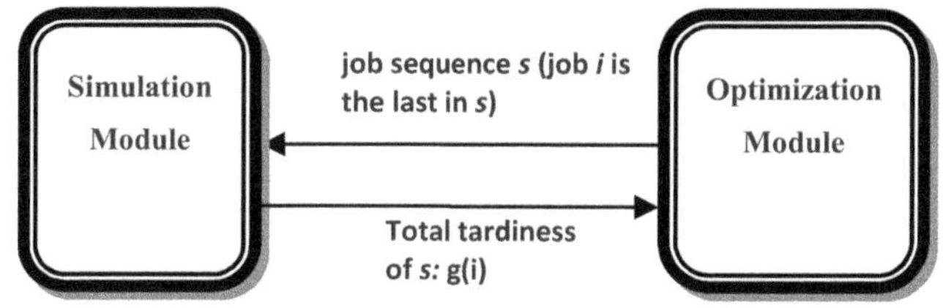

Figure 5. Optimal YC dispatching with embedded simulation.

For our YC dispatching algorithm, the optimization module and the simulation module collaborate in the way as shown in Figure 5. The same problem about the number of candidate solutions exists: we have $n!$ candidate solutions for a job sequence of n jobs. For each full length job sequence, there are n-1 partial sequences. So if there is no pruning of solutions, there will be $n*n!$ partial and complete solutions to be simulated and evaluated. The MT-RBA* algorithm discussed in the last section has pruned the solution space substantially by the heuristic function $h(i)$. However, numerous repeated simulations of partial job sequences are carried out. For each partial and complete job sequence, simulation of every job in the sequence as shown in Figure 3 is performed.

We make the observation that among the candidate (partial) solutions, there are many common prefixes. For example, job sequences 1, 2, 3, 4 and 1, 2, 4, 3 have the common prefix 1, 2. In general, when an optimization algorithm needs to evaluate a number of what-if scenarios, there will be common prefix of sequences of events that happen among these scenarios. The common prefix of sequences of events means the system starts with the same initial state and goes through the same sequence of events, arriving at the same system state after these events. Is there an effective way to avoid the repeated simulation of the common prefixes? We examine two methods of avoiding repeated simulations in evaluating partial job sequences in YC dispatching.

3.2 Approach 1

We may consider a candidate solution $x \in X$ as composed of a sequence of n decisions $\{d_1, d_2, \ldots, d_n\}$, the system S which these decisions act upon as composed of a number of m components or parts, that is,

$$S = S_1 \cup S_2 \cup \ldots S_m.$$

If we denote the system state after decision d_i of sequence x by $S_x(d_i)$, then

$$S_x(d_i) = S_{1,x}(d_i) \cup S_{2,x}(d_i) \cup \ldots S_{m,x}(d_i)$$

where $S_{j,x}(d_i)$ is the state of component j after decision d_i of sequence x. Very often, a decision d_i will not affect the whole system S but only one or two components. If the partition of S is appropriately done, it helps to keep the number of components affected by each decision low. It is also possible that multiple decisions, say, d_i and d_h, will affect the same component of the system one after another. Therefore,

$$S_{j,x}(d_i) = S_{j,x}(d_{i-1}) \qquad \text{component } j \text{ is not affected by } d_i$$
$$S_{j,x}(d_i) = \text{transform}(d_i, S_{j,x}(d_{i-1})) \qquad \text{component } j \text{ affected.} \qquad (3)$$

```
sequenceTardiness(JobList)
// JobList is the job sequence x with [i] as the last job
// job [i]'s container involves slot j
{
    If JobList has only one job      // the job sequence has just started with one job
       Sx_affected(di) = empty list;
    Else
       Sx_affected(di) = new list;       // create space for the states of affected slots
       Sx_affected(di) = Sx_affected(di-1); // make a copy of the states of affected slots so far

     If Sj,x(di-1) is not in Sx_affected(di-1)          // if slot j is affected for the first time
                                          // Sj,x(d0)is the slot status before the 1st job
       Sj,x(di) = Sj,x(d0);               // make a copy of the original state of slot j
       Sx_affected(di).insert(Sx,j(di));

     serveJob(JobList,i, Sx_affected(di));
     Calculate job_tardiness;
     update Cummulative Tardiness of Joblist
}

serveJob(JobList, k, Sx_affected(di))
{
// basically the same as serveJob() in Figure 2
// but the yard block status update is to Sx_affected(di)
}
```

Figure 6. Pseudocode for approach 1.

The function transform() is the state transformation function if decision d_i is performed on the system component j with state $S_{j,x}(d_{i-1})$.

For example, in the yard crane dispatching system, x is a job sequence; d_i is the job chosen to be the ith job in the job sequence. S includes the yard block status and the total job tardiness. $S_{j,x}$ includes the status of the jth yard slot (yard bay). A loading or unloading operation by a YC will affect only one yard slot. So each d_i will change one $S_{j,x}$. In other words,

$$S_{j,x}(d_i) = S_{j,x}(d_{i-1}) \qquad \text{if job } d_i \text{ is not in yard slot } j$$

The function transform(d_i, $S_{j,x}(d_{i-1})$) in Equation (3) will return the yard slot state of slot j after the loading/unloading job d_i is performed on slot j with state $S_{j,x}(d_{i-1})$. Sometimes, multiple jobs may be at the same yard slot j. Then $S_{j,x}$ will change multiple times.

If there are k jobs in a (partial) sequence x, the MT-RBA* algorithm discussed in the last section simulates x as requested by the optimization module from d_1 till d_k to compute the sequence dependent total job tardiness. To avoid repeating the simulation from d_1 till d_{k-1}, $S_x(d_{k-1})$ needs to be saved for the computation of the tardiness of d_k. However, saving the entire system state $S_x(d_k)$ for $k = 1, 2, n$ and all $x \in X$ will mean saving $n*n!$ system states if there is no pruning of search space. In other words, instead of simulating and evaluating $n*n!$ partial and complete dispatching solutions, $n*n!$ system states are saved, even though at any time at most n system states are saved by the recursive backtracking algorithm. A better approach will be to save the changed components of the system only. For each job sequence x including partial sequences, we divide $S_x(d_i)$ into two subsets:

$$S_x(d_i) = S_{x\_notaffected}(d_i) \cup S_{x\_affected}(d_i).$$

$S_{x\_affected}(d_i)$ contains all $S_{j,x}(d_i)$ where yard slot j is involved in a job d_k, ($k = 1, 2, \ldots, i$). $S_{x\_notaffected}(d_i)$ contains all $S_{j,x}(d_i)$ where yard slot j is not involved in any job in the sequence till d_i. Each job sequence x, including partial sequences, keeps a copy of $S_{x\_affected}(d_i)$. In other words, all the changes made to the yard slots by the jobs in the sequence till d_i are saved in each partial sequence. There will be no need to repeat the simulation of these jobs when the sequence dependent YC service time is computed for the next job. This computation just needs to refer to $S_{x\_affected}(d_{i-1})$ to get the up to date yard slot state for any slot affected by an earlier operation in the sequence, or the initial yard slot state if the slot will be affected for the first time. So only the changes made by the next job will be simulated to compute the job service time and the tardiness of the job. The pseudocode for this approach is presented in Figure 6.

Each (partial) job sequence x, in fact, each node in the search tree of Figure 1, keeps a copy of $S_{x\_affected}(d_i)$. So when the job sequence is extended from the previous job d_{i-1} to the next job d_i, $S_{x\_affected}(d_i)$ first makes a copy of $S_{x\_affected}(d_{i-1})$ in the module sequenceTardiness() in Figure 6. If slot j has not been affected by the previous jobs in the sequence and is going to be affected by job d_i, $S_{j,x}(d_i)$ will be initiated to the initial state of slot j before the job sequence and then inserted into $S_{x\_affected}(d_i)$. If slot j has been affected by a previous job in the sequence, $S_{j,x}(d_i)$ which is a copy of $S_{j,x}(d_{i-1})$ is already in $S_{x\_affected}(d_i)$. Then the module serveJob() will simulate job d_i and update the state $S_{j,x}(d_i)$ in $S_{x\_affected}(d_i)$.

3.3 Approach 2

Approach 1 removes the need of repeated simulation of jobs in a job sequence by keeping a copy of all the changed states of yard slots for each partial sequence. It does not keep a copy of the state of the entire system S, that is, $S_x(d_i)$ for all i. Therefore it does not require all $S_{j,x}(d_i)$ for all j and i to be maintained. However, there is still the overhead of keeping $S_{x\_affected}(d_i)$ for all i both in terms of allocating memory space and copying. In Approach 2, the cost of allocating memory space and copying of $S_{x\_affected}(d_i)$ for all i is further reduced to a minimum: only the state of the yard slot changed by d_i is kept in each node of the search tree, together with the references to the most up to date state of each yard slot. In other words, if d_i operates on slot j,

$$S_x(d_i) = P\_S_{1,x}(d_i) \cup P\_S_{2,x}(d_i) \cup \ldots \cup \&(S_{j,x}(d_i)) \ldots \cup P\_S_{m,x}(d_i)$$

where $P\_S_{k,x}(d_i)$ is the reference to the most up to date state of yard slot k (k = 1, 2, ..., m) in place of the actual state of the slot. Therefore if slot k has not been changed by any d_i for i = 1, 2, ..., $P\_S_{k,x}(d_i)$ will all be references to the initial state of the slot before the job sequence. Figure 7 shows the pseudocode for Approach 2.

Each node in the search tree of Figure 1 keeps an array of references to the most up to date states of the yard slots. As shown in Figure 7, before the current operation d_i is simulated, space is created for the array to store the references to the yard slot states. The entries in this array get the references to the up to date yard slot states from the previous operation (or the previous node in the search path of the tree in Figure 1). For each node (job) added to a search path in the tree, space is created for the storage of the state of the yard slot j which is going to be changed by the current operation d_i. Then $P\_S_{j,x}(d_i)$ will be the reference to this state. It should be noted that the space needed for the array of references is less than that for $S_{x\_affected}(d_i)$ in Approach 1.

4. PERFORMANE EVALUATION

4.1 Design of experiments

Experiments were carried out to evaluate the effectiveness of the proposed approaches to reduce simulation costs of embedded simulation in YC planning. We compare Approach 1 and Approach 2 against the algorithm using repeated simulation which is referred to as Approach 0. The linear gantry speed of a YC is 7.8km/hour. A yard block has a size of 36 slots. The size of a YC's working zone is an input parameter of the simulation experiments. The values used are shown in Table 1.

We assume that the vehicle job inter-arrival times follow exponential distributions. Mean inter-arrival time is an input parameter of the simulation experiments. The tested scenarios are listed in Table 1. The job deadlines are set in the same way as in [5]. They depend on the type of jobs: relatively tight deadlines for loading jobs and less tight deadlines for unloading jobs. This reflects the fact that it is more important to finish loading jobs on time than unloading jobs. Following the design of Chu [2], these deadlines are generated from uniform distributions with a width of 6 minutes for loading jobs and 12 minutes for unloading jobs. For external vehicle jobs, the deadline is 30 minutes after the truck's arrival. This follows the practice of some terminals where they guarantee that external trucks will finish their loading/unloading jobs within half an hour after their arrivals to the terminal. The slot and row numbers of the jobs are generated randomly within the zone. Other recent studies using randomized container locations include, for example, Zeng and Yang [16]. A planning window of 10 jobs for a YC is simulated. In other words, a dispatching sequence of 10 jobs is to be optimized.

Table 1. Mean job inter-arrival times and YC working zone sizes.

Mean job inter-arrival time	High traffic (180 seconds)			Medium traffic (240 seconds)		
YC working zone size	1 blk	1.5 blk	2 blk	1 blk	1.5 blk	2 blk

The types of jobs that arrive to the yard crane working zone are a mixture of vessel loading or unloading jobs and external truck loading or unloading jobs. Each container move by a YC is assumed to be 2 minutes regardless of whether it is to store or retrieve a container or to reshuffle a container to a nearby stack. For the purpose of measuring the simulation costs of the different approaches, we classify the jobs according to which tier the container is to be stored or retrieved. We tested three different

```
sequenceTardiness(JobList)
// JobList is the job sequence x with [i] as the last job
// job [i]'s container involves slot j
{
  P_Sx(di) = new array;           // create space for the references to the states of slots
  If JobList has only one job     // the job sequence has just started with one job
      P_Sx(di) = references to the initial states of the yard slots;
  else
      P_Sx(di) = copy of P_Sx(di-1) // make a copy of the references to component states

  Sj,x = new slot state;          // allocate space to store the state of slot j
  Sj,x = copy of *(P_Sx(di-1)[j]) // copy the most up to date state of slot j into Sj,x

  P_Sx(di)[j] = &Sj,x;            // P_Sx(di)[j] is now the reference to the copy of
                                  // the most up to date state of slot j

  serveJob(JobList,i, P_Sx(di));
  Calculate job_tardiness;
  update Cummulative Tardiness of Joblist
}

serveJob(JobList, k, P_Sx(di))
{
// basically the same as serveJob() in Figure 2
// but the yard block status update is through P_Sx(di)
}
```

Figure 7. Pseudocode for approach 2.

mixtures of jobs with increasing percentages of jobs not on the top tier (tier 1), as shown in Table 2. When the tier number of a job is not the top tier, reshuffling may be needed depending on the job sequence as discussed in Section 3.1. The average tier number of all jobs in the three job mixtures tested increases from 1.43 to 1.47 and then to 1.63. The average tier number is also the average number of container moves needed per job. So on average, 0.43, 0.47 and 0.63 containers respectively need to be reshuffled before each container is loaded or unloaded in the yard block for the three job mixtures.

For each experimental setting, 30 independent runs were performed.

Table 2. Job mixtures in terms of job tier numbers.

Job mixture	Tier no. of job	Percentage
1 (Average tier number of all jobs is 1.43)	Top tier	72.5%
	2nd top tier	14.5%
	3rd top tier	10.5%
	4th top tier	2.5%
2 (Average tier number of all jobs is 1.47)	Top tier	68.5%
	2nd top tier	18.5%
	3rd top tier	10.5%
	4th top tier	2.5%
3 (Average tier number of all jobs is 1.63)	Top tier	56.5%
	2nd top tier	26.5%
	3rd top tier	14.5%
	4th top tier	2.5%

4.2 Results and Discussions

All three approaches produce the same job sequences with minimum total tardiness. We examine the computational costs of these three approaches.

Figures 8-13 show the average computational times of the three approaches with varying yard crane working zone sizes for the six combinations of job mixtures and job arrival rates. For every one of these combinations, Approach 1 actually consumes more computational times than Approach 0. In other words, keeping copies of the changed yard slot states in each node of the search tree to avoid repeated simulation incurs higher computational costs than repeated simulations, in addition to the costs of extra memory space. For every one of these combinations, Approach 2 is able to reduce the computational costs significantly compared with Approach 0. So Approach 2 is effective in reducing the computational costs of embedded simulation in the optimization of YC job sequences in all the tested scenarios.

Both Approach 1 and Approach 2 save computational time by not repeating the simulation of a job in all the partial sequences and the final complete job sequence involving this job, if the search path in the tree has not been pruned. The difference between them is that Approach 1 keeps a dynamically generated list of the changed yard slot states in each node of the search tree while Approach 2 keeps a static array of references to the most up to date state of each yard slot in each node of the search tree. Approach 1 uses a dynamically generated list of changed yard slot states in each node because the number of slots affected by the jobs in a partial or complete job sequence cannot be predetermined. Approach 2 uses a static array of references that will be the pointer to the most up to date state of the yard slots in the yard crane's working zone. The number of references is predetermined by the number of yard slots in the YC's working zone. The generation of an array of a predetermined size is an one-time cost and the generation of a list which grows dynamically incurs a higher cost. Copying of $S_{x\_affected}(d_{i-1})$ to $S_{x\_affected}(d_i)$ in Approach 1 is also more expensive than copying $P\_S_x(d_{i-1})$ to $P\_S_x(d_i)$ in Approach 2.

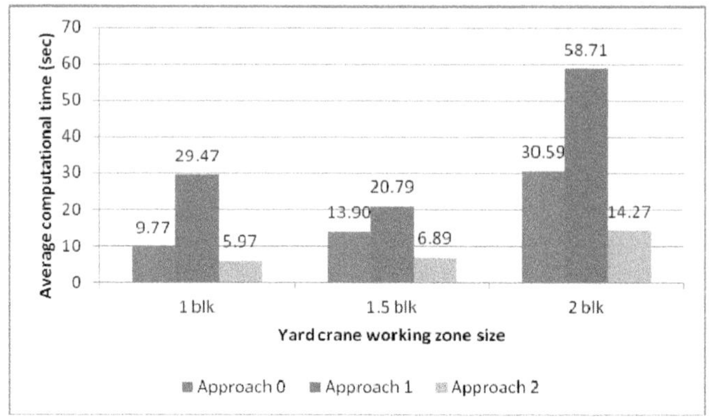

Figure 8. Average computational times for job mixture 1 (high traffic).

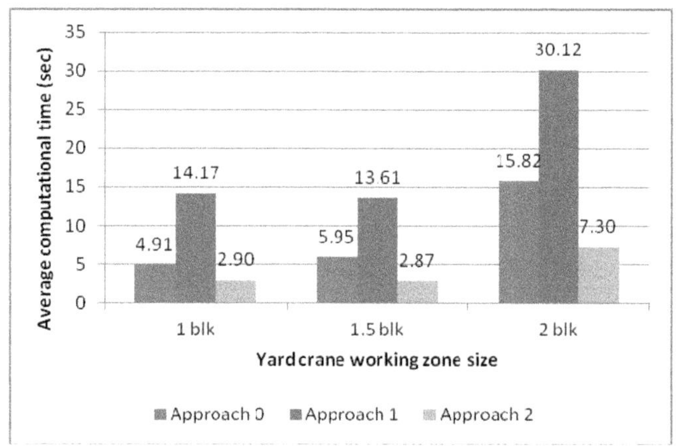

Figure 9. Average computational times for job mixture 1 (medium traffic).

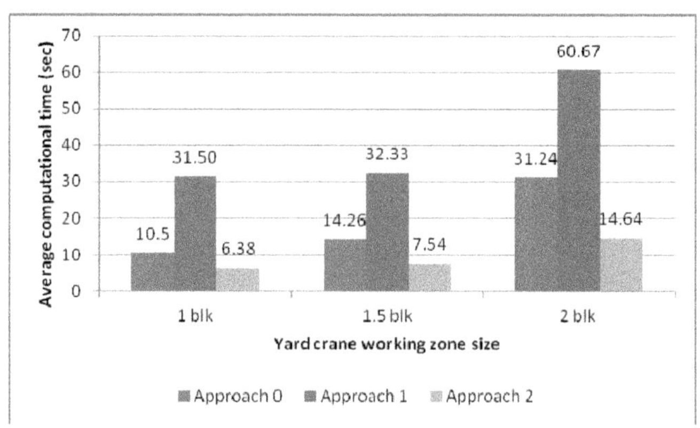

Figure 10. Average computational times for job mixture 2 (high traffic).

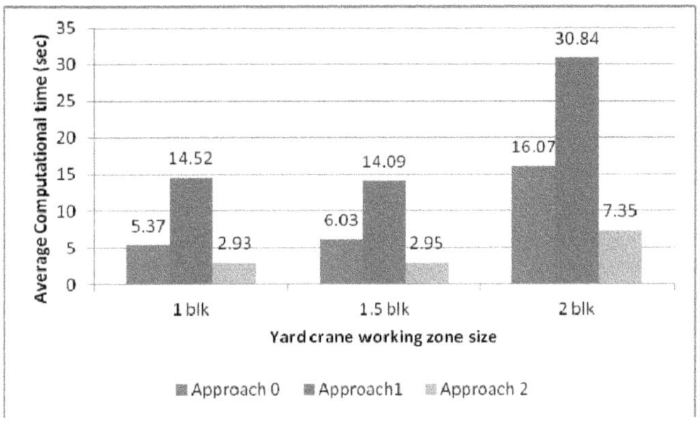

Figure 11. Average computational times for job mixture 2 (medium traffic).

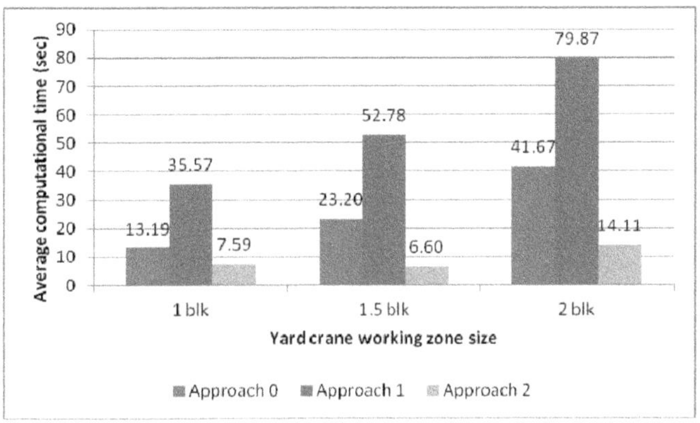

Figure 12. Average computational times for job mixture 3 (high traffic).

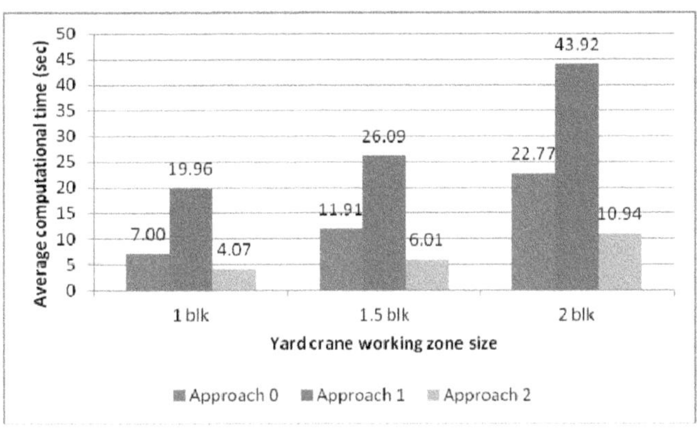

Figure 13. Average computational times for job mixture 3 (medium traffic).

Both approach 1 and approach 2 try to reduce the computational time by avoiding the repeated simulation. This is done by saving the changed yard block status in their ways as described earlier. Tables 3 and 4 show the average extra memory space in megabytes these two approaches *requested* during their execution. Since the amount of space used expands and contracts at different instances in time during execution, the amounts shown in the tables are not the maximum memory sizes used. For Approach 1 it is the sum of the space used to save the dynamically generated list of the changed yard slot states in each node of the search tree explored in the MT-RBA* algorithm. For Approach 2, it is the sum of the space used to save the static array of references and the state of the yard slot changed by the job in each node of the search tree explored. So Approach 2 actually requests less memory space than Approach 1. Since Approach 1's dynamically generated list is implemented by a vector which is a dynamic array (a vector), there is also the run time cost in supporting it.

Table 3. Average extra memory space in megabytes requested by approaches 1 and 2 compared with approach 0 (high traffic).

Job mix-ture	Approach 1			Approach 2		
	1 blk	1.5 blk	2 blk	1 blk	1.5 blk	2 blk
1	327.28	399.22	743.15	70.86	87.52	178.66
2	339.66	409.08	757.16	73.49	90.39	147.08
3	398.97	602.29	988.64	87.47	87.70	184.83

Table 4. Average extra memory space in megabytes requested by approaches 1 and 2 compared with approach 0 (medium traffic).

Job mix-ture	Approach 1			Approach 2		
	1 blk	1.5 blk	2 blk	1 blk	1.5 blk	2 blk
1	160.28	166.66	377.44	36.00	37.72	95.05
2	167.07	170.39	380.55	36.93	38.63	75.36
3	211.36	304.98	528.26	47.61	72.66	130.74

5. CONCLUSIONS

A simulation-based optimization algorithm explores a set of finite solutions $X = \{x_1, x_2, \ldots, x_n\}$ to optimize a certain objective function. Simulation helps to evaluate the objective function values of the candidate solutions which cannot be obtained accurately otherwise. But the computational costs are often very high. We propose two approaches to reduce the computational costs in embedded simulation in the algorithm MT-RBA* to compute optimal job sequences for YCs for minimizing vehicle job tardiness. Minimizing tardiness helps vehicles to support QC operations with minimal delays in the loading and unloading process and therefore reduce vessel turnaround time. Both approaches try to reduce computational costs by removing the need for repeated simulation of common prefixes of sequences of decisions among alternative candidate job sequences.

Approach 1 saves a copy of the changed system state which includes the states of all yard slots involved in every partial and complete dispatching sequence. Our experimental results show that the overhead in saving the changed system states is very expensive and it outweighs the time saved from avoiding repeated simulations. Approach 2 keeps a copy of the references to the changed system states and a copy of the changed yard slot state in each partial or complete dispatching sequence. Our experimental results show that this approach significantly reduces the computational time of the YC dispatching algorithm. It is with an overhead of extra memory space. It should be noted that if the memory space is available, saving time in computing the optimal job sequence will improve the terminal operations significantly.

This yard crane dispatching algorithm may be incorporated into a terminal operating system which is able to predict the job deadlines and vehicle arrival times at the yard blocks. Then the algorithm will be useful in real operations. An investigation into such a system is done in [6].

In general, many decision support systems need to evaluate a large number of what-if scenarios by simulation. Very often, there will be common prefix of sequences of events that happen among these scenarios. To be able to keep the simulation costs in evaluating these scenarios low will greatly increase the capability and applicability of these decision support systems. This study shows one possible approach of doing this.

6. ACKNOWLEDGMENTS

Our thanks to Lim Wei Lin and Ong Yi Long for some of the programming help.

7. REFERENCES

[1] Cao, Z., D. H. Lee, and Q. Meng. 2008. Deployment strategies of double-rail-mounted gantry crane systems for loading outbound containers in container terminals, *International Journal of Production Economics*, 115, 221–228.

[2] Chu, C. 1992. A branch-and-bound algorithm to minimize total tardiness with different release dates, In *Naval Research Logistics*, 39(2), 265–283.

[3] Guo, X., S. Y. Huang, W. J. Hsu, M. Y. H. Low. 2011. Dynamic Yard Crane Dispatching in Container Terminals with Predicted Vehicle Arrival Information, *Advanced Engineering Informatics*, 25(3), 472-484.

[4] Huang S. Y., X. Guo, W. J. Hsu and W. L. Lim. 2012. Yard Crane Dispatching to Minimize Job Tardiness in Container Terminals, *The 2012 International Conference on Logistics and Maritime Systems.*

[5] Huang S. Y., X. Guo, W. J. Hsu and W. L. Lim. 2012. Embedding Simulation in Yard Crane Dispatching to Minimize Job Tardiness in Container Terminals, *Proceedings of the 2012 Winter Simulation Conference.*

[6] Huang S. Y., Z. C. Tay and W. J. Hsu. A Framework for Automated Real Time Management of Container Handling Equipment. To be submitted to *The 2013 International Conference on Logistics and Maritime Systems.*

[7] Jung, S. H., and K. H. Kim. 2006. Load scheduling for multiple quay cranes in port container terminals, *Journal of Intelligent Manufacturing*, 17, 479–492.

[8] Kim, K. H., J. S. Kang, and K. R. Ryu. 2004. A beam search algorithm for the load sequencing of outbound containers in port container terminals, *OR Spectrum*, 26, 93–116.

[9] Kim, K. M., and K. Y. Kim. 1999. An optimal routing algorithm for a transfer crane in port container terminals, *Transportation Science,* 33(1), 17–33.

[10] Kim, K. Y., and K. H. Kim. 2003. Heuristic algorithms for routing yard-side equipment for minimizing loading times in container terminals, *Naval Research Logistics*, 50, 498–514.

[11] Lee, L. H., E. P. Chew, K. C. Tan, and Y.B. Han. 2006. An optimization model for storage yard management in transshipment hubs, *OR Spectrum*, 28, 539-561.

[12] Li, W., Y. Wu, M. Petering, M. Goh, and R. d. Souza. 2009. Discrete time model and algorithms for container yard crane scheduling, *European Journal of Operational Research*, 198, 165–172.

[13] Narasimhan A. and U.S. Palekar. 2002. Analysis and Algorithm for the Transtainer Routing Problem in Container Port Operation, *Transportation Science* 36(1), 63–78.

[14] Ng, W. C. and K. L. Mak. 2005. An effective heuristic for scheduling a yard crane to handle jobs with different ready times, *Engineering Optimization*, 37(8), 867-877.

[15] Steenken, D., S. Voβ, and R. Stahlbock. 2004. Container terminal operation and operations research – a classification and literature review, *OR Spectrum*, 26, 3-49.

[16] Zeng, Q. and Z. Yang. 2009. Integrating simulation and optimization to schedule loading operations in container terminals, *Computers & Operations Research*, 36(6), 1935–1944.

Consistent and Efficient Output-Streams Management in Optimistic Simulation Platforms

Francesco Antonacci Alessandro Pellegrini Francesco Quaglia
DIAG – Sapienza, University of Rome

ABSTRACT

Optimistic synchronization is considered an effective means for supporting Parallel Discrete Event Simulations. It relies on a speculative approach, where concurrent processes execute simulation events regardless of their safety, and consistency is ensured via proper rollback mechanisms, upon the a-posteriori detection of causal inconsistencies along the events' execution path. Interactions with the outside world (e.g. generation of output streams) are a well-known problem for rollback-based systems, since the outside world may have no notion of rollback. In this context, approaches for allowing the simulation modeler to generate consistent output rely on either the usage of ad-hoc APIs (which must be provided by the underlying simulation kernel) or temporary suspension of processing activities in order to wait for the final outcome (commit/rollback) associated with a speculatively-produced output. In this paper we present design indications and a reference implementation for an output streams' management subsystem which allows the simulation-model writer to rely on standard output-generation libraries (e.g. `stdio`) within code blocks associated with event processing. Further, the subsystem ensures that the produced output is consistent, namely associated with events that are eventually committed, and system-wide ordered along the simulation time axis. The above features jointly provide the illusion of a classical (simple to deal with) sequential programming model, which spares the developer from being aware that the simulation program is run concurrently and speculatively. We also show, via an experimental study, how the design/development optimizations we present lead to limited overhead, giving rise to the situation where the simulation run would have been carried out with near-to-zero or reduced output management cost. At the same time, the delay for materializing the output stream (making it available for any type of audit activity) is shown to be fairly limited and constant, especially for good mixtures of I/O-bound vs CPU-bound behaviors at the application level. Further, the whole output streams' management subsystem has been designed in order to provide scalability for I/O management on clusters.

Categories and Subject Descriptors

I.6.8 [**Simulation and Modeling**]: Types of Simulation—*Discrete Event, Parallel*; B.4.3 [**Input/Output and Data Communications**]: Interconnections (Subsystems)—*Parallel I/O*; D.2.8 [**Software Engineering**]: Metrics—*Performance Measures*

General Terms

Theory, Design, Experimentation, Performance

Keywords

PDES, Output Commit, Transparency, Consistency, Rollback, ROOT-Sim

1. INTRODUCTION

Parallel Discrete Event Simulation [7] is based on the partitioning of the simulation model into several (distinct) simulation objects, whose execution is undertaken by Logical Processes (LP), which are hosted (and scheduled) by one or more simulation kernel instances. Given that LPs are allowed to run concurrently, the PDES approach is natively prone to exploit the computing power offered by multi-core and/or clustered architectures in order to speedup the simulation run. The actual speed is determined by the synchronization scheme that is adopted in order to ensure causally consisted (e.g. timestamp ordered) execution of the events at each LP.

The optimistic synchronization protocol, as described in [9], has established itself as a successful support to the execution of efficient simulation runs. In particular, it entails speculative event processing schemes, coupled with rollback/recover mechanisms for squashing causally-inconsistent event processing, which are prone to maximal exploitation of the parallelism intrinsic to the simulation model. On the other hand, the optimistic protocol is well known to be difficult to deal with in terms of transparency to the modeler, given that its complexity (e.g. in terms of state restore operations and annihilation of inconsistent events' spreading across the LPs) may require the application layer to entail synchronization oriented code blocks, to be employed in synergy with the facilities offered by the underlying simulation kernel. On the other hand, masking synchronization at all to the modeler, while not sacrificing performance due to the avoidance of application vs kernel layer synergic programming schemes, would require very advanced methodologies/algorithms, and related implementations, which nowadays represent a major challenge for the diffusion of the optimistic PDES paradigm in the large. Some solutions along this direction, which have been oriented to full (or partial) transparency for what concerns state recovery of the LPs and/or mutual consistency of LPs' states and shared data can be found in [3, 16, 20, 23]. They represent a step ahead along the path of bringing the power of the optimistic PDES paradigm into the hands of ordinary modelers (namely programmers).

In this paper, we cope with the aforementioned transparency vs performance issue for what concerns the production of output streams in optimistic simulation runs. Particularly, we focus on how to efficiently and transparently tackle the output commitment problem [5] in optimistic simulation, which is related to the possibility for a simulation model (executed optimistically) to interact with the outside world, e.g. by producing output on a screen, on a network device, on a printer, or on any other device which might be unable to undo the output materialization in case a rollback operation is triggered because of a-posteriori causality inconsistency detection (see Figure 1). This timely and consistent interaction can be significant for all those simulation scenarios where the evaluation of (possibly unstable) predicates should be done on a global scale, via audit on individual LPs' state trajectories. With our approach, we explicitly free the simulation-model developer from facing the notion of *event commitment*, and allow her to rely on output calls (to be invoked within the modeler-defined event handlers), which are properly managed by the simulation kernel. More precisely, the application-level developer can rely on standard libraries calls (e.g., on the `printf()` family functions) to produce output on some streams, and the burden of materializing the actual output is placed on a specifically-targeted runtime subsystem which, at the same time, provides:

(i) *consistency*, by finalizing the actual output operation only if it is associated with an event which gets committed, and by system-wide ordering the output messages along the simulation time axis (as if they were produced by a sequential run of the same model);

(ii) *efficiency*, by inducing only a small (negligible) overhead at the side of the engine running the simulation model; and

(iii) *timeliness*, by placing only a reduced delay from the generation to the materialization of the output on the specified stream, unless for applications constantly exhibiting I/O-bound profile along the whole run.

Traditionally, PDES simulation frameworks (see, e.g., [8, 14, 19]) have relied on ad-hoc APIs for delivering consistent output related to the (progressively advancing) state trajectory while executing the simulation model, in order to (incrementally) provide, e.g., model statistics. This forces the model writer to look more deeply into the internal details of simulation supports, making the development of the application more cumbersome and more constrained to the specific programming model supported by the framework. On the other hand, in case the modeler would rely on non-consistent output production via the exploration of standard I/O libraries, the output streams would need to be post-processed for cleaning them from messages produced by events that got eventually rolled-back, and for providing a unique globally timestamp-ordered trace, if needed.

Our proposal is based on the concept of an ad-hoc *daemon*, i.e. a separate user-space process with respect to the actual simulation framework. Once equipped with our I/O-management-stub, the simulation kernel instances within the framework can communicate with the daemon process via in-memory, fast-access, shared data structures. They are used to support an additional level of temporary buffering which is biased to reduce the cost for managing output streams (and their consistency) at the side of the framework (as opposed to the typical buffering rules/schemes used by standard I/O libraries). Particularly, via this additional buffering subsystem we achieve: (i) *reduced interaction time*, by developing a non-blocking algorithm for accessing shared memory segments by the simulation kernel instances and the output daemon (hence materializing the scenario where a near-to-zero-cost (transparently consistent) logical output device is accessible by the simulation framework), and (ii) *enhanced scalability* (even at a geographical scale), allowing to process the commitment of the output on a multi-level basis; particularly, the daemon exploits Global-Virtual-Time (GVT) computation already natively performed by the framework in order to finalize the production of the output streams, which avoids the need for I/O specific consensus protocols to be run. As an additional advantage, the output daemon can run as a *stream forwarder*, allowing the user to retrieve output on a separate (dedicated) machine with respect to the cluster of machines used for model execution.

The efficiency of our proposal is daemonstrated via an extensive experimental study carried out in the context of a wireless communication system model, hosted on top of the ROOT-Sim open source PDES optimistic simulation framework [8].

The remainder of this paper is structured as follows. In Section 2, related work is discussed. Section 3 deals with theoretical aspects of output management in optimistic simulation, presenting involved issues, proposing a general design approach, and depicting our architecture/implementation, also showing how it could be simply interconnected with any existing simulation engine. Experimental data, for assessing the effectiveness of our proposal, are reported in Section 4.

2. RELATED WORK

The issue of output commitment in rollback recovery systems has been thoroughly studied in literature. An excellent survey on the proposed approaches can be found in [5]. These solutions have been oriented to fault tolerance, where rollback occurrence is due to failures, potentially causing the loss of volatile state information causally related to the output message (which might lead to un-recognize the relation between the delivered output and the actual system state, after rollback). Overall, these schemes are aimed at supporting reproducibility of state trajectories (and related outputs) in order to keep the system state aligned with what is actually observed by the external world. Instead, in optimistic PDES systems we experience the problem of masking the outcome of specific state trajectories (those that are rolled back) towards the external world. Further, the approaches surveyed in [5] deal with the Lamport's causality model [13], where no predetermination of events' ordering is imposed by pre-computed event timestamps, as instead it occurs in PDES systems. On the basis of the above considerations, our work can be considered orthogonal to these solutions.

Still in the context of fault tolerance, the work in [11] presents an innovative protocol for supporting output commitment specifically aimed at promptly delivering output data, which is one of the target of our work. It places special attention on state-information copies on stable storage, to overcome the failure of processes and minimizing the time for restarting the execution of the system in case of failure. Despite the goal differences (already discussed above), this work is based on a communication protocol which tries to minimize the time from the output generation and its materialization. Differently from this proposal, we do not explicitly rely on a special communication protocol for committing the output, rather we exploit the GVT computation protocol (endemically required by optimistic PDES systems) to get information about which portion of the generated output can be considered committed, avoiding any additional communication cost.

The work in [22] addresses the problem of external-world interactions in the context of Transactional Memories (TM). In particular, the work focuses on what a TM system (either software or hardware) should support to allow the execution of irrevocable actions, such as I/O and system calls, when the side effects cannot be rolled back. The proposed solution allows the programmer to mark a specific transaction as *irrevocable*, i.e. the interactions with the external world are immediately finalized, and the correctness is guaranteed by avoiding to abort such transactions. Whenever a transaction is marked as irrevocable, the runtime support checks whether another irrevocable transaction is currently being run. In the positive case, the new transaction's execution is delayed until the other irrevocable transaction commits. In the negative case, the transaction is immediately executed, and in case some conflict on accessed data is detected, the contention manager only aborts other transactions which are not marked as irrevocable. Differently from this proposal, we offer complete transparency with respect to the application-level programmer (i.e. non-rollbackable operations are not required to be marked), and furthermore we allow multiple interactions with the external world to run concurrently, providing ad-hoc facilities to correctly order the outcome of these operations, and to support rollback of no-longer-consistent operations by an efficient and optimized multi-level buffering architecture.

In the context of Operating Systems supports, the work in [24] proposes an architecture for enabling applications to define program-specific custom policies to carry on speculative execution, e.g. for I/O operations. Despite the clear lack of transparency (in fact, the programmer is required to manually specify policies to determine which speculative branch is correct, which ones should be rolled back, and to manually mark portions of code which can be executed speculatively, like in the TM case), this work mostly relies on system calls to communicate between the application and the Operating System, requiring a large number of mode/context changes which can significantly affect the overall performance, while we work completely in user space, thus avoiding costly mode/context changes. Additionally, speculation is implemented via an ad-hoc version of the `fork()` system call, in order to create a new speculative copy of the process, while in optimistic simulation speculation is already intrinsic in the execution model.

As hinted in the Introduction section, in the context of optimistic PDES engines, one approach to deal with I/O is based on ad-hoc API. One example along this direction is the work in [17], where the optimistic engine is able to provide the user-level software with past, committed (and globally consistent) state images. This is done by passing control (and the snapshot) to the applications via a proper callback. Once taken control, the callback can invoke output operations providing data related to the committed portion of the simulation. Compared to this approach, the present proposal does not require specific callbacks within the API. Also, in that solution the frequency of I/O production is bounded by the time period for the identification of the committed part of the computation (typically the GVT period). Hence not all the states passed through while executing the model can be observed (in terms of output stream production). Instead, with the present proposal we allow the modeler to produce output any time the event handler takes control, hence ideally at each state transition within the simulation. Further, the output is system-wide ordered, while in the approach in [17] it is ordered on a per-LP basis (hence post processing is required in order to provide a unique ordered trace along the simulation time axis).

Recently, the issue of transparency in optimistic synchronization in the context of HLA based simulations has been tackled [18], where the problem of direct external interactions (e.g. with the underlying Operating System) is also addressed. However, the provided solution is based on temporary suspension of processing activities at the federates until the interaction is conservatively (namely safely) detected to be committable, while our approach is based on post-filtering and post-manipulation of the output streams with no suspension of the actual run. Overall, we sustain pure optimism as opposed to the throttling scheme provided in [18].

A similar approach, but less transparent, has been adopted in the PDES framework in [4], where an ad-hoc API is provided to the application programmer in order to signal the kernel that a non-revocable I/O operation needs to take place. The effect on run-time is that a blocking period is experienced until the I/O is detected to be safe.

The approach provided in [10] has some resemblances with our proposal in that a special object (resembling our daemon) is used for I/O management. Any output message is routed towards this object in the form of an event, which gets processed only after GVT advancement (namely when the event is detected to be committed). However, this approach is based on ad-hoc APIs used to trigger the interaction with the special object, while we cope with the API provided by standard libraries. Also, the approach in [10] performs the I/O-event management within the simulation engine (hence leading to some I/O management latency along the execution path of the simulation kernel), while we rely on the orthogonal approach of removing most of the work for materializing the output from the simulation engine execution path.

Finally, a work related to the present proposal can be found in [6], where a scheme for optimizing checkpointing is provided in order to allow an interactive end-user to inject events prior to the commit horizon, and explore alternative paths (by resuming the computation from proper snapshots), as compared to those already established as committed. Orthogonality with our proposal lies in that we target the management of output streams, thus intrinsically coping with the typical scenarios where the input to the simulation run, e.g., in terms of simulation parameters, is provided at simulation startup and what-if analysis via simulation relies on batch processing schemes. Instead, that work targets the management of input streams, which is typical of, e.g., interactive what-if analysis approaches.

3. OUTPUT MANAGEMENT

3.1 Involved Issues

Consistent output management in optimistic simulations is a non-trivial task, due to the existence of the rollback

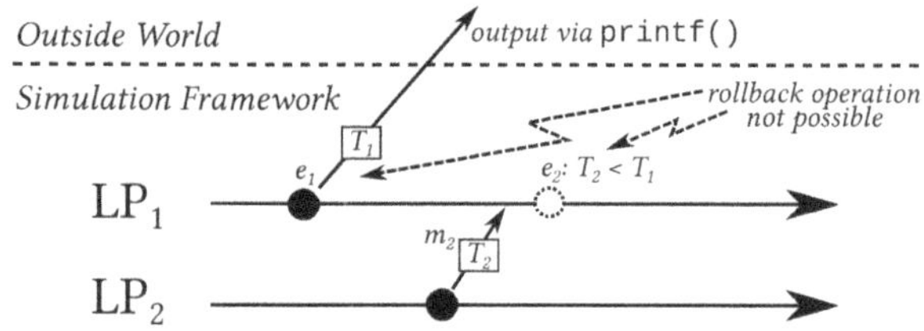

Figure 1: Interaction with the Outside World

operation, which is not handled by common libraries for managing output streams. Let us consider a simulation scenario where two LPs are present, namely LP_1 and LP_2. LP_1 is scheduled for the execution of event e_1, associated with timestamp T_1. During the execution of e_1, some output is produced via a call to the standard library's `printf()` function. After e_1's execution is completed, LP_2 generates a new event e_2 destined to LP_1, and associated with timestamp $T_2 < T_1$. According to the optimistic synchronization scheme presented in [9], e_1 is undone and the execution is restarted from e_2. However, the `printf()` invocation is already completed, the output has been already materialized on the standard output stream, and it is therefore inconsistent, as it is associated with an undone event. This is depicted in Figure 1.

The task of generating consistent output is even more complicated if we consider two different points of view on the same issue. On the one hand, the application-level programmer is interested in the *ease of use*, i.e. she does not want to rely on complex APIs which force her to be aware of the notion of rollback, and to look at the internal organization of the simulation engine. On the other hand, consistently managing output streams must not make the simulation engine pay a relevant performance penalty, in order to minimize the overhead on the actual simulation execution. This tradeoff between *application transparency* and *simulation performance* must be well balanced, in order to effectively and efficiently support the management of output streams.

In order to address *transparency*, the architecture which we hereby propose is based on compile/linking time facilities that, before creating the final simulation-model executable, redirect every output call in the application-level code from the standard `printf()` family functions to an ad-hoc simulation kernel's module, which represents the I/O-management-stub within the architecture. These facilities are present in most compiling tool-chains, and can be triggered via ad-hoc directives/scripts.

On the other hand, in order to enforce a *high performance* of the simulation execution, all the operations associated with the management of the output must exhibit an overhead—both direct and indirect—as small as possible. As for direct overhead, we have explicitly designed our proposal in order to minimize the use of system calls during the execution of the simulation for buffering the produced output until the generation-associated event is committed. In particular, at simulation startup, we pre-allocate a set of shared memory segments which are used by simulation kernel instances to store any output on any stream produced by the application-level code. These buffers are read, during the simulation run, by a separate user-space process, which we refer to as *output daemon*. This daemon is in charge of collecting all the output produced by the LPs, sort it, and—in case of a rollback operation—remove the involved strings.

Whenever a set of events gets committed, the output daemon is able to use this information in order to actually materialize the relevant (committed) output on the associated streams.

As it will be thoroughly discussed later, this explicit design choice gives us several benefits: (i) output buffering is handled completely in user space—by relying on shared memory—avoiding costly mode/context changes during the execution of the simulation; (ii) simulation efficiency is preserved, as the operations for producing the output (independently of its eventual commitment) does not involve costly procedures, giving most of the available CPU time to actual (relevant) computation; (iii) considering that each simulation kernel is assigned a private shared memory segment, and considering that kernel instances only write on it, and the output daemon only reads from it, a completely non-blocking algorithm for the interaction between kernel instances and the daemon can be implemented, providing additional benefits due to the avoidance of contention on logical data (i.e. no locking primitives must be exploited to allow kernels–daemon communication).

On the indirect-overhead side, two main issues have been addressed, namely data locality and CPU sharing. In the simulation-kernel instances, the output is produced on a contiguous buffer (i.e the private shared-memory segment), avoiding costly cache-invalidation secondary effects during the generation of output on whichever stream. The segment is used in a cache-aligned fashion, avoiding at the same time false cache sharing effects. The daemon, on the other hand, handles the output materialization relying on an efficient modified version of a calendar queue [2], which is in turn able to minimize the computing time required for sorting the output strings, and it is additionally featured with an autonomic agent which is able to determine the best activation interval for reducing CPU-sharing effects on the actual simulation, and to reduce the delay from the generation of the output to its actual materialization.

3.2 Design Approaches and Reference Implementation

Without any loss of generality, we can say that a simulation framework comprises K simulation-kernel instances, scattered across M machines, and each machine m hosts a set of K_m simulation kernel instances. Of course, K_m can be different for each m, i.e. simulation kernel instances must not be necessarily evenly distributed across the machines, depending on, e.g., the actual computing power offered by each of them. Upon simulation startup, on each machine m a separate output-daemon instance is started, and K_m shared-memory segments are created (and shared with each kernel instance). These can be seen as per-kernel private *logical devices*, on which the simulation-kernel instances write their LPs' output messages, rather than on the requested stream. In this scenario, considering the whole system, D_M^K logical devices will be installed, and each kernel k hosted on machine m will have is own device D_m^k. In particular, as mentioned before, upon the invocation of some function of the `printf()` family (which is redirected to the kernel instance's I/O-management-stub at compile time), the output subsystem stores output-related information in a variable-sized data structure for keeping the information until the associated event gets committed (or rolled back). The structure used for this intermediate buffering is as follows:

```
struct output_msg_t {
    size_t size;
    int fd;
    unsigned int era;
    unsigned int LP;
    double timestamp;
    char buffer[];
};
```

where `size` keeps the total size of the entry, `LP` associates the output generation with a specific LP in the simulation, `timestamp` keeps information about the Local Virtual Time (LVT) at which the LP has generated the output, `fd` is the file descriptor associated with the output stream, and `buffer` is the actual output payload[1]. This entry is then written—before returning control to the application-level software—into the per-kernel logical device D_m^k. We note that `timestamp` is not required to be explicitly provided by the application layer within the output message (namely as a parameter of the `printf() call`). Rather, we assume the corresponding LVT value (as well as the LP-identifier) must be provided by the simulation engine to the I/O-management-stub right before passing control to the LP for actual event processing. In this way, the application modeler is not forced to tag all (or part) of the output messages with timestamping information. She will be anyhow transparently provided with an output-stream content matching (system-wide) the advancement of simulation time.

The logical device can be implemented as a circular buffer, where kernels' output subsystems write new output messages (which are later processed by the daemon in a FIFO order) with an ad-hoc header for describing the content of the buffer. The organization of this device is described via the following structure:

```
struct logical_device_t {
   size_t size;
   unsigned int wrote;
   unsigned int read;
   unsigned char buffer[];
};
```

where `size` identifies the (current) size of the circular buffer, `wrote` is an offset pointing to the last byte in the device written by the kernel output subsystem, and `read` is an offset identifying the last byte read by the output daemon. Since these fields are updated in isolation (i.e. the field written by the kernel instance is only read by the daemon, and vice versa), a non-blocking algorithm has been developed for managing the logical device. In particular, by checking if `wrote` and `read` store the same value (either in modular or non-modular arithmetic), the daemon and the kernel are able to determine whether the buffer is full or empty, and can immediately access via displacement the correct position on which to perform a read/write operation, without the need for any synchronization primitive. If the buffer is full, then the simulation kernel must wait before finalizing the output generation procedure, unless some resize procedure, like the non-blocking one described in Section 3.3, is adopted.

On a periodic basis, the output daemon wakes up and checks whether some output message has been produced by some locally-hosted simulation-kernel instance on its private logical device (again, this can be done by comparing the values of `read` and `wrote`). In case a new output message is present, the output daemon creates a local copy of it (i.e. in its own address space), updates the `read` value, and inserts it in a specifically-modified version of a calendar queue [2], which guarantees the correct ordering of the output messages by all the output kernels. We also note that, in case the two counters match, but the actual content of a new message has already been inserted within the device (which does not impose atomicity with the update of the `wrote` counter), the demon will simply experience a false-negative on the presence of new messages, which will be resolved at subsequent iteration steps.

Overall, with the above approach, no spin-locks or other types of atomic operations (which are known to exhibit non-minimal direct and indirect costs, possibly impacting the execution speed at the side of the simulation engine) are used at all. This is done by trading-off with the actual delay for the delivery of the message at the demon.

In order for the output daemon to correctly support the execution of rollback operations, the traditional implementation of the calendar queue has been augmented with one additional operation, namely `delete`, which allows to remove elements falling in a given $[from, to]$ timestamp range. For efficiency reasons, upon the invocation of this operation, the buckets associated with $from$ and to are computed, and then a linear search for removing elements is performed, resembling the original direct search described in [2]. Of course, the delete operation removes only the elements which are associated with a particular LP, as specified in the `output_msg_t` structure. At the same time, we note that, depending on the actual simulation execution, scanning all the buckets in the $[from, to]$ range can be a relatively costly operation, if we consider that we do not want to affect the simulation's performance. To this end, the `output_msg_t` structure keeps track of the `era` field, namely a monotonic counter which is updated by every simulation kernel upon the execution of a rollback operation, on a per-LP basis. This can be regarded as a compressed information identifying every output message related to a given era comprised in between two rollback operations. The calendar queue bucket array is therefore augmented, keeping for every bucket a bloom filter [1] which is used to know whether output messages from a given era are present in the bucket. In this way, before starting to scan the list associated with any bucket in the $[from, to]$ interval, a check on the bloom filter is performed, to determine whether that particular bucket can be skipped.

To enable the execution of a rollback operation, and to enforce a timely materialization of output messages on the related streams, two control messages are placed by kernel k (namely by the corresponding I/O-management-stub) on device D_m^k, namely `ROLLBACK` and `COMMIT`. The former is a control message with a payload structured as $\langle from, to, LP, era \rangle$, which directly triggers the aforementioned `delete` operation on the calendar queue. The latter, notifies the output daemon on which portion of the per-kernel-generated output can be considered as committed[2]. Whenever a `COMMIT` control message is found on a device, the associated commitment timestamp is stored into a separate array, which keeps track of the last commitment time for each locally-hosted simulation kernel instance k. Periodically, the output daemon finds the minimum commitment time $T_{C_{min}}$ among the ones notified by the kernel instances, and invokes a `flush`

[1]We note that, if output generation entails processing a format string, this can be easily done by relying on the POSIX `sprintf()` library function.

[2]In fact, the `COMMIT` control message is generated immediately after the completion of the GVT reduction operation.

operation on the calendar queue, which iteratively dequeues elements from it until an element associated with a timestamp $T > T_{C_{min}}$ is found. Every output message dequeued during this flush operation is materialized on the associated stream, described by the `fd` field.

We note that these operations can be non-negligible in terms of CPU usage by the output daemon. In order to produce a minimal impact on the simulation's overall performance, the daemon does not process all the available messages (either output or control) from $D_m^k \forall k$ before returning to sleep. On the other hand, after having processed any message, it checks whether its execution has lasted more than a specific threshold value and, in the positive case, it returns to sleep. Of course, the overall performance can be affected by the sleep and working time. As it will be discussed later in Section 3.3, an ad-hoc solution can be adopted to autonomically self-tune these parameters for maximizing the simulation's performance, while ensuring a timely materialization of committed output messages.

As an additional note, since the proposed output message data structure identifies a particular stream using its file descriptor, the kernel instance's output subsystem intercepts calls to functions which actually open/close streams (e.g., `fopen()`-family calls) and produces on the logical device additional control messages (namely, `OPEN` and `CLOSE`) which tell the output daemon to process these operations. In this way, the daemon is the only user-space process controlling the actual output streams, for materializing committed output messages on them.

In case the simulation is executed on a distributed architecture (either a cluster, a desktop grid, or on the cloud), the daemon-based approach is able to communicate only with the kernel instances which are locally hosted on the same machine. In order to collect output messages from all the nodes in the system, the output daemon can be configured to act as a *forwarder*, i.e. whenever a set of output messages is detected to be committed, the messages are forwarded on the network to an additional (remote) instance of the daemon which acts as a *collector*. This additional instance, which can be even geographically far from the actual simulation architecture, receives all the committed messages from every daemon running in the simulation framework, and inserts them into an additional calendar queue. Whenever `COMMIT` messages are forwarded, the collector daemon relies on the same aforementioned logic for materializing the output messages on the associated streams. We note that this approach is effective in two ways: (i) over the network we transfer only committed output, thus we early process rollback operations, and avoid to pay costly network delays for exchanging output messages which might not be committed, enabling for a considerable scalability even at a geographical scale, and (ii) we can finalize the materialization of the output messages on a remote (possibly not dedicated to simulation) machine, allowing both an enhanced simulation performance (in fact, materializing output on a stream can be a non-minimal-cost operation) and the possibility to easily monitor the execution of the simulation by the user on a separate machine, without suffering a considerable delay.

As a final note, we mention that the output daemon can be flagged to work in *autocommit* mode. Using this facility, the daemon (running in the aforementioned forwarding mode) can be connected to a conservative distributed simulation framework, where the rollback issue is not present, but nevertheless for producing consistent output a timestamp-based ordering must be performed on the output messages produced by the various nodes in the system. Therefore, in this scenario, the facilities provided by our proposal would never trigger a `delete` operation, but upon receiving a message, its timestamp is considered as the last committed timestamp for the specific LP. By simply performing a local reduction across the current LVT of the LPs (which, as said is communicated by the simulation engine to the I/O-management-stub while the simulation proceeds), the set of (timestamp-ordered) output messages to be flushed is identified as the set of those messages with timestamp less than the reduction value, which are therefore immediately flushed (i.e. forwarded) for output materialization.

To give the final picture, we list the core set of APIs that are provided by the I/O-management-stub, which can be used for integration with differentiated simulation kernel layers:

`commit_time(GVT)`: This function is exposed by the output subsystem in order to allow the GVT reduction subsystem to notify the output daemon of a newly-computed GVT value. This information is used by the subsystem to generate a `COMMIT` control message to notify the output daemon.

`set_LVT(LP, timestamp)`: Using this function, the simulation kernel's scheduler can notify the output subsystem about the identity of the dispatched LP, and the timestamp of the dispatched event (hence the logical time to be associated with any output message produced as a result of processing this event).

`rollback(from, to, LP)`: Using this function, the simulation kernel's scheduler can notify the output subsystem about the reception of a straggler message or an anti-message. Using this information, the output subsystem can generate a `ROLLBACK` message for the output daemon, and instantiate a new era.

`out_msg(LP, stamp, msg, stream)`: This API is used by the simulation kernel to transfer a particular output message destined to a specified stream to the output subsystem, which will in turn write it on the kernel's logical device D_m^k.

`autocommit(flag)`: If `flag` is true, every output message received is considered as non-rollbackable, in order to support the integration with a conservative simulation engine. If `flag` is true, the daemon does not wait for `COMMIT` messages before committing output messages. The commitment is triggered by the aforementioned internal logic.

We recall that, in order to provide the application-level developer with complete transparency, calls to output generation library functions must be properly wrapped, in order to correctly redirect them to `out_msg()`. This can be easily done, as already described, by relying on compile-time facilities provided by most linkers, and by applying small changes on the application-program build rules. The interconnection with the simulation kernel, particularly the ROOT-Sim kernel we are exploiting in this study, is depicted in Figure 2.

3.3 Optimizations

In case of an output-intensive simulation model (either because a large number of events involve the generation of some output destined to some stream, or because the output messages are considerably large) the logical device might become the bottleneck of the system. In particular, since we want to ensure *exactly-once* materialization of the output

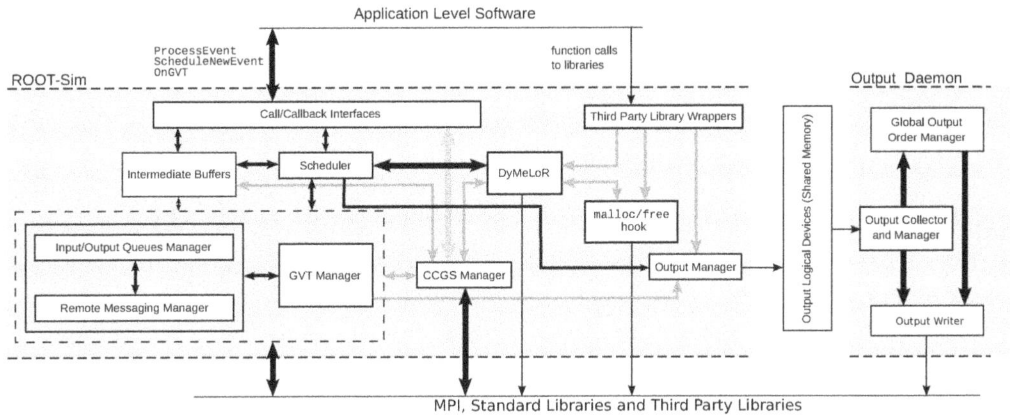

Figure 2: ROOT-Sim vs Output Daemon Architecture

messages, if the circular buffer which is used to implement the logical device gets filled, the kernel's output subsystem trying to write on it must wait for the output daemon to free some space for buffering the output.

Since this would be a non-affordable cost, we have augmented the `logical_device_t` data structure with an additional flag, namely `subst_id`, which is used by the output subsystem whenever the current circular buffer is full. In this case, the output subsystem allocates a new shared memory segment (of doubled size with respect to the old, full one), stores its id in this field, detaches from the old segment, and starts buffering output messages on this new device. Whenever the output daemon finds a logical device to be empty, it checks whether the `subst_id` field is set to a valid value. In the positive case, it attaches to the new logical device, releases the old one, and starts processing messages from the new one.

If on the one hand this approach can reduce the time spent during the execution of a simulation event inside the kernel's management subsystems, on the other it can affect memory usage if the simulation model's activity is highly output-bound. Although this can be regarded as a secondary problem, considering the large amount of memory available on modern architectures, optimizing the actual tradeoff between CPU usage by the output daemon and memory consumption by the logical device can provide benefits in terms of output materialization delay and problem feasibility.

We therefore propose an additional optimization, which addresses the amount of time the output daemon spends processing messages from the devices and sleeping, and allows the output manager to autonomically self tune its activation phase. In particular, as for output materialization delay, given that output messages are flushed on the associated streams after the GVT computation (which is, traditionally, a periodic operation), the best scenario arises when the kernels' output subsystems try to write the `COMMIT` message on their devices and find them empty. This situation happens whenever the total execution time of the output daemon is such that every message placed in the device in between two `COMMIT` messages has been processed. We therefore measure the execution time of each message (namely, output message's t_o, a `COMMIT` message's t_c, and a `ROLLBACK` message's t_r) and continuously update their mean values $\bar{t}_o$, $\bar{t}_c$, and $\bar{t}_r$ according to an exponential mean. Additionally, we rely on three counters, namely $\bar{c}_o$ $\bar{c}_c$, and $\bar{c}_m$ which describe the (exponential) average number of messages placed by simulation kernel instances in a GVT phase. By relying on these values, upon the reception of a `COMMIT` control message, the output daemon computes the expected total execution time $\mathbb{E}(T) = \sum_{x\in\{o,c,r\}} \bar{t}_x \cdot \bar{c}_x$ which is needed for emptying the logical devices during the next phase. If this value is lower than a compile-time specified threshold, it is then fragmented into several slots (resembling Operating Systems' time slices) and the sleep time is set accordingly in order to identify an execution phase which is equal to the GVT phase. The compile-time threshold ensures that, in case an application is extremely output-bound (at least in some phase of its execution), then the output daemon will not significantly affect the overall simulation performance, while trying to minimize the output materialization delay. We note that, by relying on this approach, the output daemon is able to capture variations in the actual output generation dynamics by the application-level software, thus adapting to execution phases which exhibit a higher/lower output generation rate.

The last optimization concerns timely processing of output-messages rollback, which can prevent the output daemon to process wrong data before noticing that it must be undone. In particular, upon initialization of the per-kernel logical device, each simulation-kernel instance installs a second channels for the delivery of high-priority control messages (namely the `ROLLBACK` ones) which are used to early inform the daemon that some information that it is about to process might be already uncommittable. Whenever the daemon notices that a `ROLLBACK` message is present in the high-priority channel, it starts scanning the associated logical device and marks as *don't care* every output message which should be rolled back. The circular buffer is scanned (without updating the `read` flag) until the `ROLLBACK` control message corresponding to the one found in the high-priority channel is found. When this operation is completed, the normal behavior is restored, with the exception that whenever a don't-care output message is found in the circular buffer, it gets simply discarded. We note that this rollback optimization avoids enqueueing and dequeueing the output messages which can be early detected as uncommittable, reducing the cost of the operations on the calendar queue[3]. If some events involved in the rollback operation were already

[3]This situation might result in a calendar queue's resize, which is a very costly operation.

in the calendar queue, when the processing of the logical device (which, we recall, stores messages emitted by the associated simulation kernel in FIFO order) reaches the `ROLLBACK` control message, the `delete` operation described in Section 3.2 is executed, which removes the already inserted output messages.

4. EXPERIMENTAL DATA

As hinted, we have integrated the proposed output-streams management architecture within ROOT-Sim, an open source C/MPI-based simulation package targeted at POSIX systems [8, 15], which implements a general-purpose parallel/distributed simulation environment relying on the optimistic synchronization paradigm. ROOT-Sim offers a very simple programming model based on the classical notion of simulation-event handlers, to be implemented according to the ANSI-C standard, and transparently supports all the services required to parallelize the execution. It also offers a set of optimized protocols aimed at minimizing the run-time overhead by the platform, thus allowing for high performance and scalability.

The output management subsystem has been integrated respecting the API described in Section 3.2, while the output daemon has been realized as a separate process written in ANSI-C. Upon the ROOT-Sim startup, if requested, the output daemon is launched and the output subsystem installs the logical devices (one for every simulation-kernel instance) .

The hardware architecture used for testing our proposal is a 64-bit NUMA machine, namely an HP ProLiant server, equipped with four 2GHz AMD Opteron 6128 processors and 64GB of RAM. Each processor has 8 cores (for a total of 32 cores) that share a 12MB L3 cache (6 MB per each 4-cores set), and each core has a 512KB private L2 cache. The operating system is 64-bit Debian 6, with Linux Kernel version 2.6.32.5. The compiling and linking tools used are `gcc` 4.3.4 and binutils (`as` and `ld`) 2.20.0. This hardware architecture has been used only for simulation (i.e. no other process, except for the system ones, where running during the execution), thus resembling a scenario where the hardware environment is dedicated to high performance simulation.

In order to evaluate different aspects of the proposed architecture, we have conducted experiments on a family of configurations of *Personal Communications Service* (PCS), a GSM wireless communication systems simulation model, where channels are modeled in high fidelity via explicit simulation of power regulation/usage and interference/fading phenomena on the basis of the current state of the corresponding cell. Also, the power regulation model has been implemented according to the results in [12]. Accurate descriptions of this model can be found in [21]. However, for the reader's convenience we report below some details related to the main features of the model.

Upon the start of a call destined to a mobile device currently hosted by a given wireless cell, a call-setup record is instantiated via dynamically-allocated data structures, which gets linked to a list of already active records within that same cell. Each record gets released when the corresponding call ends or is handed-off towards an adjacent cell. In the latter case, a similar call-setup procedure is executed at the destination cell. Upon call-setup, power regulation is performed, which involves scanning the aforementioned list of records for computing the minimum transmission power allowing the current call-setup to achieve the threshold-level SIR value. Data structures keeping track of fading coefficients are also updated while scanning the list, according to a meteorological model defining climatic conditions (and related variations). The employed simulation models have been developed for execution on top of ROOT-Sim in a way that each LP models a single wireless cell. Hence, the event-handler callback involves the update of individual cells' states, and cross-LP events are essentially related to hand-offs between different cells.

We have performed a set of experiments where each cell sustains the same workload of incoming calls, whose inter-arrival time is exponentially distributed, and whose average duration is set to 2 min. The expected rate for call inter-arrival has been set to achieve channel utilization factor on the order of 30%, while the residence time of an active device within a cell has a mean value of 5 min and follows the exponential distribution. For the above scenario, we have run experiments with 1024 wireless cells, modeled as hexagons covering a square region, each one managing 1000 wireless channels. These have been evenly distributed across 32 kernel instances running on the 32-core underlying machine.

For measuring the overall performance of the simulation runs, we have relied on the measurement of cumulated committed events over wall clock time advancement, i.e. a measure of how many events get committed while the simulation's execution is carried on.

To capture different aspects of the impact on execution dynamics by the output-management subsystem and the output daemon, we have modified the PCS benchmark in order to provide on the terminal statistics regarding the occurrence of the hand-off event. In particular, with a certain frequency f, the execution of the hand-off event entails the generation of an output string which tells the total amount of per-cell hand-off events so far, and the average duration of a handed-off call. We have explicitly varied the value of f so that, among all the events (not only hand-off events) executed in the simulation run, in between 1% and 35% of them involved some output generation (which corresponds, in our configuration, to a total number of generated string in between 5 millions and 35 millions).

We note that, for the above deploy/parameterization, the runs exhibited an efficiency on the order of 80%. Hence the experimentation has been carried out when considering well behaving optimistic runs (namely not affected by thrashing, which would lead the experimentation to be non-reliable), which however show an amount of rollback that is expected to provide a good test case for all the functionalities (e.g. output-message discarding functionalities) offered by our output management subsystem. Further, running the above model on top of ROOT-Sim (on the same multi-core machine used in this experimental study) has been already shown to give rise to super-linear speedup values (see the experimental data provided in [21]). Hence our experimentation is carried out via competitive parallel runs.

We have compared this execution with two different scenarios, one relying on the traditional ROOT-Sim framework (i.e. without the output subsystem and without the output daemon), and one with the I/O-management-stub working within the simulation kernel, but without any daemon listening on the other side of the logical device (in this case the device has been configured like a typical `/dev/null` device file, by simply discarding the incoming messages). We consider the former scenario as a good baseline situation, for assessing the overall overhead introduced by the output management architecture, while the latter allows us to evaluate what is the actual impact of having a separate process (the daemon) running in time-sharing on a dedicated simulation environment, for supporting the execution of additional housekeeping tasks. Further, we have also considered runs based on a modified version of ROOT-Sim where the output strings produced by the execution of an event are logged within the event queue (as a list associated with the event-buffer), and are then flushed when fossil collecting the event after GVT computation. This approach has resemblances with the solution provided in [10]. We note however that this approach does not provide global ordering of the output across the whole set of LPs.

By the results, shown in Figure 3 (obtained as the average over 10 runs done with different pseudo-random seeds), we note that the execution with the device configured like a `/dev/null` device file exhibits a reduced overhead with respect to the baseline configuration, showing that the operations internal to the I/O-management-stub (and the interaction between the simulation engine and the stub) do not impact significantly on the overall simulation performance. When the output daemon is running, on the other hand, the simulation throughput decreases when the application-level software exhibits more output-bound behavior. This is reasonable, considering that the CPU time required by the daemon for a timely processing of the messages placed into the logical device gets increased. However, the worst case for the overhead is on the order of 22%. Further, the overhead well scales vs the increase of the frequency of output production (in fact the overhead is quite similar for the cases where f is set to 12% and 35%). On the other hand, for very reduced output-message frequency (say f set to 1% or 7%), as typical of when the application is configured for primarily matching performance requirements via audit reduction, the overhead introduced by our output-management architecture is quite bounded (namely between 2% and 11%). It is interesting to notice that our proposal shows a better performance than the scenario with no output architecture activated, but with I/O calls performed while processing the events. This phenomenon is due to the fact that the `stdio` library is not optimized for integration with high performance computing, while our architecture has been oriented exactly to this scenario. Further, standard I/O calls during event processing would even give rise to non-consistent output, due to the fact that output materialization associated with rolled back events is finalized as well (in the case of optimistic synchronization), or should require an additional post processing to correctly order the output (in case of the conservative synchronization), thus requiring additional time for the end user to be able to perform its audit activities. Similar considerations can be made when considering I/O management via logging of the strings with the processed events and flush operations after GVT computation. Particularly, while this approach introduces negligible overhead with bounded frequency of output production, the overhead gets significantly increased for higher frequency of output message generation.

Another aspect which requires attention regards the overhead induced by the evaluation of parameters within a format string being passed to the output subsystem. In Figure 4, we present three different curves (whose samples are again computed as the average over 10 runs), one entailing the evaluation of a float, one of an integer, and a case where no parameters should be evaluated at all. We recall that, in our proposal, parameters are evaluated immediately within the I/O-management-stub (directly called by the application-level code through library call redirection) via the POSIX-compliant `sprintf()` library function. By the results, we can see that the overall execution time is

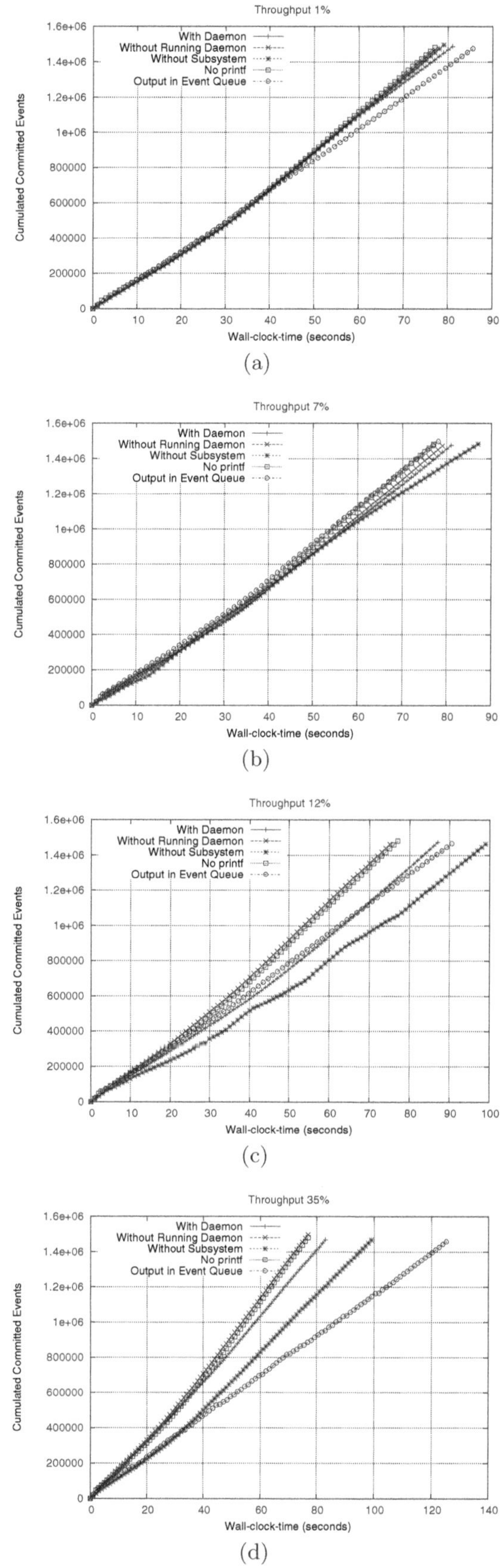

Figure 3: Throughput for Different Values of f

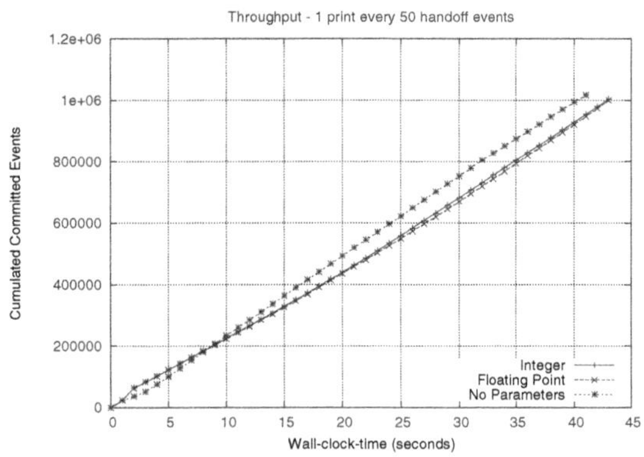

Figure 4: Throughput with Different Data Types

not significantly affected by the presence of additional (more complex) parameters to be evaluated, showing the effectiveness of our proposal even in the case of relatively complex outcome-messages from a simulation model.

To show how the CPU-usage/memory tradeoff is addressed by the output daemon, in Figure 5 we report the total amount of shared memory allocated for the logical I/O-devices during the execution of the simulation (these plots refer to one of the 10 runs, where similar behavior is anyway observed). As in the case of the throughput discussed earlier, we note that (as expected) the amount of required shared memory is increased when the application exhibits a more output-bound behavior. However, the reached bound (on the order of 16MB) represents a relatively reduced absolute value (especially when considering that optimistic simulation is known to be memory consuming on the side of the engine). Further, being such a memory virtualized by the underlying Operating System, and thanks to the fact that the shared memory segments implementing the logical I/O-device are used according to the circular rule (not in scattered mode), we may expect a reduced impact on the actual locality while the frequency of output-message generation gets increased.

In Figure 6 we present a plot which shows what is the actual output-materialization delay exhibited by the output daemon (again for one of the ten runs, which is anyhow representative of what observed in the different runs). Both the x and the y axis represent wall clock time. To the x axis we associate the time at which a specific committed output message was produced, while to the y axis we associate the time at which the same output message was materialized. For the sake of clarity, we show a 45-degree curve which represent a (theoretical) instantaneous materialization time, i.e. a situation where there is no actual delay between the generation and materialization. In this plot, the steeper the slope, the higher is the materialization delay induced by the operations by the output daemon. It is interesting to notice, by the plots, that the output materialization advances in steps. This is related to the fact that the commitment operation of output messages can be started only after a GVT calculation, which is a periodic operation. It is interesting to note that in Figures 6 (a), and (c), the autonomic self-tuning subsystem for CPU/memory tradeoff optimization is able to capture the best configuration to minimize the materialization delay. In fact, the slope of the curve, during the simulation execution, tends to get gentler. The case in Figure 6 (b) is quite different, as the

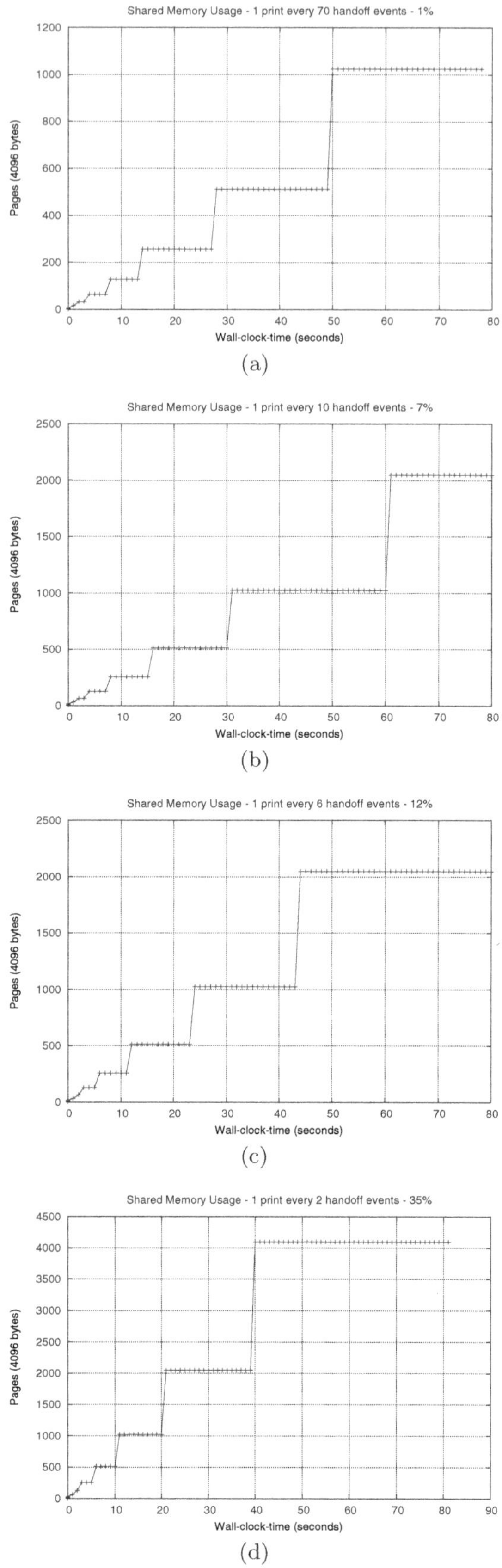

Figure 5: Shared Memory Size

daemon tries to minimize the output materialization delay, but then the CPU threshold is hit, and the daemon is not able to increase its computing power usage, in order not to significantly affect simulation performance, and therefore the curve diverges. The scenario in Figure 6 (d) shows that, considering the large amount of output messages, the calendar queue becomes the bottleneck of the system (due to an upper bound on the number of buckets, as described in [2]), and the rollbacks which are encountered during the simulation determine an amount of operations on the calendar queue to delete messages which were already stored. However, we note that for values of f from 1% to 7% (which, as said, would represent a case of orientation of the application layer to performance due to reduced audit on model execution), we get that upon run termination the output stream has been already materialized at the 75% or, at least, the 35%, which would enable pipelined treatment of the output data while the run is still in progress. The careful reader might notice that with a given generation wall-clock time, more materialization times are associated. This is related to the fact that these plots present system-wide materialization delays, where different kernel instances at the same WCT value might generate output messages from LPs running at different LVT values. This skew is therefore reflected in the commitment (wall-clock) time at which a set of messages can be safely materialized on the associated output stream.

To assess the effects of the autonomic self-tuning mechanism for daemon activation, described in Section 3.3, we present in Figure 7 a scenario where the parameter f (which describes the frequency of statistics generation on standard output) is not constant over the simulation run, rather varies in the range $[1\%, 30\%]$ in an interleaved fashion. In particular, f is set to 1% at the beginning of the simulation, and is then incremented until it reaches the value of 30%, and then again decreased. The plots show that the autonomic self-tuning system is able to cope well with the dynamics variations. In fact there is not any significant skew in the simulation throughput, despite the output daemon continuously requests for more or less computing power, depending on the actual load phase on the output architecture.

5. CONCLUSION AND FUTURE WORK

In this work we have presented design indications for the development of an efficient shared memory based output streams management subsystem targeted at optimistic simulations. It allows a simulation model to rely on standard library calls for producing output on different streams during the execution of not-yet-committed events, and to materialize this output only when the corresponding events get committed, in a system-wide timestamp ordered manner. Further, reduced overhead is introduced at the side of the simulation engine, which allows for not hampering the speedup that is expected to be achieved when executing simulation models on optimistic PDES systems. Future work entails the development of ad-hoc policies for limiting the execution's optimism in case the simulation environment is running out of memory. To complement the results of the experimental study, which has been tailored to the analysis for shared-memory multi-core architectures, we plan to investigate on the effects of our proposal in the context of distributed memory systems (e.g. clusters).

6. REFERENCES

[1] B. H. Bloom. Space/time trade-offs in hash coding

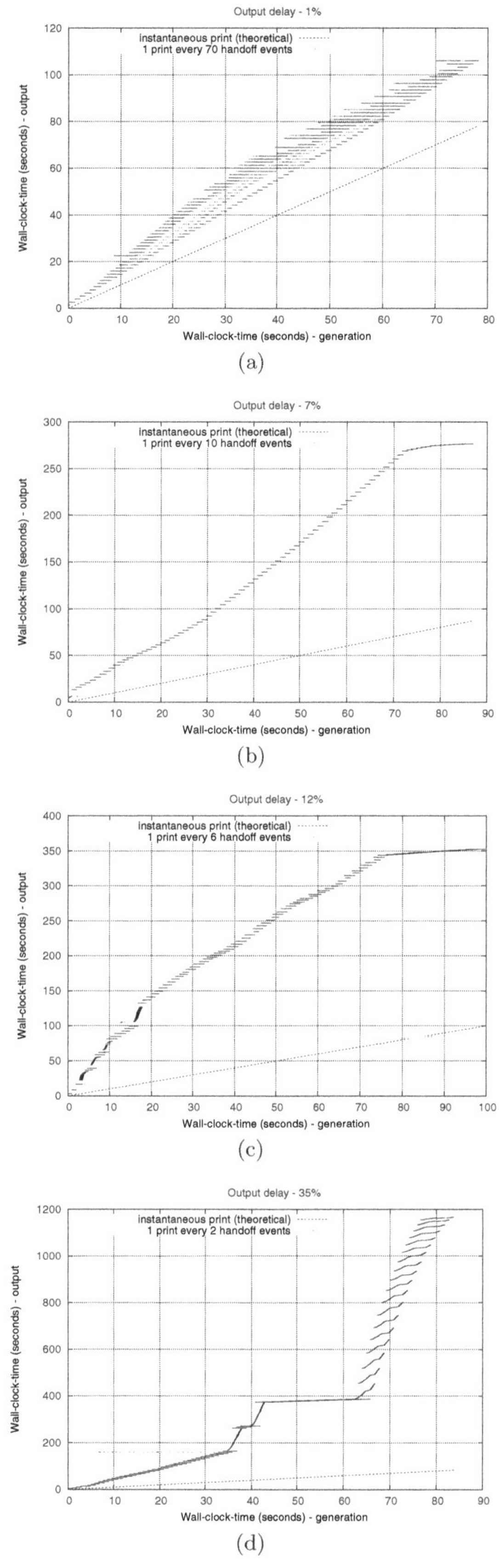

Figure 6: Generation/Materialization Delay

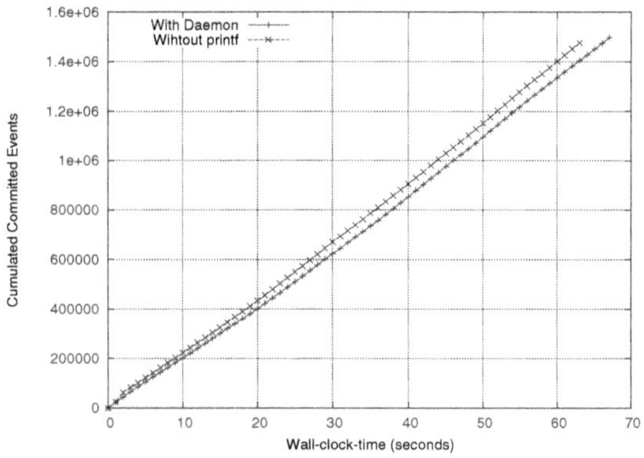

Figure 7: Frequency Variation

with allowable errors. *Commun. ACM*, 13(7):422–426, 1970.

[2] R. Brown. Calendar queues: a fast O(1) priority queue implementation for the simulation event set problem. *Communications of the ACM*, 31:1220–1227, October 1988.

[3] C. D. Carothers, K. S. Perumalla, and R. M. Fujimoto. Efficient optimistic parallel simulations using reverse computation. *ACM Transactions on Modeling and Computer Simulation*, 9(3):224–253, july 1999.

[4] S. R. Das, R. M. Fujimoto, K. Panesar, D. Allison, and M. Hybinette. GTW: a time warp system for shared memory multiprocessors. In *WSC '94: Proceedings of the 26th conference on Winter simulation*, pages 1332–1339. Society for Computer Simulation International, 1994.

[5] M. Elnozahy, L. Alvisi, Y.-M. Wang, and D. B. Johnson. A survey of rollback-recovery protocols in message-passing systems. *ACM Computing Surveys*, 34(3):375–408, sept 2002.

[6] S. Franks, F. Gomes, B. Unger, and J. G. Cleary. State saving for interactive optimistic simulation. In *Workshop on Parallel and Distributed Simulation*, pages 72–79, 1997.

[7] R. M. Fujimoto. Parallel discrete event simulation. *Communications of the ACM*, 33(10):30–53, Oct. 1990.

[8] H. R. Group. ROOT-Sim: The ROme OpTimistic Simulator - v 1.0. `http://www.dis.uniroma1.it/~hpdcs/ROOT-Sim/`, Oct. 2012.

[9] D. R. Jefferson. Virtual Time. *ACM Transactions on Programming Languages and System*, 7(3):404–425, July 1985.

[10] D. R. Jefferson, B. Beckman, F. Wieland, L. Blume, M. D. Loreto, P. Hontalas, P. Laroche, K. Sturdevant, J. Tupman, L. V. Warren, J. J. Wedel, H. Younger, and S. Bellenot. Distributed simulation and the time wrap operating system. In *SOSP*, pages 77–93, 1987.

[11] D. B. Johnson. Efficient transparent optimistic rollback recovery for distributed application programs. In *Proceedings of the 12th Symposium on Reliable Distributed Systems*, RDS, pages 86–95, Oct. 1993.

[12] S. Kandukuri and S. Boyd. Optimal power control in interference-limited fading wireless channels with outage-probability specifications. *IEEE Transactions on Wireless Communications*, 1(1):46–55, 2002.

[13] L. Lamport. Time, clocks, and the ordering of events in a distributed system. *Communications of the ACM*, 21(7):558–565, 1978.

[14] D. E. Martin, T. J. McBrayer, and P. A. Wilsey. WARPED: A time warp simulation kernel for analysis and application development. In *HICSS '96: Proceedings of the 29th Hawaii International Conference on System Sciences (HICSS'96) Volume 1: Software Technology and Architecture*, page 383. IEEE Computer Society, 1996.

[15] A. Pellegrini, R. Vitali, and F. Quaglia. The ROme OpTimistic Simulator: Core internals and programming model. In *Proceedings of the 4th International ICST Conference on Simulation Tools and Techniques*, SIMUTools. ICST, 2011.

[16] A. Pellegrini, R. Vitali, and F. Quaglia. Transparent and efficient shared-state management for optimistic simulations on multi-core machines. In *Proceedings 20th International Symposium on Modeling, Analysis and Simulation of Computer and Telecommunication Systems*, MASCOTS, pages 134–141. IEEE Computer Society, Aug. 2012.

[17] F. Quaglia. On the construction of committed consistent global states in optimistic simulation. *International Journal of Simulation and Process Modelling*, 5(2):172–181, 2009.

[18] A. Santoro and F. Quaglia. Transparent optimistic synchronization in the high-level architecture via time-management conversion. *ACM Trans. Model. Comput. Simul.*, 22(4):21, 2012.

[19] SPEEDES. `http://www.speedes.com`, 2005.

[20] R. Vitali, A. Pellegrini, and F. Quaglia. Autonomic log/restore for advanced optimistic simulation systems. In *Proceedings of the Symposium on Modeling, Analysis, and Simulation of Computer and Telecommunication Systems*, MASCOTS, pages 319–327. IEEE Computer Society, 2010.

[21] R. Vitali, A. Pellegrini, and F. Quaglia. Towards symmetric multi-threaded optimistic simulation kernels. In *Proceedings of the 26th International Workshop on Principles of Advanced and Distributed Simulation*, PADS, pages 211–220. IEEE Computer Society, Aug. 2012.

[22] A. Welc, B. Saha, and A.-R. Adl-Tabatabai. Irrevocable transactions and their applications. In *Proceedings of the 20th annual Symposium on Parallelism in Algorithms and Architectures*, SPAA, pages 285–296. ACM, 2008.

[23] D. West and K. Panesar. Automatic incremental state saving. In *Proceedings of the 10th Workshop on Parallel and Distributed Simulation*, pages 78–85. IEEE Computer Society, May 1996.

[24] B. Wester, P. M. Chen, and J. Flinn. Operating system support for application-specific speculation. In *Proceedings of the sixth conference on Computer systems*, EuroSys, pages 229–242. ACM, 2011.

Warp Speed: Executing Time Warp on 1,966,080 Cores

Peter D. Barnes, Jr.
Lawrence Livermore National Laboratory
7000 East Avenue
Livermore, CA 94550
pdbarnes@llnl.gov

Christopher D. Carothers
Dept. of Computer Science
Rensselaer Polytechnic Institute
110 8th Street
Troy, NY 12180
chrisc@cs.rpi.edu

David R. Jefferson
Lawrence Livermore National Laboratory
7000 East Avenue
Livermore, CA 94550
jefferson6@llnl.gov

Justin M. LaPre
Dept. of Computer Science
Rensselaer Polytechnic Institute
110 8th Street
Troy, NY 12180
laprej@cs.rpi.edu

ABSTRACT

Time Warp is an optimistic synchronization protocol for parallel discrete event simulation that coordinates the available parallelism through its rollback and antimessage mechanisms. In this paper we present the results of a strong scaling study of the ROSS simulator running Time Warp with reverse computation and executing the well-known PHOLD benchmark on Lawrence Livermore National Laboratory's *Sequoia* Blue Gene/Q supercomputer. The benchmark has 251 million PHOLD logical processes and was executed in several configurations up to a peak of 7.86 million MPI tasks running on 1,966,080 cores. At the largest scale it processed 33 trillion events in 65 seconds, yielding a sustained speed of 504 billion events/second using 120 racks of *Sequoia*. This is by far the highest event rate reported by any parallel discrete event simulation to date, whether running PHOLD or any other benchmark. Additionally, we believe it is likely to be the largest number of MPI tasks ever used in any computation of any kind to date.

ROSS exhibited a super-linear speedup throughout the strong scaling study, with more than a 97x speed improvement from scaling the number of cores by only 60x (from 32,768 to 1,966,080). We attribute this to significant cache-related performance acceleration as we moved to higher scales with fewer LPs per core.

Prompted by historical performance results we propose a new, long term performance metric called *Warp Speed* that grows logarithmically with the PHOLD event rate. As we define it our maximum speed of 504 billion PHOLD events/sec corresponds to *Warp 2.7*.

We suggest that the results described here are significant because they demonstrate that direct simulation of planetary-scale discrete event models are now, in principle at least, within reach.

SIGSIM-PADS'13, May 19–22, 2013, Montréal, Québec, Canada.

Categories and Subject Descriptors

C.1.4 [**Computer Systems Organization**]: PROCESSOR ARCHITECTURES—*Parallel Architectures*; I.6.8 [**Computing Methodologies**]: SIMULATION AND MODELING—*Discrete Event, Parallel*

General Terms

Experimentation, Performance

Keywords

Blue Gene/Q, Parallel Discrete-Event Simulation, Time Warp

1. INTRODUCTION

In 2009, the Time Warp synchronization protocol demonstrated highly efficient strong scaling (*i.e.*, model size held constant while processor or core count is increased) using Rensselaer's Optimistic Simulation System (ROSS) [2]. Here, we extend those results by demonstrating continued good scaling behavior at much larger scales on the new Blue Gene/Q supercomputer, *Sequoia*, located at Lawrence Livermore National Laboratory (LLNL). *Sequoia* is dedicated to the National Nuclear Safety Administrations' (NNSA's) Advanced Simulation and Computing (ASC) program for stewardship of the nation's nuclear weapons stockpile, which is a joint effort by LLNL, Los Alamos National Laboratory and Sandia National Laboratories. Jefferson's Time Warp [20] is an *optimistic synchronization protocol*. The key idea behind it is to allow the parallel *logical processes* of the simulation to execute freely and speculatively as much as possible, and to synchronize using *rollback* and *anti-messages* when necessary to correct for events executed out of order.

Since 2009, ROSS has been used in a number of large-scale modeling and simulation efforts. Most recently it has been used to model next generation exascale storage systems [23, 25]. Additionally, Liu et al. [24] created one of the first massively parallel discrete event models of a multi-dimensional torus network that is capable of model sizes in excess of 1 billion nodes. More recently, Mubarak et al. [27] demonstrated strong scaling of a highly accurate Dragonfly network model using both Blue Gene/P and Blue Gene/Q supercomputers. The dragonfly network is particularly interesting because of the use of its global channel links. One might think that these links would have the potential to induce excessive cascading rollbacks, but that was not the case. Using 65,536 MPI tasks mapped to 16,384 Blue Gene/Q cores, the efficiency was over 99% for a dragonfly network configured with 50 million nodes, and yielded an event rate in excess of 1 billion events/second. Similarly, Gonsiorowski et al. [16] demonstrate over 130x performance improvement for a 1 billion gate circuit model based off the OpenSparc T2 processor design when using 1024 Blue Gene/L processors compared with a baseline performance of a single Xeon processor. The rollback mechanism has often been viewed as the limiting factor in the Time Warp mechanism because the number and depth of rollbacks is usually not explicitly bounded [26], so that the rollback behavior is sometimes characterized as exhibiting "risk" or even considered (somewhat colorfully) as having a "dark side" [28]. However, our results to date suggest that the potential for complex rollback dynamics were not realized and ROSS continues to demonstrate highly efficient and scalable results in tackling some of today's most challenging discrete event simulations.

The key question asked in this this paper is: How much more scalability is possible? To address this we conducted a detailed experimental study of ROSS executing the PHOLD benchmark [13] model on two systems: the two-rack 32,768-core Blue Gene/Q located at Rensselaer's Computational Center for Nanotechnology Innovations (CCNI) supercomputer and *Sequoia*, a 120-rack, 1,966,080-core Blue Gene/Q supercomputer, currently the second-ranked supercomputer in the world according to the Top 500 list. In the next Section (Section 2), we describe the Blue Gene/Q architecture, followed by the design of ROSS in Section 3 and our proposed *Warp Speed* performance metric in Section 4. Section 5 presents the detailed performance results from both computing platforms. Section 6 places these results in the context of prior research and provides some thoughts on what new extreme-scale models this level of performance will enable. Section 7 summarizes these results, draws some conclusions and lays out some paths for future research.

2. THE BLUE GENE/Q ARCHITECTURE

The Blue Gene/Q is the third generation system in the IBM Blue Gene supercomputer family with the Blue Gene/L and /P coming previously in 2004 and 2007, respectively. The Blue Gene/Q has made a substantial leap in computational capabilities over these previous generations. The largest systems are currently the 48 rack *Mira* system located at Argonne National Laboratory (ANL) and the 120 rack *Sequoia* system located at LLNL. (Sequoia was recently split into a 96-rack system that retains the name Sequoia and a 24-rack system named Vulcan).

The Blue Gene/Q's A2 processor [11] (one per Blue Gene/Q node), shown in Figure 1, is a 45 nm chip comprised of 18 cores (PU's in the Figure) running at 1.6 GHz. The first 16 cores are exclusively used to execute user-level compute tasks while a 17th core is reserved to perform OS functionality. To improve overall processor manufacturing yields, the 18th core is only enabled if during final testing one of the other cores fails to operate correctly. The dedicated OS core

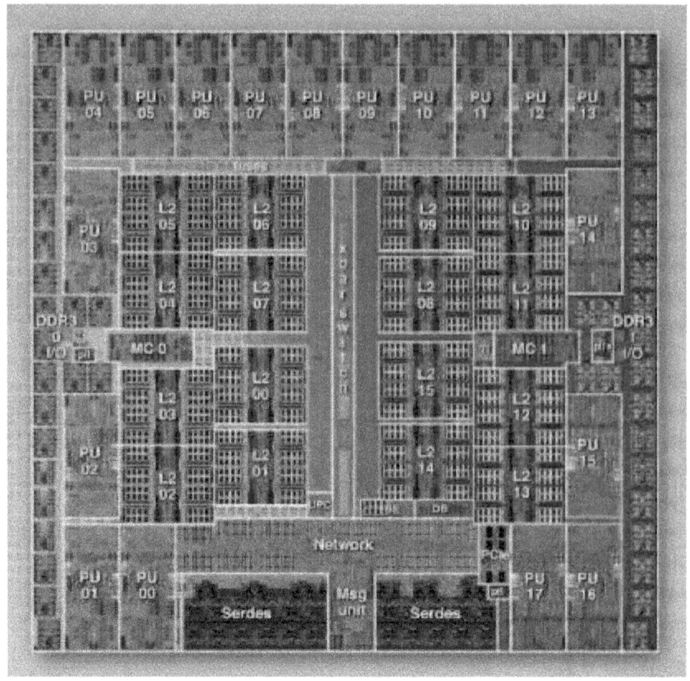

Figure 1: IBM Blue Gene/Q A2 18-way processor layout diagram from HPCWire via Google Images.

design enables the use of a much more capable compute-node OS than prior Blue Gene systems, and supports `mmap`, shared libraries, etc) without introducing OS jitter [3]. Each core supports up to 4 hardware thread or MPI task contexts, with each context having a full complement of thirty-two 64-bit registers. Each core supports up to 4-wide double precision SIMD calculations. In terms of execution models, the Blue Gene/Q supports up to 64 MPI tasks per node (up to 4 tasks per core) or a mix of MPI tasks and threads. The peak performance of the A2 processor is 204.8 gigaflops, and it consumes up to 55 watts of power. Blue Gene/Q nodes do not have GPUs as some other large scale supercomputer nodes do. In general, since the ROSS/PHOLD benchmark does not make much use of floating point operations, floating point performance is not a performance or scaling barrier.

A fully-connected crossbar switch connects all 16 cores to the 32 MB, L2 cache (realized as 16, 2 MB L2 cache units), thus all cores have a uniform cache-memory access. The amount of memory is fixed on each compute node at 16 gigbytes, with a total bandwidth of 42.6 GB/sec. In contrast to the Blue Gene/P, which only has four PowerPC 450 cores operating a 850 MHz, resulting in 13.6 gigaflops, the Blue Gene/Q provides a 15x peak floating point performance boost. However, a potential barrier to reaching that performance increase is the available node memory bandwidth. The Blue Gene/P provided 13.6 GB/sec which yields a memory bandwidth to FLOP ratio of 1. However, the Blue Gene/Q has a memory bandwidth to FLOP ratio of only 0.21.

Lowering this ratio even further relative to that of the Blue Gene/P is the doubling of the address space size from 32 bits on the Blue Gene/P to 64 bits on the Blue Gene/Q. Thus, for pointer intensive applications like ROSS, the effective pointer access rate has only improved by a factor of 1.5x (((42.6 GB/s/64 bits)/(13.6 GB/s/32 bits)) in going from the Blue Gene/P to the Blue Gene/Q. To help mitigate the lower overall memory bandwidth to FLOP ratio, the Blue Gene/Q provides an L1 cache prefetch engine for each core along with scalable atomic operations.

Connected to each node is a five dimensional (5-D) torus network with 10 serial links per node, each capable of sending and receiving 2 GB/sec [8]. An 11th link is dedicated to I/O and connects to the I/O node set. Unlike previous Blue Gene systems which have a dedicated I/O node for a set of compute nodes (*e.g*, `pset`), the Blue Gene/Q has a more flexible approach which pulls the I/O nodes outside of the primary compute fabric. In this configuration, up to eight I/O nodes, identical to the compute nodes from a hardware perspective, are grouped into a drawer. A single rack of Blue Gene/Q can drive up to 8 drawers (64 nodes) of I/O nodes. Each I/O node can service about 2 GB/sec of parallel file system data.

3. DESIGN OF ROSS

ROSS is an open source, massively parallel discrete event simulation engine supporting both YAWNS-like conservative and Time Warp optimistic event scheduling algorithms [5]. (See: `http://ross.cs.rpi.edu` for download details.) A central feature of ROSS' overall design has been its efficient use of memory and cache-aware implementation. In particular, taken from its previous shared-memory implementation [4], ROSS uses pointers to data structures as opposed to indexing into arrays. For a detailed discussion of ROSS' data structures and core algorithms used to process events, including GVT, we refer the reader to [2]. In this paper, we focus more on memory usage in ROSS and the overall event processing workflow.

In the current version of ROSS, MPI is used to spawn an instance of the model (MPI task), including all the functions for event scheduling and processing, rollback, and GVT computations. During initialization, we allocate space for the logical process (LP) state, all events (network and application), random number generator (RNG) states, and rollback support data structures. In this version of ROSS the MPI tasks use no internal threading. ROSS yields the best performance on the Blue Gene/Q system when there are four MPI tasks per core, corresponding to the four hardware contexts in each core. Thus, a node on the Blue Gene/Q will support 64 MPI tasks, each running one instance of ROSS and hosting many logical processes (LPs) of the simulation model (in this case, PHOLD).

Once memory allocations are complete, ROSS initializes each LP by first computing the correct random number generator (RNG) seed states based on the LP's id. The RNG is linear congruential with a period of 2^{121}. Each seed takes 128 bits, represented as four 32 bit integers [22]. To ensure that RNG seeds do not correlate, the start state of each seed is 2^{70} calls apart from the previous seed. Additionally, care is taken such that for any fixed LP count, the seeds are deterministicly computed irrespective of the processor count. This ensures that models runs will be deterministic and identical at different scales in a strong scaling study. Finally, we note that ROSS can support multiple RNGs per LP to avoid correlations across activities within an LP that would otherwise be independent.

Next, ROSS invokes the `init` function pointer for each LP to initialize the model's state and to schedule the start set of events for that LP. In order to schedule a new event, the application allocates a new event from the free event list. Each MPI task has its own free event list. During initialization all start events must be sent to "self" because not all LPs are initialized and installation of the mapping function between LPs and MPI tasks may not be complete.

Once all the LPs have have completed their initialization, the optimistic or conservative event scheduler is invoked. Focusing on the optimistic scheduler, there are two key parameters that control its behavior. The first is `GVT_interval`, which is the number of times through the main scheduler loop before a GVT computation will be started. As described in [2], GVT calculation in ROSS is a synchronous activity that uses the `MPI_Allreduce` collective operation. The second key scheduler parameter is `batch`. Inside the main scheduler loop, `batch` events are processed before polling the network for remote events and checking to see if a GVT computation is needed.

Polling for remote events uses a combination of asynchronous `MPI_Iprobe` and `MPI_Irecv` operations. Between successive GVT computations, on average `GVT_interval` $\times$ `batch` events will be processed by each MPI task. On the receipt of a remote message (from another task), a container is allocated pointing to the new event buffer. This container is placed in an AVL Tree [12] to facilitate fast event cancellation when an anti-message arrives. AVL Trees provide a very fast search operation, using the anti-message's timestamp, sender MPI rank, and event age as a key to find the event that must be canceled. If that event has already been processed, then the LP will be rolled back to the event just prior to the canceled event in virtual time order. The ROSS rollback mechanism uses a *reverse computation* [6] mechanism in which the model supplies a reverse event handler that reverts the LP state to the point before the event being rolled back, including the states of any RNGs that were used during event processing.

Each LP in the course of processing an event can schedule new events to be processed at some future point in virtual time. If the newly scheduled event is local (*i.e*, the destination LP is mapped to the current MPI task), then that event is immediately placed in the task's priority queue, which is implemented using a Splay Tree [34]. Otherwise, the event and its model data are sent in a contiguous memory block over MPI using the asynchronous `MPI_Isend`. ROSS manages its own `MPI_request` memory buffers which are used for the `MPI_Isend` and `MPI_Irecv` operations to ensure a sufficient number of `MPI_Isend` and `MPI_Irecv` are posted/in progress at all times.

Whenever a new GVT value is computed, all events with timestamps less than GVT are *fossil collected*. To speed up this process, ROSS creates a special container data structure called a *kernel process* (KP) which holds all the processed events in single linked list for a group of LPs. This approach reduces the amount of search require to find old event data to reclaim. Typically, each MPI task will have between 8 and 64 KPs.

4. WARP SPEED

There is a growing history of work on massively parallel simulation on state of the art supercomputer systems. The first PDES performance study to focus on the Blue Gene supercomputer platform is [29], in which PHOLD performance results for conservative, optimistic and mixed-mode PDES protocols on the Blue Gene/L were presented using the *μsik* parallel discrete event simulator. The next two Blue Gene/PDES performance studies [19, 2] demonstrated the performance of ROSS as it was in 2008. These studies were the first to demonstrate event rates from the 100's of millions to billions of events per second, and scalability to 65,536 cores. Additionally, Perumalla demonstrated epidemic models [31] using 65,536 Cray XT5 processors, and in [30] he demonstrated simulation of massively parallel MPI programs (with millions of virtual MPI tasks) using over 216,000 CrayXT 5 cores. Carothers and Perumalla [5] provided experimental results and guidance for determining when conservative or optimistic synchronization should be used for massively parallel discrete event simulation.

Thus, since 2007, our community has observed an event rate growth in PHOLD from 100 million to over 500 billion as we described in Section 5. With a nearly 5000x performance improvement in only 6 years, plotting historic speeds no longer makes sense on a linear scale. We suggest that it is time to move to a logarithmic simulator speed metric, similar to the Richter scale for earthquake amplitude, or to decibels used in many engineering domains. We propose that any discrete event simulator, whether conservative or optimistic, that achieves an overall sustained (net) event rate on the PHOLD benchmark of p events per second be described as achieving *Warp* w speed where

$$w = log_{10}(p) - 9$$

Observe that a *Warp* speed is less than zero for PHOLD event rates less than 1 billion per second. To obtain a *Warp 10.0* would require the ability to process 10 exa-events, or 10^{19} events per second.

5. EXPERIMENTAL RESULTS

Our experimental study used two separate parallel systems. The first is a two-rack, 32,768-core, 418 teraflop Blue Gene/Q system located at Rensselaer's Computational Center for Nanotechnology Innovations (CCNI). This system has 32,768 cores, 32 terabytes of RAM and is configured with 64 I/O nodes (8 drawers) making it one of the most I/O rich Blue Gene configurations for its size fielded today. The CCNI's Blue Gene/Q system is configured with driver level V1R2M0 Efix 13. This driver provides low level functionality to the Blue Gene/Q system especially related to the Parallel Active Message Interface(PAMI) [7, 21]. The MPI implementation uses PAMI to efficiently transmit messages within the 5-D torus network. The ROSS compiler settings used for all Blue Gene/Q runs were: `-qflag=i:i -qattr=full -O3`.

The second system was the *Sequoia* Blue Gene/Q system located at LLNL. Most of the time this system has been, and will be, comprised of 96 racks, 1,572,864 cores and over 1.5 petabytes of RAM, with a peak performance of 20 petaflops. In that configuration it is currently the number #2-ranked supercomputer in the world on the Top500 list (see: `top500.org`).

However, for a brief period during which this study was conducted, *Sequoia* was joined with the *Vulcan* 24-rack system to form a single 120-rack system with 1,966,080 cores and nearly 2 petabytes of RAM. While the compiler on *Sequoia* is the same as the CCNI system, the *Sequoia* experiments used two different driver levels in the OS: V1R2M0 Efix 13 and V1R2M0 Efix 15. The Efix 15 driver enabled MPI to scale to 96 and 120 racks, which was not possible with Efix 13. Additionally, for the Efix 15 runs, we had to add the following set of environment variable options in or-

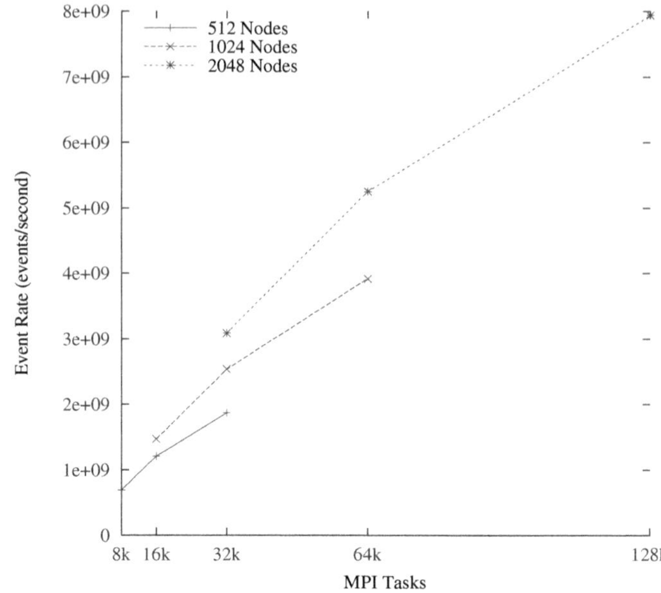

Figure 2: CCNI: PHOLD event rate performance as a function of MPI tasks for configurations of 1 rank per core, 2 ranks per core and 4 ranks per core. All runs are configured with 5,242,880 LPs, 8 `batch` events, 512 `GVT_interval` and 0.10 `lookahead`.

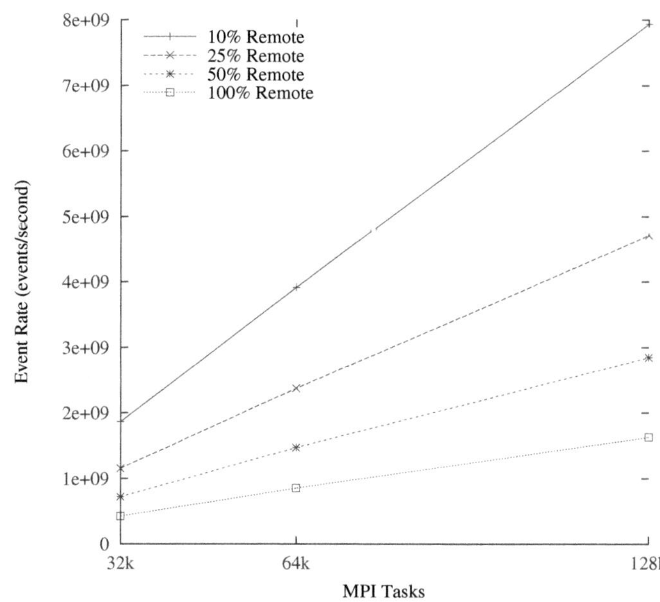

Figure 3: CCNI: PHOLD event rate performance as a function of MPI tasks for configurations with 10%, 25%, 50% and 100% remote communication fraction. All runs are configured with 5,242,880 LPs, 8 `batch` events, 512 `GVT_interval` and 0.10 `lookahead`.

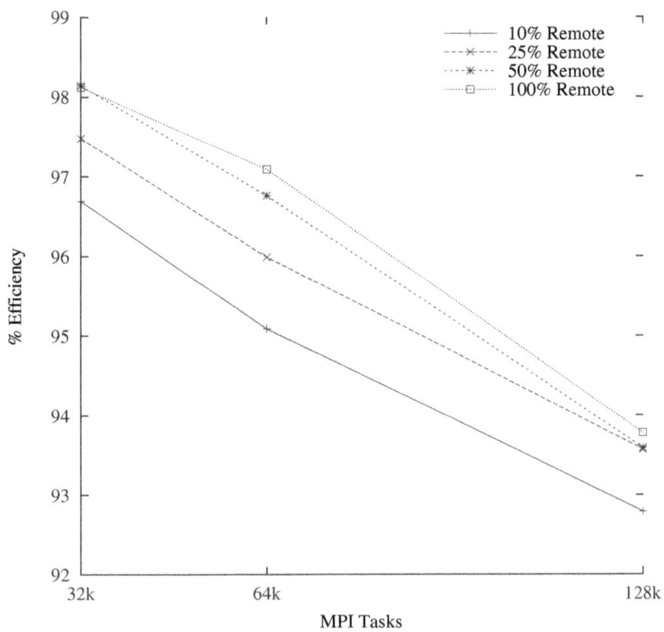

Figure 4: CCNI: PHOLD Event Efficiency (see text for definition) as a function of MPI tasks for configurations with 10%, 25%, 50%, and 100% remote communication fraction. For all data points, each node executes 64 MPI tasks. All runs are configured with 5,242,880 LPs, 8 `batch` events, 512 `GVT_interval` and 0.10 `lookahead`.

der to force PAMI and MPI to allocate the right amounts of internal memory:

- `BG_MAPCOMMONHEAP=1`
- `BG_SHAREDMEMSIZE=128`
- `PAMI_CLIENT_SHMEMSIZE=5M`
- `PAMI_GLOBAL_SHMEMSIZE=70M`
- `PAMI_SHMEM_NNODE_THRESHOLD=131072`

The PHOLD benchmark model is a derivative of the classic HOLD model [36] that was extended for parallel discrete event simulation in [13] and for reverse computation in [6]. We varied a number of ROSS and runtime configuration parameters, including: `batch`, `GVT_interval`, MPI tasks per core, and the percentage of remote communications. Each PHOLD event either schedules an event for "self" or for some other randomly selected LP, in either case with an exponentially-distributed time-stamp increment having mean of 1.0. An optional static nonzero parameter, `lookahead`, can be added to the time-stamp increment to enable direct comparison between optimistic schedulers (which can handle events scheduled with arbitrarily small positive delays) and conservative schedulers (which require a predetermined positive (nonzero) lower bound on event delays).

All *Sequoia* runs were configured with exactly 251,658,240 LPs, 16 events per LP, 8 KPs per MPI rank, 10% remote communication fraction, 0.1 `lookahead`, 8 `batch`, 512 `GVT_interval`, and 4 MPI tasks per core. The 10% remote fraction means that 90% of the events that each LP scheduled were "local" (*i.e.*, scheduled for itself) and 10% were "remote" (*i.e.*, scheduled for a different LP uniformly randomly selected from among all of the others). In case anyone wants to do a similar scaling experiment with a conservative synchronization algorithm we introduced a small amount of `lookahead`, 0.1, although the Time Warp algorithm makes no use of this. We set the mean of the exponential part of the future event time distribution to 0.90. The event itself does no substantial computational work other than random number generation for selecting the destination LP and future time-stamp. At the largest scale of 120 racks and 7,864,320 MPI ranks this yields a relatively small workload of exactly 32 LPs and an average of 512 live events per MPI rank.

We first present the results from the CCNI Blue Gene/Q and followed by our performance results from *Sequoia*.

5.1 CCNI Blue Gene/Q Results

These early CCNI tests were intended both to provide comparison to the *Sequoia* results at small scales and to mimic the same LP workloads that *Sequoia* would have at 96 racks so that we might anticipate what to expect at the largest scale. For the CCNI tests all runs were configured with 5,242,880 LPs, 8 `batch` events, 512 `GVT_interval` and 0.10 `lookahead`.

In the first series of experiments, we investigated the impact of over-committing MPI tasks to each Blue Gene/Q core. Recall that the A2 processor supports up to four hardware thread contexts per core. Thus, it is possible to support 1, 2 or 4 MPI tasks or threads per core. Figure 2 reports the PHOLD event rate performance as a function of the total number of MPI tasks for run sizes of 512, 1024 and 2048 nodes, which correspond to using a 1/2 rack, 1 full rack and 2 full racks. Unlike previous hyper-threaded architectures, such as those used by Intel [37], we observe nearly linear event rate performance improvement as each node is configured to use 2 or 4 threads. We do observe less than linear scaling when going from 2 to 4 threads but it is significantly better than we have observed on our hyper-threaded platforms. The peak event rates are nearly 2 billion/sec, 4 billion/sec and 8 billion/sec for 32,768, 65,536 and 131,072 MPI tasks respectively. In comparison to our previous peak PHOLD performance of just over 12 billion [2] on 65,536 Blue Gene/P cores, we observe here that this particular model has 5x the LPs and events, leading to greater overheads in the priority queue and event processing because of the larger memory footprint (*i.e.*, more cache misses).

The next two figures report the PHOLD event rate performance (Figure 3) and efficiency (Figure 4) as a function of the MPI Task count, varying the remote event percentages. While each remote event percentage curve has its own scaling slope, we do not observe any decrease in performance as the node count increases. This suggests that the 5-D torus network of the Blue Gene/Q enables the PHOLD model to continue to scale up to at least 131,072 MPI tasks. This is in spite of the large number of remote events; in one case 100% of the events are scheduled to remote LPs. The peak event rates at 131,072 MPI tasks for 10%, 25%, 50% and 100% remote event communications are 8 billion, 5 billion, 3 billion, and nearly 2 billion, respectively. In terms of overall speedup, we observe that the slope of the 10% remote communication line is super-linear. We attribute this scalability to better cache performance as more cores are used for the same size problem.

Cores	MPI Tasks	$Events_{Total}$	$Events_{RB}$	$Events_{Net}$	Efficiency	Time (sec)	Speed	Warp Speed
16,384	65,536	3.316E+13	1.750E+11	3.298E+13	0.9947	14964.2	2.20E+09	0.34
16,384	65,536	3.316E+13	1.750E+11	3.298E+13	0.9947	15027.2	2.20E+09	0.34
16,384	65,536	3.316E+13	1.750E+11	3.298E+13	0.9947	15027.7	2.19E+09	0.34
32,768	131,072	3.325E+13	2.678E+11	3.298E+13	0.9919	6799.6	4.85E+09	0.69
32,768	131,072	3.325E+13	2.678E+11	3.298E+13	0.9919	6822.7	4.83E+09	0.68
32,768	131,072	3.325E+13	2.678E+11	3.298E+13	0.9919	6821.5	4.84E+09	0.68
65,536	262,144	3.339E+13	4.054E+11	3.298E+13	0.9879	3128.5	1.05E+10	1.02
65,536	262,144	3.339E+13	4.054E+11	3.298E+13	0.9879	3128.2	1.05E+10	1.02
65,536	262,144	3.339E+13	4.054E+11	3.298E+13	0.9879	3127.6	1.05E+10	1.02
131,072	524,288	3.358E+13	5.988E+11	3.298E+13	0.9822	1445.1	2.28E+10	1.36
131,072	524,288	3.358E+13	5.988E+11	3.298E+13	0.9822	1447.1	2.28E+10	1.36
131,072	524,288	3.358E+13	5.988E+11	3.298E+13	0.9822	1447.1	2.28E+10	1.36
786,432	3,145,728	3.455E+13	1.562E+12	3.298E+13	0.9548	202.6	1.63E+11	2.21
786,432	3,145,728	3.455E+13	1.563E+12	3.298E+13	0.9548	200.7	1.64E+11	2.22
786,432	3,145,728	3.455E+13	1.562E+12	3.298E+13	0.9548	200.8	1.64E+11	2.22

Table 1: SEQUOIA: Raw PHOLD performance data for 1, 2, 4, 8, and 48 rack runs, each rack containing 16,384 cores. All runs were configured with 251,658,240 LPs, 16 circulating events per LP, 8 KPs per MPI task, 10% remote communication fraction (fraction of events sent to random non-self LP), 0.1 `lookahead`, 8 `batch`, 512 `GVT_interval` and 4 MPI tasks per core. The net number of events processed for all runs was exactly 32,984,968,283,642 (*i.e.*, 32 trillion), since the runs were perfectly deterministic. *Cores* **is the total number of Sequoia cores (16 per node) used in each execution;** $MPITasks$ **is the total number of MPI Tasks used, which in all cases is 4x the number of Cores;** $Events_{Total}$ **is the total number events executed, including those rolled back;** $Events_{RB}$ **is the number of events rolled back;** $Events_{Net}$ **is the number of net events executed, i.e. events committed, not rolled back;** $Efficiency$ **is** $Events_{net}/Events_{Total}$**;** $Time$ **is total wallclock execution time in seconds;** *Speed* **is** $Events_{net}/Time$ **and *Warp Speed* is** $log_{10}(Speed) - 9$ **All runs were executed between 01/24/2013 and 02/05/2013 under driver Efix #13.**

Cores	MPI Tasks	$Events_{Total}$	$Events_{RB}$	$Events_{Net}$	Efficiency	Time (sec)	Speed	Warp Speed
32,768	131,072	3.325E+13	2.679E+11	3.298E+13	0.9919	6377.8	5.17E+09	0.71
32,768	131,072	3.325E+13	2.679E+11	3.298E+13	0.9919	6378.3	5.17E+09	0.71
65,536	262,144	3.339E+13	4.053E+11	3.298E+13	0.9879	2912.4	1.13E+10	1.05
65,536	262,144	3.339E+13	4.053E+11	3.298E+13	0.9879	2912.4	1.13E+10	1.05
131,072	524,288	3.358E+13	5.986E+11	3.298E+13	0.9822	1323.8	2.49E+10	1.40
131,072	524,288	3.358E+13	5.986E+11	3.298E+13	0.9822	1323.0	2.49E+10	1.40
393,216	1,572,864	3.407E+13	1.084E+12	3.298E+13	0.9682	379.7	8.69E+10	1.94
393,216	1,572,864	3.407E+13	1.084E+12	3.298E+13	0.9682	379.7	8.69E+10	1.94
786,432	3,145,728	3.454E+13	1.554E+12	3.298E+13	0.9550	174.7	1.89E+11	2.28
786,432	3,145,728	3.454E+13	1.554E+12	3.298E+13	0.9550	174.7	1.89E+11	2.28
1,572,864	6,291,456	3.521E+13	2.222E+12	3.298E+13	0.9369	82.6	3.99E+11	2.60
1,572,864	6,291,456	3.521E+13	2.222E+12	3.298E+13	0.9369	82.6	3.99E+11	2.60
1,966,080	7,864,320	3.547E+13	2.490E+12	3.298E+13	0.9298	65.4	5.04E+11	2.70
1,966,080	7,864,320	3.548E+13	2.490E+12	3.298E+13	0.9298	65.5	5.04E+11	2.70

Table 2: SEQUOIA: Raw PHOLD performance data for 2, 4, 8, 24, 48, 96 and 120 rack runs. All runs were configured with 251,658,240 LPs, 16 events per LP, 8 KPs per MPI task, 10% remote communications, 0.1 `lookahead`, 8 `batch`, 512 `GVT_interval`, and 4 MPI tasks per core. The net events processed for all runs was 32,984,968,283,642 (*i.e.*, 33 trillion), and was fully deterministic across all job runs. Column headings have the same meaning as in Table 1. Runs were executed between 03/08/2013 and 03/11/2013 under driver Efix #15.

The PHOLD model efficiency mirrors the event rate performance as shown in Figure 4. Here, we observe that the overall efficiency ranges between 98% down to 93%. This suggests the Blue Gene/Q network is quickly moving messages between LPs so that rollback rates are low even at high remote event communication rates.

5.2 Sequoia Blue Gene/Q Results

As shown in Tables 1 and 2, we report the raw performance data collected from two distinct series of strong scaling runs on *Sequoia*. In Table 1, we show data performance for runs on 1, 2, 4, 8, and 48 racks for 3 runs each. The reason for the unusual rack scaling (not strictly powers of 2) is that these are sweet spots for the Blue Gene/Q 5-D torus network. In some other configurations the torus becomes only a mesh (*e.g.*, without wraparound) which can increase

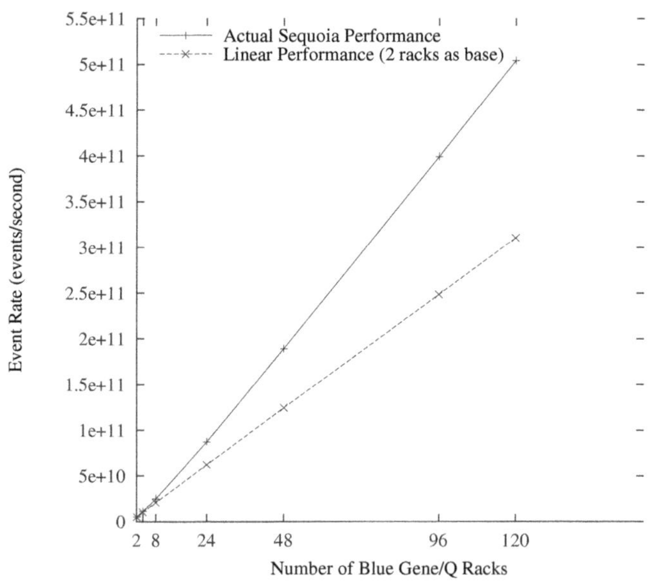

Figure 5: SEQUOIA: PHOLD event rate performance as a function of Blue Gene/Q racks for configurations of 2, 8, 24, 48, 96 and 120 racks. The linear performance curve uses the 2 rack event rate performance as a baseline. Event rate data taken from Table 2.

message latency. However, the configurations above were always using a full torus.

The performance we observed showed very high efficiencies and record breaking event rates. For example, at 1 rack (65,536 MPI tasks), the event rate is just above 2.2 billion and requires just over 4 hours (4hr, 10mins) to execute the 32 trillion events. However, as we increase the core count, we observe PHOLD's event rate not only increasing steadily, but doing so at a super-linear pace. At two racks, the event rate has more than doubled to 4.85 billion, and at eight racks the event rate is more than quadrupled again to 22.8 billion. At 48 racks the event rate is 164 billion, and the speedup from 1 to 48 racks is 74x. The overall simulator event efficiencies reflect the super-linear performance with a range of 99% down to 93%. These experiments ran during the time window of 01/24/2013 to 02/05/2013 when *Sequoia's* driver level (as designated by IBM) was Efix #13.

The second series of experiments shown in Table 2 were conducted between 03/08/2013 and 03/11/2013. At this time, *Sequoia* was running a much updated driver, Efix #15, that enabled MPI to execute on 96 and 120 rack configurations at four tasks per core. Here we observe an unprecedented level of performance. First, Efix #15 version of the driver has improved the lower rack count performance when compared with that shown in Table 1. For example, the 2-rack performance improved from 4.85 to 5.17 billion events/second which is nearly a 7% increase. Even at the higher end, our 48 rack performance has improved by over 6% (from 164.5 to 174.7 billion events/sec). However, the *piéce de résistance* comes at 96 and 120 racks. Here, we observe event rates of 399 billion and 504 billion respectively, with an overall range speedup (2 to 120 racks) of 97x, and both with an event efficiency of nearly 93%. Figure 5, plots the *Sequoia's* event rate performance compared to strictly linear performance scaling using the 2-rack performance as the base.

Data struct	Size	Used Count	Subtotal
PE struct	520 bytes	1	0.5 KB
KP struct	104 bytes	8	0.8 KB
LP struct	232 bytes	40	9.3 KB
Network data	8 bytes	7250	58 KB
AVL Tree	40 bytes	7250	290 KB
Event + model	128 bytes	7250	928 KB
Total			**1.287 MB**

Table 3: ROSS Memory Usage at 96 racks for a single MPI rank. Total memory working set per node is just 82 MB.

Now, a critical question is what accounts for the high amount of super-linear speedup across both sets of experiments? The answer lies with the A2 processor's unique memory hierarchy. Recall that the memory bandwidth is only 42.6 GB/sec. However, as more Blue Gene/Q racks are used to execute the PHOLD model, more and more of the model code and data fits within the 32 MB L2 cache on each node. This cache operates at 563 GB/sec, which is over 13x faster than main memory [11]. The memory usage of ROSS for the PHOLD model at 96 racks is shown in Table 3. Each MPI rank consumes about 1.3 MB, for a total node memory requirement of just over 82 MB. A similar analysis shows a requirement of only 65 MB at the 120 rack scale. With 32 MB of L2 cache available and a small working set of less than 82 MB, coupled with an advanced data prefetching engine, ROSS is largely executing out of L2 cache at these extremely high core counts.

These super-linear results also underscore the significant capabilities of the Blue Gene/Q network. For the 10% remote communications, each LP is sending to other randomly chosen LPs located far apart within the 5-D torus network. On a 1 million node, 5-D torus network, remote messages will travel on average 1/4 of the torus circumference in each of the 5 dimensions. Since the circumference is 16 hops, that is a mean of 5x4 = 20 hops. Thus, we are observing substantial super-linear performance in spite of a workload exhibiting a nearly worst-case, globally random communication pattern.

In comparison to previous Blue Gene/P results [2], while some degree of super-linear performance was observed, the high degree of super-linear performance shown here was not observed. Additionally, we note that the previous Blue Gene/P results yielded very high efficiency at 16 LPs per MPI ranks however at 8 LPs per MPI rank with 128K Blue Gene/P cores the amount of parallelism was insufficient and a cascade of rollbacks ensued, lowering the overall event rate performance. Consequently, we believe with our current PHOLD configuration there is additional parallelism to exploit for even greater performance. We observe that if a 240 rack Blue Gene/Q system where available, the current PHOLD model would still have 16 LPs per MPI rank and thus have a good opportunity to scale to an event rate of just over 1 trillion events per second, assuming only a linear increase in performance.

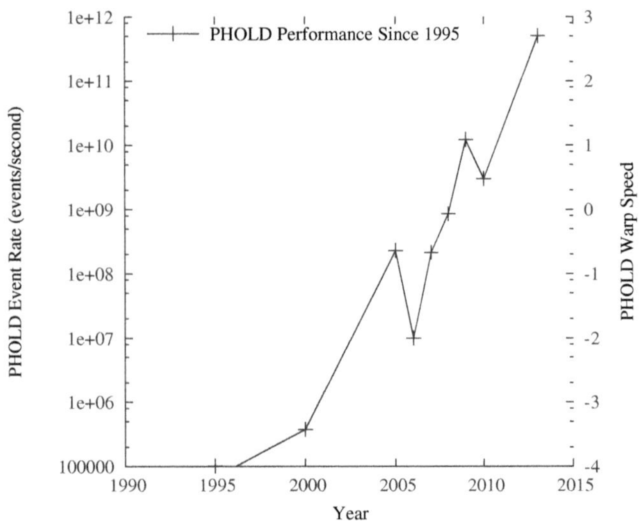

Figure 6: PHOLD History: PHOLD event rate (left side) and *Warp* number (right side) as a function of the year the performance data was published.

6. HISTORY & DISCUSSION

Year	Author/Publication	Event Rate	Warp
1990	Fujimoto [13]	N/A	N/A
1995	Fujimoto, et al. [14]	101,000	-3.99
1996	Hao, et al. [18]	95,000	-4.02
2000	Carothers, et al. [4]	375,000	-3.43
2005	Chen, et al. [10]	228,000,000	-0.64
2006	Bauer, et al. [1]	10,000,000	-2.00
2007	Perumalla [29]	214,000,000	-0.67
2008	Holder, et al. [19]	853,000,000	-0.07
2009	Bauer, et al. [2]	12,260,000,000	1.09
2010	Carothers, et al. [5]	3,000,000,000	0.48
2013	This Paper	504,000,000,000	2.70

Table 4: PHOLD History: Raw PHOLD event rate data from 1995 through present day. Note, the PHOLD configurations across these prior results vary.

The PHOLD benchmark has a long history going back to Fujimoto's Time Warp synthetic workload paper [13]. In that original paper, no event rate data was presented, but a sizable 54x speedup on a 64-way BBN Butterfly system was reported. Most papers from that era reported only speedup relative to a sequential execution, and did not single out total event rate as a key metric. On closer examination of reported performance results, we were able to find a number of event rate results going all the way back to 1995, as shown in Table 4. We hasten to note that we are only looking at PHOLD performance and do not mean to diminish the significance of high performance obtained using other models. For example, in 1994 Greenberg, et al. [17] developed a conservative synchronization algorithm that could leverage the fast SIMD features of the MasPar-1, 16K core multiprocessor system for modeling dynamic channel assignment schemes in wireless telephone networks. They obtained a speedup of 120x over a optimized serial implementation. Similarly in 2003, Fujimoto et al. [15], used 1536 processors from the Lemieux cluster at the Pittsburgh Supercomputing Center on a synthetic 10 million node campus network topology and created a traffic model that produced over 106 million network packet events per second.

Previously published results using PHOLD were usually measured on small clusters consisting typically of less than 32 nodes. It was not until Chen et al. [9] that anyone used a supercomputer of significant power for its day and reported the PHOLD event rate performance. In that case it was also using the Lemieux cluster, consisting of 750, 4-way AlphaServer processors. Of course the historic PHOLD configurations are not directly comparable given the array of different hardware systems and PHOLD configurations. Still, overall, from 1995 to the present, the event rate performance of PHOLD has increased by a factor of around 5,000,000. The exponential performance improvement is shown in Figure 6. Here, both the event rate and *Warp* number are shown on separate y-axises. We observe in both this Figure and Table 4 that the peak *Warp Speed* has increase from -4.0 in 1995 to 2.70 based on the data presented here.

With a massively parallel simulator that is capable of *Warp 2.7* (*e.g*, 504 billion events-per-second), what *big, hairy, audacious, problems (BHAPs)* might we now contemplate addressing? We submit that the Internet in all its vertical and horizontal architecture has become an integral stratum of what one might call the *human sustainability network (HSN)*. The HSN is really the network of networks on which all of our collective daily lives depend. This includes power networks (*e.g*, smart grids), fresh water networks, fuel/pipeline networks, transportation networks (air, land and sea vehicles), retail networks (Walmart, Target), financial networks (markets, banks, credit and insurance companies), manufacturing networks, and social networks. Because of the coupling of all of these networks by the Internet (via wired, wireless, cellular and satellite communication systems), we are now seeing how a drought in India can lead to a power outage impacting over 600,000,000 people [32]; how errant code in a trading bot results in a stock market flash crash [35]; and how the housing bubble results in a freeze of credit markets leading to the inability of industrial giants like General Electric to finance their daily operations [33]. All these networks are interconnected at various vertical and horizontal levels and it appears that their level of interdependence will only grow in the future.

One way of looking at the significance of the results we report here is that direct simulations of planetary-scale networks are now, in principle at least, within reach. Our *Sequoia* benchmarks had *only* 251 million LPs, because that was all we could fit in RAM at the scale of 1 *Sequoia* rack. However, at the largest scale of 120 racks, we had enough RAM available for 100 times as many PHOLD LPs, i.e. 25 billion! By comparison, there are *only* 7 billion people on Earth, and there are *only* 4 billion unique IPv4 addresses, and our infrastructure and commerce networks are generally even smaller. We are reaching the point where our simulation capability is limited more by our ability to develop, maintain, and validate models than by our ability to execute them.

7. CONCLUSIONS AND FUTURE WORK

In this paper we have demonstrated a new standard in Time Warp performance by efficiently executing the PHOLD benchmark model using the ROSS simulator running Time Warp with reverse computation on 1,966,080 Blue Gene/Q cores, yielding an unprecedented event rate of 504 billion. We emphasize that these performance results were obtained using a computational workload that generates a nearly worst-case, globally random communication patterns. This continues an exponential growth in peak PDES benchmark speed, which prompts us to propose a new performance metric called *Warp Speed* which grows logarithmically with PHOLD event rate. We are now at *Warp 2.7*.

With these results however, a number of questions still remain. First, our results used an *MPI everywhere* approach and avoided the complexities associated with using a hybrid execution model combining MPI tasks with threads. At first pass, one might think there would be an immediate and significant performance gain. However, our concern with using a hybrid execution model is that it could break the balanced workload on each MPI tasks. As previously noted, each MPI rank does a bit of all parallel simulation activity, from helping to compute GVT to managing MPI messages and polling the network. With threads it is unclear how decompose the simulator work to keep that balance. Adding to the complexity is the fact on Blue Gene/Q systems PAMI (the low level messaging layer) already creates lockless, shared-memory pools across MPI ranks that reside on the same compute node [21]. This functionality appears similar to the sender and receiver pools used by Fujimoto and Panesar [14] to greatly improve cache performance on the KSR shared memory machine. Thus, it is unclear how moving to threads will actually improve performance.

A second open question is the issue of load balancing at this scale. While a great deal of research has been done in the area of dynamic and static load distribution for parallel discrete event simulation, no research has been done for irregular systems with greater than 100,000 cores, much less millions of cores. This is a difficult open question.

Third, there is an open issue regarding efficient checkpointing as part of an overall failure recovery process for Time Warp simulation executing at this scale. While it might seem that because a Time Warp system supports a rollback and recovery mechanism, it is not immediately obvious how to adapt the reverse computation functionality for use in situations where failures can occur on any processor cycle or packet transfer instead of at well-defined event boundaries.

Finally, these results motivate us and hopefully others in the parallel simulation community to consider a wide range of new application domains that could benefit from this level of performance such as multi-network systems like the *Human Sustainability Network*, medical applications like discrete human brain models, and new computational methods like hybrid discrete-continuum models, to name but just a few.

8. ACKNOWLEDGMENTS

This work was performed under the auspices of the U.S. Department of Energy by Lawrence Livermore National Laboratory under contract DE-AC52-07NA27344, and Argonne National Laboratory ("Argonne") under Contract No. DE-AC02-06CH11357. This research used the *Sequoia* IBM Blue Gene/Q computing resources at Lawrence Livermore National Laboratory, and additional Blue Gene/Q computing resources were provided by the Computational Center for Nanotechnology Innovations (CCNI) located at Rensselaer Polytechnic Institute. Part of the CCNI's Blue Gene/Q was acquired using funds from the NSF MRI Program, Award #1126125. Prof. Carothers' time was supported by AFRL Award FA8750-11-2-0065 and DOE Award DE-SC0004875.

9. REFERENCES

[1] D. W. Bauer and C. D. Carothers. Eliminating remote message passing in optimistic simulation. In *WSC '06: Proceedings of the 38th conference on Winter simulation*. Winter Simulation Conference, December 2006.

[2] D. W. Bauer Jr., C. D. Carothers, and A. Holder. Scalable time warp on blue gene supercomputers. In *Proceedings of the 2009 ACM/IEEE/SCS 23rd Workshop on Principles of Advanced and Distributed Simulation*, pages 35–44, Washington, DC, USA, 2009. IEEE Computer Society.

[3] P. Beckman, K. Iskra, K. Yoshii, S. Coghlan, and A. Nataraj. Benchmarking the Effects of Operating System Interference on Extreme-Scale Parallel Machines. *Cluster Comput.*, 11:3–16, 2008.

[4] C. D. Carothers, D. Bauer, and S. Pearce. Ross: A high-performance, low-memory, modular time warp system. *Journal of Parallel and Distributed Computing*, 62(11):1648 – 1669, 2002.

[5] C. D. Carothers and K. S. Perumalla. On deciding between conservative and optimistic approaches on massively parallel platforms. In *Winter Simulation Conference'10*, pages 678–687, 2010.

[6] C. D. Carothers, K. S. Perumalla, and R. M. Fujimoto. Efficient optimistic parallel simulations using reverse computation. *ACM Transactions on Modeling and Computer Simulation*, 9(3):224–253, 1999.

[7] D. Chen, N. Eisley, P. Heidelberger, S. Kumar, A. Mamidala, F. Petrini, R. Senger, Y. Sugawara, R. Walkup, B. Steinmacher-Burow, A. Choudhury, Y. Sabharwal, S. Singhal, and J. J. Parker. Looking under the hood of the ibm blue gene/q network. In *Proceedings of the International Conference on High Performance Computing, Networking, Storage and Analysis*, SC '12, pages 69:1–69:12, Los Alamitos, CA, USA, 2012. IEEE Computer Society Press.

[8] D. Chen, N. A. Eisley, P. Heidelberger, R. M. Senger, Y. Sugawara, S. Kumar, V. Salapura, D. L. Satterfield, B. Steinmacher-Burow, and J. J. Parker. The ibm blue gene/q interconnection network and message unit. In *Proceedings of 2011 International Conference for High Performance Computing, Networking, Storage and Analysis*, SC '11, pages 26:1–26:10, New York, NY, USA, 2011. ACM.

[9] G. Chen and B. K. Szymanski. Dsim: scaling time warp to 1,033 processors. In *WSC '05: Proceedings of the 37th conference on Winter simulation*, pages 346–355. Winter Simulation Conference, 2005.

[10] G. Chen and B. K. Szymanski. Time quantum GVT: A scalable computation of the global virtual time in parallel discrete event simulations. *Scalable Computing: Practice and Experience: Scientific*

International Journal for Parallel and Distributed Computing*, pages 425–446, 2007.

[11] G. Chiu, P. Coteus, and R. Wisniewski. Blue gene/q overview and update. http://www.alcf.anl.gov/sites/www.alcf.anl.gov/files/IBM_BGQ_Architecture_0.pdf, 2011.

[12] C. C. Foster. Information retrieval: information storage and retrieval using avl trees. In *Proceedings of the 1965 20th national conference*, ACM '65, pages 192–205, New York, NY, USA, 1965. ACM.

[13] R. M. Fujimoto. Performance of time warp under synthetic workloads, January 1990.

[14] R. M. Fujimoto and K. S. Panesar. Buffer management in shared-memory time warp systems. In *Proceedings of the ninth workshop on Parallel and distributed simulation*, PADS '95, pages 149–156, Washington, DC, USA, 1995. IEEE Computer Society.

[15] R. M. Fujimoto, K. Perumalla, A. Park, H. Wu, M. H. Ammar, and G. F. Riley. Large-scale network simulation âĂŞ how big? how fast. In *In Symposium on Modeling, Analysis and Simulation of Computer Telecommunication Systems (MASCOTS*, 2003.

[16] E. Gonsiorowski, C. Carothers, and C. Tropper. Modeling large scale circuits using massively parallel discrete-event simulation. In *Modeling, Analysis Simulation of Computer and Telecommunication Systems (MASCOTS), 2012 IEEE 20th International Symposium on*, pages 127–133, Aug.

[17] A. G. Greenberg, B. D. Lubachevsky, P. E. Wright, and D. M. Nicol. Efficient massively parallel simulation of dynamic channel assignment schemes for wireless cellular communications. In *Workshop on Parallel and Distributed Simulation*, pages 187–194, 1994.

[18] F. Hao, K. Wilson, R. Fujimoto, and E. Zegura. Logical process size in parallel simulations. In *Proceedings of the 28th conference on Winter simulation*, WSC '96, pages 645–652, Washington, DC, USA, 1996. IEEE Computer Society.

[19] A. Holder and C. D. Carothers. Analysis of time warp on a 32,768 processor ibm blue gene/l supercomputer. In *2008 Proceedings European Modeling and Simulation Symposium (EMSS)*, 2008.

[20] D. R. Jefferson. Virtual time. *ACM Trans. Program. Lang. Syst.*, 7(3):404–425, 1985.

[21] S. Kumar, A. R. Mamidala, D. A. Faraj, B. Smith, M. Blocksome, B. Cernohous, D. Miller, J. Parker, J. Ratterman, P. Heidelberger, D. Chen, and B. Steinmacher-Burrow. Pami: A parallel active message interface for the blue gene/q supercomputer. *Parallel and Distributed Processing Symposium, International*, 0:763–773, 2012.

[22] P. L'Ecuyer and T. H. Andres. A random number generator based on the combination of four lcgs. *Math. Comput. Simul.*, 44(1):99–107, 1997.

[23] N. Liu, C. Carothers, J. Cope, P. Carns, R. Ross, A. Crume, and C. Maltzahn. Modeling a leadership-scale storage system. In *Proceedings of the 9th international conference on Parallel Processing and Applied Mathematics - Volume Part I*, PPAM'11, pages 10–19, Berlin, Heidelberg, 2012. Springer-Verlag.

[24] N. Liu and C. D. Carothers. Modeling billion-node torus networks using massively parallel discrete-event simulation. In *Proceedings of the 2011 IEEE Workshop on Principles of Advanced and Distributed Simulation*, PADS '11, pages 1–8, Washington, DC, USA, 2011. IEEE Computer Society.

[25] N. Liu, J. Cope, P. Carns, C. D. Carothers, R. Ross, G. Grider, A. Crume, and C. Maltzahn. On the role of burst buffers in leadership-class storage systems. In *In Proceedings of the 28th IEEE Conference on Mass Storage Systems and Technologies (MSST 2012)*. IEEE, 2012.

[26] B. D. Lubachevsky, A. Shwartz, and A. Weiss. An analysis of rollback-based simulation. *ACM Transactions on Modeling and Computer Simulation*, 1(2):154–193, 1991.

[27] M. Mubarak, C. D. Carothers, R. Ross, and P. Carns. Modeling a million-node dragonfly network using massively parallel discrete event simulation. In *3rd International Workshop on Performance Modeling, Benchmarking and Simulation of High Performance Computer Systems (PMBS12) held as part of SC12*, 2012.

[28] D. M. Nicol and X. Liu. The dark side of risk (what your mother never told you about time warp). In *PADS '97: Proceedings of the eleventh workshop on Parallel and distributed simulation*, pages 188–195, Washington, DC, USA, 1997. IEEE Computer Society.

[29] K. S. Perumalla. Scaling time warp-based discrete event execution to 104 processors on a blue gene supercomputer. In *CF '07: Proceedings of the 4th international conference on Computing Frontiers*, pages 69–76, New York, NY, USA, 2007. ACM.

[30] K. S. Perumalla. $\mu\pi$: A scalable and transparent system for simulation mpi programs. In *In Proceedings of the 3rd International ICST Conference on Simulation Tools and Techniques*, 2010.

[31] K. S. Perumalla and S. K. Seal. Reversible parallel discrete-event execution of large-scale epidemic outbreak models. In *In Proceedings of the 24th Workshop on Principles of Advanced and Distributed Simulation*, 2010.

[32] J. Romero. Energy-wise blog: Lack of rain a leading cause of indian grid collapse. *IEEE Spectrum*, July 2012.

[33] P. Schweizer. *Throw Them All Out*. Houghton Mifflin Harcount Publishing Company, New York, 2011.

[34] D. D. Sleator and R. E. Tarjan. Self-adjusting binary search trees. *J. ACM*, 32(3):652–686, July 1985.

[35] E. Ullman. "errant code? it's not just a bug", new york times, the opinion pages. http://www.nytimes.com/2012/08/09/opinion/after-knight-capital-new-code-for-trades.html, August 8th, 2012.

[36] J. Vaucher and P. Duval. A comparison of simulation event list algorithms. *Communications of the ACM*, 18(4):223–230, 1975.

[37] G. Yaun, C. D. Carothers, and S. Kalyanaraman. Large-scale tcp models using optimistic parallel simulation. In *Proceedings of the seventeenth workshop on Parallel and distributed simulation*, PADS '03, pages 153–, Washington, DC, USA, 2003. IEEE Computer Society.

Topological Computation of Activity Regions

Work in Progress Paper

Martin Potier
U-PEC - LACL
61 avenue du Gal de Gaulle
94010 Créteil Cedex
martin.potier@u-pec.fr

Antoine Spicher
U-PEC - LACL
61 avenue du Gal de Gaulle
94010 Créteil Cedex
antoine.spicher@u-pec.fr

Olivier Michel
U-PEC - LACL
61 avenue du Gal de Gaulle
94010 Créteil Cedex
olivier.michel@u-pec.fr

ABSTRACT

Most of the frameworks and languages available in the field of modeling and simulation of dynamical systems focus on the specification of the state of the system and its transition function. Although we believe that this task has been elegantly solved by the design of the rule-based topological programming language MGS, an interesting challenge remains in the computation of the *activity*, and its topology, exhibited by their discrete event simulation. This additional information can help in optimizing, analyzing and modeling complex systems.

Categories and Subject Descriptors

D.1.1 [**Programming Techniques**]: Applicative (Functional) Programming; F.4.2 [**Mathematical Logic and Formal Languages**]: Grammars and Other Rewriting Systems—*Parallel rewriting systems*

General Terms

Algorithms, Theory, Language

Keywords

Activity tracking, MGS programming language, spatial computing, rule-based modeling and simulation, topology of interactions

1. INTRODUCTION

Complex simulation models consist of a large number of interacting parts. In common modeling tools and languages it is not easy to extract abstractions of the dynamics of the whole system, during, before or after its simulation. The analysis of the many outputs and interactions is long and meticulous. To our knowledge, no established method exists for finding *patterns of interactions* in system structures, during a simulation. Some methods exist for particular domains (multi-agent systems, distributed and parallel simulations, image analysis, etc.), but except for the work proposed by [12] no generic methods have been developed for this purpose. In the simulation context, *activity* is usually used as a phase of the system under study. We do not consider this definition of activity here. Instead, activity is considered as a *locus of interaction* occurring during a simulation step.

We define *active regions* as contiguous active parts that are evolving according to the laws governing the model. These regions are highly dynamical, usually changing at each time step. Moreover, we are interested in giving a topological definition of the active regions and to handle them intentionally. We believe that this definition of activity and activity regions [10] can be used as a central guiding concept to construct generic structures for the analysis and specification of systems. The specification structures, driven by a measure of activity of the simulation, can be used to recognize and enhance the dynamics of sub-components in time, space, and states.

MGS is an experimental programming language dedicated to the modeling and the simulation of a special kind of discrete dynamical systems: *dynamical systems with a dynamical structure*, or $(\text{DS})^2$ [3]. Dynamical systems with a dynamical structure arise when the state space is not fixed *a priori* but is jointly computed with the current state during the simulation. In this case the evolution function is often given through local rules that drive the interaction between some system components. MGS offers a new kind of data structure, topological collections, to describe the state of a dynamical system, and a new kind of control structure, transformations, to express local and discrete evolution laws. These two notions permit an easy specification of $(\text{DS})^2$.

We focus in this paper on the computation of activity and activity regions for MGS. Section 2 introduces the required technical formalism to understand the next sections. Section 3 investigates the topological computation of activity and activity regions in MGS and preliminary results of their use are given in Section 4. Conclusions are drawn in the last section.

2. A PRESENTATION OF MGS

MGS is a domain specific language dedicated to the modeling and simulation of $(\text{DS})^2$. It makes use of topology and rewriting techniques to simulate all kind of systems. It is a rule-based declarative, functional and dynamically typed language.

2.1 Topology of Interactions

A $(\text{DS})^2$ is a dynamical system whose state space (*i.e.*, whose structure) evolves jointly with the system itself. Think for instance of a growing multi-cellular organism where cells (which are the constitutive elements of the system) divide, migrate and die: the spatial organization of the system changes with the individual cells behavior which depends on the cells locations in this organization.

The dynamical property of its state space makes difficult the specification of the global evolution function of a $(\text{DS})^2$. However by comparing two successive global states, as one could do with two successive frames of a movie, one can identify the part of the system that has evolved and the part where nothing has changed. Doing so for every pair of successive states naturally decomposes the system into elementary atomic parts. Thus a $(\text{DS})^2$ may be considered as a population of *subsystems* (the atomic parts) which interact with each other, and where the local interactions give rise to the structure of the whole system. For physical systems, subsystems are spatially localized and only subsystems that are neighbors in space can interact directly. So the interactions between parts are structured by the spatial relationships of the parts. For abstract systems, in many cases the transition function of each subsystem only depends on the state variables of a small set of parts (and not on the state variables of the whole system) and the interactions are structured by the functional relationships between the subsystems.

The idea is then to describe the global dynamics by summing up the local evolutions triggered by local interactions. And if two subsystems s and s' ever interact, it is not because they are known to interact but because they are neighbors. Considering that if a subsystem s interacts with a subset $S = \{s_1, \ldots, s_n\}$ of parts it also interacts with any subset S' included in S, it is tempting to provide the set of subsystems with a topology based on this closure property: the *topology of interactions*. It restricts the possible local evolution functions of a subsystem s: the current state of s only depends on the previous state of s and of its neighbors. Furthermore, the evolution function not only specifies the evolution of local states but also the coupled evolution of the topology itself.

2.2 Rule-Based Simulation

The MGS programming language has been developed to support the idea of interaction-based modeling of $(\text{DS})^2$. It provides *topological collections*, an original data structure for representing the state of a system based on the topology of interactions, and *transformations*, a rule-based definition of functions on collections for specifying the interaction laws of the system.

Topological Collections

A topological collection is a data structure allowing the representation of a population of subsystems.

The underlying topology of interaction is specified using an *abstract cellular complex* (ACC) which is a mathematical concept from *combinatorial algebraic topology* [9]. An ACC is a combinatorial structure made of objects of various dimensions called *topological cells*, each cell being an abstract representation of a simple part of the domain. We call *k-cell* a topological cell of dimension k: 0-cells are vertexes, 1-cells are edges, 2-cells are faces, 3-cells are volumes, etc. Topological cells are glued together and we say that a k-cell σ_1 is *incident* to a $(k-1)$-cell σ_2, denoted $\sigma_1 \preceq \sigma_2$, if σ_2 is in the boundary of σ_1. Formally the incidence relationship is a ranked locally finite partial order on the set of cells where

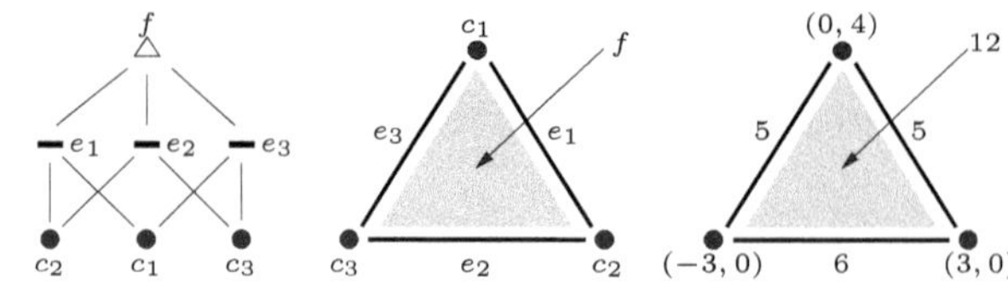

Figure 1: On the left, the Hasse diagram of the incidence relationship of the ACC given in the middle: it is composed of three 0-cells (c_1, c_2, c_3), of three 1-cells (e_1, e_2, e_3) and of a single 2-cells (f). The *closure* of cell e_1 is composed of e_1, c_1 and c_2. The *star* of cell e_1 is the set $\{e_1, f\}$. On the right, a topological collection associates data with the cells: positions with vertexes, lengths with edges and area with f.

the rank coincides with cells dimension. We call *closure* (resp. *star*) of a cell σ the set $\text{Cl}\,\sigma = \{\sigma' \mid \sigma' \preceq \sigma\}$ (resp. $\text{St}\,\sigma = \{\sigma' \mid \sigma' \succeq \sigma\}$). The incidence relation can be used in numerous ways to specify the neighborhood relationships in a topological collection. In this paper, we consider that two cells σ_1 and σ_2 are neighbors if they are not incident to each other and if they are incident to a common cell either of lower dimension or of higher dimension exclusively:

$$(\text{Cl}\,\sigma_1 \cap \text{St}\,\sigma_2) \cup (\text{St}\,\sigma_1 \cap \text{Cl}\,\sigma_2) = \emptyset$$
$$(\text{Cl}\,\sigma_1 \cap \text{Cl}\,\sigma_2) \neq \emptyset \;\oplus\; (\text{St}\,\sigma_1 \cap \text{St}\,\sigma_2) \neq \emptyset$$

The set of all neighbor cells of some cell σ is given by the *link* denoted $\text{Lk}\,\sigma = \text{St}(\text{Cl}\,\sigma) \triangle \text{Cl}(\text{St}\,\sigma)$, where $\triangle$ denotes the symmetric difference operation.

The states of the subsystems are represented as labels on topological cells: a *topological collection* C is a partial function that associates values from an arbitrary set V with cells of some ACC (see Figure 1). Thus the notation $C(\sigma)$ refers to the value/state of cell σ in collection C. We call *support* of C and write $|C|$ for the set of cells for which C is defined. Set V is left arbitrary to allow the association of any kind of information with the topological cells: for instance geometric properties ($V = \{-1, 0, 1\}$ for representing orientation or $V = \mathbb{R}^n$ for Euclidean positions) or arbitrary state of a subsystem (a mass, a concentration of chemicals, or a force acting on certain cells, etc.)

The collection C can be written as a formal sum $\sum_{\sigma \in |C|} v_\sigma \cdot \sigma$ where $v_\sigma \stackrel{\text{df}}{=} C(\sigma)$. With this notation, the underlying ACC is left implicit but can usually be recovered from the context. By convention, when we write a collection C as a sum

$$C = v_1 \cdot \sigma_1 + \cdots + v_p \cdot \sigma_p$$

we insist that all c_i are distinct[1]. Notice that this addition is associative and commutative: the order of operations used to build a topological collection is irrelevant. Using this notation, a *subcollection* S of a collection C is defined as a sub-formal sum $C = S + S'$; subcollection S' is then called the complementary of S in C and one writes $S' = C - S$. Set operations and incidence operations (Cl, St and Lk) are naturally extended on subcollections.

[1]This notation is borrowed from algebraic topology where set V is taken with a commutative group structure which gives to topological chains an abelian group structure [9]. We relax this assumption for topological collection.

Transformations

As previously mentioned, an interaction is a subset of subsystems evolving together due to the satisfaction of some local conditions: the subsystems are neighbor in the topology of interaction and their states match. We advocate that a rule-based programming style fits well the description of interaction laws and that rewriting techniques is the right computation model for modeling and simulating (DS)[2].

Transformations generalize this process to topological collections with the concept of *topological rewriting.* A transformation T is a function specified by a set $\{r_1, \ldots, r_n\}$ of rewriting rules $r_i = p_i \Rightarrow e_i$ where each p_i is a pattern and e_i is an expression. An application of such a rule selects a subcollection S matching with p_i that is then substituted by the subcollection resulting from the evaluation of expression e_i. The application of a transformation T on a collection C can be represented by the following diagram:

$$\begin{array}{ccccccccc} C & = & S_1 & + & \ldots & + & S_n & + & R \\ \downarrow T & & \downarrow r_{i_1} & & & & \downarrow r_{i_n} & & \downarrow \\ T(C) & = & S'_1 & + & \ldots & + & S'_n & + & R \end{array}$$

where each S_k is a subcollection of C matching with pattern p_{i_k} and S'_k results from the evaluation of e_{i_k}. Subcollection R consists of unchanged subsystems. The formal semantics is given in [13].

Since it may exist different ways to decompose collection C w.r.t. transformation T, only one of the possible outcomes (randomly chosen) is returned by the transformation. A *rule application strategy* is then used to control the pattern matching process.

3. ACTIVITY TRACKING IN MGS

We are now interested in investigating the concept of *activity* in MGS. Activity [11] is a measure of event occurrences or state changes in a simulation. This measure can be used for different purposes like optimizing simulation or giving a better understanding of dynamics. In the context of MGS, activity will allow us to (1) develop a more efficient pattern matching algorithm, and to (2) identify higher level structures in a model and to track them in simulations. The former will be illustrated in the next section, the latter will be discussed in the conclusion.

In this section, we present a generic way to track an active region throughout the simulation.

Context

For the sake of simplicity, we restrict ourselves to patterns involving only at most two interacting elements. For example, pattern `x, y, z` (*i.e.*, matching three elements where `y` is a neighbor of `x` and `z` is a neighbor of `y`) is out of the scope of the following study. However we conclude the section with a paragraph about the generalization.

We illustrate our idea with a simplistic but paradigmatic example, a forest fire spread. This 3-state cellular automaton is easily encoded in an MGS transformation as follows:

```
trans fire_spread = {
  'Forest as x / member('Fire, neighbors x)
        => 'Fire;
  'Fire => 'Ashes;
}
```

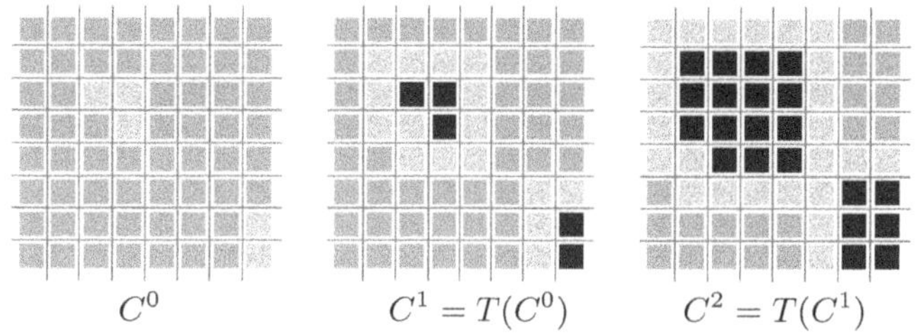

Figure 2: Evolution relation, first three steps of a forest fire simulation. Green, orange (hatched) and black represent Forest, Fire and Ashes respectively.

States are represented by three symbols: `'Forest`, `'Fire` and `'Ashes`. The first rule specifies how forest catches fire when it is neighbor of some fire and the second rule specifies that fire leaves ashes after burning. Figure 2 shows three consecutive evolution steps of this automaton on a square grid topological collection.

In the example of Figure 2, activity is located in a small piece of space – only cells in fire and forest in their neighborhoods evolve – and progresses from neighbor to neighbor. However the usual MGS pattern matching process needs to iterate over the whole collection at each application of transformation `fire_spread`. Given the small number of cells in interaction, the matching process is here quite inefficient. The following study of activity will allows us to target specifically evolving cells during pattern matching. Moreover activity enlightens an important emergent structure of fire spread models, the fire front.

Activity and Interactions

The interpretation of activity in MGS corresponds to the number of interactions occurring at each time step of a simulation. Since interactions happen whenever rules of a transformation match subcollections, activity splits naturally a collection into two parts: the *active* subcollection as the subcollection where interactions *can* occur and the *quiescent* subcollection where they cannot.

Let us define the active and quiescent subcollections in a formal and general way, using the construct of topological collections. Let C be a collection and T be a transformation. We define the *matching function* $\mathbb{M}_T$ of transformation T as the function which maps a collection C onto the set of all subcollections of C matched by a pattern of T. In other words, the matching function $\mathbb{M}_T$ represents a call to the pattern matching process. The *active subcollection* A of C is then defined as

$$A = \bigcup_{S \in \mathbb{M}_T(C)} S$$

that is the merge[2] of all matched subcollections of C. Thus, the *quiescent subcollection* Q corresponds to the complementary of A in C:

$$Q = C - A$$

Figure 3 shows the decomposition into active and quiescent subcollections for the fire spread example.

[2]The union operator is used instead of the addition since some subcollections of $\mathbb{M}_T$ may have overlapping support.

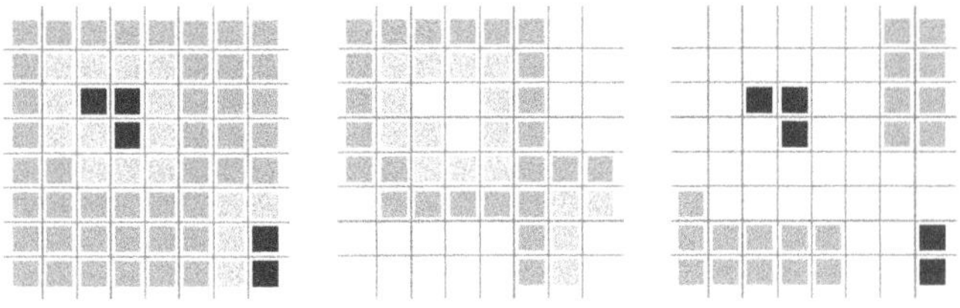

Figure 3: Decomposition of a topological collection into a set of active cells and quiescent cells. Green, orange (hatched) and black represent Forest, Fire and Ashes respectively.

Activity Dynamics

In order to track activity during the simulation of a system, we define a way to compute the evolution of the active region (grow, shrink, carve, etc.) based on the topological properties of the active subcollection.

Let us consider $(C^0, C^1, \dots)$ the trajectory of collections due to the successive applications of a transformation T, where $C^{i+1} = T(C^i)$ for $i \geq 0$. Using the active-quiescent decomposition on $C^i = A^i + Q^i$, one can notice that the application of transformation T only acts on the active part and leaves Q^i unchanged so that the pattern matching can be restricted to subcollection A^i only:

$$C^{i+1} = T(C^i) = T(A^i|F^i) + Q^i \qquad (1)$$

The notation $T(A^i|F^i)$ reflects that the restricted pattern matching process may require some information from Q^i: visiting the neighborhood of some matched element (*e.g.*, in transformation `fire_spread`: `member('Fire, neighbors x)`) does not imply that the visited neighbors are in A^i. These information are denoted F^i which is the subcollection whose support consists of all quiescent cells with a neighbor in A^i: $F^i = \mathrm{Lk}\, A^i$. The decomposition of C^{i+1} proposed in Equation (1) does not coincide with the definition of A^{i+1} and Q^{i+1}. In fact, some cells of $|Q^i|$ may become active and *vice versa*. However the tracking of the active-quiescent frontier during a simulation can be refined by making use of subcollection F^i. Indeed assuming that transformation rules involve at most two neighbor elements, any quiescent cell, at some iteration of the simulation, having no active neighbor cell will observe no change in its environment and then will remain quiescent at the next iteration step. More formally we get:

$$Q^i - \mathrm{Lk}\, A^i \subset Q^{i+1} \qquad A^{i+1} \subset T(A^i|\mathrm{Lk}\, A^i) + \mathrm{Lk}\, A^i \quad (2)$$

The second statement is trivially obtained using complementary and means equivalently that the active part cannot expand further than F^i. Equation (1) is then rewritten

$$C^{i+1} = \left[T(A^i|\mathrm{Lk}\, A^i) + \mathrm{Lk}\, A^i\right] + \left[Q^i - \mathrm{Lk}\, A^i\right] \qquad (3)$$

Optimized Pattern Matching

In the light of Equations (2), the active-quiescent decomposition of C^{i+1} is obviously over-approximated in Equation (3). As an example, on Figure 4, bold lines represent the limit of expansion of the active part at next step but some cells in this subcollection become quiescent. These cells can be identified as the cells of $T(A^i|\mathrm{Lk}\, A^i) + \mathrm{Lk}\, A^i$ which cannot be involved in any interaction at time $i+1$. In other words they are not selected by the pattern matching process:

$$\mathbb{M}_T(C^{i+1}) = \mathbb{M}_T(T(A^i|\mathrm{Lk}\, A^i) + \mathrm{Lk}\, A^i)$$

and the computation of sequence $(A^i)_{i \in \mathbb{N}}$ follows

$$\begin{cases} A^0 & = \bigcup_{S \in \mathbb{M}_T(C^0)} S \\ A^{i+1} & = \bigcup_{S \in \mathbb{M}_T(T(A^i|\mathrm{Lk}\, A^i) + \mathrm{Lk}\, A^i)} S \end{cases}$$

Notice that this recursive definition of A^i does not refer to the quiescent subcollection Q^i anymore, since the neighbor operator Lk exactly targets the interesting cells. As a consequence, activity tracking during the simulation allows us to focus on a reduced part of the collection for pattern matching. The induced optimization is discussed and illustrated in Section 4.

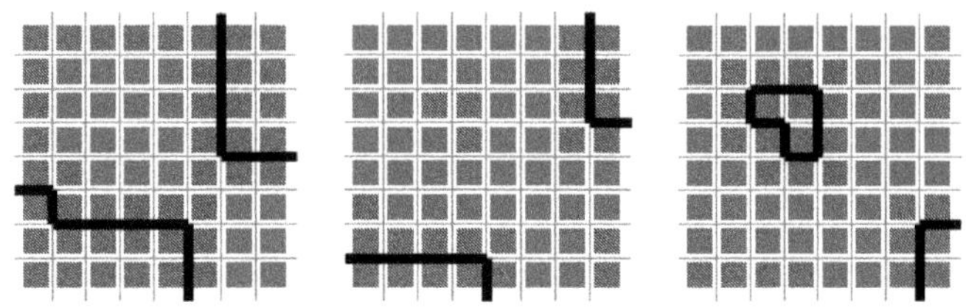

Figure 4: Evolution of the active-quiescent frontier for the three steps of Figure 2. Active cells in red, quiescent cells in light blue (hatched). The bold lines represent the decompositions induced by Equation (3).

Topological Characterization

The previous study can be generalized to transformation involving more than two interacting elements by reconsidering how far the active subcollection can expand at each time step. Let n be the *radius* of an interaction, *i.e.*, the minimum distance (in terms of hops) between interacting elements. The previous restriction was to only consider transformation of radius $n \leq 1$. Let us now consider arbitrary radius $n \in \mathbb{N}$. For example, patterns of the form `f, e / neighborsfold([...],f)` are of radius $n = 2$ since the visited neighbors of `f` can be at distance 2 of `e`.

The expansion F_n^i of A^i for a radius n is given recursively by

$$\begin{cases} F_0^i & = 0 \\ F_{n+1}^i & = \mathrm{Lk}(A^i + F_n^i) + F_n^i \end{cases}$$

This definition is analogous to the definition of the *wave operator* $W(n)$ in [1] and reveals the topological nature of activity. The wave operator is used for the elaboration of a combinatorial Morse theory; Morse theory is a mathematical tool for studying topology of spaces. Roughly speaking, this theory deals with *Morse functions* – a way to flood the space with some "liquid" – and *critical points* – where the liquid reveals basins, passes and peaks of the topography of the space. We are currently investigating the analogy between Morse theory and activity tracking: Morse functions will correspond to activity propagation and critical points to space-time positions where independent activity zones segregate or collide, pointing out important events in the model.

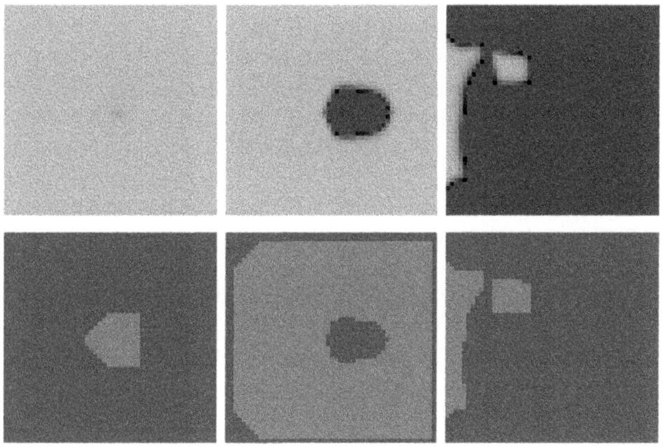

Figure 5: Fire spread (fire is orange, forest is green, ash is brown), Activity (active cells in red, quiescent cells in blue) at iterations 5 (left), 22 (center) and 95 (right) of a simulation with wind blowing from the left and a horizontal symmetrical chain of mountain landscape.

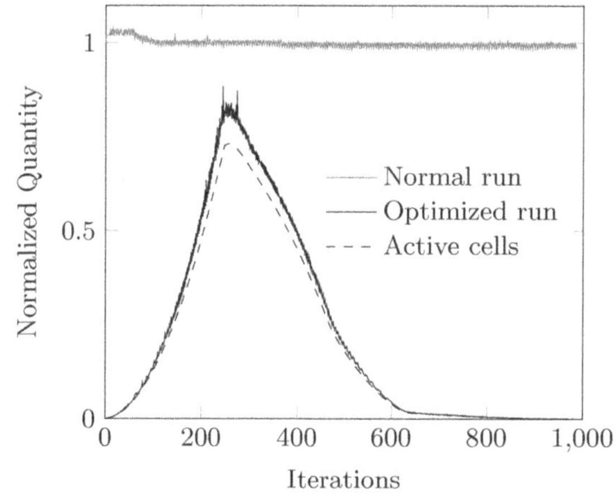

Figure 6: Amount of active cells and computation time for non-optimized and optimized algorithm per iteration on a 500×500 grid. Values have been normalized using the total size of the (250 000 cells) for amounts of cells, and the average computation time of a normal run step for computation times.

4. PRELIMINARY RESULTS

In this section, we consider a more elaborate model of forest fire spreading. Following results of Section 3, information provided by activity are used to speed up simulation by applying rules of transformation in active regions.

4.1 An Example of Forest Fire Simulation

Forest fire is a well known and paradigmatic example for the community of discrete event simulation [6]. Here, we implement in MGS a more elaborate, yet efficient, model for forest fire spreading than the basic example used in Section 3. The model is based on the work of [8] and uses the cellular automata (CA) formalism while being both simple and realistic. The forest fire spread model takes into account the main environmental effects: wind (for both speed and direction), type of fuel, and landscape topography. At any time, the state of a cell in the CA is characterized by the ratio of burnt area ranging continuously from 0 (wholesome forest) to 1 (burnt forest - ashes) where $(0, 1)$ represents burning forest. Considering a *fire front* as the *area* separating the forest from the ashes, the main concern of our model is to determine the evolution of the fire front from: the current fire front position, the distribution of rates of fire spread in the forest, the wind speed and direction, as well as the height and shape of the land.

The cyclic 2D square grid used in the CA is represented using a *GBF topological collection* [4]. A GBF is topological collection whose underlying ACC is the Cayley graph of an abelian group presentation. The elements of the group represents the allowed atomic displacements. In MGS, such a collection is specified from a presentation of the group of displacements. The definition of a Moore neighborhood grid, requires four basic displacements `n` (north), `e` (east), `ne` (north-east) and `se` (south-east):

```
gbf Land = < n, ne, e, se ;
             500 n = 0, 500 e = 0,
             ne = e + n, se = e - n >
```

The four additional equations specify that the grid is cyclic of size 500×500 and define relations between diagonal and non-diagonal directions. The reverse directions are automatically considered. Each cell of the GBF is labeled by its state (a record containing the burned out state, the wind direction, the burning rate and the altitude).

Transformation `fire_spread` of Section 3 is extended to take into account dynamics of [8]. Figure 5 shows simulations of the model at different iterations.

4.2 Benchmark

Using the classical pattern matching algorithm, the entire topological collection must be iterated over at every update. For a CA on a square grid of side length n, the process must go through the n^2 cells leading to an update step with a constant time (see Figure 6), while only a fluctuating number of cells have their values changed on the update (which correspond to only a fraction of the grid).

In this section, we use activity information to reduce the cost of pattern matching. The previous example of forest fire spread was rewritten to have the transformation rules only apply to the active region and skip the quiescent part. As with the theoretical view presented in Section 3, the cellular automaton space is split between active cells taking part in a transformation of their neighbors and quiescent cells having no role to play whatsoever in the current iteration. This results in a decent speedup of the whole computation.

Figure 6 presents a plot of the count of active cells for each iteration, and of the computation time by iteration for both the optimized and the regular run of the simulation. Time is normalized by the average computation time of the normal run so that both normal and optimized computation time can be easily compared. The occasional spikes and noise come from the fluctuating work on the test computer.

As can be deduced from Figure 5, at the beginning of the simulation, very few cells are active. Their amount increases dramatically with the spread of fire to only lower once the forest has been consumed and turns into ashes. As a cellular automaton, the computation time is linear with the number of cells: the more cells, the more time with the same computation time by cell. From the figure, we can notice that the computation time of the non-optimized run is roughly the same for every iteration: the pattern matching mechanism must explore all of the 250 000 cells to verify whether a rule applies. Whether a rule matches or not does not change the time required to compute the application of a transformation rule.

We can immediately notice that activity and computation time of the optimized run coincide: it directly depends on the amount of cells to explore, thus the shape of the curve is nearly identical to the variation of the amount of active cells. Cells are never all active at once, that is why, even at its peak, the optimized run always requires less computation time by iteration than the non-optimized one. The cost of maintenance can be read from the difference between the computation time of the optimized run and the active cell count. This optimization is data-dependent, had we changed the initial values, the graph would have been altered too. Therefore, a general or global speed-up does not make sense.

5. RELATED WORK AND CONCLUSION

This paper focuses on the computation of activity and activity regions in the context of the domain-specific language MGS. We have characterized and provided a topological framework to compute these two notions using the link operator of combinatorial topology. Activity regions have been successfully used to reduce the cost of pattern matching in the simulation of an example of fire spread. In this case, activity appears to be a data-dependent optimization technique that can be easily combined with other techniques.

While our approach could appear similar to dependency graph optimizations (as in Gillespie's SSA algorithm by [5]), it is very different since, due to the topological approach followed by MGS, the computation of activity regions described here is *generic*, unlike previously asserted in [11], page 162. Moreover, it is valid for *any kind of topological collections* available in the language. Based on the notion of *spatial interaction*, MGS provides a unified simulation framework encompassing discrete/continuous and deterministic/stochastic formalisms (as in the classical approach of rewriting-based tools in computational biology, by [7, 2] for example, that consider structureless objects - namely only chemical reactions).

The perspectives opened by this work are numerous. We have to internalize in the runtime the computation of the active regions. Indeed, we believe that it is not to the programmer to seek for complex and obfuscating optimizations but to the language (or the execution support) to provide automatic high-level techniques to reduce the execution time.

At the language level, activity regions are not first-class objects: they are computed at each time-step of the simulation, and there is no link between regions computed at two different time steps. *Reifying* the regions to first-class objects and adding operators to handle these new objects will be the key to level up the language to multi-level modeling of complex dynamical systems that exhibits behaviors at multiple levels of descriptions (like in biology the molecular level, the cellular level, the organic level, etc.).

ACKNOWLEDGMENTS

The authors would like to thanks the anonymous reviewers for their comments on a first version of this paper.

The authors are grateful to the community born during the Cargese Interdisciplinary Seminar in 2009 and to the colleagues of the spatial computing initiative. This research is supported in part by the French ANR grant "SynBioTIC" 2010-BLAN-0307-03, U-PEC, IRCAM, Univ. of Évry and ISC-Paris.

6. REFERENCES

[1] U. Axen. *Topological Analysis Using Morse Theory and Auditory Display.* PhD thesis, University of Illinois at Urbana-Champaign, Champaign, IL, USA, 1998.

[2] V. Danos, J. Feret, W. Fontana, R. Harmer, and J. Krivine. Rule-based modelling, symmetries, refinements. *Formal Methods in Systems Biology*, pages 103–122, 2008.

[3] J.-L. Giavitto, C. Godin, O. Michel, and P. Prusinkiewicz. *Modelling and Simulation of biological processes in the context of genomics*, chapter "Computational Models for Integrative and Developmental Biology". Hermes, July 2002.

[4] J.-L. Giavitto, O. Michel, and J.-P. Sansonnet. Group based fields. In I. Takayasu, R. H. J. Halstead, and C. Queinnec, editors, *PSLS'95*, volume 1068 of *LNCS*, pages 209–215, Beaune (France), 2–4 Oct. 1995. Springer Verlag.

[5] M. A. Gibson and J. Bruck. Efficient exact stochastic simulation of chemical systems with many species and many channels. *The journal of physical chemistry A*, 104(9):1876–1889, 2000.

[6] X. Hu, Y. Sun, and L. Ntaimo. DEVS-FIRE: design and application of formal discrete event wildfire spread and suppression models. *SIMULATION*, 88(3):259–279, Oct. 2011.

[7] M. John, C. Lhoussaine, J. Niehren, and C. Versari. Biochemical reaction rules with constraints. *Programming Languages and Systems*, pages 338–357, 2011.

[8] I. Karafyllidis and A. Thanailakis. A model for predicting forest fire spreading using cellular automata. *Ecological Modelling*, 99(1):87 – 97, 1997.

[9] J. Munkres. *Elements of Algebraic Topology.* Addison-Wesley, 1984.

[10] A. Muzy, L. Touraille, H. Vangheluwe, O. Michel, M. Kaba Traoré, and D. R.C. Hill. Activity Regions for the Specification of Discrete Event Systems. In *DEVS'10*, 2010.

[11] A. Muzy, F. Varenne, B. P. Zeigler, J. Caux, P. Coquillard, L. Touraille, D. Prunetti, P. Caillou, O. Michel, and D. R. Hill. Refounding of activity concept? Towards a federative paradigm for modeling and simulation. *SIMULATION*, 89(2):156–177, 2012.

[12] J. J. Shi. Activity-based construction (ABC) modeling and simulation method. *Journal of Construction Engineering and Management*, 1999.

[13] A. Spicher, O. Michel, and J.-L. Giavitto. Declarative mesh subdivision using topological rewriting in mgs. In *Int. Conf. on Graph Transformations (ICGT) 2010*, volume 6372 of *LNCS*, pages 298–313, Sept. 2010.

Software Test Automation using DEVSimPy Environment

Work in Progress Paper

Laurent Capocchi
SPE UMR CNRS 6134
University of Corsica
Campus Grimaldi, 20250
Corte (France)
capocchi@univ-corse.fr

Jean Francois Santucci
SPE UMR CNRS 6134
University of Corsica
Campus Grimaldi, 20250
Corte (France)
santucci@univ-corse.fr

Timothee Ville
SPE UMR CNRS 6134
University of Corsica
Campus Grimaldi, 20250
Corte (France)
ville@univ-corse.fr

ABSTRACT

The paper deals with test automation of GUI (General User Interface) software using simulations. The development of GUI software requires a great amount of time and cost concerning the testing aspects. In order to facilitate and speed up the testing of such GUI software an approach based on discrete-event modeling and simulation is proposed. Traditionally, the GUI software test automation approaches require the development of testing procedures which are fastidious to carry on. The idea is to perform test automation of GUI software by integrating of existing GUI software testing environments within a DEVS (Discrete EVent system Specification) formalism framework called DEVSimPy. The proposed approach is validated on a real application dealing with medical software which have to respect very strict formats defined by French governmental institutions.

Categories and Subject Descriptors

H.4 [**Information Systems Applications**]:Miscellaneous; D.2.8 [**Software Engineering**]: Metrics - *complexity measures, performance measures*

Keywords

discrete-event simulation, DEVS, medical software, Web interface testing, test automation.

1. INTRODUCTION

This paper deals with a new approach to GUI testing using a discrete-event simulation environment. Testing Automation of GUI is a process that insure the correctness of a software with a computer vision approach. Usually, a tester has to implement the generation of user interface events to invoke the changes that result in the user interface in order to validate the software. The work of the tester requires the combination of manual and automated methods. For the manual part the following steps are usually involved: (i) analyze products; (ii) design and write test code; (iii) run the test; (iv) capture and store GUI output; (v) package test code and results along with documentation process. The automated part relies on existing tools which allow: (i) to run the test code and capture the output; (ii) to compare the output with the desired output; (iii) to analyze the result of the comparison.

The blending of manual and automated testing methods is known to be the best way to perform GUI Testing. The GUI software testing traditional approaches require the development of testing procedures which are fastidious to carry on. These is due to the difficulty to manually reproduce the interaction between the interface of the software and the users.

In order to efficiently combine the manual and automated testing methods an approach based on discrete-event modeling and simulation is proposed. The idea is to perform test automation of GUI software by integrating existing GUI testing environments [13, 6, 9] with the DEVSimPy [5] framework based on DEVS (Discrete EVent system Specification) formalism [15]. DEVS has been introduced by Professor B.P. Zeigler in 1976. It is based on the system and automata theories [10] and it allows a modeling and simulation of complex systems in a hierarchical and modular way. Futhermore, with DEVS the simulation can be perform automatically due to an explicit separation between the modeling and simulation part. DEVSimPy is an easy-to-use collaborative environment allowing the development of DEVS reusable models stored in libraries.

DEVS and DEVSimPy offer intrinsic characteristics to be good candidates for the automating of the GUI test software. Indeed, the test can be viewed at multiple level of description with DEVS and DEVSimPy. This makes the testing procedure easier to maintain a series of tests when they are visually depicted using an inter-connexion of graphical blocks (DEVSimPy coupled model). With DEVSimPy, test of GUI software can be implemented using the composition of reusable DEVS models available in the libraries. Finally, DEVS and DEVSimPy add a discrete-event simulation aspect to the test of GUI software domain. With DEVS, the user can plan multiple tests in a automated way using a process dedicated to executes multiple simulations. Concerning the DEVSimPy framework, the main contribution is the implementation of a new model library dedicated to the GUI test automation. From a GUI testing point of view, we contribute also to offer a new tool to simplify the elaboration of custom test cases.

The rest of the paper is organized as follows: section 2 gives an overview of existing tools and approaches allowing to perform GUI test automation. Resulting problems are pointed out and the proposed solution has been introduced. Section 3 deals with the development of a set of DEVS models allowing the integration of GUI testing tools in the DEVSimPy framework. The validation of the proposed approach is given in section 4. A real case application coming from the health software French company is presented. Finally conclusions remarks and perspectives are given in the last section.

2. OVERVIEW

2.1 Test Automation software

2.1.1 RobotFramework

RobotFramework [12, 1] is a generic test automation framework for acceptance testing and Acceptance Test-Driven Development (ATDD). It has easy-to-use tabular test data syntax and utilizes the keyword-driven testing approach. Its testing capabilities can be extended by test libraries implemented either with Python or Java language, and users can create new keywords from existing ones using the same syntax that is used for creating test cases. *RobotFramework* is open source software and allows some interesting features like: (i)Providing support for Selenium [4, 2] for web testing, Java GUI testing, running processes, and so on; (ii) Providing easy-to-read reports (HTML or TEXT); (iii) Being platform and application independent; (iv) Offering a modular architecture for tests creation; (v) Providing a simple library API (Application Programming Interface) for test libraries.

2.1.2 Sikuli

Sikuli [14, 7] is a visual technology to automate and test GUI using images (snapshots) of the software under test. It is an open-source research project (released under MIT License) developed at User Interface Design Group, MIT computer Science and Artificial Intelligence Laboratory (CSAIL). It may be used like Selenium to control a web page. *SikuliScript* is a visual scripting API using Jython (a Java implementation of the Python language) to create automation scripts. *Sikuli* includes an IDE for writing visual *Sikuli* scripts with snapshots. The efficiency of *Sikuli* is due to: (i) the use of a powerful fuzzy based image recognition algorithm to execute actions and (ii) the possibility of using conditional statements to make complex test sequences. *Sikuli* finds on-screen matches with a reference image. It can then perform any keyboard or mouse action at or near the matches. *Sikuli* can use any kind of GUI as native, Flash/Silverlight, cross-platform. The *Sikuli* scripts can be written using its Python API by hand or in the *Sikuli* IDE. The main limitations when using *Sikuli* to perform GUI test automation are: (i) to write a wrapper to launch scripts; (ii) to handle return values; (iii) to install *Sikuli*.

2.2 Traditional approach limitations

As explained in the introduction, the main difficulty for software developers is the testing phase. In order to speed-up the development of the set of tests numerous frameworks have been developed [12, 4].

In order to develop an efficient test automation scheme for interface web software, a combination of the two first kinds

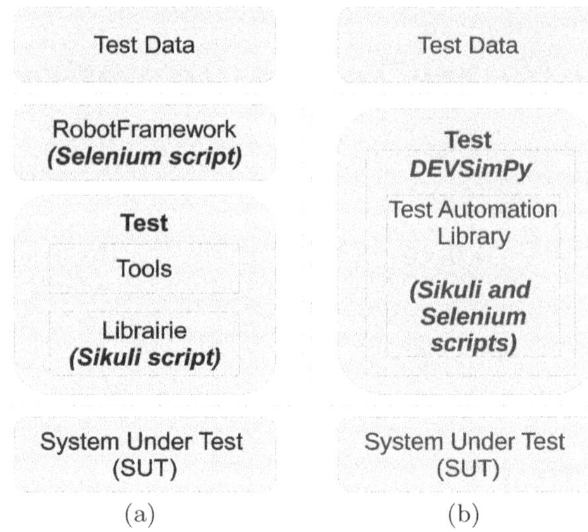

Figure 1: (a) Traditional approach dedicated to the test software (b) Proposed approach based on DEVSimPy environment

of tools (*RobotFrameWork* and *Sikuli*) are usually used. The traditional approach when developers have to test an interface web software is highlighted in figure 1(a).

The traditional approach involves the following steps:

1. From the Test Data specification the developer has to write test scripts defined using the *Sikuli* environment. The obtained scripts compose the Test Library

2. The developer has to write a set of scripts in order to visualize the results of the previous test scripts execution. These scripts are written using the *RobotFramework* environment

3. The developer has to write a launch script that will allow to both execute the test scripts of the Test Library and the visualization of the obtained results

Each step has to be repeated anytime a new test data specification has to be taken into account. Furthermore each one of these steps is time-consuming since the developer has to write manually the scripts which are very often not so easy to write.

2.3 Proposed solution

In order to facilitate the use of test automation environments combining Sikuli and RobotFramework, we propose to use DEVSimPy environment as described in figure 1(b). The use of DEVSimPy allows the automation of:

- A generation of test scripts using the simulation of models representing the test data specification

- A generation of the scripts allowing the visualization of results

- An execution of the previous test scripts and the visualization of the results through a DEVSimPy plugin

- An install of both the RobotFrameWork (including Selenium) and the Sikuli packages

Writing test GUI automation consists to create (or manipulate) new graphical models (or existing models stored in libraries) which contain elementary tests. When the user want to implement large test cases, it uses reusability for atomic model and coupled models for structuring instead of manipulate a textual syntax which can introduce additional issues. Furthermore, unit tests becomes possible on atomic models and consolidates the use of DEVSimPy for automating GUI tests. Another point to consider is the benefit provided by the DEVSimPy implementation when user must modify the test in order to validate new specifications imposed by certification organism. The delete or the add of new elementary test is performed by deleting or adding new DEVSimPy model. The order of test execution can be managed using the list of priority of DEVS models. DEVSimPy provides an dialog to manage this one and the priority is changed with a simple drag-and-drop.

We may highlight that the proposed approach is based on the combination of Sikuli and RobotFramework within DEVSimPy. This approach is different from the use of the combination of Junit with Selenium.

3. DEVSIMPY FOR TEST AUTOMATION

This part describes the DEVSimPy library of DEVS models allowing to facilitate the use of automation test software. A first sub-section briefly introduces the DEVS formalism, the second one presents the DEVSimPy framework while the last one deals with the library of DEVS models which have been developed in order to integrate GUI test software.

3.1 DEVS formalism

The Discrete EVent system Specification (DEVS) formalism introduced by Zeigler [15] provides a means of specifying a mathematical object called a system. Basically, a system has a time base, inputs, states, outputs, and functions for determining next states and outputs given current states and inputs. The DEVS formalism is a simple way in order to characterizes how discrete-event simulation languages may specify discrete-event system parameters. It is more than just a means of constructing simulation models. It provides a formal representation of discrete-event systems capable of mathematical manipulation just as differential equations serve this role. Furthermore by allowing an explicit separation between the modeling phase and simulation phase, the DEVS formalism is one of the best ways to perform an simulation of systems using a computer.

In the DEVS formalism, one must specify: (i) basic models from which larger ones are built, and (ii) how these models are connected together in hierarchical fashion. An atomic model allows specifying the behavior of a basic element of a given system. Connections between different atomic models can be performed by a coupled model. A coupled model, tells how to couple (connect) several component models together to form a new model. This latter model can itself be employed as a component in a larger coupled model, thus giving rise to hierarchical construction.

An atomic DEVS model can be considered as an automaton with a set of states and transition functions allowing the state change when an event occur or not. When no events occurs, the state of the atomic model can be changed by an internal transition function called δ_{int}. When an external event occurs, the atomic model can intercept it and change its state by applying an external transition function called δ_{ext}. The life time of a state is determined by a time advance function called t_a. Each state change can produce output message via an output function called λ.

A simulator is associated with the DEVS formalism in order to exercise instructions of coupled model to actually generate its behavior. The architecture of a DEVS simulation system is derived from the abstract simulator concepts [15] associated with the hierarchical and modular DEVS formalism.

3.2 DEVSimPy environment

DEVSimPy (Python Simulator for DEVS models) [5] is a user-friendly interface for collaborative modeling and simulation of DEVS systems implemented in Python language. Python is a programming language known for its simple syntax and its capacity to allow modelers to implement quickly their ideas [11]. The DEVSimPy project used the Python language and provides a GUI based on PyDEVS [3] API in order to facilitate both the coupling and the reusability of PyDEVS models. This API is used in the excellent multi-modeling GUI software named ATOM3 [8] which allows to use several formalisms without focusing on DEVS. DEVSimPy is an open source project under GPL V3 license and its development is supported by the University of Corsica Computer Science research team. It uses the wxPython graphic library which is a wrapper of the most popular WxWidgets C library. DEVSimPy can be downloaded at http://code.google.com/p/devsimpy.

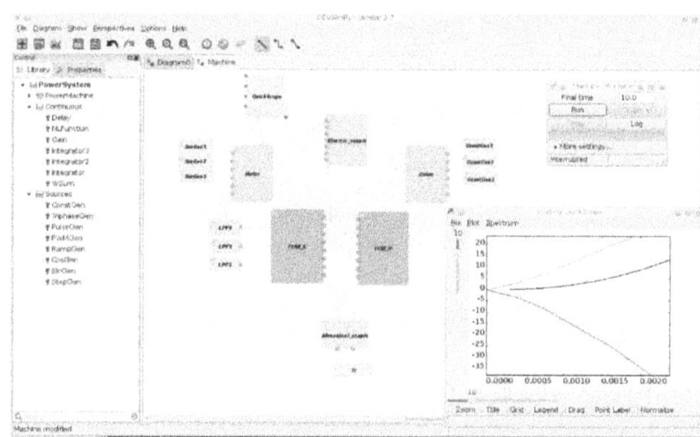

Figure 2: DEVSimPy general interface

The main goal of this environment is to facilitate the modeling of DEVS systems using the GUI dynamic libraries and the drag and drop functionality. With DEVSimPy, models can be stored in a dynamic library in order to be reused and shared (left panel in figure 2). The creation of dynamic libraries composed with DEVS components is easy since the user is coached by dialogs and wizard during the building process.

With DEVSimPy, complex system can be modeled by a coupling of DEVS models and the simulation is performed in a automatic way. Moreover, DEVSimPy allows the extension (or the overwrite) of their functionalities in using special plugins managed in a modular way. The user can enabled/disabled a plugin using a simple dialog window.

We propose in this paper the DEVS modeling of GUI test automation scenario through DEVSimPy by implementing a specific dynamic library. Thereby, this library can be reused any time GUI test automation is needed during the application development.

3.3 The TestAutom library

3.3.1 Overview

In order to facilitate the generation of test scripts when using the existing tools presented in section 2.1, the proposed approach consists in integrating these tools into the DEVSimPy framework. This integration will allow the software developers to use the previous tools in an integrated way. The scripts will be automatically generated and the different tools are automatically launched own to a simulation process. The simulation process leans on the modeling phase where the software developers have to build a DEVSimPy coupled model using some drag and drop. The drag and drop are accomplished from a set of atomic models belonging the DEVSimPy library called *TestAutom*.
The library has been developed according to two main subdivisions: the first one called *Sikuli* offers a set of models allowing to automatically generate the test scripts dedicated to the test of GUI and to automatically launch the effective test of the software; the second one called *Selenium* allows the user to complement the previous test by automatically generate log files describing the results of the previously defined tests. Figure 3 highlights the *TestAutom* library (on the left part in figure 3) and an simple example of use.

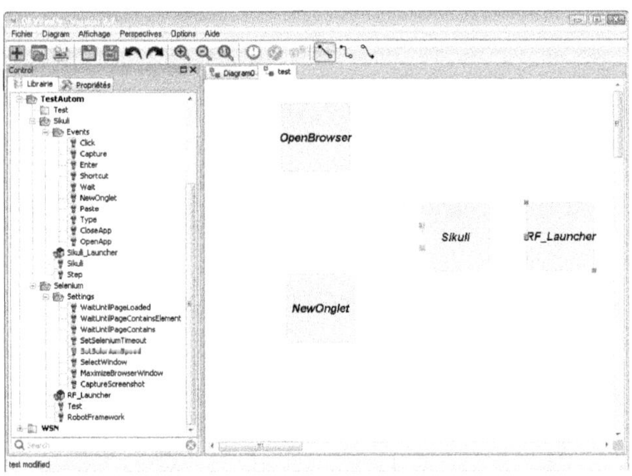

Figure 3: The *Test* model using the *TestAutom* DEVSimPy library

The *Sikuli* sub-part of the *TestAutom* library involves a set of atomic models allowing the developer of GUI to both automatically generate test scripts and easily execute them. The models are described in sub-section 3.3.2. The *Selenium* part of the library allows to generate the results of the execution of the test. This part is described in subsection 3.3.3. Finally we show on a pedagogical example how to use this library in sub-section 4.3.4.

3.3.2 The Sikuli sub-part library

The models belonging to *Sikuli* sub-part library are the basic elements (DEVSimPy atomic model) which are used to build the model which will be simulated in order to generate the test scripts. The behavior of these atomic models descibes the following user actions (left part in figure 3):

- *Click*: In order to simulate the mouse click user action
- *Enter*: To execute the *enter* key press
- *Capture*: To execute a Snapshot operation
- *Shortcut*: To execute *shortcut* keys combination press
- *Wait*: To execute a timing statement
- *NewOnglet*: To invoke a new tab in the web navigator
- *Paste*: To execute the paste function
- *Type*: To populate a text area
- *CloseApp*: To execute the closing of an application
- *OpenApp*: To execute the opening of an application

All of these models can be instantiated and combined using drag and drop functionalities in order to build a complex action.
Two other basic elements (atomic models) are playing an important role:

- *Step*: To define an complex action by combining some of the previous actions
- *Sikuli*: To aggregate the different steps involved in the definition of the test scenario

All the *Step* instances obtained from the unique *Step* model by simple Drags and Drops are connected to an *Sikuli* instance. This instance is in charge to generate the final test scripts.

3.3.3 The Selenium sub-part library

The models offered in the *Selenium* sub-part library mainly concern the possibility to generate automatically snapshots of the execution results for the test scripts generated using the *Sikuli* sub-part library. Tree atomic models are proposed:

- *RF_Launcher*: To execute both the test and visualization scripts using a plugin contained in its class
- *RobotFramework*: To execute the *Sikuli* scripts and is included in the *RF_Launcher*
- *Test*: To execute *Sikuli* scripts using a command line way (optional functionality)

Furthermore a set of atomic models belonging to the settings directory can be used by the user in order to precise some attributes when dealing with Snapshots or test format printing.
The final step consist in connecting a *Sikuli* instance to a *RF_Launcher* for the execution of *Sikuli* scripts and their visualization using DEVSimPy simulation.

3.3.4 Flexibility of the approach using the TestAutom library

In order to use the previously described library, the user (a software developer who wants to test GUI software) has to build (by some drag and drop actions) an interconnected model which will permit through a DEVSimPy simulation to automatically generate the test scripts and execute them in order to obtain the test results under Snapshots of log files format.

An example of an interconnected model is given in figure 3. This model (called *Test*) involves two atomic models: *OpenBrowser* which is an *OPenApp* model and *NewOnglet*. These two models are aggregated using the *Sikuli* model. The *RF_Launcher* model is connected to the *Sikuli* model to execute the test and visualize the results as explained in 3.3.3. Figure 4 depicts the message exchanges in chronolog-

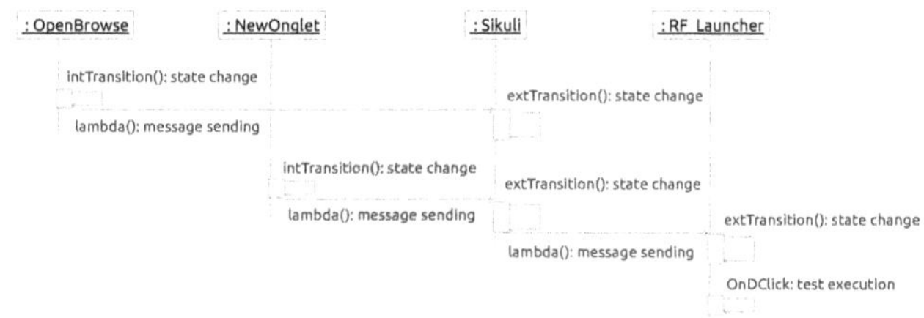

Figure 4: UML sequence diagram of the objects belonging to the *Test* model

ical order between the four atomic models composing the Test coupled model. Due to the priority list of the Test model, the *OpenBrower* model is the first model to be activated. The activation consists in sending to the *Sikuki* model a message, which contains the "open browser" associated action, through its lambda function. Then, its state is updated by executing its internal transition function. The activation of the *NewOnglet* model is performed in the same way in order to send towards the *Sikuli* model a message which contains the "new onglet" action. Each message arriving in the Sikuli model invokes the *Sikuli* external transition function in order to update its state. When the *Sikuli* model has recieved messages on all its input ports, it is ready to generate the test script with all the received events. Then, a message containing the generated test script is send to the *RF_Launcher* model which becomes active and ready to execute the test script. This execution can be performed by the user after a double click on the *RF_Launcher* model.

4. CASE OF STUDY: XPLORE TESTING

The previous *TestAutom* library has been validated on a real case application named Xplore Management software. The Xplore Management software is used in the medical domain and has been designed by a french software industry called EDL. Usually, the test cases associated with this kind of software are as follows: (i) insuring the connexion to the user database; (ii) insuring the safe edition of schedule and transport patient reports; (iii) insuring the safe access to the patient records and history manager; (iv) insuring the safe connexion to a hospital information system manager; etc.

We propose to use the previous real test case number (iii) to validate the present approach.

The test scenario consists in the search of a patient by name. It involves four steps (figure 5): (i) The launching of a web navigator (like Google Chrome) and the creation of a new tab; (ii) The private web site access by referencing the corresponding url in the navigator url area; (iii) The Backoffice access with authentication using login and password; (iv) The research of the patient called MARIN by its name following be the capture of the results under the form of a screenshot.

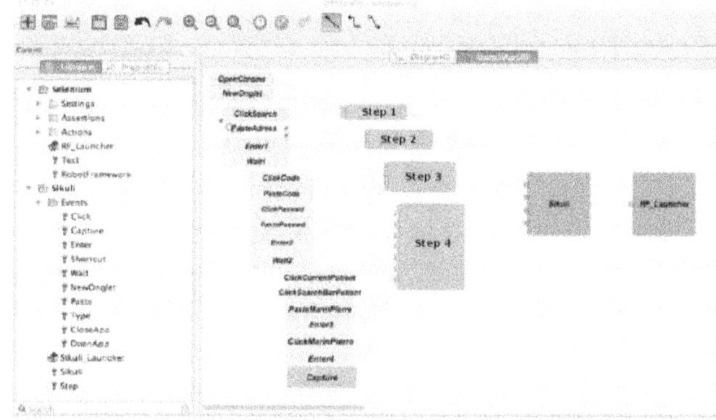

Figure 5: DEVSimPy model of the case of study

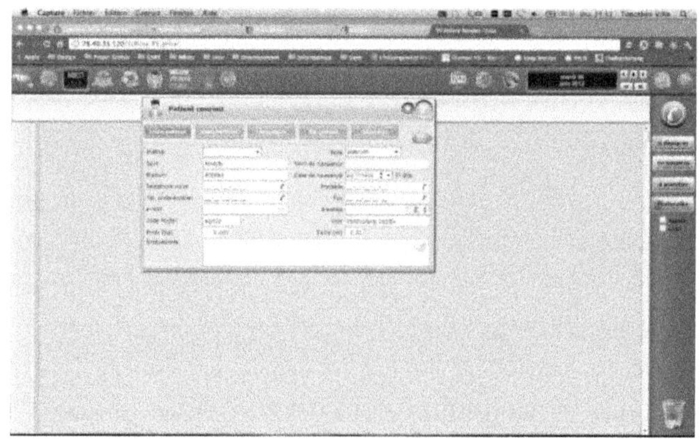

Figure 6: Screenshot of final results corresponding to the simulation of the test case study

The DEVSimPy *TestAutom* library has been employed to easily implement the test scenario using the formal constructs of DEVS. The first step is achieved by linking an instance of an *OpenApp* atomic model (called *OpenChrome* in figure 5) and a *NewOnglet* atomic model with an instance of the *Step* model (called *Step*1 in figure 5). The second step is achieved by connecting the four instances of the *Click*, *Paste*, *Enter*, *Wait* atomic models with a new instance of the *Step* model (called *Step*2 in figure 5). The third step arises from the combination of six instances of the same four atomic models enumerate in the second step. The last step is based on the inter-connexion of seven instances of the four previous atomic models and the *Capture* atomic model.

As seen in section 3.3.4, the *RF_Launcher* and *Sikuli* models are used to execute the test and visualized the final results (figure 6). The simulation final result shown in figure 6 highlight the success of the research test since the patient named MARIN has been found.

5. DISCUSSION

This section aims to discuss both the interest of using DEVSimPy for automated GUI software testing and the possible extra cost resulting by the use of the DEVS-based proposed approach rather than employing textual-based traditional approaches.

From a software engineering point of view, the testing engineer is able to implement its own models easily using the composition and hierarchy features allowed by the DEVSimPy framework. As it is shown in sub-section 3.2.2 the traditional testing approaches are difficult to be implemented due to the lack of flexibility of the textual script. With the proposed approach, the engineer benefits the DEVS composition in order to make a library of reusable models as it is explained in sub-section 2.3. The new testing model is composed by customizable and interchangeable DEVS models offering a greater flexibility faced with a text-based script model.

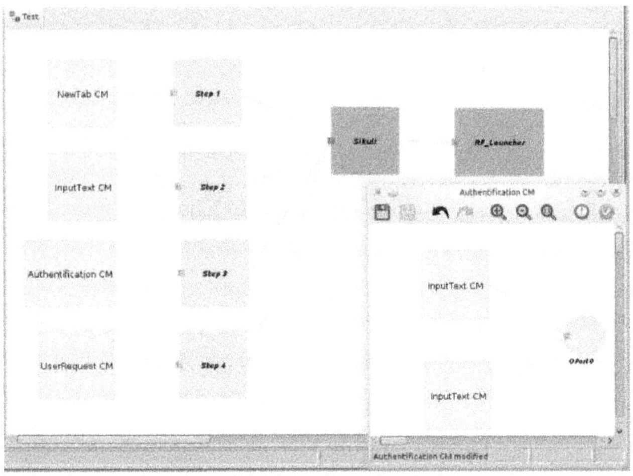

Figure 7: Reusability of DEVS coupled models

Figure 7 shows how atomic models corresponding to actions in figure 5 can be combined into reusable coupled models. Once the four coupled models NewTab, InputText, Authentication and UserRequest have been implemented and stored in library, a software tester has just to easily reuse them by a simple drag and drop. Futhermore, thanks to the DEVS description hierarchy, a coupled model can be easily composed with other defined coupled models as it is shown on figure 7 for the Authentication coupled model.

6. CONCLUSIONS

The paper deals with an efficient solution for test automation of GUI software using discrete-event simulations. We have pointed out that the DEVSimPy framework has brought a solution to the lack of homogeneous test automation environment. Furthermore, DEVSimPy simplifies the combination of test automation software as *Sikuli* and *RobotFramework*. This combination allows: (i) to automatically generate test scripts based on DEVSimPy models stored in the *TestAutom* dynamic library; (ii) to automatically execute the test scripts and visualize customizable logs using a simple click approach. The main contribution of the paper has been to extend the DEVSimPy framework with the *TestAutom* dynamic library. Furthermore, using DEVSimpy several variants of original test can be experimented and combined using simulation. A real case application has been employed in order to validate the benefits to apply DEVSimPy simulation. We plan to exploit the DEVSimPy library for GUI testing in various application domains. We envision also to embed analysis of CLR objects using DEVSimPy in order to complete the test scripts according to a code oriented view. An interesting issue is also to exploit the efficacy of explicit time DEVS formalism in revealing error types assigned to time properties as simulation of timeout connexions in web applications.

7. REFERENCES

[1] Robotframework. http://code.google.com/p/robotframework.

[2] Selenium. http://seleniumhq.org.

[3] J.-S. Bolduc and H. Vangheluwe. pythonDEVS : A modeling and simulation package for classical hierarchal DEVS. In *Rapport technique, MSDL, Universitè de McGill*, juin 2001.

[4] C. T. Brown, G. Gheorghiu, and J. Huggins. *An introduction to testing web applications with twill and selenium.* O'Reilly, first edition, 2007.

[5] L. Capocchi, J. F. Santucci, B. Poggi, and C. Nicolai. Devsimpy: A collaborative python software for modeling and simulation of devs systems. In *Enabling Technologies: Infrastructure for Collaborative Enterprises (WETICE), 2011 20th IEEE International Workshops on*, pages 170–175, June.

[6] T.-H. Chang. Using graphical representation of user interfaces as visual references. In *Proceedings of the 24th annual ACM symposium adjunct on User interface software and technology*, UIST '11 Adjunct, pages 27–30, New York, NY, USA, 2011. ACM.

[7] T.-H. Chang, T. Yeh, and R. C. Miller. Gui testing using computer vision. In *Proceedings of the SIGCHI Conference on Human Factors in Computing Systems*, pages 1535–1544, New York, NY, USA, 2010. ACM.

[8] J. de Lara and H. Vangheluwe. AToM3: A tool for multi-formalism and meta-modelling. In *Proceedings of FASE'02*, pages 174–188, London, UK, 2002. Springer-Verlag.

[9] P. Gupta and P. Surve. Model based approach to assist test case creation, execution, and maintenance for test automation. In *Proceedings of the First International Workshop on End-to-End Test Script Engineering*, ETSE '11, pages 1–7, New York, NY, USA, 2011. ACM.

[10] Z. Kohavi. *Switching and Finite Automata Theory: Computer Science Series.* McGraw-Hill Higher Education, 2nd edition, 1990.

[11] H. P. Langtangen. *Python Scripting for Computational Science (Texts in Computational Science and Engineering).* Springer-Verlag New York, Inc., Secaucus, NJ, USA, 2005.

[12] L. Pekka. Data-Driven and Keyword-Driven Test Automation Frameworks. Master's thesis, Helsinki University of Technology, 2006.

[13] J. Prabhu and N. Malmurugan. A survey on automated gui testing procedures. *European Journal of Scientific Research*, 64(3):456–462, 2011.

[14] T. Yeh, T.-H. Chang, and R. C. Miller. Sikuli: using gui screenshots for search and automation. In *Proceedings of the 22nd annual ACM symposium on User interface software and technology*, UIST '09, pages 183–192, New York, NY, USA, 2009. ACM.

[15] B. P. Zeigler, T. G. Kim, and H. Praehofer. *Theory of Modeling and Simulation.* Academic Press, Inc., Orlando, FL, USA, 2nd edition, 2000.

Discrete Event Design Patterns

Work in Progress Paper

Maamar Hamri
LSIS UMR CNRS 7296
Aix Marseille University
Marseille, France
amine.hamri@lsis.org

Rabah Messouci
LSIS UMR CNRS 7296
Aix Marseille University
Marseille, France
rabah.messouci@lsis.org

Claudia Frydman
LSIS UMR CNRS 7296
Aix Marseille University
Marseille, France
claudia.frydman@lsis.org

ABSTRACT

In this paper we highlight techniques from software engineering to design and code the behaviors of object. After a review of behavioral design patterns, we propose the state event design pattern to design basic behaviors described with state machines. In this pattern we objectify events in addition to states. Then, we generalize this pattern to DEVS behaviors. Thus, the DEVS designers may take profit from this technique to design simulations.

Categories and Subject Descriptors

D.3.3 [**Programming Languages**]: Language Constructs and Features - patterns; I.6.8 [**Types of Simulations**]: Types of Simulation - discrete event.

Keywords

Behavior of object, Finite state machines, DEVS, Design patterns, Implementation of simulation

1. INTRODUCTION

The use of Modeling and Simulation increases more and more in industry and education. In order to give simulation strong foundations, scientists defined formalisms, methods, tools and theories. One of the famous and popular theories in the field of M&S is the System theory proposed by Zeigler [9]. The DEVS formalism, that is the basis of this theory, proposes to define models by reusing existing ones in hierarchical and modular way. Then the final models will be given to an appropriate DEVS tool to make simulations.

Often, the step of modeling under a tool evokes a coding (designing) step; whereas the step of simulation is conducted automatically. The review of style of coding DEVS models shows that people use the switch-case and if-else statements to code state changes of DEVS models.

From software engineering, a code with switch-case or if-else statement, although the design is easy to do, has the following shortcomings: 1) readability: if the behavior of object to design is complex, the corresponding code becomes unreadable due to the imbrications of statements. 2) maintainability: as a consequence of 1) the designer could not add new behaviors easily to the existing code when the behavior of object to design changes. 3) reusability: portions of code can not be reused independently from the whole code; behaviors and variables are inter-related.

In order to enhance such a design, software designers propose the use of the state design pattern [4]. This pattern objectifies the different states of an object and delegates the state changes that occur at different times to the current state. Consequently we obtain a readable, maintainable and safe code.

In this paper we propose to use the behavioral design patterns to design and code DEVS behaviors in order to enhance the structure of the corresponding code and supply DEVS designers with software engineering techniques; this passes by updating the state pattern firstly. The paper is organized as follows: section 2 shows the state of the art on behavioral design patterns, especially the state one and its variants. In section 3 we discuss our proposal the state event pattern and we give two examples to analyze the efficiency of this pattern to design finite state machines; and section 4 gives a comparative study between classical design using the switch case statement and an object one based on our proposal. Sections 5 discusses the use of the state event pattern to design DEVS behaviors and finally we propose a generalized one. At the end, we conclude on this work and we underline our feature works.

2. STATE OF THE ART

In this section, we are interested on the state design pattern proposed by the Gang of Four (GoF)[4] and research works around this pattern. In fact, the state pattern is a behavioral one to describe an object in which the behavior depends on the context. It suggests objectifying the different states of the object to produce a maintainable code. Consequently, it replaces the classical approach that uses the conditional statement switch-case or if-else to describe the specific behaviors of an object in form of a statement bloc.

However, objectifying the states of an object consists on extending from an abstract class called State each possible state with a new sub-class. In addition, this abstract class specifies the interface of the object to design in form of public abstract methods that specify the different interactions of the object with its environment (context). To note that each implemented method by each sub-class should return or make the state change corresponding to the action made on the object. In fact, the context of the object receives actions to do that are delegated to the current state.

To illustrate the use of the state pattern, let us consider the Finite State Machine (FSM) of a basic door equipped with one button push to open and close it (Figure 1).

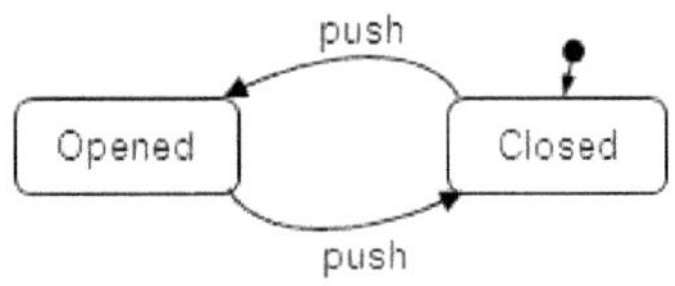

Figure 1: Door FSM.

The equivalent class diagram based on the state pattern of the specified door is shown by the figure below.

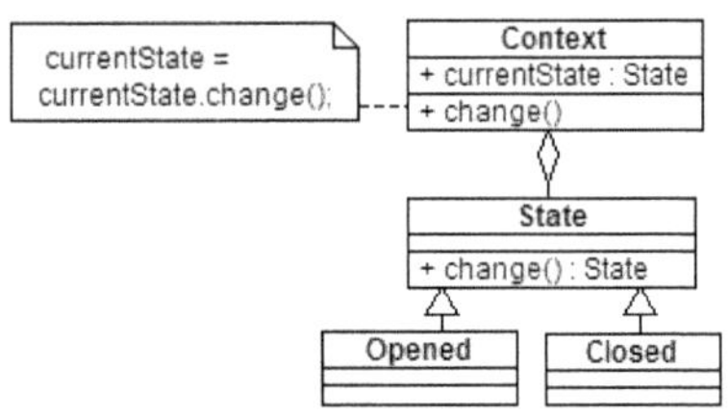

Figure 2: Class diagram of the door FSM.

Based on the state pattern of GoF, a lot of extensions were conducted to enhance it and override its shortcomings. In [3], the authors propose a catalog extending the original state pattern. Each extended one handles a specific problem. At high level, we found the original state pattern. Then this pattern is refined to produce more variants (state object, state member, etc.).

In [2], the authors propose a new variant of the state pattern called extensible state design pattern to add new behaviors i.e. add states and events without updating existing code in deep. They defined idioms to respect allowing the state pattern to support new behaviors for the designed object.

The author, in [1], addresses a complete state of the art on FSM design patterns and discusses variants that tackle the implementation of FSMs. The variant of patterns that seems more related to our proposal is archived under event pattern (Figure 3). In fact, it tackles the problem of sending/reception of events between FSMs; by encapsulating events in addition to states. In fact the event pattern defines the interface on how events make state changes through an abstract class. It classified 3 sets of events: process, ignore and handle error. This design leads to define for each concrete event class according to the current state, methods responsible of state changes. Then the object event insures making the state change and analysing input. To note that events hold the context that holds the states of FSM. However this kind of patterns is event-centric design in which other classes are less utilized.

The lack of this pattern is that the state changes are expressed with the if-else statement. The author fails to propose a maintainable design to FSMs due to the fact that we meet the classical obstacles again: code hard to update, unreadable, etc.

By refering to [1], Ackroyd proposed a variant of the event class pattern in which he integrated the state one. So that the responsibility of making state changes are allowed to

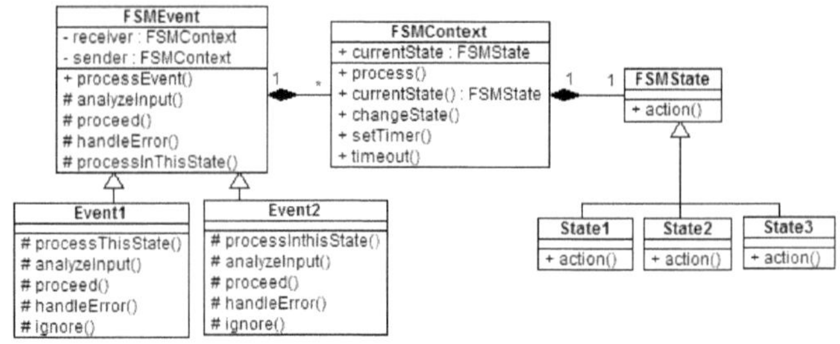

Figure 3: The event pattern [1].

state objects. The state abstract class shares an interface designed from the received events by the object. To note that event data are wrapped into event classes through a particular method to identify for the occurred event passed as a parameter which event class will handle it. Even if this design keeps our basic idea objectifying states and events, the author notes that the pattern is less flexible than the event one.

To summarize, the state pattern has the following lacks:

1) in other application fields, the event concept may be redesigned; for example timed FSMs manipulate dated events. Consequently, the designer should objectify events to allow encapsulation of event data. 2) the maintainability of the obtained code concerns only states. While new events are added to or deleted from the FSM, the code should be revised in depth due to the fact that the interface of the state abstract class should be modified. Consequently all state subclasses are modified. Only the state extensible design pattern provides such a maintainability. However it does not objectify events. 3) the methods with empty body, to code state changes that do not occur for a given state, flaw the corresponding code.

In addition, the event class pattern which is the most near to our proposal, suffers from a less flexible (upgradeable) architecture because it uses the if-else statement to link states to events. This fact let us to enhance this architecture and propose a more elaborated design pattern.

3. THE STATE EVENT DESIGN PATTERN

The state event design pattern generalizes the state one and enhances event class solution. In our proposal, we propose to objectify events with subclasses in addition to states to get an object-oriented code. Each state and event, defined in the FSM, is designed with independent subclass; still to express the state changes caused by the occurrence of events i.e. how to relate technically events to state. In fact the uniqueness of states in such a machine allows delegating the state change to the occurred event, contrary to the state pattern where the state subclasses insure the state change. However each event class should stores the list of possible state changes of the corresponding event i.e. the set of couples (source state, target state). Consequently, while an event occurs it identifies in its list of couples the future state according to the current one passed as a parameter. To note this list could be an array where indexes are source states and elements are target states.

On the other hand, to archive the state-event pattern we choose the following structure:

Problem: how to implement the behavior of an object described with a FSM, by objectifying states and events to get an object-oriented code flexible and maintainable?

Context: often the designers describe such a behavior using a FSM.

Solution: objectifying states and events with subclasses is a solution to this problem, by avoiding the use of switch-case statement to express state changes obviously. This is possible thanks to uniqueness of states in a FSM that will represent indexes of state changes. The elements of this solution are shown on the Figure 4.

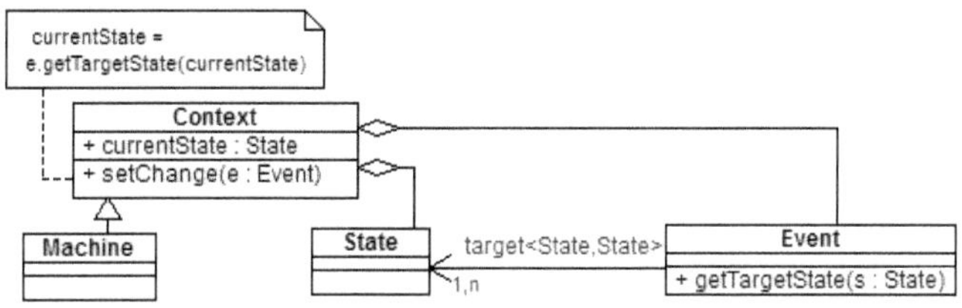

Figure 4: The state event design pattern.

State: is an abstract class. It is the parent class of each state subclass implementing a possible state of object to design. The object states may be constructed using the singleton design pattern or declared as constant.

Event: is an abstract class. It is, also, the parent class of each event subclass. It holds an array Target indexed and typed with state class. It allows saving a subset of couples (current state, future state) that concern only the event to design i.e. only a part of state changes described by the FSM. The method getTargetState() is defined at this stage. It takes the current state as a parameter and returns the future state computed from the array Target. The Target indexes may be typed as: i) integer; this implies that each state has a unique index that the designer should define. So that the array Target is a basic type of integers; or ii) state; in this case the coding language should be able to define arrays with object indexes (in java using HashMap, etc.). In our design we choose to objectify Target indexes to avoid defining for each state an index. To recall that for each event making state change on the FSM is mapped into a subclass extending the class Event; and filling the array Target according to the described state changes of the concerned event.

Context: it expresses the structure of the FSM in terms of state constants. It holds a reference of type state to get in memory the current state of the object to design. Events making state changes on the object are received through the method setChange(). This method has a parameter (event: Event). Then, the object event returns the future state by calling the method getTargetState(CurrentState) and updates the reference CurrentState. It may be responsible on defining state changes i.e. filling the array Target.

Consequences: the state event design pattern allows having a readable and expressive object-oriented code. In fact this pattern maps each state and event from the FSM into subclass. Each state subclass is a singleton; this is in respect with the FSM definition. However events are multiple occurrences and provoke state changes. At code level, each occurred event corresponds to a new instance of event. It transients through the method setChange() from the context and updates the current state. To note that this method describes the operational semantics of FSMs i.e. how events change states at conceptual level and should be transcribed in code.

In our pattern the code of the method setChange() is different from what the programmers often use in state pattern. Instead of a delegation of state change to the current state reference of the context, we opt for such a delegation to the occurred event which identifies the next state. Then the context updates its reference on the current state. This design provides an efficient and maintainable code as we will show in example 2. However, this fact leads to have a design pattern-centric event. So we can deduce that the other instances are less used.

Examples:

Example 1) let us consider the door described in Figure 1. The class diagram based on the state event pattern of this FSM is shown on Figure 5.

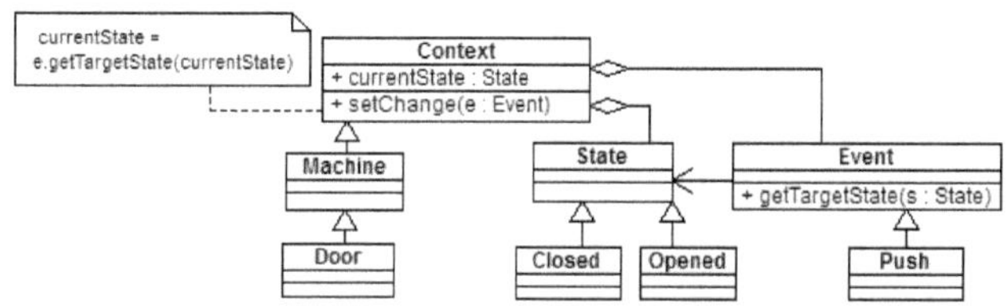

Figure 5: Class diagram of the door based on state event pattern.

The Java code obtained from the class diagram is an object code in which the states opened and closed, and the event push are mapped into Opened, Closed and Push classes respectively. For each occurred event an instance of class Push is created and transmitted to the method setChange(). This instance identifies the next state from it list of possible state changes stored in the HashMap Target; then the door context updates its current state as noted above.

```
public class Closed extends State {
   public Closed() {
     super();
   }
}
public class Opened extends State {
  public Opened() {
    super();
  }
}
public class Push extends Event {
  public Push() {
    super();
    // transition opened -> closed
    addTransition(Door.opened, Door.closed);
   // transition closed -> opened
    addTransition(Door.closed, Door.opened);
  }
}
public class Door extends Machine {
  public final static Opened opened = new Opened();
  public final static Closed closed = new Closed();
  public Door(){
    super();
    this.CurrentState = Door.closed;
  }
} ...
```

Example 2): we would add to the previous door the following behavior: while the door is in state opened, the user could maintain it opened by pushing again the button push (when it is pushed). Then, if he pushes again this button, the door will return to the normal state opened. Thus the FSM of the new door is shown in Figure 6.

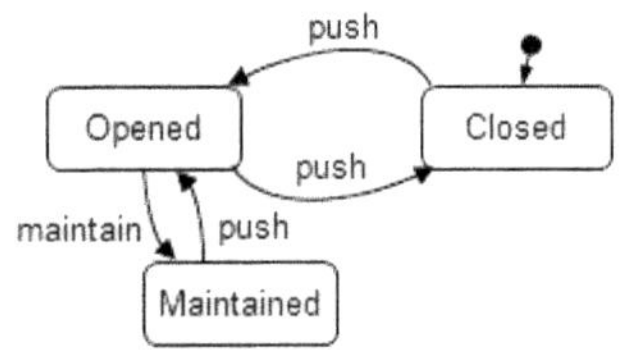

Figure 6: FSM of door with a new behavior.

The class diagram that we propose extends the initial one of the door. We add new classes Maintained, Maintain and Door2 to design the added state maintained, event maintain that express the new behavior and new door respectively (Figure 7).

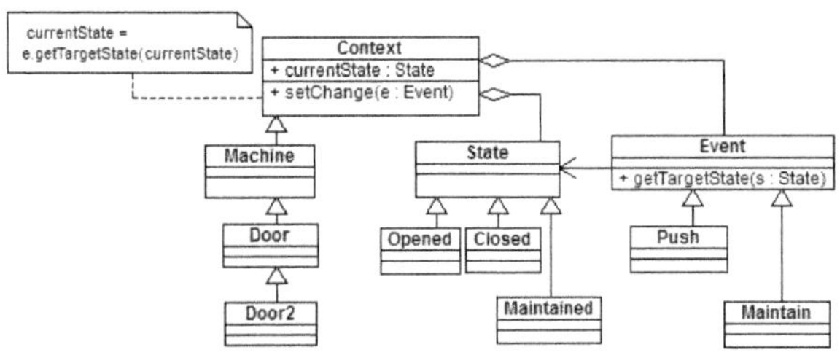

Figure 7: Updated class diagram of the new door.

The java code of the new door keeps the classes Opened, Closed and Push from the previous design with only an update of the array Target of the class Push to add the new state change (δ(maintained, push) = opened) through the class Door2. A great advantage comparing to the state design pattern that causes serious modifications to the code in order to integrate the new behaviors.

Advantages. the advantages of this design pattern are:

++) An object code in which states and events are objectified. So a structured and readable code.

++) State changes are conducted in systematic way thanks to the method setChange().

++) New behaviors could be incorporated to the existing code without affecting old classes. In addition existing behaviors could be updated at run-time.

++) Unreachable states could be deleted from code at run-time from the array Target.

++) A facility to communicate FSMs among them thanks to the objectifying of events.

Disadvantages:

-) The main shortcoming of this design pattern is the computation time for small FSMs.

-) A hard design that needs a lot of classes. A FSM with n states and m events, we need (n+m) classes to design all events and states of the FSM.

4. COMPARATIVE STUDY: STATE EVENT PATTERN VS. SWITCH CASE

In this study, we are interested in time execution and heap memory of the FSM simulation in order to compare two design techniques: switch-case and state event pattern. This study is conducted under personal computer equipped with Intel Core i3 2.2GHz, heap memory 4 GO, operating system windows 7 and java virtual machine 1.7.0-01.

In order to compare these two techniques of designing FSMs, first we define the FSM to design; then we code it for simulation. For that, the FSM will be stored under a matrix and filled randomly (matrix lines and columns define states and events respectively and crossing between a given line and column defines the future state).

Once the matrix of FSM is completely filled, we process into generating automatically the java code according to the chosen design. For the code based on the switch-case statement only one class is designed. The second code based on the state event pattern holds (lines+columns) classes. They are designed according to the previous matrix, in addition to the class Context which contains the state instances (constants) and the method setChange(event: Event).

Remain to insure the state change of the designed FSMs through a generator of events that we developed. Its main task is to produce and introduce events to the FSM codes (swith-case and pattern). Then, according to event scheduler size we measure the execution time and we track the behavior of heap memory.

From experience results (Figure 8), we deduce that the simulation of scheduler with a size less than 10^5 events, the switch-case code provides a quick simulation than the code based on the state event pattern. However this trend is reversed when scheduler exceeds this threshold value. Technically, it is allowed to code FSM with less than 75 states and 56 events (or 57 states and 75 events). More than these values, the JVM throws the java.lang.OutOfMemoryError due to the fact that the FSM class exceeds the max size of heap memory allocated to an object. However the FSM code based on our design pattern is dispatched through state and event subclasses. Consequently, this code is far to throw this heap memory error.

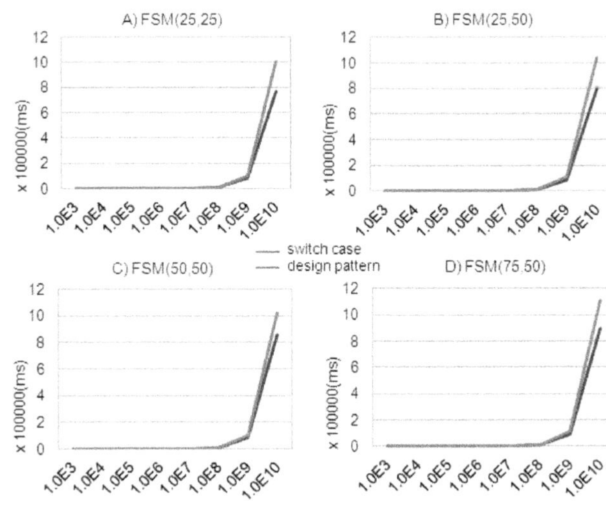

Figure 8: FSMs run-time.

To note that, we successfully generated code of FSM with 750 states and 750 events. However we met the same error when we handled FSMs with more states and events due to the fact that the class Context exceeds the max heap memory allocated to an object.

Looking to the behavior of heap memory, we remark that the state event design pattern manages it better than the code of switch case (Figure 9).

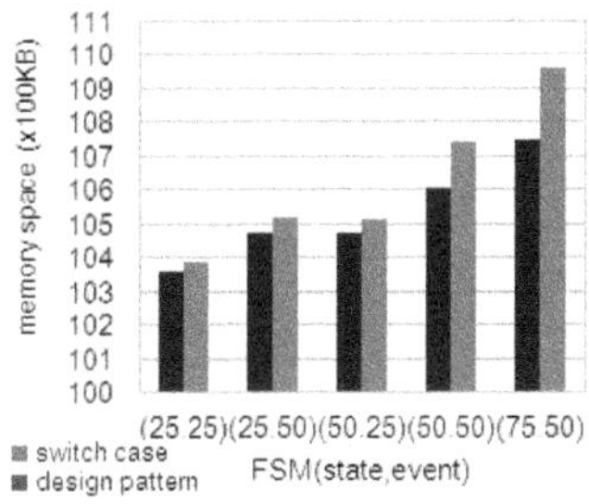

Figure 9: FSMs memory allocation.

5. THE STATE EVENT TRANSITION DESIGN PATTERN

The state event pattern in spite of its capability to design FSMs, can not be a software solution to design DEVS-phase models [8]. In fact, we hope to design conditions that define with events state changes and actions to update state variables when state changes occur in a practical way. For that, we propose the state event transition pattern in which we objectify transitions in addition to states and events. Consequently, we design each condition as a method that computes the boolean result. So to fire a transition (make a state change) when we receive an event we should identify the set of imminent transitions from the current state and then evaluate each condition associated to imminent transitions. If the condition is true, we fire the corresponding transition. Otherwise there is no transition to fire.

Problem: how to design a DEVS-phase model, to make the code abstract, readable, reusable and maintainable for states, events and transitions?

Context: the DEVS designers often recall to the if-else statement or user-friendly tools to simulate their models. In the first case, the designers meet the classical problems of coding with such a statement: code unreadable, hard to maintain, etc. In the second case, such tools provide a transformation from graphical models into formatted file and not a compilable code; except LSIS_DME, in which a transformation based on state transition pattern was introduced [5, 7]. However this design pattern does not provide a total abstract design and flexible code even if it proved its efficiency for encapsulating transitions into classes.

Solution: the design pattern that we propose extends the state event one by introducing the class Transition which objectifies the DEVS element transition (Figure 10). We modify slightly the computerization of the next state. In fact the couple (event, state) defines the transition to fire instead of the next state as in the previous design pattern, then the selected transition returns the next state. Knowing that a set of imminent transition will be selected according to the occurred event and the current state, we should identify the transition with the true condition to fire it. If it is the case, we get the next state from the selected transition and we update the current state reference. Event, State and Context: are those defined in section 3. However we allow to indexes of the array Target point on one or more transitions to design the fact from a given state there are one or more outgoing transitions. To note that the abstract class State

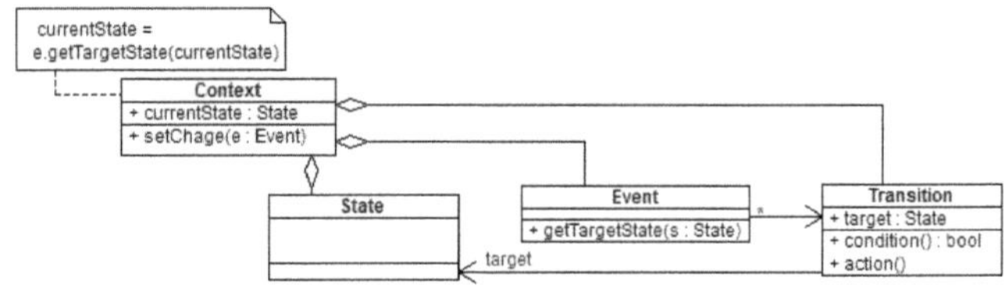

Figure 10: Class diagram of the generalized pattern.

holds the variable elapsed_time to compute the elapsed time from the last transition; and two methods get() and set() to return and update this variable. Also this class may hold the other state variables that conditions could use to define their logical expressions and actions could update them when firing transitions.

Transition: this class provides a reference on the target state that should be instanciated by each extended class to design transitions of the model. It holds two abstract methods boolean condition() and void action(). The extended transition subclasses should implement these methods to compute the diffirent conditions and actions.

In addition to make our design more practical for DEVS, we define the following abstract classes: ActiveState and PassiveState to implement active and passive states and to distinguish them; and ExtTransition and IntTransition to implement external and internal (autonomous) transitions and to overload only the IntTransition classes with the method that computes the output event for the corresponding transition.

Examples:

Example 1) let us consider an automatic door which opens for each occurred event push, remains opened for 10 u.t. (units of time), then returns to initial state closed. The DEVS model for this door is shown in Figure 11.

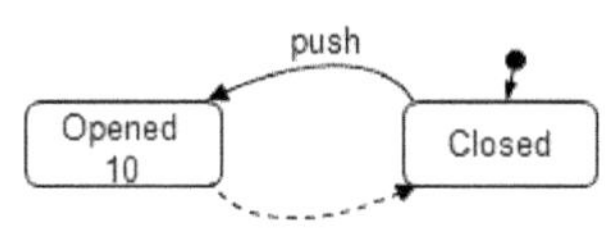

Figure 11: The DEVS model of automatic door.

The class diagram that we propose to design this model (see Figure 12) is an extension of the state event transition design pattern.

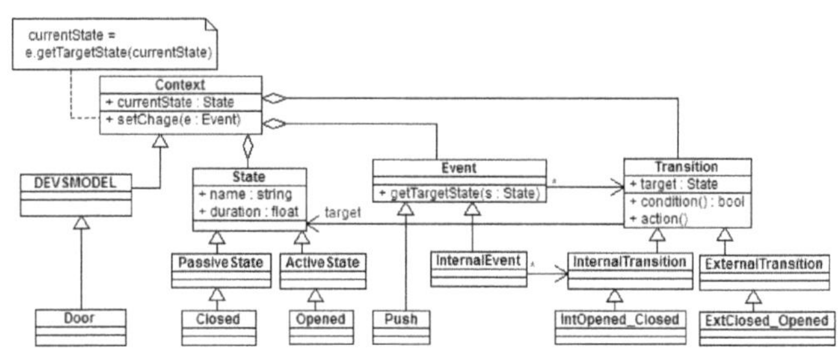

Figure 12: Class diagram of automatic door.

There are two state classes Opened and Closed to design the states opened and closed respectively; one event class Push to design the external input event and two transition classes ExtClosed_Opened and IntOpened_Closed to design the external transition closed to opened and the internal one from opened to closed to signal the fact that the door automatically makes a state change. To note that for each transition subclasses the methods condition() should return true and action() has an empty body.

Example 2) let us consider the Min Max DEVS formalism [6] in which the state lifetimes are min-max real values ($D : S \to R^{+}\text{x}R^{+}$) and the other sets and functions are similar to DEVS. However the semantics of this formalism is different, it describes the possible models for which the lifetime of each state is included in the corresponding min-max lifetime, with only one model. The behavior is given with an appropriate simulator that respects the Min Max DEVS semantics.

In order to show that the state event transition pattern can design models written with DEVS extensions, let us consider the automatic door with a new temporal constraint: the automatic closure of the door can not be defined with an accurate delay but with a min-max value [10, 12.5]. Each value from this window constitutes a possible delay to the automatic closure of the door (Figure 13).

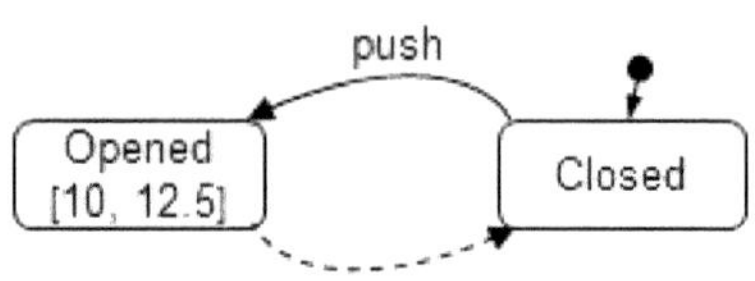

Figure 13: The Min Max DEVS model of the door.

The diagram class that we propose to design MinMax DEVS models can be easily designed from the state event transition pattern. We overload the abstract class ActiveState to MinMaxState with two attributes: MinDuration and MaxDuration. For the other elements we keep the DEVS classes without modification. If the designer hopes more clarity on class names, he can extend these classes to rename them (MinMaxEvent, MinMaxTransition, etc.).

Now we consider the new door, the diagram class that we propose reuses that we proposed for the classical door (Figure 14). We extend only the class Opened to MinMaxOpened and we reuse the classes (Closed, IntOpened_Closed and ExtClosed_Opened) to complete the MinMaxDoor class diagram. Only the class Opened is overloaded and its instance is replaced with an instance of MinMaxOpened.

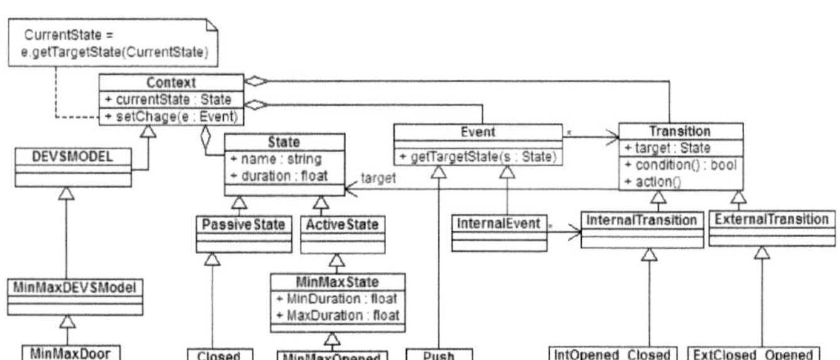

Figure 14: Class diagram of the Min Max door.

Through this example, we show the power of our proposal in terms of reusing existing designs to design new models written with a variant of DEVS.

6. CONCLUSION

In this paper we attempted to propose software architecture based on design pattern language to overcome the lacks of the state pattern. After a recall of the state pattern and its extension from the state of the art, we showed their strong and fair points. Unfortunately, these patterns can not design discrete event models, due to the fact that events are designed with methods and event occurrences with method calls. So, it is impossible to communicate models among them by sending and receiving events.

Based on existing works and our experience in developing simulation software, we propose the state event design pattern that makes the state one more general and abstract by objectifying events in addition to states. In order to avoid the use of the switch-case and if-else statements to define state changes, we decide that event classes hold the state changes. This storage takes the form of an array in which the states are the array indexes. To note this technique is less obvious, due to the fact that designers are familiar to delegate state changes to the current state and not to the occurred event.

One of the main features of our proposal is its capability to design specific discrete event models: like DEVS and some extensions. This feature makes developed models reusable and extendible by overloading classes thanks to the object paradigm. So a code based on the state event or state event transition design pattern for a DEVS model; if this model is updated to represent new elements from a DEVS extension, the initial code could be easily extended to represent the final model described with DEVS extension.

In the near future, we hope to experiment our proposal the state event design pattern to design real complex system and analyze performances of designed models and measure machine resources (heap memory, cpu time, etc.).

7. REFERENCES

[1] ADAMCZYK, P. Selected patterns for implementing finite state machines. In *Conference on Pattern Languages of Programs* (September 2004), PLOP'04.

[2] CHINE, B., AND MILLESTEIN, T. An extensible state machine pattern for interactive applications. In *the 17th Conference on Pattern Languages of Programs* (October 2010), ECOOP 2010.

[3] DYSON, P., AND PETERSON, B. State patterns. In *Pattern Languages of Programming Design 3* (July 1998), EuroPLOP'98.

[4] GAMMA, E., HELM, R., JOHNSON, R., AND VLISSIDES, J. *Design patterns: Elements of Reusable Object-Oriented Software.* Addison-Wesley, 1995.

[5] HAMRI, M., AND BAATI, L. On using design patterns for devs modeling and simulation tools. In *Spring Simulation Multi-conference-Symposium Theory of Modeling & Simulation-DEVS Integrative M&S Symposium* (April 2010).

[6] HAMRI, M., GIAMBIASI, N., AND FRYDMAN, C. Min max devs modeling and simulation. *Simulation Modelling Practice and Theory 14*, 7 (2006), 909–929.

[7] HAMRI, M., AND ZACHAREWICZ, G. Automatic generation of object-oriented code from devs graphical specifications. In *Winter Simulation Conference* (December 2012), WSC'12.

[8] PRAEHOFER, H., AND PREE, D. Visual modeling of devs-based multi-formalism systems based on higraphs. In *Winter Simulation Conference*, pp. 595–603.

[9] ZEIGLER, B., PRAEHOFER, H., AND KIM, T. G. *Theory of Modeling and Simulation.* Academic Press, 2000.

A Flexible Simulation Framework for Multicore Schedulers*

[Work in Progress Paper]

Alex Aravind† and Viswanathan Manickam
Department of Computer Science
University of Northern British Columbia
Prince George, BC, Canada - V2N 4Z9
(csalex,manickam)@unbc.ca

ABSTRACT

As multicore processors are becoming the norm, an efficient scheduling of cores to the threads is fundamentally important for multicore computing. To study the performance of a new scheduling algorithm for the future multicore systems with hundreds and thousands of cores, we need a flexible scheduling simulation testbed. Designing such a multicore scheduling simulation testbed and illustrating its functionality are the main contributions of this paper. The proposed scheduling simulation testbed is developed using Java and expected to be released for public use.

Categories and Subject Descriptors

C.4 [**Computer System Organization**]: Performance of Systems; D.2.8 [**Software Engineering**]: Metrics—*performance measures*

General Terms

Performance, Modeling, Measurement, Scheduling

Keywords

Simulation, scheduling, multicore, performance, operating systems, framework

1. INTRODUCTION

The scheduling problem in computing systems has been studied in the last several decades. With the recent arrival of multicore processors [15], the scheduling problem has gained renewed interest. The contribution of this paper is related to the scheduling problem in multicore computer systems. To meet the requirement of multicore systems, the most important component of operating systems that might need a radical change is the processor scheduler. Most developments in the operating system domain in the last several years have been on file system, security, device management, and user interface, and only minimal changes have been proposed for schedulers. Until recently, the CPU resources were considered as scarce. So, the schedulers have been focusing on effectively multiplexing the CPU among the competing threads to serve all appropriately. The arrival of multicore processors changed this situation.

The operating system literature on multicore systems is relatively limited and most of the publications are within the last five years [10, 14, 16, 19]. Of that, only a small portion is related to multicore scheduling algorithms [19]. Most of them are related to effectively dealing with resource contention.

The approaches to design scheduling algorithms for multicore systems proposed so far vary greatly, and they differ in their recommendations [3, 8, 14, 16, 17, 19]. One view is that multicore systems have in fact simplified the scheduling. That is, since we have plenty of cores, there is no need to worry about intricate time multiplexing strategies, simply giving enough cores to applications will simplify the scheduling. On the other extreme, several researchers feel that multicore systems have complicated the scheduling task, as it needs to consider several factors such as cores, caches, networks, and application requirements together in offering best possible service. A number of works suggest ideas in between these extreme cases.

Designing and evaluating a scheduling algorithm for multicore systems is a complex task. Any tool that can alleviate this complexity and aid the development of new scheduling algorithm for multicore systems would be interesting and useful. One such tool, we believe, would be a flexible simulation environment where new scheduling algorithm could be developed and studied with a little to moderate effort. That is the main motive of the work presented in this paper.

This paper contributes a generic scheduling framework, implementation, and experiments. The scheduling framework is a theoretical abstraction of the scheduling system. The scheduling simulator is an implementation of the framework. We also conducted a limited simulation study to see the performance of two popular scheduling algorithms - Linux and Solaris scheduling algorithms.

1.1 Related Work

A number of simulators for multiprocessors have been pro-

*This work was supported in part by the Natural Sciences and Engineering Research Council of Canada (NSERC) Discovery Grant (312162-10).

†Corresponding author

SIGSIM-PADS'13, May 19–22, 2013, Montréal, Québec, Canada.

posed in the literature [1, 2, 4, 5, 9, 11, 12, 18]. Among them, Simics [9], SimOS [12], SimpleScalar [4], and AMD SimNow [1] emulate the processor at the instruction set level. They differ by emulating different architectures and simulating other components such as I/O and network.

Simics simulates the hardware which can run unmodified operating systems such as Solaris, Linux, Windows XP, and Tru64. Simics supports the following processor models: Ultrasparc, Alpha, x86, x86-64, PowerPC, MIPS, IPF, and ARM. In addition, Simics simulates the device models well enough to execute the device drivers.

SimOS simulates the hardware components to boot, study, and run the IRIX operating system and the application that runs on IRIX. SimOS fastens the simulation by changing the mode of execution. There are three modes of execution proposed in SimOS – emulation, rough characterization, and accurate mode. Emulation mode models the hardware that are required to execute the workloads, leaving out other uninteresting executions such as booting the operating system, reading from the disk, and initializing the workload. This is the fastest mode. The rough characterization mode approximates the behavior of the system by simulating those uninterested executions. This mode is two or three times slower than the emulation mode. The accurate mode emulates the complete system, and therefore it is the slowest and is very time consuming. The accurate mode can be used for measuring the accuracy of the system under simulation.

AMD SimNow simualtes the AMD family processors. SimpleScalar simulates a close derivative of MIPS architecture. Turandot [11] emulates PowerPC. A recent simulator called COTSon [2] uses AMD SimNow, and employs a statistical sampling technique that can selectively turn on and off the simulation to reduce the overall simulation time.

Since all these simulators emulate machine instructions completely, they all have fine grained accuracy at instruction level. Some of them are used as virtual machines. However, they are very slow as they have to interpret each machine instruction at software level. For example, SimOS - the fastest among the group - can execute workloads only less than 10 times slower than the underlying hardware. Note that SimOS simulates other components to attain this speed. Also, as these simulators will run on host operating system, the scheduling of host operating system will further slow down the execution time of the instruction. Such fine-grained simulators are more suitable for studying low level functionalities of the processors.

These simulators are not suitable for rapid simulations aiming to get quick insight and guidance to develop new scheduling algorithms for future multicore processors. They are machine dependent and emulate only existing hardware. Implementing a scheduling algorithm in a system supported by a regular operating system is hard. Therefore, simulating a new scheduling algorithm for performance study in these simulators is time consuming and hard.

A simulator of Linux scheduler called Linshed was proposed in [5]. This simulator was designed by making changes to original Linux kernel and it runs in user mode. The objective of Linshed was to study the Linux scheduler in depth and was not intended to implement any new scheduling algorithm or comparing with any existing scheduling algorithm.

Recently, a toolset called AKULA [18] was proposed to study scheduling of threads on multicores so as to reduce their cache contention. The AKULA toolset assumes the availability of the task profile termed as *bootstrap data* on cache behaviour. Such cache behaviour can be obtained only through actual execution on a dedicated multicore system. The bootstrap data contains two information: solo execution time, which is measured when the thread runs alone in the real machine; and the degradation matrix, which is the factor of degradation that occurs when a thread is scheduled with other threads in different cores which shares the cache.

Threads can be scheduled on a multicore system in a number of ways. Consider a system with two cores and two level cache memories L1 - local to each core, and L2 shared by both. In this system, all threads can be scheduled to one core or they can be distributed between two cores in several ways. These different ways of scheduling will have different influences on both L1 and L2 level caches. To observe the cache behavior, we need to collect the cache data in all possible ways of scheduling, which will result in a large number of combinations.

AKULA collects the cache behavior for a limited set of scheduling combinations. It assumes that the threads scheduled in the cores are allotted with full L1 cache and observes the L2 level cache effect. That is, time sharing on a core is not allowed. For example, say there are four threads, *A, B, C,* and *D*, and they need to be scheduled. There are two cores in the system which shares L2 cache. The bootstrap data will have a solo execution time of threads A, B, C, and D, and the degradation matrix will have the degradation factor for the combinations of each thread with every other thread - AB, AC, AD, BA, BC, BD, CA, CB, CD, DA, DB, and DC. This is 12 combinations in total.

If the number of cores is increased to 3, then a total of 24 combination of data have to be collected. So, the size of the data increases drastically with increasing number of cores as well as increasing number of threads. Also, executing these tasks in a real machine to collect the bootstrap trace is tedious and very time consuming task. More importantly, AKULA only runs on the profile data created by actual executions; it cannot be used for testing new workloads. Therefore, it limits its usage only to the system and the workload for which the trace is collected. Even changing a single parameter such as speed, number of cores, cache, or workload will make the trace unusable. Due to this restriction, the use of AKULA is very limited.

With this background, we are now ready to present the framework next.

2. SIMULATION FRAMEWORK

This section presents the architecture of the multicore scheduling simulation (MSS) framework, which is the major contribution of this paper. The primary use of this framework is to facilitate researchers in implementing and simulating multicore scheduling algorithms to evaluate the performance visually and statistically.

2.1 Multicore Scheduler Simulation

From the system's point of view, multicore scheduling essentially has two tasks - maintaining the load among the cores and multitasking threads in each core. Generally, the first task is referred to as *load balancing* and the second task is referred to as *local scheduling*. We maintain these abstractions in our scheduling framework.

Load balancing manages the jobs across the cores, and local scheduling directs the core to switch between threads.

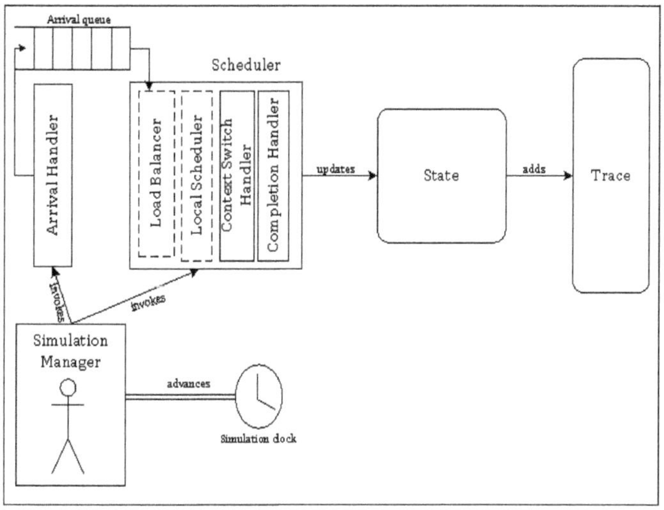

Figure 1: The Scheduler Simulator

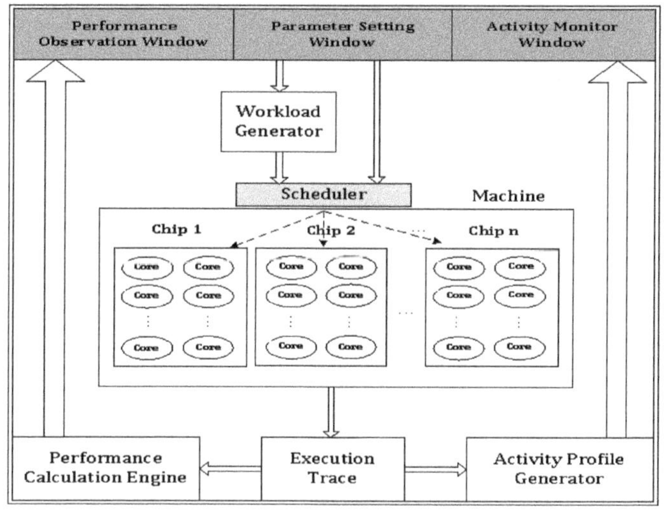

Figure 2: Architecture of MSS Framework

Thread switching (or context switching), say from T_i to T_j, requires saving the context of T_i and loading or restoring the context of T_j. Also, certain tasks must be performed when a thread completes its execution. In the simulation context, these tasks are basically updating the simulation system state. In our framework, we provide generic routines to do these tasks.

In essence, implementing the routines of load balancing and local scheduling is the programming effort needed to use our simulator to study the performance of a new scheduling algorithm. Again, to reduce the effort of implementing the scheduler further, we provide a default load balancing routine and sample local scheduling algorithm routines. These routines can be suitably modified to implement the new scheduling algorithm, unless the new scheduling algorithm is completely novel and does not follow the structure of load balancer and local scheduler combination. Even in that case, the entire scheduling can be designed from scratch with a little effort. In any case, from our experience, we are confident that, once the logic of the new scheduling algorithm is completely understood, then implementing it in our simulator is straightforward. With this background on the multicore scheduler, next we explain the overall multicore scheduler simulator, which is a part of the framework.

The simulator is illustrated in Figure 1. It has seven components: a simulation clock, a simulation manager, arrival handler, an arrival queue, a scheduler, a state space, and a trace file. The scheduler has four routines: a load balancer, a local scheduler, a context switch handler, and a completion handler.

The simulation of the system basically involves updating the state of the system at every simulation time point, and incrementing the simulation clock. Simulation clock advancement and state update could be done in an integrated fashion. But, for the modular design of the scheduling framework, we decided to keep these two tasks separate.

In our framework, we designed a component called the **Simulation Manager** to do the task of advancing the simulation clock and initiating the appropriate routines to update the system state. Updating the simulation system state typically involves recording the arrival of new jobs, and updating the state related to scheduling. To implement the arrival of new jobs, we introduced a queue called *arrival queue*, and implemented a routine to register the newly arrived jobs in the arrival queue. Updating the state related to scheduling is dependent on the scheduler logic, and it must be done as part of the implementation of the scheduler.

The simulation of the executions of jobs are recorded as simulation trace, and it is recorded at every scheduling point. To make this task generic, we have standardized the format of the execution trace and implemented a routine to add the trace appropriately during the simulation. Actually, this task of updating the trace is taken care of automatically by the context switch handler routine. With this background, we will now introduce the architecture of the multicore simulation framework.

2.2 Architecture of the MSS Framework

First, we will introduce some basic terminology used in our framework, to avoid confusion of what really refers to processor[1]. In our framework, *core* refers to the hardware execution unit, *chip* refers to an integrated circuit that contains one or more cores, and *machine* refers to a collection of chips designed to work together. *Thread* is the smallest unit that can be scheduled to a core for execution.

A higher level architecture of MSS framework is given in Figure 2. The framework has five main logical components: a workload generator, a multicore machine, a multicore scheduler, and an execution trace file, and a performance calculation engine. We explain them next.

2.2.1 Workload Generator

We have implemented the workload generator to generate two types of workloads: threads and gangs. Threads are generated for traditional applications and gangs are generated for parallel applications. The gangs of parallel threads typically execute in a synchronized manner.

The input to generate a workload of threads are: the numbers of threads, thread's mean arrival rate, and thread's mean service rate. To generate the workload of gangs, in-

[1]Before the multicore era, the term processor was used to refer to as an execution unit.

stead of the number of threads, the number of gangs is given. The number of threads within each gang is generated uniformly between the range 2 to M, where M is the number of cores. The output will be a set of threads or gangs depending on the generator chosen. Each thread will have a unique id, arrival time, execution time, I/O points, priority, and application class. Similarly, each gang will have a gang id, arrival time, execution time, and a set of parallel threads with their own ids.

The I/O points of the thread are the times when the thread will go for I/Os. For example, assume that a thread has an execution time of 50, and it will go for I/O at time 5, 20, and 30. In this case, I/O requests will be invoked after the thread is executed for 5 units, 20 units, and 30 units. The number of I/O points are generated uniformly within the execution time range, and the I/O wait time is generated uniformly within a range specified in the configuration.

2.2.2 *Multicore Machine*

The multicore machine is the computing unit that is organized in a hierarchy, starting with machine at the highest level. A multicore machine contains one or more chips, and each chip contains two or more cores. The core is the physical execution unit. In practice, a core is capable of executing one or more threads in an interleaved way, referred to as hyper-threading. In our simulator we model a core to execute one thread at a time. We believe that, with a suitable scheduling policy, the performance of hyper-threading effect can be approximately simulated using single threaded cores. A multicore machine has hierarchy of cache memories. Current multicore systems have three levels of cache memories, referred to as L1, L2, and L3. L1 is the core level, L2 is the chip level, and L3 is the machine level. The L1 cache is local to each core, cores in a chip shares the L2 cache of that chip, and the L3 cache is shared by all the cores in the machine.

2.2.3 *Multicore Scheduler*

As explained earlier, our framework implements a multicore scheduler having two logical components - load balancer and local scheduler. The load balancer is responsible for maintaining a desired balance of the system load. This task involves dispatching the new jobs to the appropriate local scheduler, and migrating jobs from one local scheduler to another when necessary. The local scheduler is responsible for scheduling jobs to the cores for execution. Generally, each core is assigned a local scheduler, but other choices are possible. In our simulation, local scheduling is implemented to have centralized control. In the simulations context, the local scheduler primarily makes a decision to choose a job for execution, determines the amount of execution time, calculates its progress rate, and produces the trace. The progress rate of a job is the crucial design factor affecting the accuracy of execution, and it is dependent on several factors such as execution speed of the core and the contention for shared resources. We have used a simple cache contention model, but it can be easily replaced with an implementation of a more refined model.

2.2.4 *Execution Trace*

During the simulation, the execution trace is recorded at every context switch to generate the activity profile and to compute the performance metrics. There are two types of traces collected: the execution trace and the I/O trace. The execution trace is a collection of quintuple: <core id, thread id, execution start time, scheduling end time, status>. The status is 0 if preempted by quanta expiration, 1 if preempted by higher priority thread, 2 if going for I/O, and 3 if completed. The I/O trace is a collection of triples: <thread id, I/O start time, I/O end time>.

The performance study primarily aims to determine how well the algorithm responds to satisfy certain criteria such as response time, fairness, and utilization of resources. The performance calculation engine calculates these values for a given set of data, and the result can be passed to the performance observation window for the users to study.

2.2.5 *Performance Calculation Engine*

The performance study primarily aims to determine how well the algorithm responds to satisfy certain criteria such as response time, fairness, and utilization of resources. The performance calculation engine calculates these values for a given set of data, and the result then can be passed to the performance observation window for the users to study. The performance criteria widely used to study scheduling algorithms are the five metrics: throughput, CPU utilization, turnaround time, waiting time, and response time [13, 7]. In addition, we have included the interactive response – the time from when a thread is ready for execution to start of execution.

2.2.6 *Statistical Measures*

For these metrics, when applicable, we calculated the minimum, maximum, average, and standard deviation. Traditionally, in this context, average and percentage are primarily used to study the performance. That is, typically, the throughput and utilization are computed in percentage, and the average is computed for the turnaround time, waiting time, and response time. We believe better measures than the average must be used in analysing these metrics.

Although the term quality of service is often used and directly related with response time, it is not well interpreted in the context of computing and communication systems. As indicated in [6], the perceived quality of customers need not be directly related with minimal response time. The study indicates that users are often unaware of the quality differences until it crosses a certain threshold. Therefore, the quality of service need not always be related to the widely used metrics such as the minimal response time or minimal average response time. Thus, we believe that a predictable response time is a more appropriate measure for the quality of service than other measures such as average response time and resource utilization.

One such measure we discussed earlier is the predictable response time. A predictable response could be measured using variance or standard deviation. Therefore, we decided to include the metric of standard deviation (i.e., square root of variance) in our framework. Predictable service is extremely important, and we believe standard deviation is a better measure of predictability than average value.

2.3 Activity Profile Generator

The activity monitor provides visualization of how the algorithm schedules the threads among the distributed cores. The activity profile generator is responsible for providing the data for the visualization. It basically derives the data from the execution trace. From the trace, it generates data for

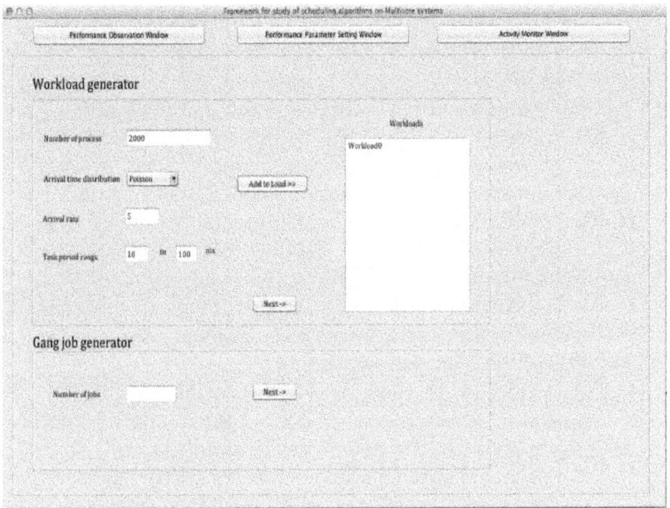

Figure 3: Parameter Setting Window

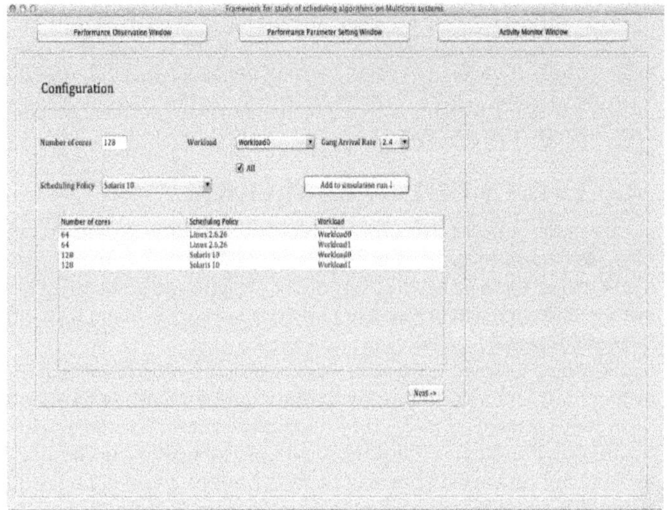

Figure 4: Simulations Run Window

every clock tick. The data contains the core status as *idle* or *occupied*. Also, if occupied, the data contains the information about the thread and its status, whether it is a newly arrived thread or preempted thread or migrated thread from different core. The activity profile generator differentiates these different states of the core by assigning different colors. The activity monitor window visualizes the derived data of core to thread allocation. Using this component, we can visually observe core utilization, load balancing, and the individual core statistics.

2.4 User Interface

The multicore scheduling simulator has three main windows, and the interface within each window is organized as hierarchical panels.

2.4.1 *Performance Parameter Setting Window*

The performance parameter setting window, shown in Figure 3, is used to configure the parameters for the simulation. It consists of two screens - upper and lower. The upper screen is used to set the workload generation parameters. It gets the number of processes/threads, arrival time distribution, mean arrival rate, and the task execution time range. The lower screen is used to generate parallel jobs. The window has the provision of creating more than one workload. We can set the above mentioned parameters and click add to workload button, which adds it to the list and the fields are cleared to create a new one.

The simulations run window, shown in Figure 4, is designed to get input for creating simulation runs. Using this window, several simulation runs can be configured. The parameters required for each run are the number of cores, workload selection, and the scheduling algorithm. Using the simulation run window, we will be able to create simulation runs with different combinations: (a) the number of cores vs. workloads with the same scheduling policy; (b) the number of cores vs. scheduling policy under the same workload; and (c) workloads vs. scheduling policy when executing with same number of cores.

2.4.2 *Performance Observation Window*

The performance observation window offers various performance metrics that can be represented in charts. The window has a list of performance metrics which can be chosen to see the observed results. Additionally, we can choose two simulation runs to compare the results. The performance metrics can be analysed with number of cores and arrival rate.

2.4.3 *Activity Monitor Window*

The activity monitor window is an interesting component in this simulator. This component displays the core usage in a graphical representation. Using this window, we can observe: (a) core utilization; (b) thread migration; and (c) the execution thread list.

The activity window clearly visualizes how the threads are distributed among the cores and how effectively load balancing happens. To see the individual core performance, there is a child window that shows a particular core's statistics.

The core monitor window has three parts. The first part (left part) is to display the threads running in that core using different colors. The second part (right upper part) is to display the statistics of busy and idle time of the core. A thread scheduled in that core could be new, preempted, or migrated from another core. The ratio of these three kinds of threads scheduled in that core is displayed in the third part (right lower part) of the window. This part shows how many threads are migrated from other cores due to load balancing. Such visual analysis is useful to capture unusual behavior and patterns.

3. SIMULATION EXPERIMENTS

To test and illustrate the functionality of the proposed simulator, we implemented the recent versions of Linux and Solaris 10 scheduling algorithms. Please keep in mind that these two algorithms are the most popular algorithms widely used in practice, and they are highly efficient. Hence, their performance closeness is not a surprising, rather confirming. From the algorithms logic, we expected Solaris to perform better than Linux.

We conducted two sets of experiments: (a) the workload is fixed and the number of cores is varied; and (b) the number of cores is fixed and the workload is varied. From the simulation experiments, we found that Solaris performs consistently better than Linux, and that confirmed our initial intuition. Due to space limitation, the experimental details are left for the full paper.

4. CONCLUDING REMARKS

Recently, multicore processors and software development for multicore systems have been receiving increasing attention from the research community. Particularly, the design of an effective scheduler for multicore systems is getting renewed interest. The contribution in this paper is related to design, implementation, and study of multicore schedulers. It has two main contributions: (i) the design and implementation of a flexible multicore scheduler simulation framework; and (ii) the illustration of the power and flexibility of the proposed framework by simulating the scheduling algorithms of Linux and Solaris operating systems.

The proposed simulator can be used for rapid simulation studies of multicore scheduling algorithms, and that can provide initial insights on how the proposed algorithm will perform in practical multicore systems. These insights will be helpful, not only in testing the performance of the proposed algorithm, but also to identify the bottlenecks and offer guidelines for improvements. Also, from our experience, we believe that the simulator can be used to develop new scheduling algorithms by experimenting and identifying the limitations of the existing algorithms.

The proposed scheduling framework for multicore systems is an important first step in the performance study of multicore scheduling algorithms. The implementation of this framework is under progress and we are expecting to have a fully functional and flexible simulator soon.

5. REFERENCES

[1] *AMD Developer Central. AMD SimNow Simulator, http://developer.amd.com/tools/simnow/pages/default.aspx.*

[2] Eduardo Argollo, Ayose Falcón, Paolo Faraboschi, Matteo Monchiero, and Daniel Ortega. Cotson: infrastructure for full system simulation. *SIGOPS Operating System Review*, 43(1):52–61, January 2009.

[3] Sergey Blagodurov, Sergey Zhuravlev, and Alexandra Fedorova. Contention-aware scheduling on multicore systems. *ACM Transactions on Computer Systems*, 28:8:1–8:45, December 2010.

[4] Doug Burger and Todd M. Austin. The simplescalar tool set, version 2.0. Technical report, 1997.

[5] John M. Calandrino, Dan P. Baumberger, Tong Li, Jessica C. Young, and Scott Hahn. Linsched: The linux scheduler simulator. In J. Jacob and Dimitrios N. Serpanos, editors, *ISCA PDCCS*, pages 171–176. ISCA, 2008.

[6] Gheorghita Ghinea and Sherry Chen. Perceived quality of multimedia educational content: A cognitive style approach. *Multimedia Systems*, 11:271–279, 2006. 10.1007/s00530-005-0007-8.

[7] Sibsankar Haldar and Alex Aravind. *Operating Systems*. Pearson Education, 2010.

[8] F. Ryan Johnson, Radu Stoica, Anastasia Ailamaki, and Todd C. Mowry. Decoupling contention management from scheduling. In *Proceedings of the fifteenth edition of ASPLOS on Architectural support for programming languages and operating systems*, ASPLOS '10, pages 117–128, New York, NY, USA, 2010. ACM.

[9] P.S. Magnusson, M. Christensson, J. Eskilson, D. Forsgren, G. Hallberg, J. Hogberg, F. Larsson, A. Moestedt, and B. Werner. Simics: A full system simulation platform. *Computer*, 35(2):50 –58, feb 2002.

[10] Jeffrey C. Mogul, Andrew Baumann, Timothy Roscoe, and Livio Soares. Mind the gap: reconnecting architecture and os research. In *Proceedings of the 13th USENIX conference on Hot topics in operating systems*, HotOS'13, pages 1–1, Berkeley, CA, USA, 2011. USENIX Association.

[11] M. Moudgill, P. Bose, and J.H. Moreno. Validation of turandot, a fast processor model for microarchitecture exploration. In *Performance, Computing and Communications Conference, 1999 IEEE International*, pages 451 –457, feb 1999.

[12] Mendel Rosenblum, Edouard Bugnion, Scott Devine, and Stephen A. Herrod. Using the simos machine simulator to study complex computer systems. *ACM Trans. Model. Comput. Simul.*, 7(1):78–103, January 1997.

[13] Abraham Silberschatz, Peter Baer Galvin, and Gereg Gagne. *Operating System Concepts,*. John Wiley & Sons, Inc., 2010.

[14] Lingjia Tang, Jason Mars, and Mary Lou Soffa. Contentiousness vs. sensitivity: improving contention aware runtime systems on multicore architectures. In *Proceedings of the 1st International Workshop on Adaptive Self-Tuning Computing Systems for the Exaflop Era (co-located with PLDI 2011)*, pages 12–21, New York, NY, USA, 2011. ACM.

[15] David Wentzlaff and Anant Agarwal. Factored operating systems (fos): the case for a scalable operating system for multicores. *SIGOPS Operating System Review*, 43:76–85, April 2009.

[16] David Wentzlaff, Charles Gruenwald III, Nathan Beckmann, Adam Belay, Harshad Kasture, Kevin Modzelewski, Lamia Youseff, Jason E. Miller, and Anant Agarwal. Fleets: Scalable services in a factored operating system. Technical report, CSAIL Massachusetts Institute of Technology, 2011.

[17] David Wentzlaff, Charles Gruenwald III, Nathan Beckmann, Kevin Modzelewski, Adam Belay, Lamia Youseff, Jason Miller, and Anant Agarwal. A unified operating system for clouds and manycore: fos. *1st Workshop on Computer Architecture and Operating System co-design (CAOS)*, 2010.

[18] Sergey Zhuravlev, Sergey Blagodurov, and Alexandra Fedorova. Akula: a toolset for experimenting and developing thread placement algorithms on multicore systems. In *Proceedings of the 19th international conference on Parallel architectures and compilation techniques*, PACT '10, pages 249–260, New York, NY, USA, 2010. ACM.

[19] Sergey Zhuravlev, Juan Carlos Saez, Alexandra Fedorova, and Manuel Prieto. Survey of scheduling techniques for addressing shared resources in multicore processors. *ACM Computing Surveys*, 45(1), 2012.

TerraME HPA: Parallel Simulation of Multi-Agent Systems over SMPs

Work in Progress Paper

Saulo H. C. Silva, Tiago G. de S. Carneiro, Joubert de C. Lima and Rodrigo R. Pereira
Federal University of Ouro Preto
{saulo.henrique.cabral, tiagogsc, joubertlima, rreisp}@gmail.com

ABSTRACT

Construction of prognoses about environmental changes demands simulations of massive multi-agent models. This work evaluates the hypothesis that the combined use of techniques such as annotation and bag of tasks can result in flexible and scalable platforms for multi-agent simulation. Although these are well known techniques, most environmental modeling platforms use other approaches to provide high performance computing. In general, the approach used is dependent of the modeling paradigm theses platforms implement. We are looking for approaches that can cope with multiple modeling paradigms. To evaluate our hypothesis, the TerraME modeling platform was extended to run over SMPs (Symmetric Multiprocessors) architectures and used in real case studies. While annotation allows modelers to implement different parallelization strategies without prevent models to run over sequential architectures, the bag of tasks provides load balancing over multiprocessors. The results demonstrated that 35% of linear speedup can be obtained for models with high dependence among tasks, when 8 processors are used. Moreover, for models that have low data or control dependencies, around 90% of linear speedup can be obtained.

Categories and Subject Descriptors

I.6.7 [**Simulation Support Systems**]: Performance and scalability of multi-agent simulation environment – Design, studies and measurement.

Keywords

Spatio-temporal, Simulation, Parallel, Multi-Agent, TerraME.

1. INTRODUCTION

The construction of prognoses about environmental changes demands simulation of massive multi-agent models. In this context, MASON [6,9,10] and Repast [4,5] platforms for agent based modeling stand out for offering parallel modeling as an alternative solution to both data intensive and high performance computing.

Control and data dependencies, imposed by the application domain, turn the automated model parallelization a challenge. Moreover, the scalability of a parallel model is determined by many variables, including the partitioning strategy that, in general, depends on the modeling paradigm used, among them: Systems Theory, Agents Theory, and Cellular Automata Theory. This way, there is a big counterpart between model performance and parallelization transparency when we develop parallel models. The less the modeler needs to deal with problems like partitioning, concurrency control, or processes synchronization and communication, in general, less will be the performance gain. Balancing performance requirements and programming simplicity is a relevant challenge, since modelers are, generally, experts in the application domain with low programming skills. In general, modelers are environmentalists, geologists, anthropologists, etc.

This work evaluates the hypothesis that the use of annotation technique for parallel model programming together with a bag-of-task technique for load balancing results on a multi-agent modeling platform with high flexibility and scalability. For this, the environmental modeling platform TerraME was extended to be efficiently executed over symmetric multiprocessors systems – SMPs, i.e., hardware architectures in which several processors share a single memory system and a single Operating System instance. We conduct experiments to analyze TerraME HPA *(High Performance Architecture)* platform performance. Results demonstrated that TerraME HPA is scalable and provides a simple application programming interface (API), enabling TerraME models portability from sequential to SMP architectures. TerraME HPA platform obtained 35% of linear *speedup* when simulates TROLL [3], an individual based model that has large sequential pieces and simulates tropical rainforest growth in 3D spaces. We also test TerraME HPA platform with low dependency models. It obtained 90.7% of linear *speedup* simulating a spatial version of prey-predator model. In TerraME HPA the modeler easily defines segments of code that have to be executed in parallel, synchronization barriers, and critical sections in which shared resources can be correctly accessed.

The remainder of this article is organized as follows: TerraME environmental modeling platform is presented in section 2. Section 3 qualitatively compares TerraME HPA approach with MASON and Repast, two promising multi-agent platforms for spatiotemporal simulation. In section 4, both TerraME HPA architecture and experiments are detailed. Section 5 presents the results of experiments. Section 6 presents the final remarks.

2. TerraME

TerraME [2] is a platform to develop dynamic spatially-explicit models which integrates multiple modeling paradigms, including agent based. In TerraME, environmental phenomena are represented by *Environment* objects. Environments can be considered micro-worlds. The landscape of an environment is defined by *CellularSpace* objects, that is, irregular grid of cells where cells may have several attributes: Land use, altimetry, temperature, etc. Actors and change processes are represented by *Agent* and *Automaton* objects embedded in the *Environment*. An *Environment* can have many *Timer* objects too. Each *Timer* is a discrete event scheduler that determines the instant in which the *Agent* and *Automaton* objects will be executed. At each event, Agent and Automaton objects percept changes in the *Environment* and react on it, changing it and themselves. A complex phenomenon can be represented by an hierarchy of *Environment* objects, in which lower level modules implements some specific properties of the phenomenon and are coordinated by higher level modules. These ideas are illustrated in Figure 1.

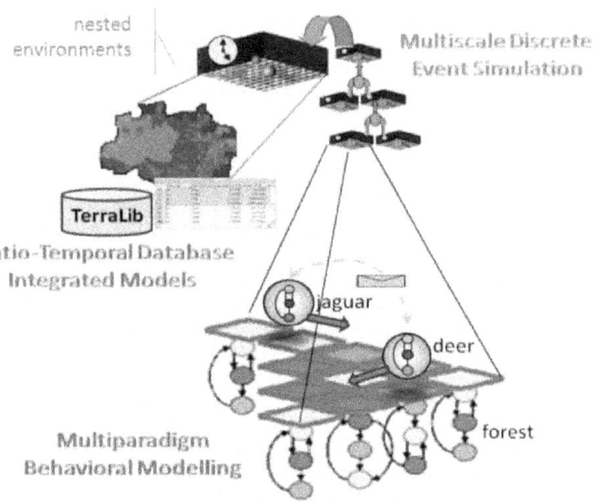

Figure 1: TerraME hierarchical concepts

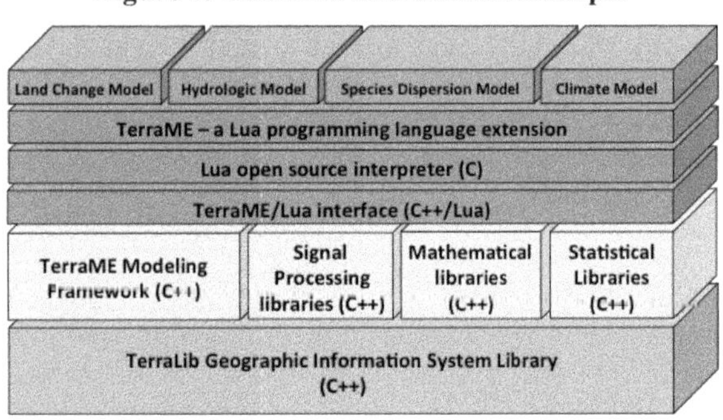

Figure 2. TerraME architecture [2]

Figure 2 illustrates TerraME tiered architecture. The user models are located on the first tier. They are written in a high level programming language named TerraML (TerraME Modeling Language), which extends Lua script language [8] with new data types. Each TerraML model instruction is interpreted by TerraME interpreter, located at second tier. It calls services of TerraME simulation engine located at the third tier. TerraME interpreter and simulation components are implemented in C++. They use TerraLib C++ library [1] to access geographic databases.

3. RELATED WORK

Although there are many agent based modeling platforms, including the pioneer Swarm [12] and the highest-level Netlogo [14], MASON [9,10] and Repast [4,5] are the most prominent high performance agent based modeling platforms used for environmental modeling. JDevs [7] is the only modeling framework that allows a wide range of modeling paradigms be expressed in the DEVS formalism. However, it does not provide a implementation for high performance computing.

The sequential version of the Repast toolkit can be programmed in Java. However, the Repast HPC is complete novel version of Repast specially designed for taking advantage of distributed memory hardware architectures. It was implemented in C++ over the MPI (Message Passing Interface) middleware, obligating modelers to explicit write senders, receivers and messages. There is no specific version for shared memory hardware architecture. This approach fits well into multicomputer architectures. However, in multicore machines and sometimes also over SMPs, MPIs implementations impose an overhead. The overhead is generated by the marshaling of message parameters and by the transmission of messages through network protocol stacks [13]. Fortunately, messages are not necessary in a shared memory system, so the use of MPI over SMPs can be unnecessary. In general, message passing based applications are more complex to be coded than shared address based applications.

Repast uses a master discrete event scheduler to iterate the simulation forward. It coordinates local schedulers spread among MPI processes. Each process is responsible for the execution of local agents. Local schedulers only execute events according to the lowest clock tick (interval between consecutive events) in the simulation. Copies of non-local agents may reside on a process, allowing agents to be shared across processes. Local agents can then interact with these copies. Processes are automatically synchronized when they require copies of agents from another process. However, in order to allow automatic synchronization, the modeler must provide the agent serialization and deserialization code.

MASON platform is developed in Java and provides a hybrid solution that can take advantage of distributed and shared memory hardware architectures. In MASON, a master process coordinates several worker processes located on different processors. The master divides the space inhabited by agents in several regions and each one is assigned to a worker. Each worker process has a discrete event scheduler that simultaneously runs agents that inhabit a particular region. In order to assure coherent computations, all communications with agents in neighbor regions (processors) are simulated before the execution of agents inside a region and the simulation is automatically synchronized at each time step. Thus, modelers have no worries about the coherency of computations. However, if several agents move to a single region, MASON may suffer from the imbalance of workload in different processors. Moreover, the number of worker processes in the simulation needs to be manually defined by the modeler. This fact can be a drawback because if the modeler defines more workers than the number of processors available in the hardware, the whole simulation performance may decrease due to workload imbalance or due to processes management overhead.

4. TerraME HPA approach

In order to allow the parallelization of models that use multiples modeling paradigm, TerraME HPA has been designed as a TerraML middleware, which is not dependent on TerraME specific data types and is capable of parallelize any TerraML (Lua) function. Decisions about problem partitioning, processes synchronization and concurrency control are left to the modeler. This approach can make model parallelization harder, but allows modelers fit parallelization strategies in order to achieve maximum performance.

TerraME HPA provide an API that allows modelers to define which functions should be run in parallel, barriers of synchronization, and critical sections. This API is provided in the form of annotations, i.e., structured comments that are inserted in the model source code. Thus, the annotated model source code can also run in a sequential version of TerraME, facilitating model verification. Before interpreting and executing a model, TerraME HPA automatically translates the annotated version of the model source code into a parallel version with explicit calls to TerraME HPA parallelization services. Then, the model is interpreted by the parallel version of TerraML (Lua) interpreter developed in this work.

Once parallel functions are called inside a model, they are instantiated and go to a bag of tasks waiting to be executed, and the model resumes its execution. This way, parallel functions are executed asynchronously by TerraME HPA threads named *workers*. In order to balance the workload among the hardware processors, TerraME HPA keeps a worker thread by processor, which continuously consumes parallel function from the shared bag of tasks. Thus, TerraME HPA attempts to ensure maximum utilization of available processors.

For while, TerraME HPA only provides services for parallel execution of functions over shared memory hardware architectures. A version for distributed memory hardware architectures is still under development.

4.1 TerraME HPA programming interface

The following methods are implemented in the TerraME HPA parallel application programming interface:

- HPA PARALLEL: Tells the interpreter that the next function found in the source code should be executed in parallel.
- HPA JOIN *Fx*: Defines a synchronization barrier, i.e., waits until all instances of the function *Fx* finish running.
- HPA JOINALL: Defines a synchronization barrier, i.e., waits all instances of parallel functions finish running.
- HPA ACQUIRE *Gl*: Sets the entry point of a critical section named *Gl* in order to ensure mutual exclusion inside the critical section. Just one parallel function get inside *Gl* until a release call is found.
- HPA RELEASE *Gl*: Indicates the end of a critical section, releases the access to the critical section *Gl*

4.2 Annotations: A flexible strategy

Annotations are structured comments in which methods of the TerraME HPA parallel API are called. Figure 3 illustrates an agent based model simulating preys and predators embedded in a *closed environment*. They are located in a unique *Cell* of a CellularSpace and can move to another during the simulation. Each predator can attack a prey using the *ag.attack(ag1)* method call, in which variables *ag* and *ag1* are predator and prey agents, respectively. During an attack, predators seek for preys in neighbor cells. If they find a prey they kill it and move to its Cell. Otherwise, they stay in the same place. Preys move randomly through empty cells.

In Figure 3, functions *execAgentPred* and *execAgentPrey* responsible for executing an given agent. Then, the model iterates over a set of agents and execute them concurrently. There are two synchronization barriers to wait all agents to finish one simulation step. Predators are always simulated before preys. The *forEachNeighbor* function iterates over cells in neighborhood of the *Cell* received as its first parameter. At each neighbor cell, it applies the function received as its second parameter. The *forEachAgent* function iterates over agents embedded in the *Cell* received as its first parameter applying the function received as its second parameter. The ag:*getLocation*() function returns the *Cell* where the agent *ag* is inserted. The command *cs = CellularSpace{ xdim = DIMENSION }* creates a squared grid of DIMENSION x DIMENSION cells, where DIMENSION is a integer constant.

```
predator = function()
    ag = {energy = 20, type = "predator"}
    ag.execute = function(self, ag1)
        attack();
    end
    ag.attack = function(self, ag1)
        forEachNeighbor(self:getLocation(), function(cell, neigh)
            forEachAgent(neigh, function(ag1)
                if ag1.type == "prey" then
                    ..DO SOMETHING TO KILL AND MOVE..
                end
            end)
        end)
    end
    ag.class = "predatores";
    ag.state = State{ id = "hunting" }
    return Agent(ag)
end
cs = CellularSpace{xdim = DIMENSION}
predatores = {}
for i = 1, POPUL_PREDATOR do
    ag = predator();  cell = cs:sample()
    ag:enter(cell);  table.insert(predatores, ag)
end

function execAgentPred(i)
    predatores[i]:execute()
end
function execAgentPrey(i)
    preys[i]:execute()
end

for i = 1, #predatores do
    --HPA PARALLEL
    execAgentPred(i)
end
--HPA JOINALL
for i = 1, #preys do
    --HPA PARALLEL
    execAgentPrey(i)
end
--HPA JOINALL
```

Figure 3: Prey-predator agent based model in TerraML.

4.3 Bag of tasks: As load balance strategy

Most modeling platform are based on a unique modeling paradigm, allowing simulation engine architects to make several design decision about parallelization, communication and synchronization strategies. This way, most tasks involved in the development of parallel models are treated transparently by the simulation engine. For instance, in agent based modeling platform, agent computations usually depends on properties of the area where they are located. So for problem partitioning purpose, it is common to divide the data structure representing the space into several regions and assign each region to a different processor. Consequently, a processor is responsible for simulating all agents inserted into its region. And therefore, the concentration of agents in a certain region may cause imbalance in the system workload.

As stated before, TerraME aims to support the simultaneous use of several modeling paradigm for the development of a unique model. This is a important requirement for integrated environmental modeling, once no modeling paradigm alone is able to represent all the complexity found in Terrestrial phenomena: Land use and cover change, global change, disease spreading, fire propagation, etc. So, a higher level of abstraction is necessary to conceive a simulation engine capable to concurrently run models based on multiple paradigms. For this reason the TerraME HPA has been developed as a TerraML (Lua) parallel middleware, i.e., a TerraML interpreter that is capable to run functions in parallel and control concurrent access to shared variables. This new interpreter has been implemented in C programming language and replaces the Lua interpreter in the TerraME tiered architecture, Figure 2.

In opposition to Lua interpreter that keeps only one execution stack in which all computation are performed, TerraME HPA keeps track of several execution stacks. The model has a main execution stack where shared variable are stored and each parallel function has its own execution stack where local variable are stored. Concurrent accesses to the main stack are transparently controlled by TerraME HPA interpreter that ensures mutual exclusion and atomicity to the operations. This way, TerraME HPA assures the coherency of computations over shared variables.

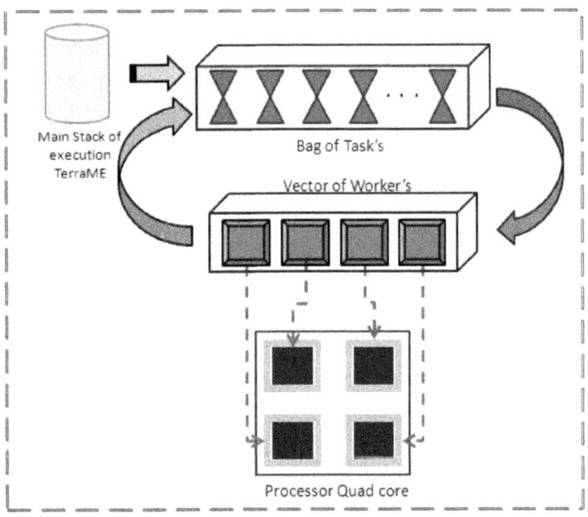

Figure 4: TerraME HPA parallelization mechanism.

When TerraME HPA interpreter starts, it creates a global data structure named bag-of-task in which parallel functions are temporally stored waiting to be executed. Also, it automatically identifies the number of available processors and starts one C++ thread by processor, avoiding a profusion of threads in the system whose exceeding context swap might slowdown model runtime. These threads are named *workers* and are responsible for continuously consume parallel functions from the bag-of-tasks, executing them one after the other, in a attempt to maintain the processors utilization near to 100% and keep the workload balanced. Figure 4 illustrate the TerraME HPA parallel architecture.

When a parallel function is called, it is instantiated and is inserted in the bag-of-tasks data structure. The interpreter collects its name, creates its local execution stack, pushes the arguments in the stack and saves the main stack address for the function returning value. Then, the model immediately resumes its execution. This way, TerraME HPA implements a asynchronous model of concurrency. In order to gather the correct result from the calling of a parallel function, the modeler must implement a synchronization barrier for waiting the end of its computation.

4.4 Agent communication

Although agents can communicate through the exchange of logical messages, the communication is implemented through shared variable. This mechanism is simple to the modeler and avoids the marshaling of message parameters and the transmission of messages through inter-process communication channels or networks protocols.

4.5 Critical Sections

Critical sections can be coded by the modelers at any granularity. A single variable or a collection of variables can be locked. Figures 5 and 6 show some snippets of the TROLL forest growth model. They illustrate how to implement coarse and fine grained critical sections in TerraME HPA. Figure 5 indicates that the interpreter will acquire the entire *summaryTable* shared variable when HPA ACQUIRE annotation will be executed. The variable *summaryTable* is a two-dimensional table that stores a integer number at each position. In contrast, Figure 6 illustrates a more efficient *summaryTable* access. Variable *lockOnePosition* indicates the finest lock granularity. Only the element in the position [cell.specie][MORTALITY_SUM_IDX] will be locked.

For each HPA ACQUIRE annotation, TerraME HPA interpreter inserts a new lock in a map of model variables. Each worker thread points to a shared map of variables. If a shared variable is acquired, the current worker waits until a notification occurs, indicating the global variable is released. This wait/notify mechanism avoids busy-waiting in TerraME HPA.

```
--example where block all positions of variable summaryTable
local lockAllPositions = "summaryTable"

--HPA ACQUIRE lockAllPositions
summaryTable[cell.specie][MORTALITY_SUM_IDX] =
summaryTable[cell.specie][MORTALITY_SUM_IDX] + 1;
--HPA RELEASE lockAllPositions
```

Figure 5: Coarse lock

```
--example where block just one position of variable summaryTable
local lockOnePosition = "summaryTable"..cell.specie..MORTALITY_SUM_IDX

--HPA ACQUIRE lockOnePosition
summaryTable[cell.specie][MORTALITY_SUM_IDX] =
summaryTable[cell.specie][MORTALITY_SUM_IDX] + 1;
--HPA RELEASE lockOnePosition
```

Figure 6: Fine lock

5. EXPERIMENTS

Two multi-agent models were used in the performance analysis experiments. In first experiment, a model with no task dependencies simulates an *Environment* formed by isolated cells in which prey-predator populations evolve with no influences of neighbor populations. This way, the modeler computes all predators in parallel firstly and then all preys in parallel. At each simulation step, there are two synchronization barriers: one to wait predators computations and a second to wait preys computations. The prey-predator implementation avoids simultaneous prey-predator executions, so it avoids costly synchronizations during a unique simulation step. Figure 3 illustrates the main part of prey-predator model in TerraML.

In the second experiment, a complex model with several synchronization points and a global variable is simulated. A *CellularSpace* is shared by *Agent* objects, which simulates the forest growth process in three dimensions. The TROLL model considers that in the interior of tropical rain forests individual trees compete for the available light shadowing each other. Therefore, the computations on a 3D cell depend on the neighbor trees [3]. In both experiments, the shared *CellularSpace* was split into several logical sub-spaces embedded into nested *Environment* objects. *Environments* were simulated concurrently.

Figure 7 illustrates the costly synchronization point of TROLL model. The function *calcLeafAreaIndex* is responsible for calculating the index of leaf area in a cell. Unfortunately, the computation of this index depends on the value of leaf area index of the neighbor cells. A partition strategy to avoid too many synchronizations can be based on height-layers. The computation is concurrently executed from the top of the forest to the bottom, the layer L1 (highest) is computed, then TerraME HPA synchronizes, then a second layer L2 is processed, then a second synchronization occurs, and so on.

```
function calcLeafAreaIndex_( p, vertical )
    --vertical parameter indicates if the forest this tilted

    if ( vertical ) then

        --[[the upper layers depend on the values of the lower
        layers is thus necessary to parallelize by layers]]
        for h, layer in ipairs(csTable) do

            --calculates to all cells in layer
            for idCell = 1, #layer.cells do
                --HPA PARALLEL
                calcLeafAreaIndex_1(p,idCell,h)
            end
            --HPA JOIN calcLeafAreaIndex_1
        end
    else
        for h, layer in ipairs(csTable) do

            for idCell = 1, #layer.cells do
                --HPA PARALLEL
                calcLeafAreaIndex_2(p,idCell,h)
            end
            --HPA JOIN calcLeafAreaIndex_2
        end
    end
end
```

Figure 7. Function *calcLeafAreaIndex* of model TROLL

The main reason to implement two models in experiments, one with low dependencies and other with high dependencies, is to illustrate that TerraME scales according to the modeler implementation. Efficient partition strategies, with few synchronizations and few serial code are always desired, but not often obtained.

Experiments were performed on a machine with OS Windows Server 2003 64-bit with 16 GB RAM DDR2 667 MHz and 2 Intel Xeon processors, summing 8 cores. Each experiment was executed 5-10 times, depending on its size. The runtime variance is calculated and then the speedup of each model experiment is calculated. The results are presented in the next section.

6. RESULTS

Figure 8 presents the reduction of simulation time for the prey-predator model. The use of two cores reduces the time by half. With 8 cores, the simulation time almost reaches the asymptotic lower bound. The parallel model scales very well, presenting 90.7% of linear speedup compared with the sequential model version.

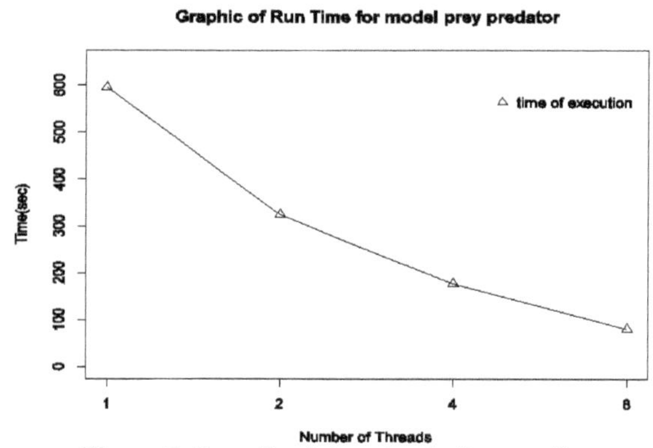

Figure 8. Prey-Predator simulation runtime

Figure 9 presents the reduction of simulation time for TROLL model. The use of two cores reduces the time by 35%. However, as the number of threads increases the concurrence also increases and the synchronization points become the bottleneck of the solution. Simulations with eight processors achieve speedup of only three. Nonetheless, it is out of scope of this paper to discuss new solutions for parallel implementations of TROLL.

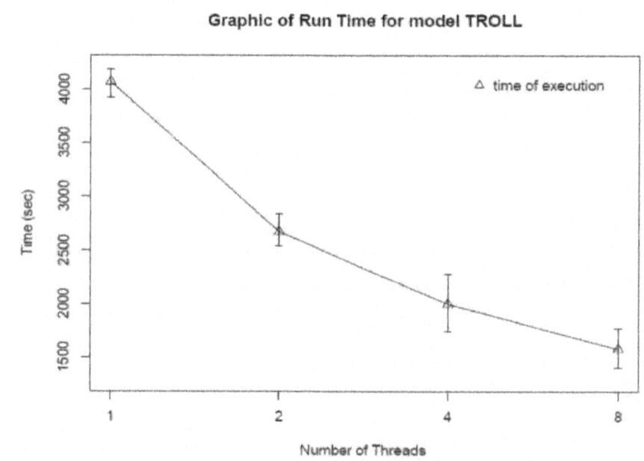

Figure 9. TROLL simulation runtime

Figure 10 shows that TerraME HPA can deliver scalability to multi-agent models, with low overhead in concurrency management. While the runtime of the sequential prey-predator model presents an exponential growth as the number of agents increases, the runtime of the parallel model presents a very slow growth.

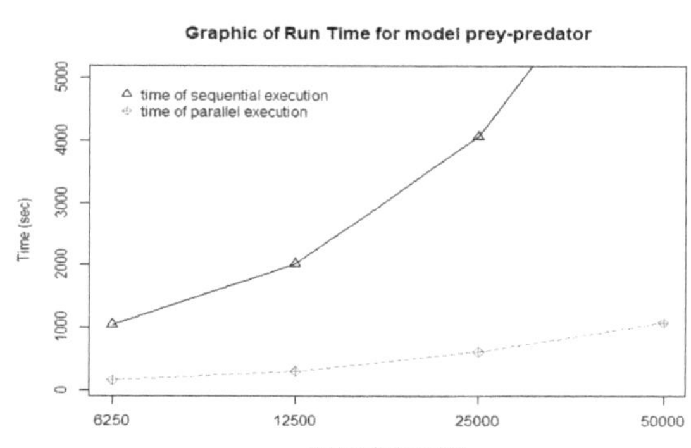

Figure 10. Prey-Predator scalability

Figure 11 shows the increasing of memory consumption as the number of prey and predator agents grows. TerraME HPA imposes a small overhead in terms of memory consumption when compared with the sequential version of TerraME. In this case, the parallel simulation was conducted with 8 worker threads. During the simulation, the average utilization of 8 available processors was 95.667%.

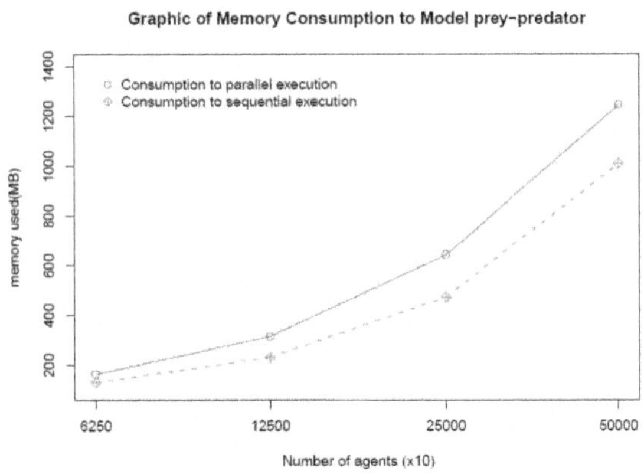

Figure 11. Prey-Predator memory consumption

7. FINAL REMARKS

The results demonstrated that the annotation technique allows modelers define model parallelization granularity and strategy without preventing that the model source code could be executed by sequential machines. Verification, debugging and validation of sequential models on sequential machines is easier than on parallel ones. Modeler has freedom to take most advantage of SMP architectures, i.e., a simple shared address space. However, the approach provides no transparency on parallelization problems and decisions

Multi modeling paradigms are addressed by TerraME HPA flexible design. Our experiments demonstrate that TerraME scales well when the modeler designs efficient parallel solutions.

The bag-of-task technique is useful for load balance among multiple processors. There is no saturation in the number of workers and they keep working task after task. Unfortunately, one task can be harder to compute then others, but for TerraME HPA they have equal priorities, so their balanced CPU usage depends only on the model design.

The results obtained by the proposed approach in multi-agent experiments can be extended to models based on other modeling paradigms, as General System Theory and Cellular Automata Theory. TROLL experiment demonstrates that TerraME is useful to real case studies. TROLL experiment also showed that very often real problems are hard to be partitioned. The first parallel and open source TROLL version can be tested against new parallel alternatives. Huge instances of TROLL can now be simulated using TerraME, opening new perspectives for better understanding tropical forests growth.

Future works include the development of solutions for distributed memory hardware architectures and GPU devices. Tests with some Operating Systems that offer SMP capabilities over multicomputer architectures are part of our actual work. We just started tests with *kerrighed* [11]. It is also necessary to develop new experiments to compare the performance and scalability of TerraME HPA with the performance and scalability of other modeling platforms.

8. ACKNOWLEDGMENTS

This work was partially funded by CAPES, CNPq (CTINFO 09/2010) and UFOP.

9. REFERENCES

[1] Câmara G., Vinhas L., et.al. TerraLib: An Open Source GIS Library for Large-Scale Environmental and Socio-Economic Applications, Open Source Approaches in Spatial Data Handling, pages 247–270. 2008.

[2] Carneiro, T. G. S. *Nested-CA: A foundation for multiscale modeling of land use and land change.* phd thesis in computer science, The National Institute for Space Research, Brazil, 2006.

[3] Chave, J. *Study of structural, sucessional and spatial patterns in tropical rain forest using troll, a spatially explicit forest model.* Ecological Modeling, 1999.

[4] Collier N. *Repast HPC Manual.* Argonne National Laboratory, Argone, IL, USA, 2012.

[5] Collier N. and North M., *Repast HPC: A platform for Large-Scale Agent-Based Modeling.* Computing Techniques for Complex System Simulation, November 29, 2011. ISBN-13: 978-0470592441.

[6] Cordasco G., Chiara D. R., et al. *A Framework for distributing Agent-based simulations.* EURO PAR 2011: PARALLEL PROCESSING WORKSHOPS, Lecture Notes in Computer Science, 2012, Volume: 7155/2012, 460-470, DOI: 10.1007/978-3-642-29737-3_51.

[7] Filippi, J., and Bisgambiglia, P.. JDEVS: an implementation of a DEVS based formal framework for environmental modelling. Environmental Modelling and Software 19(3) 261-274. 2004.

[8] Ierusalimschy, R, *Programming in Lua*, Lua.Org, ISBN 85-903798-1-7. 2003.

[9] Luke S. *Multiagent Simulation And the MASON Library.* George Mason University, First Edition, August, 2011.

[10] Luke S., Cioffi-Revilla C., et al., *MASON: A New Multi-Agent Simulation Toolkit.* Proceedings of the 2004 Swarmfest Workshop. 2004.

[11] Lottiaux, R. ; Vallee, G. ; et al., Kerrighed and data parallelism: cluster computing on single system image operating systems. Proceedings of the International Conference on Cluster Computing, 2004.

[12] Minar, N., Burkhart, R., Langton, C., Askenazi , M.,. The Swarm Simulation System: A Toolkit for Building Multi-Agent Simulation. SFI Working Paper 96-06-042. 1996.

[13] Shahid Hussain and Hassan Shabbir. *Directory scalability in multi-agent based systems.* Master's thesis in Science in Software Engineering, School of Engineering at Blekinge Institute of Technology.2008

[14] Tisue, S., and Wilensky, U.. *NetLogo: A Simple Environment for Modeling Complexity*, International Conference on Complex Systems: Boston. 2004.

An Expansion-aided Synchronous Conservative Time Management Algorithm on GPU

Work in Progress Paper

Tang Wenjie
School of Computer, National University of Defense Technology
137 Yanwachi, Changsha, Hunan, 410073, P.R.China
tangwenjie@nudt.edu.cn

Yao Yiping
School of Information System and Management, National University of Defense Technology
137 Yanwachi, Changsha, Hunan, 410073, P.R.China
ypyao@nudt.edu.cn

Zhu Feng
School of Computer, National University of Defense Technology
137 Yanwachi, Changsha, Hunan, 410073, P.R.China
zhufeng@nudt.edu.cn

ABSTRACT
The graphic processing unit (GPU) brings an opportunity to implement large scale simulations in an economical way. GPU's performance relies on high parallelism, but using synchronous conservative time management algorithm for discrete event simulation will meet the scenarios with limited parallelism. This conflict leads to bad performance even though the application itself has high parallelism. To solve this problem, we propose an expansion-aided synchronous conservative time management algorithm. It uses runtime information to enlarge the time bound of "safe" events, and uses an expansion method to import "safe" events. By interleaving a series of expansions with event computation, more events can be assembled to be processed in parallel. Moreover, a simulated annealing algorithm is adopted to control the number of expansions. It helps achieve stable performance under different conditions by finding a balance between low parallelism and unnecessary expansions. Experiments demonstrate that the proposed algorithm can achieve up to a 30% performance improvement.

Categories and Subject Descriptors
I.6.8 **[Simulation and Modeling]:** Types of Simulation—Parallel; Discrete event; C.1.2 **[Processor Architectures]**: Multiple Data Stream Architectures (Multiprocessors)—Single-instruction-stream, multiple-data-stream processors (SIMD)

Keywords
GPU; parallel discrete event simulation; conservative time management; Simulated Annealing;

1. INTRODUCTION
Modeling and simulation is an important approach to research complex systems. With the growing complexity of models, sequential simulation cannot obtain analytical results in acceptable time. Parallel and distributed simulation is a main solution to this problem [1]. Most current parallel and distributed methods are based on multiple instruction, multiple data (MIMD) machines. In other words, they are running on CPU-based high performance computing environment. Recently, the graphics processing unit has become an increasingly attractive architecture for solving compute-intensive problems for general purpose computation because of its increased computation power and relatively low cost. With newly emerged NVIDIA's compute unified device architecture (CUDA) [2], GPU has already expanded its application field from graphic community to scientific computing community. As a high performance-cost ratio parallel processor, the GPU can be viewed as a substitute for expensive clusters of workstations in a parallel simulation, at a relatively low cost [3]. In domain of simulation, some time-stepped simulations have been successfully accelerated by GPU [4].

However, harnessing the power of the GPU on discrete event simulation is relatively difficult. In previous work, some researchers [5][6][7] have implemented the synchronous conservative time management (SCTM) algorithm on GPU to control advance of simulation. Since GPU has hundreds of parallel processing units, its performance relies on high degree of parallelism to make it be fully utilized. However, traditional SCTM algorithm meets the problem of overly pessimistic in some scenarios, thereby the number of events can be processed in parallel is limited. This conflict leads to bad performance even though the application itself has high degree of parallelism. To solve this problem, we design an expansion method to increase the event parallelism (defined as the average number of events can be processed in parallel). It uses runtime information to enlarge the time bound of "safe" events and inserts a series of expansions to import "safe" events, thereby more events can be assembled together to be processed in parallel. We also prove the validity of the expansion-aided method.

Considering that the event parallelism is only a heuristic and the performance is also affected by other factors, the expansion method cannot guarantee the performance improvement always happens. Moreover, if the SCTM algorithm has already performed well so that there is little space to increase event parallelism, the overhead caused by expansion will lead to worse performance. We propose an expansion-aided synchronous conservative time management (ESCTM) algorithm, which interleaves a series of expansions with the procedure of processing event and uses a parameter to control the number of expansions. In addition, a simulated annealing (SA) algorithm is adopted to find suitable value of the parameter. It helps the ESCTM algorithm achieve stable performance under different conditions by finding a balance between low parallelism and unnecessary expansions. Experiment results demonstrate that the ESCTM algorithm can achieve up to a 30% performance improvement comparing to baseline SCTM algorithm on GPU.

The remainder of our paper is organized as follows. Section 2 introduces the background. Section 3 presents some related work. Section 4 describes our method in detail. Section 5 shows the experimental evaluation. Section 6 discusses the conclusion and presents future work.

2. BACKGROUND

2.1 GPU and CUDA

GPU is a massive parallel processor. Take Nvidia's Tesla GPU for example, it consists of a scalable number of streaming multiprocessors (SMs). Each SM contains eight streaming processor (SP) cores, two special function units (SFUs), a multithreaded instruction fetch and issue unit, a read-only constant cache, and a 16KB read/write shared memory [8]. CUDA is a general purpose parallel computing architecture — with a new parallel programming model and instruction set architecture — that leverages the parallel compute engine in NVIDIA GPUs to solve many complex computational problems in a more efficient way than on a CPU [9]. Four factors always need to be considered to develop an efficient CUDA program.

- The performance of GPU relies on thread-level parallelism to maximize utilization of its functional units. First, GPU has more than a hundred streaming processors that can execute different threads in parallel. Second, threads always take some number of clock cycles to be ready to execute its next instruction, and the warp scheduler will selects another warp which is ready to execute to hide the latency.

- When certain access requirements are met, global memory loads and stores by threads of a half warp (for GPU of compute capability 1.x) or of a warp (for GPU of compute capability 2.x) are combined into as few as one transaction. It is called coalesced access. If memory requests are not coalesced, the warp cannot be executed until all memory transactions from the same warp are served. Considering high latency of accessing global memory (400 to 800 clock cycles), it will take significantly longer waiting time than only one memory request.

- Since the warp executing on a SM share a single instruction dispatch unit, all threads in a warp execute in the Single Instruction, Multiple Thread (SIMT) processing paradigm. Any flow control instruction (if, switch, do, for, while) can significantly impact the effective instruction throughput by causing threads of the same warp to diverge (i.e. to follow different execution paths). If this happens, the different execution paths have to be serialized, increasing the total number of instructions executed for this warp. The threads converge back to the same execution path until all the different execution paths have completed.

- The peak bandwidth between the device memory and the GPU is much higher than the peak bandwidth between host memory and device memory. Hence, for best overall application performance, data transfer between CPU and GPU should always be avoided unless it is necessary.

2.2 GPU-based Discrete Event Simulator (gDES)

This section contains some background on gDES which is the simulation environment we use for our experiments. gDES is designed to support discrete event simulation on GPU. It adopts logical process paradigm to implement parallelization: The physical system can be viewed as being composed of some number of physical processes that interact in some fashion. Each physical process is modeled by a logical process (LP), and interactions between physical processes are modeled by exchanging time-stamped messages between corresponding LPs. The computation performed by each logical process is a sequence of event computations, where each computation may modify state variables and/or schedule new events for itself or other LPs. Moreover, considering that GPU is not suitable for all kinds of simulation, it must cooperate with other CPU-based simulator to achieve some complex applications. Its basic data structure of gDES is shown in Fig. 1. As traditional CPU-based simulator, logical process (*G_LP*) and event (*G_SimEvent*) are also the core concepts. However, they are not assembled into the sparse data structures, such as tree and heap. Instead, they are assembled into array-based data structure. All *G_LP* objects are stored in the *LP_Set* and all *G_SimEvent* objects are stored in the *EventPool*. During the simulation, the extracted events that have the same *lpid* will be linked together by variables before and next to construct a double linked list. This list is called event list of the LP (named EL_i if the *lpid* is i). *pending_set* structure is used to manage event list for each LP, and there is one entry per LP in the *pending_set* structure. The arrows in the figure play the same role as pointers in C++, and they are int2 or int3 variables[1] to locate the position in array-based data.

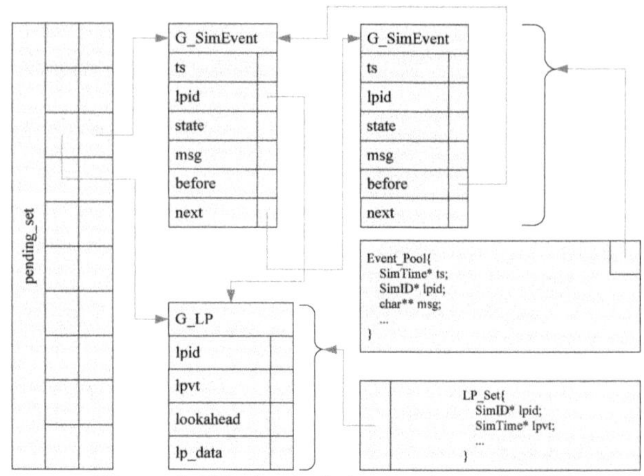

Figure 1. The basic data structure of gDES

3. RELATED WORK

Synchronous conservative time management (SCTM) algorithm moves a window across simulation time, roughly as follows. Let T_{floor} denotes the lower edge of the window, and all events with timestamp less than T_{floor} have already been processed. Let $T_{ceiling}$ denotes the upper window edge. This value is chosen in such a way that all events within $[T_{floor}, T_{ceiling})$ can be safely processed in parallel. In general, we use lookahead to introduce concurrency and avoid deadlock in SCTM algorithm. It refers to the ability of a LP to predict what will happen and what will not happen, in the future. When a LP has a local simulation time of t, it can affect other LP up to t + lookahead. A series of CPU-based SCTM algorithms have been deeply studied both in experimental way and theoretic analysis. Examples include Lubachevskey's bounded lag algorithm [10], Steinman's time bucket algorithm [11], and David Nicol's YAWNS algorithm [12].

---

[1] They are both build-in variables of CUDA

Currently, most time management algorithms implemented in GPU-based discrete event simulation is synchronous approach. In [5], Perumalla has utilized a hybrid method to run a heat diffusion simulation on a GPU. During the simulation, the algorithm selects the minimum event time from the list of update times, and uses it as a time-step to update all elements synchronously. Its event-driven method accelerates simulation and doesn't meet the problem of "limited parallelism", but it introduces unnecessary overhead since not all elements must be updated synchronously in some other simulations. Our approach adopts pure discrete event method, thereby eliminates such overhead. A more related work is from Hyungwook Park and Paul Fishwick. In [6][7], they proposed a time-synchronous/event algorithm to implement a GPU-based discrete event application framework. In their implementation, future event list (FEL) is decomposed into many sub-FELs, so they can be processed by massive threads in parallel. In order to obtain higher concurrence, events are clustered by using time interval. This time rounding technique is essentially a SCTM algorithm if we treat the time interval as the time window. Our approach differs in that we use an expansion method to increase the degree of parallelism further. Georg Kunz et al. [13] propose a parallel discrete event simulation scheme that enables cost- and time-efficient execution of large scale parameter studies on GPUs. The authors explore parallelism from two orthogonal levels, external parallelism among the inherently independent simulations and internal parallelism among independent events within each individual simulation. The method to improve internal parallelism aims to hide latency from data transfer between CPU and GPU. Because our method in this paper focuses on accelerating individual simulation purely on GPU, both of their problems are out of the scope.

4. Algorithm Description

In the following description of algorithm, events have four types of state, including *UnExtracted*, *Pending*, *Candidate* and *Committed.* When an event is created, its state is initialized to *UnExtracted.* After it is linked into an event list, its state will changed to *Pending* or *Candidate*. *Pending* state promises that the event can be processed safely when it is at the head of event list while *Candidate* state cannot guarantee that. Once an event has been processed, it will be removed from event list and its state will be changed to *Committed.* In addition, some related notations are listed in Table 1.

Table 1. Definitions

Name	Reference
ws	Window size, which equals to the maximum number of *Pending* events among all event lists
ELD_i	The set of *Committed* events which is originally in event list i
ELP_i	The set of *Pending* events in event list i
ELC_i	The set of *Candidate* events in event list i
$LTSG_i$	Lowest timestamp of events generated in current window and schedule for LP_i
$LCET_i$	Lowest timestamp of events in EL_i
T_{safe}	Lowest bound that events in event lists can affect
$T_{ceiling}$	The timestamp bound to determine whether events can be extracted

1. **while** $T_{ceiling}$ is less than end time
2. $T_{ceiling}$:= Parallel_UpdateLBTS()
3. EL := Parallel_ExtractEvents($T_{ceiling}$)
4. **for** k := 0 **to** ws
5. **forall** thread i **in parallel do**
6. ELD_i^{k+1} := process(head(ELP_i^k))
7. **endforall**
8. **endfor**
9. **endwhile**

Figure 2. Pseudo code of synchronous conservative TM algorithm on GPU

4.1 An Expansion-aided Synchronous Conservative Time Management Algorithm

Fig.2 illustrates the pseudo code of the baseline SCTM algorithm. After the initial stages of the simulation, it enters into a loop that repeatedly performs the following steps: First, a new value of $T_{ceiling}$ is generated by parallel reduction (line 2). All events, whose timestamp are less than $T_{ceiling}$, are extracted by multiple threads on the GPU (line 3). They are ordered by timestamp in its target LP's event list. Then the algorithm invokes the kernel "ProcessEvents", in which each thread chooses the head event from event list and processes it (line4-7). This kernel must be executed over and over again until all extracted events have been processed. Since we use LBTS (lowest bound on timestamp) as $T_{ceiling}$, which is defined as the timestamp of the earliest event that can be received by the system in the future, there is no *Candidate* state for any event. In this baseline algorithm, we use multiple "small" invocations instead of a single "big" invocation to implement the procedure of processing events. The choice introduces some overhead because it needs to read and write state of LP from global memory multiple times. Since one goal of gDES is to cooperate with other simulators, using "multiple small invocations" method allows for publishing information (both simulation time and system's state) frequently, and the transfer cost can be decreased because message transfer can overlap with event computation.

In DES, events are always distributed irregularly on the axis of virtual time. Hence, the number of events in each EL is different. Using baseline SCTM algorithm will meet the problem of "parallelism decrease". Fig.3 shows an example, the part (a) shows the distribution of events on virtual time of a simulation and the lookahead of each LP is set to 1. When using the baseline SCTM algorithm (part (b)), the number of events can be processed in parallel will decrease after the each invocation of "ProcessEvents". However, the dynamic characteristic of DES makes it difficult to adjust thread grid to adapt different number of events at runtime. So we have to set a fixed size for thread grid which is equal to number of LP, and let threads do idle work if its corresponding LP has no event in its EL. Though launching redundant threads leads little overhead on GPU, the computing resource cannot be fully utilized when the events are not enough. We use EP, short for event parallelism, to describe the mean number of events when invoking kernel "ProcessEvents".

$$EP = \frac{\text{Number of Events}}{\text{Number of Invoaction of "ProcessEvents"}}$$

Take part (b) in Fig.3 for example, EP of baseline SCTM algorithm is equal to 2.5. The baseline SCTM algorithm is too

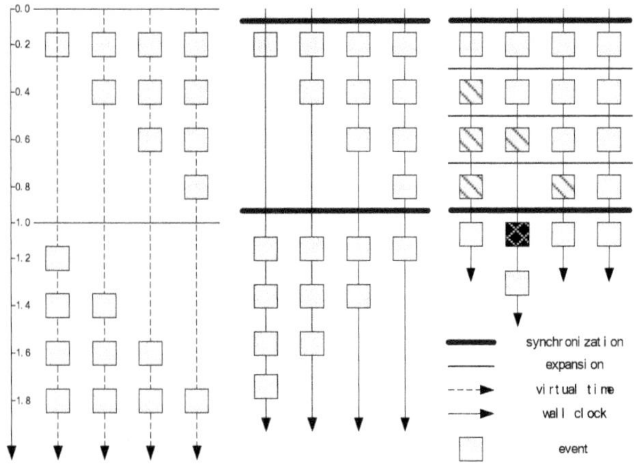

(a) event distribution (b) SCTM algorithm (c) Using expansion method

Figure 3. The event stream using different TM algorithms

pessimistic to obtain high EP. It neglects some newly updated information. In fact, the runtime LBTS has increased after processing some events. Some events, which are not safe before, can be processed safely. Meanwhile, some events are still not safe because their timestamp are greater than some newly events' timestamp. If we can use some expansions to import the "safe" events as many as possible while maintains the causal relationship, a higher EP may be obtained. As shown in part (c), blocks with slash denotes the events imported by expansions. The block with cross denotes the newly generated event which is not included in event list. The expansion method increases the EP to 3.3, about 32% improvement.

Based on such idea, we propose an expansion-aided synchronous conservative time management (ESCTM) algorithm, as shown in Fig.4. After the initial stages of the simulation, it enters into a loop that repeatedly performs the following steps: First, T^0_{safe} is computed as LBTS and $T_{ceiling}$ are generated. Then all events with timestamp less than $T_{ceiling}$ are extracted in parallel by multiple threads on the GPU (line 4). Since $T_{ceiling}$ is greater than LBTS, some events cannot be processed safely even if they have been extracted. These events are marked as *Candidate*, and some of their state may be changed to *Pending* by expansion. After extracting events, the algorithm enters into the stage of processing events (line6-14). Different from SCTM algorithm, expansion and some related operations are introduced. Runtime information, such as LTSG and T_{safe}, are collected to compute time bound, so casual relationship can be maintained when using expansion method. LTSG is updated when a new event is generated (ling9). T_{safe} is computed by parallel reduction on LCET. According to the expansion rule, an event can be expanded if it cannot affected by *Pending* events, no newly generated event to the same LP has a smaller timestamp and it is the first event in the LP's event list. Besides the expansion, ESCTM algorithm also equips with a control parameter α ($0 \le \alpha \le 1$). $ws \times \alpha$ determines the maximum number of expansions in each time window. The algorithm adopts a backward way to do expansion because it can imports most events when the number of expansions is fixed.

```
1.  while T_floor is less than end time
2.    T^0_safe := Parallel_UpdateLBTS()
3.    T_ceiling := LBTS + max{lookahead_i}
4.    EL := Parallel_ExtractEvents(T^0_safe, T_ceiling)
5.    for k := 0 to ws
6.      forall thread i in parallel do
7.        ELD_i^{k+1} := process(head(ELP_i^k))
8.        //if a newly generated event is sent to LP j
9.        AtomicUpdateMin(LTSG_j^k)
10.     endforall
11.     if ws − k < ws × α && k ≠ ws − 1
12.       T^{k+1}_safe := Parallel_Reduction(LCET^k, lookahead)
13.       ELP^{k+1} := Expansion(ELC^k, T^{k+1}_safe, LTSG^k)
14.     endif
15.     k := k + 1
16.   endfor
17. endwhile
```

Expansion rule: Assuming an event ev belongs to LP i, it can be expanded if the following conditions are met: (1) $ts(ev) < T^{k+1}_{safe}$; (2) $ts(ev) < LTSG^k_i$;(2) ev is the first event in EL_i

Figure 4. An expansion-aided synchronous conservative time management algorithm

4.2 Optimization based on Simulated Annealing Algorithm

A further question is how to determine α. As we mentioned before, α is used to control the number of expansions. Specifically, the ESCTM algorithm is equivalent to the baseline SCTM when $\alpha = 0$. Certainly, greater α usually leads to higher event parallelism. But event parallelism is only a heuristic in that we cannot guarantee that overall performance is optimized. The effect of increasing EP depends on the characteristic of applications and usually cannot be modeled by simple functions. Moreover, expansion also introduces some overhead. Hence, if the baseline SCTM algorithm has already performed well and there is little space for increasing event parallelism, such overhead leads to worse performance.

In order to solve this problem, we use the simulated annealing algorithm to find the optimal value of α. Assuming $E: S \to R$ denotes the objective function which needs to be minimized, the SA algorithm starts with an initial solution $s_0 \in S$ and tries to improve the solution by moving to its neighboring solutions. For example, if the current solution is s, the SA algorithm randomly choose a neighboring solution s'. If s' is a better solution, it will be accepted; If s' is a worse solution, it will also be accepted with a probability. This probability-based approach prevents the algorithm from being stuck in a local minima—a state that has a

```
while simulation is not over
  new_rate: = commit_events_cycle/dt
  ε: = exp{(new_rate − old_rate)/T}
  x: = random(0,1)
  if x < ε
    old_rate: = new_rate
    old_alpha: = new_alpha
  endif
  new_rate: = neighbour(old_alpha)
  ESCTM_cycle(new_alpha)
  T: = T * F_c
endwhile
```

Figure 5. Pseudo code of SA-based ESCTM algorithm

value which is greater than the global minima, but which is smaller than all its neighbors. Above process is continued for a predefined amount of time or until an acceptable value for the objective function has been determined. The probability function (Boltzmann distribution) is defined as follows:

$$P(\Delta E, T) = e^{-\Delta E/T} = e^{-(E(s')-E(s))/T}$$

where T is the current temperature.

Since our ultimate goal is to reduce the simulation time, we use the Event Commit Rate (ECR) to construct the objective function E.

$$E = -ECR_i = -\frac{NC_i}{t_i - t_{i-1}}$$

where NC_i denotes the number of committed events during i-th cycle, and t_i denotes the wall clock when the i-th cycle ends.

Fig.5 shows the way that we integrate SA algorithm into ESCTM algorithm. Each cycle is composed of 10 continuous time window. At beginning of iteration, the SA algorithm decides whether accept the current α, and generates a new α based on this decision. Using such α, ESCTM algorithm works for a cycle. After that, the algorithm decreases the temperature by multiplying cooling factor F_c.

5. Experiment Evaluation

This section presents an initial evaluation of the proposed algorithms. Experiments are tested on two platforms. One is a desktop computer equipped with a NVIDIA GeForce GTS450 GPU. The GPU has 192 stream processors and 1024MB of memory with a memory bandwidth of 57.7 GB/s. We use the PHOLD model to evaluate our work. In PHOLD simulation, each LP is initialized with some events. Upon processing an event, the LP generates a new event with timestamp increment, and sends it to a target LP. The timestamp increment is equal to the lookahead plus a random number generated by exponential distribution. In order to analyze the performance of algorithm under different conditions, we introduce some parameters to change the simulation's characteristics.

We first analyze the performance using randomly interactions. Two parameters are used to tune the model. Parameter "Space Range" determines the range of the target LP that events can be sent to. In other words, logical process can only affects another LP when the difference between their *lpid* is smaller than "Space Range". Parameter "Time Range" is the mean value of the exponential distribution. Fig.6 shows the results of PHOLD simulation with following settings: Each LP is initialized with 2 events, lookahead is set to 1 and the number of LP is set to 16384. "Space Range" is set to 50, 100, 200, 400, and "Time Range" is set to 0.1, 1, 10. Since the LPs randomly send events within "Space Range", we treat this case as random interactions. Both full ESCTM algorithm[2] and SA-based ESCTM algorithm obtain higher event parallelism, thereby they achieve higher performance than the baseline SCTM algorithm. We can also see that both "Space Range" and "Time Range" affect the performance. First, the probability of events sending to a same LP grows when "Space Range" is growing, thereby the event parallelism decreases. This kind of decrease is intrinsic since events to a same LP must be processed sequentially according to timestamp. Hence, the overall

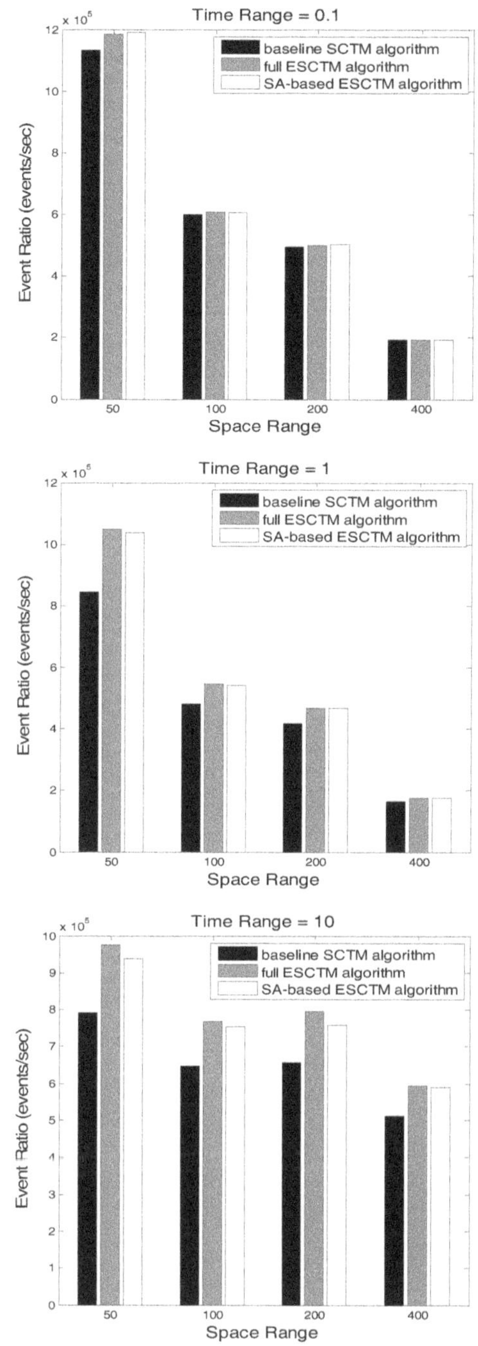

Figure 6. Comparison of event ratio among three TM algorithms using random interactions

performance decreases when "Space Range" is growing. However, the expansion method still increases the event parallelism and achieves performance improvement. Second, with higher "Time Range", the events to be processed are distributed more loosely in the axis of simulation time. Using the expansion method can assemble them together so that higher EP can be obtained. Hence, the performance improvement increases when "Time Range" is growing.

Then we consider the scenarios with simple interactions. Only the parameter "Time Range" is use to tune the model and every logical

[2] full ESTM algorithm means using expansion method after each invocation of "ProcessEvents"

process only sends events to itself. Fig.7 shows the results of PHOLD simulation with following settings: Each LP is initialized with 2 events, lookahead is set to 1, the number of LP is set to 16384, and "Time Range" is set to 0.1, 0.5, 1, 5, 10. In contrast with previous experiment, the baseline SCTM algorithm and SA-based SCTM algorithm outperform full ESCTM algorithm in most cases. This is because the event parallelism can be increased only a little by expansion and expansion also brings some overhead.

In summary, the full ESCTM algorithm always achieves the highest event ratio in the first experiment while the baseline SCTM algorithm achieves the highest event ratio in the second experiment. But in both cases, the results from SA-based ESCTM algorithm are always close to the optimal results. It means that the simulated annealing method can adaptively finds a near optimal solution.

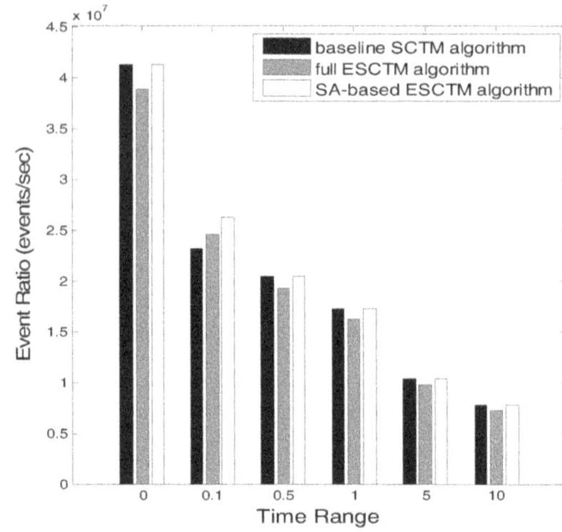

Figure 7. Comparison of event ratio among three TM algorithms using simple interactions

6. Conclusion and Future Work

The GPU has evolved into a powerful parallel computing environment with relatively low cost, so it is attractive to harness the power of GPU to support discrete event simulation. GPU's performance depends on high parallelism heavily, but using synchronous conservative time management algorithm for discrete event simulation will meet the scenarios with limited parallelism, even if the application has high parallelism. To solve this problem, we propose an expansion-aided synchronous conservative time management algorithm. It collects runtime information to import newly "safe" events to feed GPU. By interleaving a series of expansions with the procedure of processing events, more events can be assembled to be processed in parallel. Meanwhile, a simulated annealing algorithm is adopted to control the number of expansions. It helps achieve stable performance under different conditions. Experiments demonstrate that the proposed algorithm can achieve up to a 30% performance improvement.

Our future work aims at incorporating the power of GPU-based simulator with CPU-based simulator. Since not all computation are suited for GPU, letting CPU and GPU do their suitable tasks respectively is a better and necessary choice.

7. ACKNOWLEDGMENTS

We appreciate the support from National Natural Science Foundation of China (NSF) Grant (No.61170048) and the Ph.D. Programs Foundation of Ministry of Education of China (No. 201243070017). We also thank the anonymous reviewers for useful suggestions.

8. REFERENCES

[1] Fujimoto, R. M. 2000. Parallel and Distribution Simulation Systems,Wiley-Interscience, New York.

[2] NVIDIA Corporation. 2009. NVIDIA CUDA Compute Unified Device Architecture Programming Guide, 4.1 edn, NVIDIA Corporation.

[3] Owens, J. D., D. Luebke, N. Govindaraju, M. Harris, J. Krüger, A. E. Lefohn, and T. J. Purcell. 2007. A survey of general-purpose computation on graphics hardware. Computer Graphics Forum, 26(1): 80–113.

[4] Chen D, Li D, Xiong M, Bao H, Li X. 2010. "GPGPU-aided ensemble empirical mode decomposition for electroencephalogram analysis during anaesthesia". IEEE Trans Inf Technol Biomed 14(6):1417–1427.

[5] Perumalla, K. S. 2006. Discrete-event execution alternatives on general purpose graphical processing units (GPGPUs). In PADS '06: Proceedings of the 20th Workshop on Principles of Advanced and Distributed Simulation, pp. 74–81, IEEE Computer Society, Washington, DC.

[6] Hyungwook Park, Paul Fishwick. 2010. A GPU-Based Application Framework Supporting Fast Discrete-Event Simulation. SIMULATION. 86(10), 612-628.

[7] Hyungwook Park, Paul Fishwick. 2011, An Analysis of Queuing Network Simulation Using GPU-Based Hardware Acceleration. 21(3), ACM Trans. on Modeling & Simulation.

[8] E. Lindholm, J. Nickolls, S.Oberman and J. Montrym. March-April 2008. NVIDIA Tesla: A Unified Graphics and Computing Architecture. IEEE Micro, 28(2):39–55.

[9] NVIDIA Corporation. 2009. CUDA C Programming Best Practices Guide, NVIDIA Corporation.

[10] D. B. Lubachesky, 1988, Bounded Lag Distributed Discrete Event Simulation, In Proceedings of the SCS Western Multiconference on Distributed Simulation, 183-191.

[11] J. Steinman, 1991. SPEEDES: Synchronous Parallel Environment for Emulation and Discrete Event Simulation. Advances in Parallel and Distributed Simulation, SCS Simulation Series 23:95-103.

[12] D. M. Nicol, 1993 The Cost of Conservative Synchronization in Parallel Discrete-event Simulations, Journal of the Association for Computing Machinary, 40(2): 304-333.

[13] Georg Kunz, Daniel Schemmel, James Gross and Klaus Wehrl, 2012. Multi-level Parallelism for Time- and Cost-efficient Parallel Discrete Event Simulation on GPUs. In PADS 2012: Proceedings of 26th Workshop on Principles of Advanced and Distributed Simulation, 23-32.

A Context-driven Approach to Scalable Human Activity Simulation
- Work In Progress Paper -

Jae Woong Lee
Dept. of CISE
University of Florida
Gainesville, FL 32611,
United States
jwlee@cise.ufl.edu

Abdelsalam Helal
Dept. of CISE
University of Florida
Gainesville, FL 32611,
United States
helal@cise.ufl.edu

Yunsick Sung
Dept. of CISE
University of Florida
Gainesville, FL 32611,
United States
sung@cise.ufl.edu

Kyungeun Cho
Dept. of Multimedia Eng.
Dongguk University
Seoul 100-715,
Republic of Korea
cke@dongguk.edu

ABSTRACT
As demands for human activity recognition technology increase, simulation of human activities for providing datasets and testing purposes is becoming increasingly important. Traditional simulation, however, is based on an event-driven approach, which focuses on single sensor events and models within a single human activity. It requires detailed description and processing of every low-level event that enters into an activity scenario. For many realistic and complex human scenarios, the event-driven approach burdens the simulator users with complicated low-level specifications required to configure and run the simulation. It also increases computational complexity and impedes scalable simulation. Thus, we propose a novel, context-driven approach to simulating human activities in smart spaces. In the proposed approach, vectors of sensors rather than single sensor events drive the simulation quicker from one context to another. Abstracting the space state into contexts highly simplifies the tasks and efforts of the simulation user in setting up and configuring the simulation components for smart space and human activities. We present the context-driven simulation approach and show how it works. Then we present fundamental concepts and algorithms and provide a comparative performance study between the event- and context-driven simulation approaches.

Categories and Subject Descriptors
I.6.5 [**Simulation and Modeling**]: Model Development – *Modeling methodologies.*

General Terms
Algorithms, Measurement, Performance, Design, Human Factors, Theory, Verification.

Keywords
Simulation; Human Activity Simulation; Context; Context-driven Approach; Event-driven Approach

1. INTRODUCTION
For a couple of decades, the demand of smart homes and health telematics has dramatically increased as the elderly population continues to grow. As more elderly people are living alone, it has become critical to monitor their activities and recognize emergency situations through programmable and automatic recognition by computing machines. Thus, human activity recognition has become important research, and many universities and research labs are working on developing novel approaches in this area. However, it is difficult to get enough dataset used in researching human activities recognition because of high cost of building physical environment and actually performing activities. Therefore, simulation of human activities in smart home environments is becoming very important as an alternative source of datasets for researchers. Simulation offers researchers an alternative to mimic human activities virtually and generate corresponding datasets. A few simulators such as Persim [2] and DiaSim [4] have been developed for this simulation.

Existing simulators are based on an event-driven approach, which models human activities with consecutive events along a time line [7]. While simulating human activities, the events occur when sensors detect them in the pervasive space. Once an event occurs at a point in time, no event will change a sensor value until the next event occurs. For instance, once a vibration sensor on a bed detects any activity, such as a body turning left, and generates its current value, it does not respond until it detects that another activity has occurred. However, the intervals between events are not constant in event-driven simulation. Also, the value of the sensor and the type of sensor value can vary. An event-driven simulation approach could generate highly accurate datasets, which are very similar to real datasets, if the simulator can define all proper events in detail, i.e., deciding when each event occurs and what value to generate. This requires user's significant efforts in modeling space, sensors and activities as realistically as possible to generate accurate values.

User's significant efforts in capturing detailed and low level events will be required to increase realism. However, the human centric simulation can bring exploding state space, as human activities are more complex and enlarged. It challenges scalable simulation. Simulating long-lasting activities (e.g., daily activities) in an event-driven approach is complex because doing so involves significant processing of low-level events. Events still occur within an activity, and the number of events would be larger and larger, as the period of simulation is made longer. It is difficult to model all the events, and it takes much more time than desirable. These difficulties come from the extremely enlarged state space while modeling events and simulations at a low level. The approach would not scale in these cases.

To address the scalable issue, new simulation abstraction is required, or we are disable to scale simulation, eventually risk accuracy of simulation. Hence, we propose a context-driven

SIGSIM-PADS'13, May 19–22, 2013, Montréal, Québec, Canada.

approach (to be contrasted with event-driven), which reduces complexity and human efforts of simulation design, and that produces scalable simulation. The context is a higher-level structure that covers all the status information of environmental entities such as space, objects, and virtual characters, including human subjects. Because it can represent a meaningful state of the smart space, it can skip unimportant state spaces in considering during simulation. Given a context, corresponded activities are selected and scheduled. The context-driven approach is driven by vectors of entities rather than by a single event, which reduces computational complexity and leads to scalability. The simulation core advances the simulation by hopping through key contexts, each associated with one or more activities. In this paper, we present our context-driven simulation approach for scalable simulation and explain the mechanisms and principles.

The rest of this paper is organized as follows. We briefly review previous simulation researches and simulators in section 2. In section 3, we present the principles of context-driven simulation, followed by a comparative study between event-driven and context-driven simulation in section 4. Finally, we conclude the paper and present our future work.

2. RELATED WORK

There have been attempts to develop human activity simulation using event-driven approach. DiaSim [4] executes pervasive computing applications by developing simulation logic using a programming framework. The goal is to simulate applications such as fire situations and intrusions for identifying potential conflicts. In this simulator, human activities are events that are induced by stimulus procedures or services and used to check operationality of applications. Although it successfully examines the fidelity of applications, it lacks the ability to mimic a variety of human activities. Persim [2][3], which is our early work in human activity simulation, enables the design and specification of various human activities. It defines an activity by a human being as one event and predefines the relationship between such event and sensors that activates when each event is generated. Even though this early version of Persim can enable variety design of human activities, it suffers from high computational complexity as higher realism is attempted. The limitation exacerbates especially for long period simulations and for complex activities, which require massive human efforts in specifying all sensor events.

Agent-based modeling (ABM) is an alternative approach for human activity simulation. In ABM, autonomous entities called agents are modeled to drive simulation through decision-making [9]. Agents are independent subjects who perform activities and interact with other agents [10]. Every agent accesses a given situation and decides what activities he or she is performing. Simulation is driven by activities of the individual agents. Unlike event-driven simulation, it does not specify the entire events and make sensors engaged in relevant activities using stochastic equations. Instead, it describes attributes, rules for interactions of activities and histories of activities for each agent. This approach enables the user to simulate more complex activities. It makes simulation more natural and realistic than event-driven simulation. NetLogo and MASON are popular simulation platforms implemented through ABM. In these simulators, especially multi-agents characterized and parameterized for human activities realism is highly increased [8]. Even though ABM contributes to enhancing naturality and reality of simulation, it holds the same principle of event-driven approach: activity of each agent is modeled and driven through low-level events [9]. The scalability challenge therefore remains to be addressed.

To resolve the scalability challenge, we propose a macroscopic modeling and simulation approach. Rather than specifying all single events, we model vectors of information about the simulated space, sensors, virtual characters, and their activities, and model their dynamic changes carefully to drive the simulation. We refer to this simulation approach as context-driven simulation. By computing and progressing through the different contexts, computational complexity can be reduced and scalable simulation can be achieved. Also, human efforts can be better managed in high realism simulation where it is easier to specify and design around contexts than it is around low-level events.

3. PRINCIPLES OF CONTEXT-DRIVEN SIMULATION APPROACH

3.1 Context and Context Graph

In context-driven simulation, a fundamental driving element is context. Contexts are already defined in several ways [5][6], but their goal is context-awareness, which reverses simulation driven by contexts. Therefore, we define what we mean by a context in our approach. A context is a meaningful and important state space, which is defined by entities (space, human, sensor, etc.) in a pervasive space. In context-driven simulation, a context is transitioned into first, and then interaction between entities (e.g., human activities and actuation of objects) occurs within that context. Through the interaction, the entities are affected, and their state is changed and so does the overall space state. The next context is selected by the changed state space. Thus, we need to find out what status entities are in (state space) and what affects them (activities and actuations). In a pervasive space, a state space can be described by the status of sensors, objects, and human residents (refer to it with sensor values for simplicity). And for affecters of entities, we care only for human activities.

A context graph is a graph that includes all contexts that cover all scenarios of concern in a smart space. It relates all contexts via cause-effect relationships. As shown in Figure 1, an edge stands for activities, and a vertex stands for a context. In a context graph, a scenario can start with any context. A context graph shows how to get to a next context and how to traverse simulation of a scenario. Each context consists of a context label, context conditions, virtual characters, and next contexts. Context label is the unique name of the context (e.g., CONTEXT 2). Context conditions are a set of conditions over relevant sensors required to transition into the context. Virtual characters show the status of each virtual character including location, animation, interaction (with objects) and activity. Next contexts are a set of all possible next contexts that can be transitioned into. A priority scheme is used to select the next context when multiple next contexts are present.

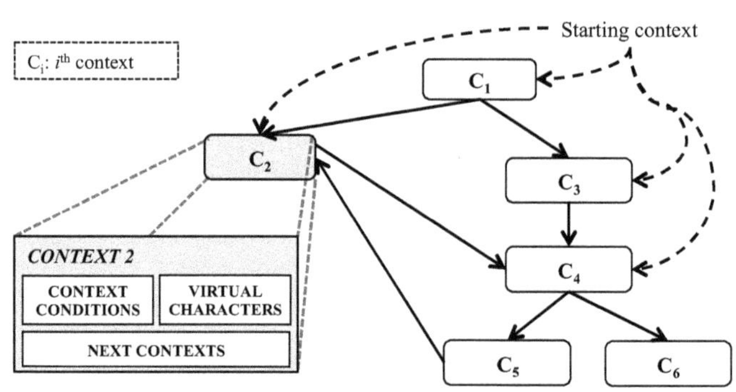

Figure 1. Context graph consisting of six contexts

3.2 Overall Approach

Context graph, activities, and state space, are key components in context-driven simulation. We refer activities that are performed in a given context as context activities. Context-driven simulation is processed by interactions between the key components. First, current state space is evaluated to decide a next context designed in a context graph. By the result of the evaluation, the context graph decides whether it drives contexts or not; if current state space is evaluated that it can transition into a next context, then the next context is driven. Otherwise, the current context continues. In a given context, a set of context activities is scheduled, propelled and performed. Performed context activity reflects its effect on state space, changing values of some sensors. When sensor values change, state space is reevaluated and decide how to drive context graph. These fundamental processes continue until simulation is terminated.

As shown in Figure 2, the processes are categorized into three modules. The *Context Handling* module evaluates state space, and selects a next context if possible. To check the availability of context transition, context conditions of each potentially next context are evaluated, and next context candidates who are deemed available to get transitioned to are decided. If more than one next context candidate exists, only one should be eventually selected. When a next context candidate is selected, it is transitioned to from the current context. The selected context is used to select and schedule context activities by the *Simulation Scheduling* module. *Simulation Propelling* module executes one of scheduled context activities, and propels it through Activity Animation. When a context activity is performed, state space potentially changes and enters into evaluating next contexts by the Context Handling module. Three modules are sequentially concatenated and repeated until simulation scenario is complete.

In a given context C, C's possible next context C_N (= {C_1, C_2, ..., C_j, ..., C_v }) should be evaluated and monitored while performing context activities of C. When a proper next context in C_N is found, the context graph drives and context C is transitioned into the found next context. We propose two transitioning modes according to consideration of changes of state space. First, in reactive transitioning mode, once the condition of one or more of C_j of C's is identified, we abort the rest of the scheduled context activities, choose a proper context from the multiple C_js, and move to the next context C_j. Another mode called latent transitioning mode is that performs the entire schedule of activities then considers and selects from all C_j during the performance of scheduled activities. To achieve higher realism, we can use reactive transitioning even though it increases calculation complexity with too many evaluations. To lower complexity, we can use latent transitioning that does not need to continuously evaluate context conditions until A_S are done. The simulation modeler is chosen one according to her motivation.

For the context evaluation method, we propose *getDistance*, which measures the difference between the current state space S and context conditions of each possible next context C_P ($\in C_N$). The state space and context conditions are defined as vectors, thus, we apply Euclidean distance to calculate those vectors for *getDistance* (see formula below). When the distance is within a specific range, Θ, it signifies no difference between the current state space and C_P, and hence, C_P becomes the next context. Note that each context has its own Θ. Some conditions may be defined with a range of values, instead of one value. In this case, in order to apply Euclidean distance, the range is represented by a median of the range.

$$getDistance(S,C_P) \leftarrow \|S - C_P\| = \sqrt{\sum_{k=1}^{\xi}(S.s_k - C_p.s_k)^2} \leq C_P.\Theta$$

(*where* $S.s_k$ *means sensor k in state space S and* $C_P.\Theta$ (≥ 0) *is a fuzzy threshold for nudging the condition of* C_P)

3.3 Context-driven Simulation Loop

Simulation loop in context-driven approach is hierarchized into two loops; inner loop for context, and outer loop for entire simulation. Simulation loop for context is shown in Algorithm 1.

Algorithm 1. ***runContext***

```
Activity Set A_G ← get context activity group
Activity Set A_S ← generate and schedule A_G
for each activity A in A_S
  A ← extract next activity from A_S
  perform a context activity A
  if (Mode is Latent Transitioning) AND (A_S != null)
    continue
  else
    Context Set C_T ← null
    C_T ← check Next Context
    if a next context activity in A_S is not available
      A_S ← regenerate and reschedule A_G
    end if
  end if
end for
return get next context from C_T
```

When a context begins, it collects context activity group A_G, schedule it, and generate a set A_S for scheduled context activities. Next, a scheduled context activity A is performed, affects virtual space, and eventually changes a state space. Every time that a state space is changed, it should be evaluated for finding a next context that will be driven. Note that in latent transitioning mode A_S should be performed first. The evaluation is processed in two phases: first, next contexts defined for the current context are evaluated, and available next contexts are collected as a set of candidates C_T; and then one of the candidates in C_T. When no next context is selected, the current context keeps processing. In this case, we should check whether or not we could propel the rest of

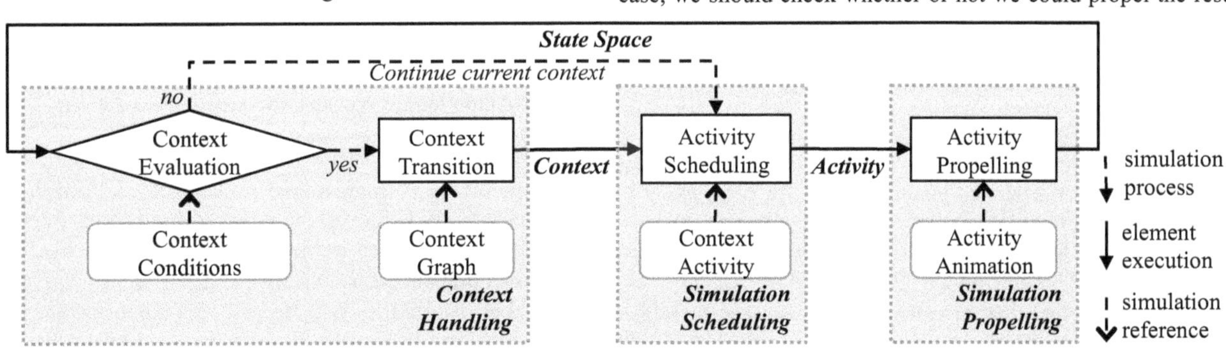

Figure 2. Context-driven framework

A_S in a changed virtual space. Unless this is available, A_G should be rescheduled. Once a next context is selected, the current simulation loop is terminated and a new simulation loop for the next context begins. The inner loop for a context is called within outer loop shown in Algorithm 2. After initializing context graph C_G, a starting context C calls Algorithm 1 and begins the inner simulation loop of Algorithm 1. The simulation of each context in C_G continues until simulation completes.

Algorithm 2. ***Context-driven Simulation Loop***

```
Context Graph C_G ← initialize Context Graph
Current Context C
C ← starting context of C_G
while (not complete simulation)
    C ← runContext(C)
end while
```

4. VALIDATION OF CONTEXT-DRIVEN SIMULATION APPROACH

4.1 Comparative Study

In this paper, while we do not attempt to provide a formal proof, we provide an argument for the correctness of our approach. The main question is that: could the shift in paradigm for event-driven simulation to context-driven simulation cause any incorrectness in the simulation? Defining contexts aims to skip unimportant space states. However, because we skip them orderly not randomly (according to the context graph), the context simulation is highly relevant and equivalent to event simulation. It is significantly accelerated though due to the skipping of events.

To strengthen our argument, we will compare it to event-driven simulation and analyze their performance. In way of overview for this comparison, we offer a metaphoric comparison first. Event-driven simulation is a microscopic simulation. It is similar to a giant ant colony. All diligent ants are working hard and maintaining the colony. Each ant's work contributes to maintain the colony, but the absence of a few ants wouldn't cause the failure of preserving it. In other words, all of the work is not always necessary. In this colony, considering every single ant's activity in detail may be excessive, especially if we mimic the system. On the other hand, context driven simulation approach conducts simulation in a macroscopic scale, where it computes the effect of relevant groups of sensors and skips many other effects. It enables the user to think only of the important contexts and focus only on involved sensors and their status, reducing human efforts and computational complexity.

In followings, we conduct a set of experiments to quantify and contrast the benefits of context-and event-driven simulation of human activities. The experiment simulates a real known scenario through both approaches to obtain synthetic datasets (simulation output), which are compared and used for validation of the context-driven approach. The scenario is based on the Amsterdam datasets [11], which have been collected for 24 days. In the scenario, 14 sensors are used to detect seven activities in a smart house. For context-driven simulation, we model five contexts: "sleeping in the bedroom," "washing in the bath room," "having breakfast in the kitchen," "having dinner in the kitchen," and "going out." The event-driven simulator used for comparison is Persim [2][3]. We modified Persim to include the core context-driven simulation loop. We refer to this "transient" simulator, designed only for this early validation, as Persim Cd.

Simulation can be analyzed for validation in two aspects: realism and scalability. To validate realism of simulation, we could analyze the similarity of a generated dataset to a real dataset. If a dataset generated through simulation is similar to a real dataset, we can infer that simulation can imitate the real world, and validate it [1][2][12] However, it cannot measure scalability that is focused in this paper. In longer and more complex scenarios, simulation may last long (i.e., daily life), occur in a large space with many sensors, and contain various and complex activities. As scenarios become longer and more complex, the complexities for computing simulation and specifying the scenarios also increase. If the degree of increase is too high, it will impede scaling simulation and make simulation useless. Therefore, we should measure the complexities for scalability.

For measuring complexities, we consider the complexities of the computation and specification. Computational complexity, which is measured during simulation, presents how many computations are required for simulation. We refer to the number of simulation loops as the number of computation. A large number of simulation loops denotes high complexity and is considered less scalable. Specification complexity shows a degree of effort that is necessary for specifying simulation. It can be measured in four terms: space complexity, sentience complexity, activity complexity, and context complexity. Space complexity is related to the size of space, the number of rooms in a space, and so on. Sentience complexity is affected by sensors that are deployed in a space. Activity and context complexity stand for efforts to design activities and contexts and context graphs, respectively. These complexities can be measured by how much efforts the user has excreted. Thus, we validate the context-driven approach by showing that a context-driven approach requires less effort by the user, and simulation loops by the computer.

4.2 Computation Complexity Analysis

Simulation is processed by repeating the simulation loop. In event-driven simulation such as Persim, a sensor event occurs at an instance of time and then generates a proper sensor value in one simulation loop. After the sensor event, a next sensor event is evaluated to check whether it can move on. Only when it is evaluated, the next sensor event is generated to repeat the simulation loop at some point in the future [2]. As a scenario gets longer and more complicated, more sensor events will occur and may increase the number of simulation loop. We can evaluate computation complexity with a Simulation Loop Count (SLC).

$$SLC_{(Event\text{-}driven)} = \sum_{i-1}^{\zeta} \sum_{j-1}^{\upsilon} |A_i||e_j| \quad (1)$$

A_i stands for i^{th} activity, e_j stands for j^{th} event occurred in A_i. SLC in event-driven simulation is the number of total sensor events, which is the sum of all the numbers of sensor events within an activity. Higher SLC means that the complexity in computation has increased and that it may be difficult to get processed quickly. It can be an impediment for scalable simulation. In context-driven simulation, SLC is derived by different domains and can return less complexity. In a simulation loop, a context activity is animated and affects a state space. Then the simulation loops ends after evaluation for a next context. Whether a next context is transitioned or the current context remains, another simulation loop is repeated if simulation is not yet over. In this mechanism, a simulation loop is repeated for each context activity.

$$SLC_{(Context\text{-}driven)} = \sum_{r=1}^{\gamma} \sum_{s=1}^{\rho} |C_r||A_s| \quad (2)$$

C_r stands for r^{th} context, and A_s stands for s^{th} activity in a given context C_r. SLC for each approach is interrelated. Suppose that all activities performed in the scenario are defined in $\mathcal{A}$. From (1), we can find out $\mathcal{A} = \{A_1, A_2, \ldots, A_i, \ldots A_s, \ldots, A_\zeta\}$, and the total number of activities is ζ. Because this number is the same as the total number of activities from (2), ζ equals $\sum_{r=1}^{\gamma} \sum_{s=1}^{\zeta} |C_r||A_s|$.

Notice that only the simulation loop number is needed to calculate computation complexity. We assume that complexity involved in a simulation loop of either approach is almost equal and able to be ignored. In other words, the complexity of deciding the event time and sensor value in an event-driven simulation and of animating an activity in a context-driven simulation are almost identical. Upon the assumption, we simulate the target scenarios and calculate SLCs over days, as shown in Figure 3. SLC for event-driven simulation increases sharply, as indicated in (a). However, SIRs (SLC Increase Ratios = (current SLC – previous SLC) / previous SLC) for each approach do not show a notable difference, as shown in (b). Therefore, both SLCs are increasingly linear. Their differences come from whether sensor events are involved or not in a simulation loop. SLC dramatically increases in event-driven simulation, while its increase is slower and much more gradual in context-driven simulation.

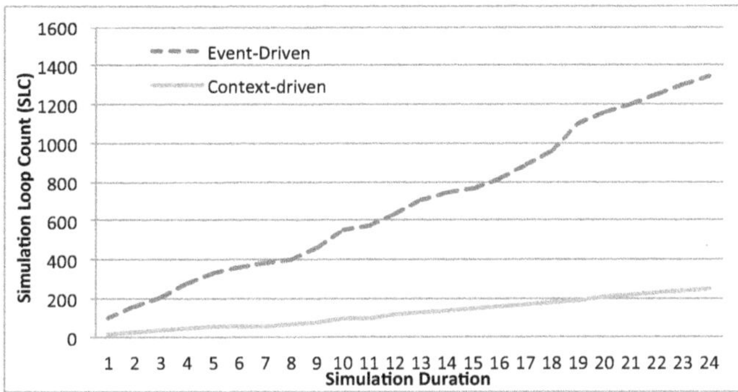

(a)

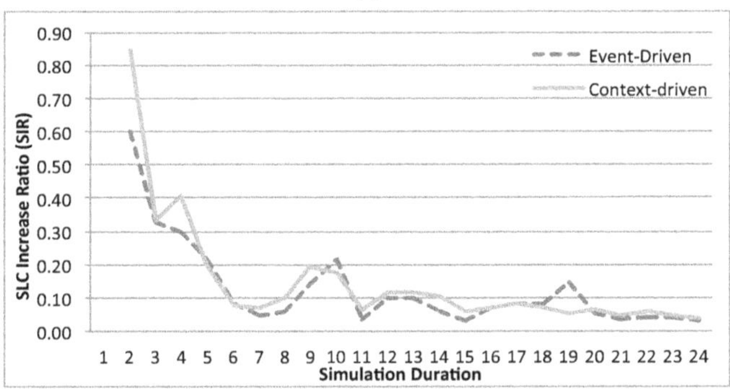

(b)

Figure 3. SLC and SIR for each simulation approach; (a) SLC (b) SIC (SLC Increase Ratio)

4.3 Specification Complexity Analysis

Alternatively, we can evaluate specification complexity by the user effort. If what has to be specified dramatically increases as the degree of scale gets deeper, a user may make mistakes unexpectedly when specifying the simulation. They can have bad effects on the accuracy and fidelity of the simulation. Therefore, users' efforts should stay constant or increase reasonably at least.

Complexity for specifying simulation can be measured by the user's efforts. To specify simulation, a user clicks icons of sensors or activity with a mouse and enters proper parameters, such as name in Persim and Persim Cd. The number of clicks and entering can indicate how much effort a user spent. However, because we assume that clicking a mouse and entering a parameter happen together, we count the number of mouse-clicks and refer it as user's efforts. For measuring users' efforts, we define User Efforts, which stands for degree of tasks to run simulation.

$$User\ Efforts\ (T, W) = \sum_{q=1}^{\omega} |t_q| w_q$$

T means tasks (={t1, t2, …, t_q, …, t_ω}) and w_q represents importance of the t_q within a scenario. We assume that each task is equally important in modeling a scenario and consider as 1. Therefore, t_q is considered in our measurement.

When deriving specification complexity using User Efforts, we can calculate in four complexities as mentioned previously: space, sentience, activity, and context. For instance, space complexity can be calculated by User Efforts (T, W) with one task, as follows:

$$User\ Efforts\ (T, W)_{(Space\ Complexity)} = \sum_{q=1}^{1} |t_q| = |t_{SC1}| = t(B)$$

B stands for a built pervasive space and t() returns user efforts to complete B. Because a target space does not change, space and sentience complexity are almost the same, as shown in Figure 4. Similarly, context complexity does not change, because almost similar living activity routines are performed daily. Thus, contexts and a context graph are specified before starting simulation, and it makes context complexity almost consistent.

On the other hand, activity complexity changes over simulation duration, because activities are rescheduled and performed differently every day. To drive activity complexity, three tasks are used. First task is to name an activity that is used (t_{AC1}). After naming all activities, a user should create sensor-activity mapping table (t_{AC2}), which can show which sensors can be triggered when a specific activity is performed [2]. Then how all the activities are scheduled and performed should be specified (t_{AC3}).

$$User\ Efforts\ (T, W)_{(Activity\ Complexity)} = \sum_{q=1}^{3} |t_q| = \sum_{i=1}^{\zeta} t(A_i) + \sum_{i=1}^{\zeta}\sum_{k=1}^{\xi} t(A_i)t(s_k) + t(R)$$

A_i and s_k stands for i[th] activity and k[th] sensor, respectively. R stands for scheduling activities and specifying them for running simulation. Once activities and a mapping table are complete, it does not have to modify them. However, activities are differently scheduled and performed every day. Even though the difference may not be big, a user has to specify all the difference. Therefore, it shows increase of activity complexity, as shown in Figure 4.

User Efforts for event-driven simulation and context-driven simulation are measured using relevant specification complexities. Only space, sentience, and activity are relevant for event-driven simulation, whereas all are used for context-driven simulation.

$$User\ Efforts\ (T, W)_{(Event\text{-}driven\ Simulation)} = \sum_{q=1}^{5} |t_q| = t(B) + t(D) + \sum_{i=1}^{\zeta} t(A_i) + \sum_{i=1}^{\zeta}\sum_{k=1}^{\xi} t(A_i)t(s_k) + \sum_{d=1}^{\rho} t(R)$$

$$User\ Efforts\ (T, W)_{(Context\text{-}driven\ Simulation)} = \sum_{q=1}^{6} |t_q| = t(B) + t(D) + \sum_{i=1}^{\zeta} t(A_i) + \sum_{i=1}^{\zeta}\sum_{k=1}^{\xi} t(A_i)t(s_k) + \sum_{r=1}^{\gamma} t(C_r) + t(C_G)$$

D, C_r and C_G stands for deployed sensors, r[th] context and context graph. ρ in event-driven simulation means the number of scenario duration (day). We compare the two approaches over the change of activity complexity, because it only makes difference for User Efforts. In lower activity complexity, User Efforts for context-driven simulation is larger than for event-driven simulation due to initial configuration for contexts and context graph. As activity complexity is higher, however, User Efforts for event-driven simulation is increasing because a user is demanded for specifying more events. On the other hand, for context-driven simulation, only a few more efforts are needed, because simulation is driven by a context graph that is already created. Rather than event-driven simulation in which a user should specify what is added, as activities are more complex, context-driven simulation algorithms cover all the difference and demand no more efforts to a user. Shown in Figure 5, event-driven simulation exceeds context-driven simulation after activity complexity is over 952. It overwhelms more, as the activity complexity gets higher.

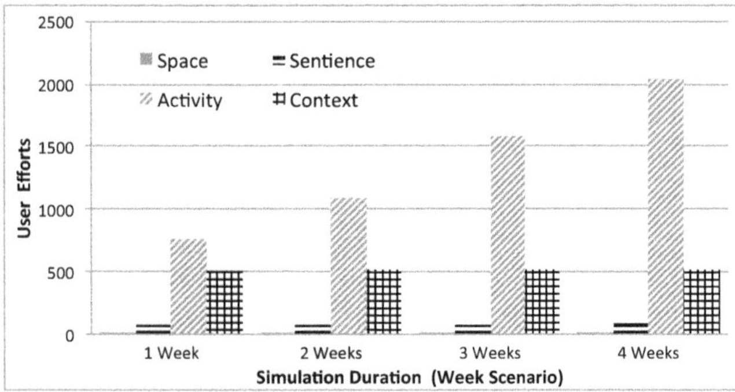

Figure 4. Four complexities over simulation duration by week

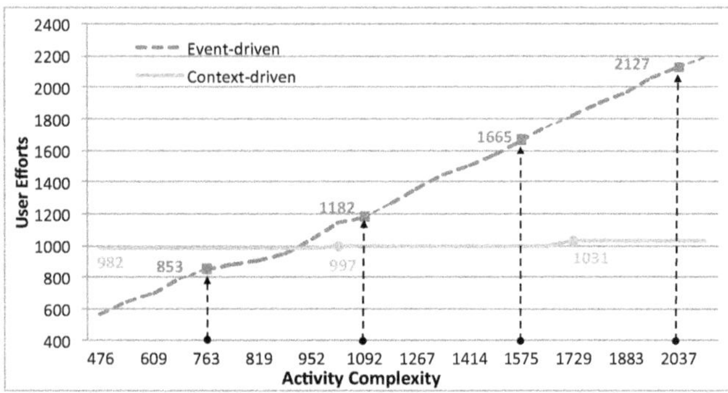

Figure 5. User Effort for event-driven simulation and event-driven simulation by activity complexity

5. DISCUSSION AND FUTURE WORK

In this paper, we introduced and validated a novel context-driven simulation approach to scale human activity simulation. By defining context as higher-level (than events), building block abstraction of simulation, and by designing context graph, we can simulate a human activity scenario with less human efforts and computational complexity than in an event-driven approach. Our approach needed some simplifying assumptions. Relaxing them poses challenges and requires further research and enhancements.

First, when a context activity is performed, we assumed that it could be performed without any interruption to completion. However, for a reason similar to why we have to reschedule context activities, during performing a context activity, a virtual environment can be changed and interrupt its currently performing activity. We can monitor this exception while performing, however it can increase computational complexity. Thus, we should handle the possible exception without increasing complexity or by increasing it to a reasonable degree.

Second, we focused on controllable effects of activities and ignored non-controllable effects that could be caused by environmental factors such as wind, light, temperature or unexpected user behavior. Their effects may be crucial in decision and scheduling of context activities. Also, they can affect the selection of a next context. Suppose that the temperature increases when a virtual character is watching TV in the living room. Obviously, it will try to cool the room by turning on an air conditioner or opening a window. Without the modeled environmental factors, or accounting for uncertain behaviors, simulation of these interactions will not be possible.

6. REFERENCES

[1] Helal, A., Cho, K., Lee, W., Sung, Y., Lee, J. W., and Kim, E. 2012. 3D modeling and simulation of human activities in smart spaces. In *Proceedings of the 9th International Conference on Ubiquitous Intelligence and Computing* (Fukuoka, Japan, September 4 – 7, 2012), 112-119. UIC '12.

[2] Helal, S., Lee, J. W., Hossain, S., Kim, E., Hagras, H., and Cook, D. 2011. Persim – simulator for human activities in pervasive spaces. In *Proceedings of the 7th International Conference on Intelligent Environments* (Nottingham, UK, July 25 – 28, 2011), 192 - 199. IE '11. IEEE Computer Society, Washington, DC.

[3] Persim Official Webpage: http://icta.ufl.edu/pervasive-enablers.htm#3.

[4] Jouve, W., Bruneau J., and Consel. C. 2009. DiaSim: A parameterized simulator for pervasive computing applications. In *Proceedings of the 2009 IEEE International Conference on Pervasive Computing and Communications* (Galveston, Texas, March 9 – 13, 2009) 1 - 3. Percom '09, IEEE Computer Society, Washington, DC.

[5] Abowd, D. G., Dey, A. K., Brown, J. P., Davies, N., Smith, M., and Steggles, P. 1999. Towards a better understanding of context and context-awareness. In *Proceedings of the 1st International Symposium on Handheld and Ubiquitous Computing* (Karlsruhe, Germany, September 27 - 29, 1999), 304 – 307. HUC '99, Vol. 1707.

[6] Yau, S. S., Wang, Y., and Karim, F. 2002. Development of situation-aware application software for ubiquitous computing environments. In *Proceedings of 26th IEEE International Computer Software and Applications Conference* (Oxford, UK, August 26 - 29, 2002), 233 – 238, COMPSAC '02, IEEE Computer Society Washington, DC,

[7] Carson, J. S. 2005. Introduction to modeling and simulation. In *Proceedings of the 37th Conference on Winter Simulation* (Orlando, FL, December 4 - 7, 2005), 16 – 23, WSC '05, IEEE Piscataway, NJ.

[8] Laclavik, M., Dlugolinsky, S., Seleng, M., Kvassay, M., Schnider, B., Bracker, H., Wrzeszcz, M., Kitowski, J, Hluchy, L. 2011. Agent-Based simulation platform evaluation in the context of human behavior modeling. In *Proceedings of the 10th International Conference on Advanced Agent Technology* (Taipei, Taiwan, May 2 – 6, 2011), 396 – 410, AAMAS '11.

[9] Bonabeau, E. 2002. Agent-based modeling: Methods and techniques for simulating human systems. In *Proceedings of the National Academy of Sciences* (May 14, 2002), 7280 – 7287. PNA '02, Vol 99 No 3.

[10] Macal, C. M., North, M. J. 2005. Tutorial on agent-based modeling and simulation. In *Proceedings of the 37th Conference on Winter Simulation* (Orlando, FL, December 4 - 7, 2005), 2 – 15, WSC '05, IEEE Piscataway, NJ

[11] Activity Datasets by Kasteren, T. V.: https://sites.google.com/site/tim0306/datasets

[12] Elfaham, A., Hagras, H., Helal, S., Hossain, S., Lee, Jaewoong, Cook, D. 2010. A fuzzy based verification agent for the PerSim human activity simulator in ambient intelligent environments. In *Proceedings of IEEE International Conference on Fuzzy Systems* (Barcelona, Spain, July 18 – 23, 2010), 1 – 8, FUZZ-IEEE '10

Data Assimilation in Agent Based Simulation of Smart Environment

Works in Progress Paper

Minghao Wang
Department of Computer Science
Georgia State University
Atlanta, USA
csloader@gmail.com

Xiaolin Hu
Department of Computer Science
Georgia State University
Atlanta, USA
xhu@cs.gsu.edu

ABSTRACT

Agent-based simulation is useful for studying people's movement in smart environment. Existing agent-based simulations are typically used as offline tools that help system design. They are not dynamically data-driven because they do not utilize any real time sensor data of the environment. In this paper, we present a method that assimilates real time sensor data into an agent-based simulation model. The goal of data assimilation is to provide inference of people's occupancy information in the smart environment, and thus lead to more accurate simulation results. We use particle filters to carry out the data assimilation and present some experiment results, and discuss how to extend this work for more advanced data assimilation in agent-based simulation of smart environment.

Categories and Subject Descriptors

I.6.0 [**Simulation and Modeling**]: Simulation types and techniques, Agent / discrete models, Data assimilation

Keywords

Agent-based Model; Data Assimilation; Particle Filter; Smart Environment

1. INTRODUCTION

Location information of occupants in building structure is valuable for scheduling efficient energy utilization, delivering conditioning air or developing evacuation strategy during emergencies. There is an increasing research interest in designing Intelligent/Smart Building architecture and applications that utilize occupancy information to automate the building's HVAC system. Agent-based simulation is a useful tool to study people's movement in building structures (see, e.g., [2][8]). It uses a bottom up approach to model individuals' behavior and their interactions with the environment. Over the years, different agent-based models with different levels of complexity have been developed, ranging from agents that model the basic movement behaviors (e.g., walking, avoiding obstacles) of pedestrians to agents that have psychological states and/or incorporate schedules (e.g., weekly working schedules) of different persons in an office environment. These simulations provide valuable information about the movement patterns of people in building structures and thus help the design of building structure and the development of egress strategies in emergency situations. Nevertheless, these simulations are typically used as offline tools that help system design. They are not dynamically data driven because they do not utilize any real time sensor data of the environment.

On the other hand, with the advances of sensor and communication technologies, more and more building environments are equipped with sensors that can provide real time occupant location information. In this paper, we refer to a smart environment as an indoor building environment equipped with sensors. In particular, we consider office environment on a building floor where people move between office rooms and corridors. With the real time data provided by sensors, how to assimilate these data into a simulation model becomes an important research topic. In this paper, we present a method that assimilates real time sensor data in agent-based simulation of smart environment. The goal of data assimilation is to provide an accurate inference of people's occupancy information from sensor data and the simulation model of occupancy dynamics. Knowing this information in real time is useful for energy control. It also supports simulations that can more accurately simulate people's movement behavior from the current time (because the simulation starts from a more accurate initial state, which is the system's current state), and thus provide useful information in real time decision making in emergency evacuation.

The quality of data assimilation depends on both the sensor data and the agent-based model. Different types of sensor devices have been used in smart environment. Typically, the sensors are sparsely deployed and provide only limited information about the environment, and thus one cannot extract the system state directly from the sensor observation. Sensing device with high resolution such as a video camera or ultrasonic radar has relatively precise measurement; however information collected by such sensors might be intrusive, and they are more expensive than low resolution sensors. In this paper, we consider binary motion sensors that provide non-intrusive information (see section 2 for more details). The quality of agent-based model will also have an impact on the data assimilation results. In general, a higher quality model captures the dynamics of the system more comprehensively and thus directing the simulation to more accurate results. In this paper, we use a relatively simple agent-based model to simulate people's movements. It is important to note that the data assimilation framework presented in this paper does not depend on the type of agent-based model and sensor data we use – it is general enough and can be adapted to other types of agent-based models and sensor data.

There are several existing works related to estimating building occupancy dynamics from models. In [6], researchers combine the sensor data, structure of the building and prior knowledge about utilization of the building together to estimate the building occupancy. In [5], Tomastik utilizes a combination of two different types of sensors and applied Extended Kalman Filter to estimate zone level occupancy information. In [3], Liao proposed a novel estimation approach which relies on an agent-based model of occupants. Our work differs from these previous works by developing an integrated approach that combines filtering technology and agent-based model to estimate the building occupancy in smart environment. We also note that while our work shares some similarities with research in target tracking, our ultimate goal is not to identify and to track each individual targets. Instead, we are more interested in estimating the overall occupancy information, i.e., the spatial density distribution of occupants, and then use that information for more accurate agent-based simulation of the smart environment.

The data assimilation algorithm we used in this research is Particle Filter (PF). PF is a set of statistical methods aiming at using observable variable to compute the latent variable linked to a Markov chain in some Bayesian model to estimate the state of a dynamic system [1]. It has the advantage that it does not have the assumption about the Gaussian property of the system and it allows the targeting posterior distribution to be multi-modal. In a standard bootstrap filter discussed in [1], the proposal distribution from which samples are drawn is constructed using the transition prior; in our work, the transition prior is the agent-based model for simulating occupants' movements.

The rest of this article is organized as follows: The framework is illustrated in section 2. Section 3 presents the experiment result and analysis. Conclusion and future work are described in section 4.

2. Data Assimilation in Agent-based Simulation

2.1 The smart environment and sensor

A smart environment is defined as any design that utilizes knowledge of the environment's context to aid occupants in accomplishing various tasks such as navigation, scheduling energy consumption, notification of activities and evacuation planning. A typical smart environment is deployed with various sensors. The data obtained by the sensing devices is then fused into a center control system for handling configurations for energy supply, air conditioner or providing building information related to the current context to the occupants.

Existing research for smart environment investigates the problem of estimating the position or distribution of occupants. ([3][4][5]) In this work, we assume that the simulated environment is deployed with sensors of the simplest form, that is, binary sensor that reports 1 as long as an occupant enters its sensing area and report 0 otherwise. It has the lowest resolution on detecting the movement of occupants entering its detection range and has the following features in terms of resolution, accuracy and ambiguity:

1. It provides anonymous position information.
2. Information it gets is ambiguous when multiple occupants are in the sensing area of single sensor,
3. Data it collects contains errors and is subject to environmental clutter.
4. Information volume is highly sensitive to the density and spatial pattern of the deployment of the sensors.

We assume that the observations generated by such sensor follow its expected basic functions described above and the model of observation error is simple.

2.2 The agent-based model

Construction of the agent-based model involves a bottom-up procedure. Specifically, the dynamics of occupants in this work are represented by the aggregation of moving behaviors of each individual occupant; agents' position at time k updates based on its current velocity and speed. A simple equation describing the physical law of position update may be used as the model of occupants' moving behavior. However, such an equation-based approach does not specify how the agent's speed and orientation are determined and fails to describe the effect of collision between agent and other object on the movement behavior.

We notice that people's movements in commercial building are generally associated with clear purposes. We model this procedure by generating a waypoint graph for the navigating behavior of each agent. The vertices of the graph represent the intersections of corridors and rooms of the building floor. With this graph, an arbitrary position in the floor can be connected to at least one of the vertices in the waypoint graph without engaging any obstacle.

The state space is therefore represented as follows:

$$\{l_k^i, v_k^i, d_k^i\}$$

And the function for determine velocity of a single agent is:

$$v_k^i = g(l_k^i, d_k^i) + Q$$

, where l ,v ,d represent the location, velocity and destination of agent i at time k respectively .

Fig 1 shows an example of a waypoint graph associates to a certain floor structure .

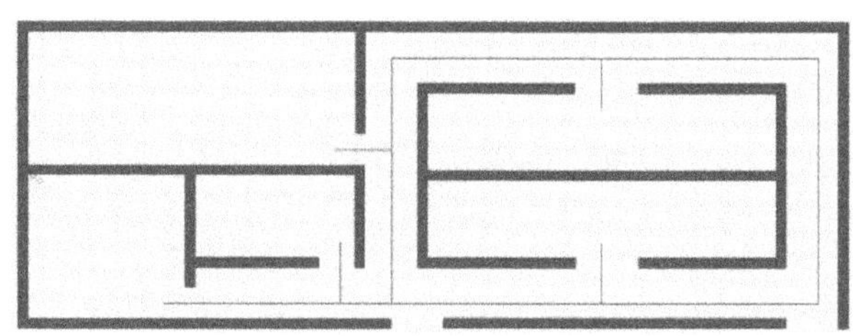

Fig 1, Floor structure with waypoint graph

According to the waypoint graph, an agent generates its route to a specific destination from its current position with the following rules:

1. Add current position to the waypoint graph by connect it to the nearest vertex such that the edge does not cross any obstacles (walls in this particular example).
2. Replace agent's current position with the destination of the agent in step 1 and repeat operations in step 1.
3. Find a shortest path from the starting position to the destination over the modified way point graph.
4. The vertices along the generated route are stored as the intermediate route points to the final destination.

By maintaining a list of intermediate route point, the speed vector of the agent is updated so that the moving direction of the agent always navigates to the final destination.

In addition to navigation, corridors and rooms in a typical building structure normally contain limited free space, which can easily result in congestion when the number of occupants is large. An agent-based model should be able to model the congestion behavior of occupants; the model otherwise fails to capture the important characteristic of people's flow pattern in such environment. Specifically, in this work, the avoidance is modeled by defining a comfortable distance for each agent. Agent will try to keep away from other individuals and reschedule a temporary route randomly to avoid potential collisions ahead.

2.3 Data Assimilation Framework

The designed agent-based model can be used as the predictive model in a data assimilation framework. Data assimilation involves incorporating observations from sensing devices into a predictive model to adjust the simulation and get the best estimate of a system's current state. Particle filter algorithms are suitable to deal with the state estimation problem in such scenario. To carry out data assimilation, we need to formulate the problem using a state-space model that contains a state transition equation (also referred to as the system transition model) and a measurement equation (also referred to as the observation model):

$$x_k \sim p(x_k \mid x_{k-1})$$
$$y_k \sim p(y_k \mid x_k)$$

,where x_k represents the posterior distribution at time k of system states evolved from states at previous time step x_{k-1} with some Markov process; and y_k represents likelihood function up to time k given posterior distribution at k. In particle filtering, the posterior state distributions are sampled into a number of weighted particles. The weights of these particles represent the likelihood of the particles. An additional resampling step is applied for eliminating particles with low weights and multiplying particles with high weights. Theoretically, by constructing an accurate easy-to-draw proposal distribution and utilizing sufficient number of particles, the estimated probability density function of system states will eventually converge to the posterior of the target system. In this paper, we draw samples only from the transition prior using the agent-based model. This means the proposal distribution is equal to the transition prior $p(x_k \mid x_{k-1})$ and the weight of the particles will be calculated from the measurement model.

2.3.1 System transition model

In our work, the state of each particle is defined as the positions of the entire set of agents. Since the agents' motions are largely driven by generated routes according to a waypoint graph, we also consider the destinations as part of the states. The system transition function is then described as follows according to the model defined in section 2.

$$S_{k+1} = a(S_k) + r_k$$

, where r_k is the noise and a is a state transition function described by the agent based simulation model described in section 2.

At each time step, samples are drawn by executing Δk steps of simulation based on the model:

$$S_{k+\Delta k} = est(a, S_k, \Delta k)$$

2.3.2 The observation model

The observations in this research are assumed to be generated from a set of binary sensors which will produce 1 if there is at least one occupant entering its sensing area and produce 0 otherwise. The error rate of the sensing device is set to 0.05 so that the probability for a sensor to report a false reading is 5%.

Assuming there are m deployed sensors; the output of the measurement is a size m array containing *0s* and *1s* to indicate whether there are agents in the sensors' detecting area.

To calculate the importance weight of a particle, the actual measurement vector SE_{real} is compared to the measurement vector of the sampled particle $SE_{particle}$ in bitwise manner, with two observation array

$$SE_{real} = [se_1^{real}, ..., se_m^{real}]$$
$$SE_{particle} = [se_1^{particle}, ..., se_m^{particle}]$$

The importance weight (likelihood) $w_k^{particle}$ of the particle is calculated as:

$$w_k^{particle} = \prod_{i=1}^{m} \omega_i$$

, where

$$\begin{cases} \omega_i = a & se_i^{real} = 1, se_i^{particle} = 1 \\ \omega_i = \sqrt[3]{a} & se_i^{real} = 0, se_i^{particle} = 0 \\ \omega_i = 1/a & else \end{cases}$$

The importance weight represents the degree of approximation of the state of a given particle i to the real state. Correct models for the noises r_k and z_k are important in constructing proposal distribution. For observation noise, we assume that the error rate is relatively low for the sensors and follows uniform distribution. The error rate of a sensor defines the probability a sensor reports false readings. For system noises, we add uniform distribution $R*u(0,1)$ to the positions of each agent, where R is a constant; we also add noise to agents' destinations as described below.

Given the destination of the ith agent, d_k^i , and a modifier lr ; the destination after adding noise is calculated as follows:

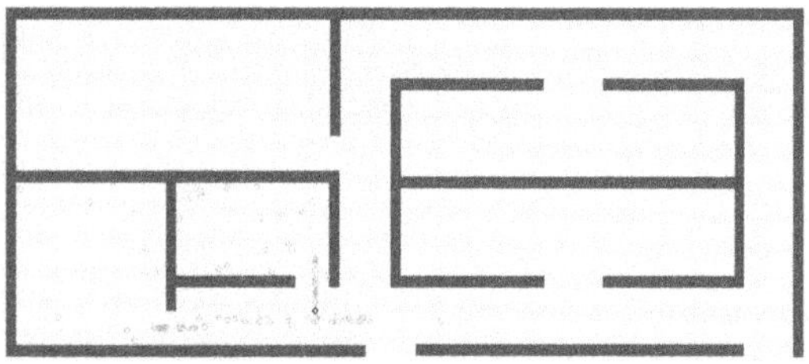

Fig 2. An example of possible destinations based on one position by adding random variance. The black circle represents the original destination and the lighter ones are the noisy destinations generated.

1. Determine the direction *angle* of d_k^i by calculating the direction from second last route point in the panned route to d_k^i.
2. According to a *probability* and *angle*; determine the direction where new destination will be extended from current destination position.
3. Let $lr' \leftarrow |GP(0,1)+lr|$ where GP is a Gaussian process with 0 mean and 1 variance.
4. $pt = d_k^i$, $pf = pt$
5. While $lr' \neq 0$ do $pf = pt$

Find the closest Vc in waypoint graph connected to $pt = Vc$

6. Select a position on the edge between pf and pt randomly as the new destination.

2.4 The Particle Filter Algorithm

With the system transition and observation models, we apply the standard bootstrap filter algorithm to carry out the data assimilation work. We note that the standard bootstrap filter has certain limitations (as will be discussed in Section 3) and we are developing more advanced particle filter algorithms, which will be presented in future work. The standard bootstrap algorithm can be summarized as in Table 1.

Table 1. The Bootstrap Filter algorithm

Algorithm 1 Bootstrap Filter Tracking Algorithm

1. <u>Initialization</u>. $t = 0$
   - For particle $i = 1,\ldots,N$, randomly assigning agents' positions and destinations in particle i; generate routes
   - Set $t = 1$
2. <u>Importance sampling step</u>
   - Add variance to the position and destination of the agents.
   - For particle $i = 1,\ldots,N$ after Δt steps of simulation based on model described by the simulation model.
   - For particle $i = 1,\ldots,N$, calculate weights
   - Normalize the weights
3. <u>Selection step(resampling step)</u>
   - Resample with replacement N particles $(x_{0:t}^{(i)}; i = 1,\ldots,N)$ from the set $(\tilde{x}_{0:t}^{(i)}; i = 1,\ldots,N)$ according to weights.
   - Set $t \leftarrow t+1$ and go to step 2.

Initially, agents in N particles are assigned with positions uniformly and randomly over the 2D space. The proposal distribution is constructed by executing the simulation for certain amount of time steps. (i.e. using the transition function to generate new samples). After this step, observation data from the binary motion sensor are utilized to calculate the likelihood of each particle. The likelihood is normalized to serve as the probability that a particle will be duplicated in the resampling step. In the selection step, we apply a roulette wheel selection [7] mechanism and select N new particles based on their normalized weights. The algorithm then goes to the importance sampling step and repeats.

3. Simulations and experiments

To verify our methods and to evaluate the effectiveness of the proposed algorithm, we have conducted a series of simulations and experiments with different number of agents. The simulation is based on a simulator which implements the system model and observation model specified in previous sections. We employ the identical twin experiment where a simulation is chosen as the "real" system that generates sensor data to be assimilated. We estimate agents' locations by assimilating these sensor data into the agent-based model and compare the estimated location information with that in the "real" system. In our experiments, the floor structure and sensor deployment information is shown in Fig 3. Initially, the positions and destinations of the agents are distributed uniformly over 800*300 2D space except the locations occupied by walls. Notice that in this research, the posterior is represented by an aggregation of all particles instead of a single one with the highest weight.

3.1 Experiment with Single Agent

This series of experiments aims at evaluating the robustness of the particle filter algorithm by tracking single agent; the evaluation of the accuracy is calculated as:

$$\frac{\sum_{k=1}^{800} | l_t^k - l_t^{real} |}{800}$$

We consider two scenarios: one is referred to as the regular route, where the tracked agent is designed to move forward through a sequence of destinations; the other is referred to as the turning back route, where the tracked agent is designed to move straight forward through a sequence of destinations, then turns back to move to its initial position. In both scenarios, the error rate of the sensor is set to 5%, which means the sensor has 5% probability to report 1 when it is supposed to report 0 and vice versa. Fig 4(a) shows these two scenarios.

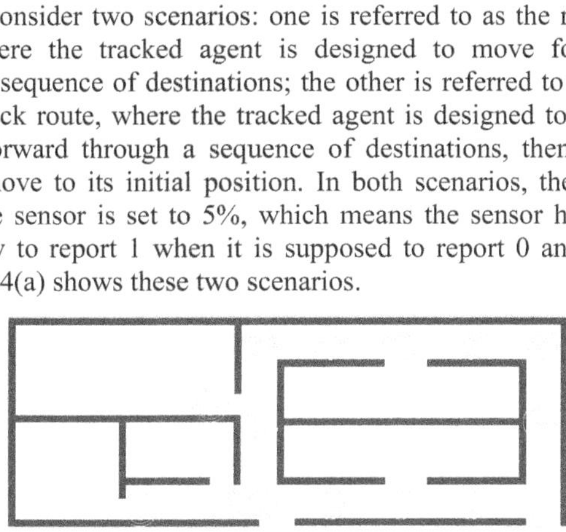

Fig 3, the simulation environment with obstacles and sparsely deployed sensors. The yellow circle represents the sensing area of deployed sensors.

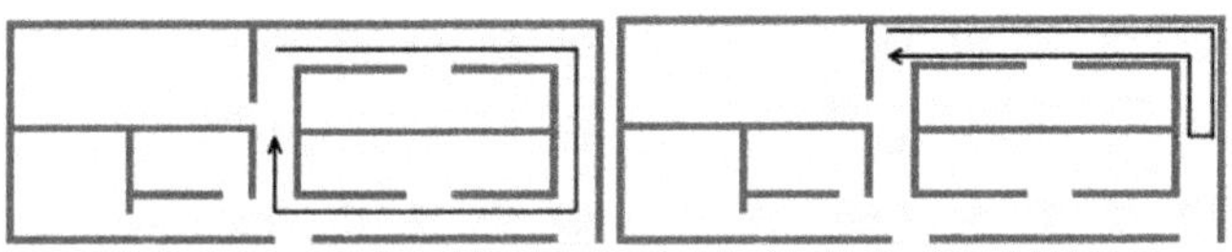

(a) The left shows regular route configuration and right shows the turning back route configuration

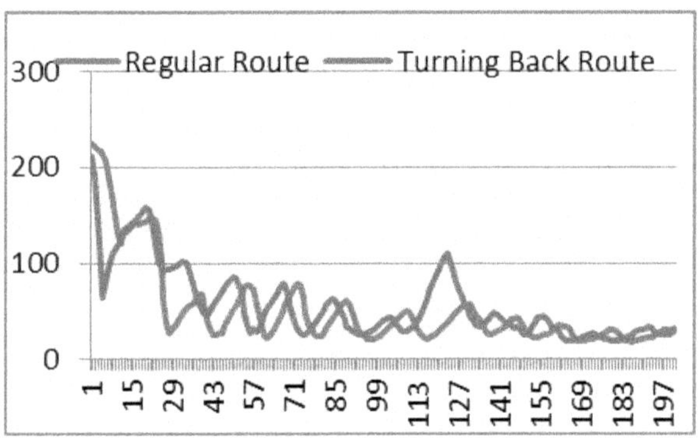

(b) Experimental results

Fig 4, estimation accuracy for regular route and turning back route.

Both of these two simulations share the same initial positions and sensor error configuration with 800 time steps of simulation. We run each of the simulations for 10 times and the error rates at each time step are averaged and plotted in Fig 4(b). In Fig. 4 (b) the vertical axis represents the error while the horizontal axis represents the iterations of the simulation. When Δt is set to 4, 800 time steps simulation consumes 200 estimation iterations. The curve presents a oscillated wave form where the error increases when the agent enters the blind area and decreases when the agent enters the sensors' detection area. The result shows that in the turning back route configuration, the error increases at the time interval where the agent is turning to an opposite direction. However, the tracking system was able to reduce this error soon after new sensor data arrive. This experiment shows that the method is working well for single agent.

3.2 Experiment with Multiple Agents

In this section, we conduct a series of simulations and experiments to compare the estimation effectiveness of the tracking algorithms to track two agents simultaneously using different number of particles. We set the route of the two agents spatially separated so that the two agents will keep a relatively long distance to each other. The initial positions of the two agents are set to be located at corridor area and have the maximum possible distance away from the nearest sensors. We modified the error measuring the accuracy calculation using 800 particles as follows:

$$\frac{\sum_{k=1}^{800} | l_t^{(1)k} - l_t^{(1)real} | + | l_t^{(2)k} - l_t^{(2)real} |}{800 \times 2}$$

The number of particles is changed from 800 to 400, 1200 and 1600 for evaluating the relationship between number of particles and the accuracy; we run each simulation for 350 time steps (95 simulation steps), average the errors of 10 simulations. This experiment is for verifying the effectiveness of the data assimilation method in multiple agent scenarios. We set the number of particles to 400,800, 1200, 1600 and calculate average error rate from time 0 to time 350 for each of these experiments. The results are plotted in Fig 5 and Fig 6, which shows that as the number of particles increases, the average estimation error decreases.

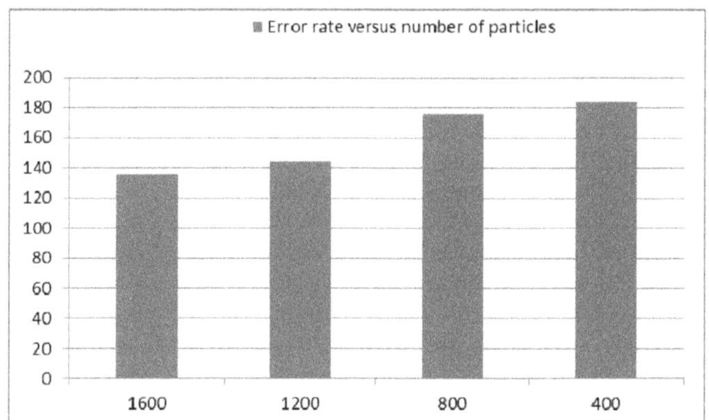

Fig 5. Average error rate using different number of particles

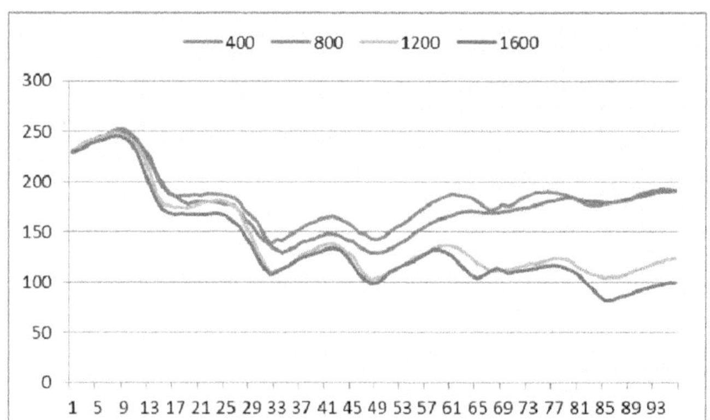

Fig 6. Average error rate per simulation step using different number of particles

In Fig 5, the vertical axis represents average estimation error in 10 simulation runs. For each run, the error is calculated by averaging the error of time step 0 to time step 350. The horizontal axis represents the number of particles initialized for estimation. When the number of particle is large, it is more likely that they will have lower estimation error. This is due to the fact that larger area of state space is covered for the initial state of the particles, therefore providing a more accurate starting point for subsequent simulations.

In Fig 6, the estimation errors over simulation time using different number of particles are presented. The error rate at a single simulation step is averaged from the error rates of 10 simulation runs at the same step. For N=400 and 800, due to the fact that in most of the simulations, the number of particles is insufficient to cover the region of the state space for providing an initial state that can lead to a global convergence; the algorithm can hardly converge to a density that is close to the posterior distribution. While the number of particle increases, this problem is solved because that larger area of the state space is covered for subsequent simulations.

The above experiment shows that there are certain limitations in the standard bootstrap filtering algorithm for inference of multiple agents. As the number of agents increases further, we expect the standard bootstrap filtering algorithm will not performance well. This is because we consider the locations of all agents as the system state. Thus a particle needs to have the correct combinations of all agents' locations in order to be selected. However, due to the irregular arrival time of the sensor data as well as the nature of the sequential importance sampling, this is not guaranteed that such a particle exists. This is especially true when the number of particles is small. In order to deal with the increasing dimensions of state space while tracking multiple agents, in future work we plan to develop an inter-state crossover resampling strategy. This strategy decouples different dimensions of the state space and regroups them together to form new particles. By doing this, combined states of agents in a multiple-agent system are relaxed and the sample space is enlarged. To avoid breaking dependencies among agents in a particle which may result in corruption of the simulation for individual particle, we plan to integrate this cross-over strategy into the standard particle filter algorithm. The new method will maintain the integrity of the system state represented by the particles and at the same time to enlarge the sample space by reconstructing new particles utilizing the crossover strategy.

4. Conclusion and Future work

In this paper, we investigate the problem of data assimilation in agent based simulation of smart environment with proximity sensors. We develop an agent-based model to represent the basic navigation and motion behavior of the occupants in building floor, and apply it in the particle filter algorithms to estimate the occupancy information of the environment at a given time. Several experiments are carried out in order to evaluate the accuracy and robustness of the algorithm. Future work will extend this work and develop more advanced methods to improve the data assimilation results.

5. Reference

[1] A. Doucet, N. De Freitas, and N. Gordon, *Sequential Monte Carlo methods in practice*. New York: Springer, 2001.

[2] D. J. Carter and B. Whitehead, "A study of pedestrian movement in a multi-storey office building," *Building and Environment,* vol. 11, pp. 239-247, 1976.

[3] L. Chenda and P. Barooah, "An integrated approach to occupancy modeling and estimation in commercial buildings," in *American Control Conference (ACC), 2010*, 2010, pp. 3130-3135.

[4] N. Shrivastava, R. Mudumbai, U. Madhow, and S. Suri, "Target tracking with binary proximity sensors: fundamental limits, minimal descriptions, and algorithms," presented at the Proceedings of the 4th international conference on Embedded networked sensor systems, Boulder, Colorado, USA, 2006.

[5] R. Tomastik, S. Narayanan, A. Banaszuk, and S. Meyn, "Model-Based Real-Time Estimation of Building Occupancy During Emergency Egress Pedestrian and Evacuation Dynamics 2008," W. W. F. Klingsch, C. Rogsch, A. Schadschneider, and M. Schreckenberg, Eds., ed: Springer Berlin Heidelberg, 2010, pp. 215-224.

[6] S. Meyn,; A. Surana; Y. Lin; S.M. Oggianu; S. Narayanan; A. Thomas, "A sensor-utility-network method for estimation of occupancy in buildings," *Decision and Control, 2009 held jointly with the 2009 28th Chinese Control Conference. CDC/CCC 2009. Proceedings of the 48th IEEE Conference on*, pp.1494, 1500, 15-18 Dec.2009 doi:10.1109/CDC.2009.5400442

[7] T. Bäck, *Evolutionary algorithms in theory and practice: evolution strategies, evolutionary programming, genetic algorithms*: Oxford University Press, 1996.

[8] V. Long, D. Quang, and K. Nahrstedt, "Jyotish: A novel framework for constructing predictive model of people movement from joint Wifi/Bluetooth trace," in Pervasive Computing and Communications

Designing Computational Steering Facilities for Distributed Agent Based Simulations

Work in Progress Paper

Gennaro Cordasco
Dipartimento di Psicologia
Seconda Università di Napoli
gennaro.cordasco@unina2.it

Rosario De Chiara
Centro Ricerca e Sviluppo
Poste Italiane
dechia24@posteitaliane.it

Francesco Raia
Dipartimento di Informatica
Università di Salerno
francesco.raia@gmail.com

Vittorio Scarano
Dipartimento di Informatica
Università di Salerno
vitsca@dia.unisa.it

Carmine Spagnuolo
Dipartimento di Informatica
Università di Salerno
spagnuolocarmine@gmail.com

Luca Vicidomini
Dipartimento di Informatica
Università di Salerno
lvicidomini@unisa.it

ABSTRACT

Agent-Based Models (ABMs) are a class of models which, by simulating the behavior of multiple agents (i.e., independent actions, interactions and adaptation), aim to emulate and/or predict complex phenomena. One of the general features of ABM simulations is their experimental capacity, that requires a viable and reliable infrastructure to interact with a running simulation, monitoring its behaviour, as it proceeds, and applying changes to the configurations at run time, (the *computational steering*) in order to study "what if" scenarios.

A common approach for improving the efficiency and the effectiveness of ABMs as a research tool is to distribute the overall computation on a number of machines, which makes the computational steering of the simulation particularly challenging.

In this paper, we present the principles and the architecture design of the management and control infrastructure that is available in D-MASON, a framework for implementing distributed ABM simulations. Together with an efficient parallel distribution of the simulation tasks, D-MASON offers a number of facilities to support the *computational steering* of a simulation, i.e. monitoring and interacting with a running distributed simulation.

Categories and Subject Descriptors

I.6.7 [**Computing Methodologies**]: Simulation and Modeling—*Simulation Support Systems*; C.2.4 [**Computer Systems Organization**]: Computer-Communication Networks—*Distributed Systems*

Keywords

Agent-Based Simulation, Distributed Systems, Computational Steering, Visualization of distributed models.

1. INTRODUCTION

Agent-Based Model (ABM) denotes a class of models which, simulating the behavior of multiple agents (i.e., independent actions, interactions and adaptation), aims to emulate and/or predict complex phenomena. An agent-based model consists of: a set of agents, a set of agent relationships and a framework for simulating agent behaviors and their interactions. For instance, ABMs can be used to represent a biological model like a school of fish, a scenario with people evacuating a building or, more in general, computational sociology experiments. ABMs have become very popular in various research fields, such as biology, ecology, economics, political science, etc..

Because of the modeling ABMs may easily comply with the KISS principle "keep it simple and short" that is simple agents may be sufficient to generate complex behaviors [25]. Unfortunately the "emergence" of such complex phenomena often requires computation-intensive software implementations. Computer science community has provided a large variety of solutions to such need to help the development and the testing of new models in each specific field, by providing tools, libraries and frameworks that speed up and make easier to manage (complex) simulations. A common approach for improving the efficiency of ABM is to distribute the overall computation on a number of machines. Several parallel implementation of ABMs frameworks have been proposed [6, 8, 12, 19].

A good parallel implementation should face several conflicting issues: (1) balance the overall load distribution; (2) minimize the communication overhead due to tasks interdependencies; (3) synchronize the evolution of the simulation among the machines that provide the computing power. A simple way to partition the whole computation into different tasks is to assign a fixed number of agents to each available worker [14]. This approach named *agents partitioning* enables a balanced workload distribution but usually introduces a significant communication overhead (all–to–all communications are required to synchronize the simulation).

Other strategies which partition the work in a smarter way [10], have been proposed in order to reduce the time due to the communication and synchronization between processes.

Parallelization and distribution of the (heavy) computational load has several important motivations in the Agent-Based Modeling field: first of all, the size of the models can be crucial to ensure that the emerging behaviour is indeed shown and made evident;

when models are too small, some of the effects might be hidden, not evident or emerge very late.

Motivations for Computational Steering. As a matter of fact, the research involving the use of simulation toolkits for ABMs is often conducted interactively, since the "generative" paradigm [15] describes an iterative methodology where models are designed tested and refined to reach the generation of an outcome with a simple generative model. In this context, given that scientists of the specific domain often are not computer scientists, usually they do not have access to systems for high performances computations for a long time, and usually they have to perform preliminary studies within their limited resources and, only later (if needed), allow extensive testing on large supercomputing centers. In social sciences, for example, the need for "*the capacity to model and make up in parallel, reactive and cognitive systems, and the means to observe their interactions and emerging effects*" [7] clearly outlined, since 1995, the needs of flexible, though powerful, tools.

This kind of facilities are well-known, in several fields. In numerical simulation field, it is known as *computational steering* and is defined as the process by which scientists interacts with a running simulation, monitoring the behaviour of the simulation, as it proceeds, and applying changes to the configuration during the execution, in order to exploit "what if" scenarios. Very often the computation steering includes some sort of online visualization tool, in order to provide the scientists adequate feedback to evaluate the effect and the impact of the modifications.

Of course, when the simulation is distributed the problem becomes rather complex and time/resource consuming. The risk is that, by imposing management and coordination, one can jeopardize the performance gains, thereby reducing effectiveness of distributed simulations.

Nevertheless, the impact of an effective and efficient computational steering is known to be very significant [21]: it closes the loop such that scientist can interactively respond to results as they occur, reducing the time between the parameter change and the visualization of the results, which makes more evident the cause-effect relationship.

In this paper, we present the design of Computational Steering for D-MASON [8, 4, 9], a distributed framework, based on MASON [17, 18].

2. RELATED WORK

Commonly used toolkits for ABMs are described in [20] and an interesting comparison of them is presented in [1, 24]. Several important issues in evaluating different platforms for ABM are speed of execution, flexibility, reproducibility, documentation, open-source and computational steering facilities.

In the following we briefly review some widespread toolkits for ABMs.

Repast HPC. Repast for High Performance Computing (HPC) [6] is a framework for agent-based simulation written in C++ and leveraging MPI as communication standard for parallel computation. It uses mostly all-to-all communication operations for synchronization and agents retrieval and migration.

NetLogo. NetLogo [26] allows the user to design the simulation by using a functional language inspired by Logo and, for this reason, it appears to be easier to be grasped by a wider audience.

FLAME. The Flexible Large-scale Agent Modelling Environment [5] is an agent-based applications generator built upon three main elements: an XMML agent specification language, the function C files and the xparser with associated templates. The basic characteristic of FLAME are those of activation (state changes) and agent-to-agent communication. Communication is implemented as a set of *message boards* (one for each message type) on which agents post messages and from which agents can read messages.

Several papers have presented techniques and tools for runtime interactive monitoring and steering on a distributed environment. These systems allow a rapid and deeper understanding of the behavior of the simulations through either the ability to view the evolution of simple and/or aggregated data of the simulations or the possibility to tune parameters at runtime [11, 27].

In [22, 16] the authors presents DIOS, a detailed infrastructure for enabling the runtime monitoring and computational steering of parallel and distributed applications. The infrastructure is designed for generic applications and allows to: (1) extend objects in such a way to export interaction interfaces that enable their state to be externally monitored and changed; (2) define a hierarchical control network for an efficient management of parallel and distributed applications.

3. DISTRIBUTED AGENT-BASED SIMULATIONS

Some aspects of ABMs implementation can be effectively parallelizable. For example, in the process of designing an ABMs there is a phase of exploration of the parameters' space. In this phase a parallel architecture can be easily exploited by letting multiple simulations run at once with different parameters settings on multiple machines [3].

Other requirements are to run massive simulation (i.e., simulating a large number of agents) and/or simulations which deal with complex agents, that is, computationally intensive agents. A common approach to the parallelization of this task is just an instance of a more general approach of parallelizing a sequential computation by dividing it into smaller computations (subtasks) and assigning them to different processes for parallel executions. This two phases represent two key steps in the design of parallel algorithms [14]. The communication and the synchronization between the different subtasks are typically some of the greatest obstacles in getting good parallel program performances.

Agent-Based Simulations are designed according to a discrete-event paradigm where the simulation time is split in steps named *simulation steps*, often but not necessarily of the same duration.

We consider a general purpose framework for discrete-event, agent-based, distributed simulations. Typically such frameworks enlist the aid of two or more workers, each replicating the functionality of the single-process simulation and taking charge of a partition of the set of the agents. Considering that most ABMs are inspired by natural models where agents are placed in a bi-dimensional (or tri-dimensional) space and agents communications/interactions are limited to a delimited area of interest (AOI) a natural way to split up the simulation between workers is to divide the space in regions, and then assigning each region, and the agents it comprises, to a worker by implementing a *space partitioning*. Since the AOI extension of an agent is small compared with the size of a region it belongs to, the communication is mostly limited to local messages within the same worker. Workers in charge of the simulation of neighboring regions, are locally synchronized in order to let the simulation run consistently (see Figure 1).

One of the main peculiarity of ABMs is their *experimental* capacity, that requires a viable and reliable infrastructure for running but also keeping the records of several experiments. In particular, models are designed using an incremental approach, from simpler to more complex ones, where the characteristics of the next model are chosen according to the results obtained from previous models. Moreover, scientists are interested in *inspecting* some data col-

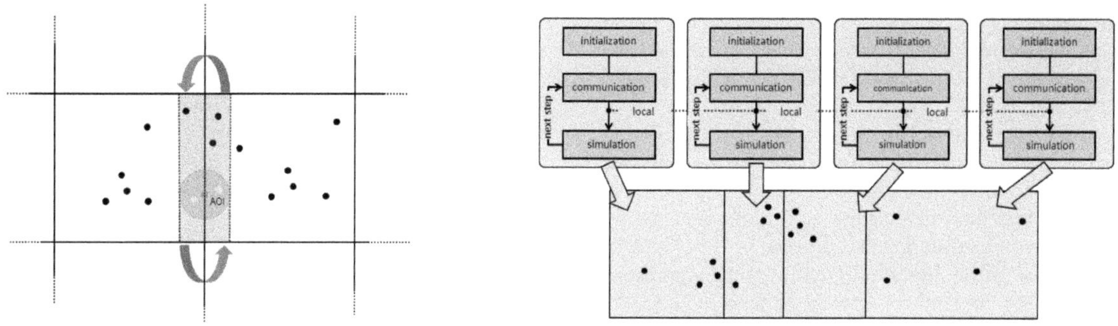

Figure 1: Space partitioning and Synchronization.

lected while running a simulation. This data may be related to a single agent and/or to the whole simulation itself.

Simulation-related data are either autonomously updated by scheduled agents or derived by the simulation framework when needed (typically once every n-th simulation step).

In a single-process simulation, the process itself acts as repository for the inspected data. On the other hand, a distributed simulation is split into several processes, so inspecting data on distributed simulations requires:

1. collect data from distributed processes (*gather*);
2. process the collected data in order to display it in a convenient manner (*reduce*).

It should be noted that, while the gathering phase requires communication from processes, the processing (or *reducing*) phase can be done on an external process dedicated to aggregation, storage (logging) and the display of aggregated data.

In some cases, the aggregate data resulting from a simulation step i are required as input for the simulation of step $i+1$ (global parameters). This is, indeed, another problem, even more difficult to approach since it requires the three following steps:

1. collect data from distributed processes (*gather*);
2. process the collected data (*reduce*);
3. deliver the aggregated data back to all the processes (*scatter*).

4. COMPUTATIONAL STEERING ON A DISTRIBUTED ENVIRONMENT

In this section we present the architecture of a computational steering tool based on a distributed ABMs. As observed in previous Section, three functionalities have to be implemented in order to allow the researcher interacting with a distributed simulation:

gather, to collect data from distributed processes;

reduce, which combine collected data into a single element;

scatter, deliver the aggregated data back to all the processes.

In some cases, for matter of efficiency, the gather step also comprises a preliminary data compression stage (see Section 6.2).

We considered several approaches ranging from centralized to fully distributed approach to implement such functions. The centralized approach implies a single point of collection named *collector*. The collector has to: (1) subscribe to all data; (2) for each simulation step it collects, combines and eventually sends back aggregated data. The main advantages of the centralized approach are its inherent simplicity and a limited impact on communication. Moreover, since data is collected at one point, it is immediately available for analysis. On the other hand, in a fully distribute approach each process acts as a collector: the scatter functionality is not needed anymore because each collector can combine data on its own but, unfortunately, this approach requires an all to all communication which is clearly not scalable. Other intermediate approaches have been considered where a gathering/scattering tree is build among processes in order to minimize the impact on communication [2]. The problem with these approaches is that both the gather and scatter phases require multiple steps (one for each level of the tree) and therefore more time. This impact negatively on the synchronization time, and then on the overall efficiency (i.e., speed) of the system.

For the reasoning above we decided to implement a very simple tool that provides the three functionalities described above (see Figure 2). The tool is based on a single collector which communicates with each worker that carries out the simulation.

The tool is completely configurable: it allows to choose which data is to be sent to the collector and which data is sent back to the worker.

Each worker, at the end of each simulation step, sends to the collector a single chunk of information containing all and only the data required by the collector. The collector aggregates the data and, if requested, sends back the aggregated data plus some information about the data to be collected in the next steps.

We implemented this architecture on top of D-MASON, that is a distributed version of MASON, a well-known and popular library for writing and running Agent-based simulations.

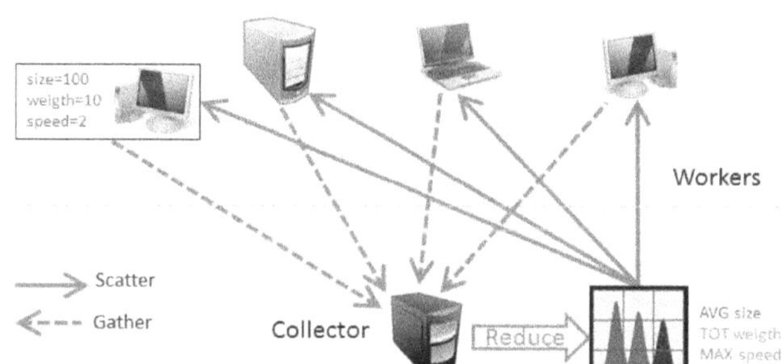

Figure 2: The architecture of a centralized computational steering tool.

5. MASON AND D-MASON

Before presenting the features of D-MASON in the next subsection we will, first, introduce MASON.

5.1 MASON

MASON [17, 18] toolkit is a discrete-event simulation core and visualization library written in Java, designed to be used for a wide range of ABMs. The toolkit is composed of two independent layers: the *simulation* layer and the *visualization* layer. The simulation layer is the core of MASON and is mainly represented by an event scheduler and a variety of fields which hold agents into a given simulation space. MASON is mainly based on step-able agent: a computational entity which may be scheduled to perform some action (step), and which can interact (communicate) with other agents.

The visualization layer permits both visualization and manipulation of the model. The simulation layer is independent from the visualization layer, which allows us to treat the model as a self-contained entity.

The main reasons that suggested the development of a distributed version of MASON are: (a) MASON is one of the most expressive and efficient library for ABMs (as reported by many reviews [1, 23, 24]); (b) MASON architecture, that clearly separates visualization by simulation, greatly helped during the process of development of a distributed version of the library [17, 18]; (c) the significant amount of research and simulations already present in MASON, which can be easily ported to D-MASON, makes it particularly cost effective for the scientists.

5.2 D-MASON

D-MASON [8, 4, 9] adds a new layer named *D-simulation* which extends the MASON simulation layer. The new layer adds some features that allow the distribution of the simulation work on multiple, even heterogeneous, machines (workers). Notice that the new layer does not alter in any way the existing layers. Moreover, it has been designed in order to enable the porting of existing applications to a distributed platform in a transparent and easy way.

D-MASON is based on a master/workers paradigm which exploits a space partitioning approach: the master partitions the space to be simulated (the field) into regions. Each region, together with the agents it contains, is assigned to a worker; then each worker is in charge of: simulating the agents that belong to the assigned region; handling the migration of agents; managing the synchronization between neighboring regions (this information exchange is required in order to let the simulation run consistently).

D-MASON uses a standard approach to achieve a consistent local synchronization of the distributed simulations: each step is associated with a fixed state of the simulation. Regions are simulated step by step. Since the step i of region r is computed by using the states $i-1$ of r's neighborhood, the step i of a region cannot be executed until the states $i-1$ of its neighborhood have been computed and delivered. In other words, each region is synchronized with its neighborhood before each simulation step.

D-MASON workers communicate via a well-known mechanism, based on the publish-subscribe design pattern: a multicast channel (henceforth topic) is assigned to each region; workers then simply subscribe to the topics associated with the regions which overlap with their AOI in order to receive relevant message updates. Other topics are also used for system management (see Section 6). The current version of D-MASON uses Java Message Service (JMS) for communication between workers. Furthermore there is a communication server, running Apache ActiveMQ Server, that acts as a JMS provider (i.e., it allows to generate and manage topics and route messages accordingly).

D-MASON is released under a Free and Open Software license and is available at [13].

6. D-MASON COMPUTATIONAL STEERING DESIGN

In this Section we describe the design of the environment for Computational Steering developed in D-MASON.

6.1 The Global Inspector

The Global Inspector (see Figure 3 (b)) is inspired by the MASON Inspector tool (see Figure 3 (a)) and is responsible for collecting, aggregating and displaying data from the workers. The Global Inspector communicates with workers using a dedicated topic for both command broadcast and data delivery. When the Global Inspector is executed, either before or while running the simulation, the gathering function is not automatically executed: instead a graphical user interface is presented with a list of inspectable parameters that can be checked individually. When the user chooses to start tracing a parameter, the Global Inspector uses its own channel to instruct the workers to begin sending that parameter and the gathering functionality is enabled.

The gather functionality. Each worker keeps a list of parameters it has to send, so at each step it (1) collects required data, (2) creates an object containing current step value and the values read for inspected parameters and (3) sends the created object to the Global Inspector through its topic.

The Global Inspector runs a special instance of the simulation whose only goal is to receive data gathered from workers and reduce them to a useful, displayable form. The procedure that will perform the actual reduction of the data collected by the Inspector deeply depends on the semantics of the simulation and for this reason, the scientist is in charge of implementing it, taking into account all of the implications. This allows a great flexibility since the scientist can decide what data are to be sent for reduction and easily perform a variety of reduction operations such as sum, mean, array operations, etc... Data gathered from workers are stored in a priority queue where the ordering key is the step number in which the such data have been generated. By exploiting such queue the Global Inspector will be able to extract data sorted by step number and to apply the reduction function to the data referring to a specific step. Reduced data are displayed through Global Inspector's user interface and can also be charted or logged to disk by leveraging such facilities that are already present in MASON.

6.2 The Global Viewer

The Global Viewer provides an efficient tool that allows visualizing a simplified representation of what is happening in the entire simulation field. A special kind of inspectable parameter is called "graphics" and allows to display an image representing agents' position within the field.

The image is composed and displayed by a component called Global Viewer, embedded into the Global Inspector. What makes graphics a special type of parameter is the fact that agents' positions do not need to be aggregated later by the Global Inspector. Instead, each worker simulating a rectangular region, for each simulation step, creates an image which represents a snapshot and summarizes some data (for example agents' position). Each image is sent to the Global Viewer, which places the image in the corresponding position of a canvas representing the whole field, without further elaboration. Each simulation step is preceded by a synchronization phase, during which each worker builds a bitmap image depicting agents' position on that regions. The bitmap image is packed into a `RemoteSnap` object together with region ID, top-left coordinates and step number. The `RemoteSnap` object is, then, published to a management topic named GLOBALS. The Global Inspector subscribes to GLOBALS so that it will receive `RemoteSnaps` from every worker at every step. The Global Inspector waits for all the `RemoteSnap` objects of the step being inspected and paints the whole image using received bitmaps, top-left coordinates and region sizes. It is important to store top-left coordinates and region sizes within `RemoteSnaps` at every step, because the load-balancing mechanism [4] can expand or reduce worker's area of concern. All these operations are implemented at framework level, so the whole process will work transparently as long as agents' positions are defined.

In order to decrease the network overhead, images are embedded into the Global Inspector's gathering procedure, so each worker, for

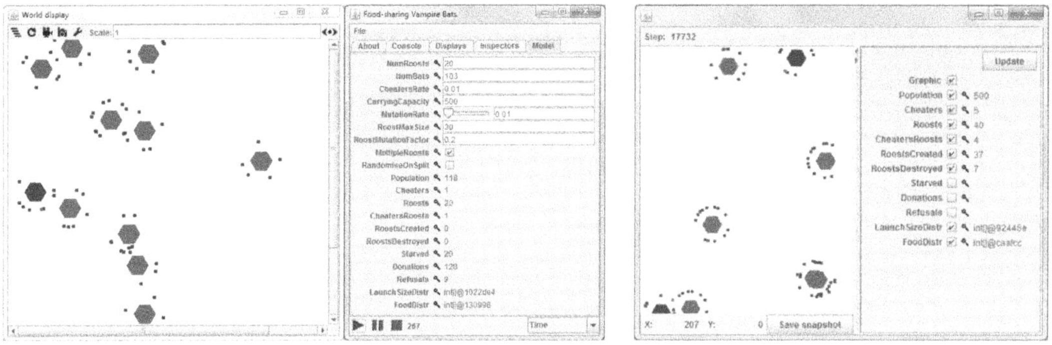

(a) (b)

Figure 3: (a) The MASON Inspector and (b) the D-MASON Global Inspector.

each simulation step, sends a single packet containing both graphics and inspected data through the dedicated topic. According to the size of regions, the level of details needed, the network speed and the computational power available on both, workers and the collector, strategies like image compression/decompression can be implemented in order to make the system more efficient.

6.3 Global Parameters

Global parameters are dynamic data which describe some aspects, about the overall simulation, and affect the evolution of the simulation. Global parameters can be derived aggregating local data, using the gathering functionality, or may be parameters editable by the user at running time.

All-to-all. A first attempt to implement Global Parameters in D-MASON was based on a single broadcast topic (e.g., GLOBALS). All the workers subscribed to GLOBALS and then, right before the simulation step, each worker publishes its own data to GLOBALS and receives a message from each other worker, thus implementing an all-to-all communication. After receiving all the messages, each worker is able to aggregate data on its own. Even if this implementation was simple because the synchronization is obtained in one single phase, it performed very poorly even using a small number of workers. With this mechanism, indeed, the number of exchanged messages needed for each synchronization phase grows quadratically as a function of the number of workers.

Two phases. Then we adopted a two phases approach. As already stated, D-MASON provides a mechanism which allows to synchronize workers that simulate neighboring regions. When we use global parameters this mechanism should be strengthened: we need data to be gathered (phase 1), reduced and scattered (phase 2) to each region before each simulation step. Inspired by other implementations, such as the *All-Reduce* operation in MPI, we decided to split the reduction task into two phases. First each worker sends its data to a GLOBAL_DATA topic, whose only subscriber is the collector. Once all data for a given step is received, the collector calculates the aggregated data and publishes it to a GLOBAL_REDUCED topic, whose subscribers are all the workers. Using this two phase approach the number of messages needed for the synchronization grows linearly in the number of workers.

We have compared the two implementations by running a benchmark consisting of running 40 000 global parameters synchronizations, obtained running an empty simulation. In this way we measured the time spent during synchronization phases. In Table 1 we report the wall clock times observed. For both the implementations, the required time is directly proportional to the number of messages sent. As the number of workers increases, the two phases approach becomes more and more efficient than the all-to-all approach; even with 5 workers the two phases approach perform better. Moreover with 16 workers, the two phases implementation is about 3.5 times faster.

# of workers	All-to-all (s)	Two phases (s)
2	7.4	10.7
3	10.8	13.2
4	15.5	16.1
5	21.4	18.9
6	29.3	21.8
8	49.9	27.4
12	115.8	39.5
16	188.2	52.8

Table 1: Comparison of Global Parameters implementations. Number of seconds to execute 40 000 synchronizations using 2 to 16 workers.

6.4 The user's view

The rationale of D-MASON is to address the quest for scalability of ABMs with a minimal impact on the development. The scientist, that design simulations, should not be directly aware of the parallelism embedded into the simulation. Indeed, one of the design goals of D-MASON is trying to to keep the distribution of sequential simulations as simple as possible. According to this goal, it is worth to mention that the Global Viewer is automatically available for the user without any intervention from the developer. Moreover, in the following, we present a description of the marginal intervention that the developer is asked to provide in order to use inspectable and global parameters.

Declaring inspectable parameters. As previously stated inspectable parameters require the developer to instruct the framework about data to be exchanged and processed. Mimicking MASON's way to annotate data, we introduce a set of methods a developer has to write in order to enable the Global Inspector for a given simulation. MASON embeds a so-called *Inspector panel* that allows the user to track parameters enabled for inspection. To enable a property the simulation class must expose a related public *getter* method.

To enable the same property on D-MASON's Global Inspector, a new public *reduce* method has to be added. This methods takes an array of parameter, where every entry is data collected from a single process using the "get" method, and performs the reduction.

Declaring global parameters. Global parameters can be aggregated local data, or parameters editable by the user.

First, a scientist must specify what parameters will be considered global. This is done by adding a related "global" method returning `true`. Before the simulation starts, D-MASON inspect the simulation class and look for *global* methods. Then, the developer has to write methods to gather and reduce this parameter from the regions. In order to avoid ambiguity, the simulation has to track two values for each global parameter: a global (simulation–wide) value obtained by the collector before each simulation step and a local (region–wide) value updated during the a simulation step and sent to the collector at the end of each step. So we need to add getter and setter methods for these values.

Simulations cannot ignore separation of local and global parameters: local parameters must be kept updated during the simulation because they will be needed for gathering and reduction, while global parameters will be used during the simulation.

7. CONCLUSION

This paper reports on an currently undergoing project, D-MASON, that has been developed with the purpose of speeding up the performances of MASON, a very well known and quite widespread framework for ABMs.

This work has been motivated by the the need for a computational steering facility that is extremely important for the development, the tuning and the analysis of complex simulations. We observed that, while this kind of facility is quite simple to be implemented in a sequential simulation (all the needed data resides in a single machine), in a distributed system it is necessary to collect and, in case, reduce the data, for each simulation step.

We have shown a simple architecture that deals with the issues presented above and we have validated the effectiveness of the strategies proposed by realizing the D-MASON Global Inspector. The Global Inspector have been designed to follow the spirit of D-MASON: an efficient tool with a marginal effort to the developer. In fact, we also shown some evidence of how easy is for the programmer to use computational steering in his/her simulation, by writing their own reduce operations that are automatically used by D-MASON infrastructure.

Future Work. Based on the same architecture, further work is already planned to increase the computational steering set of functionalities that are available to the user/programmer. For example, as described in [21] about distributed applications to be steered, it is important to provide to the user also information about the processors and network load, during the execution. Based on the work presented in this paper, the task is easily achievable and will be included in the next versions of D-MASON. About the visualization part, it is important to further investigate the trade-off between compression of the images to be assembled (smaller size but CPU (=time) consuming) and bandwidth limitation, in order to understand in Global Viewer if there exist a general solution that adapts to the available CPUs/Bandwidth the choice.

8. REFERENCES

[1] M. Berryman. Review of Software Platforms for Agent Based Models. Technical Report DSTO-GD-0532, Australian Government, Department of Defence, 2008.

[2] S. Bhatt, G. Pucci, A. Ranade, and A. Rosenberg. Scattering and gathering messages in networks of processors. *Computers, IEEE Transactions on*, 42(8):938 –949, 1993.

[3] B. Calvez and G. Hutzler. Parameter space exploration of agent-based models. In *Proceedings of the 9th international conference on Knowledge-Based Intelligent Information and Engineering Systems*, KES'05, pages 633–639, 2005.

[4] M. Carillo, G. Cordasco, R. De Chiara, F. Raia, V. Scarano, and F. Serrapica. Enhancing the performances of d-mason - a motivating example. In *SIMULTECH*, pages 137–143, 2012.

[5] S. Coakley, M. Gheorghe, M. Holcombe, S. Chin, D. Worth, and C. Greenough. Exploitation of High Performance Computing in the FLAME Agent-Based Simulation Framework. In *IEEE 14th International Conference on High Performance Computing and Communication and 9th International Conference on Embedded Software and Systems (HPCC-ICESS)*, pages 538–545, 2012.

[6] N. Collier and M. North. Parallel agent-based simulation with Repast for High Performance Computing. *SIMULATION: Transactions of the Society for Modeling and Simulation International*, online:, 2012.

[7] R. Conte and C. Castelfranchi. *Cognitive and Social Action*. UCL Press, June 1995.

[8] G. Cordasco, R. De Chiara, A. Mancuso, D. Mazzeo, V. Scarano, and C. Spagnuolo. A Framework for distributing Agent-based simulations. In *9th Intern. Wkshp. on Algorithms, Models and Tools for Parallel Computing on Heterogeneous Platforms*, 2011.

[9] G. Cordasco, R. De Chiara, A. Mancuso, D. Mazzeo, V. Scarano, and C. Spagnuolo. Bringing together efficiency and effectiveness in distributed simulations: the experience with D-MASON. *Submitted for publication*, 2013.

[10] B. Cosenza, G. Cordasco, R. De Chiara, and V. Scarano. Distributed Load Balancing for Parallel Agent-based Simulations. In *Proc. of the 19th Euromicro International Conference on Parallel, Distributed and Network-Based Computing (PDP 2011)*, 2011.

[11] T. De Wolf and T. Holvoet. Towards autonomic computing: agent-based modelling, dynamical systems analysis, and decentralised control. In *Proc. of IEEE Inter. Conf. on Industrial Informatics (INDIN 2003)*, pages 470–479, 2003.

[12] C. Deissenberg, S. van der Hoog, and H. Dawid. Eurace: A massively parallel agent-based model of the european economy. *Applied Mathematics and Computation*, 204:541–552, 2008.

[13] Distributed-Mason Project. http://www.isislab.it/projects/dmason/, 2011.

[14] J. Dongarra, I. Foster, G. Fox, W. Gropp, K. Kennedy, L. Torczon, and A. White, editors. *Sourcebook of parallel computing*. Morgan Kaufmann Publishers Inc., San Francisco, CA, USA, 2003.

[15] S. A. L. Joshua M. Epstein and S. E. Steven H. Strogatz, editors. *Generative Social Science: Studies in Agent-Based Computational Modeling*. Princeton University Press, 2007.

[16] H. Liu and M. Parashar. Rule-based monitoring and steering of distributed scientific applications. *International Journal of High Performance Computing and Networking*, 3(4):272–282, 2005.

[17] S. Luke, C. Cioffi-Revilla, L. Panait, and K. Sullivan. MASON: A new multi-agent simulation toolkit. In *Proceedings of the SwarmFest Workshop, Ann Arbor (Michigan), USA. May 9-11*, 2004.

[18] S. Luke, C. Cioffi-Revilla, L. Panait, K. Sullivan, and G. Balan. MASON: A Multiagent Simulation Environment. *Simulation*, 81(7):517–527, 2005.

[19] M. Lysenko and R. M. D'Souza. A framework for megascale agent based model simulations on graphics processing units. *Journal of Artificial Societies and Social Simulation*, 11(4):, 2008.

[20] C. M. Macal and M. J. North. Tutorial on agent-based modeling and simulation part 2: how to model with agents. In *Proc. of the 38th Conference on Winter simulation*, WSC '06, pages 73–83, 2006.

[21] J. D. Mulder, J. J. van Wijk, and R. van Liere. A survey of computational steering environments. *Future Gener. Comput. Syst.*, 15(1):119–129, Feb. 1999.

[22] R. Muralidhar and M. Parashar. A distributed object infrastructure for interaction and steering. *Concurrency and Computation: Practice and Experience*, 15(10):957–977, 2003.

[23] R. Najlis, M. A. Janssen, and D. C. Parkerx. Software tools and communication issues. In *Proc. Agent-Based Models of Land-Use and Land-Cover Change Workshop*, pages 17–30, 2001.

[24] S. F. Railsback, S. L. Lytinen, and S. K. Jackson. Agent-based simulation platforms: Review and development recommendations. *Simulation*, 82:609–623, September 2006.

[25] H. A. Simon. *The sciences of the artificial (3rd ed.)*. MIT Press, Cambridge, MA, USA, 1996.

[26] S. Tisue and U. Wilensky. NetLogo: A simple environment for modeling complexity. In *International Conference on Complex Systems*, pages 16–21, 2004.

[27] C. Wagner, A. Middel, I. Scheler, and H. Hagen. Open Problems in Computational Steering of Massive Parallel Unstructured Grid Based CFD Simulations. In *Visualization of Large and Unstructured Data Sets-Applications in Geospatial Planning, Modeling and Engineering (IRTG 1131 Workshop)*, volume 19, pages 82–89, 2011.

Research and Application on Ontology-based Layered Cloud Simulation Service Description Framework

(Work in Progress Paper)

Tan Li, Xudong Chai, Baocun Hou, Bohu Li
Beijing Simulation Center
No.52, Yongding Road, Haidian District
Beijing, China
(0086)13811058891
someone8584@sina.com

ABSTRACT

Cloud simulation system improves the ability of current network-based M&S in on-demand simulation and massive–user service. The share of multi-granularity resources and dynamic establishment of simulation services in Cloud Simulation raise new challenges to the Simulation Service Description Framework (SSDF). An ontology-based layered SSDF (OLSSDF) was proposed towards those challenges in cloud simulation, which includes the layered architecture of cloud simulation service and the ontology semantics of each layer in the framework which were defined and formalized in OWL-S. The OLSSDF for cloud simulation was applied and in the description of simulation services in certain cloud simulation system prototype of aero plane. The primary research and application show that the OLSSDF oriented to cloud simulation, which describes cloud simulation services in both attribute-semantic and model-semantic, adapts well to the various multi-granularity simulation resources and facilitates the intelligent discovery and automatic combination of simulation services in the cloud simulation mode.

Categories and Subject Descriptors

I.6.7 [**SIMULATION AND MODELING**]: Simulation Support Systems –*Environments*.

General Terms: Design, Management.

Keywords: Cloud Simulation; Simulation Service Description Framework; Ontology; Layered; OWL-S.

1. INTRODUCTION

From the in-depth applications of M&S in manufacturing and scientific research, two types of new demands emerge, which are 1) the large scale and complicated structure of the simulated systems require new distributed collaborative M&S systems; 2) users demands barrier-free M&S services through network at anywhere anytime. Those new demands push the development of the network M&S system based on modern network technology [1] [2]. Cloud Simulation System (CSS) put forward in article [3] combines cloud computing with virtualization, pervasive computing and high performance computing technology, improves the ability of current network M&S system in share of simulation resource, support of massive users, collaboration and fault-tolerance.

Share of various multi-granularity simulation resources and dynamic assemble of simulation services are the kernel features of the cloud simulation mode. Accordingly, the new features raise new challenges to the Simulation Service Description Framework (SSDF), including the demand to describe and manage fine-grained resources in CSS (including CPU core, memory, software and other sub-resources in the node), and support the on-demand automatic combination of various simulation resource services based on user demand description.

Ontology technology [4] has been widely applied in semantic web, which solves the encapsulation and combination of the web services using the abstract semantic description of them. According to the features and demands mentioned above, this paper analyzes the layered structure of the cloud simulation services based on the prime research and practice of CSS, and puts forward an ontology-based layered SSDF (OLSSDF) oriented to cloud simulation, including the layered architecture of cloud simulation service and the ontology semantics of each layer in the framework which were defined and formalized in OWL-S [5]. Then the framework is applied in the Simulation Service Description of the CSS prototype, COSIM-CSP [3], and a typical application of aero plane design is stated to verify the effects of OLSSDF. Finally, the future works of OLSSDF are presented.

2. THE CONNOTATION AND APPLICATION ARCHITECTURE OF CLOUD SIMULATION SYSTEM

Cloud Simulation System is a new kind of networked modeling and simulation system. Lead by the application demands, the background of application field, it synthetically applies modern M&S technology, advanced information technology and domain-related application technology, to realize the dynamic share and reuse on demand of various resources in the system, collaboratively cooperation on demand of resources for multi-users, and dynamic optimization of scheduling executions, etc., to support the various activities in full life cycle (from argumentation, research, design, development, test, execution, evaluation to maintenance and disposal) for existing or tentative complex systems/projects in both engineering and non-engineering field.

Cloud Simulation System is essentially the step stage of Grid Simulation, which finally implement the idea of "Simulation as a Service" (SaaS). The development of CSS brings a new simulation mode, "Cloud Simulation Mode", which utilize network and cloud simulation platform to organize various simulation resources on demand, to provide users all kinds of M&S service. In this mode, CSS identifies the different simulation task demands for each user, dynamically establishes virtualized collaborative simulation environment and automatically deploys cloud simulation services encapsulated from simulation software, models, databases and knowledge. The virtual simulation environment, namely the "Simulation Cloud", fulfills the user's demand of modeling and simulation, as shown in Figure 1.

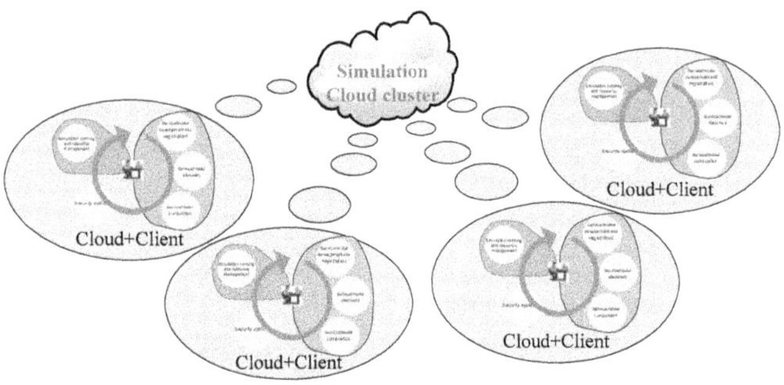

Figure 1. Cloud Simulation Mode

Based our prime practice of CSS, the application architecture of CSS is put forward in Figure 2. , which presents more technology details of the realization of CSS than the prototype architecture [3].

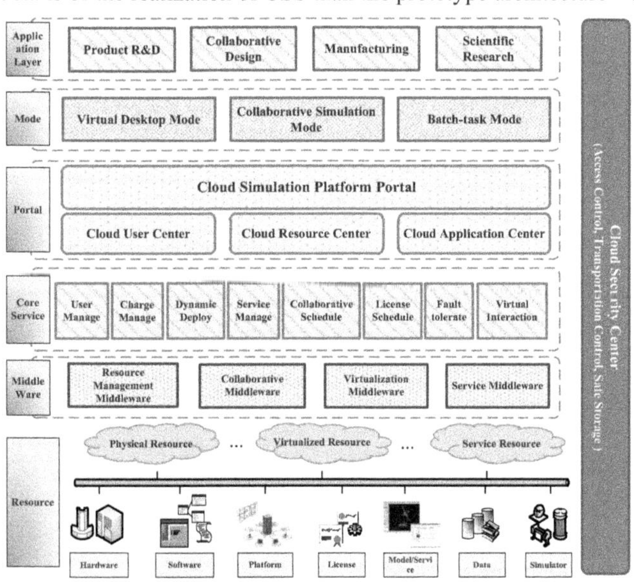

Figure 2. Application Architecture of Cloud Simulation

1) Resource Layer, which covers computing hardware resource (single/multi cores, PC/Cluster), software, platform, license, model/service and data, etc.

2) Middleware Layer integrates the infrastructure in resource layer, and provides middleware services including resource management, collaborative simulation, virtualization and service middleware, which stands for IaaS (Infrastructure as a Service) in CSS.

3) Core Service Layer provides all the application service in CSS, including user management, charge management, dynamic deployment, service management, collaborative schedule, license schedule, fault tolerance and virtual interaction, etc.

4) Portal Layer is the unified portal for the cloud simulation platform, which includes cloud user center, cloud resource center and cloud application center. The portal is accessible for web browsers.

5) Application Layer provides the massive user with three types of application modes, including virtual desktop mode, collaborative simulation mode and batch-task mode, which support the various simulation demands in product R&D, collaborative design, manufacturing and scientific research.

3. ONTOLOGY-BASED LAYERED CLOUD SIMULATION SERVICE DESCRIPTION FRAMEWORK

3.1 Layered Structure of Cloud Simulation Service

As shown in Figure 2. , despite the CSS integrates various types of M&S resource, the users acquire unified form cloud services oriented to application demands. Thus, the on-demand construction of simulation services in cloud simulation equals to the service assembling process from resources to applications.

Cloud simulation services can be sorted into three layers, which are resource service layer, function service layer and cloud application service layer. Resource service refers to the service encapsulated M&S resource in the network; Function service stands for services assembled from resource services which act impartibility functions, such as the matlab engine [6] service which is composed by specific virtual computing resource, storage service, matlab software and corresponding license service; Cloud simulation application services are services for certain simulation purposes, such as control system model service for certain product. Cloud simulation application services have the independent execution ability and are capable to be assembled with other services to carry out more complicated simulation. The layered structure of cloud simulation services is shown in Figure 3.

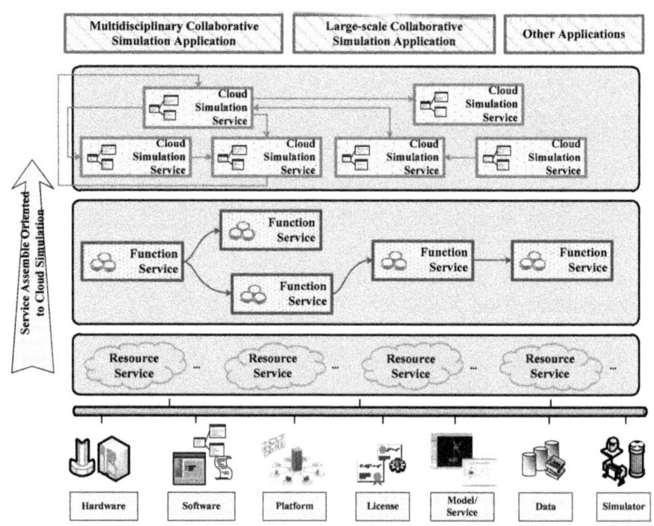

Figure 3. Layered Structure of Cloud Simulation Services

3.2 Ontology-based layered Simulation Service Description Framework

In domains like web service, grid computing, many resource service description framework have been developed, such as Resource Specification Language [7] (RSL), Web Service Description Language [8] (WSDL) and Resource Description Framework [9] (RDF), etc. Nevertheless, the current resource description frameworks are normally focus on computing resources or services, which are incapable to describe various resource in cloud simulation. Moreover, current frameworks are hard to describe the layered structure of the cloud simulation services mentioned above. Based on current resource description frameworks, this paper puts forward a new Ontology-based Layered Simulation Service Description Framework (OLSSDF) to meet the cloud simulation demands.

Corresponding with the layered structure of cloud simulation services, OLSSDF contains three layers, including resource service description layer, function service description layer and cloud simulation application description layer, as shown in Figure 4.

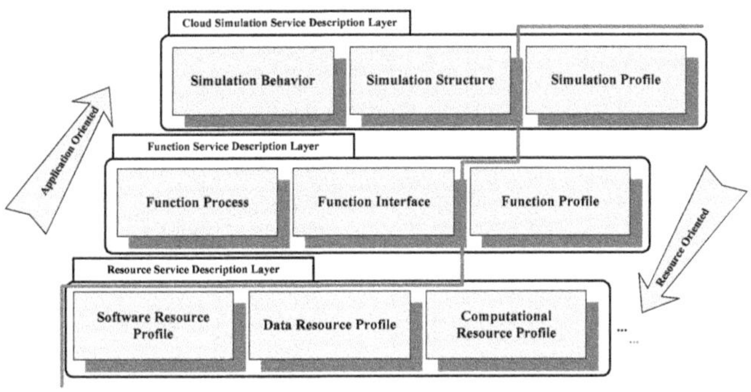

Figure 4. Layered Structure of Cloud Simulation Services

OLSSDF utilizes layered structure and maps various services into different layers in the framework for individual description. Service description for each layer contains resource-oriented attribute semantics (below the bold fold line in Figure 4.) and application-oriented model semantics (above the bold fold line in Figure 4, expect the resource service layer). The attribute semantics are description of basic information and features of services, which are the "ID" of certain service. Based on those attributes, CSS intelligently discovers and matches the simulation services. Model semantics support service modeling oriented to simulation application, which describe the content, structure, interfaces and runtime logic of the service. The model semantics equals to the assembling requirement of services in lower layer. Based on model semantics, CSS automatically carries out the discovering, matching, assembling and scheduling of the cloud simulation services. In the following semantic definition of OLSSDF, OWL-S are utilized which can better describe the static structure and dynamic behavior of the cloud simulation services.

3.2.1 Resource Service Description Layer

Resource Service Description Layer provides resource profile for all kinds of M&S resources in CSS, including basic resource attribute information such as resource identity, provider, and enrollment time and corresponding attribute description for different types of resources. For computational resources, the semantics cover CPU frequency, RAM size, storage and network performance; for software resources, semantics include version, reliance and license demands; data resource semantics include data pack size, protocol and content. Details for semantics in Resource Service Description Layer are shown in Figure 5.

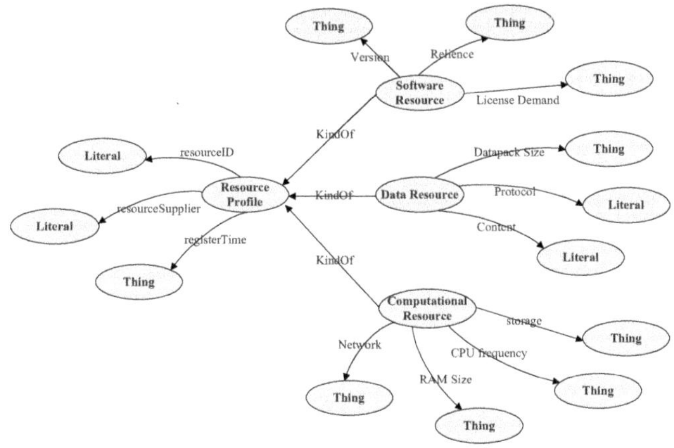

Figure 5. Semantics in Resource Service Description Layer

3.2.2 Function Service Description Layer

Semantics of Function Service Description Layer are composed by Function Profile, Function Interface and Function Process.

Function Profile describes the non-functional information, functional information and appendix features of simulation services. Non-functional information provides service identity, contact and publishing time, etc. Functional information includes input/output, precondition and effect. Appendix features includes category and QoS information of service.

Function Interface defines interface information of function services including interface type, data structure and dependency.

Process of function service is used to describe the interaction logic of resource services that make up the function, which is normally described in Workflow Language like BPEL [10].

3.2.3 Cloud Simulation Application Service Description Layer

Besides simulation profile for the description of services attributes, the semantics of Cloud Simulation Application Service Description Layer is mainly focus on the simulation structure and behavior of the function services which compose the application service.

The attributes description are used for discover of cloud simulation application services, including basic information and featured information for match and discover, which are,

1) Basic Information, including simulation name and simulation function description;

2) Service Function, including model inputs, model outputs and initial mode;

3) Service Parameters, including model classification, model type, model granularity and model precision;

4) Runtime Parameters, including service type and service address.

Model semantics covers the static structure and dynamic behavior information of the simulation services. Static structure describes the layered structure and I/O connections of the function services that make up the application service. Dynamic behavior information presents the behavior, state and procedure using

State-Machine and Workflow. Behavior description is analyzed by Simulation Assemble Service in cloud simulation platform to schedule the function services inside the application service. Model description mainly contains sub-Model set, coupling set and scheduling, as shown in Figure 6.

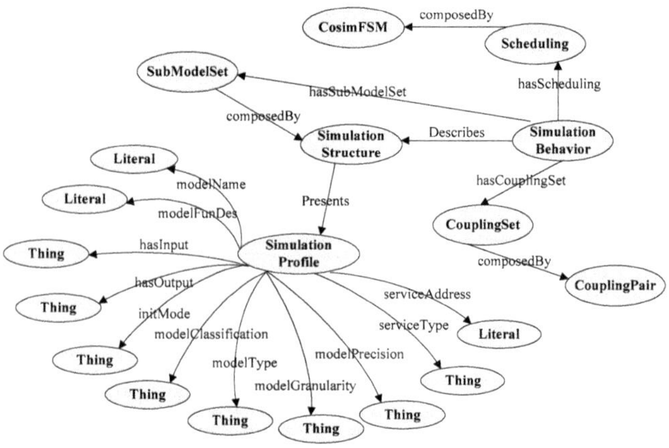

Figure 6. Semantics in Cloud Simulation Application Service Description Layer

4. APPLICATION

Intelligent Resource Discover Service and Collaborative Assembling and Scheduling Service are core services in CSS, which are realized based on the service information in the OLSSDF. This paper utilizes this framework in COSIM-CSP which is a prototype of CSS, and applies COSIM-CSP in the development of a collaborative simulation system of aero plane carriage, which realizes the intelligent discover of various resources and the on-demand establishment of cloud simulation services.

The collaborative simulation system of aero plane carriage is mainly composed of control system model, multi-body dynamics model and hydraulic model, and uses various virtual prototype design tools, such as control design tool MATLAB, dynamics design tool ADAMS and hydraulics design EASY5, etc..The structure of the virtual prototype system based on COSIM-CSP of is shown in Figure 7.

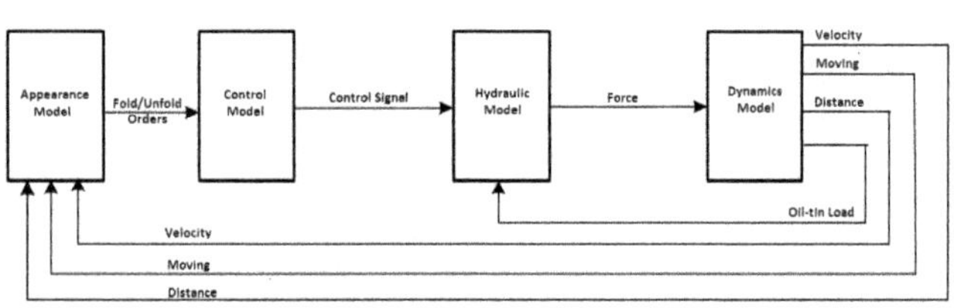

Figure 7. The collaborative simulation system structure

Before the establishment of the system, the managers of the CSS firstly describe the attributes of the computing resource and software resource in the cloud simulation platform using the resource service semantics in the OLSSDF (see in Figure 8.), and register the services in the cloud resource center for future application, as shown in Figure 9.

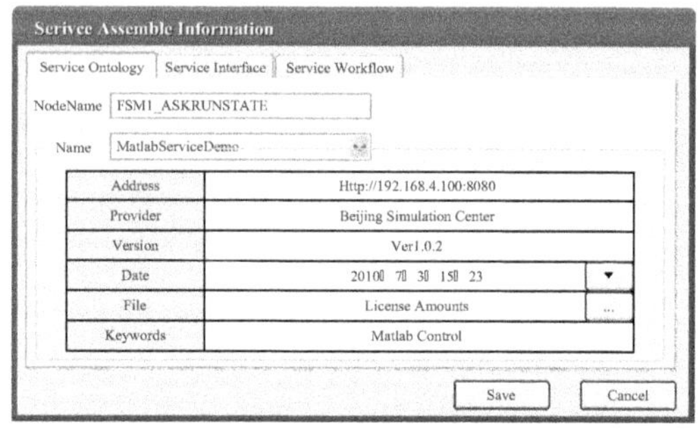

Figure 8. Service attributes description

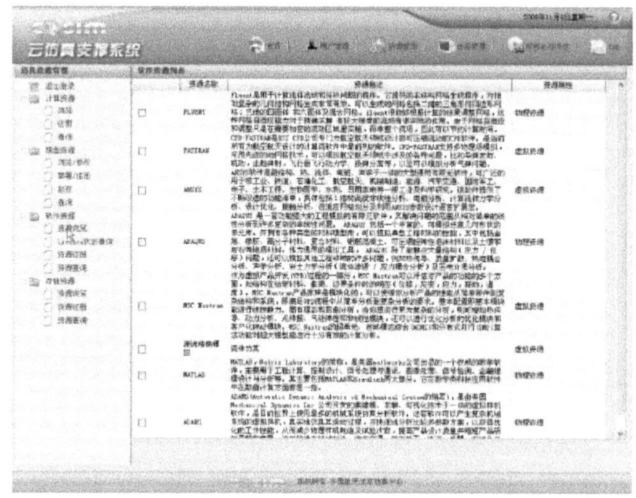

Figure 9. Cloud resource center

Based on the function service demands, the simulation engineers describe the related function service attributes, interfaces and workflow using the semantics in function service semantics. A typical function service instance using the OLSSDF semantics to describe the dynamics calculation function is shown as an example. In the former systems, the simulation attributes of ADAMS service, such as the simulation input/output interfaces, are not described in RDF.

ADAMSService (modelName.ADAMSService)
(modelFunDes.This is a Dynamics Model)
(hasInput.ActuateForce)
(hasOutput.LoadForce)
(hasOutput.ACDisInfo)
(hasOutput.UCVelInfo)
(hasOutput.UCDisInfo)
(initMode.BySimuEngine)
(modelClassification.Dynamics)
(modelType.Atomic)
(modelGranularity.Function)
(serviceType.OGSI)
(serviceAddress.http://192.168.4.56:8080/ogsa/
services/VpSimu/ADAMSService/
ADAMSServiceFactoryService)

According to the application demands of the carriage simulation, with the semantics of cloud simulation application service layer, the visualized modeling tool is provided by COSIM-CSP to describe the attribute information, static structure and dynamic behavior information of the cloud simulation application service, as shown in Figure 10.

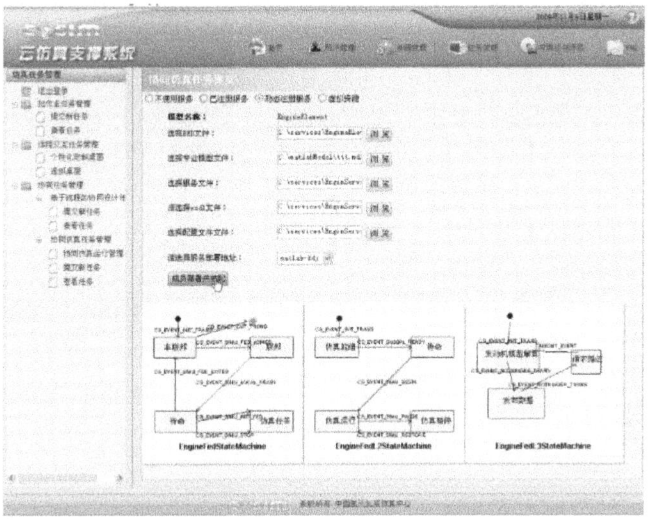

Figure 10. Visualized modeling of application services

When the simulation system starts to execute, the cloud simulation platform analyzes the cloud simulation application service description, chooses appropriate function services to form the application service. If the function service does not exist in the cloud platform, resource services in lower layer will be chose and assembled into function services on demand. After the automatic assembling of cloud simulation services in different layers, the target simulation system is established as a "simulation cloud" to support the cloud simulation mode. The runtime user-interfaces of the carriage collaborative simulation system are shown in Figure 11 and Figure 12.

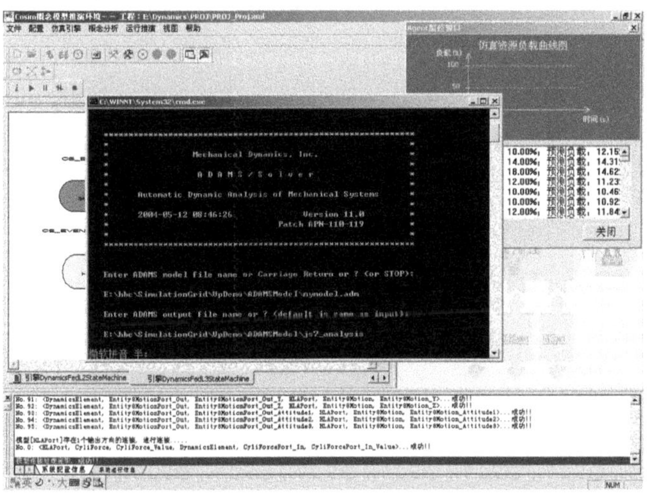

Figure 11. Adams service as a dynamics function service

5. CONCLUSION AND FUTURE WORKS

The primary research and application indicates that the OLSSDF stated in this paper is suitable to describe the various multi-granularity resources in cloud simulation system, which offers effective semantics in both service attributes and service models to describe the cloud simulation services and support the intelligent discover and assemble of the services in cloud simulation mode.

The future works of OLSSDF includes 1) Expanding the semantics in resource service layer to support the description and

Figure 12. The 3D appearance of carriage simulation

reusage of those equipment resources in new application domain of cloud simulation such as the "Cloud Manufacturing" [11]; 2) Research on the higher layer of cloud simulation service, the "Cloud Simulation Capacity Service", which pushes the development from "Simulation as a Service" to "Capacity as a Service".

6. REFERENCES

[1] R. Fujimoto, A. Malik, and A. Park, "Parallel and distributed simulation in the cloud," SCS M&S Magazine, vol. 3, 2010.

[2] G. D'Angelo, "Parallel and distributed simulation from many cores to the public cloud," in High Performance Computing and Simulation (HPCS), 2011 International Conference on. IEEE, 2011, pp. 14–23.

[3] LI Bohu, CHAI Xudong, HOU Baocun, LI Tan, et al. A Networked Modeling & Simulation Platform Based on the Concept of Cloud Computing——"Cloud Simulation Platform" [J]. Journal of System Simulation, 2009, 21(17):5292-5299(in Chinese).

[4] Chandrasekaran B., J.R. Josephson and V.R.Benjamins. What are Ontologies, and Why Do We Need Them[J]. IEEE Intelligent Systems and Their Applications, 1999, Jan/Feb: 20-25.

[5] DAM. OWL-S 1.1 Releases [EB/OL]. [2006-4-20]. http://www.Dam.org/services/owl-s/1.1

[6] Mathworks. Using MATLAB Engine. [EB/OL]. [2013-3-20]. http://www.mathworks.com/help/matlab/matlab_external/using-matlab-engine.html

[7] Globus. The Globus Resource Specification Language [EB/OL]. [2011-04-19]. http://www.hep.anl.gov/globus/RSL.html

[8] Roberto Chinnici, Jean- Jacques Moreau, Arthur Ryman, and Sanjiva Weerawarana. Web Services Description Language (WSDL) Version 2.0 Part 1: Core Language [EB/OL]. [2011-03-22]. http://www.w3.org/TR/wsdl20/

[9] W3C. Resource Description Framework (RDF) Model and Syntax Specification [EB/OL]. http://www.w3.org/TR/REC- rdf- syntax.

[10] LI Zhongjie, SUN Wei, JIANG Zhongbo, et al. BPEL4WS unit testing: framework and implementation[C]. Proceedings of the IEEE International Conference on Web Services, 2005:35-43.

[11] LI Bohu, ZHANG Lin, WANG Shilong, et al. Cloud manufacturing: a new service-oriented manufacturing mode [J]. Computer Integrated Manufacturing Systems, 2010, 16 (1): 1-7, 16(in Chinese).

Supporting End-to-End Internet QoS for DDS-based Large-Scale Distributed Simulation

Work In Progress

Akram Hakiri[1,3], Pascal Berthou[2,3], Slim Abdellatif[2,3], Michel Diaz[2,3], Thierry Gayraud[2,3]
[1]MIPS Laboratory, University of Haute Alsace, Mulhouse, France.
Akram.Hakiri@uha.fr
[2]CNRS; LAAS, 7, Avenue du Colonel Roche
[3]Université de Toulouse; UPS, INSA, INP, ISAE; LAAS; F-31077 Toulouse, France
{Berthou, Slim, diaz, Gayraud}@laas.fr

ABSTRACT

Supporting end-to-end quality-of-service (QoS) in Large-scale distributed interactive simulations (DIS) is hard due to the heterogeneity and scale of communication networks, transient behavior, and the lack of mechanisms that holistically schedule different resources end-to-end. This paper aims to cope with these problems in the context of wide area network (WAN)-based DIS applications that use the OMG Data Distribution Service (DDS) QoS-enabled publish/subscribe middleware. First, we show the design and implementation of the QoS framework, which is a policy-driven architecture that shields DDS-based DIS applications from the details of network QoS mechanisms by specifying per-flow network QoS requirements, performing resource allocation and validation decisions (such as admission control), and enforcing per-flow network QoS at runtime. Second, we evaluate the capabilities of the framework in an experimental large-scale multi-domains environment. The evaluation of the architecture shows that the proposed QoS framework improves the delivery of DDS services over heterogeneous IP networks, and confirms its potential impact for providing network-level differentiated performance.

Categories and Subject Descriptors

C.2.1 [**Computer-Communication Networks**]: Network Architecture and Design—*Distributed networks*
; I.6.8 [**Simulation and Modeling**]: Types of Simulation—*Distributed*

General Terms

Design, Performance

Keywords

Large-Scale Distributed Simulation, DDS services, QoS Framework, DiffServ, Resource Management

SIGSIM-PADS'13, May 19–22, 2013, Montréal, Québec, Canada.

1. INTRODUCTION

Large-scale distributed systems, such as mission critical systems and Distributed Interactive Simulation (DIS) applications, often comprise multiple flows that require various QoS properties affecting CPU, memory, and network resources. In particular, DIS applications take data from a large number of sensors, multimedia sources, real-time streaming systems, and remote control systems that can flood the network and reduce the user's bandwidth. As the right answer delivered too late becomes a wrong answer, achieving network QoS requirements, such as low round trip latency and jitter, is essential.

In our investigation, high performance and rich QoS policies offered by DDS-based [8] architecture are used to ensure both network centric and interoperability. In particular, DDS provides real-time, data-centric publish/subscribe (pub/sub) middleware capabilities that are used in many real-time systems. For example, DDS defines a set of *network scheduling policies* (*e.g.*, end-to-end network latency budgets), *timeliness policies* (*e.g.*, time-based filters to control data delivery rate), *temporal policies* to determine the rate at which periodic data is refreshed (*e.g.*, deadline between data samples), *network transport priority policies* (*e.g.* transport priority is a hint to the infrastructure used to set the priority of the underlying transport used to send data in the DSCP field for DiffServ), and other policies that affect how data is treated once in transit with respect to its reliability, urgency, importance, and durability. DDS policies manage QoS between publisher and subscribers, its control mechanisms are available at end-systems. Overall response time and pub/sub latencies, however, are also strongly influenced by network behavior, as well as end-system resources. As a result, DDS provides no standard QoS enforcement when a DIS applications system spans multiple different interconnected networks, *e.g.*, in wide-area networks (WANs). To cope with these issues, this paper distinguishes between DDS QoS policies provided by the middleware at each end-simulator, and network QoS to refer to the Internet QoS that should be performed at the network equipments. Therefore, the QoS-aware simulator is developed: i) close to DIS applications with DDS services, to enable autonomic adaptation

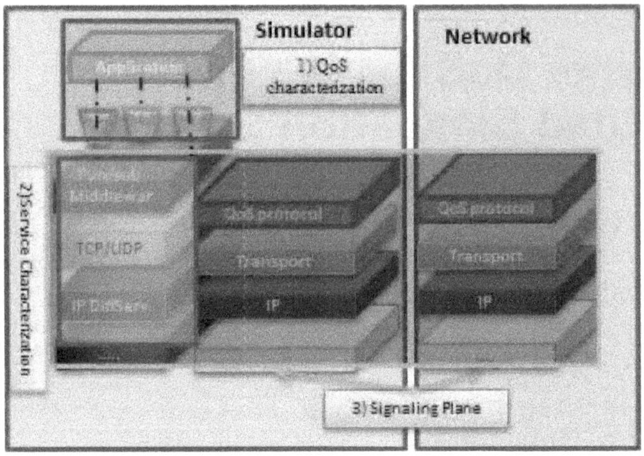

Figure 1: Enhancement of the interaction between layers

and robustness to dynamic environment, scalability, and QoS-enabled data dissemination to sets of simulators; ii) and close to the network, to provide data delivery of end-to-end QoS services across heterogeneous networks. To provision end-to-end QoS over WANs composed of heterogeneous networks, we developed a QoS policy framework called *Velox*, which enables end-to-end QoS for DIS across the Internet. Velox propagates QoS-based agreements among heterogeneous networks involving the chain of inter-domain service delivery. This paper demonstrates how those different agreements can be used together to assure end-to-end QoS service levels. To this end, as shown in figure 1,we enhanced the interaction between layers by coordinating the communication between the application and the network through the middleware in two directions: i) top-down approach: interaction in vertical plane between adjacent layers (application–middleware–routing layer); ii) end-to-end approach: interaction in horizontal plane between homologous layers to allow end-to-end QoS provisioning (end-to-end routing layers (L3)).

We focused this paper on DDS-based simulations in WANs due to our observation that many network service providers allow simulators to use MPLS over DiffServ to support their traffic over the Internet, which is the preferred approach to support QoS over WANs. We expect our Velox technique is general enough to support end-to-end QoS for a range of communication infrastructure, including CORBA, HLA and other service-oriented and pub/sub middleware. We emphasize OMG DDS in this paper since prior studies have showcased DDS in LAN environments, so our goal was to extend this existing body of work to evaluate DDS QoS properties in DIS applications over WAN environments.

The remainder of this paper is organized as follows: Section 2 describes our solution to map the applications requirements to the network throughout the middleware layer. We illustrate how Velox can schedule, negotiate, and deploy the services required by the DIS applications among multi-domain networks. Section 3 describes the testbed implementation and evaluates the performances of the presented solution. Section 4 compares our research on Velox with related work; and Section 5 presents concluding remarks and lessons learned.

2. ARCHITECTURE OF THE END-TO-END QOS PROVISIONING

This section presents the mapping of the DIS applications requirements to the network through DDS middleware and how these requirements can be communicated to the network layer. DIS applications use the underlying middleware to group their traffic flows to different classes, each class has its intrinsic QoS proprieties. Then, DDS middleware uses its QoS policies to notify the network QoS manager (Velox) about these traffic classes. Velox system enables per-flow traffic differentiation using DDS QoS to negotiate these requirements on behalf of the DIS applications.

2.1 Mapping the application requirements to the middleware

The application (called PlatSim_QoS) is composed of various data flows, each flow has its own specific characteristics. We grouped these flows to different categories (or media) by taking into account the nature of the data (homogeneity) as described in Figure 2. Each PlatSim_QoS simulator generates video streaming captured from camera to catch participant's hand gestures, audio streaming sent from micro to all other participants, and real-time simulation from virtual environment. We implemented an interface to classify those application's flows and specify their network QoS constraints. This layer defines a set of programming interfaces that can be used to serialize data flows sent by each class of traffic, and enables the interaction between the application layer and the middleware layer. To this end, we associate a set of middleware QoS policies (History, Durability, Reliability, Transport-priority, Latency-budget, Time-based-filter, Deadline, etc.) by media to classify them into 3 traffic classes, each class has its specific DDS QoS policies.

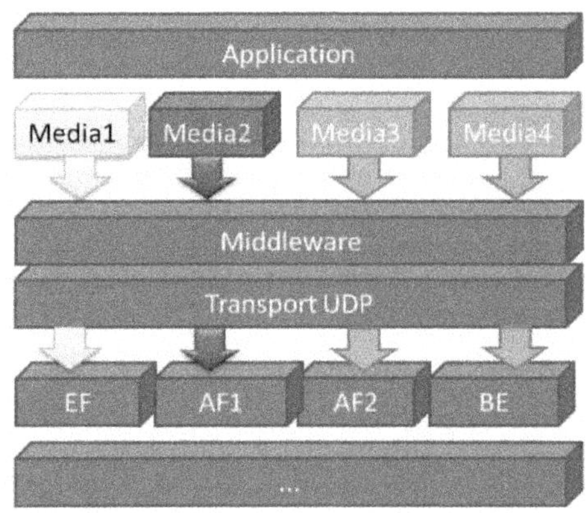

Figure 2: Mapping the application streams to the middleware flows

2.2 Mapping between the middleware and the network

DDS loads all the traffic flows the application want to send to remote simulators regarding their traffic profile. Each traffic class has its own traffic profile which specify how these flows will be enqueued and marshalled. Since DDS participants are created by the application, they attach the application's flows to DDS Topics with a specific DDS QoS policies. The *PeriodicDataTopic* is created with the QoS settings fulfilling the requirements of the simulation application. The DDS QoS policies provided by the middleware to the network (Transport-priority, latency-budget, deadline) are parsed from an XML configuration files (reported in Table 1). The Transport-priority QoS is processed by the application layer at the terminal nodes according to the value of this QoS policy, then translated by the middleware to IP packet DSCP marking(column 4 in Table 1); the Latency-budget is considered very roughly at the terminal nodes, only; and the "Deadline QoS policy" allows adapting the production profile to the subscriber request.

Topic Data	Requirements	QoS DDS	DSCP Field
Continuous Data	Constantly updating data	best-effort	12
	Many-to-many delivery	keys, multicast	
	Sensor data, last value is best	keep-last	
	Seamless failover	ownership, deadline	
States	Occasionally changing persistent data	durability	34
	Recipients need latest and greatest	history	
Alarms & Events	Asynchronous messages	liveliness	46
	Need confirmation of delivery	reliability	

Table 1: Using DDS QoS for End-Point Application Management

Table 1 shows three flows with different QoS parameters ta attach with the DDS Topics and enable the transmission of data to the network layer. These Topics have different requirements: continuous data is sent immediately using best-effort reliability settings and written synchronously in the context of the user thread, so that the DataWriter will send a sample every time-write is called. State information should deliver only previously published data samples (the most recent value) to new entities that join the network later.

Asynchronous data are used to send alarms and events asynchronously in the context of a separate thread internal to the middleware using flow controller to shape the network traffic to limit maximum data rates at which the publisher will send data for a DataWriter. The EDF flow controller buffers any excess data and only send it when the send rate drops below the maximum rate. When data is written in bursts or when sending large data type as multiple fragments, a flow controller can throttle the update rate of the asynchronous publishing thread to avoid flooding the network. Asynchronously written samples for the same destination will be coalesced into a single network packet which reduces bandwidth consumption.

Furthermore, the data produced using the local DDS service must be communicated to the remote DDS service and the other way around. The networking service provides a bridge between the local DDS service and a network interface. The application has to dimension the network properly: DDS client performs a lookup and assigns a QoS label to the packet. The QoS label identifies all QoS actions to be performed on the packet and from which queue the packet is sent. The QoS label is based on the DSCP value in the packet and decides the queuing and scheduling actions to perform on the packet.

Figure 3 describes the overall architecture for mapping the application requirements to network through the middleware. As edge router selects a packet in a traffic stream based on the content of DSCP packet header (described in column 3 in Table 1) to check whether the traffic falls within the negotiated profile, and marks packet to a particular DiffServ behavior aggregate, the application uses DDS transport_priority it can define the aggregated traffic the domain can handle separately, and each packet is marked according to the Service Level Agreement (SLA).

2.3 QoS management at the network side

The purpose of the Velox system is to implement end-to-end path for delivery of QoS guarantees over heterogeneous Autonomous Systems (AS) between remote simulation applications. Each path corresponds to a given set of limited QoS parameters (i.e., bandwidth, latency, and jitter) which specify different network Classes of Services (there are 3 CoS), controlled by different European network operators. Figure 4 shows the building blocks of the Velox system used by the invocation process. This system is composed of the following components:

- Velox provides a web interface to enable users interacting with the Velox for registration and monitoring.
- Signaling and Service Negotiation (SSN), coordinates the communication between simulators with the network. As described in Figure 5, the SSN asks the QoS manager whether or the not the network can provide enough resources to the requesting application. The AQ-SSN (Application QoS) collects the DDS QoS policies belonging to each traffic profile(or media) (Bandwidth, Latency_Budget, Reliability, Deadline, and Transport_Priority) which ask for the granted QoS level. SSN enables remote simulators contact each other to agree on the end-to-end session parameters. SSN notifies the Call Admission Control (CAC) of user authorizations, after having authenticated the user with SAAA (Security, Authentication, Authorization, and Accounting), and is also in charge of shutting down the session if faults have occurred.
- Resource Manager (RM): the RM allows resource reservation for each simulator along the end-to-end path across the different network domains, on a hop-by-hop basis between Resource Managers (RMs) of adjacent domains. Also, RM allows also handling QoS

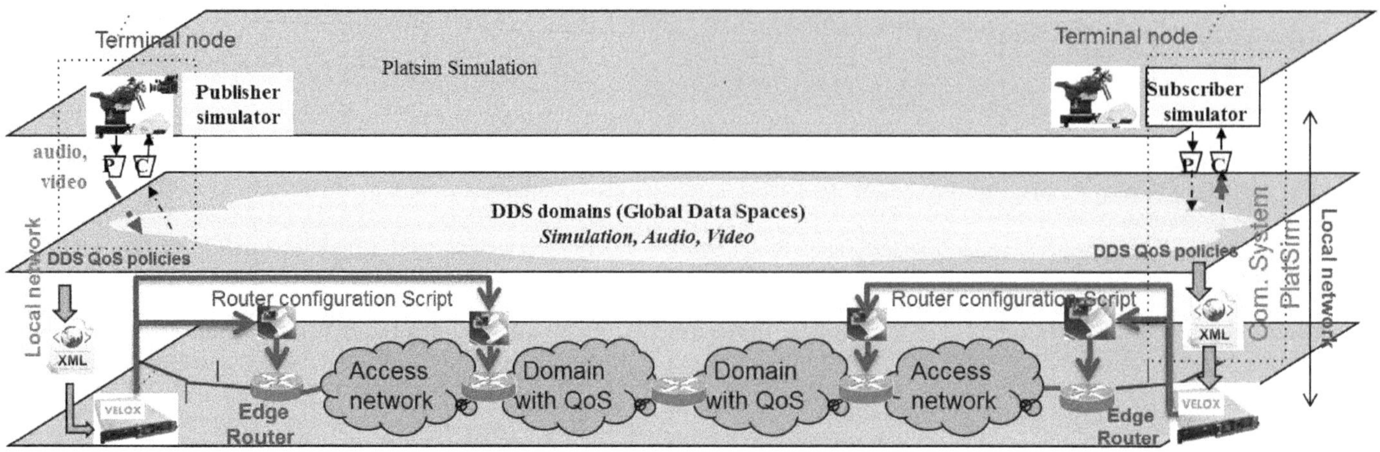

Figure 3: QoS Guaranteed Architecture

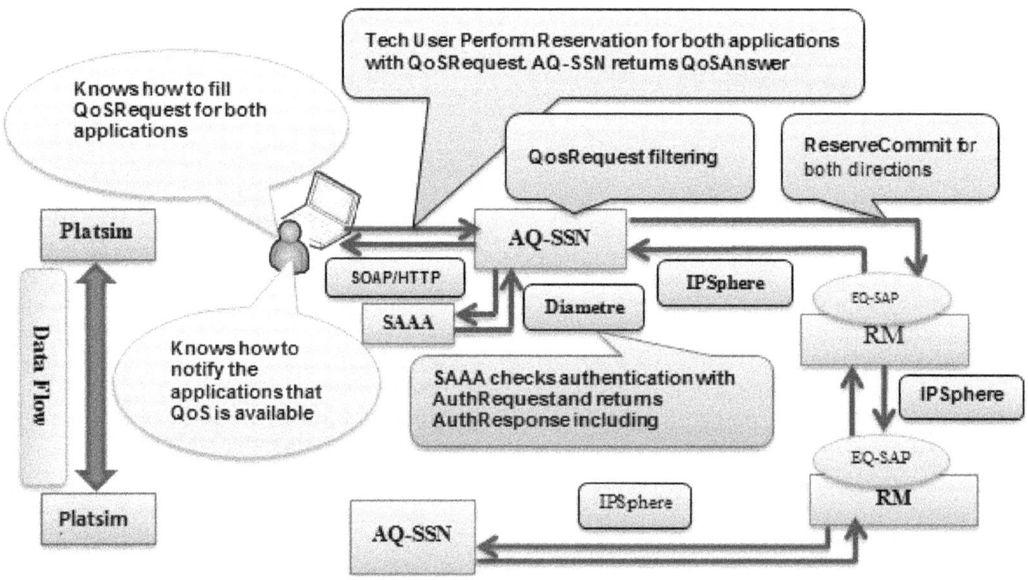

Figure 4: Velox system building blocks

requests sent by each simulator at the control plane and synchronizes those requests with the service plane for handshaking QoS invocation among domains. The process of QoS invocation is maintained by Next Steps in Signaling (NSIS) protocol [4] which enables the establishment of network services. In addition, the Resource Manager includes the Connection Admission Control algorithm.

- The Connection Admission Control (CAC) allows limiting the access to network to only the DDS-based DIS application that the QoS objectives for already-accepted flows can be maintained and protected against traffic overloading. The CAC is split into 2 services: i) for DIS applications running in single IP domain, the CAC allows the admission of those applications in each single domain; ii) for DDS applications running in heterogenous networks, the CAC looks for a path with a QoS level fulfilling the requirements of those applications in terms of bandwidth, latency and priorities.

The end-to-end path is implemented using MPLS tunnel which enables aggregation and merging from one AS to another, so that data can cross transit domains transparently. In addition, to guarantee the continuity of Per-Hop Behavior (PHB) along AS path, the Network Layer Reachability Information (NLRI) [3] is exchanged between BGP routers using NLRI field, which convey the QoS policies between remote BGP routers. Once the end-to-end path is established, the invocation process can occur: a QoS request is sent from the service plane to the first RM under some agreement (Service Level Specification) during the session establishment. The RM performs QoS commitment and checks if there is a suitable end-to-end path fulfilling the QoS requirements in term of CoS.

2.4 End-to-end resource reservation

Velox is used for managing network resources in a single domain and multi-domain network. In a multi-domain network, Velox enables deploying services with different QoS

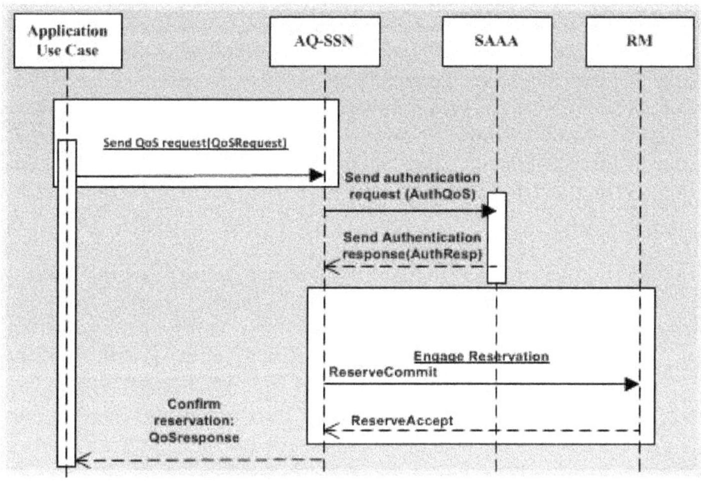

Figure 5: Signaling model

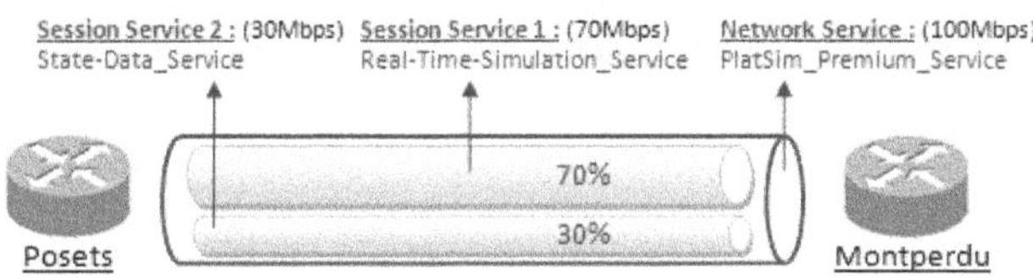

Figure 6: Resource reservation inside the MPLS end-to-end tunnel

(AF, EF) between different domains. Velox provides different services (Figure 7) to configure edge routers with the QoS required by each flow coming from each PlatSim simulator:

- Network Services: defines end-to-end paths that include one or more edge routers (see Figure 6). When the network session is created, the overall bandwidth utilization for different sessions have to be assigned to create communication channels, allowing multiple network sessions to use this bandwidth.
- Session service: Service sessions create end-to-end tunnels associated with specific QoS parameters to allow different applications communicate with the respect of those parameters. For example, bandwidth is assigned to each session as presented in Figure 6, and allocated by the network service, thereby Velox can call each service using it internal "Trigger" service.
- Trigger Service: this service is used to trigger a reservation of bandwidth available for each session of service. When the network service and session services are ready for use, the trigger service propagates the QoS parameters among the end-to-end path that join different domains.

3. PERFORMANCE EVALUATION

In this section, we present the results of experiments conducted to evaluate the network performance of the simulations exercises we conducted with the car driving simulators.

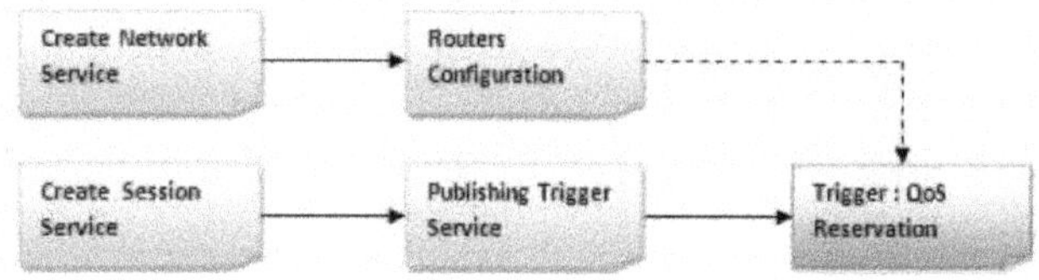

Figure 7: QoS Configuration Step automation

The results are provided for the DiffServ expedited forwarding per-hop-behavior (PHB) model [2] whose characteristics of low delay, low loss, and low jitter are suitable for voice, video, and other real-time simulation.

3.1 Impact of QoS management on the bandwidth protection

Rationale and approach. Since Velox supports QoS-sensitive traffic reliably to support delay- and jitter-sensitive applications, QoS requirements for a flow can be translated into the appropriate bandwidth requirements. To ensure queuing delay and jitter guarantees, it may be necessary to ensure that the bandwidth available to a flow is higher than the actual data transmission rate of this flow. We therefore identified two flows and used them to evaluate the impact of Velox on the bandwidth protection as follows: (1) a real-time traffic generated by the application using expedited forwarding DiffServ service with priority level 46 and (2) UDP best-effort traffic using Jperf traffic generator (`iperf.sourceforge.net`).

We performed two variants of this experiment. The first variant uses UDP network background load of forward and reverse bandwidth. For this configuration, the Velox resource manager does not provide any QoS management for the large-scale network, as the default configuration of routers uses only two queues with 95% for best-effort packets and 5% for network control packets, *i.e.*, all traffic traversing the network goes through a single best-effort queue. Subsequently, we begin sending a DDS flow at 500 Kbps followed by a UDP flow at 600 Kbps injected from Jperf to congest the queue and observe the behavior of the DDS flow.

The second variant also used the UDP computing traffic, but we enabled Velox for QoS management. The Velox resource manager configured the edge router queues to support 40% best-effort traffic, 30% expedited forwarding traffic and 20% assured forwarding traffic, and 5% for network control packets.

Results and analysis. Figure 8a shows the results of experiments when deployed applications were (1) configured without any network QoS class and (2) sending DDS flow competing with UDP background traffic. These results show the deterioration of the flow behavior as it cannot maintain a constant bandwidth expected by the DDS application due

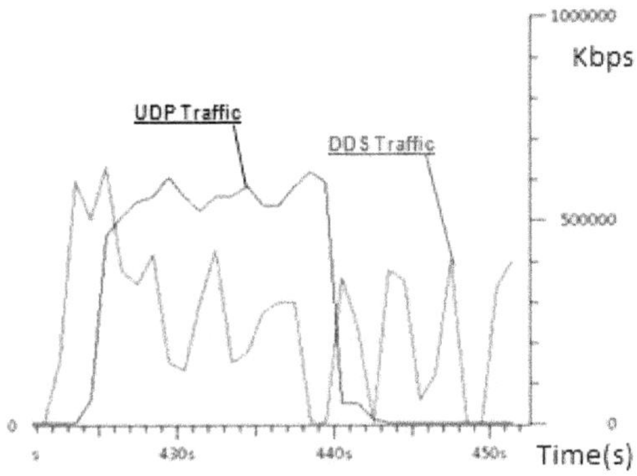

(a) without QoS

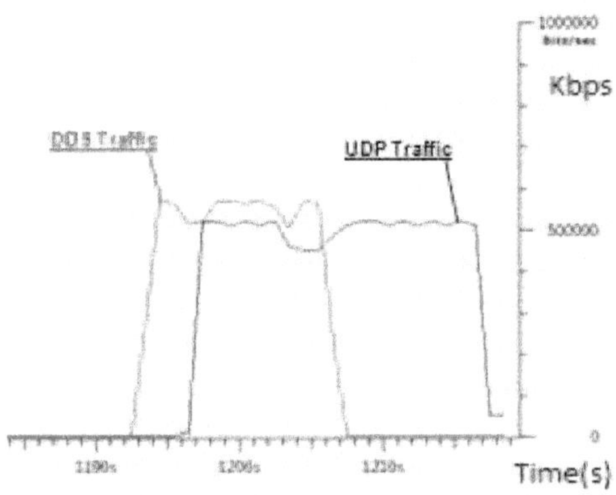

(b) with QoS

Figure 8: Impact of the QoS provisioning Capabilities on the bandwidth protection

to the disruption by the UDP background flows. Although the mapping is performed between the simulation application and the middleware, we don't see the impact of this mapping on the bandwidth protection. These results can be accepted because the DDS QoS policies don't have any impact on the end-to-end bandwidth. Because DDS resides on each end-system, it can enhance the performance of each simulator locally.

Figure 8b shows the results of experiments when the deployed applications were (1) configured with expedited forwarding network QoS class and (2) sending DDS flows competing with UDP background traffic. These results show that irrespective of heavy background traffic, the bandwidth experienced by the DIS application using the expedited forwarding network class is protected against background competing traffic. Hence, when the network becomes aware about the QoS management, the simulation traffics across end-to-end path without packet lost that can deteriorate the consistency of the simulation.

4. RELATED WORK

Though most researches on distributed simulation QoS-support focusing on solving a QoS-constrained separately from the middleware QoS policies. Authors in [7] proposed a container-based pub/sub services in the context of OMG's CORBA event service for large-scale DIS applications. Furthermore, HLA [5] was used across a full range of simulations areas [6]. While HLA enables interoperability of simulators, it does not provide support for collaborative development of simulation applications, nor does it provide any mechanism for managing the resources where the simulation is being executed.

the solution developed in this paper benefits from the rich set of DDS QoS policies that we used in the context in multi-domain network. It provides mapping the DIS applications QoS requirements to the underlying network through the middleware layer. Thus, it allows defining more flexible class of services for future DIS flows. This mapping layer enables Velox to negotiate these requirements on behalf of the application without modifying its behaviour.

5. CONCLUDING REMARKS

This paper describes the interaction between the application layer, the middleware and the network layer to provide large-scale distributed simulation. The QoS provisioning starts from the application, which notifies the DDS layer about its requirements to adapt its service to them using the DDS QoS settings. Then, the middleware negotiates the network QoS with Velox on behalf of the application. Velox policy-based management enabled end-to-end QoS provisioning for DIS applications by controlling network resources, such as a bandwidth and end-to-end delay on behalf of the simulators. Our future work will therefore focus on adding ontology-based mechanisms [1] to Velox that automate the assured configuration of DDS QoS policies, thereby adapting network resources to better meet application requirements.

6. REFERENCES

[1] R. Carlos, L. S. Rito, Álvarez Sabucedo Luis M., and C. Paulo. An ontology for managing network services quality. *Expert Syst. Appl.*, 39(9):7938–7946, July 2012.

[2] B. Davie, A. Charny, J. Bennet, K. Benson, J. L. Boudec, W. Courtney, S. Davari, V. Firoiu, and D. Stiliadis. An Expedited Forwarding PHB (Per-Hop Behavior). RFC 3246 (Proposed Standard), Mar. 2002.

[3] F. L. Faucheur and E. Rosen. Advertising IPv4 Network Layer Reachability Information with an IPv6 Next Hop. RFC 5549 (Proposed Standard), May 2009.

[4] R. Hancock, G. Karagiannis, J. Loughney, and S. V. den Bosch. Next Steps in Signaling (NSIS): Framework. RFC 4080 (Informational), June 2005.

[5] IEEE-1516. IEEE standard for modeling and simulation high level architecture (hla). *http://standards.ieee.org*, Janvier 2000.

[6] T. Lu, C. Lee, W. Hsia, and N. Sun. Supporting large-scale distributed simulation using hla. *ACM Trans. Model. Comput. Simul*, 10:268–294, 2000.

[7] C. O'Ryan, D. L. Levine, D. C. Schmidt, and J. R. Noseworthy. Applying a scalable corba event service to large-scale distributed interactive simulations. In *Proceedings of the Fifth International Workshop on Object-Oriented Real-Time Dependable Systems*, WORDS '99, 1999.

[8] G. Pardo-Castellote. Omg data-distribution service: architectural overview. *IEEE. ICDCS*, May 2003.

Grand Challenges in Modeling and Simulation: Expanding Our Horizons

Simon J. E. Taylor
ICT Innovation Group
Department of Information Systems and Computing
Brunel University, Uxbridge, UK

Osman Balci
Department of Computer Science
Virginia Tech
Blacksburg, VA, USA

Wentong Cai
School of Computer Engineering
Nanyang Technological University
Singapore

Margaret L. Loper
Information & Communications Lab
Georgia Tech Research Institute
Atlanta, GA, USA

David M. Nicol
Information Trust Institute
University of Illinois at Urbana-Champaign, IL, USA

George Riley
School of Electrical and Computer Engineering
Georgia Tech
Atlanta, GA, USA

ABSTRACT
There continues to be many advances in the theory and practice of Modeling and Simulation (M&S). However, some of these can be considered as Grand Challenges; issues whose solutions require significant focused effort across a community, sometimes with ground-breaking collaborations with new disciplines. In 2002, the first M&S Grand Challenges Workshop was held in Dagstuhl, Germany, in an attempt to focus efforts on key areas. In 2012, a new initiative was launched to continue these Grand Challenge efforts. Panel members of this third Grand Challenge present their views on M&S Grand Challenges. Themes presented in this panel include M&S Methodology; Agent-based M&S; M&S in Systems Engineering; Cyber Systems Modeling; and Network Simulation.

Categories and Subject Descriptors
I.6.0 [**Simulation and Modeling**]: General

General Terms
Algorithms and Theory

Keywords
Modeling and Simulation Methodology; Agent-based Modeling and Simulation; Modeling and Simulation Life Cycle; Cyber Systems Modeling; Network Simulation.

1. INTRODUCTION
After several decades of progress, Modeling and Simulation (M&S) continues to produce advancements in theory and practice. There continues to be innovation in existing application areas of M&S and new application areas continue to be identified. Some of these can be considered as Grand Challenges; issues whose solutions require significant focused effort across a community, sometimes with ground-breaking collaborations with new disciplines. In 2002, the first M&S Grand Challenges Workshop was held in Dagstuhl, Germany, in an attempt to focus efforts on key areas (www.dagstuhl.de/02351). In 2012, a new initiative was launched to continue these Grand Challenge efforts. The first event in this new phase of activities was the M&S Grand Challenge Panel held at the 2012 Winter Simulation Conference [1]. This discussed issues including interaction of models from different paradigms, parallel and distributed simulation, ubiquitous computing, supercomputing, grid computing, cloud computing, big data and complex adaptive systems, model abstraction, embedded simulation for real-time decision support, simulation on-demand, simulation-based acquisition, simulation interoperability, high speed optimization, web simulation science, spatial simulation, and ubiquitous simulation. The second event was another Grand Challenge Panel that took place at the Symposium on Theory of Modeling and Simulation (TMS'13) during SpringSim 2013 in San Diego [2]. This addressed a range of topics across "big" simulation applications (data, models, systems), coordinated modeling, human behavior, composability, sustainable funding, cloud-based M&S, engineering replicability into computational models, democratization of M&S, multi-domain design, hardware platforms and education.

Panel members of this third Grand Challenge present their views on M&S Grand Challenges. Themes presented in this panel include M&S Methodology; Agent-based M&S; M&S in Systems Engineering; Cyber Systems Modeling; and Network Simulation.

2. OSMAN BALCI: Developing a New Modeling and Simulation Methodology

2.1 Overview
M&S stands to be the only applicable technique in many cases for bringing solutions to many complex problems. However, M&S is currently applied in an ad hoc manner without an underlying holistic methodology. Seventeen types of M&S are used in dozens of different disciplines to show how diverse M&S is. However, despite the diversity, much of the underpinnings of the current M&S methodologies date back to 1960s. Current M&S methodologies do not sufficiently meet the requirements for solving complex multifaceted problems. Development of a holistic M&S methodology for solving such complex problems poses to be a grand challenge. This position statement justifies the need for a new M&S methodology and identifies a set of requirements for its development.

2.2 INTRODUCTION

A *Model* is a representation and abstraction of anything such as a real system, a proposed system, a futuristic system design, an entity, a phenomenon, or an idea. *Modeling* is the act of developing a model. *Simulation* is the act of executing, experimenting with or exercising a model or a set of models for a specific objective (intended use) such as analysis (problem solving), training, acquisition, entertainment, research, or education. Simulation cannot be conducted without a model and modeling is an integral part of simulation. Therefore, we refer to both modeling and simulation activities as M&S.

Many areas or types of M&S exist. Taxonomy of M&S areas is presented in Table 1. Use of the 17 M&S areas listed in Table 1 spans dozens of different disciplines for many objectives / intended uses. Each M&S area possesses its own characteristics and methodologies, is applicable for solving certain problems, and has its own community of users. Some M&S areas have their own societies, conferences, books, journals, and software tools.

For a description of the M&S areas, the reader is referred to the ACM SIGSIM M&S Knowledge Repository at http://www.acm-sigsim-mskr.org/MSAreas/msAreas.htm

2.3 THE NEED FOR A NEW M&S METHODOLOGY

Employment of M&S as a technique to solve complex problems includes the M&S of many diverse systems (problem domains), each with its own unique characteristics. In the current state of the art, the M&S methodology that is effective for one problem domain typically does not satisfy the needs of M&S for another problem domain. However, many problem domains dictate the creation of a simulation model that represents many diverse systems in an integrated manner.

Two paradigms have been primarily used for discrete M&S development: procedural and object-oriented. Under the procedural paradigm, discrete simulation models have been developed using the following conceptual frameworks (a.k.a. world views, simulation strategies): activity scanning, event scheduling, three-phase approach, and process interaction [3]. These four conceptual frameworks were created in early 1960s and some of them are still being used. It is time for new ideas!

The object-oriented paradigm originated in SIMULA simulation programming language in 1967. Smalltalk, C++, Objective C, Java, and C# followed as the contemporary object-oriented programming languages that are commonly used for software development today.

There is a need for a holistic M&S methodology to meet the grand challenges we face today. The development of the holistic M&S methodology poses to be a grand challenge because of the requirements stated below.

2.4 REQUIREMENTS FOR A NEW M&S METHODOLOGY

The Merriam-Webster dictionary defines methodology as "a body of methods, rules, and postulates employed by a discipline." The new M&S methodology should present identifiable techniques, approaches, and strategies, and provide effective guidance to M&S engineers, analysts, and managers. We provide some requirements below under which the new M&S methodology should be developed.

Table 1. M&S Areas (Types)

A.	Based on Model Representation	
	1.	Discrete M&S
	2.	Continuous M&S
	3.	Monte Carlo M&S
	4.	System Dynamics M&S
	5.	Gaming-based M&S
	6.	Agent-based M&S
	7.	Artificial Intelligence-based M&S
	8.	Virtual Reality-based M&S
B.	Based on Model Execution	
	9.	Distributed / Parallel M&S
	10.	Web-based M&S
C.	Based on Model Composition	
	11.	Live Exercises
	12.	Live Experimentations
	13.	Live Demonstrations
	14.	Live Trials
D.	Based on What is in the Loop	
	15.	Hardware-in-the-loop M&S
	16.	Human-in-the-loop M&S
	17.	Software-in-the-loop M&S

Top 10 requirements for the new M&S methodology:

(1) The new M&S methodology must be structured based on a comprehensive and effective M&S life cycle.

An M&S life cycle [4]:

- Represents a framework for organization of the processes, work products, quality assurance activities, and project management activities required to develop, use, maintain, and reuse an M&S application from birth to retirement.
- Specifies the work *products* to be created under the designated *processes* together with the integrated verification and validation (V&V) and quality assurance (QA) activities.
- Is critically needed for *project* management to modularize and structure an M&S application development and to provide guidance to an M&S developer (engineer), manager, organization, and community of interest.
- Identifies areas of expertise in which to employ qualified *people*.
- Is required to show the V&V and QA activities as integrated within the M&S development activities based on the principle dictating that V&V and QA must go hand in hand with the M&S development.
- Enables to view M&S engineering from the four Ps (Perspectives): Process, Product, People, and Project.

The author has developed such an M&S life cycle [4] based on his experience with DoD-related complex M&S development projects. The new M&S methodology can be created based on that life cycle representation.

(2) The new M&S methodology must be applicable for providing effective and integrated M&S-based solutions to complex problems.

An effective M&S-based solution is the one that is sufficiently credible, accepted, and used by the decision makers. The new methodology should assist in reducing the M&S builder's risk and M&S user's risk.

M&S Builder's Risk is the probability that the M&S application is rejected although it is sufficiently credible and acceptable. The consequences of this risk will result in higher cost and prolonged project duration.

M&S User's Risk is the probability that the M&S application is accepted in spite of the fact that it is not sufficiently credible. The consequences of this risk can be catastrophic since incorrect decisions will be made based on the M&S results.

(3) The new M&S methodology must be a holistic methodology applicable for M&S of many diverse systems in an integrative manner.

Many problem domains (universes of discourse) contain diverse systems embedded within each other forming a system of systems. Each system possesses its own characteristics, e.g., discrete, continuous, real-time, or distributed. Each system can require a type (area) of M&S listed in Table 1. The new methodology must accommodate as many M&S areas (types) as possible.

(4) The new M&S methodology must provide a unifying conceptual framework throughout the entire M&S development life cycle.

Using different conceptual frameworks from one phase of the M&S development life cycle to another increases the complexity of development and probability of inducing errors. The new methodology must employ a conceptual framework that can be used for each life cycle phase.

(5) The new M&S methodology must enable network-centric M&S application development.

Two main reasons exist for creating an M&S application as network-centric. (i) To be able to train geographically-dispersed people using M&S, the M&S application must be accessible over a network such as Internet, local area network, virtual private network, or Secret Internet Protocol Router Network (SIPRNET). (ii) M&S application execution can be improved by distributing the execution of its components on different server computers at different network nodes. The new methodology must enable the construction of a network-centric M&S application.

(6) The new M&S methodology must enable reuse and component-based M&S application development using a library of reusable components.

Undoubtedly, the reuse provides significant economical and technical benefits that cannot be underestimated [6]. The new methodology must enable the creation and use of a library of reusable components specifically created for a problem domain (universe of discourse) of interest.

(7) The new M&S methodology must facilitate verification, validation, and quality assurance throughout the entire M&S life cycle.

V&V aims to assess the transformational accuracy (verification) and behavioral/representational accuracy (validation) of an M&S application. QA aims to assess the other M&S quality characteristics such as interoperability, fidelity, credibility, and acceptability. V&V or QA is not a stage, but continuously conducted activities hand-in-hand with the development activities throughout the entire M&S life cycle. The new methodology must facilitate the effective application of V&V and QA principles [5].

(8) The new M&S methodology must support integration with real-life hardware and software systems for performing Live Exercises.

Live exercises, experimentations, demonstrations, and trials are very much needed for solving some complex problems such as emergency response management training, military training, and technology assessment. It is critically important that the M&S application be integrated with real-life systems.

(9) The new M&S methodology must support real-time decision making.

An M&S application can be embedded within a real-time decision support system to enable real-time decision making during, for example, an emergency situation.

(10) The new M&S methodology must enable the development of M&S applications for Analysis as well as for Training objectives.

Analysis (problem solving) is conducted under such objectives as comparison of different operating policies, evaluation of a given emergency response management plan, prediction, and sensitivity analysis. *Training* refers to simulation-based training of, e.g., first responders and decision makers. The same methodology must be able to be used for developing an M&S application for multiple intended uses (objectives).

2.5 CONCLUDING REMARKS

The U.S. Government is the largest sponsor and consumer of M&S applications in the world. Billions of dollars are spent annually by the U.S. Government for developing, using, and maintaining M&S applications. However, the M&S methodologies in use today date back to 1960s. It is critically important to conduct research to develop new methodologies to address the ever-increasing complexity of M&S development.

Reuse has been very difficult or in some cases impossible in the M&S discipline. However, the issue of reuse is extremely important and should be effectively addressed [6].

Component-based M&S development is an unsolved problem for stand-alone M&S applications due to differences in programming languages, operating systems, and hardware. However, network-centric M&S development promises new advances in component-based M&S engineering and should be fully investigated.

3. WENTONG CAI: Agent-based Modeling and Simulation for Complex Adaptive Systems

Traditionally M&S involves the development of a dynamic, stochastic, and discrete model of the physical system of interest. Once the model is shown to exhibit the expected behaviour for a given set of known inputs, it can be used to predict the system behaviour for a set of unknown scenarios or inputs. For many systems which are well understood, or whose behaviour can be characterized by a chronological sequence of events, this approach to modelling has been very successful. There is however a large set of systems in which a global or macro scale understanding is simply not possible to conceive. Simulating and modelling of these systems in a traditional manner is often too challenging as system level trends and properties are difficult to characterize.

At the heart of agent-based model is the principle of emergence. For studying and attempting to understand natural complex phenomena, agent-based models offer an attractive and intuitive approach of describing rules and parameters of individual entities and letting the system level properties emerge. From a modelling perspective this is an attractive method for reasoning about complex adaptive systems, where the overall behaviour of a system is the result of a huge number of decisions made by the inter-connected individual components [7]. Given this understanding it is clear to see why agent-based M&S has seen a dramatic increase in its application in a wide variety of application domains [8]. While agent-based M&S offers such great promise there are still fundamental and challenging issues.

Behaviour Modelling. The effectiveness of agent-based simulation is determined by the integrity of the simulation model with respect to its ability to capture the true characteristics of individual entities in a typical environment. An important modelling decision is the level of details: whether a simple rule-based agent model is sufficient or a complex agent behaviour model that incorporates social, psychological, and cultural factors is required. Creating a complex agent behaviour model itself also posts a great challenge. This usually requires studying theories of a specific domain and extracting the essence from the theories. With the current wealth of data availability, there is a possibility to obtain behaviour rules inductively from the data using data analytics techniques.

Verification and Validation. The major motivation for using agent-based M&S to understand complex adaptive systems has an undesirable consequence when ascertaining validity of models. The central argument for agent-based model is that the behaviour of the system emerges in some unknown and unexpected way. This unpredictable nature of the system makes tracing cause and effect relationships a very challenging issue.

The most effective approach to establishing model validity is to compare the simulation results of the model with the output data from the system being modelled. However, this approach may not be applicable for agent-based M&S for complex adaptive systems as there is usually no existing system to compare with. The complexity and arrangement of the huge numbers of agents will also typically lead to an overly parameterized model. So, even if there are data available, evolving model parameters to match the data is not a straightforward task either.

Scalability. In computational terms an autonomous agent can be viewed as an independently executing process, with its own state and thread of control. The complexity of agents can vary widely depending on their model. In agent-based M&S there is a traditional view of large numbers of simple (or lightweight) agents that are interacting with each other. However, for many applications agents themselves can have significant computational capabilities and therefore significant processing requirements. Whether agent models involve heavyweight or lightweight agents, the scale and complexity of the studied systems often makes executing these models extremely compute intensive.

Interoperability and Reusability. A large-scaled model can be constructed by sub-models created using the existing models. However, these models may not work with each other: they may operate at different levels of abstraction and created using different modelling paradigms. This makes the communication between different models difficult. In a typical crowd simulation, for example, the crowd model needs to pass along various information about the actions of individuals and also needs to understand the events in the simulated world so that the individuals can determine how to respond to these events. But, different crowd models may use different models of perception and action, and may respond to events at different level of abstraction.

The generality of agent-based M&S has seen its application across multiple disciplines. As a consequence researchers working in different communities (such as computational social science, artificial intelligence, and M&S) have addressed challenges, developed solutions and implemented systems to enable this type of computational modelling. Obviously, to deal with the above-mentioned challenges and to push the research forward in agent-based M&S for complex adaptive systems, a well-organized and orchestrated effort is required across multiple disciplines and research communities.

4. MARGARET LOPER: Modeling & Simulation in the Systems Engineering Life Cycle

Many of the most important problems facing the world are rooted in science - energy, infectious disease, climate change, and education. The National Academy of Engineering has identified a set of grand challenges in broad realms of human concern that are in need of engineering solutions [9]. All of these problems are complex systems, and finding solutions to these grand challenges will inevitably use M&S as a problem-solving technique. In order to create solutions to these problems, systems engineering is needed to focus on how complex engineering projects should be designed and managed over their life cycles.

Systems engineering is an interdisciplinary approach to translating users' needs into the definition of a system, its architecture and design through an iterative process that results in an effective operational system [10]. The systems engineering "V" process, shown in Figure 1, represents the sequence of steps in a product or project's development. The V process was designed to simplify the understanding of the complexity associated with developing systems.

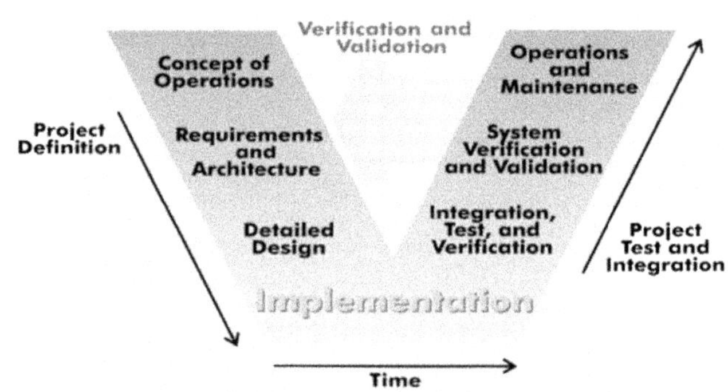

Figure 1. Systems Engineering V Process

We can also think about systems engineering from a life cycle perspective. A life cycle is a categorization of the systems development activities into distinct, controllable phases. All systems follow a general life cycle from concept definition through development and testing to deployment, operations, and deactivation. The systems engineering V process can be mapped to a simple life cycle model [11], as shown in Figure 2.

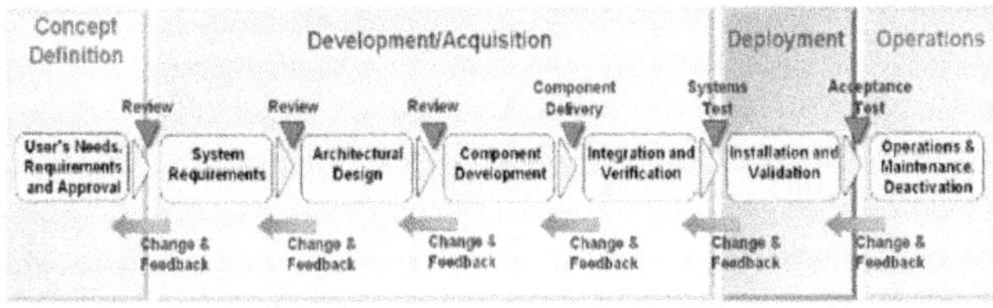

Figure 2. Systems Engineering Life Cycle

M&S has become an important tool across all phases of the systems engineering life cycle to include, requirements definition, program management, design and engineering, efficient test planning, result prediction, supplement to test and evaluation, manufacturing, and logistics support. There are many opportunities to use M&S in the systems engineering life cycle, and when appropriately applied, four major benefits can be achieved: cost savings, accelerated schedule, improved product quality, and cost avoidance [12].

To solve the grand challenge problems of our times, we need to use systems engineering to design and manage the solutions, but we as an M&S community don't have a good understanding of what types of M&S are best used/needed in each systems engineering life cycle phase (i.e., concept definition, technology development, engineering and manufacturing development, production and deployment, and operations and support). Once we do have this understanding, we can design better-integrated M&S tools and solutions across the systems engineering life cycle phases for solving these grand challenges.

For example, we commonly use low-fidelity, aggregate-level, constructive simulations (e.g., war-games) in concept definition to examine alternative solutions, look at operational effectiveness or evaluate cost of different concepts. Later in the life cycle (i.e., engineering and manufacturing development) we use high-fidelity, physics-based simulations for detailed design and for developing prototypes. Once we are in the engineering and manufacturing development phase we have committed to a design, and investments have been made in a specific solution (so no opportunity for changes). What if we had the ability to produce detailed designs and prototypes earlier in the life cycle and put them in an operational setting to see how they perform? For example, this might lead to the challenge of bringing high and low fidelity simulations together that are at different levels of resolution, in a quick and easy way. If we can do that early enough in the systems engineering process, we can design and develop more effective solutions, by letting the user actually interact with the system early-on, and have substantial input on system requirements (where now users interact with the "final" system once it has been produced and changes are cost-prohibitive to make).

A grand challenge for M&S is then to understand how M&S is used in each of the systems engineering life cycle phases, and what types of models and simulations are most effective in each phase. Once this is better understood, we will be able to develop better M&S tools and techniques that can be reused or integrated across different phases of the systems engineering life cycle.

5. DAVID NICOL: Uncertainty and Trust in Models of Cyber Systems

Model validation - determining whether a model correctly represents a system of interest - is widely recognized as a crucial and difficult aspect of M&S. Failure to properly validate may lead to disastrous results. Protective tiles on the space shuttle Columbia were damaged during liftoff by a small piece of foam insulation from a fuel tank, and the shuttle burned up on re-entry. As part of a team that reviewed NASA developed standards on model validation (in response to the disaster), I learned that the effect of the foam's impact on the tiles had actually been simulated, but the results suggested that only an acceptable level of damage would ensue. Post-disaster analysis revealed that a number of sub-models involved in the simulation were deeply flawed, and values for model parameters were unknown, while other sub-models and their parameters had acceptable validity. The faulty sub-models and parameters contaminated the end-to-end system results.

As our nation's defensive capabilities rely increasingly on computing and communication, simulation of cyber-centric systems grows in critical importance. *How trustworthy are our cyber-simulation models? How can we develop trustworthy models?* The problems are deep and can be subtle, and there are many sources for untrustworthiness to creep in, propagate, and contaminate a system model. There are serious gaps that need to be closed lest the cyber-equivalent of the Columbia disaster occur in the heat of a cyber-dependent conflict.

The first gap relates to **trust in modeling parameters and data**. Every model depends on parameters and processes data. Not all data or parameters used have the same level of certainty, trust, or meaning. Data trustworthiness depends on data provenance, on engineering accuracy and on levels of confidence in that data. Our work in simulating wireless communications has shown us how easy it is to introduce uncertainty in detailed models by simply lacking good information about the parameters called for in the models, e.g., reflective coefficients.

The second gap is **trust in model formulation**. Part of model validation needs to be quantified consideration of the degree to which the abstractions of the model match the available data or parameters. For example, why include detailed sub-models of network switches with their variations in scheduling and packet-drop policies if (a) knowledge of switches used in the system of interest is lacking, and (b) the impact of queuing policy on measures of interest (e.g., application throughput) is significant? A detailed model using uncertain parameters may be less trustworthy than a more abstract model using trusted parameters. Our work in analyzing abstractions in switching and background traffic has shown that network utilization is largely unaffected by different switching policies, but protocols involving feedback (e.g., TCP) are very much affected by packet drop policies, and different switches.

A third gap is **trust in model composition**. Data and parameters used have different levels of trustworthiness, sub-models have different levels of trust relative to the data and parameters they use. The final question asks how trustworthy is the end-to-end predictions of the "model of sub-models" that make up the entire model. This is closely related to a well-developed field of "Uncertainty Quantification" in continuous system models that seeks to explain how uncertainty and error in continuous models propagate through composition. Discrete-system models - particular those of cyber-systems - need a corresponding theory. The path forward here is difficult because classical uncertainty quantification relies on derivatives that are lacking in discrete models. The key notion though is model sensitivity, and so developing methods of quantifying sensitivity of metrics in cyber models to parameters and data may lead to a corresponding theory of uncertainty quantification for cyber simulations.

6. GEORGE RILEY: Grand Challenges in Network Simulation

The use of discrete event simulation methods to attempt to predict performance of telecommunications networks has been an important part of nearly all research in computer networks. In nearly all cases it is simply too expensive and time consuming to attempt to create an actual network to experiment with and study network behavior under controlled conditions. However, the use of network simulation tools is also fraught with pitfalls and difficulties such that it becomes difficult to draw meaningful conclusions from many simulation studies. There are several difficult problems that need solutions in order to continue the widespread use of network simulation tools.

Performance and Scale. Virtually all network simulation tools quickly run in to performance issues when modeling any non-trivial network. As the size of the network topology grows and the link capacity increases, the total number of simulation events per simulated second quickly leads to excessive running times, sometimes several hours or even days per simulated second. Clearly, meaningful research is difficult to achieve when waiting long time periods between experimental runs. Further, processor memory also grows quickly as the topology size grows, often leading to experiment failure due to memory exhausting. Distributed simulation methods on supercomputers or networks of workstations can ease this problem somewhat at the expense of extra simulator overhead for message exchanges and time management.

Accuracy of simulation parameters. The behaviors of the various models in the simulation environment are intended to reflect accurately the behavior of the same element in a real-world network. However, in many cases it is simply not known the actual internal behavior of the element in question in a real network (queuing discipline, queue size, queue size units, as an example). Thus when trying to understand the effect of proposed changes on a real network the observed metrics from the simulator might not match the actual metrics on the real network due to incorrect assumptions about how the existing network is configured.

Accuracy of simulation models. Clearly, models in a network simulation environment are intended to behave identically to the same network elements in real systems. However, models for complex protocols such as TCP are difficult to create and difficult to compare to actual networks. The number of different TCP variations and behavior in deployed systems is surprisingly large, and it is nearly impossible to determine a priori which of the many variants are in use in a network. Further, models for queuing methods also have a number of configuration parameters (see the RED queuing method for an example) for which the modeler often does not know the correct or accurate settings. In short, the behavior of nearly all network element models in network simulators is intended to mimic some real world system for which the modeler has incomplete or inaccurate information.

Modeling physical layer performance in wireless simulations. Network simulation has become nearly ubiquitous in the arena of wireless networks. It is well known that the performance of such networks is a function of many variables such as transmission power, antenna gain and orientation, network density, routing protocol in use, node mobility, and of course the network traffic demand by the applications. Of these, the physical layer characteristics are among the most important, and unfortunately accurate modeling of the PHY layer is extremely challenging and not very well understood. Many network simulation designers have created models for PHY layer behavior based on well-known theory, only to find that real-world experiments lead to vastly different results.

The field of network M&S has been active for decades, with bigger and better tools being developed. Progress has been made, but the use of network simulation to accurately predict network performance still leads to inaccurate conclusions in many cases. The above list of challenges is by no means complete, but is a good starting point for researchers wishing to create better simulation tools.

7. CONCLUSIONS

The panel members of this third M&S Grand Challenges activity present their views on why multifaceted M&S Methodology, Agent-based M&S, M&S in Systems Engineering, Cyber Systems Modeling, and Network Simulation pose serious methodological and technical challenges that are considered as grand challenges.

8. REFERENCES

[1] Taylor, S.J.E., Fishwick, P.A., Fujimoto, R., Page, E.H., Uhrmacher, A.M., Wainer, G. 2012. Panel on Grand Challenges for Modeling and Simulation. In *Proceedings of the Winter Simulation Conference 2012*. ACM Press, NY.

[2] Taylor, S.J.E., Khan, A., Morse, K.L., Tolk, A., Yilmaz, L, Zander, J. 2013. Grand Challenges on the Theory of Modeling and Simulation. In *Proceedings of the 2013 Symposium on the Theory of Modeling and Simulation*. SCS, Vista, CA. *To appear.*

[3] Balci, O. 1988. The Implementation of Four Conceptual Frameworks for Simulation Modeling in High-Level Languages. In *Proceedings of the 1988 Winter Simulation Conference*. ACM Press, NY. 287-295.

[4] Balci, O. 2012. A life cycle for modeling and simulation. *Simulation: Transactions of the Society for Modeling and Simulation International.* 88, 7, 870–883.

[5] Balci, O. 2010. Golden rules of verification, validation, testing, and certification of modeling and simulation applications. *SCS M&S Magazine*. Oct. 2010 Issue 4, The Society for Modeling and Simulation International (SCS), Vista, CA.

[6] Balci, O., Arthur, J. D., and Ormsby, W. F. 2011. Achieving reusability and composability with a simulation conceptual model. *Journal of Simulation* 5, 3, 157-165.

[7] Holland, J. 1999. *Emergence, From Chaos to Order*. Basic Books.

[8] Siebers, P. O., Macal, C. M., Garnett, J., Buxton, D., and Pidd M. 2010. Discrete-event Simulation is Dead, Long Live Agent-based Simulation! *Journal of Simulation*, 4, 3, 204-210.

[9] National Academy of Engineering. 2008. Introduction to the Grand Challenges for Engineering. Website accessed 15 February 2013: http://www.engineeringchallenges.org.

[10] Committee on Pre-Milestone A Systems Engineering. 2009. Pre-Milestone A and Early-Phase Systems Engineering: A Retrospective Review and Benefits for Future Air Force Acquisition. *The National Academies Press.*

[11] Stevens, R., Brook, P., Jackson, K., and Arnold, S. 1998. Systems Engineering: Coping with Complexity. Prentice Hall.

[12] Haskins, Cecilia (ed.). 2007. Systems Engineering Handbook: A Guide for System Life Cycle Processes and Activities, INCOSE-TP-2003-002-03.1, version 3.1.

Author Index

www.ingramcontent.com/pod-product-compliance
Ingram Content Group UK Ltd.
Pitfield, Milton Keynes, MK11 3LW, UK
UKHW051510290926
15471UKWH00008B/1545

9 781450 322812